THE
BAPTIST
HERITAGE

H. Leon McBeth

BROADMAN PRESS
Nashville, Tennessee

© Copyright 1987 • Broadman Press
All rights reserved
4265-69
ISBN: 0-8054-6569-3
Dewey Decimal Classification: 286.09
Subject Heading: BAPTISTS-HISTORY
Library of Congress Catalog Card Number: 86-31667
Printed in the United States of America

Library of Congress Cataloging-in-Publication Data

McBeth, Leon.
  The Baptist heritage.

  Bibliography: p.
  Includes index.
  1. Baptists—History. I. Title.
BX6231.M37   1987   286'.09   86-31667
ISBN 0-8054-6569-3

Preface

In a quarter-century of teaching Baptist history at Southwestern Baptist Theological Seminary, I have assigned different textbooks and various other materials for students' reading. Many of these are now out of date, no longer available, or leave serious gaps by not addressing the more recent developments in Baptist life. For these reasons I decided to arrange my own research for publication and thus offer this volume to interested readers.

Three presuppositions have guided the preparation of this work; all of them will be obvious to the reader. First, I regard the Baptist denomination as a still viable expression of the Christian faith. While I value the modern ecumenical movement and rejoice in the spirit of brotherhood which increasingly prevails among believers of different labels, I do not yet see the denomination fading away. Though I write from within the Baptist tradition, I trust that the presentation and interpretation of the data has been reasonably objective.

Second, I tried to write from a sufficiently catholic perspective to be fair to the many different Baptist groups mentioned. The nature of a general history requires brevity, and at times I settled for a sentence when a paragraph was needed. Despite this brevity, my purpose was to present each Baptist group in as complete and accurate a way as possible. I hope every Baptist group mentioned will feel that they and their emphases are fairly presented.

A third presupposition of this work is that history requires interpretation. I was not content merely to dump factual data upon the page but tried to arrange it in some order and offer my own interpretations as to its meaning and significance. My interpretations are clearly distinguishable as such, and I believe they are justified by the historical facts. I offer them with a sense of modesty, remembering Oliver Cromwell's remark to dogmatic religionists, "I beseech you in the bowels of Jesus Christ, to think that you may be wrong."

Since Baptists now have about four centuries of continuous history, writing their story chronologically, century by century, seemed feasible. Some may find it confusing to jump back and forth across the Atlantic, but other approaches have their own problems. I was not willing to tell the story of British and European Baptists up to the present before introducing

Baptist beginnings in the American colonies. One should not, I think, read about the Baptist World Alliance and the struggles of Baptists under modern Communism before even meeting Roger Williams in Colonial America.

However, within each century division, topical and geographical development are presented. Readers who prefer can realign the chapters so as to follow each Baptist group straight through from the seventeenth century to the twentieth. The century divisions are not airtight; in order to complete the story I sometimes dipped back into the previous century or overlapped a bit into the next. In chapter 16, in describing the "Larger Baptist Family," I placed the story in the present century but reached back into earlier times to trace the roots of several Baptist groups.

Though I consulted the major secondary works dealing with Baptists, I drew my materials and interpretations mostly from primary sources. To have access to these original sources, I spent considerable research time in England, Scotland, Wales, and various parts of Europe. In addition, I had admission to the major libraries and archival collections of Baptist groups in various parts of the United States. In dealing with European Baptists, especially those in Eastern Europe, inaccessibility of sources and language barriers caused me to rely more on secondary sources.

In the final preparation of these pages, I was torn between the need to avoid long quotes and the desire to allow Baptists to speak for themselves. I hope most readers will agree that I found a tolerable middle ground. For the most part, I allowed the quotes to stand exactly as they were first written, but at times I modernized spelling and punctuation for the sake of clarity.

I owe thanks to so many people for help in this project that it would be impossible to name them all here. However, they know who they are, and they know how deeply grateful I am to each one of them. Carl Wrotenbery, director of Libraries, Southwestern Baptist Theological Seminary, Fort Worth, Texas and his predecessor, Keith C. Wills, made their vast Baptist collection available to me and moved immediately to obtain any additional materials I requested. I also thank the following libraries and collections: Ron Deering, director, Boyce Centennial Library, The Southern Baptist Theological Library, Louisville, Kentucky; Lynn E. May, executive director, The Southern Baptist Historical Library and Archives, Nashville, Tennessee; The Freewill Baptist Historical Archives, Nashville, Tennessee; William H. Brackney, executive director, The American Baptist Historical Society, Rochester, New York; Barrington R. White, principal, Regents Park College, Oxford University, for admission to the Angus Collection; and the Baptist International Seminary, Ruschlikon, Switzerland, for admission to its European Baptist historical collection.

For those who read portions or all the manuscript and made helpful suggestions, I am grateful. I thank them for all the improvements they suggested and blame them for none of the remaining defects. Among those readers, I especially thank Roger Hayden of Reading, England; and two of my former teachers, Robert T. Handy of New York, and Robert A. Baker of Fort Worth.

I gladly take this occasion to thank Southwestern Baptist Theological Seminary, Fort Worth, Texas, for its generous assistance in the completion of this task. William B. Tolar, dean of the School of Theology, went the second mile in approving sabbatical leave time, allotting sabbatical travel funds for needed research, and providing extra secretarial help for manuscript preparation.

My family showed unusual patience with me during the time I was immersed in this project. They heard the typewriter clacking from my study many a late evening. I especially thank my wife, Ada, for her unwavering support in this and every other aspect of our shared lives.

HARRY LEON MCBETH

Contents

The Emerging Denomination

General Baptists. Particular Baptists.

Summary

The Early Stuart Era, to 1640

John Smyth. Thomas Helwys. Leonard Busher. John Murton

The Time of Turmoil, 1640-1648

Edward Barber. Christopher Blackwood. John Tombes.

The Saint's Regime, 1648-1660

John Clarke. Henry Denne.

The Later Stuart Era, 1660-1688

The Act of Toleration, 1689

Summary

Baptist Beginnings in New England

Roger Williams. The Providence Church. John Clarke. Swansea. Boston. Kittery.

Baptist Beginnings in the Middle Colonies

Baptist Beginnings in the Southern Colonies

A Baptist Profile

An Independent Development. Diversity. Persistent Problems. Internal Life.

Unit II: The Eighteenth Century

Decline of General Baptists

Doctrinal Problems. Matthew Caffyn. Schism and Aftermath.

The New Connection

Forerunners. Dan Taylor. Formation of the New Connection. The Articles of Religion. New Connection Progress.

Internal Life of New Connection Churches

Shared Decisions. Signing and Worship. Roles of Women. Church Discipline.

Summary

Particular Baptist Decline

Religious Liberty in the Middle Colonies

Background of Toleration. Benefits to Baptists.

Religious Liberty in the Southern Colonies

Restrictions on Religion. John Leland (1754-1841). The Baptist Petition Movement. The General Assessment Bill. Religion in the Federal Constitution.

Summary

Unit III: The Nineteenth Century

Baptists in England

The Baptist Union. General Baptists. The Baptist Missionary Society. Expansion at Home. Social Issues. The Down Grade Controversy. The Merger of 1891.

Baptists in Greater Britain

Baptists in Scotland. Baptists in Ireland. Baptists in Wales.

Baptists in the British Commonwealth

Baptists in Australia. Baptists in New Zealand. Baptists in South Africa.

Baptists in Canada

The Atlantic Provinces. The Central Provinces. The Western Provinces

Summary

The Triennial Convention

Beginnings. Society Versus Convention Plans. Expansion. Reversion to Society Approach. Foreign Missions to 1845.

The Baptist General Tract Society

Beginnings. Expansion. Relation to the South and West.

The American Baptist Home Mission Society

Early Home Missions. Survey of the West. A New Society Formed. Home Mission Achievements.

Deepening Discord Among Baptists

The Antimissions Movement. The Campbell Constroversy.

The Southern Baptist Convention

Methods of Organization. Problems in Home Missions. Slavery and Its Aftermath. Efforts at Neutrality. Two Final Straws. The Augusta Meeting.

Summary

Baptists in the North

The American Baptist Missionary Union (ABMU). The American Baptist Publication Society (ABPS). The American Baptist Home Mission Society (ABHMS). The American Baptist Education Society (ABES).

Baptists in the South

Foreign Mission Board (FMB). Home Mission Board (HMB). Sunday School Board. Baptist Colleges. Theological Education.

The Landmark Movement

Origin. Leaders. Landmark Teachings. Progress of Landmarkism. Scattered Eruptions of Landmarkism. General Assessment of Landmarkism.

Woman's Missionary Union

Summary

An Overview of European Baptists

Relation to the Anabaptist Movement. The Pietist Awakenings. Intense Persecution. Relation to Baptists in Britain and America. The Role of Laymen. European Baptists and Social Status.

Baptist Trailblazers in Europe

Johann Gerhard Oncken. Julius Wilhelm Köbner. Gottfried Wilhelm Lehmann.

Baptist Beginnings: A Geographical Survey

Central Europe. Northern Europe. Southern Europe. Eastern Europe.

At the Turn of the Century

A Measure of Growth. The German Connection. Outlook for the Future.

Unit I

The Seventeenth Century

In Europe and England the seventeenth century was a time of transition. The Peace of Westphalia in 1648 marked the end of the Reformation era and, by its limited recognition of Protestantism, marked a new era in Christian history. Enormous changes occurred in political, social, and economic areas, changes that no one could predict, affect, or even understand. In such an unsettled and volatile environment, Baptists emerged as a separate denomination.

In England, where Baptists first took root, waves of political change marked the seventeenth century. James I, the first of the Stuarts who succeeded the last of the Tudors in 1603, effectively asserted traditional royal powers. However, James's son Charles I was beheaded in 1649 for attempting the same kind of autocratic rule. After a series of civil wars, England experimented with a "rule of the saints" in which Protestant radicals dominated Parliament for a time. When this failed England moved to a Commonwealth, in which Oliver Cromwell took the title of "Lord Protector" but increasingly acted like a king. Cromwell's rule was marked by good intentions and meager achievements. In 1660 England restored its monarchy by the coronation of Charles II. The century ended, however, with yet another king deposed, but not executed, and the acceptance of William of Orange and Mary on the throne. Though England continued to have a monarchy, real political power had passed to Parliament. The rise of various dissenting religions to challenge the Church of England was in some ways the religious equivalent of the undermining of monarchy by a strong Parliament.

Along with political change came radical revisions in the social structure. One commoner with a cannon could make castles obsolete; the collapse of castles is but one example of the decline of nobility and the rise of the common man. Early stirrings of the Industrial Revolution brought new forms of employment. The opening of the American colonies focused attention on ability rather than inherited titles; this formed one more impetus to the leveling of society and the rise of the common man. Though America was "discovered" earlier, the first successful English colonies in that new land date from the seventeenth century. The enormous significance of the colonies in political and economic history may obscure their equally important impact on religion. The distant colonies provided a safety valve for diverse forms of religion, a haven in the wilderness where religions that would have been crushed in England were allowed to flourish. In effect, what was considered radical dissent in England became the established norm in America. Old and New England exercised a mutual influence upon each other; stories of religious persecution in England helped undermine that practice in the New World.

Clearly the Baptists fit the temperament of their times. Conditions were right for the emergence of more individualistic forms of religion, and the spate of new religious groups in England show that they took full advantage of the day. Not only Baptists but also Levellers, Runners, Ranters, Quakers, Independents, and others rose during this unstable time. The Puritan leaven, which for all its efforts never really reformed the Church of England, had its greatest impact among the Separated churches, including Baptists.

For Baptists the seventeenth century was a time of beginnings. Their first churches emerged during this time, and they forged their distinctive denominational structures. From the first, Baptist churches were committed to the concept of inter-church cooperation. The Baptist association and the general assembly gave both local and national structure to their church life. Through a series of confessions Baptists defined their faith, and by testimony and suffering, they hammered out their concept of religious freedom for all.

Though Baptists in the seventeenth century sprang up primarily in England and Wales, a few churches appeared in Scotland and Ireland but within a few years went into eclipse. Baptists also emerged in the New World during the seventeenth century, with churches from Maine to South Carolina before 1700. Scholars debate whether the first Baptists in America represent an offshoot from the English community or an independent beginning, but one cannot doubt the close connections that later developed between the Baptists on either side of the Atlantic. In the Act of Toleration of 1689, English Baptists achieved a measure of religious liberty but at the cost of great spiritual fatigue. In America, Baptists faced religious persecution in New England and parts of the South but found liberty and an open door for growth in the Middle Colonies.

By the end of the century, Baptists could count both pluses and minuses. They faced spiritual fatigue in England; they were doctrinally divided and vulnerable to extremist views, which would devastate them in the next century; they faced a serious shortage of prepared ministers. On a more positive note, they had defined and defended their faith, had formed denominational structures which endure to the present, and had at least glimpsed the opportunity for an aggressive evangelistic outreach.

1

Baptist Beginnings

History must look at beginnings. To know the origin of a movement or group gives a head start to understanding its present identity and significance. An effort to understand that denomination of Christians called "Baptists" must begin with Baptist history. Who was the first Baptist? When and where was the first Baptist church established? What factors best account for Baptist origins? These sound like simple questions, and one might expect straight-forward answers. The story of Baptist beginnings, however, is surprisingly complex. Additional insights surface as new evidence comes to light. This chapter will recount the historical facts of the origin of Baptists as those facts are presently known.

Overview of Baptist Origins

The modern Baptist denomination originated in England and Holland in the early seventeenth century. Baptists emerged out of intense reform movements, shaped by such radical dissent as Puritanism, Separatism, and possibly Anabaptism. Influenced by the Reformation theology of Ulrich Zwingli and John Calvin, the English Bible, and a deep desire for spiritual reform, some of these Separatists adopted baptism for believers only. They later applied that baptism by total immersion and were nicknamed "Baptists" for that practice.

Two major groups of Baptists emerged in England in the early 1600s. While they shared much in common, they differed in their views of the atonement and church organization. The earlier group was called General Baptists because they believed in a "general" atonement. They believed that the death of Christ has "general" application; that is, anyone who voluntarily believes in Christ can be saved. The General Baptists were less influenced by John Calvin, who taught that only the predestined may be saved, and more influenced by the Dutch theologian, Jacob Arminius, whose theology made room for free will. The General Baptists also, like other Arminians, taught the possibility of "falling from grace," and their church structure allowed only limited congregational autonomy, giving more power to the associations. Two primary founders of General Baptists were John Smyth and Thomas Helwys. The earliest church of this persuasion was formed about 1609.

21

A later group, known as Particular Baptists, surfaced by the late 1630s, led by such men as Henry Jessey, William Kiffin, and John Spilsbury. Under the influence of Calvinism, they taught a "particular" atonement. They believed that Christ died not for all mankind, but only for "particular" ones, namely the elect. Like Calvin, they believed that God had elected some to salvation, that the elect inevitably would be saved, and that the saved could never become "unelect" or lose their salvation. While originating a generation later than General Baptists, Particular Baptists were destined to become the larger of the two groups. The earliest church of this persuasion dates from 1638 (some say 1633). Their organizational structure gave the local congregation complete churchly power, while associations had only advisory functions.

Both groups flourished in England. By 1650 the General Baptists numbered at least forty-seven churches. They grouped these into associations, issued several confessions of faith, and had the rudiments of a national organization. The Particular Baptists, while fewer, had at least seven churches by 1644. Those churches acted together to issue a confession of faith that year. This First London Confession wielded vast influence upon the future shape of Baptist life and thought. Present-day Baptists can be traced back to these beginnings.

This summary, like one snapshot from a larger album, gives only the briefest view and leaves great gaps. We must now fill in some of those historical gaps, first by looking more closely at religious developments in England at the time Baptists emerged as a separate denomination.

Religion in England

The Christian religion came early to the British Isles. The early Celtic form of Christianity was marked by evangelical emphases and relative independence from Church developments in Europe at the time. In AD 597 the missionary monk, Augustine, introduced the Latin form of Christianity into Britain. After a time of competition, the Latin, or Roman, form of faith prevailed. Britain became Roman Catholic, but the older Celtic faith never completely disappeared. From William the Conquerer to Henry VIII, English kings alternately obeyed and defied the popes. Through the years, a number of dissenting groups, like the Lollards, arose to challenge Roman supremacy.

By the sixteenth century, England was a cauldron bubbling with revolutionary changes in economics, politics, and religion. Religion saw radical change under King Henry VIII (1509-1547). By the first Act of Supremacy (1534), Henry separated the Church of England from obedience to Rome, though it remained essentially Catholic in doctrine and practice. Many churchmen wanted more thorough reforms. Influenced by Reformers on the Continent, especially by Zwingli in Zurich and Calvin in Geneva, many agitated for more Protestant practices.

Despite his own Catholicism, Henry VIII put his son Edward VI under the training of the most Protestant of his advisers. When Edward came to the throne (1547-1553), though a mere lad, he moved England definitely toward Protestantism. As early as 1549, the Church of England adopted a new prayer book, which guided worship liturgy, and the 1552 revision of that document prescribed even more Protestant styles of worship. In 1552 the Church of England also adopted a new doctrinal standard, the Forty-two Articles (later reduced to thirty-nine), with a distinctly Calvinist flavor. Under Edward, intense Protestant sympathizers, who had been exiled during the latter years of Henry VIII, returned to England to disseminate their views, which had been made even more Protestant by contacts with Zwinglian and Calvinistic reform movements in Europe. During the Edwardian era, clergy could be married, Catholic practices were modified, doctrine and worship moved toward Protestantism of the Calvinist variety, and limited toleration allowed the rapid spread of these viewpoints. In short, while Henry VIII severed the English church from Rome, his son Edward VI made the church Protestant for the first time.

Edward's early death led to a struggle for succession to the English throne, with religion as one major factor in a series of national and international intrigues. Catholics hoped to regain England to Roman allegiance; Protestants hoped to keep and consolidate what they had gained. Mary Tudor, Catholic daughter of Henry VIII, gained the throne and ruled from 1553-1558. In a series of legislative acts, she dismantled the Protestant system of Edward and restored the Catholic system of Henry VIII, eventually restoring the Roman allegiance which had prevailed before the Act of Supremacy. She renewed several acts leading to persecution of Protestants, with the result that many went into exile as they had earlier under her father.

However, not all English Protestants conformed to the restored Catholicism or fled into exile; some merely went underground. After some years of relative freedom to worship as they felt best, some English Christians apparently continued to worship in secret congregations as early as the 1550s. These "Marian Separatists" provided models or prototypes for the later English Separatist movement. Queen Mary's vigorous efforts to rid England of all remaining Protestantism, even to the point of wholesale executions, earned her the nickname "Bloody Mary." The excesses of her persecutions, coupled with a growing English distaste for Romanism, turned England more decisively toward Protestantism.

Elizabeth Tudor, another daughter of Henry VIII, succeeded Bloody Mary and ruled from 1559 to 1603 as "ye great landlady of England." Shrewd and skilled in diplomacy, and not overly religious herself, Elizabeth had a personal preference for the colorful rituals of Catholicism, but political necessity pushed her toward Protestantism. Political developments in Europe, her condemnation by the Roman Church, and adverse English reaction to Mary's religion, determined that both Elizabeth and England would turn more toward Protestantism.

Elizabeth enacted religious laws which consciously combined elements of Catholicism and Protestantism. Centering around her own Act of Supremacy and Act of Uniformity, both in 1559, this religious system was known as the "Elizabethan Settlement." After years of fluctuation between Catholicism and Protestantism, English religion was now "settled." This settlement was a compromise, a via media, with both the strengths and weaknesses inherent therein.

Those with more intense religious views, whether Catholic or Protestant, found this system unsatisfactory; and before the turn of the century, the Elizabethan Settlement became quite unsettled. Roman Catholic pressures and political maneuvering, plus threats of assassination and military efforts to overthrow Elizabeth, forced her more firmly into the Protestant camp. The more intense Protestants also aroused the queen's ire by their desire for more Calvinist beliefs and practices. The result was that Elizabeth, beset on both sides, moved decisively to restrict both intense Catholics and Protestants and tried, with ever-decreasing success, to enforce her compromise settlement.

The Emergence of Puritanism

Church reform was in the air throughout the Western world in the sixteenth century. During this time, major upheavals occured in the Roman Catholic Church, and Protestant churches were born, such as Lutheran, Reformed, and Anglican, as well as the Anabaptists and other radical spiritual groups. Growing enlightenment from the Renaissance, the leaven of the Bible in the languages of the people, and the powerful preaching of Martin Luther, Ulrich Zwingli, John Calvin, Conrad Grebel, and others had a transforming effect.

With such reforms in progress elsewhere, a growing number of English churchmen could not be content with the halfhearted religious changes in England. Gradually a distinct party emerged to advocate further reforms. Because they sought a "pure" church, this reforming party was nicknamed the "Puritans." The word is almost as difficult to define as the movement is to pinpoint historically. For all its anti-Catholicism, modern Puritanism may root partly in the intense Catholic piety of the later Middle Ages. Later the term *Puritanism* came to designate a spirit and attitude almost as much as a set of religious beliefs. In sixteenth-century England, the Puritans did not want to break with the Church of England but to reform it. They wanted to simplify the worship patterns, modify church polity from episcopal to presbyterial and adopt more Calvinistic doctrines. The early Puritans, led by Bishop Hooker and Thomas Cartwright of Cambridge, regarded these reforms as biblical.

However, for reasons both religious and political, the Church of England resisted these changes. Queen Elizabeth had no sympathy with Puritanism and sought to enforce religious conformity by law. Bishops, not unnaturally, looked with little favor upon abolishing the episcopal system. Not all welcomed Calvinist doctrines, and some felt repelled by the Puritan tendency toward narrow rigidity and intolerance. After several centuries in which everyone was almost automatically a Christian and a church member, many in England could neither understand nor accommodate the militant new spirit which insisted upon a church so "pure" that it seemed to leave little room for human frailty. In short, the common people, church leaders, and the government did not accept the Puritan reforms completely.

Any discussion of religious dissent in England must take account of *The Book of Martyrs* by John Foxe. This vivid book, published in English in 1563, taught a generation of Englishmen to hate religious persecution and hunger for freedom for their faith. It set the stage for Protestant opposition to Catholicism and later for the Puritan-Separatist opposition to the Anglican Church. The book is mostly a collection of stories about Protestants who suffered for their faith. Many of the stories are authentic; others may be embroidered. This book helped focus the English mind upon religious reform.

From Puritanism to Separatism

Unable to purify the Church of England, many churchmen determined to separate and form their own independent congregations where they could institute what they regarded as biblical practices. Those who did this were called, naturally enough, "Separatists." Some separated out of *pragmatism;* they preferred to be part of the state church, but separated temporarily to promote reform. Others separated out of *principle;* they had come to the conviction that the church ought to be free of government connection. These "principle Separatists" figure more prominently in Baptist beginnings than do the "pragmatic Separatists."

One cannot say exactly when Separatism first began. No doubt Walter H. Burgess was correct when he wrote, "There was probably never a time in English history when men and women interested in religion did not foregather apart from the services of the official Church to confer by speech or reading about the matters that touched their lives most clearly."[1] Whatever isolated separations existed earlier, by the 1550s groups of Separatists became visible in England. Barrington R. White pointed out in his definitive work, *The English Separatist Tradition,* that many earnest Christians, accustomed to more freedom of worship under Edward VI, simply refused to

---

1. Walter H. Burgess, *John Smyth the Se-Baptist, Thomas Helwys and the First Baptist Church in England,* p. 23.

return to Catholicism as required by Mary Tudor.[2] Therefore, groups began to meet separately for worship, Bible reading, and prayer. At least two such churches met in London by the 1560s: the Privy Church led by Richard Fitz and the Plumbers' Hall congregation led by William Bonam. The Privy Church, the more separatist of the two, had left the state church "to set their hands and hearts, to the pure unmingled and sincere worshipping of God."[3] Describing themselves as "a poore congregation whom god hath separated from the churches of england," they detailed their objections to the state church, especially "the mingled and faulse worshipping therein vsed."[4] Members of both congregations were imprisoned in 1567, and Fitz died in prison. The Plumbers' Hall group was more Puritan than Separatist, at first intending no final separation from the Church of England. Their pastor promised upon his release from prison in 1569 not to observe communion "in anie howse, or other place, Contrarie to the state of religion nowe by publique authoritie established."[5]

In the excellent study, *John Robinson and the English Separatist Tradition,* Timothy George showed that great variety existed among the Separatist groups. Some debated such minor issues as whether to stand or kneel during prayer. Others objected to Calvinism, claiming "that the doctrine of predestynation was meter for develles then for christian men."[6] George placed the earliest separations in Kent, but pointed out that the London groups proved more influential.

Further evidence of early Separatism is contained in the well-known letter of Bishop Grindal to Henry Bullinger, dated in London June 9, 1568. Grindal complained:

> Some London citizens of the lowest order, together with four or five ministers, remarkable neither for their judgment nor learning, have openly separated from us; and sometimes in private houses, sometimes in the fields, and occasionally even in ships, they have held their meetings and administered the sacraments. Besides this, they have ordained ministers, elders, and deacons, after their own way.[7]

Other letters show that new separations erupted, and the authorities could not control or curtail them. B. R. White concluded, "In spite of all the efforts of the authorities, underground congregations continued to gather in London throughout the 1570s and may have survived until the activities

2. Barrington R. White, *The English Separatist Tradition.*
3. Ibid., p. 29.
4. William R. Estep, "Anabaptists and the Rise of English Baptists," *The Quarterly Review,* p. 50.
5. Ibid.
6. Timothy George, *John Robinson and the English Separatist Tradition,* pp. 10-11.
7. Champlin Burrage, *The Early English Dissenters in the Light of Recent Research,* 1:80.

in and around the capital first of Robert Browne and later of Barrow and Greenwood."[8]

For convenience, a brief sketch of Separatism can be presented around the stories of four important leaders and congregations. These are Robert Browne and the Pioneer Church (1581); Francis Johnson and the Ancient Church (1592); John Robinson and the Pilgrim Church (nucleus by 1606); and Henry Jacob and the JLJ Church (1616).

Robert Browne and the Pioneer Church

Whatever the earlier history of Separatism, most scholars regard Robert Browne (1550-1633) as one pioneer of the movement. "Troublechurch Browne," as he was nicknamed, has usually been credited with beginning the major exodus of Separatism. However, some scholars want to modify that assessment, saying that Browne may have popularized the movement but certainly did not invent it.[9] Browne's blockbuster publication of 1582, *A Treatise of reformation without tarrying for anie,* attracted widespread attention, gave an effective defense of Separatism, and attracted new converts.

Called "an ignoble prophet of a noble vision," Browne was a harsh controversialist, unduly censorious and judgmental, and a known wife beater. Later in life he withdrew from the movement he had set on foot, submitted to episcopal authority, and lived in relative comfort while his erstwhile brethren suffered persecution for practices he had taught them. Seldom does one find purer doctrine associated with a more unlovely character. It is no wonder that his followers rejected the name "Brownist."

Browne graduated from Corpus Christi College, Cambridge, in 1572, where he was probably a student of Thomas Cartwright, a leader of Puritan reform. Soon Browne came to the conviction that pastors should not be appointed by bishops, but local churches should elect their own pastors. He asked "whether the ordinarie assemblies of the professors in Englande be the Churches of Christ" and concluded in the negative.[10] He found no redeeming features in the Church of England, objecting especially to their "bablinge Prayers and toying worshippe . . . and a thousande moe abominations." In a word, he concluded, "They are not Jerusalem."[11] Browne acted upon his convictions; by April 19, 1581, he formed at Norwich a Separatist church meeting "in private houses and conventicles." The next year he

8. White, p. 27.

9. Ibid., pp. 44 *f.*

10. Cited by James Leo Garrett, "Restitution and Dissent Among Early English Baptists," *Baptist History and Heritage,* p. 13.

11. Robert Browne, *A Treatise upon the 23, of Matthew* (1582), as cited in Kenneth L. Sprunger, *Dutch Puritanism* (Leiden: E. J. Brill, 1982), p. 30.

published his famous treatise demanding reform without further delay.

Two of Browne's most intense followers, Henry Barrow and John Greenwood, carried on his Congregational Separatism in London. Barrow was described as "an ingenious and learned man, but of too warm a spirit."[12] If anything, he was even more critical of the Church of England than was Browne and carried Separatism a step further. His treatise on *Four Causes of Separation* (1587), identified false worship, false ministry, false discipline, and a false basis of membership in the Church of England as grounds for separation. Greenwood was perhaps less militant than Barrow, but he stoutly defended Separatism. His treatise on *The True Church and the False Church* (1588) listed several marks of a false church and, predictably, found all of them in the Church of England.

Both Barrow and Greenwood had also attended Cambridge, a seedbed of reform which fueled early Separatism. In 1586 both Barrow and Greenwood were imprisoned, where they remained, with some brief breaks for Greenwood, until their execution in 1593. In prison, both carried on a ministry of writing and even preaching at times. Both were rigid and intolerant. At times they advanced their faith in an unduly belligerent manner, and often elevated trifles to supreme importance. To them it was a life-or-death matter, literally, whether the church had proper ministry and discipline and whether prayers be read or prayed extemporaneously. But one must admit that to the last they had the courage of their convictions and sealed their witness with their blood. In 1592, while Barrow and Greenwood were in prison, their impromptu London meeting was formed into a Separatist church by Francis Johnson.

Francis Johnson and the Ancient Church

Another important leader of English Separatism was Francis Johnson (c.1562-c.1617). A graduate of Christ's College, Cambridge, Johnson favored reform, but for years resisted Separatism. In 1591 he obtained an order to seize and burn copies of a treatise by Barrow and Greenwood, but saved two copies out of the flames that he might study and refute them. As he studied, he was instead convinced that Separatism was both viable and biblical. Fourteen years later Johnson sought to make restitution by having the burned tract reprinted at his expense.

Johnson became a convinced Brownist, renounced his comfortable living, and went to London to confer in Fleet Prison with Barrow. In 1592 he was elected pastor of the London Separatist congregation. The executions of Barrow and Greenwood, along with John Penry, convinced the Separatists they should leave England. The Conventicle Act of 1593, providing other penalties for Separatists, also helped them decide. Most of the London congregation migrated to Amsterdam in 1593, where they came to be called the "Ancient Church." Johnson did not make the trip with them, since he

---

12. Daniel Neal, *The History of the Puritans,* 1:20.

was then in prison for his faith, but he followed in 1597. In Amsterdam the Ancient Church elected Henry Ainsworth as teacher in place of the martyred Greenwood. The peaceful and scholarly Ainsworth led the people to put out their "True Confession" in 1596, a confession said to have influenced later Baptists.[13]

Like most of the Separatists, Johnson was highly critical and censorious, a stickler on small details. This "Bishop of Brownism," as he was sometimes called, was probably more Presbyterian than Congregationalist, for he profoundly distrusted popular government in the church. His stern insistence upon the authority of the elders was one factor in his later controversies with John Smyth, the Baptist. In his twenty-five-year ministry, Johnson had to face three serious problems relating to free church, problems not completely settled to this day: the right exercise of discipline, the true nature of baptism, and the authority of the minister.

Many of Johnson's controversies centered in his own family. In London he had married a young widow, Thomasine Boys, who was beautiful but apparently quite frivolous. Described as "a bouncy girle," she had a taste for what some considered extravagant and even immodest dress, including several gold rings; and she had money from her first husband to provide these. One particularly ornate hat became the topic of church discipline for months. One gown, said to be too daring, was ordered to be produced in church that the congregation might rule on its propriety. The congregation also criticized Thomasine for allegedly remaining in bed as late as 9 AM on the Lord's Day. Francis's brother, George, led the criticism, claiming that Francis was "blinded, bewitched and besotted" by Thomasine.[14] In 1599 Francis excommunicated George, describing him as "impious, heathenish, hideous," and moreover afflicted with "crackbrainedness." Three years later he also excommunicated their father who tried to patch things up between the disaffected brothers.

Perhaps the low point of Johnson's ministry was the painful schism between himself and Ainsworth over congregational versus ministerial control of the church. The Ainsworth group pulled off to form a different church in which members could make more decisions. Their group included John Canne, considered by some the founder of the Broadmead church which later became Baptist. Another splinter of the Ancient Church went with neither Johnson nor Ainsworth but formed their own group under Elder Blackwell and sailed for Virginia about 1619.

From time to time several members of the Ancient Church were attracted to Anabaptist views and either withdrew or were excluded. In the treatise entitled *An Inquirie,* Johnson complained that of the members "divers of them fell into the heresies of the Anabaptists (which are too common in these countreys) and so persisting were excommunicated by the rest." In

13. William L. Lumpkin, ed., *Baptist Confessions of Faith,* pp. 82-97.
14. White, p. 96.

1597 Henoch Clapham had trouble with some Anabaptists in his Separatist congregation in Amsterdam and later declared that he knew of some who "blew off their baptism; one baptized himself and then baptized others." Possibly the latter was a reference to John Smyth.[15] The Ancient Church declined after the death of Johnson in 1617.

John Robinson and the Pilgrim Church

Another congregation of English Separatists, important in its own right, became even more famous as the "Pilgrim church" that migrated to Plymouth in 1620. Led by John Robinson (1572-1625), the Pilgrim church represented a milder form of Separatism. This church originated as part of the Gainsborough congregation in England led by John Smyth. When rapid growth made it unwise for such a large number to meet together, since English law forbade such "conventicles," the group divided. Some remained at Gainsborough under the pastoral leadership of Smyth; the remnant removed to Scrooby Manor, where they elected Robinson as pastor. The Robinson group included two laymen, destined to become well-known in America, William Bradford and William Brewster.

The Robinson church also migrated to Amsterdam about 1608 and, for a time, was apparently in fellowship with the Ancient Church. Later Robinson led his group to Leyden, perhaps to escape the conflicts within the Ancient Church and between that church and John Smyth. At Leyden Robinson moderated his views somewhat, away from the rigid Separatism of Smyth and Johnson, more toward the mild "semi-Separatism" of Henry Jacob. Historians debate the sources of this change, but many conclude that Robinson was influenced by Henry Jacob, who spent some years in Holland before returning to London to form an independent congregation in 1616.

Leyden proved to be an unhappy settlement for the Robinson church. They suffered economic reverses and grieved to see their children losing the English language and marrying into Dutch families. In 1620 a portion of the church, under the leadership of Bradford and Brewster, combined with other Separatists to sail for the new world on the *Mayflower*. Pastor Robinson, intending to follow them later, bade them farewell with a fervent sermon, including his oft-quoted saying, "the Lord had more truth and light yet to break forth out of his Holy Word."[16] Robinson's church became the nucleus of the "Pilgrim Fathers," pioneers of American Congregationalism, but Robinson never joined them in America, dying in Leyden in 1625.

Henry Jacob and the JLJ Church

In 1616 Henry Jacob established a Separatist church in the Southwark section of London. Like most Separatist leaders, Jacob had spent some time

---

15. James D. Mosteller, "Baptists and Anabaptists," *The Chronicle,* p. 107.
16. Cited in John H. Shakespeare, *Baptist and Congregational Pioneers,* p. 165.

in exile in Holland where he exchanged views with English and Dutch dissenters of varying emphases. Apparently Jacob disliked the narrow spirit and rigid intolerance which led to schism in Johnson's Ancient Church, and he distanced himself from that fussy church, both spiritually and geographically. Jacob developed a milder form of Separatism, which some have called "semi-Separatism," and for awhile gathered a church in Middelburg, near Leyden, on these tolerant principles.

Jacob returned to London, and in 1616 formed the church named for the initials of its first three pastors, Jacob, John Lathrop, and Henry Jessey. A more detailed account of the JLJ church will come later, for out of its membership came the first Particular Baptists in England.

This sketch provides at least the broad outlines of English Separatism. One may appreciate the movement and the commendable aspirations of its leaders without endorsing all they did. From today's perspective, they look fussy and judgmental, condemning those who differed from them even on minute details, and all too ready to separate from one another as they had earlier separated from the Church of England. They were marked, as Keith L. Sprunger noted, by "schism and bad manners."[17]

Despite these blemishes, Separatism has contributed much to the Free Church tradition. The Separatists took the Bible seriously and determined to order their lives by its teachings. They insisted upon a church made up only of the redeemed, a "gathered church." Rejecting a church polity based upon bishops, or rule from above, the Separatists favored some form of participatory church government; some were congregational, others more presbyterian. They favored a simple worship liturgy, without undue dependence upon stated forms, written prayers, or other worship aids.

Many of these concepts surfaced later in Baptist life and no doubt were absorbed from the Separatists. However, Baptists faulted the Separatists in that most of them did not go on to believer's baptism and religious liberty, two areas in which Baptists went significantly beyond the Separatists.

A variety of religious influences helped to group these Separatists into various denominations. Some of them came gradually to accept such concepts as salvation by grace, baptism of believers only, and religious liberty for all. Those who adopted such views were eventually nicknamed "Baptists," and with them this story deals.

The Baptist denomination, as it is known today, emerged by way of the English Separatist movement. The best historical evidence confirms that origin, and no major scholar has arisen this half century to challenge it. That Baptists emerged from Separatism is clear; what is less clear is exactly why. Why did a few of the Separatists go on to believer's baptism, religious liberty, and separation of church and state, when most stopped short of

17. Sprunger, p. 80.

these concepts? And what is behind Separatism that it should give rise to such a major religious movement? A more detailed look at the actual rise of the English Baptists will help answer these questions.

The Rise of General Baptists

The General Baptists represent the older and more Arminian version of Baptist faith in England. They believed that man has freedom to believe in Christ; that whoever will believe may be saved; that none are predestined to damnation; that the saved may renounce their faith and thus lose their salvation; and that all the local churches make up only one church.

John Smyth

The rise of General Baptists centers around a remarkable man, John Smyth (c.1570-1612). One historian said Smyth "stands at the fountain-head of consecutive Baptist history"; another called him a "Baptist Path-finder."[18] A contemporary described Smyth as "one of the grandees of the separation" from the church of England.[19] A capable theologian and writer, Smyth's main claim to remembrance is that he founded the first identifiable Baptist church of modern times, in Holland, about 1609.

Apparently Smyth entered Christ's College, Cambridge University, in 1586 to prepare for the ministry. After graduation in 1590 he was invited to remain as a fellow at Christ's College and served for a time as a teacher there. He was ordained an Anglican priest by the Bishop of London in 1594. Smyth was greatly influenced by a teacher at Cambridge, Francis Johnson, who later led a Separatist congregation. One historian described Smyth during this early period as "a fair specimen of a moderate Puritan," still accepting set forms of prayer, vocal and instrumental music in the church, and some degree of government regulation of religion.[20] This era of moderate Puritanism was shortlived, for Smyth was soon in trouble for his sharp criticism of the state church. One record shows he was in the "Clink," a well-known English prison, for a time for his refusal to conform to the teachings and practices of the Church of England.[21]

Not a man to compromise, Smyth often used strong language in his criticisms. He considered many Anglican priests as "too papist" (i.e., too much like Catholicism); infant baptism he equated with spiritual adultery; and he was known to rebuke prominent sinners by name from the pulpit. One historian called Smyth "too downright and absolute," yet admitted

18. A. C. Underwood, *A History of the English Baptists,* p. 45; James E. Tull, *Shapers of Baptist Thought,* p. 9.
19. Joseph Ivimey, *A History of the English Baptists,* 1:117.
20. W. T. Whitley, ed., *The Works of John Smyth,* 1:xliii.
21. Neal, 1:108.

that he was "an engaging and forceful personality."[22] Probably many would have agreed with one of Smyth's contemporaries who called him "a learned man, and of good ability, but of an unsettled head."[23] Smyth was never to escape this charge of being changeable. He progressed through the stages of being an Anglican, Puritan, Separatist, Baptist, and, eventually, tried to join the Mennonites. Before his death, he developed a distinctly ecumenical outlook, seeking to avoid all denominational controversy. After his death, most of Smyth's immediate followers merged into the Mennonite Church. His defense against the charge of being changeable was that he always changed for the better.

From 1600 to 1602, Smyth served as "city lecturer" for the town of Lincoln, in which position he received a handsome salary plus "leave to keep three kine on the commons."[24] In this position, Smyth was excused from such pastoral functions as baptizing infants, a practice he had by then rejected. Smyth was dismissed from this position in 1602; he had publicly rebuked the sins of prominent leaders. We have no detailed knowledge of Smyth's activities between 1602 and 1606, but we know that he was moving toward Separatism. His two major writings during this time, *The Bright Morning Starre* (1603) and *A Paterne of True Prayer* (1605), continued his criticisms of the state church and called for greater scriptural purity. During this time, Smyth also became a practicing physician, but this required only a few weeks of specific study.

The Gainsborough Church

By 1606 Smyth lived in Gainsborough, in the Midlands. The parish church there had an absentee pastor who, in Smyth's opinion, did not tend the flock well. Sometimes when the church met and the pastor was absent Smyth would preach. When church authorities heard this, they forbade him to preach further. This was apparently the final straw; soon thereafter Smyth broke completely with the Church of England. He became associated with a group of Separatists who met in Gainsborough and was soon accepted as a minister among them. Other leaders in this group included John Robinson, William Brewster, and William Bradford, some of whom later came to attention among the "Pilgrim Fathers" who came to America on the *Mayflower*. Another leader was the well-to-do layman, Thomas Helwys.

Persecution was a constant threat for such Separatists, for King James I had threatened to "harrie them out of the land" unless they conformed to the state church. When the group became so large and visible as to be dangerous, they agreed to meet henceforth in two groups. The Robinson-Brewster-Bradford group separated from the Smyth-Helwys group, not

22. Burgess, pp. 12-13.
23. Neal, 1:243.
24. Whitley, 1:xli.

from any doctrinal disagreement but for convenience and greater safety. Both groups migrated to Holland as religious refugees about the same time, but there their paths diverged. The Smyth-Helwys group adopted believer's baptism and became Baptists; the other group in 1620 took passage on the *Mayflower* to "ye wilderness," as America was then called, and became the nucleus of the Congregational Church in New England. Before they left England, Smyth drew up a covenant, which Bradford paraphrased as follows:

> They shooke of this yoake of antichristian bondage, and as ye Lords free people, joyned them selves (by a covenant of the Lord) into a church estate, in ye fellowship of ye gospell, to walke in all his wayes, made known, or to be made known unto them, according to their best endeavours, whatsoever it should cost them, the Lord assisting them.[25]

When Smyth and Helwys led their little band to Amsterdam in 1607, they were not yet Baptists. Their motive for migration was to escape persecution. Apparently Helwys was a leader, for one record says that if Smyth "brought oares, Helwys brought sayles." Helwys came from a landed family and was educated at Gray's Inn, London. If Smyth was the more dynamic and creative, Helwys made his contribution in clarity of thought and stability of action.

At first the Smyth group formed simply one more church of English refugees, of whom Amsterdam had many. They took lodging and employment in the old East India Bakehouse, then owned by the Mennonite merchant Jan Munter, located near the Amstel in the present Rembrandt-splein section of the city. They earned a living baking a kind of "hardtack" biscuit to supply the numerous ships using the Amsterdam harbor. The Smyth group was, at first, in fellowship with the Ancient Church. However, Smyth soon developed significant disagreements with Johnson and published these in a book titled *The Differences of the Churches of the Separation* (1608). The main differences centered around the areas of worship liturgy, the role and duties of ministers, and means for financial support of the churches.[26]

Smyth insisted that true worship must come "from the hart," and thus "reading out of a booke" in time of worship "is no part of spirituall worship, but rather the invention of the man of synne." Smyth felt that spiritual worship would be compromised by use of any written helps; he would allow no "booke before the eye" in time of worship.[27] Prayer, singing of psalms, and preaching had to be entirely spontaneous. Perhaps Smyth was reacting against the Prayer Book of the Church of England, from which some

25. Ibid., p. lxii.
26. Ibid., p. 273.
27. Ibid.

ministers merely read the prayers. To Smyth, such prescribed forms robbed the Holy Spirit of His immediate leadership. Smyth went so far in this demand for complete spontaneity that he would not allow reading from the Bible during worship, since he regarded English translations of Scripture as something less than the direct word of God.

A second area of disagreement involved the ministry. While the Ancient Church, following the teachings of Calvin, acknowledged a "triformed Presbyterie," consisting of pastors, teachers, and rulers, Smyth preferred a "uniform" ministry, in which all ministers had essentially the same function. Deacons served as lay officers, thus providing a twofold church leadership.

Smyth also differed from Johnson on church finances, insisting that "in contributing to the Church Treasurie their ought to bee . . . a seperation from them that are without."[28] This was more than fussiness on Smyth's part. He regarded giving as a part of worship, and nonbelievers were no more qualified to participate than they would in prayer or the Lord's Supper.

Smyth was moving beyond the mere Separatism of the Ancient Church. The Johnson group rejected the Church of England, regarding its every spiritual act as a "nullity," yet they did not renew the baptism of those who left that church. Smyth later argued that Johnson and similar Separatists must logically either return to the Church of England or go forward to the new ground of restoring baptism.

Developing Baptist Views

When Smyth and Helwys and their little band left England in 1607, they formed their church on the basis of an Old Testament covenant, argued for some degree of government control of religion, and made no provision for believer's baptism. Within two years they had changed on all these points, and Smyth had founded a church based on the baptism of professed believers.

Smyth startled friend and foe alike when he decided in 1609 that baptism should be applied to believers only and that this voluntary confession/baptism should form the basis of the church. While much discussion, then and now, centered around his baptism, perhaps Smyth's most basic concern was not for baptism, but for a pure church. Such a church must include only true Christians; therefore, baptism must be applied only to professed believers.

Smyth persuaded his followers to disband and reconstitute their church on the basis of believer's baptism. One writer said, "They dissolved their Church . . . & Mr. Smyth being the Pastor thereof, gave over his office, as did also the Deacons, and devised to enter a new communion by renouncing

28. Ibid.

their former baptism, and taking upon them another."[29] John Robinson, who had been associated with Smyth in England, said that "M. Smyth, Mr. Heluisse, and the rest, having utterly dissolved and disclaimed their former church state and ministry, came together to erect a new church by baptism."[30]

However, this presented a problem, for none of them, in Smyth's view, had true baptism. He had discovered two fatal flaws in their earlier baptism: it was performed upon infants, and it was authorized by a false church, the Church of England. Instead of seeking baptism from some other group, such as the Mennonites, Smyth took the novel approach of baptizing himself. He then baptized Helwys and about forty others. Some have tried to dispute this se-baptism (self-baptism). Ivimey dismissed it as "this silly charge" and claimed it was "fabricated by his enemies."[31] Others deny Smyth's se-baptism more from theological than from historical grounds; they fear that, unless his baptism had proper "historical succession," it would not be valid.

However, we have the clear testimony of Smyth himself, plus contemporary evidence, that he did indeed perform baptism upon himself. This se-baptism was often discussed during Smyth's lifetime; apparently, no one thought to question or deny it until almost a century later. John Robinson, who was on the scene, said, "Mr. Smyth baptized first him self, and next Mr. Helwisse." The scholarly Henry Ainsworth, teacher of the Ancient Church with which Smyth had formerly been in fellowship, said simply, "Mr. Sm. anabaptized himself and anabaptized others."[32] Richard Clyfton, stern opponent of Smyth, wrote at length on Smyth's se-baptism. And Richard Bernard in his *Plain Evidences* complained of Smyth that "hee is Anabaptisticall, for rebaptization; and he is a Se-baptist, because hee did baptize himselfe."[33]

If this were not enough, we have Smyth's own admission that he baptized himself, along with a spirited defense of that action. He said, "Now for baptising a mans self ther is good warrant," thus individual Christians may in unusual circumstances "put baptisme vppon themselves," and "so each of them vnbaptized hath powre to assume baptisme for himself."[34] In *The Last Book of John Smyth,* the author was still defending his se-baptism. He wrote that Christians are under no obligation to seek baptism from neighboring churches, "but may being as yet vnbaptized baptize themselves (as

29. Henry Martyn Dexter, *The True Story of John Smyth,* p. 29.
30. Ibid.
31. Ivimey, 1:115.
32. Dexter, p. 31.
33. Ibid.
34. John Smyth, *The Character of the Beast of the False Constitution of the Church,* in Whitley, 2:660.

we did) and proceed to build churches of themselves."[35]

Why did not Smyth, becoming convinced of believer's baptism, request it from the Mennonites who then practiced it? Several people during his lifetime asked that question. Perhaps the language barrier prevented them from knowing much about the Mennonites at that early time. Smyth implied as much when he said, "Seeing ther was no church to whome wee could Joyne with a Good conscience to haue baptism from them, therfor wee might baptize our selues."[36] Apparently it was somewhat later that Smyth became acquainted enough with the Mennonites to recognize theirs as a true baptism.

The method of Smyth's baptism was almost certainly by affusion or pouring; immersion did not become customary among General Baptists for another generation. One observer reported "There was some straining of courtesy who should begin," with Smyth yielding to Helwys, but Helwys insisting that Smyth go first. There is little evidence that anyone, including Mennonites, practiced immersion this early. Ainsworth said Smyth "cast water on himself." Lubbert Gerrits, a Mennonite, said his group investigated Smyth's baptism as to its "foundation and form" and concluded, "We have not found that there was any difference at all, neither in the one nor the other thing, between them and us."[37] This confirms that Smyth's baptism was by affusion or pouring, since that was the form then used by the Gerrits group.

Break with Helwys

Very soon, probably within months, Smyth came to regret his se-baptism as hasty and disorderly. Perhaps he had come to regard the Mennonites as a true church from whom they might have had baptism in orderly succession. After discussion and exchange of confessions, Smyth once again changed his religious convictions and practices. He asked the church to repudiate their baptism, as he repudiated his se-baptism and membership.

Smyth had apparently come to believe that "the Church & Ministerie must come by succession," that is, that true baptism could only be had from someone who possessed it.[38] Most of the church followed Smyth along this new twist in the road. They unchurched themselves, reported that they "confess this their error, and repent of the same, viz.: that they undertook to baptize themselves contrary to the order laid down by Christ."[39]

However, a number of the church refused to go along with these changes.

---

35. John Smyth, *The Last Booke of John Smyth, Called the Retraction of His Errours, and the Confirmation of the Truth,* in Whitley, 2:757.

36. Ibid.

37. Dexter, p. 20.

38. Ibid., p. 36.

39. Ibid.

Satisfied with their baptism and reluctant to join the Mennonites, Helwys and a small band excluded Smyth and over twenty of his followers. They did so with regret and with many affirmations of love and respect. Yet they sensed clearly, as Smyth apparently did not, that despite similarities on baptism they had more fundamental differences with the Mennonites. Helwys urged the Mennonites to use caution concerning Smyth's application. Apparently they did, for Smyth was not received during his lifetime. After a time of severe illness from "consumption," Smyth died on August 20, 1612, ending his days without membership in any organized church. After his death, the remnant of his followers were received into Mennonite fellowship on January 21, 1615, and thus disappear from history as a separate group. Smyth recovered believer's baptism, but it was the Helwys group that continued the Baptist beginnings.

Helwys's Return to England

In 1611 Helwys led his small group back to England where they established their church in Spitalfield, a section of London. Historians consider this the first Baptist church on English soil. Helwys came to believe it wrong for Christians to flee their native land because of religious persecution; for if everyone did so, true religions could be utterly driven out. The fact that his wife Joan and their children were still in England, and apparently enduring some degree of religious persecution, may also have influenced his views.

We know something of the beliefs and practices of the Helwys group from the "Declaration of Faith of English People Remaining at Amsterdam" drawn up in 1611. This confession confirms that the Helwys group continued to adhere to the Baptist principles earlier announced and then abandoned by Smyth.[40] They applied baptism to believers only, although not yet by immersion. They had departed from the Calvinism of their earlier Separate experience, making room for free will and even falling from grace. They allowed each church to elect its own officers, including preaching elders, and both men and women deacons. Perhaps under the influence of Dutch Mennonites, they embraced a semiconnectional view of the church.

Soon after their return to England, Helwys published his famous work, *A Short Declaration of the Mistery of Iniquity* (1612). This polemical attack upon the Church of England, and its defense of religious liberty for all, soon got Helwys into trouble. He apparently attempted to present a copy to King James and, failing that, wrote the king a personal note on the flyleaf and sent the book to him. Perhaps the king was offended by the bluntness of Helwys's appeal for religious liberty; at any rate, Helwys was soon in Newgate Prison, where apparently he died in 1616.

Upon Helwys's imprisonment, leadership fell to John Murton (or Mor-

----

40. Lumpkin, pp. 116-123.

ton), a furrier by trade. A native of Gainsborough, Murton made the trek to Amsterdam with Smyth, became a Baptist there, and sided with Helwys in the split from Smyth. He also suffered for his faith, spending some years in prison where apparently he died in 1626. From prison he authored two significant treatises on religious liberty. His wife Jane later returned to Amsterdam and joined the Mennonites "without further baptism."[41] By 1624 we know of at least five General Baptist churches in England. Growth was rapid, and by 1650 at least forty-seven such churches were known.

The Rise of Particular Baptists

One often hears that early Baptists in England "divided" over the doctrine of atonement, but that is misleading. They did differ sharply on that doctrine, the General Baptists holding to a "general atonement," that Christ died for all; the Particular Baptists holding to a "particular atonement," that Christ died only for the elect. They also differed at other points, including ecclesiology, eternal security, and relation to government. However, these two groups did not "divide"; instead, they had quite different origins, at different times and places, and with different leaders. The Particular group, emerging about a generation later, represent not just more Baptists, but Baptists of a significantly different kind.

Both groups of English Baptists emerged out of reforming Separatism but there the similarity diminishes. Whereas the Separatism of Smyth and Helwys was rigid, the Particular group emerged from more moderate semi-Separatist congregations. Smyth required total separation from the Church of England, which he had come to regard as Antichrist. By contrast, the semi-Separatists who later became Particular Baptists accepted the Church of England as in some sense a true church, despite its many problems and imperfections. Their relation to the Church of England, and their reasons for adopting believer's baptism, look quite different from those of the General Baptists.[42] In time, however, the Particular Baptists assumed a more sectarian stance.

Importance of Particular Baptists

Historians have tended to give more space to John Smyth and the General Baptists than to Richard Blunt or William Kiffin and the origin of the Particular Baptists. Here Underwood is fairly typical.[43] In *A History of the English Baptists,* he gave twenty-eight pages to the early history of General Baptists and barely six pages to the Particular Baptists. This historical imbalance must be corrected. Though Particular Baptists started later and

41. William R. Estep, *The Anabaptist Story,* p. 219.

42. Glen H. Stassen, "Anabaptist Influence in the Origin of the Particular Baptists," *The Mennonite Quarterly Review,* p. 323n.

43. Underwood, chapters 2 and 3.

grew more slowly at first, modern Baptists draw more of their beliefs and practices from them.

Such a careful historian as Norman H. Maring has said that General Baptists

> always represented a small part of Baptist life in England, and an even smaller part in America. Their influence upon the main currents of Baptist life in either country appears to have been slight. Indeed, if one were to concede their connection with Anabaptists, this conclusion would have little bearing upon an understanding of the mainstream of Baptist life and thought.[44]

Glen Stassen also emphasized radical discontinuity between the General and Particular Baptist witness. He said that "although Baptists had their origin in England in 1611, they had a second and independent origin in 1638-41. And it is this second, independent origin which is our primary interest."[45] Stassen called for a radical reorientation of Baptist studies, to focus upon the Particular rather than the General Baptist heritage.

We must not, however, in correcting one imbalance create another. One can acknowledge that Particular Baptists deserve more study without conceding that the General group deserves less. Modern Baptists draw significantly from both groups. Many General Baptists faded into Unitarianism or vague nonconformity, but a remnant survived in the New Connection of 1770 and continued to make their witness felt. Continued relationship between the two traditions has brought exchange of ideas, so that even the Particular Baptist witness has been leavened by contact with General Baptist views. Further, in America the General Baptist input into such reforming groups as the Separate Baptists has been considerable. The later moderation of Baptist Calvinism, increased emphasis upon human freedom and responsibility, and a tendency at times to a denominational stance more sectarian than ecumenical all testify to the continuity of emphases of the General Baptists.

Henry Jacob

Though he never became a Baptist, Henry Jacob (1563-1624) figured largely in the origin of Particular Baptists. In his thorough study, Slayden A. Yarbrough called Jacob "a moderate Separatist."[46] He apparently grew up in Kent and later graduated from Oxford, taking the B.A. in 1586. While Smyth was developing his intense Puritanism at Cambridge, Jacob was pursuing a more moderate course at Oxford. He first came to public view in 1596 when, as an Anglican clergyman, he had "some speach with certen of the separation," probably Barrowists, "concerning their peremptory &

44. Norman H. Maring, "Notes from Religious Journals," *Foundations,* pp. 91-94.

45. Stassen, p. 323n.

46. Slayden A. Yarbrough, "Henry Jacob, A Moderate Separatist, and his Influence on Early English Congregationalism."

vtter separation from the Churches of England."[47] Already Jacob revealed his irenic spirit and his unwillingness to condemn the English church completely, as Browne, Barrow, and Johnson had done, and as Smyth would later do. Jacob's correspondence with Johnson was published in 1599 under title of *A Defense of the Chvrches and Ministery of Englande.* Johnson's answer in 1600 did not convert Jacob to Separatism, as intended, but may have made him more aware of problems in the Church of England.

In 1603 Jacob signed the "Millenary Petition," calling for reforms in the Church of England, reforms ultimately thwarted by King James I and Parliament. In 1605 Jacob continued his reforming theme, short of separation, in a treatise on *Reasons taken out of Gods Word and the best humane Testimonies proving a necessitie of reforming ovr Chvrches in England.*[48] Even these moderate views were sufficiently feared by church authorities to get Jacob committed to the Clink. He was released later upon his promise not to circulate his *Reasons* further.

Upon his release, Jacob followed the same path into exile in Holland that earlier Separatists had taken. For some years he served as pastor of an independent church near Leyden. Champlin Burrage added the detail that this church was made up mostly of English merchant adventurers.[49] Though in the midst of rigid Separatism in Holland, Jacob "stuck to his non-Separatism, firmly contending that, contrary to Separatism, the Church of England was a true Church of Christ."[50] However, as Yarbrough pointed out, Jacob eventually had to distinguish between the true "churches of England," with which he was in fellowship, and the "false Church of England," from which he had to separate.[51]

Jacob's views are well expressed in *A third humble Supplication* (1605). Although not its primary author, Jacob helped shape and edit this document. While he did not totally reject the Church of England, he wanted freedom to form another kind of church and follow alternate forms of worship. Jacob and his group desired

> to Assemble togeather somwhere publickly to the Service & worship of God, to vse & enjoye peaceable among our selves alone the wholl exercyse of Gods worship and of Church government viz. by a Pastor, Elder & Deacons in our severall Assemblies without any tradicion of men whatsoeuer, according to the specification of Gods written word and no otherwise . . . And [we] shall also afterwards keepe brotherly communion with the rest of our English Churches as they are now established.[52]

47. Burrage, 1:282.
48. Ibid., 1:284.
49. Ibid., 1:290.
50. Cited in H. Shelton Smith, Robert T. Handy, and Lefferts A. Loetscher, ed., *American Christianity: An Historical Interpretation with Representative Documents,* 1:84.
51. Yarbrough, pp. 93-98.
52. Burrage, 1:286.

One might argue that while Jacob maintained nonseparatism, and professed to "keepe brotherly communion," his was, in effect, a practical separation. He desired an independent church, under the leadership of pastors, elders, and deacons instead of bishops.

Perhaps the bluntest expression of the "semi-Separatist" view was by Thomas Cartwright, who used the analogy of a human body. He said, "for if any man shuld haue both his hands & his armes cut off, his eyes put out &c. yet as long as the head standeth and other vitall parts, he is to be accompted a man, although a maymed man." So the Church of England may be "maymed," but still "it hath the due and right of the church of god."[53] In 1611, the same year the King James Bible first came out, Jacob issued a treatise called *A Declaration and Plainer Opening of certain points.* He said, "I acknowledge that in England are true Visible Churches and Ministers (though *accidentally* yet) such as I refuse not to communicate with. . . . they are . . . essentially true Churches of God and are so to be acknowledged by us, and in public not to be absolutely separated from."[54]

For contrast, one need only compare this with John Smyth's view about the same time, calling the Church of England utterly false, and "very an harlot" as the Church of Rome out of whose "loynes" she came. Smyth concluded that "although once in our ignorance we have acknowledged her a true Chu. yet now being better informed we revoke that our erroneous judgment & protest against her, aswel for her false constitution, as for her false ministry, worship, & government."[55]

The JLJ Church

In 1616 Jacob returned to England and, after conference with other reform-minded persons, Separatist and non-Separatist alike, he gathered a church in the Southwark section of London. This is often called the JLJ church for its first three pastors, Henry Jacob, John Lathrop, and Henry Jessey. This "mother church" was independent, but not in rigid or hostile separation from the Church of England. At the end of fasting and prayer,

> those who minded this present Union & so joyning togeather joyned both hands each with other Brother and stood in a Ringwise: their intent being declared, H. Jacob and each of the Rest made some confession or Profession of their Faith & Repentance, some ware longer some briefer, Then they Covenanted togeather to walk in all Gods Ways as he had revealed or should make known to them. . . . After this Hen Jacob was Chosen & Ordained Pastor to that Church, & many Saints were joyned to them.[56]

53. Sprunger, pp. 22-23.
54. Smith, Handy, and Loetscher, 1:84.
55. Smyth, *The Character of the Beast,* in Whitley, 2:565.
56. Smith, Handy, and Loetscher, 1:85.

Thus was formed the church which would later give rise to the first Particular Baptists. After several years as pastor, during which time "much trouble attended that State & People, within & without," Jacob removed to Virginia about 1622, where he ended his "Dayes" in 1624, probably near the present Jamestown.[57]

John Lathrop assumed the pastorate of the Southwark church in 1624. Lathrop, who had been a preacher in Kent, served about nine years "to their great Comfort," he being known as "a Man of tender heart and a humble and meek Spirit." Among numerous additions to the church during Lathrop's ministry were several members of more pronounced Separatist convictions. They were increasingly offended when Southwark members, following the teachings of Jacob and the original practices of the church, occasionally attended the parish church services. Church records show that several members in 1630 were "grieved against one that had his Child then Baptized in ye Common Assemblies, & desireing & urging a Renouncing of them."[58] One leader of this protest was a Mr. Dupper, who "would have them therein to Detest & Protest against ye Parish Churches." Most of the members were not willing, as Jacob had not been, to make this radical break, so Dupper withdrew in 1630 and with several others formed a new Separatist church.

Discussion continued, especially about the meaning of baptism as received in the Church of England. Whether the point of protest was that such baptism was applied to infants or that its source was the state church the records do not reveal, but probably both ideas surfaced. The imprisonment of several members in 1632 at the urging of church officials may have reinforced the views of those who regarded that as a false church. One interesting detail in the records reveals that the strict new church, led by Dupper, included the son and daughter-in-law of John Murton, an earlier leader of General Baptists.

Two factors led to further schism in the JLJ church in 1633. The church had become so large that common worship was inconvenient and dangerous, since such churches were then illegal in England. The second factor, and probably more important, was continuing unrest about acknowledging the Church of England and its ceremonies as valid in any way. On September 12, 1633, seventeen persons "desired dismission that they might become an Entire Church, & further ye Communion of those Churches in Order amongst themselves, wch at last was granted to them."[59] This group was led by Samuel Eaton and included Marke Luker, a Greek who was known to advocate immersion before 1640, and Richard Blunt, who journeyed to Holland in 1641 in an effort to recover immersion by succession.

---

57. Burrage, 1:319.
58. Ibid., 2:301.
59. Ibid., p. 299.

The most tantalizing statement in the old church minutes says that at their withdrawal in 1633, "Mr Eaton with Some others receiving a further Baptism."[60] One wishes for more detail. How many received a "further baptism," and why? Did they object to infant baptism or merely to baptism from the Church of England? By what mode was this further baptism performed? We do not know. We do know that by 1633 there was a church of Calvinist theology in London, at least some of whom had experienced rebaptism. Burrage did not hesitate to call this an "anabaptist" church, his usual name for Baptists.

Meantime, the Southwark congregation went without a pastor from Lathrop's leaving in 1634 until Henry Jessey was called in 1637. Jessey apparently sought to follow the tolerant principles of Jacob, but internal strife continued. In 1638 six more members left this church; they were said to be "of ye same Judgment wth Sam. Eaton" about baptism. Clearly they separated for the sake of baptism of believers. The records say these six joined with Mr. Spilsbury. Either Spilsbury had succeeded Eaton as pastor of the 1633 group, which is possible since Eaton was in prison, or Spilsbury headed an additional Separatist church which had adopted believer's baptism in 1638. At any rate, historians conclude on the basis of this evidence that definitely by 1638, and possibly by 1633, there was a Particular Baptist church formed in London. There is evidence of yet another such church formed in 1639, and by 1644 seven Particular Baptist churches in and near London issued a joint confession of faith.

The Recovery of Immersion

English Baptists recovered biblical baptism, as they understood it, by two stages. First, they concluded that baptism applies only to believers and not to infants. The General Baptists taught this as early as 1609, the Particular Baptists by 1638 and possibly earlier. In the second step, the Baptists restored the ancient mode of baptism by immersion, which they believed was taught in the New Testament and required by their theology of baptism. The Particular Baptists led the way in this, adopting immersion in 1640-1641. We have no definite proof that General Baptists regularly immersed before 1660, though they probably did so by mid-century.

We have shown earlier that while John Smyth recovered believer's baptism in 1609 he never immersed. Most of the Anabaptist groups baptized by affusion or sprinkling, though by 1619 a group of Collegiant Mennonites, called Waterlanders, adopted immersion. However, there is evidence that General Baptists were aware of immersion, and some apparently advocated its practice. An observer in 1611 in Amsterdam identified Leonard Busher,

60. Ibid.

a Dutchman, as "an Anabaptist of another sort," along with Smyth and Helwys.[61] Busher wrote a remarkable treatise on religious liberty, entitled *Religion's Peace,* published in London in 1614. In this treatise, Busher advocated baptism by immersion, almost thirty years before the Particular Baptists did so. Those who believe in Christ, Busher wrote, Christ "hath commanded to be baptized in water; that is, dipped for dead in the water."[62] *Religion's Peace* was revised and reprinted and for many years was known only in its 1646 edition. Many scholars doubted that the immersion reference was in the 1614 edition, but recent recovery of copies of the early edition prove that it was. However, the fact that one person advocated immersion is no proof that he or others actually put the idea into practice or that they did so as a regular custom.

Henry Jacob as early as 1610 spoke of "dipping" as the biblical mode of baptism, but apparently made no effort to restore that practice in his church. By the mid-1630s the records show several examples of individuals who advocated and/or practiced immersion, including Marke Luker of the Eaton church.

However, despite these occasional individual actions, the real recovery of immersion for Baptists occurred in 1640-1641, among the Particular Baptists. The famous "Kiffin Manuscript," which gives church minutes from the Jacob church and its Baptist offshoots, contains this notice:

1640. 3d Mo: The Church became two by mutuall consent just half being with Mr P. Barebone, & ye other halfe with Mr H. Icssey Mr Richard Blunt wth him being convinced of Baptism yt also it ought to be by dipping ye Body into ye Water, resembling Burial & riseing again. 2 Col: 2.12. Rom: 6.4. had sober conferance about in ye Church, & then wth some of the forenamed who also ware so convinced: And after Prayer & conferance about their so enjoying it, none haveing then so so [sic] practiced in England to professed Believers, & hearing that some in ye Nether Lands had so practiced they agreed & sent over Mr Rich. Blunt (who understood Dutch) wth Letters of Comendation, who was kindly accepted there, & returned wth Letters from them Io: Batte a Teacher there, & from that Church to such as sent him.[63]

After the return of Blunt, the church minutes state:

They proceed on therein, viz, Those Persons yt ware persuaded Baptism should be by dipping ye Body had mett in two Companies, & did intend so to meet after this, all these agreed to proceed alike togeather. And then Manifesting (not by any formal Words a Covenant) wch word was scrupled by some of them, but by mutual desires & agreement each Testified.:

Those two Companyes did set apart one to Baptize the rest; So it was solemnly performed by them.

61. Ibid., 1:243-244.
62. Ibid., pp. 277-278.
63. Ibid., 2:302-303.

> Mr Blunt Baptized Mr Blacklock yt was a Teacher amongst them, & Mr
> Blunt being Baptized, he and Mr Blacklock Baptized ye rest of their friends
> that ware so minded, & many being added to them they increased much.[64]

This document, so important to early Baptist history, calls for comment.
The church's arguments for immersion were both biblical and theological.
They cited Scripture which they felt specified immersion and suggested that
their theology of baptism required immersion to symbolize a burial and
rising again. Their statement that nobody was then practicing immersion
in England confirms that General Baptists had not yet adopted that practice.

Apparently the JLJ church had divided again, part under the pastoral
care of Jessey and the rest under Praise God Barebone. It was apparently
the Jessey group that sent Blunt to Holland. Not everyone accepted the new
immersion, only those that "ware so minded," so Particular Baptist churches had mixed membership from the first. Some objected or "scrupled" at
the covenant since this was the traditional Old Testament basis of forming
a church, and they wanted to move on to a New Testament basis in believer's baptism.

The Mr. Batte (or Batten) mentioned in the record was a teacher among
the Waterlander Mennonites in Holland. The record does not actually say
that Blunt was immersed in Holland. It only says that he was kindly
received and returned "with Letters from them." Many have argued that
the Particular Baptists would hardly have accepted immersion from the
Arminian Anabaptists, who themselves had received it from quite suspect
sources. They argue that Blunt received instructions about the importance
of immersion and how to perform it. Others assume, probably correctly,
that Blunt was immersed in Holland and that this is the import of the phrase
"Mr Blunt being Baptized." Indeed Blunt performed the first immersion in
the English group upon his return, and he and Blacklock then immersed
about fifty-three others.

The historian Thomas Crosby took pains to show that Particular Baptists
obtained immersion independently of the General Baptists. "Those who
follow'd this scheme," he said in reference to the Blunt mission, "did not
derive their baptism from the aforesaid Mr. Smith, or his congregation at
Amsterdam." Not all the Particular Baptists approved the Blunt mission,
and Crosby said:

> But the greatest number of the English Baptists, and the more judicious,
> looked upon all this [Blunt's mission] as needless trouble, and what proceded
> from the old Popish Doctrine of right to administer sacraments by an uninter-
> rupted succession, which neither the Church of Rome, nor the church of
> England, much less the modern Dissenters, could prove to be with them. They

64. Ibid.

affirmed therefore, and practiced accordingly, that after a general corruption
of baptism, an unbaptized person might warrantably baptize, and so begin a
reformation.[65]

Among these "more judicious" was John Spilsbury, who considered
baptismal succession neither possible nor necessary. When by the authority
of the Bible alone believers could restore the church, gospel preaching, and
the Lord's Supper, he thought it inconsistent that "as for baptism, they
must have that successively from the Apostles, tho' it comes thro' the hands
of pope Joan."[66] Spilsbury succinctly concluded that "where there is a
beginning, some one must be first." He apparently began the practice of
immersion in his church without worrying about historic succession.

Particular Baptists thus recovered immersion in two different ways. One
group sought to restore immersion through historic succession, by means
of Blunt's mission to Holland. The other group, led by Spilsbury, simply
resumed immersion on the authority of Scripture. In 1644 seven Particular
Baptist churches issued a joint statement of their faith, the famous and
formative First London Confession, which specified that baptism should be
applied to believer's only and that "the way and manner of the dispensing
of this Ordinance the Scripture holds out to be dipping or plunging the
whole body under water: it being a signe, must answer the thing sig-
nified."[67]

This is the first Baptist confession which specifies immersion as essential
to the nature of baptism. The first General Baptist confession to specifically
require immersion was the Standard Confession of 1660. However, a General confession of 1651 states that "the way and manner of baptizing, both
before the death of Christ, and since his resurrection and ascension, was to
go into the water, and to be baptized."[68] This may refer to immersion.

The large number of publications for and against immersion in the late
1640s and 1650s confirms that the Baptist practice was new in England.
Some ridiculed immersion as "a third baptism," and almost all opponents
called it a "new invention." Praise God Barebone, who later became a
Baptist, said that "the way of new Baptizing" by dipping goes back no more
than "two or three yeeres."[69] Since Barebone made that statement in 1643,
this tends to confirm the Kiffin Manuscript which puts the Baptist adoption
of immersion in 1640-1641.

Opponents of the new practice, of whom there were many if pamphlets
against immersion be any guide, argued against it on several grounds.
Immersion was, its opponents said, unscriptural, unnecessary, unhealthy,

65. Thomas Crosby, *The History of the English Baptists,* 1:103.
66. Ibid., p. 104.
67. Lumpkin, p. 167.
68. Ibid., p. 182.
69. Dexter, p. 49.

and immodest. Stories were told of people who allegedly sickened and died soon after immersion. Baptists countered with at least as many stories of people who, though immersed in rivers where the ice had to be broken, yet suffered no ill effects.

The charge of immodesty during public immersions must be mentioned. Baptists were repeatedly accused of baptizing men and women together naked and of baptizing women in immodestly flimsy garments. The more lurid stories of such baptisms may be dismissed as malicious slanders. Other charges, as Henry M. Dexter demonstrated, cannot be so easily dismissed. The evidence suggests that indeed some few Baptists, in early times, probably did immerse nude converts. One "anabaptist" preacher, as Baptists were called, insisted in 1643 that true baptism called for "all to be thus rebaptized stark naked, & diped as well head as tayle."[70] Daniel Featley, no friend of Baptists, accused them of "going naked into rivers, there to be plunged and Dipt . . . they flock in great multitudes, men and women together, to their Jordans to be dipt."[71] Some accounts describe how women on the banks would surround newly baptized women "to save their modesty."

Some Baptists denied these reports. Henry Haggar said in 1653, "I believe I have baptized and been at the baptizing of many hundreds, if not thousands, and never saw any baptized naked in my life." Probably the best answer is the cautious conclusion of Richard Baxter who said, "In diverse places some baptized naked, and some did not."[72] If Baptists ever practiced such baptisms, it was quite early, among the more extreme groups, and not continued for long. Later literature shows that Baptists went to great lengths to preserve modesty and decorum in immersion, which helps account for the prominent role of women deacons, a part of whose function was to assist at the baptism of women. The Baptists felt it necessary to add an explanatory note to their 1644 confession, specifying that immersion should be performed "with convenient garments both upon the administrator and subject, with all modestie."[73]

The Baptist Name

The name *Baptist* was not at first applied to those people who are the subject of this book. Their opponents often called them "Anabaptists," but they preferred such names as "Brethren," the "Baptized Churches," and "Churches of the Baptized way." By the early 1640s, some opponents were calling them "Baptists." The group had begun to use the name of them-

70. Ibid., p. 56.
71. Ibid.
72. Ibid.
73. Lumpkin, p. 167.

selves by the mid-1650s, but not for a full century would *Baptist* be generally accepted.

Sources of Baptist Life

The previous sections traced some facts of Baptist origins, with emphasis upon the who, what, and when kinds of information. However, this approach leaves many questions unanswered. What were the dynamic forces behind the origin of Baptists? Why did a small group of people at that time and place reinstitute believer's baptism and soon thereafter perform that baptism by total immersion? Such radical changes require powerful stimuli. Did they really begin de novo? How, if at all, were the Baptists related to earlier religious dissenters in England and elsewhere? In short, what is the story behind the bare facts of Baptist beginnings? This section will address these questions and set out possible sources of early Baptist life.

Over the past centuries historians have advanced four different explanations to account for the origin of Baptists, or four different ways of looking at Baptist history. These views are given here not because they possess equal value but to help complete the picture of Baptist beginnings. These four views hold that Baptists originated from:

1. The outgrowth of English Separatism.
2. The influence of biblical Anabaptists.
3. The continuation of biblical teachings through the ages.
4. The succession of organized Baptist churches through the ages.

Most historians lump the last two views together under the name of "successionism," but they appear sufficiently distinct to be treated separately. Some variations and overlap mark these views, and some historians do not fit neatly into any one category. While almost all recognize that early Baptists were related to the Separatists, disagreement centers around what preceded the Separatists. These views are here presented generally in the order of their appearance in Baptist history.

The Outgrowth of English Separatism

The JLJ church provided the avenue of emergence for the first Particular Baptists. This shows the importance of Separatism for understanding Baptist origins.

Highlights of this view. Many scholars explain Baptist origins as the flowering of Separatism, or following Separatist teachings to their logical conclusions. They see no need for other explanations, such as Anabaptist influence, to account for Baptist theology and practice. These scholars tend to minimize Anabaptist presence and influence in England before 1600, and they are more impressed with Baptist/Anabaptist differences than similarities. They maintain that every distinctive Baptist belief and practice is inherent within Puritanism/Separatism.

Representative writers. Some of the scholars who hold this view include

William H. Whitsitt, Henry M. Dexter, William T. Whitley, Robert G. Torbet, Norman H. Maring, Winthrop S. Hudson, William G. McLoughlin, Barrington R. White, and Robert A. Baker.

The earliest Baptists recognized their Separatist background, but later historians obscured that heritage under layers of successionist theory. Apparently, W. H. Whitsitt recovered the story of Separatist origins for modern Baptists. With a series of articles in the 1880s, and especially with his provocative book, *A Question in Baptist History* in 1896, Whitsitt showed that Particular Baptists recovered immersion in 1641. Henry M. Dexter published his important study, *The True Story of John Smyth,* in 1881, and some (including Dexter) claim he preceded Whitsitt in expressing the Separatist origins view. W. T. Whitley was a major English Baptist historian early in the present century. Known for his many books, including *A History of the British Baptists* and *The Baptists of London,* he also edited early Baptist source materials, including *Minutes of the General Assembly of the General Baptist Churches in England,* and *The Works of John Smyth.*[74] In addition, Whitley produced a steady stream of scholarly articles on various aspects of Baptist history.

In his early career, Whitley seemed to accept the idea of Anabaptist influence. In 1909 he wrote, "The General Baptists are an English outgrowth of the Continental Anabaptists," and cited what he called "the constant interaction of the Dutch Anabaptists and the English, for at least half a century."[75] However, Whitley apparently changed his judgment on the basis of further investigation. By 1923 he had rejected any major Anabaptist influence upon Baptist beginnings. His *History of British Baptists* includes a section headed "Origin Independent of the Anabaptists" in which he affirmed that "Baptists are to be sharply distinguished from the Anabaptists of the Continent, . . . Baptists moved in quite a different circle of thought." He set out what he regarded as fundamental differences between the two groups, and concluded that "it is inexcusable to-day to confound the continental Anabaptists of the sixteenth century with the English Baptists of the seventeenth."[76] For the sources of Baptist life, Whitley maintained, one must look not to the Anabaptists but to the Scriptures available in English and the desire for reform among English Christians. Whitley's approach was largely followed by Robert G. Torbet, in *A History of the Baptists,* first published in 1950.

No one has more firmly rejected Anabaptist influence upon Baptist origins than Winthrop S. Hudson in his 1953 article, "Baptists Were Not

---

74. W. T. Whitley, *A History of British Baptists; The Baptist of London 1612-1628; The Works of John Smyth; Minutes of the General Assembly of the General Baptist Churches in England.*

75. Whitley, *Minutes,* 1:ix, xi.

76. Whitley, *A History of British Baptists,* pp. 17-18.

Anabaptists." This uncompromising article helped inaugurate the contemporary dialogue among scholars about Baptist origins. Hudson insisted:

> The single most confusing element in the attempt to understand the Baptist heritage and to clarify the theological convictions which led Baptists to adopt their distinctive witness has been the identification of the Baptists with the Continental Anabaptists. Actually the Baptists and the Anabaptists represent two diverse and quite dissimilar Christian traditions. The Baptists arose within English Congregationalism and represented an essentially Calvinistic or Puritan understanding of the Christian faith. The Anabaptists stemmed from the activity of a few university-trained humanists of the sixteenth century and represented the understanding of the Christian faith which was characteristic of the Northern Renaissance and which found its most eloquent spokesman in Erasmus. The confusion introduced by the identification of the Baptists with the Anabaptists has obscured the fact that the Baptists constituted the left-wing of the Puritan movement and this, in turn, has made it difficult to recover a reasoned apologetic for the Baptist position on a wide range of theological, ecclesiastical, and political issues.[77]

In this bluntly stated article, Hudson summarized his views in five points. First, early Baptists themselves repeatedly denied they were Anabaptists, regarding the term as "a name of reproach unjustly cast upon them." Second, Baptists firmly rejected the distinctive features of Anabaptist life, such as opposition to civil magistracy, holding public office, military service, oaths, going to court, soul sleep, Hofmanite Christology, and Anabaptist "confidence in the essential goodness of man and their consequent rejection of original sin." Third, practically all of the early Baptist leaders, General and Particular, had been Separatists before they adopted Baptist views. Fourth, Baptist views represent the logical conclusions of Separatism, and "Anabaptist influence is not necessary as a hypothesis to account for the adoption of believer's baptism by the Baptists." Fifth, when John Smyth moved toward the Anabaptists, he was repudiated by the Baptist remnant that soon returned to England under the influence of Helwys and Murton, and any Anabaptist influence upon Smyth did not carry over to the Baptists. Thus Hudson traced the Baptists to the English Separatists, and no doubt would have agreed with Robinson's pungent remark that Separatists and Anabaptists had nothing in common "except for walking the same streets of the city."[78]

In "Notes from Religious Journals," Norman H. Maring reviewed several articles which had appeared on the question of Baptist/Anabaptist relationships.[79] Maring tended to minimize Anabaptist influence, saying: "There can be little doubt of his [Smyth] being influenced by the Menno-

---

77. Winthrop S. Hudson, "Baptists Were Not Anabaptists," *The Chronicle,* pp. 171-179.
78. John Robinson, *An Answer to a Censorious Epistle* (1610), as cited in Sprunger, p. 78.
79. Maring, pp. 91-94.

nites after he adopted believer's baptism, but no one has ever demonstrated influence prior to that time, . . . it is only after Smyth ceased to be identified with Baptists that the period of Mennonite influence is demonstrable." Further, Maring said General Baptists constituted such a small part of Baptist life in both England and America that "if one were to concede their connection with Anabaptists, this conclusion would have little bearing upon an understanding of the mainstream of Baptist life and thought." He concluded, "The Particular Baptists, for all practical purposes, constituted the Baptist denomination in England and America, and their origin and development were clearly within the Congregationalist movement."[80]

In *Dutch Puritanism,* published in 1982, Keith L. Sprunger gave a major chapter to "The Amsterdam Separatists and Anabaptists." While the book does not concentrate on the origin of Baptists, it sheds much light on that subject. Citing obvious contacts between Smyth and the Mennonites, Sprunger yet traced the Separatist movement to non-Anabaptist sources. He described Smyth as one of "the main recruits to Anabaptism," but, in general, found English Baptist roots more in Separatism.[81] Many historians have argued that Anabaptism prepared the way for and often led to Separatism; however, Sprunger quoted John Paget and Robert Baillie to show the stream also ran the other way, that Separatism often led to Anabaptism.

Other histories that embrace the English Separatist view of Baptist origins include John H. Shakespeare, *Baptist and Congregational Pioneers* (1906); Champlin Burrage, *The Early English Dissenters in the Light of Recent Research* (1912); and William G. McLoughlin, *New England Dissent,* 1630-1833 (1971). These represent formidable scholarship; all of them acknowledged limited Anabaptist influence upon early General Baptists but placed Particular Baptists squarely within the English Separatist movement.

Anabaptist Influence

Another group of historians seeks to relate Baptist origins more closely to the influence of biblical Anabaptists. Most of them acknowledge that Baptists emerged through English Separatism, but they believe Anabaptism both on the Continent and in England prepared the way for Separatism.

Highlights of this view. The name *Anabaptist* was applied to a large but diverse group of earnest reformers during the Reformation era. Many designate them the "Radical" Reformation, as compared to the "Magisterial" Reformation of Luther and Calvin. Though difficult to categorize, apparently Anabaptists ranged all the way from extreme mystics (much like

---

80. Ibid., p. 94.
81. Sprunger, p. 89.

Quakers) to extreme rationalists. Those who accepted only the authority of the Bible are called biblical Anabaptists, or Anabaptists proper.

Most discussions of the relationship of Baptists and Anabaptists center on a rather narrow point of contact: *some* English Baptists (the General Baptists) may have been influenced by *some* of the Anabaptists (the Dutch Mennonites) at a *specific time* (the early seventeenth century).

The Dutch Mennonites shared several similarities with early General Baptists. They not only practiced believers' baptism but also held religious liberty, separation of the church and state, and Arminian views of salvation, predestination, and original sin. Like many General Baptists, the Mennonites objected to swearing oaths, preferred a threefold ministry, and held a peculiar Hofmanite Christology which said Christ did not take His human flesh from Mary. The Particular Baptists held a more orthodox doctrine of Christ, had no objection to oaths, practiced a twofold ministry, were not pacifists, and did not require communism.

Despite these similarities, significant differences existed. The Baptists generally did not share the Anabaptists' effort to withdraw from the world, their extreme pacifism, their communal sharing of earthly goods, or their semi-Pelagian optimism about human nature.

Some historians hold that Baptists originated largely in response to the Anabaptist movement. They maintain that Anabaptists influenced the early Baptists at two points: in preparing the way for Separatism and by leading some to go beyond Separatism to believers' baptism.

Representative writers. Scholars who hold some version of this view include among Baptists A. C. Underwood, E. A. Payne, James D. Mosteller, and William R. Estep; and among the Mennonites Irvin B. Horst and Harold S. Bender. Another scholar, Michael R. Watts, has advanced an amended version of this view.

In the standard text, *A History of the English Baptists,* A. C. Underwood addressed what he called "the vexed question of the relations between the English General Baptists and the continental Anabaptists." He linked Baptists to a long line of sectarian dissent and quoted with approval the remark of Rufus M. Jones that Anabaptism forms "the spiritual soil from which all nonconformist sects have sprung."[82] Underwood concluded, "It is impossible to believe that John Smyth's contact with the Mennonites did not inoculate him with some of their ideas."[83] Underwood thought that "the General Baptists represented the English version of the sober Mennonite form of the Anabaptist movement" and that both had affinities with earlier dissenting sects. He did not claim any Anabaptist input into the origin of Particular Baptists. Underwood seems unduly influenced by Thomas Lindsay, who in his history of the Reformation, said of Menno Simons, "from

82. See details in Underwood, pp. 51-52.
83. Ibid., p. 52.

his labours have come all the modern Baptist churches."[84]

Ernest A. Payne, a well-known English Baptist historian, responded to discussion on both sides of the Atlantic in his 1961 article on "Contacts Between Mennonites and Baptists."[85] Payne advocated a "close kinship" between the two groups, based upon historical contact and doctrinal similarity. He sought to document the presence and suffering of Anabaptists in England before 1600 and reviewed the familiar account of Smyth's dealings with Mennonites in Amsterdam. He felt the Elias Tookey correspondence in the late 1620s showed that General Baptists in England still felt themselves related to Dutch Mennonites, and he cited references from Amsterdam archives showing the Mennonites received General Baptist members without question. Payne concluded, "The two communities came out of the same background . . . Mennonites certainly influenced early Baptist developments." In another article Payne said: "That one strong current of air came from the Anabaptist movement of the previous century I am convinced. Nor need Baptists be ashamed of it."[86]

In a two-part article on "Baptists and Anabaptists," James D. Mosteller added to the discussion of what he called the "knotty problem" of possible relationship.[87] In direct response to Winthrop S. Hudson's statement that "Baptists were not Anabaptists," Mosteller sought to articulate a more moderate position. "The general thesis of this paper," he wrote, "is that Anabaptists and Baptists stand in the same ecclesiastical tradition and represent the same general type of Christianity. Secondly, the Anabaptists had a direct influence upon the General Baptists at the special point of contact, namely, the Dutch Mennonites and John Smyth."[88] Mosteller amplified both of these points, but especially sought to establish doctrinal similarities between Mennonites and General Baptists.

Another scholar who accepts some degree of Anabaptist influence upon the origin of Baptists is William R. Estep, a recognized authority in Anabaptist studies.[89] Estep's views on the origin of Baptists are found primarily in his two-part article on "Anabaptists and the Rise of English Baptists," and a 1980 unpublished manuscript "On the Origin of English Baptists."[90]

---

84. Thomas M. Lindsay, *A History of the Reformation* 2 vols. (Edinburgh: T. & T. Clark, 1907), 2:469.

85. Ernest A. Payne, "Contacts Between Mennonites and Baptists," *Foundations,* pp. 39-55.

86. Ernest A. Payne, "Who Were the Baptists?" *The Baptist Quarterly,* pp. 339 f.

87. Mosteller.

88. Ibid., pp. 3-4.

89. Some of Estep's works include: *The Anabaptist Story; Anabaptist Beginnings 1523-1533: A Source Book* (Nieukoop: B. DeGraaf, 1976) and numerous journal articles on Anabaptist studies. He also translated and edited *Balthasar Hubmaier: Anabaptist Theologian and Martyr* by Torsten Bergsten (Valley Forge: Judson Press, 1978).

90. Estep, "Anabaptists."

In these articles, Estep maintained the probability of Anabaptist influence upon the rise of English Separatism, the near certainty of Mennonite influence upon John Smyth and the General Baptists, and the possibility of indirect influence of Anabaptist concepts upon Particular Baptists. In the earlier article, he cited "possible Anabaptist contributions to the rise of English Separatism," and argued specifically for Anabaptist input into the teachings of Browne and Barrow.[91] Concerning early General Baptists, he said, "That Smyth arrived at this [Baptist] position and his church followed his leadership was due in all probability to Mennonite influence." Estep concluded, "I do not believe that one can adequately explain the rise of the English Baptists simply upon the basis of English Puritanism in general or Separatism in particular."[92]

One must also take into account the recent work by Michael R. Watts, *The Dissenters.* Concerning John Smyth, he wrote that Mennonite influence "was the decisive factor in his break with Calvinism." However, Watts took the discussion a step further by affirming that "the General Baptists . . . were the principal heirs of the Lollards," an older reform movement in England.[93] Thus Watts not only attempted to trace General Baptists back to Anabaptism but also, less convincingly, to ancient Lollardy.

A somewhat different version of the Anabaptist influence theory has been advanced by Calvin A. Pater in *Karlstadt as the Father of the Anabaptist Movement.* As the title suggests, Pater argued that Martin Luther's sometime companion, Karlstadt, provided the radical ideas which gave rise to the Anabaptist movement. No doubt scholars seeking the origins of Anabaptism will have to take his work into account. However, the book sheds less light on the origin of English Baptists. Pater fell into the familiar problem of using "Anabaptist" and "Baptist" as interchangeable names, identifying Conrad Grebel, Felix Manz, and Balthasar Hubmaier as "Baptists."[94]

Most of those who accept Anabaptist influence believe it was more pronounced on the General than on the Particular Baptists. In a curious turn, however, the *Mennonite Quarterly Review,* October 1962, carried two articles which took the opposite approach. In "Anabaptist Influence in the Origin of the Particular Baptists," Glen H. Stassen argued that the Baptist interpretation of baptism "is discontinuous not only from the Congregational doctrine of baptism, but from all the Congregational doctrines." He concluded that Particular Baptists adopted believer's baptism from the *Foundation Book* by Menno Simons, thus showing direct Anabaptist influ-

91. Ibid., p. 49.
92. William R. Estep, "On the Origin of English Baptists" (1980), p. 1.
93. Michael R. Watts, *The Dissenters,* pp. 46, 283.
94. Calvin A. Pater, *Karlstadt as the Father of the Anabaptist Movement* (Toronto: University of Toronto Press, 1984), pp. 117, 134, 139, 273.

ence. In the same issue, Lonnie D. Kliever, in "General Baptist Origins: The Question of Anabaptist Influence," argued that between Anabaptists and General Baptists "no historical continuity can be claimed. . . . No Theological indebtedness is admitted. And little significant doctrine [*sic*] kinship can be discovered." Kliever placed the origin of General Baptists entirely within English Separatism and finds "no significant Anabaptist influence."[95]

Those who accept Anabaptist influence point out that John Smyth went to Holland in 1607 a convinced Separatist, soon adopted Mennonite views, and later sought to join the Mennonites. The literature of both groups, they affirm, shows significant contact, and later General Baptist and Mennonite theology and practice are too similar for coincidence. While this influence was stronger upon the General Baptists, one cannot totally rule out Anabaptist influence upon the Particular Baptists. These various facets provide sufficient evidence, say these scholars, to demonstrate Anabaptist influence upon the origin of Baptists.

Continuation of Biblical Teachings

Some historians seek to go back beyond the Anabaptist movement to trace the continuity of Baptist forms of faith through the centuries. While not claiming an unbroken succession of organized Baptists churches all the way back to Christ, many historians in this group believe that Baptist-like faith and practice never completely died out.

Highlights of this view. Those who trace Baptists back to English Separatism, with or without Anabaptist influence, regard Baptists as a new religious movement in the early seventeenth century. Some earlier historians reject this concept, preferring to interpret the origin of Baptists as merely the latest expression of viewpoints which have continued across the centuries. These historians seek to trace a *continuity of Baptist teachings* from New Testament times to the present through earlier dissenting groups.

Representative writers. Some of the historians who have held some version of this view include Thomas Crosby, Joseph Ivimey, David Benedict, H. C. Vedder, Thomas Armitage, and A. H. Newman. In some ways Thomas Crosby ranks as the earliest Baptist historian. Crosby's four-volume *History of the English Baptists,* issued 1738-1740, is valuable for its inclusion of source documents not otherwise available. This son-in-law of Benjamin Keach had access to the most important early data about Baptists. However, modern historians fault Crosby for his confusing arrangement of material, his failure to distinguish between General and Particular Baptists, and his obvious garbling of some sources.

Crosby helped develop a new explanation of Baptist origins, namely the continuity of concepts. In a lengthy preface to his first volume, he sought

95. Stassen, pp. 291, 322.

to trace believer's baptism back to the first century. One careful scholar, W. Morgan Patterson, wrote:

> Crosby's view of succession may most accurately be designated a "spiritual succession." His work reveals no disposition to harness all dissenting sects into a Baptist genealogy. He made no real effort to prove that certain ancient groups were Baptists as is characteristic of later histories. . . . There was no attempt to trace organizations, actual Baptist churches, until he reached the seventeenth century.[96]

Crosby thereby popularized a new view of Baptist history—that Baptist principles not only root in the New Testament but also can be traced through various groups since then.

Over a period of years, 1812 to 1830, Joseph Ivimey issued his four-volume *History of the English Baptists.* Intended as a corrective to the blemishes of Crosby, Ivimey nevertheless perpetuated Crosby's views on the continuity of Baptist concepts. Ivimey's first volume is essentially an effort to trace believer's baptism through the centuries. In the preface to his second volume, he wrote:

> The English Baptists, from the period of the Reformation, have been a numerous class of Protestant Dissenters. In the first Volume of this history they have been considered the descendants of the Ancient British Christians, and also of the Widkliffites and Lollards: as the latter undoubtedly were of the Ancient Waldenses. No evidence having been produced since its publication to the contrary, I may be allowed to consider it as proved.[97]

In 1813 David Benedict published *A General History of the Baptist Denomination in America and Other Parts of the World,* a work important for its early, though ill-arranged, collection of information about Baptists in America. Somewhat like Crosby and Ivimey before him, Benedict sought to trace the continuity of Baptist principles through various groups back to New Testament times. He took Johann Mosheim's remark about the origins of Anabaptists being "hid in the remote depths of antiquity" to apply to Baptists.[98] Benedict also made some use of Robert Robinson's *Ecclesiastical Researches,* which started out to be a history of Baptists but ended up in 1792 as a rambling discourse on various European dissenters. However, Benedict and others might well have paid more attention to the warning of Robinson:

> Uninterrupted succession is a specious lure, a snare set by sophistry, into which all parties have fallen; and it hath happened to spiritual genealogists as it hath to others who have traced natural descents: both have wattled

96. Morgan W. Patterson, *Baptist Successionism,* p. 20.
97. Ivimey, 2:v.
98. David Benedict, *A General History of the Baptist Denomination in America and Other Parts of the World,* 1:128.

together twigs of any kind to fill up remote chasms. The doctrine is necessary only to such churches as regulate their faith and practice by tradition, and for their use it was first invented.[99]

Thomas Armitage introduced an important shift in Baptist historiography with *A History of the Baptists,* first published in 1887. The subtitle reveals the author's views: "Traced by Their Vital Principles and Practices, from the Time of Our Lord and Savior Jesus Christ to the Year 1886." However, Armitage broke new ground in that he saw clearly the pitfalls of successionism. He pronounced churchly succession as impossible to prove, unnecessary to establish church validity, and a diversion from the more important succession, namely, "Whether true lineage from the Apostolic Churches does not rest in present conformity to the apostolic pattern."[100] Criticizing earlier historians for their tendency to try to hook "stray and casual links" into a continuous lineage of Baptists, Armitage proposed nevertheless "to follow certain truths through the ages, . . . down to their present conservators of this time, the Baptists."[101]

Some version of this approach also marks the following works: Richard B. Cook, *The Story of Baptists in All Ages and Countries* (1884); A. H. Newman, *A History of Baptist Churches in the United States* (1894) and *A History of Antipaedobaptism* (1897); and H. C. Vedder, *A Short History of the Baptists* (1892). Though Vedder sought to trace Baptist principles through the centuries, he recognized that Baptist history reached "solid ground" only in the early seventeenth century.

Succession of Baptist Churches

A fourth way of looking at Baptist history arose in the nineteenth century. Denying that Baptists originated from English Separatism and disdaining a continuity of mere principles, the Organic Successionist school would settle for nothing less than tracing actual Baptist churches from the New Testament to the present.

Highlights of this view. By use of a "trail of blood" view of history, some affirmed that earlier dissenters were simply Baptists under other names. Thus such early groups as Donatists (fourth century), Cathari (eleventh century), Waldenses (twelfth century), and Anabaptists (sixteenth century) represent an unbroken continuity, or succession, of true biblical (Baptist) churches. This view is sometimes called the Jesus-Jordan-John, or JJJ theory, that Baptists originated with John the Baptist, Jesus, or baptisms in the Jordan. This theory assumes that John the Baptist represents a denominational affiliation and that Jesus formed a Baptist church and

99. Robert Robinson, *Ecclesiastical Researches,* p. 475, as cited in Patterson, p. 21.
100. Thomas Armitage, *A History of the Baptists: Traced by Their Vital Principles and Practices from the Time of Our Lord and Saviour Jesus Christ to the Year 1886,* p. 1.
101. Ibid., pp. 8, 11.

promised in Matthew 16:18 that Baptist churches would never vanish from the world. However, even among successionists, few have been willing to go so far as one historian, who traced Baptists back to Adam!

In studying successionism, Patterson showed that there are variations within this group.[102] Some hold that organic succession can be proven and that it is essential; others hold that succession is essential and does exist, but cannot be proven; others that it can be proven, but is not essential.

Representative writers. Some historians who have advocated some version of successionism include Adam Taylor, G. H. Orchard, D. B. Ray, J. M. Cramp, and J. M. Carroll. Though not primarily a historian, J. R. Graves also held and disseminated this view, especially among Southern Baptists.

Adam Taylor published his two-volume work, *The History of the English General Baptists,* in 1818. Taylor's table of contents lists "Book I. A Sketch of the History of the Baptists from the Commencement of the Christian Era to the Reformation." He affirmed that "in all ages of the church there have been Baptists."[103] Taylor identified John the Baptist as the founder of the denomination, which has continued ever since.

A more militant successionism was taught by G. H. Orchard, who published *A Concise History of Baptists in England in 1838.*[104] Orchard sought to prove that Jesus established a Baptist church, that Baptist churches (under various names) have continued throughout history, and that such successionism is essential to church validity. Orchard began with Matthew 11:12, and the phrase, "from the days of John the Baptist until now, . . . " captures his view of Baptist history.

Orchard's book had its greatest impact in the United States. J. R. Graves, a leader of the Landmark movement, republished Orchard in 1855 and distributed it throughout the South. Graves included an "Introductory Essay," affirming that "*all* Christian communities during the first three centuries were of the Baptist denomination," that despite use of various names these Baptist churches never disappeared, and that Baptists can use this information in debates with other denominations.

Perhaps the most vivid example of successionist history is the booklet by J. M. Carroll, *The Trail of Blood.*[105] Published posthumously in 1931, this booklet has gone through dozens of editions and is still being republished. This booklet is a popularization of Orchard's ideas, but includes a vivid chart which purports to show that "according to History . . . Baptists have an unbroken line of churches since Christ." Baptists are traced back

102. Patterson, pp. 10-12.
103. Adam Taylor, *The History of the English General Baptists,* 2:1-2.
104. Published in America in 1855 by J. R. Graves; republished in 1956 by the Ashland Avenue Baptist Church, Lexington, Kentucky.
105. J. M. Carroll, *The Trail of Blood.*

through the centuries by a series of connected red dots representing the blood of those who have suffered for the true faith, thus a "trail of blood." The "false churches" (i.e., all that are not Baptist), are traced by a line graph. This chart is set forth as "Illustrating the History of the Baptist Churches from the time of their founder, the Lord Jesus Christ, until the 20th century."

Other works which embrace church successionism include J. M. Cramp, *Baptist History: From the Foundation of the Christian Church to the Close of the Eighteenth Century;* D. B. Ray, *Baptist Succession: A Hand-Book of Baptist History* (1883); and John T. Christian, *A History of the Baptists* (1922). Though not widely known, these books are still sometimes quoted. No major historian today holds to the organic succession of Baptist churches. This view was based on inadequate sources, was more polemical than historical, and made large assumptions where evidence was lacking. This interpretation arose in a time of intense denominational competition and helped reassure some Baptists that theirs was the true church. It received wide dissemination in the South by becoming identified with Landmarkism. J. R. Graves insisted that Baptists "are descended from the Waldenses, whose historical line reaches far back and connects with the Donatists, and theirs to the Apostolic Churches."[106]

Baptist Origins in Perspective

This chapter has traced the main facts about Baptist origins and summarized different ways of interpreting those facts. There remains only to set the issue into some concluding historical perspective.

Earliest Baptist Views

Though the earliest Baptists did not attempt a full history of their movement, their writings reveal their view of origins. John Smyth repeatedly denied succession of organized churches or ministers and, at one point, declared, "There is no succession in the outward church, but that all succession is from heaven." In his last book, Smyth stuck to this conviction, saying, "I deny all succession except in the truth."[107]

Thomas Helwys also discounted the possibility or necessity of historic succession. He cautioned the Mennonites, to whom Smyth had applied for admission, about the weakness of successionist beliefs, saying, "For wch way shall you ever be able to prove, that he or they from whome you [by Succession] have your beginning were the first? No man can ever prove it . . . cast it away, seeing there is not warrant in God's word to warrant it

106. J. R. Graves, *The Trilemma; or Death by Three Horns*, pp. 79, 119, 121-122.
107. Smyth, *The Last Booke* in Whitley, *Works*, 2:758.

unto you, that he or they were the first."[108] Helwys rejected succession on the grounds that it was historically untenable and that the validity of biblical faith did not depend upon it.

John Spilsbury, a Particular Baptist pastor who signed the confession of 1644, also wrote against the idea of historical succession. In *A Treatise Concerning the Lawful Subjects of Baptism,* he stated, "There is no succession under the New Testament, but what is spiritually by faith and the Word of God." Spilsbury's interpretation of Matthew 16:18 does not require the continuity of Baptist churches. One careful observer has concluded, "Organic ministerial or baptismal succession is not a landmark of the Baptists of the 17th century."[109] However, the idea of some continuity of biblical truths, or even a succession of believers, is not entirely absent as one can see from the Second London Confession of 1689. Its twenty-sixth article says:

> The purest Churches under heaven are subject to mixture, and error; and som have so degenerated as to become no Churches of Christ, but Synagogues of Satan; nevertheless Christ always hath had, and ever shall have a Kingdome, in this world, to the end thereof, of such as believe in him, and make profession in his Name.[110]

Seventeenth-Century Origins

The most reliable historical evidence confirms that the Baptist denomination, as it is known today, originated in the early seventeenth century. This does not mean, however, that Baptist *viewpoints* did not exist before that time. Those who hold the Baptist faith believe their distinctive doctrines, such as salvation by grace through faith, a "gathered church," believer's baptism, authority of Scripture, and religious liberty, reflect the doctrines of New Testament Christianity. The seventeenth-century Baptists did not *invent* these doctrines; they *rediscovered* and articulated them afresh for a new era.

By preferring the English Separatist explanation of Baptist origins, one need not reject totally the insights of other positions. Enough evidence exists to confirm that many of the distinctive views mentioned above surfaced from time to time before the Reformation era. Probably no group held all these views, and one or two of these doctrines showed up among groups otherwise quite heretical from the perspective of orthodox Christianity. Opposition to infant baptism showed up occasionally throughout Christian history, both within Roman Catholicism and in some of the dissenting sects. However, present evidence does not establish any unbroken continuity of such ideas. A devout Christian may assume that "God has always had His

108. Patterson, p. 14.
109. Ibid., p. 18.
110. Lumpkin, pp. 285-286.

people" or that "Wherever people have the Bible in their language, they will follow a biblical faith"; but one should distinguish between faith assumptions and historical evidence.

One should emphasize that these interpretations are based on evidence *presently available.* Admittedly, large gaps exist in our knowledge of Christian history over twenty centuries. Research continues, and one does well to hold one's views with modesty. These remarks have been directed to the origin of *English* Baptists, from whom Baptists in Britain and America stem. The origin of European Baptists was apparently independent of English sources, and other factors may have been present.

Are Baptists Protestants?

One sometimes hears the question whether Baptists are to be identified as Protestants. Whether one takes the shortcut answer, or goes into lengthy explanation, the answer is the same: Yes. Such important Reformation doctrines as justification by faith, the authority of Scripture, and the priesthood of believers show up prominently in Baptist theology. Further, the evidence shows that Baptists originated out of English Separatism, certainly a part of the Protestant Reformation. Even if one assumes Anabaptist influence, the Anabaptists themselves were a Reformation people. The tendency to deny that Baptists are Protestants grows out of a faulty view of history, namely that Baptist churches have existed in every century and thus antedate the Reformation.

Baptist Churches and Denomination

For convenience the early baptizing churches have been referred to as "Baptist," but that could be misleading. Not only did the name come later but also most such churches remained for a time in an extremely fluid condition, still feeling their way, so to speak. Some of those churches eventually made their way into the emerging Baptist structures, like associations and ministers' conferences, while others did not. The Baptist *denomination,* in the modern sense of that word, emerged gradually over a long period of time.

Role of the Bible

Of the different explanations of the origin of Baptists, perhaps none takes seriously enough the role of the Bible. England in the sixteenth and seventeenth centuries cannot be understood apart from the impact of the English Bible. No doubt J. H. Shakespeare was right that "the great discovery, therefore, of the age was not the New World, but a book."[111] John Wycliffe, the "morning star of the Reformation," put the Bible into English by 1382; John Tyndale issued his New Testament in 1525; Miles Coverdale put out

111. Shakespeare, p. 2.

his translation in 1535; the "Great English Bible" came out in 1539; numerous English editions of Scripture circulated during the time of Henry VIII and afterward. The famous King James Version first appeared in 1611, in the midst of Baptist beginnings.

Even the briefest glance at early Baptist writings confirms that they sought to draw their teachings directly from Scripture. Other movements may have provided a framework for their understanding, but Baptists never consciously sought to pattern their teachings from these sources. Instead, they consciously and conscientiously sought to draw every teaching and practice from Scripture. Perhaps Shakespeare is too partisan, but he made his point when he wrote that one could wipe out all the religious groups of the seventeenth century, leave an open Bible, and "there would be Baptists" tomorrow.[112]

Summary

This chapter has traced the origin of Baptists and set them in the context of their times. Having looked at how they emerged, we must now ask what kind of people the early Baptists were. The next chapter will show how Baptists defined their faith and practice.

112. Ibid., p. 4.

2

Defining the Faith

Like the denomination itself, the Baptist faith emerged gradually in seventeenth-century England. The doctrinal framework for Baptists was not erected in a day; the Baptist faith was not born full-grown. The purpose of this chapter is to trace the emerging Baptist faith and interpret it in the setting of its time.

The basics of that seventeenth-century faith will be familiar to most Baptists today. However, one should not be surprised to find varieties of belief and/or emphasis between then and now; Baptists have never regarded their doctrinal formulations as having any degree of finality. They have believed, along with John Smyth, that God "hath yet more light to break forth from his word." General and Particular Baptists are not treated separately in this chapter. Instead, their doctrinal differences are noted where they seem important to the story.

Formative Influences

A number of influences helped Baptists shape and articulate their doctrinal positions. These included public disputations, published books and treatises, and especially a series of confessions of faith in the seventeenth century.

Public Disputations

Perhaps no group in England made more use of public disputations than did Baptists. Between 1641 and 1700 at least 109 such public debates involving Baptists were held in England, with 79 of these between 1641 and 1660.[1] These debates pitted one or more Baptist champions against opponents from Anglican, Quaker, Independent, or, sometimes, Roman Catholic groups. Baptists welcomed these occasions, for they gave opportunity for declaring the gospel to large crowds, helped defend Baptists against unjust slanders, and often led to numerous conversions and the planting of new Baptist churches. Many leading Baptists of that time were converted at public disputations, such as John Tombes, Henry Jessey, and Christopher

---

1. Arthur S. Langley, "Seventeenth Century Baptist Disputes," *Transactions of the Baptist Historical Society*, 1916-1917, 5:216-243.

Blackwood. All of these became popular disputation leaders themselves, along with other Baptists such as William Kiffin, Jeremiah Ives, and John Bunyan.

Subjects debated might include baptism, whether for infants or believers and whether by immersion or sprinkling; the authority of Scripture; the nature of the church; the nature and deity of Christ; the necessity of outward ordinances; the "inner light"; and the seventh-day sabbath. Sometimes Baptists also debated among themselves on the atonement, laying on of hands, singing as a part of public worship, predestination, open versus closed communion, falling from grace, and the extent of Christian obligation to obey earthly government.

The impact of these disputations was vast. Many Baptists became skilled debaters; they cultivated a direct approach, emphasizing Scripture and clear logic. While many of their scholarly opponents obscured their points in elaborate language and pedantic form, the Baptists (with some exceptions) preferred to speak in plain "people talk." This is not to say that Baptists did not have scholars; in fact, many of the Baptist disputants were university graduates, such as Tombes, Jessey, Blackwood, and others. Some Baptists developed, one might say, "specialties" in their debates. Thus Tombes was known for his effective arguments against infant baptism and for religious liberty; John Bunyan was known for his refutation of Quakers, against whom he conducted six public disputations.

Perhaps the most famous Baptist disputation was the one held on October 17, 1642, at Southwark. William Kiffin and three other Baptists disputed against Daniel Featley, a leading minister of the Church of England. Featley later published his side of the debate under the title, *The Dippers Dipt, or the Anabaptists Duck'd and Plung'd over Head and Eares.* This piece, which was dedicated to Parliament, went through at least six editions and was widely read. Featley complained:

> this sect, among others, hath so far presumed on the patience of the State, that it hath held weekly Conventicles, re-baptized hundreds of men and women together in the twylight in Rivulets, and some armes of the Thames, and elsewhere, dipping them over head and eares. It hath printed divers Pamphlets in defence of their Heresie, yea, and challenged some of our preachers to disputation.[2]

These debates reflected keen competition, though some were conducted with good spirit. Baptists greatly benefited by these, though they suffered a few setbacks. Both sides usually claimed victory, and both sides usually published their side of the debate, thus exposing more people to Baptist views.

2. Joseph Ivimey, *A History of the English Baptists,* 1:165.

The Printed Word

Alarmed at the rapid growth of Baptists during the 1640s, opponents complained, somewhat indelicately, that every day in England "the presses sweat and groan" with new Baptist books and pamphlets; that every day, the presses "vomit forth new streams of filth" written by Baptists. While their metaphors were perhaps overly vivid, their facts were accurate. Hundreds of sermons, booklets, pamphlets, debates, and lengthy books and treatises proclaimed, advanced, defended, and explained the Baptist faith. In 1646 Thomas Edwards, a respected Presbyterian, observed, "There are more Books writ, Sermons preached, words spoken, besides plottings and actings for a Toleration, within these foure last years, . . . Every day now brings forth Books for a Toleration."[3]

During the early 1640s, the authorities made some effort to control illegal printing, but with little success. In 1643 one anonymous churchman chided the Parliament for allowing what he considered heretical tracts:

> I am not ignorant, what a numerous and almost infinite issue of bastard Books daily comes to light: Even the very streets of the most populous Metropolis or Mother-City, being spread with petty Pamphlets. . . . We are overcloyed with bookes, our eyes are pain'd with reading, and our hands with turning over leaves.[4]

A good number of these books complained of, perhaps a majority of them, were by Baptists. They dealt with many subjects and proved an effective way to spread Baptist views. These writings not only allowed Baptists to influence others but also helped shape beliefs and practices among Baptists themselves.

Confessions of Faith

Perhaps nothing did more to shape and share the Baptist faith in the seventeenth century than Baptists' many confessions of faith. Baptists have been from the first a confessional people, always ready to give an answer for the faith within them. Individuals, local churches, associations, and national assemblies have from time to time put out statements of their faith, ranging from very short summaries, scarcely a page, to lengthy and elaborate theological treatises.

Despite varieties of length, authorship, and content, all the early confessions were just that: *confessions.* Early Baptists never elevated their confessions to the status of *creeds.* Twentieth-century usage makes less difference between confessions and creeds, but the differences were both real and important to early Baptists. A confession *affirms* what a group of Baptists,

---

3. Thomas Edwards, *Gangraena: or a Catalogue of Many of the Errours, Heresies and Pernicious Practices of the Sectaries of this Time,* Epistle Dedicatory, p. 122.
4. *The Clergyes Bill of Compaint* (Oxford: Leonard Lichfield, 1643), p. 1.

large or small, believes at any given time and place; a creed *prescribes* what members must believe. Confessions include; creeds exclude. Early Baptists were careful to emphasize that confessions were merely human statements; that they might later be revised; and that in no wise could they ever approach the authority of Scripture. Several collections of these statements exist, the latest being William L. Lumpkin's useful book *Baptist Confessions of Faith.*[5] Much of the material here is drawn from Lumpkin.

General Baptist confessions. General Baptists issued the earliest Baptist confessions because they emerged first. Some of the General Baptists' leading confessions include: A Short Confession in Twenty Articles, 1609, by John Smyth; A Short Confession of Faith, 1610, by the Helwys group; A Declaration of Faith of English People Remaining at Amsterdam, 1611, by Helwys; Propositions and Conclusions, 1612-1614, by the Smyth group that later merged with Mennonites; The Faith and Practice of Thirty Congregations, 1651, the first General Baptist confession by a number of churches; the Standard Confession, 1660, issued partly to defend Baptists against charges of treason; and the Orthodox Creed, 1678, perhaps the most complete of all the General Baptist confessions.

With varying detail and intensity, these documents proclaim such General Baptist emphases as general atonement; freedom to believe without regard to predestination; the tendency to equate predestination with foreknowledge; warnings about falling from grace; baptism of believers only; pacifism; complete religious liberty; separation of church and state; and, with some exceptions, acceptance of government officers in the church without being required to resign their offices.

Particular Baptist confessions. Particular Baptists issued fewer confessions, but these confessions were usually more complete. The major confessions of Particular Baptists include: The London Confession, 1644; the Midland Confession, 1655, by an association in the West of England; the Somerset Confession, 1656, by the association of the same name; and the Second London Confession, 1677, revised and reissued in 1689.

These confessions reflect Calvinistic emphases, such as atonement limited to the elect; perseverance of the saints; and predestination of both elect and damned to their respective fates. They also reflect much in common with General Baptists, such as believer's baptism, the authority of Scripture, and religious liberty.

In 1691 Thomas Collier, called the Baptist "Apostle to the West," issued A Short Confession or a Brief Narrative of Faith whose teachings were, strictly speaking, neither General nor Particular. Collier had been a Particular Baptist, serving for years as an effective evangelist and church planter in the west of England. In later years he sought to moderate his theology to accommodate both types of Baptists. This confession also marks

---

5. William L. Lumpkin, ed., *Baptist Confessions of Faith.*

what one historian called "the remarkable current away from Calvinism" by Collier and his western churches.[6] It was apparently intended as a response to the General Assembly reaffirmation of the Second London Confession in 1689.

The Collier confession advances such General emphases as salvation for all who believe; the freedom of any to believe; believers may apostatize and so lose their salvation. It also includes such Particular emphases as the inevitability of God's decrees coming to pass; man's will is damaged by the fall; and only God can give a person the will to believe. This document also has an early Baptist statement about infants, saying, "We believe, that God hath not decreed the reprobation of any infant, dying before the commission of actual sin."[7]

Uses of confessions. How were these confessions used, and what functions did they serve? Their aim was obviously twofold: to those without, they explained, defended, and clarified the Baptist faith. To those within the Baptist fold, the confessions educated, unified, and confirmed the faithful. Any list of functions the confessions served should include the following:

1. *To clarify the Baptist faith.* Baptists were constantly accused of absurd beliefs and gross practices. Through confessions, Baptists addressed the larger world to defend their faith. Patiently refuting false charges, Baptists often used confessions not to proclaim "Baptist distinctives" but instead to show how similar Baptists were to other orthodox Christians. To show this similarity was, they said, the "Maine wheele that set us awork" in the London Confession of 1644.

2. *To inform and educate their own members.* Baptists often used confessions for instruction in the faith. Ministers and churches used the confessions to indoctrinate the lay people in the Baptist way. Thus the confessions not only *expressed* the Baptist faith but also helped *formulate* it.

3. *To provide a basis for fellowship.* Associations and later the general assemblies used their confessions as "constituting documents," providing the basis for affiliation and fellowship among churches and messengers. Local churches studied the confessions to decide if they desired to affiliate with associations; churches or individuals who deviated from the faith were often dealt with according to the confessions.

4. *To deal with controversy.* When controversy erupted in Baptist life, as it often did, Baptists usually turned to their confessions for guidance. They appealed to confessions to establish what constituted heresy, and sometimes used these standards as the basis for discipline of members, ministers, or churches. However, Baptists were careful to avoid giving the confessions too much power. In fact, efforts to use the confessions to discipline and even

6. Ibid., p. 334.
7. Ibid., p. 339.

exclude some churches probably accounts for the decline of confessions in later English Baptist life.

Relevance of confessions. Most of the early confessions are buttressed by Scripture references. If these references are often out of context, and many do not apply to the subjects addressed, nevertheless they show Baptist loyalty to the Bible. Most of these confessions are *timely,* in that they addressed issues of intense concern at that time, but which may be of less interest today. For contemporary Baptists, the issue of hymn singing has been settled; whether to lay hands on new converts is no longer an issue. Times and emphases change and doubtless will continue to do so. Many issues of urgent concern to Baptists today were not included in the early confessions, probably not even thought of by early Baptists. Even so, to a remarkable extent, the basics of the Baptist faith as proclaimed in the confessions have transcended the centuries and endure today.

Doctrinal Beliefs

Earlier discussion spotlighted the *containers* of faith (i.e., proclamations, publications, and confessions). We now proceed to the *contents* of that faith in a discussion of beliefs on specific subjects. Baptists' beliefs were explained under many headings; some of the confessions had over a hundred separate articles. If this effort to summarize their beliefs under ten headings has any defense, it is first, brevity; and second, that these ten categories actually include much that Baptist sermons and confessions spelled out under dozens of headings.

The Holy Trinity

Early Baptist confessions usually began with belief in God, who has revealed Himself to mankind as Father, Son, and Holy Spirit. That Baptist statements about God are often shorter than, say, their statements about laying on of hands, does not mean they downgraded God. Since most orthodox Christians, including Roman Catholics and the various Protestant groups, largely agreed about the nature of God, there was less occasion to spell out Baptist belief in great detail.

Baptists accepted the personality and deity of the Holy Spirit and defined His work from a biblical perspective in such areas as inspiration, comfort, and illumination of Scripture. The work of the Holy Spirit entered more into their debates with the Quakers than with more traditional Christians.

As to the nature of Jesus Christ, Baptists reflected some diversity in the seventeenth century. Judged by orthodox standards, many of the General Baptists had a rather weak Christology. Some scholars think they inherited from early Anabaptist contacts a tendency to Hofmanite Christology. Taking its name from Melchoir Hofman, this view says Jesus did not take his physical flesh from Mary His mother. According to this view, Jesus came *through* the body of Mary without partaking of her physical human nature.

This doctrine, while intended to safeguard the deity of Christ, resulted in undermining His full humanity. Clear trends surfaced in the seventeenth century showing many General Baptists moving toward a Unitarian understanding of Christ. Beginning with questions about His humanity, they ended up by doubting His deity. Although Particular Baptists had theological problems aplenty, doubts about the full humanity/full deity of Christ were not among them.

Scripture

Both groups of English Baptists agreed on the truth and final authority of Scripture. Their confessions, preaching, and public disputations all appealed to Scripture to confirm their teachings. "What does the Bible say?" and "Is it taught in the Bible?" were questions English Baptists asked of every Christian belief and practice. From John Smyth onward they refused to accept any human authority, bishop, church, or decree unless it agreed with Scripture.

Most of the early confessions include separate articles on Scripture. The Helwys confession of 1611 states

> That the scriptures off the Old and New Testament are written for our instruction, 2. Tim. 3.16 & that wee ought to search them for they testifie off CHRIST, Io. 5.39. And therefore to bee vsed withall reverence, as conteyning the Holie Word off GOD, which onelie is our direction in al thinges whatsoever.[8]

In the late 1640s Thomas Lover issued *The True Gospel Faith Declared According to the Scriptures*. A group of General Baptist churches reprinted that statement in 1654, using it as a defense against growing Quaker influence in their midst. For religious authority the Quakers depended primarily upon the "inner light," deemphasizing the "outer word" of written Scripture. They often distinguished between the "history" (written Scripture) and the "mystery" (inner illumination), giving priority to the latter. Against this viewpoint, the Baptists declared that

> We therefore do desire that whosoever read it [the confession] may weigh the Scriptures produced; and if it be according to the Scriptures, there is light in it; for its the Scriptures of the Prophets and Apostles that we square our faith and practice by, accounting that light within (not witnessed by the Scriptures without) which some so much talk of to be deep darkness. . . . Let the Scripture therefore be the rule of thy faith and practice.[9]

The two major Baptist confessions of the seventeenth century, the Orthodox Creed (General Baptists, 1678) and the Second London Confession (Particular Baptists, 1677, 1689), contain lengthy statements about the

---

8. Ibid., p. 122.
9. Ibid., p. 191.

authority of Scripture. Both are to some extent modeled after the Westminster Confession of English Presbyterians, first issued in 1647. The Orthodox Creed is unusual among Baptist confessions in that it includes the Apostles', the Nicene, and the Athanasian Creeds from the early church. However, the confession makes it clear that Scripture forms the final authority for religious belief and practice. The Orthodox Creed's article on the Bible says in part:

> The authority of holy scripture dependeth not upon the authority of any man, but only upon the authority of God, who hath delivered and revealed his mind therein unto us, and containeth all things necessary for salvation; so that whatsoever is not read therein, nor may be proved thereby, is not to be required of any man, . . . And no decrees of popes, or councils, or writings of any person whatsoever, are of equal authority with the sacred scriptures.[10]

The Second London Confession makes an even more complete statement about Baptist views of the Bible. It begins with an article on Scripture, thus fixing that order upon later Baptist confessions. It is the first Baptist confession to use the word "infallible" about the Bible. Its statement on Scripture is longer than many entire Baptist confessions of the time. The confession begins, "The Holy Scripture is the only sufficient, certain, and infallible rule of all saving Knowledge, Faith, and Obedience; . . . therefore it is to be received because it is the Word of God."[11]

Christians may receive the Bible with "full perswasion, and assurance of the infallible truth, and divine authority thereof." The proof of this divine authority comes "from the inward work of the Holy Spirit, bearing witness by and with the Word in our hearts." The confession also acknowledges that the same Spirit who inspired the writing of Scripture also illumines its present interpretation, that translations into the languages of the people are necessary, and that "the infallible rule of interpretation of Scripture is the Scripture itself." The confession also says:

> The Old Testament in Hebrew (which was the Native language of the people of God of old) and the New Testament in Greek (which at the time of the writing of it was most generally known to the nations being immediately inspired by God, and by his singular care and Providence kept pure in all Ages, are therefore authentical; so as in all controversies of Religion, the Church is finally to appeal unto them.[12]

This refers not to the original autographs of Scripture, which are not available, but to extant Hebrew and Greek manuscripts. However, because not all are able to read these ancient languages, the confession calls for translations into the languages of the people.

10. Ibid., p. 325.
11. Ibid., pp. 248, 250.
12. Ibid., p. 251.

Perhaps Thomas Collier gave the most extensive discussion of the nature of biblical authority among Baptists in the seventeenth century. Collier (d. 1691) was a pastor-evangelist among Baptists in the west of England. He was known for evangelistic fervor, effectiveness in founding new churches, organizational skills, and especially his efforts to moderate Calvinism toward a more evangelistic thrust. Collier also made one of the earliest efforts to bring General and Particular Baptists together. A prolific author, Collier published thirty-seven books and pamphlets.

In the major work, *A General Epistle to the Universal Church of the First-Born* (1652), Collier devoted a chapter to a discussion of the Bible.[13] He clearly accepted the truth and authority of Scripture. "Concerning the Scripture," he wrote, "I shall not question the truth of it."[14] However, he found little value in the various theories of the day about *how* the Scripture was inspired, the relative merits of translations and "Originalls," and whether the authority of Scripture required textual perfection. He called Scripture "a Declaration of God who is Truth: Not that I minde every letter or circumstance in it, but for the substance of it, as it declares purely the God of Truth, so its without question to me a word of Truth."[15]

Collier rejected the idea that English translations did not constitute Scripture; that only the "Originalls" were the true Word of God. "Many of those who are both Scholars, and, as they say, Teachers in England, affirm, that Englishmen never reade the Scripture, because they never reade it in the Original, that is, in Greek and Hebrew." Against such efforts to undercut the authority of English translations, Collier affirmed that the truth of God comes through the vernacular. Besides, he pointed out, "the greatest Scholars are as far from seeing the Original Copies of Scriptures, as any English Man."[16]

Acknowledging the probability of textual variations in the translations, Collier said, "Neither am I ignorant of the possibility, nay the probability of corruption in it, and in that the Greek and Hebrew too, commonly called the Original," yet these do not detract from scriptural authority. Collier said, "I can look upon the Scripture, and see . . . that it is Truth: not that it is any Article of my Faith to believe every word or circumstance there written; but what Truth God hath made known in me, that I must acknowledge."[17]

Collier's view of Scripture called for a balance between "Letter" and "Spirit," by which Collier meant that the same Holy Spirit who inspired the writing of Scripture must also guide its interpretation. Reacting against

13. Thomas Collier, *A General Epistle to the Universal Church of the First-Born.*
14. Ibid., p. 248.
15. Ibid., p. 249.
16. Ibid., p. 259.
17. Ibid., p. 250.

both the rationalists who depended entirely upon the letter of the text and the Quakers who depended entirely upon the "inner light" apart from the text, Collier called for balance. "And this is the reason," he wrote, that "men are so tost to and fro," because they attempt to understand the text of Scripture in their own understanding apart from the illumination of the Holy Spirit.[18]

Baptists accepted the sixty-six books of the Old and New Testaments, but rejected the Apocrypha. They insisted that every believer, including laymen, had the right to read and interpret the Bible for themselves. While they accepted Scripture as authoritative, in the seventeenth century Baptists developed no elaborate theories of *how* divine inspiration worked.

Atonement

On the crucial doctrine of the atonement, General and Particular Baptists reflect their sharpest differences. General Baptists believed that Christ died for every person and that all who believe in Jesus Christ can be saved. They also taught that a believer might "fall from grace." These views reflect somewhat the teachings of the Dutch theologian Jacob Arminius (1560-1609) and are thus called "Arminian."

General Baptist views reflect a rejection of Calvinism, which was the theological base of the Puritan-Separatist movement in England. Smyth rejected original sin in the Calvinist sense, insisting that God deals with people for their own sin and not for Adam's.[19] Smyth also rejected the Calvinist notion that God predestinates some for salvation and others for damnation. Smyth insisted that "as no man begetteth his child to the gallows, nor no potter maketh a pot to break it; so God doth not create or predestinate any man to destruction."[20] Thomas Helwys wrote:

> That God before the Foundation off the World hath Predestinated that all that beleeve in him shall-be saved, Ephes. 1.4, 12; Mark 16.16 and al that beleeve not shalbee damned. Mark 16..6 . . . and not that GOD hath Predestinated men to bee wicked, and so to bee damned, but that men being wicked shallbee damned, for GOD would have all men saved, and come to the knowledg off the truth.[21]

This in effect equates the foreknowledge of God with predestination, but leaves man free to choose his eternal destiny.

The General Baptists also taught the possibility of apostasy, cautioning that "men may fall away from the grace off GOD . . . And therefore let no man presume to thinke that because he hath, or had once grace, therefore he shall alwaies have grace: But let all men have assurance, that iff they

18. Ibid., p. 248.
19. Lumpkin, p. 127.
20. Ibid., p. 128.
21. Ibid., p. 118.

continew vnto the end, they shalbee saved."[22] They also believed that children dying in infancy were secure in the love of God.

The Particular Baptists, on the other hand, followed the teachings of John Calvin (1509-1564), and their views are called "Calvinistic." They believed that God before the creation of the world decided, or "predestined," the fate of every person who would ever live. Those chosen for salvation will be saved; those chosen for damnation will inevitably be damned. Both the saved and damned glorify God, one group by illustrating His grace, the other by showing His justice. God's decrees are final; a person cannot change his predetermined destiny. However, the elect are not saved automatically; they must believe in Christ. Thus the preaching of the gospel holds out hope for the elect; for the nonelect, it only foreshadows doom.

According to the Particular Baptists' view of atonement, only by the "efficacious call" of Christ can any person be saved. That call comes to the elect to draw them inevitably to Christ, but never comes to the nonelect, who cannot come to Christ whatever their own desires may be. This theology places all initiative for salvation with God and none with man.

The First London Confession affirms

> That God hath decreed in himselfe from everlasting touching all things, effectually to work and dispose them according to the counsell of his owne will. . . . And touching his creature man, God had in Christ before the foundation of the world, according to the good pleasure of his will, foreordained some men to eternall life through Jesus Christ, to the praise and glory of his grace, leaving the rest in their sinne, to their just condemnation, to the praise of his Justice.[23]

The Second London Confession added that when infants die only the elect among them could be saved. In clear detail the confession also affirmed that

> Those whom God hath predestinated unto life, he is pleased, in his appointed, and accepted time, effectually to call by his word, and Spirit, out of that state of sin, and death, in which they are by nature, to grace and salvation by Jesus Christ

> ....

> Others not elected, although they may be called by the Ministry of the word, and may have some common operations of the Spirit, yet not being effectually drawn by the Father, they neither will nor can truly come to Christ; and therefore cannot be saved.[24]

With salvation totally at God's initiative, no elect person can possibly lose his salvation. Salvation can neither be gained nor lost by any decision or

22. Ibid., pp. 117-118.
23. Ibid., p. 157.
24. Ibid., pp. 264-265.

action of man, according to the Particular Baptists. The Second London Confession said that once a person has been "given the precious faith of his Elect . . . [he] can neither totally nor finally fall from the state of grace; but shall certainly persevere therein to the end and be eternally saved."[25]

These General versus Particular views of the atonement had vast implications for preaching, evangelism, missions, and personal ethics. By the end of the century, some extreme Particular Baptists thought that preaching the gospel to the unsaved was at best a waste of time and at worst an insult to God.

The Church

Perhaps the origin of Baptists is best explained as a search for a pure church. They sought a church composed of "visible saints," that is, true believers, observing the gospel ordinances and obeying the commands of Christ. It was largely a search for a pure church that led the Puritans to dissent from the Church of England, and, in turn, led the Separatists to withdraw into their independent congregations. That search led Baptists to go a step beyond the Separatists by adopting believer's baptism.

According to Baptists, infants could not be members of the church, nor could they receive baptism. The church had to be a disciplined body, with members called strictly to account for their sins. Repentant members could be restored to church fellowship, but the unrepentant had to be excluded.

An early General Baptist confession says: "That the church off CHRIST is a compainy off faithful people . . . seperated from the world by the word & Spirit off GOD . . . being knit vnto the LORD, & one vnto another, by Baptisme . . . Vpon their owne confession of the faith."[26]

This confession also affirmed that every church, however small, had complete churchly prerogatives, but that all local congregations together formed but one church. They also cautioned that "the members off everie Church or Congregacion ought to knowe one another, that so they may performe all the duties off love one towards another both to soule and bodie. . . . And therefore a church ought not to consist off such a multitude as cannot have particular knowledge one off another."[27]

The Second London Confession goes into more detail about the church, as it does on most doctrines. Distinguishing between the "Catholic or universal Church," which consists of all the elect, and local congregations made up of "visible saints," the confession sets out the responsibilities of the latter for worship, witness, and observance of the gospel ordinances.

25. Ibid., pp. 272-273.
26. Ibid., p. 119.
27. Ibid., p. 121.

This confession acknowledges that "the purest Churches under heaven are subject to mixture and error."[28]

General and Particular Baptists agreed that the church is a company of baptized believers, that it must observe the gospel ordinances, preach the gospel, and discipline its members. However, they differed on how local churches should relate to one another. The General Baptists regarded local congregations as in some sense branches, or local units, of the larger church. They had no difficulty in speaking of the "General Baptist Church," which was composed of the local churches or congregations. Therefore, in their associations, General Baptists did not hesitate to engage in "churchly acts," such as baptism, Lord's Supper, or church discipline.

The Particular Baptists, on the other hand, regarded each local congregation as complete and independent within itself. They did not speak of the "Particular Baptist Church," but only of Particular Baptist churches. When their church messengers met together, as in associations or general assembly, they did not regard the resultant body as in any sense a "church," but only as a gathering of representatives from many churches.

The Ministry

Baptists accepted a twofold order of ministry, pastors and deacons, but General Baptists later added a third officer called a "messenger." The Baptist minister was called either "pastor" or "elder" and was expected to have a divine call before entering the ministry. The minister's duties involved preaching, teaching, administering the gospel ordinances, and leading out in worship, witness, and discipline in the church. Many of the earliest Baptists minsters were converted from the Church of England and thus had university educations, but most of the later ministers came from the laboring people and lacked classical training. Some of their opponents ridiculed them as "base, mechanical fellows who cannot turn over Arabique," thus leaving Baptists with a "mean ministry." This was mostly true, for Baptists preachers earned their livelihood as mechanics, tailors, soap boilers, brewers, tinkers, and cobblers. Baptists did in that generation what herdsmen and vinedressers did in the days of the Hebrew prophets and what fishermen and tax collectors did in the early church, namely, recovered the practice of lay preaching. To use a current term, most Baptist ministers of that time were "bivocational." While some churches acknowledged their duty to share material goods with the ministers, many of the pastors received little or no income from their church work.

The Helwys confession of 1611 says:

> That the Officers off everie Church or congregation are either Elders, who by their office do especially feed the flock concerning their soules, Act. 20.28, Pet. 5.2,3. or Deacons Men, and Women who by their office releave the

28. Ibid., p. 285.

necessities off the poore and impotent brethren concerning their bodies, Acts. 6.1-4.[29]

Propositions and Conclusions, a Baptist confession of 1612, makes essentially the same emphasis, by saying:

> That Christ hath set in His outward church two sorts of ministers: viz., some who are called pastors, teachers or elders, who administer in the word and sacraments, and others who are called Deacons, men and women: whose ministry is, to serve tables and wash the saints' feet.[30]

From these statements, we see that early Baptists distinguished between ministry of the word and ministry related to daily necessities. Both men and women served as deacons, especially among the General Baptists. Many churches would have only one man deacon and one woman deacon, but as the churches grew in membership they might have several. The deacons visited the sick, helped raise and distribute welfare to the needy, assisted in church disicplinc by admonishing the erring, and sometimes preached and exhorted. Women deacons did essentially the same kinds of ministry, in addition to assisting at the baptism of women. Most of the women deacons were widows over sixty years of age and at least some churches supplied their livelihood. Though most early Baptist confessions limited the preaching eldership to men, in fact some women preached, especially among the General Baptists. Even the women deacons were expected to speak out for their faith. At the ordination of four women deacons at the Bristol church in 1679, the church said, "It is theire duty alsoe to speake a word to their soules, as occasion requires, for support or consolation, to build them up in a spirituall lively faith in Jesus Christ; for, as some observe, there is not an office of Christ in his Church, but it is dipt in ye blood of our Lord Jesus."[31]

Most early Baptist ministers and deacons were ordained, but some were not. Many pastorates were for the lifetime of the pastor, as was true for John Spilsbury, William Knowles, William Kiffin, John Bunyan, Matthew Caffyn, and others. Pastorates of fifty-five or sixty years were not uncommon; there was little pastoral mobility. Deacons were "tyed by office" to the church that ordained them; if they moved to another church they were no longer deacons. To some extent the same was true of pastors, though they did evolve a way of limited mobility. A pastor who wanted to move to a new pastorate had to secure the approval of both churches. If the church where he was serving did not wish to release him, they simply refused to do so. Perhaps the most protracted example of such a case involved Thomas Hardcastle, a minister in Jessey's London church, who wanted to accept a

29. Ibid., pp. 121-122.
30. Ibid., p. 138.
31. Roger Hayden, ed., *The Records of a Church of Christ in Britsol 1640 to 1687,* p. 209.

call to the Bristol church. However, despite the earnest pleas of the Bristol church, and of Hardcastle himself, the Jessey church refused to release him. Though he moved to Bristol anyway, the London congregation continued to claim him.

The case of Richard Adams, assistant to William Kiffin at the Devonshire Square church in London, provides another example. At Kiffin's death, Adams succeeded as sole pastor; but due to increasing problems, he sought to relocate. He wrote to a friend, saying, "If you know a people that I may be suitable for, If they will send for me & beare my charges I will goe to them & stay one or 2 Lords dayes with them, and when wee come to have some understanding of each other wee shall better know how suitable I may be for them, & how agreeable they may be to me."[32] Adams apparently found a church which he considered acceptable but despaired of being able to move there "unless I can pceive that the Church [where he then served] will be content to pt [part] with me."[33]

This lifetime tenure and the difficulty of ministers moving to other pastorates, while lending a certain stability to Baptist work, also had its negative features. Many churches became unduly identified with the pastor, as "Kiffin's church," and some churches declined as the pastors became older and less energetic.

Some General Baptists developed a third category of ministry, the "messenger." This office grew out of the increasing associational life and the need for some minister to correlate the cooperative efforts of several churches. While the deacon and pastor were "tyed by office" to the local church and had no authority outside the local congregation where they served, the messenger was a sort of "minister at large" whose leadership extended to all the churches of a region or association. In some ways, the messenger functioned like a bishop. He had authority to arbitrate disputes, correct faulty theology, and to "set in order the things that are lacking" in local churches. However, the main work of the messenger was church extension. In today's Baptist language, he would probably be called a "home missionary," whose main task was to plant churches where none existed, strengthen weak churches, correlate the work of Baptist associations, and serve to some extent as a liason to bring churches and available pastors together.

We do not know when messengers were first introduced, but they appear well established by the late 1650s, when "Messengers, Elders, and Brethren of the Baptized Churches" was a common phrase. When Thomas Grantham, himself a General Baptist messenger, wrote his defense of the office in 1674, he claimed it was of divine origin but was careful to say that messengers were not successors of the apostles. Their main function, ac-

---

32. Richard Adams "Seeking a Change," *Transactions of the Baptist Historical Society,* 1912-1915, 3:163.
33. Ibid., p. 165.

cording to Grantham, was "to preach the Gospel where it is not known; to plant churches where there is none; to ordain Elders in churches remote, and to assist in dispensing the holy Mysteries."[34] Grantham taught that "as God hath given to His Church a fixed ministry of Bishops, Elders, Pastors, etc., to take care of particular churches, so He hath given her a travelling ministry, unfixed in respect of particular societies."[35] Like other ministers, messengers continued to earn their own livelihoods, but when they traveled in exercise of their ministry, their expenses were provided along with a stipend for the care of their families.

Observers have disagreed about the usefulness of this office. Proponents regarded it as a necessary pioneer ministry, a kind of apostolic mission to the unchurched. Opponents regarded the messenger as an unbiblical and unwarranted violation of Baptist church autonomy. Adam Taylor represented the latter by his remark, "Such an Inquisitor-general is totally incompatible with the independency of the churches."[36] The power of the office increased as General Baptists declined. By the late eighteenth century, the office had been discontinued, but its main features reappeared in the twentieth century under the name of "Superintendent."

Baptism

The baptism of believers by total immersion, and the consequent denial of infant baptism, proved the most controversial practice of English Baptists. This practice conferred their name and provided a vivid picture to distinguish them from others. Baptism was the subject of innumerable debates, treatises, and sermons and was included in all the Baptist confessions of faith. Baptists defended believer's baptism against Anglicans and Puritans, who wanted to baptize differently, and against Quakers, who did not want to baptize at all.

Just to name a few of the many treatises on the subject will illustrate Baptist emphasis on baptism of believers. Among these one finds: Samuel Fisher, *Baby Baptism mere Babism* (1653); Benjamin Keach, *The Child's Instructor* (1664); Hercules Collins, *Believer's Baptism from Heaven, and of Divine Institution; Infant Baptism from Earth and of Human Invention* (1691); Francis Cornwall, *The Vindication of the Royal Commission of King Jesus* (1643); John Tombes, *Two Treatises and an Appendix to them Concerning Infant Baptism* (1654); John Tombes, *A Plea for Anti-Paedobaptism* (1654); Christopher Blackwood, *The Storming of Antichrist, in His Two Last and Strongest Garrisons: of Compulsion of Conscience and Infants Baptisme* (1644), and *Apostolical Baptisme* (1646); Henry Danvers, *A Trea-*

34. Thomas Grantham, *The Successors of the Apostles,* p. 20, cited in A. C. Underwood, *A History of English Baptists* p. 120.

35. Ibid., pp. 16, 121.

36. Adam Taylor, *The History of the English General Baptists,* 1:415n.

tise on Baptism (1675); and John Spilsbury, *A Treatise Concerning the Lawful Subjects of Baptism* (1643). It is no wonder that this baptism discussion was called "the watery war."

Perhaps the most famous debate on baptism involving early English Baptists was that conducted in 1642 at Southwark between William Kiffin and Daniel Featley. As mentioned earlier, Featley published his side of the debate under the title of *The Dippers Dipt, or the Anabaptists Duck'd and Plung'd over Head and Eares.* In rather intemperate tones, Featley described Baptists as an illiterate and "sottish sect," who polluted the rivers with their baptism and were guilty of child abuse by witholding infants from the benefits of baptism. Featley also ridiculed Baptist ministers for their lack of formal education and their working at secular occupations.

The Baptists began their part of the debate by saying:

> Master Doctor, we come to dispute with you at this time, not for contention sake, but to receive satisfaction. We hold that the baptism of infants cannot be proved by the testimony of scripture, or by apostolical tradition. If therefore you can prove the same either way, we shall be willing to submit to you.[37]

Instead of offering the proof they requested, Featley attacked them as "Anabaptists, heretics, mechanics, and illiterate men; by whose habit he could judge they were not fit to dispute: besides, they could not dispute from authority, as they knew not the original, nor understood how to argue syllogistically in mood and figure." Featley continued in his lordly tone that, since Baptists had chosen to cast "balls of wildfire" into the bosom of the church, his duty was to "cast the water of Siloam upon it to extinguish it."[38]

However much water he cast about, Featley was not able to drown out Baptists' convictions. Two Baptists published rebuttals to Featley, Henry Denne's *Antichrist Unmasked* and Samuel Richardson's *Brief Considerations on Dr. Featley's Book* (both in 1644).

All the Baptist confessions deal with baptism. The Helwys confession of 1611 says, "That Baptisme or washing with Water, is the outward manifestacion off dieing vnto sinn, and walkeing in newness off life. Roman. 6.2,3,4. And therefore in no wise apperteyneth to infants."[39] In Propositions and Conclusions (1612), we read, "outward baptism of water, is to be administered only upon such penitent and faithful persons as are (aforesaid), and not upon innocent infants."[40] The First London Confession affirms, "Baptisme is an Ordinance of the New Testament, given by Christ, to be dis-

37. Ivimey, 1, p. 165.
38. Ibid., pp. 165-166.
39. Lumpkin, p. 120.
40. Ibid., p. 137.

pensed (a) onely upon persons professing faith, or that are Disciples," which clearly rules out infant baptism.[41]

Baptist arguments against infant baptism might be summarized as follows: The New Testament nowhere teaches that infants should be baptized or gives examples of infants being baptized; baptism is not related to circumcision, so the fact that infants were circumcised in the Old Testament in no wise proves that infants should be baptized; the New Testament does teach that believers are to be baptized, but since infants cannot yet believe they cannot be truly baptized; the nature of faith and baptism are such that they require a personal decision and commitment that infants are incapable of making.

Despite their general agreement, baptism practices varied among Baptists. If only one parent were a Baptist, that parent might agree to the baptism of an infant to pacify the non-Baptist parent. John Bunyan and William Dell are two examples of fathers who disapproved of infant baptism, yet had infants sprinkled for the sake of "pious and grieving wives."

Communion

Baptists regarded the Lord's Supper as a memorial supper to recall and reflect upon the death of Christ. Breaking bread was a major element in early Baptist services and was probably a part of each Sunday's worship. The major controversy among Baptists concerned not the meaning of the Lord's Supper but eligibility to participate. Some allowed "open communion," meaning that professed Christians could partake regardless of their baptism; others insisted upon "closed communion," meaning that only those who had received believer's baptism by immersion might join in the supper. This division was not along party lines; one finds both General and Particular Baptists on both sides of the discussion.

The First London Confession seems to have required closed communion. Certainly Benjamin Cox thought so; in his appendix to that document, he said, "We . . . doe not admit any to the use of the Supper, nor communicate with any in the use of this ordinance, but disciples baptised, lest we should have fellowship with them in their doeing contrary to order."[42] However, the Second London Confession, while much more detailed in its discussion of the theology of communion, does not mention closed communion but appears to gloss over the question of eligibility. This confirms a trend among English Baptists from early times away from closed and toward open communion. Unlike the question of infant baptism, the controversy over communion was not with outsiders but was primarily a Baptist in-house debate.

41. Ibid., p. 167.
42. Barrington R. White, "The Organization of the Particular Baptists, 1644-1660," *Journal of Ecclesiastical History*, p. 214n.

Perhaps the major seventeenth-century discussion of this issue was the celebrated literary debate between William Kiffin and John Bunyan. Kiffin (1616-1701), described by opponents as the "ringleader of the Anabaptists," was one of the earliest and most steadfast Particular Baptists. A wealthy merchant as well as a minister, Kiffin helped formulate and signed every major Baptist confession of his time. He stood firmly for closed communion and closed membership, believing the two to be inevitably linked. Bunyan (1628-1688), famous author of *The Pilgrim's Progress,* was baptized in Bedford, where he later served as pastor. Some have doubted he was a true Baptist. While Bunyan himself was baptized in the Baptist way and recommended that way for all who would accept it, he did not require it for membership in the Bedford church. Thus the church allowed open membership as well as open communion.

Bunyan published a confession of faith in 1672, including some points which alarmed Kiffin. Kiffin answered in 1673 with a work called *Serious Reflections.* Bunyan responded with *Differences in Judgment Concerning Water Baptism No Bar to Communion* (1673). Kiffin's final arguments were set forth in *A Sober Discourse of Right to Church Communion,* published in 1681.

Bunyan complained of "being assaulted for more than sixteen years, wherein the brethren of the baptized way, as they had their opportunity, have sought to break us in pieces" over baptism and communion.[43] The following statement reveals Bunyan's central ideas:

> Touching shadowish, or figurative ordinances; I believe that Christ hath ordained but two in his church, viz., Water baptism and the supper of the Lord: both of which are of excellent use to the church in this world; they being to us representations of the death and resurrection of Christ; and are as God shall make them, helps to our faith therein. But I count them not the fundamentals of our Christianity, nor the grounds or rule to communion with saints: servants they are, and our mystical ministers, . . . I therefore here declare my reverent esteem of them; yet dare not remove them as some do from the place and end, where by God they are set and appointed; nor ascribe unto them more than they were ordered to have in their first and primitive institution. It is possible to commit idolatry, even with God's own appointments.[44]

Bunyan taught that since a person could be saved, and thus be acceptable to God, without immersion or any kind of baptism, therefore, any true Christian must be welcome at the Lord's table. Otherwise, Bunyan said, Baptists would find themselves in the awkward position of rejecting those whom God accepted. He concluded, "All I say is, That the Church of Christ hath not warrant to keep out of their communion the Christian that is

43. Cited by Sydnor L. Stealey, ed., *A Baptist Treasury,* p. 79.
44. Ibid., p. 80.

discovered to be a visible saint by the word, the Christian that walketh according to his light with God."[45]

Kiffin feared Bunyan's views, not only for what he perceived as a weakening of communion but even more for the danger to strict concepts of church membership. He pointed out that in the New Testament communion comes after baptism and not before. He said: "Nor may the Lawes, Orders, and Prescriptions of Christ be altered, or varyed, in any tittle, upon any pretense whatsoever, God never having given any such Prerogative to mankind, as to be arbiters how he may be best and most decently worshipped." To Kiffin, a necessary connection existed between baptism and the Lord's Supper and to change the order would weaken both. To open communion to the unbaptized, Kiffin feared, would also open the door to "Popish Purgatory, and Monkery and ten thousand other things."[46]

To dispense with baptism, as Kiffin thought Bunyan's position would ultimately do, would be to lessen our esteem for Christ who commanded it and disregard the Bible which prescribes it. He bluntly concluded that communion belongs to the church, not to private individuals, and that only baptism is the door to the church. "None were Inchurched without water baptism," Kiffin said, and thus none could receive communion but the baptized.[47]

The short-term victory went to Kiffin, whose influence in his generation was unmatched. During Kiffin's lifetime and beyond, most Particular churches held to closed communion. Yet the long-term victory went to Bunyan, as open communion ultimately prevailed.

Relation to Government

How should Christians relate to the civil government under which they live? Baptists emerged in England at a time when civil government was hostile to them. This certainly affected Baptist attitudes. However, on this as other questions, Baptists tried to draw their answers directly from the Bible.

In the seventeenth century, General Baptists reflected more hostility toward civil government than did Particular Baptists. Many General Baptists refused to take oaths of political loyalty, to bear arms, or to allow government officials to hold membership in their churches. Some observers think the General Baptists absorbed such views from the Dutch Mennonites. The Particular Baptists, on the other hand, followed their Calvinistic heritage in giving high value to political loyalty and patriotic participation in civil affairs.

The General Baptists repeatedly affirmed their political loyalty to crown and country, but some refused to take the oaths customary in such affirma-

---

45. Ibid.
46. Ibid., pp. 82-83.
47. Ibid., p. 84.

tions. This cast suspicion upon them, for the civil officers recognized no other way of making a valid promise of political loyalty than by the oath. Many Baptists suffered severely, including fines and long imprisonments, for this conviction. They were convinced that, as an early confession put it, "Christ, the King and Lawgiver of the New Testament, hath prohibited Christians the swearing of oaths."[48] However, not all General Baptists shared this view. The Helwys group, by 1611, said, "That it is Lawful in a just cause for deciding of strife to take an oath by the Name off the Lord."[49] By the time of the Orthodox Creed, 1678, General Baptists not only allowed but even encouraged oaths under proper circumstances. They said:

> A lawful oath, is a part of religious worship, . . . when we are called before a lawful magistrate, upon a lawful matter, warranted by God's holy word; and an oath is to be taken in the plain and common sense of the words, . . . and such an oath, we believe all Christians, when lawfully called thereunto by the magistrate, may take.[50]

Many of the early General Baptists were pacifists. As early as 1610 they said, "The redeemed of the Lord, . . . do change their fleshly weapons, namely, their swords into shares, and their spears into scythes, do lift up no sword, neither hath no consent to fleshly battle."[51] However, as on the question of oaths, General Baptists tended to moderate their views. By the 1640s, many of them participated in the English civil wars.

Despite questions of oaths and pacifism, General Baptists affirmed basic loyalty to the crown. In 1610 they acknowledged, "Worldly authority or magistracy is a necessary ordinance of God," but would not allow magistrates to be church members. An early confession cautions:

> Neither hath he called his disciples or followers to be worldly kings, princes, potentates, or magistrates . . . so hold we that it beseemeth not Christians to administer these offices; therefore we avoid such offices and administrations, notwithstanding by no means thereby willing to despise or condemn reasonable discreet magistrates.[52]

A similar prohibition was voiced in 1612 by the Smyth group:

> That if the magistrate will follow Christ, and be His disciple, he must deny himself, take up his cross, and follow Christ; he must love his enemies and not kill them, he must pray for them and not punish them, he must feed them and give them drink, not imprison them, banish them, dismember them, and

48. Lumpkin, p. 112.
49. Ibid., p. 123.
50. Ibid., p. 333.
51. Ibid., p. 107.
52. Ibid., p. 112.

spoil their goods; . . . which things he cannot possibly do, and retain the revenge of the sword.[53]

However, other General Baptists would admit magistrates to membership provided they not attempt to exercise authority in the church. The Helwys group affirmed, in 1612, "Magistracie is a holie ordinance off GOD, . . . And therefore they may bee members off the Church off CHRIST, reteining their Magistracie, for no Holie Ordinance off GOD debarreth anie from being a member off CHRISTS Church."[54] Both the Second London and the Orthodox confessions affirmed loyalty to magistrates, that magistrates could be Christians and retain their offices, and that Christians could take legal oaths. The latter confession described the Christian's civil duties as follows:

> And the office of a magistrate, may be accepted of, and executed by christians, when lawfully called thereunto; . . . And subjection in the Lord ought to be yielded to the magistrates in all lawful things commanded by them.[55]

The Particular Baptists had less problems with oaths and were never pacifist. Following their Calvinism, they gave high priority to civil loyalty and many of their leaders were involved to some extent in government service. However, the Particular Baptists never wavered in their teaching that in the church the magistrate was simply another layman, under the spiritual authority of the church.

Religious Liberty

Early Baptists faced severe opposition for most of the seventeenth century from a hostile government and from religious opponents as well. Baptists developed and articulated a doctrine of complete religious liberty for themselves and for all others. Historians debate the source of these views; some assume that Baptists absorbed their views on religious liberty from the Anabaptists, while others trace Baptist views to Scripture and philosophy. The Baptists regarded their views as drawn directly from the Bible and the nature of Christian experience.

One of the earliest Baptists statements on religious liberty, and certainly one of the finest, was by John Smyth, who said:

> That the magistrate is not by virtue of his office to meddle with religion, or matters of conscience, to force or compel men to this or that form or religion, or doctrine: but to leave Christian religion free, to every man's conscience, and to handle only civil transgressions.[56]

While that statement was vastly expanded by later writings, it contains

53. Ibid., p. 140.
54. Ibid., p. 123.
55. Ibid., p. 331.
56. Ibid., 140.

the heart of the Baptist witness on religious liberty. While not using the modern terms, this statement provides religious liberty and separation of church and state.

Baptists scandalized some and frightened others by advocating liberty even for unpopular groups, such as Roman Catholics, Jews, Moslems, and even atheists. The Baptists denied that religious uniformity was essential to domestic tranquility. In perhaps the most inclusive liberty statement of the age, Helwys said, "Let them be heretickes, Turcks, Jewes, or whatsoever it apperteynes not the earthly power to punish them in the least measure" in spiritual matters.[57]

Baptists argued from Scripture, logic, and history to defend their views of religious liberty. What could be more logical, they said, than for a man to choose his own religion, seeing that he only must stand before God and give account of himself? History shows, they argued, that religious persecution has been harmful to church and civil society, while toleration has been good for both.[58] However, their major arguments were drawn from Scripture. They argued that the nature of the Christian experience is such that it cannot be compelled or coerced; to be authentic, religion must be voluntary.

The Future Hope

Baptists originated during a time when pervasive millennialism blanketed England and Europe. Many Christians of all denominations believed Christ would return soon, some said by 1660, to set up His millennial rule on earth. Of course Christians had for centuries expected the return of Christ, but events in England gave that expectation a radical new turn. A group arose who felt it was not enough to wait for Christ to bring in His kingdom; they had to take up the sword, put down earthly government by force, and thus prepare the way for the millennial kingdom. This group was called the Fifth Monarchy Movement. The name comes from the Book of Daniel, chapter 7, which describes four beasts, said to represent four major kingdoms of world history. In the seventeenth century, most interpreters identified these as the Assyrian (or Babylonian-Assyrian), Persian, Greek, and Roman empires. These earthly empires would all crumble, to be followed by an eternal kingdom. The central conviction of the Fifth Monarchy was that the time had come for the fourth monarchy, the last earthly empire, to give way to the fifth monarchy, the millennial reign of Christ. Most agreed that after initiating His kingdom, Christ would turn the actual government over to the saints. This "rule of the saints" would launch major reforms in religion, law, economics, and education. Different shades of opinion can be found among the Fifth Monarchists. Most, perhaps, were peaceful; they felt no

57. Thomas Helwys, *The Mistery of Iniquity* (London: 1612), p. 69.
58. Ibid.

call to take up the sword but were willing to wait for Christ to inaugurate His kingdom. Others agreed to take up the sword, but only at the clear call of Christ, not the call of man. The most radical urged armed revolution against earthly government. Within a few years, the latter group brought the movement into disrepute. The movement was perhaps inspired as much by crises in society as by teachings of Scripture.

The Fifth Monarchy and similar movements arose from several sources. The Protestant Reformation fueled new speculations about the end of the world; even Martin Luther came to believe he was living in the last days. The Thirty Years' War in Europe (1618-1648) and the Civil War in England (1642-1649) fanned expectations for the imminent end of all things. The beheading of King Charles I in England in 1649 released waves of pent-up millennialism that often took extremist forms. Many shared the convictions of Thomas Harrison who said, "The Worde of God doth take notice, that the powers of this world shall bee given into the hands of the Lord and his Saints."[59]

Fifth Monarchy preachers described a coming kingdom in utopian terms. Almost all the expected changes, one observes, would benefit the poor and humble. Laws would no longer exploit the poor, nor would people be hanged or imprisoned merely for debt. The universities, long the bastions of upper-class privilege, would be abolished or reformed so that common people could benefit from them. During the millennium there would be no unemployment; all would work, but labor would not be laborious. The rule of the saints, chosen by their churches, would enforce godly conduct upon all. Good health, long life, and economic plenty would prevail. Some described the millennium as a time that would be "always summer, always sunshine, always pleasant, green, fruitful, and beautiful," with plenty of "pretty robins" but no spiders. While the poor would then bask in plenty, the wealthy would lose their privileges. One Fifth Monarchist predicted that in the millennium those who had been rich would "sit bare-breeched upon Hawthorn-Bushes."[60] For a time the Fifth Monarchy worked through Oliver Cromwell and the " 'Saints' Parliament" to achieve their goals, but when the Parliament was dissolved in 1653 and Cromwell turned against their radical plots, they were forced to work outside the system. At this point, their rhetoric turned more violent. The saints proclaimed that theirs was "a smiting work" and affirmed that the sword was as much an implement of Christian ministry as the Bible. They prayed that "God would put an Axe into ye hand of some of his servants," to cut down earthly government, including that of Cromwell.[61] One Fifth Monarchist noted, "Itt is a scruple amonge the saints, how farre they should use the sworde,"

59. Louis Fargo Brown, *Baptists and the Fifth Monarchy Men in England,* pp. 14-15.
60. B. S. Capp, *The Fifth Monarchy Men,* pp. 142, 156.
61. Ibid., p. 208.

but those scruples were soon settled. At the 1656 rally of Baptists and Fifth Monarchists at Abingdon, the majority proclaimed that, at least for the time, "God's people must be a bloody people."[62] When their radical rhetoric produced nothing but uneasiness, the Fifth Monarchists determined "to trye for it with the sword." However, mostly they practiced verbal violence; their actual armed outbreaks were few and small.

The restoration of Charles II to the English throne in 1660 dealt a body blow to millennial hopes in England. The return of stable earthly government could only mean the divine kingdom was delayed. Distressed by this turn of events, Thomas Venner and about fifty armed followers marched to St. Paul's on a Sunday evening in January 1661, shouting millennial slogans. Venner, described as "a crack-brained enthusiast," provoked armed conflict which continued off and on in the streets of London for four days. Venner's followers killed perhaps a score of government officers, but more of their own fell. The revolt was crushed and many of the rebels, including Venner, were executed. This revolt marked the demise of the Fifth Monarchy. Public revulsion caused most denominations, including Baptists, to distance themselves from the movement. For a generation after 1661, a few Fifth Monarchists still promised an imminent millennium, but expectations long disappointed tended to fade. Many of the Fifth Monarchists turned quietist, and many joined the Seventh-Day Baptists, with whom they had considerable affinity. King Charles II took the Venner uprising quite seriously and used it as an occasion for a harsh crackdown on Baptist and other Dissenter meetings.

What was the extent of Baptist involvement in the Fifth Monarchy Movement? Since the movement turned out so badly, most denominations, including Baptists, minimized their connection to it. The question is further complicated by the fact that it arose at a time when Baptist identity was not yet sharply defined. Despite differences on baptism, Congregationalists and Baptists often held membership in the same churches. Many Baptist churches had members who shared the hopes and methods of the Fifth Monarchy. Fifth Monarchists preached in some Baptist churches, leading one observer to question, "Whether ever any Commonwealth will trust the Baptized Churches again."[63] In the most definitive study of that movement, B. S. Capp concluded, "The Fifth Monarchists were drawn largely from the ranks of existing Baptists and Congregationalists."[64] Such Baptists as Edmund Chillenden, Vavasor Powell, William Allen, John Simpson, Henry Danvers, and, to some extent, Hanserd Knollys and Henry Jessey were allied with the movement. However, neither of the two primary leaders, Thomas Harrison or Thomas Venner, was a Baptist.

62. Ibid., p. 116.
63. Brown, p. 194.
64. Capp, p. 172.

In the public mind the connection between Baptists and Fifth Monarchy was made easier by the old accusation that Baptists represented a new outbreak of Munster radicalism. In the 1530s a revolutionary group seized the city of Munster, Germany, and instituted radical social and religious changes. They were identified as Anabaptists, though they had little connection with authentic Anabaptism. In 1661 an author identified only as "J. B." published a book called *Munster Paralleld in the Late Massacres Committed by the Fifth Monarchists,* in which he attempted to link Munster, the Fifth Monarchy, and English Baptists as continuations of the same movement.[65]

Some Baptists, especially among the Particular churches, did share the radical Monarchist goals and methods. Vavasor Powell asked bluntly, "Lord, wilt Thou have Oliver Cromwell or Jesus Christ to reign over us?"[66] He apparently meant this in the most literal way and decided that Cromwell had to go to make way for King Jesus. When John Pendarves, Baptist pastor in Abingdon, died in 1656 of a "plague in ye gutts," his funeral became the occasion of a massive rally of Fifth Monarchists and Baptists. Before the authorities broke up that rally, the people, with Baptist participation, declared, "God's people must be a bloody people [in an active sense]."[67]

However, most Baptists tried valiantly to disassociate themselves from the more violent Fifth Monarchists. Two of the greatest Particular leaders, William Kiffin of London and Thomas Collier of the West, did their utmost to persuade Baptists to stand aloof from armed revolution as a means of doing God's work. After the Venner uprising, a group of Baptists issued *The Humble Apology of Some Commonly Called Anabaptists* to disclaim any connection with "the late wicked and most horrid treasonable insurrection and rebellion."[68] This was the first known document in which General and Particular Baptists cooperated. It was signed by such leaders as William Kiffin, John Spilsbury, Henry Denne, and Thomas Lambe. As late as 1678 Thomas Grantham was still laboring to distance Baptists from Fifth Monarchy and Munster radicals. He said most of the radicals were never "of our belief or practice about baptism," and he rejected "their conceited wild interpretations of dark prophecies."[69]

Despite the millennial milieu of the time, most early Baptists taught moderate views of the future hope. Like Christians from all times, they expected Christ to return in triumph and judgment. Most of their confessions mention this future hope, but apocalyptic speculations formed no major emphasis among them. The Helwys confession of 1611 affirms, "That

65. Harry Leon McBeth, *English Baptist Literature on Religious Liberty to 1689,* p. 207.
66. Capp, p. 101.
67. Ibid., p. 116.
68. Cited in Underwood, pp. 93-94.
69. Ivimey, 1:310.

after the resurrection all men shall appeare before the judgment seat off CHRIST to bee judged according to their workes, that the Godlie shall enjoy life Eternall, the wickeed being condemned shallbee tormented ever-lastinglie in Hell."[70] This appears to leave no room for an earthly millennial kingdom. The confession of 1612 gives a more detailed discussion of eschatology but mentions no millennium. The First London Confession, framed in the midst of intense millennial speculation in 1644, says, "That Christ hath here on earth a spirituall Kingdome, which is the Church." This influential confession proclaims Christian obedience to government and an expectancy of Christ's return, but makes no mention of any millennial kingdom.[71]

Two Baptist confessions, however, at least allude to millennial hopes though neither develops the subject. The Somerset Confession of 1656 says that at Christ's return the saints will "reign with him, and judge over all nations on the earth."[72] The Standard Confession of 1660 affirms that Christ will return as "King over all the earth, Zech.14.9. and we shall raign with him on the Earth." Now the saints suffer persecution, they said, "but when Christ shall appear, then shall be their day, then shall be given unto them power over the Nations, to rule them with a Rod of Iron." However, that confession specifically repudiates the violent plans of the Fifth Monarchy. A closing section says:

> Moreover we do utterly, and from our very hearts, in the Lords fear, declare against all those wicked, and divillish reports, and reproaches, falsly cast upon us, as though some of us (in & about the City of London) had lately gotten Knives, hooked Knives, & the like, & great store of Arms besides . . . intending to cut the throats of such as were contrary minded to us in matters of Religion . . . we do utterly abhor, and abominate the thoughts thereof, and much more the actions.[73]

As early as 1654, at the first recorded General Assembly, representatives from General Baptist churches repudiated the radical designs of the Fifth Monarchy. The Baptists defended themselves against slanders that "they were no Friends to Magistracy and Civill Government." In a clear reference to Fifth Monarchist teachings, they said, "Nor do they [Baptists] know any ground for the saints, as such, to expect that the Rule and Government of the World should be put into their hands, untill that day in which the Lord Jesus shall visibly descend from Heaven." When Christ did appear, they believed,

> the kingdoms of this World shall become the Kingdoms of the Lord and of

70. Lumpkin, p. 123.
71. Ibid., pp. 165, 169.
72. Ibid., p. 214.
73. Ibid., p. 234.

his Christ, and that then the Kingdom, . . . shall be given to the people of the Saints of the Most High, But till then they rather expect it to be their portion, patiently to suffer from the world, as the Scriptures direct them, and as the saints have usually done, than anywise to attain the Rule and Government thereof.[74]

In conclusion, most Baptists appear to have held peaceful beliefs about Christ's return. While many were caught up for a time in the millennial excitement around mid-century, most followed the nonviolent views of Kiffin and Collier. The few who embraced radical Fifth Monarchist plots attracted widespread attention and brought disrepute and suffering to Baptists. Later in the century, the Baptists, like other denominations, backed off from apocalyptic speculations. The two most influential Baptist confessions later in the century, the Othodox Creed (General, 1678) and the Second London Confession (Particular, 1689), illustrate this trend. These are regarded as definitive doctrinal statements. Both include articles on the second coming of Christ, but neither mentions an earthly millennium.[75]

Baptist Worship

The oldest record of a Baptist worship service comes from 1609, in a letter from Hughe and Anne Bromhead, who said:

> The order of the worshippe and government of oure church is .1. we begynne wth A prayer, after reade some one or tow chapters of the bible gyve the sence thereof, and conferr vpon the same, that done we lay aside our bookes, and after a solemne prayer made by the .1. speaker, he propoundeth some text owt of the Scripture, and prophecieth owt of the same, by the space of one hower, or thre Quarters of an hower. After him standeth vp A .2. speaker and prophecieth owt of the same text the like tyme and space. some tyme more some tyme less. After him the .3. the .4. the .5. & as the tyme will geve leave, Then the .1. speaker concludeth wth prayer as he began with prayer, wth an exhortation to contribute to the poore, wch collection being made is also concluded wth prayer. This Morning exercise begynes at eight of the clocke and continueth vnto twelve of the clocke the like course of exercise is observed in the afternowne from .2. of the clock vnto .5. or .6. of the Clocke, last of all the execution of the goverment of the church is handled.[76]

Though modified somewhat over the next century, this basic pattern of worship continued in Baptist churches. The services were lengthy, centered in biblical exposition and preaching, and allowed worshipers as well as speakers to confer upon biblical texts and offer their insights before the

---

74. W. T. Whitley, ed., *Minutes of the General Assembly of the General Baptist Churches in England,* 1:3-4.

75. Lumpkin, pp. 294, 334.

76. Champlin Burrage, *The Early English Dissenters in Light of Recent Research,* 2:176-177.

group. The offering for the poor and the business of the church, perhaps including matters of discipline, were appended to the end of the service. Baptist worship was usually conducted on Sunday, although there were a few Seventh-Day Baptists in England.

In the early days, few Baptist churches had their own buildings, though this became more common after 1700. They met in private homes, sometimes in public halls, and quite often out of doors in good weather. Most immersions were conducted in rivers and lakes, but some churches prepared indoor "baptisterions," or "baptismal cisterns," as they called them. Some churches with convenient baptistries levied a fee for other churches to use them, charging for converts baptized, with two shillings per head being the going rate.[77]

In addition to baptism, some Baptist churches included foot washing as part of their public worship. This practice, however, was never widespread. It endured longer among the General Baptists than the Particular. The Assembly of General Baptists left the practice optional, since it was not among the six fundamentals mentioned in Hebrews 6:1-2.

Baptists required complete spontaneity in worship, so that individuals could respond to God as the Spirit might lead them at any moment. This made Baptist worship somewhat unpredictable, for at any moment a worshiper might be given a doctrine, an exhortation, or a psalm to share with the group. Baptist resistance to set forms of worship in the Prayer Book helps explain their freewheeling style. From John Smyth onward, Baptists insisted that they could not pray out of a book but that prayer and praise must come directly "from the hart."

Modern worship practices of Baptists, with hymns, printed orders of worship, Scripture readings, and choral responses all determined in advance, would have been unthinkable to early Baptists. Even Helwys, more moderate than Smyth on many issues, said, "All bookes even the originalles them selves must be layed aside in the tyme of spirituall worshipp." Even the Bible could not be used in worship, but only "for the preparinge to worshipp."[78] Such extreme emphasis upon complete spontaneity called in question the practice of preparing or "premeditating" sermons. However, they soon allowed at least some sermon preparation, for otherwise they were likely to get "for the most part raw and undigested matter."

The Lord's Supper was an important act of worship for Baptists, being observed weekly by some, but less often by most. Many of the churches preceded the Lord's Supper with a "love feast," a church fellowship meal. Records of the Warboys congregation, for example, has this entry for 1655: "The order of love-feast agreed upon, to be before the Lord's Supper;

---

77. Thomas Crosby, *The History of the English Baptists,* 4:168.
78. From a letter of Thomas Helwys, 1608, cited in Burrage, 2:167.

because the ancient churches did practice it, and for unity with other churches near to us."[79]

The worship of Particular Baptists, like their theology, was nearer to other English Protestants. One historian has observed of the Particular Baptists, "In fact, Baptism apart, it would be difficult to distinguish their worship from that of Independents."[80]

By far, the most important Baptist contribution to worship in the seventeenth century involved the singing of hymns. At that time practically all English churches opposed hymn singing, though some would allow the chanting or even solo singing of biblical texts. At first the Baptists, like others in England, stoutly opposed singing and developed intricate arguments against this "carnal exercise." However, in later years Baptists adopted and helped to popularize singing, some of them writing hymns and publishing hymnals. Some of the early objection to singing may have grown out of reluctance to call undue attention to Baptist meeting places. Such "conventicles" were illegal, and group singing might alert passersby or the authorities that an unlawful worship meeting was taking place.

The early General Baptists rejected group singing and held adamantly to that restriction for over a century. One major statement of the case against singing was made by Thomas Grantham in his masterful book *Christianismus Primitivus*. Grantham, a messenger of the churches of Lincolnshire, was perhaps the most influential General Baptist leader in the second half of the century. He set out to trace "the singing of Psalms, Hymns and Spiritual Songs in the Christian Church, according to Scripture and Antiquity," and lamented the recent "encroachment of humane Innovations" in these areas.[81] Like other General Baptists, Grantham would allow some singing, but with severe restrictions. There were of course no musical instruments; any singing had to be by a man (women were to keep silent); any singing had to be strictly solo, with no mixed voices or "promiscuous singing" by a multitude; only biblical texts, preferably psalms, could be sung; no songs of "human composure" could be allowed; and any singing had to be done in a loud, clear voice, with "no warbling," as Grantham put it. Grantham criticized "the Custom which many have taken up to sing David's Psalms, or their own composures, in a mixed multitude of voices." He concluded "that a multitude of Christians, or a whole Congregation ought to sing together at the same time, is not at all warranted" from Scripture.[82]

To the General Baptists, group singing of "manmade" hymns carried a

79. Horton Davies, *Worship and Theology in England,* 2:504.
80. Ibid., p. 507.
81. Thomas Grantham, *Christianismus Primitivus,* 2:99-117.
82. Ibid., p. 112.

number of dangers. "Set songs" were as bad as "set prayers," or even "set sermons," and might lead to them. A singing congregation might include some non-Christians, and their particpation would pollute the worship. For all to sing the same words and same musical notes would be an obvious denial of spontaneity in worship. What if one person should be led by the Spirit to sing another word, or another note, at that time? Besides, said Grantham, few people had "tunable voices," and women were not to participate at all. The General Baptist Assembly of 1689 pronounced singing "foreign to evangelical worship."[83]

Though not as adamant, Particular Baptists also opposed hymn singing and instrumental music in worship. Their early arguments against the practice were about the same as General Baptists, though less intense. However, by mid-century some Particular Baptists regarded singing with new interest. Perhaps the Fifth Monarchy Movement, so devastating to Baptists in other ways, helped teach them to sing. Fifth Monarchy leaders quite early saw the value of rhyme and music to instruct people and motivate them to action. Particular Baptists eventually followed the lead of Independents like John Cotton who wrote about 1640, "Singing of Psalms with a lively voyce is an holy duty of God's worship. Women should not take part in this."[84]

Benjamin Keach is often credited with introducing hymn singing to English Baptists and, indeed, to all the English churches. Keach does indeed rank as an important pioneer, but others preceded him. Anna Trapnell, a Fifth Monarchy Baptist, published *The Cry of a Stone* in 1654. This was a collection of prayers and spiritual songs, which was recommended by Hanserd Knollys, another Fifth Monarchy Baptist.[85] Katherine Sutton published her collection of hymns in 1663, to which Knollys wrote an introduction recommending its use and giving further directions for the use of singing in worship.[86]

John Bunyan also wrote songs for children but could not persuade his adult congregation to sing. In 1664 Keach introduced his *Children's Primer,* which included songs for children. Keach introduced congregational singing into Baptist churches, despite what one called a "gruelling controversy" over the practice.[87] In 1673 he persuaded the church at Horsleydown to sing a hymn at the close of the Lord's Supper, allowing those who objected to leave before the hymn. Six years later the church agreed to sing a hymn on "public thanksgiving days," and fourteen years after that, to sing as part of every Sunday's worship. Keach was patient; twenty years were necessary

83. Hugh Martin, "The Baptist Contributions to Early English Hymnody," *The Baptist Quarterly,* p. 201.

84. Ibid., p. 204n.

85. Ian Mallard, "The Hymns of Katherine Sutton," *The Baptist Quarterly,* p. 24.

86. Ibid., pp. 24-25.

87. Davies, 2:509.

to complete the transition to singing. Even so, twenty-two of Keach's members withdrew to join a nonsinging church. They could not escape, however, for that church soon adopted singing, the church's new pastor making it a condition of his coming.[88] Keach put out two important Baptist hymnals, *Spiritual Melody* (1691) and *Spiritual Songs* (1696), containing about four hundred hymns, most his own writing. One observer concluded, "His hymns are best forgotten, but for his long campaign to establish hymn singing in our churches he deserves our cordial thanks."[89]

Keach's main antagonist was Isaac Marlow, a Baptist layman who wrote at least three books against singing. To refute Marlow, Keach wrote his major defense in 1691, entitled *The Breach Repaired in God's Worship, or Singing of Psalms, Hymns and Spiritual Songs proved to be an Holy Ordinance of Jesus Christ.* At the 1689 assembly, the Particular Baptists gave cautious approval to singing or at least to the concept of each congregation deciding its own practices without censure from others. With even that much approval, singing quickly caught on. By the next century, General Baptists had also adopted the practice, mostly through the influence of Dan Taylor and the New Connection.

The Emerging Denomination

To call English Baptists in the seventeenth century a "denomination" may be premature, at least in the modern sense of that word. Baptist congregations had limited contact with one another. Part of the reason for Baptist existence was the believers' insistence that churches be independent. Perhaps this hampered the development of interchurch communication and linkage.

Despite this exaggerated independence, early Baptist churches did form the rudiments of denominational structure. By mid-century the Baptist "association," a group of cooperating churches in a given region, had made its appearance. By 1660 both General and Particular Baptists had a number of associations; and before the end of the century, both had also a general assembly, a national affiliation of Baptist churches.

General Baptists

As early as 1624 five General Baptist churches took common action in responding to letters from the Dutch Mennonites. The pastor of one of these churches, Elias Tookey, wrote in the name of the several churches to repudiate Mennonite views on oaths, magistracy, and military service. This much-discussed "Tookey correspondence" does not reflect an organized association but does show Baptist churches acting in cooperation on matters of common concern.

In 1651 a General Baptist association convened in the Midlands, prob-

88. Martin, p. 207.
89. Ibid., p. 200.

ably at Leicester, and may have met even earlier. In 1651 that "association" adopted a confession of faith in the name of thirty affiliated congregations. Within a few years such associations were common among General Baptists.

Apparently the name "association" originated from military practices of the New Model Army. During the Civil War (1642-1649), the Parliamentary army organized various counties into "associations" for defense. Later each regiment in such military associations sent two representatives to confer with Parliament. Records confirm the extensive participation of Baptists in the New Model Army, both as commanders, troops, and chaplains. After the army disbanded, Baptists applied the familiar name and techniques of their army organization to church life, and the "association" caught on.

By 1654 the General Baptists had formed such a nationwide assembly, and they may have met even earlier. A manifesto appeared in 1654 on behalf of "many of the Messengers, Elders, and Brethren, belonging to severall of the Baptized Churches in this nation." They met in London "to consider how and which way the affairs of the Gospell of Christ, so farre as it concerns them, might be best promoted."[90] At this meeting, they answered slanders against Baptists, professed their civil loyalty, sought additional religious liberty, and repudiated the Fifth Monarchy Movement which was even then making inroads among the Baptists.[91]

General Baptists developed a centralized denominational structure, in which associations and the General Assembly exercised some authority over churches. They were less jealous than their Particular brethren about the autonomy of the local congregation, regarding the churches as interlocking units of the larger church. As early as 1611 the General Baptists had affirmed: "That though in respect off CHRIST, the Church bee one, Ephes. 4.4 yet it consisteth off divers particular congregacions, even so manie as there shallbee in the World, every off which congregacion, though they be but two or thre,, have CHRIST given unto them."[92] This ecclesiology was further developed in the Orthodox Creed of 1678, which says:

> General councils, or assemblies, consisting of the Bishops, Elders, and Brethren, of the several churches of Christ, and being legally convened, and met together out of all the churches, and the churches appearing there by their representatives, make but one church, and have lawful right, and suffrage in this general meeting, or assembly, to act in the name of Christ.[93]

The key phrases here are that such general gatherings make "but one

90. Whitley, 1:2.
91. Ibid., pp. 1-5.
92. Lumpkin, p. 120.
93. Ibid., p. 327.

church," with power to act in church affairs. The "Messenger," as an officer of the assembly or an association, also exercised some leadership over local churches and pastors.

Particular Baptists

Like the General Baptists, the Particular churches quite early developed associations. In 1644 seven churches acted jointly in issuing the First London Confessions, and within a few years associations emerged not only in London but also in the Midlands, Wales, and Ireland.

At its first meeting in 1652, the Abingdon Association affirmed, "Perticular Churches of Christ ought to hold a firme communion each with other in point of advice in doubtfull matters and controversies."[94] Some of their arguments for the association of local churches were:

> 1st. Because there is the same relation betwixt the perticular churches each towards other as there is betwixt perticular members of one church. For the churches of Christ doe all make up one body or church in generall under Christ their head . . . As perticular members make up one perticular church under the same head, Christ, and [so] all the perticular assemblys are but one Mount Syon.[95]

Thus the basic defense of associations was theological; the nature of the church required them to demonstrate their unity under Christ. The Abingdon Association also named certain practical reasons for linking the churches: for mutual discipline, aid in controversies, and pooling resources for more effective ministry. Churches have a duty "to keepe each other pure and to cleare the profession of the Gospell from scandale which cannot be done (I Cor. 5.5) unless orderly walking churches be owned orderly and disorderly churches be orderly disowned." Churches may benefit from "a combination of prayers and endeavors," and a church may need other churches "to quicken them when lukewarme, to helpe when in want, assist in counsell in doubtful matters."[96]

Despite this early commitment to the principle of associationalism, Particular Baptists were slower in forming a nationwide assembly. Geographical isolation, theological controversy, lack of leaders committed to unity, and a jealous obsession with local church autonomy prevented them from coming together. In 1689 messengers from 107 churches met in London, formed the General Assembly, "owned" the confession of 1677, and dealt with several pressing problems. After 1692, the assembly met twice a year, in Bristol at Easter and in London at Whitsuntide. One might regard these cities as the two poles of Particular Baptist strength.

94. Barrington R. White, ed., *Association Records of the Particular Baptists of England, Wales and Ireland to 1660,* p. 126.
95. Ibid.
96. Ibid., pp. 126-127.

Particular Baptists carefully guarded the autonomy of the local church. Their confession of 1689 affirmed:

> It is according to the mind of Christ, that many Churches holding communion together, do by their messengers meet to consider, and give advice in, or about that matter in difference, to be reported to all the Churches concerned; howbeit these messengers assembled, are not entrusted with any Church-power properly so called; or with any jurisdiction over the Churches themselves, to exercise any censures either over any Churches, or Persons: or to impose their determination on the Churches, or Officers.[97]

One can see how radically this differs from the General Baptist pattern. To the Particular Baptists, their assembly was not a churchly body and did not perform churchly functions. We do not read of baptism, ordinations, or church discipline at the denominational meetings; these were left to the local congregations. The assembly might, and often did, arbitrate differences between the churches, but their decision had to be approved by the churches.

Summary

The English Baptists came to the end of the seventeenth century with a clearly defined faith and order. This faith was expressed in a number of important confessions and in the theological writings of Baptist leaders, such as William Kiffin for the Particulars and Thomas Grantham for the Generals. Both groups had developed the rudiments of a systematic theology. They cooperated through clear channels of ecclesiastical linkage, local church, association, and general assembly. The Baptists won their long struggle for liberty in England through the Act of Toleration adopted in 1689.

Thus the Baptists came to the year 1700 with many advantages. They had worked out their theology, structured their denomination, and won the right to preach and worship freely. Surely they were on the threshold of their greatest advance. Alas, it was not to be.

---

97. Lumpkin, p. 289.

3

Defending the Faith

Most historians agree that Baptists in England, few as they were, made an important contribution to public life in their teachings on religious freedom. No group can claim more credit for the Act of Toleration, passed by Parliament in 1689. H. Wheeler Robinson says that to the Baptists belongs "the distinction of being the first to claim and the first to apply fearlessly the unfettered principle of freedom for religion."[1]

The freedom of religious belief and behavior which modern Baptists and others often take for granted was forged in the crucible of persecution in seventeenth-century England. In a time when bare toleration was refused by most and begrudged by almost all, Baptists advanced and defended the radical concept of freedom for all to believe and worship in ways they thought most pleasing to God, or not to believe or worship at all. Underhill affirmed, "To the Baptists, it will be seen, belongs the honour of first asserting in this land, and of establishing on the immutable basis of just argument and scripture rule, the right of every man to worship God as conscience dictates, in submission to divine command."[2]

The English Baptist struggle for religious liberty has significance far beyond that communion and that land. The later struggle for religious liberty in America and in other lands grows, at least in its Baptist phase, directly out of the foundations laid by English Baptist pioneers in the seventeenth century.

Because the religious situation, and thus the status of dissenters, was constantly changing, it appears best in this chapter to take a chronological approach. General and Particular Baptists are treated together for, despite their other differences, they were in substantial agreement on religious liberty.

The Early Stuart Era, to 1640

The crowning of James Stuart of Scotland as King James I of England in 1603 introduced a new era in English religious as well as political history.

1. H. Wheeler Robinson, *The Life and Faith of the Baptists,* p. 123.
2. Edward Bean Underhill, ed., *Tracts on Liberty of Conscience and Persecution,* 1614-1661, p. 2.

The death of Queen Elizabeth marked the end of the famed "Elizabethan Settlement." Dissatisfaction with the Church of England led to mushrooming sects, schisms, and separatism.

When James I came to the throne, different religious factions hoped for the king's favor. Presbyterians took hope from the fact that in Scotland he had staunchly supported the Presbyterian system. Roman Catholics hoped he would advance the Catholic cause because his wife was of that faith. Anglicans expected him to favor the Church of England because that church, ruled by bishops, was most in harmony with the new king's theories of divine right rule. The nation had not long to wait to learn what religious policies the new king would follow. He called a conference of religious leaders for Hampton Court in 1604, at which various church groups made their proposals for reform. The Puritans wanted to reform certain practices which smacked too much of Rome. The Separatists presented their views by way of the "Millenary Petition," so-called because it was said to have been signed by over a thousand persons, calling for freedom from the state church. The Hampton Court Conference also set in motion work on a new English translation of the Bible, which was issued in 1611 under the name of King James.

At Hampton Court, the king solidly supported the Church of England, though minor reforms were allowed. The idea of religious liberty horrified him. If citizens were free to hold their own views, the king feared, "Jack and Tom and Will and Dick shall meete, and at their pleasure censure me and my Councell and all our proceedings. Then Will shall stand up and say it must be thus; then Dick shall reply and say, nay, marry, but wee will have it thus."[3]

In the same conference, King James complained of dissenting ministers who prayed for him in civil affairs, "but as for Supreme Governor in all Causes and over all persons (as well Ecclesiasticall as Civill), they passe that over with silence."[4] Clearly the new king would not allow participation of the people in affairs of either church or state, and he announced his intention to act as "Supreme Governor" in religion as well as politics. In an early proclamation concerning the Book of Common Prayer, the king said it "is the chiefest of kingly duties, . . . to settle affairs of religion." James was obsessed with the idea of religious uniformity, intensified perhaps by evidence of increasing differences. Much of James's reign was spent in making good his threat to harass and exile those who refused to conform to the Church of England. Perhaps his motives were as much political as religious; his main objection to Presbyterianism was not theological but that its

3. Edward P. Cheyney, ed., *Readings in English History Drawn from the Original Sources,* p. 431.
4. Ibid.

representative church government "as wel agreeth with a Monarchy, as God with the Devill."[5]

At the death of James I, his son Charles I succeeded to the throne and ruled 1625 to 1649. Charles retained the views of kingly prerogative in religion and the political necessity for religious uniformity. Crosby said, "In short, the reign of K. Charles I. was more violent in persecuting the Puritans, than that of his father James."[6] Styling himself as the "Supreme Governour of the Church," King Charles said in 1628:

> We hold it most agreeable to this our Kingly Office, and our own Religious zeal, to conserve and maintain the Church committed to Our charge in the unity of true Religion, and in the bond of peace: and not to suffer unnecessary Disputations, altercations, or questions to be raised, which may nourish faction both in the Church and Commonwealth.[7]

The king firmly supported the Church of England, "requiring all Our loving Subjects to continue in the uniform profession thereof, and prohibiting the least difference from the said Articles."[8] He appointed William Laud as Archbishop of Canterbury, and Laud proceeded to stifle dissent and enforce Anglican uniformity.

In this oppressive environment Baptists emerged as a separate denomination. They made their early witness despite dangers, persecution, and great personal risks. Numbers of early Baptists suffered loss of goods, whippings, and imprisonments for their faith. Some were physically maimed; cutting off the ears and slitting the nose were favorite ways to impress upon Baptists the disfavor authorities felt for their views. Few suffered the fate of John James, a Seventh-Day Baptist who was executed in 1661, but no doubt many had their death hastened by being crowded into filthy and disease-ridden prisons.

John Smyth

We have seen that John Smyth formed the earliest Baptist church of modern history, early in 1609. He also put forth the earliest Baptist plea for full religious liberty. Before becoming a Baptist, Smyth held the usual Separatist view of asking liberty for Separatist views, but desiring government sanction to impose that view upon others. In *A Paterne of True Prayer,*

5. Ibid.
6. Thomas Crosby, *The History of the English Baptists,* 1:147.
7. *Articles Agreed Upon by the Archbishops and Bishops of Both Provinces . . . in the Year 1562. Reprinted by His Majesties Commandment, with his Royall Declaration Prefixed Thereunto* (London: n. p., 1628), pp. 1-2. This document is reprinted with modernized spelling in Samuel R. Gardiner, *The Constitutional Documents of the Puritan Revolution 1625-1660* (Oxford: Clarendon Press, 1951), pp. 75-76.
8. Ibid.

he said, "God's Kingdome is erected . . . when the Magistrate by law doth establish the worship of God according to the word," and even allowed that "godly Magistrates doe erect and maintaine the faith and true religion by the sword."[9] In 1608 Smyth still maintained that "the erecting of visible Churches apperteyneth to princes."

After becoming a Baptist, Smyth's views of religious liberty underwent a radical change. By 1609 he said, "Ther may be many questions made" about the authority of the magistrate over the church. He had resolved these questions by 1610 when he and his followers signed a Mennonite confession which specified that the "office of the worldly authority the Lord Jesus hath not ordained in his spiritual kingdom, the church of the New Testament, nor adjoined to the offices of his church."[10] Two years later Smyth issued a definitive confession which affirmed that

> the magistrate is not by virtue of his office to meddle with religion, or matters of conscience, to force or compel men to this or that form of religion, or doctrine: but to leave Christian religion free, to every man's conscience, and to handle only civil transgression (Rom. xiii), injuries and wrongs of man against man, in murder, adultery, theft, etc., for Christ only is the king, and lawgiver of the church and conscience.[11]

This brief statement covers all the basic points of later, more extensive treatises. The Baptists fully accepted the rightful authority of government in civil matters but would not allow the government to determine or regulate their relation to God. They insisted that reserving spiritual matters did not constitute civil disobedience. John Smyth, exiled to Holland on religious grounds, could hardly have imagined in 1612 what impact these ringing phrases would have both then and later: "to leave religion free, to every man's conscience," "Christ only the lawgiver in the church," and government limited to "civil transgressions." These concepts reshaped the modern world. They add up to what is presently called religious liberty and separation of church and state.

Thomas Helwys

Thomas Helwys assisted Smyth in forming the first Baptist church of modern history. Helwys later broke with Smyth over several issues and led a remnant back to England in 1611 to establish the earliest Baptist church on English soil. Helwys was also a major spokesman for religious liberty. He wrote *A Short Declaration of the Mistery of Iniquity* soon after returning to England. Helwys chose the inopportune time of 1612 to plead for religious liberty in England. That year Bartholomew Legate and Edward

9. W. T. Whitley, ed., *The Works of John Smyth,* 1:159.
10. William L. Lumpkin, ed., *Baptist Confessions of Faith,* p. 111.
11. Ibid., p. 140.

Wightman were burned in London for heresy, and officials threatened that others might also "frie at a Stake."[12]

The title of the book shows that Helwys was caught up in the apocalyptic enthusiasm of the times. Among Separatists the almost universal interpretation of Revelation 13 was that the first beast represented the Roman Church, the second beast the Anglican Church. In *The Mistery,* Helwys attacked the Church of England for aping Rome, the Puritans for compromise, and the Separatists for making only a partial separation. However, the book's major thrust was its consistent, courageous, and, at times, quite eloquent plea for full religious liberty for all, perhaps the first such plea in the English language. Helwys held that "none ought to be punished either with death or bonds for transgressing against the spiritual ordinances of the New Testament, and that such Offences ought to be punished onely with spirituall sword and censures."[13] He denied the validity of civil punishment for spiritual offences. He demanded for Baptists, and for all others, the "blessed liberty, to understand the Scriptures with their own spirits."

Helwys was ahead of his time in asking religious liberty for all people. In perhaps the most inclusive liberty statement of the age, Helwys said, "Let them be heretikes, Turcks, Jewes, or whatsoever it apperteynes not to the earthly power to punish them in the least measure" in religious matters.[14] Helwys's reasoned defense of liberty for such groups as Roman Catholics, Jews, and Moslems probably cost him some support he might have enjoyed otherwise.

With brilliant skill, this layman swept away the legal and biblical defenses of religious persecution. While he did not deny that Old Testament kings had supremacy over religion, Helwys, like other Baptists of that day, was not willing for the Old Testament to speak the final word on this issue. Instead he appealed to New Testament texts and expounded them with telling effect. Helwys's final argument was the example of Jesus, who would not allow the disciples to call down fire on those who differed.

Along with this plea for full religious liberty, Helwys allowed more kingly authority than later parliaments would. Let the king "comaund what ordinance of man he will, and wee are to obey it," said Helwys, but the king was to keep hands off the church for "with this Kingdom, our lord the King hath nothinge to do."[15]

Apparently Helwys made an effort to present a copy of *The Mistery* to King James in person. Failing that, he sent the king an autographed copy with this personal note in the flyleaf:

Heare O King, and dispise not ye counsell of ye poore, and let their complaints come before thee. The King is a mortall man, and not God therefore

12. Champlin Burrage, *The Early English Dissenters in Light of Recent Research,* 2:171.
13. Thomas Helwys, *A Short Declaration of the Mistery of Iniquity,* from Table of Contents.
14. Ibid., p. 69.
15. Ibid., p. 40.

hath no power over ye immortall soules of his subjects, to make lawes and ordinances for them, and to set spirituall Lords over them. If the King have authority to make spirituall Lords and lawes, then he is an immortal God and not mortall man. O King be not seduced by deceivers to sin so against God Whom thou oughtest to obey, nor against thy poore subjects who ought and will obey thee in all things with body life and goods, or let their lives be taken from ye earth. God save ye King.[16]

Helwys was imprisoned in 1612, perhaps as a direct result of this bold challenge. We know he was still alive in prison in 1614 but was dead by 1616 for his will was probated that year.

Leonard Busher

The earliest Baptist treatise devoted exclusively to religious liberty was *Religion's Peace: A Plea for Liberty of Conscience,* published in 1614 by Leonard Busher. Definite information about Busher is hard to come by. A 1611 reference, describing early Baptists in Amsterdam, mentions "Master Smyth, an Anabaptist of one sort, and master Helwise of another, and master Busher of another."[17] The learned Champlin Burrage labored to prove Busher a Dutchman; the equally learned W. T. Whitley argued that he was an English refugee in Holland, as were Smyth and Helwys. The editor of the 1646 edition of *Religion's Peace* said its purpose was to "make it appear by scriptures and sound arguments, that the only way to make a nation happy, and preserve the people in love, peace, and tranquility, is to give liberty to all to serve God according as they are persuaded is most agreeable to his word."[18]

Like Smyth and Helwys, Busher argued for religious liberty on the grounds of Scripture, logic, and history. Perhaps more than they, Busher pointed out the civil and national advantages of liberty. He was apparently the first to use a vivid illustration, much cited by later Baptists, comparing forced worship to spiritual rape. Busher said that religious persecution forces the spirit and conscience and is therefore worse "than if they force the bodies of women and maids against their wills."[19]

To Busher, religious liberty was no special favor to be granted or withheld at the whim of government. It was an inalienable God-given right. W. K. Jordan was correct in saying, "Here we have no abject pleading by a sectary for the bare toleration of his own group, but a thoughtful and noble demand for religious liberty for all men."[20]

16. From the flyleaf on an ancient copy of Helwys, *The Mistery.*
17. W. T. Whitley, "Leonard Busher Dutchman," *Transactions of the Baptist Historical Society,* p. 107.
18. Underhill, p. 10.
19. Ibid., p. 34.
20. Wilbur K. Jordan, *The Development of Religious Toleration in England,* 2:298.

John Murton

Burgess described Murton as Helwys's "chief helper" and said that after 1612 "the mantle of Helwys" fell on Murton.[21] He was apparently the main leader of the little band of English Baptists after the death of Helwys. Murton knew persecution firsthand, being described in 1613 as a "Prisoner at London," where he remained until his death years later. He wrote a treatise from prison in 1615, *Objections Answered by Way of Dialogue.* This was later revised and reissued under the title of *Persecution for Religion Judg'd and Condemn'd.*

Murton's treatise is a discussion among "Christian," who favors religious liberty; "Anti-Christian," who opposes it; and "Indifferent," who is brought in occasionally to complete the argument. Under this format, Murton answered the objections being raised against religious liberty, advanced lengthy arguments in favor of liberty, and concluded, "No man ought to be persecuted for his religion, be it true or false, so they testify their faithful allegiance to the king." Like Smyth, Helwys, and Busher before him, Murton argued that it is "heinous . . . in the sight of the Lord to force men and women by cruel persecution, to bring their bodies to a worship whereunto they cannot bring their spirits."[22]

One senses an autobiographical note in Murton's lament that many loyal Englishmen "lie many years in filthy prisons, in hunger, cold, idleness, divided from wife, family, calling, left in continual miseries and temptations, so as death would be to many less persecution."[23] Because they were often identified with Anabaptists, many of whom disallowed magistracy, Baptists felt an obligation to repeat their affirmations of civil loyalty. Murton was no exception. He claimed that Baptists "do unfeignedly acknowledge the authority of earthly magistrates, God's blessed ordinance, and that all earthly authority and command appertaines to them; . . . but all men must let God alone with his right, which is to be lord and lawgiver to the soul."[24] Murton also insisted upon separation of civil and spiritual spheres. He said, "Earthly authority belongeth to earthly kings; but spiritual authority belongeth to that one spiritual King who is KING OF KINGS."[25] A major biblical passage upon which Murton based his views was Matthew 13:24-40, the parable of the tares. According to Murton, this passage teaches that those who follow true religion and those who follow the false "should be let alone in the world, and not plucked up until the harvest, which is the end of the world."

21. Wilbur H. Burgess, *John Smith the Se-Baptist, Thomas Helwys and the First Baptist Church in England,* p. 297.

22. Underhill, pp. 95, 96.

23. Ibid.

24. Ibid., p. 100.

25. Ibid., p. 134.

In 1620 Murton issued another piece, entitled *The Humble Supplication,* repeating many of these same arguments in a more readable format. We are indebted to Roger Williams for an interesting account of the origin of *The Humble Supplication.* Williams, from his contacts in the legal offices of Sir Edward Coke where many such imprisonments for religion were argued, would have occasion to discover this inside information. He said Murton was in Newgate prison for religious convictions and wrote these arguments in milk on the paper used as a stopper for his daily jug of milk. These crumpled papers were smuggled to the Baptists, who browned them over a candle to make the words appear.[26] Thus did the imprisoned pastor continue to instruct and minister to his flock.

The Time of Turmoil, 1640-1648

In 1640 the smoldering conflict between King and Parliament intensified. The Parliament refused to obey the king's order to disband, remaining in session to pass law after law which undermined royal authority. Perhaps the climax of their reform efforts came in December 1640 with the Root and Branch Petition, so called for its intention to abolish the bishop-dominated Church of England "with all its dependencies, roots and branches." To preserve some remnant of power, the king took to the field of battle, gathering an army of Royalist supporters and making his head-quarters in Oxford. The Parliament fielded its own army, dedicated to more representative government in both church and state. Mostly, these armies marched around the countryside missing each other, but at two battles, Marston Moor in 1644 and Naseby in 1645, the parliamentary army won decisive victories. Oliver Cromwell, a leader of that army, rose to political as well as military prominence.

Parliament was unable to deal with victory as effectively as with conflict. Their most pressing task was to devise a religious settlement, but this was no easy task with the king and his Royalists plotting revenge, Baptists and a few other radicals pushing for religious liberty, and the Presbyterian party manuevering itself into a position of political power. A bewildering array of socio-religious sects arose, such as Diggers, Ranters, Quakers, Levellers, and Fifth Monarchists, to advocate changes in church and state which varied from mild reforms to radical revolution. Parliament abolished the episcopal system, and called the famous Westminster Assembly of Divines to devise an alternative form of the state church. The Parliament refused to adopt the radical precedent of leaving all the churches free and none established by law. Most Englishmen of the time could not conceive of an orderly society without an official state church. The Westminster Assembly recommended and Parliament enacted the establishment of Presbyterian-

---

26. Roger Williams, *The Bloudy Tenent of Persecution for Cause of Conscience Discussed in a Conference Between Peace and Truth,* p. 36.

ism as the state church of England. Though this act was official, and by law the Presbyterian church functioned for some years as the state church, it never gained the allegiance of the people. Henry Denne, the Baptist, said it best: "The Presbyterians found they were not like to get into the saddle."[27]

Freedom was far from the intention of the Westminster Divines. Many of them would have agreed with Richard Baxter, who said, "I abhor unlimited liberty and toleration for all."[28] They provided liberty to believe and publish the truth, but not error, and their Westminster Confession of 1647 defined the difference. They said of the civil magistrate, "It is his duty to take order that unity and peace be preserved in the Church, that the truth of God be kept pure and entire, that all blasphemies and heresies be suppressed."[29] That most Baptist views and practices fell, in the judgment of the new church leaders, in the categories of "blasphemies and heresies" could not have brought comfort to the Baptists. In fact, they suffered more severely under the new regime than the old, justifying John Milton's complaint, "New Presbyter is but old Priest writ large."

Presbyterian pamphlets of the time present religious freedom as the worst possible evil. A 1645 broadside described such freedom as "a root of gall and bitterness," and its authors proclaimed: "We detest and abhorre the much endeavoured Toleration. Our bowels, our bowels are stirred within us." Perhaps the zenith of such antiliberty treatises was the famous, or infamous, *Gangraena,* by the respected Presbyterian minister Thomas Edwards. Edwards indicted religious freedom as the midwife which brought to birth several "monstrous bastard and misshapen religious growths," and Edwards's writing leaves no doubt that he included Baptists in that category. He described religious liberty as "the grand designe of the Devil, his Masterpeece and chiefe Engine he works by at this time to uphold his tottering Kingdom." Edwards, who represented the best of conservative Calvinism, could not abide a system which might allow the Baptists to exist. He bore interesting witness to the clamour for religious liberty in his statement, "There have been more books writ, Sermons preached, words spoken, besides plottings and actings for a Toleration, within these foure last yeers, then for all other things. Every day now brings forth Books for a Toleration."[30] These books, many of them by Baptists, would ultimately have their impact.

Though sometimes described as the army of Parliament, the army and

27. Henry Denne, *The Quaker No Papist,* p. 18.

28. Cited in Joseph Ivimey, *A History of the English Baptists,* 1:169.

29. Henry Bettenson, ed., *Documents of the Christian Church* (New York: Oxford University Press, 1957), pp. 347-348.

30. Thomas Edwards, *Gangraena: or a Catalogue of Many of the Errours, Heresies and Pernicious Practices of the Sectaries of This Time,* pp. 121-122.

Parliament had different concepts of how to proceed once military victory was secured. The army regarded the Civil War as a fight for both civil and religious freedom, and they assumed that victory would bring both. Many of the officers as well as the troops were Baptists. Baptist sermons and tracts spread their viewpoints throughout the army and, indeed, to the populations where they passed. Prayer meetings were a favorite activity, and often the Baptist chaplain and the military commander were the same person. Other sectarians and independents in the army shared many of the same hopes for both civil and religious freedom after the war.

Meantime the Parliament, with incredible lack of sensitivity, sought to erect another persecuting state church in place of the one they had abolished. They planned to disband the army without back pay, without legal indemnity for acts committed during the war, and perhaps worst of all without the religious liberty the army thought it had won on the field of battle. The army refused to accept such arrangements. A turning point was reached in 1648 when Colonel Pride, on orders from Cromwell, stood at the entrance to Parliament and refused entrance to those who had opposed the army's program. "Pride's Purge," as this exclusion was called, cleared the way for a new parliament of saints, who would do the will of God, and also the will of the army. In this volatile environment, Baptists seized their de facto freedom to meet for worship but continued their agitation for full religious liberty.

Edward Barber

Described as "a gentleman of great learning," Barber was a London merchant tailor who became a Baptist perhaps in the 1630s. In 1641 he was imprisoned for denying tithes and infant baptism and, in 1642, had the distinction to advocate baptism by immersion, not yet a customary practice among the General Baptists. He was an effective minister, preacher, and writer who was, according to Crosby, "the means of convincing many, that infant-baptism has no foundation in scripture."[31]

Barber's petition, *To the Kings Majesty,* grew out of his imprisonment in 1641. His views on religious liberty were formed not in isolated theory but in the crucible of experience. Like other Baptists before him, Barber professed complete civil allegiance, denied that religious liberty led to political or social instability, cited Scripture to show that man's response to God must be voluntary to be real, and predicted that more people would accept Christianity under freedom than under coercion.[32]

31. Crosby, 3:3.
32. Edward Barber, *To the Kings Majesty: The Petition of Many of His Subjects, Some of Which Having Beene Miserably Persecuted.*

Christopher Blackwood

In two treatises, *The Storming of Antichrist* (1644) and *Apostolical Baptisme* (1645), Blackwood wrote vigorously for Baptist viewpoints. A Cambridge graduate and Anglican priest, Blackwood converted to Baptist views as a result of a public debate led by Francis Cornwall. Astonished that he and his learned colleagues could not answer the Baptist arguments, Blackwood renounced infant baptism, joined the Particular Baptists, and gathered a congregation in Kent. He served as chaplain in the parliamentary army and accompanied General Fleetwood to Ireland where he was regarded as "the oracle of the Anabaptists in Ireland." Apparently the Restoration brought him back to London, where he signed a declaration against Thomas Venner's Fifth Monarchy uprising.

Blackwood said he wrote *The Storming of Antichrist* "out of his earnest desire he hath to a thorow Reformation, having formerly seen the mischiefs of half Reformations."[33] The book is more a catalog of arguments than a systematic discussion of the topic. He asked "whether it be lawfull for any person whatsoever to compell the conscience?" In the next several pages he listed and explained twenty-nine reasons for a negative answer. Most of these arguments can be seen in earlier writings, but Blackwood did suggest one or two new ones. For example, he said, "Compulsion of conscience makes differences to rise to a great height, which if men were left to their own light, what is not of God would far more easily fall."[34]

The second part of *The Storming* examines twenty-six arguments in favor of government compelling religious uniformity. Not surprisingly, Blackwood found all of these without merit. He also advocated a lesser degree of religious liberty for Roman Catholics than for Protestants, thus falling below the high standards set by Smyth, Helwys, and Busher. He further compromised Baptist views by his "reall doubts" of the extent of liberty. He said:

> Let the reader also further enquire, whether the Magistrate have power to punish grosse idolatry, and blasphemy against God, Christ, the Scriptures, and holinesse, and seducements of persons by corrupt doctrines in fundamental points, when there is no violation of the publike peace; These being reall doubts to me, I will determine nothing on any side.[35]

Blackwood softened these doubts somewhat by his following statement, "Yet seeing there is nothing that I know of in the New Testament for the same, my conscience for the present inclines me to think, that conservation

---

33. Christopher Blackwood, *The Storming of Antichrist, in His Two Last and Strongest Garrisons: of Compulsion of Conscience and Infants Baptisme,* title page.

34. Ibid., p. 21.

35. Christopher Blackwood, *Apostolical Baptisme,* Postscript.

of peace, equity, sobriety, &c. is the adequate object of the Magistrate's power."[36]

John Tombes

A major spokesman for religious liberty in the 1640s and 1650s was John Tombes of Leominster. Although he was won to believer's baptism in a debate at Bristol in 1642, some doubt he was ever a Baptist. During the 1650s he served on the Board of Triers, a government commission to help determine ministerial appointments, and after 1672 was content to describe himself as a Presbyterian. Whitley said, "Wherever any one opposed him, whether in speech or in print, there a Baptist church sprang up at once."[37] Tombes was ejected from his living as a result of the 1662 Act of Uniformity, after which the Bishop of Hereford said of him, "The only considerable Non Subscriber is the proud Anabaptist Toms, than whom I never knew a prouder, the very child of old Marcion."[38]

Tombes wrote several treatises advocating religious liberty, and his status guaranteed a hearing for his views. *The Ancient Bounds. Or Liberty of Conscience Tenderly Stated, Modestly Asserted, and Mildly Vindicated* (London, 1645) is typical of Tombes's works. He clearly compromised the concept of full religious liberty for all. The title of his treatise implies boundaries beyond which liberty becomes license. He said, "I contend not for variety of opinions, I know there is but one truth."[39] The implication is that if one possessed full truth, untruth should not be allowed. However, since truth cannot be found without liberty, liberty must be allowed.

So long as religious differences were minor, Tombes would have the magistrate keep hands off. He would, however, allow the government to temper extremes of "the frigid Zone of deficiency" and "the torrid Zone of malignancy." That is, the magistrate could prevent total neglect of religion on one hand or too militant practices on the other. As to the division of spheres between civil and spiritual, the concept that Roger Williams and others made so much of, symbolized in the two tables of the law, Tombes said:

Wee have committed to the Magistrate the charge of the second Table. . . . But is that all? No surely; He may enter the vault even of those abominations of the first Table, and ferret the Devils and Devil-worship out of their holes and dennes. . . . Therefore, it seems to me that Polutheisme and Atheisticall doctrines, which are sins against the first Table . . . these so far forth

36. Ibid.
37. W. T. Whitley, *A History of British Baptists,* p. 70.
38. A. C. Underwood, *A History of the English Baptists,* p. 70.
39. John Tombes, *The Ancient Bounds: or Liberty of Conscience Tenderly Stated, Modestly Asserted, and Mildly Vindicated,* Preface.

as they break out and discover themselves, ought to be restrained, exploded by the Christian Magistrate.[40]

This represents a clear compromise of the full religious liberty advocated by Smyth, Helwys, Murton, and most early Baptists. However, Tombes was not consistent; in another passage he insisted, "Religion is to be perswaded and not forced upon men." At a practical level, Tombes pointed out that when truth is left free it survives, while error tends to collapse. Religious persecution not only does not control false teachings but may actually increase them, for "to forbid them, is to sowe them, and there is no readier way to make men fond of them, then to restrain them by force."[41]

One cannot but be impressed by the sheer number of Baptist treatises, sermons, and petitions for religious liberty in the 1640s. Most of them were hard-hitting demands for full liberty, growing out of the crucible of actual experience. Addressed to the common people, as well as to government leaders, they found their mark and conditioned a generation to believe that people might stand before God unfettered by government regulations in religion.

The Saints' Regime, 1648-1660

The parliamentary purge of 1648 opened the door for more radical developments in English life. The shocking execution of King Charles I in January, 1649, revealed the radical temper of the times. Until 1653 the Saint's Parliament, so-called for its pronounced Puritan tendencies, was the major legislative assembly. Several Baptists and other dissenters in that Parliament tried mightily to erect a Christian commonwealth in which Protestantism was the norm, but their dreams outran their achievements. In 1653 Cromwell dismissed Parliament, assumed sole rule under the title of Lord Protector, and toyed with the idea of assuming the crown as well as the authority of a king. Most of the Baptists had loyally supported Cromwell as leader of the New Model Army, but they were offended by Cromwell's lordly new title, his assumption of the powers and pomp of royalty, and his new tendency to compromise on religious liberty.

Two documents during this era set out the legal statute of religion in England, the *Agreement of the People* (1649) and the *Instrument of Government* (1653). These called for official establishment of Protestantism but allowed considerable liberty as to doctrine and modes of worship.

The Baptists experienced vast growth during the years 1648 to 1660. Taking advantage of the relative liberty of the times and the public favor toward evangelical Protestantism, they preached publicly, formed new churches, linked them into associations, issued confessions of faith, and published their views in a steady stream of tracts and books. A few incidents

40. Ibid., Preface, p. 7.
41. Ibid., pp. 25, 31.

of persecution mark this period; but for the most part, Baptists were free and made the most of that freedom. Even some Anglicans and Presbyterians began to advocate a limited toleration. Other problems occupied the attention of Baptists, such as eschatology, laying on of hands, relation to Quakers, and the proper day for worship. Even so, Baptists published several notable works dealing with religious liberty.

John Clarke

Though he lived in Rhode Island, John Clarke was back in England for a few years in the 1650s and while there published a tract which had profound impact on both sides of the Atlantic. This was his *Ill Newes from New-England* (1652) which described the severe punishment of Baptists in Boston in 1651. Some had claimed that the American colonies were free of religious coercion, and Clarke wrote to set the record straight.

In *Ill Newes* Clarke insisted:

> No such believer, or Servant of Christ Jesus hath any liberty, much less Authority, from his Lord, to smite his fellow servant, nor yet with outward force, or arm of flesh, to constrain, or restrain his Conscience no nor yet his outward man for Conscience sake, or worship of his God . . . every man being such as shall appear before the judgement seat of Christ, and must give an account of himself to God, and therefore ought to be fully perswaded in his own mind, for what he undertakes.[42]

Henry Denne

One of the outstanding General Baptist leaders of the Commonwealth era was Henry Denne. He had left the Anglican Church in the early 1640s and in 1644 founded and served as pastor of the Baptist church at Warboys. Sensitive to the need for reform in England, Denne was for a time loosely associated with the Leveller movement. He was described by Edwards in *Gangraena* as

> a great Sectary, . . . in the Bishops times he was a great time-server, an High Altar man, and practiced the Innovations; but now of late years an Anabaptist: This man is a great Antinomian, a desperate Arminian, . . . He was rebaptized by a Mechanick, and made a member of Lambs church.[43]

However, Edwards did admit that Denne was "the ablest man in England for Prayer, Expounding, and Preaching" and noted that his "usual Theam . . . is Christs dying for all." This reflected Denne's General Baptist affiliation.

In 1659 Denne published the celebrated treatise *The Quaker No Papist,*

42. John Clarke, *Ill News from New England: or a Narrative of New England's Persecution,* p. 10.

43. Edwards, 1:76.

in which he stoutly defended religious liberty for all, including Catholics and Quakers, two of the least popular groups in England at that time. Denne insisted that every citizen should be held accountable for civil loyalty but left free in religion. Concerning Roman Catholics he asked:

> Why do we torment their consciences, by requiring them to abjure so many other opinions, which are neither relative to this that is objected, nor such, as the maintaining of them can be dangerous to the State? What is the Doctrine of Transubstantiation and Worshipping of the Sacraments . . . in relation to Government? May not a man be a good Subject, because he thinks that Christ is in the Sacrament, and that Good Works merit salvation?[44]

Denne further objected that Catholics were denied common rights and that "everyone may abuse them, even in the streets, without offence to others, nay with satisfaction enough unto many." He made similar defenses of Quakers, a group also subject to public harassment and mistreatment. Denne felt that his own religious liberty was threatened so long as any man's liberty was not secure.

The Later Stuart Era, 1660-1688

After more than a decade of relative freedom, Baptists in England faced perhaps their most severe persecution in the generation after 1660. This harsh government crackdown touched all the dissenting groups, but Baptists were singled out for special abuse. Baptists had been most vocal in advocating religious liberty, and they had been prominent in the parliamentary army which overthrew the king and toppled the Church of England. To some extent Baptists became the scapegoat for all the problems of church and state since 1640.

By the time of Oliver Cromwell's death in 1658, disillusionment with the Commonwealth experiment had already set in. Oliver was succeeded by his son Richard, who proved harmless but inept, and by 1659 there was open talk of a return to monarchy. That was accomplished in 1660 when an English coalition, led by General Monk, called young Charles II back from exile and installed him on the throne of his father. This "Royal Restoration" marks a turning point in English religious as well as political history.

Why would England, which had abolished the monarchy and beheaded the king, restore that same system? Why would the nation that had abolished episcopacy in all its "roots and branches" restore the Church of England, returning the bishops to power as before? By way of brief answer, one must note that the Commonwealth experiment was not an unqualified success. The government of the "saints," as the nominated parliament of 1653 was called, announced impressive goals but showed minimal achievements. Their rigid religion, eschatological extremes, and narrow outlook

44. Denne, pp. 16-17.

frightened many. Charles II was not forced upon the people; most of England welcomed him gladly.

Knowing that religious differences had been a major part of English turmoil since 1640, the new king issued a statement to reassure the citizens. This Declaration of Breda, named from the Dutch town where it was first issued, gave assurance that he would not molest those who had served in the army against his father; confirmed most of the land transactions of the interregnum; and announced a policy of religious toleration. Motivated apparently by a desire for domestic peace, the new king promised

> a liberty to tender consciences, and that no man shall be disquieted or called in question for differences of opinion in matters of religion, which do not disturb the peace of the kingdom; and that we shall be ready to consent to such an Act of Parliament as, upon mature deliberation, shall be offered to us, for the full granting of that indulgence.[45]

This promise reveals both the king's desire for toleration and his limitations in providing it. Baptists seized upon the first part of the statement and constantly reminded the king of his promised liberty. However, Charles II only promised to consent to such a provision passed by Parliament, and Parliament chose not to pass such a law.

The armed rebellion of the Fifth Monarchy men in January 1661 greatly frightened the king and intensified persecution, especially of Baptists. The Thirty Years' War on the Continent and the English Civil Wars led many to believe that the end of the world and the millennial kingdom was near. To them the Stuart Restoration was a final blow. Thomas Venner, therefore, led a group of armed horsemen in rebellion on January 6, 1661. They terrorized London for about four days before the rebellion was put down. Several were killed, and of those captured about twenty of the main leaders, including Venner, were executed. In the public mind this rebellion was associated with Baptists, unfairly for the most part, and this opened the door to severe repressions. In the next few months, Baptists issued confessions, petitions, treatises, and sermons denouncing Fifth-Monarchy millennialism, disassociating themselves from that radical sect, and reaffirming loyalty to the new king. One group even sent a delegation, composed of Joseph Wright and Thomas Grantham, for a personal audience with Charles II to distance themselves from radical millennialism.

All of this was to no avail. Within weeks, meetings for Baptist worship were forbidden, Baptists were subjected to official restrictions by government and unofficial abuse by the public, and the jails were jammed with Baptists. Children of Baptists were beaten by neighborhood gangs; some Baptist families feared to light lamps at night for fear of mobs. The prevail-

45. Henry Gee and William J. Hardy, *Documents Illustrative of English Church History,* p. 587.

ing spirit seems to have been expressed by a man at a public bonfire who threw in a faggot, pretending it to be a Baptist, and then "swore and tore, and struck the ground, and said, now have at the Anabaptists."[46]

Over a period of years, Parliament erected a package of religious legislation known as the Clarendon Code. The Corporation Act (1661) provided that no person could serve in public office without conforming to the state church. Since Baptists could not do this, it effectively eliminated them from public life. However, the law provided heavy fines for citizens elected to public office who refused to serve. At times local authorities conspired to get prosperous Baptists elected, knowing they would not serve, in order to collect the fines.

The Act of Uniformity (1662) provided that all English ministers had to believe the same doctrines and conduct worship by the same liturgy. Those who refused were put out of their posts. This "Great Ejection" saw about 20 percent of English clergy excluded, including Presbyterians, Congregationalists, Independents, and about twenty Baptists who held livings. The Great Ejection tended to multiply dissent and make it more respectable.

The Conventicle Act (1664) directly affected Baptists and was perhaps aimed primarily at them. It set severe penalties for holding unauthorized worship services or "conventicles," with more than five persons present beyond the immediate family. This did not prevent Baptists from meeting but did make their meetings more dangerous. They usually avoided singing, for that might call attention to their meetings. They met in homes for the most part, with a preference for back streets, and they tried not to arrive all at the same time. They often set a lookout so the congregation and ministers might have advance warning if authorities approached. If the officers found the people sitting quietly, technically no law was broken. If the minister was not preaching, but sitting among the people, the authorities could not determine if preaching had taken place, and if so who had preached. Quite often the congregation, if they had warning, would send the minister through a trap door into a concealed basement or to an upstairs window where he could cross over into an adjoining house and thus escape. Often the Baptists would arrange to meet in an upstairs room and pack the stairway with women and children to impede the approach of authorities. We read of a few times when the lookouts, hearing the preaching, became so convinced of their own sin and need of salvation that tears obstructed their vision and they failed to sound the alarm.

The Five-Mile Act (1665) sought to plug an unexpected loophole in the Act of Uniformity. Some evicted clergy simply formed their own churches in the same town where they had previously served. Having the confidence of the people, crowds resorted to them. The new law forbade ejected minis-

---

46. Henry Jessey, *The Lord's Loud Call to England,* p. 29.

ters from preaching, teaching, or even residing within five miles of the town where they had been ejected.

The Test Act (1673) provided that those serving at the highest government levels take the Lord's Supper according to the Anglican pattern. This was probably aimed primarily at Roman Catholics, and specifically at James II, brother of King Charles II, who was a Catholic. The law failed to prevent James from coming to power, for he became king in 1685 at the death of Charles II.

During these years of persecution, Charles II made a few futile efforts to moderate the severe persecution. Charles's only success was the 1672 Indulgence, which gave dissenters a much-needed year of respite. That indulgence freed John Bunyan from Bedrord jail, where he had languished for twelve years. However, when a hostile Parliament withdrew the Indulgence in 1673, the names of ministers and members and the lists of meeting places, which had been given to qualify for toleration, became weapons to hunt down and persecute dissenters.

This atmosphere of persecution, actual and imminent, greatly affected Baptists. No doubt Whitley was correct in saying Baptists' main task was merely to exist. However, they did issue an avalanche of petitions for relief and for the most part held firmly to their convictions even during the "great persecution."

The Apology of Some call'd Anabaptists (1660) was an effort to defend Baptists against virulent but groundless rumors that they were radical revolutionaries. The authors determined "not to bring to light any new matter" but cited their previous confessions and treatises to show the civil loyalty of Baptists. The next year, 1661, several Baptists led by William Kiffin issued *The Humble Apology of Some Commonly Called Anabaptists* in an effort to distance themselves from the Fifth-Monarchy radicals. Also, in 1661 William Jeffery led in issuing *The Humble Petition and Representation of the Sufferings of Several Peaceable, and Innocent Subjects, Called by the Name of Anabaptists, Inhabiting in the County of Kent, and now Prisoners in the Gaol of Maidstone, for the Testimony of a Good Conscience.* The title tells the full story. This petition must have been successful, for shortly two of those Baptists who had been in Maidstone were at liberty and published *Sion's Groans for Her Distressed* (1661), another plea for full religious liberty. In 1664 sixteen imprisoned General Baptists issued a pamphlet entitled *The Persecuted People of God,* which not only appealed for liberty but also urged Baptists not to compromise their faith to gain freedom.[47]

Other Baptists who published defenses of religious liberty during this time include Thomas Grantham, Benjamin Keach, and Thomas Delaune.

47. See Harry Leon McBeth, *English Baptist Literature on Religious Liberty to 1689,* pp. 216 *f.*

Grantham published a major book in 1678 called *Christianismus Primitivus,* in which he expounded Baptist theology, described Baptist worship, and set out Baptist views on several controversial subjects. Book III of this massive volume deals with religious liberty, in which Grantham sought to prove "the Baptized Churches are unjustly charged with seditious principles."

Benjamin Keach wrote on many subjects, including religious liberty. He became a General Baptist in 1655 but switched to Particular by 1672. Best remembered for introducing hymn singing as a part of worship, Keach also prepared materials for the religious instruction of children, collected and preserved Baptist historical documents, and helped popularize religious allegory as a literary style. Keach had firsthand experience of persecution, being oft imprisoned and fined, his books seized and destroyed. He was once condemned to stand in the public stocks for a day. He used the time to preach to passersby.

Keach warned Baptists not to depend too much on the Indulgence issued by James II in 1687. As in the Indulgence of 1672, dissenters had to give the names of their ministers and members and the location of their meetings to qualify for relief. Remembering how these had been used against them when the earlier Indulgence was withdrawn, Keach warned fellow Baptists to be cautious. King James II proclaimed, "We do freely give them [dissenters] leave to meet and serve God after their own way and manner, be it in private houses or places purposely hired or built for that use."[48] Many Baptists agreed with the unidentified "T. W." who wrote to dissenters, "You are therefore to be hugged now, onely that you may be the better squeezed at another time."[49]

Thomas Delaune, a London Baptist and a schoolmaster and printer by occupation, published *A Plea for the Non-Conformists* in 1683. This advanced two points: that Baptists had adequate grounds for separation from the Church of England and that all denominations should be allowed complete religious freedom. Reacting to an Anglican statement that the Baptists' "wayward skittish Consciences ought to be well bridled and restrained," Delaune sought to show that Baptist views were orthodox and innocent. This treatise greatly impressed Daniel Defoe, author of *Robinson Crusoe,* who republished it in 1706, with a preface condemning "the Knocking-down-Arguments of a Gaol and Fine" in matters of religion.[50]

For religious reasons, Delaune landed in prison in 1683, where he died in 1685. No specific charges were brought against him, and efforts to obtain Delaune's release were fruitless. Even from prison, he continued writing for religious liberty. His ultimate hope was that "all who own the Name of

48. Gee and Hardy, pp. 642-643.

49. Cited by McBeth, p. 250.

50. Thomas Delaune, *A Plea for Non-Conformists,* reprinted with a preface by Daniel Defoe (London: Printed for William and Joseph Marshall, 1706), Preface, p. vii.

Christ would serve him with one Heart, and with one Soul, and not tear each other to pieces."[51] Unfortunately, he did not live to see that day.

The Broadmead Church in Bristol provides vivid examples of persecution during the later Stuart era and the strategies Baptists used to survive. Even before the Broadmead Church was formed, a few citizens who objected to the Church of England made it a point to rent houses outside Bristol to "gett out of Towne" on Sundays to avoid coerced worship. Dorothy Hazzard, a Baptist, was one of these. She used her rented house as a "lying in place" for women to give birth, that their infants, being born outside the parish, might escape infant baptism. After 1660, waves of persecution swept over Bristol as officials applied the harsh laws of the Clarendon Code with full force. Rarely could the church keep a pastor any length of time without losing him to imprisonment. However, such pastors almost invariably called a church meeting and preached on the very day of their release. Many of them came out of prison with impaired health; one was so weak he required help to baptize converts.

The Baptists tried valiantly to maintain regular church meetings through these hard times. In February 1674, church records indicate that they agreed

> to appoint some youth, or two of them, to be out at ye door every meeting, to Watch when . . . informers or officers were coming, and soe to come in, one of them and give us notice thereof. Alsoe, some of ye hearers, women and Sisters, would Sitt and Crowde in ye Staires, when we did begin ye Meeting with and Exercise, that soe ye Informers might not too Suddainely come in upon us; by reason of which they were prevented divers times.[52]

At times Baptists met in private homes which were equipped with trap doors leading to concealed basement rooms. On a July Sunday in 1675, the authorities came suddenly upon the Baptist meeting, but they "could not find ye Bro. that spake, for wee had conveyed him downe into a roome under, through a Trap made like a Biffet-Bench against ye Wall in a seate or pue enclosed."[53] In one such case, the officers almost caught the pastor, laying hold of his coat. However, the pastor "gave a Spring, and ye Coat slipt off, and he wonderfully made his Escape, tho' they pursued him."[54]

Another strategy the Bristol Baptists devised was to gather for worship at one house but to have the pastor preach from an adjoining house. They also set a flexible schedule, trying not to meet always at the same hour or place. They made it a point to wear plain clothing, "taking a great deal of Care in going and coming, ye Women wearing neither White aprons nor

51. Thomas Delaune, *A Narrative of the Sufferings of Tho. Delaune,* p. 57.
52. Roger Hayden, ed. *The Records of a Church of Christ in Bristol, 1640-1687,* p. 149.
53. Ibid., p. 170.
54. Ibid., p. 256.

Pattens" so as not to alert observers that they were gathering for worship. The members were instructed to arrive and leave singly or in small groups.

The Baptists soon learned by hard experience that setting door guards against officers from the outside was not enough; they also had to guard against informers from within. They curtained off a section of the meeting room sufficient for the minister and several trusted members. Outside the curtains was room for a number of people to sit. Any worshiper not known and trusted had to sit outside the curtain. All could hear, but only the trusted could see who preached for the minister stood up after the curtain was drawn and sat down before it was pulled back. On one occasion, however, when the alarm was given that officers were approaching, the brother appointed to pull the curtain did so too quickly before the speaker, Brother Terrill, could be seated. An informer who was present reported Terrill to the authorities.

Even these strategies did not always work, and many times the ministers and members, men and women, would be captured, haled to court, and remanded to prison with callous disregard for their basic civil as well as religious rights. On one occasion in 1674, the pastor almost escaped, but "some of ye Bishop's men gatt hold of his legges, others of his Armes, and So with much violence dragged him out, and Carryed him away."[55]

While the pastors lay in prison, the church continued to meet under lay leadership. Deacons baptized such converts as presented themselves, and laymen led the worship services, but the church would not observe the Lord's Supper in the absence of a minister. In 1674 the Baptists described their plight as follows:

> our Ministers being taken from us, one dead, and ye rest Imprissoned, and we feared their death likewise in such a Bad Prisson, and we being pursued closely . . . by ye Bishop's men . . . . For our Partes, at our Meeting, we presently made use of our ministering gifts in ye Church, (as we did in former persecutions, Contenting oursclves with meane gifts and coarse fare in ye want of Better). Wherefore we considered which way to Maintaine our Meetings, by prescrving our Speaker.[56]

As the persecution intensified, the Bristol Baptists had to abandon for a time the meetings of the entire church. Instead, they broke up into little groups, to come within the limits of the Conventicle Act, each group under the guidance of a lay leader. In a poignant letter in 1683 to their pastor who was in prison, the church inquired if their duty called for them to continue public meetings. This shows that pastors continued to guide their flocks even from prison and also that over twenty years of persecution was taking its toll upon the church. According to church records, "Our Pastour shew'd

55. Ibid., p. 154.
56. Ibid., p. 150.

it was our Duty to meet publickly, and not refrain for fear of threats." The church called a meeting, led by the influential layman Edward Terrill. The records show:

> at a Church-meeting on ye 4th of March [1683] we took our sad state into Consideration. And Br. Terrill signified that our duty lay in 3 things: - 1st. To watch over one another, that none draw back to ye World's Worship; 2nd. That every one sanctify ye Ld's say; 3rd. that we endeavour to edify one another as Members, and also do what we can for others' Souls.[57]

To accomplish these things, they "agreed to have circular meetings at 5 places where ye brethren were to exercise their gifts." They devised a round-robin of small gatherings, staggered at different times and places, with members chosen to attend first one and then another. As a result one hundred could hear the gospel on Sunday; and within five weeks, each member met with all the groups and heard all the lay leaders. Thus the church maintained contact with all the members, but never in groups of more than five.

When persecution had driven the Baptists out of the rented building and made even small group house meetings dangerous, they fled into the adjoining woods. Even there the "tything men," as they called the Bishop's officers, pursued them, sometimes on horseback. In the church records for 1681, we read, "On Ld's day, ye 11th, Br. Fowned [the pastor], being come from London, but daring to come into ye City because of ye Corporation Act, met with us and preacht in K's Wood, near Scruze Hole, under a Tree, and endured ye Rain." A few days later, "Our Pastor preacht in another place in ye Wood. Our friends took much Pains in ye Rain, because many informers were ordered out to search; and we were in peace, tho' there were near 20 men and boys in search."[58]

Despite these waves of persecution, the Bristol Baptists held firmly to their faith. Only a few returned to the world's worship, as they called the Church of England, though more "fell into Notions" (i.e., Quakerism). In time Bristol became a major center of Baptist strength in the West, rivaling London. In 1679, in the midst of persecution, they laid the basis of Bristol Baptist College. This is the oldest Baptist college in the world, and it continues to flourish in Bristol to this day.

The Act of Toleration, 1689

James II did not last long as king of England. Perhaps he moved too fast in effecting changes; perhaps England was by then too Protestant to accept a Catholic king; or perhaps persecution of Protestants in Catholic France frightened the English who feared the same might happen in England. At

---

57. Ibid., p. 259.
58. Ibid., pp. 243-244.

any rate, a powerful coalition arose to depose James in 1688. They captured the king, who was attempting to flee in disguise, but held him only briefly before allowing him with his queen and infant son to leave the country. Having killed one king in 1649, they had no desire for another regicide. This coalition invited William of Orange and Mary, rulers of Holland, to accept the English throne. William came from a strongly Protestant family, and Mary, daughter of James II, was either Protestant in her sympathies or wise enough to keep quiet.

In 1689 Parliament passed the Act of Toleration, which marks a milestone in religious freedom in the modern world. However, this act falls short of providing full religious liberty. Dissenters still had to pay tithes to the Church of England, register their meeting places with the Anglican bishop, and take the customary oaths of allegiance. They were also forbidden to meet "in any place for religious worship with the doors locked, barred, or bolted."[59] Even so, this allowed the most generous measure of religious freedom then known in England.

The motive for this toleration was at least as much practical as theological. The act set out its motive in the phrase "some ease to scrupulous consciences in the exercise of religion may be an effectual means to unite their majesties' Protestant subjects in interest and affection."[60] Apparently the act accomplished that purpose, but it did far more. It allowed English dissenters, including Baptists, to face the future with confidence, knowing that their basic rights to worship, preach, and print would be secure. Baptist response to the Toleration Act may be seen in the rejoicing of Benjamin Keach, who addressed William and Mary as follows:

> And all the time in England you have been,
> What strange amazing wonders have we seen?
> A poor sick Land divided; by Christ's power
> Made whole and all united in one hour.[61]

Summary

The Baptist emphasis upon religious liberty put them in advance of their time. They did what no other group of the time was prepared to do—advocate religious freedom not only for different sorts of Christians but also for those who followed other religions or none. A few Baptists, such as Blackwood and Tombes, taught a more limited concept of religious freedom, confirming Ivimey's remark about English Baptists: "Some of them confounded the power of the magistrate with the government of that king-

59. Gee and Hardy, p. 657.
60. Ibid., p. 654.
61. Benjamin Keach, *Distressed Zion Relieved*, Preface, To the King and Queen.

dom which is not of this world."[62] However, these were exceptions which proved the rule. By far the majority of Baptists taught complete religious liberty for all.

Unlike later philosophers who formulated theories of toleration in splendid isolation, Baptists forged their teachings in the crucible of actual persecution. Their primary source was the Bible, especially the New Testament. Baptist writings show that they had difficulty with Old Testament references to kings controlling religion, but they constantly appealed to the teachings of Christ and the apostles. The parable of the tares (Matt. 13:24-30,36-40), Christ's refusal to call down fire on those who differed (Luke 9:54-55), and Paul's regret that he had persecuted Christians (Acts 9:1-18) were among their favorites. They also appealed to the example of Christ, who called for voluntary response.

Beyond specific texts, Baptists also appealed to the nature of Christian faith as revealed in the Bible. Christianity, they said, is so personal that by its nature it cannot be coerced. Unless man's response to God is voluntary, it becomes meaningless. Describing forced religion as spiritual rape, they concluded that religious coercion "stinks in God's nostrils."

What could be more reasonable, Baptists argued, than allowing each man to choose his own religion, seeing each must stand before God for himself? The search for truth could better be conducted with freedom in inquiry, they said, than by making certain religious ideas and practices off limits.

Baptists also used a number of practical arguments to buttress their teaching on religious liberty. They argued that religious liberty increases domestic tranquility, provides a better climate for trade and economic advance, and leads to a more stable society. They appealed to history to show that religious persecution harms both church and society, while liberty proves beneficial to both.

Historians generally agree that the Baptist witness was a major factor in leading to the Toleration Act of 1689. By their preaching, teaching, and printing on religious liberty, and also by the example of their courage, and sometimes heroism under suffering, Baptists wielded an influence out of proportion to their numbers. Nor was this impact limited to England. The Toleration Act also had an impact upon Baptists in Colonial America. In the struggle for religious liberty in the new land, Baptists continued the emphases first announced by their English brethren.

At long last, Baptists had the freedom they desired. Yet their churches seemed exhausted by the long struggle to exist. The new era of religious toleration brought for the Baptists, and for most other Christians in England, a time of decline and decay.

---

62. Ivimey, 1:vi.

4

Baptist Beginnings in America

Baptists in early Armerica were few and scattered. They formed only a handful of churches in the seventeenth century, and these showed little promise of the future greatness which awaited the denomination in the new world. Of the churches formed in the colonies before 1700, most were in New England. Late in the century a few small churches sprang up in the Middle Colonies, and just at the end of the century William Screven moved the Kittery church from Maine to South Carolina to join the Baptists already present in "Charles Towne."

Most Baptists in early America stemmed from a British background. While the earliest churches were indigenous, in time the English connection became clearer. Many who joined the colonial churches had first embraced the Baptist way in England or Wales, and countless letters between Baptists in the Old World and the New helped shape similar viewpoints. Baptists in America adopted the denominational structures common among their English brethren, reproduced English confessions and catechisms, and often sent to England for ministers. One cannot regard Baptists in America as merely an extension of those in England, but neither can one minimize the connections between them.

Considerable variety marks Baptist beginnings in this country. The categories familiar in England also appeared in America, such as Particular, General, and Seventh-Day Baptists, though in time these labels tended to be modified in the new setting. Baptist mutations unknown in England cropped up in America. Two examples, both from the seventeenth century, were the Rogerenes of New England, an extreme sabbatarian group emphasizing divine healing; and the Keithians of the Middle Colonies, who combined Quaker spirituality with Baptist forms of immersion and church life. Neither of these found an enduring place in the American landscape.[1]

This chapter will trace Baptist beginnings in three major geographical areas: New England, the Middle Colonies, and the Southern Colonies.

1. A helpful analysis of various kinds of Baptists in early America is found in Robert G. Gardner, *Baptists of Early America: A Statistical History,* 1639-1790.

Baptist Beginnings in New England

The northeastern colonies called New England grew rapidly in population and exercised a formative influence upon American forms of religion, government, and general culture. Most of the early settlers in the leading colony of Massachusetts were militant Puritans, filled with godly zeal and rigid intolerance for any who differed from their theocratic concepts. They succeeded in establishing the Congregational Church as the state-sponsored religion of most of New England. This alliance of church and state called for religious conformity as a prerequisite to good citizenship. This meant harsh persecution for all who dared to differ from the official religion. In this environment of coercion, early Baptists sought to preach and practice their own distinctive concepts of Christianity. Progress amid persecution tells the story of early Baptists in New England.

Roger Williams

Extant records do not tell who was the first Baptist in America, but they do show that the first organized church was formed at Providence in early 1639 by Roger Williams. This study must include a sketch of his life and thought.

Background. Roger Williams (c.1603-1684) was born in London, the son of James Williams and the former Alice Pemberton. The exact date of Roger's birth and many other details of his youth are uncertain because the great fire of London in 1666 destroyed the records of St. Sepulchre's Parish, where the Williams family was affiliated. James Williams was a merchant tailor, middle class and ambitious, a proper member of the Church of England who reared his children in that tradition.

As a teenage boy, Roger attracted the attention of Sir Edward Coke, chief justice of the King's Bench and one of the leading jurists in England. Coke was an occasional worshiper at St. Sepulchre's and there noticed Roger Williams's unusual skill in recording the minister's sermons in shorthand. That was a skill Sir Edward could use in the law offices, and he gave the boy a job. Thus began a relationship which deeply influenced the life of Roger Williams. Through Coke Williams met many leading statesmen of England, contacts which proved invaluable later when he sought a charter for Providence Plantations. He also drew insights from Coke in framing the laws of that new government. In Coke's office, young Williams witnessed trials before the Star Chamber, many of which involved religion. There he became acutely aware of the legal risks and sufferings of religious dissenters and perhaps learned something of their teachings as well.

Coke also proved the key to young Roger's education. Coke's daughter later wrote of her father's relation to Williams, "He [Coke] seing him soe hopefull a youth, tooke such likeing to him that he put him into Suttons hospitall" in 1621.[2] Sutton's Hospital, later named the Charterhouse, was a school similar perhaps to a high school today. As a leading trustee, Coke also arranged for a scholarship to pay Williams's tuition and other expenses. Williams showed himself "a fitte scholar" and was admitted to Pembroke College of Cambridge University in June 1625. At Cambridge he had access to the best education available in England. Williams graduated Bachelor of Arts at Cambridge in 1627 and enrolled for his master's degree. After about eighteen months of further study, he withdrew from Cambridge without receiving his masters. A university record confirms "that Roger Williams . . . hath forsaken the Universitye and is become a discontinuer of his studyes."[3] Apparently religious dissatisfaction was one reason for withdrawal.

Roger Williams, Anglican. Though reared an Anglican, Williams quite early showed sympathy with religious dissenters, a tendency opposed by Williams's parents. As a lad of ten or twelve, he apparently underwent a profound religious experience which nudged him toward Puritanism. He later spoke of "being persecuted in and out of my father's house" for these views. However, at his graduation from Cambridge in 1627, Williams signed the Subscription Book, which affirmed his hearty acceptance of the major doctrines of the Church of England. These "three darling Articles," as some called the Subscription Book, affirmed that the king was by right the head of the English Church, that worship according to the Book of Common Prayer and church government through bishops were lawful, and that the Thirty-Nine Articles, the official creed of the church, expressed true doctrine. Whether Williams signed under protest, since the signature was required for graduation, we do not know.

Upon graduation Williams received ordination but did not accept a pastorate. Instead he became private chaplain to the manor of Sir William Masham in Essex County. This was not unusual; many young clergymen got started that way. The Masham estate, with its several families of workers and helpers, formed a sizeable community. The young chaplain was well liked and performed in a satisfactory manner. In Williams's early months at Sir Masham's, he advanced no radical views; but the record does reveal the usual amount of youthful mistakes, misguided zeal, and tactless blunders. Already Williams revealed that intensity of personality which would mark his later life.

After a bitterly disappointing love affair, Williams was refused permission to marry Jane Whalley, a young woman of elevated social status. Williams's reaction was extreme; he fell into severe illness, marked by deep depression and high fever, so that many despaired of his life. His nursemaid during those months of illness was Mary Barnard, a young woman of more

2. Ola Elizabeth Winslow, *Master Roger Williams,* p. 46.
3. Ibid., p. 72.

modest social status. The daughter of a minister, Mary Barnard (sometimes Bernard) was "in service" to Johanna "Jug" Altham, a daughter of Lady Masham. One of Lady Masham's letters summed up the matter: "Mr Willyams is to marrye Mary barnard, Jug Altham's made."[4] They were married December 15, 1629, a fortunate match for Williams, for Mary proved a steadfast companion.

Roger Williams, Separatist. By 1629 Roger Williams was a rigid Separatist. He had come to regard the Church of England as a false church, from which true Christians must withdraw. Several factors may have influenced Williams toward Separatism. From the first Williams's own mind was independent, and he wanted to seek out the message of the Bible for himself. He grew up in West Smithfield, in the heart of London, where within a few blocks of his home several English Christians had been martyred for their faith. Williams must have known about these cases and may even have witnessed some of these executions. Within his immediate community were known to be numerous meeting places of various kinds of dissenters. Williams must have known of these, and he may have attended some of their meetings. As secretary to Sir Edward Coke, Williams saw the seamy side of religious persecution. At Cambridge he encountered the religious thought of his day, much of which undercut the Anglican Church. These factors combined to shape Williams, and by 1629 he had moved from mild to rigid Separatism.

A young clergyman of Separatist principles faced a bleak future in England, so Williams decided to accept the "late New England call" from the church at Salem, near Boston. At first he had spurned the call, but by 1630 it looked more attractive. To escape almost certain imprisonment, Roger and Mary Williams made their way to Bristol, where they took passage on the *Lyon,* sailing December 1, 1630, for America. After a tumultuous passage of fifty-six days, they landed on February 5, 1631. Something of Williams's attitude was revealed in a letter to the daughter of Coke, recalling, "It was bitter as death to me when Bishop Laud pursued me out of this land, and my conscience was persuaded against the national church and ceremonies and bishops."[5]

Williams was eagerly welcomed to Boston. Upon Williams's arrival, Governor Winthrop recorded in his journal, "The ship *Lyon,* Mr. William Peirce, master, arrived at Nantasket. She brought Mr. Williams, (a godly minister,) with his wife, . . . about twenty passengers, and about two hundred tons of goods."[6] Williams was about thirty years of age, tall and handsome in appearance, well-educated, forceful in speech, and accounted as "a man godly and zealous, having many precious parts." Almost immedi-

---

4. Ibid., p. 87
5. James Ernst, *Roger Williams: New England Firebrand,* p. 59.
6. *Winthrop's Journal: History of New England 1630-1649,* 1:57.

ately he was offered one of the most influential church positions in America, that of teacher in the Boston church. The incumbent, John Wilson, planned to return to England and, in fact, sailed on the *Lyon* on its return voyage. Williams not only refused this generous offer but did so somewhat curtly. In a letter to John Cotton, Jr., Williams said, "Being unanimously chosen teacher at Boston, I conscientiously refused and withdrew to Plymouth, because I durst not officiate to an unseparated people, as upon examination and conference I found them to be."[7]

This was the heart of Williams's tensions with his New England colleagues: They were moderate "semi-Separates," while he had become a rigid Separatist like John Smyth. The Boston people never forgave Williams, not only for his views but also for declining their offer. By 1631 Williams also publicly denied the right of the civil magistrate to regulate breaches of the first table of the Ten Commandments (i.e., religious offenses). This division of spheres Williams would later develop into the doctrine of separation of church and state.

On April 12, 1631, Williams was installed as minister at Salem, near Boston, a church where rigid Separatist views were more welcome. However, the Boston authorities brought such pressures against Salem that Williams withdrew in the summer and went to Plymouth, as assistant to the regular minister, Ralph Smith. Williams was well-received in Plymouth. He later wrote, "At Plymouth I spake on the Lord's day and week days, and wrought hard at the hoe for my bread, and so afterwards at Salem, until I found them both professing to be an unseparated people in New England, . . . communicating with the parishes in Old (England) by their members repairing on frequent occasions thither."[8]

Williams served two years at Plymouth, 1631-1633, during which time he preached, farmed, and traded with the Indians. He began to learn various Indian languages, their "hard Rockie speech," as he called it, and by 1632 was conducting missionary work among the tribes. Governor Bradford recorded that at Plymouth Williams "was friendly entertained, according to their poore abilities, and exercised his gifts among them." However, Williams discovered that the Plymouth people were less separated than he had thought. Bradford said that in 1633 Williams "began to fall into some strange opinions, and from opinion to practice, which caused some controversie betweene ye church and him, and in ye end some discontente on his parte, by occasion whereof he left them some thing abruptly."[9] William Brewster, ruling elder of the Plymouth church, was even more specific; he said that by 1633 Williams was "venting of divers of his own singular

---

7. Cited in Ernst, p. 63.
8. Ibid., p. 81.
9. Henry Martyn Dexter, *As to Roger Williams, and his 'Banishment' from the Massachusetts Plantation*, p. 8.

opinions, and seeking to impose them upon others, he not finding such a concurrence as he expected, he desired his dismission to the Church of Salem." Brewster also feared that Williams would "run the same course of rigid Separatism and Anabaptistry, which Mr. John Smith the Sebaptist at Amsterdam had done."[10] We do not know what led Brewster to think Williams was on the way to becoming a Baptist, but he was later proven correct.

Williams returned to Salem in late 1633 and, despite pressure from Boston, was installed as minister in the church. He served until 1635, developing his views further in the direction of religious independency and political democracy.

In October of 1635 Williams was cited once more before the Boston court to answer for teachings which the authorities found objectionable. Four specific charges were lodged against Williams, that he had taught:

> *First,* That we have not our Land by Pattent from the King, but that the Natives are the true owners of it, and that we ought to repent of such a receiving it by Pattent.
> *Secondly,* That it is not lawfull to call a wicked person to Sweare, to Pray, as being actions of God's worship.
> *Thirdly,* That it is not lawfull to heare any of the Ministers of the Parish Assemblies in England.
> *Fourthly,* That the Civill Magistrates power extends only to the Bodies and Goods, and outward State of men.[11]

Williams acknowledged that he had, indeed, taught these concepts. As to the first charge: The kings of England had claimed the land in America, with power to allot it to whom they chose by a royal decree of "patent." The fact that England was Christian and the Indians pagan gave the king, the English felt, ownership of the land. Williams denied these presuppositions, insisting that the Indians were the true owners and that if others desired the land they had to purchase it from the Indians. This seemed revolutionary to New England settlers. It denied the authority of the Crown and endangered land ownership by the people.

The second charge was occasioned by the Freeman's Oath, required of settlers in Massachusetts Bay. Similar to a "pledge of allegiance," this oath was couched in the religious vocabulary of the day. To government officials, it appeared a simple promise of political loyalty; to Williams and other partisans, it appeared as a religious oath, taken in God's name, a form of government-required prayer. Non-Christians could not take the oath, said Williams, because it was coerced worship and prayer; Christians could not

10. Ibid.
11. Roger Williams, *Mr. Cottons Letter Lately Printed, Examined and Answered* (London: n. p., 1644), p. 4.

take it because only the kingdom of God and not civil states are to be established by vows to God.

The rigid Separatism of Williams formed the substance of the third charge. He insisted that Christians should not only withdraw from the Church of England but also from everyone who failed to withdraw from that church, even if a member of one's own family.

The fourth charge represented a basic part of William's teaching. As was customary then, Williams divided the Ten Commandments into the first table (duty to God), and the second table (duty to fellow man). Williams readily acknowledged the power of the magistrate to regulate breaches of the second table; he was no anarchist. However, he denied that any civil authority could regulate or punish offenses against the first table. This viewpoint was later called separation of church and state.

The court appointed Mr. Hooker to "reduce" Williams from these errors, a thankless task that Hooker tried manfully but failed to accomplish. Thereupon, in October 1635, the court passed the following sentence:

> Whereas Mr. Roger Williams, . . . hath broached & dyvulged dyvers newe & dangerous opinions, against the aucthoritie of magistrates, . . . & yet mainetaineth the same without retraccon, it is therefore ordered, that the said Mr. Williams shall dept out of this jurisdiccon within sixe weekes now nexte ensuing.[12]

The Boston court postponed the deadline for Williams's departure to the spring of 1636, on condition that he would not further disseminate his views. When they heard that Williams held private meetings, continued to preach his radical views, and had drawn away as many as twenty followers with whom he planned to set up a rival colony nearby, they moved at once to arrest him. Officials were dispatched in January 1636 to arrest Williams and put him on a ship ready to sail for England. However, Governor Winthrop, for whatever reason, secretly notified Williams of these developments, and Williams fled into the wilderness.

Had it not been for Williams's friendship with the Indians, with whom he lodged during that winter season, doubtless Williams would not have survived. Williams lost nothing in the later telling of this winter experience:

> I was unmercifully driven from my chamber to a winter's flight, exposed to the miseries, poverties, necessities, wants, debts, hardships of sea and land in a banished condition, . . . I was sorely tossed for one fourteen weeks in a bitter winter season, not knowing what bread and bed did mean. . . . exposed to a winter's miseries in a howling wilderness of frost and snow.[13]

In June 1636, Williams and several friends from Salem established the nucleus of Providence Plantations, just outside the Massachusetts Bay juris-

12. Cited in Dexter, p. 59.
13. Ernst, p. 156.

diction. He named the settlement to commemorate God's providence to him in his distress. Until Williams and the others could apply to England for a proper charter, they drew up a compact on June 16, 1636, promising to abide by "such orders and agreements as shall be made by the greater number of the present householders, . . . only in civil things."[14] From the very first the new colony provided for democracy, religious liberty, and separation of church and state. The charter of 1663 provided that

> no person within said colony, at any time hereafter shall be in any wise molested, punished, disquited, or called in question for any differences in opinion in matters of religion, and do not actually disturb the civil peace of said colony; but that all and any persons may, from time to time, and at all times hereafter freely and fully have and enjoy his and their own judgments and consciences in matters of religious concernment.[15]

The record confirms that Williams not only held these views but also lived by them. Some who doubt this may point to the case of Joshua Verlin who was exiled from Providence, much as Williams had been from Boston. But the circumstances were quite different. Verlin was known as "a young man boisterous and desperate," who would not join in the public worship at Providence nor allow his wife to do so. He beat his wife severely in an effort to prevent her attendance, citing the standard arguments for wifely submission. Verlin was never called in question for his own religious views but was disenfranchised for beating his wife and denying her civil rights. One historian regards this as an important early affirmation of the rights of women, saying:

> This new liberty gave woman an independent status and the right to leave her house without the consent of her husband. She was no longer his chattel, nor subject to his religious conscience. . . . Providence was the first civil government to recognize these feminine rights as a natural and civil right.[16]

Roger Williams, Baptist. William Brewster's remark in 1633 proved prophetic: Roger Williams was indeed moving toward Baptist views. During the first three years of Providence Plantations, the public worship could best be described as Separatist. Probably Williams and the group considered themselves still members of the Salem church. The Salem church so regarded them, for in 1639 that church presumed authority to pass a "great Censure" upon them.

Sometime before March 16, 1639, Williams and several others formed a Baptist church at Providence, the earliest Baptist church in the new world. Under that date, Governor Winthrop wrote:

14. Joseph Martin Dawson, *Baptists and the American Republic,* p. 34.
15. Ibid.
16. Ernst, p. 194.

At Providence things grew still worse; for a sister of Mrs. Hutchinson, the wife of one Scott, being infected with Anabaptistry, and going last year to live at Providence, Mr. Williams was taken (or rather emboldened) by her to make open profession thereof, and accordingly was rebaptized by one Holyman, a poor man late of Salem. Then Mr. Williams rebaptized him and some ten more. They also denied the baptizing of infants, and would have no magistrates.[17]

The Mrs. Hutchinson mentioned was Anne, who had been exiled from Boston in 1637 for speaking against rigid Puritanism in the Antinomian controversy. She was almost certainly the first woman preacher in America but never became a Baptist as is sometimes erroneously reported. She and her family settled in Rhode Island but were later massacred by the Indians in what is now New York. The Mrs. Scott mentioned was Catherine, wife of Richard Scott. Perhaps they had been Baptists in England; at any rate, she persuaded Williams to act upon his Baptist convictions. Isaac Backus suggested Williams may have considered believer's baptism earlier but searched for proper authority to confer it. The "Holyman" was Ezekiel Holliman, a layman from Salem. The denial of infant baptism is in keeping with Baptist views, but the phrase "they would have no magistrates" probably means they would not allow magistrates to regulate religious questions.

Becoming a Baptist was for Williams the culmination of several influences. He was familiar with Baptist life in England and may have come to this country already tinged with Baptist beliefs. He knew the Dutch language, and some evidence suggests he was familiar with writings of Dutch Anabaptists. His preaching at Plymouth led some, including the astute Brewster, to believe he was on the road to a Baptist destination. Later at Salem it was said that "in one year's time, Mr. Williams filled that place with principles of rigid separatism tending to anabaptism." A number of Baptists were known to be among those who migrated to Providence between 1636 and 1639; one writer said many of these came "savoring of anabaptism."[18]

Roger Williams, seeker. Williams remained a Baptist for only a few months.[19] Richard Scott, a Baptist who later joined the Quakers, writing about thirty-eight years after the event, said, "I walked with him [Williams] in the Baptists' way for about four months, . . . in which time he brake from his society, and declared at large the ground and reason for it; that their baptism could not be right because it was not administered by an

17. *Winthrop's Journal*, 1:279.
18. See Ernst; also *Winthrop's Journal*, 1:274.
19. Though some dispute it, the Providence baptisms were probably by immersion. See William Heth Whitsitt, *A Question in Baptist History;* Roger Williams, *Christenings make not Christians* in Perry Miller, ed., *The Complete Writings of* Roger Williams, 7 vols. (New York: Russell and Russell, Inc., 1963), 7:36; Roger Williams, *Letter to John Winthrop*, Jr. in Miller, 7:188; Henry Melville King, *The Baptism of Roger Williams*, p. 102.

apostle."[20] Winthrop wrote in July 1639:

> At Providence matters went after the old manner. Mr. Williams and many more of his company, a few months since, were in all haste rebaptized, and denied communion with all others, and now he was come to question his second baptism, not being able to derive the authority of it from the apostles, otherwise than by the ministers of England, (whom he judged to be ill authority,) so as he conceived God would raise up some apostolic power. Therefore he bent himself that way, expecting (as was supposed) to become an apostle; and having, a little before, refused communion with all, save his own wife, now he would preach to and pray with all comers. Whereupon some of his followers left him and returned back from whence they went.[21]

From this and other evidence, we see that Williams lost confidence in his baptism, not its mode but its authority. He took the view that for church ordinances to be valid they must be traced by unbroken succession back to the apostles. Any break in that succession would invalidate the ordinance. Only one who possessed valid baptism could confer it upon others. Clearly Holliman did not possess valid baptism; thus he could not convey it to Williams. Williams believed that when the ordinances were interrupted there could be no new beginning until Christ sent a new apostle to reinstitute them. There could be no true church, Lord's Supper, or ordination without a spiritual restoration. Perhaps Williams hoped, and even thought for a time, that he might be that apostle.

Williams later said, "If my soul could find rest in joining unto any of the churches professing Christ Jesus now extant, I would readily and gladly do it."[22] However, he never found that assurance and lived out his days as a "seeker," not in membership in any church. Though the technicality of succession prevented him from accepting any church or ordinance as valid, he retained many Baptist convictions to the day of his death.

Roger Williams, contributions. Williams was one of the most important thinkers in early America, with significance in political as well as religious history. Williams's contributions are many, of which the following summary must suffice.

1. *Missionary to American Indians.* Early Pilgrims often talked about converting the Indians, but they rarely did anything about it. Mark Twain said that the early settlers fell first upon their knees and then upon the Indians. Williams complained in 1645 that too many of the English considered the Indians as mere "Heathen Dogges." He ranged far inland, trading and preaching among the Indians. He opposed selling them guns or liquor, condemned unnecessary cruelty, and consistently defended their rights to

20. King, p. 96.
21. *Winthrop's Journal,* 1:309.
22. Reuben Aldridge Guild, "A Biographical Introduction to the Writings of Roger Williams" in Miller, 1:37-38.

the land. By Williams's own testimony, he had preached to these children of the forests "many hundred times" and affirmed repeatedly that "I long after the Native's Soul."[23] Williams mastered several Indian tongues, using these to good advantage in his trading ventures, preaching, and political arbitration among them.

However, Williams was under no illusions about Indian character; he had no "noble redman" complex. He saw the Indians as too often dishonest, crafty, and cruel—in short, much like the English. Williams's first major publication was *A Key to Languages in America,* published in 1645. It contained a wealth of material about Indian languages, customs, and life. No leader in early America was more influential among the Indians, or more trusted by them, than Roger Williams. Several times he was able to negotiate with them to avoid war and bloodshed. By this arbitration, Williams several times saved the colony that had exiled him.

2. *Religious liberty for all.* What is today taken for granted was a radical novelty in Williams's day, namely religious liberty for all. Williams preached that doctrine by the early 1630s and later built it into the law of his new colony. Almost everything Williams wrote dealt in some way with religious liberty. However, his convictions on this subject are found primarily in two publications, *The Bloudy Tenent of Persecution* (1644) and *The Bloudy Tenent Yet More Bloudy* (1652).

Williams wrote *The Bloudy Tenent* in England while seeking a charter for the Providence colony. The book shows signs of its hasty preparation. Williams acknowledged that he barely had time to "scatter his loose thoughts" into a book "in change of roomes and corners . . . in variety of strange houses, sometimes in fields, in the midst of travel."[24] Though ill-arranged and wordy, the book is a magnificent treatise for religious liberty. Williams argued that Scripture and history both prove the iniquity of religious persecution and that civil officers have only civil powers. He advocated complete religious liberty for all, including Papists, Turks, Jews, and atheists. While Williams's arguments were primarily theological, he also indicated that such liberty would tend to domestic peace and tranquility. "True civility and Christianity," he argued, "may both flourish in a state or kingdom, notwithstanding the permission of diverse and contrary consciences, either of Jew or Gentile."[25]

The Bloudy Tenent attracted immediate attention in England and America. By the end of 1649, over one hundred pamphlets had attacked it. William Prynne denounced "Master Williams in his late dangerous, licentious Book . . . so erroneous, false, seditious, detestable in itself." George

---

23. Ernst, pp. 76, 252.
24. Roger Williams, *The Bloudy Tenent Yet More Bloudy,* p. 104.
25. Roger Williams, *The Bloudy Tenent of Persecution for Cause of Conscience Discussed in a Conference between Peace and Truth,* p. 2.

Gillespie thought Williams advocated "a pernicious, God-provoking, Truth-defacing, church-ruinating, State-shaking Toleration."[26] Parliament moved too late to suppress the radical book; it was already published. The Commons *Journal* records, "Ordered, That Mr. White do give order for the Publick Burning of one Williams his Booke, intituled, & the Tolerating of all sorts of Religion."[27] They removed copies from the book stands, but a new unlicensed edition appeared almost at once. While Parliament burned the book, clearly they would have preferred to burn its author, but he was safely at sea returning to America.

John Cotton, perhaps the leading minister of the Boston establishment, attempted to answer Williams in a treatise entitled *The Bloudy Tenent Washed and Made White in the Bloud of the Lamb* (1647). Cotton said that limited religious freedom could be allowed on incidental questions but not on the more fundamental ones. The church and magistrates had a duty, he said, to see that the basic doctrines of true Christianity were accepted, even if they had to resort to force. He also argued that Williams was not persecuted for religious conscience but for sinning against that conscience after he had been instructed in the truth.[28]

In the fashion of the times, Williams answered with yet another treatise, this one entitled *The Bloudy Tenent Yet More Bloudy: By Mr Cottons endevour to wash it white in the Bloud of the Lambe* (1652). This treatise refuted Cotton's arguments and cited additional cases of religious persecution in the American colonies. Williams repeated many of the emphases from his earlier book, and in lengthy prefaces to Parliament, courts, and people urged that full liberty be put into effect.

3. *Separation of church and state.* To Roger Williams the basic principle was religious liberty, the freedom of the soul before God, but he regarded the separation of civil and spiritual spheres as essential to providing that soul freedom. In *The Bloudy Tenent* Williams, discussing Romans 13, observed, "This scripture held forth a two-fold state, a civil state and a spiritual, civil officers and spiritual, civil weapons and spiritual weapons." He further affirmed, "All the power the magistrate hath over the church is temporal, not spiritual; and all power the church hath over the magistrate is spiritual, not temporal."[29]

Williams argued that by nature and purpose a fundamental difference exists between church and state. One is civil and deals with all the citizens; the other is spiritual and deals only with its own members. Williams felt these represented different spheres. The magistrate had civil power; but in

26. Cited in Ernst, p. 247.
27. Cited in Winslow, p. 198.
28. John Cotton, *The Bloudy Tenent Washed and Made White in the Bloud of the Lamb* in James E. Tull, *Shapers of Baptist Thought,* p. 37.
29. Williams, *The Bloudy Tenent,* p. 118.

the church, he was simply another layman. The minister had churchly leadership; but in the state, he was simply another citizen. Williams illustrated this by the famous example of a ship at sea. In one sphere, at sea, the ship captain was in command and even magistrates on board came under the captain's authority. In another sphere, having landed, the magistrates were in command and the sea captain came under the magistrates' authority.

Perhaps Williams's most memorable expression of this separation of spheres was his use of the two tables of the Ten Commandments. The magistrate may regulate and punish offenses against the second table, those commandments dealing with fellowman, but not the first table, those dealing with duties to God. The modern term for this is separation of church and state.

4. *Democracy.* Though he seldom used the word, Williams clearly taught and practiced political democracy. From the first, Providence Plantations was governed by majority vote of the citizens, and Williams developed a political theory to undergird this practice. In *The Bloudy Tenent,* Williams said:

> that the sovereign, original, and foundation of civil power, lies in the people . . . and if so, that a people may erect and establish what form of government seems to them most meet for their civil condition. It is evident that such governments as are by them erected and established, have no more power, nor for no longer time, than the civil power, or people consenting and agreeing, shall betrust them with.[30]

Modern readers may skim such statements without realizing how radical they sounded at that time. England was then in a struggle to restore monarchy, and in America leading lights had pronounced that democracy is no "fitt form of government." It took a later generation to appreciate Williams's views.

5. *Founder of earliest Baptist church in America.* Though he did not long remain a Baptist, there is no reason to deny, as some writers have done, that Williams was ever a Baptist. He "brake" with Baptists over an unfortunate technicality, but Williams nevertheless formed the first Baptist church in the new world.

While Roger Williams deserves a place of honor in American history, he obviously had feet of clay. His vision of a new kind of society, with democracy and freedom for all, made him look radical to his contemporaries. However, one must admit that he often held his convictions with a tenacity resembling obstinacy and that his personality could be erratic and abrasive. John Cotton thought Williams had "windmills in his head," which with their constant turning created more heat than light. Perhaps no one has

30. Ibid., pp. 193-194, 214-215.

improved upon the judgment of William Bradford, governor of Plymouth, who called Williams "a man godly and zealous, having many precious parts, but very unsettled in judgment."[31]

The Providence Church

The original Baptist church in America had a checkered early history. It is too harsh to say, as some have done, that when one has noted its antiquity little remains to be said. Even Morgan Edwards, writing in 1771, acknowledged, "This church hath now existed for 133 years without any very remarkable events."[32] The church began on a Particular basis, but by the mid-1650s General or "six-principle" emphases prevailed. Under the pastorate of James Manning in the next century, the church returned to its Particular basis. Edwards observed, "At first they used psalmody in their worship, but afterward laid it aside" when the practice became too controversial.[33] About 1652 Thomas Olney urged the church to abandon the laying on of hands, thus reverting to a "five-principle" status. When the church refused, Olney and a group withdrew and formed a rival church. The original church continued, sometimes without a pastor, and apparently went for some time without meeting. While the two groups eventually reunited, this raises a question in the history of the church. Did the original 1639 church go out of existence, with the present church traceable only to the 1652 Olney splinter? Or can the present church be traced back to 1639, despite some lapses? Probably the latter, though little of importance for later Baptist life rests upon the answer.

The Providence church had no meeting house until about 1700, meeting in private homes and, in good weather, under a grove of trees. Their first building was erected at the expense of the pastor, Pardon Tillinghast, who also donated the land. Morgan Edwards later said that pastoral service in this church had been "a very expensive one to the ministers themselves and a very cheap one to the church." Though he received no salary himself, Pardon Tillinghast taught that pastors had the right to be supported by the church.

John Clarke

Newport, Rhode Island, was the site of the second Baptist church in America, formed by 1644 and possibly earlier. Its founder was John Clarke, minister and physician. Clarke's life was amazingly parallel with Roger Williams. About the same age, both men traveled the road from Separatism

31. Cited in *Winthrop's Journal,* 1:299.
32. Morgan Edwards, *Materials Towards a History of Baptists,* 1:167. These two volumes, prepared by Eva B. Weeks and Mary B. Warren, represent a welcome publication of Edwards's important manuscripts on early Baptist history in America.
33. Ibid.

to Baptist life, both founded colonies in Rhode Island, both established early Baptist churches, and both excelled in public service, Williams in obtaining the charter of 1644, Clarke the charter of 1663. There were also significant differences. Whereas Williams was somewhat erratic, Clarke was the soul of steadfastness. Williams remained a Baptist for only a few months, while Clarke served faithfully for more than forty years. While Williams was the more dynamic and creative of the two, Clarke was more steady and stable.

John Clarke (1609-1676) was born in Suffolk County, England, on October 3, 1609, son of Thomas and Rose Kerrich Clarke, and was baptized five days later. That he was well-educated is clear, but we do not know where. The University of Leyden shows a "Johannes Clarcq" among its students in 1635, leading some to conclude that Clarke attended that famous Dutch school and there became acquainted with Dutch Anabaptists and Baptists. This may well be true, but positive evidence is lacking. Clarke was a well-reputed physician, at times practiced law, was an able statesman and diplomat, as well as serving with remarkable success as a Baptist pastor.

With his wife, Elizabeth, Clarke arrived in Boston in 1637, the year after Williams had been exiled. The familiar combination of religious persecution in England and bright prospects in the New World probably drew Clarke to the colony. He landed in the midst of the major intellectual dispute of the century, the so-called Antinomian Controversy. This represented a substantial challenge to Puritanism, advocating in its place a "covenant of grace" which would reduce external authority, allow more individual freedom, and make religion more inward and mystical. John Cotton, called the "high priest of the Bay theocracy," was the main defender of Puritan orthodoxy. That remarkable woman, Anne Hutchinson, who had come to America specifically to follow the preaching of Cotton, became a leader of the Antinomian forces.

Described as "a woman of a ready wit and bold spirit" Mrs. Hutchinson was later excommunicated from the Boston church and exiled from the Bay colony.[34] Upon arriving in Boston, Clarke joined the Hutchinson party. He probably did not hold all their theological views but shared their commitment to religious liberty. After a brief stint in New Hampshire, Clarke in 1638 conferred with Roger Williams. The result was settlement of the Hutchinson group at Portsmouth. A year later the group moved further down the island to establish the town of Newport.

First Baptist Church, Newport. When and where John Clarke became a Baptist we do not know. Some think he had embraced Baptist views in England or possibly Holland. He was among those relieved of weapons by the Boston authorities in 1637 on suspicion of being "tinged with anabaptism," upon what evidence we do not know. Others believe Clarke became

34. *Winthrop's Journal,* 1:195.

a Baptist only after arriving in America, perhaps in the early 1640s. Clarke's conference with Roger Williams in 1638 has led to much speculation that one swayed the other to believer's baptism. *Winthrop's Journal* calls Clarke in 1638 "a physician and a preacher to those of the Island" and in 1641 refers to him more officially as "their minister."[35]

Clearly there was a church at Portsmouth by 1638, but of what nature is unclear. Winthrop recorded that "many of Boston and others, who were of Mrs. Hutchinson's judgment and party, removed to the Isle of Acquiday [Aquidneck]; and others, who were of the rigid separation, and savored of anabaptism, removed to Providence, so as those parts began to be well peopled."[36] Also he complained that "Mrs. Hutchinson exercised [preached] publicly." According to Winthrop, "they gathered a church in a very disorderly way," accepting some members of whom Boston disapproved. By 1639 reports suggested that "diverse of them turned professed anabaptists." In 1640 Robert Lenthal was employed "to keep a publick school for the learning of youth" on the island. Apart from the fact that this may be the first free public school in America, it is interesting that Lenthal had been in trouble in Weymouth, Massachusetts, as early as 1638 for advocating Baptist views.

From the first, the Portsmouth church contained two factions. One group, led by the Hutchinsons, William Coddington, and Nicholas Easton, held for the authority of the inner light and made little of outward ordinances. The other party, led by Clarke, Lenthal, and Robert Harding, held for the authority of the written Scripture. The controversy led to schism in 1641. Coddington and those who believed like him later withdrew to form a Quaker church. The Hutchinson family soon migrated northward, where they were massacred by Indians.

Apparently Clarke and others of like belief also withdrew from the Portsmouth church by 1641 and perhaps set up another church further down the island at Newport. A contemporary report speaks of "a Church were one Master Clarke was elder," at Newport. Possibly this early Newport church was, like Portsmouth before it, of mixed membership. Later it became distinctly Baptist under the leadership of Clarke and remained for the rest of the century one of the leading Baptist churches in America. When it became distinctly Baptist is unclear, whether 1641, 1644, or 1648. The first date for which we have definite documentary proof is 1648; John Comer found a membership roll of that year identifying the church as Baptist and listing fifteen male members.[37] Comer, who became pastor at Newport in 1725, discovered other information indicating that the church was Baptist by 1644. Backus added the note that "it appears as likely to be

35. Ibid., 1:277; 2:41.
36. Ibid., 1:273-274.
37. C. Edwin Barrows, ed., *The Diary of John Comer,* p. 35n.

earlier as later than that time." Though second in date to Providence, the Newport church certainly stands in first place for consistent devotion to Baptist principles, the vigor of its organization, and the zeal of its evangelistic outreach. Clarke remained pastor at Newport until he died in 1676, except for a twelve-year absence in England, 1652-1664. While in England, he preached, practiced medicine, and represented the colony in Parliament.

Serious doctrinal problems afflicted the Newport church in its early years. While Clarke and most of the members were Particular Baptists, the membership included General Baptists as well. The General Baptists were often called "Six-Principle Baptists," for their insistence upon the six points of Hebrews 6:1-2. Because the Particulars did not always practice the laying of hands upon new converts, one of the six principles, they were often called "Five-Principle Baptists." Thus the laying on of hands became the visible symbol of their differences.

As early as 1665 (some sources say 1656), the Newport church split, with twenty-one members withdrawing to form a church in which General emphases might prevail. William Vaughan led the schism and served as pastor of the splinter group. Within a few years, they formed two or three other such churches. They taught general redemption, opposed singing as part of worship, and laid hands upon new converts. James Clarke, nephew of John Clarke, was ordained pastor of this church in 1697.

Another schism occurred in 1671 over whether to observe Saturday or Sunday as the day of worship. Stephen Mumford, called the first "Sabbatarian" Baptist in America, came to Newport in 1665, joined the church, and began propagating seventh-day views. He offended many by plowing on Sunday. A persuasive man, Mumford gradually won others to that viewpoint. However, they did not at first withdraw from the church. First-day and seventh-day members worshiped together and maintained unbroken fellowship. Problems arose when some who had observed the seventh day reverted to Sunday worship. The Sabbatarians could worship with those who had never accepted the seventh day but scrupled at communion with those who once embraced and then abandoned that practice. Therefore, in 1671 the Sabbatarians withdrew to form their own church.

By the 1670s members from different Six-Principle churches in Rhode Island met periodically for fellowship and mutual edification. Some consider this the first Baptist association in America, though there is no evidence of any formal organization and the meetings did not long continue.[38]

Ill Newes from New-England. In 1652 John Clarke published a book in England about religious persecution in New England. The book deserves a place beside Williams's *Bloudy Tenent* as a courageous statement for religious liberty, and it had a similar profound impact in both countries. *Ill Newes* was triggered by an incident of harsh persecution in Boston. On July

38. William H. Brackney, ed., *Baptist Life and Thought: 1600-1980,* p. 97.

16, 1651, Clarke, along with assistant pastor Obadiah Holmes and layman John Randall, made a pastoral visit to the home of William Witter in Lynn, Massachusetts.[39] Witter, who was elderly and nearly blind, was probably a member of the Newport church. Clarke apparently preached at this private residence to several neighbors who assembled. They were arrested, transferred to the Boston court, tried and duly condemned, and sentenced to be fined or publicly whipped.

Clarke took a remark by the governor as an invitation to debate and readied four principles that he would uphold; (1) Christ is Lord of every area of life; (2) baptism should be reserved for believers only, not infants, and should be applied by immersion; (3) all believers, including unordained laymen, may speak for Christ in the church and out; and (4) religious liberty for all is a God-given right. The Boston ministers proved less eager for public discussions of these issues than the governor had intimated, and the debate never occurred.

Clarke's fine of £20 was paid by some unknown donor, Randall posted bail and was released, but the more outspoken Holmes was assessed a fine of £30. An anonymous donor offered to pay, but Holmes refused and insisted upon taking the beating. After several weeks in jail, he finally felt the lash on September 5, 1651. Holmes's hands were tied to a stake in Boston Commons, he was stripped to the waist, and the "Whipper" spat upon his hands and laid the three-corded whip "with all his strength" thirty times across the back of Holmes. Before the whipping, friends had offered Holmes wine, but he said "my resolution was not to drink wine nor strong drink until my punishment were over" lest the world say he was sustained by wine and not the Spirit. Throughout the whipping Holmes continued to preach to the crowd. When the ordeal was over, he said to the magistrates, "You have struck me as with roses."[40] He later testified that he had long believed that in the time of trial Christ stood by His own; now he had confirmed it in his own life. However, Holmes was so brutally injured that he was unable to leave Boston for several weeks, much of that time able to rest only crouched on elbows and knees. His back remained a mass of scars the rest of his life.

Clarke described that incident with telling impact in *Ill Newes.* The example demonstrated more vividly than abstract arguments could the reality of religious persecution in America.

Swansea

This settlement was the site of the earliest Baptist church in Massachusetts. Swansea lies near the Rhode Island border and was later some-

---

39. Edwin S. Gaustad, ed., *Baptist Piety: The Last Will and Testimony of Obadiah Holmes,* pp. 22 *f.*
40. Ibid., pp. 28-29.

what influenced by Baptists from Providence. There is ample evidence of Baptist sympathy in Massachusetts long before any church was formed. From the early 1630s, various records speak of people "savoring of anabaptism" in the Bay Colony. A few of these cases may be briefly noted. In 1638 Robert Lenthal, later an associate of John Clarke at Newport, was known to oppose infant baptism. In 1642 three women, Lady Deborah Moody, a Mrs. King, and the wife of John Tilton were haled before the court at Salem for denying infant baptism. In 1644 William Witter and a man named Painter came before the court for similar offenses.

Clearly, the number of people with Baptist sympathies was growing. They expressed dissatisfaction with infant baptism in a number of ways; some spoke out against the practice, others walked out of church when the ordinance was performed, others simply turned their heads away and refused to watch, meanwhile making a grimace to show their disregard. By 1644 such sentiments were prevalent enough that Massachusetts passed a law making the denial of infant baptism a crime. One such sympathizer was Henry Dunster, president of Harvard College, who was relieved of the presidency in 1654 for refusal to have his child sprinkled, and especially for refusing to keep quiet on the subject. In 1649 Obadiah Holmes and Mark Lukar were baptizing converts by immersion at Seekonk, but apparently no organized church resulted.

The earliest Baptist church was planted near Swansea in 1663 by John Miles, but the church was actually formed as early as 1649 at Ilston, near old Swansea in Wales. The 1662 Act of Uniformity put heavy pressure upon all dissenters in Britain, so Miles and his church migrated to America. Miles remained as pastor at Swansea until he died in 1683. This was one of the earliest Baptist churches in America to have its own church building.

Like most early Baptist churches in America, Swansea included both Particular and General Baptists. Those of the General persuasion separated about 1680, forming a fellowship in which they laid hands on new converts and refused to sing during worship. After a few years as an informal fellowship, they organized a church and in 1693 ordained Thomas Barnes as pastor.[41]

Boston

The First Baptist Church of Boston, formed in June 1665, was destined to exercise great influence among Baptists throughout New England. Among the many in Massachusetts with scruples against infant baptism were Thomas Gould and his wife, who refused to present their baby for that ceremony in 1655. Gould had made his objection to infant baptism well-known; he spoke of "the emptiness and nullity of that ordinance," often

41. Isaac Backus, *A History of New England with Particular Reference to the Denomination of Christians Called Baptists,* 2:434.

walked out of the church during its performance, and sometimes "used unbecoming gestures in the time of administration."[42] The church of the standing order, where the Goulds held membership, demanded they bring their infant to the font, but Gould said, "I told them I durst not do it, for I did not see any rule for it in the word of God."[43] For several years the matter rested there, with Gould refusing to conform, but not officially cast out of the church. With several friends who had been Baptists in England, the Goulds held worship meetings at their home, and in 1665 they formed a Baptist church. He later wrote:

> Now after this, considering with myself what the Lord would have me to do; . . . God sent out of Old England some who were Baptists; we, consulting together what to do, sought the Lord to direct us, and taking counsel of other friends who dwelt among us, who were able and godly, they gave us counsel to congregate ourselves together; and so we did, being nine of us, to walk in the order of the gospel according to the rule of Christ.[44]

For several years these Baptists endured a constant barrage of persecution. So severe was the opposition and so exemplary the Baptist conduct that some of the standing order petitioned for their relief. Gould was sentenced to exile; but because he would not leave, he was cast into prison for a time. The Boston church began with nine members, seven men and two women.

In 1665 the church adopted a confession of faith, undoubtedly composed by Gould, and perhaps the first Baptist confession in America. This was a courageous document and expresses the views of mild Particular Baptists. Among other things the confession affirms that

> Christ his Commission to his desciples is to teach & baptise (1) And those that gladly received the word & are baptized are saints by calling & fitt matter for a vissible Church (m) And a competent number of such joyned together in Covenant & fellowship of the gospel are a Church of Christ. . . . And have power from him to Chuse from amoung themselves their owne officers. . . . when the Church is mett to gather they may all propesie one by one that all may learne & all may be Comforted . . . wee acknowlidge Majestracy to bee an ordinance of god & to submit our selves to them in the lord not becawse of wrath only but also for Conscience sake . . . thus wee desire to give unto god that which is gods & unto Ceasere that which is Ceaseres.[45]

The confession concludes, "If any take this to bee heresie then doe wee with the Apostles Confess that after the way which they Call heresie wee worship the father of our Lord Jesus Christ."

42. Ibid., pp. 289, 293.
43. Ibid., p. 293.
44. Ibid., p. 296.
45. H. Shelton Smith, Robert T. Handy, and Lefferts A. Loetscher, eds., *American Christianity: An Historical Interpretation with Representative Documents,* 1:172.

In 1679 the Boston Baptists erected their first church building, under the leadership of John Russell and Isaac Hull who apparently functioned as copastors. They first occupied this "commodious sanctuary," as David Benedict described it, on February 15, 1679. Soon thereafter the authorities sealed off the building so the believers could not enter and in May passed an ex post facto law that "no person should erect or make use of a house for public worship, without license from the authorities," upon pain of forfeiting the property.[46] However, within a brief time the building was again open to use by the Baptists.

Kittery

William Screven (1629-1713) formed the earliest Baptist church in Maine, at Kittery in 1682. He has the distinction of beginning organized Baptist work in two states, Maine and South Carolina, and ranks as one of the foremost Baptist leaders in early America.

The few facts that are available about Screven (sometimes spelled Scriven, Sereven, Screeven, Scrivine, Serivener) may be summarized as follows. William Screven was born in Somerton, in the west of England, where he came under the influence of the great but erratic Baptist evangelist, Thomas Collier. Baptized about 1652, Screven preached for several years under the guidance of Collier as a "gifted brother," a lay status short of formal ordination. Screven must have been a leader of some prominence, for he signed the Somerset Confession of 1656. He fled to America in 1668, probably to avoid persecution for holding Baptist views, and settled in Kittery, Maine. Despite the distance, Screven was a frequent worshiper at the First Baptist Church in Boston, where he requested membership in 1681.

The church records reveal that Screven was received at Boston by baptism in 1681, and therein lies a problem. Why would Screven be baptized in 1681 if he had already been baptized in England in 1652? Some historians have assumed the Screven at Kittery was a son of the Screven in England, but the meticulous research of Robert A. Baker showed conclusively that they were the same.[47] Baker argued that several factors would hinder Screven being received at Boston on earlier baptism: The church where he was baptized was disbanded and no records were available; the minister who baptized him (Thomas Collier), though orthodox at the time, later fell into doctrinal deviation and was repudiated by the Particular Baptists;

---

46. David Benedict, *A General History of the Baptist Denomination in America and Other Parts of the World* (New York: Sheldon, Lamport, and Balkeman, 1855), p. 388.

47. See especially Robert A. Baker, *The First Southern Baptists* and Robert A. Baker and Paul J. Craven, Jr., *Adventure in Faith: The First 300 Years of First Baptist Church, Charleston, South Carolina;* see also Robert A. Baker, "More Light on William Screven," *Journal of the South Carolina Baptist Historical Society,* pp. 18-33.

Screven was a stranger in Boston, living at some distance, with no one to vouch for him.[48] Baker concluded that though Screven was a veteran Baptist minister he was rebaptized just to make sure. In 1681 the Boston church certified that

> our beloved Brother William Screeven is A member in Comunion with us and haveing had tryall of his gifts amongst us and finding him to be A man whome god hath quallifyed & furnished with the gift of his holy spiritt and grace . . . doe therefore Appoint & Approve & alsoe encourage him to Exercise his gift in ye place where he lives or else where as the providence of god may cast him.[49]

Screven preached in Kittery, gathering a number of Baptists who regarded themselves as members at Boston. In July 1682, he requested and received ordination at Boston, with the Boston Baptists' assistance for forming the Kittery band into a separate church. The distance to Boston, difficulty in attending even during good weather, and their desire that "they might become A Church . . . yt soe they might Injoy the precious ordinances of Christ," were adduced as reasons for this step. In 1682 the Kittery Baptists adopted a church covenant, perhaps the earliest in America. In this moving document the members, few and facing persecution, promised to

> give up our selves to ye lord & to one another in Solem Covenant, wherein wee doe Covenant & promise to walk with god & one with another In a dew and faithfull observance of all his most holy & blessed Commandmtts Ordinances Institutions or Appointments, Revealed to us in his sacred word of ye ould & new Testament and according to ye grace of god & light att present through his grace given us, or here after he shall please to discover & make knowne to us thro his holy Spiritt according to ye same blessed word all ye Dayes of our lives.[50]

In 1696 Screven and most of the Kittery church migrated to Charleston, South Carolina, where the earliest Baptist church in Maine became the earliest in the South. For about eighty years no further Baptist work appeared in Maine.

Baptist Beginnings in the Middle Colonies

Unlike their neighbors in New England and the South, the Middle Colonies never set up any church as the official religion of the realm. Each denomination had to make its own way in the open market of religious ideas, leaving the governments to deal only with civil matters. While these colonies did not have full religious liberty as that term was understood later, they had a generous degree of toleration. At least three factors account for

48. Baker and Craven, pp. 40-41.
49. Robert A Baker, ed., *A Baptist Source Book,* p. 1.
50. Ibid., p. 2.

this toleration. First, the Quaker influence which permeated the area encouraged freedom. Pennsylvania takes its name from William Penn who established the colony. On March 4, 1681 Charles II granted Penn a generous charter, making him sole proprietor of a large territory in America, partly to discharge a debt the Crown owed to Penn's father. Penn was a devout Quaker, and established "Penn's Woods" on a basis of religious freedom for all. His attitude was well expressed in the name given the leading settlement, Philadelphia, which means brotherly love.

Second, the religious pluralism which prevailed in the Middle Colonies prevented any denomination from gaining a majority. Many religious groups were represented but none gained the upper hand. Even without the Quaker influence, these groups had by necessity to put up with each other. A third factor was commercial enterprise. By that time, many leaders had learned that religious freedom encourages settlement and economic success; Dutch traders used that motivation to put down a brief flash of religious restriction in New Amsterdam in the years before that area was renamed New York. This atmosphere of freedom facilitated Baptist growth in the Middle Colonies.

Several Baptists were among the early settlers in Pennsylvania. Most of these were English and Welsh, with a few Irish. The first known Baptist preacher in the area was Thomas Dungan, who fled from Ireland to escape persecution. He came first to Newport, Rhode Island, but in 1684 Dungan and his family, with a few others, migrated to Cold Spring, in Bucks County, not far from Philadelphia. He gathered a Baptist church, probably in 1684, and served as its pastor until he died in 1688. Probably Dungan was already advanced in years; Elias Keach called him "an ancient disciple and teacher among the Baptists."[51] After Dungan's death the church languished.

In January 1688, Elias Keach formed the Pennepek church with twelve members; this was the first surviving Baptist church in the Middle Colonies. It is still active in Lower Dublin, a suburb of Philadelphia. Keach was a son of the London Baptist pastor, Benjamin Keach. Young Keach arrived in America in 1687, not yet a professing Christian. He was described as an exceedingly wild spark and a "stranger to divine grace." For whatever motive, he dressed like a clergyman, wearing a "band," and was invited to preach at a Baptist gathering near Philadelphia. He had heard his father often enough that giving a sermon was no great problem. However, in the midst of his sermon Keach was seized by the enormity of his sin. He stopped speaking and began to tremble. Keach's hearers thought some illness had come upon him. He confessed his deception and begged their forgiveness. He also was soundly converted—under his own preaching! He later received baptism from Elder Dungan at Cold Spring.

---

51. Albert Henry Newman, *A History of the Baptist Churches in the United States,* p. 201.

The conversion of Keach proved a great blessing to Baptist work in the Middle Colonies. He brought youth, vigor, and dynamism to the work, along with skill in organization. He represented the most progressive elements in English Baptist life, both in moderate theology and vigorous church order and evangelism. He was not involved in the divisive controversies of the time which eroded Baptist strength and hampered growth. Above all, he brought vigorous evangelistic outreach, preaching throughout the area and establishing several new churches.

Keach served as pastor at Pennepek but did not confine his preaching to that vicinity. Soon he had baptized converts in New Jersey and Pennsylvania. These converts regarded themselves as members of the Pennepek church but because of distance worshiped separately. However, each quarter the entire fellowship would assemble at one of these outposts for preaching, fellowship, and receiving the Lord's Supper. These were called Quarterly Meetings, but because they came to each outpost only about once a year the people came to call them the Annual Meeting. These informal meetings became the nucleus of the Philadelphia Baptist Association.

Over the years these preaching points became separate churches, including Piscataway in 1689, gathered by Thomas Killingsworth; Middleton, New Jersey, formed about 1688 from a nucleus of migrants from Rhode Island; and Cohansey, New Jersey, formed about 1687 from a small company of immigrants from Ireland. Obadiah Holmes, Jr., was a leading member at Cohansey. Baptists met for worship in Philadelphia from 1687 onward, but their church was not organized until 1698. A number of English Baptists migrated to the city in 1696 and 1697, augmenting Baptist strength. In its early days the Philadelphia church was troubled by internal disputes, including the sabbath question and relationship with the Keithian Quakers.

Little was recorded about Baptists in the Middle Colonies before 1700 because they developed late in the seventeenth century. However, one must not despise the day of small beginnings. Baptists in this area showed vast growth during the next century and set the tone for Baptists throughout the country. They formed the first surviving association (1707), adopted a confession of faith (1742), established a Baptist college (1764), and launched aggressive home mission work.

Baptist Beginnings in the Southern Colonies

Because Baptists predominate in the South today, many assume they have always been numerous in that area, but such is not the case. Baptists got a late start in the South; and after a hundred years of witness in America, they could number only a handful of small churches scattered over the Southern Colonies. In Virginia and parts of South Carolina the Anglican Church assumed the status of establishment, which brought severe restrictions upon other denominations. Some of the most severe persecution Baptists faced in America occurred in the South before disestablishment put all the churches on an even footing in the next century.

The area we call South Carolina was granted by charter in 1663 by Charles II to a group of proprietors headed by John Colleton and Ashley Cooper. They brought an expedition of about 150 settlers in 1670 and settled Port Royal but about 1680 moved a few miles to the bank of the Ashley River and named the settlement "Charles Towne" for the king. They allowed religious liberty and from the first the colony prospered.

Many of the early settlers came from the west of England, a Baptist stronghold, and the evidence confirms that a number of Baptists were among them. One careful historian spoke of a "Baptist Migration" to early South Carolina but admitted that it was difficult to identify these Baptists because early records of the colony identify all non-Anglicans simply as "dissenters."[52] Probably these early Baptists met occasionally for worship as a "house church." Though they had neither pastor nor formal organization, there remains a persistent tradition of Baptist worship in Charleston from the 1680s.

Baptist life in South Carolina was augmented in October 1696, when the veteran pastor William Screven moved the entire church from Kittery, Maine, to Charleston. Several factors may have triggered that move. Indian raids around Kittery made life uncertain. Screven's shipbuilding trade needed timber for topmasts, and timber around Kittery was depleted. Many of the Carolina settlers were from Somerset, England, where Screven was reared, and he probably knew some of them. Friends in Charleston may have written Screven about the economic opportunities, the warm climate, and the presence of Baptists.

Details of the early relationship between the Baptist settlers in Charleston and the transplanted Screven church are lacking. Apparently they began to worship together, and many of the earlier settlers sought membership in the new church. Baker spoke of "the rapid amalgamation of the Charleston Baptist community (which included both Particular and General Baptists) and the New England group."[53] The church secured a lot on Church Street in 1699 and had their own building sometime before January of 1701. Screven probably helped erect the first building, a 47- by 37-foot structure. Though most of the members were of the Particular persuasion, including all the Kittery people, the church continued to accept General Baptists. In June 1702, General Baptists in England sent a letter of encouragement and some money for books to "our Brethren of the Baptist perswation and of the Generall Faith who haue their aboad in Caralina."[54]

From the beginning, the First Baptist Church of Charleston regarded

52. Baker and Craven, p. 22.
53. Ibid., p. 78.
54. Ibid., p. 27.

itself as the continuation of the transplanted Kittery church and traced its origins back to 1682. No evidence suggests the Screven group ever considered reorganizing or making a new beginning of their church in Charleston. At the 150-year anniversary of the Charleston church, observed in 1832, Pastor Basil Manly, himself a careful historian, wrote:

> To the constitution, and subscription of a covenant above mentioned at Kittery, September 25, 1682, the Baptist church in Charleston traces its origin; - and from all the means of information now accessible, it is most probably concluded that their settlement about Charleston was only a transfer of the seat of worship of the persecuted flock (or a majority of it) which had been gathered on the Piscataqua.[55]

This church, the oldest Baptist church in the South, observed its 300-year anniversary in 1982 with appropriate ceremonies.

A Baptist Profile

This completes our sketch of Baptist beginnings in Colonial America. Not every church founded before 1700 is traced, but perhaps enough is given from the different areas to form a representative picture. However, this factual data alone does not tell the full story. What were Baptists like, and how did they worship? What were the issues that moved them, and what problems did they face?

An Independent Development

One might assume that because many Baptists in Colonial America had come from England, Baptist work in America was an outgrowth from English Baptists; in 1814 Thomas Baldwin referred to the English Baptists as "the stock from which the American Baptists originated."[56] Baptists in the two countries did develop close relationships, with frequent communication and exchange of messengers, with clear influence from England upon the theology, confessions, and organizational life of Baptists in the colonies.

However, most English Baptists who came to the colonies came on their own; only rarely did the denomination in England specifically appoint preachers to mission work to build up the Baptist witness in America. William McLoughlin concluded, "The Baptist movement in New England was essentially an indigenous, parallel movement to that in England and not an offshoot or extension of it."[57] In time, however, relationship between Baptists in the two areas became closer.

---

55. Ibid., p. 80.
56. Joseph Ivimey, *A History of the English Baptists,* 4:iii.
57. William G. McLoughlin, *New England Dissent 1630-1833: The Baptists and the Separation of Church and State,* 1:6.

Diversity

No one acquainted with Baptists will be surprised that they are marked by diversity! This diversity is no new thing; it can be traced to the earliest Baptist origins in America. Baptists had their existence around diverse personalities, from the volatile Roger Williams to the irenic John Clarke; in diverse regions, from the harsh persecutions of New England to the religious freedom of the Middle Colonies; and with diverse theological perspectives, from the remnants of Particular and General Baptist controversies which crossed the Atlantic with their adherents.

These diversities have left their stamp. Early Baptists in Rhode Island and Massachusetts were almost overwhelmed by harsh persecution. Under daily threat of punishment, prison, and privation, they developed a certain defensiveness. Perhaps this is one reason they put so much emphasis upon religious liberty. But they did not put the same emphasis upon church order, organization, and outreach.

The Middle Colonies, on the other hand, were spared harsh persecution. They were more free to develop their structural life and launch evangelistic outreach programs. Many of the Baptists who migrated to the Middle Colonies were from the west of England or Wales where Baptists were marked by cooperation and aggressive evangelism. This spirit also manifested itself among Baptists in the Middle Colonies, where Baptists experienced rapid growth.

Persistent Problems

The records show that Baptist churches in early America were plagued by persistent internal controversy. Most of these problems centered around four controversial doctrines and practices.

First, Baptists could not agree on the extent and nature of divine predestination. Was the eternal fate of every individual already sealed from eternity by God's decree of predestination or did individuals have freedom to accept the gospel and thus affect their own eternal destiny? Of course that was the heart of the conflict between Particular and General Baptists in England. The question goes beyond hairsplitting over trifles, however, for it affects one's attitude toward the church and the gospel. The tendency of Baptists in Colonial America was to moderate their Calvinism to allow some degree of human responsibility and response and to encourage human "effort," such as preaching, missions, and evangelism.

Second, Baptists argued over the practice of "laying on of hands" upon new converts, much as is done in ordination. General Baptists favored the practice, and sometimes took the name of Six-Principle Baptists for their adherence to the six points of Hebrews 6:1-2, which includes hands. Particular Baptists gave less importance to the laying on of hands, often abandoning the practice altogether. They were sometimes called Five-Principle

Baptists. Difficult as it may be for modern readers to believe, churches, members, and ministers often engaged in heated and divisive controversies over this question.

A third problem concerned singing during worship. Few elements in a typical Baptist worship service today are more familiar than hymn singing. However, that was a controversial practice in the late 1680s among Baptists both in England and America. Benjamin Keach introduced hymn singing among English Baptists in the 1680s, but the practice had not really caught on, especially among the General Baptists. Some churches in America allowed the singing of biblical texts, such as the psalms, but not "man-made" songs. Others would not allow singing of any kind. Many Baptist churches were kept in internal turmoil, and many were split asunder by the controversy over "psalmody."

Fourth, should Christians meet for public worship on the first day of the week, Sunday, or on the seventh day, the sabbath? This question troubled Baptists on both sides of the Atlantic. The Baptist Sabbatarians in England tended to be identified, justly or not, with radical millennialism, and sometimes with revolutionary schemes, such as the Fifth Monarchy Movement.

In Colonial America, Sabbatarianism was strongest among Baptists in Rhode Island, where they had their first church by 1671. A number of Seventh-Day churches grew up there and elsewhere. Not all Seventh-Day Baptists withdrew; many continued in unbroken fellowship in the first-day churches. However, the tendency was for Seventh-Day members to withdraw and form their own churches when their numbers justified.

Internal Life

In Colonial America most Baptist churches were small, often with no more than a dozen members. Few had their own building, and they may have gone for years without a pastor. Worship tended to be informal, with great emphasis upon the Bible. The pastors were usually mature men of natural gifts, though what education they had was obtained before coming to America. Most of the pastors would today be called bivocational, that is, they earned their livelihood by other business or employment and received little or no salary from their preaching. In fact, some Baptists made it a point of faith to regard a salaried ministry as invalid. With some happy exceptions, many of the early churches were so caught up in the struggle for their own survival against doctrinal dissension within and persecution without that they developed little effective witness to the world around them.

This chapter began with a statement that Baptists in early America were few and scattered. However, they were poised for a great leap forward.

Unit II

The Eighteenth Century

The eighteenth century promised much but delivered little to Baptists in Britain. Baptists had gained a measure of religious freedom but could not cash in on their new opportunities because of debilitating internal strife. Meanwhile, Baptists in the American colonies suddenly took a spurt of growth that laid the basis for the numerical preponderance they still maintain.

The Industrial Revolution changed the way Englishmen lived and earned a living, sweeping tens of thousands off the land into the burgeoning textile cities. The cities were not ready for them, and neither were the churches. The Church of England found itself alternately not able and/or not inclined to minister to the common multitude, thus leaving an opening for both spiritual and secular radical new movements. Many observers feel the work of the dissenting churches among the great underclass helped prevent the kind of revolution in England that rocked France and the American colonies.

The economic policies of Parliament helped provoke protests in America and in time led to armed conflict. However, the real "American Revolution" probably antedated the battles, taking place in the hearts and minds of people who came to regard themselves as "Americans." The colonists, led by George Washington, won the war against those English soldiers who came to America, though England's main military might was tied up in Europe at the time.

An intellectual revolution in the eighteenth century challenged the way people viewed God, the universe, and themselves. The theology of people like David Hume and Joseph Butler turned attention away from God's special revelation to the natural theology of the created universe. The rise of commerce and science occupied much of the energy that had previously concentrated on religion, thus laying the basis for that shifting of attention from heaven and hell to earth that people would later name *secularism*. In religion, such thinkers as Joseph Priestly undercut traditional doctrines, laying the basis for Unitarianism which has since permeated much of English religion.

The Wesleyan Revival, named for the brothers Charles and John Wesley, proved one of the most significant religious events of the century. This

151

evangelical movement reversed the earlier rationalist trends and brought evangelical emphases to most of the English churches for a half century. Though Wesley never broke with the Church of England, toward the end of the century Wesley's followers separated to form the Methodist Church. The impact of this revival spread far beyond any one denomination, bringing spiritual renewal to the Church of England and other churches in England. Baptists, both General and Particular, were direct beneficiaries of the Wesleyan Revival.

Baptists were affected by all these trends, showing a peculiar susceptibility to changing winds of doctrine. Ignoring their own earlier theologians and confessions, they drank deeply at the fountains of Anglican and Congregational thinkers. From Joseph Priestly and Matthew Caffyn, the General Baptists absorbed Unitarian Christology and their churches plunged into steep decline. From Tobias Crisp and John Gill, the Particular Baptists absorbed hyper-Calvinism, a sterile ultraconservatism that caused their churches to wither. Dan Taylor, a convert of the Methodist revivals, led a conservative reaction among the General Baptists; his New Connection of 1770 probably saved the General Baptists from extinction. Weary of "Gillism" and other strands of hyper-Calvinism, Andrew Fuller launched a more evangelical form of Calvinism that is still known as "Fullerism." In the midst of the Particular Baptist recovery, a Midlands pastor, William Carey, inspired the formation of the Baptist Missionary Society in 1792 and later was among its first appointees.

In America Baptists took a spurt of growth in the eighteenth century, stimulated by the wave of revivalism known as the First Great Awakening. Time, distance, and tensions of the American Revolution caused them to grow away from the English backgrounds and assume more independence of action and outlook. During these years, Baptists were able to link their struggle for religious liberty with the popular political independence of the time. Before the end of the century, amendments to the Federal Constitution gave them full religious liberty in America. Zeal of the Great Awakening propelled Baptists westward to the frontier and northward into Canada, thus laying the groundwork for a great Baptist empire in the new world. In 1700 Baptists had only a few scattered churches in America; by 1800 they had become the largest denomination in the land.

5

General Baptists in England

English Baptists came to their second century with high hopes. After decades of struggle, they had at last won a measure of religious freedom in the Toleration Act of 1689. In the seventeenth century, the Baptists had hammered out their faith through a series of widely circulated confessions, which gave them an identity among English dissenters. Capable scholars among them had provided a body of literature for inspiration, moral guidance, catechizing the young, and for theological instruction. More of their churches erected handsome buildings for worship, some of them equipped with "baptisterions" or "baptismal cisterns" for the more decorous observance of immersion. One would expect that as the seventeenth century gave way to the eighteenth, the English Baptists would have been ready for their greatest advance.

Quite the opposite proved to be the case. Hard on the heels of toleration came a thick fog of religious indifference and decay. This spiritual lethargy evidenced itself not only in sharp numerical decline among both branches of English Baptists but even more in the drop in their spiritual temperature. Their greatest danger was no longer external foes, but an inner decay, an aridity of the soul.

H. Wheeler Robinson described the first half of the eighteenth century as "the most stagnant and lethargic period of Baptist history."[1] Another writer described the same era as "the glacial epoch" in Baptist history.[2] An assembly of Baptist ministers in London, near the turn of the century, lamented "the spiritual decay, and loss of strength, beauty and glory, in our churches."[3] Evidences of spiritual decay "break our hearts to pieces," they said, while seeking ways to reverse these trends.

Perhaps the Baptists were emotionally and spiritually drained after decades of intense persecution. By 1700 most of their first generation of leaders had dropped by the wayside. Leaders like Thomas Grantham would be difficult to replace under any circumstances, but in the eighteenth cen-

---

1. H. Wheeler Robinson, *Baptists in Britain,* p. 20.
2. J. M. G. Owen, ed., *Records of an Old Association,* p. 37.
3. *Narrative of the General Assembly in London, 1689,* from introductory "General Epistle to the Churches," pp. 1-2.

tury Baptists were not allowed to attend the major English universities, and the earlier stream of university-trained converts to Baptist life dried up. One cannot avoid the conclusion that, with some happy exceptions, the quality of Baptist leadership declined after 1700.

Doctrinal extremes plagued the Baptists, operating perhaps as both cause and effect of their lowered spiritual vitality. More and more General Baptists compromised the doctrines of Christ and the atonement, accepting some form of Arian or even Socinian viewpoints. Local churches withered under these doctrines, and the number of volunteers for ministry diminished. Particular Baptist doctrinal extremes went in an opposite direction, but proved no less destructive. Many of their ministers and churches embraced hyper-Calvinism and even Antinomianism, which effectively severed them from evangelistic preaching, missions, and at times even from a serious commitment to moral living. "Little did they dream," said A. C. Underwood, "that the granting of their hearts' desire would be followed by a leanness in their souls."[4]

This spiritual collapse was by no means limited to the Baptists, but pervaded all of English Christendom. Underwood said:

> A cold fog of religious indifference descended upon the nation which for a century had been preoccupied with religious questions. It now began to think of other things, such as commerce and science. Religion was displaced from the centre of interest. The eighteenth century was an age of reason. The Deists whittled down the supernatural element in Christianity. . . . Philosophy became sceptical under the influence of Locke and Hume. . . . Morality sank to a low level and in all classes of society gambling and drunkenness were rife. The State Church seemed powerless and sunk in Lethargy. When Bishop Butler was offered the archbishopric of Canterbury, he declined it, saying that it was "too late for him to try to support a falling church."[5]

This dismal description fits England, and English Baptists, better in the first half of the century than the second. Even before 1750 signs of revival had surfaced. The Wesleyan movement, led by John and Charles Wesley and George Whitefield, transformed religion in England. This evangelical revival, which resulted in the Methodist movement, was also a primary factor in the revitalization of English Baptists. Through Dan Taylor, a Methodist convert, General Baptists found new life in the New Connection formed in 1770.

Decline of General Baptists

The General Baptist decline began earlier and the devastation was more complete than that of Particular Baptists. Perhaps they never recovered

4. A. C. Underwood, *A History of the English Baptists* (London: Carey Kingsgate Press, 1947), p. 117.
5. Ibid.

from the crippling effects of the Stuart persecution and the Clarendon Code. The Quakers siphoned off much General Baptist strength; some historians think George Fox drew much of his teaching, as well as a good percentage of his converts, from General Baptists. Many General Baptists who did not join the Quakers nevertheless had their Baptist faith shaken, and their tendency to put more emphasis upon the "mystery" (the inner, mystical elements of the faith) to the neglect of the "history" (the written Scriptures) could only undermine Baptist views. General Baptists were, if anything, even less able and willing to provide financial support to their ministry than the Particular group.

Doctrinal Problems

Theological decline manifested itself among General Baptists concerning the deity of Christ and the meaning of the atonement. Some scholars believe the General Baptists, more Arminian in their emphases, may have absorbed a relatively weak Christology from the Dutch Mennonites, thus making the question of Anabaptist influence upon Baptist origins of more than speculative concern. Some of the Anabaptists, such as Melchior Hofman, tended to compromise the full humanity of Christ. Some suppose that John Smyth reflected this compromised doctrine of Christ and that later General Baptists were thus preconditioned to be vulnerable to similar problems. Whatever the reasons, the fact is clear that General Baptists tended to weaken or even deny the deity of Christ, and many of their churches eventually became Unitarian.

Doubts about the deity of Christ formed a part of the rationalism which affected all Christian groups in England during the eighteenth century. Two forms of anti-Trinitarianism flourished in England at that time. The Arians accepted the preexistence of Christ and taught that He was more than a mere man but that, as a created being, He was less than God. This doctrine seems to compromise both the full humanity and full deity of Christ. The Socinians went even further to deny both the preexistence and deity of Christ, teaching that He was merely a good man. This doctrine robbed the cross of any real atonement.

Such views were widely disseminated in England among all denominations, but perhaps Presbyterians, Anglicans, and General Baptists proved most vulnerable. As early as the 1690s Thomas Firmin, a wealthy London merchant, financed a series of tracts attacking the deity of Christ and recommending Unitarianism. Thomas Emlyn, a Presbyterian, lost his pulpit by advocating Arian views in 1702. In 1712 Samuel Clarke of Westminster published his widely read *The Scripture-doctrine of the Trinity*, an Arian work that greatly influenced the dissenters.

The famous controversy at Salters' Hall revealed how far Unitarian views had progressed in England. With leading ministers of several denominations preaching and publishing in favor of the new views of Christ, leaders of the three major dissenting denominations, Presbyterian, Congregational, and Baptist, decided they had to address the issue. In 1719 representatives of the three groups met at Salters' Hall in London, and after sharp debate voted fifty-seven to fifty-three that "no human compositions, or interpretations of the doctrine of the Trinity" could be required. This was a clear victory for the Arian and Socinian factions, who had defined the deity of Christ as a "human addition" to the gospel.

On March 3, 1719, the defeated minority signed a statement affirming the deity of Christ and a Trinitarian doctrine of God. The two sides were henceforth known as Subscribers (Trinitarian) and Nonsubscribers (most of whom were or became non-Trinitarian). Most of the fourteen Particular Baptists present were Subscribers, but only one General Baptist signed the Trinitarian statement. In contrast, fourteen General Baptists and only two Particular Baptists refused to sign.[6] This trend of General Baptists away from the deity of Christ accelerated later.

Matthew Caffyn

Such views were not new to General Baptists; Matthew Caffyn (1628-1714) at the beginning of the century and William Vidler (1758-1816) at the end publicized similar views.

Caffyn became a Baptist while a student at Oxford in the 1640s and was expelled for that reason. Because he had university training, held substantial property, and had a keen native wit, he was a man of some influence as a messenger among General Baptists. Quite early, as one writer put it, Caffyn "began to puzzle himself with endeavouring to explain inexplicables" and, unable to explain the Trinity to his own satisfaction, concluded that it must not be true.[7] As pastor of the General Baptist church at Horsham in Sussex, Caffyn began to preach and publish this new Christology. He first doubted and then denied that Christ was divine and later in life openly embraced Socinian views which made Christ merely a good man. Underwood summed it up when he said that Caffyn "passed from denying the reality of Our Lord's Human Nature to a denial of His Deity."[8]

Caffyn was challenged for these deviant views as early as 1686 by Joseph Wright, pastor at Maidstone. Though a close personal friend of Caffyn, Wright preferred charges at the General Assembly, accusing Caffyn of the double heresy of denying both the humanity and deity of Christ and demanding that he be expelled from the denomination. Caffyn made a skilled defense, and the result was that the Assembly exonerated Caffyn and censured Wright for want of charity. Encouraged perhaps by the failure of efforts to purge him, Caffyn preached his views even more openly.

---

6. Michael R. Watts, *The Dissenters,* p. 375.
7. Adam Taylor, *The History of the English General Baptists,* 1:464.
8. Underwood, p. 127.

Schism and Aftermath

In 1693 the charges against Caffyn were renewed, but again the General Assembly refused to deal with the situation. Therefore, a number of churches split off, as they put it, "to clear themselves and the congregations to which they belonged of those gross errors."[9] The splinter group took the name of General Association, and published "The Reasons of our Separation from the General Assembly." They said, "We, therefore, having a due regard to the honour of God, and of our Lord Jesus Christ, the purity of the churches, and the discharge of our own consciences, so, in behalf of ourselves, and the churches which we represent, for the reasons abovementioned, dissent from, disown, and separate ourselves from this general Assembly."[10] Calling the old Assembly "Caffynites," the more orthodox insisted, "We cannot have communion with any persons at the Lords Table nor admit any to preach amongst us that are in communion with that General Assembly untill that General Assembly purge themselves from the said heresie for which wee made our separation from them."[11]

For the next thirty-four years, two General Baptist denominations existed, the more orthodox centered in Buckinghamshire and the Midlands, the less orthodox drawing its strength more from Kent, Sussex, Essex, and the West Country.[12] In 1731, after Caffyn's death, the two groups reunited on the basis of the six principles of Hebrews 6:1-2. This reunion was a compromise that, in effect, evaded the doctrinal issue by agreeing to a scriptural formulation which did not spell out the doctrines. They resolved that "all debates, public or private, respecting the Trinity, should be managed in scripture words and terms, and no other."[13] They also provided that anyone willing to reunite on the compromise basis "shall not be permitted to ask any question, neither shall any question be asked of him, upon pain of being excluded."[14] Thus the General Baptists chose denominational unity at the expense of doctrinal agreement.

Within a few years, the older General Baptist leaders were called to their reward. "When these had quitted the scene," according to one historian, "that spurious liberality and laxity of principle . . . gained the ascendancy."[15] Not many General Baptists were left who remembered the old doctrines of the full humanity and full deity of Christ and the vicarious atonement of the cross. Thus was laid the basis for the New Connection

9. Taylor, 1:468.
10. Ibid., p. 469.
11. W. T. Whitley, ed., *Minutes of the General Assembly of the General Baptist Churches in England,* 1:84.
12. Watts, p. 300.
13. Taylor, 1:470.
14. Ibid., p. 477.
15. Ibid., p. 480.

schism a generation later. According to W. T. Whitley, this debilitating controversy "destroyed the chance of General Baptists exerting any influence, and when in 1731 the two rival Assemblies did unite, . . . their attention was drawn too much to the past in which they forgot its finest ideals, while to the new needs of the new age they proved blind."[16]

Henceforth, General Baptists squandered their energies on trifles. They debated whether Christians could sing as part of worship, and if so whether standing or sitting; they condemned fox hunting, a sport of the wealthy in which few if any of their members could participate; they repeatedly condemned marriage outside the faith; and published weighty tomes on whether to eat blood. Meantime, their pastors were aging without necessary replacements; the pastors and their families were sunk in debilitating poverty; evangelism languished; churches suffered from long pastorates where the pastor might remain over fifty years and in his latter years drag down the church with his own failing health. It was not a good time for General Baptists. They fell victim to extreme liberalism. They had no gospel to preach, and they preached no gospel.

The New Connection

The distressing decline of General Baptists was halted, at least for a time, by a dynamic convert from Methodism who came into Baptist life in 1763. Dan Taylor (1738-1816) proved to be by far the most creative and energetic Baptist leader of his day. By the time of his death, he had almost single-handedly turned a General Baptist remnant back to doctrinal orthodoxy and evangelical enthusiasm.

A convert of Methodism, and for a time a Methodist preacher, Taylor embraced believer's baptism in 1763. That same year, he founded a Baptist congregation, made up largely of Wesleyan converts, which affiliated with the Lincoln Association of General Baptists. Taylor found that association disappointing. He was appalled by the pervasive spiritual dullness, the pastors with neither zeal nor vision, and abundant evidence of theological decay. When the Lincolnshire leaders showed no effort to address these conditions, Taylor and a few other young pastors withdrew to form a new denominational body in 1770. They called this the "New Connection of General Baptists" and described it as an assembly of "Free Grace Baptists."

Within a generation the Old Connection, as it came to be called, largely disappeared. Some of its churches came into the New Connection; others became Unitarian; others became nondenominational and survived more as museum pieces than as active churches; and others simply went out of existence, leaving little trace beyond an occasional minute book. In effect, the New Connection became the General Baptists, or the remnant thereof. Most discussions in the nineteenth century of proposed cooperation, and

16. W. T. Whitley, *A History of British Baptists,* p. 174.

eventually merger, between Particular and General Baptists involved the New Connection.

Forerunners

English religious life was never quite the same after 1738. That year John Wesley had his remarkable experience at the Aldersgate meeting in London, in which he felt his heart "strangely warmed." This experience was to catapult John Wesley, his brother Charles, and their friend George White-field into leadership of one of the most remarkable movements in English religious history. This movement was first called by the name of the Wesleys and later received the broader designation of "evangelical revival." Because the Wesleys followed a strict personal discipline, making much of the careful use of time, their opponents at Oxford University ridiculed their "methods" of spiritual discipline. From this developed the nickname "Methodist." The Wesleys, both loyal sons of the Church of England, never intended to separate from that church. John later gave a most reluctant blessing to his followers who did separate to form the Methodist Church.

From this awakening came a renewed moral tone and more earnest participation in missions, Sunday Schools, and evangelism. Some have even called this the nearest England came to having a genuine Protestant reformation. This evangelical movement brought renewal to all the denominations, including the Baptists. One might regard the New Connection almost as a Baptist version of the Wesleyan awakening.

Wesleyan emphases filtered into Baptist life by way of an evangelical group in Leicestershire. About 1741 David Taylor (not to be confused with Dan), connected with the household of the Countess of Huntingdon, began to preach in the villages near her residence in Leicestershire. Inspired by the Wesleys, Taylor won a number of converts who by 1745 formed them-selves into a small church. They registered as Independents but continued study of the New Testament convinced them that the scriptural mode of baptism was immersion. For a time these converts, which by 1750 numbered several churches, practiced the dipping of infants in a large tub set up for that purpose. After further study, they concluded that baptism belonged to professed believers only and not to infants. Though they baptized only believers, they developed a service of dedication for infants and their parents, in which they "brought their infants, in the time of public service, to the minister: who, taking them in his arms, pronounced an affectionate benediction on them."[17]

When these Leicestershire churches determined to adopt immersion, they knew of no Baptist who could administer the ordinance to them. Therefore, two of their ministers baptized each other and then baptized sixty or seventy of their followers in November of 1755. By 1760 they had five churches,

17. Underwood, p. 150.

with frequent communications among themselves by means of a monthly ministers' meeting and a quarterly conference for all members. Thus two movements, the Wesleyan Revival and the Leicestershire evangelicals, can be viewed as forerunners of the New Connection. Much of the Wesleyan vigor, zeal, and organizational practices showed up in the New Connection. Some of the ministers and churches of the Leicestershire movement became the nucleus of the New Connection.

Dan Taylor

Dan Taylor was born December 17, 1738, near Halifax, in York, a coal miner's son. From his youth, Taylor had unusual vigor of body and mind. He worked for some years in the coal mines, beginning at the age of five. Since he was a "low man," he later blamed his shortness of stature on being too much deprived of sunshine in the bowels of the earth during his growing years. Taylor early displayed eagerness and aptness of mind. He learned to read at an early age and often took a book with him into the mines for his few leisure moments.

The Taylor family was not overly religious, though Dan was confirmed in the Church of England at age sixteen. However, he soon became a regular hearer of Methodist preachers, including Wesley himself, whom young Dan walked miles to hear. At age twenty, he "proposed himself to the Methodists" and was received, soon becoming a lay preacher among them. He became well-acquainted with the Leicestershire evangelicals. Taylor preached his first sermon in September 1761, from Ephesians 2:8, "For by grace are ye saved." Though confirmed as a preacher among the Methodists, Taylor withdrew from them by 1762. Taylor's objection at that point was not so much doctrine but the strict discipline and almost dictatorial leadership of the movement by John Wesley, both of which offended Taylor. Having left Methodism, Taylor continued to preach and gathered a little band of converts near his home of Wadsworth, made up mostly of "mean folk," poor farmers and workmen like himself.

By 1762 Taylor became convinced of believers' baptism, led to that position, he said, by a study of the New Testament, and Dr. Hall's *History of Infant Baptism.* Though the learned Hall had defended infant baptism, Taylor reached the opposite conclusion. Taylor then, according to one historian, "applied to several ministers of the Particular Baptist persuasion; but they all refused to baptize him . . . they disapproved of his sentiments respecting the extent of the death of Christ."[18]

One Particular Baptist minister, though not willing to baptize Taylor, did tell him of some General Baptists in Lincolnshire who held to a general atonement. On February 11, 1763, Taylor and a companion set out to find these Baptists. The first night they spent in a hayrick in an open field,

---

18. Adam Taylor, *Memoirs of the Rev. Dan Taylor,* pp. 11-12.

having become lost in a rainstorm, but the second night they found a "decent inn" near Gamston. There they learned that they had passed a General Baptist church about eight miles back, and so the next day they returned. After two days of conversation and sharing their testimony, the Gamston General Baptists received Taylor, and he was baptized on February 16 in a river. Some of the Gamston Baptists returned with Taylor to Wadsworth and helped him form his little band into a General Baptist church. With his own hands, Taylor helped to erect a building on a hillside called Birchcliff, and this became the name of the church. Taylor was duly ordained on July 30, 1763, and his little church grew rapidly.

When Taylor learned of the existence of the Lincolnshire Baptist Association, he and his church readily affiliated. However, if he expected the same fervent worship and warm evangelism he had imbibed among the Leicestershire Evangelicals, he was sorely disappointed. Taylor noted that the Lincolnshire group was composed mostly of elderly pastors with neither zeal nor vision, that evangelism was frowned upon, that the churches were declining, that they tended to strife over trivial issues, and that, worst of all, the doctrines of the Arians and even Socinians were tolerated. As early as 1765 Taylor recorded in his diary, "I and my great and good friend Mr. B. are erelong to meet at Gamston, to talk upon some points wherein we differ."[19] Taylor got no satisfaction from this talk, however, occupied as it was by "impertinent quibbles." Taylor led his church to accept a more orthodox Christology, abandoned the laying of hands upon every believer as a condition of church membership, allowed and encouraged singing, even singing by women, as part of their worship, and followed after fervent evangelism. All of these practices were destined to involve them in conflict with the older General Baptists.

Formation of the New Connection

Despairing of bringing the old guard to his views, Taylor and his close friend William Thompson, pastor at Boston in Lincolnshire, turned to the churches of the Leicestershire evangelical movement for fellowship. When those churches refused to come into the Lincolnshire Association to help leaven that body, Taylor determined to withdraw and form a new body with the Leicestershire churches as a base.

On June 6, 1770, fewer than twenty ministers met in Whitechapel, London, where they formed a new body called "The New Connection of General Baptists." Describing themselves as a "free grace" group, they "called Dan Taylor to the chair" to act as moderator. For the next forty-six years, only once did Taylor fail to occupy the chair at the annual meetings of the new body.

Taylor later attended the annual session of the old General Baptists, also

19. Ibid., p. 21.

meeting in London, to explain in person the withdrawal of the New Connection churches. They thought the older group neglected vital Christianity, hampered their work by adherence to outworn customs, and tolerated doctrinal heresy. The new group had to separate, Taylor said, "to preserve themselves from the contagion of what they esteemed as dangerous heresy."[20] Taylor said bluntly:

> It is not to be doubted, if we regard the Bible, that some of the vilest errors are in this age maintained by some of the General Baptists with as much warmth and zeal as they were by any party in former ages. It behooves us, therefore, to take alarm, and, with all the little might we have, to militate against these pernicious tenets, which our forefathers so much abhorred, and which the Word of God so expressly condemns.[21]

The older body made every effort to prevent this division. At their meeting at Horsleydown, they said:

> We are very sorry that any of our Brethren in Union with us in this Assembly established on the principles of general Redemption & on Hebrews 6. 1-2 should make any particular Sentements & Interpretations of Scripture a Plea for their Seperation from us - We heartily wish for Union & Harmony & while we express our Determination not to make a Difference of private Opinion a Breach of brotherly love & Affection we recommend the Complainants to a more deliberate Consideration of their present Proposal & future Conduct, leaving them entirely at Liberty to judge and act for themselves.[22]

After adopting this one resolution, the General Assembly adjourned until the next year.

Gilbert Boyce, messenger for the Lincolnshire Association, did all in his power to dissuade Taylor from this schism. In an undated letter to Boyce, written probably just before formation of the New Connection, Taylor explained some of the reasons he felt impelled to separate. Taylor's letter deserves quotation at length since it not only seeks to justify the division but also traces General Baptist theological trends. Taylor wrote:

> In the seventeenth century the General Baptists almost universally maintained that the Death of Christ for the sins of men was the only foundation of the sinner's hope. Their churches were numerous, the zeal and piety of their ministers and people were celebrated, and the pleasure of the Lord prospered in their hands. Towards the latter end of the century, the sentiments of Arius and Socinus were countenanced by some of their leaders. Others sounded the alarm, but they were calumniated as defective in charity. Many yielded so far as to trim and to temporise, and treat the fundamental doctrines of the gospel as matters of indifference . . . The people too much lost sight of these, and

20. Ibid., p. 74.
21. Ibid., p. 76.
22. Whitley, *Minutes,* 2:141.

their relish for them gradually dwindled. Carnality and conformity to the world prevailed in the churches . . . and so one after another came to nothing, and a great number of meeting houses were lost, or converted to other uses in almost every part of the nation. In a word they degraded Jesus Christ, and He degraded them.[23]

The Articles of Religion

The purpose of the New Connection, according to a statement adopted at its formation, was "to revive Experimental Religion or Primitive Christianity in Faith and Practice." To let others know what they considered in this category, the group "proposed, agreed upon, and signed" a brief confession of faith, known as the Articles of Religion. They did not intend this as a complete confession but as a declaration of their views on six points most in dispute between themselves and the Old Connection. These articles were written by Dan Taylor, and for the first five years any ministers or churches wishing to associate with the New Connection were obliged to sign them. After 1775, however, signing was no longer required, but incoming ministers had to relate a satisfactory testimony of conversion and doctrinal orthodoxy.

The Articles dealt with the following topics: the fall of man; the nature and perpetual obligations of the moral law; the person and work of Christ; salvation by faith; regeneration by the Holy Spirit; and baptism.[24] That conservative statement sought to avoid Arian and Socinian views on one hand and the extremes of Antinomianism on the other. It affirmed that apart from Christ mankind is spiritually lost, that all men "are captives of Satan until set at liberty by Christ." The confession was evangelistic, affirming that "we ought in the course of our ministry, to propose or offer this salvation to all who attend our ministry," since "salvation is held forth to all to whom the gospel revelation comes without exception." Unlike some Baptist churches of the time, the New Connection required baptism by immersion as an "indispensible duty" and a prerequisite to church membership. Many of the older churches, both Particular and General, practiced open membership, preferring immersion but not requiring it.

Perhaps the heart of the Articles dealt with the person and work of Christ. The New Connection affirmed faith in the complete deity and complete humanity of Christ and the effectiveness of the atonement He wrought on the cross. While affirming the view that Christ "is God and man," they admitted that "we pretend not to explain" the depths of His divine-human nature. They further affirmed that Christ "suffered to make a full atonement for the sins of all men—and that hereby he has wrought

---

23. W. E. Bloomfield, *The Baptists of Yorkshire,* p. 105.
24. William L. Lumpkin, ed., *Baptist Confessions of Faith,* pp. 342-344.

out for us a compleat salvation."[25] This salvation is received by faith but only that quality of faith which produces good works.

Those of the older group who still hoped the schism might be healed met with New Connection representatives during 1770-1771. When presented with a copy of the Articles of Religion, many ministers and churches refused to sign, objecting to one article or another, or to the principle of signing any confession. However, some who found the Articles satisfactory came into the New Connection.

New Connection Progress

Between 1770 and 1800, the relationship between the Old and New Connections remained ambiguous. The New Connection continued to have communication with the General Assembly and, at times, apparently was regarded as merely one more association in fellowship with the national body. The two groups cooperated in some projects; and almost every year until 1803, Dan Taylor attended the General Assembly as a voting member and frequently was "called to the chair" (i.e. to preside). Part of this was due, no doubt, to reluctance to accept the schism as permanent. Leaders of the Old Connection hoped to woo the Taylorites back; Taylor and his New Connection hoped to win their former brethren to what they regarded as more evangelical positions. However, when after extensive debate the Old Connection in 1803 admitted William Vidler, an avowed Unitarian and Universalist, to their fellowship, Taylor served notice that he would no longer participate or even attend their meetings.

Under Taylor's aggressive leadership, the New Connection grew rapidly. They began in 1770 with only 7 churches and about 1,000 members. By 1786 the group numbered 31 churches and 2,357 members.[26] Until his death in 1816, Taylor was undoubtedly the primary leader, justifying the comment of one observer that Taylor "carried the New Connection upon his back." Before 1800 they provided a collection of hymns, along with instructions on the importance, methods, and justification for singing as a part of worship. They prepared a catechism for the instruction of children and youth, along with the rudiments of what would today be called Sunday School curriculum materials. They raised up candidates for the ministry and opened an academy in 1798 in London for their instruction, under the tutelage of Taylor. In 1797 Taylor launched a paper called *The General Baptist Magazine* (later, *The Baptist Repository*) to inform Baptists of the New Connection and to bind the churches in more cooperative endeavors.

In 1783 Taylor moved from Wadsworth to Halifax and in 1785 to London, where he spent the remainder of his years. However, one condition he put in accepting the London pastorate was that "Mr. T. should be left to

25. Ibid., p. 343.
26. *Minutes,* Association of General Baptists held at Leicester, 1786, pp. 8-9.

his full liberty respecting his journeys" among the New Connection church-es.[27] He exercised this liberty, though the church later complained of Taylor's frequent absences. His function among his followers was quite similar to that of John Wesley among the Methodists, whose influence he reflected.

During his busy ministry, Taylor published forty-five pieces, from brief sermons and tracts to several major works, such as *Fundamentals of Religion* (1775, revised and reissued 1802) and treatises on baptism, worship, and church discipline. In his writing, Taylor sought great "plainness of speech" in order to appeal to the common people who made up most of his followers. He wrote numerous associational letters, participated in thirty-eight ordinations, and traveled thousands of miles a year. Today Taylor would probably be called a "workaholic." In his diary he counted any day wasted in which he did not preach one or two sermons, visit different churches, and write several pages on some treatise.

Such was Taylor's status that his word was almost an oracle; nothing could be done without him or against him. When an occasional New Connection minister strayed too close to Arian or Socinian views, Taylor could and did reprimand and, if necessary, depose him. Though he never had the title, he functioned largely as a bishop among the churches.

Even so, Taylor did not escape some opposition and criticism among the faithful. Some accused him of "too much stiffness about indifferent things."[28] Several times Taylor had to defend himself against charges of dictatorial leadership.

Internal Life of New Connection Churches

The New Connection churches tried to be timely and relevant. They sought to escape the outmoded practices of the Old Connection, relaxed some of the more rigid social customs, and conducted far more lively and interesting worship services. Consequently they had greater appeal to younger people, though they continued to draw primarily from the lower socioeconomic levels of society.

Shared Decisions

New Connection pastors in the early days did not change pastorates often. Like other Baptists, they tended to compare pastorates with marriage and regard both as lifetime commitments. However, as early as 1783, Taylor was invited to move from Wadsworth to nearby Halifax. After a year of discussion, Taylor made the move and thus set a precedent in the New Connection which allowed pastors to move and probably added a note of freshness to some churches. However, Taylor did not presume to make this

27. Taylor, *Memoirs,* p. 170.
28. Ibid., p. 80.

decision himself but submitted the matter to the decision of the association. When Taylor moved to London two years later, opposition was more severe. He had already moved once, and the brethren feared he would set a precedent by which Baptist pastors would move every few years. However, such was the need in London that in April 1785, the association voted nineteen to eight "that it would be most for the glory of God for Mr. T. to remove to London."[29]

Even such personal decisions as marriage were not left entirely to individual decision, as we see in the experience of Dan Taylor. When the first Mrs. Taylor died in 1794, leaving him with nine children, all agreed that the pastor should remarry; and straightway the church began seeking a wife for him. But when the church "could not easily agree who was the most proper person," Taylor offended some by hastily marrying without waiting for the full approval of the church. At Taylor's third marriage, many years later, some church members were so scandalized that they sought his removal from the pulpit, and failing that some thirty withdrew from the church. They were offended that Taylor married an extremely young widow and, what was perhaps worse, he refused to heed the counsel of the church against the marriage. As the years passed, the New Connection churches exercised less control over personal and family decisions of the members.

Singing and Worship

Perhaps the major difference in worship between churches of the Old and New Connections is that the latter accepted music and singing as a part of worship. England in the late eighteenth century seems to have experienced a resurgence of popular and folk music, a renewed emphasis upon singing in homes and families, and the growth of "music halls" as a form of public entertainment. Naturally the question arose as to the place of music and singing in public worship.

The older General Baptists sternly forbade singing in church, describing it as carnal, worldly, and frivolous. Gilbert Boyce, messenger of the old Lincolnshire Association, wrote repeatedly against singing. He objected that not all have "tuneable voices" for effective singing; that public singing allows the "carnal" (i.e. unconverted), to participate; that singing "set" songs is as bad as preaching set sermons and praying set prayers; that public singing tempts women to participate, which would violate Pauline prohibition that women remain silent in church; that singing may lead to a worldly rather than a somber spirit in worship; and that the smiles and enjoyment which often accompany singing might insult God. Further, Boyce claimed that the New Testament presents no clear instruction that Christians should sing as part of worship and no clear example of New Testament Christians doing so.

29. Ibid., p. 128.

Dan Taylor published a major treatise in 1786, called *A Dissertation on Singing in the Worship of God,* in direct response to the restrictions of Boyce. Taylor defended singing, arguing that both Scripture and Christian history afford ample justification for the practice and that Christians sang for centuries "before Mr. Keach . . . came into existence."[30] Along with Boyce, Taylor admitted that the unsaved might join in singing but said that this might lead them to accept the gospel; in fact, singing might affect them more readily and powerfully than the sermon.

As to women singing, Taylor said, "Women, as well as men have rational capacities; . . . they, as well as men, are the creatures of God," and thus have equal freedom to participate in worship.[31] In fact, these "daughters of musick" often sing better than men. Taylor admitted that "there are others, whose capacities, both of voice and ear, are very slender" but said that did not excuse them from doing their best to praise God with the voice. Though Taylor opposed instrumental music in the church, he approved of children being taught to sing and allowed them to join in congregational singing, though such children were as yet unconverted.

Taylor did, however, insist upon plain and simple songs for congregational singing. He disapproved involved anthems, saying, "I cannot think them a proper part of the public worship of Almighty God." "Few can join in the singing of *Anthems;* nor have they sufficient time or skill to learn them," he observed and concluded that "however it may please the ear, experience teaches that the singing of Anthems is not so edifying to the soul."[32] Taylor also taught that public worship songs should generally be familiar to the congregation. New tunes should "be learnt at another time, and not in public worship." He concluded, "I cannot see how we can justify a person who leads the song, in fixing upon a tune generally unknown."[33]

Roles of Women

Women probably enjoyed more freedom in the New Connection churches than among the Old Connection or the Particular Baptists. In this area, as all others, Dan Taylor set the standards. In Taylor's book on singing, he defended the right of women to speak in church. He said:

> When a church undertakes anything of peculiar importance or difficulty in which the women may have occasion to be concerned; or to the expense of which they may have a call to contribute; or in the good, or bad effects of which, they may be, at least, as much interested as the men are; it is right they should give their voice in it, and their advice concerning it; and it appears

30. Dan Taylor, *A Dissertation on Singing in the Worship of God,* p. 18.
31. Ibid., p. 33.
32. Ibid., p. 62.
33. Ibid., p. 70.

to be intolerant not to allow them this privilege.[34]

He pointed out that women in the New Testament church served as deaconesses and prophetesses and concluded, "I am persuaded there are many things which some of the women understand better than some of the men." He interpreted the statement in 1 Corinthians 14:34 to mean only that women should not speak in a disorderly manner.[35]

Church Discipline

Perhaps the most pervasive and most serious matter for church discipline among General Baptists had to do with marriage. For years General Baptists had forbidden marriage outside the fellowship and had strictly enforced that decree even to their own hurt. They assumed that marriage required the approval of the church as well as consent of the two partners, and unless both were Baptists the church withheld its consent. This led to a plethora of discipline cases, distracted the church from more important matters of ministry, led many to leave the fellowship, and caused no end of human misery among those who genuinely wanted to remain in the good graces of the church but found their domestic situation contrary to community expectations.

In 1704 the General Assembly of General Baptists reaffirmed a policy statement from 1668, saying:

> That the Genall Estimacon that the Scriptures make . . . for a Believer to a Marry an Unbeliever is a Sin against the Law of God & for those So Marryed yett to live together as a man & wife when Repented of as sin. . . . It is Agreed that the Sin before mentioned Shall be Called a Marrying out of the Lord or out of the Church.[36]

This stern provision defined such a marriage, even when repented of, as a continuing in sin and further provided that "a Beliver Marrying with an Unbeliver as aforesd. Contrary to the Law of God & the Declared Judgmt of the Church or his own Agreemt ought to be withdrawn." Ample evidence shows that this rule of exclusion was enforced.

Gradually this stern stance was modified. Later Baptists, while continuing to oppose such mixed marriages, allowed that after proper repentance the continuation of such marriages need not be defined as sinful. Even in 1704 the minutes state of such a relationship, "It is Agreed that I shall not call it fornication to the trouble of my Bror nor he Say it is not fornication to troubell me."[37] The assembly responded to an inquiry from the Norwich church in 1721 about "Mixt Marriages" and concluded, "Wee cannot say

34. Ibid., p. 36.
35. Ibid., p. 40.
36. Whitley, *Minutes,* 1:93.
37. Ibid.

that the Holy Scriptures do Warrt. persons Baptized to Marry with those Unbaptized Neither can we say that when it so happens Every Such person so Marrying Should be Excumunicated."[38] They did agree that mixed marriages have ill consequences, that the Scripture seems to disallow them, and therefore, "We do veryly Conclude them to be inExpediant and that every such person as Marrying as aforesd. is worthy of Blame."[39] While disapproving, that fell far short of the outright condemnation expressed in 1704.

A more moderate view seemed to prevail a generation later, brought about perhaps by the practical consequences of enforcement of the strict rules. In 1744 in answer to a question from a church in Kent, the General Assembly said, "It is agreed on all hands, that Mix'd Marriages are not only inexpedient but dangerous, and some times lead to very bad consequences, and, as Such are to be prevented as much as may be, by all seasonable advice, watchfulness and Caution." However, when such marriages do occur, the church should be more redemptive than punitive. The assembly said, "The only difficulty is; how the Church ought to deal with those Members who, after all, marry out of our Fellowship? . . . But to make it a general rule, to suspend from Communion all, without exception, is what I could never find defensible by the Word of God."[40]

The Baptist approach to mixed marriages, according to the statement of 1744, should major on prevention rather than excommunication. "It deserves to be consider'd," they said, "whether suspension from Comunion for so marrying be, in point of prudence, a proper method to reclaim offenders or promote the Baptist interest?" They cited instances where persons treated with such severity had left the church never to return and others who had been prevented from becoming Baptists because they feared their marriages would be opposed. Kind and generous treatment, on the other hand, won many back to the church, often including the non-Baptist marriage partner.

Besides, the report continued, partners within the communion are not always available. Must persons, therefore, upon pain of excommunication, "refuse every sober, virtuous, Christian-like person merely because he has not happened to be baptized by immersion?" They concluded in the negative and agreed that "the case of marriage cannot be brought under any one Strict invariable rule by the Xitian church."[41] Not all agreed with this softening of church discipline, and some churches still tried to enforce the old rules. However, after mid-century, most Baptist churches followed the more moderate course.

38. Ibid., p. 135.
39. Ibid., pp. 135-136.
40. Ibid., 2:72-73.
41. Ibid., p. 74.

Summary

The eighteenth century proved devastating for the General Baptists. Theological problems, antiquated church practices, and failure to recruit new leaders of stature hampered their growth. The New Connection brought spiritual renewal to the General Baptists, at least for a time. It sought to recover doctrinal orthodoxy, spiritual vitality, and meaningful worship. Its success in these areas was destined to be but partial, and within a century the New Connection embodied many of the same problems it originated to protest. The movement never attained numerical success, and its growth rate diminished after the death of its vigorous early leaders.

General Baptists had always tended to draw their members primarily from the poorer classes, and the New Connection followed that trend. Like other Baptists of the time, and perhaps even to a greater degree, they enlisted poorly qualified ministers, provided inadequate training for either lay or ministerial leadership, and forced their pastors into secular employment which drained time and energy, and eventually their interests, away from ministry. The 1770 separation proved to be the death knell for the old General Baptists; within a generation or two they had largely disappeared.

6

Particular Baptists in England

Like General Baptists, the Particular Baptists found the eighteenth century mostly an uphill pull. The two groups had many problems in common: the overall decline of evangelical religion in England; continuing threats to religious liberty; Baptist exclusion from the major universities; a tendency for the churches to focus on what now appear as minor issues; and difficulty in enlisting a leadership equal to the times. Like the General Baptists, Particular Baptists' first generation of leaders had dropped by the wayside: Thomas Collier and Hanserd Knollys in 1691; William Kiffin in 1701; and Benjamin Keach in 1704. Unfortunately, some of the new leaders who took their places lacked the balance, both in theology and churchmanship, which had marked these men.

While General Baptists had fallen into extreme liberalism, the Particular group fell victim to extreme doctrinal conservatism. Both extremes proved equally devastating to Baptist life and vitality. The seventeenth-century leaders like Benjamin Keach and Hanserd Knollys had balanced their conservative Calvinism with a warm and fervent evangelism. That wholesome balance, however, was not to endure. In the eighteenth century, many Particular Baptists became theologically narrow, rigid in sterile orthodoxy, and with a faith more rationalistic than biblical.

However, before the end of the century, this dismal picture brightened considerably. Particular Baptists recovered more theological balance and, through Robert Hall and Andrew Fuller, modified the extreme Calvinism of John Gill to recover a "gospel worthy of all acceptation." William Carey led the Particular Baptists to launch a world missionary effort, and the "call to prayer" of 1784 proved both cause and effect of a surge of spiritual renewal among the churches.

Particular Baptist Decline

Particular Baptists shared fully in the decline which decimated Baptists, though both their practical and doctrinal problems took a different turn from the General group. Only rarely do we read of Particular Baptists doubting the deity of Christ; the one Particular church said to embrace such views died out. Staunch Calvinism protected the Particular Baptists against

171

Arian and Socinian views, but alas that same Calvinism led them to opposite extremes.

Rise of Hyper-Calvinism

Early in the eighteenth century, many Particular Baptists hardened their theology to "hyper-Calvinism." They so exaggerated certain aspects, such as election and predestination, that these came to dominate their entire theology and all else had to be judged in that light. Because they gradually put more stress on the Calvinistic aspects of their faith, and less upon the evangelical, they gradually lost their zeal for evangelism and vital church life. At their most extreme, Particular Baptists would not preach or apply the gospel to the unsaved. Some of them also fell into Antinomianism, an extreme form of Calvinism which assumed that even personal behavior was foreordained, thus excusing individuals for any lapses in moral conduct. It should be noted that, while much Particular Baptist theology tended to Antinomianism, most of their leaders claimed they did not intend this.

Calvinism was not new among Particular Baptists in the eighteenth century. From their beginnings, this branch of the Baptist family tended to follow the theology of John Calvin, absorbing such views from their Puritan-Separatist backgrounds. Their early confessions committed them to such views as election, predestination, and perseverance of the saints. However, along with these views, they practiced vigorous evangelism. Local churches sent their pastors to evangelize in surrounding areas. Their associations raised money to send out preachers, as in 1649 when London Particular Baptists sent a delegation to evangelize in Wales. Their printed sermons and tracts, while staunchly orthodox in doctrine, breathed a spirit of concern for the spiritual welfare of their own people and a caring outreach to bring others to the Christian faith. Their faith was, one might say, an evangelical Calvinism.

The change came not so much in the doctrines as the tone and spirit in which the doctrines were held, or the degree of emphasis election and predestination received in relation to other doctrines. Gradually these doctrines overshadowed all else. In the confession of 1689, Particular Baptists identified themselves as those "holding personal election and perseverance." Their first major denominational fund, the Particular Baptist Fund, formed in 1717, limited its aid to those holding strict Calvinist views. Gradually they put less emphasis upon evangelism. Finally their theologians and pastors issued learned treatises explaining why they should not address the gospel to the unsaved.

One historian listed 220 Particular Baptist churches in England in 1715, but by 1750 that number had been reduced to only 146. This was not quite so severe a decline as the General Baptists suffered, who fell from 146 churches to 65 in the same time.[1] Many congregations were like the one at Norwich, which reported 52 members in 1723 but only 27 in 1750. Joseph Ivimey concluded, "There is no reason to doubt that our churches were far more prosperous and numerous at the Revolution in 1688, than at this period, sixty-five years afterwards; so that prosperity had indeed slain more than the sword."[2] In the call for a general meeting of the Particular Baptists in 1689, spokesmen said, "We cannot but bewail the present condition our churches seem to be in; fearing that much of that former strength, life and vigour, which attended us is much gone; and in many places the interest of our Lord Jesus Christ is much gone."[3] The numerical decline was matched by a sharp drop in financial support.

The 1689 statement went on to lament that congregations were languishing, ministers and ministry were neglected, and few people volunteered as ministers. They called for a conference to plan for the future and to lift "our sinking and drooping spirits."[4] The decline accelerated as the eighteenth century progressed. One reason, most historians agree, was the increasing tendency toward hyper-Calvinism among Particular Baptists.

Sources of Hyper-Calvinism

Where did the Particular Baptists get their extreme Calvinism? They would have said from the Bible; and of course, their doctrinal heritage from the first had been Calvinistic. However, two influential non-Baptist theologians helped lead the Baptists into more extreme forms of Calvinism.

Tobias Crisp (1600-1642), an Anglican rector in Wiltshire, preached and published extreme Calvinism even before the Civil War. In 1690 Crisp's son published *Christ Alone Exalted: Being the Compleat Works of Tobias Crisp.* Several Baptists, including Hanserd Knollys, helped sponsor this edition of Crisp, and Crisp's views greatly shaped the Baptist mind-set of the time. The Baptist John Gill later reissued the works of Crisp, with a highly complimentary memoir of his life. This ultraconservative Anglican became the fountain of much of the hyper-Calvinism that marked Baptists later. Much of the later works of John Gill read like a baptized version of Crisp.

Crisp advocated not only extreme Calvinism but also Antinomianism. While a complicated set of teachings, one aspect of Antinomianism tended to free the Christian from obligations to moral conduct by emphasizing that no sin can possibly threaten the secure spiritual status of the elect. Crisp said, "The state of the unconverted elected person, is as sure from danger

1. H. Wheeler Robinson, *Baptists in Britain,* p. 21.
2. Joseph Ivimey, *A History of the English Baptists,* 3:279.
3. Ibid., 1:479.
4. Ibid., pp. 478-479.

of final miscarriage as the estate of a Saint in glory."[5] He said of believers, "Whatsoever sins they do commit, being Believers, their sins shall do them no hurt."[6] In a sermon on John 14:6, Crisp said, "God doth no longer stand offended nor displeased; though a Believer after he be a Believer, doth sin often, yet I say, God no longer stands offended and displeased with him, when he hath once received Christ." That did not mean that God tolerated sin but that for the elect God directed His wrath at Christ, who suffered on the cross. For the nonelect, however, God directed His wrath toward the sinner. Thus, according to Crisp, whatever sins the elect commit, God had no more complaint against them "than he hath to lay to the charge of a saint triumphant in glory." Such a system, said Joseph Ivimey, "tended to lull persons to sleep in sinful security."[7]

Another source of ultraconservatism was the Presbyterian Joseph Hussey. As a pastor in Cambridge in 1691, Hussey took Calvinism so seriously that he refused to offer God's grace to sinners lest he offend God by inadvertently including the nonelect in the invitation. That teaching had a profound effect upon John Skepp, a member of the Cambridge church who absorbed Hussey's views. Later Skepp became a Baptist and helped impart these views into Baptist life. While moderate Calvinism had from the first been a part of the Particular Baptist heritage, the hyper-Calvinism which marked them for a time in the eighteenth century came primarily from non-Baptist sources.

Skepp and Brine, Particular Pioneers

The Particular Baptist detour into extreme Calvinism followed two strict spokesmen, John Skepp and John Brine. Skepp (d. 1721) became the major avenue by which the extreme views of Crisp and Hussey filtered into Baptist life. Skepp was pastor of the Particular Baptist church at Cripplegate by 1715 and was one of the orthodox Subscribers at Salter's Hall in 1719. He had been a member of Hussey's church before becoming a Baptist. Skepp lay for some years under a cloud for scandalous conduct but was later rehabilitated. He wrote one work, published after his death, entitled *Divine Energy: or the efficacious Operations of the Spirit of God upon the Soul of Man.* This proved quite influential among Baptists. John Gill gathered many of his views from Skepp, and he republished the work in 1751 with a laudatory preface. The work was also republished in 1815.

Designed as an antidote to "the Pelagian errors" of the time, Skepp's *Divine Energy* was basically a Baptist version of the earlier emphases of Crisp and Hussey. He developed the concept that conversion came from God's initiative and was not affected by human decision. That is the point

---

5. Tobias Crisp, *Christ Alone Exalted: Being the Compleat Works of Tobias Crisp,* p. 579.
6. Ibid., p. 549.
7. Ivimey, 3:55.

of Skepp's title, showing that conversion results not from human decision but from "divine energy" operating by way of predestination and election. He devoted chapter 3 to showing the insufficiency of "moral suasion," by which Skepp meant "an endeavour, by proper methods and arguments, to persuade a man, in a natural and unrenewed state" to become a Christian.[8] That would completely invalidate preaching to and extending "gospel invitations" to the unsaved. Skepp frankly said of gospel invitations that "this method [is] not only deficient but culpable, and founded altogether upon an old mistake."[9]

Skepp argued that exhortations to sinners to persuade them to become Christians were at best a waste of time and at worst might violate the sovereignty of God. They are pointless in that the nonelect, and even the elect who are not yet energized by God's grace, not only *will not* but *cannot* respond. When such invitations include the nonelect, whom God had not invited to salvation, they fly in the face of divine sovereignty. Skepp insisted that invitations were "of little use to such a dead or disabled soul; . . . [invitations] amount to no more than a dead and helpless exhortation."[10] One might as well ask a paralytic to decide to stand up and walk. In a vivid complaint, Skepp lamented, "This is the helpless, lifeless way of preaching and reasoning now in vogue with our high and mighty rationalists, and doctors of free-will . . . their lifeless motive and spiritless exhortations and offers are as ineffectual as the prophet's staff in Gehazi's hand."[11]

Though Skepp appears to have embraced Antinomianism, he was by no means as extreme as Crisp. He did teach man's "moral impotence," showing that man's will was so damaged by the fall, and remains so captive to Satan, that man has lost all moral freedom to decide and effect any good thing. Comparing freedom of the will to gangrene, Skepp concluded that man is truly passive in the presence of divine energy and that "not one vital spiritual act can be put forth" by man either before, during, or after conversion.[12]

John Brine (1703-1765) succeeded Skepp in the pastorate at Cripplegate, though there were a few years between them. As a youth, Brine became a friend of John Gill when both were members of the same Baptist church near Kettering. Brine was called to the ministry by the Kettering church and later served as pastor at Coventry. He received aid from the Particular Baptist Fund to assist in his education and to purchase books. He went to

8. John Skepp, *Divine Energy: or the efficacious Operations of the Spirit of God upon the Soul of Man,* p. 58.
9. Ibid., p. 59.
10. Ibid., p. 81.
11. Ibid., p. 82.
12. Ibid., p. 163.

London about 1730 and for many years was a close friend and confidant of Dr. Gill. "Mr. Brine was of great weight in the denomination," said one historian, and "he was also a very considerable writer."[13] In 1732 he published *A Defence of the Doctrine of Eternal Justification,* and in 1734 *The Covenant of Grace Opened.* After 1734 seldom did a year pass that Brine did not publish some work, ranging from sermons and brief treatises to more substantial works.

For the most part, Brine avoided the ostentations and literary flourishes which spoil so much of the writing of that time. The result was that Brine's works, rather brief for the most part and plainly written, were widely circulated. Along with Skepp and Gill, Brine did much to fasten hyper-Calvinist views upon his denomination. His church, Curriers' Hall in Cripplegate, had already begun to decline under Skepp and under his ministry diminished to fewer than thirty members.[14]

Like his predecessor, Brine continued the "noninvitation, nonapplication" style of preaching, and "contented himself with what he considered clear statements of doctrinal truth, without making any application of his subject."[15] Though largely free from the harsh spirit of Skepp, Brine allowed no room for evangelism in his preaching. As one historian complained, "Even in sermons where the subjects, it might have been expected, would have led him to address the unconverted, . . . there is not a syllable addressed to them on any topic."[16]

John Gill, Leading Hyper-Calvinist

The famed John Gill (1696-1771) was perhaps the most eminent Particular Baptist of his age and is almost universally considered the leading Baptist spokesman for strict Calvinism. Reared and educated at Kettering, Gill in 1719 began a pastoral tenure at the historic Horsleydown church in Southwark, London, which would last for more than fifty years. For twenty-seven years, he held an endowed lectureship on Wednesday evenings at the Great Eastcheap which attracted the intelligentsia of London of all denominations. Acknowledged as one of Baptists' most profound scholars, Gill published many works, including *The Doctrine of the Trinity stated and Vindicated* (1731); *An Exposition of the Old Testament* (6 vols., 1748-1763); *A Body of Doctrinal Divinity* (1769); and *A Body of Practical Divinity* (1770). He was so jealous to maintain the sovereignty of God that he refused "to offer Christ" to unregenerate sinners and taught others to make the same refusal.

Gill was greatly influenced by both Skepp and Brine and perhaps did

13. Ivimey, 3:367-368.
14. Ibid., p. 373.
15. Ibid., p. 271.
16. Ibid., p. 272.

more than both of them to spread hyper-Calvinism among the Particular Baptists. Gill, more than any other, "produced a very powerful influence among the Baptist Ministers, and gave the tone to their preaching." Gill's massive works, wrote John Fawcett, were "considered as almost an essential part of the library, not only of ministers, but of private Christians of the [Particular] Baptist denomination," and "were read almost exclusively, to the neglect of other works on divinity."[17]

A representative sample of Gill's teaching might come from his *Body of Doctrinal Divinity,* where he contrasted election to life and its opposite, rejection or reprobation from God's grace. Election to eternal life was from eternity and did not depend upon nor begin with the believer's faith or perseverance in faith. Election was "free and sovereign; God was not obliged to choose any; and as it is, he chooses whom he will, . . . and the difference in choosing one and not another is purely owing to his will."[18] God's election was "immutable and irrevocable"; God never changed His mind. God made His choices in eternity past and absolutely nothing could change that outcome. Election was "special and particular," that is, God chose specific *persons.* When God was pleased to call His chosen, they could know their election and find spiritual security therein.[19]

God's special election of others to damnation was just as intentional and just as binding, according to Gill. Gill said, "I shall prove that there is non-election, or rejection of some of the sons of men, when others were chosen."[20] God had made "a decree, by which he has rejected some of the race of Adam from his favour," not because they sinned, for all have sinned, but just because He decided to do so. The cause of their election to damnation was not sin, but "the good pleasure of his will."[21] No human cause or conduct could "move God to choose one and reject another." That came entirely from His sovereign will and the final purpose of the damnation of the nonelect was to spotlight the glory of God. The nonelect could do nothing to change their dismal status and future. Indeed, their fate was sealed not only before they were born but in the eternal counsels of God before the creation of the world, for "if some were chosen before the foundation of the world, others must be left, or passed by, as early."[22]

Since the nonelect "are persons who are foreordained to condemnation, whose names are left out of the book of life," it would hardly make sense to preach the gospel to them, urge them to repent of their sins, and issue "gospel invitations" to them to receive Christ and become Christians. That

17. John Fawcett, *An Account of the Life, Ministry and Writing of the Late Rev. John Fawcett* (London: Baldwin, Cradock, and Jay, 1818), p. 97.
18. John Gill, *A Body of Doctrinal Divinity,* 1:311.
19. Ibid., p. 312.
20. Ibid., p. 315.
21. Ibid., p. 321.
22. Ibid., p. 322.

rigid "noninvitation" style of theology and preaching, while ringing with impressive logic, brought the kiss of death to Particular Baptists.

To see how far hyper-Calvinism had affected Particular Baptists, one has only to compare the emphases of Gill, as cited, with the earlier teachings of Hanserd Knollys. In *The World that now is, and the World that is to come* (London, 1681), Knollys had, despite his Calvinism, earnestly appealed for sinners to be converted. "O, ye unconverted sinners, both professors and profane, will you accept of, and receive now a word in season of spiritual counsel," he cried. If so, the preacher continued, "Then I will instruct you how you that are miserable may become happy, and you that are in a damnable state, may get into the state of salvation." Citing several evangelistic Scriptures, and urging his readers to apply them to their own hearts, Knollys concluded with an appeal that sinners work out their own salvation with fear and trembling.[23]

Revival Among Particular Baptists

After 1750 the Particular Baptists experienced a powerful spiritual recovery. Like the similar movement among General Baptists, this revival sought recovery of more vital theology, preaching, and evangelism. Like the New Connection, the Particular renewal drew from the larger evangelical awakening of the Wesleyan movement. Unlike the New Connection, however, the Particular revival did not lead to schism. This revival was so connected with one man, Andrew Fuller of Kettering, that it often bears his name, "Fullerism." Influential as Fuller was, others were also involved in the reaction against sterile hyper-Calvinism among Baptists.

The views of Gill reigned supreme for years, but at last they were challenged. Ironically, the most effective challenge came from Kettering, Gill's home church, where a new pastor, Andrew Fuller, led a renewal movement back toward a more evangelical form of faith. The records reveal a growing discontent among Particular Baptists about the deadening effects of the theology of Skepp, Brine, and Gill. Churches declined, evangelism waned, and the entire denomination withered. Voices calling for return to the older, more evangelical Calvinism were heard by 1750 and reached a crescendo by the 1780s.

Many Baptists came to agree with John Fawcett, a Particular Baptist pastor who profoundly disliked doctrinal wrangling which drained away spiritual energies from more meaningful ministry. Fawcett never preached against hyper-Calvinism; he simply lived it down. He preached the gospel and many responded, especially young people. Some have said that Fawcett led the first "youth revival" among Baptists.[24] Fawcett's views are well-expressed in a poem he wrote, which ended as follows:

23. Cited in Ivimey, 3:364-365n.
24. Fawcett, pp. 168-169.

> To be brief my friends, you may say what you will,
> I'll ne'er be confined, to read nothing but Gill.[25]

Forerunners of Revival

In 1752 Alvery Jackson, a Particular pastor in Yorkshire, published a book attempting to refute hyper-Calvinism. A few years later Abraham Booth, also a Particular Baptist, published *The Reign of Grace* (1768) with similar emphases. Booth grew up in Nottinghamshire and was converted among the fervent evangelicals who later helped form the New Connection. In fact, Booth was for a time a General Baptist but changed to Calvinist views. However, he never lost the fervent evangelism he had absorbed from these earlier contacts. In *The Reign of Grace* he said:

> Complete provision is made for the certain salvation of every sinner, however unworthy, who feels his want, and applies to Christ. The Gospel is not preached to sinners, nor are they encouraged to believe in Jesus, under the formal notion of their not begin elected. No: these tidings of heavenly mercy are addressed to sinners, considered as ready to perish.[26]

This book combining staunch Calvinism and fervent evangelism was released the year before John Gill in London issued his most influential treatise, *A Body of Doctrinal Divinity,* which advanced quite different and less hopeful views. Booth reinforced his treatise a few years later in *Glad Tidings to Perishing Sinners* (1796), whose subtitle described its emphasis: "the genuine Gospel a complete warrant for the ungodly to believe in Christ." Booth remained a Calvinist, believing in election, but his understanding allowed him to call upon sinners to repent. He rose to leadership among Particular Baptists, helped support the missionary society in the 1790s, took the lead in forming the Itinerant Society in 1797 which sponsored home mission work, and, though uneducated himself, was a factor in the formation of Stepney College. Booth introduced the erratic Dr. John Thomas to Fuller and Carey. Booth was also known for his antislavery views, when such views were far from common in England.

One would hardly predict that Booth would lead Particular Baptists toward spiritual renewal. Though uneducated, he was a careful student of Scripture and was utterly devoted to the people he served. "He appeared always willing to give up almost everything to the decision of the church; the consequence was that the church gave up almost everything to his decision."[27] An advocate of a simple life-style, Booth once gave a brother minister a plain meal in his kitchen and warned him, "If you do not take care, my friend, you will spend twenty pounds a year at your tea-table."

25. A. C. Underwood, *A History of the English Baptists* (London: Carey Kingsgate Press, 1947), p. 173.

26. W. T. Whitley, *Calvinism and Evangelism in England,* p. 35.

27. Ivimey, 4:375.

Though Jackson and Booth are rarely noticed, the older histories do take note of the 1770 circular letter of the Northamptonshire Association. This powerful epistle, put out the same year the New Connection was formed, has often been described as the opening shot in the battle against hyper-Calvinism. One historian called this "the first stirrings of new life, after the winter of hyper-Calvinism."[28] That letter affirmed that "every soul that comes to Christ to be saved from hell and sin by him, is to be encouraged. . . . The coming soul need not fear that he is not elected, for none but such would be willing to come and submit to Christ." In the mid-1770s the younger John Ryland, then pastor in Northampton, read *Inquiry into the Freedom of the Will* by Jonathan Edwards and was deeply influenced by its insights. Sensing that the American pastor-evangelist had found a way to combine orthodox Calvinism with warm evangelism, Ryland recommended the works of Edwards to his colleagues, including Robert Hall, pastor in Leicestershire, and Andrew Fuller of Kettering.[29] Edwards had been influenced by an evangelical movement in Scotland and had published a piece on prayer which also influenced the Particular Baptists of the Midlands. Perhaps this was the inspiration for their 1784 prayer call in the Northampton Association, which had such impact upon the revival and helped lead to the missionary movement a few years later.

In 1779 Robert Hall, Sr. (1728-1791), preached the Northampton Association sermon from Isaiah 57:14: "Cast ye up, cast ye up, prepare the way, take up the stumblingblock out of the way of my people." Hall portrayed hyper-Calvinism as a barrier which prevented sinners from approaching the forgiving Christ. He described the sermon as "an attempt to remove various stumbling-blocks out of the way, relating to doctrinal, experimental and practical religion."[30] One is struck with the similarity to the announced purpose of the New Connection a few years earlier, "to revive experimental religion."

The Northampton Association sermon had the effect of a bombshell upon Particular Baptists in the Midlands. In response to pressing demands, Hall printed the sermon in 1781 under the title of *Help to Zion's Travellers,* affirming that "the way to Jesus is graciously laid open for everyone who chooses to come to him." One could hardly overestimate the impact of that sermon. William Carey later said, "I do not remember to have read any book with such raptures," and one must assume this helped prepare Carey for his missionary ministry. Ivimey did not exaggerate in saying that sermon

28. Underwood, p. 160.
29. Michael R. Watts, *The Dissenters,* pp. 459-460.
30. Underwood, p. 160.

and its publication marked "the commencement of a new era in the history of our denomination."[31]

Andrew Fuller and "Fullerism"

The stirrings of revival and recovery among Particular Baptists reached its zenith in the ministry and writings of the remarkable pastor at Kettering, Andrew Fuller (1754-1815). The son of a Cambridgeshire farmer, Fuller was a big, broad-shouldered man over six feet tall. Possessed of incredible strength, Fuller as a youth had been a wrestler. Years later, so tradition says, when he met another strong man he would give him an appraising glance and mentally calculate if he could still defeat such a man.

Fuller was converted at the age of sixteen and was baptized into the Soham church in Cambridgeshire. Within a year he was preaching and at the age of twenty was ordained pastor at Soham. In 1783 he moved to the pastorate at Kettering, where he served the remainder of his life. Fuller's early ministry showed little promise of his later fame. The Soham people, he complained, "were inclined to find fault with his ministry, as it became more searching and practical, and as he freely enforced the indefinite calls of the Gospel."[32] They expressed their displeasure by extreme stinginess in his salary, forcing him to keep school and also to open a shop to support his family.

Fuller grew up in a hyper-Calvinistic church where the gospel was never addressed to sinners. Having been thoroughly indoctrinated in that extreme system, Fuller said that he "durst not, for some years, address an invitation to the unconverted to come to Jesus."[33] However, during a visit to London in 1775, Fuller said, "I met with a pamphlet, by Dr. Abraham Taylor, concerning what was called *The Modern Question.*" Reading this treatise, he said, "revived all my doubts on what was called the High Calvinistic system, or the system of Dr. Gill, Mr. Brine, and others, as to the duty of sinners, and of ministers addressing them."[34] The example of Jesus, John the Baptist, and the apostles, more than Taylor's arguments, convinced Fuller. He saw that, despite Gill's logic and arguments, Christ and His early followers did, indeed, address the gospel to sinners and invite them to believe.

Fuller also had the advantage of a stimulating circle of friends in the Northampton area, including Robert Hall of Arnsby, John Sutcliff of Ol-

31. Ivimey, 4:41.
32. Underwood, 163.
33. John Ryland, *The Life and Death of the Rev. Andrew Fuller*, p. 26.
34. Ibid., p. 28.

ney, John Ryland, Jr., of Northampton, and William Carey of Moulton. "In them," Fuller wrote, "I found familiar and faithful brethren . . . (who) had begun to doubt of the system of False Calvinism."[35] Fuller's diary for July 16, 1784, reveals his aversion to hyper-Calvinism. After a trip to Arnsby, he wrote, "Came back, and heard an aged minister (deeply tinged with False Calvinism) with grief. Surely the system of religion which he, with too many others, has imbibed, enervates every part of vital godliness."[36]

Opposition forced Fuller to think through his views carefully; and in his maturity, he became perhaps the greatest theologian English Baptists ever produced. A self-taught man, he showed great depth and power as a thinker but did not clutter his work with the ornate flourishes so prevalent at the time. Fuller's insights were fresh and vital, and he cared little for idle speculations. Modest to a fault, when the Baptist College of Rhode Island conferred upon him a Doctor of Divinity degree, Fuller remarked pleasantly, "Now I must learn Latin in order to read it." A man of incredible energy, Fuller slept little, worked tirelessly, and took little thought for rest or ease. While some majored on the devotional aspects of religion, Fuller's strength turned to the intellectual and practical aspects of the faith. While engaged in his study and writing, he was reluctant to be disturbed by casual visitors. When such appeared, Fuller would block the door with his massive frame, deal with them as quickly as possible, sometimes by pointing to a plaque on the wall reading, "He who steals my purse steals money; he who steals my time steals my life."

Fuller's own theological development was accelerated by an unfortunate experience in the Soham church the year after his conversion. Finding a fellow church member frequently drunk, young Fuller chided him. The drunkard excused himself by citing hyper-Calvinist views that he could not help himself and, therefore, should not be held accountable. The ensuing dispute in the church, which led to the dismissal of the pastor, revealed that most church members accepted hyper-Calvinism. Later as Fuller served as pastor of this rather unlovely church, their opposition to his more evangelical views forced him to clarify his thoughts.

The classic statement of the new evangelical doctrine, which would take the name of "Fullerism," was *The Gospel Worthy of All Acceptation.* Fuller had begun this while still at Soham, partly to clarify his own views, but did not publish it until 1785. It must be reckoned one of the most influential Baptist books of the century. It turned Particular Baptists around, brought a new style of preaching, helped stave off the paralysis of hyper-Calvinism, developed a theology of moderate conservatism which made possible the missionary movement embodied in William Carey, and laid the groundwork for Baptist advance in the nineteenth century.

Upon being called to the Kettering church in 1783, Fuller provided them

35. Ibid.
36. Ibid., p. 86.

with an extensive written confession of his faith, a practice fairly customary among pastors assuming a new work. In that confession, Fuller embraced a modified Calvinism which affirmed election and predestination but called for the gospel to be preached to all. He said:

> I believe, it is the duty of every minister of Christ plainly and faithfully to preach the gospel to all who will hear it. . . . I, therefore, believe free and solemn addresses, invitations, calls and warnings to them, to be not only consistent, but directly adapted, as means, in the hand of the Spirit of God, to bring them to Christ. I consider it as a part of my duty, which I could not omit without being guilty of the blood of souls.[37]

Two years later Fuller published a more complete work on this subject, which he entitled *The Gospel Worthy of All Acceptation.* In this work, Fuller set out a theology which preserved Calvinist orthodoxy but made room for evangelism and missions. He urged that the gospel be presented with compassion to all hearers, that all be invited to receive Christ, and that efforts to identify whether specific persons were among the elect be left to God. He said, "It is the duty of ministers not only to exhort their carnal auditors to believe in Jesus Christ for the salvation of their souls; but it is at our peril to exhort them to any thing short of it."[38] In the same work, Fuller assessed the impact of hyper-Calvinism upon preaching among Baptists and found it bad news. Such lifeless preaching, he said, is one reason "that sinners of every description can sit so quietly as they do, year after year, in our places of worship." Fuller's remark that "hearers of this description sit at ease in our congregations" brings to mind the fact that in the first ten years he attended the Baptist church at Soham he did not see a single baptism. Fuller concluded, "I conceive there is scarcely a minister amongst us whose preaching has not been more or less influenced by the lethargic systems of the age."[39] In *The Gospel Worthy* he not only called Baptists back to a more biblical theology but also appealed for recovery of a biblical style of preaching. In *The Atonement of Christ,* Fuller gave his final exhortation to his fellow ministers, urging them to "hold up the blessings of his salvation for acceptance, even to the chief of sinners. . . . The gospel is a feast, and you are to invite guests."[40]

Rise of the Missionary Movement

No history of Baptists can overlook the life and contributions of William Carey (1761-1834). Indeed, volumes have been written about Carey and the Baptist missionary movement he launched, and yet the story is not exhausted. Along with the two Robert Halls, father and son, John Sutcliff, John

---

37. Ibid., p. 58.
38. Joseph Belcher, ed., *The Complete Works of the Rev. Andrew Fuller,* 3 vols. (Philadelphia: American Baptist Publication Society, 1845), 2:387.
39. Ibid.
40. Andrew Fuller, *The Atonement of Christ, and the Justification of the Sinner,* p. 208.

Ryland, and Andrew Fuller, William Carey was one of the Particular Baptists who shared in the evangelical renewal of the northern Midlands in the latter part of the eighteenth century. If he was never quite the theologian that Fuller became and never the pastor that Ryland was, Carey yet made world-changing contributions in a new area—foreign missions.

William Carey in England

William Carey was born in 1761, in the Northampton village of Paulerspury, son of a village schoolmaster. Carey was reared in nominal affiliation with the Church of England. As a boy William had an eager, enquiring mind and was nicknamed "Columbus" for his boyhood hero Christopher Columbus. He was fascinated by the tales of his uncle, Peter Carey, a sailor and world traveler, and later was an avid reader of *Captain Cook's Voyages.* These influences helped acquaint Carey with the larger world.

At age fourteen, Carey was apprenticed to a shoemaker in a neighboring village. One of the other apprentices, John Warr, persuaded Carey to attend a Dissenter meeting where he heard a Baptist preaching. In 1779 at age eighteen, Carey made a profession of conversion but did not immediately seek baptism. Carey's own study of the Bible and a reading of Robert Hall's treatise, *Help to Zion's Travellers,* persuaded him to become a Baptist. Accordingly, he was baptized on October 5, 1783, in the river Nen by the younger John Ryland. Ryland entered into his diary for that day, "Baptized today poor journeyman shoe cobbler."

Carey began to speak at Baptist meetings and became convinced that he should preach, though he was never considered a good speaker. Slight of stature, prematurely balding, and wearing an ill-fitting red wig, Carey made a distinctly unimpressive personal appearance. He preached for the entire summer of 1785 at the church at Olney and did so poorly the church refused to recommend him for ordination. On one occasion he gave, according to one hearer, a message "as weak and crude as anything ever called a sermon." Carey persisted, and the next year the church voted reluctantly to recommend that he be ordained to "preach wherever God in his providence might call him." The church appointed one of its members, a Miss Tressler, to canvass the community to raise money to buy Carey a black suit to be ordained in. He was later called as pastor of the church at Moulton.

In addition to being a pastor, Carey continued to cobble shoes. To support his growing family, he also opened a school. He thirsted for knowledge and showed remarkable ability to learn, especially languages. He kept a book propped upon his cobbler's stand and thus learned Greek, Hebrew, Dutch, French, Latin, and several other Indo-European languages. Later in India, Carey would display this same remarkable linguistic ability, mastering several Indian dialects and putting the Bible and other Christian literature into those tongues.

One of Carey's interests was map making. The story is often told of his taking shoe leather from the cobbler's shop to stitch a make-shift globe with various continents made of leather tanned different colors. In teaching geography, Carey thought of world populations without Christ. During class he would often pause and say to himself, "Pagan! Pagan!" That concern for world conversion welled up in Carey's soul to become a consuming passion. It was the subject of his conversation, his preaching, and his writing. In 1787 Carey, attending the Ministers Fraternal of the Northampton Association, proposed the following topic for discussion: "Whether the command given the apostles to teach all nations was not binding on all succeeding ministers to the end of the world." The revered Dr. Ryland, Sr., was said to have retorted, "Sit down young man. You are an enthusiast! When God pleases to convert the heathen, He will do it without consulting you or me."

Carey sat down, but he did not stop thinking about missions. He put his thoughts into a remarkable book, called *An Enquiry into the Obligations of Christians to use means for the Conversion of the Heathen* (Leicester, 1792). This book proved to be the charter of the modern missionary movement and had vast impact on two continents.

The Baptist Missionary Society

In May 1792, Carey preached from Isaiah 54:2 at the association meeting at Nottingham. Carey's sermon had only two points: 1. Expect great things from God, and 2. attempt great things for God. Called the "deathless sermon," it provided a turning point in Baptist history. The sermon was inspiring, yet it appeared that Fuller, who was presiding, would close the meeting without specific action. Carey tugged at Fuller's coat and pleaded, "Oh, sir, is nothing to be done? Is nothing again to be done?"

That emotional plea turned the tide. The association adopted the following resolution, "Resolved, that a plan be prepared against the next Ministers meeting in Kettering, for forming a Baptist society for propagating the gospel among the Heathen." Pursuant to that call, fourteen persons met on October 2, 1792, at the home of Widow Martha Wallace in Kettering, an active member of Fuller's church. After prayer and discussion, the group voted to form the "Particular Baptist Society for the Propagation of the Gospel among the Heathen." The group was popularly known by the shorter name of Baptist Missionary Society or just BMS. At the initial meeting, they took up an offering of cash and pledges amounting to £13.2.6. The collection was temporarily stashed in one of Andrew Fuller's snuff-boxes. Fuller was elected secretary of the group and for the next twenty-two years gave masterful leadership in promotion, fund raising, and planning for the society.

William Carey in India

The BMS became aware of Dr. John Thomas, a Baptist physician in England who had spent many years in India and who wanted to return to that land. Probably unwisely, the BMS appointed Thomas as their first missionary. However, before Thomas could sail, the BMS also decided to appoint Carey. Carey's domestic situation complicated his appointment, for his wife Dorothy flatly refused to go. She was never in sympathy with her husband's mission interests and never shared his world vision. In five generations, no member of her family had ever moved more than ten miles from their native village. She was a kind and good-hearted village girl, an affectionate wife and caring mother; and she probably deserves more sympathy than some historians give her. At times she thought her husband might actually be going insane for considering such a preposterous plan to move to India.

Carey accepted appointment as a missionary to India, and the date for sailing was set before Dorothy was even told about it. Carey urged her to go with him, but she at first refused. So Carey took their oldest child, Felix, and set out for the ship. However, the sailing was delayed, and Carey took the opportunity to rush back home and plead once more with Dorothy to join him. With many tears, she yielded and had only a few hours to pack all her possessions for herself and four children, bid farewell to family and friends, and leave England forever. She was scarcely aboard ship when she came to regret her decision, and she adapted poorly in India. The heat and humidity took their toll, and she was subject to severe fevers. Their grinding poverty, the uncertainty of their existence, and the death of one child proved more than she could cope with, and she lapsed into deep and debilitating depression. For the last thirteen years of her life, she lived in a single room, with padded walls, behind a locked door. Somewhere in missionary history a word of compassion should be written for Dorothy Carey, who paid a high price for Baptist missions and never knew why.

The first few years in India were a nightmare to the Careys. Dr. Thomas squandered their entire annual allowance within a few weeks, and they had to find secular employment or face starvation. In his naive hopes, Carey had expected multitudes in India to turn to the gospel, and he was shocked at the utter indifference and occasional hostility his preaching met. To earn a living, Carey became a planter, managed an indigo factory, and later became a teacher at a university. He preached frequently but with little response. Carey found the social and religious culture of India so intertwined with the caste system that persons of status feared to become Christians.

For the first few years in India, Carey was essentially in missionary orientation. He had no precedents to guide him, no sizable body of missionary literature to offer insights, and few missionary colleagues with whom to compare notes. Carey's work was trial and error until after a few years he hammered out a missionary strategy to go with the missionary theology he had developed in England. The methods Carey developed, emphasizing not only preaching but also Scripture translation and the printed word, along with efforts to move the mission churches toward indigenous status, are worthy of note in missionary history. On the mission field, Carey also developed a more open attitude toward other denominations, helping to lay some foundations for Baptist participation in the later ecumenical movement.

On the first day of the new century, 1800, Carey and his family moved to Serampore. There he was joined by two other Baptist missionaries, John Marshman and William Ward, with their families. Thus began a famous missionary partnership and the Serampore Mission. Marshman was the preacher; Ward the printer; Carey the translator.

Internal Life of Particular Baptists

Doctrinal issues hardly tell the full story of English Baptists in the eighteenth century. They sought to carry on a full range of church activities, both in local congregations and active associations. They won converts, formed new churches, called pastors and established schools for their training, disciplined members, and spoke out on social and moral issues of the day. General and Particular Baptists faced many similar issues.

After their successful national meetings of 1689 and 1691, the Particular Baptists did not follow through in organizing a national assembly as the General Baptists had done. They continued to function through the associations, various coffee-house fellowships, and local ministers organizations, particularly in London. The London Baptist Association, when functioning, and the London Ministers Meeting exercised influence and leadership whose impact was nationwide. However, not until early in the next century did Particular Baptists form a national organization. Perhaps their independent connectionalism, carried over from their Separatist origins, caused them to exaggerate local independence and to fear a national structure.

The Particular Baptist Fund

In 1717 a group of London ministers formed the Particular Baptist Fund to provide salary supplements for needy pastors, minimal allowances for retired pastors and their widows, and scholarship aid for student ministers of their communion. This was the first organized fund in English Baptist life and is still operating today. In describing the need for such a fund, its sponsors gave a dismal picture of conditions among English Baptists at the time, a picture whose accuracy need not be doubted. Their "Paper of Proposals for raising a Fund" noted "the great want of able and well-qualified persons to defend the truth, and to supply those churches which are in want of ministers; [and] the poverty and distress which some em-

ployed in that sacred office are exposed to for want of a competent maintenance for themselves and families."[41] These pioneers deplored that impoverished pastors often had to appeal to wealthy individuals for aid, that such
individuals were not always able to judge the merits of the case, and that
such gifts often allowed individuals too much power over ministers.

The fund was administered by trustees chosen by contributors, At their
first meeting on June 4, 1717, representatives from six Particular Baptist
churches laid down rules for the use of the fund. One provision proved quite
controversial: Applicants were limited to Particular Baptists only. The
trustees said:

> By Particular Baptists are intended those that have been solemnly immersed
> in water, upon a personal confession of faith; and who profess the doctrines
> of Three Divine Persons in the Godhead—eternal and personal election—
> original sin—particular redemption—efficacious grace in regeneration and
> sanctification—free justification, by the imputed righteousness of Christ—
> and the final perseverance of the saints—according to the Confession of Faith
> that was published in London, by the Calvinistic Baptists, in the year 1689.[42]

Benjamin Stinton, though an ardent supporter of the fund, opposed that
restriction and urged that its benefits be available to all Baptists. He argued
that some Baptists do not fit neatly into either category of General or
Particular; that to restrict the fund would make Baptists look fussy and
narrow, and would thereby repel churches and individuals who might
otherwise contribute; that other dissenting denominations had established
similar funds without such restrictions; and that limiting beneficiaries to
those who hold personal election and perseverance of the saints unduly
elevates those doctrines.

However, Stinton was outvoted, and the restriction remained. The years
fully justified Stinton's fears, for we read of ongoing hassles to determine
who did or did not qualify doctrinally for aid. More than once the trustees
were embarrassed by the necessity of turning down needy widows and
orphans on doctrinal grounds and, as one might predict, the questionnaire
developed to test the doctrinal views of applicants aroused much antago-
nism.

For more than two and a half centuries, the fund has operated among
English Baptists, benefiting countless persons. As the beginning of organized benevolence in the denomination, the effort was laudable, for it addressed needs that could not be ignored. One melancholy fact, however,
requires notice; this marked the beginning of the trend of many English
Baptist churches depending upon others for the support of their pastors.

41. Ivimey, 3:150.
42. John Rippon, *A Brief Memoir of the Life and Writings of the Late Rev. John Gill,*
p. 3n.

Early managers of the fund were aware of that danger. They urged churches whose pastors qualified for some supplement not to thereby "lessen their contributions," for that would result in "a very great abuse and perversion of the generosity of others."[43]

Several General churches and individuals wished to contribute to the fund but were unable to do so because of its restrictions to Particular Baptists. Therefore, a similar fund was established among General Baptists. They did not restrict its benefits to their group. Thus an early opportunity for cooperation between the two branches of the Baptist family was lost.

Threats to Toleration

The legal status of English Baptists remained somewhat ambiguous in the eighteenth century. In the first flush of victory in 1689, they tended to see the positive benefits of the Act of Toleration, which allowed Baptists to exist and worship in their own churches. However, as the century unfolded, Baptists had ample occasion to discover the limitations that yet remained upon the free exercise of religion in England.

For one thing, Baptists along with other free churchmen were permanently tagged as "Dissenters." That word carried negative overtones and, in effect, reduced its wearers to a distinctly second-class status. Parts of the Clarendon Code remained in force, particularly the Corporation and Test Acts, which effectively sidelined Baptists from meaningful participation in public life. Dissenters were also excluded from the universities. Granted that at this time Oxford and Cambridge were themselves in serious decline, and that some of the dissenting academies offered educational opportunities as good or better than the two universities, the fact remains that Baptists suffered from a lack of able and prepared leaders. Just as England entered an era of intense intellectual searching, the Baptist clergy were, for the most part, ill-equipped to participate in the religious dialogue of the time. While the Baptists had many caring pastors who nurtured their flocks, their leaders were usually drawn from persons of diminished vision, lesser preparation, and smaller expectations, and the denomination paid a heavy price.

The provisions of the Act of Toleration were scrupulously kept by William of Orange until his death in 1701. However, the accession of Queen Anne (1701-1714) marked the resurgence of the High Church party, along with persistent efforts to undermine and eventually repeal the religious freedoms afforded to dissent under that law. During Queen Anne's time, Baptists, Presbyterians, and Congregationalists, who had before acted separately for the most part, formed committees to act in concert as the "three denominations" in response to a common threat.[44]

During the latter part of her reign, the queen moved decisively to abbrevi-

---

43. Ivimey, 3:156.
44. Ibid., p. 43.

ate religious freedom in England. The historian was correct who wrote that under Queen Anne, "the situation of the Dissenters, . . . became very perilous."[45] Many felt it was only a matter of time until dissent would be curtailed, and therefore

> the spirit of envy and persecution was revived among the people; and those encroachments that were made upon the Act of Toleration, caused some to fear, and others to hope, that in a little time it would be wholly taken away. And the more zealous were hereby encouraged to threaten the Dissenters with demolishing their places of worship, driving their teachers into corners, and banishing out of the land all that dared to dissent from the church.[46]

The proposed legislation which would, in effect, repeal the Act of Toleration was called the "Schism Bill," though many called it the "Occasional Bill." Though Baptists were less directly affected by the prohibition of "occasional conformity," they suffered from other restrictions in the bill. They, along with other dissenters, wrote numerous petitions to the queen, pointing out that the proposed bill would undo parts of the Toleration Act, force Baptists to educate their children as Anglicans or leave them in ignorance, further deprive Baptists of an educated clergy, renew religious factions and fusses in England, and damage both the spiritual and civil health of the nation. They urged the queen to withhold her approval. Notwithstanding such outcries, the queen signed the bill.

However, on the very day the bill was to go into effect, August 1, 1714, Anne died suddenly, at age fifty. The dreaded bill died with her. Crosby probably expressed the reactions of most Baptists accurately, if somewhat indiscreetly, by saying that "providence, and its inevitable decrees, took the whole work out of their hands."[47] Even more pointedly, Benjamin Stinton, son-in-law and successor to Benjamin Keach, preached a sermon entitled "A Discourse of Divine Providence," based on Daniel 2:20-21, part of which says that God "changeth the times and the seasons: he removeth kings, and setteth up kings."[48]

George I came to the throne in 1714, thus continuing a line of monarchs who were at least Protestant if somewhat unimaginative. Though Baptists still went under that dreadful name of "Dissenters" and continued to suffer disabilities that reduced them to second-class status, the monarchs did not again try to reverse the Toleration Act.

Baptist Buildings

In 1700 few Baptist churches had their own buildings. They met for the most part in rented halls, often with long-term leases, or in homes or out

45. Ibid., p. 67.
46. Ibid., p. 104.
47. Thomas Crosby, *The History of English Baptists,* 3:81.
48. Ivimey, 3:104.

of doors. However, after 1700 more churches enjoyed the luxury of their own buildings, modest though most of them were. Later observers thought the early Baptist buildings "unattractive and uncomfortable" and described the high-backed pews as "a sort of religious penance."[49] The Baptists found it prudent, in a land dominated by a state church, to locate their churches inconspicuously. Even today a few Baptist churches in England are hidden away on back streets, behind other buildings, or otherwise concealed. As one writer put it, "To avoid observation of enemies they [buildings] were built in obscure situations."[50]

These generalizations must not obscure the fact that during the eighteenth century many Baptist churches erected large and handsome buildings, some to seat upwards of a thousand persons. Such churches were more numerous in London and some of the larger towns, but the dissenters had nothing to compare to Saint Paul's or Westminster Abbey. Having their own church buildings, some say, provided a mixed blessing to Baptists. While they benefited from having permanent meeting places, the ministers tended to be more localized, and itinerant and village preaching probably declined.

Pastors and Religious Education

During the eighteenth century, Baptist pastors received relatively less financial support than did ministers of the other dissenting churches and far less than clergy of the standing church. While many received supplementary grants from the Particular Baptist Fund, and comparable funds in General and New Connection circles, many pastors either eked out a poverty-level existence or, what was more likely, gave themselves more to secular employments. This bivocational approach to ministry tended to distract the energy and attention of the pastors more to their daily work and less to their ministry. A few pastors, such as John Gill, had independent means, and did not concern themselves about salaries.

Most of the English Baptist pastors were called *minister* or *elder.* Toward the end of the century the title *reverend* became more common. For example, in 1776 the Eastern Association voted to use the title *reverend* "in order to express our notion of the lawfulness of the ordination of nonconformist ministers against the preposterous claims of a clergy who ordain one another after the manner of the papal hierarchy."[51] Some Baptist pastors wore the clerical collar, especially in the pulpit, to emphasize that they took their ministry just as seriously as did the Anglican priests.

Throughout the century, Baptists made continuing efforts to provide

---

49. Fred Trestrail, *The Past and Present,* p. 25.
50. Ibid.
51. C. F. Stell, "The Eastern Association of Baptist Churches, 1775-1782," *The Baptist Quarterly,* p. 16.

training for their ministers, mostly through local academies kept by Baptist ministers. Not only the law but also costs kept Baptists out of Oxford and Cambridge. As early as 1702, Hercules Collins set the tone of Baptist emphasis upon education in his treatise, *The Temple Repair'd.* He urged the churches and pastors to watch for and encourage young men for ministry and also to stir up and equip a lay ministry.

Collins insisted that a church is still a church even without pastors but that it can do its work more effectively with a capable, called, and trained ministry. He noted a preference among the churches for pastors "such as have had Human learning; and there hath been too great a slight put upon such as had it not, tho no way inferior in spiritual Gifts."[52] He complained that many churches needing a pastor sought one abroad, when they might better call out one from among themselves. Churches were vulnerable, Collins said, "where there is but one Gift in exercise" (i.e., only one pastor). He suggested that neighboring pastors come together once a month or more often for instruction, citing the schools of the prophets in 2 Kings 2.

Collins rejected the idea, sometimes heard among Baptists then and now, that the preacher need not study but should rely upon the immediate inspiration of the moment for his preaching. Instead, he recommended careful study and preparation, though academic and literary exactness could never take the place of spiritual depth. He admitted, "It is possible to . . . give an exact Grammatical Construction of the same [Scripture], yet if the Man be void of the Spirit of Christ, he cannot know or understand the Mysteries contain'd in God's Word." Collins often quoted a saying that, "Tho I understood Latin and Greek, Philosophy, Logick and Rhetorick, etc., yet before conversion I was as ignorant of Christ as a wild Ass's Colt."[53]

As to practical matters, Collins recommended that sermons be relatively brief, with a limited number of "points," that they be delivered in a clear natural voice without notes, well-prepared but not with learned ostentation, and that pastors dress and act decently in the pulpit. Of sermon length, Collins pointed out that it was better to leave the people "longing than loathing." Pastors should give attention to sermon preparation before Saturday night, he said, "else we may be at a loss, and have very poor and lean Discourses." Above all, Collins urged, "let us have no indecent Behaviour, nor uncomely Garb" in the pulpit.[54] He complained that some pastors went into the pulpit "with their Hair and Shoulders covered with Pouder."

52. Hercules Collins, *The Temple Repair'd: or, An Essay to revive the long-neglected Ordinances, or exercising the spiritual Gift of Prophecy for the Edification of the Churches; and of ordaining Ministers duly qualified,* p. 12.

53. Ibid., pp. 19, 20.

54. Ibid., pp. 29-31.

Even young men wore white wigs or sifted white powder into their hair to affect an appearance of age and thus garner more respect from the church.

By far the most important advance in Baptist education occurred at Bristol, in the West of England. In 1679 Edward Terrill left a substantial bequest to support a pastor who was "well skilled in the tongues" and who would spend part of his time teaching others. That wealthy layman realized the importance of ministerial education and wanted to help remove any reproach that Baptist ministers lacked proper intellectual preparation. The school thus modestly begun, and which still exists in Bristol, is the oldest surviving Baptist college in the world. In its early days its tutors and students had to resist some antieducation sentiment among Baptists. In 1639 a Baptist minister, Samuel How, had written a treatise on *The Sufficiency of the Spirit's Teaching without Humane Learning: or, a Treatise Tending to prove Humane Learning to be No Help to the Spiritual Understanding of the Word of God.* Even Thomas Collier, energetic but erratic leader of Baptists in the west, argued in 1651, "It is the spirit of Antichrist that seeks after humane help to supply the room or want of this Spirit of Christ and having gotten it they grow proud of it."[55] Despite such suspicion of an educated ministry, the churches learned to prefer the well-prepared pastors for their obvious advantages in preaching, teaching, and overall leadership.

Bristol College was strengthened under the dynamic leadership of Bernard Foskett (1685-1758). Foskett arrived at Bristol in 1720 and, by example and precept, demonstrated the advantages of a trained ministry. The school was supported not only by the Terrill bequest but also by the Particular Baptist Fund and the Bristol Baptist Fund, both established in 1717. According to the style of the day, the students lived in the home of the pastor-tutor, shared at his table, and not only studied theology but shared to some extent in the practical duties of the pastorate, thus combining academic and practical training. Between 1735-1740 the Bristol College sent out approximately a dozen graduates to serve churches in England and Wales. Altogether some sixty-four students studied under Foskett, who must be reckoned a major factor in Baptist ministerial training in the eighteenth century.

At Foskett's death in 1758, the Bristol church called Hugh Evans and his son Caleb, who served as copastors for twenty-three years. The senior Evans, who had primary responsibility for the college, announced his purpose was "not merely to form substantial scholars but as far as in him lay he was desirous of being made an instrument in God's hand of forming them

55. Cited in Norman S. Moon, *Education for Ministry: Bristol Baptist College 1679-1979,* p. 2.

able, evangelical, lively, zealous ministers of the Gospel."[56] Thus the school combined academic preparation, spiritual formation, and practical training in ministry.

The college was stabilized in 1770 with formation of the Bristol Education Society, which appealed for wider financial support from the Baptists of England. Almost at once enrollment doubled from nine to eighteen, and the course of study was expanded to four years. The society statement of 1770 justifying expansion of the college deserves quotation, partly because it provides an insightful comment upon conditions in Baptist life of the time. The society said:

> It has long been a matter of complaint that there is a great scarcity of ministers to supply the congregations of the Baptist denomination. Many of those who have been called to the ministry among them have been unable, for want of provision for their support, to prosecute preparatory studies which would have enabled them to exercise their ministerial gifts with more general acceptance. To supply this defect a small number of pupils have for many years past been instructed in various branches of knowledge in Bristol. But many of them . . . have been obliged to break off their studies very abruptly to make room for others. Notwithstanding which disadvantage it is presumed that Baptist churches in various parts of the Kingdom have experienced the utility of the institution.[57]

After 1770 the expanded college set itself to "supply destitute congregations with a succession of able and evangelical ministers," to assist promising young men in obtaining an education, and to encourage evangelistic work in the churches. Among students at Bristol were John Rippon, John Sutcliff, John Collett Ryland, Thomas Blundell, and William Staughton, all destined to become outstanding Baptist leaders.[58] The effective work of its graduates convinced the churches of the value of education. The work of Hugh Evans bore fruit, who in a sermon on *The Able Minister,* said, "The able minister needs to possess a tolerable share of endowments, . . . and he needs the improvements of human learning."[59] When Particular Baptists elsewhere sank into hyper-Calvinism, Bristol graduates continued their evangelical preaching. They were like Andrew Gifford (1700-1784), Bristol graduate and former teacher, who "would offer Christ to sinners." No doubt Bristol College was one factor in the rise of Fullerism; some even suggest a direct influence from Caleb Evans upon Fuller.[60]

In addition to ministerial education, many Baptists saw the need for Christian training for lay members, especially the religious training of

56. Ibid., p. 11.
57. Ibid.
58. Ibid., pp. 19-21.
59. Ibid., p. 15.
60. Ibid., p. 20.

youth. The minutes of numerous associations and assemblies reveal the efforts made to meet this need. Letters to the associations confirm that this was a primary concern among the churches. They devised various plans for Bible instruction either on Sundays or weekday evenings and even tried at times to provide curriculum materials suitable for the religious instruction of children. Of course, such daily education as was available to the children of Dissenters would include religious instruction.

Most historians agree that the architect of the present Sunday School was an Anglican layman, Robert Raikes, who began Sunday instruction for disadvantaged children about 1780. Raikes's classes included secular subjects, primarily reading and writing, and depended upon employed teachers. Baptist layman William Fox turned the Sunday School more to religious instruction. Amid various efforts at the religious instruction of youth among English Baptists, one notes the lack of emphasis upon Bible study for adults. Since the sermons of the time were lengthy, hortatory, and heavily laced with biblical and doctrinal content, perhaps they depended upon that avenue for indoctrinating adults more firmly in the faith.

Laying on of Hands

From early times, the General Baptists, and sometimes the Particulars, debated the importance of laying on of hands. All agreed that hands must be laid upon candidates for ordination, but whether to lay hands upon every new convert was hotly disputed.

Among Baptists the transition from "the world" to the church involved several steps. After an intensely personal experience of inner anxiety and turmoil about one's sins, sometimes called being "under conviction," the inquirer would profess a conversion experience and relate to the church, often at great length, the autobiography of awakening to sin and struggle through to faith. If that experience were judged authentic, the church members voted to receive the new convert, who was then baptized by immersion. However, immersion did not complete the process. The next step was to join the church. Most General Baptist churches and a few Particulars required the new convert to have the laying on of hands as a prerequisite to church membership. Usually the convert would kneel while the church members filed by, laying both hands on the head of the new convert in a gesture of prayer. For those who practiced it, this completed the process into full church membership.

Conditions of Communion

More serious perhaps was the communion controversy, which erupted again by mid-century after a generation of relative quiet. The practice of open versus closed communion had long troubled Baptists. They experienced a major controversy in the seventeenth century between William Kiffin (closed) and John Bunyan (open), and the nineteenth century would see a further controversy between Joseph Kinghorn (closed) and Robert Hall (open) which would involve the entire denomination. The controversy was fanned to new heat by the publication of Abraham Booth's book in 1778. Like many books of that time, to read the lengthy title is to get the gist of the book. Booth called his work, *An Apology for the Baptists. In which they are Vindicated from the Imputation of Laying an Unwarranted Stress on the Ordinance of Baptism; and against the Charge of Bigotry in refusing Communion at the Lord's Table to Paedobaptists* (London, 1778).

Booth's book was a major theological work, tightly reasoned and well-written for the time. Booth developed several of the ideas Joseph Kinghorn would advance in the next century. Though his arguments focused on baptism and communion, Booth's greater concern was for the doctrine of the church. He feared that if the Lord's Supper, the primary spiritual privilege of church membership, were extended to the unbaptized, it would lead to contempt for baptism and ultimately for the church. It might lead, he feared, to admission not only of the unbaptized but also the unconverted to church membership. This would undercut the concept of a gathered church made up "visible saints." Many of the Particular Baptists and most of the New Connection Baptists preferred closed communion, limiting eligibility to the Lord's Supper to baptized (immersed) members. The old General Baptists preferred open communion, and the moderate Particular Baptists of the Fuller variety tended in that direction.

Church Discipline

In matters of discipline, the eighteenth-century English Baptists kept a tight ship. In addition to the usual moral lapses common to humanity, Baptists could be called to account for loose doctrinal beliefs, questionable social practices, and economic offenses ranging from idleness to bankruptcy. Such offenses as "returning to the world," (going back to the Church of England); "falling into notions," (joining the Quakers); and "doubting the eternal decrees" (questioning the tenets of hyper-Calvinism), could and did result in offenders being called before their churches to explain, recant, and/or be excluded. For minor offenses, one might be only reprimanded; for the more serious ones, exclusion was the penalty. Pastor John Gill of London wrote in his own scrawling script in the Horsleydown churchbook an intricate theological formulation which no mortal could possibly understand and required all the members to agree to it or be cast out. Probably not one layman in a dozen had the faintest idea what the doctrine meant, but they loved and trusted the pastor so they agreed.

Those Baptists who attended fox hunts, public dances, music hall entertainments, theater plays, or lingered overlong at the public inns could expect such deviant behavior to come to the attention of the church. Most Baptists opposed these practices though some of the New Connection gave cautious approval to strictly chaperoned dancing and group singings, so long as the songs were not too worldly. One cannot avoid the conclusion that the practices Baptists opposed revealed their own social status. Those amusements which marked the privileged upper classes, activities beyond the means of most Baptists, seemed to offend them most, while they found ways to justify their own modest social amusements.

Status of Children

The records reveal some change in the religious status of children among Baptists in the eighteenth century. One major emphasis of Baptists from their origin was a rejection of infant baptism. However, some Baptists apparently devised a substitute service of infant dedication. From such sketchy records as remain, the service appears as much a dedication of parents as of infants. Such dedications may have been practiced, at least occasionally, in the seventeenth century and became more common as the years passed.

Also in the eighteenth century, Baptists began to accept conversion of children at earlier ages. Most Baptists had felt that conversion should ordinarily occur in adult years and rarely younger than sixteen or eighteen. The conversion of a child as young as twelve would be considered so unusual as to be reported to the association among the "remarkables" of that year. One church reported the conversion of a girl of nine. This was apparently opposed by some, for the church felt called upon to offer an elaborate defense, citing hers as an admittedly unusual case.

Role of Women

One also finds that the church roles of Baptist women changed somewhat in the eighteenth century. Whereas in the previous century women had served as deacons, sometimes designated as "deaconesses," that role diminished in the eighteenth century. By then one does not read much of Baptist women preaching. Indeed, Ann Dutton in the 1740s found it necessary to defend the practice of women writing for publication, teaching publicly in the church, or even giving the lengthy public confession of faith or "testimony of experience" by which new converts were received into the church. She herself was a prolific writer and able speaker who apparently chafed under restrictions put upon her freedom to exercise those gifts in the church.

Social Issues

English Baptists spoke out on social and moral issues but not always with a single voice. Some of their early writers defended slavery, while others condemned both slavery and the slave trade as unspeakable evils. In 1711 the Western Association received a question from the First Baptist Church of Charleston, South Carolina, asking advice about whether to discipline a member who had severely punished a slave for running away. In their response, the association took a strongly proslavery stance. They concluded that the practice of slavery is lawful, that buying and selling slaves is nowhere forbidden by Scripture, and that owners may enforce whatever punishments are necessary to retain their property. They said of slaves, "We finde by Scripture, that 'tis lawfull to buy them, Gen: 17.13,23,27. And if lawfull to buy them 'tis lawfull to keep them in order, and under government; and for Self preservation, punish them to prevent farther Mischief."[61]

In time these harsh views were challenged and changed. Several of the Baptist associations after mid-century took a stand against slavery, and some formed local abolition societies and raised money to seek, as they put it, "the abolition of the abominable slave trade."[62] Robert Robinson, an influential Baptist leader in Cambridge, preached and wrote against slavery and in 1788 helped to frame an early resolution to Parliament against the practice.

Perhaps the most powerful Baptist voice raised against slavery in the eighteenth century was that of Abraham Booth, who published in 1792 his treatise, *Commerce in the Human Species, and the Enslaving of Innocent Persons, Inimical to the Laws of Moses and the Gospel of Christ.* Booth forcefully condemned slavery not only as a violation of the teachings of both Testaments but also as a deprivation of the natural rights of mankind. He called slavery "this outrage on the sacred rights of liberty" and condemned those who captured slaves and those who purchased them, for "if there were no receivers, there would be no thieves."[63] Booth concluded, "The traffic in man is unjust and cruel, is barbarous and savage" and the basic human rights were as valid in Africa as in England.[64]

Summary

The eighteenth century was a fateful time for English Baptists. They had won a measure of religious freedom in 1689 but seemed too spiritually depleted to take advantage of their new opportunities. They were unable to replace their aged leaders, and the churches either went without pastors or depended upon men of lesser caliber. The Baptists never developed the grace of Christian stewardship; most were quite poor, but they never supported their churches even to the extent they could have. The founding of various denominational funds, though necessary and achieving laudable good, nevertheless fixed upon the churches the idea that the support of the ministry should come from elsewhere. Sensing perhaps that the lay people counted the ministry of little value, many of the ministers may in subtle ways have shared that impression. At any rate, many of them were so

61. Cited in Robert A. Baker, ed., *A Baptist Source Book,* p. 31.
62. Ivimey, 4:63.
63. Abraham Booth, *Commerce in the Human Species,* pp. 4-5.
64. Ibid., p. 13.

distracted by secular employments that they could give little time to their ministry, and consequently the churches went untended.

The churches were also devastated by doctrinal extremes which sapped vitality and warped Baptist outlook. The General Baptists fell into extreme liberalism, Arianism, and Socianism, and the denomination languished. Some General emphases survived in the New Connection schism, but General Baptists never recovered from the devastation of the eighteenth century. Particular Baptists fell into extreme conservatism, hyper-Calvinism, and Antinomianism, and their churches withered under the arid blasts. They demonstrated that extreme conservatism can be as damaging to spiritual vitality as extreme liberalism.

The Baptists entered the eighteenth century with good prospects and high hopes; but as the century unfolded, the prospects diminished and the hopes faded. They came to the nineteenth century chastened by reverses, with the denomination split into factions, diminished in number, and depleted in spiritual vitality.

7

Revival Fires: Baptists in America

The eighteenth century proved a turning point for Baptists in America. In 1700 they could count only 24 churches with 839 members.[1] That number included all kinds of Baptists, fewer than half of them Regular or mainline Baptists. As late as 1720, a Baptist writer lamented "the paucity of those of our denomination in New England."[2] One cannot say that those scattered churches in 1700 formed a "denomination." They had no organized association, sponsored no societies for missions or evangelism, and probably had limited awareness of one another.

The small beginnings abruptly gave way to a surge of growth, beginning with the sweeping revival of the 1730s which historians have called the First Great Awakening. Though not begun by Baptists, and at first opposed by many of them, they became its chief beneficiaries. Waves of revivalism, immigration of English and Welsh Baptists to America, and a social environment that gave status to Dissenters, all contributed to the spurt of growth among Baptists.

By the end of the century, Baptists had become the largest denomination in America, according to one historian.[3] By 1790 they numbered 979 churches, with 67,490 members, grouped into at least 42 associations, and were discussing plans to form a national organization. The Baptists adopted a confession of faith in 1742, formed a Baptist college in 1764, struggled for and achieved religious liberty, and worked out an evangelical theology of moderate Calvinism. Baptists grew rapidly in the South, where by the end of the century the Separate Baptists of the frontier and the Regular Baptists of the coastal regions found common ground.

Seen in the classic before-and-after framework, Baptists in America were hardly the same people in 1800 as they had been a century earlier. Their outward progress was more than matched by corresponding inward changes. The spiritual lethargy and "dullness of spirit," often complained of before 1740, gave way to new vitality and vigor. The tendency to bitter

1. Robert G. Gardner, *Baptists of Early America: A Statistical History,* 1639-1790, p. 63.
2. Isaac Backus, *A History of New England with Particular Reference to the Denomination of Christians Called Baptists,* 2:487.
3. Winthrop S. Hudson, *Religion in America,* p. 218.

quarrels over trifles, so devastating in the 1600s, abated for a time in the 1700s as Baptists gave themselves to evangelism and the struggle for religious liberty. Their increasingly attractive buildings, capable ministers, and above all their patriotic participation in the Revolutionary War improved the public image of Baptists, and no doubt their self-image as well. One recalls the "candid old lady" who about 1750 described Baptists as "an outlandish sect" but later acknowledged that "they are much more like other folk than when I was young."[4] Baptists had less occasion to defend themselves against such familiar charges as these: "That we are disorderly persons, and walk disorderly. . . . That we are disturbers of the Publick Peace."[5] Some felt Baptists had gone too far toward respectability. A young backwoods preacher, upon seeing the ornate Baptist churches and polished ministers of Boston in the 1790s, whose pulpit robes had sleeves "as wide as the meal bags used in Vermont," complained that elaborate chandeliers, pew "cushing," and powdered wigs distracted from spiritual worship.[6]

The First Great Awakening

For Baptists the Matterhorn of the eighteenth century was the First Great Awakening; nothing else comes close in its impact upon the future shape of the denomination. The waves of revival which swept through the American colonies in the 1730s and 1740s affected all the churches. Their impact, said one historian, was "to mold the various denominations to a common pattern," thus imprinting most of American Protestantism with common evangelical beliefs and practices.[7] No isolated movement, the American Awakening was interconnected with similar revivals elsewhere, such as the Pietist movement in Europe and the Wesleyan Revival in England.

A time of coldness and spiritual decline preceded the awakening when, as C. C. Goen observed, "saints were in short supply."[8] The zeal of the first Pilgrims had cooled, and the new generation expected to inherit the kingdom along with the family pewter. The declension is nowhere more evident than in the "Half-Way Covenant" of 1662. Earlier, the New England churches had allowed infants of church members to receive baptism, and thus church membership, though they were expected to make their own profession of faith later. A question arose about the status of infant children of the next generation, whose parents had never made the expected profession of faith. The question involved more than religion, for social and

4. William Warren Sweet, ed., *Religion on the American Frontier: The Baptists 1783-1830*, p. 10n.
5. William H. Brackney, ed., *Baptist Life and Thought: 1600-1980*, p. 112.
6. Ibid., pp. 136-137.
7. Hudson, p. 60.
8. Clarence C. Goen, *Revivalism and Separatism in New England, 1740-1800*, p. 3.

economic benefits were attached to church membership. The decision of 1662 allowed the third generation, infants of moral parents who claimed no religious conversion, to be received into the church by infant baptism. They had all the social privileges of church membership but could not receive communion unless they made their own professions of faith. Thus they were "halfway" members, and most never went beyond that status. In effect, this abandoned the earlier ideal of a regenerate church membership.

To exaggerate the importance of the Great Awakening would be difficult, not only for religious reasons but also for its contributions to American political self-identity and general culture. Some consider the awakening the real American Revolution. H. Richard Neibuhr pointed out that America had an "awakening to God that was simultaneous with its awakening to national self-consciousness." He described the awakening as "a new beginning; it was our national conversion."9

Four leaders are usually credited with guiding the revival. Theodore Freylinghuysen (1691-1747) had served as a pastor in the Netherlands. About 1720 he migrated to the Raritan Valley of New Jersey to minister among Dutch Reformed churches. An eloquent preacher, Freylinghuysen sought spiritual renewal through fervent preaching, strict church discipline, and personal visitation.

Gilbert Tennent (1703-1764), a Presbyterian, began preaching similar revivalist views in the Middle Colonies, influenced perhaps by Freylinghuysen. The eldest son of William Tennent, founder of the "Log College" forerunner of Princeton, the younger Tennent is best remembered for his fiery sermon on "The Danger of an Unconverted Ministry" (1740). Though intemperate in tone, that sermon was printed and circulated widely and not only furthered the revival but also helped split the Presbyterian church into "Old Side" and "New Side" factions in 1741. The sermon attacked the churches and ministers for their coldness and indifference in religion, accused them of elevating formality above spirituality, and advocated a more emotional style of preaching.10

Jonathan Edwards (1703-1758) was the theologian of the revival. A graduate of Yale, Edwards later served as assistant to his grandfather, Soloman Stoddard, and in 1729 succeeded him as pastor of the Congregational church at Northampton, Massachusetts. Edwards was known for his powerful preaching. Most people know Edwards's famous sermon, "Sinners in the Hands of an Angry God," though that was hardly typical of his preaching. More important perhaps was his "great Thursday lecture," given at Boston in 1731, in which Edwards set out his view of man's total

9. H. Richard Niebuhr, *The Kingdom of God in America* (New York: Harper and Row, 1937), p. 124.

10. Robert L. Ferm, ed., *Issues in American Protestantism* (Garden City, N. Y.: Doubleday and Company, Inc., 1969), pp. 73 *f.*

dependence upon God.[11] At Northampton, spiritual renewal first appeared among the youth who had previously, according to Edwards, been "much addicted to night walking, and frequenting the tavern."[12] By late 1734 "the Spirit of God began extraordinarily to set in," leading to a revival of major proportions. Over three hundred were converted in a year, about one hundred of them on one Sunday. Similar awakenings were reported in other churches in the Connecticut Valley. However, the movement at Northampton faded as rapidly as it had arisen; in the early 1740s, the church went several years without a single conversion.

Similar revivals were reported in scattered churches in New England and the Middle Colonies. While a few traveling evangelists, like the eccentric James Davenport, carried word from one place to another, it fell to George Whitefield (1714-1770), the English evangelist, to tie these scattered awakenings together into one concerted movement. An associate of John Wesley, Whitefield made at least five tours of the American colonies where his fervent preaching, evangelical ecumenism, and evangelistic zeal made a deep impact. Whitefield made the colonies more aware of each other; his followers formed the first intercolonial leadership in America.

Revival zeal proved as divisive as it was dynamic. Not everyone favored the "new exercises." Perhaps many agreed with Charles Chauncy's penetrating critique in his "Letter Concerning the State of Religion in New England."[13] Chauncy, pastor in Boston, portrayed the revivals as shallow, overly emotional, and without lasting effect. Criticizing Tennent and Whitefield by name, Chauncy huffed that their sermons contained "mere Stuff," though delivered with much shouting and wild gestures. For a time those who favored the revival and those who opposed tried to exist in the same churches. But when this proved impossible, many Congregational churches split into "Old Lights" (antirevival) and "New Lights" (prorevival).

While Baptists had little to do with initiating the awakening, they reaped much of its benefits. Not only were Baptist churches caught up in the revivals, with their resultant growth, but over a hundred of the New Light Congregational churches eventually moved into Baptist life. Many such churches also found themselves nearer the Baptists in social status and political views, which aided in their transition to Baptist affiliation. In that way, Baptists gained not only a number of churches but also some outstanding leaders like Isaac Backus and Shubal Stearns, to name only two. Since people tend to carry baggage when they move, these New Lights turned-

11. Ibid., pp. 61 *f.*
12. Peter G. Mode, ed., *Source Book and Bibliographical Guide for American Church History*, p. 214.
13. Ferm, pp. 83 *f.*

Baptist also brought new ideas which affected Baptist theology as well as the emerging structure of the denomination.

Baptists went through their own revival divisions. Their factions took the names of *Regular,* mostly the urban churches that shied away from the revival emotions, and *Separates,* who saw the revivals as a genuine work of God. One of the first identifiable Separate Baptist church originated in a split of First Baptist, Boston, in 1743. George Whitefield had preached in Boston in 1740, and as one historian reported, "A torpid community was aroused as by the trump of God."[14] Jeremiah Condy, pastor of First Baptist Church, disapproved the revival, abhorring its theology and disdaining its emotionalism. However, a few of his members caught the new excitement and became discontented with Condy's solemn ministry. "They regarded his preaching as grievously defective," said one report, and complained of "a cold, cadaverous formalism." The disaffected members began to meet separately, and in 1743 they "proceeded to make arrangements for a separate and independent organization."[15] Seven members formed the Second Baptist Church (Separate), called Ephraim Bound as pastor, and entered their own building in 1746. The church increased to 120 members in five years. Later Thomas Baldwin helped launch the Baptist missionary movement as pastor of this church.

One can almost trace the course of Separate Baptists in New England through one church. In the heat of revivalism, a New Light Congregational church was formed near Middleborough in 1748, with Isaac Backus as pastor. In 1749 the church engaged in serious discussions of baptism, and Backus first accepted, and then backed away from, the concept of believer's baptism. However, the question would not die down. In 1751 Backus received immersion as a Baptist and immersed others who accepted it but continued to accept non-baptized members. A conference of ministers at Exeter, Rhode Island, ruled in 1753 that either form of baptism, the sprinkling of infants or immersion of believers, was acceptable. However, a similar conference ruled the next year at Stonington, Connecticut, that these two forms of baptism were incompatible and that churches had to choose between them. In a pungent statement, the Stonington ministers concluded, "Either B sins in making infants the subjects of baptism, or A in cutting them off."[16] By 1756 Backus had given up efforts to coexist with the Congregationalists. Gathering his Baptist adherents, he pulled out and on January 16, 1756 formed a distinctly Baptist church which he served as pastor the rest of his life.

W. G. McLoughlin described the New Light Congregational status as a

---

14. David Benedict, *A General History of the Baptist Denomination in America and Other Parts of the World* (New York: Sheldon, Lamport, and Blakeman, 1855), pp. 392 *f.*

15. Ibid., pp. 392, 393.

16. Backus, 2:114.

halfway house on the road to becoming Baptists.[17] David Benedict called such churches "nurseries of baptists."[18] Perhaps half of the New Light Congregationalists became Baptists; the records detail church after church which made the transition. Until then Baptists in America had not shown much vitality. Backus said, "Declension and stupidity had long prevailed in the land," with Baptists providing their share of both.[19] The influx of New Light Congregationalists helped to revitalize what one described as "the dormant Baptist denomination."[20]

Denominational lines were less sharply drawn in the early 1700s, and the effort of Baptists and Congregationalists to exist in the same churches seemed feasible. They were remarkably similar in all doctrines except baptism. One Baptist pastor said that "different sentiments about baptism were no more to him than their different complexions or stature, or the color of their clothes."[21] When John Comer, who later became pastor at Newport, received immersion in 1725 his pastor recommended against it but assured Comer that his Baptist views would not affect his standing in the Congregational church. The churches made determined efforts to make coexistence work. "Council after council and conference after conference recommended it, and there seemed to be no voice against it, and yet it failed," said Backus.[22] At least three reasons may be cited for the failure of Congregational and Baptist coexistence. First, the inherent incompatibility of infant baptism and believer's baptism could not be forever concealed or papered over. Second, the evangelistic zeal of those who preferred immersion drew multitudes to their position; in some cases the Congregationalists had to withdraw for self-preservation. Third, the adherents of alternate forms often differed in worship styles, an area which proved more divisive than doctrine.

Different as they were, Regular and Separate Baptists in New England never really divided. For one thing, there was no denomination to divide. Some historians have labored to prove the Regular/Separate distinctions more sociological than theological, pointing out that Regular Baptists were more urban and urbane and preferred orderly worship led by educated ministers. The Separates, on the other hand, congregated on the frontier and in small towns, came from the lower classes, and worshiped and converted more noisily. There is some truth in this, but it can be overdone; efforts to explain the awakening as a clash of frontier versus urban cultures have been largely abandoned. In the South, however, Regular and Separate Baptists

17. William G. McLoughlin, *New England Dissent 1630-1833: The Baptists and the Separation of Church and State,* 1:424.

18. Benedict, p. 549.

19. Backus, 1:495.

20. McLoughlin, 1:425.

21. Backus, 2:442n.

22. Ibid., p. 115n.

formed more distinct groups; they became, for a time, separate denominations.

Rapid Expansion

With the awakening as the main catalyst, Baptists by mid-century entered a period of rapid growth. While statistics are elusive and tell only part of the story, they do illustrate the larger trends affecting Baptists. Robert G. Gardner's statistical study, the most thorough recent analysis of Baptist growth patterns, shows that Baptists increased from 60 churches in 1740 to 979 in 1790; from 3,142 to 67,490 members in the same half century.[23] Other historians give slightly different figures. Gardner includes most immersionists, even the Keithians and Rogerenes, whom many would not count as authentic Baptists. By any standards, this represents an unprecedented explosion of Baptists in the new land. That growth was reasonably well distributed geographically, though the South at first lagged behind New England and the Middle Colonies. The following sketches are incomplete but are intended to illustrate Baptist expansion in the major areas.

New England

Baptists experienced their earliest surge of growth in the six states of New England. In areas where the Congregational church was established by law, Baptists faced legal restrictions and opposition which varied from harrassment to severe persecution.

Rhode Island. In Rhode Island Baptists never quite lived up to early expectations. They formed the first Baptist church in America in Providence in 1639 and in 1764 located their first college there, thinking that state would be predominantly Baptist. Perhaps their extreme diversity hampered growth, for Rhode Island Baptists included Regular, General, Six-Principle, Seventh-Day, and Separates. For a time the Separate churches outnumbered the Regulars, but their reluctance to participate in associations and the tendency of Regular churches to reclaim some of the Separate members hampered their witness.

Massachusetts. Despite heavy opposition from the standing order, Baptists prospered in Massachusetts. The progress of churches in the Bay Colony entitle them to be placed "at the head of the American Baptists," according to one early historian.[24] The Regular Baptists predominated. Of ninety-one Baptist churches in Massachusetts by 1790, seventy-three were Regular, and they contained 82 percent of the Baptists of that colony.[25] The others were distributed among Separates, Six-Principles, and two Indian

---

23. Gardner, p. 63. Not all of these are the exact figures printed in Gardner's book; some reflect penciled corrections which Gardner made in the author's copy.
24. Benedict, p. 366.
25. Gardner, pp. 72-74.

churches. In no other area, perhaps, did Regular Baptists make a greater comeback against the inroads of Separate influence. Of forty-six Separate Baptist churches formed in Massachusetts, thirty had switched to Regular Baptists by 1790.

No person better illustrates Baptist progress in eighteenth-century Massachusetts than Hezekiah Smith (1737-1805). Called "the Baptist Whitefield," Smith combined pastoral duties, evangelistic tours, and denominational service, particularly as a trustee of the Baptist college in Rhode Island. In New England, Smith ranked perhaps next to Isaac Backus as a Baptist spokesman for religious liberty. Smith's service as a chaplain in the Revolutionary War won additional converts to the Baptist cause.

Converted and baptized by John Gano, Smith entered the Hopewell Baptist Academy in New Jersey in 1756 and graduated from Princeton in 1762. At the time he was one of only five college-educated Baptist ministers in America, only three of whom (Smith included) were considered orthodox in theology. After college Smith made a fifteen-month preaching tour of "the Southern governments." He formed a firm friendship with Oliver Hart, pastor in Charleston, where Smith was often invited to preach. Hart ordained Smith to the ministry in 1763. Ready for settlement, Smith preached in most of the Baptist churches in Rhode Island but was not uniformly well-received. After one sermon in Providence, he recorded in his journal, "God only knows whether I did any good in Providence, or whether I had any business there."

On a tour of western Massachusetts, Smith found few Baptists in the 1760s, but the New Light Congregationalists heard him gladly. He preached for several months at Haverhill and, following a familiar pattern, by 1765 those who preferred the Baptist way withdrew to form a church. Remarkably, Benedict noted, the church building was located "in the centre of the town; a rare occurrence in those days, when the denomination seldom made any efforts but in remote situations."[26] Smith served as their pastor for the next forty years. However, he often "itinerated in the wilderness," spending only a few months of each year in Haverhill and the rest of the time on home mission preaching tours. He was almost a home mission society within himself, credited with forming thirteen additional churches.

On those frequent preaching tours, Smith left his growing family, as well as the work on their farm and orchard, to the care of his young wife, Hephzibah, or "Hephsy" as she was called. Though a young woman of grace and charm, she was, one biographer noted, "a stranger to experimental religion." In Smith's letters to her, amid instructions about gathering the apples or overseeing the rent houses, he would make some touching comment like, "My dear Hephsy, have you yet found the comforts of true religion?" Unfortunately, we do not have her reply.

26. Benedict, p. 402.

Smith excelled not only as a pastor and evangelist but also as a major architect of the emerging denomination. He was one of the leading founders, and a longtime trustee, of the Rhode Island College. The Haverhill church was one of four that formed the Warren Association in 1767. In 1769 the college requested Smith "to solicit and receive benefactions." Smith stated it more bluntly, "The corporation voted me to go into the Southern governments to beg for the college." In 1802 Smith helped form the Massachusetts Baptist Mission Society, the first of its kind in America and forerunner of the nationwide Home Mission Society formed in 1832.

Maine. The earliest Baptist church in Maine was that formed by William Screven at Kittery in 1682. After Screven moved the church to Charleston, South Carolina, in 1696, no other Baptist church appeared in Maine for almost seventy years. No doubt, a few Baptists lived in the area, most probably holding membership with churches in Massachusetts or New Hampshire. A number of Baptists were among the surge of new settlers in Maine in the 1760s, and by 1764 Joshua Emory had formed a church at Berwick and served as its pastor. For a number of years this remained the only known Baptist church in the state.

What Benedict called the "re-entry of Baptists" into Maine was led by Hezekiah Smith of Haverhill.[27] Smith's itineration took him into Maine, where he gained a few converts, gathered up some immigrating Baptists, and as elsewhere drew away a number of New Light Congregationalists. The Baptist presence in Maine took a radical upturn by 1780, and in 1790 Baptists listed a total of 32 churches with 912 members.[28] Those were about evenly divided between Regular and Separate persuasions.

New Hampshire. In New Hampshire persons with Baptist views are found quite early, but no church was formed until 1755 when Walter Powers gathered a small congregation at Newtown. Hanserd Knollys preached in the Dover area in 1640 and upon his return to England in 1641 became a well-known Baptist minister. Whether he had embraced Baptist views as early as 1640 cannot be determined. The first known Baptist in the state was Mrs. Rachel Thurber Scammon who moved to Stratham before 1730. Though without a church, she remained a committed Baptist and tried to win others to the faith. In forty years, she gained one convert, a woman who went to Boston to receive baptism from Ephraim Bound of Boston's Second Church.

Coming upon a little book advocating Baptist principles, known simply as *Norcott on Baptism,* Mrs. Scammon purchased a hundred copies and distributed them in New Hampshire. From that bread cast upon the waters came many returns. One who chanced upon the book was Dr. Samuel Shepherd, a physician who straightway accepted Baptist principles. He was

27. Ibid., p. 505.
28. Gardner, p. 67.

baptized at Brentwood and later ordained in Boston. For years Shepherd was much respected in New Hampshire both as a physician and Baptist pastor. However, Baptists faced severe opposition. Perhaps nowhere else did the state church make a more determined effort to keep them out or such strong efforts to retain their own members who leaned to New Light emphases.

An early historian said: "In 1770 commenced a new era in the history of our denomination in New Hampshire. About this time there was an almost simultaneous visit made by a number of ministers to different parts of the State."[29] Among the ministers was Hezekiah Smith, who in one town in 1771 baptized 38 persons, including the Congregational pastor. Most of the Baptist itinerants were Separates, who could appeal effectively to the New Lights among the Congregationalists. That, plus the new waves of immigration, allowed Baptists to grow rapidly after 1770. However, many of the Separate Baptist churches tended in time to adopt Regular views, perhaps in reaction to the Freewills. At any rate, by 1790 New Hampshire had a total of 38 churches with 1,740 members.[30] Three churches formed the New Hampshire Association in 1785, the first in the state, though a few churches had affiliated with associations in neighboring states.

Vermont. Many of the early Baptist churches in Vermont were formed from New Lights, particularly around Bennington in the southwest corner of the state. Baptist families and ministers also migrated to the Green Mountain area where several churches were formed in the 1780s. Perhaps the earliest Baptist church in the state was that formed at Shaftsbury in 1768, led by Bliss Willoughby and his son Ebenezer. Jonas Galusha, one-time governor of Vermont, was said to be a member of this church; his son Elon later became an outstanding Baptist leader.

Despite their lack of numbers, the Vermont churches formed several associations, most of them tiny and probably ill-advised. The Shaftsbury Association was first, formed in 1780 with five churches; followed by the Woodstock in 1783; and the Vermont in 1785, formed "in Elder Joseph Cornell's barn."[31] As elsewhere, Baptists in Vermont benefited from the postwar revival. By 1790 they reported 1,796 members in 39 churches, most of them Regular Baptists.[32]

Connecticut. In Connecticut the earliest known Baptist was Mrs. Theophilus Eaton who held her Baptist views with sufficient militancy to get her ousted from the Congregational Church in New Haven in 1657. About twenty years later, Seventh-Day Baptists appeared in the state, some of whom formed a Rogerene church at Groton in 1677. However, a more

29. Benedict, p. 499.
30. Gardner, p. 70.
31. Benedict, p. 489.
32. Gardner, p. 71.

durable Baptist beginning dates from 1705 at Groton and is connected with
the famous Wightman family. In 1705 Valentine Wightman (1681-1747)
moved from Rhode Island to Groton, near New London, and formed a
church on the Six-Principle order. For more than twenty years, it was the
lone Baptist church in Connecticut, until another was formed in New
London in 1726.

About 42 Separate Baptist churches were formed in the state, but 19 of
them switched to Regular and most of the rest died out. By 1790 Connecticut numbered a total of 58 churches and 3,298 members, over two-thirds
of them Regular Baptists. A few Separate and Seventh-Day churches survived, and at least one Rogerene church was included in this total.[33] Three
Connecticut associations were formed before 1800, the Stonington in 1772;
the Groton Union Conference in 1788; and the Danbury in 1790.

Common Patterns. Despite regional differences, a common pattern of
Baptist development emerged in much of New England. Baptists were
extremely scarce before mid-century, but thereafter drew converts from two
main sources: New Light Congregationalists and Baptist immigrants, both
conditioned by sociological as well as religious factors to be receptive to the
Baptist witness. The Separate Baptists practiced a fervent evangelism that
brought rapid growth. However, their churches showed a tendency, once
settled, to move toward more orderly Regular Baptist theology and practices, perhaps in reaction to the Freewill Baptists. Before 1790 men greatly
outnumbered women in Baptist churches in most areas of New England.
The membership was predominantly white, but one reads occasionally of
black or Indian members and even an occasional Indian church. When the
churches were numerous enough, and sometimes before, they linked into
associations, which gave stability and provided an avenue of church extension through home mission itineration.

The governments in Colonial New England were aristocratic in tone, a
spirit which the state church tried to copy. However, the immigrants who
swarmed over New England after the 1760s tended to be, for the most part,
energetic but poor, people on the rise, people who respected achievement
more than privilege. No church corresponded to this egalitarian spirit more
closely than Baptists, and no church benefitted more from the revival of the
1780s.

The Freewill Baptists, whose northern branch arose under Benjamin
Randall in New Hampshire, challenged the stern Calvinism of the day.
They probably impacted upon the mainstream Baptists in an least two ways,
which may seem paradoxical. First, they nudged Separate Baptists toward
the Regular position, to distinguish themselves from the Freewills. At the
same time, the Freewill emphasis, along with the revivalism of the 1780s,

---

33. Ibid., p. 81.

probably led to a softening of Calvinist extremes among the Regular Baptists.

Middle Colonies

Baptists in the Middle Colonies enjoyed far more religious freedom during the eighteenth century than in either New England or the South. The Congregational Church was established by law in the North, while the Anglican Church was set up by law in the South. By contrast, the Middle Colonies had no state church, though for a time the Dutch Reformed in New York sought to gain a favored position and restrict others. Probably the Quaker influence from Pennsylvania and the great religious pluralism helped prevent any church from gaining an upper hand in this region.

Pennsylvania. By 1700 Pennsylvania already had a diverse Baptist population, including Regular Baptists, whose churches at Pennepek and Philadelphia were prominent; Keithians, who came to attention in the 1690s; Mennonites, who settled in Germantown by 1692; and Tunkers (or Dunkers), who sprang from German Pietist sects which had adopted immersion. From these latter the Ephrata sect grew in the 1730s, led by Conrad Beissell. The English-speaking Seventh-Day Baptists formed churches at Newtown and Nottingham in 1700, which later grew to five churches. However, as the Regular Baptists gained strength, most of the other groups declined; by 1711, for example, all four of the Keithian churches were extinct.[34]

Philadelphia provided the major area of Baptist concentration. The important Philadelphia Baptist Association was formed in 1707. It was the first organized Baptist association in America. In 1742 that association adopted a confession destined to shape Baptist theology in America for more than a century and in 1749 issued a carefully reasoned explanation of the power and limitations of an association. By 1770 this association had founded a Baptist college (in Rhode Island), sent out home missionaries, provided a cohesive center for Baptist life throughout America, and was entertaining plans for a Baptist organization to cover the entire country.

Baptist churches in the Middle and Southern Colonies drew heavily from the extensive Welsh migration in the eighteenth century. The Welsh provided not only members and ministers for the Baptist churches in this country but also shaped their spirit, doctrines, worship patterns, and organizational practices. That story is told best by Gwyn A. Williams in his fascinating book, *The Search for Beulah Land.* In what Williams called "a millenarian migration," multitudes of Welshmen succumbed to "the rage to go to America."[35] Economic and political conditions in both countries encouraged that migration, though Williams added that "the American

34. Ibid., p. 91.
35. Gwyn A. Williams, *The Search for Beulah Land: The Welsh and the Atlantic Revolution,* pp. 1, 23.

demand for preachers was . . . a major factor in the Welsh migrations."[36]

Welsh Baptists formed several of the early churches in Pennsylvania, including Pennepek and First Baptist, Philadelphia, and provided leadership for others. Such leaders as Jenkins Jones, Abel Morgan, and Samuel Jones testify to the influence of the Welsh in their new country. One of their greatest contributions was in the person of Morgan Edwards, a Monmouthshire man and graduate of Bristol College. He served for years as pastor of the Philadelphia church, was a prime mover in forming Rhode Island College, helped inaugurate home mission work through the Philadelphia Association, and lent doctrinal and spiritual stability to Baptists.

In tracing the progress of Welsh Baptists in this country, Williams concluded that "the Welsh grew in considerable strength, planting significant offshoots in the Carolinas, particularly at the Welsh neck on the Peedee river, South Carolina. Missionary waves reinforced the southern settlements, but Pennsylvania remained the Welsh heartland."[37]

A number of Welsh pastors opened academies, thus contributing to early Baptist educational efforts. They also showed a willingness to organize, with none of the reluctance of New England Baptists. The Philadelphia Association bore a distinctly Welsh flavor in its early days. The Welsh also brought their tradition of great preaching and their love for singing. But most of all, perhaps, the Welsh influenced Baptists in America by their warm and fervent evangelism.

New York. The Dutch Colony of New Netherlands (later New York) had a few Baptists by the 1650s, probably migrants from Rhode Island, but no organized church appeared until 1714. Later New York became a pivotal state for Baptist growth throughout the Northeast, providing leadership in education, church extension, and missions.

Data about early Baptist activity comes from a paper on "The State of Religion" in New Netherlands, prepared in 1657 by two Reformed ministers. They reported:

> Last year [1656] a fomenter of evil came there. He was a cobbler from Rhode Island . . . and stated that he was commissioned by Christ. He began to preach at Flushing, and then went with the people into the river and dipped them. This becoming known here, the constable proceeded thither and brought him along. He was banished the province.[38]

The cobbler was William Wickendon, pastor of the historic Providence church. Not only was Wickendon fined and banished but also the sheriff of Flushing who had permitted Baptist services was removed from office. Around 1700 another company of Baptists gathered at Oyster Bay, on

---

36. Ibid., p. 21.
37. Ibid., p. 20.
38. Albert Henry Newman, *A History of the Baptist Churches in the United States,* p. 233.

Long Island, and heard occasional preaching by William Rhodes, a Six-Principle Baptist from Rhode Island. The records do not reveal when their church was organized, but it was probably shortly before 1724 when Robert Feeks was ordained their pastor.

More stable Baptist beginnings center around Nicholas Eyres, who migrated from England to New York City in 1711. He became interested in the Baptist way and invited Valentine Wightman of Groton, Connecticut, to hold services in the loft of his brewery as early as 1712. Wightman's preaching garnered about a dozen converts. From fear of persecution, the five women converts were immersed before daylight, but at the last moment the seven men disdained such secrecy as a lack of faith. Eyres determined to baptize them publicly and appealed to the governor for protection. The governor not only granted protection but also attended the baptismal service and later reportedly said, "This was the ancient way of baptizing, and in my opinion much preferable to the practice of modern times."[39] The First Baptist Church was formed in 1714 in Eyres's home, and he was ordained its pastor.

New Amsterdam alternated between religious toleration and restriction. Eyres registered his home as "an Anabaptist meeting-house within the city," gave assurances of his "good behavior and innocent conversation," professed his willingness to abide by the Act of Toleration, and requested the governor "to grant and permit this petitioner to execute the ministerial functions of a minister within this city to a Baptist congregation, and to give him protection therein."[40] The church met in homes and rented quarters until entering their own building in 1728. This Arminian church was plagued by doctrinal problems and later the membership scattered.

In 1745 Jeremiah Dodge, a Calvinistic Baptist from Fishkill, settled in New York City. Not finding fellowship with the Arminian Baptists, he held prayer meetings in his home with others likeminded, with occasional preaching as ministers passed through the city. In 1762 the Dodge band had sufficient strength, with help from immigrants from the Scotch Plains church in New Jersey, to form the first Regular Baptist church in New York City with twenty-seven members. They "owned" the Second London Confession and the same day called John Gano as pastor. He served twenty-six years, though he was often absent on extensive preaching tours and spent some years as a chaplain during the Revolutionary War, during which time the church ceased to function. Gano must be ranked as one of the most outstanding Baptist leaders in early America. Theologically balanced, well-educated, mission-minded, and with a keen sense of denominational cooperation, Gano helped turn the scattered Baptist churches of America into a

39. Benedict, p. 575.
40. William Cathcart, ed., *The Baptist Encyclopedia* (Philadelphia: Louis H. Everts, 1881), p. 846.

denomination. A moderate Calvinist, Gano helped bridge the diversity among General, Six-Principle, Regular, and Separate Baptists. Gano's vigorous preaching attracted hearers, and soon he built the New York church to over two hundred members.

However, Gano never confined his work to New York City. He preached throughout the country and established churches in several states. An entry in Isaac Backus's diary records the kind of missionary journeys Gano undertook:

> People apear to be somewhat stirred up in Boston; and one means of it I find was Mr. Gano's preaching who has been as far as Haverhill and Newbury, and in 11 days preacht 18 sermons besides all his travel and last Wednesday he went from Boston to Providence and preacht . . . his preaching seems to be as much admired as Mr. Whitefields.[41]

That confirms the observation of Benedict that Gano made his church in New York "a central point of operations for the denomination throughout a wide circuit around."[42] After the Revolutionary War, Gano returned to find the members scattered and the building damaged from use as a stable by British troops. His vigorous ministry soon had the church rebuilt to its former strength.

After the Revolution, Baptist growth in New York accelerated. Increased immigration upstate and to the west, more complete religious freedom, the improved image of Baptists, a moderating of doctrinal divisions, and a more abundant supply of ministers, partly from the massive Welsh immigration, all aided this growth. The revival of the 1780s, little noted by historians who have not designated it one of the "great" awakenings, greatly revitalized Baptist life.

Leaders like Gano and others laid foundations for a strong Baptist life in New York and from there to adjoining states. New York Baptists later distinguished themselves as leaders in education; some of the earliest and strongest Baptist academies, colleges, and seminaries were planted there. They also led the way in home missions, with a strong state society for that purpose. By 1790 New York had 66 Baptist churches, with 4,149 members.[43]

Delaware. Baptists were in Delaware as early in 1703 when the Welsh Tract church, which had been formed two years earlier in Pennsylvania, moved there. It remained the only Baptist church in Delaware until 1779, when three Separate Baptist churches were formed. By 1790 Delaware had eight churches, five of them affiliated with the Philadelphia Association. Perhaps the most influential of these was the Welsh Tract church, which

41. William G. McLoughlin, ed., *The Diary of Isaac Backus,* 1:583.
42. Benedict, p. 575.
43. Gardner, p. 87.

in 1710 adopted a covenant and rules of discipline which later served as a pattern for other churches.[44]

New Jersey. Baptist work progressed more slowly in New Jersey. For some reason, the Great Awakening had less impact there, and by 1790 the state had only 30 churches and 2,247 members.[45] However, these churches, for the most part, reflected doctrinal and spiritual stability, with a greater degree of cooperation between the churches.

When the Dutch relinquished New Netherlands in 1664, one effect was to open the Jersey territory to greater settlement. Four of the original twelve participants in the Monmouth Patent were Baptists, one of them Obadiah Holmes, Jr., son of the Newport pastor. Baptists show up in other settlements from 1665 onward, but no church was organized until 1688. In that year Thomas Killingsworth, recently arrived from England, formed several Baptist families into a church at Middletown. Like Elias Keach, who preached in Pennsylvania and New Jersey at about that time, Killingsworth traveled extensively. He helped organize several other churches, including Piscataway, 1689; Burlington, 1689; and Cohansey, 1690. These churches later became the nucleus of the Philadelphia Baptist Association. Most of the churches were Regular Baptists, though a few professed some form of General Baptist doctrines. The Seventh-Day Baptists formed a church in New Jersey in 1705, and within a few years had five such churches. As elsewhere, most of these had their origin from the Sabbatarians of Rhode Island.

The Cape May church illustrates the nature of Baptist life at the time. At its formation in 1712, the neighboring Cohansey pastor preached on the nature of the church, defining it as "a society or congregation of persons called out of the world . . . by the word of God and the Spirit of Christ . . . unto obedience of faith."[46] Citing their obligation to "give themselves to the Lord and to one another according to the will of God," the minister asked, "Are you willing and desirous to be united in a gospel bond and to be a church of Jesus Christ according to his order?" Another interesting feature was that the minister asked the prospective members if they knew one another well enough to know their mutual needs, to be able to minister to one another. Members agreed to "give up ourselves to the Lord in a church state" and promised to exercise watchcare over each other, to bear one another's burdens, to submit to the discipline of the church, to attend the stated services, and to obey the duly appointed ministers.[47] Later, after a time of doctrinal disputes, some churches adopted the practice of asking

---

44. *Recordes of the Welsh Tract Baptist Meeting,* 2:4 f.
45. Gardner, p. 91.
46. Norman H. Maring, *Baptists in New Jersey,* p. 18.
47. Ibid., p. 19.

the members, as well as the pastor, to sign a Baptist confession, usually the Second London Confession.

Such familiar Baptist disputes as laying on of hands, singing in church, Sabbatarianism, and Calvinistic-Arminian doctrines surfaced less among New Jersey Baptists. However, the growth of Universalism plagued many of their churches. When Elhanan Winchester, Baptist pastor in Philadelphia, embraced Universalism, his influence extended into New Jersey. Among seven ministers attending a Universalist conference in 1790, three were Baptists from New Jersey, who later spread these views among their churches. The Philadelphia Association took notice, warning about "the leprosy of universal salvation" which had infected a number of Baptist churches. The association reported in 1790:

> This Association lament they have occasion again to call the attention of that part of Zion we represent, to another awful instance of departure from the faith once delivered unto the saints. Mr. Nicholas Cox, late a brother in the ministry, having espoused, and artfully, as well as strenuously endeavored, to propagate the fatal notion of the universal restoration of bad men and devils from hell. As such, we caution our churches, those of our sister Associations, and Christian brethren of every denomination, to be aware of him.[48]

The Middle Colonies became the primary center of Baptist growth and leadership during the eighteenth century. They benefitted from capable leaders, and the Philadelphia Association provided a framework for doctrinal identity, church extension, and the sense of fellowship so important under frontier conditions. Baptists also benefitted from the religious toleration of that area.

The Southern Colonies

Since Baptists have become so numerous in the South, some find it hard to believe they had their slowest beginnings in that region. Some reasons for the slow start include a sparse population, severe restrictions upon Dissenters in areas where the Anglican Church was established, and a general spiritual lethargy which marked the region in early days. Baptists planted a few churches in the Southern Colonies, but not until the Separate Baptists migrating southward from New England in the 1750s brought the fervor of the Great Awakening did Baptists begin to assume any numerical importance there. The Regular Baptists planted their churches along the coastal areas, in such centers as Charleston, Richmond, and Savannah. On the other hand, the Separate Baptists grew more rapidly on the frontier, where cultural as well as doctrinal factors tended to give them a distinctive identity.

48. A. D. Gillette, ed., *Minutes of the Philadelphia Baptist Association, From A.D. 1707 to A.D. 1807,* pp. 256-257.

South Carolina. Baptists came to "Charles Town" by 1672 and occasional worship services probably date from shortly thereafter. The arrival of William Screven in 1696 greatly strengthened Baptist work in Charleston and adjacent areas. By 1740 there were only five Baptist congregations in South Carolina, most of them beginning as branches of the Charleston church.

By 1708 William Screven, the pastor of First Baptist Church, Charleston, listed its membership at about ninety. The church already had assumed a place of leadership among Baptists in South Carolina and throughout the South. Almost every new venture for good among South Carolina Baptists first arose in that congregation, including the earliest efforts at ministerial education, formation of the first Baptist association in the South, organized home mission efforts, and efforts to promote Sunday School work among Baptists in the South. Several problems afflicted the church during the eighteenth century, including doctrinal divisions between Particular and General members, disputes about ownership and control of the church lot and buildings, and attitudes toward the First Great Awakening. For the most part, the church had the benefit of eminent pastors, among whom must be named William Screven, Thomas Simmons, Oliver Hart, and Richard Furman. By 1796 the Charleston church reported 248 members, of whom most were black. That year they reported 15 baptisms, out of only 36 baptisms reported in the entire association of 27 churches.[49]

From the first, the Charleston church included members of both Particular and General persuasions. As early as 1702 the General Assembly, the national organization of General Baptists in England, noted:

> Whereas our Brethren of the Baptist perswation and of the Generall Faith who haue their aboad in Carlina haue desierd us to Supply them wth a Ministry or with books, we being not able at present to doe the former haue collected ye Sum of Seuen pounds twelve Shillings wch wth wt can be farther obtain'd we haue put into the hands of our Bror S Keeling to Supply ym wth ye latter. & yt ye sd Bror Keeling doe wright a letter to them in the name of this Assembly.[50]

At times the two groups coexisted in peace. The pastors usually held the Particular faith, suggesting that group formed the majority. One exception was Thomas Simmons, pastor from 1725 to his death in 1747, who while not Arminian was decidedly cool toward strict Calvinism. Several schisms rocked the church under Simmons's leadership, the membership at one time declining to only three persons. Simmons alienated many by his opposition to George Whitefield and the Great Awakening.

49. *Minutes,* Charleston Baptist Association, 1796, p. 3. However, not all of the churches sent reports.

50. William T. Whitley, ed., *Minutes of the General Assembly of the General Baptist Churches in England,* 1:75.

Additional churches were formed in the vicinity of Charleston, including Euhaw, Ashley River, and Stono. At first these were considered "arms" of the Charleston church, a pattern not unusual at the time in which a central church might establish branches in neighboring communities. While such members were still related to the central church, they might erect their own buildings and call their own pastors. Such was the pattern that developed around Charleston.

William Screven had preached as early as 1700 in the Euhaw area, baptizing a number of converts. They increased enough to erect their own meeting house in 1726 and ordained one of their members, William Fry, as their local pastor in 1731. Apparently distance and convenience of worship led these Euhaw Baptists to worship separately.

Different motives led to forming branches at Ashley River and Stono. A concentration of Baptists on Ashley River held more strictly Calvinistic views, but under Screven and succeeding pastors they continued in fellowship with the Charleston church. However, the coming of Pastor Simmons, known to be cool to Calvinism, was apparently more than they could endure, and the Ashley River arm distanced themselves from the main body in Charleston. They erected their own meeting house in 1727 and about 1733 called Isaac Chanler (or Chandler) as their pastor, a man known to share their strict views. Relations between Chanler and Simmons deteriorated, and in 1736 Ashley River constituted a separate church. A bequest of funds in 1752 revealed the sharpness of the doctrinal differences, when an Ashley River member left a generous grant to the church

> as a Perpetual fund for and towards the support of the Gospel Ministry among the Christian Congregation of People (at Ashley River) . . . who by Profession are Antepedo Baptists denying Armenyanism and owning the Doctrine of Original Sin Personal Election and final Preserverance . . . no such Minister shall be entitled to all or any part thereof unless such Minister hold Profess Preach and Defend the aforesaid Doctrines.[51]

Leah Townsend reported that when George Whitefield, the revivalist, reached South Carolina about 1740, "Charleston was the place of his greatest success and of the greatest opposition."[52] Chanler welcomed Whitefield and invited him to preach at Ashley River. Simmons, while not openly opposing Whitefield, criticized some of his revival tactics.

At about the same time, another "arm" of the Charleston church pulled away to establish its separate worship at Stono, erecting their meeting house in 1728. One is tempted to describe Stono as the "left arm," while theologically the Ashley River group formed the "right arm." One motive for separation at Stono was their General Baptist theology. As the doctrinal

51. Cited by Joe M. King, *A History of South Carolina Baptists,* p. 27.
52. Leah Townsend, *South Carolina Baptists 1670-1805,* p. 18.

conflicts increased, they drew away some of the more General members from Charleston and eventually formed a separate church.

Another strong church was formed at Welsh Neck in 1738, composed of Baptist migrants from the Welsh Tract in Delaware. This established a second major center of Baptist influence in South Carolina. The Welsh settled on the Pee Dee River, formed their church in 1738, and in 1743 ordained Philip James as pastor. He and his successors not only cared for their own flock but also preached up and down the rivers of that section, assisted weak churches, and formed new ones. The Welsh brought a moderate doctrinal stance, paying more attention to their witness than to theological intricacies. The Welsh Baptists sided strongly with the Charleston church in efforts to provide organization and education for Baptists in the South.

In *Saints of Clay*, a history of Baptists in South Carolina, Loulie Latimer Owens names the coming of Oliver Hart to Charleston in 1749 and the conversion of Richard Furman to Baptist views in 1770 as two of the "major events that profoundly influenced the course of South Carolina Baptists."[53] Both were creative leaders, and while Furman is better known, Hart laid strong Baptist foundations. Oliver Hart (1723-1795) was converted to Baptist views at the age of seventeen and five years later was set aside to preach at the insistence of the church. He attended the 1749 sessions of the Philadelphia Association, at which a letter from the Charleston church was read, outlining their fruitless two-year search for a pastor to succeed Simmons, who had died. The brethren present agreed that Hart should go. Without a call from Charleston, he quietly moved to the town and about two months later was installed as pastor, a relationship that lasted thirty years.

In 1751 Hart led four churches, Charleston, Euhaw, Ashley River, and Welsh Neck, to form the Charleston Association, the first in the South. For years he had been active in the Philadelphia Association and had seen its benefits. He consciously patterned the Charleston body after its northern neighbor in confessional stance and mode of operation. One could hardly overestimate the importance of this association to Baptists in the South. It provided their major forum for discussion of issues, ventures in church extension and home missions, efforts in ministerial education, and served as a clearing house for churches and pastors seeking settlement. Like the Philadelphia Association, it dealt with issues which troubled the churches, often offering assistance in matters of discipline.

Though not formally educated himself, Hart realized the importance of education and by his own reading made himself one of the best-informed citizens of Charleston. His manner of preaching was both instructive and inspiring, and he lent dignity to the services by wearing a pulpit gown and

---

53. Loulie Latimer Owens, *Saints of Clay: The Shaping of South Carolina Baptists*, pp. 28, 32, 46.

bands in the more formal Calvinist pattern. Hart led the Charleston Association to form a fund in 1755 to assist in the education of young men called to ministry. This fund has been described as the first organized effort of Baptists in the South on behalf of ministerial education.[54]

Because of his political activities, Hart was driven out of Charleston by the Revolutionary War. He accepted the pastorate at Hopewell, New Jersey, intending to return to Charleston when conditions allowed. During Hart's absence, the Charleston church declined severely from lack of leadership and from ravages of the war. The association did what it could to obtain temporary supplies for the Charleston pulpit, but often the church simply did not meet. When peace returned, the church made repeated entreaties to Hart to return, but by then he was established at Hopewell and remained there until his death.

The Charleston church called Richard Furman as pastor, installing him in office in 1787 at age thirty-two. He served for thirty-eight years, during which time his became the final word among Baptists in South Carolina. More than any other person, Furman devised and implemented the organizational concepts that have since characterized Southern Baptist denominational life. Furman (1755-1825) was born in New York, grew up in Charleston, and moved to High Hills of Santee in 1770, where he was converted to Separate Baptist views by Joseph Reece. Furman later served as pastor at High Hills. Unlike Hart, who opposed slavery, Furman both owned slaves and articulated Southern Baptists' most widely quoted defense of that system. Furman later became quite wealthy from land and other investments.

During Hart's enforced absence, Furman had often preached at Charleston, so his move there, though with many tears at leaving friends at High Hills, brought him into a familiar world. Like "Father Hart," whom he so admired, Furman continued the practice of wearing a pulpit robe and bands. Though converted among the Separate Baptists, Furman made the transition easily to Charleston. By that time, the sharp doctrinal and social barriers between the two groups had moderated. Furman brought a fervent evangelism to the Regular church and perhaps absorbed from them a more formal style of preaching and worship. Unlike many of his Separate brethren, Furman valued education and became its apostle among Baptists throughout the South. He dominated the Charleston Association during his lifetime, in the best sense of that word, and helped effect a national organization of Baptists in America in 1814. The first Baptist college in the South located at Greenville, South Carolina, bears his name. Furman died in 1825 and lies buried only a few feet from the magnificent pulpit of the church he helped to build in Charleston.

54. Leon McBeth, "Southern Baptist Higher Education" in William Estep, ed., *The Lord's Free People in a Free Land: Essays in Baptist History in Honor of Robert A. Baker,* p. 118.

The story of Separate Baptists occupies a section later, but suffice it to say here that their presence was vigorous in South Carolina. Gardner lists forty-four such churches formed before 1790, but as elsewhere most of them moved toward the Regular position. Of the Regular churches in the state, fully 40 percent of them came from a Separate background. This unique combination of emphases in theology, practice, and worship styles helped create the distinctive blend later to appear in the Southern Baptist Convention.

Virginia. Nowhere was the Anglican Church more firmly established than in Virginia, and nowhere were Dissenters more harrassed. While individual Baptists probably lived in Virginia before 1700, the first organized church was formed in 1714 in Prince George County. Robert G. Torbet pointed out that early Virginia Baptists stemmed from three sources: (1) General Baptists from England; (2) Baptist immigrants who came down from Maryland in the 1740s, mostly Calvinistic; and (3) New Englanders, converted to Separate Baptist views, who settled in the back country after 1760.[55]

Evidence confirms the presence of Baptists in Virginia before 1700. Thomas Story, an English Quaker, in an account of his visit to America, wrote: "On the 23d (January, 1699) being the First of the Week, we had a meeting in York City, at the home of Thomas Bonger, a Preacher among the General Baptists."[56] This clearly implies the existence of a company of General Baptists to whom Bonger preached, though whether they had formed a church or merely held occasional meetings is not known.

Apparently the General Baptists in Virginia appealed to the General Assembly in England for aid. That body noted in 1714 a plan "To Stir them [the English churches] Up for Some Assistance for Robt. Norden and Thos. White who are Appointed & Approved by this Assembly to go to Virginia to propogate the Gospell of truth." At the same meeting they "agreed the persons Appointed to go to Virginia go with all Conveniant Speed."[57] Only Norden survived the ocean voyage, and shortly after his arrival formed the Prince George church, just across the James River from Jamestown. He preached extensively, forming other churches, until his death in 1725. Most of these General churches either became extinct or moved to the Calvinist position as a result of missionizing efforts from the Philadelphia Association.

By 1790 Virginia had the largest Baptist population of any state in America, with 210 churches and 20,861 members.[58] Not only the revival activity of the Separates in the 1760s but also the awakening of the 1780s

55. Robert G. Torbet, *A History of the Baptists,* pp. 215-216.
56. Reuben Edward Alley, *A History of Baptists in Virginia,* pp. 18-19.
57. Whitley, 1:125.
58. Gardner, p. 103.

greatly augmented Virginia Baptists, with growth running as much as elevenfold in one decade. Virginia Baptists represented a peculiar mix of Regular-Separate emphases. While the Separates had formed numerous churches, by 1790 about 98 percent of the churches were Regular; all but three of the Separate churches had made the transition to modified Calvinism. About 57 percent of Regular churches and 71 percent of Regular members came from a Separate background, indicating that Separate emphases were not lost.

Separate Baptists passed through Virginia in the 1750s, but prospects did not seem promising; they went on to North Carolina. By 1760 their work had backtracked into Virginia, when Daniel Marshall and Philip Mulkey formed a church on the Dan River. It was the first Separate Baptist church in Virginia and was composed of sixty-three white and eleven black members. One of their converts was Samuel Harris (or Harriss), a leading citizen who became an effective Separate evangelist, sometimes known as an "Apostle" among the Separates. At first the Virginia churches affiliated with the Sandy Creek Association in North Carolina but in 1770 formed their own General Association.

North Carolina. In the 1770s Morgan Edwards wrote, "Next to Virginia, southward, is North-carolina; a poor and unhappy province. . . . In this wretched province have been some baptists since the settlement in 1695."[59] A letter from a Church of England missionary in 1710 gives further evidence of Baptists in North Carolina, complaining that two vestrymen had turned "professed Anabaptists."[60]

Organized Baptist work in the state apparently began with Paul Palmer, a General Baptist who arrived about 1720. He preached at various places but gathered no church until 1727 at Chowan. John Comer's *Diary* helps establish the date of the Chowan church, apparently the first in North Carolina. In September 1729, Comer wrote, "This day I received a letter from ye Baptist church in North Carolina, settled about two years (in ye year 1727) since, by Mr. Paul Palmer, . . . This church consists of 32 members, it meets in Chowan."[61]

Palmer was a native of Maryland but became a Baptist in the Welsh Tract area of Delaware. He also preached in Maryland, where he established the earliest Baptist church in that state at Chestnut Ridge in 1742. In North Carolina he gathered several groups of Baptists, but settling down to one pastorate was not his style. Palmer had difficulty getting along with the churches, and he was once accused of stealing a slave. He did win Joseph Parker to the Baptist way; Parker apparently provided some of the stability

59. Morgan Edwards, *Materials Towards a History of the Baptists,* 2:79.
60. Torbet, p. 218.
61. C. Edwin Barrows, ed., *The Diary of John Comer,* pp. 84-85.

which the volatile Palmer lacked. Yet Palmer is known as "the father of the General Baptists in North Carolina."

A second church, and the oldest surviving Baptist church in the state, was formed at Shiloh. Faded records make the founding date somewhat uncertain, but examiners have made it out to read September 5, 1729. Within a few years, the church sent out nine ministers and formed six additional churches.

A third church was formed at Meherrin, perhaps by Joseph Parker when he left Chowan. The accepted date for this church is 1729, but the earliest documentary evidence comes from notice of the building in 1735. A division in the Meherrin church about 1740 apparently led to yet another early congregation.

Another important Baptist settlement centered around Kehuckee Creek in Halifax County. A company of General Baptists went there from Virginia in 1742, where they established a strong church. By 1790 at least twenty-five General churches had been formed in North Carolina, but in the "reformation" of the 1750s and following, almost all of them switched to Regular emphases. Gardner said the General churches were "invaded by missionaries from the Philadelphia Baptist Association," a rather blunt but accurate statement of the case.[62] After the 1750s, Regular Baptists got a start in the state, planting by 1790 about forty-eight churches of their own, plus those they won from the Generals.

Perhaps the most dynamic event among North Carolina Baptists in the eighteenth century was the coming of the Separate Baptists in 1755. Shubal Stearns and Daniel Marshall, brothers-in-law from New England, embraced the Separate Baptist faith in the early 1750s. Both men, already in middle life, desired to preach. Finding little reception in New England, they with their families and a few friends migrated southward, first to Virginia, and in 1755 to Sandy Creek, North Carolina.

Thus from the first North Carolina Baptists included three major groups: the old General Baptists of the Paul Palmer type; the Regular Baptists who settled first along the Kehuckee; and Separate Baptists who came with Stearns and Marshall. Differences between these included not only theology but also cultural variations and diversities of worship style.

Most of the North Carolina churches eventually found common ground, but some went to extremes, provoked perhaps by sharp reaction to each other. Some of the General churches refused to be "reformed," sticking with their Arminianism. Some claim these North Carolina churches as the earliest Freewill Baptists, antedating the New England beginning under Benjamin Randall.[63] The Regular Baptists around Kehuckee went to the opposite extreme, embracing extreme Calvinism. Early in the next century

---

62. Gardner, p. 108.
63. William F. Davidson, *An Early History of Free Will Baptists, 1727-1830,* pp. 131 *f.*

the Kehuckee became an antimission association, providing a major center of "Primitive" Baptist life in the South. In fact, the term "Kehuckeeism" became a synonym for "Hardshell" or "Primitive" Baptist.

Georgia. At least two Baptists were on the boat with James Oglethorpe, who formed the Georgia colony in 1733. Other Baptists migrated to that area, and from time to time worship services were held, but no organized church resulted for years. By 1770 scholars estimate that well over one hundred Baptists lived in Georgia, but their only church, a Seventh-Day church formed in 1759, had died. Nicholas Bedgegood, who had been baptized by Oliver Hart at Charleston, preached in Georgia in the 1760s, baptizing a number of converts, but never formed a church.

Separate Baptists from South Carolina settled near Augusta by 1762. Daniel Marshall joined them later and led in forming the Kiokee (or Kioka) Baptist Church in 1772, the first surviving Baptist church in Georgia. In the next several years, perhaps a dozen other Separate churches were formed, but true to patterns elsewhere most of them later switched to Regular.

Regular Baptists got a start in Georgia in 1773 when Edmund Botsford established a church near New Savannah, now known as the Botsford Church. By 1790, they had forty-eight churches, some of which they had established and some they had absorbed from the Separates. Black Baptists founded a church near Savannah in 1777, but before then blacks had held membership either in the Silver Bluff church in nearby South Carolina or in the predominantly white churches. Under the leadership of Andrew Bryan (c.1716-1812), a much-persecuted black pastor, the Savannah church grew rapidly, being received into the Georgia Association in 1788. By 1790, at least 641 black Baptists were known to live in Georgia, about 61 percent of them in predominantly white churches.[64] Georgia listed a total of 53 churches, with 3,260 members, in 1790. The earliest association was the Georgia, formed in 1784 and including most churches in the state. By the end of the century, that association was making plans to sponsor statewide mission work.

Kentucky. Squire Boone, brother of Daniel, was a Baptist and preached in Kentucky probably by the early 1770s. However, the first Baptist sermon of record in that state was preached by William Hickman at Harrodstown in 1776. The mass migration through the Cumberland Gap in the late 1770s included a number of Baptists, many of them Separates from Virginia. During 1781 two churches were organized in Kentucky, and a third migrated there as a body. The earliest was the Severns Valley church, now located in Elizabethtown, formed in 1781 with fifteen white and three black members. The Cedar Creek church was formed a few weeks later, near Bardstown. The third church, known as the "traveling church," settled on

64. Gardner, p. 119.

Gilbert's Creek and took that name. It had been formed in Virginia in 1767. Under their pastor, Lewis Craig, the entire church made the five-month trek to Kentucky. Their wagon train always stopped over Sunday, and Craig conducted services, baptizing converts not only from their group but also from other wagon trains they encountered. They arrived in Kentucky with the church intact, with about two hundred members. Gilbert's Creek was Separate, while the other two were Regular.

As migration increased, Baptist churches sprang up rapidly. By 1790, at least 43 Baptist churches existed in Kentucky, with 3,209 members.[65] Of these, well over 200 members were black. Blacks conducted their own worship services in Lexington by 1790, but no organized church resulted for several years.

Separate-Regular divisions were never as sharp in Kentucky as in the Carolinas. At its formation in 1785, the Elkhorn Association, first in the state, took the name "Regular" but never made an issue of it. Later that year churches in the western part of the state formed the Salem Association, also Regular. Other churches formed the South Kentucky Association of Separate Baptists in 1787. However, within a few years these distinctions diminished, and churches with Separate and Regular backgrounds cooperated in the same associations. A gradual process of exchanging ministers and members gradually drew the two groups together. Having little else to change, they simply changed their name.

The faith and practice of Baptists on the frontier may be glimpsed in the constitution adopted by the Beaver Creek church in Kentucky at its formation in 1798. This church of seven members set out careful rules concerning discipline, conduct of church business, reception of new members, and conditions under which a member could be "debar,d." The church also adopted a confession of faith, as follows:

> First, We believe in one only true and living God and that their are three persons in the God-head. the Father Son and Holy Spirit.
>
> 2nd We believe that the Scriptures of the old and new Testaments, are the word of God, and the only rule of faith and practice.
>
> 3rd We believe that we are saved by grace thro faith and that not of ourselves it is the gift of God.
>
> 4th We believe in the doctrine of original sin.
>
> 5th We believe in mans impotency to recover himself from the fallen state he is in by nature.
>
> 6th We believe that sinners are justiyd [*sic*] in the sight of God, only by the imputed righteousness of Christ.
>
> 7th We believe that the saints shall persevere and never finally fall away.
>
> 8th We believe that baptism and the Lord's Supper are ordinances of Jesus

65. Ibid., p. 123.

Christ, and that true believers and them only are the fit subjects of these ordinances, and we believe that the true mode of baptism is by immersion.

9th We believe in the resurrection of the Lord and universal Judgement,

10th We believe the punishment of the wicked will be everlasting and the Joys of the righteous will be eternal.[66]

Tennessee. By 1790 Tennessee had 17 Baptist churches, with 770 members, and most of that growth had occurred in the last decade. However, Baptists were among the first settlers in the state, and they formed a church on the Clinch River by 1765, plus one or two others before 1780. Most of the early churches were Separate and held fellowship with the Sandy Creek Association in North Carolina. Regular Baptists formed their first church in Tennessee in 1786, followed soon by others. Baptists there followed the familiar pattern; while most of the early churches came from a Separate background, they soon switched to Regular emphases.

Mississippi. Only one tiny Baptist church was formed in Mississippi in the eighteenth century, though Baptists lived in Jefferson County by 1780. Seven of them formed the Cole's Creek church in 1791.

Summary. This brief summary of Baptist beginnings in the South shows some common patterns. First, Baptist growth occurred through migration, not organized mission activity. Families were on the move, seeking new homes and economic opportunity. Among these were Baptist families and a good sprinkling of Baptist preachers. As they settled new areas, they formed their own churches, usually calling one of their fellow pioneers as pastor or "raising up" a pastor from the laymen in their midst.

Second, in many cases Baptists went through a period of years in which they met and worshiped in what might be called "fellowship groups" before they formed churches. Scarcity of numbers, lack of available pastors in some cases, and distances among scattered frontier settlers help account for this. Some of these "fellowships," however, assumed "churchly" functions; some of them baptized, observed the Lord's Supper, and admonished one another in the rudiments of church discipline.

Third, the records show a variety of Baptist churches throughout the South, including General Six-Principle, Seventh-Day, Separate, and Regular Baptists. The Seventh-Day churches were relatively few in the South, too far removed, perhaps, from their primary sources in Rhode Island. The Separate churches, with their greater evangelistic zeal and less stringent membership requirements, often entered new areas first and established more churches.

However, almost invariably, the Regular churches drew Separate Baptist churches over to a modified Calvinistic basis. This change cannot be accounted for on the basis of doctrinal preference alone. To some extent the

66. Sweet, pp. 258-260.

Methodists, organized in America at Baltimore in 1784, preempted much of the ground formerly occupied by Separate Baptists. Their zeal and circuit-riding evangelism, their informal worship, and above all their emphasis upon man's free will, closely resembled the early emphases of Separate Baptists. Perhaps Separates moved toward the Regular Baptists to distance themselves from their major frontier competitors. Further, cultural factors may have influenced the tendency of Separates to shift. The Regular Baptists emphasized an educated clergy, dignified and orderly worship, and did not encourage women to pray or prophecy in public, whereas early Separates took opposite positions on all of these.

Fourth, Baptist churches in the South welcomed the opportunity to link their churches into associations. The "unassociated" churches were relatively few, and usually represented those who had no association nearby. Unlike Baptists in the North, those in the South had no fear that associations would compromise the independence of the local church. From the first a greater degree of denominational identity and cooperation marked the Southern churches, a fact which would later be underscored as churches North and South moved toward national organizations.

Separate Baptists in the South

Though they have been mentioned in passing, Separate Baptists in the South require further comment. They exercised an enormous influence upon Baptist beliefs and behavior in that region and, while they later merged with the Regular Baptists, much of the Separate style of churchmanship carried over. Understanding the later development of the Southern Baptist Convention apart from the contributions of Separate Baptists would be impossible. The best study of this movement is found in William L. Lumpkin's *Baptist Foundations in the South*. His subtitle indicates the thrust of the book: "Tracing through the Separates the Influence of the Great Awakening, 1754-1787."

The Sandy Creek Church

The Separate Baptists originated in New England out of the revival fervor of the First Great Awakening. Sometimes called "New Lights" because they favored the preaching of George Whitefield, the name "Separate" was the one that stuck. The more staid and urban Baptists, who felt little enthusiasm for the awakening, took the pejorative description of "Regular" Baptists.

The two persons most responsible for transplanting Separate Baptist teachings into the South were Shubal Stearns and Daniel Marshall. Stearns (1706-1771) was born in Boston but later moved to Connecticut where he joined the Congregational Church. Deeply influenced by Whitefield's revival preaching, Stearns became a "New Light" in 1745 and in 1751 made the further step of receiving immersion and ordination as a Baptist. Marshall

(1706-1784) followed an almost identical pilgrimage, becoming a Baptist by 1754. He married Martha Stearns, sister to Shubal, a remarkable and gifted woman who fully shared the evangelistic zeal of her husband and brother. She may, in fact, have been a major influence in their embracing the Separate Baptist way.

By 1754 both Stearns and Marshall had migrated with their families to the Opekon area of Virginia. Finding little response there, and hearing of communities in North Carolina that would welcome their emotional style of worship, eight families migrated on to North Carolina in 1755. Settlers were pouring into North Carolina, but at that time the area was considered a "religious vacuum."[67]

The Stearns-Marshall group settled on Sandy Creek, in present Randolph County. They formed the first Separate Baptist Church in the South in 1755. The church proved vastly influential. Within a few years, it had grown from 16 to 606 members and, according to the custom of the time, had established "arms" in several localities. Morgan Edwards observed:

> Sandy-creek church is the mother of all the Separate-baptists. From this Zion went forth the word, and great was the company of them who published it: it, in 17 years, has spread branches westward as far as the great river Mississippi; southward as far as Georgia; eastward to the sea and Chesopeek bay; and northward to the waters of Potowmack: it, in 17 years, is become mother, grand-mother, and great grandmother to 42 churches, from which sprang 125 ministers, many of which are ordained and support the sacred character as well as any sett of clergy in America.[68]

Without doubt, Shubal Stearns was the most dynamic leader of early Separate Baptists. Edwards said:

> Mr. Stearns was but a little man, but a man of good natural parts and sound judgment. Of learning he had but a small share, yet was pretty well acquainted with books. His voice was musical and strong, which he managed in such a manner as, one while, to make soft impressions on the heart, and fetch tears from the eyes in a mechanical way; and anon, to shake the very nerves and throw the animal system into tumults and purturbations. All the Separate ministers copy after him in tones of voice and actions of body; and some few exceed him.[69]

Daniel Marshall had less conspicuous gifts, but by his zeal and tireless travels established several churches. Edwards described him as "a weak man, a stammerer, no schollar."[70] In the early 1770s Marshall moved his

67. William L. Lumpkin, *Baptist Foundations in the South,* p. 36.
68. Edwards, 2:92.
69. Ibid., p. 93.
70. Lumpkin, p. 39.

family to Georgia, thus helping perpetuate the Separate Baptist movement when the North Carolina center diminished.

Other important leaders included the Craig brothers, Lewis and Elijah; Dutton Lane; John Waller, known before his conversion as "Swearing Jack"; Samuel Harris, called the "Apostle to Virginia"; and Philip Mulkey, an eloquent preacher who later came "under a cloud" for allegedly scandalous conduct. Few of these served as settled pastors; instead, they were the missionary vanguard who planted Separate churches and emphases throughout the South.

Beliefs and practices. Differences between Separate and Regular Baptists centered partly in doctrine but perhaps more in manner of preaching, evangelism, and overall style of churchmanship. The first covenant of the Sandy Creek church reflected a moderate Calvinism, including "particular election of grace by the predestination of God."[71] In time that early Calvinism gave way to more emphasis upon human freedom and responsibility to believe the gospel. Their confession, adopted in 1845, affirmed that "election is the gracious purpose of God," but added that "the blessings of salvation are made free to all by the gospel; that it is the immediate duty of all to accept them by a cordial and obedient faith; and that nothing prevents the salvation of the greatest sinner on earth, except his own voluntary refusal to submit to the Lord Jesus Christ."[72]

The Sandy Creek covenant shows that Separate Baptists represented Calvinism with a difference. They believed that men are condemned apart from Christ, that Christ is a sufficient Savior for all, and that sinners may freely choose the way of life or the way of death. This gave an urgency and zeal to their evangelism, which has carried over among Baptists in the South. A comparison of confessions adopted in 1816 and 1845 by the Sandy Creek Association indicates that in time their evangelistic *practices* tended to determine their theology rather than their *theology* guiding their practices.

However, like the General Baptists, the Separates were subjected to some "reforming" from the Philadelphia Association. John Gano visited the Sandy Creek Association, probably in 1759, and, after some hesitation, was invited to preach. Edwards recorded that Gano

> ascended into the pulpit and read for his text the following words, "Jesus I know, and Paul I know but who are ye?" this text he managed in such a manner as to make some afraid of him, and others ashamed of their shiness. Many were convinced of errors touching faith and conversion, and submitted to examination. One minister hearing this (who stood well with himself) went to be examined, and intimated to his people, he should return triumphant. Mr. Gano heard him out and then turned to his companion and said, "I

71. Ibid., p. 62.
72. George W. Purefoy, *A History of the Sandy Creek Baptist Association*, pp. 204-205.

profess, brother, this will not do: this man has yet the needful to seek." Upon which the person examined hastened home, and upon being asked, How he came off? replied "The Lord have mercy upon you; for this northern minister put a 'mene tekel' upon me!" Three years after Messrs. Miller and Vanhorn were sent among them who reformed their churches agreeable to the churches belonging to the philadelphian association.[73]

Perhaps the most distinctive feature of the Separates was their emotional style of preaching and worship. Morgan Edwards seemed at pains to defend them against charges of emotional excesses. He minimized "the outcries, epilepsies and extacies attending their ministry" and offered his opinion that "I believe a preternatural and invisible hand works in the assemblies of the Separate-baptists bearing down the human mind."[74] Shouting, weeping, and falling down in a faint were not uncommon. John Leland observed that among the Regulars "the work [worship] was solemn and rational; but the Separates were the most zealous and the work among them was very noisy."[75] Another observer described their preaching as "warm and pathetic," "accompanied by strong gestures, and a singular tone of voice."[76] Their preachers slipped naturally from praying to preaching, and often the people could not tell the difference.

In 1758 one of the Separate churches asked if "the new exercise, called dancing, be a bar to communion." This had no reference to social dancing, but to "dancing in the spirit" in worship. The association cautioned against excess but refused to make such dancing and other emotional outbursts a bar to membership. "Many pious persons were very much tried in their minds" about such things, it was reported, but "finally tolerated them, because they saw that, . . . there was a genuine work of grace among the people."[77]

Most of the Separate churches observed the "nine rites," including baptism, Lord's Supper, love feast, laying on of hands, foot washing, anointing the sick, the right hand of fellowship, the kiss of charity, and dedicating children. However, a number of churches abbreviated the list. Gradually foot washing, for example, came to be regarded as a "social rite" between Christians, but not a "church rite."

For the most part the Separate preachers were innocent of formal education, whether from necessity or choice. If God wanted educated preachers, they reasoned, he would call educated persons. Since he apparently called those without formal training, they should "abide in the same condition wherein they were called." An opponent in 1761 accused the Separate

73. Edwards, 2:79-80.
74. Ibid., pp. 92-93.
75. Lumpkin, p. 67.
76. Purefoy, pp. 46-47.
77. Ibid., p. 75.

Baptists of "preaching up the inexpediency of human learning . . . and the great expediency of dreams, visions, and immediate revelations."[78] Along with anti-education, most of the Separates opposed ministerial salaries. They observed that an educated clergy is usually a salaried clergy and so opposed both. To them, to preach Christ for money was just a notch above Judas who denied Him for money. Edwards's description of the Separate churches usually included the phrase, "No salary. No estate." Some churches did provide for their pastors occasional gifts of goods or cash, but most earned their livelihood in the same ways the people did, by farming, trading, or day labor. Among people who criticized state church clergy for their oppressive "church rates," this economic independence added greatly to the Separates' appeal.

The Separates apparently helped popularize what is now known as the "evangelistic invitation."

> At the close of the sermon, the minister would come down from the pulpit and while singing a suitable hymn would go around among the brethren shaking hands. The hymn being sung, he would then extend an invitation to such persons as felt themselves poor guilty sinners, and were anxiously inquiring the way of salvation, to come forward and kneel near the stand.[79]

The Separates thus devised a method of encouraging on-the-spot religious decisions, to the singing of a hymn, well before the revivals of Charles G. Finney, who is often credited with inventing the invitation. Steve O'Kelly said, "This may be the earliest known record of an invitation of this type being given in American church history."[80]

Women assumed a larger church role among the Separate Baptists than among the Regulars. In describing the Sandy Creek church, Morgan Edwards said, "Ruling elders, eldresses, and deaconesses are allowed."[81] Similar statements were made about most of the Separate churches. Eldresses and deaconesses assisted at baptisms, especially of women, at the Lord's Supper, and some of the other church rites, as well as visiting among church families, especially in cases of illness among other women. Some women also preached among the Separate Baptists in the South. Martha Stearns Marshall, sister of one Separate leader and wife of another, was known to preach quite fervently. Described as "a lady of good sense, singular piety and surprising elocution, in countless instances [she] melted a whole concourse into tears by her prayers and exhortations."[82] Margaret Meuse Clay and Hannah Lee also preached among the Separates. This aroused opposi-

78. George W. Paschal, *A History of North Carolina Baptists*, 1:308.
79. Robert I. Devin, *A History of Grassy Creek Baptist Church*, p. 69.
80. Steve O'Kelly, "The Influence of Separate Baptists on Revivalistic Evangelism and Worship," p. 130.
81. Cited in Leon McBeth, *Women in Baptist Life*, p. 43.
82. Purefoy, p. 63.

tion among Regular Baptists, who called the Separates "a disorderly set, suffering women to pray in public." This extensive ministry of women later proved to be one barrier that delayed the merger of Regular and Separate Baptists.

When their buildings proved too small, the Separate Baptists met out of doors and thus anticipated the "camp meetings" of the Second Great Awakening a generation later. Semple said, "It was not uncommon at their great meetings for many hundreds of men to camp on the ground, . . . There were instances of persons traveling more than one hundred miles to one of these meetings."[83]

Expansion of Separate Baptists. Nine Separate churches met in 1758 to form the Sandy Creek Baptist Association, the second such in the South and third in the country. One observer noted, "At their association their chief employment was preaching, exhortation, singing, and conversation about their various exertions in the Redeemer's service."[84] Often large crowds would gather, and association meetings turned into occasions for fellowship, preaching, and evangelism.

At first the association elected no moderator; the messengers simply waited for God to reveal what He wanted them to do. Some felt that Stearns, perhaps from his Congregational background, exercised dictatorial control. Apparently, in their unstructured sessions God usually led to actions which Stearns favored. The overpowering influence of one person was probably a factor in the threefold division of the association in 1770: the Congaree for churches in South Carolina; the General Association in Virginia; thus leaving the Sandy Creek with churches only in North Carolina. In the early 1770s, trouble with the "Regulators" and the Battle of Alamance caused multitudes to migrate westward to Tennessee. The Sandy Creek church, which had mushroomed from 16 to 606 members, dwindled to only 14. However, by that time the Separate leaven had so permeated the South that the weakening of the original center had little impact.

Separate Baptist statistics are hard to come by because many churches refused to send in reports lest they incur the wrath of God as King David did for numbering Israel. However, by the middle 1770s Separates made up more than half of all Baptists in South Carolina and probably had as many in other areas.[85] No doubt many would have agreed with the Anglican minister who complained, "Religion and the Chh lye bleeding . . . overrun with Sectaries, especially ye New Light Baptists."[86]

Union of Separates and Regulars. From the first, some on both sides worked toward rapprochement of Regular and Separate Baptists. The

83. Cited in O'Kelly, p. 157.
84. Purefoy, p. 63.
85. Lumpkin, p. 54.
86. Ibid.

Charleston Association made overtures for cooperation as early as 1763, sending Oliver Hart and Evan Pugh to meet with Separates in North Carolina and welcoming Philip Mulkey to the Charleston meetings. Despite these overtures, the Separates remained cool. "Excuse us in love," they said, "for we are acquainted with our own order but not so well with yours; and if there is a difference we might ignorantly jump into that which might make us rue it."[87]

Barriers which delayed union included Regular objections to several Separate practices: their allowing women and untrained men to preach; their manner of preaching and worship; their objections to the use of confessions; their use of the nine rites; and some of their strict social customs, especially about plain clothing. For their part, Separates objected to having to endorse the Philadelphia or any other confession; the emphasis upon education among the Regulars; their keeping women in silence in the churches; and the fact that Regulars tolerated more expensive and elaborate forms of clothing.

Most of the Separate Baptists feared that confessions might supplant the direct authority of Scripture. John Leland said, "Confessions of faith often check any further pursuit after truth," and exclaimed, "Why this Virgin Mary between the souls of men and the scriptures?"[88] In time this anticonfessional stance softened, and Regular and Separate Baptists united on the basis of the Philadelphia Confession, but both agreed the Separates "should retain their liberty with regard to the construction of some of its objectionable articles." After debating whether to adopt any confession, they agreed as follows:

> To prevent the confession of faith from usurping a tyranical power over the conscience of any, we do not mean, that every person is bound to the strict observance of every thing therein contained; yet that it holds forth the essential truths of the gospel. . . . Upon these terms we are united, and desire hereafter, that the names Regular and Separate be buried in oblivion; and that from henceforth, we shall be known by the name of the *United Baptist Churches.*[89]

Eventually those factors that separated the two groups receded in importance, while factors drawing them together increased. Several individuals helped bridge the gap, like Richard Furman, converted a Separate but serving with distinction in a Regular pulpit. The struggle for religious liberty in the South was shared equally by Regular and Separate Baptists, and that drew them closer. The two groups voted to merge in Virginia in 1787 and in North Carolina in 1788. In South Carolina, Georgia, and

87. Ibid., p. 69.

88. L. F. Greene, ed., *The Writings of the Late Elder John Leland,* p. 114.

89. David Benedict, *A General History of the Baptist Denomination in America and Other Parts of the World,* 2 vols. (Boston: Manning and Loring, 1813), 2:62.

Kentucky, the barriers gradually eroded; they merged by a gradual process rather than by formal vote.

Continuing Impact

The influence of the Separate Baptists lingers to this day. The merged group in some areas took the name of "United Baptists," but the name never stuck. Some of the emphases of both groups were muted by the merger, but other emphases continued. Even today some characteristics of Southern Baptists can be traced to the Separate influence in their heritage: warm preaching, fervent styles of worship, emphasis upon conversion, moderate Calvinism that makes room for a personal decision for Christ, and a liking in some churches for the gospel song tradition.

With keen insight, Walter B. Shurden painted the Regular and Separate Baptists as a contrast between the expression of ORDER and ARDOR.[90] He described the "Charleston Tradition," with its grace and dignity, as emphasizing *theological* order in their confession of faith; *ecclesiological* order in their "Summary of Church Discipline" and their emphasis upon the churches in association; *liturgical* order with their dignified worship and stately hymns; and *ministerial* order in their emphasis upon a trained ministry. Shurden concluded, "The word for Charleston is ORDER."

The "Sandy Creek Tradition," on the other hand, would have found such order too restrictive. Shurden described them as a people of ARDOR. Their worship was *revivalistic:* "Faith was feeling and every Sunday was a camp meeting." Their ministry was *charismatic;* preaching was a calling and never a profession, and preachers needed little human learning since their purpose was not to inform but to alarm. The Sandy Creek *ecclesiology* was independent; their *theological* approach biblicist. They formed associations, but not so much to express church connectionalism as to provide mass meetings for evangelism. They accepted the Bible as authority and opposed confessions lest they become creeds. Not until 1816 did the Sandy Creek Association adopt any kind of confession, and it ran less than one page.

Both the order of Charleston and the ardor of Sandy Creek contributed to the synthesis that made up the Southern Baptist Convention. Creative elements from both traditions have enriched Southern Baptist life and, like two streams merging into one river, currents from each can still be identified and traced. The merging of these traditions brought tensions which continue today; Southern Baptists are still trying to maintain balance between two streams of their heritage, the order of Charleston and the ardor of Sandy Creek.

Lumpkin listed a number of ways in which the Separate Baptists left a

90. Walter B. Shurden, "The Southern Baptist Synthesis: Is It Cracking?" *Baptist History and Heritage,* pp. 2-11.

continuing impact.[91] Among other things, they (1) brought the Great Awakening to the South, (2) fixed an evangelical stamp upon American Protestantism, (3) provided religious leadership for the American frontier, (4) contributed to the struggle for religious liberty in America, (5) helped prepare the American people for the Revolution and the coming of political freedom, (6) contributed to winning black people to Christianity, (7) brought great numerical gains to Baptists, and (8) provided significant antecedents for the Southern Baptist Convention in doctrine, styles of evangelism and worship, and strong biblicism.

Baptists and Education

Though Baptists sponsor multitudes of schools today, education did not appear a major priority to Baptists in the eighteenth century. The scarcity of Baptists limited their ability to promote major projects. Some Baptists also harbored a lingering suspicion of an educated clergy, lest learning sap spirituality. The persecuting state church clergy were both learned and salaried, facts not lost upon Baptists.

Baptist attitudes toward education are revealed in a letter of 1720 to Elisha Callendar, pastor in Boston. The writer was Edward Wallin of London, but no doubt he expressed the consensus of Baptists on the American side of the Atlantic as well. Wallin said, "Surely a man blessed with good natural genuis, who has been brought to a true sense of sin, and the saving knowledge of Jesus Christ, though he should want the advantage of human literature, must be better capable than one that has it, and is destitute of the other, to guide souls into the way of salvation." Wallin concluded, "Therefore, though I have a high esteem for human learning, and wish every minister had the advantage of a good degree of it, yet I conceive it is far from being necessary to a man's being employed in the public ministry."[92] Separate Baptists on the frontier were even more opposed, lest human learning lead to "a disestum [disesteem] of the Bible."[93]

Baptist ministers who desired education had three choices. They could return to England, which a few did before the Revolution made that less feasible; they could read on their own; or they could attend Harvard or Yale, especially later in the century. However, Baptists faced harrassment and second-class treatment at these schools. Further, many were proselyted to the state religion before graduation, giving rise to the saying that you could send a Baptist to Harvard but could not get one out.

In the eighteenth century, Baptists established a number of academies in the Middle Colonies, and Charleston Baptists established a fund in 1755 for the education of young ministers. However, the crowning educational

91. Lumpkin, pp. 147 *f.*
92. Backus, 1:487-488.
93. Sweet, p. 480.

achievement of the century was the founding of Rhode Island College in 1764, the first Baptist college in the new world.

Baptist Academies

In 1756 Isaac Eaton established an academy at Hopewell, New Jersey, where he was pastor. Eaton, who had been educated in England, sought to involve the Philadelphia Association in this project. Its minutes for 1756 state: "Concluded to raise a sum of money towards the encouragement of a Latin Grammar School for the promotion of learning amongst us, under the care of Brother Isaac Eaton."[94] However, shortly the association turned its attention to the college and its support for the academy waned.

However, the Hopewell Academy served a great need. Its success must be judged by the accomplishments of its graduates, which included such outstanding leaders as James Manning, Samuel Jones, Hezekiah Smith, William Williams, and others. In 1760 a number of members of seven congregations in Pennsylvania and New Jersey, concerned for the "languishing of learning" among Baptists, met to devise a plan to strengthen Hopewell. This was a lapse to the society method and probably resulted from failure of the association to carry through on its earlier support. Before 1800 a number of other Baptist academies had been founded at different places, usually by pastors who had some education and realized its importance and who needed to supplement their income.

The Baptist associations at Philadelphia, Charleston, and Warren all established funds and/or committees for the encouragement of education. The evidence suggests Baptist students have changed little since Hopewell days. Students were expected to attend worship at Eaton's church. One student recorded in his diary for a winter Sunday in 1757, "As Mr. Eaton had a sore throat, he fortunately stopped at the end of an hour and a half, and I confess I was glad to hear him say 'Amen.' "[95]

The Charleston Fund

In 1755 Oliver Hart led the Charleston Association to establish a fund for the education of pious young men inclined toward the ministry. That same year Charleston Baptists formed "The Religious Society," a group without official connection to the association, to promote education. These were the first definite educational efforts among Baptists in the South. Their first collection in 1755 amounted to about £133, and the churches augmented the fund from time to time.

At that time Baptists in the South had no thought of establishing a school. The funds were used to send students to schools elsewhere and later to acquire a theological library and commit it to the keeping of some willing

94. Gillette, p. 74.
95. Cited in Maring, p. 25.

minister who would accept young men to "read theology" with him. Students would live in the minister's home, share his table, and observe and sometimes participate in his ministerial duties, thus combining the advantages of classical and practical learning. Oliver Hart, Joseph Reece, and, above all, Richard Furman, took custody of this library and the young ministers who followed it. Later those books became the nucleus of the library of Furman University, and some of them went in 1859 to Southern Baptists' first theological seminary. It was Furman's idea to transfer the education work from the Religious Society to the association itself, and in 1790 the association formed a "General Committee" for that purpose.

Another leader in Baptist education in the South was John M. Roberts. He had attended Rhode Island College as a beneficiary of the education fund and, in 1799, became pastor at the High Hills church and chairman of the General Committee. With Furman's encouragement, he established an academy at High Hills, probably in 1799. This was apparently the earliest educational institution sponsored by Baptists in the South. Meanwhile, most Separate Baptists kept their distance from such educational efforts.

Rhode Island College

A number of Baptist pastors in Colonial America had attended Bristol College in England, one of whom was Morgan Edwards, who became pastor of Philadelphia's First Baptist Church in 1762. He conceived the idea of forming a Baptist college in America, patterned on the Bristol plan. The Philadelphia Association, according to its minutes for 1764, "Agreed, to inform the churches to which we respectively belong, that, inasmuch as a charter is obtained in Rhode Island government, toward erecting a Baptist College, the churches should be liberal in contributing towards carrying the same into execution."[96]

The college was located in Rhode Island because there was as yet no college there, and that colony had a large Baptist population. Ezra Stiles estimated in 1760 that there were about 22,000 Baptists in all of New England, and about 80 percent of them lived in Rhode Island.[97] The college opened in 1764 at Warren but moved in 1770 to Providence, although Newport competed strongly for it. The founders could not agree on how closely the college should be related to Baptists. The charter provided that while Baptists might compose the majority, the trustees should include representatives of other denominations as well, and that "Sectarian differences of opinions shall not make any Part of the Public and Classical Instruction." Jeremiah Condy, pastor in Boston, "desired the College might be on a broad bottom; and that the direction of it might not be confined

96. Gillette, p. 91.
97. McLoughlin, 1:492.

to any particular denomination."[98] The urban and urbane Baptists, led by Condy, wanted a more liberal college basis, with a nonsectarian approach. Perhaps their purpose was to demonstrate broad and tolerant religious principles by creating a sort of Baptist Harvard. Most people assumed Condy would be chosen president.

However, the more conservative Baptists prevailed at several points. They elected James Manning president instead of Condy; they altered the proposed charter to make the college more distinctly Baptist; and the move to Providence instead of Newport was also a victory for the more evangelical party. Financial support came from the Rhode Island legislature, from wealthy donors, and from smaller gifts raised by traveling agents.

Baptists in the South also supported Rhode Island College; Hezekiah Smith and John Gano found the South fertile territory for raising both contributions and students. Some had their doubts, of course, like Frances Pelot of Euhaw, South Carolina, who wrote to Hezekiah Smith in 1771 that, while he favored the college, he hoped its graduates would not turn out to be "learned graceless wretches."[99] Others, while not too enthusiastic, saw that a college was necessary; one wrote in 1770 that when the old ministers died off he foresaw "a new Succession of Scholar Ministers: . . . it has got so far already as scarcely to do for a common Illiterate Minister to preach in the baptist meetg at providence."[100]

Manning moved to Providence with the college in 1770 and was soon called, as expected, as pastor of the First Baptist Church there. For two or three years his preaching aroused little response, but in the mid-1770s a revival broke out that strengthened both church and college. Manning "reformed" the church back to a modified Calvinistic doctrinal basis and led in the erection of the magnificent meetinghouse that still stands. It was completed in 1775, at that time the most magnificent Baptist building in America, dedicated as "a meeting house for the public worship of Almighty God, and to hold commencement in."[101] The first bell in the 196-foot tower, weighing 2,500 pounds, had engraved upon it the motto:

> For freedom of conscience the town was first planted
> Persuasion, not force, was used by the people;
> This church is the eldest and has not recanted,
> Enjoying and granting bell, temple, and steeple.[102]

The significance is that in England the dissenters, including Baptists, could have neither bell nor steeple on their buildings. This deprived Baptists

98. Ibid., pp. 495-496.
99. Ibid., p. 499.
100. Ibid.
101. Benedict, 1855 ed., p. 455.
102. Ibid.

of the most impressive religious sight and sound of the time. But in America they had freedom to enjoy both.

Rhode Island College proved an immense benefit to Baptists. It provided a trained leadership; many of the most outstanding Baptist leaders in America graduated from the Providence school. The college raised Baptists' image and also stimulated Baptist expansion. In the next century the famous Brown family of Providence made generous contributions to the college, whereupon its name was changed to Brown University. Over the years its relation to the Baptist denomination, never secured by any structural ties, diminished. Presently the university has no relationship to the Baptist or any other religious denomination.

In retrospect, many have puzzled over why Middle Colony Baptists, who conceived and established the school, should have located it in New England. While Baptists made up a majority of the Rhode Island population at that time, they were soon reduced to a rather small minority. Meanwhile, Baptists in Philadelphia and the Middle Colonies grew rapidly in numbers and influence and represented perhaps more nearly the heart of the Baptist denomination spiritually and theologically.

Baptists came to the end of the eighteenth century with a few academies, a number of "lesser schools," and one major college. Much of the old prejudice against learning was eroding, and Baptists came to the new century with a new educational vision. They saw more clearly that schools were important, that they need not sap spirituality but indeed might enhance it, and that the growing denomination had the means to provide schools for its people.

Baptist Associations

Baptists in Colonial America developed several associations of churches. Emerging denominational structure provided another clear example of British influence; both name and concept of a grouping of churches in association was imported from England. Baptists also talked of a national organization, but that had to wait for the early nineteenth century. The associating of churches proceeded more rapidly in the South.

By 1800 Baptists in America had at least forty-two associations, but most of them originated after 1780 in the surge of post-Revolutionary Baptist growth. Three leading associations are spotlighted here, one from each major region. They illustrate the motives, methods, and functions of early associations.

The Philadelphia Association (1707)

Historians have named the Philadelphia Association as the first Baptist association in America and dated its origin at 1707. Both points could be debated. Robert Gardner has shown that a few General Six-Principle churches in Rhode Island probably held "yearly meetings" as early as

1670.[103] The question turns upon one's definition of an association; the Rhode Island meetings were apparently mostly for fellowship with no continuing organization. As to the date, the Philadelphia Association originated out of a circle of churches planted in the late 1680s by Elias Keach and Thomas Killingsworth. Keach formed the Pennepek church in 1687, but an ancient record states, "the church had several distant places to meet in," and members "held their communion at the Lord's table at these several places."[104] However, members of these "arms" came together for united worship about once a quarter. The leaders called these Quarterly Meetings, but since they came to each locality about once a year, the people referred to them as the Annual Meeting. Thus, by 1688 a group of Baptist congregations in the Philadelphia area met regularly for fellowship, worship, and discussion of mutual concerns. However, in 1707 the body was more definitely organized, elected a moderator, and took its present name. Certainly the Philadelphia Association is the oldest surviving Baptist association in America, and no other comes close in importance in the Colonial era.

In time the Philadelphia Association affiliated churches from New England to the South, spanning a distance of several hundred miles and several states. It became, to all practical purposes, a national body, and in 1770 Morgan Edwards urged that it be recognized as such. Edwards proposed that the Philadelphia Association be incorporated and a delegate from each of the other associations be admitted to the corporation, thus forming a national body. In 1767 Samuel Jones, moderator of the Philadelphia body, wrote to James Manning in Rhode Island, pointing out that

> as particular members are collected together and united in one body, which we call a particular Church, . . . so a collection and union of churches into one associational body may easily be conceived capable of answering those still greater purposes which any particular Church could not be equal to. And, by the same reason, a union of associations will still increase the body in weight and strength, and make it good that a three-fold cord is not easily broken.[105]

A meeting of Baptists was called to convene in Virginia in 1776 to form a "Continental Association," but unsettled times prevented the meeting. In 1799 the Philadelphia Association issued another call for a national meeting, noting that

> many advantages may result from a general conference, composed of one member, or more, from each Association, to be held every one, two, or three years, as may seem most subservient to the general interests of our Lord's

103. Gardner, p. 137.
104. Gillette, p. 11
105. William Wright Barnes, *The Southern Baptist Convention, 1845-1953*, p. 2.

kingdom; this Association respectfully invites the different Associations in the United States to favor them with their views on the subject.[106]

The Philadelphia plan called for a "union of associations," with stair-step representation from local churches to associations, and from associations to the national body in a kind of presbyterial pattern. That plan never materialized; when national union came early in the next century, it was on a modified society basis that within a few years repudiated the principle of church representation altogether.

At least three reasons account for the failure of the Philadelphia plan for national union: They cited no clearly defined purpose for such a union; Baptists were then preoccupied with achieving unity within the states; and some feared a national union might threaten the independence of the churches.[107]

After returning to England, Elias Keach and his famous father revised the Second London Confession for their church, adding two articles approving hymn singing and laying on of hands. In 1712 when a New Jersey church faced doctrinal disputes, they were advised to "subscribe to Elias Keach's Confession of Faith."[108] The Welsh Tract church also used the Keach confession both in English and in a Welsh translation made by Abel Morgan. In 1724 the Philadelphia Association, in reply to a question about the sabbath, referred to "the Confession of faith, set forth by the elders and brethren met in London, 1689, and owned by us."[109] A major step came in 1742 when the Philadelphia Association formally adopted the Keach version, which became known in this country as the Philadelphia Confession. It fixed for generations the doctrinal character of Baptists in this country as evangelical Calvinism, providing a bulwark against both the Arminianism of the Freewills and the determinism of the Hardshells. The 1742 edition was printed in Philadelphia by Benjamin Franklin, who commented favorably upon its contents.

The added article on hymn singing affirmed:

> We believe that . . . singing the praises of God, is a holy Ordinance of Christ, . . . it being injoined on the churches of Christ to sing psalms, hymns, and spiritual songs; and that the whole church in their public assemblies, as well as private christians, ought to 'heb 2 12 jam 5 13' sing God's praises according to the best light they have received.[110]

For all practical purposes, that settled the singing controversy in America;

106. Gillette, p. 343.
107. Walter B. Shurden, *Associationalism Among Baptists in America: 1707-1814*, pp. 223-224.
108. William L. Lumpkin, ed., *Baptist Confessions of Faith*, p. 349.
109. Gillette, p. 27.
110. Lumpkin, *Confessions*, p. 351.

henceforth, Baptists would be a singing people.

The Charleston Association (1751)

The second Baptist association in America, and first in the South, was formed at Charleston, South Carolina, by Oliver Hart in 1751. Hart had been active in the Philadelphia Association, and clearly that body provided a model for the Charleston effort. Only four churches made up the association in 1751, with twenty-six affiliated by 1796. From the first, some of the churches treated the association lightly. Available minutes later in the century show that rarely more than half of associated churches sent reports to the annual meeting, and fewer sent messengers. In 1788, for example, only four of seventeen ministers in the association attended its meeting, and those present took occasion to complain of the "general backwardness respecting our associational meetings."[111] "These meetings are a great means of union and common interest," they said, and "that union will be weakened and those interests suffer, in proportion as neglect prevails."

Several associations in the South adopted the Philadelphia Confession, beginning with Charleston in 1767. The Philadelphia Confession served as the major doctrinal statement for Baptists in the South until the rise of the New Hampshire Confession in 1833.

The Charleston Association sponsored two major projects in the eighteenth century: ministerial education and home missions. As set out elsewhere, the association established a scholarship fund in 1755 to aid young ministers. For some years the fund was managed by the Religious Society, led by Charleston Baptists but not actually connected with the association. In 1790, however, the association assumed direct management of the fund. From the beginning, the association helped churches obtain pastors, arranged pulpit supplies for churches temporarily without pastors, and later in the century sent preachers to frontier areas to preach and establish churches. Thus they fixed in the South the concept of missionary work through denominational channels. In all of these endeavors, of course, they followed the lead of the Philadelphia Association.

The Warren Association (1767)

The first Regular Baptist association in New England was formed at Warren, Rhode Island, in 1767. Before then most of the New England churches remained "unassociated," though a few had lined up with the Philadelphia Association. More than elsewhere in America, New England Baptists shied away from associations; they had seen close-up how the once voluntary Congregational associations had assumed power over local churches. Isaac Backus noted in his diary for September 8, 1767, "We went to Warren, where a general conference was appointed, . . . The design of

---

111. *Minutes,* Charleston Baptist Association, 1788, p. 5.

this meeting was to inquire into the state of the churches, and to see if they would come into the method of annual associations."[112]

Ten churches were represented, but only four agreed to affiliate with the newly formed association. Backus, though chosen clerk of the meeting, refused to join. He said, "I did not see my way clear to join until 1770, when the benefits of the association were clear and its supposed dangers had been laid somewhat to rest." Backus "waited until they could be satisfied that this Association did not assume any jurisdiction over the churches." Gradually other churches overcame their apprehensions, and by 1772 a total of 21 had affiliated, representing 960 members.[113] Most of these churches were in Massachusetts.

The Warren Association made important contributions in two areas: They provided a degree of sponsorship for the Rhode Island College, and they correlated Baptist efforts in the struggle for religious liberty in New England. In 1769 the association appointed a "Grievance Committee," headed by Isaac Backus after 1772, whose task was to collect cases of persecution of Baptists, have them "well attested," and take such evidence to courts and legislatures seeking redress. In this way the Warren Association made a major contribution in the struggle for religious liberty in America.

The Power and Function of Associations

What authority does an association have, and how can it exercise that authority without compromising the independence of affiliated churches? Those questions surfaced in both England and America but were seldom faced so frankly as by the Philadelphia Association at its 1749 session. By mid-century, the association referred to churches as "belonging to this association," offered advice to churches on both doctrinal and practical issues, sent "helps" or representatives to assist in cases of local church discipline, and helped to accredit, and when need be to discredit, ministers. Naturally, the question arose as to the association's authority in these areas. The association asked Benjamin Griffith to prepare an essay "respecting the power and duty of an Association." They unanimously adopted Griffith's brief *Essay* and inserted it into the minutes in 1749 "that it may appear what power an Association of churches hath, and what duty is incumbent on an Association; and prevent the contempt with which some are ready to treat such an assembly, and also prevent any future generation from claiming more power than they ought—lording it over the churches."[114]

Griffith's *Essay* provides a model of balance and restraint, setting out clearly the authority of both churches and association. He said:

112. McLoughlin, *Diary,* 2:670-671.
113. Benedict, 1855 ed., p. 470.
114. Gillette, p. 60.

> That an Association is not a superior judiacature, having such superior power over the churches concerned; but that each particular church hath a complete power and authority from Jesus Christ, to administer all gospel ordinances, provided they have a sufficiency of officers duly qualified, . . . and to receive in and cast out, and also to try and ordain their own officers, and to exercise every part of gospel discipline and church government, independent of any other church or assembly whatever.[115]

This confirmed church ordinances, discipline, and ordination as local church and not denominational functions. However, churches should associate with others when possible for mutual counsel and strength. According to the *Essay,* the churches should

> choose delegates or representatives, to associate together; and thus the several independent churches being the constituents, the association, council or assembly of their delegates, when assembled, is not to be deemed a superior judiacature, as having a superintendency over the churches, but subservient to the churches, in what may concern all the churches in general, or any one church in particular; and, though no power can regularly arise above its fountain from where it rises, yet we are of opinion, that an Association of the delegates of associate churches have a very considerable power in their hands, respecting those churches in their confederation; . . . that a defection in doctrine or practice in any church, in such confederation, or any party in such church, is ground sufficient for an Association to withdraw from such a church or party.[116]

The *Essay* made it clear, however, that the association had only the power to withdraw its fellowship; they might urge the churches to exclude members involved in erroneous practice or teaching, "but excommunicate they cannot." That power belongs only to the church. W. W. Barnes pointed to the Philadelphia Association moving from a union composed of representatives to a union composed of churches as a major turning point in the development of Baptist ecclesiology.[117]

The *Essay* set out what an association *should* do; the Philadelphia minutes reveal what they *did* do. For the most part, the two harmonize. From the first, the churches sent "queries" to the associations, seeking advice on knotty points of doctrine or on sticky matters of practice and discipline. The associations performed several functions.

First, the association served as a doctrinal monitor. In time, most of the associations adopted a confession of faith, and some made adherence a condition of affiliation. Churches that departed significantly from Baptist doctrines were to be dealt with by the association and excluded if they did not recant. Often a church facing doctrinal disputes appealed to the associa-

115. Ibid., pp. 60-61.
116. Ibid., p. 61.
117. Barnes, pp. 13 *f.*

tion to send "helps," ministers and brethren who went to the troubled church and helped arbitrate the issues. While each church was independent, such "helps" and the voice of the association carried considerable weight.

Second, the association advised on Baptist practices. Such issues as singing in worship, the marriage of slave members, dealing with divorce and remarriage, what offenses merit church discipline, whether members who have not moved may move their membership, the role of women in church, whether the pastor should receive a salary and, if so, how it should be raised, how to choose deacons and how to define their duties, whether to dedicate infants, whether to accept non-Baptist immersion, and how to use "vacant" days of worship (when no preacher was present) were typical issues faced by associations.

In 1765 the Smith's Creek church asked "whether it be proper to receive a person into communion who had been baptized by immersion by a minister of the Church of England, if no other objection could be made?" The Philadelphia Association replied, "Yea, if he had been baptized on a profession of faith and repentence."[118]

The following query was sent to the Philadelphia Association in 1746, "Whether women may or ought to have their votes in the church?" After lengthy discussion, the brethren agreed that women as members of the church at least had "liberty to give a mute voice, by standing or lifting up of the hands" to vote. Under some conditions, a woman might have a spoken voice, as to confess her faith, praise God, or testify in cases of church discipline. The brethren concluded:

> Therefore there must be times and ways in and by which women as members of the body, may discharge their conscience. . . . And a woman may, at least, make a brother a mouth to ask leave to speak, if not ask it herself; and a time of hearing is to be allowed, for that is not inconsistent with the silence and subjection injoined on them by the law of God and nature, yet ought not they to open the floodgates of speech in an imperious, tumultuous, masterly manner.[119]

Third, associations served as clearing houses in personnel matters. Churches seeking pastors and pastors seeking settlement often worked through the associations. The associations also aided "vacant" churches by helping them find temporary supply preachers, often by rather arbitrarily assigning neighboring pastors to take turns supplying. Associations helped "credential" preachers by endorsing them and, conversely, warned churches against unworthy or unorthodox preachers. The Charleston Association, for example, in 1790 warned the churches to avoid Philip Mulkey, formerly a leading Separate Baptist minister, but then "under the awful sentence of

118. Gillette, p. 95.
119. Ibid., p. 53.

excommunication," and "degraded from the rank of a minister."[120]

Fourth, the associations promoted benevolent work, primarily in the three areas of Chrisian education, the struggle for religious liberty, and home missions. As early as 1722, the Philadelphia Association raised money for education and, in 1764, helped sponsor the Baptist college. By 1755 the Charleston Association raised an educational fund, and many other associations did likewise. The Warren Association correlated Baptist efforts for religious liberty in New England, a function performed in the South by several groups, including the General Committee of Virginia. One purpose of associations was to extend the gospel to destitute areas, and by the 1760s the Philadelphia Association employed an "evangelist at large" to plant new churches in needy areas.

Fifth, associations provided fellowship for lonely Baptists. In areas sparsely settled, with Baptists at best unpopular and at worst severely persecuted, the opportunity to share with others like-minded was important. At their associations Baptists received inspiration and encouragement, heard reports of progress elsewhere, and felt a part of a significant movement. As Robert Semple wrote, "We conceive it is no inconsiderable advantage that an opportunity should be offered for brethren to see each other."[121]

Sixth, the associations provided models for preaching. Preaching was always a major feature of association meetings, and churches put forward their best preachers. The younger ministers, and the less capable, heard Baptist preaching at its best and learned thereby. Of course, the associations might also spread bad preaching practices. However, perhaps more young ministers learned the natural but forceful preaching of John Gano than picked up the holy whine of Shubal Stearns.

Internal Life of Baptist Churches

What were Baptists like in the eighteenth century? How did their churches operate, and what did it mean to be a Baptist in Colonial America?

The Baptist Faith

In the eighteenth century, as in all others, the Baptist faith varied. It included Calvinism and Arminianism; Saturday worship and Sunday worship; belief in eternal damnation of the lost and belief in universal salvation; belief in open communion and closed communion. Sometimes religious faith was conditioned by ethnic background; the German Dunkers, for example, differed from the Welsh evangelicals. Most Baptists, however, harbored a keen awareness of sin. Baptists' confessions reveal an overpowering need for forgiveness and spiritual healing. Their faith in the Bible was

120. *Minutes,* Charleston Baptist Association, 1790, p. 2.
121. Robert Baylor Semple, *History of Baptists in Virginia,* p. 63.

firm but not doctrinaire; they believed the Bible, but modern theories of inspiration would have been unfamiliar to most Baptists. While their faith had a basic other-world orientation, they never forgot the Christian obligation to live in the here and now.

Anti-Catholicism formed a staple of Baptist preaching in the eighteenth century, as it did for most denominations. Perhaps most would have agreed with Elisha Paine, Baptist pastor on Long Island, who wrote in 1752, "We all own that the pope or papal throne is the second beast."[122] Most Baptists believed the world was created about 4000 BC. While they did not stress the millennium, most held views similar to what is now called postmillennialism; premillennialism had few followers in America until after the Civil War. While most Baptists held orthodox Christology, Hofmanite views surfaced at times, and Unitarian and Universalist views cropped up occasionally.

The Baptist Minister

The Baptist minister of the eighteenth century might not recognize his counterpart two centuries later. One became a Baptist minister then not from personal choice, but in response to an overwhelming sense of divine call. Some Baptists distinguished between the "providential call," by which God endowed individuals with necessary gifts, and the "outward call," by which the church acknowledged those gifts. The churches often took the initiative in calling persons into ministry, and they always evaluated the person's gifts. The "call to preach" was much less subjective then; the church shared in it.

Ordination was a lengthy process that usually began with a church authorizing a young candidate to "improve" or exercise his gifts locally. If those efforts proved fruitless, the church usually advised the person to give up the ministry. If local efforts proved successful, the person might be authorized to preach in wider circles and eventually undergo formal ordination. Ordination in the eighteenth century varied. It might be to a specific pastorate or a more general ordination to an "itinerant ministry." When pastors moved to another church, they were often reordained to the new pastorate. Some pastorates proved brief, but the ideal was a lifetime pastoral commitment.

The attitude toward ministerial support varied. Roger Williams had spoken strongly against financial support in his widely quoted *Hireling Ministry None of Christ's*. A conference of Baptist leaders in Massachusetts in 1727 asked, "Whether ministers of the gospel ought to be maintained, in the least, by goods taken away by force from men of contrary conscience." The brethren answered in the negative. Baptists seemed to have little acquaintance with the concept of freely given offerings; they were

122. Backus, 2:100n.

obsessed with the idea of distrained goods taken by force by the state church.[123] The Separate Baptists, especially, spoke against ministerial salaries.

Other Baptists objected to a *stated* salary but often shared with the preacher such commodities as they had, including crops, livestock, and sometimes cash. The fact that some churches agreed to pay a salary was no guarantee the preacher would actually receive it; the records are replete with examples of pastors who could not collect what had been promised. Withholding salary was one way a church had of showing dissatisfaction with a pastor. Some Baptists, like Joseph Hencks, argued that "it is not only lawful for a minister or elder that preaches the gospel to receive (by way of contribution) a competent maintenance, but also the duty of the church, according to their ability, to afford it to him."[124] Some pastors signed contracts with churches, specifying both duties and benefits; and some went to court to enforce such contracts. Money for pastors was seldom raised in church, but usually came from a canvass or subscription conducted outside the church. The idea of an offering as a part of worship was little known among Baptists of the time.

The concept of retirement is a recent invention; in the eighteenth century most Baptist preachers simply worked until they died or their health failed. Neither denomination nor government offered anything like modern retirement provisions. Most elderly people were cared for by relatives, though occasionally a beloved pastor or his widow might be cared for voluntarily by some family in the church. Few Baptist pastors in the eighteenth century were *full-time* as that term is now used; most of them supplemented their needs by working at other jobs, farming, or engaging in business.

The Baptist pastor exercised considerable authority in the eighteenth century. Most of this authority was of a spiritual nature, since the churches had little business to conduct. Laymen probably exercised less leadership in the churches; they deferred to the ordained to discover and articulate the will of God. Such terms as *ruling elder,* the responsibility of the pastor to *govern the church,* and the duty of members to *follow and obey the pastor* occur frequently in Baptist sources of the times. For a layman (and even that term was rarely used) to go contrary to his pastor on any matter of religious teaching or duty was a rare occurence. Laymen came into more power in later generations when churches acquired more property to manage, more funds to raise and allot, and more secular "business" to conduct.

The Local Church

Not all churches had buildings, and those that did usually had only a plain, one-room frame structure. In Morgan Edwards's account of Baptist

123. Ibid., 1:520.
124. Ibid., 2:22.

churches in the 1770s, "30' by 40' " appears so often one almost assumes that was a customary size for Baptist buildings. The pastor often held catechizing or teaching sessions, and sometimes school classes were held in the church building during the week, but all meetings/classes took place within the one large room. No Sunday School rooms were provided for the simple reason that the churches had no Sunday Schools. The pulpit was usually elevated more than is customary today and was reached by stairs. Most of the churches had no musical instruments; they were either not available, too expensive, had a worldly "saloon" image, or were opposed as not being scriptural. In time Baptists outgrew their anti-instrument bias, as they had earlier overcome their antisinging prejudice.

Baptists, like other denominations, often distinguished between the "church," made up of baptized members, and the "congregation," which included regular hearers who were not members. Both groups had rights. The "congregation," which might be two or three times as large as the "church," often participated in the call, installation, and support of a pastor, but they could not receive communion. Most people joined the church as adults, but youths as young as sixteen might also be converted and baptized. In time the average age at conversion dropped. At conversion a person might receive the right hand of *Christian* fellowship but only after baptism would receive the right hand of *church* fellowship. Some churches received new members with a laying on of hands, similar to present ordination practices.

Most early Baptist buildings had neither heating nor lighting, though in the cities and towns a few had both. They usually conducted two services each Sunday in summer, but only one in the winter. The popularity of Sunday night services increased with the improved lighting that came in the nineteenth century.

Since most Baptists were common people, they were sensitive to social status, having been looked down upon by many of the state church people. While some Baptist churches, especially in New England assigned pews by social rank, most did not. However, quite early they recognized an "amen corner" where the most fervent, or at least the most vocal, of their members tended to congregate, thus setting aside a section for the spiritual elite instead of the social elite.

Churches that sang mostly made a dismal affair of it, if surviving hymn texts and descriptions of their performance furnish any guide. Given these conditions, one is not surprised that some argued against singing altogether. For the most part, their hymn texts now appear dreary, trivial, polemical, or all of these, though there were happy exceptions. Mostly the minister would "line out" the hymn, with the people singing after him. The idea of a professional music leader was, of course, unheard of among Baptists of the eighteenth century. Many of the Baptist hymns centered around baptism and the Lord's Supper, and many found ways to refute other denominations as well as to praise God. One favorite in *The Newport Collection* of 1766, perhaps the earliest Baptist song book in America, had a stanza proclaiming

> Some call it baptism and think it will stand,
> a few drops of water dropt from a man's hand,
> In the face of the infant who's under the curse,
> But we find no scripture that proves it to us.[125]

Behavior at church proved a problem at times, not only among youth but also among adults who sometimes talked out, laughed, or simply went to sleep. Backus complained that before the revival of the 1780s "the church was in low circumstances for some time, and young people got to be so extravagant in vanity, that they could hardly be kept civil in times of public worship."[126] However, the revival and an awful sense of sin came upon the congregation, causing the "giddy youth" to settle down.

Special Occasions

Baptists in the eighteenth century made much of baptism and the Lord's Supper, and some churches emphasized other rites as well. The baptisms were always public; different associations ruled that "private immersions" were "nullities." Baptism might take place in a river or lake, with witnesses both from the church and the world gathered on the banks. Quite often groups of rowdies came to shout and mock and sometimes tried to break up such baptisms. The minister would usually preach a sermon, and often people would be converted on the spot, go into the baptismal waters, and walk home in their wet clothing. Toward the end of the century, a few churches began to install baptismal pools in the church building. The Lord's Supper was usually a solemn occasion, and until the twentieth century most Baptist churches used wine. To use any other liquid would have been unthinkable to Baptists who took the Bible seriously.

Easter and Christmas were not only not observed by Baptists but also both were opposed as worldly and popish. When Samuel Jones was a student at Hopewell Academy, he wrote in his diary on December 25, 1757: "Christmas day! But our school goes on as usual. The only difference was that we had two big turkeys for dinner. Mr. E(aton) told us that he did not observe Christmas as he was certain that our Saviour was not born on the twenty-fifth or any other day in December."[127]

Others were even more militant, regarding Easter as pagan, and Christmas as "the superstitious relique of the scarlet whore."

Most Baptist church members got their religious education from the

---

125. Cited by O'Kelly, p. 182.
126. Backus, 2:429.
127. Maring, p. 25.

pastor's sermons. Sunday Schools were nonexistent, and religious literature was scarce. However, several associations adopted catechisms as well as confessions, and pastors were expected on occasion to "catechize" the children. Churches of the Philadelphia Association were encouraged to use the catechism prepared by Benjamin Keach, and in 1738 the association ordered more to be printed. In 1794 they voted, "That it be recommended to the different churches in this Association, to institute the chatechising of children in their respective congregations, at stated seasons."[128]

Conclusion

The eighteenth century transformed Baptists in America. They entered that century with a handful of churches, divided in doctrine, disspirited by persecution, and despised by most observers. They had formed no associations, sponsored no mission efforts, and launched no schools. By 1800 they were a different people with a different spirit. Their *outward* transformation to become the largest denomination in America seems less significant than their *inward* transformation into a confident, aggressive, evangelistic people. The scattered churches had become a denomination. They had discovered purpose in evangelism, missions, and education and had organized to pursue those objectives.

Without doubt, the event which did most to transform the Baptists was the First Great Awakening. Their greatest achievement was their struggle for religious liberty.

---

128. Gillette, p. 297; see also Tom J. Nettles, *Baptist Catechisms.*

8

Baptists in Colonial America: The Struggle for Religious Liberty

For almost four centuries Baptists have insisted upon complete religious liberty not only for themselves but also for others. In no other area has Baptists' witness proved clearer and more consistent than in their struggle for the right of persons to answer to God and not to government for religious beliefs and behavior. Baptists were born in travail for freedom to differ from a state church, and they have resisted every effort, whether from civil or ecclesiastical authorities, to force them into religious conformity. Though its details and implications continue to be worked out, the basic struggle for religious freedom in America culminated in the Bill of Rights, added to the federal Constitution in 1791. The First Amendment guarantees that "Congress shall make no law respecting an establishment of religion, or prohibiting the free exercise thereof."

Baptists in America drew upon their English heritage for ideas and strategies in the long campaign for freedom of religion. They defended their views with arguments drawn from English Baptist confessions, petitions, and treatises. As early as 1612 an English Baptist confession declared "that the magistrate is not by virtue of his office to meddle with religion, or matters of conscience, to force or compel men to this or that form of religion, or doctrine: but to leave Christian religion free, to every man's conscience, and to handle only civil transgressions."[1] Though later amplified, explained, and enlarged in countless tracts and treatises, that pioneer statement contains the basic ingredients of the Baptist witness for religious liberty. Baptists also took up the arguments advanced by Roger Williams and John Clarke in the 1600s and applied them with telling effect in the next century. Some political leaders debated whether the Act of Toleration, passed by Parliament in 1689, should extend to the English colonies. That act, when acknowledged at all, was applied reluctantly and unevenly in America.

Restrictions upon Baptists varied at different times and places from mild harrassment to severe persecution. No Baptist is known to have been executed for religion in America. However, many Baptists were severely whipped, forced to pay taxes to support the state church, had property

---

1. William L. Lumpkin, ed., *Baptist Confessions of Faith*, p. 140.

confiscated, paid fines, and suffered lingering imprisonments. They also faced public harrassment; Baptist preachers endured occasional indignities, public baptisms were often mocked or disrupted by onlookers, and Hezekiah Smith complained that "a beetle was cast upon him" as he walked a public street.

Some consider religious liberty and separation of church and state the major American contribution to the science of statecraft. Religious liberty's sources, spiritual and secular, are many. The philosophy of John Locke with its emphasis upon toleration; the enlightenment thought of Thomas Jefferson with its desire for personal liberties; the awakening theology of Isaac Backus with its call for personal decision; and the biblical views of John Leland who insisted that man remain free before God, all added their contribution. Political thinkers like Thomas Jefferson, James Madison, Patrick Henry, and to a lesser extent George Washington, gave a kind of secular blessing to religious freedom. If some acted more out of religious indifference than conviction, the result was much the same: to leave people alone in their religion. To this must be added the contribution of people who advocated liberty from religious motives. These primarily included the Baptists and Presbyterians, though Quakers, Mennonites, and others also spoke for freedom. However, for their numbers probably no denomination made a greater contribution to achieving religious liberty in America than did the Baptists. While Baptist churchmen provided many of the basic concepts, they lacked political power to get them enacted into law. Political leaders, on the other hand, could pass religious legislation, but their ideas of what to enact were significantly shaped by input from religious groups. Therefore, no religious group, including Baptists, can claim exclusive credit for religious liberty in this country.

Nor were the motives uniform among those who advocated religious liberty in Colonial America. Some wanted freedom in order to escape religious influence over the government. Perhaps that was a major motive for leaders like Jefferson; this position has been called freedom *from* religion. Others, like the Baptists, sought the same freedom, but for different reasons. They wanted freedom *for* religion, freedom to worship, preach, and practice according to their own convictions. American religious and political leaders reached a radical but creative solution: They separated church and state, thus giving all persons freedom to believe and practice the religion of their choice but refusing to force others to share either those convictions or practices. The government would attend to civil matters and remain neutral in religion.

Commenting on the First Amendment, President Jefferson wrote to a group of Baptists in Danbury, Connecticut, in 1802:

> Believing with you that religion is a matter which lies solely between man and his God, that he owes account to none other for his faith or his worship, that

the legislative powers of government reach actions only, not opinions, I contemplate with sovereign reverence that act of the whole American people which declared that their legislature should "make no law respecting the establishment of religion, or prohibiting the free exercise thereof," thus building a wall of separation between church and state.[2]

Though first coined by Roger Williams, the "wall of separation" metaphor was popularized by Jefferson. It has proven both helpful and, at times, troublesome. While emphasizing the reality of separation, the "wall" has implied a more complete division than has existed in reality. Other metaphors have been used to describe church-state relations: "neutrality" of government in religion, popularized in 1872 by Judge Alphonzo Taft, and "no excessive entanglement" of government and religion, as announced by Chief Justice Warren Burger in 1970.[3] An earlier description by James Madison, describing "a line of separation" may have been more accurate.

Two movements radically affected religious freedom in America, setting the stage and influencing the nature and extent of that freedom. These were the First Great Awakening, which peaked before 1750, and the Enlightenment, which reached full force a generation later. Alan Heimert in *Religion and the American Mind* showed how both the conservative awakening and the more liberal Enlightenment furthered the cause of religious liberty.[4] The revivalists' calls for personal decision in religion directly undercut not only the inherited Calvinism of the Puritans but also the concept of a state church imposing religious belief and behavior upon the citizens. While many of the "Awakeners" may not have wished it, their work led to more voluntaryism in religion.

The Enlightenment, on the other hand, expressed a desire for individuals to search and decide issues for themselves. In politics the Enlightenment strengthened the emerging concepts of democracy, giving each citizen a voice in determining public issues. In religion the movement called for toleration, an end to religious coercion, and in effect a reduction of the central role of religion in both public and private life. One must face frankly the role of religious indifference, as well as conviction, in gaining religious freedom in America. After all, those who persecute others for religion must be deeply convinced that religion is vitally important, that they alone are right, and that others are certainly wrong. The Enlightenment challenged all those concepts, and thus undercut the basis for religious persecution. It diminished the role of religion, making religious persecution hardly worthwhile; it called in question the dogmatic certainty which religious persecu-

2. George C. Bedell, Leo Sandon, Jr., and Charles T. Wellborn, *Religion in America* (New York: Macmillan Publishing Co., Inc., 1975), p. 74.

3. Ibid., pp. 77-85.

4. Alan Heimert, *Religion and the American Mind* (Cambridge: Harvard University Press, 1966).

tion requires; and, at the very least, it made religious persecution a matter of bad taste, beneath the dignity of the enlightened. Thus both religion and irreligion contributed to religious liberty in America, creating a unique system which has protected the rights of both.

In that pluralistic environment, Baptists made their pitch for soul freedom. Affected by both awakening and Enlightenment, drawing from English Baptist arguments, and appealing directly to the Scripture, Baptists like Isaac Backus in Massachusetts and John Leland in Virginia articulated a case for spiritual freedom which eventually bore fruit.

Conditions varied between the major geographical sections, with different laws and leaders affecting religion. Therefore, it seems best to trace religious liberty by a regional rubric, in New England, the Middle Colonies, and the South. These form several stories, but they later merge into one story—the achievement of full religious freedom for all.

Religious Liberty in New England

The "Pilgrim Fathers" who first settled New England represented a Congregational form of religion. Obsessed by Old Testament patterns and Reformed theology, they felt obliged to establish a kind of theocracy. Through the Cambridge Platform of 1648 and other legislation, they established the Congregational Church by law, taxed all the citizens to support that church, and restricted alternate forms of religion. Ironically, settlers who had just come from dissenter status in Old England established themselves as the official church in New England and persecuted those who dissented from them.

In "Liberty of Conscience," John Cotton affirmed that people could hold diverse views in religion so long as they met two conditions: the points at which they differed from the state church had to be peripheral and not fundamental, and they had to hold those views quietly and not to seek to win others to them. "In things of lesser moment," Cotton allowed, "whether points of Doctrine or Worship, if a man hold them forth in a spirit of Christian meekness and love . . . he is not to be persecuted, but tolerated, till God may be pleased to manifest his truth to him."[5] However, if any "should blaspheme the true God and his true Religion, they ought to be severely punished."[6] Of course, the state church would define which points were eligible for toleration and which must be suppressed.

Cotton seemed genuinely astonished at Roger Williams's objections to such narrow "freedom." By then Williams had arrived at the radical notions that government should leave religion alone, that truth would prevail by its own strength without being propped up by the civil arm, and that

5. Robert L. Ferm, ed., *Issues in American Protestantism* (Garden City, N. Y.: Doubleday and Company, Inc., 1969), p. 12.
6. Ibid.

complete freedom in religion was not only demanded by theology and Scripture but on a practical level would result in a more tranquil society. Though Williams, John Clarke, and other Baptists advocated these radical views, such ideas did not receive a wide hearing until the Revolutionary era.

Restrictions on Religion

In 1679 when members of the First Baptist Church of Boston sought to meet for the first time in their new building, they found the doors nailed shut and a sign posted forbidding them to use the building. Though the building was open by the next Sunday, that was typical of the kind of restrictions New England authorities, both civil and ecclesiastical, placed upon Baptists. Public calamities, such as disease epidemics or Indian raids, were especially hard on Baptists because some ministers of state churches in their "election day" sermons interpreted those as God's punishment upon the people for allowing Baptists and other dissenters to exist.

The law required all citizens, Baptists included, to pay taxes to support the Congregational Church which was established by law in most of New England. Those who did not pay had their goods seized and sometimes sold at a "public outcry" (auction) for a fraction of their worth. Some dissenters were cast into jail until they paid their apportionment to support the official ministers, a practice which at some places so backfired that the ministers themselves paid the fines just to be rid of prisoners who were winning such a favorable hearing by preaching from jail windows.

The case of Sturbridge, in western Massachusetts, provides an example of financial exploitation of Baptists. The Separate Baptists formed a church there in 1748 and met all requirements for exemption from religious taxation. However, according to Backus, "They were all again taxed to Mr. Caleb Rice, a [Congregational] minister in that town."[7] When Baptists were slow to pay, the authorities "made distress" upon their goods. According to Backus, they "took a good cow from David Morse, a ruling elder in said Baptist church, for a tax of one pound, one shilling and four-pense." Backus reported that they also "took a pair of oxen from him, valued at eleven pounds, for a tax of less than five dollars. Such havoc did they make of their neighbors' goods, under religious pretenses!"[8] Backus gave a summary of these exactions:

> They stripped the shelves of pewter, of such as had it; and of others that had not they took away skillets, kettles, pots and warming-pans. Others they deprived of the means they got their bread with, viz., workmen's tools, and spinning-wheels. They drove away geese and swine from the doors of some others; from some that had cows; from some that had but one they took that

7. Isaac Backus, *A History of New England with Particular Reference to the Denomination of Christians Called Baptists,* 2:94.
8. Ibid.

away. They took a yoke of oxen from one. Some they thrust into prison, where they had a long and tedious imprisonment. One brother was called from us and ordained a pastor of a Baptist church, and came for his family; at which time they seized him and drew him away, and thrust him into prison, where he was kept in the cold winter until somebody paid the money and let him out.[9]

Similar confiscations took place elsewhere. One man complained that the authorities had taken from him "a good riding beast" and petitioned that they, like the good Samaritan, would set him upon his own beast.[10] Ashfield, a new town on the western frontier of Massachusetts, was settled mostly by Baptists who formed and supported their own church. Later, Congregational settlers arrived and levied taxes upon the Baptists to establish a Congregational Church. When Baptists refused to pay, Backus reported that in April 1770,

> the assessors of Ashfield met, and sold three hundred and ninety-eight acres of the Baptists' land to support the worship of the opposite party. For a demand upon the Baptist minister of one pound, two shillings, they sold ten acres of his home lot. His father had one of the best apple orchards in the town, which is of special service in a new place; yet twenty acres of improved land, containing the main of his orchard, with a burying-yard, and a small dwelling-house, were struck off to Elijah Wells, for thirty-five shillings; who . . . forcibly entered upon it, and pulled up a number of the smaller apple trees and carried them away, and offered to sell the house.[11]

Probably the state church made one of their biggest mistakes when they imprisoned Elizabeth Backus, a widow and mother to Isaac Backus, the major Baptist spokesman for religious liberty in New England. Mrs. Backus, like her son, had left the state church to become a Baptist and was behind on her church taxes. When the officers came for her late one night, she was sick, wrapped in quilts to promote perspiration, sitting by the fire reading her Bible. They hauled her away to jail despite her condition. Her letter to Isaac says:

> Norwich, November 4, 1752
>
> MY DEAR SON: I have heard something of the trials amongst you of late, and I was grieved, till I had strength to give up the case to God, and leave my burthen there. And now I will tell you something of our trials. Your brother Samuel lay in prison twenty days. October 15, the collectors came to our house, and took me away to prison about nine o'clock, in a dark rainy night. Brothers Hill and Sabin were brought there the next night. We lay in prison thirteen days, and then set at liberty, by what means I know not. Whilst I was there a great many people came to see me. . . . though I was bound when

9. Ibid., pp. 94-95n.
10. Ibid., p. 179.
11. Ibid., p. 153.

I was cast into this furnace, yet was I loosed, and found Jesus in the midst of the furnace with me. O then I could give up my name, estate, family, life and breath, freely to God. Now the prison looked like a palace to me. I could bless God for all the laughs and scoffs made at me. . . . We are all in tolerable health, expecting to see you. These from your loving mother,

Elizabeth Backus[12]

Probably few letters from a mother to her son had greater impact. The Widow Backus was well-respected, and her case attracted widespread attention, all unfavorable to the standing order. Apparently the state minister was only too glad to see Mrs. Backus released and her damaging witness momentarily silenced. One may only surmise the extent to which this family incident hardened the resolve of Isaac Backus to break the state church monopoly over religion.

The Exemption Laws

Beginning in 1727 several of the New England states passed a series of "Exemption Laws" in religion, whereby Dissenters could apply to have their church taxes refunded under specified conditions. To qualify for exemption, such persons had to prove that they regularly attended and supported their own church and that they lived within five miles of their church and to present certificates from at least three other churches of their order confirming that theirs was, indeed, a church in good standing in that denomination. Baptists who met these conditions could apply for refund of their church rates. The authorities in both church and state thought these provisions sufficiently generous and could not understand the Baptist demand for more freedom.

However, Baptists found many problems with the Exemption Laws. They allowed government to legislate about religion, a premise that Baptists rejected even when it went in their favor. Further, the laws were temporary; they would lapse, be renewed, lapse again, and not be renewed for a year or so, to be renewed yet again in slightly different form. Baptist churches were scattered, especially on the frontier, and many faithful members lived more than five miles away. The laws referred to Baptists as "Anabaptists," a name they rejected. Some of the Separate Baptist churches had difficulty in obtaining certificates of fellowship from neighboring churches if those happened to be Regular Baptist churches. Further, the certificates of exemption, even when one met all the red tape to obtain them, required a substantial fee. Backus later commented that "a copy of which [certificate] could not be had without four-pence of our money, which is three-pence

12. Ibid., pp. 98-99.

sterling; the very tax upon a pound of tea that brought on the American war."[13]

The red tape connected with these certificates was formidable. A Baptist who met all the requirements and yet was not placed on the official exemption list had no recourse. Further, Baptists feared that some might be tempted to join a church to avoid taxes, or as Backus put it, they might be tempted "to come under the water when they have not been under the blood."

Isaac Backus (1724-1806)

Many regard Isaac Backus as the greatest Baptist spokesman for religious liberty in America. Backus applied many of the pioneer arguments of Roger Williams to the freedom struggle in the late eighteenth century. He could quote Jonathan Edwards or John Locke with equal ease, thus combining the strengths of awakening and Enlightenment views. As chairman of the influential Grievance Committee of the Warren Association, Backus was in the forefront of every important Baptist statement and strategy on religious liberty during the formative years of the Revolution. Backus's extensive writings form a body of literature on the subject still relevant today.

Backus was born in 1724 of well-to-do parents and brought up in the Congregational Church. An admirer of George Whitefield, Backus experienced an emotional conversion at age seventeen and soon thereafter affiliated with the prorevival New Lights. Though shy and introverted as a youth, Backus's early efforts to preach proved fruitful and confirmed his sense of inner call to that vocation. By 1751 Backus received immersion as a Baptist but for five years tried to maintain an open church that included both immersed and nonimmersed. In 1756 he abandoned that effort and formed a new church on strict Baptist principles, which he served as pastor for the rest of his life. Though lacking formal schooling, Backus read widely. His writings show acquaintance with events and authors of his own time, plus an avid awareness of Christian history. Backus was asked by the Warren Association in 1769 to write a history of Baptists in America; his three-volume work, with volumes appearing in 1777, 1784, and 1796, ranks as the earliest published history of the denomination in this country. This work is best known in its two-volume format, published almost a century later.

Backus showed considerable influence from the Enlightenment, especially the works of John Locke. Unlike Jefferson who found in Locke a substitute for revelation, Backus found there a buttress for revelation. In

13. Ibid., p. 182.

various treatises, Backus appealed often to Enlightenment concepts, as well as to Scripture. He remained a convinced Calvinist, quoting from "our excellent Edwards" as he called the theologian of Northampton.[14] However, Calvinism was on the wane in America; some argue that Backus and Calvinism died at about the same time. In old age Backus was troubled by an assistant pastor who held a modified Calvinism, but Backus at least credited him with winning many converts. Though he had only seven years of schooling, mostly in the winter months, Backus said, "Let none think me to be an enemy of learning." However, he complained, "It is too notorious to be denied that many scholars that have come out of college of late are rank Arminians."[15]

Though a Separate Baptist, Backus was not extreme, and he probably prevented the Baptists in New England from splitting into distinct Regular and Separate denominations as they did in the South. Gradually he pulled many of the Regular churches into at least moderate forms of revivalism, especially after the awakening of the 1780s. Perhaps more than any other person, Backus set the tone for New England Baptists during his lifetime in theology, evangelism, and churchmanship.

However, Backus is best remembered for being a leader in the struggle for religious liberty. His position as chairman of the Grievance Committee, his substantial but sometimes unexciting sermons, and his extensive writings allowed him to advance, defend, and publicize Baptist views. Modern readers consider two of his most effective treatises on that subject to be *Government and Liberty Described; and Ecclesiastical Tyranny Exposed* (1778) and *An Appeal to the People of the Massachusetts State against Arbitrary Power* (1780).[16] In both treatises, Backus responded to efforts of Massachusetts to include state control of religion in its state constitution after the Revolutionary War.

In 1778 Massachusetts leaders issued a proposed constitution, hastily compiled, which made no significant changes in the laws which had oppressed Baptists for generations. Backus had described the Revolution as a fight on two fronts, against the British troops for civil liberty and against establishment legislators for religious liberty. The proposed constitution appeared to limit the victory in the first category and negate the second altogether. At the request of the Grievance Committee, Backus prepared the treatise *Government and Liberty.* Defining "true religion" as a voluntary obedience unto God," Backus restated the familiar Baptist demand that government simply leave religion alone.[17]

Backus cleverly turned the authorities' arguments against them. He quot-

14. William G. McLoughlin, ed., *Isaac Backus on Church, State, and Calvinism: Pamphlets, 1754-1789,* p. 16.
15. Ibid., p. 30.
16. Ibid., pp. 345 *f.* and 385 *f.*
17. Ibid., p. 351.

ed Charles Chauncy, Congregational minister of Boston, who opposed the idea of an Anglican bishop exercising authority over others. Yet, said Backus, that was precisely what the Congregationalists sought to do to Baptists. To political leaders Backus showed clearly that Baptists also suffered taxation without representation when they were forced to support churches they did not attend and in which they did not believe. Backus quoted Roger Williams in favor of religious liberty, recalling that Williams "founded the first civil government, that ever established equal religious liberty, since the rise of Antichrist."[18] Apparently Backus regarded the struggle for religious liberty as the fundamental issue of the Revolution. He said, "It is well known that contests about the matter kindled this bloody war."[19] The proposed constitution of 1778 was defeated. Many credit Backus and the Baptists with large influence in that result.

In 1779 Massachusetts made another attempt to frame a state constitution, calling a convention of 293 delegates, including 5 Baptists, for that purpose. The resulting document appeared contradictory in that Article II seemed to provide religious freedom, while Article III specifically allowed, and under some circumstances required, the government to tax all citizens for the support of Protestant ministers. Once again, the Baptists asked Backus to be their spokesman in opposing the continued alignment of church and state. By conference and correspondence, Backus sought to influence the delegates to alter Article III; failing that he wrote *An Appeal to the People* in an effort to persuade the voters to reject the constitution. Though the constitution was adopted, and the article on establishment remained in effect until 1833, Backus made a strong case for the Baptist position.

In *An Appeal to the People,* Backus reviewed the Baptist arguments and efforts for religious freedom over the past generation. Noting that the authority of the civil magistrate should be limited to civil things, Backus agreed that ministers should be supported but by voluntary contributions and not by forced taxation.[20] To those who said Article III could benefit religion, Backus replied, "It asserts a right in the people of this State to make and execute laws about the worship of God, directly contrary to the truth which assures us that we have but ONE LAWGIVER in such affairs."[21] Backus also noted that the authorities "have raked up the German Anabaptists" to prove that Baptist views are dangerous and had described Baptists as "furious blind bigots." Backus dealt with these complaints by patiently reaffirming Baptists views of religious liberty.

McLoughlin raised a question about the basis for Backus's claims for religious liberty. He said:

18. Ibid., p. 355.
19. Ibid., p. 356.
20. Ibid., p. 391.
21. Ibid., p. 392.

The attitude toward separation of church and state held by Backus and the Separate-Baptists for whom he spoke evolved gradually from self-interest and experience. It had at first little relation either to the contemporary struggles and principles of English Baptists and other dissenters in Britain or to the struggles of Roger Williams.[22]

This would interpret Baptists' arguments for religious liberty, at least in New England, as based more on pragmatism than principle. According to this view, Backus at first saw no fundamental problems with religious establishment so long as all were treated equitably. In time, however, Backus came to see that Baptists would fare better on their own and what began as a matter of pragmatic preference gradually matured over the years to embody a principle of religious liberty for all.

There is no doubt that Backus, like others, formed some judgments gradually. He appealed often to Enlightenment concepts and pointed out the practical benefits of religious liberty. In this he followed in the footsteps of other Baptists, notably Thomas Helwys in England and Roger Williams in America, both of whom emphasized the benefits of liberty to society. However Backus arrived at his early convictions, one can hardly doubt that his mature position represented more than pragmatism, that a deeply held principle was involved.

Baptists Organized for Liberty

From the time of Roger Williams, Baptists in New England protested religious discrimination, but not until 1769 did they form a specific organization to give a united voice and concerted action to the struggle for liberty. In that year the Warren Association formed its famous Grievance Committee to direct the Baptist struggle for freedom. After 1772 Isaac Backus headed that committee, a post which made him the primary Baptist spokesman for religious liberty in New England. The Grievance Committee gathered data on Baptist sufferings, presented petitions for redress to various courts and legislatures, and pushed for legislation to alleviate religious discrimination. That committee probably qualifies as the first organized religious lobby in America. Baptists in America have a tradition not only of preaching and practicing religious liberty but also of monitoring government legislation to protect the interests of Baptists and others.

For a time Backus led the Grievance Committee to follow a brushfire approach; wherever persecution broke out, they tried to alleviate it. Through travel and correspondence, Backus gathered innumerable cases, had them "well-attested," and presented evidence before courts, judges, and assemblies. However, that process was time consuming, and the few victories won did not affect the system itself. In a bold move, Backus developed

22. Ibid., p. 17.

two new strategies. The first involved the idea of appealing not just to local authorities but to London itself. Backus placed the following notice in the *Boston Evening Post* of August 20, 1770:

> To the Baptists of the Province of Massachusetts Bay, who are, or have been oppressed in any way on a religious account. It would be needless to tell you that you have long felt the effects of the laws by which the religion of the government in which you live is established. Your purses have felt the burden of ministerial rates; and when these would not satisfy your enemies, your property hath been taken from you and sold for less than half its value. These things you cannot forget. You will therefore readily hear and attend, and when you are desired. . . . and bring or send such cases to the Baptist Association to be held at Bellingham; when measures will be resolutely adopted for obtaining redress from another quarter than that to which repeated application hath been made unsuccessfully.[23]

This appeal to "another quarter" was clear, and it caught the attention of Colonial authorities. For many reasons they wanted no discussion of their case in London. Many London leaders would have been only too happy to seize any pretext, including religion, to invalidate the Colonial charters. Thus the Baptist threat to present their appeals in London carried significant pressure. Baptists never actually carried out this threat, though at one time they raised money to send an agent to London.

An even more courageous course was adopted in 1773 when the Baptists decided simply to stop paying church taxes and stop applying for the exemption certificates altogether. They decided to ignore the human law in obedience to a higher law, the law of God. The record shows that, by that policy of civil disobedience, Baptists made more progress toward religious liberty in a year than they had made in the previous decade. The new policy apparently grew out of a meeting of the Grievance Committee in Boston on May 5, 1773, when several members reviewed the cases of Baptists who had obtained exemption certificates and still could not recover their church taxes. In a subsequent letter to the association, Backus complained that "liberty of conscience, the greatest and most important article [of] all liberty is evidently not allowed as it ought to be in this [cou]ntry" and offered that the root of these difficulties lies in "civil rulers assuming a (power) to make any laws to govern ecclesiastical affairs." He concluded:

> Therefore these are to desire you [to conside]r, whether it is not our duty to strike so directly at this root, [as to refu]se any conformity to their laws about such affairs, even [so much as] to give any certificates to their assessors; . . . . and if we may be enabled to treat our oppressors with a christian temper, would make straining upon others under a pretense of supporting religion,

23. Backus, 2:155.

appear so odious, that they could not get along with it.[24]

Some Baptists resisted the new policy; they had been law-abiding too long to take lightly to civil disobedience. However, in the end the Backus policy prevailed and won numerous concessions. Of course, the growing spirit of revolution in the colonies aided Backus's bold move. The concept of "taxation without representation" had become a battle cry against England. Baptists showed that the state church was treating Baptists and other Dissenters exactly as England was treating the colonies and that Baptists were taxed to support churches which they did not attend and in which they did not believe, "and that even by the very men who are now making loud [com]plaints of encroachments upon their own liberties."[25] Backus later said, "The worst treatment we [Baptists] here met with came from the same principles, and much of it from the same persons, as the American war did."[26] That point was reinforced by a resolution before the Warren Association in 1775 which said:

> Our real grievances are, that we, as well as our fathers, have, from time to time, been taxed on religious accounts where we were not represented;
> . . . . Is not all America now appealing to heaven against the injustice of being taxed where we are not represented, and against being judged by men who are interested in getting away our money? And will heaven approve of our *doing the same thing* to your fellow servants? No, surely.[27]

The growing spirit of revolt against England in the 1770s helped Baptists in a number of ways. First, American leaders wanted to head off any plan of Baptists to send agents to London to argue against the Colonial governments. Second, patriot complaints against English oppression were precisely the same as those of Baptists against state church oppression, as many came to realize. Third, Baptists had become so numerous that their support was essential if war came. The Colonial legislatures, faced with these factors plus Backus's flaunting of their certificates, had little choice but to make concessions to the Baptists.

In September 1774, the Warren Association sent a delegation, headed by Backus, to present their appeals for religious liberty before a committee of the Continental Congress then sitting in Philadelphia. In his *Diary* Backus recorded that "Mr. Manning and Mr. Hezekiah Smith were arnest [earnest] with me to go to Philadelphia, and see if something might not be done to secure our religious liberties beyond what we have yet enjoyed." The association unanimously backed this project and contributed money for expenses. "So I purchased a beast for the purpose," Backus wrote, "and

---

24. William G. McLoughlin, ed., *The Diary of Isaac Backus,* 3:1595-1596.
25. Ibid., p. 1595.
26. Backus, 2:197.
27. Ibid., p. 203n, emphasis his.

Monday Sept. 26, Tho' in an infirm state of Body, yet being persuaded of duty, I set off, and met with elders Gano and Van Horn at Providence."[28]

The Baptist delegation received discouragement from several sources, including both the Quakers and Baptists of the Philadelphia area, both of which groups urged the Backus delegation not to appear before the Continental Congress. Before 1776 Baptists of the Philadelphia Association appear much cooler toward the patriot cause than their fellow churchmen in New England and the South, due perhaps in part to the influence of Morgan Edwards. The Backus delegation persisted, though they did not obtain a hearing before the full Congress. They appeared before a subcommittee composed of Massachusetts delegates John Adams, Samuel Adams, Robert T. Paine, and Thomas Cushing. James Manning led off by reading a *Memorial* from the Warren Association, setting out Baptist sufferings and concluding that, "as a distinct denomination of Protestants, we conceive that we have an equal claim to charter-rights with the rest of our fellow-subjects; and yet have long been denied the free and full enjoyment of those rights."[29] After particularly reviewing Baptist mistreatment at Sturbridge and Ashfield, the *Memorial* concluded:

> It may now be asked, *What is the liberty desired?* The answer is. As the Kingdom of Christ is not of this world, and religion is a concern between God and the soul, with which no human authority can intermeddle, consistently with the principles of Christianity, and according to the dictates of Protestantism, we claim and expect the liberty of worshipping God according to our consciences, not being obliged to support a ministry we cannot attend, whilst we demean ourselves as faithful subjects.[30]

However, the delegates stoutly denied the Baptist claims, seeking to show they had no cause for complaint. Both John and Samuel Adams made long speeches, both of whom said, "There is, indeed, an ecclesiastical establishment in our province; but a very slender one, hardly to be called an establishment."[31] In his *Diary*, Backus later recorded:

> Mr. S. Adams tried to represent that regular baptists were easy among us, and more than once insinuated that these complaints came from enthuseasts who made a merit of suffering persecution, . . . And Mr. Paine said there was nothing of conscience in the matter; twas only a contention about paying a little money.[32]

The conference concluded about 11:00 PM, with the delegates promising to look into the Baptist complaints more fully. However, John Adams

28. McLoughlin, *Diary*, 2:913.
29. Backus, 2:200n.
30. Ibid., p. 201n, emphasis his.
31. Ibid.
32. McLoughlin, *Diary*, 2:917.

warned that "[Baptists] might as well expect a change in the solar system, as to expect they would give up their establishment." Thus far the solar system has endured, but religious establishment in Massachusetts gave way in 1833, over forty years after adoption of the First Amendment.

Freedoms Achieved

Backus lived to see Baptists achieve religious liberty in practice, if not always in law. He struggled unsuccessfully against Article III in the Massachusetts constitution of 1780, which gave the government some jurisdiction over religion. However, the federal Constitution adopted in 1789, and especially the Bill of Rights added in 1791, gave the Baptists more legal basis for religious freedom.

Not all favored the proposed Constitution when it first appeared. The citizens were sharply divided between those dubbed "rats" (for ratification) and "anti-rats" (who opposed). Backus was a strong "rat," though many Baptists were "anti-rats." Backus is usually credited with helping achieve ratification in Massachusetts and, indeed, in other New England states. The force of the new Constitution and its amendments; the achievement of religious liberty in the other states, particularly in Virginia; the commendable support of the Baptists in the Revolutionary War; and the growing unpopularity of religious coercion, combined to help Baptists achieve their goal of liberty. However, some state church leaders felt quite peevish about the new liberties, and they conducted a rear-guard harrassment of Baptists for over a generation.

Religious Liberty in the Middle Colonies

An entirely different situation prevailed in the Middle Colonies, where no church was established by law and, for the most part, religious freedom obtained from the first. For a time the Dutch in what was then called New Netherlands sought to restrict others, but that proved a passing thing. At times the less conventional forms of religion, such as held by Jews, anti-Trinitarians, and atheists, faced problems even in the tolerant Middle Colonies, but these were exceptions that proved the general rule of toleration. At times Baptists had to license their meeting houses, as in early New York, and faced some public harrassment; but they enjoyed greater freedom in Pennsylvania than perhaps anywhere else in the country. Therefore, Baptists had a place to develop their strength and theology largely without hindrance, providing spiritual stability that later spilled over to other areas.

Background of Toleration

Two factors best account for the broad religious freedom allowed in the Middle Colonies: the Quaker influence and the religious pluralism that prevailed in that area. William Penn, who had turned Quaker, received a vast land grant in America from King Charles II in payment for a debt owed to Penn's father. The fertile territory quickly attracted settlers of all sorts. Penn brought a large contingent of Quakers, establishing Philadelphia as the "city of brotherly love." True to their heritage, the Quakers both preached and practiced religious freedom in the new area, welcoming those who differed with them.

Quite early the Middle Colonies included both Catholics and Protestants of several varieties, but none had a majority sufficient to dominate. Such pluralism made religious toleration a practical necessity.

Benefits to Baptists

Baptists were among those who benefited from toleration. In two ways the Middle Colonies furthered the Baptist struggle for religious liberty. First, this area provided a model, a living laboratory of society as Baptists claimed it could be organized. There religious liberty was not mere theory but daily practice, and society flourished. Many had argued that government-sponsored religion was essential to a well-ordered civil state, that church, commerce, and government could not survive without religious establishment. The Middle Colonies, especially Pennsylvania, provided a convincing example to the contrary.

Second, the Middle Colonies provided a haven where Baptists could flee when persecution became too severe elsewhere. From this area, much of the Baptist evangelization of the South was launched, particularly from churches of the Philadelphia Association. The area functioned to some extent as a safety valve for Baptist pressures to the North and South, and as such it was not particularly popular among authorities in either area. For a stern New England Puritan, to "go to the Dutch" (i.e., to move to the easygoing New Amsterdam settlements) represented a moral as well as a geographical removal and contributed a vivid metaphor to the language.

Religious Liberty in the Southern Colonies

The religious situation in the South differed greatly from the other two major regions. The Anglican Church (Episcopal) was established by law, with its main strength limited to Virginia and parts of South Carolina. Elsewhere it was established more in name than in fact and lacked power to enforce its system. From its earliest settlement, Virginia passed laws harshly restricting Dissenters, but the laws were not always strictly enforced. However, by the 1750s opposition escalated to severe religious persecution, directed primarily against the Separate Baptists who entered the South in numbers at about that time.

Baptists and Presbyterians led the struggle for religious liberty in the South, along with statesmen like Thomas Jefferson, James Madison, and Patrick Henry. Baptists endured severe hardships, especially the Separates, but won a significant victory that affected the entire nation. Virginia adopted religious liberty by 1786, several years before the federal Constitution was ratified. The Virginia example led a number of other states to write religious liberty into their constitutions and probably influenced the inclusion of similar provisions in the federal Constitution and Bill of Rights that followed.

Baptists faced problems on the requirement to register their meeting-houses, the refusal of authorities to recognize the validity of Baptist-performed marriages, and their requirement to pay tithes in tobacco and other crops for the support of Anglican ministers. John Leland was the primary Baptist spokesman for religious liberty in the South, and the General Committee of Virginia, first formed in 1784, provided the major organization through which Baptist efforts were correlated.

Restrictions on Religion

Anglican worship came to Virginia with the first settlers. Captain John Smith later recalled, "When I went first to Virginia, I well remember wee did hang an awning (which is an old saile) to three or four trees to shadow us from the Sunne, our walles were rales of wood, our seats unhewed trees, our Pulpit a bar of wood nailed to two neighboring trees." Even in these primitive circumstances, Smith continued, "wee had daily Common Prayer morning and evening, every Sunday two sermons, and every three moneths the holy Communion, till our Minister died."[33] As early as 1611 Governor Thomas Dale instituted strict laws requiring all citizens to conform to the Anglican Church in belief and conduct. Incoming settlers were required to "repair unto the Minister," there to "give up an account of his or their faith, and religion."[34] Whippings, fines, and bodily mutilation were prescribed for those who failed to attend church or spoke against its doctrines. These laws proved fiercer on the books than in practice but left no doubt that religious dissent would not be tolerated.

Throughout the 1600s, the Virginia colony added various laws to reinforce the Anglican Church and plug any loopholes which might have allowed Dissenters to gain a foothold there. A new law in 1624 required "an uniformity in our church as neere as may be to the canons in England," and each "tithable" (head of family) was required to contribute so much tobacco and other crops to support the clergy. Later laws spelled out that "noe minister be admitted to officiate in this country" except those "conformable to the orders and constitutions of the church of England."[35] The Tobacco Laws, by which the clergy were supported, proved especially unpopular. After the restoration of the English king in 1660, the laws in Virginia were

33. Peter G. Mode, ed., *Source Book and Bibliographical Guide to American Church History*, p. 10.
34. H. Shelton Smith, Robert T. Handy, and Lefferts A. Loetscher, eds., *American Christianity*, 1:44.
35. Ibid., p. 50.

tightened even more. Some settlers who felt little enthusiasm for the Anglican Church were obliged to leave the colony, and Quakers were severely punished and exiled. In 1662 the Colonial government passed the following statute, leading some to believe that a few Baptists had arrived by that time.

> Whereas many schismaticall persons out of their aversenesse to the orthodox established religion, or out of the new fangled conceits of their owne hereticall inventions, refuse to have their children baptised, Be it therefore enacted by the authority aforesaid, that all persons that, in contempt of the divine sacrament of baptisme, shall refuse when they may carry their child to a lawfull minister in that county to have them baptised, shall be amerced two thousand pounds of tobacco; halfe to the informer and halfe to the publique.[36]

In spite of such statutes, dissent grew, both within and without that church. In time the Act of Toleration was applied in Virginia; in 1699 Francis Makemie, a Presbyterian, was granted a license to preach in Virginia.[37]

From 1700 to about 1750, the records reveal little public turmoil over religion in the South. The few dissenters in the South were not growing and thus represented no threat to the established church. They adhered generally to terms of the Act of Toleration. Therefore, they were usually left alone, especially in frontier settlements where they provided some buffer against hostile Indians.

However, religious persecution took on a new intensity in the 1750s, which continued to the end of the Revolution. In this wave of persecution, Baptists suffered most. Two trends help account for the escalation in religious coercion. First, Revolutionary sentiment had put the Anglican Church on the defensive. Its monopoly was threatened, and its connection with England hurt at a time when England was increasingly unpopular. Most of the Anglican clergy were worldly or worse, and their financial exactions created an undercurrent of resentment and resistance. Church leaders felt it necessary to move vigorously to reassert their historic dominance.

Second, the Separate Baptists entered Virginia in force in the late 1750s and early 1760s. The new Baptists, unlike some of the older dissenters, proved aggressive and militant. They swarmed over the country, appealing to the common folk. They disdained the state church and its license laws, preaching in obedience to a higher law. And worse yet, they grew rapidly. The stately Anglican churches, with their allegiance to England, were almost emptied as the new dissenters won multitudes of converts. These factors combined to introduce a generation of intense religious persecution in the South, centering in Virginia. Baptists, who were perhaps the chief cause of the escalation, bore the brunt of its fury.

---

36. Cited in Lewis P. Little, *Imprisoned Preachers and Religious Liberty in Virginia,* p. 6.
37. Ibid., p. 12.

Beginning in the 1760s, Baptists in Virginia were whipped, fined, beaten by mobs, jailed, and/or exiled in an attempt to control them. Between 1768 and 1777, at least thirty Baptist preachers in Virginia were imprisoned, whipped, or stoned. Most of these were Separates. Apparently Lewis Craig was the first Baptist preacher hauled before the court for preaching in Virginia. At his indictment, Craig said: "I thank you, gentlemen of the grandjury, for the honour you have done me. While I was wicked and injurious, you took no notice of me; but since I have altered my course of life, and endeavored to reform my neighbors, you concern yourselves much about me."[38]

The grand jury that indicted Craig included John Waller, known as "Swearing Jack" before his conversion. The testimony of Craig deeply impressed Waller, who soon professed conversion and joined the Baptists. In 1768 Waller was included with Craig and several other Baptists who were cast into the Fredericksburg jail in Spotsylvania County for preaching. This was the first recorded imprisonment of Baptists in Virginia, but many other examples followed.

David Thomas, one of the ablest of Virginia Baptist preachers, endured his share of persecution. Historian David Benedict said:

> Outrageous mobs and individuals frequently assaulted and disturbed him. Once he was pulled down as he was preaching, and dragged out of doors in a barbarous manner. At another time a malevolent fellow attempted to shoot him, but a by-stander wrenched the gun from him, and thereby prevented the execution of his wicked purpose.[39]

Thomas served as pastor of the Broad Run church, where he was later succeeded by Amos Thompson. The circumstances of their friendship were unusual. In his old age Thomas became less patient with the mobs who often beat him up for preaching, so he called for help from the young preacher, Amos Thompson. Thompson was described as a man of gigantic frame, whose strength was prodigious. Thomas had been threatened with a severe beating if he preached again, so he invited Thompson to preach in his place. The records state that "a great multitude had assembled, some to hear the preacher, and some to see the sport, for the ruffians had sworn that they would beat up old Thomas."[40] But it was not "old Thomas" they faced. An observer reported, "A company armed with bludgeons entered the house, and took their position just before the pulpit; but when they saw the brawny arm and undaunted appearance of the preacher, they became alarmed and

38. Ibid., p. 54.

39. David Benedict, *A General History of the Baptist Denomination in America and Other Parts of the World,* 2 vols. (Boston: Manning and Loring, 1813), 2:30-31.

40. Little, p. 43.

permitted the service to go on to its conclusion."[41]

Samuel Harris, the Separate Baptist "Apostle to Virginia," also faced persecution. On one occasion, he was arrested while preaching in Culpeper County and charged with disturbing the peace. In court he was called "a vagabond, a heretic, and a mover of sedition every where," but was told that he could be released upon his agreement not to preach in that county again for a year and a day. Harris agreed, saying that since he lived over 200 miles away it was unlikely he would be back that way in a year. After his release, Harris attended a meeting where other Separate Baptists were preaching. This proved too much, for

> the word of God began to burn in Col. Harris' heart. When they finished, he arose and addressed the congregation, "I partly promised the devil, a few days past, at the courthouse, that I would not preach in this county again for the term of a year; but the devil is a perfidious wretch, and covenants with him are not to be kept, and therefore I will preach."[42]

Not only were Baptist preachers subject to arrest but those who allowed them to preach on their property could also be subject to heavy fines. Once when James Ireland was to preach at the home of a certain Mr. Manifa, who had been threatened with a fine of £20, Ireland set a table directly across Manifa's property line. When the authorities came, he simply retreated to the other end of the table and claimed, quite rightly, that he was not preaching on Manifa's land. This strategy attracted a large attendance but did not prevent the arrest of Jamie Ireland. He said:

> I heard a rustling noise in the woods and before I could open my eyes [from prayer] to see who it was, I was seized by the collar by two men while standing on the table—they told me that I must give security not to teach, preach, or exhort for twelve months and a day or I must go to jail. . . . They browbeat me . . . would admit of no defense I could make, but ordered me to hold my tongue and let them hear no more of my vile, pernicious, abhorrible, detestable, abominable, diabolical doctrines, for they were nauseous to the whole court.[43]

From jail Ireland preached through the bars to throngs who assembled to hear the "tabletop" preacher. The Anglican authorities were especially embarrassed by this and sought to break up the crowds of listeners. Horsemen would gallop through the crowds gathered in the street, and at times black slaves would be beaten until the preacher agreed to cease. On one occasion, the mob tried to blow up the jail and later placed "Indian red pepper" near the door and set it afire so the "killing smoke" would enter the tightly enclosed cell. However, Ireland put his mouth to cracks in the

41. Ibid.
42. Ibid., p. 48.
43. Cited in Benjamin P. Browne, *Tales of Baptist Daring*, p. 40.

wall and thus drew in fresh air from outside to survive.[44]

A typical example of Baptist suffering occurred in Middlesex County in the summer of 1771. In a letter from the Urbanna Prison, John Waller described the incident as follows:

> At a meeting which was held at Brother McCan's, in this county, last Saturday, while Brother William Webber was addressing the congregation from James ii., 18, there came running toward him, in a most furious rage, Captain James Montague, a magistrate of the county, followed by the parson of the parish and several others, who seemed greatly exasperated. The magistrate and another took hold of Brother Webber, and dragging him from the stage, delivered him, with Brethren Wafford, Robert Ware, Richard Faulkner, James Greenwood and myself, into custody. . . . Brother Wafford was severely scourged, and Brother Henry Street received one lash from one of the persecutors. . . . the parson and some others, carried us one by one into a room and examined our pockets and wallets for fire-arms, &c., charging us with carrying on a meeting against the authority of the land.[45]

Similar examples could be multiplied at length. Almost always the imprisoned preachers took opportunity to preach through the jail bars to crowds who assembled on the streets outside. Given the growing Revolutionary sentiment, the connection of the Anglican Church with England, and the almost universal unpopularity of the Anglican clergy, one is not surprised that the preaching of these earnest men won a wide hearing. Their jail-house preaching proved so popular that many authorities dismissed the prisoners early or even contrived for them to "escape." Others tried to curtail such preaching by refusing the prisoners food, but when the people heard they brought so much food to the jail that the preachers had an abundance to share with the poor of the area. The Baptists also won some powerful political allies, including the Virginia lawyer Patrick Henry, who is said to have defended Baptist preachers on several occasions.

Scholars are not certain that any law in Virginia really allowed the imprisonment of anyone for preaching, and yet about thirty or more Baptists suffered that fate. Alarmed by the decline of the state church and the rapid growth of Baptists, both civil and ecclesiastical authorities "strained every penal law in the Virginia code to obtain ways and means to put down these disturbers of the peace."[46] Though arrested while preaching and for preaching, many of the Baptists were imprisoned or fined for other offenses, such as disturbing the peace or creating a public nuisance. Some parents were fined for "parental cruelty" in withholding their infants from baptism, and the authorities also dusted off old and seldom-used laws requiring all citizens to attend the Anglican Church.

44. Ibid., p. 41.
45. Cited in Robert Baylor Semple, *History of Baptists in Virginia*, pp. 481-482.
46. Ibid., p. 29.

Under provisions of the Act of Toleration, Baptists, along with others, were eligible for toleration so long as they registered their meetinghouses. In fact, most of the Presbyterians and Regular Baptists used this means to avoid the worst of persecution. However, it was not so simple for the Separates. For one thing, those who applied for registration were often scolded by their own people for having yielded to Caesar. Further, the law provided for the registration of dissenter meetinghouses, but many of the Separates had no such houses; they met in homes, barns, and even under trees. The Anglicans would often certify only one dissenter meeting in each county, usually allotting it to Presbyterians. Further, Baptists who applied for the registration had to ride to Williamsburg where the court sat. Sometimes they waited in vain for days, only to be told that the court had recessed and would not reconvene for a half year. Most of the Separates, like their fellow-Baptists in New England, decided to ignore the certificates and preach the gospel in obedience to a higher law. To this extent they were legally lawbreakers.

Another point at which Baptists felt severely restricted was in the refusal of the authorities to recognize the validity of Baptist-performed marriages. Baptist couples had to be married by an Anglican minister, who would sometimes use pressure to proselyte them away from Baptists. The marriage fee required by such ministers also seemed quite exorbitant. Both from lack of money and lack of access to Anglican ministers in parts of the backcountry, Baptist young people were almost prohibited from forming legal marriages. Many feared that if they accepted Baptist marriage, their children would be disqualified from inheriting or holding property. However, Patrick Henry advised the Baptists to perform their own marriages and fill up the country with Baptists, so that the state would be forced to recognize their validity.

John Leland (1754-1841)

John Leland ranks as the primary Baptist spokesman in the South for religious liberty. He was born in Massachusetts and lived there most of his life, except for fifteen fruitful years in Virginia from 1776-1791. Those happened to be the most crucial years in the struggle for religious liberty, and Leland helped organize the Baptists and articulated their views on that subject. Known as a shrewd, witty, and somewhat eccentric man, Leland embraced with fervor the views of Separate Baptists. Leland's gifts fitted him best for the role of traveling evangelist and agitator, though he served briefly as pastor. Though he lacked formal education, Leland possessed a keen mind and read widely, making himself one of the best-informed Baptist ministers of the time. During his years in Virginia, he preached 3,009 sermons and baptized 1,278 converts.[47]

47. Jack Manly, "Leland, John," *Encyclopedia of Southern Baptists* (Nashville: Broadman Press, 1958), 2:783.

In 1776 Leland married Sallie Devine, a gifted young woman who fully shared his beliefs. She once saved his life by grabbing the arm of a man who sought to cut Leland down with a sword while he preached.[48] In Virginia, Leland also worked toward improving the lot of slaves and eventually toward emancipation, composed hymns, and wrote on devotional and theological subjects. He proved a capable interpreter of Jeffersonian politics and ideals to the common folk of the time. As his writings make clear, Leland combined the best of both the awakening and the Enlightenment. In theology he held a Calvinism more modified than some Baptists preferred. He often said that the best theology had enough Calvinism to believe man was lost and enough Arminianism to believe he could be saved. As a messenger of the Philadelphia Association, Leland helped spread moderate views among Baptists in the South. After his return to Massachusetts, Leland turned more to writing. In his diary, he expressed amazement that he had lived so long, describing himself as "an old grey-headed sinner."[49]

Perhaps Leland's major treatise on religious liberty was *The Rights of Conscience Inalienable,* first published in 1791. This hard-hitting defense of full religious liberty represented the mature culmination of Leland's thought. The longer title is quite descriptive: *The Rights of Conscience Inalienable, and Therefore, Religious Opinions not Cognizable by Law; or, The High-Flying Churchman, Stripped of His Legal Robe, Appears a Yaho.*[50] In this treatise, Leland argued three basic points: (1) that the rights of conscience are inalienable, not subject to either government permission or restriction; (2) that establishment of religion by law always damages religion; and (3) that the real motives for establishment are not to benefit religion but to buttress the power of civil rulers and augment the purses of ambitious clergy.

Leland said the rights of conscience are inalienable, for "every man must give an account of himself to God, and therefore every man ought to be at liberty to serve God in a way that he can best reconcile to his conscience."[51] One must not surrender to man what should be kept sacred to God, and especially one must not bind the consciences of those yet unborn. "Religion is a matter between God and individuals," concluded Leland, with "the religious opinions of men not being the objects of civil government, nor in any way under its control."

Religious establishments always corrupt both church and state, Leland said. They make the "uninspired, fallible" systems of men the final measure of faith. Such establishments alienate the people from each other, and

---

48. L. F. Greene, ed., *The Writings of John Leland* (New York: Arno Press, 1969), p. 27.
49. Ibid., p. 35.
50. First published in New London, Connecticut, 1791. Reprinted in Greene, pp. 179-192.
51. Ibid., p. 181.

ultimately from God himself. They tend, Leland said, to "metamorphose the church into a creature, and religion into a principle of state, . . . while preaching is made a trade of emolument."[52]

To those who feared Christianity would perish without state support, Leland maintained, "It is error, and error alone, that needs human support."[53] The real motive for establishments, he said, was a desire "to dictate to others. . . . to have a halter around the necks of others." By using government to favor the church, the Emperor Constantine did more harm than all the persecuting emperors, thought Leland.

Leland agreed that government could punish persons whose behavior broke out in "religious phrenzy" to harm others, but only for their actions, not their beliefs. Truth can take care of itself, needing no civil ruler to steady the ark of God. Leland concluded:

> Government has no more to do with the religious opinions of men, than it has with the principles of mathematics. Let every man speak freely without fear, maintain the principles that he believes, worship according to his own faith, either one God, three Gods, no God, or twenty Gods; and let government protect him in so doing.[54]

The Baptist Petition Movement

As one means to push their case for religious liberty, Baptists presented numerous petitions to the Virginia legislature. These varied from a few paragraphs to a few pages and dealt with one or more grievances Baptists faced in the restrictions upon their religious activities. Occasionally an individual church might send a petition, especially on behalf of an imprisoned pastor, but most petitions were framed by one of the four Baptist associations in the state. In 1784 Virginia Baptists agreed to send a number of delegates from each association to form a General Committee and, for the sake of making a greater impact by speaking with one voice, agreed that henceforth only the General Committee would petition the legislature. The General Committee was authorized to work on behalf of religious liberty and other causes of interest to the denomination at large. It commanded greater allegiance in the former than the latter; after the winning of religious liberty, the committee lapsed.

The Baptist petitions, numerous as they were, usually followed a common format. They identified the group for whom they spoke and included a profession of civil loyalty and allegiance. They then set out specific problems Baptists faced in restrictions upon their religious practices, such as taxation to pay the Anglican clergy, requirement to register their meeting-

52. Ibid., p. 183.
53. Ibid., p. 185.
54. Ibid., p. 184.

houses and the endless red tape involved, and refusal of the authorities to acknowledge the validity of their marriages.

Having set out the problems, the petitions then set out proposed solutions. The Baptists always asked that the government leave religion alone. They no more wanted laws favoring than laws opposing them. They asked for no government encouragement, preference, or assistance. They asked that the government attend to its proper civil and economic duties and simply leave religion alone. To Baptists that seemed both scriptural and practical; but to many reared in the state church tradition, it seemed too radical to comprehend.

In August 1775, the General Association, convened at Dupuy's meeting-house, addressed the following petition to the Virginia Convention, then sitting at Richmond. Having identified themselves and claimed the rights common to loyal citizens, the Baptists said:

> Alarmed at the shocking Oppression which in a British Cloud hangs over our American Continent, we, as a Society and part of the distressed State, have in our Association consider'd what part might be most prudent for the Baptists to act in the present unhappy Contest. After we had determined "that in some Cases it was lawful to go to War, and also for us to make a Military resistance against Great Britain, in regard of their unjust Invasion, and tyrannical Oppression of, and repeated Hostilities against America," our people were all left to act at Discretion with respect to inlisting without falling under the Censure of our Community.[55]

Such an affirmation of military participation did not come easy for Baptists. A few opposed war, and others felt they might win more concessions by pitching in on the British side. However, the loyalty professed in this petition was important to Colonial political leaders who had a war to fight and needed recruits. The Baptists used this advantage to press for more concessions. The same petition continues:

> And as some [Baptists] have inlisted, and many more likely to do so, who will have earnest Desires for their Ministers to preach to them during the Campaign, we therefore deligate and appoint our well-beloved Brethren in the Ministry, Elijah Craig, Lewis Craig, Jeremiah Walker and John Williams to present this address and to petition you that they may have free Liberty to preach to the Troops at convenient Times without molestation or abuse.[56]

Nothing better illustrates the Baptists' use of political pressure, in the South as well as in New England, to gain a greater measure of religious liberty. Given their need for loyal troops, the Colonial legislature had little choice but to grant the Baptist petition, which they speedily did. All the fulminations of state church clergy and the cautions of conservative churchmen in

55. Semple, p. 493.
56. Ibid.

the legislature could not overcome the practical need of the hour, which was for a united American front against Britain. Many of the Baptist victories in their quest for freedom came not as a result of doctrinal persuasion but simply as practical and political necessities.

A similar petition was presented to the Virginia Convention by "sundry persons of the Baptist Church in the county of Prince William," who said:

> at a time when this Colony, with the others, is contending for the civil rights of mankind against the enslaving schemes of a powerful enemy, they are persuaded the strictest unanimity is necessary among ourselves; and, that every remaining cause of division may, if possible, be removed, they think it their duty to petition for the following religious privileges, which they have not yet been indulged. . . . That they be allowed to worship God in their own way, without interruption; that they be permitted to maintain their own ministers, and none others; that they may be married, buried and the like without paying the clergy of other denominations; that, these things granted, they will gladly unite with their brethren to the utmost of their ability to promote the common cause.[57]

A petition from the Baptist Association meeting at Sandy Creek in Charlotte County, October 1780, showed that the end of the war left Baptists still with some grievances. While grateful for the "heaven-born Freedom" which had already been obtained, Baptists pointed out limitations that still denied them full religious liberty. They said:

> As Religious Oppression, or the interferring with the Rights of Conscience, which God has made accountable to none but Himself, is of all Oppression the most inhuman and insupportable, and as Partiality to any Religious Denomination is its genuine offspring, your Memorialists have with Grief observed that Religious Liberty has not made a single Advance in this Commonwealth without some Opposition.

They called for "the Completion of Religious Liberty" and concluded by asking the government to "consign to Oblivion all the Relicks of Religious Oppression."[58]

The legislature took the petitions seriously. They realized that Baptists were numerous and growing, that their political loyalty could be assured if only they might enjoy religious liberty, and that Baptists raised many of the same arguments against an oppressive church establishment that the colonies advanced against England. In that atmosphere, the Baptist petitions clearly exercised a significant impact.

57. Ibid., pp. 494-495.
58. Ibid., pp. 497, 499.

The General Assessment Bill

In their search for a compromise between establishment and radical demands for religious liberty, some suggested the idea of a "general assessment" for religion. All citizens would be taxed for the support of religion but could designate the denomination to which their taxes would go. The idea of a general assessment had been considered off and on since the 1770s, but resurfaced as a serious option in 1784 when the legislature considered "a bill establishing provision for the teachers of the Christian religion." The bill passed the first two readings and seemed on the verge of becoming law. Had it succeeded, the relation of church and state in this country might have turned out quite differently.

The general assessment bill gained broad support, including Patrick Henry and George Washington among the statesmen and leaders of both Presbyterian and Anglican churches. Henry thought the bill eminently fair to all. The Presbyterians seemed as eager to support an establishment that included them as they had been to oppose one that shut them out. The Anglicans generally supported the idea, not as the ideal but as the best they could do in the Revolutionary environment of Colonial America. They felt their church would still occupy a favored place under that system, as no doubt it would have.

However, the Baptists never wavered in demanding separation of church and state. They spoke out as strongly against a government assessment that might benefit them as they had against earlier assessments to their hurt. Most historians credit the opposition of the Baptists with derailing this popular proposal. Robert Semple recorded the response of the General Committee of Virginia Baptists:

> Resolved, That it be recommended to those counties which have not yet prepared petitions to be presented to the General Assembly against the engrossed bill for a general assessment for the support of the teachers of the Christian religion, to proceed thereon as soon as possible; that it is believed to be repugnant to the spirit of the Gospel for the Legislature thus to proceed in matters of religion; that no human laws ought to be established for this purpose; but that every person ought to be left entirely free in respect to matters of religion; that the holy Author of our religion needs no such compulsive measures for the promotion of His cause; that the Gospel wants not the feeble arm of man for its support; that it has made, and will again through divine power, make its way against all opposition; and that should the Legislature assume the right of taxing people for the support of the Gospel, it will be destructive to religious liberty.
>
> Therefore, This committee agrees unanimously that it will be expedient to appoint a delegate to wait on the General Assembly with a remonstrance and petition against such assessment.[59]

59. Ibid., p. 96.

In opposing a general assessment for religion, Baptists had the firm support of James Madison. In 1784 he brought out "A Memorial and Remonstrance on the Religious Rights of Man."[60] This magnificent statement gathers up the best American thinking on church-state relations to that time. Madison outlined fifteen arguments against general assessment and in favor of complete religious liberty, citing a "fundamental and undeniable truth" that "religion, or the duty which we owe to our creator, and the manner of discharging it, can be directed only by reason and conviction and conscience of every man."[61] Though the term *separation of church and state* was not yet in common usage, that is what Madison called for in his statement that religion should be "wholly exempt" from the realm of government.[62] Madison's arguments, stated in language simple but profound, sounded the death knell for general assessment in Virginia and probably in several other states as well.

The next year, 1785, Thomas Jefferson introduced a "bill for Establishing Religious Freedom" in Virginia. It passed the legislature with the support of Madison, having also been strongly supported by the Baptists. That bill was one of only three accomplishments for which Jefferson wished to be remembered, along with the Declaration of Independence and establishing the University of Virginia. Noting that "Almighty God hath created the mind free," this bill said:

> Be it enacted by the General Assembly, That no man shall be compelled to frequent or support any religious worship, place or ministry whatsoever, nor shall be enforced, restrained, molested, or burthened in his body of goods, nor shall otherwise suffer on account of his religious opinions or beliefs; but that all men shall be free to profess, and by argument maintain, their opinions in matters of religion, and that the same shall in no wise diminish, enlarge, or affect their civil capacities.[63]

The bill passed handily and settled the issue of religious liberty in Virginia. Details remained to be worked out, particularly relating to the glebe lands of the Anglican Church, but the basic issue of disestablishment and full liberty for all was no longer in doubt. Virginia's action provided a powerful precedent which influenced a number of other states and helped bring similar liberty throughout the new nation.

Religion in the Federal Constitution

The task of linking a group of independent colonies into one united nation proved more difficult than many expected. When the military portion of the American Revolution ended with victory for the patriot cause, the task of

---

60. Printed in Ferm, pp. 120-127.
61. Ibid., p. 120.
62. Ibid., p. 121.
63. Cited in Reuben E. Alley, *A History of Baptists in Virginia*, pp. 372-373.

creating a new nation had just begun. After extensive writing and rewriting, the proposed new federal Constitution first appeared in 1787, and the country was divided on its merits. Baptists were shocked that the document said nothing about religious liberty, indeed, that it said so little about religion at all. They had widely regarded the war as a struggle for both civil and religious rights and feared that the new Constitution did not adequately guarantee either.

The Constitution itself, other than two or three incidental references to the "Deity," contains only one statement of substance relating to religion. Article VI provides that "no religious Test shall ever be required as a Qualification to any Office or public Trust under the United States." To the leaders who framed the Constitution, that seemed a broad and sufficient guarantee of religious freedom. Significantly, there is no recorded discussion of a broader provision at the Constitutional Convention. This relative silence about religion in the Constitution was apparently intentional. John Adams had expressed the hope that "Congress will never meddle with religion further than to say its own prayers, and to fast and give thanks once a year."[64]

Baptist opposition to the new Constitution surfaced immediately. When their Virginia General Committee met on March 7, 1788, one of the questions considered was: "Whether the new Federal Constitution, which had now lately made its appearance in public, made sufficient provision for the secure enjoyment of religious liberty." After extensive study and discussion, "it was agreed unanimously that, in the opinion of the General Committee, it did not."[65] The next year, 1789, the committee appointed John Leland to write President Washington about Baptists' concerns. Leland wrote:

> When the Constitution made its first appearance in Virginia, we, as a society, had unusual strugglings of mind, fearing that the liberty of conscience, dearer to us than property or life, was not sufficiently secured. Perhaps our jealousies were heightened by the usage we received in Virginia under regal government, when mobs, fines, bonds and prisons were our frequent repast.[66]

Baptists feared further oppression, according to Leland, since "religious liberty is rather insecure in the Constitution." However, they staked their hopes on the character of President Washington. Leland wrote, "The Administration will certainly prevent all oppression, for a *Washington* will preside."[67]

Washington's gracious letter of reply to the Baptists' General Committee

64. Madison Papers, Library of Congress, quoted in Leo Pfeffer, *Church, State and Freedom* (Boston: Beacon Press, 1953), p. 110.
65. Semple, p. 102.
66. Cited in Joseph M. Dawson, *Baptists and the American Republic,* p. 116.
67. Ibid., p. 116, emphasis Dawson's.

sought to reassure them. "If I could have entertained the slightest apprehension," he wrote, "that the Constitution framed in the convention, where I had the honor to preside, might possibly endanger the religious rights of any ecclesiastical society, certainly I would never have placed my signature to it."[68] Washington repeated his own confidence that the Constitution adequately protected the religious rights of all and concluded, "I beg you will be persuaded that no one would be more zealous than myself to establish effectual barriers against the horrors of spiritual tyranny, and every species of religious persecution."[69]

However welcome those assurances, they missed the point of the Baptists' concern. Baptists were troubled by the fact that the Constitution itself did not spell out the rights that Washington affirmed and well they knew that Washington would not always preside.

At first Madison appeared to share the judgment that the Constitution provided adequate guarantees of religious liberty. In January 1789, he wrote, "I have never seen in the Constitution as it now stands those serious dangers which have alarmed many respectable citizens."[70] Thomas Jefferson, however, felt some concern about omissions from the Constitution. Writing from Paris, he commended the overall document but said, "I will now add what I do not like. First, the omission of a bill of rights providing clearly and without the aid of sophisms for freedom of religion, freedom of the press, . . . [A] bill of rights is what the people are entitled to against every government on earth."[71]

Virginia Baptists felt strongly enough about the omission of overt guarantees of religious liberty that they mounted a campaign to prevent ratification of the Constitution. Exactly what the Baptists did is not clear. Some accounts say John Leland entered the race for election to the ratifying convention, while others name James Barbour as the candidate chosen to oppose Madison. In several counties Baptists controlled the "swing" vote; many thought Madison, and the Constitution, could be defeated. At the request of James Barbour, Leland wrote a list of Baptist objections to the Constitution. To Madison's request for a copy, Leland wrote, "Sir, According to your request I here send you my objections to the Federal Constitution, which are as follows."[72] The list included ten objections, centering around the lack of a bill of rights and written guarantees of religious liberty.

Much has been written about a supposed meeting between Madison and Leland in March 1788 and a "deal" between them to gain Baptists' support for the Constitution. The most recent and thorough discussion of the inci-

68. Ibid., p. 117.
69. Ibid.
70. Ibid., p. 114.
71. Pfeffer, p. 112.
72. Alley, p. 107.

dent is found in Reuben E. Alley, *A History of Baptists in Virginia.*[73] Older sources state that Madison visited Leland's home where the two men discussed the Constitution for several hours. At the close of that discussion, Leland withdrew from the race for the ratification convention and threw Baptist support to Madison. In return, Madison agreed to introduce amendments to the constitution, spelling out the freedoms which Baptists desired. While Alley showed that much of that information comes from secondary sources and the memory of participants years after the facts, it still bears the stamp of authenticity. Such a meeting, whether at Leland's home or elsewhere, seems likely. Baptists did throw their support to Madison, who was elected and led Virginia to ratify the Constitution.

As a member of Congress, Madison spoke often of the "public clamor" for a bill of rights. On May 4, 1789, only four days after the inauguration of President Washington, Madison announced to the House of Representatives that "he intended to bring on the subject of Amendments to the Constitution." He further explained:

> It cannot be a secret to the gentlemen of this House that, . . . there is a great number of our constituents who are dissatisfied with [the Constitution], ... There is a great body of the people falling under this description, who at present feel much inclined to join their support to the cause of Federalism, if they are satisfied on this one point.[74]

Historians generally agree that Baptists were included among the "great number of our constituents" and that the "one point" on which they desired further guarantees involved religious liberty. Madison introduced ten proposed amendments, to be known as the Bill of Rights. Their wording was modified in committee, but Madison's basic ideas survived. The First Amendment was rewritten several times and finally emerged as follows: "Congress shall make no law respecting an establishment of religion, or prohibiting the free exercise thereof; or abridging the freedom of speech, or of the press; or the right of the people peaceably to assemble, and to petition the Government for a redress of grievances." For almost two centuries, that amendment has provided the major legal guarantee for religious freedom to all Americans.

The First Amendment prohibits Congress from establishing or restricting religion at the federal level; it says nothing about the states, and for over forty years some New England states continued to maintain their established churches. In the twentieth century, religious liberty cases have been adjudicated on the basis of the First Amendment, as made operative in the individual states by the Fourteenth Amendment, which provides that "no

73. Ibid., pp. 106 *f.*

74. Charles F. James, *Documentary History of the Struggle for Religious Liberty in Virginia,* p. 166.

State shall make or enforce any law which shall abridge the privileges or immunities of citizens of the United States." Provisions relating to religion in the federal Constitution are extended to all levels of government.

Summary

In tracing the emergence of religious liberty in America, Joseph Dawson concluded, "If the researchers of the world were to be asked who was most responsible for the American guarantee for religious liberty, their prompt reply would be 'James Madison.' " However, Dawson continued, "If James Madison might answer, he would as quickly reply, 'John Leland and the Baptists.' "[75] If that sounds too partisan, overlooking the role of other denominations, it does focus upon Baptists' great contribution in winning religious liberty in America. Baptists provided many of the ideas undergirding religious liberty, and they spearheaded the public agitation which led to the Bill of Rights.

Of course, the Bill of Rights did not close off all relations of church and state in America, as continuing court cases amply testify. As Glenn T. Miller pointed out in *Religious Liberty in America,* the churches helped construct a kind of "religious nationalism" which provided both symbols and reality of spiritual unity which transcended the denominations.[76] That spirit later developed into a "civil religion" which has existed alongside the "denominational religions." In the past two centuries whenever the First Amendment has been under attack, or up for proposed revision, Baptists have been its steadfast defenders. In the late twentieth century, however, some evidence suggested that Baptist commitment to religious liberty might be weakening. Baptists who bore the scars of religious persecution struggled to achieve religious liberty; it remains to be seen whether Baptists who live in comfort can preserve it.

75. Dawson, p. 117.
76. Glenn T. Miller, *Religious Liberty in America,* p. 79.

Unit III:

The Nineteenth Century

Church historians generally call the time from 1800 to 1900 "the Great Century" for Christian advance. That description certainly holds true for Baptists. During that time they escalated in numerical growth, perfected organizational structures which endure to the present, overcame divisive controversies, and made the transition from a small dissenting sect to a major world Christian communion.

In England, Queen Victoria gave her name and viewpoints to much of the century in political, economic, and social realms. The nineteenth century was the age of reform. England abolished slavery, at least discussed prison reform, and put into place a system of public education. Baptists found it a heady time. For the first time, they could be admitted to the major universities, hold commissions in the military, and rise to political power in the nation. Their churches grew and multiplied, and a number of their preachers attained national prominence.

The Baptist Missionary Society, formed in 1792, flourished during the nineteenth century. In addition to its overseas work, settlers opened a Baptist witness in the larger British Empire, such as New Zealand, Australia, and South Africa. Baptists also made new beginnings in Scotland and Ireland. In all those places, not only churches but also vigorous denominational unions emerged in the nineteenth century. In England the Great Century began with formation of the Baptist Union in 1812 and concluded with the merger of Particular and General Baptists in 1891.

However, as English Baptists achieved more organizational union, they seemed to lose their spiritual and theological unity. Toward the end of the century the Down Grade Controversy shook the Baptist Union and raised questions about Baptists' doctrinal and spiritual identity. The century ended on a crest of growth and progress.

Baptists in Canada shared in the advance of the nineteenth century. The full century was needed for them to span the nation. Baptists' first churches in the Maritime Provinces date from the 1770s, but they gradually moved through the Central and Prairie Provinces and in 1871 established their first church at Victoria in British Columbia. During the nineteenth century, Canadian Baptists formed regional unions, launched both home and foreign missions, and formed several schools. Internally, they searched for identity.

Two forces tugged at them: their British heritage and the pull of American Baptists to the south. In time, they embodied elements of both English and American heritage but worked out their own distinctive Canadian identity. By the end of the century, a number of Baptists from America, especially from the Washington and Oregon area, had migrated into Western Canada. Many of these were Southern Baptists, thus laying the background for the question of relationship between Canadian and Southern Baptists which became troublesome in the twentieth century.

During the nineteenth century, the United States took its place in the world community of nations. The War of 1812 confirmed the continued existence of the United States as a separate nation, and the Civil War of the 1860s determined that it would be one nation rather than two. The Louisiana Purchase, the political ambitions symbolized by the slogan of "Manifest Destiny," completion of the transcontinental railroad, and the flood of immigration greatly enlarged the nation and strained the vision and resources of the churches.

Baptists in America shared both the growth and the pains. Their growth and westward expansion, and even their internal tensions and schisms, provide a rough ecclesiastical parallel to similar experiences of the nation itself. In 1800 Baptists in America had many churches but no organization of national scope; by 1900 they had more national organizations than one could conveniently count. Between 1814 and 1832, American Baptists achieved national unity, but in 1845 they lost it in the great schism which divided Baptists North and South. Though in 1845 Baptists proclaimed themselves still brethren, those brethren increasingly lived in different worlds, faced different issues, and developed different approaches which made Northern and Southern Baptists, if still brethren, certainly more distant brethren.

In the North, Baptists faced a compact industrial society. Their primary mission challenge consisted of the millions of European immigrants who, especially after 1880, flooded into the northern cities. Most of the immigrants had neither background nor interest in evangelical forms of religion, and the Baptist growth rate dropped. Meantime, to address the needs of their industrial society, Northern Baptists shared in the development of the Social Gospel which, in time, came to be associated with more liberal theological concepts.

In the South, the floods of immigrants came largely from a Scotch-Irish background. Their earlier connection with evangelical forms of Protestantism made them prime candidates for conversion to the Baptist way. That responsive population, plus the adaptation of camp-meeting styles of revivalism, help account for the rapid growth of Baptists in the South.

In both North and South, alternate forms of Baptist life appeared and persisted. Whether formed on the basis of ethnic origin, doctrinal differences, or the force of strong personalities, Baptists in America by 1900 reflected a mosaic of diverse patterns of belief and worship.

A new community of Baptists emerged in the nineteenth century on the continent of Europe. With distant echoes of the earlier Anabaptist witness, but fueled primarily by waves of evangelical Pietism, Baptists formed continuing churches first in Germany and from there throughout Europe. Their Pietist background made them more quietist than their American counterparts, and continuing confrontation with hostile state churches and civil governments hampered their witness. The diversity of languages on the Continent delayed the formation of a Baptist union to embrace all of Europe. By the end of the century Baptists in Western Europe had achieved a measure of freedom, while those in the Eastern countries were on the eve of the greatest challenge to Christian faith since the Roman caesars—the rise of Communism.

9

Baptists in Greater Britain

One might describe the nineteenth century as the best of times for Baptists in Great Britain. Baptist churches grew and multiplied, the modern denomination took shape and launched numerous programs of ministry, overseas mission work flourished, and they produced outstanding leaders who commanded national attention. The 1800s were as hopeful for British Baptists as the 1700s had been discouraging. Even before 1800 signs of recovery surfaced among both General and Particular Baptists.

During the Victorian era, wrote one historian, "Baptist principles were striking root in every part of the new empire."[1] As the new century dawned, William Carey was in India developing a missionary enterprise which would give Baptists a world outlook; Andrew Fuller was in Kettering pulling Baptists back toward a more evangelical theology; Dan Taylor was in London helping create for General Baptists of the New Connection a denomination complete with churches, schools, publications, and societies for missions and other Christian work. Things were definitely looking up for the Baptist cause.

The Victorian age brought changes in society which benefited Baptists. For generations power and influence in England had concentrated in the hands of the upper classes. However, after 1830 various reforms shifted political and economic advantage to those social classes where Baptists were more numerous. The repeal of the Test and Corporation Acts in 1828 allowed Baptists to enter careers in public service and to be admitted to Oxford and Cambridge.

These advances were not unmixed blessings. Careers in secular and public life lured away many capable young people who in earlier days might have entered the service of the church. Every Baptist student at Oxford or Cambridge meant one less enrolled in the Baptist schools which had done such heroic work during the era of their disability at the universities. Even so, the new social situation provided more advantages to Baptist life and witness than at any time since the Commonwealth.

Baptists seized these new opportunities with zeal. In addition to the

---

1. W. T. Whitley, *A History of British Baptists* (London: Charles Griffin & Company, 1923), p. 281.

network of associations, they formed an amazing array of societies for various forms of ministry. These societies ranged from local to regional in scope, from narrow to comprehensive in purpose, and some, like the Baptist Missionary Society (BMS), gained nationwide acceptance. To correlate their multiple ministries and to express their growing sense of oneness, Particular Baptists formed a national denominational body in 1813. The Baptist Union, after a rather slow start, gathered up earlier programs and funds and gave a more unified approach to Baptist life. Toward the end of the century, in 1891, the General Baptists of the New Connection united with the Baptist Union, thus merging the General and Particular Baptist traditions which had remained separate since the early 1600s. Not only in England but in greater Britain, such as Scotland, Wales, Ireland, and elsewhere Baptists experienced a new spurt of growth.

Along with new opportunities, the Victorian era brought new problems and challenges to the churches. Developments in science seemed to many to undermine traditional religious concepts. New methods of historical and literary study were applied to the Bible with startling results, causing some to regard the Bible in a less authoritative light. Economic development, both in England and its colonies, brought new levels of prosperity and perhaps turned the attention of some from the meetinghouse to the countinghouse. The growing acceptance of the theater, novels, popular magazines, and similar amusements forced the churches to reexamine earlier teachings and strict life-style.

British Baptists also suffered some reverses during the Great Century. Not all the Particular Baptists went into the Baptist Union of 1813; others refused to go along with the General-Particular merger of 1891. The result was that Baptists produced yet another separate group, complete with divisive spirit and wearisome controversy, which took the name of Strict and Particular Baptists. Baptists also sustained major damage toward the end of the century in the "Down Grade Controversy," which engendered much strife and bitterness, and at last caused Charles Haddon Spurgeon, without doubt the greatest Baptist preacher of the century, to withdraw from the Baptist Union. Further, the quickened pace and changing customs of the late Victorian era caught many Baptists unprepared. Their continued adherence to old, familiar ways, while comforting to some, alienated others and hampered the Baptist witness. Changing views of life and moral values, often lumped together under the generic name of secularism, grew rapidly during the late Victorian era and made many Baptists uncertain about religious practices and teachings.

Amid these complex problems and possibilities, Baptists in England sought to apply their traditional teachings. One historian said that "a wonderful change came over Baptists" during the nineteenth century.[2]

2. Ibid., p. 245.

Baptists in England

The Baptist Union

Particular Baptists took a giant step forward in 1813 by forming a union of churches and ministers, thus giving them for the first time a national organization. Though rather slow in winning support, toward the end of the century the Baptist Union gathered momentum. The new organization underwent frequent name changes, but it seems best to refer to it by the name that later stuck, the Baptist Union.

In forming the Baptist Union, leaders had to overcome the historic reluctance of Particular Baptists to organize on a national level. They had linked their churches into associations since the 1640s, and from time to time pastors in such centers as London and Bristol had formed more or less organized coffeehouse "fraternals" in which they heard papers on various issues, discussed theology, and planned local church activities. In 1689 and for a year or two following, the Particular Baptists convened well-attended national assemblies in London, but efforts to effect a continuing organization came to nothing. They projected two annual meetings, one in London and one in Bristol. The London meeting fizzled out, and the Bristol assembly became indistinguishable from meetings of the Western Association. Failure to organize nationally may be attributed at least partially to such causes as theological differences, jealousy for the independence of each local church, reluctance on the part of outlying areas to see Baptist power concentrated in London, lack of adequate information and awareness of one another, and above all lack of some motivating cause or mission to demand unified effort. Baptists had been, as one historian said, "busy as beavers" in their work but "unsociable as otters" in their isolation.[3]

By 1800, however, sentiment was growing for a more unified organization, motivated partly perhaps by success in the mission societies. In June 1811, Joseph Ivimey published a paper entitled "Union Essential to Prosperity," in which he extolled the advantages of union and proposed specific plans to that end.[4] Ivimey showed that "some general bond of union" need not compromise the independence of local churches. The *Baptist Magazine* took up the cause, saying in 1811, "We are anxious to see such a Union prevail in our Denomination as shall most effectively combine all our efforts in the cause of Truth and Righteousness at home, and give ten-fold vigour to our exertions on behalf of the heathen abroad."[5] Joseph Ivimey and John Rippon may be regarded as the primary founders of the new organization. About sixty ministers from as many churches answered Ivimey's call for

3. Ernest A. Payne, *The Baptist Union*, p. 79.
4. Joseph Ivimey, *A History of English Baptists*, 4 vols. (London: Printed for the author, 1811-1830), 4:122 f.
5. Whitley, p. 263.

a meeting in the summer of 1812 to plan the union. They met at Rippon's church in Carter Lane and agreed that a "more general Union of the Particular (or Calvinistic) Baptist churches in the United Kingdom is very desirable." They invited churches, ministers, and associations to send representatives to London in June 1813 to form a "General Union." The purposes of the new body were to include "the promotion of the cause of Christ in general: and the interests of the denomination in particular; with a primary view to the encouragement and support of the Baptist Mission."[6] The new body would also promote Christian education, Sunday Schools, village preaching, and funds for construction of new church buildings. An annual assembly would convene, according to Rippon, to consider *"whatever* relates to the real interests of the denomination at home and abroad."[7]

The Baptist Union was formed in 1813, with forty-six ministers as charter members. This represented only a fraction of the Baptists in England. The new union got off to a slow start, with few members, limited financial support, and tacit opposition from some. The influential Andrew Fuller did not at first support the new union, partly because it was headquartered in London and partly because he saw it as competing with his beloved Baptist Missionary Society. In its early years, the Baptist Union was sometimes opposed or lightly supported, but mostly it was ignored. Perhaps W. T. Whitley was too harsh in saying that the early union "had no practical aim, no permanent officers, no inspiring leader."[8]

At its formation the Baptist Union adopted a statement of principles which may be regarded as its original constitution. Described as a "Society of ministers and churches," its theological base was summarized as belief in:

> three equal persons in the Godhead; eternal and personal election; original sin; particular redemption; free justification by the imputed righteousness of Christ; efficacious grace in regeneration; the final perseverance of real believers; the resurrection of the dead; the future judgment; the eternal happiness of the righteous, and the eternal misery of such as die in impenitence, with the congregational order of the churches inviolably [*sic*].[9]

The constitution also provided that "this Society disclaims all manner of superiority and superintendence over the churches; or any authority or power, to impose anything upon their faith and practice."[10] Thus from the first the union sought to safeguard the freedom of local congregations.

In 1832 the Baptist Union underwent a reorganization so thorough that it may be regarded as a new beginning. Even so, widespread support was

6. Payne, p. 21.
7. Ibid., p. 22.
8. Whitley, p. 266.
9. Payne, p. 24.
10. Ibid., p. 25.

not forthcoming. In the 1830s perhaps fewer than half of English Baptist churches were affiliated with any association. Many contributed to one society or another, but a truly denominational spirit had not yet emerged. Union meetings were frequently described as "thinly attended," and perhaps many would have agreed with the delegate in 1847 who asked himself, "For what *purpose* are we gathered? . . . Are the authorities themselves quite clear upon the matter?"[11] The union continued to be overshadowed by older and larger societies, especially the BMS. Its London headquarters prejudiced some against the union. The spirit of independency prevented many of the churches from cooperating meaningfully with any denominational body.

At its fiftieth anniversary in 1863, the Baptist Union underwent yet another reorganization and thereafter gained steadily in the support of churches and ministers. Though still in the shadow of the BMS, for years occupying office space in BMS facilities, the union gradually gathered within its orbit other smaller societies and funds. Conditions allowed the union to act as an integrating force in Baptist life. By 1877 it had absorbed the home mission work, and even the Particular Baptist Fund (1717) and the Baptist Building Fund (1824) came within union oversight if not control. A number of Baptist newspapers continued on an independent basis, but both the *Baptist Magazine* and the more recent *Freeman* came under union influence and actively promoted union causes.

Capable secretaries (and cosecretaries in some years) like Joseph Belcher (1832-1840), William H. Murch (1834-1846), John Howard Hinton (1841-1866), James H. Millard (1863-1877), and especially Samuel Harris Booth (1877-1879 and 1883-1898) advanced the union greatly.[12] Whitley observed that "with 1863 the Union began to be a real factor in denominational life."[13] Its executive committee included the heads of most of the other Baptist societies in England. Booth was the first full-time paid secretary of the union. Though the words may sound uncomplimentary to modern ears, an observer meant it favorably when he said that the revitalized Baptist Union meant that "an ecclesiastical 'machine' has loomed on the horizon, and a bureaucracy has begun to take shape."[14]

Even before 1863, a number of General Baptist churches (of the New Connection) sought affiliation with the Baptist Union, thus anticipating the full merger between the two groups which was finalized in 1891. The union modified its doctrinal base in 1873, partly to reflect its own changing emphases and partly, no doubt, to encourage affiliation of the General Baptist churches. The articles of strict Calvinism were softened, and both

11. Ibid., p. 67.
12. Ibid., p. 262, for tables of Baptist Union leaders and their dates of service.
13. Whitley, p. 318.
14. Ibid., p. 323.

closed and open communion were accepted. The earlier reference to "evangelical sentiments" was removed in favor of the following Declaration of Principle: "In this Union it is fully recognized that every separate church has liberty to interpret and administer the laws of Christ, and that the immersion of believers is the only Christian baptism."[15] That marked the movement of the Baptist Union away from a confessional to a more functional basis. While it succeeded in achieving a larger union numerically, it probably diminished the core of spiritual unity among Baptists and set the stage for doctrinal debates a generation later.

In the last quarter of the nineteenth century, the Baptist Union was definitely on the rise. Under the effective leadership of Samuel Harris Booth, the union assumed management of several other societies and funds. There was even talk of merging the BMS into the union network of benevolences, but that proved a vain hope. In fact, the BMS continued to outdraw the union in attendance, financial support, and overall interest by rank and file Baptists. Many still regarded the BMS as the center of Baptist denominational life. Toward the end of the century, the union devised new programs, launched new funds, and spoke for Baptists in the emerging ecumenical movement.

General Baptists

The General Baptists had their own problems in adjusting to the new realities of the nineteenth century. The "Old Connection," as the original group came to be called, continued its slide into doctrinal extremism and numerical decline. As its Unitarianism became more pronounced, its adherence to outworn methods more intransigent, the old General Baptists, to quote one Baptist historian, "subsided into insignificance."[16] Meanwhile the New Connection prospered, though its growth leveled off somewhat from its early days. In 1811 the New Connection assembly registered 81 delegates from 58 churches, and reported a total membership of 5,471 with 339 baptisms that year.[17]

The New Connection underwent fundamental reorganization in the 1830s. New Connection leaders sought to streamline the denominational machinery, outgrowing the stamp of Dan Taylor. In addition to home and foreign missions, the New Connection also sponsored several printing efforts, including the *Repository,* the *Missionary Observer,* a hymnbook, and a tract society. Against sharp opposition, the group voted to keep its headquarters in Leicestershire rather than move to London.

Before their own societies were in place, New Connection Baptists sought to cooperate with Particular Baptists in missionary work. As early as 1795, they requested the privilege of contributing to the BMS but were refused. Thus rebuffed, they formed a Foreign General Baptist Mission in 1816 and opened work on patterns similar to the BMS. One of their greatest missionaries was James Peggs, who began work among the Oriyas on the Bay of Bengal. When he was obliged to return to England, he helped arouse and inform England through preaching and writing to the evils of crass idolatry, slavery, and murder of widows and children.[18]

Despite these marks of dynamic life, the New Connection enjoyed no great numerical success. At their centenary in 1870, they reported 20,488 members in 153 churches, mostly in the Midlands.[19]

Though no one emerged to dominate the New Connection as had Dan Taylor, perhaps their most capable nineteenth-century leader was John Clifford (1836-1923). Born in Derbyshire, Clifford was educated at the Midland Baptist College at Leicester and later at the University of London. He came to London in 1858 to serve as pastor of the Praied Street and Westbourne Park church, where he continued for fifty-seven years. From 1870 to 1883 he edited *The General Baptist Magazine*. Clifford rose rapidly to become a major spokesman not only for Baptists but for all of English dissent. A man of ecumenical sympathies, Clifford served in 1898-1899 as president of the National Council of Evangelical Free Churches in England. Clifford had led in the 1891 merger of the New Connection into the Baptist Union.

The Baptist Missionary Society

That the BMS should require a separate section in this history reveals its place of priority in English Baptist life in the nineteenth century. No other society or agency so captured the interest and financial support of English Baptists as did the "heathen society," as some called it. For example, in 1863 the BMS received contributions of almost £31,000. That same year the Baptist Union received only £90 from all sources. That trend was still obvious by 1874 when churches in Lancashire and Cheshire contributed only £24 to the Baptist Union, but £2,312 to the BMS.[20]

Such strong loyal support enabled the BMS to "lengthen its cords and strengthen its stakes," to paraphrase one of its founders. In addition to the famous triumvirate of William Carey, John Ward, and William Marshman, the BMS sent out nine foreign missionaries before 1800. By direct evangelism, Bible translations, educational work, and by means of the printed page, they sought a foothold for the gospel in India and elsewhere. Although Carey did not baptize his first convert for seven years, thereafter conversions were more numerous.

18. Whitley, pp. 254-255.
19. A. C. Underwood, *A History of English Baptists*, p. 214.
20. Payne, pp. 91-92, 106.

In no area did the BMS excel more than in Bible translation and printing. Carey was a brilliant translator and writer; Ward was an expert printer. By 1812 they had published gospel tracts in twenty languages and portions of the Bible in eighteen.[21] They also opened new fields of service in Java, Burma, and elsewhere. New missionaries from England staffed the new stations, augmented by the second generation of BMS pioneers, as in the person of Carey's son, Felix.

Other societies, though technically separate, augmented the work of the BMS. In 1814 the influential Baptist Irish Society was formed, led primarily by Joseph Ivimey, to sponsor mission work in Ireland. In 1831 Baptists formed a "Society for diffusing the Gospel through the Continent of Europe." Though these operated separately for years, their work eventually came under the oversight of the BMS, which in 1875-1877 began work in parts of Europe, Africa, and China.

What first appeared as a great tragedy in 1813 quickly turned into a blessing in disguise for the BMS. A disastrous fire wiped out mission property at Serampore, the major BMS station, and mission work came to a halt. When this became known in England, a groundswell of concern was matched by the most generous financial offerings any Baptist agency had ever received. In only two months, English Baptists had subscribed enough to replace all the Serampore losses. One historian noted that the response was so general and generous that "the society was shifted from a Northamptonshire basis to a British," commanding national rather than regional allegiance.[22]

However, leadership remained firmly in the hands of Northamptonshire men who resisted all efforts to share leadership with London. Andrew Fuller was typical of those who thought no good could come from that metropolis. In 1813 he had predicted little success for the Baptist Union, partly because it would be headquartered in London. In a letter of 1812, Fuller noted, "There is talk among the denomination of a general union, and of an annual meeting in London." In a letter to Joseph Ivimey, he advised against any such plan, saying, "You will only show the poverty of the denomination by such a meeting."[23] In a letter to missionaries on the field, Fuller wrote in 1812, "The seat of the Society will, it is hoped, continue in the association where it originated."[24] A close friend remarked upon Fuller's "strong (and the writer thinks) and unfounded prejudice against the business of the society being managed in London."[25] No such transfer of society headquarters occurred during Fuller's lifetime; when it

---

21. Whitley, p. 253.
22. Ibid.
23. Payne, p. 17n.
24. Ivimey, 4:129.
25. Ibid., p. 529.

did occur after his death, it helped provoke serious controversy in the mission work.

A letter to missionaries upon the twentieth anniversary of the BMS reveals the close relationships which prevailed between the society at home and its workers on the field. The letter, likely the work of Fuller, greeted the missionaries, called many of them by name, and inquired of their well-being and work. The letter assured the missionaries of the continued support of the society, promised new appointments to assist the veterans, and generally revealed a warm personal regard for the missionaries. The letter said:

> You can hardly conceive how intimately we are acquainted with you, who went out from us. . . . Our thoughts rove with delight from station to station. We seem to be present with you in all your domestic circles, rising seminaries, and religious assemblies.[26]

Much of the leadership of the BMS fell upon the broad shoulders of Andrew Fuller. He was pastor of the church where the society was formed, served as its managing secretary until his death, traveled tirelessly raising money for its needs, and wrote countless letters to actual and potential contributors. One need not be surprised that he developed a kind of proprietary regard for the society, jealous of others who sought to share the leadership, and opposed to any attempt to alter its operation or headquarters. John Ryland, another founder of the society, wrote of Fuller:

> In short, the whole weight of its concerns lay far more upon him than any man in England, and he cared for it night and day, and most disinterestedly laid himself out for its welfare, from its commencement to his death. While on a journey with a confidential friend, he once remarked, . . . Our undertaking to India really appeared to me, on its commencement, to be somewhat like a few men, who were deliberating about the importance of penetrating into a deep mine, which had never before been explored. We had no one to guide us, and while we were thus deliberating, Carey, as it were, said, "Well, I will go down if you will hold the rope." But before he went down (continued Mr. Fuller) he, as it seemed to me, took an oath from each of us, at the mouth of the pit, to this effect, that "while we lived, we should never let go the rope."[27]

One regrettable incident marred BMS history early in the nineteenth century. The "Serampore Controversy," named for the major mission station in India, alienated veteran missionaries and for a number of years caused schism in the mission work. Several factors led to that unhappy conflict. Upon Fuller's death, leadership passed to younger hands, and BMS headquarters were moved to London in an effort to enlist nationwide sup-

26. Ibid., p. 131.
27. Ibid., p. 529.

port. The new leaders did not personally know Carey, Ward, and Marshman. They also held quite different views of mission administration. Whereas Fuller had treated the missionaries as trusted friends and colleagues, leaving all important policy decisions to be made on the field, the new leaders took a more directive approach.

In 1818 John Dyer of Reading was employed as corresponding secretary and, thus, became one of the first Baptist ministers to hold a full-time paid denominational post. Dyer wrote rather curt and commanding letters to the missionaries, who were not accustomed to be so addressed. Carey later complained that Dyer's letters "resembled those of a Secretary of State."[28] Clearly the trend was toward greater control and policy making at the home base rather than on the field.

One point in dispute was control of mission property. Carey and the other pioneers had to shape their mission methods and policy de novo, by trial and error. They had no backlog of missionary history or precedent to draw on, no earlier colleagues on the field to guide them. Unlike most modern foreign missionaries, they made learning trades a priority so they could earn a livelihood and become financially independent of the sponsoring society as soon as possible. All of the Serampore triumvirate earned far more than a living, and they plowed the excess back into printing presses and other mission property. While all property was used for mission work, the missionaries insisted upon retaining title and control over properties purchased from their own earnings. To what extent society funds may have gone into properties held by the missionaries was sharply disputed.

The new leaders made rather sweeping accusations; in retrospect, their charges seem unnecessarily harsh. Carey, Ward, and Marshman were accused of having "amassed extensive property, and thereby enriched themselves and their families, while they had been unmindful of the great cause to which they originally devoted themselves."[29] Marshman and Ward returned to England to meet with the officials, but their efforts at peace proved fruitless. Carey wrote, "We are your brothers, not your hired servants. We have always accounted it our glory to be related to the Society . . . and we shall rejoice therein so long as you permit us, but we will come under the power of none."[30] In 1827 the BMS and the Serampore Mission parted ways. Never again was Carey in fellowship with the society he had helped to form.

For ten years the schism between the BMS and the Serampore Mission continued, giving English Baptists, in effect, two rival foreign mission societies. The Serampore men continued to solicit funds under a new organization called "The Society in Aid of the Serampore Mission." The schism was

28. Underwood, p. 197.
29. Ibid.
30. Ibid., p. 198.

healed in 1837, on the day after the burial of Marshman, the last of the original triumvirate. One must acknowledge that the society management won its point. Thereafter, the home office exercised more direct control over mission affairs. But, on the other hand, missionaries came to rely more upon society salaries and generally diminished their efforts to become self-supporting. This helped introduce the era of the career missionary.

Expansion at Home

Home mission work also flourished in England during the nineteenth century. Though lacking the emotional appeal of the foreign mission, with its far away places with strange sounding names, local missions, village preaching, and bands of lay preachers sought to preach the gospel and plant churches in destitute places in the homeland. While the statistics on their efforts are not startling, a measure of success crowned their work.

Efforts at organized home mission work among English Baptists date back at least to the 1640s when various associations sponsored preaching tours in England, Wales, and Ireland. The success of the foreign society in 1792 quickly raised the question of a comparable society for work in the homeland. Some Baptists objected to expending all their efforts abroad when England had such spiritual needs. "It has been objected to us," wrote the BMS committee, "that while we are seeking the good of heathens abroad, we are not sufficiently attentive" to needy people in England who "are heathens in reality, nearly as much so as the inhabitants of India and Africa."[31] Diligent regard to foreign missions stimulated and encouraged greater attention to home missions.

As early as 1796 Bristol College sponsored a summer missions experiment by which they sent out student preachers to Salisbury, Broughton, and Cornwall. The students fanned out over these areas, preaching in churches, town halls, private homes, and out of doors. Their success was immediate and gratifying. Within a few weeks, a new association was formed in Essex to emphasize missionary and evangelistic work. One benefit of the student preachers was to free the regular pastors for summer itineration.

These and other experiments in home missions bore fruit with the 1797 formation in London of the Baptist Society for the Encouragement and Support of Itinerant Preaching. This "Itinerant Society," later to be known as the Home Mission Society, eventually came under the leadership of the Baptist Union. It sent out home missionaries and itinerant preachers, helped train bands of lay preachers and coordinated their efforts, and cooperated with the various colleges in sponsoring a variety of programs to bring the student preachers to the villages.

Perhaps the most ambitious program of the Home Society was the 1887 launching of the Jubilee Fund. Within a year over £1,773 was contributed

31. Whitley, p. 266.

to aid home missions. Social and economic changes were drawing more people to the cities, leaving the village churches destitute. The Jubilee Fund helped to maintain a Baptist witness in villages unable to support a Baptist church.

The nineteenth century was a time of growth for English Baptists. John Rippon in his *Annual Register* for 1794 reported 326 churches in England and 56 in Wales. The Religious Census of 1851 reported 1,374 Particular Baptist chapels in England and 3 in Wales. The Old Connection in 1851 still had 93 chapels in England, most of them Unitarian. The "sittings" in Baptist chapels totaled 752,343, but less than half were occupied on any given Sunday.[32]

Even with due account for the vagaries of religious statistics, these figures reveal significant Baptist growth in the first half of the nineteenth century. The *Baptist Handbook* for 1874 reported a total of 2,606 Baptist churches of which 1,946 were in England, 528 in Wales, 96 in Scotland, and 36 in Ireland. They were reported to have a total Baptist membership of 244,416.[33] "The Revival Decade" is the name some give to the responsive era of the 1860s. One observer wrote, "During this decade the Baptist denomination . . . steadily increased in numbers and influence."[34]

Social Issues

The story of British Baptists in the nineteenth century requires a word about their witness on social issues. Whitley complained that Baptists tended to "protest and protest" but did little of substance to correct ills in society.[35] In at least two areas that was not true. In the abolition of slavery and in temperance, Baptists provided both arguments and national leaders to effect significant change.

Slavery was abolished in the British Empire in the 1830s and in the United States in the 1860s. Long before that time, some Baptists in both areas had spoken out vigorously against this evil. William Ward, a missionary colleague of Carey in India, began his ministry as a speaker and writer against slavery. However, the English Baptist who did most to abolish slavery was William Knibb (1803-1845). As a missionary to Jamaica, Knibb became an impassioned defender of the human rights of blacks.

Perhaps Knibb's greatest contributions, however, were made in England, where his flamboyant speeches aroused the people against slavery. After slavery was abolished by an act of Parliament in 1833, Knibb helped blacks adjust to their new opportunities in freedom. Perhaps Knibb is best remembered for the dramatic service in Jamaica in which he led a crowd to place

32. Payne, p. 19.
33. Ibid., p. 102.
34. Ibid.
35. Whitley, p. 289.

leg irons and slave shackles in a coffin, to be buried at midnight on the day slavery was officially outlawed, shouting, "The monster is dead! The monster is dead!" A set of similar shackles hangs on the wall by a portrait of Knibb in an assembly room of the Baptist Church House in London.

Distressed by the practice of slavery in America, and encouraged by their victory in Jamaica, the English Baptists in 1833 began a correspondence with Baptists in America on the subject of abolition. On December 31, 1833, the Baptist Union sent a lengthy letter to the Triennial Convention in America in which they condemned "the slave system . . . as a sin to be abandoned, and not an evil to be mitigated."[36] They urged Baptists in America to do all in their power to "effect its speedy overthrow."

On September 1, 1834, the acting board of the Triennial Convention responded with a letter that did not defend slavery but pointed out several economic and political factors which made abolition more complex in the United States than in England. They included a resolution by the acting board that while they regarded themselves as not deficient to the English brethren in human compassion, "they cannot, as a Board, interfere with a subject that is not among the objects for which the Convention and the Board were formed."[37] That letter, penned by Lucius Bolles, pointed out that Britain had earlier encouraged the slave trade to America and concluded that "it is not the duty of the Baptist General Convention or of the Board of Missions, to interfere with the subject of slavery."[38] A more sympathetic letter, however, was sent by C. P. Grosvenor on behalf of several American Baptists who shared the British antipathy to slavery.

To follow up the correspondence with American Baptists, in late 1834 the Baptist Union appointed Francis A. Cox and James Hoby a committee to visit Baptists in America "to promote the sacred cause of negro emancipation."[39] Both Cox and Hoby were prominent pastors in England, and Cox had long been active in British abolition circles. After some months of travel among Baptists in the United States and Canada, Cox and Hoby returned to England where the Baptist Union in 1836 expressed disappointment that they had not pushed abolition with more insistence. The correspondence and visit helped to surface the tensions over slavery, already present among American Baptists, which led to the great schism of 1845 which brought the Southern Baptist Convention into existence.

Temperance in the use of alcoholic beverages became a major topic of social reform in the nineteenth century. Baptists took a prominent role in this reform, and many went the next step to advocate total abstinence. Many Baptist pastors served as officers of various temperance societies.

36. A. T. Foss and E. Matthews, *Facts for Baptist Churches*, p. 18.
37. Ibid., p. 21.
38. Ibid., p. 23.
39. Ibid., p. 297.

Local churches often switched from wine to grape juice in the Lord's Supper, and some associations advocated temperance and published the names of pastors who had taken the pledge.

One lesser-known Baptist spokesman in social causes was Charles Stovel, pastor in London. His range of concern was wide. In 1852 he preached a sermon on *The Sin of Exacting Excessive Labour,* in support of the Early Closing Association which was advocating a forty-hour week for workers. He said that for the benefit of family, health, spiritual well-being, and the good of society there must be for "persons who are employed in subordinate stations, a limitation of the hours of business."[40] In *The Duty of the Church in Relation to the Evils of Intemperance,* Stovel spoke out against "the malignant ravages of intemperance" and defended the duty of the church to speak on moral issues. A teetotaler himself, Stovel complained that many Baptist pastors drank; he knew one, he said, who was a "two-bottle man."[41] Stovel, a chain smoker, also spoke against the opium traffic, aggressive war, and corrupt government.

English historian W. T. Whitley pointed out that English Baptists appeared more eager to reprove than to be reproved about moral issues. Not long after the English had admonished Baptists in America about slavery, the Americans urged that English pastors consume less beer at ordinations and association meetings. The English took offense and, according to Whitley, the incident created a greater breach between the two groups than had the Revolutionary War.[42]

The Down Grade Controversy

Clearly the "Down Grade" was the most serious controversy facing English Baptists in the late nineteenth century. The controversy broke out in London in 1887 and swirled around two outstanding Baptist leaders, Charles Haddon Spurgeon and John Clifford. Historians reckon that the controversy ended with the death of Spurgeon in 1892, but its consequences have continued.

Some have found the seed of the controversy as early as 1873, when the Baptist Union modified its constitution away from a doctrinal to a more functional base. Unhappy conservatives had complained for years about doctrinal deterioration in the union but attracted little notice until they gained the powerful voice of Spurgeon. The controversy broke out with the publication of a series of articles in Spurgeon's paper, the *Sword and Trowel.* The first article, in March 1887, was entitled "The Down Grade" and gave the name to the controversy. Although not written by Spurgeon, the article probably expressed Spurgeon's views. It painted a dismal picture of moral

40. Charles Stovel, *The Sin of Exacting Excessive Labour,* p. 1.
41. Charles Stovel, *The Duty of the Church in Relation to the Evils of Intemperance,* p. 14.
42. Whitley, pp. 277-278.

and doctrinal decay in the denomination, with prayerless churches, indifferent laity, and unbelieving pastors who spent their time in worldly pursuits like the theater rather than in Bible study and fervent preaching. Spurgeon later took up the writing and published some article on the controversy almost every month until his death five years later.

Spurgeon's early complaints centered around three problems as he perceived them: the decline of prayer meetings among Baptist churches, the worldliness of ministers in attending the theater and sometimes even having dramas or other "intertainment" presented in their churches, and doctrinal decay.[43] Gradually the first two receded, and the controversy centered on alleged doctrinal problems among English Baptists. Spurgeon charged that a number of Baptist pastors held Socinian views of Christ, Universalist views of salvation, and infidel views of the Bible. This controversy exploded at a time when English theology was undergoing a revolution in its understanding of the origin, literary and textual criticism, and authority of the Bible. In some ways, one may regard the Down Grade Controversy as part of the Baptist response to those new and sometimes disturbing trends in biblical studies.

Spurgeon clearly was shocked at the response his articles received. He had not expected such a controversy, and he was no doubt chagrined by the slight support and extensive criticism he personally encountered. He stepped up the attack, and subsequent articles became ever more intense. Affirming that doctrinal conditions were ten times worse among Baptists than he had first thought, Spurgeon lamented, "A new religion has been initiated, which is no more Christianity than chalk is cheese."[44] In September 1887, he wrote:

> No one has shown that prayer-meetings are valued, and are largely attended; no one has denied that certain ministers frequent theatres; no one has claimed that the Broad School newspapers have respected a single truth of revelation; and no one has borne witness to the sound doctrine of our entire ministry. Now we submit that these are the main points at issue. . . . Others may trifle about such things; we cannot, and dare not.[45]

Citing the "wretched indifferentism" that caused some to remain silent, Spurgeon summed up his conviction that "many ministers have seriously departed from the truths of the gospel, and that a sad decline of spiritual life is manifest in many churches."[46] When the Baptist Union demanded that Spurgeon name names rather than level anonymous blanket charges, he refused to do so, although it was well known that he objected to the views

43. Charles Haddon Spurgeon, *The "Down Grade" Controversy: Collected Materials Which Reveal the Viewpoint of the Late Charles Haddon Spurgeon,* pp. 513-514.
44. Ibid., p. 17.
45. Ibid., p. 21.
46. Ibid., p. 28.

of Samuel Cox, pastor in Nottingham. In his 1877 book, *Salvator Mundi,* Cox had embraced the "larger hope," as he called his view of universal salvation.[47]

Spurgeon's refusal to name those who had embraced heresy may have grown out of several factors. If he named them, Spurgeon felt he would be accused of introducing personalities into the discussion. Further, he pointed out that the Baptist Union had no doctrinal standard except a belief in immersion and thus the doctrinal deviations he cited were not actually grounds for discipline in the union. No doubt he was also reluctant to invite possible legal response from those named. Apparently Spurgeon also had a kind of "gentleman's agreement" with Samuel Harris Booth, secretary of the Baptist Union, who had supplied Spurgeon with some of his information about growing heresy in the ranks but swore him to confidentiality. Spurgeon wanted the Baptist Union to adopt a conservative doctrinal statement, which would give them definite grounds to discipline those who held variant beliefs. The union consistently declined to adopt such a statement.

Calling the union a conspiracy of evil and pronouncing that fellowship with doctrinal looseness is sinful, Spurgeon announced in November 1887, "We retire at once and distinctly from the Baptist Union."[48] At the same time he withdrew from the London Baptist Association. His son, Thomas, and a few friends also withdrew, but his brother James, associate pastor at Metropolitan Tabernacle, remained in the union.

Less excitable leaders made every effort to win Spurgeon back to the denomination. They sent delegations to wait upon him and even drew up a proposed doctrinal statement which might at one time have satisfied Spurgeon. However, things had gone too far; the issues had become more personal than theological, and the proud Spurgeon was deeply stung by the lack of support he had received among the brethren. Some suggested that the smaller churches and their pastors were by then so economically dependent on the Baptist Union that they no longer had the luxury of speaking against it. Instead of drawing him back into the fold, the council and later the entire union passed a rather severe censure against Spurgeon in 1888. He never recovered from the sting of this rebuff.

Perhaps most surprising is that so few churches followed Spurgeon out of the union. In 1889, for example, five churches pulled out but sixty-one new ones joined.[49] In some ways Spurgeon was larger than the denomination; he could well do without the union, but most of the other pastors could not. Several friends urged Spurgeon to lend his influence to the formation of some alternate denominational, or even interdenominational, grouping of churches. Apparently, he seriously considered that. Had he done so,

47. Payne, p. 125.
48. Spurgeon, p. 36.
49. Payne, p. 144.

perhaps more of the dissident Baptists would have joined him. Spurgeon urged other churches not to withdraw from the union, but his later writings reveal a note of loneliness and subtle suggestions that perhaps others churches would also like to stand boldly for the truth as he had done.

After his exit from the union in 1887, the Down Grade Controversy became an obsession with Spurgeon. Described by one historian as "a sad, isolated, and sick man," Spurgeon had clearly overestimated his power to control Baptist life in England.[50] Spurgeon's preaching and writing thereafter seemed obsessed with the issues of the Down Grade Controversy, repeating his accusations and in subtle ways defending his actions, all the while professing no need to do so. Serious illness overtook Spurgeon, and he died in 1892 at the age of fifty-seven. Some, including both Spurgeon and his wife, were convinced that the rigors of the controversy had robbed the robust pastor of his health.

To sketch the course of the controversy is easier than to interpret its meaning. Some tried to make it a personal struggle between two strong men, the conservative Spurgeon and the less conservative John Clifford. Both men rejected that view and, despite their theological differences, remained warm personal friends. Others have painted this as another chapter of the old conflict between Particular and General Baptists. Spurgeon was a Particular Baptist, though his Calvinism may have been suspect at points, and Clifford was a General Baptist with the usual Arminian views associated with that group. These two groups of Baptists had been moving closer together for almost a century, and their merger was completed in 1891 during Spurgeon's lifetime. Many of the points at dispute in the controversy had long been important between Particular and General adherents, and the move toward merger would have surfaced them again. Further, Spurgeon emphasized evangelism as the only hope of society, while Clifford was the major Baptist spokesman for social reform.

Some have raised a question about the role of Spurgeon's illness in the controversy, suggesting that the growing physical and emotional ailments that left him sick and depressed may have turned him to his pessimistic outlook on Baptist life. Spurgeon repeatedly repudiated such suggestions, pointing out that when he first leveled his charges he was in robust health.

In retrospect, Spurgeon's charges pointed out real and serious doctrinal deviations among English Baptists. His exit from the denomination was hasty and ill-advised, did not have its desired effect, and left Spurgeon isolated and disappointed. The refusal of the Baptist Union to declare its faith seems incomprehensible in light of the Baptist confessions of earlier times. One recent historian concluded, "The Baptist Union emerged from

50. Ibid., p. 142.

the Down Grade Controversy shaken but not shattered."[51] That assessment may not stand up. Like an earthquake that weakens the foundations of buildings left standing, the Down Grade Controversy may have done more damage than first appeared.

The Merger of 1891

General and Particular Baptists had originated separately in the early 1600s and had followed different courses. However, a few signs of cooperation between the two groups surfaced from time to time. In 1792 some Generals had asked tentatively about sharing in Carey's new missionary society; by 1800 others had expressed an interest in working together in home missions. New Connection pastors participated in the Baptist Union from the first; in 1842 a New Connection pastor presided over that body. As doctrinal debates gave way to more practical questions in Victorian England, General and Particular Baptists exchanged pastors and members. The confessional basis of the Baptist Union was modified to make it easier for General Baptists to participate, and by 1863 fully one-third of affiliated churches were of the New Connection.

In 1857 the union met by invitation at Nottingham, the heart of New Connection strength. While gratefully acknowledging "the vital unity which (presently) prevails among them," leaders of both branches clearly hoped for greater cooperation.[52] At its centennial observance in 1870, a New Connection leader said:

> The union of Baptists is especially to be sought. I mean a much closer one than now exists. For our present semi-separate state is neither satisfactory nor seemly. No doubt we have our distinctive opinions still, but they are so seldom made prominent that the bulk of the people do not understand them. For all practical ends what might be called the Calvinism of one party is exactly the same as the supposed Arminianism of the other.[53]

Thereafter, leaders of both groups urged union; the 1873 meetings heard a call for "a complete amalgamation of the two sections of the Baptist body." That might have taken place almost at once, but for two factors. The Northern churches of the New Connection, always the more conservative of that group, required more convincing. Further, some Particular Baptists had made incautious remarks, welcoming the General Baptists to the Calvinist faith. Most of the General Baptists, including John Clifford, had no intention of embracing Calvinism as the price of merger.

In what is probably too simple a summary, one historian attributed the merger to three factors: (1) the continued decline of Calvinism among

51. Ibid., p. 144.
52. Underwood, pp. 213-214.
53. Ibid., p. 214.

Particular Baptists, (2) the growth of open communion among both groups, and (3) the development of the Baptist Union which provided them with a common platform.[54] However reasons for the merger are summarized, issues which had long separated the English Baptists became less important and forces drawing them together became more important.

On June 25, 1891, after a four-hour discussion, Baptists voted 155 to 39 to merge the two groups. The General Baptist structures were dissolved and the churches parceled out among the Particular associations. The two mission societies were merged, and various funds were combined. Colleges of both groups were accepted by the enlarged body. One historian concluded, "With remarkable ease and amity, the older distinctions passed from the mind of the denomination as a whole."[55] One is tempted to say that, while Particular Baptist structures prevailed, the General Baptist theology continued in the merged group.

English Baptists came to the end of the nineteenth century with an air of optimism. Their churches were still growing. The *Baptist Union Handbook* listed for 1899 a total of 2,697 Baptist churches in England, Wales, Scotland, and Ireland, with 355,218 members. These churches baptized 16,805 new converts that year.[56] Their mission work flourished at home and abroad.

However, not all was well in the Baptist Zion. Already secularism, so rampant in the twentieth century, was making its presence felt. Though General and Particular Baptists had managed to merge in 1891, they seemed to lose much of their soul in the devastating Down Grade Controversy. Further, Baptists' days of rapid growth were coming to a close and soon the numerical charts would turn downward. The swirling currents of new biblical studies, and new concepts in the physical and behavioral sciences, seemed to question many traditional religious concepts, and Baptists in 1900 were on the brink of perhaps the most serious crisis of faith in their history. The albatross of Dissenter status, being limited to "chapels" in a land of "The Church," eventually wore down the Baptist spirit.

Baptists in Greater Britain

While not specifically "English," early Baptist life in Scotland, Ireland, and Wales was closely related to that of England. A common overall pattern emerges in relation to Baptist origins and development in these areas. Baptist beginnings date from the 1650s, in the burst of Baptist activity surrounding the English Civil Wars, either from Cromwellian soldiers or from early Baptist missionary evangelists like Vavasor Powell. After the Restoration of 1660, the political situation which encouraged Baptist work

54. Ibid., p. 202.
55. Payne, p. 147.
56. *The Baptist Union Handbook,* 1899, p. 147.

was reversed and outpost churches languished. A few survived to eke out a tentative existence for decades, but in the early 1800s Baptist work enjoyed such a revival that it might almost be considered as new beginnings.

The churches in these areas formed local associations and at times attempted larger unions which failed to survive. In the first half of the nineteenth century, many of them affiliated with the Baptist Union in England. That relationship was marked by tension, and later in the century Baptists formed their own unions in Scotland, Ireland, and Wales.

Baptists in Scotland

The stern John Knox dominated the Reformation in Scotland and vigorously resisted those views which would later mark the Baptists. Knox described believer's baptism and religious liberty as "maist horribill and absurd," and some of his disciples described Baptists as "pests."[57]

Yet Baptists gained a foothold in Scotland in the 1650s. Baptist army officers used their influence to found and encourage churches. Many of the soldiers were also Baptists, several from the Fenstanton and Hexham churches in England. The Hexham church sent one of their members, Edward Hickherngill, to minister in Scotland in 1652. He later reported, "There were divers honest Scots . . . that long to be gathered into the same Gospel order with us, but they want a faithful pastor."[58] The Hexham church immediately sent out Thomas Stackhouse to meet this need.

The army was parceled out in eighteen garrison towns, as far north as Inverness. Churches were founded in most of these towns, but records remain of only a few. A Baptist church met at Leith by 1652, in Fife by 1652, in Perth by 1653, and a church met alternately at Leith and Edinburgh by 1653. Samuel Oates helped found Baptist work in Aberdeen about the same time, and by 1656 records speak of a church composed of "those dipping themselves in water" as far north as Sutherlandshire. In 1653 Scottish Baptists owned the 1644 London Confession as their doctrinal standard.

The Scots objected to the elevation of Oliver Cromwell to Lord Protector in 1653 and formed resistance groups that bordered on revolt. Cromwell, in turn, set up a system of spies among them and purged the army of Baptist officers. The churches presented a petition with two hundred signatures to Parliament in 1659 seeking toleration, but in vain. The army left Edinburgh in late 1659, further depleting the churches. After the Restoration, as historian George Yuille put it, "active Baptist life in Scotland disappears."[59]

General Monk, who took over the Scotland command, harshly restricted

---

57. George Yuille, *History of the Baptists in Scotland,* p. 24.
58. Ibid., p. 27.
59. Ibid., p. 34.

Baptists. In 1662 parents with unbaptized infants over thirty days old could be subject to heavy fines. An act of Parliament lumped Baptists with Quakers and Fifth Monarchists, referring to them as "the sneaking sect of Anabaptists," and allowed officers to seek out and silence them.[60]

Two streams of evangelical renewal in the 1700s brought a new beginning for Baptists in Scotland, but the streams issued into quite different forms of Baptist life. The first surfaced as early as the 1730s when John Glas and Robert Sandeman broke with the prevalent Scottish Presbyterianism and formed churches with views similar to Baptists. In 1750 William Sinclair, who had been baptized in England, gathered some converts and remnants from the Glas and Sandeman groups and formed a church at Keiss. For several years it was the only known Baptist church in Scotland. In the 1760s Archibald McLean and Robert Carmichael formed a Baptist church in Edinburgh. Carmichael went to London to receive baptism at the hands of the esteemed John Gill.

The second stream of evangelical renewal drew from James and Robert Haldane, wealthy brothers who devoted their lives and fortunes to the gospel, especially in Scotland. Called the "Wesley and Whitefield of Scotland," the Haldane brothers sponsored missionary societies, formed schools to train Scottish pastors and evangelists, and encouraged the travels of Andrew Fuller in Scotland which tended to tie their churches to the English. The Haldanes arrived in Scotland in 1808, and by 1810 a score of new Baptist churches had been formed through their efforts.

Baptist churches from the Glas/Carmichael background were often called "Scotch" churches. They were ultraconservative, strictly Calvinistic, suspicious of ministerial education, and opposed to a salaried clergy, preferring to administer their churches under a group of lay elders. The Scotch churches were reluctant to organize into associations or larger unions, though they did form missionary societies. Churches of the Haldane background, on the other hand, were often called "English" churches. This was a misnomer, for they were not English, but they did follow more nearly the doctrinal and pastoral patterns of Baptist churches in England. Their Calvinism was more moderate; they favored ministerial education, sought to link their churches into associations and larger unions, and preferred to have each church under the ministry of an ordained pastor, usually salaried.

Despite differences and sometimes hostilities, the Scotch and English churches gradually learned to work together. The Baptist Union of Scotland formed in 1869 included churches of both groups. However, over the years the Scotch churches tended to diminish. Some of them adopted the English patterns, some remained independent, and a significant number merged eventually into the Church of Christ movement, with which they had much in common.

60. Ibid., p. 37.

Efforts to organize Baptists in Scotland can be summarized, at least in the early years, as a story of good intentions, valiant efforts, and meager results. The missionary societies led the way, stirred into life no doubt by the missionary awakenings to the south and especially by the preaching and fund-raising tours of Andrew Fuller. Churches of the English pattern formed a Baptist Itinerant Society in 1808, whose missionary, Dugald Sinclair, evangelized successfully in the Gaelic Highlands. This society was enlarged in 1824, taking the name of Baptist Home Missionary Society for Scotland. It represents an early effort at cooperation between churches of the two patterns. By the 1830s they had about thirty home missionaries at work in various parts of Scotland.

Efforts to form the churches into associations were less successful. Their scattered locations, an exaggerated sense of local church independence, diversity in organizational patterns between the Scotch and English, and perhaps a limited vision of the purposes or advantages of cooperation, tended to discourage organizational efforts. One historian observed, "In the circumstances, associated work was not possible, and the majority of the Churches were so weak that, separately, they could make little or no contribution toward Church extension."[61] The beginnings of associational life stem primarily from churches of the English pattern.

The pioneer of Baptist organization in Scotland was Francis Johnstone. In 1835 he led a few churches to form the Scottish Baptist Association, renamed the Baptist Union of Scotland in 1843 in an effort to form a national body. Johnstone wrote an article in 1843, "An Inquiry into the Means of Advancing The Baptist Denomination in Scotland." He advocated a union of churches to provide pastoral aid for weak churches, the appointment of itinerant evangelists, forming a school to train Baptist pastors for Scotland, a building fund to assist churches to erect or repair buildings, and publication work to encourage Sunday Schools.

Much of this work had actually been launched, though on a small scale. The "first union," as it was later called, failed in 1856. One observer complained that of the Baptist churches "few concerned themselves with matters beyond their own immediate interests."[62] The larger churches held aloof, and without their support the union was doomed. The Home Missionary Society, anxious to preserve its own sources of support, did not encourage the union. Not all Baptists in Scotland favored all the causes proposed; ministerial education proved especially troublesome. However, during its life the union did much good, with several missionaries appointed, two magazines under publication, and much encouragement to Sunday School work. Johnstone himself tutored about twenty young candidates for

61. Ibid., p. 76.
62. Ibid., p. 236.

the ministry. Johnstone's return to England in 1856 was an insurmountable loss, and the union folded.

A more successful Baptist Union of Scotland was formed in 1869 at Glasgow and has continued to this day. Fifty-one churches formed the Union, with 109 affiliated by 1900. Theological differences had by 1869 moderated enough to allow Scotch and English churches, open and closed communion churches, and churches with varying degrees of Calvinism, to cooperate. The large and influential churches in Scotland affiliated with the 1869 union, as they had not done with the earlier union. A rising tide of revivalism among Baptists in Scotland, influenced by the preaching and example of Charles Spurgeon, also encouraged union. By 1869 even the most cautious Baptists in Scotland saw the values of broader cooperation.

The first secretary of the new Baptist Union of Scotland (BUS) was William Tulloch. Son of a Highlands missionary, Tulloch was pastor in Edinburgh and continued there until his retirement in 1893. In 1869 the BUS listed four objectives: (1) to strengthen home mission work throughout Scotland, (2) to provide financial aid for weak churches, (3) to prepare young men for ministry, and (4) to obtain information about Baptists and foster fellowship and brotherly cooperation.[63] The BUS sponsored a Provident Fund in 1873 to aid retired pastors or their widows, a Building and Loan Fund in 1876 to aid in the erection and/or repair of church buildings and manses, formed the Sabbath School Association in 1885 to encourage Sunday School work, and formed a Scottish Baptist Total Abstinence Association in 1881, for a while employing a "temperance evangelist."[64] This association led the drive to persuade Scottish churches to switch from wine to grape juice in the Lord's Supper, published a list of churches which did so, and posted the names of pastors who promised to be total abstainers. By 1900 most of the Scottish churches had switched to grape juice but not without resistance. Some churches continued to offer two trays at communion, one with juice, one with wine.

The driving force of the BUS was evangelism. In addition to home missionaries, the union developed a system of itineration whereby settled pastors could be released for a few weeks each year for mission work in unchurched areas. Support for foreign mission work continued to be directed, for the most part, through the BMS of England.

Less successful were efforts to provide training for ministry candidates. Ministerial education was one of the main purposes for formation of the union. Suspicion and even opposition to ministerial education lingered, especially among churches of the Scotch tradition. Educational enterprises were expensive, and some feared colleges would detract from missions and church extension. The seemingly inevitable suspicions of doctrinal "liberal-

---

63. Derek B. Murray, *The First Hundred Years: The Baptist Union of Scotland,* pp. 37-38.
64. Ibid., p. 68.

ism" among Baptist teachers cooled the zeal of some. Further, the Baptists could never agree on *how* they would provide education, whether by pastor-tutors who would take in a few students; establishing their own theological college with full-time tutors; or simply by raising money to send their students to England. All of these plans were tried at one time or another, and none succeeded well or won widespread support. Finally in 1894 the BUS, in apparent frustration, washed its hands of direct sponsorship of education. It did, however, encourage its students to attend the Baptist Theological College of Scotland, established as an independent effort with no official relationship to the union. By 1900 Scotland reported 16,905 Baptists, gathered into 118 churches.[65]

Baptists in Ireland

During the decade of the 1650s, at least eleven Baptist churches were formed in Ireland, but only five or six survived into the nineteenth century.[66] These churches were of the Particular persuasion, though they differed somewhat among themselves on doctrine, discipline, and communion. Most of them were founded and sustained by officers and soldiers of Cromwell's army stationed in Ireland. In addition to military leadership, London Baptists sent, or at least encouraged, a number of preachers to go to Ireland. Some of the Baptist pastors known to be active in Ireland in the 1650s include Thomas Patient, William Allen, Christopher Blackwood, and John Vernon.[67] Patient formed a Baptist church at Waterford and by 1652 was preaching in Dublin. In 1653 the first Baptist meeting house in Ireland was erected under Patient's leadership. Most of the early members, if one may judge by the names, were English or Welsh.

The so-called "Irish Correspondence" between Baptists in England and Ireland in 1653 reveals much about early Baptist witness in that island. The Irish churches felt their isolation and sought closer relationship with Baptists in England, apparently hoping also for evangelistic aid from that source. They requested of English churches "that you would send two or more faithfull brethren, well acquainted with the discipline and order of the Lord's house and that may bee able to speak seasonable woords suiting with the needes of his people, to visit, comfort and confirme all the flock of our Lord Jesus."[68]

For their part, the London Baptists seemed cautious, seeking further information that they might know "what churches and societies [in Ireland]

65. *Scottish Baptist Year Book,* 1900, p. 17.
66. I. J. W. Oakley, "A History of the Baptist Irish Society," *Irish Baptist Historical Society Journal,* p. 55.
67. Barrington R. White, "Thomas Patient in England and Ireland," *Irish Baptist Historical Society Journal,* pp. 36 f.
68. Barrington R. White, ed., *Association Records of the Particular Baptists of England, Wales and Ireland to 1660.* (London: The Baptist Historical Society, 1974), Part 2, p. 115.

wee may groundedly communicate with, according to the rule of Christ, and what not."[69] Distance and doctrinal differences help account for this caution, especially the Irish tendency to radical millennialism. William Kiffin of London sought to lead the Irish away from the militant Fifth Monarchy Movement toward a more moderate view of Christ's second coming. The practice of Baptist preachers in Ireland accepting government grants for preaching may also have inhibited close fellowship.

In response to the London request for more information, the Irish sent a list of "the churches of Christ in Ireland walking together in the faith and order of the Gospell."[70] Ten churches were listed—at Dublin, Waterford, Clommell, Killkenny, Corke, Lymrick, Galloway, Wexford, Kerry, and Carrick Fergus. The pastor, if any, was listed with each church, along with leading laymen. Brief remarks on the spiritual condition of each church were also included. While their overall spiritual condition was sturdy, several of these small churches, it was reported, "may bee in a decaying condition for want of able brethren to strengthen them."

Along with their letter to London, the Irish Baptists listed twelve matters "requiring prayer by the churches." This list of spiritual priorities reveals much of the internal life of the churches at that time, with emphasis upon prayer for spiritual growth, more intense Bible study, closer personal communion with God, and more personal discipline in the Christian life. To keep those needs before them, they had set aside the first Wednesday of each month as a day of fasting and prayer. The Irish spoke much of their spiritual deficiencies, but one suspects that their laments may be overdrawn, such as when they exclaimed, "Alas, alas, what meanes the dull, cold, estranged frame of heart wee beare each to other . . . with constant complaynings, with little sense of our victory over our leanese, our dryalnese and barrenese."[71]

The Restoration of 1660 dealt the Irish Baptists a serious blow, for "most of the brethren . . . have relation to the army and therefore are subject to be called away."[72] The army left in 1660 and with it much support for the Baptist cause. The churches also suffered from continuing doctrinal problems, isolation from the mainstreams of Baptist life, lack of ministerial and lay leadership, and renewed opposition from the Irish population which cultivated the unfortunate habit of identifying Baptists with the English. Renewed persecution of Baptists followed the Restoration. Many opponents of Baptists would have agreed with the later writer who predicted that Baptists would not prosper in Ireland because of "the peculiarity of their

69. Ibid., p. 111.
70. Ibid., pp. 119 *f.*
71. Ibid., p. 113.
72. Ibid., p. 119.

scheme [doctrines] and the uncomfortableness of their dipping."[73] The result was that the Baptist witness largely died out in Ireland, surviving only in a few tiny churches.

A spirit of revival marked Baptists life in Ireland after 1800, aided by several factors. The conversion of Alexander Carson to Baptist views gave the Irish one of their greatest leaders of the century. He spent more than thirty years in Ireland, much of that time as pastor of the influential Tobermore church. By the time of his death in 1844, Carson had established four more churches in Ulster. The new vitality among English Baptists had spilled over to Ireland.

The Baptist Irish Society was formed in a London tavern on April 19, 1814, "for the propagation of the Gospel in Ireland." The two main founders were Andrew Fuller and Joseph Ivimey. Though separate from the BMS, the new society enjoyed support from the older mission body and functioned essentially as an arm of that society for Baptist work in Ireland. This led to an infusion of funds and personnel into Baptist life in Ireland. At its first meeting the Baptist Irish Society adopted a resolution that "the principal object of this Society is to employ Itinerants in Ireland, to establish schools and to distribute Bibles and tracts."[74] This society served well for many years, but having its headquarters in England eventually led to friction.

The Irish Baptist Association was reorganized in 1862 to become, in effect, a national body. It voted in 1865 in Dublin to form an Irish auxiliary to the BMS and over the years appointed a number of Irish missionaries, including the grandson of Alexander Carson. Like the Baptist Union of Scotland, the Irish Association worked in close relationship with the Baptist Union in England. However, as ties between the two areas weakened, the Irish formed independent denominational structures. The Irish Baptist Foreign Mission absorbed the earlier Baptist Irish Society but kept headquarters and control in Ireland. In 1895 the Irish Baptist Association voted "that in order to express our independent position and freedom from all external control we form ourselves into a Society entitled 'The Baptist Union of Ireland,' thus ending our existence as 'The Irish Baptist Association.' "[75]

Two main factors led to the separation of the Irish from English Baptists. The first was a desire for independence, pronounced among the Irish Baptists from the first. The second was theological. The Irish sided strongly

73. H. D. Gribbon, "The Cork Church Book 1653-1875," *Irish Baptist Historical Society Journal*, p. 71.

74. R. C. McMullan, "Baptist Education in Ireland," *Irish Baptist Historical Society Journal*, p. 21.

75. Joshua Thompson, "The Origin of the Irish Baptist Foreign Mission," *Irish Baptist Historical Society Journal*, p. 17.

with Charles Spurgeon during the Down Grade Controversy. Hugh D. Brown, pastor in Dublin and a close friend of Spurgeon, led the Irish to pass resolutions supporting Spurgeon's position. In 1888 Brown presented to the Irish Association a doctrinal statement, largely in response to the Down Grade situation in England. This "Declaration of Belief" reads in part:

> While desiring to extend to all believers the fullest and freest liberty of conscience we yet expect from all members of the Association an adhesion to the following doctrines of our faith as understood in a simple, straightforward and evangelical sense. The Inspiration and all-sufficiency of the Holy Scriptures, the Trinity in Unity of the Godhead, the fall of Man through sin, the perfect Divinity and perfect Humanity of our Saviour, the justification of the sinner through faith in the Lord Jesus, the Atonement through the blood-shedding of Jesus Christ, the personality of the Devil, the resurrection of the body, the immortality of the soul, the everlasting security of the believer, the everlasting punishment of those who die impenitent, the perpetuity of the ordinances of baptism and the Lord's Supper "till He come," the priesthood of all believers and the obligation resting upon all saved souls to live soberly, righteously, and godly in this present world.[76]

While modified somewhat before adoption, the statement reveals the continuing conservatism of the Irish Baptists. They did what the English declined to do—adopt a specific statement of faith.

Irish Baptists were apparently affected by the so-called "Prayer Meeting Revival" in America in the late 1850s. The first notice of this movement in Ireland surfaced in a letter of 1859 from the pastor at Tobermore, who wrote, "Just at this time we began to hear of the glorious revival in America; and suddenly, as by a touch of the Divine hand, we found ourselves earnestly desiring something of the kind at Tobermore."[77] The revival spread throughout Ireland, especially in the north, and opened the way for wider distribution of Baptist views.

The impact of the Prayer Meeting Revival can best be traced at the Tobermore church, since its experiences were probably typical of others. The church formed prayer meetings, attendance swelled, numerous souls came under conviction and professed conversion, and membership soared with 99 new converts from March 1859 to March 1860. The previous year the church had had only 10 additions. However, the new converts proved susceptible to numerous moral and ethical problems, and not a few had to be excluded. The revival zeal passed almost as quickly as it came. Membership at Tobermore dropped from 269 in 1860 to 223 in 1865, and in 1869 the church had no additions. The pastor later wrote, "As it now appears, . . . that [Revival] movement was anything but a blessing. Out of some

---

76. Cited from *Irish Baptist Magazine* (1888), p. 102.
77. D. P. Kingdon, "Irish Baptists and the Revival of 1859," *Irish Baptist Historical Society Journal*, pp. 19 *f.*

eighty or ninety individuals received at that time, scarcely one remains to us at this moment."[78] By 1874 only 154 members remained.

In the days before public education, Irish Baptist churches helped educate children of Baptists and non-Baptists alike. The good image of their schools, usually connected with churches, helped offset some of the anti-Baptist hostilities present in Ireland from Commonwealth days. With the introduction of public education in 1831, Baptist schools quickly declined. As to theological education, some local efforts were made toward ministerial training in the 1820s. For a time Irish Baptists raised funds to send students to England for training but, like the Baptists in Scotland, found that method less than satisfying. A Baptist seminary operated at Bellina from 1830 to about 1840, under the leadership of James Allen, and Alexander Carson taught a few ministry candidates at Tobermore. However, a major breakthrough came in 1892 when John D. Rockefeller of the United States provided money for the Irish Baptist Training Institute, located in Dublin. This was later renamed the Irish Baptist College and moved to Belfast.

Baptists in Wales

An early tradition places Baptists in the Olchon Valley of Wales as early as 1633; others trace Welsh Baptists to a "gathered church" at Llanfaches in 1639, but positive evidence is lacking in both cases.[79] Early records mention a soldier in the Civil War who in 1646 had been allegedly "for divers weeks last past in Wales . . . apreaching and dipping, where he hath vented many doctrines of Antinomanianisme (sic) and Anabaptisme and rebaptized hundreds in those counties."[80] William Thomas and Hugh Evans are said to have been connected with this early Baptist work, but such information is sketchy and largely undocumented.

John Miles may be regarded as the founder of Baptist work in Wales, beginning in 1649. In 1650 the English Parliament passed an "Act for the better propagation and preaching of the Gospel in Wales," to be in effect from 1650-1653, and named Miles among those qualified for that task. However, even before that act went into effect, Miles and Thomas Proud were already evangelizing in Wales. They went to London in the summer of 1649 and apparently received immersion at that time. They arrived just as London Particular Baptists were ready to launch a mission "into the dark corners and parts of this land."[81] They were commissioned to return to

---

78. Ibid., p. 28.
79. Thomas Myrfin Bassett, *The Welsh Baptists,* p. 14.
80. Ibid.
81. B. R. White, "John Miles and the Structures of the Calvinistic Baptist Mission to South Wales 1649-1660" in Mansel John, ed., *Welsh Baptist Studies,* p. 36 hereafter cited as "John Miles").

Glamorganshire to preach and gather churches, and by October 1650 Miles and Proud baptized their first converts, two women. While regretting these were not men, they agreed that God was "thereby teaching us not despise the day of small things."[82]

Within a few weeks, Miles and Proud formed congregations at Ilston, Hay, Llantrisant, Carmarthen, and in 1652 at Abergavenny. These churches were closely disciplined, embraced Calvinist theology, and conducted lengthy worship services each Sunday, plus other meetings during the week. Miles served as pastor at Ilston, clearly the bellwether church of early Wales, but itinerated among the other churches. These churches provided preaching both in English and Welsh, observed the Lord's Supper once a month, and held meetings on the Saturday preceding communion "to satisfy doubts, to reconcile differences, to call offenders before them."[83]

In 1654 the Welsh Baptists issued a lengthy statement about the ministry. They listed six kinds of church officers and their duties as follows: the pastor, whose work was to preach, exhort, and administer the ordinances; the teacher, to expound Scripture and refute error; the ruling elder, to oversee the lives and conduct of the members; the deacon, to serve the physical and financial needs of the church; the widow, for the assistance of the deacons in looking after the poor and sick; and prophets, for the further edifying of the church.[84] Apparently the widows served in the capacity of deacons or deaconesses.

Miles not only formed churches but also linked them into close fellowship and cooperation. Some have accused him of following a kind of presbyterianism in which the general meeting or association exercised authority over local congregations. Many decisions about church policy, discipline, and even pastoral placement were made at the association meetings, but these were usually confirmed by local congregations. Miles devised a system by which both minister and leading laymen could itinerate among the churches for mutual help. At times historians have had difficulty determining whether these should be regarded as separate churches or merely branches of the Ilston church. Even the separate churches, if separate they were, would sometimes split up into subgroups or "house churches" in various parts of the community. However, Miles was careful to cultivate a spirit of unity by making occasions for all the members to come together periodically for worship, communion, and discussions.

Items discussed at the general meetings reveal some of the concerns and problems of early Welsh Baptists. Miles favored closed communion and closed membership, as did most of the Particular Baptists at that time. Thomas Proud, however, not only favored open communion but also

82. Ibid.
83. Ibid., p. 51.
84. B. R. White, *Association Records,* Part 1, 2.

sought to win others to that viewpoint. The general meetings often discussed that issue; in fact, Proud was for a time excluded. Other questions which came up, and the church response, included: must new converts be received by laying on of hands (no); may widowed church officers remarry (yes); should a church include singing as part of its public worship (no); and should speaking in unknown tongues be regarded as a valid part of worship (no).[85]

Several questions of church doctrine and order arose first at Abergavenny, which appears to have been a problem church. John Tombes preached there in 1653 and fixed upon them his open communion/open membership views. Tombes took a strong stand for believer's baptism, preaching "that infant baptism was a nullity, a mockery; no baptism but by dipping or plunging was lawful."[86] The Ilston leaders frowned upon the singing at Abergavenny and said, "considering the several frailties of the church . . . it was desired that they would forbear to sing psalms in the manner they now practice."[87] At the general meeting in August 1654, the Welsh Baptists agreed that unknown tongues, miracles, and gifts of healing were given in apostolic times for special purposes, but "all those offices and gifts were extraordinary, and therefore are now ceased."[88]

Another Baptist pioneer in Wales was Vavasor Powell, known for his connection with the Fifth Monarchy Movement. When he became a Baptist is uncertain; some suggest that he did not receive immersion until about 1655. One record states:

> In August, (1660) the Congregations in North Wales, collected and taught by Mr. Vavasor Powell, were ordered to be broken up. That excellent man was called a seditious sectarist, and his people restless and rebellious spirits, neglecting the places of the worship of God.[89]

Powell spent most of the remainder of his life in one prison or another, until his death in 1670. Though he spent little time in Wales, he sent several letters and assisted in encouraging Baptist preachers to move westward. Apparently Powell never fixed his radical millennialism upon the Welsh Baptists, who were distinguished rather for practical ministry and evangelism.

Unlike Baptist experiences in Scotland and Ireland, where Baptist churches planted during the Commonwealth era soon died out, Baptist life in Wales continued throughout the seventeenth and eighteenth centuries. Though statistics are hard to come by and must be handled with caution,

85. Ibid.; see also B. R. White, "John Miles," p. 36.
86. White, "John Miles," p. 61.
87. Ibid., p. 63.
88. White, *Association Records,* Part 1, p. 10.
89. R. Tudur Jones, "The Sufferings of Vavasor," in Mansel John, ed., *Welsh Baptist Studies,* p. 80.

perhaps 500 to 550 Baptists were in Wales by 1689. They had increased to perhaps 1,600 by 1760 and 9,000 by 1800.[90] Welsh Baptists reached a turning point about 1775 with the growth of population and industry, especially the coal mining industry, which attracted craftsmen and workers who proved remarkably open to Baptist views. Throughout the 1700s the Welsh churches had only one association, but in 1790 it was divided into three, the Southwestern, the Southeastern, and the Northern.

The Welsh Baptists tried, with considerable success, to hold the churches to traditional Particular Baptist theology. For years some associations specified that each church had to read the London Confession of 1689 twice a year in the churches and certify that they continued to accept it. However, in the 1800s, under the influence of revivalism, doctrinal strictness tended to wane. From time to time, the Welsh churches were troubled by Campbellism, Sabbatarianism, open communion, and Arminianism. The views of Scotch Baptists, placing the churches under a lay eldership rather than pastors, also surfaced occasionally in Wales.

In foreign and home missions, the Welsh churches cooperated with the English societies or formed their own, depending upon the degree of tension with the English at any given time. For years the Welsh churches took only one annual mission offering, dividing it between home and foreign work. By 1850, however, most of the churches took separate offerings, channeling the home portion through a confusing array of local and regional societies. Baptist work grew in Wales, due more perhaps to population and industrial growth than any concerted home mission strategy. People flocked to the ironworks, mines, and industrial centers; Baptist churches sprang up in these new centers. Welsh churches also spread beyond Wales, with churches in London, Liverpool, and Manchester; as one observed, "Wherever a Welshman went in the nineteenth century he took his religion with him."[91] Welshmen also populated many of the Baptist churches in America during this period, especially in the Middle and Southern Colonies.

The Welsh Baptists became known for their outstanding preaching. Unlike the English preachers, known for their painstaking division of the text into innumerable "heads," the Welsh preachers used homely examples from daily life and enriched their preaching with stories, anecdotes, and vivid illustrations. Perhaps the best example of such preaching among the Baptist was Christmas Evans (1766-1838). Born in Cardiganshire on Christmas day, Evans worked as a farm hand in his early years. Evans's formal schooling was scant, but he was blessed with a vivid imagination and natural gifts of oratory. Ordained in 1789, Evans served as an itinerant evangelist and later, 1791 to 1826, was pastor in Anglesey. He returned to North Wales in 1832 and spent his remaining years there, until his death at Swansea. He emphasized evangelism and practical theology. His dramat-

---

90. Bassett, p. 93.
91. Ibid., p. 236.

ic sermons made him a popular preacher, though he was said to have moved the heart more than he informed the mind. With his emphasis upon evangelism and practical theology, Evans helped soften the strict Calvinism of Welsh Baptists.

The Welsh churches, like the English, adopted singing as part of worship, though not without a struggle. They went through the familiar process of debating whether to sing at all, whether to sing only biblical psalms or "man-made" songs, whether to sit or stand to sing, and whether to allow instrumental music to accompany the singing. Gradually singing "human composures" gained general acceptance; toward the end of the nineteenth century, many Welsh Baptist churches installed organs or other musical instruments. Some churches even brought in professional musicians. By the 1880s, groups of churches in some areas met for "music festivals."[92]

Baptist church buildings in Wales tended, in the early days, to be small and somewhat nondescript. The improving economic scene allowed more churches to have their own buildings but brought a corresponding burden of debt. Some novel plans helped finance these buildings, but the usual pattern was for the pastor to go on preaching tours, collecting for the building as he went. Baptists in Wales were credited with 845 chapels in 1891, and fully 200 of them had been built between 1867 and 1887.[93]

By the 1860s a few women were preaching among the Welsh Baptists. Rachel Paynter was preaching and lecturing by 1865, and while the Anglesey Monthly Meeting sought repeatedly to silence her, she continued to preach with good acceptance as far afield as Monmouthshire. She later went to America where she served for a time as an evangelist. There was some talk of ordaining her, but no record remains of any such move. A number of other women preached among the Welsh Baptists, but they never won general acceptance. Some opposed them; others tried to ignore these examples of the "gospel in crinoline." However, one historian summed up their impact by saying, "In spite of all objections, the women were popular in the churches; their preaching and singing had an evangelical appeal which pleased the congregation."[94]

The Welsh Baptists usually took a strict view of morality, social entertainment, and recreation. One historian spoke of the "dull grey hue of Nonconformity" in Wales, and the Baptists were apparently as dull and gray as any. They tended to condemn most sports and games, including some which look rather innocent by contemporary standards. The attitude of Baptists toward such activities, according to one observer, "had more starch than humour in it."[95]

92. Ibid., p. 270.
93. Ibid., p. 242.
94. Ibid., p. 280.
95. Ibid., p. 365.

In the nineteenth century, the Welsh Baptists gradually shifted their teaching and practice on the use of alcoholic beverages from moderation to total abstinence. Many had become embarrased by the sometimes immoderate use of alcohol by Baptists. Associations often adjourned to the local taverns where ministers as well as laymen lingered long over their cups. By 1879 Welsh Baptists formed a Temperance Society, which promoted first moderation and finally total abstinence. They also led the churches to abandon the use of wine in communion and printed annually the names of ministers who promised to be total abstainers.

One continuing problem for the Baptists in Wales was to provide a trained ministry for the churches. To this end they formed three Baptist colleges, at Llangollen (moved to Bangor in 1891), Pontypool (moved to Cardiff in 1892), and Haverfordwest (moved to Aberystwyth in 1894 and closed in 1899). These colleges operated independently of the Baptist Union of Wales. Repeated efforts to consolidate their resources into one strong school, or at least to one college in the north and one in the south, failed to win support. The colleges were handicapped by limited financial support, doctrinal controversies, and the ongoing debate about the use of the Welsh or English language in instruction.

While Baptist churches existed in Wales from early times, the organized denomination was slow in emerging. Suspicion of centralized organization, lack of communication, fierce local independence, and lack of any overall vision of the function of a denomination hindered Baptist unification. The associations developed early and maintained a near monopoly, next to the local churches, over Baptist work. The associations met annually, but quarterly and even monthly meetings of ministers and leading laymen came to exercise considerable authority of their own, often at cross-purposes with the associations. A confusing array of societies, local and regional, added a kind of structural chaos to Welsh Baptist life in the eighteenth and nineteenth centuries. These societies had no uniformity in funding, allocation of tasks, or means of reporting. The most one can say is that dozens of such societies existed, no doubt many of them rendered worthwhile service, but in the process they distracted the churches with appeals too numerous to answer and probably delayed the emergence of any effective denominational life in Wales.

The Welsh Baptist Union was formed in 1866. At first this effort at a national structure won little acceptance, but toward the end of the century it gradually pulled into its orbit the various Baptist societies. In 1902 Edwyn Edmunds relinquished his pastorate and became the first full-time secretary of the union.

Despite problems and setbacks, the nineteenth century was a time of rapid growth for Baptists in Wales. The churches multiplied, a denominational order gradually emerged, the Baptist colleges gave such training as they could to young ministers, and the churches benefited from frequent periods of revival.

Baptists in the British Commonwealth

While not completely satisfactory, especially for more recent history, the term *British Commonwealth* provides a category in which to sketch Baptist origins and development in such areas as Australia, New Zealand, and South Africa. Several common threads unite Baptist work in these areas. Early Baptists came primarily from British immigrants, the churches and denominational structures largely reproduce the British patterns, and most of the early pastors came from England.

The early nineteenth century was a time of expanding empire for the British, but problems abounded at home. The shortage of land, labor dislocations caused by the Industrial Revolution, and efforts to absorb English soldiers returning from the Napoleonic Wars into an already troubled economy, led to widespread recession. These problems combined with the lure of British outposts where land was plentiful, wages high, and the economic outlook seemed bright. Those factors took waves of British immigration to such places as South Africa, Australia, and New Zealand. Like Britishers the world over, they took their religion with them. Among the modern migrants were a number of Baptists who formed churches and, when they became numerous enough, linked the churches into associations and unions.

A common pattern emerged from Baptist settlements in British outposts. Most of the early churches were founded by laymen, and for years they suffered a chronic shortage of pastors. Their few pastors came from England, with Spurgeon's College providing most of those who had ministerial training. Baptists in these areas faced such issues as ecumenism, the charismatic movement, and tensions over doctrine. They tended to be more conservative than Baptists in England.

Baptists in Australia

Conditions were hardly promising for early Baptists in Australia. Originating as a penal colony and serving as a dumping ground for misfits and debtors, as well as hardened criminals of English society, early Australia was marked by religious indifference, high crime, and excessive drunkenness. As late as 1834 almost 43 percent of the population was made up of transported convicts. Yet, a Baptist witness was established in Australia even under such adverse circumstances. Baptist work in Australia included, as one described it, both "troubles and sweet deliverances."[96]

The earliest known Baptist worship service in Australia was conducted by John McKaeg on April 24, 1831, in the Long Room of the Rose and

---

96. J. D. Bollen, *Australian Baptists: A Religious Minority* (London: Baptist Historical Society, 1975), p. 43.

Crown Inn of Sydney, New South Wales. Probably a small group of Baptists had been meeting there for some weeks, but no organized church resulted. McKaeg was a militant preacher from a strict Particular background. He had grown up in Scotland and later served as a missionary in Ireland. Lack of success in Ireland forced him to England, where he served a pastorate for a few years at Bingley with disastrous results. In Australia McKaeg collected a following among the scattered Baptists and other dissenters. His shouting style of preaching, his wild gestures, and theological peculiarities brought ridicule from some but seemed to have a strange appeal to many of the lower-class population. Some complained that in the pulpit, "he was not as sober as he ought to have been."[97]

McKaeg conducted the first Baptist immersions of record in Australia in Woolloomooloo Bay on August 12, 1832, to the amusement of an unfriendly crowd. The following account of that baptism by the *Australian*, a Sydney newspaper, shows that Baptists were not a popular group.

> Salt Water Baptism—Between two and three o'clock on Sunday afternoon, Mr. McKaig, Baptist Preacher, baptized two Females, who appeared to be a mother and daughter, in the presence of about 70 spectators. . . . After Mr. McKaig who was habited in a black garment that flowed down to his heels, garnished with a belt fast girded round his waist, had harangued the spectators for some time with extraordinary energy and violent gesticulations, he took hold of the female who appeared to be the mother of the other that stood by to be baptized, and leading her into the water to the depth of about three feet, divested her of a shawl which he tied round his own neck, and then fastening both hands in one of his hands, and throwing his right arm around her neck transversely to her waist, proclaimed her baptized in the name of the Holy Trinity, accompanying his words by throwing her backwards into the water once, from which she rose, completely drenched. The other female . . . was soused in like manner.[98]

Despite such energy and zeal, McKaeg came to a bad end. One account says simply that he "gave way to immorality, fell into public and private disgrace, and was at last imprisoned for debt."[99] Never a balanced personality, McKaeg had at various times to defend himself against charges of doctrinal extremism, insanity, dishonesty, gambling, and drunkenness. In addition to preaching, he launched a snuff and tobacco business, whose failure cast him into debt which led to imprisonment. In prison McKaeg had access to liquor, stayed drunk most of the time, and gambled heavily. Even McKaeg's despairing attempt at suicide was a failure, and we have no record of his actual death. He was a man of good intentions, but his aberrant

97. Ken R. Manley and Michael Petras, *The First Australian Baptists,* p. 45.
98. Ibid.
99. Ibid., p. 49.

personality and flawed character doomed him to defeat. Yet, in some ways, McKaeg illustrates the erratic beginnings and troubled history of Baptists in Australia.

A different kind of Baptist preacher arrived in Sydney on December 1, 1834, in the person of John Saunders. Saunders was everything McKaeg was not: balanced, well-educated, from a successful ministry in England, and able to win the confidence of upper classes. At age twenty-eight Saunders was at first unimpressed with Sydney and its people, whom he described as "so thin, so sunburnt, and many of them so drunk."[100] Saunders became the virtual founder of Baptist work in Australia. In September 1835 the land previously given to the McKaeg group was transferred to Saunders, and a chapel was opened on Bathurst Street with seating for 400 worshipers. On December 15, 1836 the Bathurst church was formally constituted with nine charter members. Obviously these were too few to raise the £1400 for such a building. By means of the Church Act of 1836, most of the cost of both the land and the building was borne by the government. Government subsidy of churches caused the Baptists of Australia much trouble before the provisions were abolished in 1862.

Founding documents describe the Bathurst group as, "A Church of Christ of the Particular Baptist Denomination," but "admitting of Open Communion and Fellowship."[101] Although the pastor had to be a Baptist, other members could be received by immersion, sprinkling, infant baptism, or no baptism. Saunders was ecumenical by nature and by policy, deliberately avoiding all sectarian topics. While he recommended believer's baptism, he did not insist upon it; he cooperated equally with Baptists and other dissenting denominations. By downplaying Baptist distinctives, Saunders won friends in high places and improved the public image of Baptists. In time Saunders's church was made up of people without much Baptist identity and with little zeal to perpetuate the Baptist cause. Under Saunders the Bathurst church grew to 124 members in 1848, of whom one fourth had been immersed.

Saunders resigned in 1848 because of ill health. He was succeeded by John Ham of Melbourne, who served until 1853. Ham was succeeded by James Voller, who served from 1853 to 1870. Voller led the Bathurst church, and Australian Baptists generally, to embrace more distinctly Baptist teachings and practices.

Space does not allow detailed description of other Baptist congregations in Sydney and throughout New South Wales. There were 11 churches in 1868 and only 16 in 1882. There were 6 Baptist pastors in New South Wales in 1868 and only 10 in 1882. In the same time, membership rose from 359 to 848. Voller led in forming an association of churches in 1858, but it

100. Ibid., p. 54.
101. Ibid., p. 56.

lapsed, to be renewed with more success in 1868. In 1872 this association was renamed the Baptist Union of New South Wales.[102]

Baptist work in Australia moved generally from east to west, beginning in New South Wales and proceeding to the other states of Tasmania, Victoria, South Australia, Queensland, and Western Australia. Henry Dowling, a Strict Baptist minister from England, arrived in Hobart, the capital city of Tasmania, in 1834. He formed a Baptist church at Launceston the next year, where he ministered for thirty-four years. In Victoria, the first Baptist worship service was held in a tent in Melbourne in 1838, led by two laymen, Peter Virtue and James Wilson. They brought the Scotch Baptist influence. John Ham formed a Baptist church in Melbourne on July 20, 1843, the first in Victoria. In 1850 W. P. Scott formed another church in Melbourne, on closed communion lines. This ultimately became the Albert Street Church, later the headquarters of the Victoria Baptist Union.

The first Baptist church in South Australia was formed in Adelaide, in July 1848, with only thirteen baptized members. An important event for South Australian Baptists was the coming of Silas Mead in 1861. He formed the influential Flinders Street church in North Adelaide, where he continued for thirty-four years. Observers agree that Mead brought aggressive ministry and doctrinal stability to Baptists in that area.

On August 5, 1855 the first Baptist church was formed in Queensland. Western Australia was the last of the states in which Baptist work took root. There was no Baptist work there until 1896, when J. H. Cole, a lay preacher from Victoria, formed a church at Perth.

Most observers agree that Baptist work in Australia has been less than successful. One writer cited "a strong and unanimous feeling of failure in the colonial period."[103] Perhaps this picture has been overdrawn. It fails to take into account several obstacles which confronted Baptist life in that subcontinent.

Perhaps the major obstacle to early Christian witness in Australia was its general atmosphere of irreligion. Saunders described early Sydney as a place where "Satan's seat is." He was appalled at the violence, immorality, and drunkenness of the early colony, which he described as "a vast whirlpool of iniquity and pollution."[104] While many of the convicts dumped in Australia were debtors or convicted of what today would be considered minor crimes, a good number were hardened criminals. None of the churches, including Baptists, had much chance of progress until voluntary immigration increased.

Divisions among Baptists provided another handicap to their progress.

102. Bollen, pp. 17, 19.

103. J. D. Bollen, "English-Australian Baptist Relations 1830-1860," *The Baptist Quarterly*, p. 290.

104. Manley and Petras, pp. 19-20.

All the varieties of English Baptists showed up in Australia, but the bitterness and divisiveness were, if anything, intensified. One reads of Particular, General, Strict, and Scotch Baptists, Fullerites, Plymouth Brethren, and Millerites, plus others who held some combination of the views of Alexander Campbell, the Haldane brothers, and/or John Gill. At times these competing groups existed in the same churches, at other times they formed separate churches, and one is at a loss to say which arrangement was worse. One must agree with H. E. Hughes that Australian Baptists exhibited "a most unhappy tendency to quarrel over their beliefs and practices and to separate from one another without really sufficient reason."[105] These diversities prevented the emergence of any unified denominational witness.

Baptists in Australia also suffered from neglect by their brethren in England. Australian leaders pleaded for aid from English Baptists, but experience taught a Victorian pastor to remark on "how useless it is to expect help from England."[106] Appeals to the BMS received the response that "the society only contemplates the heathen."[107] Reports that parts of Australia were quite as "heathenish" as anything in the distant islands fell on deaf ears.

Not all agreed with the policy of concentrating mission money on heathen lands to the neglect of English colonies. Some individuals sent funds, and even the BMS occasionally sent tiny amounts and at times encouraged likely pastors to emigrate to Australia. In 1836 a few Baptists, primarily addressing the situation in Canada, formed the Baptist Colonial Missionary Society (BCMS). Its purpose was to do for the English colonies what the larger BMS sought to do for heathen lands. Founders of this largely forgotten society argued that biblical missions must not neglect "our kinsmen according to the flesh." They said, "the self-exiled Briton is not to be forgotten. . . . He is still our brother."[108] Spokemen argued that work in the colonies would pay good dividends in souls saved, churches planted, and the increase in Baptist strength would in the long run result in more missions to the non-Christian world. The BMS, reacting perhaps to favorable response to the BCMS, changed its constitution to allow work in the colonies, whereupon the BCMS was abolished in 1843. However, the changes were largely cosmetic, and the BMS gave little aid to places like Australia. One historian has observed, "The B.M.S. went on after 1843 much as before . . . the constitutional change had led to no change in B.M.S. priorities."[109] A recent observer concluded, "The absence of any great

105. Bollen, *Australian Baptists,* p. 27.
106. Bollen, "English-Australian Relations," p. 290.
107. Manley and Petras, p. 18.
108. Bollen, "English-Australian Relations," p. 294.
109. Ibid., p. 298.

achievement was really the price Australian Baptists paid for English neglect and indifference."[110]

Lack of pastors and undue dependence upon lay preachers formed another handicap to early Australian Baptists. Pastors were few indeed, with only six in New South Wales in 1861. Until late in the Colonial period, ministerial training had to be obtained in England since there were no suitable Baptist schools in Australia.

A further obstacle arose out of the identification of Baptists with the lower classes of Australian society. J. D. Bollen made much of what he called "the burden of minorityhood" of Baptists in Australia, pointing out that this status was more than numerical; it was also spiritual and psychological. Noting that Baptists in Australia in the late 1800s "were a people under stress," he cited the dream of an Australian Baptist who visited the United States: "To be in a place where the Baptists are somebody and the Anglicans nobody."[111] For most of the Colonial period, Australian Baptists were destined to function more on the fringes of society than at its center.

When one takes account of these obstacles, the wonder appears not that Australian Baptists have not achieved more but that they have achieved so much. They came to the end of the nineteenth century, according to reports in the *Baptist Union Handbook,* with 18,261 members in 236 churches, served by 169 ordained ministers. In 1899 they had baptized 1,252 new converts.[112]

Baptists in New Zealand

Located "at the end of the world," some said, the beautiful islands of New Zealand stand out of the Southwest Pacific not far from Australia. Baptist interest in this area surfaced quite early. In October 1792, at the second meeting of the newly formed Baptist Missionary Society in England, New Zealand was mentioned as a possible field for missionary labors. In his *Enquiry* the previous year William Carey had expressed concern for the "poor, barbarous, naked pagans of New Zealand," a reference to the native Maoris.[113] However, economic opportunity and not missionary zeal first drew Baptists to these islands. A few Baptists were among those who met the high standards of "no riff-raff or convicts," thus qualifying for a place in the early settlement.[114]

Baptist beginnings. For the first several years Baptists in New Zealand

110. Manley and Petras, p. 91.
111. Bollen, *Australian Baptists,* p. 22.
112. *Baptist Union Handbook,* 1899, p. 539.
113. Paul Tonson, *A Handful of Grain: The Centenary History of the Baptist Union of New Zealand,* 1:25.
114. Ibid., p. 2.

worshiped mostly with other denominations, such as Plymouth Brethren and the Church of Christ. When Baptists became numerous enough, they formed separate "meetings," many of which later became churches. Laymen presided over these meetings and formed most of the early churches for the simple reason that ordained ministers were not available. Most of these pioneer efforts bore good fruit, but some of the laymen introduced doctrinal aberrations which hampered Baptists later. Churches served by lay pastors also showed a tendency toward independence; few would cooperate in early efforts to form an association or Baptist union.

The first Baptist minister in New Zealand was Decimus Dolamore who arrived in 1851 and that same year formed a church in Nelson, the first in New Zealand. Nine Baptist ministers had arrived by 1876, and thirty-seven by 1882, though most remained but a short time. Of the few who had ministerial training, most came from Spurgeon's College in London, thus fixing upon New Zealand Baptists the evangelical conservatism which has marked them to this day. One of the most notable was Thomas Spurgeon, son of the London pastor, who ministered about eleven years in New Zealand.

In time, Auckland and Wellington on the North Island, and Christchurch and Dunedin on the South Island, developed major centers of Baptist strength. Most of the early Baptist churches began with fewer than twenty members. Like their counterparts in Australia, and with as little result, the pioneer churches appealed to English Baptists for aid. In 1861 James Thornton, minister in Auckland, wrote:

> We have special claims upon the churches at home. You are constantly sending out your flocks for us to feed, and it is only fair that you should send us a little of your abundance wherewith to feed them. The class of persons you send are not those who have much to spare but those who come hither to better their condition.[115]

The early Baptist church buildings in New Zealand were painfully plain observers said. In 1882 one described the new chapel at Sydenham as "so plain that even the most puritanical among us would be satisfied." However, most of the Baptists were glad to have any building at all. Some of the larger churches formed preaching points nearby, with services conducted by gifted laymen or ministerial students. Called "branches" or "multichurches," many of these centers later grew into churches.

The Baptist Union. As early as 1852, Decimus Dolamore suggested that New Zealand churches join in a Baptist union with Australian churches, but nothing came of the suggestion. With small churches scattered over large areas, some doctrinal strife, limited leadership, and a scarcity of funds, one is not surprised that denominational organization came slowly to New

115. Ibid., pp. 8-9.

Zealand Baptists. The first structure was the Canterbury Baptist Association, formed by six churches in 1873. Its announced aim was "to advance the cause of the Lord Jesus Christ by promoting the formation of Christian Churches, by the sustenance of Evangelists, by the assistance of Pastors, by giving counsel if requested, touching matters connected with any of its associated churches."[116]

Of particular note was the "Canterbury Plan" of itinerant preaching, developed by the association on a circuit basis. Within a few years, thirty volunteer preachers had gone out under the plan, most of them laymen. In 1876 the association employed its first full-time evangelist, George Johnston. Also in 1876 they launched a newspaper which, after a series of name changes, became the *New Zealand Baptist* and is still published.

The success of the Canterbury Association led to plans for a larger union to include all the churches in New Zealand. In 1880 Charles Dallaston of Christchurch, called "the Father of the Baptist Union," called a conference which agreed "that it is desirable to form some practical Union among the Baptist churches in New Zealand . . . to promote the formation of new and the help of weak churches." This was favorably received, and the Baptist Union of New Zealand was formed at Wellington in 1882. It was a small beginning. Eight pastors and seven laymen from ten of the twenty-five churches agreed to form the union. Twenty-two churches became foundation members, three remaining aloof.[117]

The Canterbury Association disbanded in 1884, handing over its functions and its paper, the *New Zealand Baptist,* to the new union. In addition to promoting unity among the churches, the new body launched ambitious plans in home and foreign missions, ministerial education, and Sunday School work. The constitution of 1882 provided for a list of accredited ministers, no doubt reflecting problems the churches had experienced in the past with unsuitable leaders, lay and ordained alike. The new union was hampered by the refusal of some churches to participate and by limited funds. In 1888, for example, the union received only £105 for its entire work for the year.[118]

Even so, the Baptist Union of New Zealand accomplished a great deal. In the 1880s, home missions were launched among the native Maori population and among the new settlements on the West Coast. Like the Canterbury Association before it, the union sent out traveling evangelists. The most successful of these was Thomas Spurgeon, who from 1882 had been pastor in Auckland where the church grew to almost five hundred members, the largest in the land. In 1890-1891 Spurgeon covered New Zealand

---

116. Ibid., p. 106.
117. Ibid., pp. 108, 110.
118. J. Ayson Clifford, *A Handful of Grain: The Centenary History of the Baptist Union of New Zealand,* 2:74-75.

on preaching tours, gathering large crowds and recording impressive numbers of converts. In 1885 the union formed its own Baptist Missionary Society, which opened work in India. Realizing that the itinerant evangelist system, called "evangelism at the gallop," would not do, they also formed a Home Mission Society.

Internal dissension caused the union some anxiety. The small churches felt overshadowed, with major decisions being made by the few larger churches; "aided churches" resented having to consult the union about whom to call as pastor; and union leaders were unwilling for small churches to have the same vote as larger churches which, they said, would put Baptists "in danger of being governed by the most loud-lipped and ignorant of their members."[119] By 1890 almost half of the Baptist membership was in three large churches.

One of the most successful efforts of the Baptist Union was the promotion of Sunday School work. Until the turn of the century, many churches conducted Sunday Schools far larger than the church membership itself. A series of "Bible Clubs" brought Bible study opportunity to scores of young men and women. Efforts to introduce the all-age Sunday School failed.

A persistent problem for New Zealand Baptists was the shortage of qualified ministers. When the union was formed in 1882, almost one third of the churches were pastorless, with little hopes for improving their situation. Trained pastors were scarce, and one with a college degree was truly a novelty. In 1885 the union voted, "That steps be taken at once for the training of young men for the ministry," placing this work in the hands of a Student Committee.[120] No Baptist school was formed until 1924. Until then the few ministerial students were placed under the tutelage of some successful pastor, who led them to "read theology" and receive practical experience by assisting in ministry.

Doctrinal issues. Like Baptists everywhere, those in New Zealand faced doctrinal diversities. For the most part the General/Particular distinctions seemed less crucial in New Zealand, but Baptists were troubled by other problems such as millennialism, open versus closed communion, ecumenism, and the propriety of state aid for churches. From the first, many Baptists worshiped with other denominations. Beginning as a necessity, it later became a preference for those who wished to avoid a strictly denominational approach. The 1880 census showed 9,159 Baptists in New Zealand, but only 2,314 were worshiping in Baptist churches.[121]

Most of the New Zealand churches began on a closed communion basis; but by the 1890s, most had moved to open communion. As in Australia, many New Zealanders opposed government aid to churches, though a few

---

119. *New Zealand Baptist* (December 1892), p. 179, cited in Clifford, p. 13.
120. *New Zealand Baptist* (November 1886), p. 169, cited in Clifford, p. 32.
121. Tonson, p. 108.

accepted it. William Birch, pastor at the Tabernacle Church in Auckland, found himself in a minor tempest when he attempted to introduce infant dedication services in 1890. He called this "a Presentation Service for the little lambs of God's people," but this plus his open communion, Keswick-type holiness emphases, and the "Arminian flavour" of his doctrines led to his dismissal.[122] A few New Zealand Baptist churches absorbed emphases from the Church of Christ movement which had recently sprung from Scotland and reached fuller development in America.

Probably the most serious doctrinal problem facing New Zealand Baptists came from the Plymouth Brethren, a group formed in England in the 1830s.[123] Led by Anthony N. Groves and John Nelson Darby, the Plymouth Brethren developed fundamentalist doctrines, antichurch attitudes, and one branch of the movement adopted charismatic practices similar to later Pentecostalism. However, the Brethren were best known for their peculiar eschatology, involving a dispensational form of millennialism and a two-stage second coming of Christ, known as the *rapture*. Similar views were developed at about the same time by Seventh-Day Adventists in the United States.

Brethren teachings created problems for New Zealand Baptists throughout the nineteenth century. Some churches left the Baptists to join the Brethren; some pastors adopted Brethren views, left their churches, and drew away a number of Baptists with them. For example, after two years of struggle the Baptist church at Matakohe splintered; the *New Zealand Baptist* reported in 1878, "Plymouthism has practically broken it up."[124] The same fate befell a number of Baptist churches. William Biss, a leading lay pastor, fell into Brethren views and he who had previously founded Baptist churches found himself undermining others. A much more serious problem was the gradual infiltration of Plymouthism into Baptist life until it became accepted by some as historic Baptist doctrine. In 1884 Charles Carter, president of the Baptist Union, used the presidential sermon to combat the growing Plymouthism in Baptist ranks. A hearer said that Carter "shot scholarly holes through dispensationalism," but apparently it was not fatal for such views have survived among Baptists to the present.[125] Decimus Dolamore, assessing Baptist progress, said "but for strife and division we would have been five-fold what we are."[126]

Growth rate. Despite their vigor, New Zealand Baptists remained a small denomination. Only twenty-two churches formed the Baptist Union in

122. Clifford, p. 29.
123. For a good survey of the origin and teachings of the early Plymouth Brethren, see F. Roy Coad, *History of the Brethren Movement* (Grand Rapids: Wm. B. Eerdmans Publishing Company, 1968).
124. *New Zealand Baptist* (February 1881), p. 3, cited in Tonson, p. 68.
125. Clifford, p. 18.
126. Tonson, p. 53.

1882, and they had the misfortune to launch their most ambitious programs on the eve of serious economic recession. This led to massive out-migration in the 1880s, as people returned to England or moved to Australia. Thomas Spurgeon noted in 1888, "The Churches have suffered severely. Many of our members have been out of work for weeks and months. . . . Our sheep have scampered away from us. Literally by shiploads they have departed. Some of our best workers are not."[127]

Most of the churches consistently added members by baptism, but they tended to lose almost as many as they gained. The problem of "census Baptists," those who claimed the Baptist faith but refused to join any of the churches, continued to plague Baptists. The years 1882-1892 are known as the "dismal decade," with decline setting in at some places. Records for 1890, after almost a half-century of Baptist witness, show 29 churches affiliated with the Baptist Union of New Zealand, with 2,915 members, and fewer than 20 accredited ministers.[128]

Baptists in South Africa

In 1820 over four thousand English formed a new settlement in South Africa. A number of Baptists from Joseph Ivimey's church in London were among the settlers.[129] Within a few years, several Baptist churches emerged in the Cape Colony at the tip of Africa. The churches were without ordained ministers until William Davis arrived in the early 1830s. The church at Grahamtown is known as the "Mother Church" of South African Baptists.

Internal dissension troubled the pioneer Grahamtown church, and for fifteen years it met in separate branches. Tensions between Calvinistic and Arminian Baptists provoked schism when a later pastor, Alexander Hay, preached from the text, "God be merciful to us." Hay's thesis was that God uses the witness of redeemed persons to lead others to salvation, a concept not acceptable to Calvinistic church members. However, the church later reunited, and strict Calvinism tended to be modified in South Africa.

An early constitution of the Mother Church reveals more about the theological complexion of the first African Baptists. The church constitution said:

> Believing that Baptism, as instituted by our Lord Jesus Christ, is an immersion on a profession of faith in Him as the one and all-sufficient Saviour of sinners, we would receive into Church membership only those who have been thus baptized, but as we would not judge any man's conscience who may differ from us, we would cordially welcome at the Lord's table all who afford

127. *New Zealand Baptist* (December 1888), pp. 178-179.
128. Clifford, p. 13.
129. Sydney Hudson-Reed, ed., *Together for a Century: The History of the Baptist Union of South Africa 1877-1977*, p. 10.

satisfactory evidence that they love the Lord Jesus Christ in sincerity.[130]

This open communion/closed membership stance has marked the South African Baptists ever since, although there have arisen periodic protests against open communion, especially among the German immigrants.

In addition to the English, German and Dutch immigrants also settled in South Africa. Among the Germans who came in the late 1850s were a number of Baptists, including Carsten Langhein and his wife Dorothea. Langhein, who had more zeal than gifts for ministry, had been won to Baptist views in Germany. At the German town of Frankfort in South Africa, Langhein formed a Baptist church in 1861, with sixty-one members. While recognized as an elder, Langhein could not cope with the growing pastoral needs. The church appealed to the German patriarch, Johann Oncken, for aid. Oncken urged them to patience, saying, "Such men [as you request] do not grow on apple trees, nor are they produced as a baker produces loaves of bread."[131]

The German Baptist Assembly at Hamburg in 1867 appointed Carl Hugo Gutsche to South Africa. Gutsche, who had served as assistant to Oncken, provided stable leadership for German Baptists in South Africa for a generation. He gathered the scattered German Baptists and formed "the church of baptized believers in British Kaffraria" in late 1867. When Gutsche arrived, Baptists had no church buildings in British Kaffraria; within twenty-five years he had built twenty-five churches. Emphasizing "planned giving," he never opened a church that was not debt free. By the time of formation of the Baptist Union in 1877, the German Baptists slightly outnumbered the English.

In late 1867 a Dutch farmer, J. D. Odendaal, was converted to Baptist views. The church minutes record that Odendaal "acknowledges before the congregation that he is a poor lost sinner, and could be saved only by the blood of Christ. . . . He desires to join us and be baptized."[132] He was baptized by Gutsche and for some years acted as a lay preacher among German and Dutch immigrants. In 1875 the German church, led by Gutsche, ordained Odendaal and in 1886 he founded *Die Afrikaanse Baptiste Kerk* of Dutch Baptists. However, the Dutch Baptists never grew as rapidly as did the English and Germans.

Never content just to cling to the tip of Africa, the Baptists from the first had dreams of taking the gospel to the interior even before the famous David Livingstone opened that vast land to European influence. As early as 1873, four churches founded a "Baptist Sustentation Fund" for home missions, the first effort at denominational structure. The formation of the

130. Ibid., p. 117.
131. Ibid., p. 19.
132. Ibid., p. 21.

Baptist Union of South Africa in 1877 seems in retrospect almost accidental. The occasion was the installation of a new pastor at the Grahamstown church, where pastors and deacons from six churches met in July 1877. After the induction, one of the pastors "suggested that the opportunity be taken to form the Baptist Union of South Africa," which they immediately did. The next day a new constitution was adopted, and six churches, four English and two German, formed the new union. Their historian described them as "small in numbers, scant in wealth, devoid of theological training, bereft of home support . . . [and] scattered over vast distances."[133] They launched a work that in six years had grown to include sixteen ministers and thirteen churches, in all twenty-six places of Baptist worship.

The success of the new union is more surprising in that it combined English and German churches, with their different views. The English followed open communion, while the Germans kept a restricted table. More important, perhaps, were their differing views of ecclesiology. Out of their seventeenth-century origins, English Baptists had developed an autonomous view of the church, fearful of ecclesiastical control and jealous for the freedom of each congregation. The Germans, with different origins and different experiences in their *Bund* structures, preferred to concentrate power in the denomination. In the presidential message to the Baptist Union in 1881, Gutsche said, "All our German Churches form one Church."

The nineteenth century was for the British an age of empire and an age of missions, and often the two went together. This spirit was absorbed by the Baptists in South Africa. In 1892, the centennial of the BMS, Baptists in South Africa formed their own missionary society and launched plans more ambitious than their abilities warranted. Baptists had more response among European imigrants than among the native African population. By 1898 they reported 3,033 "European" members and 172 "Native" members of union churches.[134] This does not comprise all the Baptists in Africa, however, for a number of churches had not affiliated with the union. In 1894 *The South African Baptist* was established, and it still functions as the official voice of the denomination.

Baptists in Canada

Canada, it is said, is a nation formed in defiance of geography. This vast stretch of British North America, divided into ten states or provinces, forms an area larger than Europe or the United States. In 1867 the Atlantic and Central Provinces formed a confederation, called the "Dominion of Canada," which the Western Provinces later joined to form the modern nation. In addition to a concentration of French Catholics in Quebec, Canada has been settled by immigrants from the United States, England, Scotland, all

---

133. Ibid., pp. 25, 42.
134. From annual handbooks, cited in Hudson-Reed, p. 84.

the major European countries, and also has sizable communities of Chinese and Japanese. The Baptist witness in Canada dates from the 1770s, and since then the work has grown to form one of the major world Baptist communities. As in the United States, Baptist work in Canada has moved from east to west and has grown more from the migration of settlers than the work of appointed missionaries.

Canadian Baptists reflect considerable diversity, accounted for by several factors. First, the vast extent of the Canadian landscape meant that Baptists often remained isolated, with little contact with outsiders or other Baptists in the Dominion. Second, Baptists in Canada reflect their various origins, with some stemming from England, others from America, some from Scotland, others from various European backgrounds. Black people, fleeing slavery in the South, also formed a Baptist witness in Canada, especially in the Atlantic Provinces.

Third, a major theme of Canadian Baptist history revolves around differences between American and English patterns of Baptist belief and practice. The "search for identity" about which Canadian Baptist historians have written comes down to a choice between English and American patterns of churchmanship; doctrinal beliefs, as between different levels of Calvinism; church practices, as in the open versus closed communion controversy; and structural patterns, whether missionary work should be conducted through denominational boards or by separate societies. In general, Canadian Baptists have drawn from both English and American patterns but have forged their own distinctive Canadian form of Baptist life.

Baptists in Canada can best be presented, perhaps, in terms of the three major geographical divisions: the *Atlantic Provinces* of Nova Scotia, New Brunswick, Prince Edward Island, and more recently Newfoundland; the *Central Provinces* of Ontario and Quebec; and the *Western Provinces* of Manitoba, Saskatchewan, Alberta, and British Columbia.

The Atlantic Provinces

Nova Scotia and New Brunswick nurtured the earliest Baptist churches in Canada. Migrations from New England brought Baptists, or people with Baptist sympathies, to these areas from the 1760s onward. Some migrants came on the waves of the First Great Awakening; others were among the farmers and fishermen known as the "Planters" who came after 1760; and after the Revolutionary War, a number of English loyalists left what they regarded as a rebel nation to return to British rule in Canada. From these various groups, early Baptists were recruited.

Paradoxically, one major founder of Baptist work in Canada was not a Baptist. Henry Alline (1748-1784) was a "New Light" Congregationalist from Rhode Island. He conducted a number of preaching tours of the Atlantic Provinces, preaching a fervent form of revivalism, and gathered converts into churches. Later, as in New England, many of these churches became Baptist. Ebenezer Moulton (1709-1783), a Baptist preacher from Massachusetts, formed a Baptist church at Horton (now Wolfville), Nova Scotia in 1763. This church lapsed when Moulton returned to the States, but it was reconstituted in 1778 and is now recognized as the oldest Baptist church in Canada. The Horton church is sometimes called "the mother church of Baptists in Canada," for at least twenty other churches grew out of it.

A group of churches in 1798 formed the "Baptist and Congregational Association," the first such association in Canada. This shows the close relationship between Baptists and New Light Congregationalists. However, since Baptists were a majority, *Congregational* was dropped in 1800, leaving a Baptist body composed of twelve churches in Nova Scotia and six in New Brunswick. A few years later they voted to "consider themselves a regular close communion Baptist Association" and withdrew fellowship from churches that allowed either open membership or open communion.[135] In 1821 the association divided into two, one for churches in Nova Scotia and one for New Brunswick churches.

Baptists beginnings in Prince Edward Island stem from the work of John Scott and Alexander Crawford, laymen from Scotland, who formed a few churches in the early 1800s. The Nova Scotia Association also sponsored some church extension work in Prince Edward Island, but growth was not rapid. In 1826, for example, there were 15 ministers for 28 churches and a membership of 1,347 in New Brunswick, and 17 ministers for 29 churches and a membership of 1,711 in Nova Scotia.[136]

The first efforts at a larger union came in 1846, when the various associations were grouped into the Baptist Convention of Nova Scotia, New Brunswick, and Prince Edward Island. Its main purpose, according to the founders, was "to advance the interests of the Baptist denomination and the cause of God, generally." The new convention represented a constituency of 88 ministers, 173 churches, and 14,152 members.[137] In 1879 the name was mercifully shortened to the Baptist Convention of the Maritime Provinces. As the convention gained acceptance, it assumed leadership in missions, education, and Sunday School promotion, work previously done by the associations or separate societies.

Since foreign missions was specifically assigned to the new convention, one of its first acts was to establish a board for that work. By the end of the century, the Maritime Convention was sponsoring 20 missionaries and almost 100 native workers in 7 mission stations in India. They reported 8

135. George E. Levy, "The United Baptist Convention of the Maritime Provinces," in Davis C. Woolley, ed., *Baptist Advance,* p. 141.
136. Cited in Robert G. Torbet, *A History of the Baptists,* 3rd ed., p. 139.
137. Levy, "The United Baptist Convention of the Maritime Provinces," in Woolley, p. 145.

overseas churches with a membership of 415, plus additional work in 15 outstations and 65 villages.

Home mission work had been a hodgepodge of efforts by interested individuals, local churches, associations, and several societies. After formation of the convention 1846, Maritime Baptists consolidated their home mission work in the unified Home Mission Board. Their work bore fruit, with 106 churches formed in the two decades from 1850 to 1870. Especially remarkable was the work of Silas T. Rand (1810-1889) among the Micmac Indians of the Maritimes.[138] Witness among the Acadian French and the Gaelic-speaking settlements in Cape Breton proved less successful. Several women's mission circles were formed as early as 1870, primarily by Miss Maria Norris. The circles were merged into the Woman's Baptist Missionary Union in 1884, later known as "The Woman's Convention."

From the first, Maritime Baptists realized the need for an educated clergy and laity. A schism in one of the Anglican churches in Halifax in the 1820s brought a number of educated new members into Baptist life. They intensified the already growing sentiment for a Baptist school. In 1828 Baptists formed the Nova Scotia Education Society. The society formed the Horton Academy at Wolfville, and in 1838 they formed Queen's College, which has survived as the present Acadia College. The New Brunswick Baptists established a seminary in Fredericton in 1838, which lasted until 1872.

About 1880 a move was made to have the Baptist Theological Seminary at Toronto transformed into a central training center for all of Canada. To that end the theological departments of other schools, including Acadia College, were for a time transferred to Toronto. However, the experiment failed to win acceptance. Distance, expense, regional loyalties, and, above all, the tendency for Canadians to enroll in theological schools in the States caused the project to fail. The handsome gifts of Senator William A. McMaster (1811-1887) transformed the Toronto school. It later moved to Hamilton, taking the name of McMaster University.

A number of black people settled in the Maritimes, including immigrants from Africa as well as blacks fleeing slavery to the south. The earliest known black Baptist in Canada was David George (b.1742), an escaped slave who traveled the underground railroad to Canada. He preached and formed churches among the black population in Nova Scotia. At first these congregations joined existing associations. However, in 1854 Richard Preston, a former slave who had escaped from Virginia and had been ordained in London, gathered about a dozen black churches into the African Baptist Association of Nova Scotia. This association later was received into the Maritime Convention. By the time of confederation in 1867, about half of the blacks in Canada lived in the Halifax area, most of them Baptists.

Nothing better illustrates the influence of New England Baptists upon

138. Ibid., p. 147.

their northern neighbors than the growth of Freewill Baptists in Canada (sometimes written Free Will). In New England, the Freewills emerged in New Hampshire in the 1780s, led by Benjamin Randall. They rebelled against the stern determinism of the Calvinist system; the "Free" in their name referred to their belief in man's freedom to choose his eternal destiny. Different groups were known variously as Free Baptists, Freewill Baptists, or Free Christian Baptists. Though the differences were negligible, at least to outsiders, they were not able to merge into one group in Canada until the 1860s. The pioneer leaders of the movement in Nova Scotia were Jacob Norton (1792-1868), Asa McGray (1780-1843), and Thomas Crowell (1768-1841). They enjoyed their greatest success in areas where Henry Alline's revivalism had undermined rigid Calvinism. In 1819 Norton organized the first church of this type in Nova Scotia under the name of Free Christian Baptist, and in 1821 McGray wrenched a Calvinist church at Barrington away from the association and transformed it into a Free Baptist Church.

The Freewill movement had several churches in New Brunswick by 1826, most of them stemming from Maine. In 1832 a half dozen churches formed a Free Baptist Conference. All the churches met in a "yearly meeting," while the local areas held "quarterly meetings." Among the Freewills, the denomination exercised a degree of influence, at times even control, over the local congregations which would have been intolerable among the Regular Baptists.

Rapid growth marked the Freewill Baptist movement, for it came just as Calvinistic determinism was losing much of its appeal. One of the Freewill leaders observed, probably correctly, "They [the Regular Baptists] embraced the highest Calvinistic views and injured their influence . . . and the hearts of many were turned against them."[139] By 1900 the New Brunswick Conference had 156 churches with 12,352 members, whereas in Nova Scotia there were 23 churches and 3,391 members.[140]

The Central Provinces

Baptist advance was slow in Quebec due to the prevalence of French Catholics, but Ontario proved a more fertile field. The first Baptist churches in the Central Provinces were found in three clusters: in the eastern townships of Quebec; in the Niagara area of western Ontario; and along the northern shore of Lake Ontario from Toronto to the Bay of Quinte. Most of these churches were formed by ministers from the States, representing the Regular Baptist position. Before forming their own associations, some of these churches affiliated with the Danville Association in Vermont.

"The Baptist Church of Christ in Caldwell's Manor," formed in 1794 on the shores of Lake Champlain by Elisha Andrews, probably ranks as the

139. Ibid., p. 151.
140. Ibid.

first Baptist church in the Central Provinces.[141] The church was composed mostly of immigrants from Connecticut. One of its members, William Marsh, received ordination in 1795 and formed several other churches in the area. In the Niagara area, the first church was formed at Beamsville. Some claim it was founded as early as 1776, but extant records do not confirm its existence before 1807.[142] The first church in northern Ontario was apparently formed in 1799 at Hallowell (now West Lake) by Reuben Crandall. Three neighboring churches in this area formed the Thurlow Baptist Association in 1802, the earliest denominational organization in the Central Provinces.

About 1816 another type of Baptist witness came to central Canada with the arrival of Scottish Baptists in the Ottawa Valley. They brought a style of piety and church life learned in the Scottish Highlands from the Haldane revival influence. With aid from Britain, they also formed a Baptist college in Montreal in 1838. John Edwards, a convert of James Haldane, arrived in Canada in 1819 and soon formed several small congregations. In 1829, while in Scotland, he enlisted John Gilmour and William Fraser to come to Canada as missionaries. Gilmore settled in Montreal, while Fraser went to Breadbane. By 1836 these various efforts had resulted in enough churches to form the Ottawa Baptist Association.

Efforts at larger organization among Baptists of the Central Provinces proved frustrating. Between 1833 and 1851 several societies, conferences, and fellowships were founded, only to lapse almost as quickly. Doctrinal differences, diverse national origins, and distance were among factors which prevented unification. Perhaps the most devastating issue was the communion controversy, which divided Central Baptists for most of the nineteenth century. One historian has interpreted this as basically a tension between British and American patterns of Baptist life.[143]

However, unification eventually came. In 1851 the Regular Baptist Missionary Convention of Canada, West was formed with its first meeting held in Hamilton, Ontario. In 1858 the churches east of Lake Ontario formed the Canada Baptist Missionary Convention, East. Satellite societies, newspapers, women's work, and youth organizations grew up around each convention. In 1888 these two groups merged into the Baptist Convention of Ontario and Quebec, with boards for various kinds of ministry. In the years 1890 to 1900 the churches increased from 388 to 464, and membership from 33,000 to 44,000.[144]

141. G. Gerald Harrop, "The Baptist Convention of Ontario and Quebec," in Woolley, p. 159.
142. Ibid., p. 160.
143. Ibid., p. 168.
144. Ibid., p. 162.

The Western Provinces

The prairie provinces of Manitoba, Saskatchewan, and Alberta, plus the coastal province of British Columbia, make up the majority of the land area of Canada, but a minority of the population. Baptists got a later start in that area. After confederation in 1867, most people anticipated increased immigration to the Northwest Territories, as the prairie provinces were then known. The Ontario Convention sent Thomas L. Davidson and Thomas Baldwin to scout the region and report on prospects for Baptist work. As a result of their report, Alexander McDonald (1837-1911) was sent to Winnipeg in 1873 and in 1875 formed a church of seven members. He was commissioned by the Ontario Baptists to bear a distinctive Baptist message to the Western Frontier: "You will preach not only the gospel, but also the doctrines peculiar to us as a people. We claim that we have a mission among the denominations, . . . That mission is to maintain the ordinances in their purity, and to keep them as they have been delivered to us."[145] Upon arriving in Winnipeg, "Pioneer" McDonald was asked by clergymen of other denominations why he had come to an area with so few Baptists. "To make more Baptists," was his confident reply. By 1878 the Winnipeg church had eighty-nine members and was self-supporting. Several other churches sprang up in this area and later formed the Red River Association of Regular Baptist Churches.

The Baptist Convention of Manitoba and the Northwest Territories was formed in 1884 and, small as it was, at once undertook work in foreign and home missions, started a denominational paper, and laid plans for a Baptist college in the west. The Canadian Pacific Railway opened that area to further settlement, and Baptist work shared in the increase. Churches sprang up at Calgary (1888), Medicine Hat (1890), Edmonton (1892), and Stratcona (1895). By 1900 there were 99 churches and 170 preaching stations in the prairie provinces.

Baptist witness in British Columbia, which became a province only in 1871, began independently of work on the prairies. Coastal Canada was more closely linked to the United States than to Maritime Canada. Many of the members who made up the early British Columbia churches, and the pastors who served them, had migrated northward from the States. One early observer said, "Much of the material [members] of the . . . Victoria churches was first gathered in Seattle."[146] Before their own structures evolved, some churches in British Columbia affiliated with associations in Washington.

---

145. Jarold K. Zeman, *Baptist Roots and Identity*, p. 33.
146. Gordon H. Pousett, "Formative Influence on Baptists in British Columbia, 1876-1918," *Baptist History and Heritage*, p. 15.

Alexander Clyde, who migrated from Ontario, formed the first Baptist church at Victoria in 1876. Of the original fifteen members, eight were black. A number of blacks, some of them Baptists, had migrated to Canada from California as early as 1858. The biracial church at Victoria disbanded in 1883 and reorganized as the Calvary Baptist Church, with the declaration that in the church "no distinction shall ever be made in respect to race, colour or class."[147]

Robert Lennie was another important early Baptist leader in British Columbia. Trained in England, Lennie laid the groundwork for the First Baptist Church of Vancouver in 1887. Other important leaders include the "Stackhouse Triumvirate," of J. H. Best, Ralph Trotter, and W. T. Stackhouse. These forceful and creative men gave leadership to Baptist work in British Columbia through the important decade of the 1890s. Much of their work involved the planting of new churches and was carried on through the British Columbia Baptist Church Extension Society, formed in 1896. In 1897 the Baptist Convention of British Columbia was formed with 11 churches and 1,050 members.[148]

The Baptist Convention of British Columbia tended at times to exercise more leadership than similar bodies in Atlantic Canada. One writer attributed that to geographical and economic factors in the far West which "combined to produce unstable congregations, lack of steady leadership, and financial weakness, which have in turn made it necessary for the denomination and its structures to be strong."[149] The convention often held property for the churches, paid their debts, and examined candidates for ordination. Tension arose out of the fact that in the 1890s a number of Maritime Baptists migrated to British Columbia, bringing their preference for more British patterns of church life.

Jarold K. Zeman, a recent president of the Baptist Federation of Canada, has described Canadian Baptist history as "a search for identity."[150] Caught between the pervasive influences of American Baptists to the south and their British Baptist backgrounds, Baptists in Canada have struggled to find their own path. As with most Baptists, Canadians have faced tensions between the seemingly paradoxical Baptist traditions of cooperation and independence. In the first half of the nineteenth century, independence was paramount, but after 1850 cooperation came to the fore.

The controversy over communion, perhaps the most severe doctrinal conflict among Canadian Baptists in the nineteenth century, involved far more than the Lord's Supper. Closed communion churches usually repre-

---

147. Ibid., p. 19.
148. William C. Smalley, "Baptist Work in Western Canada," in Woolley, p. 178.
149. Pousett, p. 22.
150. Jarold K. Zeman, *Baptists in Canada: Search for Identity Amidst Diversity.*

sented Calvinist theology, along with an emphasis upon the independence of local churches. Open communion churches, on the other hand, often held a more optimistic Arminian theology and encouraged the churches to cooperate. At another level, perhaps the communion controversy illustrates the fundamental question facing Canadian Baptists in the nineteenth century: Would they follow the British Baptist pattern of church life (including open communion), or would they follow the pattern of their aggressive brethren in the United States (including closed communion). Canadian Baptists drew from both traditions, though open communion gradually prevailed.

Summary

British Baptists fanned out over the globe during the nineteenth century. Wherever Baptists went they formed churches and, in time, local associations and national unions. Baptists' common background gave them an underlying unity, while their response to doctrinal differences in various lands created a mosaic of Baptist diversity.

10

United for Mission: Baptists in America, 1800-1845

The early 1800s marked not just a new century but a new era in American history. The Revolutionary War severed the colonies from England, and the War of 1812 confirmed the existence of the United States as a separate nation. Abundant raw materials, a vigorous transatlantic trade, the opening of the American West, and a growing population brought prosperity and optimism. The Louisiana Purchase in 1803 and the Lewis and Clark expedition in 1804-1806 accelerated westward migration, and the "Manifest Destiny" of the 1830s showed that Americans intended to occupy the land from coast to coast. The advancing railroads helped to expand the new nation from a narrow ribbon of real estate along the Atlantic seaboard to a vast empire poised for greatness.

All of these trends affected Baptists. Baptists' support for the Revolution greatly improved their public image, winning them friends in high places and low. Presidents Washington and Jefferson both wrote to Baptist groups expressing appreciation for their loyal support of the patriot cause. The various revivals so augmented Baptist growth that by 1800 they had become the largest denomination in America.[1] The "Second Great Awakening" in the early 1800s further extended Baptist growth and brought for the first time numbers of black people into the Baptist fold.

The foreign mission movement took early root in America. The newsy letters of William Carey were read at church and association meetings. English Baptist missionaries en route to India often came by way of America. During their weeks or months of layover they lived in Baptist homes, spoke in Baptist churches, and their zeal for missions proved contagious. Concern for the "aborigines," as the American Indians were called, and spiritual needs of settlers who followed the wagon trains westward, awakened a corresponding zeal for home missions. Church growth called for more pastors which, in turn, encouraged formation of training schools. The early 1800s also saw a moderating of Baptist theology toward more evangelistic emphases, and the newly won religious liberty allowed Baptists to expand their witness.

The early 1800s also brought conflict and controversy for Baptists. De-

---

1. Winthrop S. Hudson, *Religion in America*, 3rd ed., p. 118.

spite widespread adherence to the Philadelphia Confession of 1742 and creation of a new confession in New Hampshire in 1833, Baptists could not achieve theological consensus. Unitarians and Universalists claimed a few Baptist adherents, while others proved susceptible to the claims of Mormonism and Campbellism. Membership in secret lodges troubled some, while others debated the merits of Saturday versus Sunday worship. Some Baptists saw no place for human effort in religion and thus fathered the antimission movement; others favored missions but could not agree on how to organize the work. However, the greatest controversy which faced Baptists was slavery. This issue divided Baptists North and South in 1845 in a schism which continues to the present.

Against this background of progress and problems, perhaps the most important events from 1800 to 1845 center around the formation of the "Three Great Societies," for foreign missions (1814), tracts and publications (1824), and home missions (1832).

The Triennial Convention

On May 18, 1814, at the First Baptist Church of Philadelphia, thirty-three delegates met to form the General Missionary Convention of the Baptist Denomination in the United States for Foreign Missions. This was the first organization of national scope for Baptists in America. Although the cumbersome name called it a "convention," in constitution and function it was basically a society for foreign missions. Minutes of the formative meeting set the convention's purpose as "diffusing evangelistic light through benighted regions of the earth."[2] Most people referred to the new body in verbal shorthand as the General Convention, or more often as the Triennial Convention since it met every three years. The day-by-day work was carried on by a Managing Board from the Philadelphia area which met more frequently. The first delegates came mostly from the North, with only nine from the South, one of whom was chosen president—Richard Furman of Charleston. Thomas Baldwin of Boston was elected recording secretary and William Staughton of Philadelphia corresponding secretary.

Several developments prepared for this important new Baptist organization. The awakening of missionary zeal in England and America has been cited. At Williams College (Congregational) in Massachusetts a group of students led by Samuel Mills became interested in missions and met regularly for prayer and discussion. They formed a group, known as the "Brethren," to promote missions. On a sultry Saturday in 1806 five of these students, caught in a sudden thunderstorm, took refuge under the sheaves of a haystack near the campus and continued their prayer. This "Haystack Prayer Meeting," some say, marked the birth of the foreign mission movement in America, for there the students resolved to go beyond talk to action.

2. *Proceedings,* Baptist Convention for Missionary Purposes, p. 6.

One of the Brethren, Luther Rice, though not at the haystack prayer meeting, later said, "I have deliberately made up my mind to preach the gospel to the heathen, and I do not know but it may be Asia."[3]

After graduation from Williams College most of the Brethren went to Andover Seminary, where they came under the leadership of Adoniram Judson, a recent graduate of Brown University. Judson shared their missionary zeal. Deeply moved by a sermon entitled "Star in the East," which made a powerful appeal for missions in India, Judson had knelt in the snow on a February day in 1810 and dedicated himself to missions in heathen lands.[4]

Upon the urgent appeal of Judson, the Congregational leaders in 1810 formed the American Board of Commissioners for Foreign Missions, the first organized foreign mission body in America. Baptists, as well as others, contributed to the new work. The Board appointed Judson and Mills, with their wives. After some delay Rice was also appointed, though his intended bride canceled their wedding when she learned of his mission plans. Judson married Ann Hasseltine on February 5, 1812. At Judson's ordination a few days later, Ann so much wanted to share in her husband's commitment to ministry and missions that she slipped quietly out of the pew and knelt in the church aisle while the ministerial council laid ordaining hands upon her husband. The new missionaries sailed on February 19, 1812.

On the long sea voyage the Judson and Mills couples kept busy with study, witnessing to the ship's crew, and exercising to maintain their health (dancing was their favorite exercise, according to Ann). Knowing that they would meet the Baptist veteran, William Carey, Judson studied his Greek New Testament on the subject of baptism, coming to the startling conclusion that immersion of believers is the biblical form of baptism. In a later letter Ann said, "Mr. Judson's doubts began on our passage from America. . . . I tried to have him give it up, and rest satisfied in his old sentiments, and frequently told him, if he became a Baptist, I would not."[5] Apparently Ann later changed her mind, as both were immersed as Baptists in Calcutta by William Ward. Luther Rice, arriving in India on a separate ship, also embraced Baptist views. After a brief hesitation, the newly convinced Baptists saw the necessity to resign from the Congregational board. They decided that Rice, being single, should return to America to enlist Baptist support for the mission venture. Neither Rice nor Judson expected this would take more than a year or two, whereupon Rice expected to return to the heathen field. Rice never returned, ending his days in promoting

---

3. Evelyn Wingo Thompson, *Luther Rice: Believer in Tomorrow*, p. 36.

4. Claudius Buchanan, "Star in the East," *Massachusetts Baptist Missionary Magazine* (September 1809), pp. 202-206, in American Baptist Historical Society (ABHS), Rochester, N.Y.

5. Cited in Robert A. Baker, ed., *A Baptist Source Book*, p. 53.

foreign missions and education in America, a change of plans Judson never approved and which for years brought coolness between the two.

Beginnings

Rice did his work well. Backed by letters from Judson and Carey, Rice's eloquence led Thomas Baldwin of Boston's Second Church to form a local society to aid the Judsons. Rice traveled among the churches and associations, spellbinding audiences with his exciting message on missions. As one observed, "He was the only one who had gone out into the darkness of paganism and returned to tell us what existed there."[6] Rice helped form a number of mission societies and discovered others already in existence, forming a link of communication and cooperation between them. The Massachusetts Baptist Missionary Society, formed in 1802, expressed interest. Though primarily a home mission body, its constitution provided for preaching in the United States "or farther, if circumstances should render it proper."[7] Before the end of 1813, at least seventeen local and regional Baptist societies had agreed to share in the foreign mission work. Rice conceived the plan of drawing delegates from these groups to form one nationwide mission agency, influenced thereto by his own Congregational background and perhaps by suggestions by William B. Johnson of South Carolina. Rice said:

> While passing from Richmond to Petersburg in the stage, an enlarged view of the business opened upon my contemplation. The plan which suggested itself to my mind, that of forming one principal society in each state, bearing the name of the state, and others in the same state, auxiliary to that; and by these large, or state societies, delegates be appointed to form one general society.[8]

This plan came to fruition in the Triennial Convention of 1814. One could scarcely overestimate its importance. From this small beginning, Rice envisioned a great denomination united for multiple ministries at home and abroad. He later wrote to Judson, "My mind became impressed with the importance of a general combination of the whole baptist interest in the United States, for the benefit alike of the denomination here, and the cause of missions abroad."[9] The dream of a united denomination led by a full-time general secretary proved premature; it later came to pass but not during Rice's lifetime.

6. Thompson, p. 88.

7. Cited in William H. Brackney, ed., *Baptist Life and Thought: 1600-1980*, p. 158.

8. Cited in Thompson, p. 97.

9. William H. Brackney, ed., *Dispensations of Providence: The Journal and Selected Letters of Luther Rice, 1803-1830*, pp. 118, 155.

Society Versus Convention Plans

Despite being committed to missions, the delegates in 1814 sharply disagreed on methods of organization. The disagreement subjected the proposed constitution to several revisions and delayed its adoption for several days. Most of the Northerners preferred to work through an independent *society* unconnected to the churches, while the Southerners unanimously favored an *association* or *convention* plan based upon the churches. The constitution finally adopted was a compromise, with elements of both plans. Both society and convention plans had strong advocates, but the "swing vote" apparently was that of Francis Wayland, outstanding Northern Baptist theologian and later president of Brown University. For almost a decade he favored the Southern plan, during which time the Triennial Convention gradually took on the functions as well as the name of a convention. By 1823 that body sponsored not only foreign missions but also home missions, publications, and education. However, by the mid-1820s Wayland had changed his mind and turned against the unified convention approach. Partly through Wayland's influence, by 1826 the Triennial Convention had reverted completely to a society basis and removed its headquarters from Philadelphia to Boston, thus further diminishing Southern participation. Sharp differences had arisen between Northern and Southern Baptists before the slavery issue became crucial among them. Wayland later wrote:

> An attempt was made, pretty early in the history of this organization [the Triennial Convention], to give it control over all our benevolent efforts. It was proposed to merge in it our Education Societies, Tract Societies, Home Mission Societies, and our Foreign Mission Societies, so that one central Board should have the management of all our churches, so far as their efforts to extend the kingdom of Christ were concerned. After a protracted debate, this measure was negatived by so decided a majority that the attempt was never repeated, and this danger was averted. We look back, at the present day, with astonishment that such an idea was ever entertained.[10]

Wayland concluded, "I now rejoice exceedingly that the whole plan failed," but he did not emphasize his own role in the plan's earlier success nor its later failure.

Whoever fails to grasp the differences between society and convention methods will never understand Northern and Southern Baptists.[11] The *convention* concept is based upon *churches,* which send messengers (or delegates, as they were then called) and contributions to a central body to plan and carry out Christian ministries beyond the local churches. The

10. Francis Wayland, *Notes on the Principles and Practices of Baptist Churches* (New York: Sheldon, Blackman & Co., 1857), p. 185.

11. For an extended discussion of the society vs. convention plans, see Robert A. Baker, *The Southern Baptist Convention and its People 1607-1972,* pp. 97-101.

convention (or association) usually covers a specific geographical area, as a county or state. Further, the convention may sponsor multiple ministries, limited only by its vision and resources, the same convention appointing different boards for foreign missions, home missions, Sunday School publications, Christian education, or whatever. While contributions are obviously essential, the convention plan is *church based;* its representatives come from churches and its work is to some degree the work of the churches combined. This plan emphasizes a strong central denomination. In essence, this is a plan whereby cooperating churches work together.

The *society* plan, by contrast, is based upon the voluntary participation of interested *individuals.* Membership in a society is determined mostly by financial contributions. The fact that most members of Baptist societies were also members of Baptist churches was never a key concern because the societies had no official connection with the churches. Most societies were *cause centered;* and interested individuals from any place might join by paying the membership fee, though a few also had geographical limits. An important difference is that the society took a single-barreled approach, with a separate society for each cause. Thus societies for foreign missions, home missions, or Christian education were separate, with different leaders, different members, and separate meetings. The society involves not churches, but individuals working together.

Each plan has both advantages and disadvantages. The society is simpler, requires no extensive denominational machinery or approval for its work, maintains more local control, and has the advantage of a committed membership. Those not interested in the society's cause simply do not join. To its adherents, it also seems to protect the autonomy of the churches. However, the society plan does not enlist the involvement of churches, seldom builds denominational identity and loyalty, and makes overall denominational planning and correlation difficult.

The convention plan tends to enlist the churches, build denominational identity and loyalty,and allows correlation and balance between the various causes sponsored. Its adherents feel it preserves the autonomy of the churches, though it does call for a degree of centralization. However, at times the convention plan proves cumbersome since the whole body must deliberate and decide on all kinds of work. Problems arise when some voting members have greater interest in one cause, like foreign missions, and lesser commitment to others. This sometimes leads to rivalry as leaders seek to enlist support for the causes they represented. In general, the convention plan calls for more denominational machinery. The convention plan emphasizes the denomination more, and it creates more denomination to emphasize.

At times Baptists have used both plans. As early as the 1650s Baptist associations in England encouraged itinerant preaching as far as Wales and Ireland. William Carey tried to persuade the Northampton Association to sponsor foreign missions, and only when they refused did he fall back to form a missionary society independent of the churches. William Staughton, one of those who helped form the BMS, later came to America where he was one founder of the Triennial Convention and for years a strong proponent of the denominational approach. In America, the Philadelphia Baptist Association, formed in 1707, became a general denominational body. Covering several states from New England to the South, representatives from affiliated churches established a college, sponsored home missions, and employed an "evangelist at large" to preach and form churches in emerging frontier communities. The Shaftsbury Association formed a similar plan by 1802. Thus the associational plan had considerable precedent among Baptists.

The society plan also has historical precedent. The primary pattern for this style of structure comes from the Baptist Missionary Society of England in 1792, a body vastly influential among Baptists on both sides of the Atlantic. Picking up some patterns of English culture, where people tended to cluster into interest groups to push for certain political or economic viewpoints, the typically English *society* was thus adapted to religious use, as the earlier political concept of *association* was also adapted into Baptist usage. The Massachusetts Baptist Missionary Society, formed in 1802, provides an American example of the society method.

Given these two plans of Baptist work, why should the North so strongly prefer the society while the South almost unanimously chose the convention? Both from theological and historical backgrounds, early Baptists in the North feared that denominational structures might endanger local church autonomy. Most absorbed exaggerated views of local church independence from their Particular Baptist background. In New England, Baptists had seen how Congregational "consociations" had gained a measure of control over local churches. For example, though Isaac Backus was one founder of the Warren Baptist Association in 1767, Backus's own church was so skittish they would not affiliate for some years.

On the other hand, as W. W. Barnes has pointed out, three important factors conditioned Baptists in the South to favor the convention plan.[12] First, many early Baptists in the South came from a General Baptist background, with traditional General concepts of a strong denomination. Second, the Philadelphia Association influenced Baptists south of the Potomac, conditioning them to accept its methods as well as its theology. Third, the rapid growth of Separate Baptists after 1750 helped fix a centralizing trend upon Baptists in the South. Early Separate associations functioned as ecclesiastical bodies, superintending numerous ministries, such as ordination, itinerant preaching, church extension, and at times church discipline.

Probably social conditions also influenced Southerners' preference for a

12. William Wright Barnes, *The Southern Baptist Convention: 1845-1953*, pp. 6-8.

convention. New England was from the first intensely democratic. Its town meetings encouraged every citizen to express his views, and its small factories and isolated farms defied centralization. Southern society, on the other hand, reflected a more centralized plantation social structure which was at times almost feudal. The South had no equivalent of the town meeting. Add to these factors the powerful advocacy of such Southern leaders as Richard Furman, W. B. Johnson, Robert B. Semple, and Jesse Mercer, to say nothing of Luther Rice, and Southern preference for a more unified denominational approach becomes clearer.

Expansion

The first annual report of the Triennial Convention managing board noted that "the Board undertook the patronage of Rev. Luther Rice as their missionary, to continue his itinerant services in these United States for a reasonable time; and also the patronage of Rev. Adoniram Judson, now in India, as a missionary under their care and direction; for whose use they ordered one thousand dollars to be transmitted to India by the earliest opportunity."[13] The board in 1815 appointed printer George H. Hough and his wife to join the Judsons at Rangoon but requested Rice to delay his return overseas. They said that " such is the actual posture of the missionary business in this country, . . . as, in the judgment of the Board, imperiously to require his longer detention and farther labors here—therefore, Voted that brother Rice for some time longer continue his labours as an agent of this Board."[14] For his work, Rice was allowed eight dollars a week plus expenses, a sum he was not always able to collect. Year after year the board repeated the request for Rice to remain a little longer in America, for they felt no one else could arouse Baptist sentiments for missions as he could. The criticism Rice faced later for not returning to India seems unjustified, though clearly with each passing year he lost some of his early zeal for going back.

Promoting foreign missions. The journal and letters of Luther Rice reveal his methods of work. The board furnished him with "credentials," or letters of introduction to churches and associations. Wherever he went, Rice produced the credentials and invariably was invited to preach. He was an extremely effective preacher, able not only to expound the missionary message of the Bible but also to draw upon anecdotes and his own overseas experiences, thus making a profound impact upon audiences. He always took a missionary offering wherever he spoke, and where possible helped form local missionary societies auxiliary to the Triennial Convention. Rice also had a gift for enlisting others in the missionary task.

13. *First Annual Report,* Baptist Board of Foreign Missions, Philadelphia, 1815, p. 10, in ABHS.
14. Ibid., p. 11.

The endless travel was not easy for Rice. At first he used public transportation but later rode horseback (and bested John Wesley's record of one day's horseback travel by three miles, ninety-three to ninety). Later in life he acquired a more comfortable one-horse sulky, a kind of two-wheeled buggy. Rice swam rivers, braved snowstorms, endured the heat, and at times detoured to avoid hostile Indians or bandits, lodging in homes along the way when he could find them, under the open sky when he could not. Whether in crude frontier cabins or the fine homes of Richmond or Boston, Rice felt equally at home. He would usually read from the Bible, sing a hymn, pray with the family, and speak at least a brief testimony for missions wherever he stopped overnight. Though immensely popular, Rice also had his detractors. Some complained of his ready wit and use of humor in preaching, feeling that such levity was unbecoming in the pulpit. Some of his hostesses along the way expressed amazement at the number of cups of tea and coffee he could drink at one sitting.

The board faced an unusual situation in 1815 with the application of Charlotte H. White, a widow, for foreign appointment. She had given the first recorded missionary contribution to the Triennial Convention in 1814, the sum of fifty dollars.[15] Realizing the board would not send out a woman alone, Mrs. White asked to be appointed with the Hough family. She wrote, "My wishes are to reside in their family in the character of a sister to Mrs. Hough and a sister in the Lord; with them to pursue such studies as are requisite to the discharge of missionary duties."[16] Her work would consist, she said, "either in taking management of a school, or to hold private meetings should there be opportunity, with native females, to instruct them in the principles of the gospel."[17] That statement reveals not only the dedication of Mrs. White but also something of the work of women missionaries of the time, their sphere largely restricted to women and children. Judson welcomed Hough, for he needed a printer, but he was dismayed at Mrs. White's coming. Shortly after arrival, she married Joshua Rowe, an English Baptist missionary recently widowed, and accompanied him to his new station at Digha. In a letter to Lucius Bolles, marked "private," Judson said somewhat ungallantly that "Mrs. White very fortunately disposed of herself in Bengal. Fortunately, I say, for I know not how we would have disposed of her in this place. We do not apprehend that the mission of single females to such a country as Burmah, is at all advisable."[18] Perhaps Judson was concerned that when a single woman lived in a missionary family, no amount of explanation could avoid the impression of polygamy, so common among the Burmese.

15. Cited in Leon McBeth, *Women in Baptist Life,* pp. 83-84.
16. *Second Annual Report,* Baptist Board of Missions, Philadelphia, 1816, p. 112.
17. Ibid.
18. McBeth, p. 84.

During these early years, a powerful stimulus to Baptist missions, second only to the work of Luther Rice perhaps, was the lively correspondence of Ann Judson. Ann's vivid description of missionary life and labors in "heathen lands" both informed and inspired Baptists in America. These epistles were read in homes, churches, association meetings, and published in Baptist and other religious papers. These letters plus her personal visit to the States in 1822-1823 gave wide publicity to foreign missions. The later accounts of her sufferings along with Mr. Judson, her heroic efforts to protect him and preserve his New Testament translation, and her early death quickly gave "Ann of Ava" the status of a martyred saint. American women were especially moved by Ann's poignant remark in 1813 that "there are no English families in Rangoon, . . . there is not a female in all Burmah with whom I can converse."[19]

The constitution of the Triennial Convention provided not only for the appointment of foreign missionaries but also, if necessary, "to take measures for the improvement of their qualifications," thus holding out the possibility of a theological school in the future.[20] Both Richard Furman and W. B. Johnson went to Philadelphia in 1814 with proposals for a general denominational body sponsoring multiple forms of ministry. In the presidential address, Furman urged that Baptists form "a general theological seminary." He said, "It is deeply to be regretted that no more attention is paid to the improvement of the minds of pious youths who are called to the gospel ministry."[21] He concluded:

> The effects of the present convention have been directed chiefly to the establishments of a foreign Mission; but, it is expected that when the general concert of their brethren and sufficient contributions to a common fund shall furnish them with proper instruction and adequate means, the promotion of the interests of the churches at home will enter into the deliberations of future meetings.[22]

Home missions. However, the first expansion of the Triennial Convention came not in education but in home missions. By 1800 several local home mission societies were already at work, and strong associations such as the Philadelphia and Charleston had for some years sent out preachers to destitute areas. In 1817 the Triennial Convention officially launched a home mission effort. They added to their already lengthy name the phrase, "and other important objects relating to our Redeemer's Kingdom," and changed the constitution to authorize the board "to appropriate a portion

19. Letter to Parents, July 30, 1813, printed in *First Annual Report,* Baptist Board of Foreign Missions, p. 39.
20. *Proceedings,* Baptist Convention for Missionary Purposes, p. 4, in ABHS.
21. Richard Furman, "Address," *Proceedings,* Baptist Convention for Missionary Purposes, p. 42, in ABHS.
22. Ibid.

of the funds to Domestic Missionary purposes."[23] A major catalyst for this expansion was John Mason Peck, a young pastor in the New York Catskills. Like Rice, John and Sally Peck were converts from Congregationalism. Peck wrote in his diary:

> Friday Evening, June 25, 1813. Received the last number of the Baptist Missionary Magazine. The missionary accounts from India are very interesting. . . . Oh, how I wish I was so circumstanced in life as that I might be able to bear the gospel into some distant pagan lands where it has never yet shined. A large part of the American continent is also involved in darkness. Yes, under the immediate Government of the United States, there is an abundant field for missionary labor.[24]

Peck felt that his lack of theological education and his growing family responsibilities would disqualify him from foreign missions. However, in 1815 he made a three-week missionary tour, mostly in upstate New York, which was crowned with success and confirmed Peck in his commitment to missionary work. In June 1815 he first met Luther Rice when both attended the Warwick Association. Peck was thrilled with the message of Rice and invited him to spend the night at the Peck home, where the two young men talked far into the night. That night Peck committed himself to home missions, and Rice committed himself to persuading the Triennial Convention to sponsor home missions. In January 1816, Peck wrote to William Staughton, corresponding secretary, about possible appointment:

> By communications from Brother Rice I learn that it is in contemplation to establish a mission in the Missouri Territory. On this subject I found in my own mind such a correspondence of feeling and sentiment that I could not forbear opening my mind to him. Ever since I have thought upon the subject of missions, I have had my eye upon the people west of the Mississippi. . . . I have had serious thoughts of making a tender of myself to the Board.[25]

Encouraged in this direction, Peck spent several months in Philadelphia studying in the small theological school conducted by Staughton and preaching in area churches as opportunity presented. On May 17, 1817, Peck wrote in his diary: "This day, I suppose, will decide my future prospect. . . . Six o'clock. The long agony is over. The Board have appointed Mr. Welch and myself as missionaries to the Missouri Territory. . . . In this I think I see the hand of God most visibly."[26]

For 129 days in 1817, the Pecks made their way westward to Saint Louis

23. Cited in John M. Murdock, ed., *The Missionary Jubilee: An Account of the Fiftieth Anniversary of the American Baptist Missionary Union*, p. 101.
24. Cited in Rufus Babcock, ed., *Memoir of John Mason Peck*, p. 38.
25. Ibid., p. 48.
26. Ibid., pp. 67-68.

by wagon, boat, and on foot. When they arrived in Saint Louis, Peck had to be carried ashore on a stretcher, too sick with fever to walk. As soon as he was able, Peck began to preach in the area, gathered children for a school, began evangelistic work among the black population, and made excursions into surrounding area to preach and distribute Bibles and tracts.

A man of vision and energy, Peck laid foundations for the strong Baptist witness which still prevails in the Midwest. He saw that millions of settlers would surge westward. He spied out the land and published a "Gazeteer" which both encouraged and guided settlers. Not afraid of new methods, Peck pioneered in founding Sunday Schools, women's mite societies, and missionary societies. He founded the earliest Baptist churches west of the Mississippi; published the first newspaper in that area; and founded Alton Seminary, which became Shurtleff College, the first college in the West. Such were his many ministries that Peck was later nicknamed "the man with twenty hands."[27] Peck served two terms in the Illinois state legislature, where he is credited with helping keep slavery out of that region.

A glimpse of Peck's work can be seen in the following diary entry in 1825:

> I have been absent from home fifty-three days; have travelled through eighteen counties in Illinois and nine in Indiana, rode nine hundred and twenty-six miles, preached regular sermons thirty-one times, besides delivering several speeches, addresses, and lectures. I have been enabled to revive three Bible societies, . . . to establish seven new societies; . . . aided in forming three Sabbath-school societies, and in opening several schools where no societies exist.[28]

In 1820 the Triennial Convention voted to close the Western Mission, not from lack of confidence in Peck but from a desire to concentrate on foreign work. The board directed Peck to transfer to Fort Wayne to assist Isaac McCoy in the Indian Mission. However, Peck resigned instead. He said:

> The field around me appears too important to be thus early vacated. . . . It really seems to me as if the voice of Providence was saying to me: "Stay where you are," . . . I do not see how I could leave this region; for St. Louis must not be relinquished by the Baptists.[29]

For the next several years, Peck remained in the Saint Louis area, though moving his headquarters a few miles northward into Illinois. The Massachusetts Baptist Mission Society provided about five dollars a month for the Peck family, a fraction of what was provided for the Judsons, and Peck eked out the rest of their living by teaching, publishing a paper, and occasionally by day labor.

Theological education. Another area into which the Triennial Conven-

27. Benjamin P. Browne, *Tales of Baptist Daring,* p. 96.
28. Babcock, pp. 208-209.
29. Ibid., pp. 168-169.

tion expanded its work was theological education. One tour among the Baptist churches convinced Rice that a better trained ministry was essential and that without improvement in this area no Baptist venture could succeed. Therefore, almost from the first Rice promoted Baptist education, not in competition with missions but as an essential part of missions. William Staughton, a graduate of Bristol in England and who for years taught young ministers in his home, also knew the value of education as did Furman of South Carolina and Mercer of Georgia.

At its 1817 meeting, the Triennial Convention amended its constitution to provide that "when competent and distinct funds shall have been received for the purpose, the board from these, without resorting at all to mission funds, shall proceed to institute a classical and theological seminary.[30] This amendment became the source of much confusion and conflict in the years ahead. How "competent" should the funds be before launching a seminary? How "distinct" must these funds remain from the mission treasury? With characteristic optimism, Rice believed that whatever *should* be done *could* be done; and he proceeded apace with ambitious educational plans. Already several strong Baptist educational societies were at work in Philadelphia, New York, and South Carolina. It was agreed that the school kept by Staughton in Philadelphia would become the convention's seminary, that it would be relocated to Washington City, and that Staughton would become president and Irah Chase would serve as professor. The board appointed a committee which drew up a "Plan," providing that the new institution, to be named Columbian College, would offer two years of classical studies, eventually with full courses in medicine and law, plus two advanced years in theological studies. Thus Rice nurtured a dream of a great Baptist university combining classical and theological studies, centrally located in the nation's capital, which would unite the Baptists throughout America and advance their cause at home and overseas. The failure of that dream and the subsequent separation of university and seminary training had a far-reaching impact upon Baptists in America.

Some felt the board rushed the school beyond its convention's authorization and certainly beyond its means. Even Richard Furman led the Charleston Association to protest the seeming haste and inadequate planning behind the venture. In 1817 the board purchased forty-six acres of choice land in Washington, about a mile northwest of the Capitol, made plans for a building, and employed a president and a professor. Agents scurried about America, England, and Europe raising pledges, gathering a library, and buying suitable "apparatus" for the scientific and mechanical classes. The 1820 Triennial confirmed those actions, and that year a five-storied building 117 feet by 47 feet, was completed. Theological classes opened in the fall of 1821, with classical studies to commence the next year. Student enroll-

---

30. Cited in Thompson, p. 117.

ment exceeded expectations, and the college became the talk of Washington, attracting the favorable attention of congressmen, senators, and even the president.

Unfortunately, Baptists had not raised enough money to pay for all that was built nor for the reportedly lavish "public occasions" that President Staughton sponsored for publicity value. Clearly Rice and the board had not observed the convention's caution to proceed only with adequate funds in hand. Instead, they proceeded on pledges, and financial reverses in the 1820s rendered many of these uncollectible. Despite the accumulating debt, the college continued to recruit more students, thus obligating the college to "board" them. Perhaps the final folly was a plan to erect yet another building as large as the first, also on borrowed money.

Baptists leaders did not learn the true financial conditions of the college until probably too late to save it. In 1826 the convention voted to sever all connections with Columbian, though expressing the hope that the school might remain Baptist in emphasis. Rice spent the rest of his life in a desperate effort to save the college for Baptists. He traveled incessantly, juggled funds, and in the end damaged his own reputation in his heroic but losing efforts. Eventually Congress bailed out the school. The college changed its name to George Washington University and in 1904 severed its last remaining links to the Baptist denomination.

Several factors help explain why Baptists fell short on their first educational effort of national scope. In the 1820s economic hard times reduced Baptist contributions for all causes, and schools were even then notoriously expensive. Some antieducation bias lingered among Baptists. Not all Baptists wanted to combine collegiate and theological training in the same school; most Baptist schools founded after the failure of Columbian separated the two. Further, regional ties commanded great loyalty in the early 1800s. Perhaps the idea of one central school to unite Baptists North and South was simply premature. The decades from 1830 to 1850 saw waves of Baptist colleges founded in the various states, with regional appeal and loyalties.

Publications. Yet another area into which the Triennial Convention expanded after 1814 was publications. A great "print hunger" marked Americans in the nineteenth century. Newspapers and magazines were read and passed along to others until they literally wore out. Even the dullest published sermons found eager readers, and not always just among the faithful. Many a traveler squinted at a book over a Western campfire. Judson in Burma often appealed for tracts, and home missionaries like John Mason Peck stuffed their saddlebags with tracts and Testaments for the frontier communities. The Sunday School, quite new in America in the early 1800s, began to catch on and provide a growing market for Bible lessons and teacher aids. In 1818 the Triennial Convention founded the *Latter Day Luminary,* a paper published in Washington City and soon boasting a circulation of about eight thousand copies a month. The paper promoted all the various denominational mission and education efforts, adding its voice to the several privately printed Baptist papers of the time, including its neighbor in Washington, the *Columbian Star*. The latter paper was established in 1822 and eventually became the *Christian Index* of Georgia, the oldest Southern Baptist paper still published.

Reversion to Society Approach

By 1826 the Triennial Convention had "cleansed its constitution" of every provision except foreign missions. By a large majority, the convention voted to drop every "superadded enterprise," thus severing all ties with home missions, Columbian College, and the *Latter Day Luminary*. It replaced Staughton as corresponding secretary, dismissed Rice as traveling agent, moved the convention headquarters from Philadelphia to Boston, and took action to guarantee that the convention would henceforth remain firmly under the control of New England Baptists. Lucius Bolles, the new corresponding secretary, called the 1826 session "revolutionary" and said the convention "is now a simple body, with one undivided object, and that object is the promulgation of the Gospel among the heathen."[31] Clearly the Triennial Convention had undergone a general housecleaning, and the reversion to the society method was complete.

Those who favored the society method had not been silent during the decade the Triennial Convention blossomed into a general denominational body; indeed, they resisted that development every step of the way. However, the society forces could not prevail against the crowds of Southern delegates who attended when the Triennial meetings were held in Central and Southern states. Nor could they prevail against the powerful voices of Francis Wayland in the North and Richard Furman in the South, especially during the ebullient days when every new work appeared to prosper beyond all expectations. However, all that changed. New England delegates managed to move the 1826 meeting from Washington to New York and then worked carefully to assure a large attendance from the North. By that time, Wayland had changed his mind and advocated the society method which he had previously opposed. Furman was dead, Staughton disspirited, and Rice discredited. More important, perhaps, was the undeniable evidence that expansion into other forms of ministry had detracted from foreign missions. Baptists in the North also distinctly disapproved of the trend to concentrate denominational headquarters, institutions, and leadership in the South.

Baron Stow, who called the 1826 meeting "a stormy session," pointed out that in the years 1820-1823 the board had sent no new missionary to Burma. As early as 1815, the board had plans to enter Brazil and Africa, but they

31. Murdock, p. 107.

had to be shelved for lack of funds. Meantime, Isaac McCoy's mission to American Indians sometimes cost more in one year than the entire Burma mission, due partly to McCoy's refusal to abide by the financial restrictions voted by the board.[32] The immediate increase in foreign mission funds and personnel after 1826 confirms the views of society advocates who argued that foreign missions could prosper best on its own. However, long-range comparisons show that ultimately the strong denominational plan raises more money for foreign missions as well as for other forms of ministry.

Theologically, some Baptists found their doctrine of the church in conflict with the concept of a denominational convention. Apparently enough people shared that view to lead the 1826 Triennial Convention to reaffirm that, "as fears have existed to some extent . . . that at some future day this body might attempt to interfere with the independence of churches—therefore, Resolved, In accordance with its former views, and with well-known and long established Baptist principles, this Convention cannot exercise the least authority over the government of Churches."[33] The appearance of state conventions in the 1820s, and the trend in some quarters to assume a stair-step representation from churches to associations, to state conventions, and to a general convention, fanned these fears.[34]

The theology underlying the society concept was best expressed by Francis Wayland. Basing his view upon the "absolute independence of the churches," Wayland said, "I do not see how it [a church] can possibly be *represented.*" He noted that "Jesus Christ left his church without any general organization. . . . Is it not probable that as he left it, so he intended that it should continue to the end of time?"[35] He recalled that the Triennial Convention had become for a time a denominational body but looked back with astonishment that such a thing should have been tolerated. Similar views on the primacy of the local church took root in the South, combined with a few other ingredients, and produced the Landmark movement.

Wayland insisted that the various societies in no way represented or involved the churches, a viewpoint which continued among Northern Baptists well into the twentieth century. Wayland's position not only undercut the convention form of denominational organization, but in effect negated any *denomination* at all. Some antimission Baptists used arguments similar to Wayland's to invalidate the entire missionary effort.

In various writings, Roger Hayden, an English Baptist pastor-historian with no vested American interests, documented the sectional strife among

32. Baptists did not supply all this money for Indian missions; much of it came from the government.

33. *Annual Report,* Triennial Convention, 1826, p. 20, in ABHS.

34. See Winthrop S. Hudson, "Stumbling into Disorder" *Foundations,* pp. 45*f.*

35. See Wayland, pp. 157 *f.,* 177, 180.

Baptists in America before 1845.[36] As the Baptist population in the South and West multiplied, and as Rice concentrated in Washington such Baptist institutions as the denominational board, seminary, newspaper, and for awhile the publication work, Northern Baptists saw their power erode. Further, as Winthrop S. Hudson pointed out in his provocative article, "Stumbling into Disorder," these institutions conflicted head-on with newspapers and seminaries in the North.[37] "Preoccupied as they were with their own educational ventures," Hudson wrote, "the Baptist leaders of Massachusetts and New York tended to regard with something less than enthusiasm" the establishment of a rival seminary in Washington.[38] Similarly, Wayland, editor of the *American Baptist Magazine,* led the struggle to drop the *Latter Day Luminary* of Washington and make his own New England paper the voice of the convention. Hudson concluded that Baptists in the North deliberately packed the 1826 meeting and, with this regional control, proceeded to dismantle the convention, sacrificing national Baptist unity and cooperation to regional interests. Of sixty-three delegates present in 1826, twenty-three were from Massachusetts and seventeen from New York, giving Northerners a clear majority on every vote. The reorganized convention, according to Hudson, himself a Northern Baptist, put control firmly in the hands of a few elite leaders and assured that those leaders would be drawn mostly from New England. While these facts are clear, an interpretation less judgmental than Hudson's is possible.

One of the less lovely aspects of the 1826 meeting was the discrediting and dismissal of Luther Rice as agent of the convention. Actually, he had already begun to give less time to convention tasks and more to Columbian College. In retrospect, Rice was apparently a man of great virtues and equally great faults. His vision for Baptists was vast, but he attempted to bring it to reality too rapidly. With him, expansion quickly became overexpansion; whatever needed to be done he tried to do at once, confidently expecting the money would come later. Time and time again, he appears to have gone beyond convention authorization in various projects. Repeatedly the convention instructed Rice not to proceed until the cash was in hand; just as repeatedly, he branched out on pledges and sometimes just on hopes. Rice's vague financial records concerned some. At times as debts mounted, Rice would allot funds given for one cause to some other cause, always intending to replace them. Some thought the college benefited at the expense of foreign missions.

36. See Roger Hayden, "Kettering 1792 and Philadelphia 1814," *Baptist Quarterly;* "William Staughton: Baptist Educator and Missionary Advocate," *Foundations;* and the more extensive work, *William Staughton: Baptist Educator, Missionary Advocate and Pastor;* copy in ABHS.

37. Hudson, "Stumbling into Disorder," pp. 45 f.

38. Ibid., p. 53.

Some Baptists even accused Rice of dishonesty in handling funds. That prompted Rice to demand an investigation of his own conduct, both personal and official. The "Committee on the Conduct of Mr. Rice," chaired by Lucius Bolles, one of Rice's critics, seemed determined to discover some serious transgression but found none. Their 1826 report criticized Rice as "a very loose accountant," called him "too loose in all his dealings," and set out in painful detail the "many imprudences . . . laid to his charge." However, the committee concluded, "We can find nothing censurable in Mr. Rice, . . . nothing like corruption or selfish design."[39] Perhaps the crowning indignity came when even Rice's friends agreed that, while he could continue to *raise* funds, the *disbursement* of the funds had to be taken out of his hands. Thus publicly discredited, even though officially exonerated, Rice gradually withdrew from denominational leadership.

Rice died in 1836, exhausted in body and soul. He labored to the last for his beloved college; on his deathbed he instructed friends to sell his horse, Columbus, and his sulky and give the proceeds to the college. He died as he lived, alone. Though he had proposed marriage to different women, none accepted him. While his old colleagues overseas, the Judsons, were elevated to a status near sainthood, Rice, who labored at home to build a strong denomination, was vilified by many. Rice's faults were glaringly real, but the twentieth century has seen a renewed appreciation for his pioneer contributions in transforming scattered churches into a great denomination.

The 1826 reversion to a society basis had far-reaching consequences. Baptists North and South were committed to different patterns of work which would make continuing cooperation almost impossible. While slavery was the major factor in the 1845 schism, the events of 1826 paved the way for division and probably made schism inevitable.

Foreign Missions to 1845

The records show a remarkable increase in foreign mission funds and personnel after 1826. In 1832 the Baptists had 14 missionaries in Burma, 5 ready to sail, and another 5 in school awaiting appointment. By the mid-1830s they had opened missions in France, Germany, Greece, and China, and by 1844 had 10 missionaries in Europe.[40] In 1835 the convention reported 72 missionaries, the opening of additional fields, and the appointment of single women as missionaries. At the next Triennial Convention, the number of missionaries had risen to 98, and in 1844 to 111. Of these, 10 served in Europe, 6 in West Africa, 63 in Asia, and 32 in North America, mostly among the Indians, a work which continued under the foreign board until 1865.

---

39. Brackney, *Journal,* pp. 157-158.

40. *Thirtieth Annual Report,* Board of Managers, Baptist General Convention for Foreign Missions, carried in *The Baptist Missionary Magazine* (July 1844), p. 216, in ABHS.

Baptist growth also continued in the United States. By 1844, according to the best records available, Baptist strength stood at 720,046 members, gathered in 9,385 churches, with 6,364 ministers. This represented a 360 percent increase in the 30 years since 1814.[41]

The Baptist General Tract Society

Beginnings

The second society of national scope among American Baptists was the Tract Society, formed in Washington City, D.C., in February 1824. It was literally an idea drawn from a hat. On one occasion Samuel Cornelius removed his high-crowned hat, from which bundles of gospel tracts fell to the floor. Cornelius had obtained the tracts from another denomination and carried them in his roomy hat rather than his pocket. Noah Davis witnessed this incident, and it led him to reflect upon the potential for a tract ministry among Baptists. Davis wrote to his friend, James D. Knowles, editor of the *Columbian Star,* saying, "I have been thinking for some time how a Tract Society can be got up in Washington. . . . I now feel very much the necessity of having tracts to scatter in destitute places. It is a plan of doing good which is scarcely known among Baptists."[42]

In the February 14, 1824 edition of the *Star,* the editor inquired if others might be interested in such a project. Response was immediate and positive. Eighteen men and seven women met on February 25, 1824, at the home of George Wood where, after prayer by Luther Rice, they formed "The Baptist General Tract Society." Its constitution specified that "its sole object shall be to disseminate evangelical truth, and to inculcate sound morals, by the distribution of tracts."[43] In time the Tract Society developed into one of the major religious publishing houses in America. From the first its basis was to be distinctly Baptist, yet not narrowly sectarian. The society basis of this new venture was a forecast of the reversion to that method effected two years later in the Triennial Convention.

During its first year of operation, the Tract Society received only $373 in offerings but managed to issue nineteen tracts dealing with doctrinal, devotional, and moral topics. Most of the tracts were brief, from 4 to 12 pages, and included such titles as "Life of Bunyan," "Friendly Advice," "The Death Bed of a Medical Student," "Address to the Sinner," and "The Dreadful Superstition of the Hindoos."[44] By 1830 the Tract Society had issued almost 100 titles, for a total of 1,394,000 tracts with 15,393,000

41. Cited in Albert Henry Newman, *A History of the Baptist Churches in the United States,* p. 442.

42. Murdock, p. 362.

43. Daniel G. Stevens, *The First Hundred Years of the American Baptist Publication Society,* p. 114.

44. *First Annual Report,* Baptist General Tract Society (BGTS) Washington, 1825, p. 21.

pages.[45] Many tracts emphasized a temperance theme; the Tract Society played a major role in the development of the temperance movement among Baptists.

These "silent messengers" had great potential because they were eagerly read by saints and sinners alike. In the first annual report, Tract Society leaders noted, "Not the least advantage of the tracts is, that they enable every man to become a preacher of righteousness." Such ink-and-paper witness enabled the gospel to penetrate to destitute places which could not sustain a preacher. The *Baptist Tract Magazine,* a monthly launched in 1827, carried frequent testimonies and examples of persons converted from reading tracts. One pastor wrote:

> I have often known a tract to be read repeatedly, . . . And when I have conversed with a man who has no interest in Christ, and left him alarmed at his condition as a sinner, I wish to put into his hand a tract that may be the means of directing him to his Saviour. But I am grieved, from day to day, that I have no tracts.[46]

The Tract Society also helped to unify American Baptists. The vast extent of the country, the scattered churches, and difficulty of communication hampered the emergence of common views and practices. By its publications, the Tract Society led Baptists along the path of unity, helping them to develop common viewpoints on doctrinal and moral questions and more uniform styles of worship. In the early 1830s, the society bound several of its most popular tracts into a single volume under the title of *The Baptist Manual,* with a goal to place a copy in every Baptist home in the Mississippi Valley. The society also issued a hymnal, *The Psalmist,* in 1843, which not only helped through its large sales to sustain the society but also, according to reports in 1845, "has already done more to produce uniformity in the use of hymn books, and correct the taste of the churches, than its projectors ever anticipated."[47] *The Psalmist* never proved popular in the South, however, and its publication marks an important turning point in which the styles of worship between Baptist churches North and South began to develop in different directions.[48] By 1845 about fifty thousand copies of this hymnal had been distributed.

In 1827 the Tract Society moved from Washington to Philadelphia, over the strong objections of Luther Rice who wanted to maintain the Baptist concentration in the capital. However, Philadelphia offered advantages in shipping. At least half of the tracts sent out had to be shipped first to Philadelphia anyway and from there redirected to their destination. George

45. *Sixth Annual Report,* BGTS, 1830, p. 11.
46. *First Annual Report,* BGTS, 1825, p. 8.
47. *Sixth Annual Report,* BGTS, 1845.
48. Hugh T. McElrath, "Turning Points in the Story of Baptist Church Music," *Baptist History and Heritage,* p. 10.

Wood resigned as secretary to remain in Washington, to be succeeded by Noah Davis.

Expansion

The Tract Society underwent a major reorganization in 1840 when its name was changed to the American Baptist Publication and Sunday School Society. The name change reflected the expansion of the work beyond tracts and showed the growing importance of Sunday School literature. The society also received a bequest from the will of Jesse Mercer to issue the complete works of Andrew Fuller in three volumes. Other books by 1845 illustrate the range of materials offered, including such titles as the *History of Baptism* by I. T. Hinton; *The Mode and Subject of Baptism* by M. P. Jewett; *The Pilgrim's Progress* by John Bunyan; *The Reign of Grace* by Abraham Booth; *Church History of New England* by Isaac Backus; and *Baptism in its Modes and Subjects* by Alexander Carson.[49]

Another growing need which they supplied was for Sunday School lesson helps, especially for children and youth. The Sunday School was quite new in this country in the early 1800s. Rufus Babcock recalled that, as a boy growing up in a pastor's home, at age fifteen he had never heard of a Sunday School. In 1819 as a college student at Providence, Babcock and a few other students organized a Sunday School in the First Baptist Church. At first it included only children and youth, and the leaders struggled with questions of organization, teacher training, and above all where to find suitable lesson materials. One of the students involved was James D. Knowles, later to become one of the founders of the Tract Society. When Baptist Sunday Schools were ready for lesson helps, the Tract Society was ready to supply them, a fact of great significance.

From the first, the Tract Society also provided materials for overseas distribution, both in English and native languages. Indeed, the repeated calls of Judson for more tracts in Burma provided one motive for forming the society in 1824. Judson's letters often commented upon the tracts he received, described how he had used them and to what effect, and always requested more. By the late 1830s, the society also provided tracts in French and German. Johann G. Oncken, Baptist pioneer in Germany, wrote in 1834:

> I feel greatly endebted to the Directors of the Baptist General Tract Society, for the many excellent books sent me, most of which are already in circulation, especially those on baptism. . . . The English language is now studied, so that I can always make good use of books and tracts in that language.[50]

Oncken also noted that believers' baptism was just then under intense

---

49. *Sixth Annual Report,* American Baptist Publication Society (ABPS), 1845, pp. 8-9.
50. *Eleventh Annual Report,* BGTS, 1835, p. 19.

study in Germany and pointed out the importance of having another tract upon that subject translated into German and published as early as possible. By the 1840s, the society also produced a number of language tracts for immigrants to this country, mostly in French and German.

Perhaps the most ambitious effort of the society by 1845 was the plan to produce complete collections or "libraries" of books and pamphlets, in three categories: for Sunday Schools, for families, and for ministers. The Sunday School collection may be regarded as a forerunner of modern church libraries. The family library at first consisted of eight volumes, including doctrinal, devotional, and biblical topics, along with biographical studies of distinguished Christians. The society hoped to place a collection in every Baptist home in America. The minister's library included many of the same works, plus several others. Realizing the lack of theological training that prevailed among Baptist ministers in the South and West, the society hoped to provide this minimal library to every pastor. As resources allowed, they provided these free or at reduced costs. This helped carry out the hopes of John Mason Peck, secretary of the society 1843-1846, who wrote in 1843, "The paramount object of the Society . . . is to make our denomination, and all others over whom we have influence, a reading, thinking, working, and devotedly religious people."[51]

From the first the Tract Society sustained a unique relationship to churches in the South and West. Most of its founders and early supporters were from the South; and even after its move to Philadelphia in 1827, it remained geographically more accessible to Southerners than the other societies located in New York and Boston. Several local literature societies already supplied the needs of many Baptist churches in the North; Thomas Baldwin had formed such a society in Boston by 1811. Before the Tract Society was two weeks old, a sympathetic reader in Providence wrote that the new society would do well to "extend its operations more particularly to the southern and western parts of the Union."[52] The early leaders felt that the witness of tracts was more essential where ministers were few. Statistics of 1845 show that while Baptist churches in New England totaled 2,156 as compared to 6,282 in the South and West, most of the latter tended to be smaller and a greater proportion of them lacked pastors or even itinerant preaching.[53]

Relation to the South and West

In 1826, the year the Triennial Convention moved to minimize its relation to the South, the Tract Society urged:

51. Stevens, p. 18.
52. *Columbian Star,* March 6, 1824.
53. *Annual Report,* ABPS, 1845, p. 18.

Cast your eyes over the wide fields of the South and the West. They are already white for the harvest, but where are the laborers? Alas! Many of our churches are destitute of pastors, enjoying only occasional opportunities of hearing the word of life dispensed; and many extensive portions of our Southern and especially of our Western States, are seldom visited by preachers of the Gospel. We cannot send them preachers, nor are they able to support them if sent. But can we not send them these silent, though efficient messengers of truth, which cost but little and consume nothing?[54]

No evidence of the growing estrangement of Northern and Southern Baptists appears in Tract Society reports. The slavery controversy, so prominent in the two mission societies, was strangely absent from the Tract Society. The schism of 1845 did not extend to the Tract Society; in fact, one could not learn from its 1846 report that any such schism had taken place. Baptist churches in the South continued to patronize the Publication Society until the late 1890s.

Very quickly the Tract Society (later called Publication Society) won widespread acceptance in Baptist life, both North and South. It was a service organization, its products were popular, and it tended to be noncontroversial. It operated with little financial demand upon the churches, raising its own revenue by sales. In 1846 society leaders were no doubt correct when they affirmed "that the American Baptist Publication Society is of equal importance in its place with the Foreign, the Home, and the Bible Societies."[55]

The American Baptist Home Mission Society

Formation of the Home Mission Society in 1832 completed the trilogy of Baptist benevolent societies. For the remainder of the nineteenth century, American Baptists carried on their denominational ministries primarily through these three organizations: the American Baptist Missionary Union (ABMU, the old Triennial Convention, since 1826 located in Boston); the American Baptist Publication Society (ABPS, the old Tract Society, since 1827 located in Philadelphia); and the American Baptist Home Mission Society (ABHMS, located in New York City). Not until 1888 was a fourth national society added, The American Baptist Education Society (ABES), and it never won a niche in the denomination equal to the other three.

Early Home Missions

One must not assume that Baptist concern for home missions began only in 1832. As early as the 1630s Roger Williams preached to the Indians, and in the 1700s pastors like Hezekiah Smith spent several weeks of each year "itinerating in the wilderness" to preach the gospel and form churches in

---

54. Handwritten report for 1826, pp. 12-13, ABHS.
55. *Annual Report*, ABPS, 1846, p. 8.

frontier communities. The Philadelphia Association employed an "evangelist at large" to travel in destitute areas to preach and form new churches. Two major state mission societies were at work quite early, the Massachusetts Baptist Mission Society, formed in 1802, and the New York Baptist Mission Society, formed shortly thereafter. From the late 1770s the Charleston Association had sponsored home mission work through its General Fund, sometimes far beyond its associational boundaries. When the South Carolina state convention was formed in 1821, one of its tasks was to sponsor home mission work throughout the state. The several state conventions formed through the 1820s usually engaged in home missions; in fact, many of them, though called "conventions," were in reality home mission societies, a fact which Francis Wayland recognized and urged them to name themselves accordingly.[56] Despite these many efforts, there was, except for a brief period under the Triennial Convention, no organized home mission work of a national scope.

When it was barely a year old, the Triennial Convention showed interest in home missions. Its first annual report in 1815 mentioned the "native tribes in the West" and agreed "that something should be done for these unhappy natives."[57] In 1816 the board spoke of "the priority of originating a Western Mission, on a large scale, embracing the country beyond the Mississippi," and appointed a committee to plan for "a mission westward." Early home mission zeal led to the appointment of John Mason Peck and James Welch to the Missouri Territory in 1817. That same year the Triennial Convention appointed a Mr. Ranaldson to preach in New Orleans and named Isaac McCoy to establish a mission station among the Indians near Fort Wayne. To make that possible, the convention amended its constitution to say "that the Baptist Board of Foreign Missions for the United States, have full power at their discretion to appropriate a portion of the funds to domestic missionary purposes."[58]

However in 1820 the convention dropped its home mission work, keeping only the Indian station under McCoy. In a letter to Peck in Saint Louis, informing him the mission would be closed, the board gave three reasons for the action:

1. The want of ample funds for its vigorous prosecution.

2. A supposition on the part of the Board that this region would be soon supplied by the immigration into it of preachers from the Middle and Eastern States.

3. The opposition in the West was also urged as a reason for its being abolished. The triennial convention had accordingly recommended this

---

56. Wayland, p. 184.
57. *First Annual Report,* Baptist Board of Foreign Missions, 1815, p. 53.
58. *Annual Report,* Triennial Convention, 1817, p. 131.

course, which the Board, as in duty bound, thus carried out.[59]

The shortage of funds and opposition in the West were real enough, but Peck strongly dissented from the second reason given for closing the mission. He said:

> They [the Board] widely mistake when they deduce their reason "from the numerous emigrations of ministers to our Western settlements, that the period has arrived when it is no longer necessary to support any brethren as missionaries at these places." But one Baptist preacher has emigrated to Missouri, . . . since our arrival, and we heartily wish him back again.[60]

Peck reported that he found many of the farmer-preachers unfit, not always sober, and not always better when they were sober. In light of the spiritual needs of the Saint Louis area, Peck elected to resign rather than transfer to the Indian mission to assist McCoy. For a few years he was partially supported by the Massachusetts Baptist Mission Society.

Peck never gave up the dream of organized home missions in America. In 1826 he went East to try to persuade Baptists to renew that effort, but tensions in Baptist ranks that year ruined the timing and he never raised the subject. In a kind of Baptist equivalent to "let them eat cake," the Triennial Convention voted in 1826 that "if they [Baptists] desire to give for missions at home, let a Home Missionary Society be formed."[61]

Survey of the West

In a brilliant stroke, Peck invited Jonathan Going to visit the Western states in the summer of 1831. Going was the influential pastor in Worcester, Massachusetts. For almost three months the two men traveled by buggy throughout Kentucky, Indiana, Illinois, and Missouri. By the end of that tour, Going had agreed to use his influence to help form a mission society. Easterners had read of spiritual destitution in the new states, but written reports could not convey the depth of need. The two men saw countless frontier families with no Bibles and no opportunities to hear the gospel; small churches without pastors and no hope of obtaining pastors; overworked pastors trying to stretch their time to serve four to six churches at once; many churches without buildings, and others with inadequate buildings. Statistics in 1833 showed that at least 40 percent of all Baptist churches in America were without pastors, and in the West the ratio was much higher.[62] However, the destitution of the Western churches was probably even worse than the figures suggest. While many of the Eastern churches

---

59. Cited in Babcock, p. 166.
60. Ibid., p. 168.
61. *Annual Report,* Triennial Convention, 1826, p. 171.
62. *First Report of Executive Committee,* American Baptist Home Mission Society (ABHMS) (New York 1833), p. 8, in ABHS.

had full-time pastors, most pastors in the West were bivocational, devoting only a fraction of their time to ministry and often dividing that among several churches. Thus a church in the West that had preaching as much as once a month was counted with a pastor.

During the 1830s, Easterners became more concerned about spiritual conditions in the West. In 1835 Lyman Beecher issued his famous "Plea for the West," which proved a stimulus to home mission work in all denominations. Many feared that the frontier population, removed from church and cultural influences, would fall into barbarism and thus subvert the American culture. Baptists also noted that other denominations were making headway in the West, especially Roman Catholicism. At that time, American Protestants harbored an intense fear of Catholicism, and the desire to prevent Romanists from establishing a strong empire in the West provided one motive for Protestant home mission work.[63]

A New Society Formed

John Mason Peck and Jonathan Going laid the groundwork well for the new society. They first secured the cooperation of influential Baptist organizations and individuals in the East and then placed in the Baptist papers a call for a meeting in April 1832 to consider forming a home society. Delegates from fourteen states and one territory met in New York and voted unanimously to form the American Baptist Home Mission Society (ABHMS or HMS). Already a Provisional Executive Committee had been formed, a proposed consitution drawn, and fields of labor laid out. The delegates confirmed these arrangements with minor changes. The constitution provided that "the great object of this Society shall be to promote the preaching of the gospel in North America."[64] This field was inclusive, but the society noted that its concentration would be "more especially the Valley of the Mississippi." From the first the society adopted the motto, "North America for Christ."

The new HMS issued an Address to the Public, explaining its work and appealing for support. Pointing out the strategic importance of the West and noting that "this wide space" already contained one-third of the nation's population and would within a few years contain the majority, the society maintained that the West had to be converted and civilized or the nation was doomed. The new society was not in competition with foreign work but was part of the same world missions task. "Every tie which we have recognized as binding us to seek the salvation of the heathen in foreign

63, Terry G. Carter, "Baptist Participation in Anti-Catholic Sentiment and Activities, 1830-1860." See esp. chapter 3, "Baptist Missiology and Education During the Anti-Catholic Crusade."

64. *Proceedings of the Convention Held in the City of New York for the Formation of the American Baptist Home Mission Society,* 1832, p. 2, in ABHS.

lands, attaches us with yet greater strength and closeness to these our compatriots," the leaders said.[65] Perhaps some people had raised a question about the need for a Baptist society since the interdenominational American Home Mission Society was so active, for the HMS leaders pointed out that "while they would dread and abjure the spirit of sectarianism, which seeks merely to count the number of its proselytes, and is less anxious for the essence than the forms of Christianity, they recognize it as their duty to disseminate, with all candour and kindness, their own views of Christian doctrine and practice."[66]

The new society elected Jonathon Going corresponding secretary. Going served 1832-1837; he was succeeded by Luther Crawford, 1835-1839; and next came Benjamin Hill, 1839-1862. The years do not correspond exactly, for some served as assistant secretaries or cosecretaries.

Southerners participated little in the Home Mission Society. Baptists from the South had practically nothing to do with the society's formation, provided none of its major leaders, and made only minimal contributions to its work. This is in contrast to the overwhelming Southern participation in the Tract Society formed 8 years earlier. An 1834 report showed 34 life directors of the HMS, of whom only 1 was from the South (Tennessee) and he had not paid the dues but was given that status "for services rendered." Of 129 life members in 1834, only 2 were from the South, Thomas Cooper of Georgia, who had paid his own dues, and William B. Johnson of South Carolina, whose dues were paid by "the females of his church."[67]

In light of Southern awareness of home mission needs and Southerners' intense efforts to keep the Triennial Convention involved in that work, how can this lack of support for the HMS be explained? For one thing, distance proved a barrier. Travel in the 1830s was difficult and sending delegates to the "New York Society," as it came to be called, was slow and expensive. When combined with the need to attend meetings of the foreign mission and publication societies, this called for more travel than most Southerners could afford or endure. Second, by the 1830s a number of strong associations and state conventions in the South were engaged in their own home mission work, and these tended to win support and divert attention from the New York Society. Third, Baptists in the South had felt severely rebuffed at the breakup of the Triennial Convention in 1826. Though final division did not come until 1845, the "era of good feeling" clearly ended in 1826 when Baptists in the North, in effect, withdrew from national cooperation.

The work of a home missionary in the 1830s was not easy. In vivid letters

65. Ibid., p. 14.
66. Ibid., p. 15.
67. *Second Report of the Executive Committee,* ABHMS (New York, 1834), pp. 3-4.

to the board, Jacob Bower described problems he faced in Illinois.[68] He encountered cholera and other epidemics, swam raging rivers, dodged hostile Indians and bandits, traveled constantly, and slept many nights under the stars. The missionary also faced frequent opposition. Many in the West opposed all mission work, ridiculed the "beggar societies," and opposed Sunday Schools and a paid clergy. Bower wrote in 1833, "Some people love much in word and in tongue, but not in deed and in truth. They say, 'we like to hear you preach. . . . come and preach for us.' But only mention their duty, that the labourer is worthy of his hire, and they will be offended, and say, money-hunter, beggar, missionary, etc." Bower traveled that year 1,247 miles, preached 191 sermons, baptized 43 new converts, and formed countless new Sunday Schools. This faithful witness bore fruit, for Bower later wrote, "The good cause is evidently gaining ground, though its progress is slow; . . . . Opposers are not so saucy and violent as they were two years ago."[69]

Home Mission Achievements

The achievements of the Home Mission Society were truly remarkable. During the first year of operation, it reported 89 appointments to 10 states, territories, and provinces, including 2 collecting agents, 7 missionary agents, and 5 grants to churches.[70] Not all those appointed actually served, and some served for only a few weeks, but nevertheless this shows a strong beginning. By 1844 the society had 97 missionaries under appointment and, with the help of its auxiliaries, supplied 327 churches and mission stations. By 1844 HMS workers had organized a total of 551 new churches and baptized 14,426 new converts.[71] Practically every strong Baptist church in the Midwest was in some way indebted to the HMS for its origin or survival.

Though concentrating its early efforts in the West, the HMS never swerved from its original goal: "North America for Christ." Some of the society's personnel and resources were directed toward needy areas in the East, and for years HMS appointees worked in Canada and Mexico. However, in time "North America" came to mean the United States. The society had the good fortune to be launched during the height of the Second Great Awakening which greatly enhanced response to its labors.

Deepening Discord Among Baptists

By the 1830s American Baptists had completed their structures for missions and other benevolences. Despite problems common to such organizations, all three of the major societies were doing good jobs and winning

---

68. *First Annual Report of Executive Board,* ABHMS (1833), p. 15.
69. Ibid., pp. 13-14.
70. *First Annual Report of Executive Board,* ABHMS (1833), p. 15.
71. Henry L. Morehouse, ed., *Baptist Home Missions in North America, 1832-1882,* p. 551.

widespread acceptance. Yet the denomination lacked the inner spiritual and theological unity to match its outward structures. A number of divisive controversies kept Baptists off balance, distracted them from their ministry, and at times required them to struggle to preserve historic Baptist principles and practices. In the helpful book, *Not a Silent People,*[72] Walter B. Shurden advanced the idea that Baptists have been shaped by their controversies. During the early nineteenth century, two internal controversies revealed deep discord in Baptist life and shaped the denomination for years to come. These concerned missions and the emerging Disciples movement. These were by no means the only conflicts Baptists faced. They also disputed over Masonic Lodge membership, whether the Bible society should translate or transliterate the Greek word for *baptize,* slavery, and many other issues.[73]

While theological controversy was not peculiar to Baptists, they, more than some denominations, seemed ill-equipped to handle it. Each Baptist church was independent, and the denomination had never adopted any authoritative creed. Such an idea was repugnant to Baptists, and no denominational body had the authority to devise such a creed, much less enforce it. By the 1830s American Baptist groups had adopted two confessions of faith, and some local churches had prepared their own doctrinal statements. The two general confessions, one adopted by the Philadelphia Association in 1742 and the other by the Baptist State Convention of New Hampshire in 1833, did not protect Baptists from doctrinal diversity. The two confessions themselves differed, and some Baptists refused to use any statement but the Bible.

The Antimissions Movement

Not all Baptists shared the zeal for missions which led the majority to form the missions and tract societies. By the 1820s, articulate spokesmen arose to undermine missions; what began as scattered dissent mushroomed into a full-fledged antimission movement.[74] Its adherents believed that conversion was God's task alone, that mission societies and conventions were mere human inventions, and that missionaries were mostly hirelings. The earliest Baptist mission efforts had encountered few objections. John Mason Peck, called "the field marshal of Baptist home missions," was well-received at the Illinois Association in 1818. Minutes of that body reported, "Brother Peck presented the plan of a society to employ missionaries, . . . which we desire to see carried into effect, and which we recom-

72. Walter B. Shurden, *Not a Silent People.*

73. For a good discussion of these several controversies, see Robert G. Torbet, *A History of the Baptists,* esp. chapter 10, "Dissension and Strife."

74. For an excellent discussion on this movement, see William Warren Sweet, ed., *Religion on the American Frontier: The Baptists* 1783-1830, esp. chapter IV, "The Rise of the Anti-Mission Baptists: A Frontier Phenomenon."

mend to the churches." The next day Peck preached a missionary sermon, received an offering, and formed a mission society. Similar success marked Peck's trail throughout the West in the early days. However, in 1820 one of the churches in that association voted that "the church is not willing for any of her members to have anything to do with the bord of Western missions."[75]

Baptist sentiment moved quickly from support to uncertainty to adamant opposition to missions. The Wabash Association received a "query" from a church in 1818 asking, "Are the principles and practices of the Baptist Board of Foreign Missions, in its present operations, justifiable and agreeable to gospel order?"[76] A year later the association answered, "It is not agreeable to gospel order." However, not all churches accepted such associational decisions. In 1820 the Maria Creek Church requested the association to "point out the wickedness of the Baptist Board of Foreign Missions." They must have found the association's response unconvincing, as the church was later excluded "for holding and justifying the principles and practices of the Baptist Board."[77] In 1824 the Illinois Association huffed, "Money and Theological learning seem to be the pride, we fear of too many preachers in our day."[78]

The Apple Creek Association wrote antimissionism into their constitution:

19. We as an association do not hesitate to declare an unfellowship with foreign and domestic missionary and bible societies, Sunday Schools and tract societies, and all other missionary institutions.

....

21. No missionary preacher is to have the privilege of preaching at our association.

....

23. We advise the churches to protest against masonic and missionary institutions, and not to contribute to any such beggarly institutions.[79]

Amid these scattered expressions, perhaps the two most important Baptist antimission statements were the Kehuckee Declaration and the Black Rock Address.[80] In October 1827 the large and influential Kehuckee Association of North Carolina issued "A Declaration Against the Modern Missionary Movement and Other Institutions of Men." They voted to "discard

75. Ibid., pp. 61-62.
76. Ibid.
77. Ibid., pp. 62-63.
78. Ibid., p. 65.
79. Ibid., p. 64.
80. Both of these have been reprinted in W. J. Berry, comp., *The Kehuckee Declaration and Black Rock Address, with Other Writings Relative to the Baptist Separation between 1825-1840.*

all Missionary Societies, Bible Societies and Theological Seminaries" and to exclude any who favored these institutions.[81] In 1832 delegates from churches of the Baltimore Association, meeting at Black Rock, Maryland, issued a more extensive address to "Old School Baptists," as the antimission forces were then called. They condemned several "modern inventions," such as tract societies, Sunday Schools, Bible societies, missionary societies, colleges and seminaries, and revival meetings, on the grounds that none of these are authorized in the Bible.[82] Such Baptists also opposed Masonic Lodges, sermons prepared in advance, and a salaried ministry.

The antimission movement had several leaders, of whom the most prominent were Daniel Parker, John Taylor, Joshua Lawrence, and Alexander Campbell. Parker (1781-1844) was the great enemy of missions on the frontier. A man of slight build and unkempt appearance, his beard often streaked with tobacco stains, Parker had a keen mind and piercing blue eyes. He served for several years as a pastor in Tennessee. Parker's own lack of formal education seemed to deepen his hostility to theological schools. While serving as moderator of the Concord Association in 1815, Parker openly condemned missions, theological education, Bible societies, and all other human efforts for the gospel. These views spread rapidly in Tennessee. In 1817 Parker moved to Illinois and in 1833 to Texas, thus spreading his views in several states.

In 1820 Parker published a pamphlet against missions, widely circulated and often reprinted. For two years, 1829-1831, he published a monthly paper, the *Church Advocate,* wrote other books, and traveled widely. Perhaps no person did more to fix antimissions upon Baptists. He formed the Pilgrim Predestinarian Regular Baptist Church in Illinois and in 1833 moved it to Texas. At that time, Baptist churches could not legally be formed in the Mexican province of Texas, but importing one was not technically illegal. From the Pilgrim Church other similar churches developed. Some of them continued in the Primitive movement, others joined fundamentalist groups in the next century, and eventually many of them affiliated with the Southern Baptist Convention. While their antimissionism has long since faded, these Parker churches left a deposit of ultraconservatism that has flavored Texas Baptist life to the present.

In 1826 Parker published *Views on the Two Seeds,* a major treatise which advocated his peculiar doctrine of "two seeds in the spirit." Drawing upon Genesis 3:15, Parker said, "It is evident that there are two seeds, the one of the serpent, the other of the woman." He concluded that "the woman's seed . . . was Christ and his elect," while "the Serpents seed here spoken

81. Ibid., p. 14.
82. Ibid., pp. 25 *f.*

of, I believe to be the Non-elect."[83] Eve's sin allowed Satan "to beget the wicked, sinful principle and nature in her," thus allowing both the seed of Satan and the seed of Christ to enter the human bloodstream. Satan's seed is represented in the covenant of works, Christ's in the covenant of grace. The elect seed can be redeemed, but the nonelect cannot. This was another version of determinism in religion and had great appeal at the time. That branch of the Primitive Baptists which grew from Parker's movement held that no missionary efforts were needed or could bear fruit.

Parker's ecclesiology also discouraged organized mission work. He allowed some church-centered mission preaching but opposed missionary societies and all other "extra-church" efforts. His opponents may have seen more antimission implications in his two-seeds doctrine than Parker intended.[84]

A more moderate antimission leader was the respected John Taylor of Virginia. Taylor (1752-1835) grew up in the backwoods of Virginia and became, despite lack of schooling, a popular traveling preacher. Later as a prosperous farmer in Kentucky, he developed strong opposition to missions, ministerial education, and salaried pastors. Two incidents served to harden Taylor's views. Taylor resented the statements of John Mason Peck and others in the home mission movement that Baptists would languish in the West without appointed missionaries since resident Baptist preachers were of such low quality. Taylor also reacted adversely to two young mission appointees who spent the night at his house. With incredible presumption, the two young men asked Taylor how much income he derived from preaching and offered the opinion that if he would preach more on missions he could increase his own salary. The young missionaries, who were not Baptists, observed that "many poor ministers could scarcely get their bread before, but by stirring up the people in the mission cause, and getting them in the habit of giving their money," such ministers were now "richly supplied."[85]

However, Taylor's sharpest criticisms were reserved for Luther Rice whom he had heard several times. Calling Rice "a Tetzel, . . . and his motive about the same," Taylor ridiculed Rice's missionary sermons, impugned his motives, and rejected all human societies for Christian ministries. He said, "My object is, if possible, to drive these presuming men out of Baptist associations."[86]

Joshua Lawrence provided effective leadership for antimissions in North

83. Daniel Parker, *Views on the Two Seeds,* pp. 4-5.

84. For an excellent study of Parker's views, see O. Max Lee, "Daniel Parker's Doctrine of the Two Seeds."

85. From the pamphlet by John Taylor, *Thoughts on Missions* (1820), as cited in Baker, *Source Book,* pp. 79-80.

86. Ibid., p. 81.

Carolina, Georgia, and Alabama. A veteran pastor, Lawrence published a pamphlet in 1820 which helped turn the Kehuckee Association against missions and made "Kehuckeeism" a synonym for antimissions.

Another influential spokesman against missions was Alexander Campbell (1788-1866). Though he was a Baptist for only seventeen years, 1813 to 1830, Campbell had a great impact upon the denomination. In 1823 he launched a paper called the *Christian Baptist* (changed in 1829 to *Millennial Harbinger*) in which he attacked mission societies, Bible societies, associations, confessions of faith, use of the title *reverend,* and many other things he considered nonbiblical. Taking the name of "Reformers," these Campbellite Baptists sought to cleanse the churches of all "human traditions" and return to "primitive order."

One of Campbell's most frequent attacks had to do with the expense of mission societies. In his paper, he printed missionary expense reports in an effort to show that operating costs were excessive. He accused some societies of greed, dishonesty, embezzlement, and outright stealing. The Campbell movement represented a serious threat to Baptists in several areas, of which antimissions was only one. Eventually the "Reformers" almost wrecked the Baptist denomination in the West, sowing seeds of discord wherever they appeared.

Several reasons can be cited for the widespread antimission movement among Baptists. Theology played a role, especially with Daniel Parker. While the Second Great Awakening in the early 1800s tended to soften Calvinist theology, thus encouraging missions and evangelism, some Baptists on the frontier held to such strict predestination that missions societies and all other "human effort" agencies seemed improper. If human destiny is already determined, then missionary effort loses its theological base.

Another reason for antimissions might be called "biblicism." "Biblicism" refers to the concept that no organization or effort can be permitted in the church but what is specifically named in the New Testament. Parker often ridiculed the idea of a mission society, saying, "It has neither precept nor example to justify it within the two lids of the Bible."[87] He observed that God required no mission society to send Jonah to Nineveh. Campbell used similar biblicism to invalidate theological seminaries, mission boards, ministerial titles, and stated salaries for pastors. Campbell's convictions on the latter subject increased somewhat after he had married into a well-to-do family. Having witnessed a commissioning service for two foreign missionaries, Campbell wrote a clever parody of the biblical appointment of "the Rev. Saulus Paulus and the Rev. Joses Barnabas." Developing his motto, "Where the Bible speaks, we speak; where the Bible is silent, we are silent," Campbell rejected any organization for mission work beyond the local church. Both Parker and Campbell would have agreed with the Illinois

87. Sweet, pp. 69-70.

Association statement that "the Bible knows of no society but the Church of Christ."[88] Similar views surfaced later in the South under the name of Landmarkism in the 1850s and Gospel Missionism in the 1880s.

Sectional jealousies provided another reason for antimissionism. Frontier Baptists were keenly conscious that the mission societies were headquartered in Boston and New York. John Taylor said that he "did begin strongly to smell the New England Rat" in the mission operation, and many feared that the Eastern churches might somehow gain control over the whole denomination. Further, one is not surprised that frontier ministers, educated mostly "between the handles of a plow," would resent the more favored missionaries, graduates of theological seminaries, whose sermons proved so attractive to the people. No one expressed this dimension of antimissionism more bluntly than the farmer-preacher who said,

> Well, if you must know, Brother Moderator, you know the big trees in the woods overshadow the little ones; and these missionaries will be all great men and the people will all go to hear them preach, and we shall all be put down. That's the objection.[89]

Though largely confined to the frontier, the impact of antimissionism was vast. The *Baptist Register* for 1847 reported 655,536 "Regular" Baptists, and 68,068 "anti-mission" Baptists in America. Of the antimission adherents, only 245 were in New England, while Georgia and Tennessee had over 10,000 each, followed by Alabama and Kentucky with 6,417 and 7,085 respectively. In Alabama, this conflict was known as "the big split," and in 1836 about 40 percent of all Baptists in Missouri opposed missions. The "anti" movement swept through Tennessee as it did few other areas. One observer remarked that antimission prejudice reached such a fever pitch that

> not a man ventured to open his mouth in favor of any benevolent enterprise or action. The missionary societies were dissolved, and the Association rescinded all their resolutions by which they were in any way connected with these measures, and, in this respect, the spirit of death rested upon the whole people.[90]

Antimission churches and denominations have generally remained few in number and limited in influence.

The antimission movement bias may be best understood as an example of ultraconservatism confronting the progressive spirit of mainline Baptists. In the name of biblical authority, the antimission movement undercut biblical teachings and practices. Lingering opposition to denominational programs, continuing suspicion of theological education, and rigid biblicism

88. Ibid., p. 65.
89. Ibid., p. 74.
90. Newman, pp. 437-438.

represent the legacy of the antimission movement. Baptists in areas where antimissionism flourished have inherited a pronounced susceptibility to other ultraconservative movements. A. H. Newman observed that the aftermath of antimissions retarded Baptist growth, for "a large proportion of the Baptists of the Southwest were so perverse in doctrine and so unamiable in spirit" that potential converts were repelled.[91] The "missionary Baptists" ultimately prevailed, but at great cost.

The antimissions movement gave Baptists in America their first major experience with a divisive internal doctrinal controversy. What began as objections to mission methods soon expanded to include other issues, such as the nature of biblical authority, distrust of denominational leaders and programs, and a suspicion of any new ideas or methods. Many of the antimission leaders also developed unlovely dispositions and rigid spirits.

The Campbell Controversy

For Baptists Alexander Campbell has significance far beyond the antimission movement. In the 1820s, he led an ultraconservative "Reformation" which challenged historic Baptist teachings and ultimately split the denomination. Hundreds of Baptist churches left the denomination to line up with Campbell's "Reformers," who after 1830 formed a new denomination known as Disciples of Christ or Church of Christ. Historians estimate, for example, that fully half the Baptist churches of Kentucky switched to the new Disciples movement.[92]

The Campbells came from Scotch-Irish Presbyterianism, migrating to this country from Ireland in the early 1800s. Both the father, Thomas, and his son, Alexander, left the Presbyterian ministry, though for somewhat different reasons. Alexander spent a year at the University of Glasgow, where he absorbed elements of Scottish philosophy, along with the strict biblicism of men like Greville Ewing, John Glas, and Robert Sandeman. From these sources young Campbell developed rationalistic views of faith, insistence upon every Sunday communion, distaste for confessions of faith, and belief in baptismal remission of sins. To this volatile mix was added, primarily by Thomas, an ecumenical effort to move beyond all denominational names and distinctives to be "Christians only."

Having left Presbyterianism, the Campbells formed the nondenominational "Christian Association of Washington" (Pennsylvania) in 1809 and in 1811 transformed this gathering into the Brush Run Church so they could observe the Lord's Supper. The birth of a baby to Alexander and Margaret Campbell raised the question of whether the infant should be baptized. After careful study of the New Testament, Campbell concluded

91. Ibid., p. 440.
92. A good history of this movement, from a Disciples perspective, is W. E. Garrison and A. T. DeGroot, *The Disciples of Christ* (St. Louis: Christian Board of Publications, 1948).

not only that infants should not be sprinkled but also that professed believers should be baptized by immersion. On June 12, 1812 Thomas and Alexander Campbell, with their wives and several other Brush Run members, were immersed in Buffalo Creek by Matthew Luce, a neighboring Baptist preacher. Soon other members of Brush Run accepted immersion; those who did not withdrew.[93]

Baptists pressured the new immersionist church to join the local Redstone Baptist Association, which they did in 1813. The move proved hasty and ill-advised. Beyond immersion, the Campbells and Baptists had almost nothing in common. The years would confirm that the similarities were shallow, the differences deep. The first serious confrontation developed from Alexander Campbell's famous "Sermon on the Law" at the association meeting of 1816. In effect, Campbell dismissed the Old Testament as no longer authoritative. The next year some Baptists tried, without success, to have the association repudiate that sermon. Campbell was an excellent speaker and held numerous well-publicized debates with Methodist and Presbyterian champions, as well as with fellow Baptists. He also used the pages of his paper, the *Christian Baptist,* to challenge traditional Baptist teachings and practices.

In time, several areas of disagreement between Campbell and the Baptists came into focus. First, on the nature of saving faith, Campbell had absorbed the rationalism of Scottish realism. To him simply to *believe,* in the most rationalistic sense of that term, that Jesus is the Christ was sufficient for salvation. Campbell taught that "faith is only an historical belief of facts stated in the Bible."[94] Thus he would settle for what some have called "head belief," or "mental assent." The Baptists, on the other hand, felt that biblical faith should include an element of personal trust or life surrender to Christ. This "heart faith" sometimes led to emotional expressions at conversion. Campbell once snapped his fingers and said, "I would not give that much for the conversion of a person who weeps." He taught that "the belief of one fact, . . . is all that is requisite as far as faith goes, to salvation. The belief of one fact, and submission to one institution, expressive of it [baptism], is all that is required." That one historical fact, said Campbell, is "that Jesus, the Nazarene, is the Messiah."[95] This view of salvation ruled out what Baptists called "an immediate work of God's grace in the heart." In an insightful remark, Robert B. Semple described Campbell's view as "exploding experimental religion in its common acceptance."[96]

Second, Campbell taught that baptism by immersion completes the process of salvation. Whether Campell taught that baptism actually washes

---

93. Ibid., p. 160.
94. *Minutes,* Franklin Baptist Association (Kentucky), 1830, p. 7, in ABHS.
95. Ibid., p. 12.
96. Baker, *Source Book,* p. 77.

away sins and brings salvation, as some of his writings imply, or that the only saving faith is that which leads to obedience in baptism, as others understand him, makes little difference. In either case, salvation is not complete apart from baptism. As early as 1827, Campbell wrote in the *Christian Baptist:*

> We have the most explicit proof that God forgives sins for the name's sake of his Son, or when the name of Jesus Christ is named upon us in immersion: —that in, and by, the act of immersion, so soon as our bodies are put under water, at that very instant our former, or "old sins," are washed away, provided only that we are true believers.[97]

This seems to confirm the understanding of Campbell's views as held in Kentucky, where the "Reformation" was strong. In 1829 the Franklin Association in an extensive analysis of Campbellism said:

> They contend there is no promise of salvation without baptism—that it should be administered to all who say they believe that Jesus Christ is the Son of God, without examination on any other point,—that there is no direct operation of the Holy Spirit on the mind prior to baptism,—that baptism procures the remission of sins.[98]

Third, Campbell's view of Scripture differed from that of most Baptists. The essence of Campbell's controversial "Sermon on the Law" in 1816 was a rejection of the binding authority of the Old Testament upon Christians. Semple chided Campbell for "casting off the Old Testament," but Campbell felt he was doing for modern Christians what the apostle Paul did for the early church, that is, liberating them from the authority of the old dispensation.

Campbell embraced a stark literalism which required that all church practices have precept or precedent in Scripture. By that hermeneutic, he rejected missionary societies, instrumental music in worship, the use of written confessions, regular salaries for ministers, the use of ministerial titles, and many other practices.

Fourth, Campbell rejected all use of confessions of faith. The Redstone Association had adopted the Philadelphia Confession and asked each affiliated church to own that confession as generally expressing their views. An exception was allowed in 1813 for the Brush Run church, an early indication of problems to come. The Campbells persisted, against all evidence, in describing the Philadelphia Confession as a binding creed. However, ample evidence confirms that Baptists regarded it as a general guide in no way approximating, much less displacing, biblical authority. The Franklin Association (Kentucky) devoted its circular letter of 1826 to the

97. Alexander Campbell, *Christian Baptist*, (1827), 5:416, as cited in James E. Tull, *Shapers of Baptist Thought*, p. 113.
98. *Minutes*, Franklin Baptist Association, Kentucky, 1829, p. 5.

Baptist view of confessions in answer to Campbell's objections. "To deny any religious society the privilege of expressing their views of the Bible in their own words and phrases is a violent interference with the rights of conscience—it is tyranny."[99] The circular letter acknowledged that "our confessions are human productions, they may all require revision, and be susceptible of amendment, but to erase them from our books, our memory and our practice, is to make . . . a leap into chaos." Further, such confessions serve a positive good in declaring to the world what Baptists believe. "It is vain to say, that the Bible is sufficient for that purpose," the letter concluded, for most false doctrines grow out of faulty intepretations of the Bible. While Baptists accepted the authority of the Bible, they found value in some minimal statement of what they found in the Bible. Without some such general understanding of their beliefs, "the Church is constrained to receive into her bosom, . . . the enemies of truth. . . . reduced to the cruel necessity of harboring under her wings the vilest heresies."[100] In summary, Campbell rejected confessions because he thought them binding creeds; Baptists used confessions as general guidelines but never elevated them to creedal authority.

Campbellism severely disrupted Baptist life, splitting churches and associations. Campbell's appeal to biblical authority fell on receptive ears, thus confirming Baptists' peculiar susceptibility to those who loudly affirm the authority of Scripture even while teaching contrary to it. Many a Baptist church became a Church of Christ, such as the First Baptist Church of Nashville.[101] Sometimes entire associations defected to the Disciples, as the Mahoning did in 1830. After hearing Campbell preach in 1825, Robert B. Semple wrote to him, "Your views are generally so contrary to those of the Baptists in general, that if a party was to go fully into the practice of your principles, I should say a new sect had sprung up, radically different from the Baptists, as they now are."[102] Those words proved prophetic. Within a few years, Campbell did, indeed, form a new denomination.

The two ultraconservative movements of antimissionism and Campbellism represented major schisms among American Baptists. However, as Campbell and his disciples completed their exit from Baptist life, another controversy loomed on the horizon which would shatter the denomination in a sectional schism that endures to this day.

99. *Minutes,* Franklin Baptist Association, Kentucky, 1826, p. 6.
100. Ibid., p. 7.
101. Lynn E. May, Jr., *The First Baptist Church of Nashville, Tennessee, 1820-1970* (Nashville: First Baptist Church, 1970), pp. 30 *f.*
102. Cited in Baker, *Source Book,* p. 78.

The Southern Baptist Convention

In May 1845, a delegation of Southern Baptists met in Augusta, Georgia, to discuss the formation of separate mission agencies for Baptists in the South. They did more than discuss; they formed the Southern Baptist Convention, adopted a constitution, and established mission boards to begin work at once.

At least three factors led to that fateful schism: disagreements on methods of organization, problems in home mission work, and the slavery controversy. While each of these played an important role, they were not of equal weight; slavery was the final and most decisive factor which led Southern Baptists to form their own convention.

Methods of Organization

Baptists disagreed about society and convention methods of organization, the Southerners prefering the convention method. However, more than mere *method* was at stake. Differences in ecclesiology between Baptists North and South help explain why they structured benevolent work in different ways.

Practical considerations also pushed Southern Baptists toward a unified convention approach. While New England was compact geographically, making travel more convenient, the vast distances of the South and the Southwest made travel expensive and time-consuming. Southern Baptists simply could not attend the sessions of three separate societies meeting in distant Northern cities. Distance alone determined that Southern representation remain minimal. Baptists in the South preferred a denominational structure with *one* meeting, at which all their work could be managed. Changes in the Triennial Convention in 1826 meant that Baptists in the South could no longer share meaningfully in the Northern societies.

Problems in Home Missions

During the 1830s a question arose about appointments by the Home Mission Society. Baptists in the South felt that, although they contributed to the society, they did not receive their fair share of home missionaries. The alleged neglect of the South, whether valid or not, provided one major motive for the division of 1845. This issue led to calls for a separate Southern work as early as 1835 on the grounds that the New York society could neither know nor address needs in the South. Careful analysis of this issue by Robert A. Baker has shown that in the decade 1832-1841 the states of the deep South contributed $28,149 to the HMS and had only $13,646 expended by the society in their states.[103] However, if such border states as Kentucky, Tennessee, and Missouri are considered Southern rather than

103. Robert A. Baker, *Relations Between Northern and Southern Baptists,* p. 35.

Western, then the entire South received in missionary aid slightly more than it contributed. The Northern states contributed far more than was expended in their areas, so Baker concludes, "It is not correct to say, then, that Southern contributions during this decade were applied to the evangelization of northern fields."[104]

In personnel the Southern fields fared poorly. The society drew most of its missionary volunteers from Northern areas and appointed most of them to the upper Midwest. In the decade 1832-1841, the HMS appointed 506 missionaries to the 4 Northwestern states of Illinois, Indiana, Michigan, and Ohio. During the same decade, the 6 Southwestern states of Kentucky, Louisiana, Mississippi, Arkansas, Tennesse, and Missouri, with about the same total population, received only 127 missionaries. However, the HMS tried to remedy this imbalance. It made special appeals for Southern volunteers and in some cases paid higher salaries to missionaries who agreed to serve in the South. Even with such inducements, few Northerners wanted to work in the South, citing such problems as slavery, climate, distance from their families, and lack of welcome on the part of Baptists in the South. In summary, Baptists in the South apparently got about as much home mission aid as they paid for. Whatever the reality, the *perception* by Southern Baptists that they were being neglected by the HMS clearly contributed to the schism of 1845.

Slavery and Its Aftermath

Slavery was the main issue that led to the 1845 schism; that is a blunt historical fact. Other issues raised barriers and, in time, might have led to division, if not North-South, possibly East-West. However, slavery *did* lead to division.

Slavery had an early and inglorious beginning in America. John Rolfe of Jamestown, Virginia, reported casually in 1619, "About the last of August came in a Dutch man-of-Warre that sold us 20 negars."[105] These probably were not slaves but indentured servants, a status shared by many whites. After serving the allotted time, the indentured servants were to go free. However, it did not work out that way for blacks. If dishonest masters kept them beyond their obligated service, who would come to their aid? Their high visibility made running away almost impossible. The result was that within a few years the system of indentured or temporary servanthood hardened for blacks into perpetual slavery. In 1637 a black man named Punch, who had tried to run away, was sentenced by Colonial authorities to serve *durante vita,* or for the duration of his lifetime. Two major pieces of legislation provided that a child born of a slave mother took the mother's

104. Ibid., p. 36.
105. Cited in Daniel P. Mannix and Malcolm Cowley, *Black Cargoes* (New York: Viking, 1962), p. 60.

status (1662) and that "the conferring of baptism does not alter the condition of the person as to his bondage or freedom" (1667).[106] The last law addressed a fear of Southern planters who hesitated to allow their slaves to be Christianized lest it require their freedom. Other states passed similar laws.

Robert A. Baker distinguished three periods of American slavery during which attitudes toward the "peculiar institution" changed.[107] Before 1830 slavery was viewed primarily as an *economic* system; from about 1830-1840, an era of moral reform in America, slavery was seen as a *moral* issue; and after 1840, the *political* aspects of slavery came to the fore and ultimately led to the Civil War. However, from the first, many opposed slavery on principle, and some Baptists were among them.

Before 1800 slavery had not become a sectional issue. One might find antislavery viewpoints in both North and South; indeed, the evidence confirms more antislave societies in the South before 1800. The immense profit in importing slaves accrued more to the North than the South. That importation was outlawed in 1807. The invention of the cotton gin in 1792 made slave labor more profitable in the South, whereas Northern industry profited less from slave labor. Thus, around the turn of the century, the slave system lost its profitability in the North just as it gained new profitability in the South. These related realities must be assessed in any evaluation of evolving attitudes toward slavery in the two regions.

Before 1830 considerable antislavery sentiment existed among Baptists in the South. In 1785 the Baptist General Committee of Virginia pronounced slavery "contrary to the word of God."[108] Two years later the Ketockton Association called slavery "a breach of divine law" and suggested a plan of gradual emancipation. When several churches protested, in 1788 the association "resolved to take no further steps in the business." In 1790 the General Committee of Virginia adopted a statement calling slavery "a violent deprivation of the rights of nature, and inconsistent with a republican government; and therefore [we] recommend it to our brethren to make use of every legal measure, to extirpate the horrid evil from the land."[109] However, many of the churches did not share these views, and after 1800 more Baptists defended slavery.

A strong antislavery movement emerged among the Baptists of Kentucky, led primarily by David Barrow (d.1819). When Barrow's abolition views forced him out of the North District Association in 1807, he led

106. Mortimer J. Adler, ed., *The Negro in American History* (Encyclopedia Brittanica Educational Corporation, 1969), 3:445.

107. Baker, *Relations,* pp. 18-25.

108. H. Shelton Smith, *In His Image, But . . . : Racism in Southern Religion, 1780-1910* (Durham, N.C.: Duke University Press, 1972), p. 47.

109. Ibid., p. 48.

messengers from nine churches to form the "Baptized Licking Locust Association, Friends of Humanity." They made antislavery a condition of affiliation, and for awhile the movement flourished. Later many Baptists left for Illinois to get away from slavery. Among those Baptists was Thomas Lincoln, whose son Abraham never joined a church but sometimes swept out the meeting house and doubtless heard many antislavery sermons among the Friends of Humanity.

In the Carolinas and Georgia, no significant antislavery movement developed among Baptists; in South Carolina, for example, such outstanding Baptist preachers as Richard Furman, Peter Bainbridge, and Edmund Botsford were among the larger slaveholders. Furman wrote a detailed defense of slavery in 1822, a document which influenced Baptists throughout the South. Though Furman used logic and history, the heart of his argument is that "the right of holding slaves is clearly established in the Holy Scriptures, both by precept and example."[110] The slave rebellions, particularly the Denmark Vessey uprising in South Carolina in 1822 and the Nat Turner movement in Virginia in 1831, tended to silence any remaining antislavery voices in the South. In 1835 the Charleston Association adopted a militant defense of slavery, sternly chastising abolitionists as "mistaken philanthropists, and deluded and mischievous fanatics." Antislavery efforts, the association said, "will be perfectly futile, so long as they [the Baptists who favor slavery] have the Bible in their hands." They regarded abolition as "not only officious and unfriendly, but incendiary and murderous in its tendency," and warned "of the consequences which must grow out of any continued interference with this question."[111]

While the South moved toward militant defense of the slave system, the older Northern states one by one outlawed slavery, and the newer Northern states refused to allow the system to be introduced into their areas. The issue was thrust into the forefront of Baptist life by the 1835 visit of Francis Cox and James Hoby, English Baptist abolitionists who came to America to urge Baptists to abandon slavery. This visit and subsequent correspondence tended to polarize Baptists. Baptist abolitionism took a new turn in 1840 with the formation of the American Baptist Anti-Slavery Convention in New York. The convention made two general addresses to the public. To Baptists in the North, it appealed for support, urging that the mission agencies be cleared of any taint of slavery. The address to the South condemned slavery in militant terms, outdoing even the Charleston Association in flaming rhetoric and judgmental tones. Asserting that slaveholders stand under the "contempt of mankind" and the "displeasure of God," the New York convention called upon Southern Baptists to "confess before heaven

110. Cited in H. Shelton Smith, Robert T. Handy, and Lefferts A. Loetscher, eds., *American Christianity*, 2 vols. (New York: Charles Scribner's Sons, 1960), 2:184.
111. *Minutes,* Charleston Baptist Association, 1835, p. 6.

and earth the sinfulness of holding slaves; admit it to be not only a misfortune, but a crime." If necessary, it said, Baptists should leave the South and "forsake, like Abraham, your fatherland, and carry your children . . . to the vast asylum of our prairies." Moreover, the convention warned, if Baptists in the South ignored such warnings and persisted in the practice of slavery, "we cannot and we dare not recognize you as consistent brethren in Christ."[112] Later the same year, 1840, a group of Baptists in Boston formed the American Baptist Free Mission Society on abolitionist principles, largely in protest against the Triennial Convention in which both Northern and Southern Baptists cooperated. The purpose of the society, according to its constitution, was to "separate ourselves now and forever from all connection with religious societies that are supported in common with slaveholders."[113] Thus the issue was joined, placing Baptists North and South in confrontation.

Efforts at Neutrality

Leaders of the Baptist societies sought to work together in missions despite their differences on slavery; many leaders North and South dreaded division and did all they could to avoid it. At the triennial meetings in 1841 and 1844, both mission societies voted policies of official neutrality on slavery. Acknowledging that members held strong views on both sides, the societies agreed that since their constitutions committed them to mission work, other questions fell outside their jurisdiction. In 1841 the Home Society voted that "our cooperation in this body does not imply any sympathy either with slavery or anti-slavery."[114]

At the 1841 meeting in Boston, the Triennial Convention also adopted a statement of neutrality on slavery. Noting the convention's purpose was foreign missions, the convention delegates said, "The Board are unable to discover any sufficient reason for the withdrawal of support on the part of any of their contributors, in view of facts . . . wholly extrinsic and irrelevant."[115] They said that while individuals might hold and express whatever views they wished, "as a Board of the Convention for Foreign Missions, they can say and do nothing." They also deplored the confusion caused by "the unseasonable diversion of our thoughts to irrelevant subjects."

These efforts to maintain neutrality proved fruitless. Militant abolitionists in the North and equally militant proslavery Baptists in the South drowned out the more moderate voices. As the rhetoric became more inflamed, cooperation became more difficult. The Charleston Association voted in 1840 to consider "the necessity of the formation, at as early a period

112. Cited in Baker, *Source Book,* pp. 93-94.
113. Ibid., p. 94.
114. Ibid., p. 97.
115. *Minutes,* Baptist General Convention for Foreign Missions, Boston, 1841, pp. 80-81.

as practicable, of a Southern Baptist Board of Foreign Missions."[116] As early as 1839, similar calls were heard for a separate Baptist mission society in the West; in fact, one was actually formed but endured only for a short time.

The 1844 meeting of the Home Mission Society proved decisive. A "Brother Adlam," not otherwise identified, introduced a resolution that owning slaves would "prove no barrier" to appointment by the HMS. Perhaps Adlam expected the resolution to fail and thus, in effect, place the society on record as opposed to slavery. Richard Fuller of Charleston moved a substitute that "whereas, the question has been proposed— whether the Board would or would not employ slave-holders as missionaries of this Society," that the society reaffirm "that to introduce the subjects of slavery or anti-slavery into this body, is in direct contravention of the whole letter and purpose of the said Constitution, and is, moreover, a most unnecessary agitation of topics with which this Society has no concern."[117] Fuller's motion then repeated the earlier neutrality statement of 1841: "Our cooperation in this body does not imply any sympathy either with slavery or anti-slavery, as to which societies and individuals are left free and uncommitted as if there were no such cooperation."

After extensive debate, the society adopted the Fuller statement by a vote of 123 to 61. However, this represented no victory for continued cooperation, for in the very next action the society approved a motion "to take into consideration the subject of an amicable dissolution of this Society." The process of division had begun.

Two Final Straws

Two events in 1844 hastened the schism, serving as the final straws, so to speak, that broke the back of Baptist unity. These were the "Georgia Test Case" and the "Alabama Resolutions." Georgia Baptists, not convinced by the repeated assurances of neutrality, introduced a test case to the Home Mission Society. They nominated James E. Reeve, a slave owner, for appointment as a home missionary and, according to the custom of the time, also raised the money for his support. They frankly admitted that the nomination was intended "to stop the mouths of gainsayers" and answer once for all whether the society would appoint a slave owner. In response to Reeve's nomination, the board reaffirmed its commitment to neutrality, said that to act on a test case either way would violate that neutrality, and voted that "we deem ourselves not at liberty to entertain the application for the appointment of Rev. James E. Reeve."[118] Thus the board neither

116. *Minutes,* Charleston Baptist Association, 1840, p. 4.
117. *Minutes,* ABHMS, 1844, p. 6.
118. Baker, *Source Book,* p. 106.

appointed nor rejected Reeve; it simply declined to act upon the matter. Evidence suggests the board acted in good faith.

The second "final straw" involved a bluntly worded inquiry from the Baptist State Convention of Alabama to the Board of the Triennial Convention, asking if slaveholders could be appointed as foreign missionaries. More was at stake than slavery. In effect, the "Alabama Resolutions" questioned the appointive powers of the board, suggesting that churches shared that power. This emphasis also surfaced later in the Landmark movement. The board's response was as sharply worded as the inquiry. It said, "The appointing power, for wise and good reasons, has been confided to the 'Acting Board,' " and would remain there.[119] The response repeated the familiar neutrality statements, but added, "one thing is certain; we can never be a party to any arrangement which would imply approbation of slavery." Some observers felt this sentence violated neutrality. The board itself was divided on how to respond to the Alabama inquiry. Members who favored a stern reply threatened to withdraw from the board and the convention if their wishes did not prevail. In such a case, some feared, "the Acting Board, itself reduced perhaps to a minority of its present members, will be left with a minority of northern supporters and contributors to cooperate with southern contributors in sustaining our missionary operations."[120]

Thus the board faced a serious dilemma: It could placate the South and lose Northern support or satisfy the North and lose Southern support. Either way division was inevitable. Either Northern Baptists would divide among themselves or they had to separate from the South. The board chose the latter.

Southern Baptists put the worst construction upon responses to the Georgia and Alabama cases, but they were not agreed on what to do. This diversity is illustrated in two major newspaper articles. In a lengthy article on March 13, 1845 the *Religious Herald* of Virginia called the response to the Alabama Resolutions "an outrage of our rights" and recommended immediate withdrawal. The paper reported recent resolutions adopted by the Virginia Baptist Missionary Society, as follows:

> 1. *Resolved,* That this Board have seen with sincere pain the decision of the Board of the Baptist Triennial Convention, ... and that we deem the decision unconstitutional and in violation of the rights of the Southern members of the Convention; and that all farther connection with the Board, on the part of such members, is inexpedient and improper.
> 2. Resolved, That the Treasurer of this Board be requested to deposit ... any funds which may be in hands or which may come into them, to be disposed of as the Society, at its annual meeting, may direct.

119. Ibid.
120. *Minutes of Acting Board,* American Baptist Missionary Union, February 24, 1845, 74, in ABHS.

3. Resolved, That this Board are of the opinion that . . . those brethren who are aggrieved by the recent decision of the Board in Boston, should hold a Convention to confer on the best means of promoting the Foreign Mission Cause, and other interests of the Baptist denomination in the South.

4. Resolved, That in the judgment of this Board, Augusta, Geo., is a suitable place for holding such a Convention, and that Thursday before the 2nd Lord's day in May next is a suitable time.[121]

These resolutions, probably framed by J. B. Taylor, looked toward immediate separation. Though foreign missions would be of primary concern, the proposed Southern organization would also deal with "other interests of the Baptist denomination in the South."

However, J. L. Waller, editor of the *Baptist Banner and Pioneer* of Louisville, Kentucky, took quite a different approach. In an article on "A Southern Convention," Waller urged caution and delay. He proposed that if a Southern convention were called, its purpose should be "not for the inevitable purpose of effecting a separation, but for the purpose of ascertaining whether the causes of difficulty cannot be removed and the union of the denomination preserved." Waller held out the hope that the majority of Baptists in the North would repudiate the actions of their managing boards and that, therefore, separation would be avoided. He attributed recent board actions to the efforts of militant abolitionists "to drive off the South." "They know," Waller said, "that if the South does not withdraw, the North will divide, and the abolitionists must go to themselves." He also saw, prophetically, that division of the churches might hasten a division of the nation. Waller concluded, "We wish to preserve the Union, . . . and if the Abolitionists cannot be still in such company, *let them withdraw.*"[122]

The Augusta Meeting

Caution did not prevail. The Virginia Baptists renewed their call for a consultative meeting, and on May 8, 1845, delegates from various Southern Baptist bodies met in Augusta. These 327 delegates included only 293 persons since some represented more than one church or society, a fact which has created no end of confusion in reporting. This was hardly a representative assembly; of the 293 present, 273 came from the three states of Georgia, South Carolina, and Virginia. Significantly, the American Baptist Publication Society had representatives in Augusta, which means that one of the Northern Baptist agencies helped form the Southern Baptist Convention. Francis Wayland, whose ideas had helped set the stage for division, wrote to J. B. Jeter:

You will separate of course. I could not ask otherwise. Your rights have been

---

121. *Religious Herald,* March 13, 1845.
122. *Baptist Banner and Pioneer,* May 1, 1845.

infringed. I will take the liberty of offering one or two suggestions. We have shown how Christians ought not to act. Put away all violence, act with dignity and firmness and the world will approve your course.[123]

The principal architect of the new convention, and its first president, was William Bullein Johnson of South Carolina. Johnson had been deeply influenced by Richard Furman and the Charleston tradition. He served on committees to prepare constitutions for three important Baptist bodies: the Triennial Convention of 1814, the State Convention of South Carolina in 1821, and the Southern Baptist Convention in 1845. Johnson tried to establish all three bodies upon convention rather than society basis and succeeded in the latter two and for a time even in the first. In a lengthy message to the South Carolina Convention a week before the Augusta meeting, Johnson said:

> I invite your attention to the consideration of two plans: The one is that which has been adopted for years past, viz: Separate and independent bodies for the prosecution of each object. . . . The other proposes one Convention, embodying the whole Denomination, together with separate and distinct Boards, for each object of benevolent enterprise, located at different places, and all amendable to the Convention.[124]

It was clear which plan Johnson favored; in fact, in his coat pocket he already had a draft of a constitution which would set the new Southern body clearly on the convention plan, and in Augusta his proposed draft was adopted with minor changes. The constitution included both foreign and home missions, plus "other important objects connected with the Redeemer's kingdom." Article V specified, "The Convention shall elect at each triennial meeting as many Boards of Managers, as in its judgment will be necessary for carrying out the benevolent objects it may determine to promote."[125] The constitution also staked out the convention's home field as including the entire United States. In later years the phrase "and its territories" was added. With this "judicious concentration," Johnson said, "the whole Denomination will be united in one body for the purpose of welldoing."

Thus, from the first the Southern Baptist Convention (SBC) had a regional name and a national field of work. Before 1900 some sought to adjust this anomaly by bringing the constitution into line with the name or by adopting a national name. In fact, in 1861 the constitution was changed to limit the home field to the Confederate States of America, but after the war the original wording was quietly restored.

123. *Daily Chronicle and Sentinel,* Augusta, Ga., May 10, 1845, cited in Baker, *Source Book,* p. 116.
124. Baker, *Source Book,* p. 114.
125. *Proceedings,* Southern Baptist Convention, 1845, p. 3.

The new convention authorized an address to the public to explain its actions. Though prepared by a committee, the address shows the hand of W. B. Johnson. Acknowledging that "a painful division has taken place," the address nevertheless affirmed that "we do not regard the rupture as extending to foundation principles, nor can we think that the great body of our Northern Brethren will so regard it."[126] The address emphasized three basic points. First, the division grew out of Northern violation of the constitutions of the mission societies. Those constitutions made no mention of slavery, and from the first slave owners and nonowners enjoyed equality. Given that background, for Northerners to make slavery a test of mission appointment was, in the view of Southerners, a unilateral violation of earlier agreements. Many Northerners, like Francis Wayland, agreed.

Second, the address claimed that the Southerners were restoring the original basis of Baptist missionary work. "We have but enquired for 'the old paths.' " "The Constitution we adopt is precisely that of the original union." Having been, as the Southern Baptists felt, "thrust from the common platform of equal rights, between the Northern and Southern churches, we have but reconstructed that platform." However, that was not entirely accurate, for the SBC constitution abandoned the society plan in favor of the convention method. The delegates did, to some extent, duplicate the Triennial constitution in 1823 but made a radical departure from the one in effect in 1845.

Third, the purpose of the new body, the public address continued, was not the defense of slavery or "the upholding of any form of human policy," but simply "the extension of Messiah's kingdom." That statement reflects Southern sensitivity to the fact that some would view them as a "slave convention."

The events of 1845 must have looked different from Northern and Southern perspectives. In the view of the Baldwin-Wayland tradition, there was no real denomination to divide; the SBC was viewed as simply one more among several Baptist mission societies. In the South, on the other hand, the sense of schism was stronger. Influenced by the Furman-Johnson tradition, Baptists in the South held more intense denominational views and thus saw the events of 1845 as splitting the Baptist denomination.

By the terms of the division, the SBC received none of the assets of the Northern societies but assumed none of their debts. The Boston Board voted that "inasmuch as brethren from the south have retired from the General Convention, and formed a new organization for themselves, the property and liabilities of the General Convention should remain with that body."[127] As for missionaries on the field, the Boston board agreed that "if any of them should prefer to change their relation from us to the Southern

126. Ibid., pp. 17-20.
127. *Proceedings*, First Triennial Meeting of the Southern Baptist Convention, 1846, p. 22.

Board, they should, in the spirit of fraternal regard, be allowed every facility for doing so."[128] A few elected to switch, including John Day, a black American missionary to Liberia, and John Lewis Shuck and Issachar J. Roberts, both in China. Shuck had inherited slaves through his wife's Virginia estate and had also encountered several incidents which soured his relation with the Boston board.

At its organization in 1845, the Southern Baptist Convention numbered 4,126 churches and 351,951 members. Baptisms totaled 23,222 that year.[129]

Summary

As 1814 marked the beginning of an era for Baptists, 1845 marked its end. Baptists who had tried to unite the denomination saw it succumb to schism. Whatever official names they have used, Baptists since 1845 have required some regional prefix; they were no longer just "Baptists" but "Northern" and "Southern" Baptists.

128. Ibid., p. 21.
129. Lewis Wingo, "Little Known Facts about the Southern Baptist Convention," *Quarterly Review* (April-June 1984), pp. 40-41.

11

Going Separate Ways:
Baptists in America, 1845-1900

The schism of 1845 which divided Baptists into Northern and Southern branches looks bigger now than it must have looked then. In a Baptist landscape already crowded with various societies, the formation of one more in the South hardly seemed earthshaking. Adoniram Judson, who attended an early meeting of the Southern Baptist Convention, congratulated its leaders upon the formation of yet another society to strengthen foreign missions. To Judson, and doubtlessly to many others, the events of 1845 seemed not so much a division of the denomination as an expansion to include other strong societies.

However, in retrospect it appears that the separation was one of the most crucial events in American Baptist history. Instead of healing the breach after 1865, as many in both sections apparently expected, Baptists widened the gap. For the next half century Baptists North and South grappled with different issues. Baptists in the North faced massive European immigration, the rise of organized labor, and the development of an industrial economy. In that environment, they developed different methods of evangelism and different emphases in theology, particularly in the Social Gospel which emerged late in the century.

Meanwhile, Baptists in the South confronted a newly freed black population of about four million whose physical and spiritual needs were overwhelming. Political turmoil, economic devastation, sharecropping, and poor health care were facts of life in the postwar South. Scotch-Irish immigration into the South provided ready converts to the Baptist way. Most of the blacks who accepted Christianity became Baptists. The camp meetings, though used more extensively by other denominations, tended to fix a certain evangelical style upon Southern religion which Baptists turned to their own advantage. These factors contributed to the numerical growth of Southern Baptists.

In explaining the division of 1845, Southern Baptists affirmed, "Northern and Southern Baptists are still brethren. They differ in no article of the faith."[1] If true in 1845, those hopeful sentiments were less true by 1900. Regional isolation, war bitterness, and differing emphasis in theology cre-

---

1. *Proceedings,* Southern Baptist Convention, 1845, p. 17.

ated chasms by the end of the century which leaders of an earlier generation could not have anticipated.

Baptists in the North

This section will trace Northern Baptist work in missions, publication, and education, with some attention to other issues, up to the twentieth century.

The American Baptist Missionary Union (ABMU)

The old Triennial Convention took the occasion of the schism to change both its name and its constitution. The new name was the American Baptist Missionary Union (ABMU), devoted exclusively to foreign missions. Its new constitution limited membership to individuals who paid one hundred dollars, which made them "life members." The individuals represented only themselves and not the churches or mission societies which may have sent them and in some cases paid their dues. A group of life members were named "Directors," and a smaller group of Directors served as an "Executive Committee."

Clearly the constitution of the ABMU reinforced the society method. The removal of "representation" from the membership was intended to protect the autonomy of the local church; but, in effect, it removed the work of missions from the church and placed it in a nonchurch society, an approach which anticipated the parachurch organizations of the twentieth century. The new constitution did not win universal acceptance; some Baptists regarded it as too removed from the churches and too elitist, being limited to members who could pay one hundred dollars at one time. In 1854 the constitution was changed to allow any individual who gave ten dollars to be a delegate for that year. With minor adjustments, that remained the membership policy of ABMU for the rest of the century.[2]

Advance on every front marked the work of ABMU after 1845. The withdrawal of Southern Baptists apparently had little impact. Receipts had been around $80,000 in 1845, and exceeded $100,000 in 1846 and almost $121,000 in 1851. To illustrate the level of growth, annual receipts in 1900 amounted to $543,048, and during a special drive in 1893 had topped $766,782.[3] Missionary personnel and mission stations show similar increases. In 1846 the union had 99 missionaries and assistants, 155 native workers, and 82 overseas churches, with about 5,300 members.[4] By 1900 that had increased to 474 missionaries, of whom 171 were ordained; 3,482 native helpers, of whom 301 were ordained; and 928 churches, of which 596 were self-supporting. These churches had 102,216 members, with 6,739

---

2. See Robert G. Torbet, *Venture of Faith*, p. 144.
3. *Eighty-sixth Annual Report,* ABMU, Detroit, 1900, p. 225, in ABHS.
4. Robert G. Torbet, *A History of Baptists,* 3rd ed. p. 338.

added by baptism in 1899.[5] The union reported at the turn of the century 94 mission stations in 6 areas: Burma, Assam, South India, China, Japan, Africa, and the Philippines.

Areas of unusual response. Amid this half-century of progress, 4 areas of remarkable response call for special attention. First, the Karen people of Burma showed great interest in the gospel after 1850. The Karens' efforts to evangelize their own people, plus the continuing labor of missionaries, led to great success. By 1900, 47 tribes in Burma had been touched by the gospel, with over 35,000 Karens accepting Christianity. Most of their churches were self-supporting.[6]

Second, Baptists opened work in Assam, a province in Northeast India, in the 1830s but setbacks limited its success for the first years. Later several tribes received the gospel. By the end of the century, indigenous churches had been established and over 4,000 tribesmen had become church members. Missionary work continued in several stations, with people supposed to be quite savage showing widespread openness to the gospel.

Perhaps the most dramatic example of mass conversions in Baptist mission work occurred among the Telugus in Ongole, India. Baptists opened work there in 1836 with Samuel S. Day. At first the work was so discouraging that the union considered closing the station. Instead, they sent additional personnel, including John E. Clough in 1864. Clough, whose skills included engineering, contracted to build four miles of the Buckingham Canal, a project that employed hundreds in the famine-plagued district. When the laborers were not at work, the missionaries and native preachers read the Bible and preached to them. Those converted tended to share their new faith back home and on Christmas Day 1877 about 2,300 persons presented themselves for baptism. Clough was cautious, fearing that some hoped by baptism to prolong their jobs, so he delayed the baptisms until the project had been completed. Then Clough's careful examinations convinced him the conversions were genuine. In July 1878, 6 ordained native preachers baptized 2,222 converts in 1 day, the ministers working in relays of 2 at a time. By 1879 the number of converts had reached 10,500.[7] This remarkable response spread to other districts in India and helped tilt Baptist mission methods toward direct evangelism and away from the earlier concentration upon schools.

Africa provided the fourth area of unusual response to Baptist missions in what has been called the "Pentecost of the Congo." A wealthy Englishman had established a mission in the Belgian Congo, a work taken over by the ABMU in 1884. Henry Richards was appointed to that station; in less than a year, he reported response similar to that among the Karens and

5. *Eighty-sixth Annual Report,* ABMU, 1900, opposite p. 216, in ABHS.
6. Torbet, *A History,* pp. 340-341.
7. Ibid., p. 342.

Telugus. More than 1,000 of the Congo population piled their idols in a heap and professed faith in Jesus Christ. By 1900 there were over 1,500 church members and 57 native preachers, and their enthusiasm was spreading to other Congo missions.[8]

Northern Baptist foreign mission work benefited from outstanding home leadership in the nineteenth century. Secretaries included Edward Bright (1845-1855); Jonah G. Warren (1855-1866); and John Nelson Murdock (1866-1893). The Murdock era especially was marked by growth and stability, with entrance to several new fields and strengthening of old ones.

By the 1870s a question arose as to the relation of Baptist women to the denomination's overseas ministry in church life.[9] Delegates to the Triennial Convention often represented women's societies; as early as 1815 the convention appointed a woman in the person of Charlotte H. White. In 1861 a group of women from several denominations formed the Woman's Union Missionary Society of America for Heathen Lands.[10] Its primary purpose was to send single women as missionaries. In time, this ecumenical effort gave way as women in each major denomination formed their own groups.

About two hundred Baptist women met in Boston in 1871 and formed the Woman's Baptist Foreign Mission Society. The constitution set their purpose as "the Christianization of women in foreign lands," primarily by appointing women missionaries through the ABMU. A month later, Baptist women in Chicago formed the Woman's Baptist Missionary Society of the West. In a joint meeting of representatives in 1872, the Boston group pushed for union, but the Chicago women elected to keep their own organization. In 1874 Baptist women in California formed the Woman's Baptist Foreign Missionary Society of the Pacific Coast, based in San Francisco. For about twenty years, Northern Baptist women worked through these three regional societies. In 1893 the San Francisco group merged with the Chicago society, and the remaining two merged in 1914.[11]

Two forces brought the women's societies into existence: the desire of women for more involvement in Christian work and the need for women missionaries on the field. On mission fields, especially in Asia and the Orient, male missionaries had limited access to the homes. By the 1870s missionaries, and in some cases groups of women converts overseas, began to call for more women missionaries. The women's societies raised their own funds and appointed their own missionaries, in what some described as "woman's mission to woman." However, the women's societies cooperated closely with the ABMU. In 1875 the ABMU acknowledged the impor-

8. Ibid., p. 343.

9. For a discussion of this development, see Leon McBeth, *Women in Baptist Life,* pp. 49 *f.*

10. Torbet, *Venture,* p. 190.

11. Ibid., p. 440.

tance of the women's societies in raising the level of missionary giving among Baptists.[12]

Major trends. Several major trends mark the foreign mission work of Northern Baptists from 1845 to 1900. Four are noted here.

1. *Home office versus field direction.* Early in Baptists' foreign mission work the Triennial Convention sent the Judsons money and prayers but few instructions. While the work was new and missionaries few, this hands-off policy largely continued. On such things as where a mission would be opened, where the missionaries would live, how much money they should requisition, and how the missionaries would spend their time, the home board might offer advice; but most actual decisions were made on the field. There developed a strong feeling of independence among some missionaries; even before 1820 George H. Hough felt free to separate from the Judsons at Rangoon and move to a distant city without consultation with the society.

In 1841 the society included in its report a section on "Relation of the Board to its Missionaries," affirming that "when a brother is accepted it is the duty of the Board to assign his station, [and] to give general direction to his duties and labors."[13] What seemed to the society simply good administration seemed to some missionaries a dictatorial take-it-or-leave-it attitude. The basic issue revolved around control of the mission enterprise: Would policies and expenditures be decided at the home office or on the field? One or two of the missions split off and operated independently for a few years, but in the end home direction largely prevailed.[14]

2. *Education versus evangelism.* For years Baptists debated the priority of education versus direct evangelism in converting overseas populations. Those who favored education felt it would prepare people for the gospel and provide trained lay and ministerial leadership needed for strong indigenous churches. They thought foreign missionaries could never convert the nations; only indigenous churches could do that, and the churches required training. Thus it is hardly accurate to say, as some have done, that the missionaries wanted to substitute education for evangelism. Most of those who pushed for schools believed that would lead to more effective evangelism. Others, however, warned of "a preoccupation with education at the expense of preaching" and later cited mass conversions among the Telugus and in the Belgian Congo as proof that direct evangelism was more fruitful. Some Baptists feared that education would absorb too large a percentage of missionary funds and personnel and that the boarding schools might

12. *Sixty-first Annual Report,* ABMU, as carried in the *Baptist Missionary Magazine,* July 1875, p. 213, in ABHS.

13. *Minutes,* Tenth Trienniel Meeting of the Baptist General Convention, Boston, 1841, pp. 27-28.

14. For a fuller discussion of this issue, see Torbet, *Venture,* pp. 133 *f.*

accustom the pupils, especially potential national pastors, to life-style expectations which could rarely be fulfilled. They also pointed out that many of the pupils never professed conversion.

More than once the union indicated its intention to put direct evangelism ahead of education, but a study of annual reports raises questions as to how effectively that priority was implemented. A study in 1894, led by Alvah Hovey, showed a total of 1,246 mission schools under the care of the union, compared to only 44 in 1841.[15] Of 474 total foreign missionaries in 1900, only 171 were ordained, most of the nonordained working in some phase of education.[16] However, toward the end of the century, more of the schools were turned over to nationals; and in 1893 less than 25 percent of union expenditures went to education.[17]

3. *Development of indigenous churches.* Long before the much-heralded "indigenous church movement" of the twentieth century, Northern Baptists adopted specific policies to encourage overseas churches to become self-supporting and self-directing as soon as possible. They had no interest in perpetuating "Northern Baptist" churches overseas. By 1898, 524 out of a total of 853 mission churches were entirely self-supporting, and only about one-third of the mission schools received direct mission funds.

4. *The role of women missionaries.* Among Baptists the role of missionary wives was unclear. At times the society debated whether to apply the term "missionary" to the wives and once even voted not to call one missionary wife "sister" until it could learn more about her conversion. However, the dynamic Ann Judson clearly regarded herself as much a missionary as her husband and was so regarded by others. Whether Charlotte White, appointed in 1815, had full missionary status is unclear. In 1832 Sarah Cummings and Caroline Harrington, both single, were appointed to Burma with full missionary status. Four years later Eleanor Macomber was appointed to work among the Karens. Unlike the other single women, Macomber insisted upon living alone, although many expressed dismay that a woman should be left, as one put it, "with no strong arm to lean on." Before her premature death in 1839, Macomber became an effective evangelist and church planter, most of her converts being baptized by Judson. In 1836 the respected Rufus Anderson no doubt expressed the opinion of most Baptists when he said: "It has been urged upon missionary societies to send out unmarried females. . . . Few however appear to be aware of the difficulties of placing the single female in circumstances to live and labor happily in pagan

15. See the *Twenty-seventh Annual Report,* Board of Managers of the Baptist General Convention for Foreign Missions, Boston, 1841, p. 71; see also Torbet, *Venture,* p. 167.
16. See the *Eighty-sixth Annual Report,* ABMU, Detroit, 1900, p. 215, in ABHS.
17. Torbet, *Venture,* p. 167.

lands."[18] Because of this reluctance, Baptist single women had "to slip quietly into missions without attracting much notice," as one historian put it.[19]

However, after the Civil War, the policy of appointing women missionaries began to change. In 1866 the executive committee of the ABMU voted that "large discretion should be given to the Corresponding Secretary in discouraging or encouraging applications from unmarried women."[20] After an 1867 survey showed that qualified women missionaries would be welcomed on the field, the executive committee in 1870 reversed its earlier policy and actively sought women appointees. The rise of the women's societies no doubt augmented that trend; by 1900 the women's societies had appointed 113 women missionaries and supported 284 native "Bible women."[21]

Of course, the story of Baptist missions was not all advance and achievement. There were also problems, some of which were frankly discussed in the annual report for 1875.[22] Some of the churches contributed nothing to foreign missions, while others contributed to nothing else. Some churches sent and supported their own missionaries, which led to endless confusion and conflict on the field. Other churches "adopted" native preachers and helpers, thus leading to different levels of support which caused inequities and jealousy. The union discouraged designated gifts and urged the churches not to appoint their own missionaries but to work through the union. Adequate funding remained a perennial problem: The report for 1900 called for twenty-five new mission appointments, but shortage of funds prevented that. The report noted that "these years have witnessed a retrenchment; only needs that were most urgent have been met."[23] Despite impressive achievements, Northern Baptists came to the end of the century with diminished enthusiasm for overseas ministries. Perhaps the challenging spiritual needs at home helped redirect their efforts.

The American Baptist Publication Society (ABPS)

No Baptist agency had a broader assignment than the ABPS, which had grown out of the old Tract Society. Its constitution declared that "the object of this Society shall be to promote evangelical religion by means of the Bible, the printing press, colportage, and the Sunday-School." In further explaining its task, the society said in 1879, "It is at once a Bible Society, Book Concern, Tract Society, Colporteur Agency, and Sunday School Union of

18. Cited by R. Pierce Beaver, *All Loves Excelling: American Protestant Women in World Missions,* p. 61.

19. Torbet, *Venture,* p. 187.

20. Ibid., p. 191.

21. Ibid., p. 199.

22. *Sixty-second Annual Report,* ABMU, Buffalo, 1875, p. 215 *f.,* in ABHS.

23. *Eighty-sixth Annual Report,* ABMU, Detroit, 1900, p. 20, in ABHS.

the Baptists in the United States."[24] Perhaps this agency did more than all the colleges and seminaries to increase the religious education of Baptists, simply because its work touched so many.

The schism of 1845 hardly touched the Publication Society; its minutes of the time make no mention of the division. Indeed, there *was* no division in the publication work for another half-century. The SBC "Address to the Public" in 1845 had specifically noted that the division involved only the mission societies. The new SBC turned down suggestions to form its own publication agency in 1845, and Southern churches continued to use ABPS literature into the 1890s.

Benjamin Griffith, secretary of the ABPS 1857-1893, described the agency as "preeminently a Sunday School Society," and no doubt its greatest contributions came in that field.[25] In the early 1800s, the Sunday School was new among Baptists in America, unknown to many and opposed by some. The ABPS formed countless new Sunday Schools, while its staff in Philadelphia issued a steady stream of lesson helps for pupils and teachers. As early as 1830 Noah Davis, then an agent for the Tract Society, had observed that "the time may come when the number of schools in our denomination will be so great as to require . . . a series of Sabbath-school books suited to their wants."[26] Baptists were among the first to support B. F. Jacobs's plan for a "uniform lesson," by which several denominations studied the same Bible passages each week.

Printing materials is one thing; getting them into the hands of the people is quite another. Baptists accomplished the latter through a system of colporteurs who sold publications house to house and church to church. In 1851 the society had twenty-seven "colporteur missionaries" in seven states; by 1855 the number had risen to sixty-nine.[27] Some colporteurs received salaries, while others paid their way by profits on their sales. The goal of ABPS was to have such "print missionaries" visit "every church, every Sunday school, and every family in the land."[28]

Bible distribution formed another aspect of the society's work. A report in 1856 noted that "among the families visited by our colporteurs within the last two years, no less than 4,746 were found without a Bible."[29] For a time, Baptists cooperated with the nondenominational American Bible Society but in 1837 formed their own American and Foreign Bible Society to publish Baptist translations of Scripture. In 1850 this Baptist agency further split, resulting in a new group called the American Bible Union. Neither won a permanent place in Baptist life. In 1883 a "General Baptist

24. Cited in William H. Brackney, ed., *Baptist Life and Thought: 1600-1980*, p. 310.
25. Daniel Gurden Stevens, *The First Hundred Years of the American Baptist Publication Society*, opposite p. 39.
26. Ibid., p. 15.
27. Ibid., pp. 31, 32.
28. Ibid., p. 31.
29. Ibid., p. 48.

Bible Convention" voted that "the Bible work of Baptists should be done by our two existing Societies—the foreign work by the American Baptist Missionary Union, and the home work by the American Baptist Publication Society."[30] Efforts to produce a "Baptist Bible" came to little.

One of the most creative ministries of the ABPS was its chapel car work. This involved outfitting a railway car as a "church on wheels," complete with pews, hymnals, a small organ and a pulpit, as well as living quarters for a missionary couple. The chapel cars could go wherever the railroad went and stop on sidings for a day or a month in communities with no permanent church. The first car, *Evangel,* was put in service in 1891, and was soon followed by *Emmanuel, Glad Tidings, Good Will, Messenger of Peace, Herald of Hope,* and *Grace.*[31] A chapel car syndicate in New York, including John D. Rockefeller and James B. Colgate, guaranteed the cooperation of the railroads, most of which moved the cars free wherever they wanted to go. In its first year, *Evangel* visited 88 communities, held 424 sessions, with 474 sermons, 400 conversions, and 4 Sunday Schools and 8 new churches formed.[32] A number of strong churches grew out of the chapel car ministry, including, for example, the First Baptist Church of Van Nuys, California.[33] Other variations of this work included colportage wagons, chapel buses (in the twentieth century), and even a few "gospel cruisers," special boats outfitted as chapels. Such efforts enabled hundreds of communities to have Sunday Schools, Bible classes, worship services, and evangelistic meetings which would not have been possible otherwise.

Nothing better illustrates the overlap of the Publication Society and the Home Mission Society than the chapel cars. Over the years the two Baptist societies found themselves doing similar work, sometimes in cooperation, sometimes in competition. In 1874 the ABPS described itself as "strictly and eminently a missionary Society" and did not hesitate to call its appointees "Sunday-school Missionaries."[34] By contrast, they described the HMS as a *"church* missionary society," whose agents worked primarily to establish and strengthen churches. The ABPS's work was not primarily with churches, but with families and Sunday Schools. The distinction was clearer on paper than on the field, where the actual work of home missionaries and Sunday School missionaries seemed much the same. In 1860, for example, ABPS missionaries formed 34 new churches and baptized 722 converts.[35]

---

30. Ibid., p. 51.
31. Lawrence T. Slaght, *Multiplying the Witness: 150 Years of American Baptist Educational Ministries,* pp. 49-50.
32. Stevens, p. 103.
33. Slaght, p. 50.
34. Stevens, p. 69.
35. Ibid., p. 100.

Efforts to delineate the tasks of each agency succeeded in February 1899 when the ABPS agreed to concentrate on literature and Sunday Schools, leaving the more distinctly missionary work to the HMS. The Publication Society retained the chapel car ministry but agreed to consult with the HMS about places to visit and refer the baptism of converts, forming new churches, and building church houses to HMS personnel.

As noted earlier, the Publication Society provided Sunday School lesson materials for Baptist churches, including Southern Baptists and the growing number of black churches (grouped after 1880 into the National Baptist Convention). By the 1890s both Southern and National Baptists launched agencies to provide their own literature. The ABPS resisted this loss of Southern markets, citing its unbroken record of cordial and effective service in the South. Despite the publications of the newly formed Sunday School Board of the SBC, many churches continued to buy literature from the Philadelphia society. However, ABPS secretary A. J. Rowland made what now appears to have been a tactical error at the SBC meeting in Wilmington, North Carolina, in 1897. Instead of emphasizing the advantages of ABPS, which were considerable, he attacked the Sunday School Board. Southern leaders reacted negatively, and from that moment the Publication Society lost its place in the South.[36] The last organizational tie between Baptist churches North and South was thus severed.

The American Baptist Home Mission Society (ABHMS)

This was the only one of the three great Baptist societies which did not change its name during the nineteenth century, though its work expanded vastly in geographical extent and types of ministries. In the early 1800s, as noted earlier, many Baptists considered foreign missions as *the* Baptist task, with home missions an afterthought. That had changed by 1900. Under the dynamic leadership of secretaries like Henry L. Morehouse, the HMS played a more central role in Baptist life. Such factors as European immigration, the spiritual needs of Southern freedmen, and population explosion in the West focused new attention upon home missions. Of the three great societies, perhaps none had a more sharply defined task, or less internal dissension in carrying out its work, than the HMS. The Jubilee Report of 1882 said, "The Society is practically a triune organization. The missionary, church edifice and educational work . . . [are] intertwined and independent."[37]

Baptists particularly felt the challenge of the West. One Baptist reported

36. For a discussion of this, see James M. Frost, *The Sunday School Board of the Southern Baptist Convention: Its History and Work,* ch. xi, "The Opposition and What Became of It," pp. 78 f.

37. Henry L. Morehouse, ed., *Baptist Home Missions in North America, 1832-1882,* p. 363.

that "the first six houses will not go up in . . . a new town, but one of them will be a saloon; and a man might venture his life upon the certainty that the first railroad that thunders through those streets will have a cargo of whiskey and beer on board." Baptists concluded that "while sin is moving West by steam, it will never do for Christianity to go afoot."[38] Nor did the HMS missionaries go only by foot; they went by wagon, horseback, rail, and even by boat. The HMS's announced objective was nothing less than "North America for Christ," and if it fell short of this ambitious goal, its achievements were considerable.

By 1900, after 68 years of ministry, the HMS calculated that a total of 24,242 home missionaries and teachers had been commissioned. Those missionaries and teachers had preached over 2,000,000 sermons, had baptized 163,361 converts, and had organized 5,387 new churches.[39] The number of missionaries under appointment rose from 352 in 1871 to 513 in 1882 and to 1,180 at the turn of the century. Total income reached $580,891 by 1900.[40] The HMS maintained far more missionaries than the foreign society did on comparable funds because home missionary salaries were only about half that of their overseas colleagues.

Church edifice work. Quite early the HMS saw the need for church buildings to stabilize Baptist work in new areas. In 1882 the society reported at least 2,500 "houseless churches" among Baptists, mostly in the South and West.[41] The 7 states of Montana, Idaho, Wyoming, Nevada, Utah, Arizona, and New Mexico had only 9 Baptist buildings among them. The society reported that "300 church edifices ought to be built annually for the Baptists of this country" because, "without a house of worship, money for missionaries' support is often almost thrown away."[42] Such buildings as did exist often proved no credit to Baptists. While touring with John Mason Peck in 1831, Jonathan Going, standing before the building of the First Baptist Church of Columbus, Ohio, exclaimed "Pity! Pity!"[43]

The first recorded action related to edifice work by the HMS came in 1850. The executive committee reported that "the subject of devising a plan for aiding feeble churches in building meetinghouses was introduced."[44] In 1854 the society established its Church Edifice Fund and launched a drive to raise $100,000 to fund the work. That year the society received $5,678 and erected 2 buildings.[45] The original plan called for loans for a maximum

38. Ibid., pp. 55-56.
39. *Annual Report,* ABHMS, Detroit, 1900, p. 68.
40. Ibid., pp. 31, 69.
41. Morehouse, p. 40.
42. Ibid.
43. Ibid., p. 6.
44. Ibid., p. 371.
45. For an excellent discussion of this work, see Robert A. Baker, *Relations Between Northern and Southern Baptists,* 2nd ed. (Fort Worth: Marvin D. Evans Printing Company, 1954), pp. 125 *f.*

of 3 years, but some of the loans proved difficult to collect. Of 213 churches aided by 1880, only 63 kept the loan less than 5 years, and 39 kept it longer than 10 years. Some could not pay even the interest on their loans. When the HMS forgave or discounted some loans, other churches expected similar concessions. This led to a change of policy in 1881, whereby the society made outright grants up to $500, provided twice that amount was raised in the local community. Aided churches had to show good title to their property, and no church costing over $10,000 could receive a grant. The society added the not unreasonable requirement that aided churches send an annual contribution to the work of the society. In the South, this tended to tie churches more to the Northern Society than to the Home Mission Board of the struggling SBC. The Edifice Fund aided white, black, and immigrant churches; in 1868 for example, 24 meeting houses were begun among black churches with HMS funds. By the turn of the century, hundreds of Baptist buildings had been built or repaired through the Edifice Fund. The low point was reached in 1880 when only 6 buildings were erected; the high point was 1892, when 121 were built.[46]

An unexpected feature of the edifice program developed during the Civil War. As Southern civilians fled before the advancing Union armies, they left scores of abandoned Baptist buildings. In 1864 the society noted, "In almost every city, town and village taken by our army there has been found a deserted Baptist meeting-house. In many places these houses have been stripped of all that was movable, or converted into hospitals, stables, store houses."[47] In some cases, the church buildings were pulled down for firewood or diverted to non-Baptist use. In an effort to preserve the buildings for Baptists, the HMS asked the War Department in Washington for authority to take over *abandoned* Baptist buildings in the South. On January 14, 1864, the War Department notified its military commanders, "You are hereby directed to place at the disposal of the American Baptist Home Mission Society all houses of worship belonging to Baptist Churches South, in which a loyal minister does not now officiate."[48] Clearly the society received far more authority than they had asked. J. W. Parker of Boston, appointed by the HMS to oversee this work, reported that about half of the Baptist meetinghouses in the South had been abandoned; and the HMS proceeded to take custody of many of them.

In effect, the War Department gave authority to the HMS to seize almost any Baptist building in the South, for "a loyal minister" by Washington definition could rarely be found. In a few cases, the society took over functioning Baptist churches, in effect dismissing pastors and scattering congregations. Further problems surfaced in restoring the confiscated

46. *Annual Report,* ABHMS, Detroit, 1900, p. 69.
47. Morehouse, pp. 373-374.
48. Ibid., p. 374.

churches to local ownership after the war, a process delayed by endless red tape. It took years, for example, for the Coliseum Place Baptist Church in New Orleans to return to local ownership. Such experiences added to Southern Baptist bitterness after the war and sometimes obscured the overall benefits of the society's efforts to preserve Baptist buildings for Baptist use.

For a few years after the 1845 schism, the Northern Baptists largely withdrew from work in the South. However, in 1862 the HMS reentered the Southern field, reaffirming "its original birthright to the cultivation of this entire continent."[49] In 1863 the HMS divided the nation into four areas, one of which, the Southern District, included all of the area south of New York. By 1869 the society had stationed one-third of its total home mission force in the South. This is more remarkable in light of the society's inability to send missionaries to the South a generation earlier, one factor which provoked the schism. However, the overwhelming spiritual needs among both black and white people in the South could not be denied, and the Home Board of the Southern Convention could not effectively address those needs.

Work with freedmen. In 1863 the HMS established its Freedmen's Fund to sponsor evangelistic and educational work among Southern blacks. After the war, thousands of black Baptists withdrew from the predominantly white churches to form their own. The black churches grew rapidly but faced a serious leadership vacuum. The society tried to address this need in two ways. First, it devised the "Freedmen's Institute," a kind of traveling study course by which HMS leaders went to an area, gathered all the black ministers and deacons they could, and taught the rudiments of Baptist doctrine and church life. The institutes might run from a few days to a few weeks and were repeated throughout the South. In 1879 S. W. Marston was appointed superintendent of Missions to Freedmen. During that first year, he reported 33 institutes, involving 1,119 ministers and deacons, with at least 1 institute in each Southern state. In 1881 this work was made a summer program connected with the black colleges.

In a second approach to the educational needs of freedmen, the HMS established a string of black colleges in the South. By 1894 the society helped sponsor 32 such schools, with 177 teachers and 5,357 pupils, including 432 ministerial students.[50] Many of these schools served their time and lapsed, but others matured into major black colleges, such as Morehouse College in Atlanta and Bishop College in Marshall, Texas (later moved to Dallas).

Southern Baptists were less than thrilled at the renewal of Northern Baptist activity in the South. Reports of spiritual needs implied that South-

49. Cited in Baker, p. 92.
50. Ibid., p. 123.

ern Baptists had done a poor job, and HMS work tended to tie the churches to the Northern societies and undercut the SBC. Some looked with disfavor upon the black colleges and urged the "pretty yankee girls" who came South to teach to return home. The society's evangelistic efforts encountered less opposition than its edifice and educational work.

By 1865 Southern Baptists had developed a strong territorial identity. They regarded the South as "our territory" and did not hesitate to use the term *invasion* to describe Northern Baptist work there. In 1865 Virginia Baptists passed a resolution protesting the "pretensions and usurpations" of the society in sending missionaries to the South and urged the churches to offer neither cooperation nor fellowship to these "brethren from abroad."

The SBC voted in 1867 that since the Northern Society wished to work in the South, "the Domestic Mission Board be directed to make known to that Society our willingness to receive aid in this work by appropriations made to the Boards of this Convention."[51] Thus the Southern Baptist concept was for the North to supply the money and the South to appoint the missionaries, a plan quite different from what the society had in mind.

In a conference between leaders of the two sections in 1868, John A. Broadus suggested that "no missionaries should be sent among the Southern people except those selected by the Southern Board, or if selected by the Home Mission Society, approved by the Board."[52] Edward Bright of the HMS responded that such a plan would "shut out of the South every laborer that a Southern organization does not endorse" and insisted that "Northern Baptists . . . purpose not to relinquish the right of sending any man to any place."[53] In time the hostility diminished. Many Southern Baptists came to agree with Basil Manly, Jr., who remarked in an address before the society, "We ask for help and cooperation, but if you repell our confidence, . . . we will at least not oppose whatever you may choose to do."[54]

Ministry to immigrants. Ministry to immigrants provided another challenge to Northern Baptists in the nineteenth century. From 1790 to 1820 about 250,000 people emigrated to America, according to best estimates. In the 1820s, immigration averaged no more than about 15,000 a year.[55] Complex social and economic conditions, both in Europe and America, combined to increase this trickle to a deluge. Between 1880 and 1900 about 20 million new immigrants arrived for an average of about 1 million a year.[56] Most of the "new Americans" came from nonevangelical back-

51. *Annual,* SBC, 1867, p. 79.
52. Morehouse, p. 426.
53. Ibid.
54. Cited in Baker, p. 98.
55. From Bureau of Labor Statistics, cited in Morehouse, p. 116.
56. *Annual Report,* ABHMS, Detroit, 1900, p. 65, in ABHS.

grounds and proved resistant both to Christian conversion and assimilation into traditional American cultural patterns.[57] Noting the tendency of the new Americans to cluster in Northern cities, the HMS warned in 1900 that "under the influence of this tremendous force our Republican institutions are subjected to an enormous strain while our religious life is being slowly but surely and sadly corrupted."[58] Comparing the American influx to the barbarian migrations that overran the Roman Empire, the HMS no doubt expressed the nativist fears of many Americans that the new immigrants, unless converted and assimilated, would radically change the soul of America.

Some Baptist voices were among those that clamored for a limit to immigration and that blamed immigrants for the social unrest and violent labor confrontations of the late nineteenth century.[59] A Baptist group in West Virginia worried that "Infidels, Catholics, Formalists and all other classes of Gospel-haters are coming"; and some Baptists called the newcomers "European refuse," "sabbath-breakers," and described them as a "beer-guzzling" people.[60] At first Baptists seemed confident of their ability to convert and assimilate the newcomers, but as the influx reached floodtide, according to one careful scholar, "Baptists joined in the hysteria that swept the country" and later advocated legislation to restrict immigration after World War I.[61]

Whatever Baptists may have thought of immigration policies, they made heroic efforts to convert the newcomers. At one time the HMS sponsored ministries among twenty-one different nationality groups in as many languages.[62] Baptists were ever on the lookout for candidates among the ethnic groups whom they might appoint as missionaries, and they assisted generously in forming churches and supplementing pastoral salaries among the language groups. Most immigrant churches organized their own "fellowships" on an auxiliary relationship with the Northern Baptist agencies. Baptists provided tracts and other literature in various languages, but at times debated whether such ministries were best conducted in English or the immigrant tongues.

Baptists also provided training for ethnic pastors, mostly by forming "language departments" in several seminaries. Baptists opened a German department at Rochester in 1858 under August Rauschenbusch, a department for Swedish, Danish, and Norwegian students at Chicago in 1871, a

57. For a careful study of Baptist ministries to immigrants, see Lawrence B. Davis, *Immigrants, Baptists, and the Protestant Mind in America;* for a breakdown of religious affiliations of these immigrants, see p. 41n.

58. *Annual Report,* ABHMS, Detroit, 1900, p. 65, in ABHS.

59. Davis, pp. 41 *f.*

60. Ibid., pp. 45, 53.

61. Ibid., p. 57.

62. Winthrop S. Hudson, *Religion in America,* 3rd ed., p. 248.

French department at Newton in 1889, and an Italian department at Colgate Theological Seminary in 1907. Later this work was gathered up in the International Baptist Seminary in East Orange, New Jersey, which rendered valuable service before immigrant ministers and members picked up English as their major language. When that time came the International Seminary was closed, the ministers attended regular seminaries, most ethnic churches worshiped in English, and many members and even entire churches simply merged into the mainstream of Northern Baptist life.

German Baptist work in this country dates back to 1842 with the conversion of Conrad A. Fleischman. He formed a church in 1843 which affiliated with the Philadelphia Association. In 1846 John Eschman gathered a German Baptist church in New York City with 12 members. From these small beginnings the churches multiplied; by 1882 the Germans numbered 10,334 members in 137 churches. They formed local mission societies to cooperate with the HMS and obtained some of their literature from a small German publication society in Cleveland.[63] In 1853 Fleischman launched a periodical, *Der Sendbote des Evangelium* or *Gospel Messenger*. Johann Gerhard Oncken, Baptist pioneer in Germany, visited America in 1854 and greatly encouraged Baptist work among his countrymen here. In 1859 the German Baptist Conference divided into Eastern and Western branches, and because of vast distances the Western Conference further subdivided in 1881 into three regional conferences. By 1882 German churches stretched from New England to Texas, with a total of 48 home missionaries at work among them (though not all sponsored by the HMS).[64]

Immigrants from the Scandinavian countries (Sweden, Denmark, and Norway) proved open to Baptist witness, and the HMS reported in 1882, "Our missions among the Scandinavians . . . were never more encouraging than now."[65] Many of the Swedes, especially, were Baptists before coming to America. The first Swedish Baptist church in America was formed by Gustaf Palmquist in Rock Island, Illinois, in 1852. Palmquist was appointed a home missionary to the Swedes in 1853, gathering churches throughout the Midwest before returning to Sweden in 1857. The second Swedish church was formed in 1853 in Minnesota by F. O. Nelson, who had become a Baptist in Sweden upon the witness of G. W. Schroeder, who, in turn, had been won to the Baptist faith and baptized in a Seaman's Mission in New York in 1845. By 1882 the Swedes reported 104 churches, 41 ministers, and 4,980 members, mostly in the Midwest.[66] One of their great leaders was J. A. Edgren, who edited the *Evangelisk Tidskrift* and taught in the Scan-

63. Morehouse, pp. 30-31, 475.
64. Ibid., p. 30.
65. Ibid., p. 31.
66. Ibid., pp. 477-478.

dinavian department of the Baptist Theological Seminary in Chicago, where at one time as many as 78 students studied.

The first Norwegian Baptist church in this country was formed in Illinois in 1848 by Hans Valder. Baptized in 1842 and ordained two years later, Valder preached among Norwegians despite opposition from those who wished to retain their inherited Lutheranism. Following a pattern repeated frequently among ethnic groups, Valder was appointed a missionary of the HMS. In 1849 he reported, "Our little church has increased . . . from seven to nineteen, seven of the number by baptism and five by experience. We ask all to pray for the Norwegians in Illinois."[67]

Lewis Yorgenson, converted in Denmark, formed the first Danish Baptist church in America in 1856 in Wisconsin.[68] Like Valder, Yorgenson was appointed by the HMS and on his travels formed nine other Danish churches. More Danish Baptists arrived in this country, led by P. H. Dam, who also ministered under the HMS. In time most of the Norwegian and Danish churches merged. By 1882 the combined group had about 2,000 members, gathered into 30 churches, under the care of 22 ordained ministers. They published a periodical, *Oliebladet,* in Chicago.

French immigration to America, some by way of Canada, increased after 1850. The Home Mission Society became directly involved in work among the French in 1849 when they assumed major support of the Grande Ligne Mission in Canada. The mission originated among French evangelicals who had been driven to Switzerland and eventually to Canada because of their Baptist views. They came under sponsorship of the Canadian Baptist Missionary Society in 1845, but lack of funds soon severed that tie. In 1849 they appealed to the HMS, saying, "We are Baptists of your own faith and order; . . . we are cut off from our former sources of aid because we are Baptists. What shall we do? Can you do anything for us?"[69] For eleven years, 1849-1860, the HMS helped support the Grande Ligne work, which gave them a head start when many of the French Baptists migrated southward into New England. Beginning in 1853 the HMS appointed missionaries among the French, with eight at work in 1882. Though a number of separate churches were formed, most of the French joined English churches.

Chinese immigrants provided a special missionary challenge on the West Coast. The gold strike of 1849 and the extension of rail lines to the West drew Chinese immigrants. The HMS had missionaries in California as early as 1849, but the great need was for Chinese Baptists who could preach among their own people. The Home Board of the SBC appointed J. Lewis Shuck, former missionary to China, in 1854. He established a Chinese mission, and later a church, in Sacramento, where he also served as pastor

67. Ibid., p. 478.
68. Ibid.
69. Ibid., p. 481.

of the First Baptist Church. In 1870 the HMS appointed John Francis and Fung Seung Nam to work in the San Francisco area. The Sunday School they gathered in the basement of the First Baptist Church soon enrolled 150 Chinese children. Later the society asked the Foreign Board of the SBC to release R. H. Graves, veteran missionary in China, for two years to put the Chinese mission work on firm footing. Though this arrangement never worked out, the work expanded along the coast from California to Oregon, and to a lesser extent on the East Coast. Problems continued to plague the Chinese mission, including the resistance of the Chinese to conversion, lack of suitable buildings, shortage of Chinese-speaking preachers, disagreement about whether to conduct the work in English or Chinese, and the tentativeness many Chinese felt because of their intention to return to their homeland.

By the 1830s the mission needs of the Southwest, including Mexico, Texas, and New Mexico came to HMS attention. In 1840 Mr. Wilder's Sunday School class in Albany, New York, sent eight dollars to assist mission work in the Republic of Texas. Shortly afterwards, the HMS sent two home missionaries, James Huckins and William Tryon, to Texas. In 1849 it sent H. W. Read to New Mexico, probably the first Protestant missionary in that state (he was heading for California but became weary and stopped in Santa Fe). In Monterey, Mexico, Thomas W. Westrup, a businessman from England, was baptized in January 1864, along with several Mexican converts. The same day they formed the First Baptist Church of Monterrey with five members. Within months they had increased to twenty members, and in 1870 the HMS appointed Westrup its missionary to Mexico. At that time among Northern Baptists, missions to Mexico as well as to Canada came under the home society. Evangelistic and printing work was conducted by a Mexican Baptist Mission Society, and in the 1880s Baptists in Texas also sponsored missions south of the border. By 1900 the society had eighteen missionaries in Mexico, four in Cuba, and six in Puerto Rico.[70]

Indian missions among Northern Baptists passed from the foreign to the home society in 1865, but at the time only two missions were active, one among the Cherokees and the other among various tribes in Indian Territory (now Oklahoma). The HMS appointed E. E. L. Taylor in 1865 as associate corresponding secretary for the Indian Department, but in the next several years more was said than done. A number of factors complicated Indian missions, such as whether Baptists should seek or accept government money for their mission schools, how they should relate to missionaries of the SBC on the same fields, and how much emphasis to allot to the two focuses of Indian missions, namely to "convert" and "civilize"

---

70. *Annual Report,* ABHMS, Detroit, 1900, pp. 67-68, in ABHS.

them.[71] The major institutional survival of the work was the "Indian University" first established in 1880 at Tahlequah in the Cherokee Nation, now the highly respected Bacone College near Muskogee, named for Almon C. Bacone who taught at Tahlequah and led in the relocation and strengthening of the school. John D. Rockefeller was one of the major donors to the reorganized school.[72] The story of Indian missions throughout this period was marked by the heroic efforts of a few, the apathy of many, and limited response by the Indians.

Toward the end of the century, the major emphasis in Northern Baptist home mission work shifted westward. By 1882 the HMS spent almost as much mission money in the West as in the rest of the nation combined, and of 1,180 home missionaries in 1900, 799 worked in Western states.[73] Needs in the West, plus increasing demands of immigrant ministries in the East and Midwest, probably help account for Northern Baptists willingness to curtail their work in the South toward the end of the century.

One problem that plagued Baptist home missions, both North and South, was a spirit of "localism." One observer pointed out that while Landmarkism (big L) spread in the South, landmarkism (little l) remained in the North. At any rate, an exaggerated sense of the local church continued to mark Northern Baptists. A network of local societies stretched across the North, most of them auxiliary to the HMS. However, some did not cooperate; instead, they appointed their own home missionaries, which created overlap, duplication, and no end of confusion as missionaries on the same fields jockeyed for position. Planning an overall home mission strategy was made more difficult by such localism.

The American Baptist Education Society (ABES)

From 1764 American Baptists have sponsored colleges. In fact, the school they launched that year came out of more comprehensive planning and enjoyed more united support than most of those formed during the next century. During the 1800s Baptists formed countless colleges, seminaries, academies, and "normal schools," most planted by local education societies, poorly supported, and appealing to a limited constituency. Many were badly located and overly dependent upon one or two affluent donors. Many had to merge with others or lapse unlamented. Of course, these schools came out of the noblest motives and no doubt accomplished much good, but the lack of educational planning and correlation created a hodgepodge that wasted both human and financial resources and yet left vast sections of the constituency beyond easy access to a Baptist school. The Baptist right

71. Morehouse, p. 20.
72. See William A. Carleton, "Bacone College," in Davis C. Woolley, ed., *Encyclopedia of Southern Baptists* (Nashville: Broadman Press, 1958), 1:102 (hereafter cited as *ESB*).
73. *Annual Report,* ABHMS, Detroit, 1900, pp. 67-68.

hand did not know what the left hand was doing in educational work, and neither hand could reach the pocketbook. Over the years all three of the great societies became involved in education, with the attendant duplication; but in time the Home Mission Society related most closely, though not always willingly, to the Baptist schools.

The *Columbian Star* in its issue of March 20, 1824, carried two articles about education. It noted that "a society has been formed in the city of New York, called the Baptist Female Association. The object of the Society is to aid pious young men, called to the work of the Gospel Ministry, in obtaining an education." The same page also carried a comment that "God alone can judge and determine what gifts are wanting, and what gifts will best promote the interests in his kingdom," and therefore "it is His prerogative alone to furnish them." Thus one page spotlighted two of the most serious problems facing Baptist schools in the nineteenth century: sponsorship by isolated societies and lingering opposition to education. Of the two, the former seemed harder to overcome in the North, the latter in the South.

For years Baptist leaders had seen the need for more correlation, but it remained for Henry L. Morehouse to do something about it. A statesman of major stature, Morehouse as head of the HMS called for a meeting to discuss education. Noting that "Baptists have no [educational] organization. There is no comprehensive plan," Morehouse asked, "Is it not time for the denomination to have a defined policy and better methods in . . . the establishment of denominational schools?"[74] Response was favorable and led to a meeting in Washington in May 1888, which formed the American Baptist Education Society (ABES). Its constitution defined its purpose as "the promotion of Christian education, under Baptist auspices, in North America." At the time Northern Baptists sponsored twenty-five academies, nineteen colleges, and five seminaries, but these numbers increased by the turn of the century.[75] During its first year, the new society had requests for aid from about fifty schools.

From the first the ABES included Southern Baptists. J. B. Link of Texas made the motion to form the society, and its early sessions were addressed by Southern leaders like John A. Broadus, B. H. Carroll, J. B. Gambrell, and T. T. Eaton. Broadus spoke of "our new Education Society" and urged, "Let us all, . . . from the North and the South, from the East and the West, gladly contribute to the Society's treasury, and co-operate with its efforts to promote the great work of education."[76] In 1890 A. C. Dixon noted that the ABES, "without any war history," could serve as a rallying point for Baptists in the two sections. The next year B. H. Carroll rejoiced that "this

74. *Minutes,* The National Baptist Education Convention, Washington, 1888, pp. 7-8, in ABHS.
75. Ibid., pp. 3, 16.
76. Ibid., p. 62.

National Education Society . . . knows no North, no South, no East, no West."[77] In its early years, the ABES aided Southern as well as Northern schools, including Furman University in South Carolina, Carson-Newman College in Tennessee, Mississippi College, and The Southern Baptist Theological Seminary in Kentucky.[78] For years the society followed its plan to meet in alternate years in Northern and Southern cities, though its leaders showed minimal enthusiasm for J. B. Link's invitation to meet in "Fort Worth City" in 1890; they went to Chicago instead. The society was first headquartered in Washington, D.C., specifically to be accessible to both North and South, but later moved to New York City.

Perhaps the society's greatest achievement, and at the same time its greatest failure, was the establishment of the University of Chicago in 1890. No one can doubt that the establishment of this university represented a milestone not only for Baptists but also for American higher education. The achievement is clear. The failure lay in several areas. By its obsession with Chicago and diversion of funds to this one school, the society never effectively addressed the educational needs of the West. Its conviction that a major school in Chicago could serve the needs of the entire West proved erroneous. By not securing the school to Baptist control, the society eased the way for the university to move outside Baptist life. From the first, the school expressed doctrinal views which provoked controversy and schism, spawned a number of rival protest schools, and played a major role in the rise of the Fundamentalist movement in the next century.

Using the money of John D. Rockefeller and the brains of William Rainey Harper, Baptists launched the present University of Chicago on land donated by Marshall C. Field. It replaced an earlier school of the same name which had perished by fire. The secretary of the ABES, F. T. Gates, said in 1889, "Nothing great or worthy can be done for education in the West until this thing is done."[79] As it turned out, little was done by the society *after* that thing was done. Baptists in the West found the state conventions more responsive to their needs, and the ABES lapsed in 1903. Northern Baptist schools continued to flourish, though the effort to form national planning and funding failed. Even before 1900 Southern Baptist participation had diminished, and one more hopeful avenue to bridge the chasm created in 1845 came to naught.

Baptists in the South

Chapter 10 sketched the formation of the Southern Baptist Convention in 1845. At its formative meeting the infant SBC appointed boards for foreign and home missions. Delegates also discussed publication and educa-

77. *Annual Report,* ABES, 1890, pp. 31, 71.
78. Ibid., p. 12.
79. *Annual Report,* ABES, 1889, p. 31, in ABHS.

tional work but caution prevailed and entrance into these areas were delayed.

Foreign Mission Board (FMB)

On May 10, 1845, in one of its earliest official actions, the SBC passed the following resolution: "*Resolved,* That the Convention appoint a Board of Managers for Foreign Missions, and also one for Domestic Missions, and that a committee be appointed to nominate the members for such boards."[80] The Foreign Mission Board got off to good start and for years tended to overshadow the other agencies. One might say that at first the FMB in effect *was* the convention. The official convention record books, there being then no denominational headquarters or executive committee, were kept at the Foreign Mission Board in Richmond.

To avoid undue centralization, the SBC located its boards in different cities. Richmond, Virginia, was chosen as the home of the FMB, where it remains. Richmond was the approximate center of Baptist strength along the Atlantic Seaboard, had early become a strong missionary center, and was known for its excellent banking facilities. Virginia was also the home of the *Religious Herald,* one of the strongest Baptist papers, and several Baptist giants like J. B. Jeter and J. B. Taylor labored there. Richmond also formed a center of economic strength in the South and, though not on the coast, proved convenient for overseas shipping and travel.

J. B. Jeter of Richmond served as acting secretary of the FMB until a permanent leader was enlisted. That proved no easy task, since the first six men to be offered the post declined. Finally the board persuaded James Barnett Taylor (1804-1871) a Richmond pastor, to accept the office. He agreed "to devote two entire days in each week, to the duties of the Secretaryship, and, if it be necessary, . . . to take a journey to the South."[81] Taylor had been active in the Triennial Convention, was a member of the Virginia society that called the 1845 meeting, and was elected one of four SBC vice-presidents at its 1846 meeting. When he took office, the board had two missionaries; when he laid down the mantle a quarter century later, the board had eighty-one missionaries in China, Africa, and Italy.

Taylor's work did not long remain part time. His travels, correspondence, and editing the *Southern Baptist Missionary Journal* (a monthly, begun July 1, 1846) took all his time. In a tour of several states in 1846, Taylor "found a considerable readiness among many churches and individuals to

80. *Proceedings,* Southern Baptist Convention, 1845, p. 14.

81. *Minutes,* Foreign Mission Board (December 29, 1845), 1:24, cited in Baker James Cauthen and others, *Advance: A History of Southern Baptist Foreign Missions* (Nashville: Broadman Press, 1970), p. 26.

respond to the claims of the mission cause."[82] He was especially gratified to find a number of students in Southern schools ready to seek missionary appointment.

The early FMB was practically autonomous; little if any of its funds came through the SBC. The board placed in the field "an efficient corps of solicitors" who traveled among the churches and associations, presented the needs of missions, and urged Baptists to forward their foreign mission contributions to Richmond. W. B. Johnson, first president of the SBC, was released for a time from his Edgefield pastorate to travel among the churches, explaining the new convention and appealing for its support. He met hearty response wherever he went. The board also requested J. Lewis Shuck to delay his return to China in order to speak among the churches, accompanied by Yong Seen Sang, a Chinese convert. This remarkable team of missionary and convert made a deep impact and helped fix China as the major mission field of Southern Baptists for the rest of the century.

During its first year, the board received $11,735 and reported that "a much larger contribution would have been made by the churches, had immediate necessity demanded."[83] Little money was expended in that first preparatory year. The board moved slowly, seeking to establish enduring foundations for the future. Its original vision was extensive. C. D. Mallary reported for the Committee on New Fields of Labor in 1846 as follows:

> Resolved, That whilst for the present it would be unwise for the energies of our Foreign Board to be diverted from China, and our contemplated mission in Africa; yet it is proper that they should direct their preliminary enquiries to other fields, and especially to Mexico, South America and Palestine, with a view to the future establishment of missions in those regions, if their means should justify it.[84]

In fact, funds did not allow expansion for some years. The board opened missionary work in China in 1845; in Liberia, 1846; in Nigeria, 1850; in Brazil, 1859 with T. J. Bowen, and reopened 1881 with William B. and Anne Bagby; in Italy, 1870; and Japan, first missionaries appointed 1860, work actually opened 1889. Space allows only a brief survey of pioneer beginnings in these various fields.

China. The first and major mission field of Southern Baptists was China. J. Lewis Shuck and his wife, Henrietta Hall Shuck, were the first Baptist missionaries in that vast land, appointed by the Triennial Convention in 1835. The Shucks opened work in Hong Kong, baptized their first convert in 1837, and formed the first Baptist church in China at Hong Kong in 1843. Upon the death of Mrs. Shuck in 1844, he returned briefly to the

82. *Proceedings,* First Triennial Meeting of the Southern Baptist Convention, 1846, p. 22.
83. Ibid., p. 23.
84. Ibid., p. 18.

United States and was later appointed by the new SBC. He helped form the first Baptist church of Shanghai in 1847, serving as its pastor. Upon the death of his second wife in 1851, Shuck returned to the States and served from 1854-1861 with the Home Mission Board, establishing work among the Chinese on the West Coast. He established the first Chinese Baptist church in America in Sacramento.[85] Shuck later returned to China with his third wife.

Within weeks of its formation, the FMB named "China as the province where our forces ought to be chiefly concentrated."[86] Samuel C. Clopton was appointed to China on September 1, 1845; he has the distinction of being the first missionary appointed by the FMB. In November, George Pearcy was appointed, and in 1846 the two couples sailed for Canton.

From the beginning, the South China mission was the strongest Southern field. Before the end of 1846 a physician, J. S. James, and a teacher, Francis C. Johnson, were also appointed. Harriet Baker came in 1849 to open a school for girls. Also in 1849 B. W. Whilden joined the mission, and two of his daughters later became China missionaries. Problems plagued the South China Mission, not the least being health concerns. Within months of his arrival, Clopton died of fever; Dr. and Mrs. James drowned in Hong Kong harbor; and in 1850 Mrs. Whilden died. Personal conflicts developed, and the Pearcys and Miss Baker moved to Shanghai. By 1861 the South China mission again had five missionaries one of whom was Rosewell H. Graves.

R. H. Graves was one of the most remarkable missionaries in Southern Baptist history. A physician from Maryland, he served in China for fifty-six years, 1856 to 1912. Only the W. B. Bagbys in Brazil had a longer tenure with the FMB. Graves brought stability to the mission and rendered effective service as a preacher, teacher, and writer. Graves's medical skills helped give Baptists a good image in China. He also led in expanding the work to other cities in South China.

The Central China Mission opened in 1847 when Matthew T. Yates and his wife, Eliza, arrived in Shanghai. Mr. and Mrs. Thomas W. Tobey joined them before the year was out, along with J. Lewis Shuck and his second wife, and they formed a church in 1847. The Tobeys did not remain long because of Mrs. Tobey's health. Yates served forty-one years in central China, lending the kind of stability that Graves had brought to the south. The Taiping Rebellion cut the missionaries off from contact with America, and they were unable to receive funds from the FMB. During that time, Yates worked as a translator, earning a livelihood for most of the personnel of the mission. They were aided also by the Baptist Missionary Society of England; over a century later the FMB gladly took occasion to return the

85. J. B. Hipps, "Shuck, John Lewis," *ESB,* 2:1201-1202.
86. *Proceedings,* First Triennial Meeting of the Southern Baptist Convention, 1846, p. 10.

favor by aiding a group of English missionaries. By 1881 there were enough Baptist churches in the Shanghai area to form a Baptist association, the first in China.

The third Southern Baptist mission in China opened in 1859 when Mr. and Mrs. Jesse B. Hartwell and Mr. and Mrs. J. L. Holmes, arrived in the Shantung province. Tengchow became a major center, but the work branched out to other northern cities, including Pingtu, where Lottie Moon served. One of the leading missionaries of North China was Tarleton Perry Crawford (1822-1901), first appointed to Shanghai in 1852 but switched to North China in 1863. Mrs. Crawford became adept at teaching the Chinese language; many of the new appointees came to her for language studies. Mr. Crawford served in China for about forty years, almost thirty in North China. Though a man of deep convictions and great energy, Crawford's growing Landmark views led to his severance from the board in the early 1890s in the "Gospel Mission Controversy." He came to believe that missionaries should be sent directly by churches rather than a mission board. He also said that missionaries should receive no salaries beyond an initial grant to get them established, after which they should earn their own way. Crawford's own successful investments which provided him financial security may have influenced his views.

Edmonia Moon was appointed to Tengchow in 1872, and her older sister Lottie arrived in 1873. Another sister, Orianne, served for a time in Jerusalem as a medical missionary with the Church of Christ. Although the FMB had appointed single women since the 1840s, they were still few and the Moon sisters rank among the pioneers. Edmonia, or "Eddie," helped form the Baptist Ladies Missionary Association in Richmond in 1872 and, in so doing, became enamored with the work and applied for appointment. Within weeks she sailed, arriving in Tengchow at the age of twenty-one, though personally much less mature than that age might suggest. She put pressure on her sister Lottie to join her in China. She enlisted the aid of T. P. Crawford who, in turn, urged the secretary of the FMB, J. B. Taylor, to recruit Lottie for the mission cause. After four years Edmonia's health, physical and emotional, forced her home. Joining the Catholic Church years later did not bring the peace she sought, and in 1908 Edmonia took her own life.[87]

Charlotte Diggs Moon (1840-1912) became Southern Baptists' most famous missionary. "Lottie" Moon grew up in a devout Virginia home, but she scoffed at religion until her conversion at age sixteen. At a time when most girls received little or no schooling, the Moon sisters attended the best schools available. Both parents insisted that their daughters have every educational opportunity available to their sons. An older sister, Orianne,

87. Catherine B. Allen, *The New Lottie Moon Story*, p. 258.

became the first woman physician in Virginia and rendered heroic service as a surgeon in Confederate hospitals during the Civil War.

Lottie proved a brilliant student, especially adept at languages. Barely over four feet tall, she remained sensitive about her size all her life. She refused to be photographed standing and, in fact, tried to avoid all photographs. After the war she became a teacher in Kentucky and later in Georgia. In February 1873, after her pastor had preached a fervent missionary sermon, Lottie Moon went forward and said, "I have long known that God wanted me in China." She was appointed in July 1873. From the first Lottie displayed the gifts of an effective missionary. Mrs. Crawford noted, "Miss L. Moon is a highly cultivated, very pious, self-sacrificing woman," and Mr. Crawford wrote the board, "She will prove a true missionary, or I'm a poor judge of character."[88] By contrast, the missionaries recognized at once that Edmonia could not endure; that she lasted four years was due to the supportive presence of Lottie.

Lottie Moon served at first in Tengchow, among other duties keeping a school for girls. Later she transferred to the remote city of Pingtu, where for years she was the only missionary. She later wrote the board, "I hope no missionary will ever be as lonely as I have been."[89] She served fourteen years before receiving a regular furlough. However, during her infrequent trips back to the States, her appearances in Chinese dress, her dramatic speeches, and her display of interesting Chinese articles kindled great missionary interest among Southern Baptists. In Pingtu and surrounding villages, Moon distributed Christian tracts and told the story of God's love in Christ. As curious crowds gathered, she would sometimes stand in her rickshaw and raise her voice to be heard. Some of the men claimed she was "preaching," a charge that infuriated Moon. She retorted that if they did not like what she was doing, let them send men to do better. At mission meetings, the women kept mostly to their tea and knitting, while men discussed and decided mission policy. Moon not only insisted upon attending such meetings but spoke out to express her own views. She insisted that "simple justice demands that women should have equal rights with men in mission meetings and in the conduct of their work."[90]

An article by Lottie Moon published in 1884 in Virginia caused some Baptists to fear she was advocating too active a role for women. Even the FMB passed a resolution against the article, whereupon Miss Moon wrote:

It seems to be the purpose of the committee to relegate me henceforth to the first class [of women troublemakers]. I distinctly decline from being so relegated. Will you be so kind as to request the Board to appropriate the proper

88. Ibid., p. 92.
89. E. C. Routh, "Moon, Lottie (Charlotte)," *ESB,* 2:923.
90. Allen, p. 142.

sum, say $550, to pay my return passage to Virginia? On arrival, I will send in my resignation in due form.[91]

Fortunately the board refused this offer of resignation. The men accepted Lottie's active role, and in later years her counsel was both sought and valued. One male colleague, in an effort to compliment her, said she "had a very masculine mind."

Lottie Moon twice considered marriage, in 1861 and again in 1877. Both engagements were to the same man, Crawford H. Toy, who had been appointed a missionary to Japan in 1860 but did not sail, possibly for lack of funds. Both times Lottie broke off the engagement. Toy's doctrinal views may have influenced her decision the second time. Two years later, in 1879, he was forced to resign from his professorship at The Southern Baptist Theological Seminary. He finally married at age fifty-six, but Lottie never married.

Though overdue a furlough, Moon refused to leave the Pingtu work unless a replacement could fill in and shortage of funds made that impossible. In 1887 she suggested to the Baptist women of Virginia the idea of a special Christmas offering. Its original purpose was to provide help for Moon so she could take her furlough and apparently was not at first intended to continue as an annual event. Learning that Methodist women planned to observe a week of prayer before Christmas, with a missionary offering, she suggested a similar plan to the Baptist women. She wrote:

> Need it be said why the week before Christmas is chosen? Is not the festive season, when families and friends exchange gifts in memory of The Gift laid on the altar of the world for the redemption of the human race, the most appropriate time to consecrate a portion from abounding riches and scant poverty to send forth the good tidings of great joy into all the earth.[92]

The Woman's Missionary Union, formed in 1888, took up the challenge and proclaimed a week of prayer and a special Christmas offering for 1888. It adopted a goal of $2,000 and requested a grant of $100 from the FMB for postage and publicity, of which only $72.82 was spent. Actual receipts amounted to $3,315.26.[93] The week of prayer and Christmas offering became an annual emphasis among the Baptist women.

In her advancing age, broken in health and under the hardships of the Boxer Rebellion, Lottie Moon fell victim to the depression that seemed to run in her family. She thought the Chinese girls in her school would starve, so she refused to eat so they could have food. Though times were hard, actual starvation was probably not imminent. However, if the crisis loomed larger in Moon's mind than it was in reality, that takes nothing from her heroism and courage. The board sent Cynthia Miller, a nurse, to escort

91. Ibid.
92. Ibid., p. 170.
93. Ibid., p. 177.

Lottie home. They made it as far as Kobe, Japan, where Moon fell into a coma and died on Christmas Eve 1912. In her last moments, she clasped her hands in traditional Chinese greetings, calling the names of dear Chinese friends who had been dead for years. Her body was cremated, as required by law, and the ashes delivered to the FMB in a small brown package. After a brief memorial service in Richmond, Lottie Moon was buried at her home church near Crewe, Virginia. Her simple monument includes the words, "faithful unto death."

Miss Moon's death, and stories of her starvation, captured the imagination of Southern Baptists. As a memorial to "Lottie's first Christmas in heaven," the 1913 offering was larger than ever. In 1918, at the suggestion of Annie Armstrong, the annual offering was named the Lottie Moon Christmas Offering for Foreign Missions. At first largely limited to the WMU, it has since become a churchwide project. In the ninety-five years since she first suggested it, more than a half-billion dollars have come to the FMB through the Lottie Moon offering, not a bad return on that one hundred dollars appropriated for promotion back in 1888.[94]

Africa. In 1846 the FMB reported that "another important position which the Board consider themselves as specially invited to occupy, is Africa. They are only waiting to secure men of suitable qualifications to enter the field. Africa is doubtless to be evangelized."[95] Southern Baptist interest in Africa dated far back, for as they noted, "Many of her sons are among us." Black Baptists formed the African Baptist Missionary Society in Richmond in 1815, and in 1821 that society, assisted by the American Colonization Society and the Triennial Convention, sent Lott Cary and Collin Teague to Liberia. In its early days, Baptist missions to Africa cooperated closely with the ill-fated colonization society, whose goal was to return blacks to Africa. The Triennial Convention had sent several white missionaries to Africa before 1845, most of whom died within the first year or two, thus giving Africa the nickname of "White Man's Graveyard." Actually, it was the white women who most quickly succumbed to the graveyards. The FMB concluded that American blacks, though growing up in this country, might have retained enough natural immunities to make them adjust better to Africa. In 1846 the board appointed John Day, who had been in Africa for years under the Northern board. In 1849 the FMB reported thirteen missionaries at work in Liberia, all of them American blacks. In 1856 Northern Baptists transferred their work in Liberia to the Southern board.

A mission in Central Africa was opened in 1849 with the appointment of Thomas Jefferson Bowen, who made his way to Abeokuta, in the Yoruba

---

94. For a most perceptive discussion of Miss Moon's life and impact, not always favorable, see also Irwin T. Hyatt, Jr., *Our Ordered Lives Confess*, Part II deals with Lottie Moon.

95. *Proceedings*, SBC, 1846, p. 24.

country of what was then called Nigeria. Within the next few years several missionary couples joined the Yoruba mission, but within months most of them either died or returned broken in health. In 1856 Mr. and Mrs. Bowen returned to the States. In 1859 Bowen established a mission in Brazil among Yoruba slaves, from which he sought to launch out to a larger mission to Brazil. This effort proved a failure, and not until 1881 did Southern Baptists launch a successful mission to Brazil.

The Civil War disrupted SBC missions to Africa, and in the late 1860s Nigeria had its own civil war. Most of the Baptist missionaries moved from Abeokuta to Lagos. A new beginning was made in 1875 with the arrival of William J. David and W. W. Colley. Sensing that conditions favored a renewal of the Yoruba work, David closed the Liberian Mission and reopened strong centers at Abeokuta and Ogbomosho. Resigning from the FMB in 1879, Colley returned to the States and led black Baptists to form their own national organization in 1880. As first secretary of the new board, Colley led a group of missionaries back to Liberia, which became a major mission station for National Baptists.

The death of his wife and infant daughter, the first baby born to white missionaries in Africa, sent W. J. David home in discouragement. However, he returned in 1885 with the new Mrs. David, plus materials for a beautiful church building at Lagos, where a talented African convert, Moses Stone, served as pastor. A disagreement with David in 1888 caused Stone to withdraw from the church, taking most of the members with him. Though painful at the time, this schism probably accelerated the development of indigenous Baptist work. Health conditions, the slave trade, and tribal wars seriously curtailed Baptist work in Africa. By 1899 the Africa mission reported 6 missionaries, 6 churches, with 341 members and 211 pupils enrolled in Sunday Schools. There were 2 ordained African preachers and 4 day schools with 140 pupils.[96]

Italy. As early as 1850 the SBC considered opening missions in Europe, but funds disallowed it. However, in 1870 the board voted that "while we attach great importance to China, India, and Africa, we believe that Italy, Spain, Germany, Mexico and Ireland are not less inviting."[97] William N. Cote was appointed to Italy that same year.

Cote, who was probably the first Protestant missionary in Rome, established a Baptist church there in 1871 with 18 members. For the first few years, Baptists met in rented quarters, until their own building was completed in 1878. By 1872 the board reported 271 members in several Baptist churches in Rome and other Italian cities. However, the work did not prosper. A scandal split the church in Rome, leading to Cote's recall by the FMB, though no moral blame attached to him. Baptist work in Italy

96. *Annual,* SBC, 1899, Appendix A, p. 1xix.
97. Cauthen, p. 188.

achieved more stability, however, with the appointment of George Boardman Taylor in 1873. The son of J. B. Taylor, secretary of the FMB, the younger Taylor served in Italy for thirty-four years, until his death in 1907. He brought personal maturity and wisdom to the Italian work, strengthening the churches and establishing a theological training school in Rome. He helped extend a Baptist witness to other cities, including Florence, Milan, Venice, Bari, and Naples. By the turn of the century, the Italian mission reported 624 members gathered into 24 churches, with 72 baptisms in 1899-1900.[98]

Mexico. As early as 1846, the FMB named Mexico as a promising mission field and acknowledged that, by its geographical location, that land had special claims upon Southern Baptists. Expecting that Mexico "is sooner or later to be redeemed" and that pure Christianity would one day resound through the "halls of the Montezumas," the SBC acknowledged that as of 1846 the only thing it could do for Mexico was pray. The SBC opened work in Mexico in 1880, but Baptists had been there earlier. John Hickey from Ireland formed the First Baptist Church of Monterrey in 1864, apparently the first evangelical church in Mexico. Two brothers from England, Thomas and John Westrup, became Baptists from the ministry of Hickey. John O. Westrup, who had earlier worked under the Northern HMS, accepted appointment under the Southern board in 1880, baptizing converts and strengthening churches in the state of Coahuila. However, within weeks of his appointment he was killed. Because of the proximity, Baptists in Texas monitored the Mexico work and sent William D. Powell to investigate Westrup's death. Just before his untimely death, Westrup had reported a total of thirteen Baptist churches in Mexico. Powell read the last entry in Westrup's diary: "Four baptisms today. Go back and teach them next week." This note, plus evidence of churches needing guidance and new converts yet untaught, gripped Powell's mind, resulting in his taking Westrup's place in Mexico.[99]

At first the Mexican work flourished, with strong churches and schools in Saltillo, Torreon, Chihuahua, and elsewhere. However, serious disruptions in the 1890s, involving disagreements among the missionaries, almost destroyed the work. Several missionaries left the field; but, even so, by 1900 Mexico reported 1,232 members in 32 churches, with 175 baptisms that year.[100]

Brazil. The vast land of Brazil had long appealed to Baptists; the old Triennial Convention had often discussed but never entered that field. As noted earlier, T. J. Bowen attempted to open Southern Baptist work there in 1859 but his effort was soon abandoned. A strange set of circumstances

98. *Annual,* SBC, 1900, unnumbered statistical page, opposite Appendix B.
99. Cauthen, p. 272; *Annual,* SBC, 1881, p. 39.
100. *Annual,* SBC, 1900, unnumbered statistical page, opposite Appendix B.

led Southern Baptists to reopen mission work in Brazil in 1881. After the Civil War, a group of exiled Southerners established a colony in Sao Paulo, where a group of Baptists formed a church in 1871. An ex-Confederate general, A. T. Hawthorne, another exile, was converted on a trip back to the States. He urged the SBC to send missionaries to Brazil. The board appointed William B. and Anne Luther Bagby during Christmas week of 1880, thus beginning the incredible saga of the "Bagbys of Brazil." Anne served sixty-one years, until her death during Christmas week of 1942, the longest tenure of any SBC missionary. Of the five surviving Bagby children, all became missionaries.[101]

The Bagby's were soon joined by Zachary C. and Kate Taylor. These two couples enjoyed unusual success in their missionary efforts. They opened work in the city of Bahia and formed a church in 1882, the first Baptist church in Brazil made up of Brazilians. One of the early converts in that church, John Baptist, became a pastor and evangelist. Bagby formed a church in Rio de Janeiro in 1884 with only four members, but it grew rapidly. Bagby and Taylor followed the policy of starting work in the larger cities, training Brazilian pastors as quickly as possible, and turning the work over to national leaders. Rio became the Baptist center for South Brazil, while work in the North centered in Salvador (and later Recife).

Other missionaries were appointed to Brazil, including Solomon L. Ginsburg and Erik A. Nelson who ranged farther afield and formed the first Baptist church in the Amazon Valley in 1897. The fascinating account of Ginsburg's missionary travels and experiences, under title of *A Wandering Jew in Brazil,* was widely read in the States and further kindled Southern Baptist interest in Brazil. Brazilian churches grew rapidly, doubling in membership approximately every decade and becoming before the turn of the century Southern Baptists' most responsive mission field. The 1900 report showed 1,922 members in 27 churches, with 431 baptisms that year. The work of 18 missionaries was augmented by 19 Brazilian preachers, of whom 7 were ordained.[102]

Japan. In 1854 the Japanese government, influenced by Commodore Perry, opened a narrow door to the West. In 1859 Japan opened five major port cities to American residents. Southern Baptists took that as a divine call and appointed four missionaries to Japan in 1860. John Roher and his wife, Sarah, sailed in August, along with another Southern Baptist couple appointed to China, but the ship was lost at sea. Mr. and Mrs. J. L. Johnson, also appointed to Japan, were expected to sail with the Rohers, but illness caused them to miss the ship. The board also appointed Crawford H. Toy

101. For the story of this the remarkable Bagby family, see Helen Bagby Harrison, *The Bagbys of Brazil* (Crawford, Texas: Crawford Christian Press, n.d.).

102. *Annual,* SBC, 1900, unnumbered statistical page, opposite Appendix B.

to Japan in 1860, but Toy's departure was delayed, possibly due to shortage of funds in Richmond. Toy never made it to Japan.

Matthew T. Yates of China saw the strategic importance of Japan and during the 1880s urged the SBC to enter that field. In 1888 the death of Yates called new attention to his appeal, and the FMB noted that Japan was "a most valuable strategic territory for the capture of the boundless regions beyond." The board reported, "The Committee especially recommend to the Convention the establishment of a mission in the long-neglected but progressive empire of Japan."[103] It appointed Mr. and Mrs. J. W. McCollum and Mr. and Mrs. John A. Brunson, who arrived in Yokohama in 1889 and continued to Kobe for a year of language study. The Brunsons resigned after two years but by the turn of the century others had arrived, making a total of eight missionaries, with six Japanese preachers. The seventy-five Japanese converts were scattered over a number of preaching stations, but only two organized churches, at Osaka (formed in 1891) and Fukuoka (formed in 1900). The Japanese Mission was formally organized at Fukuoka in February 1900.

From this brief survey, it is clear that Southern Baptists took foreign missions seriously. By 1900 they reported 6,537 members in 113 churches in six nations, with a total of 94 foreign missionaries.[104] They had been served by 3 outstanding corresponding secretaries, James Barnett Taylor (1846-1871), Henry Allen Tupper (1872-1893), and Robert Josiah Willingham (1893-1913).

Problems plagued the work both at home and abroad. At home apathy, lack of information, doctrinal controversy, and antimission opposition hindered. Further setbacks came with the Civil War and its aftermath. During the war Southern Baptists, because of the Union blockade, had difficulty conveying funds to their overseas personnel. Northern Baptists assisted by sending some Southern funds to SBC missionaries. On the field, a number of missionaries secured secular employment, while others were assisted by the English Baptist society. In other daring ventures, the FMB sometimes invested in long-staple cotton, committing it to shippers who would attempt to slip through the Union blockade. Those who succeeded could sell it for three times their investment, for the English textile mills were hungry for Southern cotton. The money could then be transmitted from England to the various fields.

Perhaps the worst problems, however, came after the war. During the war the problem was how to send money; after the war there was no money to send. The work suffered severely, curtailing what could be done on existing fields and limiting the opening of new fields. However, by the

103. *Annual,* SBC, 1888, p. 22.
104. *Annual,* SBC, 1900, unnumbered statistical page, opposite Appendix B.

1880s, a measure of recovery marked the South and the mission work fared better.

Additional problems cropped up on the fields, chief being missionary health. The roster of SBC missionaries before 1900 reads like a giant obituary. Africa was not the only graveyard; deaths by disease, accident, and martyrdom marked the various missions. Other problems included personality conflicts, doctrinal differences (as with T. P. Crawford in China), scandal (as in Italy in the 1870s), hostile governments, building restrictions, and disagreements about the payment of native assistants. Despite these problems, later events would confirm that at the turn of the century, Southern Baptist foreign mission work was poised for a great leap forward.

Home Mission Board (HMB)

At its initial meeting in 1845, the SBC also formed a Board of Domestic Missions, to be located in Marion, Alabama. Over the years, the board's name varied, according to the work assigned to it. In 1874 the board took its present name, Home Mission Board. The board remained in Marion until 1882, when it was moved to Atlanta, its present site. The Marion location seemed favorable; it placed one board in the Western part of SBC territory, while the other remained in the East. Marion was a strong Baptist center, with two Baptist colleges, and provided a gateway to the Mississippi Valley. The board remained there for thirty-seven years, much of that time housed in a basement room of the Siloam Baptist Church. Later the economic devastation of Alabama in the Civil War, and the image of failure at Marion, made a new location necessary if the board were to survive.

The Southern field. The Home Mission Board faced a challenging field of labor, including fourteen states with a population then of about eight million. "To supply this vast multitude," the board said, "we have, connected with our denomination about 2,000 preachers, including the superannuated, and those of feeble and broken constitutions."[105] The majority of Baptist pastors then were bivocational, leaving relatively few who gave their full time to ministry. From the first the board felt the challenge of the Mississippi Valley and the expanding states of the Southwest, especially Texas. The spiritual needs of this area were overwhelming. Travelers encountered families who had never owned a Bible and persons who had never attended a church or heard a gospel sermon. One home missionary reported that in "districts which I visited, Baptist ministers are few, preaching seldom, churches cold and inactive, . . . In traveling a distance of seventy-five miles, I met with but one Baptist, a lady, and she was not living in connection with any church."[106]

As in the foreign work, home missionaries on the field could choose to

105. *Proceedings*, SBC, 1846, p. 34.
106. Ibid., pp. 34-35.

remain with the Northern society or come under the new HMB. Some switched, including James Huckins and William M. Tryon in Texas and Isaac T. Hinton in New Orleans. A few later switched back to the Northern agencies, including M. T. Sumner who had served from 1862-1875 as secretary of the HMB.

Problems facing the HMB. Early in its life, the HMB faced problems that nearly caused its collapse. Its first annual report included a sentence that, while grammatically incomplete, expressed the attitude of many Southern Baptists: "Some confidently affirming that its first regular meeting would number its days, and furnish materials for its entire history."[107] Throughout the nineteenth century and into the twentieth, the Home Mission Board had to struggle not only for funds to pursue its ministries but also to maintain its place in the life and work of Southern Baptists.

From the first, the board faced a crisis of leadership. Its first president, Basil Manly, Sr., and its first secretary, J. L. Reynolds, both resigned shortly after the 1845 meeting. Of course, this stymied the board; its first report noted, "These changes in the acting officers of the Board, almost paralyzed its efforts, and at one time threatened its overthrow." At length Daniel P. Bester was persuaded to become corresponding secretary, but he resigned after only five months. He said:

> I have learned by visiting many, and by an extensive correspondence, that our brethren prefer carrying on their domestic missionary operations, through their Associations and State Conventions. They approve, invariably, of our Southern organization; but I cannot persuade them to act efficiently in its support. Some one should be employed who can be more successful than I have been; who can induce the churches and Associations to unite with the Board, and to pour their funds into a common treasury.[108]

Bester's remarks spotlight a basic organizational problem facing early Southern Baptists. They had not yet worked out the relationship of local church, association, state convention, and Southern Baptist Convention. Many identified home mission work as the task of associations and state conventions. To them the Home Mission Board seemed at best unnecessary duplication and at worst a rival to local work.

In addition to several who declined the office, eight men served as corresponding secretary of the HMB up to 1900: Daniel Perrin Bester, 1845; Russell Holman, 1845-1851, 1857-1862; Thomas F. Curtis, 1851-1853; Joseph Walker, 1853-1856; Martin T. Sumner, 1862-1875; William H. McIntosh, 1875-1882; Isaac T. Tichenor, 1882-1899; and Franklin H. Kerfoot, 1899-1901. Of these, several resigned in discouragement, one returned to Northern Baptist work, one was said to have "lapsed from the Baptist

---

107. *Proceedings,* SBC, 1846, p. 29.
108. Ibid., pp. 29-30.

faith," and one remained in office almost two years though too sick to work. Not until Baptists enlisted aggressive leaders who remained at the post for several years did the HMB gain stability.

In addition to leadership and localism, a third problem facing the infant HMB was an empty treasury. The churches were slow to forward money, and the leaders took the cautious approach of avoiding debt. This meant that at first they did nothing, which fixed upon the HMB an image, not altogether deserved, of not being aggressive or effective. A fourth problem was the antimissionism which, dividing churches and associations, blanketed much of the South in spiritual anemia and noneffort theology. While some debated *how* to do missions, all too many opposed missionary work however it might be done.

Despite these problems, at the end of its first year, the HMB reported a cash income of $1,824, with six missionaries at work, including two in Texas, and one each in Virginia, Florida, Alabama, and Louisiana. Of these receipts, the board spent $1,284. The extent of localism can be seen in the fact that during the same time "Auxiliary relations [local and state work], so near as ascertained, have expended in their own bounds $8,460."[109]

In 1855 the convention made the domestic board responsible for "the conduct and management of all matters appertaining to Indian missions." That work had previously been conducted by the American Indian Mission Association. With this transfer, the Home Mission Board inherited not only a major task but also about twenty-five missionaries and a debt of over $6,000. The Civil War disrupted most of this work; but after the war, Henry F. Buckner and Joseph Samuel Murrow made outstanding contributions in mission work in Indian Territory, now the state of Oklahoma. Some of the Indian work was jointly sponsored by Northern and Southern Baptists.

Disruption of a war. The work of the HMB suffered great disruption during the Civil War. In both domestic and Indian departments, the board retained only thirty-two missionaries.[110] The promising work in California had to be dropped, and for a time the HMB ceased its Indian missions. The states across the Mississippi were largely cut off from the Marion board, and missionaries had to seek other employment when the board could no longer provide their meager salaries. At one time, the home mission force, except for those preaching in the Confederate armies, dropped to a total of six.[111]

At the outbreak of the war, the SBC, like most of the state conventions, passed a resolution of support for the Confederate cause. Though lightly attended, the convention met in 1863 in Augusta. The messengers heard

109. Ibid., pp. 33, 36.
110. See statistical tables in Arthur B. Rutledge, *Mission to America: A Century and a Quarter of Southern Baptist Home Missions,* p. 245.
111. See J. B. Lawrence, *History of the Home Mission Board,* p. 46.

dismal reports of SBC work, but of course the worst was yet to come. One report said:

> Colleges have suspended, some of them indefinitely. . . . the students of most of our colleges have enlisted in the Confederate army. . . . Our female schools, in several localities, show signs of distress. Some six or seven Baptist papers have gone down in the past six months, . . . our Foreign Missions are paralyzed, our Home Missions almost suspended, and our state organizations unable to carry on their work. Ministers have been forced through stern necessity to leave their fields of usefulness in order to provide bread for their families.[112]

Most of the ministry conducted by the home board during the war years was directed toward the Confederate armies, which included many Baptists. Several outstanding revivals broke out among the troops, with hundreds of baptisms. W. W. Barnes said, "Perhaps there was never an army in which a greater religious work was done than in the Army of Northern Virginia," an anomaly for an army dedicated to the perpetuation of human slavery.[113] The soldiers also had an immense hunger for Bibles, Testaments, and gospel tracts. One missionary reported, "There is a great thirst for reading among the soldiers . . . they will read—read anything." In 1865 the board spent almost $1,700 for Bibles and Testaments, but could not keep up with the need. One account says "not less than 5,000,000 pages of tracts" were distributed among the Confederate troops.[114]

After the war, the South was left with worthless currency, a flattened economy, insufficient labor to produce crops, and extremely low prices for crops that were produced. The home board found itself not only unable to respond to the needs of its field but also facing head-on competition from a strong Northern Baptist agency. As noted earlier, after the war the Home Mission Society of New York assigned about one-third of its total mission force to the South and opened aggressive evangelistic, educational, and church edifice work among both white and black populations of the South. The HMB offered verbal resistance because they could offer no other. The Northern society gradually won the allegiance of Southern churches, associations, and state conventions.

Reorganization of HMB. What to do with the Home Mission Board remained a controversial question throughout the 1870s. Three options emerged. First, they could simply abolish the board and allow the work to be conducted by associations, state conventions, and the Northern society. Those who favored the reunion of Baptists felt attracted to that solution. Second, some suggested the two SBC mission boards be merged, with home

---

112. *Annual,* SBC, 1863, pp. 34-35, as cited in Robert A. Baker, *The Southern Baptist Convention and Its People 1607-1972,* p. 227.

113. William Wright Barnes, *The Southern Baptist Convention: 1845-1953,* pp. 48-49.

114. Ibid., p. 49.

missions becoming simply one department of the foreign board. In 1880 the convention appointed a committee "to inquire into, and report upon, the expediency of consolidating the work of the Home and Foreign Boards, and of appointing but one Board upon Missionary work, which shall be known as the 'Missionary Board of the Southern Baptist Convention.' "[115] That merger was not implemented, although the suggestion was renewed from other motives around the turn of the century.

The third option, and the one adopted, was to seek to revitalize the home board. That seemed possible, for one unexpected side effect of the war was to draw the associations into closer cooperation with the HMB. In a report given in 1867, the Home Mission Board noted that among the associations, "Hitherto many of them have deemed it advisable to act independently of any connection with this Board," but in light of "the present scarcity of money, [they] have therefore thought it best, and indeed necessary, to obtain the assistance of the Domestic Board."[116] Experience showed that cooperation need not threaten but indeed could augment local efforts.

The convention took radical action in 1882. Messengers voted to dismiss not only the secretary of the HMB but the entire elected board of trustees and move the headquarters to Atlanta immediately. The convention felt its home mission work could never succeed at the Marion location. The Committee on the Condition of the Home Mission Board, said:

> Your Committee . . . beg leave to report that we find a want of enthusiasm on the part of the denomination in the work of this Board, and since from the experience of a series of years, it seems impossible to arouse this enthusiasm without making material changes, your Committee . . . recommend the following resolutions, viz;
>
> 1st. That the Home Mission Board be removed . . . to Atlanta, Georgia, as soon after the adjournment of this Convention as such transfer can be made.[117]

The work of I. T. Tichenor. The new board elected Isaac Taylor Tichenor (1825-1902) as its secretary. Perhaps no better choice could have been made; Tichenor brought to the work a new energy, vision, creativity, and above all a consuming commitment to the Southern Baptist Convention. He served until 1899, thus giving him enough years not only to devise an effective program but also to put it into effect. Of course he also benefited from the improving Southern economy after the end of Reconstruction. He had served as paster of the First Baptist churches of Montgomery, Alabama, and Memphis, Tennessee, and came to the HMB from the presidency of what is now Auburn University. He joined the movement to establish Southern Baptists' first theological seminary at Greenville, South Carolina,

115. *Annual,* SBC, 1880, p. 15.
116. *Annual,* SBC, 1867, p. 36.
117. *Annual,* SBC, 1882, p. 29.

in 1859 and preached its first commencement sermon. He served as a chaplain to the Seventeenth Alabama Regiment during the Civil War, earning a reputation as a sharpshooter during the Battle of Shiloh. Tichenor had a highly developed sense of denominational unity. He was among those who helped form the first Board of Sunday Schools in 1863 and must be ranked along with J. M. Frost as one of the primary founders of the present Sunday School Board in 1891.

Under Tichenor, the home mission work expanded in several directions. Sensing the need for more Sunday School materials suited for Southern Baptists, Tichenor expanded the publication work to include lesson materials for various age groups. He thus showed the need for such material and, in time, urged the convention to establish a separate Sunday School agency to pursue this work. He also opened mission work in new fields, including Cuba. In 1884 Tichenor led the HMB to launch a church building fund, which later became a major ministry of the home board.

In the 1880s two Baptist giants collided: Henry L. Morehouse, head of the Home Mission Society in New York, and Isaac T. Tichenor, head of the Home Mission Board in Atlanta. Both were dynamic, creative men of vision; clearly each was among his denomination's most outstanding leaders of that generation. Morehouse cherished the national scope his agency had charted from its beginning, and he had no intention of withdrawing from the South. Perhaps he also hoped that the two groups might eventually reunite. Tichenor, on the other hand, held and communicated to others an intense loyalty to the SBC and its work. In 1882 E. T. Winkler, new president of the HMB, published an article bluntly challenging the right of the Northern society to work in the South. He chided Southern states and associations for their continuing affiliation with Northern Baptist work and pointed out that this would eventually undermine the SBC. This led to an extensive controversy in the Baptist papers of both regions and probably did more than any other one thing to alert Baptists in the South to the long-range implications of what Winkler called Northern Baptist "intrusion" in the South.

Morehouse was not slow to respond; he reaffirmed that the HMS was not just Northern but national and that they had both constitutional right and historic precedents for working throughout the country. Noting that it had missionaries in forty-five states and territories, continued to enlist contributors and life members in the South, and planned to hold some of its future meetings in the South, Morehouse reaffirmed that the society was in the South to stay. This defense, plus the suggestion the HMB was no longer needed and ought to be disbanded, led to an intense backlash in the South.

One of Tichenor's first tasks in 1882 was to survey the field, a task which yielded discouraging results. He found most of the Baptist state conventions in the South in some degree of affiliation with Northern Baptist work. His report concluded, "The entire territory west of the Mississippi River had passed out of the hands of the Board. . . . A survey of the field indicated a great defeat and a lost cause."[118] Baptist work in Texas was typical of the times: Texas was then divided into five overlapping state conventions, four receiving aid from the Home Mission Society and the fifth paralyzed by its own dissensions. However, the aggressive work of the home board bore fruit. Tichenor reported that

> such were the earnestness of its efforts and the happy results of its policy, that in five years there was not a missionary to the white people of the South who did not bear a commission from either the Home Mission Board of the Southern Baptist Convention, or one of our State Boards in alliance with it. Its territory had been reclaimed. . . . The Board had demonstrated its right to live and had won the confidence of the denomination.[119]

The Fortress Monroe Conference. Toward the end of the century, the Northern society found its resources taxed to meet the growing demands for ministry in the West and among European immigrants. Those factors, plus the growing ability of the SBC to address needs in the South, brought a new era in which cooperation replaced confrontation. This led to a joint conference in 1894 at Fortress Monroe, Virginia, which marks a significant milestone in the relations of Northern and Southern Baptists.

The Fortress Monroe conference grew out of Southern Baptist desire to be more involved in ministry to blacks, especially in education, along with Northern Baptist willingness to share the load of that work which they had carried virtually alone for thirty years. Noting that "the time has come when it should enlarge its work among the colored people of the South," the Home Mission Board sought a conference with the Northern brethren to discuss ways of cooperation. The joint conference of HMS and HMB leaders that met September 12-13, 1894, included Henry L. Morehouse and Isaac T. Tichenor. At the meeting cordiality prevailed, as it had not for a generation in Baptists' North-South relations. Every vote was unanimous but one: Northern brethren insisted a Southern brother preside, while Southerners deferred to a Northerner, J. L. Howard, who was elected chairman.

The joint committee determined "to avoid discussion of past issues" and confine themselves "to the task of securing for *the future* such cooperation as may be found practicable."[120] After full discussion, the committee agreed on three items. First, on schools for blacks, the members agreed that basic control would remain with the HMS, but Southern Baptists would cooperate by helping raise funds, appointing local committees to advise on

118. *Annual,* SBC, 1892, Appendix A, p. xi.
119. Ibid.
120. *Annual,* SBC, 1895, p. 15, emphasis theirs.

administration and faculty additions, and recruiting students. Second, the HMS and HMB agreed to cooperate in mission work among blacks.

Third, as to territorial limits, the committee heard reports that "it is inexpedient for two different organizations of Baptists to solicit contributions or to establish missions in the same locality." Members agreed that "in the prosecution of their work already begun on contiguous fields or on the same field, all antagonisms be avoided," but that "in opening new work, to direct their efforts to localities not already occupied by the other."[121] When ratified this represented a significant milestone, for it recognized the territorial integrity for which the SBC had been pushing since the 1840s. In effect, the Northern society agreed to work in the North while the SBC would work in the South. This introduced a new era of comity agreements; several similar comity conferences were held early in the twentieth century.

Several factors help explain Northern concessions at Fortress Monroe. For years the HMS had desired more Southern help in its freedmen ministries; that was its main victory at Fortress Monroe. The increase in home mission needs in the West and among European immigrants placed heavy demands upon HMS resources, and at Fortress Monroe, according to Torbet, the HMS recognized the danger of overextension unless it reduced its earlier level of work in the South.[122] Perhaps there was also some hope that the agreement might mark a first step on the road to eventual reunification of the two branches of the Baptist body.

One must not assume that Fortress Monroe marks the beginning of Southern Baptist ministries among black people. In fact, Baptist efforts to evangelize the black population antedate the SBC. At its formation in 1845, the convention voted, "*Resolved,* That the Domestic Mission Board be instructed to take all prudent measures for the religious instruction of our colored population." At its first meeting after the end of slavery, the convention voted, "*Resolved,* That in our changed relations to the colored people, we recognize as heretofore our solemn obligation to give religious instruction to them by all those means which God has ordained for the salvation of men." The 1894 convention reported that not a year had passed since 1845 in which "the religious needs of these people did not claim a share of the thought and interest" of the SBC.[123]

However, the records show less actual ministry than the reports might suggest. Several reports urged the *oral* instruction of blacks in Sunday Schools, a tacit recognition that because of restrictive laws many of them could not read the lesson materials. The HMB also spent much time explaining why so little had been done. The reports also show the paternalism

121. Ibid., pp. 14-16.
122. Torbet, *A History,* p. 374.
123. All cited from *Annual,* SBC, 1894, Appendix B, p. lvii.

and racial prejudice that marked the era; perhaps the worst example of white paternalism was the report for 1891, in which the HMB said:

> Our work among the COLORED PEOPLE has by no means reached the proportions its importance demands. . . . The race problem, as it is called, has been deemed by statesmen the most perplexing of all questions affecting our society. . . . We venture the assertion that it can and will be found of easy solution.
>
> Nothing is plainer to any one who knows this race than its perfect willingness to accept a subordinate place. . . . Whenever it shall understandingly and cheerfully accept this condition, the race problem is settled forever.
>
> ....
>
> We do not hesitate to affirm our confident belief that an expenditure under the best conditions by our Home Mission and State Boards of fifty thousand dollars a year for the next ten years will settle this race question forever.[124]

However, despite the problems of war, economic depressions, and what now appear as serious misunderstandings, the achievements of the Home Mission Board by the turn of the century were substantial. Its report for 1900 shows 671 missionaries under appointment, with 5,696 baptisms that year, 195 new church buildings erected and 63 others improved, and 639 new Sunday Schools organized.[125]

Sunday School Board

Not until 1891 did the SBC form its present Sunday School Board, thus in effect completing the schism of 1845. Many churches in the South had continued to buy Sunday School materials from the American Baptist Publication Society in Philadelphia. Not all Southern Baptists wanted it that way. A group whom Baker called "Southern denominationalists"[126] argued strongly for a complete break in 1845, with the new convention setting up its own theological seminary and publication work, as well as the two mission boards, but that group was voted down. However, many assumed the denominationalists would eventually prevail. When John Mason Peck of the ABPS inquired about sending an agent to Georgia in the summer of 1845, he was informed that Southern Baptists would likely soon form their own publication ministry.

A slow start. Several factors help explain Southern Baptists' reluctance to launch a printing program in their early history. First, many saw no need to separate from the ABPS. That society had originated in the South, had its early leaders and primary support before 1845 from the South, and "admidst the ravings of Abolition phrenzy [sic]," as a South Carolina group

---

124. *Annual,* SBC, 1891, Appendix B, p. xxxvi.
125. *Annual,* SBC, 1900, Appendix B, pp. cxxii-cxxiii.
126. Robert A. Baker, *The Story of the Sunday School Board,* p. 11.

expressed it, the society had carefully avoided taking sides.[127] No doubt J. L. Waller, editor of *The Western Baptist Review* of Kentucky, expressed the views of many when he wrote in 1845, "We are opposed to any more divisions. We wish to see no further alienation of feeling between the North and the South. Discord has already done enough."[128]

Second, probably fewer than 500 Baptist churches in the South had Sunday Schools in 1845, and thus the majority felt little interest in a Southern publication board. As late as 1892, J. M. Frost reported that barely half of Southern Baptist churches had Sunday Schools.[129] Third, the lingering impact of the depression of 1837 made Southern Baptists wary of overexpansion. Everyone knew that publications could be costly, and economic prudence prevailed. A fourth reason the SBC delayed its entrance into publication work was that a number of private companies already supplied the market.

Despite the setback in 1845, Southern Baptist denominationalists persisted. At its first session in 1846 the SBC was asked again to consider "the expediency of organizing Boards of Managers, for Bible and Publication operations." It refused. The committee to study the proposal reported, "As the Convention has no connection with any Publication Society, your committee submits the following resolution: *Resolved,* That this Convention does not deem it advisable to embarrass itself with any enterprise for the publication and sale of books." However, they added, "This Convention regards with approbation Southern enterprises for the publication and diffusion of a religious literature," a reference perhaps to the private enterprises.[130] These mixed signals reflect the confused situation of the time.

Four broken threads. In reporting to the SBC in 1892, J. M. Frost, head of the Sunday School Board, said, "We take up a broken thread in the history of the Southern Baptist Convention, reviving a work begun and fostered more than twenty-five years ago. . . . we stand, brethren, in a royal line."[131] The "broken thread" to which Frost referred was the first Board of Sunday Schools of 1863, but there were other threads in Southern Baptists' ongoing efforts to create their own publication ministry. In the first quarter century of the SBC, Southern Baptists tried four times to establish a printing program and four times failed. These included (1) the Southern Baptist Publication Society, Charleston, 1847-1863; (2) the Bible Board of the SBC, Nashville, 1851-1863; (3) the Southern Baptist Sunday School Union, Nashville, founded 1857, lapsed sometime after the war; and (4) the

127. *First Annual Report,* Southern Baptist Publication Society, Charleston, 1848, p. 8, in ABHS.

128. Cited by Baker, *Sunday School Board,* p. 7.

129. *Annual,* SBC, 1892, Appendix C, p. lix.

130. *Proceedings,* SBC, 1846, pp. 14, 20.

131. *Annual,* SBC, 1892, Appendix C, p. lvi.

Board of Sunday Schools, 1863-1873. Two of these were officially sponsored by the SBC (the two boards), and two were independent societies which grew up alongside the convention. The failure of these efforts fostered a defeatist attitude among many Southern Baptists on the subject of publications. Each of these four efforts requires a brief word here.

When the SBC in consecutive sessions refused to enter the publication field, a group of interested individuals formed the Southern Baptist Publication Society (SBPS) in 1847 and located its operations in Charleston, South Carolina. Noting that many Southern Baptists were saying, "Give us a Southern Society, or we will patronize none," the SBPS organizers announced that the object of the new body "shall be to publish and distribute such books as are needed by the Baptist Denomination in the South."[132] This revealed two things: how deeply some felt the need for an indigenous Southern literature and how much of the society mind-set survived in the South. Under the leadership of Richard Furman, Jr., general secretary, the SBPS encouraged the formation of new Sunday Schools and supplied tracts and lesson materials. During its first year, it published 2,000 copies of "The Advantages of Sabbath School Instruction" by C. D. Mallary, along with a "A Defense of Strict Communion" by J. B. Taylor, and 1,500 packets of "S.S. Bible Cards" for small children. Noting that "Sabbath Schools are constantly rising at new points," the SBPS stepped up its publications in 1851. It published a catechism by John A. Broadus and several books on doctrinal issues.[133]

At its 1857 meeting, the SBPS noted, "This Society has a special vocation assigned to it, in preparing works suited to the wants of the Sunday Schools in the South, and also for preparing such works as are adapted to the oral instruction of our colored population." Perhaps that was an effort to stake out its field against a new competitor, the Southern Baptist Sunday School Union, formed that same year in Nashville. The Charleston society came under heavy criticism from J. R. Graves of Nashville for its doctrinal views. The SBPS folded in 1863, a victim of diminishing support and war devastation. The first thread was broken.

A second effort was made when the SBC formed a Bible Board in 1851. Its original task was to print and distribute Bibles, but in 1856 the convention broadened its assignment to include publication of Sunday School materials. This board, located in Nashville, had as its first secretary William C. Buck, who served until 1854. Buck was succeeded by Amos C. Dayton, who served 1854-1858. Dayton came under the influence of J. R. Graves, and the board opened the way for Landmark views to be circulated over the SBC. Thus by the 1850s Southern Baptists had two competing publication efforts: the SBPS in Charleston, representing more mainline Southern

132. *First Annual Report,* SBPS, Charleston, 1848, pp. 8, 10.
133. *Second Annual Report,* SBPS, Athens, Ga., 1849, p. 11.

Baptist viewpoints, and the Bible Board in Nashville, representing ultraconservative views. This conflict, plus shortage of funds, undercut the Bible Board. Dayton was asked to resign in 1858, and at the convention of 1859, W. C. Buck moved, "That the Bible Board be abolished." Failing that, he moved, "That the nominating committee be instructed to nominate a Bible Board at Macon, Ga.," an effort to take the board out of the hands of the Landmark faction. That motion also failed.[134]

However, the Bible Board never regained the confidence of the denomination. In 1861 the SBC attempted to merge the Bible Board with the Publication Society, but their diverse views made that unfeasible. The Bible Board ceased operations when the Union Army took Nashville in 1862, and the next year the SBC officially abolished it. The second thread was broken.

In 1857 a group of Nashville Landmarkers, led by J. R. Graves and A. C. Dayton, formed the Southern Baptist Sunday School Union. This body originated out of a called Sunday School Convention in Nashville attended by delegates from several states, many of whom had no idea that a new organization was intended. Most of the delegates were ardent supporters of Graves and the opposition, led by R. B. C. Howell, was outvoted by a large majority.

All the Baptist papers in the South opposed the Sunday School Union, except the *Tennessee Baptist*, edited by Graves. Final formation was scheduled for 1858 in Americus, Georgia, but the controversy became so bitter that the Americus church declined to host the meeting. The group was therefore diverted to Memphis, where organization was completed; operations began in Nashville in 1859. The SBSSU helped polarize Southern Baptists, fanning a major theological controversy. This union, plus Graves and his paper, helped spread Landmarkism throughout the West and Southwest, laying the groundwork for internal tensions which afflict Southern Baptists to the present. Baptists in the older sections of the South never favored Landmarkism, and thus the controversy introduced sectional as well as doctrinal tensions into SBC life. The Sunday School Union never won widespread support. It was decimated in the Civil War and eventually ceased operations, with great financial loss to Graves and his partners.

In 1863 the SBC formed a Board of Sunday Schools, in Greenville, South Carolina. This constituted a fourth try at a Southwide publishing work. The fact that the convention authorized this move immediately after abolishing the Bible Board shows that Southern Baptists had not given up on a publication ministry but had lost confidence in the Nashville-based Bible Board. The new board was essentially an outgrowth of The Southern Baptist Theological Seminary, then located in Greenville, and represented an effort to bring Baptist publications back to the East and back to mainline SBC viewpoints. The first secretary of the new board was John A. Broadus and

---

134. *Annual*, SBC, 1859, pp. 23, 24.

its first president was Basil Manly, Jr., both professors at the seminary. Their names were later combined to form "Broadman Press," a division of the Sunday School Board to this day.

In what Walter B. Shurden calls the "Manly Manifesto," Basil Manly addressed the 1863 convention on the place and importance of Sunday Schools in the life of the denomination. "All of us have felt," he said, "that the Sunday School is the nursery of the Church, the camp of instruction for her young soldiers, the great missionary to the future."[135] It seems significant that this early effort to provide training for church members came from the seminary, dedicated to the education of ministers.

Though formed in the midst of war, the new board got off to a good start. In its early years it published the *Confederate Sunday School Hymn Book*, and a *Little Sunday School Hymn Book* for children, plus *A Brief Catechism of Bible Doctrine* by James P. Boyce, *A Sunday School Primer, Little Lessons for Little People*, and other materials for Bible study from children to adults. However, their most famous publication was *Kind Words for the Sunday School Children*, known simply as *Kind Words*. This was a little paper for small children, with pictures, Bible verses, and a brief Bible story. It achieved wide circulation, and eventually included materials for different age groups. For a time, the Woman's Missionary Union provided content for a section of *Kind Words*, thus disseminating missionary information. This little paper survived from 1866 to 1929 and provided what Baker called "the golden thread" that bound together the 1863 Board of Sunday Schools with its successor established in 1891.[136] *Kind Words* was published successively in Greenville, South Carolina; Memphis, Tennessee; Marion, Alabama; Atlanta, Georgia; and Nashville, Tennessee.

From the mid-1860s J. R. Graves had attempted to merge his languishing Sunday School Union with the Board of Sunday Schools. In 1868 the SBC voted this merger, and the board moved to Memphis in what proved to be its death knell. J. B. Jeter spoke for those who insisted the board not come under the control of Landmarkers, but the location almost guaranteed that it would. Little was done after the move to Memphis, and the future looked bleak for what one historian called "the stepchild of the Convention."[137] In 1873 the SBC reluctantly abolished its Board of Sunday Schools. Thus ended the fourth effort to provide a published ministry in the South; the fourth thread was broken. The board, like its predecessors, fell victim not only to the war but also to doctrinal controversy, sectional strife, suspicion of the seminary, and competition of private printing concerns.

---

135. *Annual*, SBC, 1863, p. 45, cited in Walter B. Shurden, *The Sunday School Board: Ninety Years of Service*, p. 13.
136. Baker, *Sunday School Board*, p. 20.
137. Ibid., p. 23.

In 1873 the SBC transferred its print ministries to the Domestic Board, giving it the cumbersome name of Domestic and Indian Mission Board and Sunday School Board (the next year the name was shortened to the Home Mission Board). Though strapped for funds, the HMB carried this extra assignment for eighteen years. Conditions forced the HMB to reduce the publication work, which allowed the American Baptist Publication Society to recapture much of the Southern market. However, under the aggressive leadership of I. T. Tichenor, the Home Mission Board in 1885 began to expand its publications. Tichenor called for Sunday School literature in "a graded series reaching from our infant classes to mature age" so that "none of our people would look either North or West for any Sabbath-school literature." At the same convention, Tichenor emphasized the importance of Southern literature for Southern churches and asked, "Should this wide field of usefulness and future influence be surrendered to others?" Meeting with positive responses, by 1886 Tichenor brought out a full line of Sunday School literature for pupils and teachers in every age group. This brought him into head-on competition with the Northern society.

The present Sunday School Board. Tichenor faced the question of whether the HMB should continue to issue literature or whether a separate publishing board should be established. He opted for the latter. One of his first converts was James Marion Frost (1848-1916), scholarly pastor in Richmond. In 1889 Frost and Tichenor discussed the issue until past midnight. As Frost later reported that conversation, "Rather he talked and I listened. I was sympathetic, but unable to follow his sweep of thought in outlining the future, showing what the Baptists of the South might accomplish, and the imperative need that a people make their own literature."[138]

A few months later Frost awakened from sleep with a sudden flash of insight, with a clear plan in mind for the new work. When morning dawned, he committed the plan to writing, later published it in the Baptist papers, and went to the convention in Fort Worth in 1890 ready to present six resolutions. The first said, "Resolved, That to the Boards already existing we add another, to be elected at this session of the Convention, and to be called the Board of Publication of the Southern Baptist Convention."[139] Opposition to this move was intense, both from the Northern society and from Southerners who had had enough of publishing ventures. The SBC appointed not a board but a Sunday School Committee with limited functions. The next year in Birmingham the question surfaced again, and a committee of one from each state grappled with the issue. That committee named a subcommittee of two, James M. Frost of Virginia, who favored the

138. Frost, p. 11.
139. *Annual,* SBC, 1890, p. 9.

board, and J. B. Gambrell, then of Mississippi, who led the opponents. After a daylong conference, the two agreed that Frost would write the report if Gambrell could add a closing paragraph. Frost agreed, providing that to Gambrell's closing paragraph he could add one closing sentence.

Frost wrote a detailed report recommending establishment of the new board. In his closing paragraph, Gambrell added:

> there are widely divergent views held among us by brethren equally earnest, consecrated, and devoted to the best interest of the Master's Kingdom. It is therefore recommended that the fullest freedom of choice be accorded to everyone as to what literature he will use or support, and that no brother be disparaged in the slightest degree on account of what he do in the exercise of his right as Christ's freeman.[140]

To that cautious paragraph Frost added one encouraging sentence: "But we would earnestly urge all brethren to give to this Board a fair consideration, and in no case to obstruct it in the great work assigned to it by this Convention." Somewhere between 1890 and 1891 the name of the proposed board had changed; it was founded not as a Publication Board but a Sunday School Board. Perhaps this made it sound less like a direct challenge to the American Baptist Publication Society.

When Frost came to give the report, the convention was so packed he had to be lifted through a window to make his way to the platform. When he had read the report, brethren lined up to argue pro and con, but the venerable John A. Broadus, who had headed the first Sunday School Board, urged them to vote without discussion. Only thirteen negative votes were cast. Broadus, one of the greatest Southern Baptists of his day, buried his head in his hands and wept. It seemed to him, and to other Southern Baptist denominationalists, that the SBC had been given yet another chance to grow a great denomination.

Nashville was chosen for the site of the new board. That city had become a major printing center, was near the center of the westward-expanding convention, and the center of the troublesome Landmark movement had shifted somewhat when J. R. Graves moved his operation to Memphis in 1867.

When Lansing Burrows turned down the post as secretary of the board, Frost reluctantly accepted it. With his own small desk, money borrowed from his wife's inheritance, and a small rent-free room, he set up operations in Nashville, describing his first Sunday there as "the loneliest day of my life." By the end of the first year, the board had developed an attractive line of Sunday School literature, had won favorable response from the churches, and, perhaps most importantly, had a few hundred dollars left over. Frost waxed eloquent in the first annual Sunday School Board report in 1892. He said:

140. Cited in Baker, *Sunday School Board,* pp. 44-45.

Coming with its first report the Sunday-school Board greets the Convention with bright face and cheerful heart. . . . We are glad to report that [our publications] are in growing demand with our people, and their circulation is steadily and rapidly increasing.[141]

Frost pointed out that the convention could make the publications "an engine of tremendous working force." In an obvious reference to the private companies, Frost emphasized that "these periodicals are the property of the Convention; they have no private interest for any one, and in fostering them the Convention fosters its own property." And best of all, Frost said, "Instead of the Board's being distractive and a stirrer-up of strife, it now promises to be a unifying element in our denominational life and enterprises."[142]

Frost was certainly correct about the unifying effect of the board. Perhaps no agency has done more to unify Southern Baptist people in heart and mind than the Sunday School Board. It originated out of a growing denominational consciousness and, in turn, has strengthened that consciousness. For years Baptists in the South were, as Shurden remarked, just that, Baptists in the South. The Sunday School Board helped turn them into Southern Baptists.

Confrontation with ABPS. For several reasons the ABPS in Philadelphia took little pleasure in the success of the Baptist Sunday School Board (BSSB) in Nashville. ABPS begrudged the loss of Southern markets for its own products, and the rising tide of Southern Baptist partisan spirit threatened to widen the gap between Northern and Southern Baptists which some had hoped to narrow. Further, those who pushed the Southern literature often did so by implying that the Northern Baptist material was doctrinally unsound.

The ABPS tried, understandably, to continue its work in the South. It placed despositories in several Southern cities, employed Southern Baptist ministers as agents, offered literature discounts which the Southern board could not match, and made annual well-publicized grants to SBC causes. In 1896 the head of the ABPS, A. J. Rowland, himself a Southerner, offered proposals for cooperation which amounted to disbanding the Sunday School Board. Frost responded with indignation, saying, "We have no thought whatever of surrendering the work entrusted to us by the Southern Baptist Convention."[143]

At the convention of 1897, a representative of the Northern society made an open attack upon the Sunday School Board. The SBC reaction was immediate and intense. Frost later observed, "I never saw so many heavy guns unlimber so quickly and get ready for action." William E. Hatcher,

141. *Annual,* SBC, 1892, Appenix C, pp. lv, lviii.
142. Ibid., p. lviii.
143. Cited in Shurden, pp. 28-29.

influential pastor in Richmond, gained the floor and after an impassioned defense of the BSSB, concluded, "I have been a life-long friend of the Publication Society, but it must not come here to interfere with our work. We have our way of doing things and woe betide the man who crosses our path."[144] Hatcher's message in effect ended the society's long ministry in the South. Intense Southern Baptist loyalty responded to what it perceived as a challenge, and even churches which had persistently used ABPS materials switched to the Southern Board. By 1910 the society had withdrawn all its branch depositories from the South. The Sunday School Board had secured its place.

Perhaps no agency has done more to foster intense *Southern* Baptist identity and loyalty than has the BSSB. Its Sunday School quarterlies shaped the biblical views of lay people, its books shaped the minds and sermons of pastors, and its hymnals brought a measure of order and uniformity to Southern Baptist worship. By the late 1890s, it had encouraged formation of the Baptist Young People's Union, the famous BYPU, and provided literature for the emerging youth movement in Baptist churches. This movement later expanded to include all ages, was renamed Baptist Training Union (BTU), and after still other name changes, remains a part of the Sunday School Board work. No Southern Baptist, from the cradle to the grave, escapes the influence of the Sunday School Board.

Baptist Colleges

Baptists in the South have been somewhat ambivalent about education. On one hand, they have produced some outstanding advocates of education, such as Richard Furman and James P. Boyce, and by 1845 had established an impressive string of academies and colleges throughout the South. The Southern Baptist Theological Seminary was formed in 1859, another evidence of Southern Baptist commitment to education. On the other hand, many opposed education, fearing the schools would sap Baptist spirituality, divert mission money, lead to a hireling ministry, and/or produce "learned dunces and third-rate preachers."[145] For the most part, the Regular Baptists along the Southern seaboard favored education, while the Separate Baptists in the back country remained more suspicious. The merger of these two groups late in the eighteenth century helps account for the ambivalence which has left Southern Baptists deeply committed to higher education, while at the same time retaining considerable suspicion of their own schools.

Early efforts. The first organized effort of Baptists in the South for education dates from 1755, when Oliver Hart led the Charleston Association to form "The Religious Society" to raise and disburse funds to assist

---

144. Frost, p. 82.
145. William Warren Sweet, *Religion in the Development of American Culture* (Gloucester, Mass.: Peter Smith, 1963), p. 170.

"pius young men" to obtain ministerial training. Hart's later successor in the Charleston pastorate was Richard Furman, known as the "apostle of education" among Baptists in the South. Furman led the association to form the General Committee in 1790 to administer its educational funds. Charleston Baptists provided scholarships for some to attend the Baptist college in Providence; others they put to study under competent pastors who led a few young ministers to "read theology" and assist in pastoral duties. Some time after 1800 John Roberts formed an academy at the High Hills of Santee church. In 1802 the Charleston Association voted to purchase "a complete library" and deposit it with Roberts on condition he would take in a few students. This early Southern Baptist book collection was later given to Furman University.

As first president of the Triennial Convention in 1814, Richard Furman sought to include Baptist education as part of the convention's work. His presidential message of 1817 advocated education. An observer said, "From a heart surcharged with concern on the subject of education, especially that of the rising ministry, he [Furman] made an address, the effect of which was powerful and instantaneous. From that day a great idea was born in the Baptist public mind."[146] William Staughton and Luther Rice shared Furman's commitment, and after 1820 they persuaded the Triennial Convention to sponsor Columbian University in Washington, D.C. Baptists in the South sent both students and funds for its support.

The environment. Several factors led to a mushrooming of colleges in America after 1800. The wars with England put a stop to the practice of sending students to English schools. The religious awakenings led to the founding of colleges, and the rise of the mission movement, home and foreign, had a hothouse effect upon the schools. Luther Rice saw Baptist colleges as an essential part of the mission movement, and the first college of the West grew out of the home mission work of John Mason Peck. Westward expansion included colleges; one man remarked, "A settler could hardly encamp on the prairies, but a college would spring up beside his wagon."[147] As part of that westward expansion, Baptists shared fully in the college movement.

Any description of the Southern educational environment must take account of the widespread antieducation bias. Prejudice against schooling surfaced quite early among Baptists. Some early Baptists boasted that they had "never rubbed their backs against college walls." Perhaps this prejudice stemmed partly from Baptist resentment at the persecuting state-church ministers, whose qualifications often seemed more academic than spiritual. Resistance to education became widespread in the South. In 1798 the

---

146. See Leon McBeth, "Southern Baptists and Higher Education," in William R. Estep, ed., *The Lord's Free People: Essays in Baptist History in Honor of Robert A. Baker,* p. 122.
147. Ibid., p. 116.

Marble Creek church in Kentucky asked "whether it is consistent with our duty to God . . . to read Books of human institution" and whether human learning might lead Baptist minds "into a disestum [disesteem] of the Bible." About the same time the Kehuckee Association voted that "education is not essential to the qualifications of a gospel minister."[148]

Many early preachers in the South prided themselves that they were "mostly educated between the handles of a plow." "Plough handle" preachers were suspicious of human learning for, they said, "There ain't no Holy Ghost in it."[149] In "Address to the Churches" in 1822, W. B. Johnson of South Carolina defended education, refuting several grounds of opposition. Among these were a fear that educated ministers might require a salary for their services and that untrained pastors might be displaced by "a race of learned but graceless preachers" who would be "incapable of work . . . caring more for the fleece than the flock . . . tempted rather by the loaves and fishes, than influenced by the good of souls."[150] Johnson concluded that, while talent is a gift, God expects each person to develop his talent to its highest potential.

Several factors helped overcome Baptists' antieducation prejudice. People soon saw that educated men made good pastors and that they could better defend the faith against such challenges as the Campbell movement and antimission attacks. With acceptance of the concept of a salaried clergy, Baptist opposition to education diminished. The Manual Labor plan also helped overcome some antieducation prejudice, even if it had little other benefits. This was a plan whereby colleges were located on farms, with students and teachers alternating between academic study and manual labor. It was generally abandoned before the Civil War. Baptist colleges in the South also became effective agents of revival and evangelism. Many of them held "seasons of revival" in which classes were suspended while all gave attention to matters of the soul. This gave rise to that familiar institution, the "campus revival." These and other factors gradually eroded earlier opposition to schools. Before the Civil War, Baptist historian David Benedict could observe, "Our people began more generally to favor a systematic course of ministerial education."[151]

The college movement. The first Baptist college in the South was formed in South Carolina, a fact not surprising since that state had been the center of proeducation efforts among Baptists since the 1750s. The constitution of the Baptist State Convention of South Carolina, formed in 1821, named as its "grand objects" the promotion of missions and education. In its first

148. Ibid., p. 117.
149. Cited in Walter B. Posey, *The Baptist Church in the Lower Mississippi Valley 1776-1845*, p. 22.
150. Cited by Joe M. King, *A History of South Carolina Baptists* p. 176.
151. David Benedict, *Fifty Years Among the Baptists*, p. 299.

year, the convention announced plans to found "a seminary of learning in this state," to promote the "education of indigent, pious young men, designed for the gospel ministry."[152] At its 1825 meeting, the South Carolina convention authorized "the establishment and maintenance of a respectable institution" at Edgefield. The location was chosen partly in hope that Georgia Baptists would share jointly in the school. The school was moved to Greenville in 1851 and renamed Furman University.

The next few years saw a string of Baptist colleges established throughout the South from Virginia to Texas. The slavery controversy and growing estrangement between North and South encouraged this trend, leading to what one writer called "educational sectionalism." A convention in Savannah voted before the Civil War "that the education of southern youth in northern seminaries, is to be strongly deprecated as unnecessary, impolitic, and having a tendency to taint their minds with disloyalty to the South. . . . The people of the South owe it to themselves and their interests to give their patronage to southern journals and southern books as far as possible."[153]

Kentucky Baptists chartered Georgetown College in 1829. North Carolina Baptists formed their state convention in 1830 to sponsor education and chartered Wake Forest Institute four years later on the Manual Labor plan as a "good cheap school." Under the leadership of Jesse Mercer, Georgia Baptists opened Mercer Institute, which later moved to a new location and took the name of Mercer University. Virginia Baptists advocated schools as early as 1788, but none was established until 1832 when Robert Ryland founded a Manual Labor school which later moved to Richmond and took its present name, University of Richmond. In 1842 Alabama Baptists chartered Howard College, which became Samford University. Carson-Newman College in Tennessee dates from 1850, and the same year Mississippi Baptists assumed control of a school which had operated since 1826, renaming it Mississippi College. In 1849 Missouri Baptists formed their first college, naming it for Dr. William Jewell, a physician who had given a generous grant. In 1845 Texas Baptists formed Baylor University at Independence, but later relocated at Waco. Others could also be named; these are only examples of a string of Baptist colleges in the South that antedated the Civil War.

No social institution suffered more from the Civil War than the colleges; many closed never to open again. However, after the end of Reconstruction, the Baptist colleges had a new surge of life. Existing colleges were strengthened and additional ones founded, such as Stetson University in Florida (1883) and Ouachita Baptist University in Arkansas (1886). Texas provides

152. William J. McGlothlin, *Baptist Beginnings in Education*, p. 50.
153. Cited in Edgar W. Knight, ed., *A Documentary History of Education in the South Before 1860* (Chapel Hill: University of North Carolina Press, 1953), 5:302.

further examples of the late-century surge, for in the 1890s alone no less than fifteen new Baptist colleges were established in that state, but not all survived. Baptist academies also enjoyed a surge of growth after 1880, and by 1900 probably six hundred academies had been established under Baptist auspices in the South. Baptist schools faced new competition from state schools after the Civil War. The Morrill Act of 1862 put the state into education as never before. After the turn of the century, Baptist academies greatly diminished, replaced by public high schools.

In the South, most Baptist colleges were sponsored by state conventions, which elected trustees, provided a portion of their support, and thus retained a measure of direct control. Control was not always wisely exercised, and many colleges collapsed from lack of support. Colleges among Northern Baptists, on the other hand, tended to be sponsored by independent educational societies not organically connected to the denomination. Many of those schools later severed their loose ties to Baptists.

Theological Education

From the first, Baptists in the South sought to provide not only collegiate education but also training in theological studies. Most of the early Baptist colleges included Bible or religion departments, and one major purpose of their existence was the training of ministers. However, many Baptists saw the need for a separate theological seminary. In 1835 Basil Manly, Sr., suggested a southwide seminary but received little response outside South Carolina.

As early as 1833, plans called for a seminary in the West, and the Western Baptist Convention was formed to sponsor such a school. At its first session, John Mason Peck said, "It is essential to the interests of Western Baptists that a theological institution be established in some central portion of the Mississippi Valley."[154] This led to formation of the Western Baptist Theological Institute, which opened in 1845 at Covington, Kentucky, a joint operation of Northern and Southern Baptists. The school closed after only three years. The faculty, composed of Northerners, held antislavery views, which caused Southerners to withdraw. However, this school whetted the appetite of Southern Baptists for a seminary of their own.

At its formation in 1845, the SBC steadfastly refused to extend its work beyond the two mission boards; the messengers specifically declined to establish either a publication work or a theological seminary, both of which were earnestly advocated. Friends of theological education pursued their goal outside the convention. R. B. C. Howell convened a meeting of interested persons in Nashville in 1847, who issued a statement that a southwide seminary "is absolutely necessary." At the 1849 convention such leaders as Basil Manly, Sr., and W. B. Johnson spoke earnestly for a seminary, but

---

154. William A. Mueller, *A History of Southern Baptist Theological Seminary*, p. 6.

again the convention declined. Some opposition came from the Baptist colleges who feared that a seminary might compete with their Bible departments. Manly and Johnson emphasized the need for a seminary and argued that it would contribute to denominational unity.

After repeated failure to persuade the SBC to establish a seminary, its advocates fell back to a society approach. An Education Convention met in Augusta in 1856, with most of its delegates from South Carolina and Georgia, the two states most in favor of a theological school, which determined to establish a seminary. Later, the South Carolina Convention offered to turn over the theological department of Furman University, plus $100,000, on condition that other states raise a matching amount and that the school be located in Greenville. Despite the urgent claims of other schools, the offer was accepted. Plans were finalized in 1858, and The Southern Baptist Theological Seminary opened in the fall of 1859 with four professors and twenty-six students. James P. Boyce was elected chairman of the faculty, which included also John A. Broadus, Basil Manly, Jr., and William Williams. The new office of president was created later, and Boyce was elected to that office shortly before his death in 1888. He was succeeded by Broadus (1889-1895) and William H. Whitsitt (1895-1899).

In the inaugural address as professor of theology at Furman University in 1856, Boyce set the direction for future theological education among Southern Baptists. He suggested three principles: (1) that Baptist schools of theology provide a suitable course of study for students who had not completed college, (2) that the schools provide on another track the very highest academic theological education, and (3) that the faculty be asked to sign a statement of Baptist faith. These principles have guided SBC theological seminaries to the present.

The seminary charter of April 30, 1858, provided that

> Every professor of the Institution shall be a member of a regular Baptist Church; and all persons accepting Professorships in this Seminary, shall be considered by such acceptance, as engaging to teach in accordance with, and not contrary to, the Abstract of Principles hereinafter laid down.[155]

Boyce was commended by Francis Wayland, president at Brown University, for requiring an affirmation of faith by the faculty. Without this, he said, such seminaries "have I think proved to be, after a generation or two, schools of heresy."[156]

Basil Manly, Jr., drafted a brief "Abstract of Principles" in twenty articles, adopted by the trustees, to be signed by the faculty. This 1859 abstract is thus the oldest confessional statement prepared and adopted by any Southern Baptist group, and faculty members at Southern Seminary still

155. Ibid., p. 238.
156. Baker, *Source Book,* p. 137.

sign that statement. The abstract recognized Baptist diversity by using general terms and by refusing to speak dogmatically on areas where Southern Baptists were not agreed.

The seminary grew up not within but rather alongside the convention, basically on a society basis. However, from early days it was regarded as a vital part of the denomination and gave reports at SBC meetings. Eventually the convention "adopted" the seminary and charter alterations gave the convention more input into the election of trustees and funding.

During the Civil War, the seminary closed and many feared it would never reopen. The survival of the school owes much to the determination of James P. Boyce and the original faculty. In an oft-quoted statement, they agreed that the school might die but that they would die first. At its first session after the war, the school enrolled only seven students. Many thought Boyce visionary when he suggested the day might come when the seminary would enroll as many as five hundred students. However, the economic devastation of South Carolina, augmented by the depression of the mid-1870s, almost did the seminary in. This led to its relocation from Greenville to Louisville, Kentucky, in 1877, leaving Baptists in the Southeast, the historic center of proeducation leadership, without a Southern Baptist seminary until the mid-twentieth century. At Louisville the school prospered, with support not only from Southern Baptists but also a significant number of students and funds from Baptists in the North.

The seminary confronted two serious internal problems in the nineteenth century, when controversy swirled around Crawford H. Toy in the 1870s and William H. Whitsitt in the 1890s. Toy (1836-1919), a graduate of the seminary, joined its faculty as professor of Old Testament in 1869, the first faculty addition to the original four. A close friend of Lottie Moon, Toy had been appointed a missionary to Japan but never sailed. While still a professor at the University of Virginia, he had spent a two-year sabbatical studying theology and Semitic languages in Germany. By the mid-1870s Toy's views of the Old Testament had become controversial, and in 1879 he was forced to resign. He became a distinguished professor at Harvard University but later withdrew from evangelical church life.

William Heth Whitsitt (1841-1911) was elected professor of church history at the seminary in 1872. In 1895, upon the death of John A. Broadus, he became its third president. A graduate of the seminary, Whitsitt had also studied at the universities of Leipzig and Berlin. The "Whitsitt Controversy" grew out of articles he published in *Johnson's Universal Cyclopedia* in 1886. At a time when most Baptists assumed that Baptist churches could be traced in unbroken succession from New Testament times to the present, Whitsitt affirmed that Baptists as a denomination had emerged from English Separatism in the early 1600s. This view challenged one of the most crucial views of Landmarkism and embroiled the seminary in such controversy that Whitsitt was forced to resign in 1899. He taught at Richmond College (University of Richmond) until his death in 1911.

These controverseries hardened Southern Baptist suspicion of seminary education and tended to drive a wedge between the churches and the schools. In 1877 the Franklin Association of Kentucky surveyed the several Baptist schools in the state and concluded, "There are now abundant facilities offered for education. What we need is more appreciation and enthusiasm for this grand work."[157]

The Landmark Movement

One distinguished historian has called Landmarkism Southern Baptists' "greatest internal crisis" of the nineteenth century.[158] Perhaps no movement has done more to shape the self-identity and intense denominational loyalty of Southern Baptists. Though Landmarkers failed in their efforts to take over the SBC, they injected their viewpoints deep into the bloodstream of Southern Baptists. It would be impossible to understand Southern Baptists apart from Landmarkism.

Origin

Though reaching its fullest development in the Southwest, early Landmark ingredients originated in New England, perhaps as exaggerated expressions of the views of Francis Wayland. J. R. Graves, the "father of Landmarkism," formed some of his views in Vermont. Landmarkism also owes much to the Baptist effort to refute the Campbell movement by using intense argument and logic to prove the validity of the Baptist cause. Landmark-like views surfaced in the New Hampshire Confession of Faith adopted in 1833 and later widely dispersed in the South.

Although the various ingredients of Landmarkism existed earlier, in the 1850s J. R. Graves stirred them together into a new mixture. As editor of the *Tennessee Baptist,* a paper widely circulated throughout the South and Southwest, Graves fixed Landmarkism upon Southern Baptists, many of whom accepted it as historic Baptist orthodoxy. It reached its greatest strength in the Southwest, where intense denominational rivalries prevailed among Baptists, Methodists, Presbyterians, and Disciples. Landmarkism became the main method by which Baptists convinced themselves that theirs were the only true churches and all others mere human societies without valid ministers or ordinances.

---

157. *Minutes,* Sixty-Third Annual Session, Franklin Association of United Baptists, August 1877, p. 4.

158. Baker, *Southern Baptist Convention,* pp. 208 *f.*

Leaders

The most important early leaders of Landmarkism were James Robinson Graves (1820-1893), Amos Cooper Dayton (1813-1865), and James Madison Pendleton (1811-1891). W. W. Barnes described Graves as the warrior of the movement, Pendleton as its prophet, and Dayton as its sword bearer.[159] Graves was the primary founder and exponent of the movement; in the early years Graves *was* Landmarkism. Perhaps no other person exercised as much influence upon Southern Baptists in the nineteenth century as did Graves.

Graves grew up in Vermont, where he left his Congregational background to become a Baptist at age fifteen. He was deeply influenced by his pastor, who had developed a militant defense against Campbellism. Graves had a keen mind, an inquiring spirit, and unusual powers as a speaker. Despite his scanty schooling, Graves served for a time as a teacher in Ohio, where he was also ordained to preach. Graves's lack of formal education contributed no doubt to the imbalance and rigidity of the Landmark system. Graves arrived in Nashville in 1845 and joined the First Baptist Church. He soon after became pastor of the Second Baptist Church (later called Central). In 1846 Graves was elected assistant editor of the *Tennessee Baptist,* succeeding to the editorship in 1848 when R. B. C. Howell resigned. For almost forty-seven years Graves edited the paper, which became a major avenue for the spread of Landmark views.

Quite early Graves realized the importance of the Sunday School and for thirty years made determined, but ultimately unsuccessful, efforts to gain a monopoly on providing lesson literature for Baptist churches. Graves became a severe critic of the Southern Baptist Publication Society and sought to displace it with his control of the Bible Board or his own private publishing ventures. Graves's literature, of course, expressed Landmark views; and he sought doggedly to undercut his competitors, whether denominational agencies or other private businesses. However, the Civil War intervened and probably prevented Landmarkism from gaining more influence. Graves had to move his publishing company from Nashville to Memphis, but the crash of 1873 brought bankruptcy from which he never recovered. Formation of the present Sunday School Board in 1891 put the production of Sunday School literature back into the hands of the denomination.

Like many successful debaters, Graves loved conflict and where none existed he tried to create it. He often held audiences spellbound for over three hours at a time and was without doubt one of the most powerful preachers and debaters of his time. He was also a writer of note. In addition to the Baptist paper, periodicals, and published sermons, Graves authored

159. Barnes, p. 103.

a number of books. One of the smallest of these proved to be one of the more important, entitled *Old Landmarkism: What Is It?* In this brief book, Graves gave a popular exposition of the Landmark system, buttressed by vivid anecdotes and plentiful Scripture citations. First published in 1880, this book went through many editions and was widely circulated throughout the South. A disabling stroke in 1884, followed by a fall, left Graves an invalid the last several years of his life. He continued to write and travel, making "chair talks" from his wheelchair. After his financial and physical reverses, Graves apparently came to terms with life and developed a gentler spirit.

J. M. Pendleton, pastor in Bowling Green, Kentucky, helped establish Landmarkism, though he never embraced the total system as did Graves. In 1854 Pendleton wrote a pamphlet urging that Baptists abandon their custom of pulpit exchange with other denominations. Pendleton's point was simple: Only Baptist ministers were valid gospel ministers, while the leaders of other denominations were mere functionaries. At first Pendleton tried to restrict Landmarkism to this one emphasis. Graves, who had become acquainted with Pendleton when he preached a revival at Bowling Green, published Pendleton's tract under the title *An Old Landmark Re-set,* which gave the name to the movement. However, Pendleton's major influence came through his popular *Church Manual,* first published in 1867 and still available. Pendleton's *Manual* advances Landmark views of Baptist life on closed communion, alien immersion, and Baptist successionism. Through this manual, generations of Southern Baptist pastors have absorbed Landmarkism, often without knowing it.

A third member of the "Landmark Triumvirate" was A. C. Dayton, a Presbyterian dentist converted to Landmark Baptist views. Dayton wrote a number of books and articles advancing Landmark views. He served four years as head of the Bible Board in Nashville and later headed some of Graves's other publishing efforts. Perhaps Dayton's most influential work was a fictional novel, *Theodosia Ernest, Or Heroine of Faith.* This book, which reflects better polemics than literature, traces the struggles of a beautiful young Presbyterian girl, Theodosia Ernest, and some of her friends, as they gradually conclude that Baptists represent the only true church. Using Bunyan-like symbolism, Dayton named his heroine "Theodosia" (love of God), and she proved "earnest," indeed. The liberal protagonist is named Dr. Thinkwell, and the book abounds with subtle antiintellectualism, with many a sharp dig at "learned clergy" and "doctors of divinity." The clear message of the book is that ministerial education is dangerous. Of course, the novel includes romance between beautiful Theodosia and a handsome young lawyer, Harold Percy, who also converts to Baptist views and becomes a preacher. The characters are thoroughly unbelievable, with the young couple and friends spending endless hours in tedious doctrinal discussions, the teenage Theodosia explaining Greek and

Hebrew passages, revealing a detailed knowledge of ancient church history, and expounding intricate questions of theology. Many regard the book as largely autobiographical, tracing Dayton's own pilgrimage to the Baptist position.

Theodosia Ernest made a profound impact. A public hungry for reading material gobbled it up, and it provided just enough drama and romance to appeal to, and yet be permissible for, Baptists still suspicious of novels. It went through twenty-eight editions in two years. Later one of Dayton's daughters, Lucie Dayton Phillips, condensed the original two volumes to one, thus giving *Theodosia* an extended life.

Despite poor eyesight, Dayton was a prodigious writer. In a span of ten years, he wrote thirteen books. During his lifetime, he was said to have published at least a thousand articles in twenty different periodicals.[160] He edited *Children's Friend,* a Sunday School paper for children which was a precursor of the famous *Kind Words* series. He also published *How Children May Be Brought to Christ* (1860) and *A Catechism for Little Children* (1864).

Landmark Teachings

Lengthy books can be written, and have been, on Landmark teachings; but the system boils down to one bedrock concern: the doctrine of the church. Landmarkism is a system of high church ecclesiology with implications for every area of doctrine and church practice. The following list of emphases is by no means complete, but all of them grow out of one taproot, the doctrine of the church.

1. Baptist churches are the only true churches in the world. The Landmark system was exclusive; in this view, Baptists alone represented the true church. Drawing perhaps from Dayton's "marks of the true church" in *Theodosia Ernest,* Graves concluded that only Baptist churches had all these marks. According to this view, the church established by Jesus and the apostles was a Baptist church. James E. Tull, a recognized authority on Landmarkism, said Graves would even put the word *Baptist* before the kingdom of God, since that kingdom was composed of true (i.e., Baptist) churches.[161] Because Baptists have the only true churches, it follows that they have the only true ministers, ordinances, and preaching.

2. The true church is a local, visible institution. According to Landmarkism, the only "church" is a local organization. No room is made for any "invisible" or "universal" church. Graves emphasized that the New Testament church was "a single congregation, complete in itself, independent of

---

160. James E. Taulman, "The Life and Writings of Amos Cooper Dayton 1813-1865," *Baptist History and Heritage.* p. 41.

161. James E. Tull, *Shapers of Baptist Thought,* p. 137.

all other bodies, civil or religious, . . . amenable only to Christ."[162] As Miss Theodosia expounded at length, the word *ecclesia* is used over one hundred times in the New Testament, almost always designating one local congregation. Each church was self-governing under Christ, and each maintained its own discipline (thus no right of intercommunion). Baptist structures, such as associations and conventions, were in no wise "churchly" and had no churchly functions. Calling the idea of an "invisible church" an exercise in "invisible nonsense," Graves affirmed that

> the only church that is revealed to us is a visible church, and the only church with which we have anything to do, or in connection with which we have any duties to perform, is a *visible* body. . . . Christ never set up but one kingdom; and if this is visible, he has no invisible kingdom or church, and such a thing has no real existence in heaven or earth. It is only an invention to bolster up erroneous theories of ecclesiology.[163]

3. The churches and the kingdom of God are coterminous. This is one of the most distinctive doctrines of Landmarkism. Graves said "church" and "kingdom" are used as "synonymous terms" in the Bible. "The kingdom embraced the first church, and it now embraces all the churches. The churches of Christ constitute the kingdom of Christ."[164] Therefore, the kingdom of God is made up of the sum total of Baptist churches. Graves illustrated this concept by noting that the individual states compose the United States, and no one can become a citizen of the United States without also becoming a citizen of one of the constituent states thereof. Since the only way to enter the kingdom is to enter one of the units thereof (a Baptist church), it appeared that Graves meant that only Baptists could be saved, and he was forced to protest many times that he did not mean that.

4. There must be no "pulpit affiliation" with non-Baptists. From early times, Baptists in America had participated with other denominations in joint endeavors. Among these were "union revivals," in which ministers of different denominations would take turns preaching, with converts free to join the church of their choice; ministers of Baptist and non-Baptist churches exchanging pulpits on special occasions; and joint participation of Baptists and non-Baptists at services of ordination and pastoral installation. For the first decade of the Southern Baptist Convention, the messengers would pass the customary motion to "invite visiting brethren of other denominations to seats in this convention." Though such non-Baptists had no vote, they were encouraged to participate in the discussions.

The Landmarkers abhorred such ecumenical acceptance of non-Baptists. Since such brethren represented "human societies" instead of churches,

---

162. J. R. Graves, *Old Landmarkism: What is It?* p. 38.
163. Ibid., p. 32.
164. Ibid., p. 33.

they had no valid ordination and no commission to preach. To invite them to preach in Baptist churches, even on special occasions, was tantamount to recognizing them as valid ministers, which, in turn, was tantamount to recognizing their churches. Within a generation, Landmarkism effectively halted most pulpit exchanges among Baptists.

5. Only a church can do churchly acts. Certain acts or functions are by their nature "churchly," such as baptism, the Lord's Supper, and preaching. All of these acts have been committed by Christ to His church; no organization but a church can validly perform them. Since Baptist churches alone are true, the only valid baptism, Lord's Supper, or preaching is that authorized and performed by Baptists. Out of this doctrine grew the Landmark advocacy of closed communion and opposition to "alien immersion" and missions boards.

The "water ceremonies" of non-Baptists were not considered baptism by Landmarkers. Since they had no valid church, no valid ministers, and no valid commission from Christ, the Methodists, Presbyterians, Disciples, and other "human societies" could not perform valid baptism. Therefore, when members of these churches joined Baptist churches, they were required to undergo Baptist baptism. All other baptism, even immersion of a believer, was considered "alien," that is, coming from an organization other than a church. By the same teaching, Landmarkers opposed all alien or non-Baptist communion and preaching.

Only a true church can set the Lord's table, said the Landmarkers, and only church members can validly approach that table. This resulted in "closed communion" by which non-Baptists were not eligible to partake of the Lord's Supper in Baptist churches, nor Baptists in non-Baptist churches. Though one of the less significant points theologically, this became one of the most prominent and most offensive in practice because it acted out the Landmark exclusivism. Some Landmarkers, including Graves, took this one further step to "double closed communion," meaning that communion must be restricted to members of the local church observing the supper, with visiting Baptists of like faith and order ineligible. Some required that such visitors refrain; other Landmarkers would extend "transient communion" as a privilege but not as an inherent right. This grows out of the Landmark emphasis upon the local nature of the church and the idea that a church's communion should not exceed its discipline.

Landmarkism rejected not only alien immersion and alien communion but also alien preaching. Preaching is a gospel act which can be authorized only by a church. Therefore the "speeches" of non-Baptists cannot be considered valid preaching. The Landmark faction rejected even Baptist preaching except as authorized by a *church*. This led them to oppose the work of the mission boards. Landmarkers denied the right of boards, especially the Foreign Mission Board, to examine, appoint, and direct the work of missionaries. All of these tasks, they said, belonged exclusively to the churches. After a full day of debate, the SBC in 1859 declined to dismantle its Foreign Board as Graves had insisted. The issue came up again in the 1890s in the "Gospel Mission Controversy," but once again the SBC kept its Foreign Mission Board. The Landmark objection was not to missions per se but to the *method* of working through boards, which it claimed represented a capitulation to episcopacy.

6. Baptist churches have always existed in every age by an unbroken historical succession. Each Landmark emphasis or teaching is closely related to its central doctrine, the nature of the church. This one is no exception. Since it is unthinkable that the kingdom of God could ever go out of existence, even for a short time, and that kingdom is composed of Baptist churches, then it follows that there must always have been Baptist churches. Landmarkers acknowledge that these churches may not always have been called by the name Baptist but insist they had all the essential marks of a gospel (i.e., Baptist) church. Graves said:

> Landmark Baptists very generally believe that for the Word of the Living God to stand, and for the veracity of Jesus Christ to vindicate itself, the kingdom which he set up "in the days of John the Baptist," has had an unbroken continuity until now.[165]

While repudiating the concept of apostolic succession, the Landmarkers taught that Christ "must always have had true and uncorrupted churches, since his kingdom can not exist without true churches." Graves understood such Scripture passages as Daniel 2:44 and Matthew 16:18 to promise the unbroken continuity of Baptist churches. This is one reason Landmarkers created such a controversy when W. H. Whitsitt suggested that the modern Baptist denomination originated in the early 1600s. Graves republished G. H. Orchard's *History of Baptists* in 1855, to emphasize Landmark historiography. Perhaps the most popular exposition of the Landmark view of Baptist history was the pamphlet by J. M. Carroll, *The Trail of Blood*, which is still in print.

From these doctrinal teachings, one can detect the exclusive nature of Landmarkism. Some considered it a Baptist form of popery, with church succession in the place of apostolic succession. It reached its height in an atmosphere of intense denominational competition and rivalry. Many Baptists eagerly embraced the system because it offered spiritual compensation; it made them not only *a* true church but the *only* true church, thus affording feelings of superiority to people to whom that was not overly abundant.

Progress of Landmarkism

Graves dated the rise of Landmarkism to questions he raised in 1832 about the meaning of baptism. He had seen a pedobaptist minister who at

---

165. Graves, p. 121.

one service immersed several converts (including Graves's mother and sister), poured upon another who knelt in the stream, and sprinkled others who stood on the bank.[166] How could these different acts constitute the "one baptism" of the New Testament? Can an unbaptized person perform valid baptism? Troubled by these questions, Graves concluded that only Baptist immersion constitutes valid baptism. He required his mother to be immersed again when she joined his church in Nashville years later.

A newspaper controversy first brought Landmarkism to public discussion among Southern Baptists. Graves said,

> In 1846 I took charge of 'The Tennessee Baptist,' and soon commenced agitating the question of the validity of alien immersions, the propriety of Baptists recognizing, by any act, ecclesiastical or ministerial, Pedobaptist societies or preachers as *churches* and ministers of Christ.[167]

John L. Waller, editor of *The Western Baptist Review* in Kentucky, took an anti-Landmark position on these issues. In early 1848 Richard B. Burleson of Alabama had directed the following question to Waller: "Is the immersion of a person in water into the name of the Trinity, upon a credible profession of faith in Christ, by a Pedo-Baptist minister who has not been immersed, a valid baptism."[168] In replying, Waller gave a qualified affirmative. The faith of the person being baptized is more fundamental, he said, than the qualifications of the administrator. If the validity of baptism depends upon the "baptizedness" of the administrator, then no one can be sure he is baptized. Waller said:

> If any link in the succession [of baptism] be broken, the most skillful spiritual smith under the whole heavens cannot mend the chain. . . . An improper administrator twenty generations removed, is as fatal to the genuineness of the ordinance as such a one but one generation removed.[169]

Waller concluded that such questions should be left to the individual churches which alone had the right to decide.

Graves ridiculed Waller's response, deploring what he called "this sort of gassing."[170] In a series of strongly worded articles, Graves held for the validity of Baptist baptism alone. This newspaper controversy led to a called meeting at Cotton Grove in West Tennessee, on June 24, 1851, "of all Baptists willing to accept and practice the teachings of Christ and his apostles in these matters." This meeting discussed five issues, known as the "Cotton Grove Resolutions."

The Cotton Grove Resolutions of 1851 represent the earliest organized

166. Ibid., p. ix.
167. Ibid., p. xi.
168. *Western Baptist Review* (March 1848), p. 267.
169. Ibid., p. 269.
170. *Tennessee Baptist,* (June 1848).

expression of Landmark views and reveal the first traces of a potential denominational division over these issues. The minutes of that meeting record that:

> Rev. J. R. Graves offered the following queries:
>
> 1st. Can Baptists, consistently with their principles or the Scriptures, recognize those societies not organized according to the pattern of the Jerusalem Church, but possessing different *governments,* different *officers,* a different class of *members,* different *ordinances, doctrines* and *practices,* as churches of Christ?
>
> 2d. Ought they to be called gospel churches, or churches in a religious sense?
>
> 3d. Can we consistently recognize the ministers of such irregular and unscriptural bodies as gospel ministers?
>
> 4th. Is it not virtually recognizing them as official ministers to invite them into our pulpits, or *by any other* act that *would or could be* constructed into such a recognition?
>
> 5th. Can we consistently address as *brethren* those professing Christianity, who not only have not the doctrine of Christ and walk not according to his commandments, but are arrayed in direct and bitter opposition to them?[171]

These "queries" were all answered in the negative, except the fourth. Graves was probably correct that many Baptists of Tennessee, and multitudes all over the South, endorsed those resolutions. He exaggerated, however, in regarding them as the most influential statement of religious reformation since Luther's *Theses.*

The Graves-Howell controversy of 1857-1859 proved crucial to the fortunes of Landmarkism. It was more than a personal conflict between two strong leaders who were allergic to one another. It spotlighted the denominational conflict in miniature, and the failure of the Landmark faction to capture the First Baptist Church of Nashville was perhaps prophetic of their failure to capture the Southern Baptist Convention.

Robert Boyte Crawford Howell (1801-1868) helped lay the foundations of the SBC and was one of its greatest and most loyal leaders until his death. In 1835 he went to Nashville as an appointee of the American Baptist Home Mission Society and soon accepted the pastorate of the First Baptist Church. The church was shattered, having lost its pastor and building, and most of its members, to the Campbell movement in 1828. Howell saw at once that the Great Valley of the Mississippi could become a Baptist empire, that Nashville was the key to that valley, and that strong publications provided one way to win Baptist adherents. Within a month of arriving, he put out the first issues of *The Baptist,* the paper that still survives as the *Baptist and Reflector,* the Baptist state paper of Tennessee. Howell served eight years, 1851-1859, as SBC president. In addition, he served as president

171. Graves, pp. xi-xii.

of three of the convention boards, the FMB, the Bible Board, and the first Sunday School Board. Howell also wrote a number of books which shaped the thought and theology of early Southern Baptists. Among these was *The Deaconship* (1846), which included a role for both deacons and deaconesses. Howell deplored controversy and in *The Baptist* determined to maintain an irenic spirit. He hoped to restore the good image of Baptists in the West, who had been torn by the three great controversies of Hardshellism, antimissions, and Campbellism. In 1850 Howell resigned the Nashville church to accept a pastorate in Richmond, where he remained until 1857.

For fifteen years, 1835-1850, Howell had been perhaps the most influential Southern Baptist leader in the West. During Howell's tenure as a Virginia pastor, J. R. Graves moved into the leadership role, consolidating power by his writing, preaching, and control of the Bible Board. Repeatedly, the Nashville church urged Howell to return, and he did so in 1857, partly, no doubt, to conteract the growing influence of Landmarkism. From the moment of Howell's return, these two great Baptist leaders were set on a collision course and both seemed to realize it.

The conflict broke into the open early in 1858 over the proposed Southern Baptist Sunday School Union which Graves established in direct competition with the existing Southern Baptist Publication Society in Charleston. Graves was a constant critic of the SBPS, finding fault with its policies, literature, and leaders. Howell supported the Charleston group and opposed Graves's efforts to take over Southern Baptist publications. In response, Graves made a series of personal attacks upon Howell, his pastor. On September 8, 1858, two members of First Baptist Church called for a church trial to discipline Graves. In five charges, Graves was accused of slandering the pastor, seeking to divide the church, publishing "sundry foul and atrocious libels," using his paper to attack other Baptist leaders, and uttering and/or publishing falsehoods in nine specifications."[172] At a meeting on October 12, Graves demanded that the church drop the charges. After five hours of discussion, the church voted about midnight by ninety-one to forty-eight to proceed with the trial. After nine subsequent meetings, in which Graves was neither present nor represented, the church voted unanimously to convict him on all charges and exclude him from the church. During the next year forty-six of Graves's remaining followers were also excluded.

Graves refused to make his defense before the church. When the church refused to drop the charges, he and twenty-three of his followers remained for a post-midnight session in which they declared themselves the "true and orderly First Baptist Church," claiming the majority had forfeited their standing as a church. They later took the name of State Street Baptist

172. See Joe W. Burton, *Road to August: R. C. B. Howell and the Formation of the Southern Baptist Convention,* p. 135.

Church. Graves's popularity is seen in the fact that at meetings of the association and state convention, messengers from his church were seated and Howell's excluded. Graves called a council attended by representatives from twenty churches in the Concord Association in March 1858, thus in effect appealing beyond the authority of the local congregation. This conference was made up of Graves's supporters and, as expected, they exonerated him of all charges.

Flush with these local victories, Graves indicated his intention to confront Howell at the SBC in Richmond in 1859. However, not only did the convention seat messengers from Nashville's First Baptist Church but they also reelected Howell as president on the first ballot. After extensive debate, the messengers refused to dismantle the FMB, thus dealing Landmarkism a double defeat. After his election, Howell resigned the presidency in an effort to bring peace to the troubled denomination, and the SBC further mollified the Landmarkers by agreeing to help those churches who preferred to appoint their own missionaries by transmitting funds for them. This incident also confirmed that fellowship in one Baptist body does not depend upon status in another, but that each Baptist body is autonomous in its own sphere.

The Civil War interrupted the progress of the Landmark movement. Southern Baptists had also begun to tire of the constant controversy and attacks against their leaders. As the true nature and spirit of Landmarkism became clearer, it lost much of its appeal.

Scattered Eruptions of Landmarkism

The death of Graves in 1893 deprived Landmarkism of its greatest leader and cohesive center of unity. By the turn of the century, however, Landmarkism erupted in several scattered incidents, each spotlighting a different dimension of its teachings. The first of these was the "Gospel Mission" movement, or "Crawfordism," an anti-convention movement led by T. P. Crawford, veteran SBC missionary to China. Crawford attended the 1859 meeting of the SBC and heard Graves's attack upon the Foreign Mission Board. He apparently absorbed much of Graves's teachings. Later Crawford advocated that missionaries be appointed by churches, not boards, and that missionaries become self-supporting as soon as possible. In 1892 he published a booklet, *Churches to the Front!,* attacking the SBC and its mission boards. He was eventually dismissed, and his movement won little support.

The Whitsitt Controversy of the 1890s, mentioned earlier, represented another outbreak of Landmarkism. William H. Whitsitt, professor of church history and president of The Southern Baptist Theological Seminary in Louisville, published articles in the 1880s which affirmed that Baptists as a denomination had their beginnings in the early 1600s. In 1896 he published *A Question in Baptist History,* which spelled out his conclusions in greater detail. The Whitsitt Controversy spread through local associations and state conventions, seriously undermining support for the seminary. Whitsitt resigned under pressure in May 1898. The Landmarkers, led by T. T. Eaton and John T. Christian, felt they had won a victory, though the remainder of the seminary faculty informed the trustees that they shared Whitsitt's views.

A third appearance of Landmarkism centered around Samuel A. Hayden of Dallas, though its implications stretched far beyond one state. Hayden moved to Dallas in 1883 as pastor of the Live Oak Baptist Church, which had originated in a split from the First Baptist Church in 1879.[173] The Live Oak split represented basically a Landmark minority, encouraged by J. R. Graves who spoke there occasionally. They adopted extreme Landmark practices and teachings in the local church. Despite these problems, however, Hayden led a reunion with FBC in 1884, leaving R. T. Hanks as pastor of the united church, with Hayden as a sort of unofficial assistant pastor. Hayden also owned and edited *The Texas Baptist,* which competed with the *Texas Baptist Standard* edited by J. B. Cranfill. In 1886 Hanks led a unification of the various overlapping conventions into one Baptist General Convention of Texas (BGCT), established on a missionary basis. Almost at once Hayden attacked the new body, and his opposition intensified over the years.

In 1894 Hayden proposed reforms which amounted to adoption of Landmark practices by the BGCT. When the convention refused, Hayden used his paper to attack, ridicule, harass, and (some said) slander Texas Baptist leaders. In 1896 the executive board of the Texas convention fought back, accusing Hayden of "undermining the mission work, drying up the mission spirit, and sowing down our once fertile fields with salt." It was time, the board said, for Texas Baptists to fight back. "Shall we wait until the mission cause, now bleeding, is stamped out of existence?"[174] In 1897 and again in 1898, the state convention denied Hayden a seat. On April 28, 1898, he filed a lawsuit in the Dallas courts, seeking an injunction against the convention and $100,000 in damages. His primary contention, and the center of "Haydenism," was that the state convention was made up of *churches,* and the convention could not refuse to seat delegates without violating the autonomy of the local church. The convention voted, however, that "the Convention is composed of persons chosen by churches, associations, and missionary societies as their messengers, and that when said persons are

173. For an account of this church split, see Leon McBeth, *The First Baptist Church of Dallas: Centennial History 1868-1968,* p. 73 f.

174. Robert A. Baker, *The Blossoming Desert: A Concise History of Texas Baptists,* pp. 159-160.

convened they, and not the churches are the Convention."[175] Hayden later added other lawsuits against various individuals, including J. B. Cranfill. These dragged on for several years, with various verdicts, reversals, and appeals. They were finally settled out of court, primarily to deny Hayden the benefit of the continuing publicity. Hayden's followers formed a rival state convention in 1899, which later merged with another Landmark splinter group, and took the name of Baptist Missionary Association (BMA). Hayden affiliated with the new body, and though he continued as a member of First Baptist Church of Dallas, it was a troubled relationship.

A fourth "outcropping" of Landmarkism may be seen in the Ben Bogard movement in Arkansas in the late 1890s. In some ways this was the Arkansas equivalent of Haydenism in Texas. A group of Landmark Baptists, led by Ben Bogard of Searcy, sought to turn the Arkansas convention to Landmark principles. Failing that, they split off to form the General Association of Baptist Churches in 1902 at Little Rock. Seeking to impose upon the entire SBC what they had failed to fix upon their own state convention, the Bogard group issued an ultimatum to the SBC to switch to a Landmark basis of operation or else. When the SBC refused to make the demanded changes, representatives from 107 churches in several states met at Texarkana in 1905 to form a Landmark body, which later took the name of American Baptist Association.

General Assessment of Landmarkism

Perhaps the Landmark movement is best understood as a Baptist equivalent of nineteenth-century Roman Catholicism. The two groups show remarkable similarity in doctrine and spirit. For Landmark Baptists, the principle of church succession plays the same role as apostolic succession for Catholics, validating their claims to be the only true church. Both claimed to have the only true ordinances or sacraments, and both embraced a doctrine of "high churchism."

For all its dogmatism and ironclad certainty, the Landmark movement also appealed to an underlying insecurity among frontier Baptists. How could they be sure among the competing denominations that theirs was right? Landmarkism answered that question by a dogmatic system proving not only that Baptist churches were valid but also that they were the only valid churches.

The Landmark view of Baptist history is based upon an assumption, not upon the evidence of historical research. Landmarkers assumed on the basis of doctrine that Baptist churches *must* have existed since New Testament times, no matter what the evidence may show. Instead of drawing conclusions from the historical data, they looked for historical evidence to support their a priori conclusions.

175. Ibid., p. 162.

Like most ultraconservative movements, Landmarkism had a low tolerance for ambiguity. Followers felt a need to project absolute certainty on every question, however scanty or inconclusive the evidence. To admit uncertainty on any religious issue or, worse yet, to tolerate a diversity of views, proved emotionally and doctrinally difficult for Landmarkers. Perhaps uncertainty on even one point would have threatened the entire system.

Many Southern Baptists in forming the SBC in 1845 had tried to build a complete *denomination*. This denominational concept was threatened by the society system of the North and by the Landmark system in the South, two movements which despite their differences in spirit and doctrine nevertheless have much in common. While the society system called for benevolent work to be done outside the church, Landmarkism took the opposite approach of centering all religious work in the local church. Both in effect preferred an *independent* method which left no room for a strong denomination. Thus for different reasons, both anticipated the modern "independent" Baptist movement.

Like most Baptists caught up in controversy, the Landmark faction claimed to represent the ancient or historic Baptist positions. The name "old Landmarkism," somewhat like "Primitive Baptists," lays claim not only to truth but to historic precedent as well. However, despite its claims to antiquity, the actual origin and teachings of both groups prove surprisingly modern. John L. Waller considered Landmarkism "a new kink" in Baptist life, and W. W. Everts, pastor in Louisville, said, "It is a strange assumption that this new high church dogma should be claimed as an old land-mark of our denominational estate. We regard it rather as a new stake, which can be set down and maintained only in sectarian arrogance."[176] The evidence confirms that the movement was more nearly a "new stake" than an "old landmark."

Landmarkism must also be seen against the backdrop of the Alexander Campbell movement. The Campbell controversy decimated Baptist life with its claims of primitivism and exclusive biblical truth. Perhaps W. M. Patterson was correct that "in some degree the Landmark movement was a defensive reaction to the agitation and schism fostered by Alexander Campbell and his followers."[177] In this case, however, the defense ultimately hurt as bad as the attack. Despite its polemics against Campbellism, Landmarkism shows many similarities to the Disciple movement.

One must not overlook the regional character of Landmarkism in Baptist life. In the Southwest Campbellism and denominational rivalry reached their height and called forth the most vigorous Landmark response. J. R.

---

176. Tull, p. 144.
177. W. Morgan Patterson, "The Influence of Landmarkism Among Baptists," *Baptist History and Heritage* p. 45.

Graves did his work in Nashville and later in Memphis. Baptists in the older states, such as Virginia, Georgia, and the Carolinas, generally followed the older Baptist patterns and never showed much interest in Landmarkism. This introduced regional tensions into Southern Baptist life that are still evident today.

Though Landmarkism failed to capture the SBC, Southern Baptists absorbed and still retain much of its spirit and emphases. The continuing Landmark legacy can be seen in several contemporary Southern Baptist traits and practices. These include an exaggerated emphasis upon local church autonomy, continuing tensions over alien immersion and closed communion, a suspicion of other denominations, refusal to participate in organized ecumenical conferences, SBC representation which is now limited to messengers from churches, and a continued emphasis among a few Southern Baptists upon a successionist view of Baptist history.

On a more positive note, Landmarkism helped build Southern Baptist identity and loyalty. Its teachings provided doctrinal reasons to be Baptist and, as one observed, it "put iron into the Baptist bloodstream." In his careful study of the movement, Harold S. Smith concluded that along with all the weaknesses of his system Graves

> performed a valuable service for nineteenth century Baptists. He helped to awaken them to a needed self-consciousness in a day when the loss of denominational identity appeared to be imminent . . . he emphasized the need for education and encouraged the organization of schools. The theological dimension which he gave to his Baptist paper illustrated the need for and the broad possibilities of doctrinal publications.[178]

Woman's Missionary Union

In the decade after the Civil War, the women of most American denominations formed their own national organizations. Southern Baptist women were somewhat slower to organize. The earliest general meeting of Southern Baptist women was held in Baltimore in 1868 when a number of the wives of messengers attending the SBC gathered in the home of Mrs. Ann Graves. She read to them excerpts of letters from her son Rosewell, a missionary doctor in China, pointing out the need for women missionaries. After 1868 Baptist women continued to meet in connection with the convention. In 1872 the SBC took its first recorded notice of the mission work of women when it asked the FMB to include a report of the work of "Bible Women."

An earlier chapter traced the rise of women's mission societies after 1800. However, these hundreds of local groups had little correlation until the formation of a Central Committee of Baptist women in each state, beginning with South Carolina in 1876. The local societies funneled mission contributions to their state Central Committees, which, in turn, forwarded

178. Harold Stewart Smith, "A Critical Analysis of the Theology of J. R. Graves," p. 330.

funds to the appropriate SBC mission board, with the Foreign Mission Board usually receiving the lion's share. In 1882 the SBC suggested that the mission boards elect "some competent woman as Superintendent of the State Central Committees, whose duty it shall be to collect and disseminate information and in other ways to stimulate and strengthen woman's work for women in all lands."[179] The FMB dragged its feet, however, and no such leader was elected. Perhaps Southern Baptists feared that women might form a separate organization, as other churchwomen in America had done, or that the move would be too controversial in drawing women into leadership roles.

No doubt the formation of a national organization by Southern Baptist women was hastened by an incident at the SBC meeting of 1885, at which women messengers from Arkansas were disqualified. At that meeting, the convention revised its constitution to substitute the word "brethren" for "messengers" in Article III on membership. For thirty-three years, until 1918, this restriction remained in the SBC constitution, forbidding women to serve as messengers. In response, Southern Baptist women who had been hesitant to form their own organization became determined to do so.

At the 1887 meeting of Baptist women in Louisville, Annie Armstrong of Baltimore set the stage for national organization by calling for each state Central Committee to send delegates to the 1888 meeting in Richmond. At the 1888 meeting Fannie Stout of South Carolina pointed out, "The question of organization of Southern Baptist women for mission work has been exciting thought and discussion for years." She listed benefits that could result from such an organization, concluding, "We organize simply for greater efficiency in work and our work is the work of the Convention. We do not desire a separate work, but if in some particulars we separate ourselves as women, it is that we may gather greater momentum with which to push forward our united work."[180]

Another who encouraged a national organization for Baptist women was Lottie Moon. Though half a world away, her letters informed, inspired, and guided Baptist women in the South. In late 1887 she wrote that "until the women of our Southern Baptist churches are thoroughly aroused, we shall continue to go on in our present hand-to-mouth system. . . . I am convinced that one of the chief reasons our Southern Baptist women do so little [in missions] is the lack of organization." However, Miss Moon warned against a separate organization, such as Northern Baptist women had formed. She said:

> What we want is not power, but simply combination in order to elicit the largest possible giving. Power of appointment and of disbursing funds should

179. *Annual,* SBC, 1882, p. 25.
180. Cited in McBeth, *Women in Baptist Life,* p. 96.

be left, as heretofore, in the hands of the Foreign Mission Board. Separate organization is undesirable, and would do harm; but organization in subordination to the Board is the imperative need of the hours."[181]

In 1888 the Baptist women formed the Woman's Missionary Union, Auxiliary to the Southern Baptist Convention. The first president was Martha McIntosh of South Carolina, and Annie Armstrong of Baltimore was elected corresponding secretary. Although linked in a cooperative auxiliary relationship, the new WMU was not technically a part of convention structure. The women elected their own officers and planned their own programs. Though sustaining the same name and structural relationships to the present, in reality the relation of the WMU to the SBC has grown much closer. Until the twentieth century, the annual WMU reports to the convention, though prepared by women, were presented only by men. The new organization was first headquartered in Baltimore but later moved to Birmingham. No group has done more to stimulate and channel Southern Baptist mission interest and support. The WMU has long since outgrown its early tendency to support only the foreign mission work and has become a stalwart supporter of the entire work of the SBC.

Many of the men opposed the WMU for fear that women would be tempted to speak and teach in church. Most, however, were content for the women to do whatever they wished, so long as it involved only women and children.

Summary

Baptists in America entered the nineteenth century with scattered churches and a few associations but no general organization. The rise of the mission movement stimulated Baptists to form national structures, but the brethren North and South could never agree on the kind of denomination they wanted. This tension, plus the slavery controversy, shattered the Baptist structures; by mid-century Baptist North and South separated to go their own ways, developing diverse styles of organization and emphases in theology. Despite several efforts at continuing cooperation, and even talk of reunion, the chasm seemed wider in 1900 than it had in 1845. However, each group had vastly multiplied its benevolent work, as if provoking one another to good works. Not just their isolation from each other, but the impact of different socioeconomic forces shaped Baptists in the two regions into separate molds. Both entered the twentieth century with strength, but their strengths were different, as were their weaknesses.

181. Cited in Alma Hunt, *A History of Woman's Missionary Union*, p. 24.

12

Baptist Beginnings in Europe

"Baptists in Europe wear a coat of many colors." This apt description by a recent historian sums up the diverse origins, differing doctrinal views, and varied church practices of almost a million Baptists scattered over twenty-five or more countries of Continental Europe.[1] Their diversity is real. Though close geographical neighbors, Baptists in various European countries emerged from different racial and linguistic backgrounds, grew up under various political and economic systems, and gradually developed forms of faith which fuse the historic Baptist witness with the unique spirit and flavor of their own national heritage. Despite their diversity, however, European Baptists share much in common. Their confessions reveal local differences but an overall commonality of faith. They form one of the major Baptist communities of the world.

From the first, Continental Baptists have marched to their own spiritual drummers. They not only differ somewhat among themselves, a trait not uncommon among Baptists, but are also both similar to and yet different from those who bear the same name in other parts of the world. They emerged about two centuries later than did British and American Baptists in response to quite different spiritual forces. European Baptists are less a product of Puritanism and more an outgrowth of the Pietist awakenings which swept the Continent in the early 1800s. That heritage has stamped European Baptists with a Christian life-style more inward and quietist, often more reflective than activistic.

An Overview of European Baptists

J. H. Rushbrooke made the sharp contrast, "In the year of Waterloo [1815] there was no Baptist church on the mainland of Europe, and, in the year 1850 there were only about 4,000 church members. In 1900 the number had increased to some 220,000."[2] This section will introduce some of the factors which have shaped the European branch of the Baptist family.

1. G. Keith Parker, *Baptists in Europe,* p. 26.
2. J. H. Rushbrooke, *The Baptist Movement on the Continent of Europe* (London: Kingsgate Press, 1923), p. 5.

Relation to the Anabaptist Movement

Most European Baptists see themselves in close kinship with the earlier Anabaptist movement. Many European historians portray Baptists as direct descendents of the Anabaptists and thus emphasize a European origin for all Baptists. Despite some similarity, evidence to trace any historical linkage between the two groups remains scanty.

Though Keith Parker spoke of Baptist "re-beginnings" in Europe, he is on solid ground when he said:

> Some Baptists in Europe, especially in Eastern Europe where masses of Anabaptists fled during the Reformation, make closer historical connection with that early radical movement in Zurich in the sixteenth century than do most Anglo-American historians. Their point is that those refugees made a long-lasting impact upon society and spirituality in their lands, a fact that cannot be denied. Although admitting no clear historical continuity between Anabaptists and the nineteenth-century Baptist movement in their lands, some Baptists note the deep identification with their forefathers and the context of modern Anabaptist descendants, such as the Brethren and the Mennonites.[3]

Further evidence of Anabaptist influence is seen in the fact that many Mennonites in Europe, direct descendants of earlier Anabaptists, have joined Baptist churches. Especially in Russia the Mennonites made up a major part of the early Baptist movement. The similarity between European Anabaptists of the sixteenth century and Baptists of the nineteenth cannot be denied. In light of this, one must conclude that European Baptists probably sustain a closer relation to the Anabaptists than is true of Baptists in Britain and America. However, the evidence falls short of proving direct historical linkage between the two groups.

Regardless of what historians may conclude, however, many European government officials and individual Baptists assume uncritically that modern Baptists represent a new appearance of Anabaptists. Some Baptists, thinking they are Anabaptists, have tended to act as if they were. What is worse, some officials have written Baptists off as another eruption of radical Anabaptism, thus fastening upon the European Baptist community a heavy and undeserved burden. Many European citizens, if they have heard of Baptists at all, consider them a radical sect and some connect them with the Munster revolution, which broke out in central Germany in the 1530s. The "Munster fiasco," as historians describe it, became identified in the popular mind as an Anabaptist movement. Though some of the Munster radicals did rebaptize, the movement was a far cry from the biblical Anabaptists who flourished at about the same time and who condemned the Munster revolution as vigorously as anyone. Europeans have often done

---

3. Parker, pp. 21-22.

Baptists a double disservice by identifying them not only with Anabaptists but also with the most radical and revolutionary fringe of that movement.

The result has been that European Baptists have had to struggle for identity as part of the authentic Christian community. That is perhaps one reason they have so often included the Apostles' Creed as a part of their confessions of faith. Identification with Anabaptism provided a major handicap to Baptist advance in the nineteenth century, especially in Germany. However, it became less a factor in the present century.

The Pietist Awakenings

In 1674 Philip Spener of Germany published his *Pious Wishes,* a fervent reaction to the cold creedalism and lifeless churches which had engulfed much of German Protestantism of the time. Spener sought to reaffirm Christian experience as well as theology, to recover lay participation in church life, to revitalize preaching which had become largely polemical, to reaffirm the priority of a conversion experience, and to reassert the role of emotion in religion. To accomplish these and similar goals, he gathered lay people into small groups or "cells" for Bible study, singing and praise, and the mutual sharing of Christian testimonies. From *Pious Wishes,* which set out reforms he wished to see in the church, Spener's movement was nicknamed "Pietism" by its opponents.

Gradually the impact of Spener's movement waned in Germany, though others like August Hermann Francke and Count Nikolaus Zinzendorf took similar teachings to other areas. Other groups, such as the Moravian Church, arose to carry on much the same emphases. In time the opposition of a strong state church and, above all, the rise of rationalism, tended to undercut the Pietist movement. However, the early nineteenth century saw a strong resurgence of Pietism in Europe. Out of this ferment came a new emphasis upon personal religion, including Bible study, prayer, and a personal relation to God through conversion. The movement called for a voluntary church as opposed to the state churches and more personal forms of ministry that related primarily to persons rather than to institutions.

Pietist resurgence provided the major avenue for the emergence of Baptist churches in Europe. Many Pietist groups, gathered for Bible study and prayer, came to the conviction of believer's baptism before they ever heard of Baptists. Some early Baptist missionaries, encountering such baptizing groups in Europe, pronounced them Baptists and reported that their own work consisted not only in forming new churches but also in gathering existing churches into the Baptist fold and instructing them more fully in the faith.

The Pietist environment placed a distinctive stamp upon European Baptists. Pietist heritage helped shape forms of worship, methods of evangelism, emphases in theology, and daily Christian life-styles. European Baptist antecedents are quite different from those of Baptists in Britain and America. Baptists on the Continent have little connection with Puritanism, with its obsessive zeal to reshape the world. The Great Awakening which stamped a revivalist spirit upon Baptists in America provided but little input into European Baptist life. They have grown up in a different soil, been called forth and nurtured by spiritual forces of their own time and place.

Intense Persecution

Baptists are no strangers to persecution. In early England, Baptists crowded the prisons; in Colonial America, they felt the lash. However, the most overt forms of religious persecution ended in England by 1689 and in America by a century later, though at times more subtle forms of discrimination have continued. In Europe, however, Baptists originated in persecution and have continued therein in many places to the present. They have faced perhaps the longest Baptist persecution in history and some of the most severe. That they have survived, and in many places flourished, is a marvel. However, such intense opposition over a long period has left its mark upon them.

Two powerful agencies spearheaded the effort to stamp out Baptists on the Continent: the state churches and civil governments. Whether Roman Catholic, Lutheran, or Reformed, the state churches threw considerable influence against the emerging Baptist groups throughout Europe. The state churches fanned fears of sectarianism, dredged up the old accusations of Baptist connection with revolutionary Anabaptism, and stirred up government officials to move against Baptists. Hostile governments took opportunity to imprison Baptist leaders, disperse congregations, levy fines and other financial penalties, and arrange for Baptists to lose their jobs. In some cases, children were taken by force from their parents and christened in the state church. Baptists in Europe emerged in areas that had little acquaintance with religious liberty and where such liberty was greatly feared.

By the late nineteenth century, secular governments emerged as a major opponent of Baptists, often at the behest of established churches. While some governments seemed willing to tolerate Baptists, allowing them to register as a recognized religion, others determined to stamp them out entirely. Such governments exercised authority to close meetings, imprison leaders, forbid Baptists to own church buildings, and control printing and distribution of literature.

Even after most European governments adopted official policies of religious toleration, some restrictions upon Baptists remained. In some areas Baptists have been allowed to register with their government as "approved" churches and have been permitted to carry on their church life with minimal government restrictions. In other places, particularly in Eastern Europe, Baptists were long denied access to the approved list, and some have not made it yet. The Revolution of 1848 eased religious restrictions somewhat in Western Europe. The Communist Revolution of 1917, whose impact reached far beyond Russia, at first brought a remarkable increase in religious freedom. Not until about 1929 did the Communist lands launch the intense persecution of Christianity which has left such an impact upon the twentieth century.

Many of the state churches in Europe have been disestablished; some have found themselves in the same boat with free churches, both seeking survival in the face of hostile governments and growing secularism. However, even in disestablishment many of the state churches, by virtue of endowments and accumulated prestige, have found ways to continue to cast stumbling blocks in the Baptists' path.

In some cases persecution probably helped spread the Baptist witness by calling attention to the group, scattering their pastors and people, and creating public sentiment for a suffering people. Dean Kirkwood said, "In a sense, imprisonment was the government's unintentional 'authentication' of the Baptist believers' depth of conviction and courage. Instead of stamping out the movement, unjust punishment spread it."[4] While that was true in many local cases, the overall impact of persecution no doubt severely limited Baptist growth. In Russia, for example, Baptists by 1940 numbered only a fraction what they had around the turn of the century.

In addition to such outward influence upon growth rates, sustained opposition over many generations has had a more subtle inner impact. The history of Christianity worldwide offers abundant examples of the power of persecution to introduce abberations, to distort theological priorities, and affect both self-image and public image of the persecuted group. Even in those parts of Europe where Baptists are no longer persecuted, they continue to bear emotional and spiritual scars of their long ordeal. Perhaps outsiders who wonder that Continental Baptists are not more aggressive in proclaiming their faith do not realize what a victory it appears to some Baptists just to exist.

Relation to Baptists in Britain and America

The records reveal extensive contacts between European Baptists and fellow believers in Britain and America. This relationship is illustrated in the life of Johann Gerhard Oncken, who first met evangelical Christianity in Scotland, was converted in London, was later baptized by an American, and throughout his long ministry was sponsored by various societies in Scotland, England, and the United States. Though the Baptist Missionary Society worked mostly in Asia, it also launched a witness to Europe and encouraged other societies in England to do the same. From the 1830s a witness in Europe formed a major section of the missionary work of American Baptists. After the schism of 1845, the new Southern Baptist Conven-

---

4. Dean R. Kirkwood, *European Baptists: A Magnificent Minority,* p. 33.

tion launched mission work in Italy, but SBC European involvement during the nineteenth century never approached the level of their Northern Baptist counterparts.

Despite the many societies in Britain and America dedicated to planting the Baptist witness on the Continent, for the most part they have not appointed "missionaries" in the traditional sense. While they have sent some ministers to Europe, they have preferred to assist Europeans to carry out their own Baptist witness. An American professor, Irah Chase, wrote in 1833 that "the sum necessary to support for one year a missionary sent from America would, if duly managed, educate a native French preacher."[5] While never formally adopted, this "Chase Philosophy" has largely guided the European mission involvement of Britain and America ever since.

The Role of Laymen

At a 1984 convocation on the laity, Gerhard Claas, executive secretary of the Baptist World Alliance, was reported as saying, "Eighty percent of [Baptist] ministers in eastern Europe are lay ministers."[6] While the percentage is not so high in Western Europe, this is no new trend. European Baptists have from the first depended upon the help of unordained leaders.

The great fire of Hamburg, Germany, in 1842 provides an example of the role of laymen and workers in the spread of Baptist witness. After fire destroyed much of the city, workers flocked to Hamburg from other cities and countries to take up the job of rebuilding. Johann Gerhard Oncken, who had formed a church there in 1834, evangelized among those workers with considerable success. When the jobs were completed, many of the workers carried their newfound Baptist faith back home and established churches there. Some of the most effective early missionaries in Europe would be considered laymen by today's standards. Many of them found ways to witness in connection with their daily work.

Not only men but also women helped to carry the Baptist message in Europe. From the earliest times, many Baptist communities established "deaconess houses," where Baptist women devoted their lives to witness and ministry, largely among the sick and needy. In time, their work expanded to include orphanages, schools, hospitals, and welfare centers, in addition to home visitation.

European Baptists and Social Status

"Not many mighty, not many noble" find their way into the Christian faith, observed Paul of Tarsus in the first century (1 Cor. 1:26). That has largely been true of Baptists, who the world over have drawn their converts

---

5. Ibid., p. 92.
6. Jack U. Harwell, "New Orleans Convocation on Laity," *Baptist Message* (January 5, 1984).

mostly from the common folk. One observer noted, "From the beginning of the Baptist movement in Europe, the response came predominantly from the peasant and lower classes, with some individual exceptions."[7] This trend has continued, though modified somewhat in the twentieth century.

The tendency to recruit largely from one social category has had an impact upon Baptists. Though people have sponsored a number of schools, a suspicion of education lingers in some places. Baptists in Europe have not generally had access to large funds, which has hampered them in providing buildings, sponsoring schools, and financing the work of a full denominational program. Difficulties in appealing to status-conscious youth and retaining in Baptist affiliation those members who have attained greater worldly success have at times been a problem among Baptists.

Baptist Trailblazers in Europe

Three men played outstanding roles in planting the Baptist witness in Europe. This triumvirate consisted of Johann Gerhard Oncken (1800-1884), Julius Wilhelm Köbner (1806-1884), and Gottfried Wilhelm Lehmann (1799-1882). Known as the *Kleeblatt* (cloverleaf) of early Baptist witness, these men preached, won converts, and established Baptist churches not only in Germany but also throughout the German-speaking areas of both Western and Eastern Europe. Other pioneer leaders, such as Frederick O. Nilsson in Sweden and Vasili G. Pavlov in Russia, also deserve to be ranked among the pioneer trailblazers of the Baptist on the Continent.

Johann Gerhard Oncken

Without doubt, the greatest pioneer of the Baptist faith in Europe was J. G. Oncken. He stands head and shoulders above all others; some have suggested that Oncken's life and ministry could form the framework for the history of Baptists in Europe.[8] Known as the "Father of Continental Baptists," Oncken served as a one-man mission society, theological seminary, and literature distribution center. Seldom has one person contributed so much to the development of a denomination, nor left his stamp more indelibly upon it. Not only in Germany but also throughout Europe much of the Baptist work stems either directly from Oncken or from others whom he trained and sent out. He served in an almost apostolic role, making extensive missionary tours of his own, writing letters to win new converts and confirm others in the faith, and sending out missionaries and ministers to sustain the work thus begun.

Barnas Sears, an American Baptist, said of Oncken, "He is a German, a little more than thirty years of age, married in England, has two children, is perfectly master of the English language, . . . and though not a man of

7. Kirkwood, p. 8.
8. Parker, p. 53.

liberal education, has a very strong, acute mind, has read much, is a man of much practical knowledge, and is very winning in his personal appearance and manners."[9] These abilities made Oncken a remarkably effective minister and church planter.

Early life and conversion. Oncken was born at Varel (Oldenburg) in 1800. After his father's exile for political reasons, young Oncken was apprenticed to a Scottish merchant and worked for several years in Edinburgh. In Scotland he came in contact with evangelical Christianity, influenced particularly by the Haldane movement. Oncken experienced personal conversion in London and at once became zealous in sharing his evangelical faith with others. Distribution of tracts and personal witnessing were Oncken's major methods, though he also preached. Many times he ate only a penny roll for a meal in order to use his limited funds to purchase more tracts.

By 1823 Oncken was back in Germany, appointed by the Continental Society, a British group that majored in distribution of Bibles and other Christian literature. In 1828 he was appointed by the Edinburgh Bible Society and for the next half century made the sharing of Scripture and gospel tracts a major part of his ministry. He reported in 1879 that by then he had given out no less than two million Bibles in Europe.[10]

Conversion to Baptist views. Though Oncken became a Christian in London, there is no evidence of direct contact or influence from English Baptists. He apparently came to Baptist convictions gradually over a number of years, primarily from personal study of the Bible. By 1826 he confessed that he had doubts about infant baptism and refused to present his own infant for that ceremony. Oncken's continuing Bible study firmed those doubts into convictions and he sought to be immersed but had no one to perform that rite for him. After returning to Germany, he corresponded with James Haldane of Edinburgh, who advised him to baptize himself, as John Smyth had done in Holland two centuries earlier. However, Oncken recoiled at that suggestion, considering it quite disorderly. He preferred to wait for a "Philip" who would come to baptize him in his new faith.

During his years of waiting, Oncken shared his story with a sea captain, Calvin Tubbs, who later reported the incident to the American Baptist Triennial Convention. An American professor, Barnas Sears, went to Germany on sabbatical in 1833 and made a point to contact Oncken. After careful inquiries into the faith of seven persons, including Oncken and his wife, Sears baptized them in the Elbe on April 22, 1834. The next day he formed them into a church which called Oncken as pastor. While not the first formed, this is the oldest surviving Baptist church in Europe. It grew rapidly, with sixty-eight members by 1836, before persecution broke out the

9. *Proceedings,* Baptist General Convention, 1835, p. 26.
10. Rushbrooke, p. 21.

next year. From this little group grew a vast network of Baptist witness throughout the Continent.

Missionary extension. In 1842 Hamburg suffered a devastating fire that destroyed much of the city. The helpful spirit shown by the Baptists to the homeless gained the respect of officials and brought at least a temporary halt in persecution, which allowed the church to witness in relative peace. Growth was rapid, both among Hamburg residents and the countless workers who migrated there to work in the rebuilding. Baptisms reached 273 by 1843 and totaled over 300 for each of the next two years.[11] The Hamburg church opened its own chapel in 1847.

Oncken adopted the motto *"Jeder Baptist ein Missionar"* (every Baptist a missionary), and he put that motto to practice in his own life. The details of his travel are incredible. He crisscrossed Germany many times and also conducted preaching tours in Switzerland, France, Prussia, the Balkans, Hungary, and Russia, plus making extensive tours of Britain and the United States. A man of vast energy, Oncken also had a gift for organization. He left a string of newly formed Baptist churches wherever he traveled and enlisted and trained workers to serve them.

Oncken faced considerable persecution and was himself imprisoned a number of times. The early immersions in Germany had been conducted at night or in private, but in 1837 Oncken first baptized openly. That boldness provoked opposition which did not subside until the crisis of the great fire. The police chief of Hamburg once told Oncken, "As long as I can lift this little finger, you will feel the force of it." Oncken replied, "I see a greater arm, and that is the arm of God. So long as that arm moves, you will never silence me."[12] However, changes in the constitution in 1848 and 1850 assured German citizens a measure of religious freedom. As a result, the churches could emerge from hiding, and the gospel could be preached openly. With new freedom, the German Baptist movement figuratively exploded throughout much of Europe, often because of German immigrants living in various countries.

From the first Oncken believed in the power of the printed word to spread the gospel, and for much of his life he was a colporteur. In 1848 he helped to found the first regularly published Baptist paper in Europe, *Das Missionblatt*. Oncken also helped form the seminary in Hamburg. Students gathered around Oncken from the first, but not until about 1849 were anything like organized classes held. In 1880 a permanent seminary was established, offering a four-year course in theological studies.

The Oncken stamp. Oncken's influence was like a pebble dropped into a pond, with ever-widening ripples extending in every direction. His importance for early Baptists cannot be overemphasized. His spirit and zeal

11. Ibid., p. 31.
12. William L. Wagner, *Growth Patterns of Baptists in Europe,* p. 8.

proved contagious. In theology Oncken was fairly conservative, with a decided preference for Calvinistic emphases, and he injected that viewpoint into early Baptist confessions in Europe. His methods of preaching, distributing Bibles and literature, and personal witness were also followed by others. While favoring theological education and helping to sponsor the Hamburg seminary, Oncken always put priority upon spiritual gifts and preparation, rather than academic. His work and witness truly made Germany the center of European Baptist witness.

Julius Wilhelm Köbner

A worthy colleague to Oncken was J. W. Köbner, known as a "songful theologian" for his hymns. The son of a Danish rabbi, Köbner became a Christian in 1826. He was won to the Baptist faith and baptized by Oncken in Hamburg in 1836. Köbner traveled with Oncken, as well as making several missionary journeys of his own. He also helped establish the theological seminary in Hamburg and played a major role in planting the Baptist witness not only in his native Denmark but throughout the Scandinavian area.

Gottfried Wilhelm Lehmann

Another of Oncken's most able associates was G. W. Lehmann, born in Hamburg but reared in Berlin. After his father's business failure in Berlin, young Lehmann lived with an uncle in the Netherlands, where he came under the influence of Mennonites. As an adult he returned to Berlin, working as a copper engraver. Disillusioned with the state church, Lehmann gathered a small group in his home for Bible study and devotions. His interest in Bible distribution brought him into contact with Oncken of Hamburg, and the two men formed a close friendship before either became Baptists.

Oncken's immersion in 1834 brought tensions to this friendship, for Lehmann had no such intentions. However, he invited Oncken to Berlin to share with a group of spiritual seekers his concept of baptism and church order. Oncken made his usual dynamic impact, and the result was that most of the group accepted Baptist views. On May 13, 1836, Lehmann and his wife, along with four others, were baptized by Oncken in Rummelsburg Lake, just outside Berlin. The next day they were formed into a Baptist church with Lehmann as pastor.

The Berlin church grew rapidly under Lehmann's creative leadership, providing another major center of Baptist life along with Hamburg. However, like Oncken and Köbner, Lehmann traveled widely throughout Europe winning converts, forming churches, and gathering into the Baptist fold churches already formed on the basis of believer's baptism. Joseph Lehmann, son of G. W., also became a Baptist leader. He helped stabilize the seminary in Hamburg and prepared some of the study materials for students there. The elder Lehmann was intensely missionary. In light of the challenge of evangelizing Europe, Oncken for awhile urged the German Baptist Union to allot all its resources to missions in Europe. Lehmann disagreed. He said, "So long as I have two pfennings, I will give one to our mission and one to the heathen."[13]

Baptist Beginnings: A Geographical Survey

Though far from complete, this section will trace the emergence of Baptists in different parts of Europe. Of course Europe has changed radically since the 1830s when Baptists first appeared, with territories divided, national lines drawn and redrawn, and in many cases new names assigned to the resulting nations. No attempt is made here to follow in detail this complex political story, and for the most part the more recent territorial names are used.

Baptists emerged in Europe in areas long dominated by strong state churches, areas that had little or no heritage of religious liberty. During the Reformation the Free Church groups were largely stamped out on the Continent, a fact with far-reaching significance not only for the later history of Baptists but also for retarding the development of democracy there. Economic and political turmoil marked the generation from 1830 to 1860 in much of Europe, and in that revolutionary environment Baptists got their first toehold.

Central Europe

Baptists first emerged and made the greatest progress in the central part of Europe. A few churches originated elsewhere at an earlier date, but Germany itself provided the major center of Baptist expansion. The unsettled social conditions of the time triggered massive migrations of people, which scattered German-speaking populations into most of the other European nations. Among people of that dispersion, the Baptist message found its earliest acceptance.

Germany. Some highlights of Baptist beginnings in Germany have been sketched in connection with the life of J. G. Oncken. By 1850 the church in Hamburg supported three missionaries, raised annually a considerable sum for local poor relief, contributed to various Bible and missionary societies, and when Oncken was present conducted classes for young ministers. Though their own meetings were held in a converted warehouse, the Hamburg church helped raise funds to build more than twenty Baptist buildings in Europe.

In 1835 Oncken was appointed as a missionary of the Triennial Convention in the USA. In his first annual report, Oncken took note of "the formation of an apostolic church in this city" (Hamburg) and said that

13. Ibid., p. 33.

laymen regularly visited house to house, distributing tracts and Bibles, "accompanied with suitable exhortations."[14] He also reported his own missionary journeys in Germany and beyond. Oncken made it a point to visit ships, always distributing tracts and Bibles, hoping to scatter the gospel to many places. As part of his ministry, Oncken visited the Mennonites and other evangelical Christians, leading some of them into the Baptist way. This earned him the nickname of *Sammler,* or collector of existing Christians.

From the first, Baptists in Europe felt a need to organize for fellowship and also for more efficient witness. In 1848 Lehmann called for messengers from Prussian churches to meet in Berlin, where they formed an association. As one of its earliest actions, the association established a fund for mission work. The members' first decision was that two-thirds of the fund should be devoted to "home" missions in Germany, while one-third should be devoted to "foreign" mission work through the Triennial Convention in America. Their second decision was to appoint Wilheim Weist as the first traveling home missionary to represent an association in Europe.

Desiring a wider fellowship, fifty-six representatives met in Hamburg in 1849 where they organized the Union of Associated Churches of Baptized Christians in Germany and Denmark. This was the first attempt at a more general organization of Baptists in Europe. The new body was modeled after the Triennial Convention in America and adopted similar methods of work. Purposes of the new structure included preparation of a confession of faith, encouraging fellowship, promoting missionary work, and gathering statistical data on the churches. Most of the early meetings were held in Hamburg; in fact, many came to regard this as a Hamburg society. A report in 1886 said:

> The meeting of our churches [was] held in Berlin. . . . Never before have our churches convened anywhere else for their triennial gatherings than at Hamburg. Some were therefore beginning to look upon Hamburg as a Baptistic Jerusalem, or a Mohammedan Mecca, to which Baptists must make a pilgrimage from time to time. A meeting outside of Hamburg was beginning to be felt to be a necessary thing.[15]

Several factors account for the prominence of the Hamburg church. It developed quite early and, from the first, showed an aggressive missionary spirit. However, the main reason was no doubt the presence of Oncken, who overshadowed other Baptist leaders during his lifetime. Oncken's missionary methods, his conservative theology, and his views on local church life and theological education tended to prevail. No wonder Hamburg became the center of European Baptist life. The evidence suggests that Oncken at

14. *Annual Report,* American Baptist Board of Foreign Missions, 1836, p. 15.
15. Kirkwood, pp. 99-100.

times found it difficult to share leadership with colleagues and had only limited patience with those who did not see things as he did.

In addition to receiving tracts from England and the United States, Oncken established a printing business in Germany, which he later gave to the Baptist Union. In 1878 Philip Bickel, who had aided the beginnings of German Baptist work in the United States, returned to Germany to take over the publishing ministry that Oncken had launched. Bickel, and later his son Karl, turned the *Oncken Verlag* into a major aspect of Baptist witness in Europe. From this source came materials for Bible study, missionary enlistment, devotional inspiration, and doctrinal instruction. It also provided a source of inner cohesion for the scattered churches, since most were using the same materials.

Oncken apparently had mixed feelings about ministerial education. As early as 1849, the new German Baptist Union laid plans for a seminary, and from that time Oncken held classes in Hamburg whenever he could. Yet he feared "priestcraft" and opposed any tendency to set educated preachers apart from lay preachers. He often warned, "A great danger is that the young people who are trained, taught, and blown up are then totally incompetent for the missionary work."[16]

In the 1870s a serious disagreement erupted between Oncken and other Baptist leaders in Germany. This led to the *Hamburg Streit,* or argument. Oncken felt that all the churches should be branches of the Hamburg "mother church," while both Köbner and Lehmann felt the local churches should be independent and relate to the German Union on a voluntary basis. The *Streit* was aggravated by the fact that Oncken had simply removed some deacons he disapproved. These incidents reveal Oncken's increasing autocratic tendencies in his later years.[17]

From early days German Baptists, like fellow Baptists in England and America at that time, recognized a biblical role for women as deaconesses. They established *Haus Bethel* in 1887 to give order and structure to the deaconess ministry. Over the years, many forms of deaconess ministry developed in such areas as nursing, social work, work with orphans, and homes for the aged. Similar ministries grew up also in other European centers.

Switzerland. Oncken, who seems to show up everywhere in Europe, made a preaching tour of Switzerland in 1847. He found a number of "house churches" already in existence practicing believer's baptism. One such group at Hochwart was pronounced by Oncken as an authentic Baptist church. In addition to gathering existing churches into the Baptist fold, Oncken also baptized a number of new converts and distributed Bibles and other literature.

16. Wagner, p. 24.
17. Ibid., p. 18.

Oncken commissioned Friederich Maier, his colporteur assistant in southern Germany, to extend his missionary orbit into Switzerland. By 1849 Maier formed a church in Zurich, which grew rapidly and became the major center of Baptist life in Switzerland. By 1870 the few churches in Switzerland joined the German Baptist Union, which also affiliated churches from other non-German lands.

Early Baptists faced some persecution in Switzerland, but it was of short duration. The constitution of the Swiss Confederation in 1848 provided religious freedom for "recognized Christian confessions," and in 1874 a revised constitution expanded that provision to guarantee complete "freedom of faith and conscience" for all citizens. Oncken wrote of a spiritual awakening in Switzerland, with houses crowded with eager hearers. Such was the popularity of Baptist meetings, Oncken wrote, that "the ale houses are deserted" and missionaries were implored to remain for longer stays. Despite these opportunities, however, Baptist growth in Switzerland remained slow.

Austria. A number of craftsmen and their families left Austria to work in Hamburg after the great fire, and some of them came under the spell of Oncken. Two families, particularly, became active in Baptist witness and upon their return to Austria in 1846 held devotional meetings and distributed gospel tracts. They invited Oncken to visit Vienna in October 1847, where he preached and baptized a number of converts. Oncken visited Vienna twice more in 1848, but his converts had to remain largely underground to escape the wrath of the state church and civil government.

In 1851 the British and Foreign Bible Society appointed Edward Millard to Vienna. He won and baptized a number of converts and held home fellowship meetings for worship and Bible study, but opposition prevented formation of a church until 1869. Millard was forced to leave Austria for a number of years but later returned. Yet another visit by the aging Oncken gave new inspiration to the work, and in 1869 Millard formed a Baptist church with ten members. About ten other Baptists scattered in surrounding country towns often worshiped in the Vienna church.

During the absence of Millard, the Baptists around Vienna could do little other than meet secretly to comfort and edify one another. They often met at the home of Karl Rauch, who had been baptized in Hamburg. Rauch's refusal to have his children sprinkled brought him to the attention of the authorities. On April 20, 1850, police raided his home and arrested the nine men and eight women present and imprisoned them as criminals. The Rauch children were taken forcibly to the state church and christened according to the official Lutheran rites.

Religious liberty did not come to Austria until early in the twentieth century; despite these hardships, the faith gradually spread from Vienna to other Austrian centers. By 1900 the Vienna church had 224 members, and sustained 6 additional preaching stations in the area. W. S. Oncken, son of the great pioneer, ministered effectively for a number of years in Austria.

Netherlands. The earliest Baptist church of modern history originated in Amsterdam about 1609. However, after the Helwys portion of that church returned to England in 1611 and the Smyth group later merged with the Mennonites, the Baptist witness disappeared from Holland, not to reappear for over two centuries.

In the 1840s J. E. Feisser, minister of the Dutch Reformed Church, experienced a traumatic conversion which led him to emphasize the importance of Bible study and personal relation to God. Feisser's own study led him to question the validity of infant baptism. His refusal to christen infants led, understandably, to his removal as a Dutch Reformed minister in 1843. Feisser's writings on baptism attracted the attention of German Baptists, and Oncken sent Köbner to meet with the Dutch pastor. Feisser, as it turned out, had never heard of Baptists, but his continued contacts with Köbner led him to accept the Baptist position. He and six others were immersed by Köbner on May 15, 1845, and formed into a church with Feisser as pastor. This church later moved from Gasselte-Nijveen to Stadskanaal, where a modest chapel was erected. Over the years it established a number of preaching points, many of which eventually became churches.

The second Baptist church in Holland was formed in the small town of Zutphen, in the province of Gelderland, later in 1845. This church grew from the leadership of Mennonite minister Jan de Liefde. Contacts with Feisser and Köbner almost persuaded Liefde to become a Baptist, but his millennialist views made him hesitant to affiliate with Baptists. However, during Liefde's absence, most of his followers requested and received immersion and formed a church in 1845. Upon his return Liefde refused to join the church and later left the area. The church soon expired.

A third church grew up in Amsterdam. From about 1840 a small group had met for prayer and Bible study in the Dutch capital, and the subject of baptism had come up. By 1845 most of them had concluded for believer's baptism. Hearing of this group, Köbner and Feisser visited Amsterdam in 1845 and baptized four members who accepted the Baptist way. Two years later they had sufficient strength to form a church in Amsterdam. In 1849 Jan de Liefde, who had held aloof from the church in Zutphen, joined the infant church in Amsterdam. This brought a spirit of controversy and division since Liefde attempted to introduce the radical millennial views which John Nelson Darby had recently developed in England. Eventually the church received government sanction to exist and, after a reorganization in 1866 to exclude Darbyism, counted that year as its official beginning.

In 1881 H. Z. Kloekers led in forming a Baptist union which affiliated the several scattered churches in the Netherlands. At first the churches at Franeker and Amsterdam, which were strictly Calvinistic, held aloof from the union because of its Arminian tendencies introduced by Kloekers, the first president. However, a few years later, the Amsterdam church did affiliate. As one of its first projects, the Dutch Union founded *De Christen,* a Baptist paper which is still published under the same name.

For years the Dutch churches were troubled by various controversies, the most serious of which involved Calvinism versus Arminian theology, Darbyite millennial views, some inroads of Socinianism, and tinges of early Pentecostalism of the Irvingite variety. By the turn of the century, Dutch Baptists numbered about one thousand.[18]

Northern Europe

In the Scandinavian countries of Denmark, Sweden, Norway, and Finland, an evangelical awakening gained headway during the 1830s. With emphases similar to the Pietism which blanketed much of the rest of Europe, these northern areas were prepared for the emergence of different forms of evangelical churches, including Baptists.

Denmark. In the late 1830s Julius Köbner, a Danish convert and colleague of Oncken, returned to Denmark to establish contact with several home Bible study groups of whom he had heard reports. After this extended visit, Köbner and Oncken returned to Copenhagen where they baptized eleven converts, including Peder C. Mønster. This little group formed a Baptist church in 1839, the first in Denmark or in any part of Scandinavia.

The Danish Baptists met immediate and severe opposition, Mønster was jailed for several weeks and then ordered out of the country. Oncken wrote, "Our brethren [in Denmark] will be charged with being Anabaptists, and the antiquated laws against that deluded sect will be brought forth against them."[19] His prediction proved only too accurate; and despite persecution, the Baptist witness grew, with preaching points established at several areas around Copenhagen, some of which eventually grew into churches.

Constitutional changes in 1849, while still affirming Lutheranism as the state church, provided some religious toleration for non-Lutherans. This led to two categories of Danish churches, those "recognized" by the government and those only "tolerated." The former could own property, conduct weddings for their members, and maintain their own records. The "tolerated" groups, which included Baptists, could do none of those things. Not until 1952 did Danish Baptists finally gain the more favored status of being "recognized" by the government.[20]

Despite restrictions, the Baptist faith made progress in Denmark. In 1900 Baptists reported 28 churches, with 19 pastors, 278 baptisms for the previ-

18. Parker, p. 85.
19. *Proceedings,* American Board of Foreign Missions, 1841, p. 55.
20. Parker, p. 93.

ous year, and a total membership of 3,906.[21]

Internal problems plagued the Danish churches. By 1850 Mormon influence had seeped into the Copenhagen church, causing several to forsake their Baptist views, apparently including Mønster. When Köbner moved to Copenhagen to become pastor in 1865, little was left of this original Danish church, but it began a period of renewed vitality under his leadership. His successor, Marius Larsen, proved the ablest Danish preacher of the period; and under his ministry the work expanded. Aid from the American Baptists allowed a number of young Danes to study at the Danish-Norwegian department of the seminary at Morgan Park, Illinois. Their return gave the work a boost; over 3,500 baptisms were recorded from 1833 to 1899.[22]

Norway. A group of earnest Christians involved in group Bible study in Norway became convinced of believer's baptism before they had heard of Baptists. A Lutheran pastor, G. A. Lammers, came to such a conviction and in 1856 he and several others formed an "Apostolic Free Church." In time a number of such "Lammers" churches sprang up, but they split over Lammers's teaching that while new converts were to be immersed upon their profession of faith, those baptized in infancy need not be baptized again.

Into this environment came Fredrick L. Rymker, a Norwegian converted in America and returned to witness in his own country. Rymker gathered those with Baptist views, won and baptized numerous converts of his own, and on April 22, 1860, organized the first Baptist church in Norway. Preaching missions by Swedish Baptists helped spread the faith in Norway, as did literature from Sweden. Anders Wiberg's book on baptism was widely circulated in Norway, where it influenced many toward believer's baptism.

Like Baptists everywhere, those in Norway reached out hands of fellowship to others of their faith. Their first association dates from 1872, and five years later they formed a Norwegian Baptist conference affiliating 14 churches. At that time, they reported only 12 ministers and a total of 511 members.[23] Several lay preachers were active in the churches, which met mostly in homes. Lack of trained leadership hampered the work, but by 1900 they reported 32 churches, 16 ministers, and 2,671 members.[24]

Sweden. Baptists progressed in Sweden more rapidly than anywhere else in Scandinavia. From their first church in 1847, they reported in 1900 a total of 564 churches with 40,759 members. One key to this growth was the

21. *Proceedings,* American Baptist Missionary Union (ABMU), 1900, p. 217.
22. Rushbrooke, p. 81.
23. Ibid., pp. 104-105.
24. *Proceedings,* ABMU, 1900, p. 217.

fact they had 749 ministers in 1900 and had reported 1,447 baptisms for 1899.[25]

Educational reforms in Sweden in the early 1800s required all young people to attend school; and under the Pietist awakenings, the people used their new reading skills for personal Bible study. This provided a stimulus for the emergence of Free Church groups, including Baptists.

Frederick Olaus Nilsson (1809-1881) was born in Sweden. As a young man, he went to sea. He jumped ship in New Orleans. In 1835 he was converted and worked for some years distributing tracts and doing personal witnessing in New York City. He returned to Sweden about 1839, appointed by the American Friends Seaman's Society. Further study led him to accept Baptist views and in 1847 he and five others were baptized at Hamburg by Johann Gerhard Oncken. This little group of converts formed a church near Gothenburg in 1847, the first in Sweden.

As in other places, Baptists in Sweden faced severe opposition from authorities of both church and state. By 1850 Nilsson was banished from Sweden. The official document of Nilsson's banishment merits quotation because of its succinct summation of his work and the degree of his success. The official order of April 26, 1850, read:

> The Royal Court has taken into consideration what concerns this question, and for that Frederick Olius Nilsson has freely confessed to having embraced the positions, that child-baptism, not being commanded in holy Scripture, is only a human institution; that baptism, therefore, ought only to be administered to men arrived at full knowledge of Christian doctrine; and then only with immersion of the whole body in water; and also that the holy communion can be received worthily only by persons of this persuasion; and for that Nilsson, having caused himself to be re-baptized at Hamburg, has in a society there founded, been received as an elder and teacher of the Baptists here in this realm; . . . and has caused forty-seven or forty-eight persons to receive his doctrines, and form a separate congregation, to the members whereof, he, in the character of teacher, administers baptism and the holy communion; . . . and having been admonished by the chapter of Gothenborg; yet has persisted in disseminating these his doctrines; . . . because, therefore, Nilsson has made himself guilty of the misdemeanor referred to in the code of offences . . . the Royal Court, in virtue of the said last command, justly condemns Nilsson, for that wherein he has offended, to be banished from the Kingdom.[26]

After being exiled Nilsson went to Copenhagen and later to America where he helped settle Swedish and Norwegian immigrants and established

25. Ibid., p. 217.
26. Cited in Kirkwood, pp. 40-41.

Baptist churches among them. He later returned to Sweden, where he played a leading role in forming the Baptist Union of Sweden in 1857. However, Nilsson found himself increasingly at odds with another Swedish Baptist leader, one of his own converts, Anders Wiberg.

Wiberg had left the Lutheran ministry to adopt believer's baptism and was immersed by Nilsson in 1852. He became pastor of the church in Stockholm in 1854, and that city rapidly became a major center of Baptist work in Sweden. Nilsson and Wiberg held quite different concepts of how Swedish Baptist work should be structured. Nilsson preferred a more democratic and indigenous work. While he had no objections to outside aid, he insisted that the Swedish churches maintain their independence and more than once he declined appointment by the American Baptist Publication Society. Wiberg, on the other hand, both thought and acted like a bishop and set up an extensive network of churches and societies dependent upon American funding. Wiberg's centralized views more nearly prevailed because of his zeal, organizational ability, and his influential writings which helped to mold Swedish Baptists both in Sweden and America. Wiberg, who married an American, spent his last several years in the United States as a pastor and agent for the American Baptist Publication Society. Toward the end of his life, Wiberg drifted away from the Baptist faith.

Bethel Seminary, established in 1866 in Stockholm, was the first regularly organized Baptist seminary on the Continent, though informal classes had been held earlier in Hamburg. This school has, through the years, provided a point of unity and stability for Baptist work in Sweden and beyond. It has been, next to Hamburg perhaps, one of the most influential Baptist schools in Europe.

A denominational structure emerged in Sweden over a period of years, out of various local and regional societies and conferences beginning in 1857. These overlapping organizations led to confusion and competition for mission funds, so they combined all their work into the Swedish Baptist Union in 1889. The union had separate committees for various causes, such as home and foreign missions, but all the work was coordinated through the one union.[27]

In 1861 the Stockholm church drew up a confession of faith, motivated both by an effort to define their doctrines more sharply and also to win more freedom from Swedish authorities who were more inclined to persecute than to tolerate Baptists. The confession bears the stamp of Wiberg, whose conservative views it embodies on Calvinism and closed communion.[28]

Baptist work in Sweden has been divided since the 1890s, when the Orebro Mission split off from the Swedish Baptist Union. Heavily in-

27. Ibid., p. 100.
28. This confession, as translated by Erik Ruden, is printed in Parker, pp. 100-102 and in William L. Lumpkin, ed., *Baptist Confessions of Faith,* pp. 408-410.

fluenced by Pentecostalism, the Orebro Baptists accepted women pastors, followed more vigorous foreign mission work, and in general accepted some of the more dramatic charismatic practices. John Ongman, who had embraced Pentecostal views in America, returned to Sweden to wean away many Baptist churches to his views. Since 1892 when the movement in Orebro began, the two groups of Baptists have been separate, with the Orebro group conducting their own mission work and their own seminary at Orebro.[29]

Finland. Baptists in Finland, like those in neighboring Sweden, also are divided into two separate groups, but for language rather than doctrinal differences. Baptist missionaries from Sweden went to work among the Swedish-speaking Finns. They formed their first church in 1856 and a tiny Baptist union in 1883. Work progressed more slowly among the Finnish-speaking peoples, with a church formed by 1870 and the Finnish Baptist Union organized in 1903.[30]

C. J. Mollersvard, a Swede, preached in Aland by 1854. Two years later the first Baptist church in Finland was formed there but met stern persecution from authorities "in order to prevent proselytism and the speaking of false doctrines." However, waves of awakening had prepared the way for the Baptist witness, and other Finnish churches sprang up at Jacobstad (1870), Vasa (1881), and Helsinki (1885). All of these churches maintained close ties to Stockholm and depended upon their Swedish brethren for help in evangelism, missions, and the supply of pastors. For a time they sponsored their own theological school at Vasa, but later Finnish students went to Bethel Seminary in Stockholm. Partly because they emerged after the most severe persecution had abated, the Baptists in Finland faced less opposition than those in other areas. The "Dissenter Law" of 1889 allowed them a generous degree of freedom.

Baptist work among the Finnish-speaking population dates from the 1870s when Esaias Lundberg preached and baptized at Luvia. At about the same time a Lutheran pastor, John Hymander, renounced infant baptism, received immersion in Stockholm, and returned to Finland to form a Baptist church at Parikkala in 1870. The Finnish Baptists launched a paper in 1896, along with Sunday Schools and mission efforts.

The Finnish Baptists drew up a confession of faith in 1891, partly to help win government recognition as an officially registered religious community and thus become entitled to a broader measure of religious freedom. The confession reveals the influence of Anders Wiberg, who ministered in Stockholm. Marked by conservative theology and evangelistic zeal, the confes-

29. Parker, p. 103.
30. Ibid., pp. 105, 110.

sion proclaims that the Baptist way "makes it possible for every church member to do something for spreading the good news either by means of a financial gift or work."[31]

Lack of preachers and what one observer called "the great emigration to America" hampered Baptist progress in Finland. "This people are begging to hear the Gospel message," the report continued in 1900, "but we are lacking men to carry it to them."[32] Even so, by the turn of the century, Finland reported 31 churches, with 2,030 members, and 244 baptisms in 1899.[33]

Southern Europe

The earliest Baptists on the Continent appeared in Southern Europe, but the work never prospered as it did in Germany and Sweden and thus has attracted less attention. In central and northern Europe, the free churches faced opposition from the Lutheran establishment, but this opposition tended to moderate after mid-century. In Southern Europe, where the Roman Catholic Church held sway, the opposition proved more persistent and more effective.

France. In the village of Nomain near the Belgium border, a French farmer in 1810 found an old Bible in an unused corner of his house and began to read it eagerly. He gathered a little Bible study group, one of many that emerged from the Pietist awakening then sweeping Europe. In late 1819 Henri Pyt, the first Baptist to preach to the Nomain group, spoke to about 140 persons. Pyt was a Swiss evangelist who had been brought to the Baptist faith by contact with Robert Haldane of Edinburgh. He preached in Nomain for over a year, winning many to Baptist convictions. In 1820 Pyt baptized a number of converts secretly for fear of persecution. They formed a small Baptist church, the first in France and probably the first in Europe since the days of John Smyth. However, the church did not long survive.

In 1831 Howard Malcolm, a Baptist pastor from Boston traveling in France, heard of Baptists there. After making contact with remnants of the Pyt group, and sensing great evangelistic opportunity there, he appealed to the Triennial Convention to send aid. The 1832 report of that convention reported:

> Mr. Malcolm presented the claims of France on the Christian Community, and urged the expediency of commencing a mission there. In compliance with the general sentiment of the Board, Rev. Prof. Peck, formerly of Amherst College, and Mr. Rostan, a native of that country [Marseilles], are immediately to engage in an agency for the Board for two years, to investigate *on the*

31. The confession is printed in Parker, pp. 106-109, as translated by Anneli Kothavnori and Antti Marjaren.
32. *Proceedings,* ABMU, 1900, p. 214.
33. Ibid., p.217.

ground, the possibility and propriety of attempting to diffuse among that oppressed people the blessings of an enlightened Christianity.[34]

The "Mr. Rostan" referred to was Casimir Rostan, a brilliant Frenchman who had become a Baptist in America. He began his work in Paris, making great progress among the educated classes until his untimely death in 1834. He brought visibility to the Baptist cause in France, especially among intellectuals. Rostan was succeeded by Isaac Willmarth, an American who had been converted in Paris. After five years, Willmarth was succeeded by Erastus Willard who became an outstanding Baptist leader in France during the next twenty-one years. A church was formed at Douai in 1835, and in the next few years others followed.

In 1849 Willard formed a Baptist association, the first in France, which affiliated a total of fifteen churches. Distance soon dictated a division of this body into the Department of the North (north of Paris), and the Department of the South (south of Paris). A few churches in Belgium and Switzerland were included. In 1879 French Baptists launched their first paper, *L'Echo de la Verite* (*Echo of Truth*), and the next year they formed a theological school, though informal ministerial training had been conducted off and on from the 1830s.[35] The founding of the French Republic in 1871 brought a larger measure of freedom for Baptists. However, they were not able to capitalize upon the opportunity, largely because of doctrinal dissension which decimated the churches by the turn of the century.

Italy. The evangelical awakening came somewhat later to Italy, but by mid-century Bible study groups hungering for personal religion had emerged even in Rome. Baptist work began in Italy by 1863 with the coming of two English Baptist missionaries, James Wall and Edward Clark, who began work at Bologna and La Spezia. An edict of King Carlo Alberto in 1848 had provided limited religious toleration to Protestant groups, a liberty which expanded by the turn of the century. In 1875 the Baptist Missionary Society of England sent an additional worker in the person of W. K. Landels, who opened work in Turin.

The Southern Baptist Convention entered the "papal field," as it called Italy, and in 1873 appointed George B. Taylor who served thirty-four years in that land. American Baptists also showed an interest in this field. The earliest Baptist church in Italy was formed in Rome in 1871, and by the turn of the century a number of others had grown up throughout Italy. However, Baptists were plagued by internal problems, lack of trained ministers, and difficulties arising from Roman Catholic opposition. From the first the Baptists made extensive use of the printed word, distributing tracts printed in England and America and also forming their own periodicals. This

34. Cited in Kirkwood, p. 15.
35. Ibid., p. 109.

included *Il Testimonio* (*The Witness*) and *Il Seminatore* (*The Sower*), both of which included evangelistic appeals and efforts to confirm the faith of believers. A witness to the effectiveness of these periodicals is that the Roman church placed them under a ban.

Spain. The infamous Spanish Inquisition largely wiped out the Reformation in Spain, and Protestant forms of Christianity have found uphill going there ever since. As recently as 1855, a Spanish Protestant was condemned to death on religious grounds; although the sentence was commuted, it indicates the continuing intolerance.[36] Limited toleration was allowed by the turn of the century, but even in the twentieth century Free Churchmen in Spain have faced severe government restrictions upon the practice of their faith.

The Brethren were among the earliest evangelicals to get a toehold in Spain. Rushbrooke calls these "Semi-Baptists."[37] Since their churches practiced believer's baptism, they worked closely with students who later came to Spain from Spurgeon's College. A more official Baptist work began with the arrival of William Knapp in 1868. Knapp, an independent who later cooperated with Northern Baptists, baptized thirty-three persons and formed them into a Baptist church in Madrid in 1870. This was the earliest Baptist church in Spain, but others soon grew up at Alicante, Valencia, Barcelona, and elsewhere. About 1880 Eric Lund, a Swedish Baptist missionary and talented linguist, began work in Spain and over the years conducted an effective literature ministry, especially in the Barcelona area. However, by the end of the century, Baptists in Spain numbered only 115 members, gathered into 10 churches, with 6 ministers.[38]

Portugal. No specific Baptist witness was known in Portugal until 1888, when Joseph Jones began to preach and baptize in Oporto. Jones, an English layman, had been baptized by Charles Spurgeon in London. Other foreigners joined with Jones in sharing their faith; while many individuals received baptism, no Baptist church was formed until after the turn of the century.

Belgium. Baptists from adjoining areas extended their witness into Belgium, and a few churches were founded before the turn of the century. However, the work remained small, and the churches usually were included in the associations or unions of the adjoining countries. The Baptist Union of Belgium dates from the twentieth century and continues to maintain close ties with its neighbors, especially France.

36. Rushbrooke, pp. 189-190.
37. Ibid., p. 190.
38. *Proceedings,* ABMU, 1900, p. 217.

Eastern Europe

The Baptist witness came somewhat later to Eastern Europe and only toward the end of the century did it gain momentum. Lutheranism prevailed as the state church in much of the East and provided the usual obstacles to free church growth. In Russia the Orthodox Church, established by law and allied with the repressive tsarist regime, provided overwhelming opposition to the emerging free churches, but the population was so large and the area so vast that they could not stamp out the new leaven. Though coming a bit later than in the West, a similar Pietist awakening swept over Eastern Europe, leading to similar results and by similar means, namely countless Bible study groups.

Poland. The national boundaries of Poland have undergone frequent revision in the past century, resulting in a population with diverse languages and cultures. However, almost all of these diverse peoples have had one thing in common, their devout allegiance to the Roman Catholic Church. In the popular mind, to cease to be a Catholic was almost to cease to be a Pole, a factor which hampered the advance of Baptists and other free church groups. The earliest Baptist witness emerged among groups which did not speak Polish and was usually brought by people from nations considered hostile to Poland. These factors did not help the progress of Baptist principles.

The earliest Baptist church in Poland was formed in the village of Adamow in 1858, when a teacher, Gottfried Alf, baptized twenty-six converts among German-speaking Poles. For some months Alf had conducted a home Bible study, which had grown out of local Pietist awakenings. On his own he had come near to Baptist convictions but openly accepted that label only after contact with a Baptist pastor from Prussia. Alf met immediate opposition, not only with persecution by officials of church and state but also rejection by his own family.[39] He persevered in the faith despite ten periods of imprisonment.

A second center of Baptist work developed at Kicin (or Kiciny), beginning in 1860 among Mennonites. Gottfried Alf had moved there, and his preaching led a number of Mennonites, including their leader, to accept Baptist views. By 1900 there were reported 4,162 Baptists in Poland, but government opposition and linguistic diversity hampered their growth and prevented any degree of unity.[40]

Hungary. What Joseph Lehmann called Baptists' "feeble beginnings in Hungary" can be traced to two groups, Hungarian carpenters converted in Hamburg in the 1840s and British-sponsored missionaries who came to Hungary in the 1870s. A number of workers from Hungary who helped

39. Parker, p. 171.
40. Kirkwood, p. 66.

rebuild Hamburg after the great fire came under the spell of Oncken and embraced the Baptist faith. Joseph Lehmann later said, "There is a new opening for the gospel at Bucharest, in Hungary. Five converted Hungarians all left the Catholic church together, and were baptized at Hamburg in 1845. They have formed a Tract Society to which eight families have contributed."[41]

Upon returning to their native land, these new converts bore witness to their faith, although quietly for fear of the authorities. Oncken not only won them to faith but also instructed them in beginning Baptist work in their homeland. According to one early account, "They endeavoured to secure a footing by distribution of tracts and Bibles, and by holding meetings, but were obliged to act with utmost prudence in view of the severity of the law."[42] Frederich Oncken, son of the great pioneer, also ministered for a time in Hungary, partially sponsored by mission societies in Hamburg. By 1846 a church of nine members was formed in Budapest, apparently the first in Hungary, but persecution drove it out of existence within a few years. Almost twenty years later G. W. Lehmann, pastor in Berlin, made a preaching tour of Hungary, baptizing several converts in the Danube near midnight to escape persecution. These converts either did not gather an organized church or, if they did, it did not long endure.

A second group of Hungarian Baptists grew out of the work of Heinrich Meyer, a missionary sent by Oncken but also for a time sponsored by a British society. Meyer settled in Budapest where he baptized a number of converts and formed a church in 1874. He also preached at Gyula, where he baptized eight persons, among whom were Mihaly Kornya and Mihaly Toth. Both became fellow workers of Meyer and, though lacking formal education, both had great zeal and good native abilities. They traveled widely, becoming known as the "peasant prophets" of the Hungarian Baptist Mission. Toth helped erect the first Baptist church building in Hungary. Kornya was said to have baptized over eleven thousand persons during his thirty-year ministry in Hungary and part of the area now known as Romania.[43]

During the first twenty years, most of the churches were regarded as outposts of the Budapest congregation, and Meyer was regarded as "pastor of the Baptists in Hungary." Most of the preaching and worship were conducted in German. In 1893 two young preachers, who had completed their studies at the Hamburg seminary, introduced non-German Baptist work in Hungary. While reaching new people, this led to tensions with the Meyer group and unfortunately divided the churches for a few years. During his first ten years in Hungary, Meyer had baptized over six hundred

41. Ibid., p. 61.
42. Joseph Lehmann, *History of the German Baptists,* as cited in Rushbrooke, p. 149.
43. Rushbrooke, p. 153.

persons, and by 1893 the Baptist membership in Hungary had reached about thirty-two hundred.[44]

Czechoslovakia and Yugoslavia. These modern nations were formed after World War I, patching together a mosaic of diverse ethnic and language groups and combining several earlier territorial divisions. Baptist missionaries and colporteurs had preached in these areas by the 1860s, but organized churches emerged a few years later.

In the 1860s a German Baptist, A. Knappe, preached in Bohemia, which is now part of Czechoslovakia. As in so much of Europe, the Baptist witness first took root among the German-speaking population. Knappe baptized a few converts but formed no church. A missionary of the British Bible Society, A. Meereis, also preached in Bohemia, baptizing converts and laying foundations for the later growth of Baptists. Perhaps the most effective Baptist pioneer in early Czechoslovakia was Henry Novotny, who was influenced toward the Baptist way by Meereis. Novotny was baptized in Poland and upon returning to Czechoslovakia formed a Baptist church with sixteen members near Prague in 1885. Baptist work flourished in that area, and the Novotny family played a leading role in Baptist life for several generations.

Historians have identified three sources of Baptist churches in modern Yugoslavia.[45] First, many were converted abroad and brought their new faith back when they returned to Yugoslavia. An early example was Franz Tabory of Novi Sad who, with his wife, was baptized in Bucharest in 1862. Second, missionaries sent by Bible societies in England and Germany helped plant the Baptist faith. For example, Oncken sent August Liebig to Yugoslavia in 1863, and a decade later Heinrich Meyer expanded his work in Hungary to include Novi Sad where he baptized several converts. Adolf Hempt was converted there in 1875 and later served as a missionary for the British and Foreign Bible Society, traveling widely in Bosnia and Serbia. A strong Baptist work grew up among the Slovak population, led primarily by laymen. By 1900 the Slovaks made up about 30 percent of the total Baptist population of Yugoslavia. A third source of Baptist life stemmed from the work of Vinko Vacek, a Croatian, who was for a time supported by the Southern Baptist Convention. He was able to unite the five major language groups to form a Baptist Union of Yugoslavia in 1920.

Romania. The first known Baptist to enter what is now called Romania was Karl Scharschmidt, who had been baptized by Oncken in Hamburg in 1845. A carpenter by trade, Scharschmidt came to Romania in 1856 after several years of witness in Hungary. Within a few years, he baptized enough converts to form a church among the German-speaking population of Bu-

44. Ibid., p. 152.
45. Parker, p. 202.

charest, the first Baptist church in Romania. In 1863 Oncken sent August Leibig as pastor, and Oncken himself visited the church in 1869.

Evangelical immigrants who came down from southern Russia into Romania provided another source of Baptist witness. By 1862 several had adopted Baptist views and formed a church aided by Liebig. One of the most able of the Romanian Baptist leaders was Constantin Adorian, who had studied in the Hamburg seminary and later returned to minister in Bucharest. Baptist growth in Transylvania proved quite rapid also, stemming largely from the work of Antal Noval who served as a colporteur for the British and Foreign Bible Society.

These pioneers laid a strong foundation for later Baptist growth. The impact of the Pietist awakenings, the immigration of Baptists from surrounding areas, and the effective leadership of Baptist pioneers laid the foundation for the remarkable expansion of Baptist witness in Romania in the twentieth century.

Bulgaria. Baptists first appeared in Bulgaria in the 1860s. Some of them, like Vasili Pavolvo, were religious refugees fleeing persecution in Russia. Some Bulgarian workers who traveled abroad returned with Baptist views, and several Bible societies also turned their attentions to that land. As elsewhere in Europe, home Bible study groups prepared the way for the witness of Baptists and other evangelicals. German Baptists in the United States sent P. E. Petrick to Bulgaria as their missionary.[46] Despite these forerunners, the earliest Baptist church in Bulgaria did not arise until 1880 in Ruse. Another church in the capital city of Sofia opened in 1897, and Bulgarians also formed the first known Gypsy Baptist church.

Russia. Under cover of darkness on August 20, 1867, Martin Kalweit, a German Baptist, immersed Nikita Voronin in a creek near the Kura River in the Caucasus of southern Russia.[47] Voronin, a Russian merchant, had come to Baptist convictions some time earlier but could find no one willing to take the risk of baptizing him. This was the first known Baptist immersion in tsarist Russia. However, within a short time, Baptists appeared at other locations, in central Russia around Kiev and far to the north in the capital city of Saint Petersburg. From these small beginnings, Baptists grew rapidly and, by the twentieth century, ranked as the third largest Baptist community in the world. They have attracted world attention for their extensive persecution both under the tsars and under Communism.

At least four factors, all interconnected, helped prepare the way for Baptists in Russia. These include the Pietist movement, the Russian Bible Society, the Molokan sect, and the Stundist movement. In Russia, as in other parts of Europe, the Pietist movement of the early nineteenth century brought a hunger for more personal religion. Home Bible study groups

46. Ibid., p. 231.
47. Walter Sawatsky, *Soviet Evangelicals Since World War II,* p. 27.

sprang up, and the Russian Orthodox Church gave the people adequate grounds for spiritual dissatisfaction. "Generally speaking, the Russian Orthodox Church was in a sorry condition by the middle of the nineteenth century," said one historian, who also spoke of the "cold confessionalism" of that church.[48] The Orthodox Church was allied closely with the tsarist regime and was a full partner in the oppression and exploitation which marked that era. The Pietist groups fostered belief in the authority of the Bible, the reality of personal conversion, and a sense of devotional nearness to God. This provided an important seedbed for later conversions to the Baptist way.

The British and Foreign Bible Society formed a branch in Russia and by 1819 issued portions of Scripture in Russian to meet a remarkable hunger for Bibles evident in that land to this day. By 1826 the Bible society was forced to close and not until late in the century did the complete Bible appear in Russian. However, those early portions of Scripture helped prepare the way for Baptist advance.

The Molokan sect, concentrated mostly in the Caucasus, formed an important seedbed for later Baptist growth. The Molokans, or "milk-drinkers," separated from the Orthodox Church in the eighteenth century and held largely evangelical views. They were a reform group who sought to recover the practices of the early church.[49] They preached equality of all people, rejected militarism, and many of them held apocalyptic millennial views. They differed from Baptists primarily in that they rejected water baptism, preferring a "spiritual" baptism much like the earlier English Quakers. By 1900 there were probably about two hundred thousand Molokans in Russia.[50]

After the 1860s, Baptists persuaded many of the Molokans to accept baptism. Such leaders as Nikita Voronin, Vasili Pavlov, Ivan Prokhanov, Jacob Zhidhov, and Alexander Karev all came into Baptist life from the Molokans.[51] The Russian historian A. I. Klibanov spoke of the "Baptization of the Molokans" and observed that by 1900 "almost half of today's Baptists consisted of yesterday's Molokans." He also described the Molokans as "the soil for the success of Baptist teaching" in Russia.[52] However, many of the baptized Molokans brought with them a nondenominational orientation, which created tensions with the more strict Baptists.

The Stundist movement provided yet another preparation for the emergence of Baptists in Russia. Concentrated primarily in the Ukraine, the

48. Ibid., pp. 30-31.
49. A. I. Klibanov, *History of Religious Sectarianism in Russia, 1860s-1917,* Ethel Dunn, trans. (Elmsford, New York: Pergamon Press, 1982), pp. 153 *f.*
50. Ibid., p. 222.
51. Sawatsky, p. 32.
52. Klibanov, pp. 224-225.

Stundists were greatly influenced by German Mennonites who desired a more personal religious life than that afforded in the state church. They were named after the German word for *hour (Stunde)* because of their practice of holding weekly meetings of about an hour for Bible study and testimony. While "practicing their hours," as their meetings were described, many of the Stundists came to Baptist views. Later the ideas of Oncken of Germany made headway among them, reinforced by a personal visit of Oncken. The Orthodox Church found the Stundists such a threat that they formed a specific society to try to stamp them out.[53]

Influenced by these factors, Baptists emerged almost simultaneously in different parts of Russia in the late 1860s. Historians have identified at least three main streams of Baptist life in Russia. Baptists appeared first in the Caucasus, in southern Russia, in the baptism of Voronin as noted. Drawing primarily from the Molokan movement, these Caucasus Baptists founded an influential church at Tiflis. The church sent Vasili Pavlov to study with Oncken at Hamburg, and upon his return, he evangelized widely and introduced the Oncken confession into Russia. Pavlov and the Tiflis church thus represented the more specifically Baptist wing of the south Russia movement.[54] Another wing of the Caucasus movement was led by Ivan Prokhanov, who was less committed to strictly Baptist views. In time this wing became known as the Evangelical Brethren but maintained outward union with Baptists.

A second center of Baptist life emerged in the Ukraine, around Kiev, drawing converts largely from the Stundist movement. One leader was Peter Lysenko, who had adopted Baptist views earlier but was not baptized until 1875. He made a practice of walking through the streets of his village shouting, "Repent and turn to the gospel."[55] Abraham Unger, who came from a Mennonite background, baptized the first Stundist, Efim Tsymbal, in 1869. From that time Baptist growth accelerated among the Stundists.

A third stream of Russian Baptists centered in the capital city of Saint Petersburg, led at first by an English nobleman, G. A. W. Waldgrave (better known as Lord Radstock), who came from a Plymouth Brethren background. Because they represented an upper-class elite, though with Pietist views, Radstock's early followers are often called "drawing room Stundists."[56] In 1874 Lord Radstock began preaching in Saint Petersburg and soon a group of prominent Russians gathered around him, holding worship in homes of the wealthy. Among the Englishman's most important converts were Baron M. M. Korf and Colonel Vasili Pashkov. Pashkov became such a zealous and effective leader that the movement soon took the name of

53. Sawatsky, p. 35.
54. Parker, p. 150.
55. Sawatsky, p. 34.
56. Parker, p. 150.

"Pashkovism."[57] From the first the Pashkovites took a nondenominational stance, drawing from the background of English Plymouthism. Pashkov was a leader in the effort to form a Baptist union in the 1880s to include all the baptizing groups in Russia.

From the first, the Russian Baptists included believers of many shades of doctrine and church practice. Some were specifically Baptist in the Oncken tradition and were, in fact, directly influenced by Oncken. Others practiced immersion but held more nondenominational views from the Molokan heritage or from the Plymouthism of the Saint Petersburg group. These also tended to hold rather vivid millennial views, not shared by the more strictly Baptist members. To this mix was added the significant Mennonite leaven of the Stundists and, in the twentieth century, Baptists absorbed a large influx of Pentecostals. The result has been that Russian Baptists reflect considerable variety of belief and practice.

From early times, the Russian Baptists sought to bring their scattered churches into some kind of cooperative union. Leaders of the Tiflis church, representing the specifically Baptist tradition, called a meeting in 1879 to attempt formation of a Baptist union. However, that came to nought. Another effort, led by Pashkov and meeting first in his home, formed the Russian Baptist Union in 1884, but it had a short life. Not until the twentieth century did a continuing Russian Baptist Union emerge, and it included evangelicals of various shades.

Russian Baptists suffered intense opposition in the nineteenth century. Both the tsarist government and its ally the Orthodox Church identified the Baptists as a threat to their system. One writer observed, "The danger to Russian Orthodoxy from 1,500 Baptists is greater than from 8,000 Molokans."[58] Though the "Baptist sect" was granted legal existence in Russia in 1879, freedom was intended to apply to foreign residents only, such as the German Mennonites. Only in 1905 did the persecution of Russian Baptists let up for a few years, but Baptists grew rapidly despite restrictions. Available information does not reveal how many Baptists were in Russia by the turn of the century, but estimates place the number at over 100,000 by 1905. Others place the number much higher.[59]

At the Turn of the Century

By 1900 Baptists had made their appearance in most of the European countries and went about extending their witness by local preaching, evangelistic tours, and extensive use of tracts and other Christian literature. They also worked at Bible distribution and published a number of national language Baptist papers.

57. Sawatsky, p. 34.
58. Klibanov, p. 222.
59. Sawatsky, p. 27; Parker, p. 152.

A Measure of Growth

One informed source calculated the number of Baptists in Continental Europe at about 220,000 by the turn of the century.[60] However, growth was far from uniform. Perhaps Germany and Sweden provided the most receptive soil for Baptist growth, with sizable communities also growing up in Russia and other Eastern countries. In other areas, such as Italy, Protestantism of any kind found less acceptance. In Albania, there were no known Baptists even late in the twentieth century.

The German Connection

Even a scanning of the story of Baptist beginnings in Europe reveals the importance of German missionaries who went first to the sizable German-speaking population in the various countries. The aggressive German Baptists, led by J. G. Oncken, used that dispersion as an avenue to extend their witness throughout the Continent. The disadvantage was that Baptist churches, having their beginnings among German immigrants, seemed somewhat "foreign" in many of the European countries. That not only hampered their witness at places but also tensions erupted between leaders of the German-speaking churches and later converts who began Baptist work in the national languages.

Outlook for the Future

An observer of Baptist life in Europe at the turn of the century would have had reason for guarded optimism. Though the Baptists still faced opposition in places from both civil governments and state churches, the worst persecution had moderated at least in Western countries. Still plagued by lack of unity, and sometimes with competing Baptist groups within the same country, Baptists nevertheless possessed an inner vitality that was perhaps their greatest asset.

Conclusion

At the time of Waterloo, Rushbrooke reminded us, Baptists had no church on the continent of Europe. By mid-century they had appeared in most of Western Europe, borne on the waves of Pietism, personal Bible study, and spiritual hunger not being satisfied in the state churches. By the turn of the century, Baptists had largely completed their sweep of Europe and stood poised for a great leap forward in the twentieth century.

---

60. Rushbrooke, p. 205.

Unit IV:

The Twentieth Century

In *Future Shock,* published first in 1970, Alvin Toffler said that more history has unfolded within living memory than during the rest of recorded history combined. Some people pinpointed 1945, the beginning of the atomic age, as the midway point of history. Since then we have been "future shocked" with successive "ages," such as the nuclear age, the television age, and the computer age. One might now argue that more has happened *since* Toffler wrote than before; history continues to "telescope" and the midway point keeps gaining on us.

If history means "happenings," and not merely the passing of time, then more Baptist history stems from the twentieth century than all previous times combined. However, space allotments in this book cannot reflect that assessment for several reasons. First, recent Baptist history becomes meaningless if severed from its earlier roots. What *is* grows out of what *was,* and today takes its significance, at least in part, from yesterday. Second, for all its bulk, recent history bristles with problems. As in photography, we lack the depth of field to bring events into sharp focus. The historian can list endless facts but may lack the insights to put them into perspective, dividing the mountains from the molehills. Third, with the recent past, the historian describes his own times and becomes vulnerable to subconscious biases and imbalances. The reader shares this vulnerability, for one also reads of one's own times.

"A great people have come to a great time." That description of one Baptist group entering the twentieth century could be applied to the entire Baptist family. This century has been unprecedented both in problems and progress. Some parts of the Baptist family grew rapidly, while others fell into steep decline, and historians have not been able to give satisfactory explanations for either trend. While Baptists in the English-speaking world took religious liberty for granted, and some even began to undermine the historic Baptist position on that subject, Baptists in parts of Europe faced the most severe and sustained persecution which Christians have seen since the caesars.

The world has seemed less secure in the twentieth century. Two world wars, countless other conflicts, the development of atomic and nuclear weapons, advances in transportation and communication, and opening of the space age have radically transformed the global village. Hunger, war, and pollution have seemed to compete as the most likely agents of destruction. These world changes have been matched by changes in the realm of religion. The resurgence of Eastern religions, the rise of curious new cults, the violent revivals within Islam, renewal of Catholicism, and the rise of fundamentalist tensions in most of the Protestant bodies have shown that the twentieth century will not be an irenic time. The rise of new theologies, increased social awareness, and the ecumenical movement have been among the major trends affecting Christianity. Permeating this entire atmosphere, and providing perhaps the one greatest challenge to twentieth-century Christianity, has been the rise of secularism. Baptists, of course, have shared in all these developments.

Among the British Baptists perhaps the primary internal development in the present century has been numerical decline. Social conditions that favored the Free Church tradition in the Victorian era changed, and Baptists found themselves facing an uphill pull. English Baptists have participated in the world ecumenical movement, experimented with closer relationships with other English Free Churchmen and have made various theological restatements. English Baptists took the lead in forming the Baptist World Alliance in 1905, a body which gave for the first time a world structure to the Baptist family.

In Canada, Baptists have achieved a national union but have lost much of their inner unity in a series of doctrinal and regional tensions. The Fundamentalist movement, often identified with the United States, ravaged the Canadian Baptists as well. After mid-century, the growing Southern Baptist presence in Canada raised important questions for future directions of Baptists both in America and Canada.

In the United States, Baptists in the twentieth century have formed a confusing but dynamic picture. Baptists in the North tinkered with the denominational machinery, forming a "convention" in 1908, and changed their name to "American" in 1950. They abandoned the convention structure in the 1970s, adopting a more ecclesiastical structure. During this century, American Baptists were fragmented by Fundamentalism, challenged by ecumenism, and concerned by the massive movement of Southern Baptists into the North. The American Baptists have been actively involved in the Social Gospel and other social ministries since 1900.

Early in the twentieth century, Southern Baptists achieved a high degree of internal unity, symbolized by formation of the Cooperative Program in 1925, but a half century later appeared to lose much of that unity in the rise of Fundamentalism within the denomination. Once confined to the states of the deep South, Southern Baptists in the twentieth century have expanded to the entire nation and appear ready to annex Canada as Southern Baptist territory. Beginning in the 1920s with the development of large programs of ministry, and large sums of money to fund them, Southern

Baptists entered an era of centralization in which money and decision making moved inward to the denominational center. By the 1970s, however, a process of decentralization had appeared, with renewed vitality at associational and state levels of Baptist work.

Black Baptists in the United States entered the twentieth century organized into one major body, the National Baptist Convention. That convention split in 1915 over ownership and control of convention property and again in 1961 over the Civil Rights movement. Toward the end of the century, however, they seemed to achieve a high degree of spiritual unity despite organizational disunity. Black Baptists entered the century in segregation and suppression; toward the end of the century, a National Baptist pastor attracted widespread attention and support in his bid to run for the presidency of the United States.

For Baptists in Europe, the twentieth century has brought mixed blessings. For the most part, Baptists in the Western countries on the Continent have achieved religious freedom, but their sectarian status has prevented their making a major impact upon the population. Nothing comparable to the Wesleyan Revival of England or the Great Awakenings of America occurred in Europe. Those evangelical movements had paved the way for Baptist advance in their respective countries. The nearest European equivalent was the Pietist movement and when that faded, the European Baptists were left with no spiritual vehicle of sufficient force to carry them forward.

More than Baptists in other countries, Baptists in Europe felt directly the devastation of the world wars. Those conflicts and the subsequent realignment of political borders, economic systems, and language groupings affected Baptists. Amid these challenges, the Baptists not only survived but also have flourished in many areas. In this century, they have perfected their national Baptist unions, supported several strong theological seminaries, participated in the world Baptist community through the Baptist World Alliance, and about the middle of the century formed the European Baptist Federation which brought a measure of commonality among the twenty-five or so different Baptist groups of Europe.

The one overwhelming reality faced by Baptists in Eastern Europe during the twentieth century has been the rise of Communism. Though officially committed to atheism, the Communism which first arose in the Soviet Union allowed Baptists more freedom than the tsars had done. Later the Communist government cracked down and Baptists suffered severe and sustained periods of persecution. With the enlargement of the Soviet empire, late in the century about two-thirds of all European Baptists lived behind what the West calls "the iron curtain." Some of the major challenges these Baptists have faced include: how to survive the systematic Communist persecution; how to be good citizens and yet true to their faith; how to teach their faith with a shortage of Bibles and printed materials and with restrictions upon preaching; how to provide ministers in the absence of seminaries and restrictions upon study abroad; and how to maintain their own unity in the face of internal strife and schisms.

Toward the end of the century the Soviet Baptists have become more visible to the outside world. Because they represent the major Protestant group in Eastern Europe, Baptists have attracted widespread and sympathetic attention in the West. This high visibility and sympathetic awareness probably provides their greatest bulwark against future government efforts to eradicate the church.

13

British Baptists

"Larger Horizons and New Problems" is the title A.C. Underwood gives to his discussion of English Baptists in the twentieth century.[1] Certainly the horizons for Baptists, indeed for the whole world, have been vastly enlarged in the present century. However, it appears that rapidly as the horizons have expanded, the problems have grown even more rapidly.

A recent general secretary of the Baptist Union, E. A. Payne, reduced to one word the story of English Baptists at mid-century: *hesitancy.* This hesitancy expressed itself in theology, ecumenical relations, and perhaps most of all in the life of the local churches.

In this century English Baptists have confronted a declining membership, efforts to restructure the denomination, ecumenical dialogue, serious questions about theology and belief patterns, and a growing sense of discouragement. Yet, amid these challenges, English Baptists continue to bear witness to the faith. This chapter will sketch briefly the highlights of their recent heritage.

The Baptist Union

J. H. Shakespeare

The Baptist Union entered the twentieth century two years early with the election of John Howard Shakespeare as general secretary in 1898. A man of remarkable vision and statesmanship, Shakespeare (1857-1928) served until 1924 and gave the denomination its present structure and shape. As a youth he had come under the preaching of James Thew of Leicester, a man less traditional than most Baptist preachers of the time. A student at Regent's Park College and later a graduate of the University of London, Shakespeare's only pastorate was at St. Mary's Chapel in Norwich. His outstanding gifts as a preacher and organizer led to his election in 1898 to succeed Samuel H. Booth as head of the Baptist Union.

Shakespeare occupies a secure place in English Baptist history. At least five major achievements are credited to him: (1) He led the Baptist Union

---

1. A. C. Underwood, *A History of English Baptists* (London: Carey Kingsgate Press, 1947), pp. 238 *f.*

in major fund drives, including the Twentieth Century Fund in 1899 and
the Sustentation Fund in 1914; (2) he led in construction of the Baptist
Church House, the handsome denominational headquarters in London; (3)
he restructured the denomination under the leadership of general superintendents; (4) he led Baptists into serious ecumenical dialogue with other
denominations; and (5) he helped form the Baptist World Alliance in 1905.

Shakespeare's first task as general secretary was to lead the Twentieth
Century Fund, the largest financial drive English Baptists had mounted to
that date. As early as 1896, people had suggested a major fund; in 1899
those suggestions became official when the union voted "that a special Fund
be formed, to be called 'The Baptist Union Twentieth Century Fund,' to
raise at least a quarter of a million pounds."[2] Half of the money would be
used for church extension, particularly in urban areas where Baptists were
weak. Part of the fund would supplement the salaries of village ministers,
augment the Annuity Fund for retired ministers and their dependents, and
strengthen various educational ministries. The remaining funds provided a
suitable denominational headquarters building, something the union had
never possessed. Under the leadership of Shakespeare, Alexander Mclaren,
president of the union, and John Clifford, the most influential pastor of the
time, the fund was completed by 1902.

The success of the fund provided a good beginning for Shakespeare's
leadership and launched the Baptists into the twentieth century. It convinced them they could accomplish major goals. Unfortunately, as some
English Baptists were to observe a half century later, it also had the effect
of making the pastors more dependent upon the denomination for their
support. This continued a trend noted as early as 1717 with the formation
of the Particular Baptist Fund. The trend was accelerated in 1914 with
completion of the Sustentation Fund, an effort to raise an additional
£250,000 to supplement pastoral salaries.

For years Baptist individuals in England had published an array of papers
and periodicals, but the denomination had no official voice. As early as
1891, the council suggested it was time for an official weekly newspaper.
In 1899 Shakespeare led the union to purchase the *Freeman,* which had
been privately published since 1855. The union also acquired another independent paper, *The Baptist,* and merged these in 1910 as the *Baptist Times.*
In recent years this has become the official English Baptist newspaper.

Baptist Church House

In 1903 the Baptist Church House opened in London. The handsome
structure gave the Baptist Union its own facilities for the first time. This
building forms an attractive headquarters in the heart of London. It has

2. J. H. Shakespeare, *The Story of the Twentieth Century Fund,* p. 5.

been far more important than just a place of operation; it has given to the Baptist Union an identity and status which had been lacking.

Reshaping the Church

With the Sustentation Fund, Shakespeare gave renewed emphasis to the "accreditation list," an official listing of recognized ministers which had been established in 1896. Only listed ministers could participate in the Sustentation Fund and the later Baptist United Fund. For generations English Baptists had been troubled by itinerant preachers and evangelists who sometimes did more harm than good, and the accreditation list was an effort to address that problem. In time, the list tied both pastors and churches more closely to the Baptist Union.

In 1916 Shakespeare launched the most radical restructuring of the Baptist denomination since the seventeenth century. Drawing perhaps from the Lutheran model, he led the union to divide England and Wales into ten districts, or "areas," and set over each a general superintendent. The superintendent became a "pastor to the pastors" of his area, responsible for both spiritual and administrative well-being of the churches.

Combined with the superintendent system was the Ministerial Settlement and Sustentation Scheme, with responsibility "for the removal and settlement of ministers."[3] Thereafter, churches seeking pastors or pastors wanting placement would deal with the area superintendent. Gradually the superintendents came to function much as bishops; in fact, Shakespeare had no objection to them being called bishops, suggesting that *superintendent* and *bishop* are merely different words designating the same function. Perhaps most English Baptists today would agree with W. M. West, who wrote, "There can be little doubt that the Baptist General Superintendents of today represent a twentieth century interpretation of the Messengers who functioned three hundred years ago."[4] The new structure took root slowly among English Baptists, though it is considered essential today.

The superintendents keep several lists: active pastors who would welcome a move, recent ministerial graduates to be placed, and churches seeking pastors. While larger churches may deal directly with prospective pastors, most of the churches work through the area superintendent. The superintendent's task is to match up church and pastor, though the church retains the right of formal "call." He also recommends the level of pastoral salary supplement to which each church is eligible. The superintendents are elected to a five-year term and are eligible for reelection.

Shakespeare also introduced English Baptists to serious ecumenical dialogue. For years he had lived with a growing conviction that the Baptist

3. Underwood, p. 5.

4. W. M. S. West, "Baptist Church Life Today," in *The Pattern of the Church*, Alex Gilmore, ed., p. 52.

pattern of independent congregations was too individualistic for modern conditions. Shakespeare's first goal, apparently, was to merge Baptists with the other Free Churches, like Congregationalist and Presbyterian, to form a "United Free Church of England." Perhaps he saw the superintendency system as preparing for that merger. However, this Free Church merger was only one step along a path which Shakespeare saw leading to eventual reunion with the Church of England. Unlike most Baptists, he had no hesitancy in accepting episcopacy as one price of that merger.

In his impassioned book, *The Churches at the Crossroads* (1918), Shakespeare expressed an intense ecumenical commitment which he had long held but had concealed from his Baptist brethren. "I passionately desire the goal of Church Unity," he said, insisting that "the days of denominationalism are numbered. There is nothing more pathetic or useless, in this world, than clinging to dead issues." He compared denominations to "men, wrapped in graveclothes of dead controversies, [who] utter battle cries which have lost all their power." Warning that "if we are simply denominations and not a united Church, we are doomed," Shakespeare said: "The plain fact is that the vast tree of sectarian divisions is rapidly becoming hollow: it is propped up by iron bands of trust deeds and funds. . . . One day, in a general storm, the hollow tree will come down with a crash."[5]

Grasping what Roger Hayden called "the nettle of episcopacy,"[6] Shakespeare frankly admitted, "It is no use concealing my conviction that reunion will never come to pass except upon the basis of episcopacy." That would, in effect, invalidate Baptist ordinations and require reordination in the episcopal pattern. This issue has been the most formidable barrier to Baptist participation in ecumenical mergers in England.

These views aroused a storm of protest, and Shakespeare's plans did not prevail among Baptists. Some observers felt the resulting tensions damaged Shakespeare's health and cut short his tenure as general secretary. After a year of interim leadership by John C. Carlile, Shakespeare was succeeded by Melbourn E. Aubrey, who served from 1925 to 1951. Though Aubrey sought to steer Baptists away from preoccupation with ecumenism, Shakespeare's vision gripped English Baptists and has deeply influenced their ecclesiastical thinking in the twentieth century.

New Leadership

M. E. Aubrey (d.1957) came to leadership after Baptist decline had already begun. Aubrey's was a work of consolidation, seeking to deal with

---

5. J. H. Shakespeare, *The Churches at the Crossroads: A Study in Church Unity*, pp. 79, 82.

6. Roger Hayden, "Still at the Crossroads? Revd J. H. Shakespeare and Ecumenism," *Baptists in the Twentieth Century*, K. W. Clements, ed. (London: Baptist Historical Society, 1983), p. 38.

the aftermath of World War II and raise the various funds needed to strengthen Baptist work. His steady if unsensational leadership restored Baptist confidence and led to closer cooperation between different units of Baptist life, particularly the associations and the Baptist Union.[7]

Ernest A. Payne was elected general secretary of the Baptist Union in 1951 and served until 1967. Payne had been a pastor and spent some years on the staff of the BMS. He also taught for a time at Regent's Park, the Baptist college in Oxford. Though he presided over the usual denominational meetings and raised needed Baptist funds, the pressing priority of Payne's life was ecumenism. For all his quiet ways, Payne rose to prominent leadership in the World Council of Churches, serving as vice-president of that body. He first came to notice as a youth for his highly favorable review of Shakespeare's book, *The Churches at the Crossroads*.[8] If anything, he went beyond Shakespeare in devoting his time and energy to the ecumenical vision.

Payne led the Ter-Jubilee (1959-1963), surely one of the highlights of his ministry. The celebration marked the 150-year anniversary of the Baptist Union, formed in 1813, and provided English Baptists with an opportunity to rediscover their heritage and launch bold new plans for the future.

The Ter-Jubilee began with a reissuing of the famous Prayer Call of 1784, out of which came the missionary movement. Along with new efforts in giving and witnessing, the Baptist Union called for massive prayer support to revitalize the denomination. Goals were adopted for evangelism, church extension, and finance. The Ter-Jubilee Fund sought to raise £300,000 to build and repair churches and manses, to strengthen ministerial training, and to augment the home mission fund. By late 1964 receipts stood at £281,463.

The Ter-Jubilee was far more than just another effort to raise funds; it also addressed the continuing numerical and spiritual decline of English Baptists. It led to the "Swanwick Statement" of 1961, so called because it emerged from meetings at the Hayes Conference Center at Swanwick, in Derbyshire. With input from representatives from all aspects of English Baptist life, the Swanwick Statement has been regarded as a kind of state-of-the-churches message. It particularly expressed concerns of some younger pastors who feared that the persistent numerical decline reflected a corresponding spiritual decline. The statement was presented in seven categories, which might be summarized as follows:

1. The historic independency that has marked Baptist churches needs to be supplemented by a recognition of the interdependency of Baptist churches, both on biblical and pragmatic grounds.

7. W. M. S. West, *To Be a Pilgrim: A Memoir of Ernest A. Payne*, p. 77.

8. W. M. S. West, "Baptists in Faith and Order: A Study in Baptismal Convergence," in Clements, p. 56.

2. Baptist associations continue to be relevant, though some lines may need to be redrawn.

3. There must be changes in the present methods of settlement of ministers, the status of deaconesses, the recognition and ordination of men over 40, clearer distinctions between full-time and part-time ministers, and changes in the training and stipends of lay preachers.

4. In light of the "spiritual and numerical weakness which is evident in certain areas," pastors and churches should experiment with pilot programs of grouping neighboring churches under one pastor.

5. There is an urgent need for better training of lay members, and for better literature in such areas as biblical studies, doctrine, denominational ministry, and Baptist heritage to accomplish this goal.

6. That the Baptist Union take appropriate steps to appoint Commissions for further study and implementation of these goals.

7. That both pastors and laymen be led to deeper understanding of the world scene, including ecumenical discussions.[9]

The Swanwick Statement had a large impact, provoking widespread discussions among English Baptists. It apparently led to a more complete acceptance of women in ministry. It also marked the emergence of a group of militant younger ministers who were no longer content to accept the drift and decline which they felt marked the recent history of Baptists in England.

Perhaps one stands too close yet to evaluate the times of such recent general secretaries as David S. Russell (1967-1982) and Bernard Green (since 1982). Both have dealt with such factors as steep inflation, continued numerical decline, the increased fragmentation of the union into various interest groups, intense theological controversy, a growing charismatic movement, and, of course, the old problem of Baptists' proper response to the ecumenical movement. Current observers note that Green is the first general secretary of the twentieth century to come to office from significant pastoral experience, and it appears he is attempting to steer the union back to local church concerns.

Baptist Colleges

In the twentieth-century restructuring of English Baptist life, some people apparently hoped to bring the colleges into closer relationship with, and perhaps under supervision by, the Baptist Union. However, this has not happened. For generations the colleges have been independent centers of Baptist life, and their principals are usually leaders of some influence locally and nationally. The union does allot some of its funds but not enough to constitute effective control. The British government provides a cash scholarship for a "first degree" in a college or university for any of its young

9. Ronald W. Thomson, *The Story of the Ter-Jubilee of the Baptist Union,* pp. 21-25.

citizens gaining admission. Students may attend Baptist colleges on these scholarships to prepare for ministry. Presently English Baptists conduct four colleges. They are Bristol College, the oldest, founded in 1679; Regent's Park in Oxford, founded 1810; Spurgeon's College formed in London in 1856; and Manchester, formed in 1964 by the merger of Rawdon (1804) and Manchester (1866). Of these, Spurgeon's is the largest. In addition, Welsh Baptists operate colleges at Bangor and at Cardiff, and Scottish Baptists have their college in Glasgow.

In summary, one might say that English Baptists formed an ecclesiastical body in the twentieth century, whereas before they had only a loose collection of churches and individuals. The congregations became to some extent local units of the larger church, and the pastors were tied more closely to the Baptist Union by various funds and salary supplements. As in similar developments among Baptists in other nations, this shift came not so much from new convictions in ecclesiology as from a search for greater efficiency in the practical world.

The Baptist Missionary Society

The continued separate identity of the BMS reveals the degree of disunity that remains despite the twentieth-century push for unity among English Baptists. Some consider the BMS the world evangelism arm of the Baptist Union, but the relationship exists more in rhetoric than in reality. The two bodies maintain distinct headquarters, budgets, staffs, and leadership. As the older and usually stronger organization, the BMS has successfully resisted all efforts to pull it into the orbit of the union.

The BMS provides an example of the independent society approach to Baptist work, as contrasted with more centralized denominational approach. The evidence suggests that Carey's preference, and certainly his first effort, was to have missionary work done through the associations. However, upon failing to enlist the denomination in missions, Carey fell back upon the plan of working through an independent society of interested individuals.

Dissatisfaction with the extreme independence of the BMS is no new thing. In 1863 Spurgeon curtly refused to support the BMS, writing of "my desire to be in no way identified with your Society." Spurgeon said, "It seems to me that *our churches* are responsible for the spread of the Gospel and not a Society *as such.*"[10] He felt the policies of the missionary society were not responsive to the denomination. An important part of the vision for a unified Baptist denomination in the twentieth century involved bringing the foreign mission work under denominational oversight. Some felt that independence made missions seem a kind of optional appendage to

---

10. Brian Stanley, "Spurgeon and the Baptist Missionary Society, 1863-1866," *The Baptist Quarterly,* p. 321, emphasis his.

Baptist witness. One writer said, "This [isolation] we regard as regrettable. The missionary work of the churches must find expression side by side with other aspects of the life of the churches within the association." The writer urged the merger of the missionary agency into the denominational structure and concluded "Whether it comes quickly or slowly this [integration] must be our goal."[11]

The sturdy old BMS vetoed on several occasions the proposal to move into a common headquarters with the Baptist Union, preferring to maintain its separate location and separate identity. Quite early the BMS set its policy of keeping its distance from the union and has never budged from that stance. At times it has tended to picture the union as divided in its priorities, theologically suspect, moving toward an ecumenism that might threaten Baptist identity, and presiding over a severe case of numerical and spiritual decline. The missionary body has shown no desire to come into the larger family to compete for support with home missions, Baptist colleges, and other denominational programs. Closer affiliation with the Baptist Union might also threaten its support from the Scottish churches and from the sizable body of non-Baptist donors.

The twentieth century has brought to the BMS increased financial support, expanded programs at home and abroad, and slow but steady church growth on its overseas fields. With a constitution committing the society to "the diffusion of the knowledge of the religion of Jesus Christ throughout the whole world beyond the British Isles," it had in 1981 a total of 191 foreign missionaries, plus another 130 retired missionaries.[12] In addition to planting churches, it reported missionary work in such areas as Christian education, ministerial training, medical work, agricultural work, and other social ministries.[13]

The Candidate Board of the society accepted twenty-five new applicants in 1982, signaling an upturn in interest on the part of young people seeking appointment to overseas ministries. The society operates its own printing facilities at its headquarters at 93 Gloucester Place in London, some distance from the Baptist Church House. Countries in which the society had work in 1982 included India, Bangladesh, Sri Lanka, the Republics of Zaire and Angola, Tanzania, Jamaica, Trinidad, Brazil, and Hong Kong. The concentration of missionary personnel was then in the African countries and Brazil, with only eleven appointees in India, the land of Carey.[14] In

11. Gilmore, p. 151.

12. *Directory and Financial Report, 1982* (London: Baptist Missionary Society, 1982), pp. 7, 10.

13. *Ardent in God's Service: Baptist Missionary Society Annual Report 1981-1982* (London: Baptist Missionary Society, 1982), pp. 4 f.

14. *Directory*, 1982, p. 10.

1959 the society reported over twenty-five hundred overseas congregations, with a combined membership of about one hundred ten thousand.[15]

Patterns of Growth

One of the most persistent and puzzling problems facing English Baptists in the twentieth century has been their steady numerical decline, which since 1906 has been consistent and sometimes drastic. A veteran Baptist leader recently charted the extent of that decline. He said:

> In 1921 there were 3068 churches in the Baptist Union with a total membership of 442,000; in 1981 there were 2058 churches with a total membership of 170,000. A 57% decline in membership. In 1921 our Sunday Schools had 518,000 scholars; in 1981, 157,000: a decline of 70%.[16]

Ernest A. Payne, whose lot it was to preside over the worst of this decline, gathered statistics which confirm these grim findings. English Baptists have faced this problem, studied and analyzed it, offered several explanations for its presence, and above all have mounted countless campaigns to reverse these trends. Although it appeared after 1980 that at last there might be some better news, one cannot yet say that the decline has been arrested.

In April 1977, the Baptist Union voted "to set up an inter-departmental commission to examine the causes for the numerical and spiritual decline in our denomination." This commission, chaired by John H. Y. Briggs, reported in March 1979. Its findings were published under the title of *Signs of Hope*.[17]

Taking note of "a dispirited air" about the denomination, the commission found many Baptists felt that "decline is inevitable." The commission set out to document the extent of decline, to assess whether it was merely numerical or included spiritual erosion, and to suggest steps to reverse these adverse trends. As to the extent of decrease, the commission found plenty of bad news. It found that decline had been steady since 1906 but had plummeted since the early 1950s. Its figures cited a 28 percent decrease of churches and membership in the quarter century, 1952-1977. Though this decline may be exaggerated by omitting churches that still exist but have withdrawn from the union, the rate is still alarming. Baptisms hit a peak in 1956 during the Billy Graham crusades in England and fell to a new low in 1970.

The Briggs Commission reported that English Baptist churches have

15. Ernest A. Payne, *The Baptist Union: A Short History*, p. 268.

16. L. G. Champion, "Baptist Church Life in the Twentieth Century: Some Personal Reflections," in Clements, p. 4.

17. John H. Y. Briggs, *Signs of Hope: The Report of the Denominational Enquiry Group*. It represents by far the most thorough study of growth patterns ever undertaken among English Baptists. Much of the material in the following paragraphs comes from that report.

about twice as many women as men members. In the under 40 group, the proportion is about 1 to 1.5; in the 41 to 60 age group, it is 2 to 1; and over 60, it rises to about 3 to 1.[18]

This analysis, and others like it, have also shown that while the churches are becoming fewer they are also becoming smaller. N. B. Jones led a study, authorized by the council of the Baptist Union, that analyzed patterns of church growth in 1968. He showed that of affiliated churches, 70 percent had a membership of fewer than 100 members, and 90 percent had fewer than 200 members. Even more surprising, perhaps, is that fully one third of the affiliated churches had fewer than 40 members, making it difficult to maintain any regular ministry. The average per capita gifts of English Baptists in 1978 was reported to be £53.20.[19]

The Briggs Commission found it difficult to distinguish between numerical and spiritual decline but professed to find both among English Baptists. "All too easily," they wrote, "the living experience of one generation can become a hollow and second-hand form for the next."[20] Warning that "there is a danger in our denominational life of holding to out-dated structures and practices," the commission acknowledged, "We have to accept that some of our churches are open to the criticism that they have become closed in outlook, backward-looking, concerned to maintain a legacy from the past in terms of church plant and former glories, uncertain how to throw off the shackles of yesterday in giving themselves in totality to the mission of today."[21]

What has caused this decline? The Briggs report cited changes in society and the erosion of interest in evangelical religion as helping set the environment for decline. More specifically, it pointed to "theological polarization, the charismatic movement, [and] ecumenical commitment" as specific factors in the Baptist decline.[22] The report noted also a subtle psychological tendency to expect decline, with a result that Baptist preaching, planning, and church activities are subconsciously geared to expect and accept decline as the norm.

Most observers relate the decline of religion in Britain to the rise of social and economic forces which have made the church seem increasingly irrelevant. In his astute analysis, *The Making of Post-Christian Britain,* Alan D. Gilbert developed his thesis of "the relationship in modern Britain between the decline of religion and the emergence of a complex urban-industrial society."[23] The earlier functions of the churches have either been dropped as no longer needed or performed more efficiently by government or other

18. Briggs, p. 16.
19. Ibid., p. 11.
20. Ibid., p. 17.
21. Ibid.
22. Ibid., p. 1.
23. Alan D. Gilbert, *The Making of Post-Christian Britain,* p. 15.

social agencies. For many people, the importance of religion diminished. A 1977 report, headlined in the *Baptist Times,* said "Britain is not only becoming less Christian, it is increasingly anti-Christian."[24]

While this throws light on the larger picture of religion in England, specific problems faced the Baptists and no doubt contributed to their numerical downtrend. Baptist life in England has long been beset with internal tensions. The Briggs report cited at least three such tensions: theological polarization, the charismatic movement, and the ecumenical movement. These will be discussed more fully in the next section, but their impact on growth patterns may be briefly noted here.

Some feel that the Down Grade Controversy of the 1880s prepared the way for Baptist decline. Continuing conflicts over the authority of Scripture, the person of Christ, and the meaning of salvation have distracted Baptists. These continuing controversies damaged Baptists' public and self-images and fragmented the Baptist Union into any number of interest groups organized to push some particular point of view. Perhaps the most serious problem has been not heresy but a doctrinal vagueness which has not commanded a loyal following and perhaps cannot.

The charismatic movement has undermined the Baptist witness, though decline was far advanced before the appearance of this latter-day Pentecostalism among Baptists. Churches that adopt charismatic practices often grow, but they tend to embrace non-Baptist theological views, downgrade the role of pastor, restructure the church around authoritative elders, and quite often withdraw from participation in the Baptist Union. Many churches have split over this issue, while others are lured away from their Baptist moorings.

The Briggs Commission bluntly identified the ecumenical movement as a factor in Baptist decline, thus in effect challenging denominational preoccupation with that movement since the days of J. H. Shakespeare. In 1963 some of the most progressive thinkers among English Baptists wrote that church reform is essential, but no denominational reform is possible apart from reunion with others. A chapter entitled, "Towards Church Union," affirms that "the time for Free Church union has long since passed," and the future demands ultimate reunion not only of the free churches, but also with the Church of England. According to this view, by its nature a *denomination* is partial and, therefore, a false church.[25]

Whatever its value or legitimacy, the practical effect of this emphasis has been to undercut the Baptist denomination. The Briggs report defended Baptist participation in ecumenism but admitted it was for many churches "a ground of suspicion." One of the churches cited in that study reported, "It was progressing much better now that it had given up trying to get involved with churches of other denominations and so losing its distinctive

24. *The Baptist Times* (December 8, 1977), p. 1.
25. Gilmore, p. 21.

Baptist emphasis."[26] Some Baptists who favor ecumenism admit that it hinders the advance of distinctly denominational emphases, but they feel that church reunion, whatever its cost, is demanded by the gospel.

The Baptist Union has launched a number of special campaigns to reverse these trends, such as "Baptist Advance" in the 1950s, the Ter-Jubilee in the early 1960s, the "Simultaneous Movement for Evangelism" in 1968, and the "Wholeness of the Gospel" movement of the 1970s. They have also improved the training and accreditation of lay preachers and provided better Bible training for all lay members. Pastors have sought to enrich the worship services with new hymns, new liturgy, and experiments with such concepts as "Family Church," and "All Age Sunday Schools." The denomination and some of its churches have cautiously adopted certain features of the church growth movement currently popular in the United States. Whether or not a result of these efforts, the rate of decline has slowed and some areas are now showing modest gains.

Doctrinal Developments

Some say that people no longer care about religious doctrines, but that has not proved true of English Baptists, though they are far removed from the early days of intense confessionalism. One is tempted to generalize that the 1891 merger left the Baptist Union with a Particular Baptist organization infused with General Baptist theology. Present theological tensions within Baptist life mirror ancient polarities which go back as far as John Smyth for the General Baptists and William Kiffin for the Particulars.

In the twentieth century, English Baptists have lived with minimal doctrinal moorings. Pastors and laymen alike have enjoyed remarkable freedom in framing and expressing their theological views. As the Down Grade crisis revealed in the late 1880s, Baptists had little inclination and almost no means to hold individual Baptists to any kind of confessional stance. The Baptist Union maintained only minimal doctrinal standards, devised partly to accommodate the General Baptist merger of 1891.

In 1904 the union adopted the Declaration of Principle, which affirmed that:

> The basis of this Union is:
> 1. That our Lord Jesus Christ is the sole and absolute authority in all matters pertaining to faith and practice, as revealed in the Holy Scriptures, and that each Church has liberty to interpret and administer all His laws.
> 2. That Christian Baptism is the immersion in water, into the Name of the Father, the Son and Holy Ghost, of those who have professed repentance toward God and faith in our Lord Jesus Christ, Who "died and rose again the third day."

26. Briggs, pp. 18, 25.

3. That it is the duty of every disciple to bear personal witness to the Gospel of Jesus Christ, and to take part in the evangelization of the world.[27]

In a move that might have pleased Charles Spurgeon, the union in 1906 added the phrase "our God and Savior" after "our Lord Jesus Christ" in the first clause. This was changed a generation later to "God manifest in the flesh."

Desire for a more comprehensive confession of faith surfaced in the 1970s. Many felt that English Baptists had retreated too far from the difficult task of defining their doctrines. Repeatedly in the nineteenth century, and especially during the Down Grade crisis, they had declined to spell out their faith for fear such a document might lead to creedalism. More recently fear of doctrinal looseness seems to be gaining on fear of doctrinal rigidity, resulting in calls for a new confession.

For convenience the following sketches treat English Baptist doctrinal development under various categories. However, we must recognize the interrelatedness of theology and the fact that in real life the lines are not so sharply drawn.

Growing Polarization

Whether one describes them as liberal and conservative, evangelical and sacramental, or even progressive and traditional, at least two major groupings are evident among English Baptists in the twentieth century. For this section, the terms *evangelical* and *sacramental* are preferred because they seem less pejorative and more accurately describe the viewpoints represented.

These groups exist only informally; they have little if any structured existence, no membership lists; and some individuals may agree with one group on certain topics and with the other group on other topics. The sacramental group generally favors ecumenism while the evangelicals would prefer to reaffirm Baptist viewpoints. Perhaps the greatest difference would be in baptism. The sacramental party would, in general, accept different forms of baptism, would affirm the validity of infant baptism under some circumstances, require no baptism under others, and teach that baptism conveys specific grace. The evangelical group, on the other hand, would disagree on most of these points.

Adherents of both groups have cooperated cordially in the Baptist Union, and both are represented on its boards and commissions. Perhaps the nearest these two groups have come to an organization has been in the Baptist Revival Fellowship (for the evangelicals) and the Baptist Renewal Group (for the sacramental party). Each group has undertaken studies,

27. Cited in Payne, p. 162.

sponsored conferences, and published materials to advance its interpretations of Baptist life.

A pioneer restatement of Baptist theology in England was Robert C. Walton's *The Gathered Community* (London: Carey Press, 1946). Three books edited by Alec Gilmore have proven provocative, including *Christian Baptism* (Philadelphia: Judson Press, 1959), *The Pattern of the Church: A Baptist View* (London: Lutterworth Press, 1963), and *Baptism and Christian Unity* (London: Lutterworth Press, 1966). These and similar works have advocated a generally sacramental view of baptism and the Lord's Supper, a favorable view of ecumenism, and a recovery of infant baptism or something like it to symbolize the status of infants of believing parents. More conservative viewpoints are advanced in Arthur Dakin's *The Baptist View of the Church and Ministry* (London, 1944) and a small but important book by several authors, *Liberty in the Lord* (London, 1964). Books expressing more moderate theological views include Ernest A. Payne, *The Fellowship of Believers* (London: Carey Kingsgate, 1944) and H. Wheeler Robinson, *The Life and Faith of the Baptists* (London: Carey Kingsgate, 1946).

The Church

Perhaps no doctrine has been more crucial, and more controversial, for English Baptists than ecclesiology. Clearly such related issues as ministry, ecumenism, and to some degree sacraments depends upon how one views the church. "The Baptist Doctrine of the Church," an extensive statement adopted by the Baptist Union in 1948, is only one of many efforts to explore Baptist ecclesiology. Other studies, such as "The Report of the Commission on the Associations" (1964) and "The Child and the Church" (1966), also deal with the church.[28]

Baptist diversity on the church was sharply focused by two books in 1944 which advanced opposite views. Dakin's *The Baptist View of the Church and Ministry* emphasized the local congregation and reaffirmed Baptist distinctives in a rather exclusive way. Reading that work with dismay, Ernest A. Payne offered the same year his small book on *The Fellowship of Believers.* This presented the church, along with sacraments and ministry, in their more universal rather than local dimensions. This emphasis more nearly agreed with Robert C. Walton who challenged Baptists to "rethink our doctrine of the Church."[29] While some would reaffirm early individualism and local church autonomy, the recent tendency is to emphasize the interrelatedness of the churches.

Some envision a "Baptist Church" with local congregations as constituent units, while others regard the denomination as "churchly" in nature and function. This view of the church would relate ministers to the whole

28. All of these are found in Roger Hayden, ed., *Baptist Union Documents 1948-1977.*
29. Robert C. Walton, *The Gathered Community,* p. 112.

church, not just to a local congregation. In turn, the entire church would have a stake in pastoral placement and a responsibility in pastoral support. This ecclesiology would elevate the general superintendents to a sort of bishop status and lead to more decisions by the denomination rather than by local churches, moving the locus of authority from local to national levels.

The second half of the twentieth century has revealed among English Baptists a variety of experiments in alternative forms of the church. Only a few can be described here. Some stand alone as completely independent communities; others form more or less definite links with similar groups elsewhere. Some maintain affiliation with the Baptist Union and local associations; others tend to withdraw from organized Baptist life; and a few maintain only a paper relationship to the denomination as required by property deeds. Most of these alternative groups have been influenced by the charismatic movement or by "Bannerism," an ultraconservative group known as the Banner of Truth.

The "Community Church" is the name attached to a group of Baptist churches which have sought to reorganize their life, work, and worship. These churches elect elders in place of deacons. They generally reduce the role of pastor to layman, often volunteer and unpaid, and dispense with the church meeting since all decisions are made by the elders. They often follow an intense form of "discipling," with each member responsible even in daily decisions to an elder. Opponents regard this as a departure from Scripture and early Baptist practices. Those who favor it argue that it recovers the original Baptist emphasis upon church elders.

The "House Church," as the name implies, groups people not in church buildings but in private homes. Partly because of a pervasive antichurch prejudice and partly to evade what they regard as clerical domination, some Baptists gather in private homes. One can hardly deny the biblical as well as early Baptist precedents for such meetings. Advocates of church renewal also point out that these house churches, or small Christian cells, formed the nucleus of earlier Methodist and other Pietist groups in England. Some of the more traditional churches also divide their membership into small groups for home fellowship, Bible study, and worship.

The "Restoration Church" is more radical, essentially a Baptist form of communalism. A few Baptists have formed themselves into a kind of commune. Ruling elders assign to each person and family their appropriate tasks and allotment of goods. Where possible, the members live together, and church meetings for worship and community meetings for business are hardly distinguishable. Perhaps the best known of the restoration churches is at Bugbrooke, near Northampton, where Ernest A. Payne served some years as pastor.

Though they differ among themselves, these alternative forms of church share certain characteristics. Most reveal charismatic tendencies in their worship, structure, and theology. Most are profoundly antiecclesiastical. Disillusionment, and even hostility, toward the more traditional churches provides their primary recruitment motivation. Along with an antichurch stance, most of these groups are openly anticlerical. They either eliminate the pastoral office or reduce it to insignificance, putting administration into the hands of volunteer laymen. Another mark of such groups is their extreme authoritarianism. Elders make decisions, give authoritative teachings, and mediate the will of God to the membership, whose role is not to search and consider, but to receive and obey. These groups keep women in silence and subjection; among most of them women could not be elders or exercise a leadership or teaching role. These groups are almost completely turned in upon themselves. Their orientation is not outward, toward ministry in the world, but inward, toward cultivation within the narrow group.

Sacraments

Their view of baptism most nearly gives the sacramentalists their name. They affirm that "the Lord's Supper and Baptism are sacraments in which God acts and not merely ordinances which the Christian obeys."[30] Flexible as to the forms of baptism, the sacramentalists could under some circumstances accept the immersion of believers, the sprinkling of believers, or the sprinkling of infants. Many regard baptism as part of the process of salvation. In rejecting infant baptism in the seventeenth century, the sacramentalists say, the early Baptists never worked out a consistent theology of the child's relation to the gospel and the church. They have sought to carve out what might be called a "theology of childhood." They affirm that a child can be related to God by the faith of the Christian community; that there is a fundamental difference in the spiritual status of the infant of believing parents and the infant of unbelieving parents; and that there should be a ceremony, infant baptism or something similar, to symbolize the infant's relation to the church.

While some sacramentalists would accept infant baptism, others would stop at the half-way house of infant dedication. Though Baptists still debate whether the focus of the service is the dedication of the infant or the dedication of the parents, its growing popularity is clear. A prominent English Baptist leader has written that after dedication "the child stands in a new relationship . . . to the church community."[31] In this view, dedication puts the infant "on track" in the process which will culminate, presumably, in baptism and church membership.

Other trends show that many Baptists regard baptism as part of the salvation experience; a 1977 report adopted by the Baptist Union speaks of

30. Ibid., p. 158.
31. West, "Baptist Church Life Today," p. 15.

baptism as "a personal transition from death to life."[32] In 1983 one English Baptist scholar spoke of the rescue of "the sacrament of baptism out of the Zwinglian shadows" and described baptism as "a place of rendezvous between God and man, an integral part of that process of conversion."[33] There is also a trend to separate baptism and church membership, with the result that many who are baptized never follow through by joining any church. While some British Baptists regard baptism as part of the salvation experience, others consider it merely a ceremonial relic which is optional for modern Christians.

The communion controversy, so intense in the nineteenth century, is all but forgotten today; practically all the Baptist churches practice open communion. The theology of communion has changed some, influenced by the Oxford Movement of the nineteenth century and the ecumenical movement of the twentieth. However, the question of open versus closed membership still arises. Some churches require the immersion of believers as the basis of membership. Others require the minister to be immersed, and any baptisms performed in the church must be by immersion, but they accept into membership those baptized by other forms. A third group, which might be described as "wide open," will accept members by any form of baptism or with none.

Ministry

The Baptist ministry has not escaped the myriad changes of the twentieth century. This was made clear in a paper by L. G. Champion, a senior minister whose life spans the century.[34] According to Champion's observations, the Baptist ministry has become less clearly defined as to function, diminished in importance, subject to increased denominational demands beyond the local church, and increasingly imbued with a spirit of professionalism. Recent pronouncements have insisted that the ministry belongs not just to local congregations but to the whole church. That is, a minister in one church has responsibilities to the whole church, and they to him or her. Emphasis upon the role of laity in ministry, according to Champion, has "diminished the significance of the minister's place in the life of the church."[35]

At least four forces have helped shape Baptist concepts in ministry, in addition, of course, to such basic sources as Scripture and theology. First, because the Oxford Movement put such exaggerated emphasis upon sacerdotalism, ordination, and ministerial authority through historic succession-

---

32. "The Child and the Church," in Hayden, *Documents,* p. 212.
33. Michael J. Walker, "Baptist Worship in the Twentieth Century," in Clements, p. 25.
34. L. G. Champion, "Baptist Church Life in the Twentieth Century," in Clements, pp. 7 f.
35. Ibid.

ism, Baptists tended to react to the opposite extremes. At times they almost reduced the ministry to lay status, avoided ministerial garb and titles, and eschewed formal ordination. One recalls, for example, that Charles H. Spurgeon refused any kind of ordination, claiming that a commission from God outranked any from men.

Second, the modern ecumenical and liturgical movements have helped reverse earlier Baptist reaction to Oxford formalism and have pushed them further into sacerdotalism. Formal ordination is back in style, and the ministerial collar and pulpit robe are quite common among English Baptists.

Third, the general social environment, and particularly the economy, has profoundly affected the ministry. Champion said ministers are more aware of working conditions, salary and pension provisions, and housing. He spoke of the "growth of what, with some hesitation, I call professionalism."[36] Despite heroic efforts by the denomination, salaries for English Baptist pastors have fallen behind inflation. This has probably had an impact upon recruitment of ministerial candidates, as well as helping shape attitudes and actions in the manse. A 1969 report warns that "the ministry has sub-consciously gained the outlook of a depressed class. What this fact has cost the churches would be difficult to calculate. A depressed class is rarely renowned for vision and imaginative leadership."[37]

The ordination of women to full ministry status among English Baptists marks a fourth development in the doctrine of ministry. We have seen that a number of Baptist women preached in the early seventeenth century, and women deacons and deaconesses were numerous, but ministerial ordination came later. In the early days of the BMS, women missionaries were "valedicted" rather than ordained, but in recent years some have administered baptism and the Lord's Supper. The Baptist Union officially accepted the Order of Deaconesses in 1919, an order originally established by the London Association in 1890. A shortage of men pastors after World War I pressed the deaconesses into more distinct ministerial roles. In 1922 a woman's name first appeared on the list of probationary ministers, and by World War II women served regularly in pastoral functions. In 1979 the deaconess order was discontinued, with remaining deaconesses ordained to full ministerial status. At that time there were over fifty ordained women ministers among the English Baptists; indeed, the Ministerial Recognition Committee was headed by a woman.[38]

Baptists in England have made extensive use of lay pastors, as one might expect in the land of Wesley. The Baptist Union maintains a list of accredit-

---

36. Ibid.

37. "The Ministry Tomorrow," in Hayden, *Documents,* p. 101.

38. "Report of the Sub-Committee on Women in Ministry" (Glasgow: Baptist Union of Scotland, 1983).

ed lay pastors and has launched an ambitious program for their training through correspondence and periodic conferences. Most lay pastors supply remote village churches which would not otherwise have preaching.

Christology

The doctrine of Jesus Christ has been troublesome for Baptists from their earliest origins. One recalls the attraction of Hofmanite Christology for some early General Baptists and the almost total collapse of old General Baptists in the Socinian controversies of the eighteenth century. Though Dan Taylor reaffirmed the full deity and humanity of Christ in the New Connection schism of 1770, problems continued. With the merger of Particular and New Connection Baptists in 1891, the exchange of ministers and members spread General Baptist Christology throughout the denomination. Theological trends of the times called for a reevaluation of traditional Christology. A tendency to Unitarian views of Christ among Baptists was one of the issues raised but never settled during the Down Grade. Controversial views of Christ have persisted among English Baptists to the present.

The Christology controversy moved to center stage with an address by Michael Taylor at the Baptist Union Assembly of 1971. Taylor, who was president of the Northern Baptist College, was specifically assigned to speak on the subject "How much of a man was Jesus Christ?"[39] To say that Taylor's message was a bombshell would be mild. In a later published version, entitled "A Plain Man's Guide to the Incarnation," Taylor referred to his message as "the cutting-down-to-size of Jesus Christ."[40]

"It is unbelievable," Taylor said in his published address, "that God became a man when Jesus was born."[41] Therefore, "we don't believe in miracles and we don't believe in the intervention to crown all interventions, namely the Incarnation."[42] Noting that even those who accept the incarnation have never been able to explain it, Taylor said it was time to give up the impossible task; it cannot be explained. Perhaps readers were most startled by his comparison of belief in the deity of Christ to a child's belief in the tooth fairy, innocent in children but to be outgrown by adults. The Jesus who emerges from the Taylor address is still one revealer of God, though by no means "divine."

In light of the unbelievable incarnation, Taylor said Christians could take one of four alternatives: "You can go on saying the same thing, or you can say something different, or you can allow more than one thing to be said, or you can say very little at all." Taylor showed a preference for the last

39. West, *Pilgrim,* p. 173.
40. Michael H. Taylor, *A Plain Man's Guide to the Incarnation,* p. 1.
41. Ibid.
42. Ibid., p. 2.

alternative, because, as he concluded, "Who Jesus was (God or man or both) matters less than what he was like . . . all the arguments about the Incarnation are a lot of fuss about nothing."[43]

While not unknown among Baptists, such views had seldom been stated so bluntly. Reactions to the speech were intense, but some hearers felt it was their publication which catapulted the incident into a full-blown controversy. An effort was made to have the union repudiate Taylor's views. This move was blocked by the president, Ernest A. Payne, who hoped perhaps to contain the controversy and also to preserve freedom for Baptists to speak honestly of their religious convictions. In November 1971, Payne once again blocked an effort to censure Taylor's views, though the council reaffirmed the Declaration of Principles with its more orthodox Christology and in 1972 the Baptist Union Assembly reaffirmed its faith.

However, the controversy has continued. About thirty or forty pastors led their churches to withdraw from the union, including several large and influential churches. For example, of sixteen leaders of the Baptist Revival Fellowship who protested Taylor's views in 1971, only four were known to be still in affiliation with the Baptist Union in 1983. For a time this incident occupied the headlines of the *Baptist Times,* but after airing the matter thoroughly the editor closed its pages to further comment. Several attempted to answer Taylor's views, of which perhaps the most widely circulated was "The Christological Controversy in the Baptist Union" issued by George R. Beasley-Murray in 1972. Beasley-Murray cautioned that Taylor's views would undercut not only Baptist theology but also worship of Christ, hymns about Christ, and baptism and the Lord's Supper.

The Ecumenical Movement

English Baptists have been among the pioneers of the modern ecumenical movement. As early as 1678 Thomas Grantham, General Baptist "Messenger," wrote: "When it shall please God to put it into the Hearts of the Rulers of the Nations, to permit a Free and General Assembly, of the differing Professors of Christianity, for the finding out of Truth, we trust that some of the Baptized Churches will (if permitted) readily make their appearance with others to help on that needful work."[44] In 1805 William Carey proposed a conference of Christians of all denominations to meet in Capetown in 1810 and every few years thereafter. The next year Carey renewed this suggestion. In a letter from Calcutta to Andrew Fuller, secretary of the BMS, Carey said:

Would it not be possible to have a general association of all denominations of Christians, from the four quarters of the world, kept there [Capetown] once

43. Ibid., pp. 7-9.
44. Thomas Grantham, *Christianismus Primitivus,* book II, chapter 10, p. 143.

in about ten years? I earnestly recommend this plan, let the first meeting be in the Year 1810, or 1812 at furthest. I have no doubt but it would be attended with very important effects; we could understand one another better, and more entirely enter into one another's views by two hours conversation than by two or three years of epistolary correspondence.[45]

That suggestion was dismissed in England as "another of brother Carey's pleasant dreams," and nothing came of it. However, Baptists were present at the first meeting of the Evangelical Alliance in 1846 and at subsequent meetings of that interdenominational body. They also participated in the ecumenical conference at Edinburgh in 1910 and helped form the World Council of Churches in 1948 at Amsterdam. John H. Shakespeare and Ernest A. Payne, both of whom served as general secretary of the Baptist Union in this century, led English Baptist into closer ecumenical cooperation.

Few English Baptists today would question the need for ecumenical dialogue, cooperation, and even mutual recognition and intercommunion. But at the point of denominational mergers, some Baptists resist; and in recent years this has provoked a sizable reaction. The "Nottingham Call" of 1964 proposed that the various denominations in England covenant or unite by 1980. The Baptist Union's response in 1967, entitled "Baptists and Unity," showed interest but concluded, "That so far no plan of church union or scheme for basically altered Church Relations has been put forward in Britain to which Baptists could unitedly or near unitedly give assent."[46] In 1975 the Church Unity Commission, an arm of the ecumenical movement, issued *Ten Propositions,* the first of which said, "We reaffirm our belief that the visible unity in life and mission of all Christ's people is the will of God."[47] These proposals provided for mutual acceptance of various forms of baptism, intercommunion, and mutual acceptance of ordination, though provision was also made for reordination.

The first official response of any major denomination to the *Ten Propositions* was by the Baptist Union in 1977. The union's statement, "Visible Unity in Life and Mission," concluded, "It is our clear judgment that at present no unqualified recommendation to accept the Ten Propositions can be made."[48] The possibility of having to undergo episcopal reordination proved a barrier to most Baptists.

English Baptists are on record as favoring greater ecumenical cooperation, and their practice confirms this commitment. They are not adverse to

45. Cited in Ruth Rouse and Stephen Charles Neill, eds., *A History of the Ecumenical Movement 1517-1948* (Philadelphia: Westminster Press, 1967), p. 355n. The original letter is preserved in St. Mary's Baptist Church, Norwich, England.

46. Hayden, *Documents,* p. 187.

47. Ibid., p. 191.

48. Ibid., 193.

eventual reunion of the denominations, but the majority apparently do not believe an adequate basis has yet been found for such reunion that would preserve the Baptist heritage.

The Charismatic Movement

Modern Pentecostalism, stemming from the famous Azusa Street revival in Los Angeles in 1906, has become a worldwide phenomenon. In addition to spawning countless Pentecostal denominations, this style of religion (under the more recent name of charismatic movement) has established beachheads in most denominations. The Fountain Trust, an independent group, spread charismatic practices in the Church of England in the early 1970s; from there, according to most observers, the movement spread to other churches, including English Baptists.

The extent of charismatic presence among English Baptists cannot be minimized. Few churches are unaffected; one association reported that two-thirds of its churches were caught up in the movement. Pastors and denominational leaders alike name this as one of the most serious issues facing English Baptists in the 1980s. Baptists caught up in this movement emphasize livelier forms of singing and worship, pray for divine healing, restructure their churches to reduce the role of pastor and deacons, encourage congregational participation in worship, and seek to decide daily issues, even rather mundane ones, according to the will of God. A church that goes charismatic often loosens or severs its ties to the Baptist Union. Some churches that withdraw from the union remain independent; others link themselves with similar churches elsewhere or find fellowship in such noneclesiastical circles as the Dales Bible Week.

Sponsored by an interdenominational charismatic group, called Harvestime House, the Dales Bible Week is an annual conference drawing over ten thousand persons. Much like the old Keswick conferences, the group emphasizes worship, Bible study, and cultivation of a deeper spiritual life. Meetings are held in the Dale Mountains of northern Yorkshire, thus the name. Many families camp out, combining spiritual renewal with vacation. A number of Baptists attend these conferences, including a few union leaders. Those who attend often return to their local churches to spread their charismatic discoveries.

Baptist attitudes toward the charismatic movement, as toward everything else, run the gamut from one extreme to another. At best, say some, it is psychological drivel; at worst, demonic. Others praise the movement as a God-given revival of spiritual dynamic. Still others take a wait-and-see attitude. Baptists have prayed for revival for years, they say; should they now reject a movement that at least shows potential for renewal?

Other Baptists in England

This chapter has sketched primarily those English Baptists affiliated with the Baptist Union. However, from the union's beginning in 1813, a number of churches remained aloof, and into the twentieth century perhaps a fourth or more of the Baptist churches in England remained independent. Some of these cooperated with local associations, but others stood alone. Many of these nonaligned churches were small and isolated. However, the development of the great denominational funds in the twentieth century tended to tie more of these churches to denominational cooperation. Under the new system, they needed the denomination for help in pastoral placement and support. Even so, a number of churches have never come into the Baptist Union.

The number of non-union churches has in recent years been augmented by ex-union churches, those that had been in the union but withdrew. The most often mentioned reasons for leaving the union have been dissatisfaction with the ecumenical movement, divisions caused by the charismatic movement, dissatisfaction with some Baptist Union policy or program, or doctrinal disagreement.

There are other Baptist groups in England, of whom at least two may be mentioned here. The Strict and Particular Baptists continue in existence and have enjoyed growth in some quarters. Led by such conservative stalwarts as William Gadsby, John Warburton, and John Kershaw, the Strict and Particular Baptists emerged gradually into separate status in the mid-nineteenth century, growing largely out of their resistance to the Fuller movement. Grouped around two newspapers, *The Gospel Advocate* and *The Gospel Herald,* they accept the 1689 London Confession and regarded themselves as heirs of the original Particular Baptists.[49]

In the twentieth century, Strict and Particular Baptists have formed a number of associations and a general union of their own. There were in 1982 perhaps one hundred Strict and Particular churches, with about fifteen thousand members, mostly in London and areas to the south.[50] For a time they contributed to the BMS but more recently have formed their own Strict Baptist Mission. Theologically they have advanced as far as Fullerism, but not beyond. Their worship is simple, usually without musical accompaniment, and women are expected to dress with extreme modesty and keep silent in the church. Their social practices are as strict as their theology, for some of this group do not read daily newspapers, listen to the radio, or watch television. In some ways, they represent an effort to preserve the simple life-style, as well as the strict theology, of earlier times.

More recently another group has emerged, known as the Reformed Evan-

---

49. For an overview of this group, see S. F. Paul, *Historical Sketch of the Gospel Standard Baptists.*

50. Hayden, *Documents,* p. 115.

gelical Baptists. They also accept the confession of 1689 and regard themselves as in line of succession from the earliest Particular Baptists. They represent renewal of Calvinist theology, emphasizing human depravity, the predestination of both saved and damned, and the eternal security of the elect. In 1976 they formed the London Reformed Baptist Seminary, based at Metropolitan Tabernacle, Spurgeon's old church. Ultraconservative in doctrine, methods, and social practice, this group condemns the Baptist Union and its churches. Regarding the Baptist colleges as "seminaries of uncertainty," they reject even Spurgeon's College. Railing against "liberal ecumenists" and "carnal-idiom music and methods" in union churches, their literature shows that on most subjects they hold a fundamentalist outlook. Perhaps the feelings of futility and helplessness so prevalent in society contributed to the revival of this kind of determinism in religion. The attitude of many of this group, according to their own literature, is "Let go, let God."[51] This seems to fit better the theology of John Gill whom they ignore than Charles Spurgeon whom they idolize.

The Baptist World Alliance

Though an international organization, the Baptist World Alliance (BWA) may best be introduced in connection with English Baptists. It was founded in London in 1905, its first president was English, and from 1905 to 1941 it was headquartered at Baptist Church House in London. Nazi bombs threatened these facilities early in World War II, forcing the BWA to take temporary headquarters in Washington, D.C. in 1941. Six years later that move was made permanent. A European headquarters was retained in London but later moved to Copenhagen, Denmark.

Perhaps the earliest call for a world conference of all Baptists was in 1678, when Thomas Grantham said, "I could wish that all congregations of Christians of the world that are baptized according to the appointment of Christ would make one consistory at least sometimes to consider matters of difference among them."[52] Over a century later, in a 1790 editorial, John Rippon wrote:

> To all the baptized ministers and people in America, England, Ireland, Scotland, Wales, the United Netherlands, France, Switzerland, Poland, Russia, and elsewhere, with a desire of promoting a universal interchange of kind offices among them, and in serious expectation that before many years elapse (in imitation of other wise men) a deputation from all these climes will meet

51. See the booklet, "London Reformed Baptist Seminary" (Elephant and Castle, London: Metropolitan Tabernacle, n.d.).
52. Cited by Louie D. Newton, "Baptist World Alliance," *Encyclopedia of Southern Baptists* (Nashville: Broadman Press, 1958), 1:127-28 (hereafter cited as *ESB*).

probably in London to consult the ecclesiastical good of the whole, which is now submitted to their superior wisdom.[53]

Though nothing came of these early suggestions, they show that the concept of a world gathering of Baptists goes far back. At the turn of the twentieth century, the idea was suddenly revived. Presbyterians and Congregationalists had formed world fellowships, and this doubtlessly influenced the Baptists to do likewise. One of the earliest expressions of this revived interest came in *The Baptist Argus* (later *The Baptist World*), edited by J. N. Prestridge of Kentucky. Professor A. T. Robertson of The Southern Baptist Theological Seminary in Louisville had suggested that one issue of the *Argus* be devoted to the theme of "Baptist World Outlook." That issue, focusing attention on Baptists around the world, aroused intense interest.

The *Argus* carried Robertson's follow-up editorial, "Why Not a World's Baptist Conference?" on January 14, 1904. Described as "The editorial that started it," marked copies were sent to Baptist leaders around the world. Robertson wrote:

> We suggest, for what it may be worth, that next summer, say in London, the Baptists of the World send some of its mission and education leaders for a conference on Baptist world problems. . . . If such a conference led afterwards to a Pan-Baptist Conference, well and good.[54]

Although the conference contemplated would pass no "legislation," it would allow opportunity for Baptists to grow in fellowship and learn much from each other. According to Robertson:

> The responses came thick and fast from all over the world and great interest was aroused. In particular in London Dr. J. H. Shakespeare, editor of *The Baptist Times and Freeman,* caught the vision of the thing and he threw into it his own great gifts for organization.[55]

In addition to Shakespeare, such leading English Baptists as Alexander Maclaren and John Clifford supported the idea. In July 1904 the English Baptists extended to the Baptists of the world an invitation to meet in London the next year. Representatives from Baptist groups in twenty-three countries met at Exeter Hall July 11-19, 1905 and formed the Baptist World Alliance. The first president was the famed London preacher, John Clifford.

The name *Alliance* puzzled some Baptists, who were more familiar with such terms as *association, convention,* or *union.* The name was chosen to show that the new organization had no intention to assume the functions of any existing organization. Despite the name, it has more nearly func-

---

53. Cited by F. Townley Lord, *Baptist World Fellowship: A Short History of the Baptist World Alliance,* p. 2.
54. Carl W. Tiller, *The Twentieth Century Baptist,* p. 2.
55. Lord, p. 3.

tioned as a world fellowship. Its purposes have been to promote mutual awareness, fellowship, inspiration, and to speak out on matters of mutual concern such as religious liberty, world peace, and distribution of relief funds in emergency areas. The constitution, as modified in 1955, says:

> The Baptist World Alliance, extending over every part of the world, exists in order more fully to show the essential oneness of Baptist people in the Lord Jesus Christ, to impart inspiration to the brotherhood, and to promote the spirit of fellowship, service and cooperation among its members; but this Alliance may in no way interfere with the independence of the churches or assume the administrative functions of existing organizations.[56]

Article II of the constitution, under the category of "Nature and Functions," merits quotation at length.

> Serving as the nerve center and corporate will of Baptists throughout the world the Alliance shall:
>
> (1) Have as one of its primary purposes the safeguarding of full religious liberty everywhere, not only for our own constituent churches, but also for all other religious faiths.
>
> (2) Serve as an agency for propagating Baptist principles and tenets of faith, objectives and distinctive principles throughout the world.
>
> (3) Serve as an agency to make surveys throughout the world with a view to furnishing facts to the various Baptist groups and counselling with them in establishing work in new fields when such service is requested.
>
> (4) Serve as a world-wide agency in making such use of the radio and press as may be practicable in preaching the Gospel, propagating Baptist principles, and promoting common tasks of Baptists throughout the world.
>
> (5) Arrange and conduct preaching missions throughout the world.
>
> (6) Co-operate with Baptist groups in instituting and administering relief funds as occasion may require.
>
> (7) Gather news by means of correspondence in the various Baptist groups, and disseminate it by use of bulletins, Baptist and other papers, and radio; and, when feasible, by a Baptist world publication.[57]

Though its intention has been to meet in world congress every five years, wars and other world crises have sometimes forced postponement of meetings.

The driving force of the BWA in its early years was J. H. Shakespeare of London, who in addition to his other duties served as its general secretary from 1905 to 1925. From 1923 James H. Rushbrooke gave full time to alliance work in Europe; in 1928, he became its first full-time secretary. For years it was customary to elect a general secretary from England and an associate secretary from the USA. However, as the work expanded, its leadership was placed under one general secretary and a number of full-time

56. Cited by Newton, p. 128.
57. Josef Nordenhaug, ed., *The Truth that Makes Men Free: Official Report of the Eleventh Congress, Baptist World Alliance, 1965,* p. 545.

associates for various interests and areas. In 1955 the committees for work with youth and women were expanded to department status, each with its own associate secretary, and the same expansion marked work with Baptist men in 1960. General secretaries have included J. H. Shakespeare, England, 1905-1925; James H. Rushbrooke, England, 1928-1939; Walter O. Lewis, USA, 1939-1948; Arnold T. Ohrn, Norway, 1948-1960; Josef Nordenhaug, Norway, 1960-1969; Robert S. Denny, USA, 1970-1980; and Gerhard Claas, West Germany, since 1980.

The president of the alliance has often spent much time visiting Baptist groups in various parts of the world. The president's role has been primarily in inspiration and public relations, while the day-to-day work of administering the various programs falls to the general secretary and the associate secretaries.

The BWA allows Baptists to pool their resources to do large tasks. It provides inspiration, especially for the smaller Baptist groups, to see they are part of a vast world movement of Baptist faith. It allows Baptists to speak more effectively to world issues, especially in religious liberty. It provides Baptists from over 125 countries, with their cultural and theological variety, a moving demonstration that their common ties in Jesus Christ are more important than their various doctrinal and social differences.

Signs of Renewal

Numerical decline and doctrinal diversity do not tell the full story of English Baptists in the twentieth century. Signs of renewal are evident and may yet bring some degree of recovery. Among the hopeful signs were a growing supply of promising young ministers, a recovery of evangelism in the churches, increased church participation of youth and young couples, renewed interest in Bible study, upgrading of Baptist styles of worship, and a trend toward reaffirming the historic Baptist witness in an ecumenical age. Throughout Britain, observers said, a renewed interest in the spiritual life seemed to follow the widespread feeling of futility at the failure of the secular society to meet the most basic of human needs.

Baptists, like Wesley in his day, seem to be discovering the potential for renewal in small groups or spiritual "cells." One article concluded, "All over the country there are signs of a fresh stirring of the Spirit that has at last broken the failure syndrome and is giving fresh hope for the future."[58] While perhaps a bit too optimistic, this article reveals a new spirit among English Christians. In 1979 the Baptists formed a group called "Mainstream Baptists for Life and Growth" to encourage these signs of renewal.

58. Monica Hill, "God Is Doing a New Thing in Britain: Twelve Signs of Growth," *Church Growth Digest* (Spring 1983), p. 6.

Baptists in Greater Britain

While specific economic and political relationships with England have changed in this century, for Wales, Scotland, and Ireland the term *Greater Britain* still provides an acceptable category under which to sketch the highlights of Baptist work in those areas. The unyielding demands of space allow little beyond the major Baptist highlights.

Baptists in Wales

Wales lies to the west of England, bordering on the Irish Sea. A land of legend, Wales was populated by ancient Celts who struggled heroically, but in the end unsuccessfully, to repel the Anglo-Saxon invader-immigrants. Though they are now linked with England in politics and economy, the Welsh maintain identity as a people apart. About 20 percent still speak the Welsh language.

The fortunes of Baptists in Wales follow closely the fortunes of the land. When Wales prospered, Baptists prospered; when Wales declined, Baptists shared fully in that decline. Welsh Baptists entered the twentieth century on a high note, with the great revival of 1904-1905. They approach the end of the century paralyzed with spiritual lethargy, in need of another such renewal.

The revival of 1904-1905. Wales has a long history of revivalism. One recalls, for example, the great revival of 1859 and the earlier work of Christmas Evans. Another such awakening broke out in 1904 when a twenty-six year old miner, Evan Roberts, began to preach and thousands flocked to hear him. Roberts, a Methodist, is usually considered the founder of the Welsh revival, but he was perhaps as much a product as the creator of that movement.

The first reference to a stirring among the Baptists came in July 1904. By October the revival was in full force, with emotional services and numerous baptisms reported. In the two-year period, thousands of converts were baptized and scores of lapsed members restored to active church life. For example, in the Monmouthshire Association alone the 68 affiliated churches reported 5,100 baptisms and 1,236 restored by late 1905.[59]

The Welsh revival was largely a lay effort and had many anticlerical overtones. It was marked by prayer, singing, and sharing of personal testimony. "The movement has its origin," one historian wrote, "in the masses and especially among women and young people."[60]

By late 1905 the revival disappeared as suddenly as it had appeared. Professional evangelists blew upon the embers, but to no effect, and by 1907 the churches began to record losses in number and coldness of spirit. The

59. Thomas Myrfin Bassett, *The Welsh Baptists,* p. 378.
60. Ibid.

churches had no effective means to disciple the new converts, who soon drifted away. Wales has not seen another such revival in this century, though the two world wars brought brief flurries of spiritual kindling.

Four groups of Baptists. At least four groups are discernible among Welsh Baptists. In South Wales, a number of English-speaking churches are affiliated with the Baptist Union of Great Britain and Ireland. These "English churches," as they are known, count over fifty churches organized into three associations. Their affiliation with the English union is perhaps as much cultural as theological, since many of their members come from English immigrants to the area. At times the situation creates tensions, and certainly limits communication, between the English-related churches and the bulk of Welsh Baptists.

A second group is made up of churches that are English-speaking, 172 in 1983, but affiliated with the Baptist Union of Wales. They share much of the cultural and political loyalty of the Welsh but are unable or unwilling to use the Welsh language. At one time these churches had their own separate union, but in the twentieth century they merged to form one arm of the Welsh Union.

The over four hundred Welsh-speaking Baptist churches that affiliate with the Baptist Union of Wales form the third group of Baptists in Wales. Most of these churches are small and face the persistent problem of obtaining pastors able to preach in Welsh. The blunt truth is that the Welsh language is disappearing despite all efforts to preserve and perpetuate it. Of the 20 percent of the population now using the language, many are among the highly educated elite. Among the working people, from whom Baptists in Wales largely recruit, the percentage who use the language is said to be less than 5 percent. By 1983 there were fewer than one hundred Welsh-speaking full-time Baptist pastors and only a handful in the colleges to take their place. A Welsh church that loses its pastor can hardly expect to obtain another. They have to devise alternate ways of worship, led by laymen who present a message or read one in Welsh. Some who attend the Welsh churches do not understand the language but go for the cultural value or to learn the language.

Remnants of the "Scotch" Baptists have about ten surviving churches in northern Wales. This fourth group represents a continuation of McLeanist and Campbellite forms of Baptist life whose adherents migrated to Wales from Scotland and still maintain a tiny presence.

In addition to language problems, the Welsh Baptists have been plagued by their inability to achieve unity either of outlook or organization. Extreme doctrinal conservatism and exaggerated local church independence mark many of the churches, and a resurgent Calvinism has made itself evident at some places.

The Baptist Union of Wales. Formed in 1866, the Baptist Union of Wales has been restructured in the twentieth century. For years Welsh and

English-speaking churches had separate unions, but these have since been merged into one union with two distinct wings, one for the English-speaking churches and one for the Welsh-speaking. Each branch has its own council and annual assembly. However, one general secretary serves both branches.

Headquartered in Swansea, the Baptist Union of Wales publishes *Seren Gomer,* a Welsh-language quarterly, in addition to the *Messenger,* an English newspaper. They produce and distribute other types of Christian literature, operate a book store, and have in recent years published new hymnals in both Welsh and English. The union has only one full-time staff member, the general secretary, but plans in the 1980s to add a minister to work in evangelism and church planting.

Welsh Baptists operate two colleges. The South Wales Baptist College was first formed under another name at Abergavenny in 1807. It was moved to Pontypool in 1836 and to Cardiff in 1893. It enrolls about twenty-five students. Bangor College was formed at Llangollen in 1862 and moved to Bangor in 1892. Several proposals to combine the colleges have as yet come to nothing.

The Baptist Union has made ongoing efforts to adapt its ministry to the changing conditions in Wales. The reports of two special study groups may be briefly noted here. In 1964 the union appointed a committee to study Baptist work in Wales, with special attention to the years 1945 to 1965, and to report findings as a basis for possible policy changes. The report in 1967 described Baptist life in Wales as "tottering precariously these days under the weight of social change and religious apostasy."[61] The committee called for improvements in the quality and training of ministers, more adequate financial support for pastors, and updated teaching methods in Welsh Sunday Schools. Other suggestions included bringing the colleges under closer denominational oversight and above all a renewal of evangelism in the denomination. The report concluded, "Unless we evangelize in earnest, our days, as a *Denomination in Wales,* are surely numbered."

On the ordination of women, the 1967 report affirmed that while the Scripture did not forbid it, "in practice, we fear that the ordaining of women to the full ministry would not be acceptable at present to the majority of our churches."[62] The Baptist Union has since acknowledged women ministers, but few have applied for ordination.

For a small denomination, the Baptist Union of Wales sustains a confusing array of funds for various causes, all worthwhile no doubt and all competing with the others. Efforts of the study commission to consolidate these brought only limited results, and efforts to upgrade pastoral benefits floundered on the rocks of poverty combined with the low level of financial

61. "*Adroddiad Comisiwn Y Weinidogaeth,*" or "The Report of the Commission on the Ministry" (Swansea: Baptist Union of Wales, 1967), p. 5.
62. Ibid., pp. 9, 15.

stewardship which has long marked the Welsh churches. "We are Britain's Meanest Baptists," proclaimed one headline in the Baptist *Messenger,* describing per capita giving of Baptists in Wales, which measured only about one third as much as in England and one fourth that of Scotland.[63]

"A Step Further" was the title of the report of another study group, which reported to the Baptist Union in 1980. Under the chairmanship of Robert J. Young, this commission made perhaps the most detailed analysis of Welsh Baptist life since mid-century. Citing the failure to evangelize, the commission portrayed a picture of small and discouraged churches. "A sense of hopelessness has grown in our churches," the report said, "where men are few and young people even fewer," and most of the membership is made up of aged pensioners. In blunt fashion, the report said, "We have spent so much time thinking about our problems that we have forgotten God. As a result our congregations are vague in doctrine and therefore uncertain in practice."[64]

Between 1945 and 1965 Baptist membership in Wales declined by 50 percent, while the number of churches declined by only 15 percent. This left a lot of small churches; the average membership in a Baptist church in Wales was 55 in 1965 and between 40 and 50 in 1983. Over 80 percent of the Welsh churches, according to the 1980 study, report no converts and no baptisms in a typical year. Recognizing that "yesterday's chapels were erected for services of worship alone; [while] today's church needs to do so much more," the report also complained that the "drab colours and hard seats" of present buildings leads to "congregations with stiff necks and cold feet." Noting that "the record of Welsh Baptists in financial giving is appalling," the report urged Baptists to adopt a spirit of "thank-offerings" to God rather than "grudge-giving" to keep the churches alive.[65]

Suggestions for the future included a renewed emphasis upon evangelism, better recruitment and preparation for ministers, improved literature for teaching children and lay persons, grouping several small churches under one pastor, and allowing some dying churches to die while concentrating available funds to plant churches in more promising new population centers.

Patterns of growth. Nowhere in Britain has Baptist decline been more disastrous than in Wales since World War I. This is more surprising in that Wales was a leader in Baptist advance in the nineteenth century. D. Islwyn Davies, general secretary, warned in 1978, "The denomination is disappearing before our eyes." He continued:

There is hardly need to spell out the dramatic drop in the membership of our

63. *The Messenger,* Baptist Union of Wales (Autumn 1977), p. 1.

64. R. J. Young, ed., "A Step Further: The Report of the Baptist Union Working Group," Baptist Union of Wales (May 1980), p. 3.

65. Ibid., p. 7.

Churches nor the fall-out of Ministers of the Word and Shepherds of souls. One set of statistics will suffice to illustrate. In 1950 the membership of the Baptist Union of Wales was 81,622; in 1978 about half that number—41,228. In 1950 the Union had 330 ministers in charge of Churches; in 1978 about half that number—161.[66]

In some places the decline was even sharper. In the Aberdare Valley Baptists in 1926 had 4,443 members; in 1963 they had only 893. Sunday School enrollment dropped from 3,675 in 1926 to 965 in 1963.[67] In 1983 the Baptist *Y DYDDIADUR A LLAWLYFR* (*Diary and Handbook*) reported further decline, to 36,120 members in 613 churches in all of Wales.[68]

Welsh Baptist leaders have pointed out what outsiders would hesitate to suggest: This numerical decline has been accompanied by a corresponding inner decay of spiritual vitality. "All religions are slowly fading out," lamented one Welshman, and "chapels are being turned into garages."[69] A Baptist Union report confessed in 1980 that Welsh Baptists give only "half-hearted obedience" to the gospel. After citing the usual socioeconomic explanations for Baptist decline, one Baptist leader added, "But there is something more, something deeper, a crisis of the spirit."[70]

Those who like "explanations" will find at least five major reasons advanced to account for the decline of Welsh Baptists: changes in the economy, changes in the political structure, Baptist controversy and conservatism, refusal to switch to the English language, and the neglect of evangelism. In the nineteenth century, Wales became almost totally dependent upon the coal industry, which drew millions of workers to Wales, most of them sympathetic to evangelical religion and prime prospects for Baptist affiliation. However, after World War I the Welsh coal industry collapsed, leading to massive depopulation, as unemployed workers left Wales in despair. Since mines and chapels were often located together, the closing of one meant the closing, or at least the decimation, of the other.

Second, political changes have also had an impact upon Baptists. In his *Chapels in the Valley,* D. Ben Rees says that political changes, in effect, turned Dissenters into an "out class." One result has been a tendency for Baptists, laymen and ministers alike, to move out of Baptist life when they achieve some measure of economic or cultural success.

A third reason advanced for Baptist decline is the traditional Welsh Baptist conservatism and controversy. Welsh Baptists were born in contro-

66. *The Messenger,* Baptist Union of Wales (Spring 1978), p. 1.

67. D. Ben Rees, *Chapels in the Valley* (Wirral, Merseyside: The Feynnon Press, 1975), pp. 76-77.

68. D. Islwyn Davies, ed., *The Diary and Handbook, 1983* (Swansea: Baptist Union of Wales, 1983), p. 44.

69. Rees, p. 115.

70. Personal interview at Ilston House, Swansea, July 6, 1983.

versy and have lived therein ever since. Their conservatism has been not only doctrinal but also extends to social and cultural mores. Fourth, the adamant refusal of the majority of Welsh churches to shift to the English language has put them out of touch with the population around them. In what some describe as a decision for their native tongue over the gospel of Christ, the churches have preferred to die in Welsh rather than live in English.

A fifth and perhaps major explanation of Baptist decline centers around the neglect of evangelism. For some years the annual reports show that only about 20 percent of the Welsh churches report any converts during the year. In a booklet that formed part of the 1966 centennial celebration of the Baptist Union, Raymond Williams said:

> We might say that every empty pew, all irreligion and ignorance, every emptiness and meaninglessness in the life of people, every "falling away" from the Faith underlines the need for Evangelism. . . . The Churches must Evangelise in the fullest sense of the word, or perish with the passing of the years.[71]

In summary, for Welsh Baptists in the twentieth century the good news seemed eclipsed by the bad. A few leaders professed to see glimmers of hope on the horizon; others who failed to see those signs hoped the leaders were correct.

Baptists in Scotland

Life for Baptists has not been easy in a land blanketed with the repressive spirit of John Knox and dominated by the state church of Scotland (Presbyterian). Scottish Baptists have shared many of the same trends which have marked English Baptists during the present century. Since mid-century they have experienced a measure of church growth, financial advance, and renewed spiritual vitality.

The Baptist Union of Scotland. From its beginnings in 1869, the Baptist Union of Scotland (BUS) was served by part-time general secretaries. In 1919 W. B. Nicholson became the first full-time secretary, followed by Thomas Stewart (1920-1930), James Scott (1930-1949), G. M. Hardie (1949-1966), Andrew D. MacRae (1966-1980), and Peter H. Barber (since 1980). Of these, MacRae proved the most controversial, and perhaps also the most innovative.

The union is divided into three departments: Department of Church Life, dealing with union funds and internal affairs; Department of Mission, dealing with church extension; and Department of Publications, responsible for an extensive list of periodicals, reports, booklets, and other Christian literature. *The Scottish Baptist,* official magazine of the BUS, came into denominational ownership in 1943 from the Tulloch family. The union also

---

71. Raymond Williams, *Evangelism Now* (Swansea: Baptist Union of Wales, 1966), p. 6.

publishes *Scottish Baptist News,* a monthly newspaper, and sponsors the Atholl Baptist Centre at Pitlochry. Like other British Baptists, the BUS maintains a list of accredited ministers. The "unaided churches," those receiving no supplementary funds from the denomination, may call whom they will as pastor, but "aided churches" must call pastors from the accredited list. In 1983 the union redefined the role of general secretary and added to the staff a "general superintendent" to work with pastors in counseling, ministerial education and certification, and pastoral placement. David Eric Watson was chosen for this new office.

Closely associated with the union, but under separate management, is the Baptist College of Scotland, with an enrollment of twenty-two in 1982.[72] In 1981 the college moved to spacious new facilities on Aytoun Road, Glasgow, next door to the union building. Scottish leaders expect the physical proximity to lead to closer cooperation between the denomination and its college.

One of the major efforts of organized Baptist life in Scotland has been to provide for an educated ministry. Various plans have been tried, including putting students with a pastor-tutor, sending them to English Baptist colleges, and attempting to establish a college of their own. While none of these has been without problems, the latter has been the way of the present century. Theological tensions as well as scarcity of funds handicapped earlier efforts, as in 1894 the Baptist Union relinquished educational work and the Baptist Theological College of Scotland was formed as an independent effort separate from the union. One historian has concluded, "The education story [in Scotland] is not altogether a happy one, and some of the wounds were to be a long time in healing."[73]

In 1909 the Baptist women of Scotland formed the Women's Auxiliary to the Baptist Union, with the fourfold aim of (1) organizing women for the spread of evangelical truth and Baptist teachings, (2) assisting the Baptist Union work in Scotland, (3) appointing and supporting an order of deaconesses, and (4) organizing women's work locally in the churches. The first president was Mrs. George Yuille, wife of the union secretary. While several Baptist unions elsewhere formed deaconess orders, Scotland never did, although several individual churches have maintained deaconesses. The auxiliary did for a time support a woman evangelist.

During the first half of the twentieth century, the Baptist Union of Scotland was reorganized, its constitution brought up to date, and more orderly lines of communication established between local churches, associations, and the national union. The union adopted the Declaration of Princi-

---

72. *The Scottish Baptist Year Book* (Glasgow: Baptist Church House, 1981), p. 60.
73. Derek B. Murray, *The First Hundred Years: The Baptist Union of Scotland* (Dundee: The Baptist Union of Scotland, 1969), p. 75.

ple, in effect a doctrinal statement, which had been voted by the Baptist Union of Great Britain and Ireland in 1906.

Home and foreign missions had long been conducted separately from the Baptist Union. For years Scottish Baptists contributed foreign mission offerings through the Baptist Missionary Society; Andrew Fuller traveled regularly among the Scottish churches raising funds. The home mission society was also separate, antedating the Baptist Union by a full generation. However, in the twentieth century the Baptist Union exercised its gravitational force and mission work was drawn into its orbit.

Patterns of growth. Statistics may fail to capture the inner dynamic, but they can illustrate outward conditions, as we see in the case of Scottish Baptists. In 1900 Scottish Baptists reported 118 churches, with 16,905 members, and 929 baptisms.[74] In 1982 they reported 158 churches, with 14,656 members and 571 baptisms. This did not include reports from about 10 Baptist churches not affiliated with the BUS, with about 1,760 members.[75] Both world wars triggered spurts of Baptist growth, especially in the cities, but postwar recession brought its toll of dislocation and decline. For example, Glasgow reported 5,700 Baptists in 1941, portioned out in several strong churches; in 1981 the Baptist population had dropped to about 2,800, an almost 50 percent decline in forty years.[76]

In the fifteen years between 1965 and 1980, membership declined about 12 percent despite the fact that hundreds of new members were baptized each year.[77] Some Baptists joined the Church of Scotland while others dropped out of church life altogether.

Andrew D. MacRae set about in the late 1960s to reverse these trends. Somewhat enamored of the church-growth school of thought in the United States, MacRae made it a point to import innovative approaches. In particular he initiated closer relations with the Southern Baptist Convention, known for its evangelism and growth. He took thirty Scottish pastors to the States to preach and to observe SBC methods, encouraged Southern Baptists to spend time in Scotland in youth work, teaching, and church planting. MacRae led the union in 1977 to adopt a goal of 50 percent increase in church membership within three years, with a 100 percent increase in contributions. In general, he saw encouraging uptrends in most aspects of Baptist life. Some pastors, however, were less comfortable with the "American connection" and found some of the methods unacceptable.

Following MacRae, Peter H. Barber modified some methods but kept the emphasis upon church growth. He led the BUS to adopt a major evangelis-

74. *The Scottish Baptist Year Book* (Glasgow: Baptist Church House, 1900), p. 17.
75. Ibid. (1983), p. 30.
76. David Watts, "Baptists in Glasgow: The Twentieth Century Challenge of Urban Growth and Decline," in Clements, p. 18.
77. *The Scottish Baptist Magazine,* Glasgow (Aug. 1982), p. 8.

tic campaign, known as "Scotreach," for the years 1984-1986.[78] From a 1966 lament that "the life of the church is languishing," one senses a different spirit in a 1979 report which affirms:

> The past few years have seen many new developments in the life of the denomination, and have assured us that God is truly at work amongst us. The blessings of Simultaneous Evangelism; the influx of young people into our churches; the rise in the number of men entering the ministry; the development of new churches . . . the unprecedented growth in support for the denomination's budget . . . are all signs of God's living presence among us.[79]

Issues facing Scottish Baptists. Several controversies have plagued Baptists in Scotland in the present century. As always, some have centered around Baptist schools and accusations of false teaching by certain professors. Nowhere in the world where Baptist have operated schools have they been able to avoid this kind of conflict. By the late 1940s tensions were so sharp in the Baptist Union that a few pastors withdrew to form a rival Evangelical Baptist Fellowship, which for a time sponsored its own school.

Another controversy led to the Commission of Enquiry, which presented its preliminary report in 1939. Noting that many pastors were leaving the denomination, the commission sought to find reasons and recommend changes to stop the flow. Citing such factors as low salaries, constant doctrinal conflict, and low spirituality as some of the causes for leaving, its suggestions for change looked radical to many Baptists. It called for higher minimum salaries, more authority for the denomination over the settlement of pastors, and less independence for local congregations. Its recommendations would, in effect, have brought the congregations under denominational control. After vigorous discussion at the 1944 meeting of the union, the report was shelved.

A third area of controversy arose out of the ecumenical movement. The Baptist Union sent representatives to the Missionary Conference in Edinburgh in 1910 and the World Council of Churches in Amsterdam in 1948. However, Scottish Baptists were not agreed on the extent of their participation in the church union movement. By a bare margin, the union voted to join the World Council, but controversy lingered.

Influential leaders urged the union to quit the World Council, and a number of churches threatened to withdraw from the union unless that was done. One objection claimed, "The World Council will not commit itself to bow to the final authority of Scripture."[80] After years of intense discussion, the union voted in 1956 to "withdraw affiliation for 7 years in the hope that the basis of the World Council of Churches be brought nearer our own

78. Ibid. (June 1983).
79. "Basis for Advance" (Glasgow: Baptist Union of Scotland, 1979).
80. Murray, p. 116.

faith and practice." At the end of the seven years, the union voted more than four to one to "continue in disaffiliation with the World Council of Churches."[81] It did, however, retain ties with the British Council, as well as with the Scottish Churches Council.

Scottish Baptists have confronted several other crucial issues in recent years. Among these are the charismatic movement, the ordination of women to ministry, and the status of divorced pastors. These can be sketched only briefly and, since they are currently under discussion, a final word on Baptist response must await the future.

Whether the charismatic renewal movement, which the Scots abbreviate as CRM, has "afflicted" or "blessed" the churches depends upon the perspective of the one describing the phenomenon. Like most denominations, the Baptist Union has been profoundly affected, with a number of churches, pastors, and lay persons caught up in Pentecostal practices and beliefs. This has led to tension between charismatic churches and the union, though few to date have withdrawn from affiliation. The pages of the *Scottish Baptist Magazine* and the *Scottish Baptist News* have been open for articles, letters to the editor, and the exchange of testimonies pro and con. At a deeper theological level, the Department of Mission issued a thorough study in 1983 under title of "Scottish Baptists and the Charismatic Renewal Movement: Report and Guidelines." With remarkable balance, the report surveyed the extent of charismatic infiltration into Baptist life, summarized scriptural and theological aspects of the movement, and assessed both positive and negative results. The report urged caution and patience, outlining ways in which both opponents and proponents might cooperate and reduce the risk of church schisms.

Scottish Baptists met the issue of women in ministry not in theoretical discussion but in the person of a young woman who enrolled in the Scottish Baptist College in 1981 and applied for ministerial status. The Baptists appointed a "Sub-Committee on Women in the Ministry," including one woman and six men, to study the matter. Its report in 1982 comprised a rather thorough study of biblical, historical, and theological dimensions of the question of women in ministry, along with a brief survey, not always accurate, of the status of women in other denominations. A majority of the committee favored admitting women to ordination, but a substantial minority opposed. The matter was referred to the Union Council and ultimately to the assembly in 1983. In both of these mostly male forums a clear majority favored ordaining women, but the vote failed of the two thirds required to implement such a decision.

The status of divorced pastors also troubled Scottish Baptists. In December 1982, the union received a report on "The Nature of Marriage and Problems of Divorce," noting that divorce had become prevalent among

81. Ibid., p. 118.

Baptists and was not unknown among pastors. Rejecting the indiscriminate marriages of divorced persons in church, and the equally indiscriminate refusal of some pastors to perform marriages for any divorced persons, the union suggested that each case be decided on its merits, with a church wedding approved for some divorced persons.

In an appendix on "Marriage and the Ministry," the report reaffirmed a 1979 assembly decision that disqualified divorced pastors from the list of accredited ministers. Frankly admitting that it required a higher standard for ministers than for laity, the assembly voted that "breakdown of marriage in which there is no apparent prospect of reconciliation shall normally be considered a bar to approval for Baptist ministry."[82] Later discussions have brought a number of modifications and exceptions. One is struck by the similarity between these modern discussions and those among the General Baptists in the early 1700s, and prospects are that the outcome will be much the same.

In summary, one may say that Scottish Baptists in the twentieth century present the classic good-news-bad-news syndrome. The good news includes a new note of spiritual vitality, a good supply of able ministers, aggressive and capable denominational leadership, a reversal of numerical decline, and renewed interest on the part of young people. The bad news includes remnants of the "Scotch" and "English" church controversy from the previous century, continued domination of Scottish society by the Church of Scotland, economic recessions to which Baptists are particularly susceptible, and doctrinal diversity that at times threatens to turn divisive. Most observers, however, feel that the good news predominates.

Baptists in Ireland

Baptists in the Emerald Isle have a small but vigorous presence. From small beginnings in the 1640s, they have over the years withstood such obstacles as famine, resistance from a strong Roman Catholic population, legal handicaps placed by hostile government, doctrinal dissension, and not least a sense of isolation from other parts of the Baptist family. Despite these problems, the Irish Baptists have come to the last decades of the twentieth century with a sense of inner spiritual vitality. With 85 churches and 7,941 members in 1981, they have experienced steady growth throughout the century.[83]

For years the Baptists in Ireland affiliated with the larger body in England, but early in the present century, the Irish formed their own denominational union. For a time they continued to funnel their foreign mission contributions through the London-based BMS but in 1926 severed this last

82. "The Nature of Marriage and Problems of Divorce" (Glasgow: Baptist Union of Scotland, 1983), cited from "Appendix: Marriage and the Ministry," p. 8.

83. *Assembly Handbook* (Belfast: Baptist Union of Ireland, 1982), p. 29.

official tie by forming their own missionary society. The present social and political unrest in Northern Ireland has further widened the gap between English and Irish Baptists.

The Baptist Union of Ireland. In 1862 the Irish churches grouped themselves into the Irish Baptist Association and affiliated with the English Baptists. They reorganized in 1895, taking the name of the Baptist Union of Ireland and stood alone. A desire for independence in home mission work, plus a sense of doctrinal alienation, probably motivated this move. J. H. Shakespeare earnestly sought reunion, but in 1908 the Irish once again voted to remain separate. For a time a few Irish churches maintained dual affiliation.[84]

Relations between Irish and English Baptists were further strained in 1918 by Shakespeare's book, *The Churches at the Crossroads.* This book advocated more ecumenical concessions than Irish Baptists and, as it turned out, English Baptists were willing to make. The years 1920-1921 were known among Irish Baptists as the "troubled times."[85] Always more conservative than English Baptists, the Irish fell into doctrinal conflict among themselves and also found time to criticize such English Baptists as H. Wheeler Robinson for his biblical views. In 1921 the Irish Baptist Union passed with applause a move to designate foreign missionary money only to "approved missionaries," thus showing some suspicion of the BMS.[86]

Relations with the BMS remained strained, and in 1925 the Irish formed their own separate agency, called the Irish Baptist Foreign Mission. The new body was committed to "the establishment and control of Irish Baptist Foreign Mission fields, staffed by missionaries who accept and adhere to the Basis of Doctrines of the Baptist Union of Ireland."[87]

Home mission leaders have raised funds to plant new churches, especially in the northern cities, obtain sites for future church locations, and assist churches in erecting new buildings or repairing old ones. The 1981 home mission report, for example, described a number of tent revivals, home Bible study fellowships, and house-to-house evangelistic visitations.

The foreign mission work has been concentrated in only a few fields, primarily Peru and two or three countries of Europe. Much of the foreign mission support, amounting to £94,000 in 1981, comes from the Baptist Women's Fellowship. This missionary society has "branches," as they are called, in seventy-two of the eighty-five Irish Baptist churches, with regular meetings to study and promote missions.

Efforts to sponsor a Baptist college in Ireland go back at least to 1892

84. Joshua Thompson, "The Origin of the Irish Baptist Foreign Mission," *The Irish Baptist Historical Society Journal,* p. 21.
85. Ibid., p. 26.
86. Ibid., p. 28.
87. Ibid., p. 35.

when the Irish Baptist Training Institute opened in Dublin. Funded primarily by John D. Rockefeller of the United States, the school opened with five students under the tutelage of Hugh D. Brown. The announced purpose was to provide for "training Irishmen for pastoral and evangelistic work in their native land."[88]

From the first the churches showed little interest and gave limited support. The college considered relocation as early as 1919 and in 1964 did move to Belfast to be nearer the center of the Baptist constituency. The school remained small, with an enrollment throughout the 1920s and 1930s of fewer than ten. A decision in 1921 opened the college to women students, though none enrolled until the 1960s. At the move to Belfast, the college was reconstituted and brought under the direction of the Baptist Union. This has led to greater interest by the churches, more generous financial support, and less suspicion of an educated ministry.

In 1976 the Baptist College of Ireland was fully accredited as part of the Irish university system, though not without some anxiety on the part of Baptist leaders. Some registered fear lest the school "be invaded by Marxists, Hindoos, I.R.A. terrorists, etc." who would be "all littering the place with beer cans and cigarette butts."[89] If any of these dire predictions materialized, the records do not mention them.

Patterns of growth. The Irish Baptists have largely escaped the numerical decline which has marked other parts of the British Baptist family in the twentieth century. This does not mean they have grown large; they remain the smallest of the British Baptist groups. However, they have shown steady growth, rising from a membership of 3,498 in 1940 to 7,941 in 1981.[90] Of their 85 churches, 78 are in Northern Ireland, with 24 in Belfast alone.

In addition to statistical growth, the evidence suggests an inner spiritual dynamic among Irish Baptists. They are marked by aggressive evangelism, a unified denominational program, relative doctrinal harmony, and a more conservative theological stance than prevails among most British Baptists. In the Down Grade Controversy, the Irish sided strongly with C. H. Spurgeon against the English Baptist Union. Hugh D. Brown, a close friend of Spurgeon, led the Irish Baptists to spell out a conservative doctrinal confession. At times the Irish have been troubled by Campbellism, an ultraconservative form of Baptist life stemming primarily from Scotland. Interestingly, the theological textbook of the Irish Baptist College in its early days was the famed *Systematic Theology* of Charles H. Hodge of Princeton, often regarded as a primary source of doctrinal fundamentalism in both Britain

88. R. C. McMullan, "Baptist Education in Ireland," *Irish Baptist Historical Society Journal,* p. 30.

89. Ibid., p. 40.

90. "Membership of Affiliated Churches 1940-1981," *The Irish Baptist* (June 1982), statistical section, no page number listed.

and America.[91] Following Spurgeon, the Irish for years refused the title of *Reverend* but in recent years have accepted it. Irish Baptists do not ordain women but they list a number of "Lady Workers" alongside accredited ministers.[92]

Like other Baptists, the Irish have been confronted with the charismatic movement, especially since the 1970s. The 1981 home mission report included the blunt notice that "the work in ATHLONE suffered a set back when over half the people who met regularly for worship left to meet with a newly formed Pentecostal group."[93] Other churches faced similar problems, but the charismatic movement appeared not to have the appeal for Irish Baptists that one finds, for example, in England. Perhaps this is at least partly explained by doctrinal conservatism, lively worship services, and strong denominational identity among the Irish.

The time of troubles. Northern Ireland has been caught up in political unrest and violence that borders on civil war. While the recent crisis roots in ancient conflicts, the levels of hostility and violence have escalated, especially since the 1960s. The basic conflict is whether Northern Ireland shall remain a part of Britain or pull away to form a separate nation. The southern part of Ireland has already pulled away, forming the Republic of Ireland. The fact that Northern Ireland is predominantly Catholic and England predominantly Protestant has added to the problem, but must not obscure the fact that at its root the conflict is about political independence.

Apparently Baptists have been less affected by the Irish conflict than one might have expected. Paul Doherty conducted a study, entitled "A Survey of the Effects of 'the troubles' on Irish Baptist Churches." Upon the basis of questionnaires from 78 of the 85 churches, Doherty reported in 1978 that 17 churches, about 20 percent, had sustained some damage to their buildings, 5 churches had members killed in conflict, while another 9 had members injured. Several churches reported members moving their families to safer areas, especially away from Belfast. Some reported decreased attendance, but others reported increases. Much to Doherty's surprise, he reported, "The main finding of the survey would seem to be that the troubles have had little or no effect on the vast majority of Irish Baptist churches."[94]

Baptists of the British Commonwealth

In the nineteenth-century expansion of the British Empire, Baptists migrated to Australia, New Zealand, and South Africa. They established

91. McMullan, p. 31.

92. *Assembly Handbook* (Belfast: Baptist Union of Ireland, 1982), statistical section, no page listed.

93. Ibid., p. 15.

94. Paul Doherty, "A Survey of the Effects of 'the troubles' on Irish Baptist Churches," *Irish Baptist Historical Society Journal* (1977-1978), pp. 63-64.

indigenous churches which, though independent, maintained strong cultural and denominational ties with Britain. These churches originated primarily among migrant British nationals seeking a new life in a new country.

Baptists in Australia

Perhaps *unification* is the word that best describes Baptist work in Australia since 1900. Baptists began the century with regional unions in New South Wales, South Australia, Victoria, Queensland, Tasmania, and Western Australia. Each union published its own paper and sponsored separate efforts in home and foreign missions. Little communication, much less cooperation, existed across these state lines. A strong spirit of localism dominated Australian Baptist life.

Factors which encouraged growth included organized home mission work, evangelism, and immigration. Obstacles for Baptists included divisions, lack of denominational awareness and identity, the casual ease with which Baptists joined other denominations, the "tyranny of distance" which inhibited close fellowship, and what some writers have called the "burden of minorityhood."[95]

Toward the end of this century, however, Baptists have developed a stronger common identity and a central Baptist Union of Australia in which the state unions cooperate. The Baptist Union, sometimes called the Federal Union, sponsors two theological colleges, directs the work of united home and foreign mission boards to which all the state unions contribute, and publishes the *Australian Baptist,* the united voice of the denomination.

The state unions. Baptist work developed just as the various states of Australia were asserting their independence of each other, and this localism carried over into Baptist life. Distance, difficulty of travel and communication, and the problems of vast, sparsely populated areas added their impact, and the result was a series of regional Baptist bodies with little knowledge of each other. Each state union sponsored its own work, and these various ministries tended to overlap and even compete.

Gradually the Baptist work in New South Wales outgrew the other areas, due largely to rapid economic development and population growth. This expansion, especially when combined with decline in South Australia and Victoria, has given New South Wales a dominant voice in Baptist affairs. Not only did its institutions flourish and its leaders exert widening influence but also its theological views tended to prevail.

The federal union. From the first a few Baptist leaders recognized the disadvantages of regional isolation. As early as 1861 a correspondent to *The*

95. Michael Petras, *Extension or Extinction: Baptist Growth in New South Wales 1900-1939,* pp. 9, 15-39 passim.

Australian Evangelist suggested a national union of Baptist churches.[96] Such suggestions were common by the 1880s, but nothing was done largely because the political situation favored strict separation of each state. A further effort in the 1890s to create a "Federal Council" of representatives from each state union also failed. One editor commented tersely, "The unification of Baptists by the surrender of individual powers will indeed be a triumph of grace."[97]

Three forces combined around the turn of the century to pull the fragmented Australian Baptists into closer cooperation. First, the political situation changed. On January 1, 1901, the separate states came under a unified national constitution, in effect creating the nation of Australia. Whereas separateness had been the political stance earlier, unity now moved to center stage, and Baptists tended to follow their host culture. Second, the Baptist World Alliance, formed in London in 1905, captured the attention of Baptists and demonstrated the value of wider cooperation. The BWA led to a series of Australian Baptist Congresses, and these in turn led to unification of Baptist work. The third force pulling Baptists together was practicality. To make a running start on the new century, almost all the state unions planned major campaigns of fund raising, church extension, and ministerial training. The advantages of cooperation became obvious.

The first Australian Baptist Congress, held in Sidney in 1908, set in motion forces which eventually led to Baptist unification.[98] A second congress in 1911 at Melbourne made further progress, and by 1913 Baptists had agreed upon a common publishing house for all Australian Baptists; one newspaper, the *Australian Baptist;* and a united Baptist Foreign Mission Society. Full unification was delayed by World War I, but additional Baptist congresses in 1922 and 1925 completed the process. At Adelaide in 1925, Baptist leaders agreed upon a constitution, the state unions ratified it, and in early 1926 the Baptist Union of Australia came into existence.

This new body did not, however, follow the British pattern as closely as some had hoped. It was not a union of churches, but a union of unions. The state unions continued to conduct most of their ministries through the state bodies rather than through the national body. At first, the union set up only three boards, for home missions, youth work, and education. Later the foreign mission work came under direction of the union. The central denomination has continued to grow; in 1958, for example, no fewer than forty different boards and committees reported to the Baptist Union.

For a time the Baptist colleges, and other scattered "pre-college" educa-

96. Basil S. Brown, *Members One of Another: The Baptist Union of Victoria 1862-1962,* p. 108.

97. Ibid., p. 110.

98. Alan C. Prior, *Some Fell on Good Ground: A History of the Beginning and Development of the Baptist Church in New South Wales, Australia, 1831-1965,* pp. 204 f.

tional efforts, remained independent of the new Baptist Union. They had, in fact, limited organic relationship to the state unions, being operated mostly by local education societies which were often under the control of generous donors. However, in time the two major colleges at Melbourne and Sidney came into closer relationship to the union.

Lack of trained pastors proved a persistent problem for Australian Baptists; one writer described it as a "damaging deficiency" which reached well into the present century. The numerous efforts from the 1850s onward to provide ministerial training are remarkable for their surprising number and their common failure. Shortage of funds, disagreement about the kind of education required, and lingering suspicion of an educated ministry helped scuttle early educational efforts. The result was that few Australian pastors had any specific theological training; as late as 1921, for example, of seventy-four pastors in New South Wales, only two had earned college degrees.

The Baptist College of Victoria was formed in 1891 at Melbourne. Its first principal, W. T. Whitley, served for eleven years, and then moved back to England where he later distinguished himself as a major historian of British Baptists. After 1908 the Victorian Baptists agreed to admit students from the other provinces, thus providing, in effect, a common college center for all Australian Baptists. When economics forced the curtailment of this provision, Baptists of New South Wales established their own Baptist Theological College in 1916. With more hopes than achievements at first, the principal could as late as 1922 describe it as "a splendid possibility rather than an accomplished fact." Its students, sometimes fewer than ten, met in homes or churches, but in 1934 the college occupied its own building. In 1962 the college moved to its handsome new campus, with an enlarged faculty and expanded curriculum.

The Australian Baptist Foreign Mission Board, like the state boards before it, concentrated its work largely in India and Pakistan. In 1949 New South Wales opened a work in New Guinea, inspired by needs observed by World War II chaplains; but in 1951 they turned it over to the denominational board. In home missions, the Australian Baptists have tried to balance their efforts between the burgeoning cities of the south and the sparsely populated regions of the north. Since World War II the denomination has sponsored a number of foreign language missions, an opportunity made possible by government policy which has encouraged immigration into Australia.

Issues facing Australian Baptists. Among issues common to Baptists everywhere, two or three of the problems faced by Australian Baptists in the twentieth century merit mention here. They met the ecumenical issue in the 1830s when Baptists were forced into varying degrees of cooperation with others, especially Congregationalists. Their mixed membership churches often contained only a minority of baptized members, and many of the early schools were joint endeavors with others. Government assistance on church building funds, a practice frowned upon by Baptists but usually accepted when offered, sometimes cast Baptists into joint church building ownership and use with other denominations. Some early pastors, like John Saunders, made it a point to downplay Baptist distinctives in an effort to cooperate with other denominations. However, none of this precedent really prepared Australian Baptists for the extensive ecumenical proposals of 1919-1920.

In 1919 proposals were presented for the merger of Australian Methodists, Presbyterians, Congregationalists, and Baptists. Baptist leaders in South Australia pushed hard for acceptance, but the opposition was led by New South Wales.[99] When the scheme came to naught, one effect had been to increase the prestige of NSW to the detriment of South Australia. At the Australian Baptist Congress of 1922, a few proecumenical voices were stifled by a strong reaffirmation of Baptist distinctives. A Baptist paper asserted, "The best contribution which we can make to the Christianizing of Australia will not be in conferring with other Christians, but by converting the non-Christians."[100]

In pushing for the proposed merger, the Baptist Union of South Australia passed a resolution in three points:

> 1. Church membership shall be for those who profess faith in Jesus Christ and obedience to Him. 2. Baptism shall not be essential to Church membership. 3. The subjects of baptism to be left open. The fact that some hold the proper subjects of baptism are believers, and some infants presented in Christian faith, shall not be regarded as a barrier to Church Union.[101]

Most of the Australians, however, thought this went too far. They wanted to be "distinctively Baptist," and a later observer wrote that "while baptism is not essential to salvation from sin, it is essential to the salvation of our denomination."[102] Given this background, one is not surprised that the Baptist Union of Australia, by a decisive vote of 220 to 67, declined to join the World Council of Churches in 1948. Deploring any approach that was "interdenominational, undenominational or non-denominational," the union opted instead to be "positively and distinctively Baptist; unitedly and interdependently Baptist."[103]

Like Baptists everywhere, the Australian Union has faced times of theological tension. Of the few Australian pastors with college training from England, most were from Spurgeon's College, and they tended to bring to Australia the issues of the Down Grade Controversy. One such Spurgeon's

99. J. D. Bollen, *Australian Baptists: A Religious Minority,* p. 33.
100. Ibid., pp. 34-35.
101. Ibid., p. 53.
102. Ibid., p. 35.
103. Ibid., p. 41.

graduate was C. J. Tinsley (1876-1960), who served for more than a half century as pastor of the Stanmore church in NSW.[104] A staunch conservative, Tinsley is often called "the Spurgeon of Australia"; another common expression is that he "Spurgeon-ized Australian Baptists." With several terms as president of the Baptist Union of NSW, and later of the national union, Tinsley exerted a powerful influence. Once described as "an evangelist immune to doubt," Tinsley defended his view of Baptist distinctives against ecumenists, progressive biblical scholarship, and other liberal tendencies. He was one of those who brought the Canadian fundamentalist, T. T. Shields, to Australia for extensive preaching tours. F. J. Wilkins, a Baptist theologian and college leader in Victoria, offered a more liberal alternative to Tinsley's strict views, but he gained only a limited hearing.

Patterns of growth. Many observers consider 1910 a turning point in the life of Australian Baptists. At that point, the new-century enthusiasm waned, and numerical decline marked the next half century. "The ugly fact must be faced," said one observer in 1937, "that we have made no progress, if figures tell the truth, in the last quarter of a century."[105] The number of baptisms in 1950 was fewer than in 1900, and not all who accepted baptism joined one of the churches. As late as 1970 Baptists in Victoria lamented that "the close connection between conversion-baptism-Church membership is very far from being as strong as we might have thought."[106]

In early years, Australian Baptists showed a certain fascination with Baptist growth in America and sought for themselves the kind of growth that had marked "British America." However, it was not to be; as Bollen said, they had waited for a "revival that has never come."[107] This relative slowness of growth has not been for lack of effort. One could list at length the special evangelistic campaigns, like the Gypsy Smith crusades in 1927 and the Billy Graham crusades more recently, all to little avail. Some have accused the Australian Baptists of harboring an "obsessive concern" for growth; if that assessment is accurate, such concern has not paid the expected dividends. However, at least modest growth has marked the recent history of Baptists in Australia. Their reports to the Baptist World Alliance listed 52,148 members in 1980, up from 48,520 in 1970.[108]

Baptists in New Zealand

One historian described the early twentieth century as a time of "break-

---

104. *The Australian Baptist* (Jan. 3, 1939), p. 1.

105. Hughes, Henry Estcourt, *Our First Hundred Years: The Baptist Church of South Australia* (Adelaide: South Australia Baptist Union, 1937), p. 301.

106. *The Australian Baptist* (Feb. 18, 1970), cited in Bollen, p. 53.

107. Bollen, p. 58.

108. *ESB*, III (1971), 1604; and IV (1982), 2115.

through" for New Zealand Baptists.[109] Their achievements include not only measurable external successes but also less tangible growth in spirit and confidence. Since 1900 they have more than quadrupled the number of churches, a growing membership, an adequate supply of trained ministers, a strong theological college, vigorous programs of church extension at home and missions abroad, and vastly improved financial support. Their recent records reveal a growing theological maturity, a better self-image as a part of the Christian world, more confident participation in ecumenical dialogue, and a growing sense of confidence in their future in New Zealand.

The Baptist Union. Recent general secretaries of the Baptist Union have included P. F. Layon (1940-1955), L. A. North (1955-1966), Hugh Nees (1966-1975), and S. L. Edgar (since 1975). The union offices, at first just a room at a church, were in 1945 located in rented quarters. In 1963 they moved to their own building in Wellington.

From 1885 when they formed the Baptist Missionary Society, New Zealand Baptists have conducted a small but vigorous foreign mission work in India. The end of British rule in 1947 brought division to India, with the emergence of West Pakistan and East Pakistan. Missionaries remained until 1973, but they had gradually turned mission work over to Indian leadership. Despite problems in Bangladesh, New Zealand Baptists had more missionaries in that country in 1981 than ever before.

After an intensive study, New Zealand Baptists adopted an important new policy in 1967. Called "Other Avenues of Service," they set out a plan of "seconding" appointees to other missionary bodies. They felt that in light of their total resources, they could make a greater impact by placing their missionaries in strategic centers sponsored by other bodies than by launching new missions of their own.[110] Under this policy, New Zealand Baptists have placed, and supported, appointees with such groups as the BMS of England, the BMS of Australia, the American Baptist Convention (now, American Baptist Churches USA), and some non-Baptist evangelical groups. They thus yield control and also tend to receive less news and promotional contact from mission fields. Some leaders feel this is a creative and unselfish way for a small denomination to make a difference. Others fear it may lead to a decrease of missionary awareness and involvement among New Zealand Baptists.

Unlike the foreign society, which in 1985 celebrated its centennial, home mission work among New Zealand Baptists has struggled to find a suitable structure for its work. While its purposes have remained fairly constant, strengthening weak churches and planting new ones, its methods and struc-

109. J. Ayson Clifford, *A Handful of Grain: The Centenary History of the Baptist Union of New Zealand,* 1882-1914, 2:71.

110. S. L. Edgar, *A Handful of Grain: The Centenary History of the Baptist Union of New Zealand,* 1945-1982, 4:74-76.

tures have varied considerably. At times local churches have encouraged their pastors to preach in outlying areas, forming "missions," to use an American term, or branches of a "multi-church." Later the Baptist Union, and local associations when they had resources, employed traveling evangelists who literally covered the country. However, suggestions for a home mission society fell on deaf ears.

Part of the problem lay in the Baptist ambivalence between national and local control of home mission work, a conflict seen in many parts of the Baptist family. In New Zealand most of the associations sponsored church extension efforts, and they were loath to yield this to the national union. While localism has its own benefits, it hampers the planning and prosecution of a unified nationwide policy. Another problem which affected New Zealand home mission work was its mundane nature, lacking the romantic appeal of foreign missions, with its faraway places with strange sounding names.

The union launched a "Trans-Pacific Crusade" in 1965, bringing a team of 103 ministers from churches of the Southern Baptist Convention to hold revivals in 104 New Zealand churches. Numerically the results were good; of 1,488 baptisms, 1,040 new members joined the churches. However, some New Zealanders felt the visitors showed inadequate understanding of local Baptist customs and culture and assumed perhaps too readily that American methods would work equally well in other lands.[111]

New Zealand Baptists have faced a mixed response to their Sunday Schools and related organizations in the twentieth century. The traditional Sunday School, meeting on Sunday afternoon, has declined sharply. Up to World War I, most of the Sunday School enrollment came from the non-Baptist and often non-Christian population and thus served as a prime source for new Baptist converts. That trend has been reversed in recent years with most of the Sunday School enrollment made up of the children of Baptist members.

Beginning in 1957 under a program of "Bible Teaching for All," New Zealand Baptists made an all-out effort to introduce the "all-age" Sunday School. J. J. Burt visited the States to study the Sunday School work of Southern Baptist churches, and W. L. Howse, a leader in the Baptist Sunday School Board in Nashville, spent three weeks in New Zealand in 1958 to introduce all-age Sunday Schools. By 1963 almost half the churches in New Zealand had adopted this method, but the movement soon lost favor. The rise of the charismatic movement shifted the focus away from knowledge and understanding of Scripture to the priority of experience. Despite their determined efforts, the New Zealand Baptists could not overcome their British heritage of identifying Sunday School for children only. This proved particularly difficult for youth who resisted what they regarded

111. Ibid., pp. 33-34.

as a children's program. The adults fared little better; most churches abandoned the program, and by 1981 only eleven churches in all of New Zealand reported more than twenty in their adult Bible classes.[112] Meantime, in an effort to make the all-age program work, the churches had neglected other efforts, such as the youth Bible Class Movement. It proved difficult to revive these once the new experiment was abandoned.

From their beginnings in the early 1840s, New Zealand Baptists had a shortage of trained ministers. The supply of preachers from England was never adequate, though Spurgeon's College furnished more than most. From the 1880s New Zealanders addressed this need by placing ministerial candidates to study with leading pastors. However, in 1924 they took a giant step forward by founding their own Baptist Theological College in Auckland. Despite limited financial support in the early days, inadequate facilities, and a minor controversy in the 1950s when the president was accused of theological liberalism, the college has grown and won an enduring place in the work of the Baptist Union.

New Zealand Baptists have concentrated their social ministries mostly in three endeavors: a children's home, a home for girls, and youth camps and hostels. The Manurewa Children's Home dates back to 1893, begun when Baptists found two abandoned children living in a barrel. By 1946 it provided care for sixty-seven children, most of them orphans. In 1947 they founded "Arahina," with room for six girls, but closed it in 1956 when it appeared the state could meet the needs better.

Weekend camping has always been important to New Zealand youth, and Carey Baptist Park, first acquired in 1945, has provided attractive facilities for camping, retreats, and various conferences both for youth and adults. New Zealand Baptists began a home for the aged in 1952 when Mrs. H. M. Hughes, an Auckland widow, gave her home for that purpose and continued as its first resident. One official remarked, "The denominational conscience concerning the need for social service of this nature is outrunning the vision of our Baptist people concerning such work as a sphere of Christian service for them."[113] Translated, that means Baptists see the needs but cannot agree whether the church should address them.

New Zealand Baptists have devised more orderly methods of raising and dispensing denominational funds in the twentieth century, and certainly they have had more funds to handle. In addition to such major efforts as the Sustentation Fund to aid new churches and supplement pastoral salaries, and the Annuity Fund established in 1900, the union has sponsored a number of special campaigns. In 1955 it tried a new approach, called "Baptist Forward Move." For the three summer months of that year, pastors were urged to lead their members to give a tithe of their income.

112. Ibid., p. 60.
113. Ibid., p. 48.

Any receipts over the same period in 1954 were to be forwarded to the Baptist Union to expand its work. This led to record income for 1955, but tithing through the local church has not replaced the special offerings. One reason is that the denomination has been uneasy about support funneled through the churches rather than directly to the union by means of special offerings.

Theological trends. In theology New Zealand Baptists have had much variety but few divisions. Always among the more conservative of British Baptists, those in New Zealand took a new turn toward conservatism in the 1930s and 1940s. A minor doctrinal controversy forced the resignation of the college principal in 1952, but he was hardly liberal by modern standards. D. B. Forde Carlisle, an ultraconservative pastor, published a small paper called *The Contender* in which he accused most of the denominational leaders of one heresy or another. Carlisle undermined Baptists' confidence in their leaders and his overall impact must be recorded as negative.

New Zealand Baptists have encountered the ecumenical movement at two levels and at both have shown openness to cooperation with others but a determination to preserve their Baptist identity. Early in the twentieth century a number of Baptists worshiped in other churches, none of their own being near. One lamented in 1906 that "though working in other churches, we remain Baptist. But what about our children?"[114] Amid efforts to unite the five major Protestant denominations in New Zealand, Baptists discussed the issue but never agreed to be part of it. Later the entire effort broke down. Baptists preached a more enthusiastic ecumenism than they ever practiced. As early as 1883 the union president, Charles Carter, called for "one grand Union of all Christian churches in N.Z. of all who love our Lord Jesus Christ in sincerity and truth."[115] Similar views were expressed from time to time, but no action was taken. In 1904 it appeared that Baptists might merge with the Church of Christ, but that fell through because of their differing views of baptism.

Despite cautious approaches to local ecumenism, the New Zealand Baptist Union has participated in the larger ecumenical movement. In 1941 the union joined the New Zealand Council of Churches and as early as 1944 applied for membership in the World Council of Churches, then in process of formation. This participation has been repeatedly challenged by some who wanted no ecumenical ties and by others who preferred to join the fundamentalist International Council of Christian Churches (ICCC). A recent historian observed that younger pastors have "criticized any drumming up of denominational loyalty" among New Zealand Baptists, a trend

114. Clifford, p. 81.
115. Ibid., p. 96.

he attributes to the ecumenical movement.[116]

Open communion has long been the customary practice among New Zealand Baptists, but the question of open membership is still debated. This issue took center stage at the assembly of 1911, when strong advocates pleaded for both sides. With arguments reminiscent of John Bunyan 250 years earlier, some insisted a closed membership was inconsistent with an open table. Others insisted that baptism of believers by immersion was a Baptist essential, without which their churches might as well close.

The earliest Pentecostal practices among New Zealand Baptists date from the 1920s but did not become widespread until the 1960s. A recent historian said the movement brought the Baptists "much hurt and little lasting good."[117] Charismatics broke up a number of churches, some of which left the Baptist Union and some later went out of existence entirely. "What happened to these churches," an observer said, "made many people fearful of even restrained expressions of the charismatic movement in their own churches."[118]

In 1967 the Baptist Union launched a thorough study of the charismatic movement as it affected Baptists. In a balanced report, it urged traditional Baptists to be more tolerant of charismatic enthusiasm and cautioned charismatics to observe their devotions privately if need be to avoid disrupting the churches. The study bluntly suggested that any charismatic who could not observe these restraints should "move to a section of the Christian church where these matters are given the prominence he wishes."[119] This report reduced confrontation between the two groups, but some agitation continued. Some hoped to link the charismatic Baptist churches and withdraw from the union to form another denomination, but that failed. The 1967 report said that among the Baptist churches "only a small minority was seriously affected."[120] That assessment may need revision in a few more years.

Changing roles of women. True to their general conservatism, New Zealand Baptists have allowed only limited church roles for women. The primary leadership of women has been in Sunday School and in missionary education and fund raising. Women also served as missionaries; Rosalie MacGeorge was the first appointee of the New Zealand BMS in 1885.[121] The fact that women missionaries performed a ministry, including proclamation and teaching, that did not differ significantly from that of men missionaries appeared not to trouble the churches.

116. Edgar, p. 90.
117. Ibid., p. 82.
118. Ibid., p. 83.
119. Ibid., pp. 83-84.
120. Ibid., p. 83.
121. Clifford, p. 92.

In 1903 the women formed their Baptist Women's Missionary Union, and eventually branches sprang up in most churches. Expanding its educational role, the WMU formed an auxiliary for younger women in 1916, known as "Shareholders," and a society for children in 1925, called "Ropeholders."[122] A growing number of women who felt they should do something more than give programs on missions formed the Baptist Women's League in 1947 in Auckland, and within a few years a national organization had been formed. By 1966 branches of the league were active in 110 churches of the Baptist Union. While the WMU studied and gave programs, the BWL acted, thus involving women more in the actual work of churches.

Soon after the Baptist Union was formed in 1882, a question arose as to whether women could serve as delegates to that body. The term *delegate* in the constitution was officially defined in 1891 as an "adult male," but agitation continued. In 1893 the nation gave women the vote, and in 1894 the Canterbury Association seated women delegates. A motion to seat women at the assembly was hooted down in 1904 "amidst a thunder of merriment and applause."[123] That decision was reversed in 1908 when the union accepted women delegates on the same basis as men.

Following the British pattern, a number of Baptist women in New Zealand were appointed to serve the churches as deaconesses. By 1956 there were enough deaconesses to merit a special course of instruction being added to the theological college to prepare them for their work, including "theological and biblical subjects . . . religious education in schools, practical church work under supervision, home nursing and home craft, visitation, singing, blackboard work and elementary automobile mechanics."[124] The first student was Patricia Preest, followed by thirteen others by 1982. In 1972 Miss Preest returned to college for additional study and ordination to full ministerial status. Another woman, Margaret Motion, was ordained in 1978, joined by several others since then. The first to be called as full-time pastor was Ngaire Brader at Epsom.

Growth rate. Though still a small denomination, New Zealand Baptists have grown rapidly in the twentieth century. In 1981 they reported 170 churches, with 152 active pastors, plus a number of ordained ministers in denominational work.[125]

Baptists in South Africa

As with most Baptists elsewhere, those in South Africa entered the twentieth century with high optimism. They had launched the program called "Forward Movement" in 1899 to provide funds for church extension

122. Edgar, p. 79.
123. Clifford, p. 93.
124. Edgar, p. 71.
125. Ibid., p. 14.

and planned to employ a full-time general secretary as well as "missioners" or traveling missionary-evangelists. However, those hopes were dashed by the South African War of 1899-1902, which dealt severe setbacks to Baptist work. The crisis did, however, lead to more assistance from England through the Baptist Colonial Society.[126]

Four new ventures of 1910-1911 showed that Baptists had recovered from the war and were ready to move forward again. They established a Sunday School department to encourage formation of Sunday Schools in all of the churches. This proved extremely successful. Second, in 1911 a meeting of "lady delegates" laid plans to form a South African Baptist Women's Association, which they completed in 1912. Like similar societies among Baptists everywhere, this one led to heightened missionary awareness and support. Third, the union launched a successful annuity plan, a step which they hoped would enable them to provide more and better ministerial leadership for the churches. Fourth, they formed a "Book Depot" to provide the churches with literature for Sunday Schools, lay training, and inspiration.

In 1908 another effort surfaced to change the shape of the Baptist Union. In that year F. B. Meyer, influential English Baptist leader, suggested on one of his visits to South Africa that the Baptists reform their loose union into "The United Baptist Church of South Africa." The primary motive, apparently, was to give the denomination more direct control over the placement and tenure of pastors. The union assembly agreed in 1908 to recommend this plan to the churches and in 1910 learned that thirty-six churches favored the plan while only one opposed. They agreed that until they could become unanimous, the "United Baptist Church shall be a federation of churches within the Union," which amounted to a church within a union of churches. By 1919 this plan had lost favor and was abandoned.[127]

The 1920s proved a time of doctrinal ferment for most Baptists, and those in South Africa were not exempt. The Declaration of Principle, adopted from the Baptist Union of England, had served since 1877. However, new challenges led South African Baptists to spell out their faith in greater detail. The new "Statement of Faith" was adopted in 1924 and later incorporated into the union's constitution. Its preamble says, "Resolved, That having no authority to accept a doctrinal statement on behalf of our Churches, but knowing there is unsettlement in some of our Churches, we agree to commend this statement to them for their consideration as a general expression of our Baptist belief." One important article affirmed "the Scriptures of the Old and New Testaments in their original writings

126. Sydney Hudson-Reed, ed., *Together for a Century: The History of the Baptist Union of South Africa 1877-1977*, p. 80.

127. Ibid., pp. 80, 88.

as fully inspired of God" and said they constitute "the supreme and final authority for faith and life."[128] Theological problems arose again in the 1950s when a Baptist college principal was dismissed for deviation from these views.

As elsewhere, Baptists in South Africa suffered from a shortage of trained ministers. In 1898 G. W. Cross reluctantly admitted, "The time has not yet come for establishing a Theological School here." Such students as presented themselves were placed under the tutelage of established pastors. In 1935 the Ministerial Education Committee oversaw the studies of fifteen ministerial students but reported that only two of them were working hard at their studies. Ernest Baker formed the "Baptist Bible School" in 1928, largely at his own initiative, and in 1931 it was reported that "the relationship of the Baptist Bible School to the Union was still under consideration." By 1932 that question had become moot as the school had lapsed.

The postwar "Forward Movement" included more determined efforts to provide ministerial training. In 1949 the union registered fifty-nine votes in favor of forming a school, with only six against. However, the thirty-five abstentions showed lack of unity, and the union wisely delayed the project. The problems were worked out and in 1951 the union opened The Baptist Theological College of Southern Africa. The school, aided by a grant from the Southern Baptist Convention, was located in Johannesburg. The first full-time principal was A. J. Barnard, from Birmingham, and within two years the college registered twenty-one full-time students.

Problems arose in 1954 when union leaders learned that Barnard neither held nor taught "the doctrine concerning the inspiration of the Scriptures which the majority of the Executive requires to be taught in the College, which the majority of the ministers of the denomination believe." By his own admission the principal was "seriously at variance with those beliefs."[129] Barnard was dismissed at once and the school closed. It reopened, however, with C. M. Doke serving as acting principal before the election of J. C. Stern in 1956. Two years later J. D. Odendaal became the first full-time tutor in addition to the principal. Never large, the school has continued to provide trained pastors for Baptists in Africa and beyond. In 1973 it opened a branch campus at Capetown.

Throughout the twentieth century, South African Baptists have kept an emphasis upon evangelism and church extension, employing various plans and funds to advance that work. In 1922 the union appointed a "missioner" in the person of Ernest Baker but did not provide his support. In 1935 the assembly set up "The Evangelisation and Extension Committee" and the next year appointed J. C. Stern to "visit our churches to conduct evangelistic campaigns and for the deepening of Spiritual Life." Thus Stern became

128. Ibid., p. 36.
129. Ibid., p. 108.

the first full-time worker supported by the union, other than missionaries. A "Children's Missioner and Sunday School Organizer" was added to the staff in 1958. A number of pastors from the Southern Baptist Convention conducted "simultaneous revivals" in South African churches in 1967; baptisms for that year doubled the total of the previous year.

As elsewhere, the Southern Baptists recommended their own form of Sunday School. Clifton J. Allen and Gaines S. Dobbins, Southern Baptist educators and Sunday School leaders, visited South Africa where they "warmly commended to the churches the All-Age Sunday School." However, this plan never caught on.

Ecumenism and the charismatic movement have troubled South African Baptists less than most. One reason for formation of the union of 1877 was to have a vehicle for friendly cooperation with other denominations, which aim has been amply realized at the local level. Though the union never joined the World Council of Churches, it did for a time hold membership in the Christian Council of South Africa. By 1967 it changed its relationship from membership to "observer status" and, in 1975, by a large majority voted to sever even that slight relationship.[130] Theological liberalism and harsh condemnation of apartheid, both associated with the council, contributed to this severance.

As late as 1960 most of the churches affiliated with the Baptist Union were made up mostly of white membership, but since then Baptists have become more multiracial. During the 1960s such racial groups as the South Africa Baptist Alliance, the Indian Baptist Mission, and the Bantu Baptist Convention were received into affiliation with the Baptist Union. The assembly voted in 1976 that "the Baptist Union is open to all churches which qualify in terms of its constitution, regardless of race or colour." In 1976 total membership was reported to be 51,305.[131]

Baptists in Canada

Canadian Baptists entered the twentieth century in an expansive mood. Baptist work had achieved stability and a measure of growth in the Atlantic and Central Provinces, and already churches were springing up across the vast Western territories. There was abundant diversity of doctrine, and Baptist organizations in the various provinces lacked uniformity of structure and function. Efforts at national organization had proven unfruitful; but by the early twentieth century, Canadian Baptists were clearly moving toward greater unity.

The twentieth century brought new challenges and intensified some old ones. First, Canadian Baptists have had to face the ecumenical issue in more than theory. In 1925 several Protestant groups formed the United Church

130. Ibid., p. 124.
131. Ibid., pp. 136, 139.

of Canada, one of the more successful church merger attempts to date. Baptists had to determine their relationship to this close-up ecumenism, as well as deciding whether to work with the World Council of Churches and its Canadian expression, the Canadian Council. Second, Canadian Baptists were fractured by the Fundamentalist controversy of the 1920s. While often identified with the United States, Fundamentalism had its Canadian equivalent and devastated Baptist churches and conventions, particularly in the Central and Western Provinces.

A third challenge of the new century has been the advance of Southern Baptists into Canada, especially in the west. Migrants from Washington and Oregon helped populate the Western Provinces, and they tended to bring their own forms of Baptist life. Many Southern Baptists regarded Canada as an eligible place for SBC expansion, but many Canadians feared that Southern Baptist affiliation would undermine their Canadian identity. Since the 1780s Baptists in Canada had been torn between English and American patterns of Baptist life. The growth of Southern Baptists added to that diversity.

The Atlantic Provinces

At the beginning of the new century, Baptist work in the east centered in the Baptist Convention of the Maritime Provinces, formed in 1846. Local associations and regional conventions grouped the churches of Nova Scotia, New Brunswick, Prince Edward's Island, and later Newfoundland, into cooperative units. The Atlantic Baptists sponsored a number of schools, including Acadia College and a seminary in New Brunswick.

A trend toward unification marked the Maritime Baptists early in this century. The union of Freewill and Regular Baptists had been discussed for years but was delayed by differences in doctrinal belief and disagreement about denominational affiliation. The first major example of cooperation between the two groups was the joint sponsorship of the Union Baptist Seminary in 1884. In 1905 in New Brunswick and 1906 in Nova Scotia the two groups merged and changed the name of the resulting body to the United Baptist Convention of the Maritime Provinces. Their various missionary societies, organizations for women and youth, and newspapers also merged.[132]

World War I disrupted the work of Baptists in many ways. Construction workers especially tended to migrate to the Central and Western Provinces, a factor which slowed the growth rate for Baptist churches in the Maritime area. The war also speeded the process of Baptist organizational unity. In 1919 the Maritime Convention formed the Board of Home Missions,

---

132. For a discussion of this merger, see F. H. Sinnott, "The Union of the Regular and Free Will Baptists of the Maritimes, 1905 and 1906," Barry M. Moody, ed., *Repent and Believe: The Baptist Experience in Maritime Canada,* pp. 138-150.

through which the provincial conventions worked. In the same year they formed the Maritime Religious Education Council to promote Sunday School, summer camps, and leadership training for teachers. In 1920 the Board of Social Services was formed to give voice to Baptist views on matters of public and social concern. Previously these functions had been carried out in the conventions of each province, but now they were transferred to the larger convention covering all of the Atlantic Provinces. The Maritime Convention has been headquartered in Saint John, New Brunswick, since 1960. In 1962 the convention reported 611 churches with a membership of 68,832.[133]

The Central Provinces

The Baptist Convention of Ontario and Quebec came into the twentieth century with about 44,000 members in 464 churches.[134] With strong Roman Catholicism in Quebec and the popular United Church of Canada in Ontario, Baptists in the Central Provinces have not had an easy road. Their churches have been weakened by out-migration, and Baptists in this area have been more prone to doctrinal controversy. The Fundamentalist controversy of the 1920s had its most devastating impact in Ontario. Decline has continued, with only 380 churches reported in 1980, with 46,340 members.[135]

The Western Provinces

Baptist work in the Western territories began later but has shown considerable progress. Population influx from Eastern and Central Canada, as well as from the Western United States, brought a variety of Baptist life to these emerging areas. Doctrinal controversy has been a prominent feature in Baptist history in Western Canada, with several schismatic groups formed. Southern Baptist presence has also been greater in the west than in other parts of Canada.

The population of the four areas of Manitoba, Alberta, Saskatchewan, and British Columbia increased over 400 percent from 1901 to 1913 and continued to grow thereafter.[136] The Baptist Convention of Western Canada, formed in 1907, coordinated the work of the conventions in the four provinces. In 1909 the name was changed to the Baptist Union of Western Canada, with headquarters later moved from Winnipeg to Edmonton.

In 1937 and again in 1967 the Western Union was reorganized. Over the

133. George E. Levy, "The United Baptist Convention of the Maritime Provinces," *Baptist Advance,* Davis C. Woolley, ed. (Nashville: Broadman Press, 1964), p. 159.

134. G. Gerald Harrop, "The Baptist Convention of Ontario and Quebec," in Woolley, p. 162.

135. Jarold K. Zeman, "Canadian Baptists," *ESB,* 4:2145.

136. Margaret E. Thompson, *The Baptist Story in Western Canada,* p. 136.

protests of many, the union assumed more centralization and authority, taking over some functions of the provincial conventions. As a part of its 1967 restructuring, the union adopted a statement of faith which established it as perhaps more conservative than comparable bodies in Eastern and Central Canada.

Baptists in the Western Provinces have made numerous efforts to provide schools, beginning with Prairie College in Manitoba as early as 1880, but without notable success. Okanagan College in British Columbia lasted from 1907 to 1915, when it closed for lack of funds and enrollment. Brandon College was established in Manitoba in 1899, in some ways a continuation of efforts started earlier at the Prairie College. In the 1920s Brandon suffered a serious blow in the Fundamentalist controversy. Though the union repeatedly reaffirmed its confidence in the college and its faculty, the school closed in 1938.

The loss of Brandon College proved a serious blow to Western Baptists. Their students had to go long distances for theological training, either to other Canadian schools or to the United States. Many felt they could not go so far away, and others who attended distant schools never returned to Western Canada. These needs led to the 1949 formation of the Baptist Leadership Training School, located in Calgary. While neither a college nor seminary, this school has provided basic training in biblical and pastoral studies. The Canadian Baptist Theological College in Saskatoon, Saskatchewan, offers additional training opportunities.

Numerical decline has marked the Baptist Union of Western Canada in recent years. However, these statistics can be misleading for there are numerous other Baptist groups in that area, so that the total Baptist presence in Western Canada has increased. The Fundamentalist controversy of the 1920s led to the withdrawal of many churches. In British Columbia alone, for example, the schism of 1927 reduced membership in Baptist Union churches by about 35 percent.[137]

The Baptist Federation of Canada

Canadian Baptists took years to complete their denominational structure, moving patiently from one step to the next. When their churches and associations grew strong enough, they formed *provincial* conventions in each province, such as Nova Scotia, New Brunswick, or Ontario. These were comparable to state conventions in the USA. The next step was to group these provincial bodies into three *regional* conventions for the Atlantic, Central, and Western Provinces.

However, Baptist leaders had long cherished a desire to form some *national* structure to unite all the Baptists of Canada. Such a suggestion was first made in the 1840s, but no action was taken until 1880 when a Baptist

137. Ibid., p. 158.

Union of Canada was formed. Despite its name, this was largely limited to the Central Provinces; in 1888, it was more realistically renamed the Baptist Convention of Ontario and Quebec. In 1900 at Winnipeg, Baptist leaders from all parts of Canada formed the National Baptist Convention of Canada, but for some reason it never met again.[138]

Unable to unite the regional conventions, Canadian Baptists moved toward national cooperation in home and foreign missions. In 1912 they formed the Canadian Foreign Mission Board, which allowed the several regional conventions to pool their resources for a united effort in foreign missions. Later a comparable body was formed for home mission work. The effect was that Canadian Baptists were actually functioning in national cooperation before there was formal organization.

Toward mid-century Canadian Baptists made another effort at national organization, this one successful. Delegates met in Toronto in 1943 to draw up a proposed constitution, which was adopted in 1944, to form the Baptist Federation of Canada. One of its announced objectives was "to express the common judgment of the constituent churches and organizations on matters of national, international, or interdenominational importance." The new body was also intended "to create among Canadian Baptists a more active denominational consciousness, a closer sense of fellowship, and a fuller sense of responsibility in the work of the kingdom."[139] This gave Canadian Baptists their long-sought national organization. In 1980 the Baptist Federation reported 127,270 members in 1,115 churches.[140]

The Fundamentalist Controversy

Fundamentalism made deep inroads into Canadian Baptist life in the 1920s, particularly in Ontario and the Western Provinces. The leader of Fundamentalism among Canadian Baptists was Thomas Todhunter Shields (1873-1955), pastor for forty-five years of the Jarvis Street Baptist Church, once Toronto's most influential congregation. A close friend of W. B. Riley of Minneapolis and J. Frank Norris of Fort Worth, Shields imitated their methods, raised similar issues, and made common cause with them in an effort to link Baptist Fundamentalism in Canada and the USA into one united movement. He joined in calling the 1923 meeting that formed the Baptist Bible Union and served as its first president.

Shields called himself a "fighting fundamentalist" and was described even by his friends as "too eager to do battle with modernism."[141] Though a premillennialist, Shields rejected dispensationalism and often denounced

---

138. Watson Kirkconnell, "The Baptist Federation of Canada," in Woolley, p. 132.
139. Ibid., p. 134.
140. Zeman, *ESB*, 4:2145.
141. Jarold K. Zeman, ed., *Baptists in Canada: Search for Identity Amidst Diversity*, pp. 202-222.

what he called "Schofieldism."[142] However, the Shields group later fell
under the influence of radical dispensational millennialism, and while keeping the Baptist name became, in effect, independent Fundamentalists. In
1922 Shields suffered a setback when his own church split, with 341 members withdrawing. Most of these were influential members of long-standing,
and their departure permanently changed the character of the once-
prominent church.

Charges of doctrinal liberalism centered in McMaster University, then
located in Toronto and on whose board Shields served. Apparently a liberal
tradition had emerged there by the 1880s when William Newton Clarke
taught for about five years in the Toronto Baptist College, the school which
preceded McMaster. Clarke's influence continued when his students
became teachers and leaders in McMaster.

The controversy took a new turn in 1919 when the *Canadian Baptist*
carried an editorial on "Inspiration and Authority of Scripture" which
seemed to undercut historic Baptist teachings. Shields wrote to the editor,
"I am resolved to avail myself of the first opportunity of testing the attitude
of the Denomination toward the position taken in your article."[143] Shields
wrote editorials in his paper, *The Gospel Witness,* preached fiery sermons,
and introduced convention resolutions of censure against McMaster, and
more than once the sponsoring Baptist convention urged the school to
adhere to traditional positions.

Shields's failure in 1925 to prevent the election of a professor whom some
thought to be liberal led to division. The convention of 1926 voted to
censure Shields, asked him to resign from the McMaster board, and notified
the Jarvis Street Church that he would no longer be welcome to participate
in the convention. Shields thereupon withdrew and formed his own rival
school, the Toronto Baptist Seminary, and his own convention. In 1928
representatives from seventy-seven churches sympathetic with Shields met
in Hamilton where they formed the Union of Regular Baptist Churches.
This group soon split again, and the Independent Fellowship of Baptist
Churches was formed in the 1930s. In 1949 what was left of the Regular
Union split again when Shields created a crisis by ousting the dean of his
Toronto school. Remnants of the Regular Union later merged into the
Fellowship of Evangelical Baptist Churches, which represented a more
moderate spirit.

This painful schism was probably inevitable. Shields represented, according to one historian, "the Norris-Riley type of belligerent fissiparous fundamentalism."[144] He could not be placated. On the other hand, it appears in
retrospect that some of Shields's charges were justified, and there is little

142. Ibid., p. 220.
143. Ibid., p. 211.
144. Ibid., p. 173.

evidence that mainline Baptists took them seriously or made any substantial efforts to face or correct potential doctrinal problems.

Fundamentalism also proved divisive in the Western Provinces. In British Columbia, the familiar attacks upon Baptist professors centered around Brandon College. When the Fundamentalists were rebuffed in several convention votes, about seventeen churches withdrew to form the Convention of Regular Baptists.[145] Similar schisms occurred in other Western Provinces; only about one-third of the Baptist churches in British Columbia, for example, remained with the Baptist Union.[146]

Southern Baptists in Canada

From the late 1880s, a number of Southern Baptists migrated into Western Canada, usually via Washington-Oregon. At first no organized Southern Baptist work resulted since most affiliated with Canadian churches. After 1950 Southern Baptist work took a new turn in Canada, with organized churches and the beginnings of a denominational structure.[147]

As early as 1949 Ross McPherson and Jim Yoder, young pastors among the Regular Baptists in Vancouver, became interested in the SBC. They arranged an invitation for R. E. Milam, executive secretary of the Baptist General Convention of Washington-Oregon, to visit Vancouver in 1951. A number of Regular pastors, whose churches had descended from the 1927 Fundamentalist schism, voted to "survey the Southern Baptist program to see if it would be practical . . . to affiliate with them."[148] They were attracted by the conservative theological stance of the SBC, the highly organized church educational structures, available church literature, and perhaps also by the possibility of church aid through the Home Mission Board. In 1952 the Emmanuel Church (later renamed the Kingcrest Southern Baptist Church) declared itself Southern Baptist and affiliated with the Baptist General Convention of Washington-Oregon. By 1953 several other churches had taken similar action.

Problems arose from two sources. First, the Canadian Baptists protested what they regarded as an unwarranted "invasion" by Southern Baptists. Second, messengers from the Canadian churches, though affiliated with a state convention of the SBC, could not be seated in the SBC itself. The constitution limits direct affiliation in the SBC to the United States and its territories. Efforts to change the constitution have not succeeded.

Numerous conferences between Canadian and SBC leaders have pro-

---

145. Thompson, p. 157.
146. Ibid., p. 158.
147. For a summary of this movement, see Roland P. Hood, *Southern Baptist Work in Canada* (Portland: Baptist General Convention of Washington-Oregon, 1968).
148. A. Ronald Tonks, "Highlights of the Relationships of Southern Baptists with Canadian Baptists," *Baptist History and Heritage*, p. 9.

duced limited agreement on the nature and extent of SBC activity in Canada. In general it was agreed that, while local Baptist churches are free to seek whatever affiliation they wish, the SBC would not directly sponsor work in Canada nor seek to recruit existing churches into SBC affiliation. Within these limited agreements, the Home Mission Board and Sunday School Board of the SBC found ways to aid Southern Baptist churches in Canada.

The SBC and its affiliated state convention in Washington-Oregon, since renamed the Northwest Baptist Convention, have shown different attitudes toward Southern Baptists in Canada. The state convention has been eager to assist and affiliate such churches, has sent money and personnel into Canada to extend their work, and has spearheaded the effort to persuade the SBC to extend full recognition. The SBC itself, on the other hand, has been reluctant to recognize the Canadian churches.

Southern Baptist work in Canada began on a small scale, with four churches in 1953, two in British Columbia, one in Alberta, and one in Saskatchewan. Soon these churches multiplied. In 1954 William Fleming, a wealthy Texas oil man, gave generous grants earmarked for Southern Baptist expansion in Canada. Southern Baptist pastors like Austin Hunt in Vancouver, Jack McKay in Edmonton, and Eugene Laird in Winnipeg, extended SBC work. In March 1956, the South Park Church in Edmonton purchased a site for a mission, and Jeff McBeth of Texas was called as mission pastor in August. He led in forming the Argyll Baptist Church on November 11, 1956, with twenty-two members.

In 1963 the Canadian Southern Baptist Conference was formed, largely for fellowship and inspiration. Reports showed 53 Southern Baptist churches in Canada in 1979, with 3,154 members.[149] In the 1978-1979 school year, the Southern Baptist Theological Seminary in Louisville enrolled 21 Canadian students and had 44 graduates serving in Canada.[150]

Other Baptists in Canada

In addition to the Federation Baptists, Regular Baptists, Southern Baptists, and various independent groups, Canada also has a number of other Baptist groups. The Fellowship of Evangelical Baptist Churches (FEBC) is the second largest Baptist group in Canada, with 405 churches and membership estimated at about 47,000.[151] This body was formed in 1953 by a merger of remnants of various Fundamentalist groups which had withdrawn from the Convention of Ontario and Quebec in 1927. The Union of Regular Baptists (formed in 1927 by the Shields Fundamentalists) and the Fellowship of Independent Baptist Churches in Ontario (a rival group

149. James G. Yoder, "Canadian Southern Baptists," *ESB,* 4:2147.
150. Tonks, p. 8.
151. Zeman, *ESB,* 4:2146.

formed in 1933), merged to form the FEBC. Though beginning in Central Canada, this body now has affiliated churches throughout the nation.

The North American Baptist Conference (NABC) reported about 105 congregations in 1980, with about 15,000 members, mostly in the Western Provinces. The North American churches grew out of a German-speaking Baptist church established in Ontario in 1851 by August Rauschenbusch, father of the more famous Walter Rauschenbusch. With increasing immigration from Germany, similar congregations sprang up across Ontario and into the west. Though some of these churches still conduct worship in German, most have made the transition to English and appeal to a cross section of Canadians.

The Baptist General Conference (BGC) originated among Swedish Baptists in Canada. A small Swedish church was formed in Quebec in 1892, but the major growth was in the Western Provinces where a Swedish church was formed in Winnipeg in 1894. By 1930 there were 23 Swedish churches, reporting a membership of 929. By 1980 estimates place their numbers at about 6,500 members in 85 churches.[152] Though organized into their own regional conferences, their primary affiliation was for about a half a century with the Baptist Union of Western Canada. However, in 1948 they voted to affiliate exclusively with the Baptist General Conference in the United States.

The Primitive Baptist Conference of New Brunswick (formed 1875), the Alliance of Reformed Baptist Churches (formed 1888), and the Association of Regular Baptist Churches (formed 1957) represent some of the other small Baptist groups in Canada.

The Baptist Federation of Canada gave Baptists a national organization in 1944, but unity of outlook and effort has proven more elusive. Canadian Baptists find themselves divided over doctrine, methods, and affiliation. They continue to bear the scars of the Fundamentalist movement, and modern ecumenism and social issues have provided additional tensions.

The original alternatives between British and American patterns of Baptist life continue in Canada and fuel some of the present controversies. One might say that the Baptist Federation generally represents the British tradition, while the Regular Baptists, the Evangelical Baptists, and more recently the Southern Baptists, embody American patterns.

The several strong Baptist groups nearby in the United States have proven both a blessing and a bane to Canadian Baptists. On the positive side, the Canadians have drawn immigrants, pastors, and funds to aid their work. On the other hand, they have at times had difficulty in maintaining the indigenous nature of Canadian churches when so many of their pastors have been trained outside the country.

152. Ibid.

Summary

This chapter has sketched Baptists in Britain and traced other British Baptists who fanned out to other parts of the world. Despite the variety of localities, Baptists have faced a number of the same issues and made similar responses. They also display diversity, but the following generalizations may be applied, with some exceptions, to Baptists of a British background wherever they are found.

British Baptists value the independence of local congregations. They show preference for loose-knit societies over the more centralized denominational structures. While in some places the denomination is gaining power at the expense of local churches, that trend has usually been resisted. British Baptists emphasize the role of ministers and often place educational requirements for ordination. Generally, they make a lesser role for laymen, though recent emphasis upon the "elder" may modify that trend.

With some exceptions, British Baptists seem open to more liberal forms of theology and find value in ecumenical cooperation. In England the Baptists have resisted adopting any modern confession of faith, though some British Baptists in other areas have formulated doctrinal statements. Largely unaffected by the various "awakenings" which shaped Baptists in America, those of a British background have generally followed less aggressive forms of evangelism. They have also lived, for the most part, in areas of the world where secularism was quite advanced, which has affected their outlook.

New trends in theology and witness often appear among British Baptists before they reach other parts of the Baptist family. In the world Baptist community, those of a British background have exercised influence beyond their numerical strength.

14

Northern Baptists

Northern Baptists entered the twentieth century on a wave of optimism and growth. The work of their three major societies had followed an upward spiral, showing progress on every front. The word *forward* shows up on many of their committee and planning reports. The Northern Baptist schools prospered, placing their graduates in leading roles in American life and religion. Perhaps the ultimate in Baptist optimism was expressed in the name given the Northern Baptist fund-raising drive in 1919: the New World Movement.

Out of a desire for greater unity and efficiency, the Northern Baptist Convention was formed in 1908, bringing the societies for missions and education under one umbrella for the first time in their history. Twice more in this century Northern Baptists took a new name and a new denominational shape: American Baptist Convention, 1950; and American Baptist Churches, USA, 1972. These changes went deeper than nomenclature; the restructuring of 1972 represented a radical reshaping of the denomination which has yet to win full acceptance among its own adherents.[1] Early in the century, prominent scholars like Augustus H. Strong, William Newton Clarke, and Walter Rauschenbusch articulated an able Baptist scholarship. The denomination absorbed the Freewill Baptists of the North in 1911, conducted ongoing reunion talks with the Disciples until the mid-1950s, and made overtures for eventual reunion with Southern Baptists. The Northern Baptists also joined the Federal Council of Churches in 1908, helped transform it into the National Council in 1950, and throughout the century have played a leading role in both American and world ecumenical ventures.

However, the new century brought new problems and intensified old ones. Nowhere has the secularization of American society proceeded more rapidly and more thoroughly than in areas of Northern Baptists' home base. In New England, historic home of the early Puritans, immigration and the growth of Roman Catholicism modified the earlier efforts at a Protestant

1. For a low-key defense of that restructuring, see Philip E. Jenks, "In SCODS We Trusted," *American Baptist Quarterly,* December 1983, pp. 292 *f.* The same issue carries a number of briefer articles critical of the results of the SCODS.

empire. The three major overhauls of Baptist denominational machinery in one lifetime have taken their toll; many of the churches and pastors, jealous for local church independence, have felt little denominational identity and offered limited cooperation with the national body. Rumblings of doctrinal discontent after the turn of the century erupted in the 1920s in a major theological earthquake which fractured both fellowship and organization. Participation in the ecumenical movement has cost Northern Baptists, leaving a legacy of resistance and resentment among a sizable portion of their constituency. Modern Baptist theologians, like William Hamilton, helped announce the death of God in the 1960s, while another Baptist, Harvey Cox, proclaimed *The Secular City.* Some Northern Baptists felt that traditional forms of evangelism should give way to social action, a trend favored or feared, depending upon the views of observers. As if these did not provide challenge enough, for much of the present century Southern Baptists have planted aggressive churches throughout the Northern states, appealing not only to migrating Southerners but to native Northerners as well.

In such an environment, and amid such crosscurrents, the history of Northern Baptists since 1900 must be sketched. That story includes both problems and progress.

The Northern Baptist Convention

From early times, two styles of benevolent organization competed among Baptists in the North. The more centralized denominational plan appeared in the Philadelphia Association (formed in 1707), a plan by which churches cooperated to launch various forms of ministry. By contrast, the single-barreled society approach surfaced in the Massachusetts Baptist Missionary Society in 1802. Of these two approaches to Baptist organization, Northern Baptists generally preferred the society because it seemed to better preserve the independence of the local churches.

However, in time Baptists in the North became more aware of the problems of the society method, and at the same time their churches lost some of their historic hesitation at the idea of denominational cooperation. The several societies overlapped in some of their work, duplicated efforts, and fragmented the denomination by going their separate ways. The society machinery provided no handle for overall denominational planning and promotion. The triplicate societies, which in early days seemed to guarantee Baptist freedom, seemed by 1900 to guarantee instead inefficiency and waste. *Efficiency* was a big word to Baptists at the turn of the century, both North and South. "Efficiency Committees" and "Efficiency Study Groups" surfaced in both groups. This desire for greater efficiency and better coordination led Baptists to form the Northern Baptist Convention in 1908.

The formation of the Northern Baptist Convention represented a turning point in several ways. First, Baptists in the North accepted for the first time a regional name, whereas previously all their ministries had claimed both a national scope and a national name. Second, this represented a switch from the single-society approach to a unified convention, a change more far-reaching than it may sound. Third, the change called for a general convention managing board or executive committee (it has gone by various names) to direct the work of the whole denomination. For the first time, a layer of leadership was placed over the societies, a new dimension which many had difficulty accepting. For legal reasons the societies had to remain intact, but they were intended to function basically as program boards of the Northern Baptist Convention for foreign missions, home missions, publications, and education.

The idea for a unified denominational body for Northern Baptists goes back at least to the 1890s and went through several steps before it took shape in 1908. As early as 1896, a Commission on Systematic Beneficence led the three societies to cooperate in fund raising. This venture led F. M. Ellis of Baltimore to declare, "We have unified the denomination at the contribution box, and that is next to the throne of grace."[2]

Various other moves toward unification followed, and by 1897 the women's societies had added their voices for greater unity. In 1900 at Detroit a Commission on Coordination was formed, with representatives from all the Baptist societies. The next year the chairman, Stephen Greene, addressed a rally on "Coordination." That rally of 1901 was the first general meeting of the denomination in the North. Greene urged specific steps to draw the societies into cooperative ministries, with common delegates and common budget planning. An editorial in *The Baptist* later judged that it was Greene's address that "set in motion forces which eventuated in the formation of the Northern Baptist Convention."[3] The formation of the Baptist World Alliance in 1905 furthered the trend toward consolidation. In response to a landslide of resolutions from Baptist groups large and small from all across the constituency, the heads of the three major societies, H. L. Morehouse, ABHMS; T. S. Barbour, ABFMU; and A. J. Rowland, ABPS; called for a consultative meeting on May 16, 1907, at the Calvary Baptist Church in Washington, D.C.

That provisional meeting, attended by representative Baptist leaders, appointed a committee of fifteen to draw up a proposed constitution for a Northern Baptist Convention. The structure informally agreed upon in Washington in 1907 was formally adopted in 1908 in Oklahoma City, though incorporation was not completed until 1910.

In the years following, the three societies, now program boards of the new convention, prospered and expanded their work. After some years the American Baptist Education Society became the Board of Education of the

---

2. Cited in William H. Brackney, ed., *Baptist Life and Thought 1600-1980*, p. 284.
3. *The Baptist*, July 10, 1920, p. 835.

new body. However, a certain "leveling" took place, as home missions, publications, and Christian education received more attention and funds, alongside foreign missions, which had long exercised a dominant emotional tug upon Baptist purse strings. Just as some Baptists could not accept the move to a more general denominational body in 1817 and 1820, so some opposed the new unified convention and for many of the same reasons. Problems with the new structure probably added to the Baptist unrest of the 1920s which the Fundamentalists so skillfully exploited. When the Fundamentalists later pulled out from the NBC, they grouped their churches into alignments significantly different from the Northern Baptist Convention. Escape from excessive "denominational machinery" was one reason they gave for their withdrawal. In explaining formation of a conservative foreign mission society in 1943, Earle V. Pierce said, "There are few who realize how far we [Northern Baptists] are board- and secretary-controlled."[4]

In retrospect, however, the Northern Baptist Convention apparently erected no more "machinery" than was needed for its tasks and, in some cases, perhaps not enough. Though adopting a convention plan, clearly much of the old society mind-set continued among Northern Baptists. The Northern Baptist churches, lacking any sustained tradition of denominational cooperation, failed to rally thoroughly around the new convention, and the societies, though now called boards, behaved much as before.

The New World Movement

One can hardly fathom the American optimism which marked the end of World War I. It was, after all, a "war to end all wars" and "a war to make the world safe for democracy." America was thrust into major world leadership for the first time and, most importantly, was on the winning side of the war. At home the economy seemed strong. The churches fully shared the optimism of the times. In the heady months after the war, several denominations launched major fund drives, including Methodists, Presbyterians, Disciples, and both Northern and Southern Baptists. All of them drew upon the techniques popularized in the successful war bond drives during the war years. Certainly it appeared a propitious time for major financial campaigns.

At their Denver convention in 1919, the NBC launched the New World Movement (NWM). This was an effort to pledge and collect $100 million over a five-year period, 1919-1924. The money was to be used to strengthen Baptist work at home, extend Baptist missions overseas, and to share in several ecumenical projects. From the first, the NWM faced obstacles. For one thing, since the societies had for years raised their own budgets, North-

4. Earle V. Pierce, "Northern Baptist Foreign Missions—Part II," *Watchman-Examiner,* p. 818.

ern Baptists had little experience in coordinated denominational fund raising. Second, the NBC may not have had enough time to prepare for the campaign. In 1918 the Education Board had launched its own drive to raise $1 million for Baptist schools. The Northern Convention rather suddenly escalated the campaign from $1 million for one cause to $100 million for all causes. This allowed about six months of preparation.

A third obstacle was the economy; it proved less solid than had appeared in 1919. Postwar economic adjustments, many unanticipated, weakened Northern industry; at the same time, drought and fluctuations in overseas demand for raw materials undercut Southern agriculture. The result was that in the 1920s all the denominations found it difficult to collect the pledges so cheerfully given in 1919.

A fourth obstacle to the NWM, and one which proved well-nigh fatal, was its early connection with the Interchurch World Movement (IWM). This was an ecumenical effort of about thirty denominations to combine their resources, cooperate in ministries at home, and parcel out their overseas efforts to avoid overlap and duplication. One motive was to assist in rebuilding war-torn Europe and reestablishing ties with European Christians. For all its worthy motives, most observers now concede that the Interchurch Movement was premature, poorly planned, and structurally flawed. For whatever reasons, it failed to enlist the necessary cooperation, and its failure almost pulled down the Baptists' New World Movement in its wake. Though Northern Baptists had for years shared in ecumenical ventures, many of their constituents neither understood nor favored the movement. Northern Baptist reaction to linking the NWM to an ecumenical effort was so overwhelmingly negative that by 1920 the convention voted reluctantly to pull out of the Interchurch Movement.

However, instead of easing the problem, withdrawal from the IWM further complicated things. Many who favored the ecumenical linkage lost enthusiasm for the entire fund drive. Many who opposed the ecumenical connection seemed to think that withdrawal from the Interchurch Movement canceled the entire movement, thus releasing them from their pledges. Others accused the convention, with some basis, of continued contributions to Interchurch projects even after the vote to withdraw.

By 1924 the convention had received $45,009,378.04 for the New World Movement campaign, though constituents had pledged about 20 percent more.[5] Failure to receive all the expected funds was not the most damaging result of this first great united effort of the Northern Baptist Convention; none of the other denominations received all their pledges either. The confusion and bitterness attending the campaign, suspicion of denominational leadership, resistance to the kind of organization required to conduct

---

5. *Annual of the Northern Baptist Convention,* 1924, p. 133 (hereafter cited as *Annual, NBC*).

such a campaign, and above all the coalescing of Fundamentalists in concerted opposition to the campaign boded ill for the days ahead and left Northern Baptists severely weakened. Ten years later Northern Baptist leaders were still trying to explain and defend the New World Movement.

Amid such problems, one must not forget the positive accomplishments of the New World Movement. By any standard, $45 million for Christian work ranks as a major achievement. The money was disbursed as follows:[6]

National Societies and Boards	$22,447,651.78
Schools and Colleges	7,814,322.83
State Conventions	6,747,394.34
State Missionary Societies	2,739,729.00
General Board of Promotion	3,158,656.70
Interchurch Movement	1,781,978.11
Transferred to Board of Missionary Cooperation	3,948.05
Miscellaneous	315,697.23
	$45,009,378.04

The Fundamentalist Movement

Doctrinal disagreement is no new thing to Baptists in America, nor did the twentieth century provide Baptists' first taste of it. The denomination had faced the rise of Sabbatarian Baptists in Rhode Island, Freewill Baptists in New Hampshire, Primitive Baptists in Illinois, and Campbellite Baptists in the Midwest, to name only a few family fractures on the American side of the Atlantic. The eruption of the 1920s among Northern Baptists was new, however, in some of its issues and especially in its intensity and bitterness.

Early Tremors

Though the full doctrinal quake hit in the 1920s, distinct tremors could be felt even before the turn of the century. Some date the crisis from the founding of the University of Chicago in 1890. William Bell Riley, a major Fundamentalist leader, later recalled that while a pastor in Chicago, as early as 1893, he was shocked at doctrinal views advanced at the Monday pastors' conference by such Chicago men as William R. Harper and George B. Foster. It was there, Riley later recalled, that "I first faced organized modernism in my denomination." He described the views of Harper and Foster as "this attempt of Unitarianism to capture our Baptist body."[7]

The Baptist Congress, an informal but important discussion forum, heard

6. *Annual*, NBC, 1924, p. 145.

7. W. B. Riley, "The Foreign Mission Board Controversy," *Watchman-Examiner*, p. 1131.

papers on new views of the Bible, the validity of conversion, new forms of the psychology of religion, and alternate views of the life and work of Christ well before 1900. In 1909 T. O. Conant spoke at the Baptist Congress on "Recent Tendencies to Change Denominational Practice" and defended traditional Baptist views on the authority of Scripture, the independence of local churches, and the requirement of immersion for membership against what he regarded as trends to change these emphases.[8] At the anniversary of the American Baptist Publication Society in Detroit in 1900, Ira M. Price gave an address on "The Bible and Its Critics" which indicated that newer approaches to the biblical text and its interpretation had won some following among Baptists.[9] In 1897 A. K. Parker, pastor in Chicago, told the scholarly congress bluntly, "The denomination contains within itself two quite distinctly defined schools or parties."[10]

Two books by Baptist theological professors further agitated the conservatives among Northern Baptists. George B. Foster (1858-1918), of the University of Chicago, published *The Finality of the Christian Religion* in 1906, and Walter Rauschenbusch (1861-1918), of the Rochester Theological Seminary, issued his *Christianity and the Social Crisis* in 1907. Foster seemed to conservatives to compromise several Baptist doctrines, most importantly perhaps, the traditional understanding of the person and work of Christ. "The church's theological Christ," he said, "still supplants the real Jesus of history."[11] Foster also seemed to question the reliability of Scripture and regarded Paul more than Jesus as the founder of Christianity. In the resulting outcry, which saw over 225 churches in southern Illinois withdraw and later join the Southern Baptist Convention, Foster was shifted from the divinity school to the university's department of philosophy. In his book of 1907, which many regard as perhaps the finest statement of the Social Gospel, Rauschenbusch indicted the church for producing what he called priests instead of prophets and accused the church of forsaking the message *of* Jesus, the coming kingdom of God, for a Hellenized message *about* Jesus. Rauschenbusch also tended to see a tension between Jesus who offered a kingdom and Paul who structured the church. Many conservatives responded negatively to both books.

Even the unlikely Henry C. Vedder, a Baptist historian, was suspected of heresy. He published a defense, entitled "My Teaching About the Atonement," which perhaps raised more questions than it settled. Affirming the atonement itself, Vedder said he only denied Fundamentalist theories about

8. *Twenty-Seventh Annual Session,* The Baptist Congress, Madison Avenue Baptist Church, New York City, 1909, pp. 112 *f,* in ABHS.

9. Ira M. Price, "The Bible and Its Critics," *Seventy-Sixth Anniversary,* American Baptist Publishing Society (ABPS), Detroit, 1900, pp. 32 *f.*

10. Baptist Congress, 1897, p. 87.

11. George B. Foster, *The Finality of the Christian Religion* (University of Chicago Press, 1906), p. xii.

the atonement. He concluded, "I do not believe in the transference of penalty from one person to another," which he dismissed as "clan ethics."[12] Augustus H. Strong, who could not be considered either a Fundamentalist or a liberal, had to defend his views on evolution and higher criticism, both of which he accepted, but in their more conservative forms. A part of Strong's defense, interestingly, was his claim, "I am both a premillennialist and a postmillennialist."[13]

These few examples are enough to illustrate that doctrinal diversity preceded the Fundamentalist uproar of the 1920s. Enough dissent had surfaced to call into existence a new conservative school, the Northern Baptist Theological Seminary in Chicago in 1913 and to make it a success.

Against this backdrop, the NBC at Denver in 1919 launched its New World Movement and, despite sharp opposition, insisted on linking it with the ecumenical Interchurch Movement. The Fundamentalists at Denver were soundly put down but laid plans to make their voices heard the next year.

Fundamentalist Rallies

Men like William Bell Riley, John Roach Stratton, Frank M. Goodchild, and J. C. Massee hit upon the plan of holding regional rallies of conservative sympathizers, culminating in a large preconvention rally of dissidents in Buffalo in 1920. This two-day rally before the Buffalo convention was well-attended. Under the chairmanship of Bell, Fundamentalists aired their grievances, doctrinal and procedural, heard a series of militant messages on fundamental issues, and even voiced a few threats; Cortland Myers, pastor of Tremont Temple in Boston, said, "If you don't get rid of the Interchurch Movement, and your Baptist newspaper, and some of your secretaries and missionaries, something is going to happen."[14]

And something did happen. Dominating the Buffalo convention, the well-organized Fundamentalists forced withdrawal from the Interchurch Movement, passed a motion to investigate Baptist schools, and so disrupted the convention that some scheduled speakers and reports were either delayed or deleted. The conservatives escalated their informal gathering into the Fundamentalist Fellowship, elected a small committee to arrange regional conferences and an annual preconvention rally, and laid plans to capture the Northern Baptist Convention. While the term *fundamental* had long been used to describe basic doctrines, and two wealthy Presbyterian oil men had bankrolled publication of a series of booklets called "The Fundamentals," the term had usually referred to doctrines and not persons.

12. *The Baptist,* November 20, 1920, p. 1458.
13. A. H. Strong, "My Views of the Universe in General," *The Baptist,* May 29, 1920, pp. 625-626.
14. *The Baptist,* July 3, 1920, p. 800.

Curtis Lee Laws, editor of the *Watchman-Examiner,* an independent conservative paper, after the Buffalo convention wrote an editorial in which he applied the term "Fundamentalist" to those who were ready to "do battle royal" for certain doctrines, thus in one stroke naming the movement and documenting its belligerent spirit.

The Buffalo rally was also addressed by J. W. Porter, one of the more conservative Southern Baptists, who was then editor of the *Western Recorder* of Kentucky. He offered to publish all the Fundamentalist papers given at that rally, an offer that was declined. No doubt Porter was one avenue by which Northern Fundamentalist views made inroads among Southern Baptists, leading to the 1925 adoption of the New Hampshire Confession, slightly revised, as the SBC confession. The Fundamentalist Fellowship had earlier adopted the same confession.

Areas of Attack

The Fundamentalist attack upon the NBC proceeded on three major fronts, charging heresy in the schools, among the missionaries, and in the literature issued by the Board of Publication. Questions about the schools surfaced first. In what one called "an outburst against our colleges and seminaries," a series of Fundamentalist speakers at Buffalo attacked Baptist teachers and teachings. Some later said J. C. Massee was propelled into the Fundamentalist movement when his son came home from a Baptist school with his faith shaken.[15] John Roach Stratton, in his attack upon the Baptist seminaries, read a statement of what he regarded as dangerous heresy being taught, only to have the convention applaud, thus in effect endorsing the suspect views as their own.

However, enough concern existed for the convention to establish a Committee of Nine to investigate the Baptist schools, making Frank M. Goodchild, a moderate Fundamentalist, its chairman. The convention resolution noted, "There are many rumors and charges concerning the teachings and teachers in the secondary schools, colleges, and seminaries in the territory of the Northern Baptist Convention." It charged the committee to investigate teachings in the schools, the methods of choosing trustees, and

> to give special attention to the question of whether these schools and individual teachers are still loyal to the great fundamental Baptist beliefs as held by the denomination in the past, with particular reference to the inspiration of the Word of God, the Deity of Christ, the atonement, the resurrection, the return of the Lord, the spiritual nature of the church, the necessity for a regenerated baptized church membership, . . . and the imperative responsibility of carrying out the great commission.[16]

15. Ibid., July 24, 1920, p. 909.
16. *Annual,* NBC, 1920, p. 48.

The work of that committee, after a year of travel, interviews, and questionnaires, proved quite revealing. It turned out that many of the colleges had long since severed their slight connection with the denomination, and others were so offended by the investigation that they also withdrew from any remaining connection with the NBC. The society basis of their origin and their independent sources of support allowed these schools almost complete independence from the denomination. Some of the schools, like Brown University, the first Baptist college in America, simply declined to respond to the committee's questions on the grounds of the historic freedom of thought among Baptists.

The Board of Education of the Northern Baptist Convention valiantly defended the schools in its 1921 report. Noting that "our schools and colleges have been under severe storm of criticism during the past year," the board concluded that "the charges which have been made are largely false."[17] The report deplored the attacks, feared they would undermine confidence in the schools just when Baptists seemed to be taking a renewed interest in Christian education, and concluded that such unfounded accusations bordered on the criminal. However, the board did not respond to several alleged problems in specific schools.

Little of practical consequence issued from the investigation of Northern Baptist colleges, universities, and seminaries. The report did pinpoint some of the seminaries as more liberal than others. One indirect result of the investigation and its inconclusive report was to encourage the founding of more conservative Northern Baptist seminaries at Philadelphia and Los Angeles.

The next point of Fundamentalist attack focused upon foreign missionaries, a fact surprising in itself. Baptists have a long tradition of attacking their teachers, but their foreign missionaries have usually stood above suspicion, doctrinal or otherwise. In 1922 the foreign board acknowledged that many were calling in question the theological veiws of missionaries, as well as the doctrinal positions of churches on the foreign field. Accusations that missionaries were "teaching and preaching other than the evangelical gospel" had been widely reported and had produced a drop in missionary contributions. The board affirmed its confidence in the missionaries and the appointment procedure, attributed the unrest to postwar social anxieties, and cautioned against missionary contributions with strings attached. This last was prompted by the offer of a substantial sum from a wealthy donor if the board could guarantee it would go only to conservative missionaries.

Not satisfied with the Foreign Mission Board's general report, Fundamentalists sought access to missionary letters to the board in order to document their claims of doctrinal deviation. Not surprisingly, the board

17. *Tenth Annual Report,* Board of Education of the Northern Baptist Convention, 1921, pp. 6-7.

denied access on the grounds of confidentiality, but somehow the disaffected group obtained a number of damaging quotations allegedly from missionary letters and circulated them widely. W. B. Riley published what purported to be a number of statements from Northern Baptist missionaries in which they denied biblical inspiration, the virgin birth, the deity of Christ, and the resurrection.[18] One missionary, when pressed about his beliefs, was asked

> whether or not he believed in the virgin birth: "I think not." His reply when asked if he believed in miracles, "I think not." When asked if he believed in the bodily resurrection, his final answer was "I think not," and when asked if he believed in the inspiration of Scriptures he said, "I think not."[19]

The Fundamentalists said they found one missionary who believed there was no such thing as salvation, that death brought annihilation; while another was a universalist, believing that all would have salvation.

Those and similar charges, if substantiated, would obviously represent a problem, but at first the Foreign Mission Board resisted the idea of a full investigation. By 1924 it agreed, however, to an investigative committee. Earle V. Pierce, writing some years later, accounted for that change as follows. A foreign missionary had apparently denied several Baptist doctrines, a fact known to the Fundamentalists. Pierce, a leader of the Fundamentalists, said he was approached by two Baptist leaders who said, "If you Fundamentalists will agree not to spring the Hartley matter on the floor of the Convention, we will stand with you for an investigation of the entire Foreign Mission situation and personnel, for there's something rotten in Denmark."[20]

Whether or not due to this scenario, the Milwaukee convention in 1924 appointed a Commission of Seven to investigate "the conduct, policies, and practices of the Board of Managers of the American Baptist Foreign Mission Society and of its secretaries in the selection of missionaries to the foreign field."[21] They were also to consider what to do with missionaries "who do not accept or have repudiated or abandoned the evangelical faith as held historically by Baptists." The commission, chaired by A. W. Beavan, conducted a thorough study and did turn up perhaps a half-dozen missionaries who had either forsaken the faith or stated their faith so carelessly as to raise questions, though the commission generally exonerated the missionaries.[22]

During the troubled years 1920-1928, Frederick L. Anderson, professor

18. W. B. Riley, "To All Baptists Who Believe the Bible to Be God's Word," *Watchman-Examiner,* 1925, pp. 1497 *f.*

19. Ibid., p. 1497.

20. Pierce, p. 794. Hartley was the name of the missionary in question.

21. *Annual,* NBC, 1924, p. 51.

22. *Watchman-Examiner,* October 22, 1925, p. 1362.

at the Andover Newton Theological Seminary, served as chairman of the managing board of the foreign mission work of Northern Baptists. He led with statesmanship and dignity, listened to all complaints, and tried to preserve balance which could continue to enlist the support of the whole denomination. In a 1924 speech, which became known as the "Anderson Statement," he said:

> Your Board has sought to find the common ground on which we all or nearly all stand. Guided by the facts that Baptists have always been known as evangelicals, and that the gospel is the most important message of the Scriptures, we have demanded that all our officers and missionaries be loyal to the gospel. We will appoint only suitable evangelical men and women; we will appoint evangelicals, and we will not appoint nonevangelicals.[23]

In amplifying this "evangelical policy," Anderson affirmed that since the Northern Baptist constituency included a broad theological spectrum, the board would appoint missionaries from all across that spectrum so long as they came within the broad boundaries of the announced policy. In what must rank as one of the most unfortunate phrases of the twentieth century for Northern Baptists, this was dubbed the "inclusive policy." The Fundamentalists made the most of their criticism of the "inclusive policy," claiming that it included radical liberals. Whether fairly represented or not, Fundamentalist attacks upon the inclusive policy struck a vital nerve among the churches, put the foreign mission leaders on the defensive, and figured prominently in the schisms of 1933 and 1947.

Meanwhile, the Beavan Commission reported to the Seattle convention in 1925: "About the vast majority of our missionaries there is no question. We have been led to renewed conviction as to their evangelical faith and efficiency in service."[24] However, the commission noted, "We do feel there is ground for criticism that in some cases there has been evidenced a tendency to underestimate the value in a missionary of thoroughly sound, evangelical Christian views."[25] Citing evidence that the managing board did not inquire closely into the doctrinal views of candidates, and in other cases appointed persons with needed skills without much regard to theology, the commission called for more careful screening in the appointment process.

As to missionaries on the field, the commission found a few cases of genuine doctrinal deviation. Citing from missionary letters, without naming the writers, the commission cited examples of missionaries who apparently denied basic Baptist beliefs.[26] The commission called not only for more

23. Cited in Robert G. Torbet, *A History of Baptists,* 3rd ed., pp. 399-400.
24. *Annual,* NBC, 1925, p. 81.
25. Ibid., p. 83.
26. Ibid., pp. 88-90.

careful appointment procedures but also for some method of monitoring the continuing faith of the missionary after appointment.

There the matter might have rested, but W. B. Hinson of Portland moved that "our Foreign Mission Boards are hereby instructed to recall immediately every representative, whether in evangelistic or educational work, who is found on investigation to deny any of the great fundamentals of our faith" and that no one be elected to the mission board who could not pass the same doctrinal scrutiny as the missionaries.[27] However, R. V. Meigs of Illinois moved a substitute: "That we urge upon our Foreign Mission Board such action, in the light of the facts reported by the Commission, as seems to them will best conserve our denominational interests."[28] After intense debate, the substitute prevailed by a vote of 742 to 574. In effect, the commission spotlighted the problems, but the convention left it to the mission leaders to address the problems.

The closeness of the vote assured continuing agitation. The Fundamentalists felt they had won a victory by forcing the commission to document and the convention to acknowledge that doctrinal problems did exist. However, the moderates won perhaps a greater victory by leaving the solution in the hands of the board without specific instructions from the convention. The Fundamentalists felt the problem had been aired but not cured; the moderates felt that the convention and its missionary board had been saved from Fundamentalist control. Under these conditions, one is not surprised to learn that tensions continued.

The Publication Board became the arena for another skirmish, but far less serious than that which plagued the schools and foreign mission work. As in the slavery conflict of the 1840s, the Publication Board tried to serve all sides and, indeed, published several Fundamentalist works, including *Baptist Fundamentals,* the messages of the preconvention conference at Buffalo in 1920.[29] Even so, Fundamentalists alleged that some of the Sunday School literature taught liberal views and by the mid-1920s were making plans to obtain their church curriculum materials elsewhere or produce their own. In 1925 W. B. Riley, for example, announced plans of the Baptist Bible Union, composed of the more militant Fundamentalists, to bring out a new line of church literature, to be called the "Whole Bible Sunday School Lesson Course," with lesson notes to be written by T. T. Shields of Toronto.[30]

While by no means as sensational as the attacks upon the teachers and missionaries, the gradual undermining of confidence in the convention's curriculum has continued over the years, with serious cumulative effects.

27. Ibid., p. 5.
28. Ibid., p. 174.
29. J. C. Massee, ed., *Baptist Fundamentals* (Philadelphia: ABPB, 1921).
30. Riley, "To All Baptists," 1:497.

A report in the 1980s stated that a minority of American Baptist churches then used the Judson curriculum materials, with other churches using SBC materials, materials from one of the independent presses, preparing their own, or using none at all.

Other conflicts arose between Baptist Fundamentalists and moderates not specifically related to one of the program boards. The General Board of the newly formed Northern Baptist Convention bought and combined several earlier papers to form *The Baptist,* published weekly as the voice of the convention.[31] Baptists in America have a long tradition of newspapers, often expressing diverse views. Throughout most of the nineteenth century, each society issued its own paper. However, *The Baptist* (still published as *The American Baptist,* or TAB) was the first attempt at an official paper for Northern Baptists. Fundamentalists felt the paper was slanted to liberalism, pushed the denominational party line uncritically, and alternately ignored or distorted Fundamentalist emphases. At the Buffalo convention, J. C. Massee moved, "That the Convention now instruct the Board of Promotion to sell *The Baptist* to the highest bidder."[32] While this did not pass, W. B. Riley promised "guerilla warfare" against the paper, saying, "We do not believe that we have any adequate representation of our orthodox views."[33] The *Watchman-Examiner,* ably edited by the moderate conservative, Curtis Lee Laws, gave more favorable attention to Fundamentalism, but for the most part preserved an independent stance, while allowing expression of both liberal and Fundamentalist viewpoints on its pages. The editorial stance of Laws, however, was consistently conservative.

A Proposed Confession

One agenda of the Fundamentalists in the 1920s was to commit Northern Baptists to a confession of faith, preferably the New Hampshire Confession of 1833, with a premillennial understanding of the last article. They found it difficult to prove teachers and missionaries heretical in the absence of specific doctrinal standards, just as Spurgeon had discovered in the Down Grade Controversy in England a generation earlier. At the Indianapolis convention in 1922, W. B. Riley, citing "unquestioned defection" from the historic Baptist faith throughout the denomination, moved adoption of the New Hampshire Confession, one of the more conservative confessions ever framed by Baptists in this country.[34] Riley's motion did not actually call for the convention itself to adopt any confession, but to recommend it for adoption by the churches. While not a major point, perhaps, this does reveal

31. *Annual,* NBC, 1920, pp. 72-73.
32. Ibid., p. 124.
33. *The Baptist,* July 3, 1920, p. 810.
34. *Annual,* NBC, 1922, pp. 129-130.

a dimension of Northern Baptist ecclesiology, somewhat different from that prevalent in the Southern Baptist Convention, which in 1925 did adopt the New Hampshire Confession in a slightly modified form but said nothing about local churches adopting it.

Cornelius Woelfkin of New York offered the substitute motion that "the Northern Baptist Convention affirms that the New Testament is the all-sufficient ground of our faith and practice and we need no other statement."[35] The substitute passed by a vote of 1,264 to 637. Even some who favored the confession found it difficult to vote against the New Testament. The very next entry in the convention records, after this confession conflict, says, "President E. Y. Mullins, of Kentucky, offered prayer." Three years later Mullins, president of the SBC, served on the committee which led the Southern Baptist Convention to adopt the New Hampshire Confession in modified form as its own statement of *The Baptist Faith and Message.*

Amid the plenitude of doctrinal emphases pushed by the Fundamentalists in the 1920s, one kept bobbing to the surface: premillennialism. Some thought this the main issue which drew the Fundamentalists together; many of them in fact embraced the dispensational form of that doctrine. One thoughtful scholar has traced the entire modern Fundamentalist movement to millennial speculations.[36] A more balanced view, which shows other sources for Fundamentalism, can be found in George M. Marsden, *Fundamentalism and American Culture.* Dispensationalism probably infiltrated into Baptist thought from nondenominational sources, such as the Plymouth Brethren, and through a popular study Bible issued by Cyrus I. Scofield in 1909. By the twentieth century, many of the more conservative, both North and South, had come to regard it as a part of Baptist orthodoxy.

Two Streams of Fundamentalism

From the first, two separate streams of Fundamentalism assailed the Northern Baptist Convention, and failure to distinguish them leads to endless confusion. One stream arose *within* the convention and, although pushing for reforms, intended to remain within NBC life and loyally support its programs. Led by men of broad culture and generous spirit, such as J. C. Massee, Frank M. Goodchild, and John Roach Stratton, the group campaigned vigorously but courteously for change. Deploring the radical schism of 1933, the group remained in the convention until 1947 when the members felt themselves forced out. When over a quarter century of effort failed to produce the changes they wanted, they pulled out in 1947 to form the Conservative Baptist Association of America (CBAA).

A more militant Fundamentalist stream arose *outside* the convention, but

35. Ibid., p. 133.

36. See Ernest R. Sandeen, *The Roots of Fundamentalism: British and American Millenarianism 1800-1930.*

eventually pulled in many convention leaders and churches. Drawing from such diverse sources as English Baptist Fundamentalism, American non-denominational Fundamentalism, and Fundamentalism among Southern Baptists (J. Frank Norris of Fort Worth was one of the leaders), a different sort of Fundamentalists formed the Baptist Bible Union in 1923. A number of factors pulled the Bible unioners together, especially the refusal of the NBC to adopt the New Hampshire Confession in 1922. In general, they represented a narrower educational and cultural base, a firmer commitment to premillennialism, a persistent nondenominational flavor, and above all a meaner spirit. However, they saw more clearly than their calmer conservative brethren that the Northern Baptist Convention would not change. Acting with the courage of their convictions, they cut their ties in 1932 and organized in 1933 as the General Association of Regular Baptist Churches (GARBC).

Though neither stream of Fundamentalism captured the Northern Baptist Convention, each inflicted gaping wounds which have never healed. A fact of far-reaching significance in American religious history is that while Fundamentalism invaded most major denominations in the 1920s it captured none of them. These successive defeats drove some Fundamentalists underground and others into schism or interdenominational alliances where their disappointments festered and their troops regrouped to make another, better organized, run on American religion after World War II.

Impact of Fundamentalism

A half-century of bitter conflict and schism left its mark upon Baptists of the North, both in the convention and in the schismatic groups. Each has caused the other to intensify, and perhaps thereby to exaggerate, its positions. To some extent their dire predictions for each other have been self-fulfilling. Though partisan leaders may fail to see it, their schisms have loosened restraints on both sides. Fundamentalists have been free to implement extreme and sometimes bizarre policies, though in recent years a second generation of leadership in the GARBC and CBA have toned down both the rhetoric and the policies. On the other hand, the draining off of conservatives left the main body largely without effective brakes on leaders who wanted to veer sharply to the left.

The American Baptist Convention

A New Name

The denominational overhaul which formed the Northern Baptist Convention in 1908 was never fully successful. Always "a family of missionary societies," under the NBC the societies were called boards but continued to function in relative independence. Like bushes tied together at the top, their structural unity did not extend to the roots of Baptist benevolence.

Problems with the Interchurch Movement and the theological crisis further hampered the new convention, and the historic local church independence of Northern Baptists fueled resistance to a strong central board and executive leadership which might have made the convention more effective. Throughout the twentieth century, Baptists in the North have tinkered with their denominational machinery, with changes ranging from minor tuning to major overhauls. The change from the Northern Baptist Convention to the American Baptist Convention in 1950 was major.

In 1947 the NBC appointed a Commission of Review, chaired by former president Edwin T. Dahlberg. The commission's assignment was "to make a thoroughgoing study of our whole denominational structure, with a view to making it more efficient, democratic, and responsive to the will of the churches."[37] It made a preliminary report in San Francisco in 1949, recommending far-reaching changes. These included changing the name to American Baptist Convention, improving convention fund raising and promotion, creation of a stronger general board, closer relations with colleges and seminaries, and of course closer cooperation between the program agencies, a goal sought since the 1820s. The commission also recommended creation of the office of general secretary; Reuben E. Nelson was the first to hold that office when the changes were effected in 1950 at Boston.

Many of the Baptists had never liked the regional name of the Northern Baptist Convention. For most of the nineteenth century, the several societies had used *American* as part of their title, and they regarded the 1950 change as taking back their old name rather than adopting a new one. Perhaps the forty-two-year interval with a sectional name grew partly out of comity agreements with Southern Baptists, beginning in 1894, in which Baptists North and South basically agreed to recognize each other's territory and work their own. The passing of the comity era and the aggressive expansion of Southern Baptists, especially in California in the 1940s, was a factor in the decision to reaffirm ministries of national scope.

The convention seemed sensitive to the fact that other Baptist groups, by virtue of being in this country, also had some claim to the name. They said, "We hold the name in trust for all Christians of like faith and mind who desire to bear witness to the historic Baptist convictions in a framework of cooperative Christianity."[38] Perhaps this was addressed partly to the Disciples, with whom Northern Baptists were then in merger talks, as they had been off and on since the turn of the century. Two motions came from the floor during the preliminary report of 1949, apparently unexpected and perhaps discomfiting to the commission. One moved, "to invite the Southern Baptist Convention to unite with us in the American Baptist Conven-

37. *Year Book,* NBC, 1947, p. 115.
38. Ibid., 1950, p. 55.

tion."[39] The other moved, "to invite all organized Baptist conventions and conferences in the continental United States, including the bilingual groups and the two Negro national conferences, to unite with us in the American Baptist Convention."[40] The fact that both motions passed overwhelmingly showed that many Baptists hoped to unify the Baptist family, or at least create an umbrella under which all Baptists in the country could rally.

In its final report the next year, the commission cautiously modified these motions. Pointing out that nine of the bilingual groups were already "associated" with the Northern Convention, and while others would be welcomed to this undefined relationship, "the possibility of *merger* of other Baptist conventions with ours" would take cautious and lengthy negotiations.

For whatever reasons, Southern Baptists regarded the 1950 name change and the invitation for other Baptists to gather under that umbrella as an aggressive act.[41] They responded with rather aggressive actions of their own. Already their annual conventions were set for Chicago in 1950 and San Francisco in 1951, hardly within traditional SBC territory. In Chicago the SBC announced that all comity agreements had expired and Southern Baptists would feel free to establish churches throughout the nation. Actions of the two conventions in 1950 introduced a decade of tension between Baptists North and South, tensions which began to abate by the mid-1960s.

A New Headquarters

In the continuing search for unity and efficiency, the American Baptist Convention decided in the mid-1950s to bring all its program agencies together in the same city, expecting that would both express and further the desired unity. Three cities emerged as leading contenders for headquarters: New York, at the new Interchurch Center which housed the National Council of Churches; Chicago, near the center of the constituency; and Valley Forge, near Philadelphia where national Baptist organization had begun in 1814. New York was the clear choice of denominational leaders; the Headquarters Commission voted 8 to 4 for that city. However the "people's convention" of 1958, as some called it, rejected the Interchurch site by a 65 percent margin. Those for Chicago could muster only 51 percent and the convention had agreed it would take 55 percent to move. When several votes continued deadlocked between New York and Chicago, Valley Forge emerged as a compromise site "acceptable if not agreeable."[42] The

39. Ibid., p. 160.
40. Ibid.
41. Some say that Southern Baptists intended to recommend that their convention switch to the name "American Baptist Convention." See James L. Sullivan, *Baptist Polity as I See It,* p. 104.
42. See Brackney, p. 387.

convention occupied its impressive new facilities at Valley Forge in 1960, bringing foreign missions, home missions, education, and publication work, in fact, all denominational offices except the Ministers and Missionaries Benefit Board, under one roof for the first time.

SCODS: The New Shape of Baptists

In 1972, for the third time in this century, Baptists in the North changed their name and reorganized their denomination. In many ways the 1972 overhaul was the most radical of all. The new name became "American Baptist Churches in the USA." The Study Commission on Denominational Structure (SCODS) was appointed in 1968. Its final report, accepted in 1972, called not only for a new name, which omitted the convention concept, but a radically revised decision structure, giving extensive power to a general board of about two hundred members. The entire body would henceforth meet biennially rather than annually and would deal mostly with inspiration and fellowship, leaving most actual policy decisions to the general board. The new name was not easily chosen. The term *convention* was discarded because it means merely a meeting and carries no churchly overtones. The constituency preferred "The American Baptist Church." The name chosen, using "Churches" in the plural, carries the desired churchly overtones and yet avoids the hierarchical overtones of the first alternative.

Restructuring the Denomination

More important than the name were the new lines of representation and reasons for them. Previous surveys showed that only about 20 percent of the ABC churches sent delegates to the national convention, thus leaving 80 percent of the churches unrepresented, including almost all of the smaller churches. The SCODS study was intended, among other things, to devise a representative system by which all the churches could make their voices heard. To this end the country was divided into ten areas or regions, covering more or less geography depending upon the number of ABC churches there. Each area was headed by an "area minister," elected by the denomination and functioning somewhat like the area superintendents among English Baptists. Each area was in turn divided into several "election districts," following the same principle of concentration. Local churches sent delegates to the election district, which in turn elected delegates to the general board and to the biennial sessions. Some areas are coterminous with the old state conventions, while others comprise several states; some election districts are identical with the old associations, while others cover only part of an association or several associations, depending on the number of churches involved. The long-range expectation is that the state conventions and associations will eventually give way to the new structures.

Structural Problems

Robert T. Handy pointed out that some problems with the new structure have surfaced.[43] Some find the election districts artificial and prefer to work through associations. Pastors feel their voice and power in the denomination have been diminished, with more power gravitating to professional staff of the agencies. The general board is composed of clergy, laymen, and women in equal numbers. After a ten-year "shakedown cruise," one defender of the new system acknowledged that most churches place little importance upon electing their representatives to the election district, that clergy feel disenfranchised, and that conservatives feel they have no way to make their views felt in the denomination.[44] By 1983 it was no longer possible to ignore growing dissatisfaction with the new structures. Ray Jennings observed that SCODS "produced an undercurrent of acrimonious dissatisfaction which has yet to be fully evaluated or understood."[45] He concluded, "The concept of 'election districts' has not proven an effective way of keeping local churches involved" in denominational life, and local pastors and members feel they have been relegated to sideline status. Another respondent to the 1983 biennial, Brian A. Nelson, said that the disenfranchisement of pastors means that "the single most important group of leaders for the denomination is outside the structure" and that "local churches are already simply ignoring what the denomination does."[46]

These criticisms must not obscure the positive aspects of the 1972 reorganization. The new plan, for example, gives a greater voice to black Baptists, who by 1983 composed one-third of the ABC, and women, who outnumber men in the membership. However, if the criticisms continue, one may expect further adjustments in denominational polity among American Baptists.

Baptist Ministries

Reports of structuring and restructuring must not occupy the full story, however. Under whatever name, Baptists in the North have conducted extensive ministries in the twentieth century in foreign missions, home missions, and Christian education.

43. Robert T. Handy, "American Baptist Polity: What's Happening and Why," *Baptist History and Heritage,* p. 21.

44. Jenks, pp. 297-298.

45. Ray Jennings, "The Biennial as 'Family Gathering'" *American Baptist Quarterly,* p. 355.

46. Brian A. Nelson, "The '83 Cleveland Biennial: A Personal Perspective," *American Baptist Quarterly,* December 1983, pp. 358-361.

Board of International Ministries (BIM)

After World War I, Northern Baptists recognized that a changed world called for changed missionary methods. They sought to prepare national leaders to exercise indigenous leadership in overseas churches. This tended to shift the priority from direct evangelism to education and to reduce missionary visibility. These methods had less emotional appeal; one seldom received the kind of letters that Ann Judson used to write, full of vivid accounts of spiritual conquests.

Even before strong Fundamentalism and a weak economy teamed up to undercut the work in the 1920s, Northern Baptist foreign missions faced setbacks. The "intensive policy" of 1912 became another name for retrenchment; the foreign board announced that it would enter no more fields but intensify its work in fields already occupied. Shifting theological views, changing conditions overseas, competing priorities at home, and ecumenical teamwork reduced the overseas missionary force and reordered its functions.

Statistical reports show a decrease in the number of Northern Baptist foreign missionaries from a total of 474 in 1900 to 203 in 1982.[47] Ordained ministers among these numbered 171 in 1900, in 1982 only 57. In 1900 the largest concentration of missionaries was in Asia, with 168 in Burma alone. By 1982 they had fewer missionaries in Asia, none in Burma, with the greatest concentration in Zaire.

Taken by themselves, these statistics can be misleading. The overseas budget rose from $543,048 in 1900 to $6,900,000 in 1982.[48] If the number of direct missionaries decreased, the number of trained national workers increased from 3,482 in 1900 to almost 20,000 in 1982. In the same years, the number of overseas Baptist churches related to Northern Baptists increased almost tenfold, membership almost thirteenfold. The BIM can claim significant overseas achievements, partly by channeling more resources into national leadership and increasingly turning its institutions over to national control.

There is no escaping the fact, however, that Northern Baptists have placed less emphasis upon overseas ministries in the twentieth century than in the nineteenth. In the nineteenth century, foreign missions provided the major motive which drew the scattered churches into cooperation and consumed their primary attention and funds. The present century has seen other forms of ministry compete for attention and funds in the overall Baptist witness. Leading Northern Baptists were "re-thinking missions" long before a formal study by that title burst upon the denomination in

---

47. *Annual Report,* American Baptist Missionary Union (ABMU), Detroit, 1900, p. 215; *Year Book,* ABC, 1982, p. 135.

48. Ibid., pp. 235, 129.

1932. Countless speeches at the Baptist Congress, the annual autumn talk-fest which ran from 1888-1913, dealt with missions. The speeches often explored such topics as the utility, economy, methodology, and theology of foreign missions, many with negative conclusions. Those were augmented by a controversial study in 1932 which questioned many of the basic principles on which Baptist mission work had rested for over a century.[49] The joint study by seven Protestant denominations, including Northern Baptists, called for fundamental changes in the motives and methods of foreign missions.

Board of National Ministries (BNM)

One could hardly name a tougher task than that faced by home mission agencies in twentieth-century America or name a group that pursued its work with more courage and zeal than the Home Mission Society of Northern Baptists. The name of the group changed twice, to Home Mission Board in 1908 and to Board of National Ministries in 1972; and its methods have changed even more in pursuing its unchanging goals. "North America for Christ" has been more than a motto; the home board has made an all-out effort to plant churches and extend the gospel throughout this changing nation.

Facing new challenges. That the nation has changed since 1900 seems an understatement. Two world wars catapulted the United States into world leadership, rearranged the economy, led to reevaluation of moral standards, and made heavy demands on the churches for ministry to military personnel and their families. The massive shifts in population left many churches emptied, while burgeoning new communities called for new churches faster than they could be provided. In the first quarter of the present century, European immigration brought millions of "new Americans," most of whom settled in Northern states. These hyphenated Americans comprised a foreign mission field at home, and a difficult one, for later waves of immigration brought mostly people with neither background nor interest in evangelical Protestantism. The emergence of urban America, with the growth of middle-class suburbs, left crowded but crumbling inner cities with overwhelming spiritual needs that seemed impervious to traditional forms of church life. The Baptist home mission heritage grew out of rural America in the early 1800s, based upon "itineration in the wilderness" and taking the gospel to "frontier outposts." That rural orientation had to be adapted to the new realities of urban America. These changes affected all Baptists, of course, but they hit Northern Baptists earlier and harder, challenging not only traditional methods of evangelism but at times its underlying theology as well.

49. William E. Hocking, *Re-Thinking Missions: A Laymen's Inquiry after One Hundred Years.*

Racial and economic conditions siphoned millions of blacks out of the South to the North where they competed with foreign immigrants, both lured by the industrial complex caught in a labor shortage caused by World War I. Southern whites also migrated northward and westward, driven by the dust bowl and the Great Depression and drawn by the defense plants of the North and the vineyards and vegetable fields of the West. The Southern invasion set up additional challenges to Northern Baptists and led to a series of territorial comity agreements. By mid-century the agreements were largely abandoned, with Northern Baptist churches multiplying in the South and SBC churches dotting Northern areas.

A change of directions. External changes were fully matched by inner developments which challenged the methods, priorities, and sometimes the theology of earlier Baptist home missions. Nowhere was that more evident than in the gradual shift from direct personal evangelism to social action forms of evangelism among Northern Baptists. The shift grew out of changing conditions in society, especially the cities, and changing theology, especially as articulated by Walter Rauschenbusch and other Social Gospel leaders. The rise of the institutional church, majoring on social ministries, the growth of community centers, and the formation of ministries for youth, the aged, and immigrants addressed crucial needs and absorbed more home mission money and personnel. A second important internal change involved the ecumenical movement. Northern Baptists were charter members of the Federal Council of Churches in 1908, the National Council of Churches in 1950, and the World Council of Churches in 1948. The growing ecumenical involvement affected home mission work, with efforts to cooperate with other denominations in common projects. Northern Baptists cooperated in the interdenominational Home Missions Council formed in 1909 and in 1925 sought to coordinate their own overlapping local and regional home mission agencies with the national board of an organization called the Associated Baptist Home Mission Agencies. In 1955 the Woman's American Baptist Home Mission Society, originally formed in 1871, merged with the national board.

The depression of the 1930s devastated the home mission work of Northern Baptists, as it did other groups. By the time it began its second century in 1932, the home society operated on a reduced budget, faced mounting debts, and was forced into a policy of retrenchment at a time when needs and opportunities were mushrooming. In 1925 the home mission budget was $1,100,000; by 1933 it had dropped by half and continued to decline until an upturn came in 1942.[50] During those difficult days, the society did not replace resigning or retiring missionaries, lowered salaries, sharply reduced the home office staff, curtailed services, and rode out the storm.

50. G. Pitt Beers, *Ministry to Turbulent America: A History of the American Baptist Home Mission Society Covering its Fifth Quarter Century, 1932-1957,* p. 25.

When the executive secretary, Charles A. Brooks, died in 1931 even he was not replaced. For almost four years the society operated without an executive secretary until the election of G. Pitt Beers in 1934. The 1933 annual report observed that "the Home Mission enterprise, as indeed the whole Christian Church, finds itself in a day of confusion."[51]

However, despite these conditions Northern Baptists carried on their work. At the turn of the century, the home society listed 1,180 missionaries, deployed from coast to coast and from Canada to Mexico. Of these only 44 worked in New England, 67 in the central states, and 231 in the South. The Western states had the largest concentration with 799 missionaries, with a few in Canada, Cuba, Mexico, and Puerto Rico.[52] Of that force, fewer than half worked among Anglo-Saxon Americans; the majority was divided among Indians, freedmen, and various language immigrants.[53]

Amid the Great Depression, a slimmed-down society launched a program of advance. The first step was enlistment of G. Pitt Beers, pastor of First Baptist Church of Patterson, New Jersey, to head the work in 1934. One of Beers's first moves was to enlist a full-time secretary of evangelism and to emphasize work in the cities.

World War II brought multiplied ministry needs which Northern Baptists sought to address. The society formed the General Commission on Chaplains to recruit and certify Baptist chaplains. Altogether, Northern Baptists provided 976 military chaplains during World War II, second only to the Methodists.[54] Northern Baptists also launched major ministries to servicemen and their families, often in cooperation with other denominations. The Department of Christian Ministry to Service Personnel administered the work, continuing well beyond the end of the war. Similar, though less extensive, ministries were provided during military actions in Korea, Vietnam, and elsewhere. Unlike some denominations, Northern Baptists helped protect the rights of conscientious objectors to war. Working closely with the historic "peace churches," they placed about 150 Baptists in the noncombatant camps and aided their reentry into society after the war.

In 1945 the NBC launched the World Mission Crusade to raise $14 million to strengthen their work. Some wanted to seek $50 million, but the convention, perhaps remembering the $100 million campaign a generation earlier, scaled the plans down. Led by C. Oscar Johnson, pastor of Third Baptist Church of Saint Louis, and Luther Wesley Smith, secretary of the Board of Education and Publication, the effort proved a great success. Northern Baptists pledged over $16 million and by 1947 had collected

51. Ibid., p. 28.
52. *Annual Report,* American Baptist Home Mission Society (ABHMS), 1900, pp. 67-68.
53. Ibid., p. 60.
54. Beers, p. 36.

$15,212,355.[55] Although the home board received only $1,206,884 of that amount, it allowed modest advances to be made.

Nothing challenged the home society more than the need for church planting in the new instant communities which sprang up in mobile America. A 1953 survey revealed that about 7,000 American communities, most with a population of 2,500 or more, had no place of worship of any kind.[56] In 1951 denominational leaders declared church extension a major priority, and two years later they launched a campaign, called "Churches for New Frontiers," to raise $8 million for new churches. Though the campaign fell short of the goal, the society was able to provide loans and grants for new building, especially in the West, and to supplement pastoral salaries until the new churches could become self-supporting.

No group in America tried harder to minister to non-English speaking immigrants than did Northern Baptists. In an important study entitled *Immigrants, Baptists, and the Protestant Mind in America,* Lawrence B. Davis traced Baptist attitudes and actions toward immigrants in the crucial years 1880 to 1924.[57] Baptists participated fully in the dialogue over whether immigration represented a mission or a menace to America. Shaken by the Haymarket Riot of 1886, which was widely blamed on immigrants, many Northern Baptists joined the harsh chorus which adopted the dregs-of-society theory of immigration and deplored making America the "dumping ground" of Europe. However, an articulate group of Baptist leaders refused to succumb to such jingoism. In a speech before the Baptist Congress in 1888, Walter Rauschenbusch set the tone for pro-immigration forces when he said:

> I am not in favor of any restriction on immigration. I do not believe it is right to restrict immigration. . . . I believe in throwing open this country to all who will come, for I believe God made it for all. Who are we that we should close this country against the rest of the world?[58]

World War I increased hostility toward Europeans, and many Baptists probably approved the 1924 National Origins Act which restricted immigration. Like most of their countrymen, Baptists showed a clear preference for those immigrants most likely to embrace Protestant religion and its related moral standards and cultural mores.

Whatever their attitudes, Northern Baptists acted to evangelize the new Americans. At the peak of this effort, Northern Baptists presented the gospel in at least twenty-five languages. By 1939 more than a thousand churches related to the NBC were an outgrowth of ministry to immi-

55. Ibid., p. 44.
56. Ibid., p. 53.
57. Lawrence B. Davis, *Immigrants, Baptists, and the Protestant Mind in America.*
58. *Seventh Annual Session,* The Baptist Congress, Richmond, 1888, pp. 86-87.

grants.[59] Language ministries included Swedes, Danes, Germans, Norwegians, and Russians from Europe, plus Japanese and Chinese from the Orient. Gradually a common pattern emerged among most of these groups. What began as foreign language churches became in one generation bilingual and by the next generation worshiped primarily in English, with only a few language services retained for older members. Most of the churches eventually merged into the American Baptist Convention, though retaining conference status with other ethnic churches mostly for old times' sake. Two groups which did not follow that pattern were the Swedes and Germans; they withdrew in the 1940s to form separate denominations.

Changes in the training of ministers for immigrant churches paralleled the changes in the churches themselves. At first ministers were trained in the various languages. The Germans established a study center in Rochester; the Swedes formed Bethel Seminary in Saint Paul; the Hungarians had a school in Scranton, Pennsylvania; Slavic training was provided in Chicago and Russian in New York. Older seminaries established language departments, like the French Department in Newton Theological Institution and the Italian Department at Colgate Seminary. In 1920 most of the individual efforts were combined in an International Baptist Seminary in East Orange, New Jersey. However, in time, most of the immigrant churches and their pastors used English, and the International Seminary was closed in 1941.

From 1832 the Home Mission Society staked out its field as "North America," but over the years it drew the boundaries at different places. In its more expansive days, the HMS sponsored work in Canada, Mexico, Cuba, Puerto Rico, El Salvador, Nicaragua, and Haiti. Missionaries for the Latin countries were generally trained in Los Angeles at the Spanish-American Baptist Seminary, established in 1921 as a western branch of the International Seminary. In time, the work in those areas diminished due to limited funds, changed conditions in the Latin countries, and perhaps also to a narrower understanding of "North America."

The original language group addressed by Northern Baptist home missions was, of course, the American Indians. That ministry has continued in the twentieth century on a smaller scale and with meager results. At the turn of the century, J. S. Murrow gave a dismal description of Baptist work among the Indians. Murrow served at different times under the auspices of both Northern and Southern Baptists and probably was, next to Isaac McCoy, the best-known Baptist missionary to the Indians. From his station in Atoka, Indian Territory (now Oklahoma), Murrow in 1900 reported a declining Indian population, chronic poverty, serious health problems, fragmented families, and acute spiritual needs. He wrote, "I regret to say that all mission work among the full-bloods, is also retrograding. There are

59. Beers, pp. 60-61.

fewer churches and members now than five years ago."[60] Of twenty-two Baptist associations in the Indian Territory, three were composed of Indian churches. Murrow concluded his report by writing, "They [the Indians] recognize in the Home Mission Society one of their best friends. . . . I trust the Society will continue its interest in the work among the full-blood Indians of these five tribes."

Murrow's report was discouraging in light of the major investment of the society in Indian missions. In Indian Territory alone, it spent $76,323 for evangelism and education, plus another $14,018 for church buildings, between 1890-1900.[61] The total investment from 1865, when the Indian work passed into the hands of the home society, stood at $610,016. In 1908 the society reported confidently that "every important point had been occupied" among the Indian populations. However, for several reasons, the work did not prosper. Those reasons include the historic Indian resistance to Christianity, reduced emphasis on Indian missions, and the confusion, and at times tensions, arising between Northern and Southern Baptist work on the same or adjacent Indian fields.

One recent trend has been to reevaluate the meaning and methods of evangelism, not only in the BNM but throughout the ABC. While far more complex than one brief statement can cover, much of the new trend shifted the focus from personal redemption to social ministries. Among American Baptists, that shift has often been associated with the name of Jitsuo Morikawa. A Japanese-American, Morikawa served several years as associate pastor, and later as pastor, of the First Baptist Church of Chicago where he compiled an outstanding record. In 1957 he was called from that pulpit to head the Division of Evangelism of the Home Mission Society. For twenty years, Walter E. Woodbury had held that post, having come as part of the rebuilding effort of the postdepression 1930s. For the most part, Woodbury had encouraged the churches to practice the more traditional forms of Baptist evangelism.

In electing the more innovative Morikawa, the home board apparently made an intentional change of direction. Its report pointed out that "the year 1956 may prove to be a turning point in the evangelistic history of the denomination when one notable era came to a close and a new era still uncertain began."[62] The report cited Woodbury's commitment to "personal involvement in witnessing and conducting crusades and campaigns," plus his emphasis upon "visitation evangelism." Having honored the past, the report said, "The new era into which we have entered seems to point a searching finger in the direction of a needed recovery of a profound theology

60. *Annual Report,* ABHMS, 1900, p. 99.
61. *Annual,* NBC, 1908, p. 45.
62. *Year Book,* ABC, 1957, p. 313.

of evangelism."[63] Morikawa headed the Division of Evangelism until the reorganization of 1972, when he became associate secretary for the BNM. The new structure did not provide for a division of evangelism as such; that work was included in the Personal and Public Witness Unit. For over fifteen years Morikawa occupied a sensitive post where he could affect the theology and practice of evangelism for Northern Baptists.

In 1969 Morikawa called a conference of twenty-five key American Baptist leaders "to explore new forms of evangelism."[64] For some years he had promoted ecumenical projects, sensitivity training, and a new understanding of personal conversion. He led not only his department but also, by his visibility and personal charisma, the entire denomination to reevaluate the older theology and methods of evangelism in light of new social conditions and new theology. The changes encouraged more ecumenical involvement with other denominations and a shift away from the older direct evangelism to newer forms of social action evangelism. Some American Baptists felt that the shift was demanded by the gospel and that it arose from the churches rather than from denominational leadership. Others saw it as a weakening of the historic Baptist witness and blamed it for declining growth rates.

Board of Educational Ministries (BEM)

For years Northern Baptists operated separate societies for Sunday School literature and for the promotion of higher education. Later those societies became boards of the Northern/American Baptist Convention. In time, the two boards' inherent similarity led to their merger into one board which was named the Board of Educational Ministries in 1972. This section will trace briefly the two major prongs of its work, publication and higher education.

An earlier chapter sketched the origin of the Baptist Tract Society in 1824, created to supply study helps for the emerging Sunday School movement among Baptists and to provide books and periodicals for a print-hungry society. No agency did more than the Publication Society to create denominational awareness and unity. One must agree with a report in 1900 that said, "This Society has been a bond of union for the denomination in America, stronger than popes, bishops or presbyters, and our unity in faith and practice is due more largely to its influence than to any other earthly power."[65]

Competition and diversity. However, nagging problems faced the society as it entered the twentieth century. First, it faced serious competition. Southern Baptists formed their own Sunday School Board in 1891, and by

63. Ibid.
64. Ibid., 1969-1970, p. 285.
65. *Annual Report,* ABPS, 1900, p. 16.

1900 SBC churches that had Sunday Schools used its literature. The National Baptist Convention established a publishing arm in 1895. Those two new ventures quickly won the support of churches in the South and deprived the ABPS of a significant part of its market.

A second problem facing the ABPS concerned theology. The publishing board was brought into the Fundamentalist controversy through accusations of liberal teachings in its various publications. The American Baptists appointed a number of committees over the years to study the complaints. At times ABPS reacted defensively, denying that such allegations were valid; at other times, it changed the materials or produced alternate series to try to appeal to different kinds of churches. Neither approach worked well because of diversity among the churches.

In 1934 a group of more conservative Baptists requested copies of a full year of publications of the Board of Education. The study concluded that the materials retained a "conservative and evangelical basis, yet there is mixed in with this material a considerable amount of troublesome and adventurous interpretations of Scripture which, far from clarifying the truth, rather lead to complex and inharmonious conclusions."[66] Whether such charges were valid is another question entirely. However, they were *perceived* so by many, and one Northern Baptist historian indicted the board for its failure to address the charges.[67]

When confidence in Northern Baptist literature further eroded, the board in 1938 brought in an outside professional study team, headed by Henry E. Cole, to assess its work. By that time 30 percent of Northern Baptist churches had dropped the denominational literature and another 50 percent used only parts of the curriculum.[68] One historian said of Cole's study:

> His report was devastating. It was declared that the greatest weakness in the Publication Society had been the failure to serve the people through the Sunday school literature. The investigator noted that the churches demanded a greater biblical and evangelistic witness than was being provided. . . . Needless to say, the Cole report was shocking.[69]

By 1945 the board published the Judson Keystone Graded Series for children, introduced in 1909, plus the International Uniform Lessons. In 1947 they introduced a new Judson graded series, which proved quite popular. In the 1960s American Baptists participated with fifteen other denominations to create the Cooperative Curriculum Project. Some of the groups took the basic curriculum, added some denominational emphases of their own, and published it under their own names. Others, including

---

66. Lawrence T. Slaght, *Multiplying the Witness: 150 Years of American Baptist Educational Ministries*, p. 120.
67. Ibid.
68. Ibid., p. 121.
69. Ibid.

American Baptists, experimented for a time by issuing an ecumenical curriculum jointly with other groups. By 1982 the BEM offered four curriculum series, plus elective adult discussion resources. These were Uniform Bible Series; Children's Bible Series; Bible and Life Graded Series; and Living the Word.[70]

The BEM also sponsors a major book publishing agency, under the name of Judson Press. The 1972 restructuring of the denomination also brought under the Board of Educational Ministries such diverse groups as American Baptist Men, American Baptist Women, the Division of Communications, and the American Baptist Historical Society. The latter was formed in 1853, perhaps at the suggestion of John Mason Peck who had lost his own extensive collection in a fire. Its impressive historical collection is now located at the Colgate Rochester Divinity School in Rochester, New York, a collection made famous in the twentieth century by the curator, Edward Starr. The society has since 1978 been ably headed by William H. Brackney. The conference center at Green Lake, Wisconsin, also falls within the scope of the BEM. The center was established in the 1940s by Luther Wesley Smith, creative leader of the Board of Education, who had been a frequent speaker at the Southern Baptists' Ridgecrest Baptist Conference Center in North Carolina.[71]

Collegiate education. Another major area of BEM work involves oversight of Baptist higher education. From the 1750s American Baptists have sponsored schools, but in the 1820s and 1830s, the Baptist college movement mushroomed. The old Triennial Convention undertook for a time to support a Baptist university. Most of the early Baptist schools were founded by local or regional education societies. The schools had, for the most part, no official relationship to each other or to the denomination, and thus no overall policy of planning or coordination was possible. Later when doctrinal diversity led some schools away from traditional Baptist positions, the denomination discovered that it had no effective control over them.

As early as 1867 Sewell S. Cutting of the University of Rochester had proposed an American Baptist Education Society on a par with the three major societies. Nothing came of that suggestion until 1888, when such a society was formed. However, it never caught on and had largely lapsed by the end of the century. Henry L. Morehouse, the great home missions leader, led in the formation of a Board of Education in 1912 as part of the Northern Baptist Convention. In time, the legal complications were worked out to allow, in essence, the merger of the Education Society of 1888 and the new Education Board of 1912. As the similarity of their work became more evident, the Publication Board and the Education Board were merged in 1944.

---

70. *Directory,* ABC, 1982, pp. 30-31.
71. Slaght, p. 137 *f.,* 145.

The Education Board of 1912 proceeded with vigor to provide what Northern Baptists had never had, namely central oversight, planning, and funding for efforts in higher education. In 1914 at Boston it launched what was described as "the greatest forward movement ever undertaken by the denomination," an effort to raise several million dollars to strengthen the schools. Divided more equally among the schools, the money might have made a greater impact, but about two-thirds of it went to the newly formed University of Chicago.

At the collegiate level, Baptist schools included such institutions as Brown University, Rhode Island (1764); Colby College, Maine (1813); Colgate University and the University of Rochester, New York (1820, moved to Rochester 1850); George Washington University, Washington, D.C. (the old Columbian College, 1821); Bucknell University, Pennsylvania (1846); Shurtleff College, Illinois (chartered 1835, closed 1957); Denison University, Ohio (1830); Kalamazoo College, Michigan (1833); and William Jewell College, Missouri (1849, at first jointly sponsored by Northern and Southern Baptists, but later related to Southern Baptists). These schools and others like them have individual stories worth telling if space allowed. Increasing costs, a diminishing of the older Baptist college vision, and above all the growth of state colleges and universities have reduced the role of Baptist colleges in the twentieth century.

Theological schools. Most of the early Baptist colleges included departments of theology, and a primary purpose, if one may believe their public appeals for support, was the training of ministers. The dream of combining a university and theological school is nowhere better illustrated than at Columbian College, nor was its failure anywhere more spectacular. The classical and theological studies, so logically related in theory, never made good campus comrades, at least in the early days. The theological department of Columbian was moved to Newton Centre, Massachusetts, in 1825 and named the Newton Theological Institute (later Andover Newton, from merger with a similar school from nearby Andover). It was the first separate theological seminary among American Baptists offering a standard three-year degree. It set a precedent for separating classical and theological studies which has been followed largely by Baptists both North and South. The University of Chicago, established in 1890, may be seen as an effort to reestablish the tie between classical and theological studies. Though the division of labor is far from complete, many observers view the university divinity school as more academic, while the theological seminary fulfills a role more professional.[72]

Northern Baptists also planted a number of newer theological schools in the twentieth century. Efforts at geographical balance, plus doctrinal dis-

72. See Claude Welsh, *Graduate Education in Religion* (Missoula: University of Montana Press, 1972).

satisfaction, fueled most of the new ventures, two of which grew rather directly out of problems with the University of Chicago. It soon became evident that for many reasons that university could not supply Baptist ministers for the growing Midwest. In 1901 a small group founded the Kansas City Seminary (now known as the Central Baptist Theological Seminary). For years the school was jointly sponsored by Northern and Southern Baptists before voting single alliance with the North in 1956. From the first, it provided training for students both with and without collegiate backgrounds.

Another school which grew out of the Chicago situation was the Northern Baptist Theological Seminary. In 1913 John Marvin Dean was called as pastor of the conservative Second Baptist Church of Chicago and the same year formed the seminary. The school first met in the church's Sunday School rooms, and early trustees were laymen from the church. Reacting to the emerging Fundamentalist movement, and specifically to its neighbor, the University of Chicago, the school adopted the New Hampshire Confession and set a conservative course from which it has not wavered. By the time of its thirtieth anniversary in 1943, Northern had become the largest seminary related to the NBC. Of 126 pastors in the Chicago area, 56 were Northern graduates.[73] That concentration of conservatives probably formed one of the obstacles which prevented the denomination from choosing Chicago as its headquarters in the early 1960s.

The Eastern Baptist Theological Seminary was founded at Philadelphia in 1925, primarily in response to the Fundamentalist crisis. Founded to provide pastors with conservative theological training, spiritual warmth, and evangelistic zeal, friends of the school believe it has achieved a good measure of success in all these areas. In his incisive account, Norman H. Maring attributed the founding of Eastern Seminary to the moderate conservatives.[74] The first chairman of trustees was Frank M. Goodchild, and the first president was Charles T. Ball, a Southern Baptist. Maring said, "Convinced that liberalism could not be checked in the older institutions and disturbed by the growth of Bible schools, a group of the Fundamentalists concluded that a new seminary should be established in the East."[75] Concern for the schools had been heightened by this statement by A. H. Strong in 1918: "The theological seminaries of almost all our denominations are becoming so infested with this grievous error [liberalism] that they are

73. John W. Bradbury, "Northern Seminary's Thirtieth Anniversary," *Watchman-Examiner,* November 25, 1943, p. 1.

74. Norman H. Maring, "Conservative but Progressive," *What God Hath Wrought: Eastern's First Thirty-Five Years,* Gilbert L. Guffin, ed. (Philadelphia: Judson Press, 1960), pp. 15 f.

75. Ibid., p. 35.

not so much organs of Christ as they are organs of Antichrist."[76] Curtis Lee Laws, a member of the first board of trustees, promised, "Those in charge of the new seminary purpose founding a school of the prophets in which loyalty to the Scriptures shall be conspicuous" and the "crown of deity" would not be removed from Christ.[77]

Without doubt the extensive study, *Theological Education in the Northern Baptist Convention,* issued in 1945, represents the most thorough evaluation of ministerial training ever undertaken by Baptists in this country. The Commission of a Survey of Theological Education, led by Hugh Hartshorne and Milton C. Froyd, was appointed in 1943 and made its final report in 1945. Basically the commission sought answers to four questions: (1) What is the job of the minister? (2) Who are the candidates for the ministry? (3) How are these candidates being trained? (4) How can this training be improved?

As to the first question, the commission traced the emerging role of the Baptist minister from the seventeenth to the twentieth century, showing changes that had occurred. One was a tendency to regard the ministry more as a profession than a calling, though 44 percent of pastors still cited a sense of divine call as their reason for becoming ministers.[78] The commission also discovered certain discrepancies relating to the concept of the minister's task as perceived by lay people, as perceived by seminarians, and as it actually worked out on the field. The study also found that ordination was no longer "restricted to the local church, with about two-thirds of the affiliated Northern Baptist state conventions having adopted at least minimum ordination standards."[79]

As to the candidates for ministry, the study provided a few surprises. The small churches in rural areas made up about two-thirds of NBC churches but provided far fewer ministerial candidates. The Baptist seminaries were then graduating approximately two hundred students a year, about half the number needed to staff the churches. Therefore, many Northern Baptist churches had to settle for untrained pastors or turn church leadership over to persons trained outside NBC ranks.

The report bluntly affirmed that current theological training was inadequate but blamed it as much on mediocre students as on an outmoded curriculum.[80] Noting that the denomination was seriously short of qualified pastors, the report added, "The ministry is not getting the share of competent young men it should have." The commission calculated that of current

76. Ibid., p. 21.

77. Ibid., p. 36.

78. Hugh Hartshorne and Milton C. Froyd, eds., *Theological Education in the Northern Baptist Convention,* p. 133.

79. Ibid., p. 97.

80. Ibid., pp. 162 *f.*

pastors, fully two-thirds fell below what was "commonly accepted as the standard for professional training."[81] It insisted that "the fact must be faced that the church, by and large, has not been able to attract its most competent young men to the ministry. . . . [thus] leaving the ministry with an increasingly mediocre quality of leadership."[82]

Having pinpointed the problems, the commission gave the least space, and some think its least creativity, to suggestions for improvement. Beyond the usual recommendations for better recruitment and revamped seminary curriculum, the major conclusion was that Northern Baptists should move toward uniform ordination standards based upon the familiar "seven-year course," namely, four years of college and three of seminary. Over the forty years since the release of that study, the denomination has tried to hold that standard, yet with limited success. For one thing, the denomination does not have enough churches of sufficient strength to provide positions for such graduates. Further, a number of ministers ignore the denomination's standards, attend non-Baptist (and sometimes nonaccredited) schools, are ordained, and called to ABC churches anyway. The denomination has little choice in recognizing such pastors. If not accepted, such pastors might lead the churches out of the denomination, a practice all too common.

Despite these problems, American Baptists continue their commitment to higher education and specifically to the concept of an educated ministry. The Hartshorne-Froyd study concluded on a hopeful note, foreseeing improved training opportunities at both seminary and continuing education levels.[83]

Twentieth-Century Trends

Other recent developments and trends among American Baptists must be noted. The most important of these fall in the areas of theology, ecumenism, local church life, relation to other Baptist groups, and a search for identify.

Trends in Theology

Northern Baptists produced a number of major theologians who have shaped doctrines in the denomination and beyond. Such people as William Newton Clarke, Augustus H. Strong, Walter Rauschenbusch, George B. Foster, Shailer Mathews, and Harry Emerson Fosdick must be named, though the list could be extended. Some made their mark from the classroom as teachers and authors, others from the pulpit and platform as preachers and popular speakers.

William Newton Clarke (1841-1912) published his *Outline of Christian Theology* in 1898, a book which expressed the evangelical liberalism which

81. Ibid., p. 162.
82. Ibid., p. 164.
83. Ibid., pp. 233 *f.*

had been in formative stage for a generation or more.[84] Described as a "systematic theologian of theological liberalism," Clarke accepted the concepts of evolution, biblical criticism, and the priority of Christian experience over rational dogmatism. Claude L. Howe concluded that Clarke's "theological system was basically a traditional orthodoxy, modified by new views of the Bible and the universe, reinterpreted in the light of Christian experience."[85]

Clarke grew up in a Baptist parsonage and served some years as a pastor before becoming a professor, first in Canada and later at Colgate. Clarke's first book "brought down on him the invectives of the orthodox" but was well-received by others. One described it as "an epoch-making book, for it was the first broad survey of Christian theology which frankly accepted the modern views of the world."[86] Clarke realized he was moving beyond traditional Baptist thought. He wrote, "I do not regard myself as a champion of denominational orthodoxy, but I do regard myself as a Baptist and as a humble champion of my Master's truth."[87] For Clarke, theology was not static but ever-changing as conditions in society changed. Perhaps most troublesome for the more conservative was Clarke's view that some Bible statements "express truth in forms that cannot be of permanent validity."[88] Some of Clarke's other books include *Can I Believe in God the Father?* (1899); *The Use of the Scriptures in Theology* (1906); *The Christian Doctrine of God* (1909); and *Sixty Years with the Bible* (1912). Clarke led many Baptists to accept a more developmental view of Scripture, a more optimistic view of mankind, a less traditional view of Christ, and a more hopeful view of the emerging physical sciences. He must be regarded as a major source for the moderate forms of theological liberalism which came to prevail among Northern Baptists. It was largely Clarke's views to which the Northern Baptist Fundamentalists responded in the 1920s.[89]

Augustus Hopkins Strong (1836-1921) served for years as president and professor at the Rochester Theological Seminary. Strong's major work, *Systematic Theology,* was first issued in 1886 but over the years underwent numerous revisions and was still being republished well into the twentieth century. More conservative than Clarke, Strong nevertheless sought to reformulate Christian theology in terms of modern thought. His *Systematic Theology* exercised a formative influence on Southern as well as Northern

84. For a study of Clarke's contributions, see Claude L. Howe, "William Newton Clarke: Systematic Theologian of Theological Liberalism," *Foundations* pp. 123-135.

85. Ibid., p. 123.

86. Ibid., p. 131.

87. Ibid., pp. 128-129.

88. William Newton Clarke, *Sixty Years with the Bible,* pp. 210-211, cited in Brackney, p. 266.

89. See "William Newton Clarke" in James E. Tull, *Shapers of Baptist Thought,* pp. 153 *f.*

Baptists. Strong held traditional Baptist views on most points, but his great contribution lay in giving new and powerful expression to those views in the context of modern thought. Perhaps Strong attracted most attention for his views of ethical monism.[90] He also felt a commitment to keeping the denominational seminaries orthodox, at times complaining, "We [the seminaries] are losing our faith in the Bible and our determination to stand for its teachings."[91] Strong felt equally committed to academic freedom. The work of Walter Rauschenbusch, who taught on the faculty at Rochester where Strong served as president, severely challenged Strong's dual commitment. After much agony of spirit, Strong refused to silence or restrict Rauschenbusch.

Walter Rauschenbusch (1861-1918), son of a German pastor who embraced Baptist views, radically reoriented theology in America from his post at Rochester Theological Seminary, where he served from 1897 until his death. Known as the "Father of the Social Gospel," a distinction which perhaps should be shared with Washington Gladden and Josiah Strong. Rauschenbusch, as a pastor in the "Hell's Kitchen" area of New York City, became aware of the social and economic problems of laboring people and their families. Distressed by the harsh treatment of laborers by industry, unsanitary health conditions, child labor, and other problems of the emerging industrial society, Rauschenbusch became convinced that the message of Jesus applies to society as well as to individuals. With others likeminded, he formed the Brotherhood of the Kingdom in 1892 to apply the gospel to modern needs. The Social Gospel addressed primarily the problems of Northern industrialism. It is no accident that the Social Gospel was articulated by persons from an immigrant background and that it addressed primarily those social problems of industrial America that bore heaviest upon immigrant laborers. Social problems of the South, such as race, sharecropping, and health care, were largely ignored by the Social Gospel.

In two powerful books, Rauschenbusch made his greatest impact. His *Christianity and the Social Crisis* (1907) and *A Theology for the Social Gospel* (1917) set out his distinctive views. The central message of Jesus, said Rauschenbusch, was the kingdom of God. Rauschenbusch understood this kingdom not just as a future eschatological state, but as potentially present in human society. He urged church and society to work together to bring society closer to kingdom ideals. Decrying what he termed "despotic churches and unbelievable creeds," Rauschenbusch accused the church of corrupting the original message and mission of Jesus.[92] Despite linking the Social Gospel to certain liberal doctrines, Rauschenbusch retained many conservative emphases. Some of his followers, however, tended to abandon

90. See Brackney, pp. 263-264.
91. Cited by Maring, p. 21.
92. Walter Rauschenbusch, *A Theology for the Social Gospel,* p. 43.

these conservative vestiges. The twentieth-century trend of Northern Baptists to emphasize social action owes much to the legacy of Rauschenbusch.

Other leaders who influenced Northern Baptists include Shailer Mathews of Chicago and Harry Emerson Fosdick of New York. Mathews (1863-1941) served for twenty-five years as professor in the Divinity School of the University of Chicago where he was said to have moved beyond liberalism to modernism. He saw modernism as a positive factor which could help people believe in God, whereas traditional creeds were no longer believable. His major book, *The Faith of a Modernist*[93] (1924) established Mathews as a major spokesman for the new theology and set him up as a target for its opponents. As a theologian, he sought to get behind religious dogma to religious experience which, like Friedrich Schleiermacher, he regarded as primary. Mathews defined modernism as "the use of the methods of modern science to find, state and use the permanent and central values of inherited orthodoxy in meeting the needs of a modern world."[94]

Mathews refused to place boundaries on religious truth, insisting that "Modernism has no Confession" and is therefore not bound by viewpoints of the past. However, Mathews's own affirmations included belief in God, Christ, the Holy Spirit, and the Bible, but in terms quite different from earlier Baptist teachings. Perhaps the use of old terms with new meanings gave rise to the oft-repeated quip: "What is modernism? What Shailer Mathews preaches in the North. What is fundamentalism? What Shailer Mathews preaches in the South."

Harry Emerson Fosdick (1878-1969) served for a time as professor at Union Theological Seminary but made his greatest impact as pastor of the impressive Riverside Church in New York. Though not primarily a theologian, Fosdick became a major target of Fundamentalism in the 1920s, partly because of his ability to popularize modernist thought. After a pastorate in Montclair, New Jersey, and some years as "stated preacher" at the prestigious Fifth Avenue Presbyterian Church in New York, Fosdick in 1925 succeeded Cornelius Woelfkin as pastor of the Park Avenue Baptist Church. Fosdick's close friendship with John D. Rockefeller, with whom he was in theological agreement, led Rockefeller to provide funds to move the Park Avenue church to Riverside Drive, change its name, and build the fabulous building that led some to call it "the cathedral church of American Protestantism."

Fosdick sought to express the Baptist faith in terms of new social and scientific views. His head-on challenge of 1922, "Shall the Fundamentalists Win?" proved one of the more thoughtful critiques of the new right wing. This sermon, according to one historian, "set off the hottest controversy

93. Shailer Mathews, *The Faith of a Modernist* (New York: Macmillan, 1924).
94. Cited in Edwin S. Gaustad, ed., *A Documentary History of Religion in America Since 1865*, p. 398.

that ever raged about any sermon in American history."[95] Fosdick's books include *The Manhood of the Master* (1913); *The Meaning of Prayer* (1915); and *On Being a Real Person* (1943). In later years his autobiography, *The Living of These Days* (1956), influenced many. This title comes from a line in Fosdick's famous hymn, "God of Grace and God of Glory." He also adopted parts of the Social Gospel, less strict views of Scripture, and a fervent form of pacifism, best expressed in his moving sermon on the unknown soldier.[96]

Best known for eloquent preaching, Fosdick published a number of inspiring sermon books. When his name became anathema, generations of preachers were forced to quote him under the camouflage, "As someone has said. . . ." Later in life, he modified some of his earlier optimistic, modernist thoughts. Chastened by World War I and the Great Depression, Fosdick issued a statement in 1935 entitled "Beyond Modernism."[97] He indicted modernism for its obsession with the purely intellectual aspects of the faith, its sentimentalism, its neglect of the doctrine of God, and its loss of ethical authority by too easy accommodation to its surrounding culture. However, he wanted to go beyond modernism, not abandon it. Fosdick said:

> We have largely won the battle we started out to win; we have adjusted the Christian faith to the best intelligence of our day and have won the strong minds and the best abilities of the churches to our side. Fundamentalism is still with us but mostly in the backwaters. The future of the churches, if we will have it so, is in the hands of modernism. Therefore, let all modernists lift a new battle cry: We must go beyond modernism![98]

Gradually these and other pacesetters among Northern Baptists tilted the denomination distinctly leftward in theology. Conservative voices remained but were hampered by several factors. The denominational boards and machinery remained largely in the hands of more liberal leaders. The schisms of 1933 and 1947 drained off most of the more conservative leadership; indeed, many individual pastors and churches had left the denomination before the major schisms occurred. Further, the eminence and eloquence of the modernists, plus their apparent atunement to the times, gave their viewpoints great appeal.

Trends in Ecumenism

Baptists in the North have maintained a stance of cordial cooperation with other denominations throughout the twentieth century. The roots of

95. Shelton H. Smith, Robert T. Handy, Lefferts A. Loetscher, eds., *American Christianity: An Historical Interpretation with Representative Documents,* 2:295.

96. See Brackney, pp. 372-376.

97. Cited in Robert L. Ferm, ed., *Issues in American Protestantism* (New York: Doubleday & Co., 1969), pp. 303-313.

98. Ibid., p. 313.

Baptist ecumenism in America, however, go back much further. In the early 1700s, Baptists, Congregationalists, and Presbyterians helped install one another's pastors and at times apparently regarded themselves as different expressions of one church. Baptists linked arms with other denominations in the early ecumenical era of 1800-1825 to form several interdenominational societies for home and foreign missions, the American Bible Society (1816), the Sunday and Adult School Union (1817), the American Sunday School Union (1824), and others.

Interdenominational emphasis has accelerated in the twentieth century. The Northern Baptist Convention was a charter member of the Federal Council of Churches in 1908 and in 1950 helped transform that body into the present National Council of Churches. Northern Baptists participated in the Edinburgh Conference of 1910 and enrolled as charter members of the World Council of Churches in 1948. The Northern Baptist Convention first joined and later withdrew from the Interchurch Movement, an important but premature ecumenical effort after World War I. In the 1960s, the ABC participated with eight other denominations in the Council on Churches Uniting (COCU), an attempt to merge several denominations into one major Protestant church, an effort not formally abandoned but gone dormant in recent years. In 1911, as noted earlier, the Freewill Baptists in New England merged with the Northern Baptists. Merger talks with Disciples of Christ through much of the twentieth century have as yet borne no fruit. However, this brief sketch demonstrates that American Baptists have long held and acted upon ecumenical convictions. As early as 1868, George R. Bliss gave an address before the American Baptist Historical Society on "The Place of Baptists in Protestant Christendom," in which he placed Baptists squarely in what he called the "vanward" center of Protestantism.[99]

No practice of American Baptists has engendered more criticism than their participation in ecumenism. The ecumenical ties of the New World Movement of the early 1920s must be reckoned a major barrier to the success of that movement. This dealt a serious blow to the denomination and helps explain later struggles within the Northern Baptist Convention. A number of churches have withdrawn from the ABC over the ecumenical movement, like the First Baptist Church of Wichita, Kansas, long a bellwether church among Northern Baptists. By 1982 the ABC *Directory* listed a total of 510 churches which had requested to be named under the heading: "Churches Which Have Recorded the Desire to be Listed as Not Approving Affiliation with or Providing Financial Support for the National Council of Churches of Christ Through the American Baptist Churches in the

99. Printed for the society, 1862, in ABHS.

USA."[100] Since this listing originated in the mid-1970s, under protest by denominational leaders, the number of churches requesting to be included has grown steadily.

In 1966 the ABC created an Office of Ecumenical Relations, headed for several years by Robert G. Torbet, more recently by Pearl McNeil, and since 1981 by Martha Barr. The Rochester convention of 1960 strongly reaffirmed American Baptist commitment to ecumenism, and a Committee on Christian Unity, appointed in 1967, was authorized by the general board to "enter into conversation with other Christian bodies in the interest of Christian unity." American Baptist leaders are aware of opposition to ecumenism among parts of their constituency, primarily in the West and Midwest, but have held firmly to their own deep convictions and practices. Some have become a bit disillusioned, however, in that the ecumenical movement has so far produced so little concrete results.

Relation to Other Baptists

In what might be called "family ecumenism," American Baptists cooperate with a number of other Baptist bodies, especially in the Baptist World Alliance and its regional affiliate, the North American Baptist Fellowship. They also shared in the Baptist Jubilee Advance, 1959-1964, and help sponsor the Baptist Joint Committee on Public Affairs (BJCPA) in Washington. In 1950 they invited any interested Baptist group to form a cooperative relationship under the name of American Baptist Convention. Some Baptist groups in essence maintain dual alignment, in their own group, plus affiliation with the ABC. Presently the National Progressive Baptist Convention and the Church of the Brethren, plus a number of bilingual ethnic groups, hold this relationship.[101]

The relationships between the American Baptists and two groups which pulled out, the General Association of Regular Baptist Churches (GARBC, 1933) and the Conservative Baptists of America (CBA, 1947), have remained cool. To some extent, these groups have driven each other to extremes, as each tries to be as unlike the other as possible. Some observers feel that distaste for the doctrinal emphases and styles of churchmanship represented by these two groups has become a major barrier to those within the ABC who would like to reaffirm more traditional Baptist doctrines and practices but do not wish to be associated with the schismatic groups.

Like the Southern Baptist Convention, the ABC has founded and funded any number of cooperative endeavors with the three National Baptist conventions. Historically, many of these efforts have been in the realm of education; the ABC to this day maintains ties with some predominantly black colleges in the South. A number of individual black churches have

100. Listed on pp. 189-191.
101. *Directory,* ABC, 1983, pp. 69-70.

aligned with the ABC and, as noted, the Progressive Convention is an "Associated Organization" with the ABC. Robert C. Campbell, general secretary for ABC churches, reported in early 1984 that blacks make up over one-third of the ABC constituency.[102]

The relationship of Northern and Southern Baptists since 1900 has alternated between rocky and smooth, sometimes bitter and sometimes better. However, despite their noisy separation in 1845, a considerable amount of cooperation has continued between these two branches of the Baptist family. One lesser-known avenue of mutual exchange of views was the Baptist Congress which met annually from 1882 until it lapsed after formation of the Baptist World Alliance. Southern Baptists regularly attended and spoke at its sessions. Some Southerners, pointing out that the congress had no "war history," openly hoped that the congress might prove an avenue of reconciliation. The Southern Baptist Theological Seminary has drawn students and financial support from the North as well as the South; its old New York Hall was so named for its major contributors. Although a proposal in 1920 for an "All American Baptist Council," to include Northern, Southern, and Canadian Baptists came to naught,[103] the two groups did jointly issue the *New Baptist Hymnal* in 1925.

The geographical expansion of Southern Baptists, a story told in the next chapter, put great strain upon Baptist relationships in this century. The expansion began early in the century, creating tensions in Missouri, Illinois, New Mexico, Oklahoma, and Arizona before World War I and spreading throughout the nation by mid-century. Expansion first arose out of the migration of Southern people, not from any denominational sponsorship, but when the "exile" churches appealed for aid the SBC responded readily enough and eventually such churches were received into SBC affiliation. Northern Baptists felt this "invasion" violated earlier comity agreements. Some Southerners maximized the tensions by locating their churches near the Northern churches, stressing the word *Southern* in their church name, and sometimes even canvassing the membership rolls of Northern Baptist churches seeking to draw out members who had come from the South. The Northern Convention protested, but these were for the most part the actions of zealous individuals over whom the SBC had no control. When the SBC itself became involved in promoting the expansion, primarily through its Home Mission Board, guidelines were established to correct these abuses.

By the 1970s a better relationship prevailed between the two branches of Baptists. Southern expansion into the North had been balanced, on a lesser

102. "Campbell: Identity of ABC is Evangelical, Ecumenical, Interracial, and International," *Capital Baptist*, February 16, 1984, pp. 1, 8.

103. *The Baptist*, July 3, 1920, pp. 803-804.

scale, by Northern churches in the South.[104] Southern Baptists in the North also developed more sensitivity to existing Baptist work in that area. Further, Baptists from both groups came to realize that the awesome challenge of evangelizing the nation was a greater task than either or both could accomplish. Both learned to say with the apostle Paul that, despite some contention, "Christ is preached; and I therein do rejoice" (Phil. 1:18).

Of course, no one can predict what the future relationship may be between Northern and Southern Baptists. In its 1845 Address to the Public, the newly formed SBC said, "Northern and Southern Baptists are still brethren. They differ in no article of the faith."[105] That hopeful statement is probably less true now than then. Not only have significant doctrinal differences developed but also diverse patterns of organization, different priorities of ministry, different methods and understandings of evangelism, and what, for want of a better term, might be called alternate styles of churchmanship have both accentuated and perpetuated the separateness of the two bodies. However, in 1983 the First Baptist Church of Boston, one of the oldest in the nation, voted a resolution asking the ABC to enter at once into conversations with the Southern Baptist Convention looking toward eventual reunion, hopefully by the end of the century. At the Cleveland biennial meeting, this resolution barely failed passage but gathered enough support to show considerable interest in the topic.

During the merger conversations with the Disciples in the 1930s and the 1950s, one recurring reason given for opposition by some Northern Baptists was that such a move might further alienate them from their Southern Baptist brethren. Curtis Lee Laws noted in 1929:

> Southern and Northern Baptists are nearer each other than this sister denomination [Disciples]. They are one denomination. It may be a question of either one or the other. As we draw near the Disciples we may estrange ourselves from our Southern Baptists. Will there be a gain?[106]

Frederick L. Anderson, who could hardly be considered one of the more conservative Baptists, took a similar view. Having noted that Baptists and Disciples divided about 1830 over serious doctrinal differences and that those differences continued to exist, Anderson opposed reunion also. His reason was that it "would in large measure estrange our Southern brethren, and would engender division in our own ranks."[107]

These various examples show that, while tensions and troubles have pushed them apart, Northern and Southern Baptists have never completely lost the sense of unity they once shared. The nineteenth century was a time

---

104. See "ABC Goes South," *The American Baptist* (May 1971), p. 6.

105. *Annual,* SBC, 1845, pp. 17-20.

106. Curtis Lee Laws, "As to Union with the Disciples," *Watchman-Examiner,* p. 955.

107. Frederick L. Anderson, "A Minority Report of the Committee on Relations with Other Religious Bodies," *Watchman-Examiner,* p. 472.

of conflict and division. The twentieth century has seen both groups trying to carve out a distinct territory and, failing that, learning to coexist on the same fields. What the twenty-first century may hold for these two branches of the Baptist family is yet unknown.

Church Life

Like all Baptist groups, churches affiliated with the ABC follow diverse styles of worship. Some follow a formal liturgical order, with weekly worship largely guided by the Christian calendar, with robed ministers presiding in formal sanctuaries with divided chancels. Other churches prefer more informality, with lively congregational singing and worship centered in a biblical sermon delivered from a central pulpit. The Lord's Supper is observed monthly or quarterly in most churches and is generally open to all; the old Baptist debates about open versus closed communion have long since given way to other concerns.

Baptism continues to spark dialogue and even occasional controversy, particularly on whether immersion is essential for membership. The question is far from new. One of the earliest Baptist churches in England adopted immersion in 1641 but did not require it of all members. The records reveal that this question came up frequently in speeches and discussions at the Baptist congresses in the 1880s and 1890s, with leading voices taking each side. By the 1920s Harry Emerson Fosdick had decided to build, with Rockefeller money, a great Baptist church in New York in which baptism by immersion would be available for those who desire it but not required for membership. This became even more pointed in 1925 when the Seattle convention voted, despite the wealth and influence of the Fosdick-Rockefeller group, to maintain immersion as a requirement for church membership. Citing the New Testament as a guide, the convention affirmed that "this law of Christ permits believers only as members of his churches, and that it recognizes nothing as baptism save the immersion of a believer in water upon profession of faith."[108] However, after lengthy debate, the Fosdick representatives were seated because they had only announced the new policy and had not yet put it into effect. Fosdick pointed out that making immersion optional had historical precedent as far back as John Bunyan and that many leading Baptist churches in England followed that practice. The practice would, he felt, allow Baptist churches to appeal to a broader constituency and place emphasis upon spiritual rather than ceremonial aspects of the Baptist faith.

In 1926 the convention voted an even stronger resolution:

The Northern Baptist Convention recognizes its constituency as consisting

108. Cited by Curtis Lee Laws, "The Seattle Convention," *Watchman-Examiner*, July 16, 1925, p. 909.

solely of those Baptist churches in which the immersion of believers is recognized and practiced as the only Scriptural baptism; and the Convention hereby declares that only immersed members will be recognized as delegates to the Convention.[109]

Several times since 1926 Northern Baptists have gone on record as favoring immersion, most recently in 1970 when the ABC voted to reaffirm its commitment to the baptism of believers by immersion, described as "the historic and continuing practice" of Baptist churches. The statement concluded by saying that the ABC "urges all of its churches to strengthen their witness to this principle in their faith."[110] However, the "urging" of 1970 fell short of the "requirement" of 1926, and delegates to the biennial sessions are no longer scrutinized as to their form of baptism. Frequent references to the subject suggest that many of the ABC churches now quietly follow the Fosdick practice. In some cases, recent styles of Baptist church architecture have removed the baptistry from the sanctuary; and immersions, when performed, are not witnessed by the congregation.

The Charismatic Movement

Like most mainline denominations, the American Baptists have a small group of churches and individual members who have adopted charismatic styles of belief and behavior. While existing since the mid-1960s, this group was apparently first organized in 1968 as a fellowship within the ABC. They had so grown by the time of the 1971 convention in Minneapolis that 175 persons attended their prayer breakfast, and their afternoon seminar was so crowded it had to be repeated the next day. Led in the 1970s primarily by Kenneth L. Pagard of California, the American Baptist Charismatic Fellowship (ABCF) sponsored meetings, seminars, and exhibit displays at convention meetings.[111] Since the late 1970s, this movement has declined among American Baptists, as it has in most other mainline groups. Perhaps most American Baptists would have agreed with Culbert Rutenber's low-key assessment of the group and his half-humorous appeal for tolerance. Surely, Rutenber said, a few charismatics could be tolerated in a denomination "which, in the name of unity-in-diversity puts up with the widest spectrum of bigots and broadminded, fundamentalists and liberals, orthodox and heretics, saints and barely-saved-if-at-all (not to mention a good sprinkling of plain kooks and crackpots.)"[112]

109. *Annual,* NBC, 1926, pp. 80-81.
110. *Year Book,* ABC, 1969-1970, p. 82.
111. See *The American Baptist* (April 1971), p. 7.
112. *The American Baptist* (October 1971), p. 7.

Patterns of Growth

Membership in churches affiliated with the ABC increased from 1,412,879 in 1928 to 1,607,268 in 1982.[113] For most of the twentieth century, membership has ranged around a million and a half, sometimes under, more recently a bit over. However, the number of affiliated churches has declined, as have Sunday School enrollments and the number of baptisms. The number of affiliated churches dropped from 8,292 in 1928 to 5,703 at the end of 1982, and baptisms for the same years dropped from 66,410 to 27,815.[114] Decline has been most pronounced in Sunday School enrollment, a traditional source of church converts, from 1,139,613 in 1928 to 417,134 at the end of 1982.[115]

These facts call for some sort of interpretation. Secularism has proceeded most rapidly in Northern urban America. The Fundamentalist crisis of the 1920s and subsequent schisms in the 1930s and 1940s drained off hundreds of churches and thousands of members who might otherwise have been a part of Northern Baptist growth. Southern Baptist presence in the North has, no doubt, attracted some who might otherwise have joined ABC churches. Further, the twentieth century has brought basic changes in the population base of states where the ABC has worked. Since the 1880s immigration has brought millions of "new Americans" with no previous background or interest in Baptist forms of faith. This has meant an uphill struggle for American Baptists as they seek to bear their witness in an environment seldom friendly, and sometimes hostile, to evangelical Christianity.

In the ebullient 1950s, which some consider yet another "great awakening" in American religion, American Baptists did not share fully in the rapid growth that marked many other groups. Denominational officials pointed this out in 1957:

> Each day since 1950, American Baptists have been losing 1.2 members per hour.
>
> On each successive Sunday, during the past six years, there have been almost 201 fewer people in our membership. American Baptists have been losing 10,473 members per year. . . .
>
> If the trend of the past six years continues, within a decade over 100,000 members and 500 churches will be lost.[116]

Robert C. Campbell, general secretary of ABC churches, suggested in early 1984 that American Baptists are caught up in a search for identity.

---

113. *Annual,* NBC, 1928, p. 27; *Directory,* ABC, 1983, p. 100.
114. Ibid., pp. 27, 100.
115. Ibid.
116. Cited in Anthony Campolo, "A Denomination Looks at Itself," *The American Baptist,* June 1971, p. 21.

"Most American Baptists think our primary identity is pluralism. That's a lousy identity," Campbell observed. A better identity, he said, would be to view the ABC as evangelical, ecumenical, interracial, and international.[117]

The current American Baptist structure bears little resemblance to the earlier shape of the denomination. Some suggest that American Baptist theology and mission have changed at least as much as the denominational form. The earlier image of American Baptists as solidly upper middle class may also be changing. In a perceptive article entitled, "A Denomination Looks at Itself,"[118] Anthony Campolo cited a growing gap between the image and reality of American Baptist social status. Campolo, chairman of the Department of Anthropology and Sociology at Eastern Baptist College, analyzed a survey of the denomination conducted by Roper Research Associates in 1968. That survey confirmed that ABC members tended to be upper middle class. But the churches were not effectively appealing to others of that class because they were *perceived* as being lower on the social scale. Thus upwardly mobile people tended to gravitate to other churches. At the same time, ethnic Americans and inhabitants of the inner cities perceived American Baptists as higher on the social scale and, therefore, showed limited interest in ABC programs. While acknowledging that other factors affected ABC growth, Campolo portrayed American Baptists as a denomination caught between the categories of society, lacking a clear-cut constituency. He said that the result is that, while 35 percent of those who join ABC churches come from other denominations, even more leave for other denominations.

Summary

American Baptists are no strangers to problems and challenges. They continue to show spiritual vitality and vigorous ministry amid changing times. The evidence suggests they will continue to be a vital force in the Baptist family, and in American and world Christianity, in the twenty-first century.

117. See "Campbell: Identity of ABC."
118. Anthony Compolo, *A Denomination Looks at Itself* (Valley Forge: Judson Press, 1971), p. 25 *f.* The article cited above is distilled from this book.

15

Southern Baptists

For Southern Baptists the twentieth century has been a time of remarkable growth, of geographical expansion throughout the nation, and of rapid development of institutions and programs for ministry in this and other countries of the world. Evangelistic zeal and missionary fervor have marked Southern Baptists. For a large group, they have enjoyed a substantial degree of inner spiritual and theological cohesion, a cohesion threatened in recent years by the growth of doctrinal dissent.

The Southern Baptist Convention formed in 1845 would be hardly recognizable today; its organizations and methods of work have changed radically. Over the years the SBC has, sometimes by trial and error, worked out more effective ways of raising and disbursing funds, enlisting people in support of its work, and instilling a sense of denominational identity and loyalty in its people.

The Emerging Denomination

The 103 messengers at the 1849 meeting of the SBC in Charleston would have been shocked at the 45,519 registered at Dallas in 1985, to say nothing of thousands of visitors. Not until the twentieth century did SBC attendance exceed 1,000; the attendance of 1900, for example, was 646. The custom of meeting in local churches largely prevailed well into the present century. Few cities can now accommodate the SBC meeting, making it increasingly difficult for the convention to follow its custom of meeting in different sections of the country. More denominational awareness by local churches and pastors, controversial issues at the meetings, ease of travel, and the tendency for pastors' families to combine convention attendance with a family vacation have been among factors contributing to this mushrooming attendance.

These changing patterns reflect, and perhaps also helped to cause, corresponding changes in the way the convention is organized and pursues its work. The SBC entered the twentieth century with three general boards, no standing committees, and no continuing commissions. The president simply presided at the annual sessions; between sessions the office hardly existed. The convention had no "headquarters" and no continuing officers to occupy it if they had. The Executive Committee did not exist before 1917 and

609

had little to do before its enlargement in 1927. As the convention crowds grew, deliberative sessions became almost impossible and the convention evolved a system of committees and trustees to conduct the actual work of the agencies. After the turn of the century, convention agencies multiplied. At this writing they include no less than twenty-five separate organizations, including four general boards, seven commissions, and several standing committees, plus the auxiliary Women's Missionary Union. Immediate control is vested in its boards of trustees and professional leaders employed by the trustees. Ultimate control rests firmly with the convention, except for the auxiliary, through election of trustees, allocation of funding, and approval of policy.

Search for Efficiency

Southern Baptists greeted the new century with optimism. The worst of Reconstruction was past, economic recovery allowed the churches and denomination to expand their ministries, and pressing needs elsewhere had reduced the competition of Northern Baptist work in the South. A Baptist editorial observed in 1901, "There is a new South among Baptists."[1] The decline of Landmarkism, and especially the withdrawal of the most intense Landmark faction in 1905, gave the SBC almost two decades of relative peace before the next major controversy exploded, a time Southern Baptists used to strengthen their work in missions, evangelism, and Christian education. Perhaps J. B. Gambrell best captured the new-century spirit of Southern Baptists when he called them a great people who had come to a great time.

The new-century spirit included a search for more efficient ways of conducting Southern Baptist work. In 1898 the SBC reacted favorably to a suggestion from Georgia to form a Centennial Committee for proper observance of the new century. What began as a celebration of past achievements quickly turned toward the future, laying plans "to better organize and equip [Baptists] for the mighty work which lies before them in the century to come."[2] The Centennial Committee contained the first germ of what later became the Executive Committee.

The Centennial Committee made an elaborate report in 1900, the substance of which probably exceeded the committee's assignment. Dreading lest their work "dwindle into a mere celebration" (which is what their original assignment called for), the committee suggested a continuing Committee on Co-operation to devise more efficient ways for Southern Baptists to raise and disburse funds for benevolent causes. In a blunt assessment, the Centennial Committee said:

1. *Baptist Argus,* May 30, 1901, cited in W. W. Barnes, *The Southern Baptist Convention 1845-1953* p. 167.
2. *Annual,* SBC, 1898, p. lxvi.

Fifty-five years ago the Convention came into existence, and adopted a constitution declaring . . . that the purpose of the Convention's existence was "to carry into effect the benevolent intentions of its constituents by . . . eliciting, combining, and directing the energies of the whole denomination in one sacred effort for the propagation of the gospel." More than a half a century has been spent, and the plan adopted has not yet enlisted one-half of our churches, nor one-tenth of our members. Is it not time to re-examine a plan which, after such a trial of its merits, has come so far short of accomplishing its avowed purpose? Is not this turn of the century a good time for earnest enquiry into our whole plan of work?[3]

The committee, chaired by J. B. Gambrell, was continued to 1901 when it presented a briefer but even more radical report. It recommended that the SBC establish a Committee on Co-operation, composed of fifteen members, with authority to employ a full-time secretary to help correlate the work of the SBC and its various boards.[4] Funding would be provided jointly by the SBC, the Sunday School Board, and the Baptists of Maryland (on condition that the committee be headquartered in Baltimore). That was more than a move to correlate the work of the SBC; the committee said, "We earnestly invite every State Association or Convention, and every State Board, to co-operate with us in a vigorous, specific movement" toward greater cooperation involving every level of Baptist life. From that time, *cooperation* assumed a large place in the Southern Baptist vocabulary. However, the convention was not yet ready to take that step. The messengers thanked the Baltimore brethren for their generous offer but rejected the proposals.[5] No similar proposal surfaced for over a decade.

However, a feeling persisted that Southern Baptists needed to streamline their work. Increased attendance made careful deliberation more difficult; by 1909 a perceptive editorial pointed out, "It must be frankly admitted, however, that the real work of the Convention is no longer done by the Convention itself. . . . We are coming rapidly to the place, if we have not already reached it, when we must rely wholly upon the Boards and standing committees to do our thinking for us." The editorial continued, "It is not best for us, . . . that our great representative body should degenerate into a mere celebration, a place for set and formal reports and addresses, a sort of spectacular gathering, full of holy enthusiasm, it may be, but lacking utterly the deliberative element."[6]

In 1913 John E. White of Georgia called for a study to discover the means "for securing the highest efficiency of our forces." Noting that the complexity of SBC tasks had grown far beyond the simple machinery erected

3. Ibid., 1900, p. 22.
4. Ibid., 1901, pp. 33-34.
5. Ibid., p. 35.
6. *Religious Herald,* May 20, 1909, p. 10.

in 1845, White suggested that a commission make "a thorough examination of the organization, plans and methods of this body."[7] This action revealed the growing influence of laymen in SBC work, with insistent calls for "more business in religion." J. B. Gambrell, himself an advocate of improved methods, countered with a call for "more religion in business." The Commission on Efficiency, which grew out of White's resolution, reported in 1914. It resisted heavy pressure to merge the two mission boards into one, recommending instead that the general boards retain their separate identities and locations. However, the report recommended "that the Convention herewith expressly instructs the general Boards, including the Seminary, to maintain affectionate relations with each other, keeping in view the unity of their common cause and the necessity of their cooperation with each other and the avoidance of any appearance of competition between them."[8]

The report also called for closer cooperation between state boards and the SBC and suggested the SBC adopt an annual budget, launch a campaign for proportionate giving, and devise means for proportionate distribution of income among association, state, and national bodies. In a most important but somewhat unrelated report, the committee spelled out the rudiments of a confession of faith and recommended that the SBC concentrate on strengthening its denominational programs rather than becoming deeply involved in ecumenical efforts.[9]

Consolidation was in the air in the early twentieth century, and Baptists breathed that air. The state conventions led the way; the Baptist General Convention of Texas, for example, consolidated all of its work under one executive board in 1914, and within a few years most states had made similar moves. One observer noted "the increasing tendency of the state boards to take over the work of the Convention Boards."[10] Clearly the SBC was losing out in a competition between doing Baptist work from a national basis versus a states' rights approach. Suggestions to revamp Baptist work took several forms. Some wanted to reunite all Baptists in America; others proposed that the SBC be divided into regional conventions, with a triennial meeting of all; others favored consolidation, with existing boards becoming, in effect, departments of one executive board.

The Executive Committee

Until 1916 there had been much talk but little action about restructuring the work of the convention. The Centennial Committee (1898), the Commission on Co-operation (1900), and the Commission on Efficiency (1914) had recognized the problems, considered and discarded a number of

7. *Annual,* SBC, 1913, p. 70.
8. Ibid., 1914, p. 71.
9. Ibid., pp. 73 *f.*
10. *Religious Herald,* May 11, 1916, p. 10.

proposed solutions, and laid the groundwork for future changes. Talk of reorganization led to action, however, when the SBC created its present Executive Committee in 1917. That grew out of a resolution by M. H. Wolfe, a Dallas layman, who in 1916 moved, "That Articles V to X of the Constitution of this Convention be amended and revised so as to create one strong Executive Board which shall direct all of the work and enterprises fostered and promoted by this Convention."[11] The committee appointed to study that proposal was asked to report in 1917, with a plan to bring "our denominational machinery . . . to the highest possible degree of efficiency."[12] In its report in 1917, the committee, though chaired by Wolfe, recommended that the convention boards remain separate but that a standing Executive Committee be formed to oversee all SBC ministries. The report, which was adopted, said:

> There is a strong sentiment in favor of greater unity in the general direction
> of the Convention's affairs . . . we recommend that an executive committee
> of seven, representing the different parts of the territory of the Convention,
> be elected annually by the Convention . . . that this committee shall act for
> the Convention ad interim on such matters . . . not otherwise provided for
> in its plans of work.[13]

This represented an important turning point for the SBC. Before 1917 the SBC had no structure for correlating its work; in effect, the three boards were practically autonomous. The SBC heard many reports but determined little policy. In fact, one might argue that legally the SBC existed only during the few days it was in session; during the rest of the year, with no continuing organization, it went out of existence, or at least went dormant. The Executive Committee changed all that. It gave the SBC an existence and a voice between sessions; it gave the hitherto independent boards a group to whom they must not only report their actions but justify them, and it gave messengers an agency to help channel funds for convention ministries. Of course, the Executive Committee of 1917 was to the present Executive Committee as the acorn is to the tree, but a new direction was set.

The first Executive Committee had no employed staff. The committee was enlarged in 1927 and its functions expanded. The Seventy-Five Million Campaign, 1919-1924, brought added funds into SBC coffers and such expanded budgets required more management. In 1919 the membership was expanded to include the SBC president and secretary, one member from each general board (named by the board), and one member from each state (elected by the SBC), with the SBC president as chairman. Had this trend

11. *Annual,* SBC, 1916, p. 18.
12. Ibid., p. 57.
13. Ibid., 1917, p. 34.

continued, the power of the SBC president might have developed differently than it has. While the president still holds ex officio membership, he no longer chairs the Executive Committee. In 1926 the powers of the committee were expanded, giving it authority "for fixing total objectives, for allocating funds to its various agencies and recommending same to the Southern Baptist Convention for adoption."[14] The Executive Committee employed a full-time secretary in 1927; Austin Crouch was the first to hold this post, serving from 1927 to 1946. Others have been Duke K. McCall (1946-1951), Porter W. Routh (1951-1979), and Harold C. Bennett (since 1979).

The convention created the Inter-Agency Council (IAC) in 1948, since expanded, to allow representatives of the various boards and agencies to coordinate their work. Unlike the Executive Committee, the IAC has little power but provides a forum for communication, mutual planning, and calendar correlation.

Convention Representation

Who can be a voting messenger at the meetings of the Southern Baptist Convention? The answer to that question has changed over the years, especially in the twentieth century. The opening sentence of the 1845 constitution spoke of "the delegates from Missionary Societies, Churches, and other religious bodies of the Baptist Denomination," and Article III said the "Convention shall consist of members who contribute funds, or are delegated by religious bodies contributing funds."[15] Over the years the "other religious bodies" which sent delegates included not only missionary societies but also associations and state conventions. Membership was set on a financial basis; the more contributions, the more delegates. In fact, the system could allow one individual to represent more than one group, or to represent large contributions, and thus cast more than one vote. Early Southern Baptists had no hesitation in using the word *delegate* to designate voting members of the convention. Preference for the term *messenger* came as a reaction to Landmarkism and was intended to make the point that the member of the SBC votes his own convictions and does not come with "delegated" authority from the church, nor does he carry back to the church any official or authoritative instructions from the convention. Landmarkers, of course, preferred *delegates* since they felt the churches were directly represented in the convention. However, since each Baptist body is independent in its own sphere, the term *messenger* was thought to convey

14. Cited in Porter Routh, "Executive Committee of the Southern Baptist Convention," *Encyclopedia of Southern Baptists* (Nashville: Broadman Press, 1958), 1:429-433 (hereafter cited as *ESB*).

15. *Proceedings,* SBC, 1845, p. 3.

best the element of communication and cooperation without overtones of authority.

Rober A. Baker spoke of a "chronic tampering with the basis of representation" in the SBC, which clearly reflected problems with the existing system but also inability to devise one satisfactory to all.[16] Most agreed in their criticisms of a purely financial basis, but such alternatives as association, state, numerical, and church representation presented their own problems. In 1885 the word *members* in Article III was changed to *brethren* to prevent women from serving as voting members, but the financial basis of representation remained. In 1918 the convention changed *brethren* to *messengers,* thus allowing women to vote. From time to time, the *amount* of money necessary to obtain a vote changed, but the most basic alteration of the financial basis came after World War I.

In 1924 the SBC appointed a Committee on Basis of Representation, basically to deal with problems involved in the increased attendance at convention sessions. In its 1926 report, under the chairmanship of E. Y. Mullins, the committee noted problems of crowded attendance, reports too numerous and lengthy to digest, difficulty of deliberation, the tendency to limit discussion to a few appointed speakers, and the imbalance created by disproportionate attendance of persons near the convention site. Some proposed solutions included limiting convention membership to a few hundred, with one thousand as a maximum; dividing SBC territory into three areas, each to hold an inspirational meeting annually, with the convention itself limited to about three hundred members meeting triennially; increasing the Executive Committee to about three hundred members meeting annually to hear reports from the boards and agencies, with the convention meeting every three years; and extending the SBC meeting to include a full week.[17] However, the committee rejected all of these, reporting instead, "We reaffirm our conviction that the financial basis of representation is sound and scriptural. . . . We recommend that no essential change be made at the present time in the basis of representation."[18]

However, the question would not be dropped. Another committee in 1931 recommended a twofold pattern of representation: (1) a representative from each association, and (2) messengers selected on the basis of money contributed, either (a) an individual Baptist who contributed $500, (b) messengers elected by churches which had contributed $500, or (c) messengers from state conventions which had not already filled their quota in the

16. Robert A. Baker, "The Southern Baptist Convention, 1845-1970," *Review and Expositor,* p. 138.

17. *Annual,* SBC, 1926, pp. 31-33.

18. Ibid., p. 33.

first two categories.[19] That plan was voted down. The convention adopted instead a substitute motion by E. C. Routh of Oklahoma:

> The Convention shall consist of messengers who are members of missionary Baptist churches co-operating with the Southern Baptist Convention on the basis of one messenger for every church contributing to the work of the Convention and one additional messenger for every $250 actually paid to the work of the Convention during the calendar year . . . provided no church shall be entitled to more than three messengers.[20]

With minor changes, the SBC since 1931 has followed this modified church-financial basis of representation. No one can be a messenger except as elected by a local church; associations, state conventions, and missionary societies cannot send messengers. However, later changes allow a church to send one additional messenger for each additional 250 members, as well as for each additional $250 contribution, up to a maximum of ten from any one church.

The majority of SBC messengers are pastors and other church ministers and their spouses; the records show a decreasing proportion of laypeople attending. As travel costs escalate, many of the smaller churches, especially those with bivocational pastors, have not been represented at all. The "chronic tampering" which Baker described may continue; the present mammoth convention meetings are clearly not representative since a typical SBC meeting has messengers from no more than 20 percent of the churches.

While suggestions to limit messengers to no more than 1,000 found no favor, over the years the SBC has erected a committee substructure which involves about that many persons doing the actual work of the agencies. Each board, commission, institution, or other agency of the SBC is entitled by constitution by-law to have a certain number of trustees, elected by the convention, from each cooperating state. Detailed planning and careful deliberation mark the work of these trustees and then their reports must survive the scrutiny of the convention in session. Thus Southern Baptists have evolved a way to have the needed deliberation yet maintain the ultimate authority of the convention itself.

Recent proposals have surfaced to alter the SBC constitution to call for meetings only every two years. Motives for such a change include financial economy and an effort to quiet the constant controversy which seems to surround convention meetings.

Financing Southern Baptist Ministries

Through the nineteenth century, Baptist churches in the South followed the most informal system of fund raising, if system it may be called. Many

19. Ibid., 1931, p. 44.
20. Ibid.

pastors received no stated salary, though the churches usually took up a subscription for them in cash or goods. Worship services rarely included an offering; indeed, many Baptists felt that fund raising should remain separate from worship to protect the spirituality of the church. The records speak of a Kentucky church which "agreed to raise twenty-five dollars for the use of the Church and that Brethren Wm Samuel, Blanton & Settle be appointed to proportion the same among the White mals [male] Members and report nex [next] meeting."[21] A church budget would have been not only unknown among most Southern Baptists in the 1800s but also vigorously opposed. Some churches, reflecting their rural heritage, raised only two offerings a year, called the spring and fall roundups.

Informal methods of local church finance were reflected also at the denominational level. The boards of state conventions, as well as the SBC, employed "agents" to preach among the churches, raising money for their particular cause. Judging from its frequent defense, this method must have been much criticized. It was inefficient, with costs of raising the funds sometimes amounting to almost half the amount raised. The agents also created problems for the churches, often one or more of them showing up unannounced and expecting pulpit time to make an appeal for his cause, a pattern disruptive and often demoralizing to pastor and people alike. The method also led to imbalance. The boards which got to the churches first with the best speakers raised the most money; those caught by bad weather or bad roads, or who followed hard on the heels of others, raised less money, however worthy their cause. By raising its own funds, each board was practically independent and the convention itself more an observer than a determiner of Baptist ministries.

Quite early Baptist leaders saw the need for better fund-raising methods for Southern Baptist ministries. An 1884 report to the SBC on "Plans for Systematic Giving" noted that fewer than half of Southern Baptist churches contributed anything to missions and that total missionary giving amounted to only about thirty-five cents per year for each Southern Baptist.[22] Most Southern Baptists were farmers, with crop income bunched at certain seasons. Few were regular wage earners and, therefore, the practice of weekly offerings was slow to catch on.

In stewardship, as in several other areas, Baptist women led the way. Long before most men adopted these views, Baptist women taught tithing, regular weekly offerings no matter how small the amount, and most importantly the inclusion of the offering as a part of the worship of God.[23] By their Christmas mission offering, later to bear the name of Lottie Moon, Southern Baptist women also pioneered in special offerings for missions.

21. W. W. Sweet, ed., *Religion on the American Frontier: The Baptists 1783-1830* p. 350.
22. *Annual,* SBC, 1884, p. 20.
23. See Leon McBeth, *Women in Baptist Life* pp. 104 *f.*

Despite this progress, it was not until after World War I that Southern Baptists generally adopted more systematic methods of financial stewardship.

The Seventy-Five Million Campaign

After the turn of the century, prosperity and optimism prompted Southern Baptists to project larger programs. World War I focused their attention on world needs as never before. The sale of Liberty Bonds during the war showed that vast sums could be raised for a worthy cause. Many of the denominations pushed major fund drives, including the "Men and Millions Movement" (Disciples, 1913, $6 million); the "Methodist Centenary Fund" (1916, $115 million); the "New Era Movement" (Presbyterian, 1918, $13 million); "The Progress Campaign" (Reformed Church, 1918); and the "New World Movement" (Northern Baptist Convention, 1919, $100 million).

In 1919 Southern Baptists launched their "Seventy-Five Million Campaign," an effort to raise $75 million for Baptist causes over a five-year period, 1919-1924. By far the most ambitious fund-raising effort of Southern Baptists to that time, it began as an effort to strengthen Baptist education but mushroomed into a campaign to aid all Baptist causes.

In 1919 at Atlanta, the Committee on Financial Aspects of Our Denominational Program reported as follows:

> In view of the needs of the world at this hour, . . . we suggest, (1) that in the organized work of this Convention we undertake to raise not less than $75,000,000 in five years.
>
> (2) We recommend that the Executive Committee of the Convention in conference with the Secretaries of the General Boards and the State Boards be requested to distribute the amounts among the different objects fostered by the Convention . . ., and apportion the amount to the various states.[24]

Goals for raising the funds, and their distribution, were agreed upon.

To implement such an ambitious program, the convention appointed a Campaign Commission of fifteen, chaired by George W. Truett of Dallas. They elected L. R. Scarborough as southwide director, for which he received a leave of absence from his post as president of Southwestern Baptist Theological Seminary in Fort Worth. The campaign structure was completed with directors for each state, association, and local church. Baptist pastors and editors supported the campaign enthusiastically. The Campaign Commission launched the most intense campaign of publicity and promotion Southern Baptists had ever known, with the campaign calendar set as follows: July, preparation; August, information; September, intercession; October, enlistment; November, stewardship; and November 30 to Decem-

24. *Annual,* SBC, 1919, p. 74.

	Goals		Projected Distributions
Alabama	$ 4,000,000	Christian Education	$20,000,000
Arkansas	3,200,000	Foreign Missions	20,000,000
Dist. of Col.	400,000	Home Missions	12,000,000
Florida	1,000,000	State Missions	11,000,000
Georgia	7,500,000	Ministerial Relief	5,000,000
Illinois	1,200,000	Orphanages	4,700,000
Kentucky	6,500,000	Hospitals	2,125,000
Louisiana	3,325,000	National Memorial	175,000
Maryland	750,000	Total	$75,000,000
Mississippi	3,500,000		
Missouri	2,925,000		
New Mexico	250,000		
North Carolina	5,500,000		
Oklahoma	2,500,000		
South Carolina	5,550,000		
Tennessee	4,000,000		
Texas	16,000,000		
Virginia	7,500,000		
Total	$75,000,000		

ber 7, victory week. During those months, pastors preached on the campaign and the causes it would strengthen; thousands of Baptist laymen were enlisted as "four-minute speakers" (a method adapted from the Liberty Bond drives); and Baptist papers blitzed their readers with information, appeals, and reports. By the end of victory week, pledges exceeded the goal and by the cut-off date totaled $92,630,923. Southern Baptists were ecstatic. They proclaimed their 1920 meeting as "Victory Convention," and Scarborough confidently reported that this response represented the greatest victory since Pentecost.[25] On the strength of those pledges, most SBC agencies expanded their work at once, on borrowed money.

However, the seventy-five million dollars proved easier to pledge than to collect. An economic recession hit the South in 1920, with agricultural prices, driven up in World War I, dropping sharply. Crop prices dropped by about 50 percent, and total farm income in the South plummeted from almost ten billion dollars in 1919 to less than four billion dollars in 1921.[26] By 1922, not over half of Southern Baptists had participated in the campaign, about a half million new members added since 1919 had not been enlisted, and Baptists who moved often considered their pledges can-

25. Ibid., 1920, p.50.
26. Cited in Donnie Gerald Melton, "The Seventy-Five Million Campaign and Its Effects upon the Southern Baptist Convention," p. 188.

celed.[27] Individuals signed pledge cards, indicating how much they would give each year for five years. In case of financial reverses, the pledges could be adjusted, a provision which seemed unclear to some. The collections were also hampered, perhaps, by an erroneous impression that part of the funds would go to the Interchurch Fund, an ecumenical effort which found no favor among most Baptists in the South. The bottom line showed that at the end of the campaign, Baptists had collected only $58,591,713.69 of the amount pledged.

That this percentage was far better than most other denominational funds had achieved provided scant comfort to SBC agencies plunged into debt. Carping criticism arose, which had remained muted during the glory days of the campaign. The financially troubled SBC received another jolt in 1928 at the revelation that Clinton S. Carnes, treasurer of the Home Mission Board, had embezzled $909,461 from that agency. That cost more than money; it dealt a severe blow to the image of the convention and the confidence of its people. The stock market crash of 1929 signaled an industrial depression, which augmented the agricultural depression Southerners had faced since 1920; the despair of the nation, and of Baptists, was complete. The two mission boards cut their work to the bone in massive retrenchment; other SBC institutions, especially the seminaries, faced imminent foreclosure; and the SBC and its entire assets could probably have been thrown into bankruptcy proceedings had the creditors desired.

However, the convention fought back. Frank Tripp led in forming the Hundred Thousand Club in 1933, composed of Baptists who pledged to give one dollar a month over and above their regular contributions to pay off convention debts. Loans were renegotiated at lower interest rates, but Southern Baptists declined offers, common at the time, to settle their debts for less than face value. George W. Truett, by the vast respect in which he was held and on his own signature, renegotiated some loans, but he promised that, given time, Southern Baptists would repay their debts in full. The convention adopted a goal of paying off their debts by 1943; "debt free by '43" became a popular slogan. They barely missed the deadline, as the last of the debilitating indebtedness was paid off in 1944.

Assessing the far-reaching impact of the Seventy-Five Million Campaign, Donnie G. Melton concluded, "Some effects were bad, others were good, but no one could deny that after the Seventy-Five Million Campaign the Southern Baptist Convention would never be the same again."[28] The bad effects were real enough. The campaign provided tempting targets for Fundamentalist attack, especially by J. Frank Norris. Pressure to pay pledges,

27. *Annual,* SBC, 1922, p. 30. This refers to individuals. Other reports showed that 16 percent of SBC churches were not participating in the campaign as of 1922. See Melton, p. 191.

28. Melton, p. 222.

or embarrassment at inability to pay, fueled a fear of pledging that plagues some Baptist stewardship efforts to this day. Some thought the intense promotion turned the convention too much toward Madison-Avenue techniques, and disputes between state conventions and the SBC about distribution of funds created some tensions. The resulting overexpansion severely crippled Southern Baptist work for over a decade.

However, the benefits of the campaign proved overwhelming. Despite the shortfall in receipts, Southern Baptists gave over three times as much to their various causes from 1919 to 1924 as in the preceding five-year span. Their per capita contributions rose from $5.08 in the five years before the campaign, to $9.37 during the campaign, and to $10.52 in the next five-year period.[29] Even from a financial standpoint, the campaign cannot be put down as a failure.

The overall benefits, however, far exceeded any financial gain. During the campaign, Baptist churches experienced a major spiritual renewal. They baptized more converts than ever before and enlisted thousands of young men and women as volunteers for Christian service, over four thousand on one Sunday in a southwide emphasis that Scarborough described as "calling out the called." As a result, Baptist schools were crowded with new students, and after graduation these new pastors and other church ministers led a period of unprecedented Baptist growth. The campaign also brought a new spirit of unity, convincing Baptists they could accomplish big things. Baptists became more stewardship conscious, and many churches adopted the budget system to regulate local church finances. Campaign leaders waxed eloquent, saying in 1921:

> Besides all this which we can tabulate, He has wonderfully unified, solidified, organized, informed and inspired our people. The tides of spiritual and evangelistic and missionary power which have swept over our churches, bringing hundreds of thousands into the fold, the mighty vision which He has given to our people, . . . the deepening of the prayer life of our churches, the calling out of more than 10,000 of our young people in the spirit of voluntary service to give their lives to Him, the development of a great denominational consciousness, . . . The question is whether or not we will be big enough for our day.[30]

The Cooperative Program

In 1920 the SBC appointed a Conservation Committee to preserve the results of the campaign. Clearly Southern Baptists did not regard the Seventy-Five Million Campaign as a one-time shot. Out of it came a permanent convention financial plan startling in its simplicity, yet revolutionary in its impact. Launched in 1925 and called the Cooperative Program (CP), the

29. Barnes, p. 224.
30. *Annual,* SBC, 1921, p. 33.

plan called for churches to send their offerings for denominational ministries to their state conventions. The states, in turn, would retain a portion of the funds for work within the state, forwarding the rest to the SBC office in Nashville. There the Executive Committee, made up of representatives from each state, would recommend percentage allotments for the work of each agency, the final decision to be ratified by the convention.

Cooperative is the right word to describe this stewardship program, and it shows the near canonization of both the word and the concept among Southern Baptists. The *Encyclopedia of Southern Baptists,* the first volumes issued in 1958, has no fewer than eleven articles on various aspects of Baptist cooperation. To be "noncooperative" is a serious thing to Southern Baptists, and to be "independent" has become a severe criticism. The leaders insisted the Cooperative Program was both scriptural and fair. It depended upon a high degree of trust and mutual confidence and a willingness to forego most designated gifts and special offerings in favor of casting most Baptist funds into a common pot for convention distribution. Often described as "the life-line of Southern Baptist ministries," the Cooperative Program has been a major factor in the growth of missions, evangelism, and Christian education among Southern Baptists. The SBC began, according to its constitution, as a plan for "eliciting, combining, and directing the energies of the denomination for the propagation of the gospel"; no method has even remotely approached the effectiveness of the Cooperative Program in achieving that objective.

Benefits of the program include economy, balance, and perspective. Unlike the old agent system, the Cooperative Program requires only a fraction of its funds for administration. Further, in the old days the more emotional causes always raised more money, but the Cooperative Program allows ministries that may work behind the scenes or in less glamorous, but equally important, areas to receive funding. The churches gain perspective by participating not just in some but in all the denomination's ministries, and pastors need not fear their services will be constantly interrupted by traveling agents who want to commandeer their pulpits. The agencies receive funds regularly. They can better plan for the future and require less borrowed money.

Any assessment of the Cooperative Program must include its drawbacks. However noisome the traveling agents, they did share information and emphasize the importance of various ministries. Their hearers were informed. Modern Baptists, whose contributions are funneled through the Cooperative Program, may hear fewer sermons on the causes it supports; indeed, some speak of giving *to* rather than *through* that program, as if it were an end in itself. Further, the program has raised some tensions between states and the SBC. In the late 1920s, some states sought to withhold CP funds from Nashville, but later decisions established that they had no right to use that kind of pressure. Some Baptists chafe when the program funds ministries that they, for some reason, oppose. The goal has been a fifty/fifty division between state and SBC work. For the past several years, the actual division has been nearer 65 percent to state causes and 35 percent to SBC causes, though a few states have reached the fifty/fifty goal.

Geographical Expansion of Southern Baptists

With formation of a church in Vermont in 1964, Southern Baptists had churches in all fifty states, from Florida to Alaska, from Charleston on one coast to Seattle on the other. Despite its regional name, the SBC has become a national denomination. A convention once limited to fourteen states of the old South has spread its work throughout the nation in a modern diaspora. With growth of Southern Baptist churches in Canada in recent years, the SBC may become international, a possibility with enormous implications.

We must distinguish between numerical growth and geographical expansion. During the twentieth century, Southern Baptists have experienced both. At the turn of the century, records showed a total of 1,586,709 members in 18,873 churches.[31] These churches were grouped into 16 state conventions, all but 2 in the South. By 1983 reports showed 14,208,226 members in about 36,500 churches, gathered into 37 state conventions, many of them outside the South. However, almost three-fourths of Southern Baptists still lived in the states of the old Confederacy.[32] At the turn of the century, the name *Southern Baptist Convention* reflected accurate geography. Today it can be defended, if at all, only as a doctrinal or programmatic description.

Two factors have been constant in the SBC's geographical expansion. Other factors may be present, but these have never been absent. Robert A. Baker observed:

> The development of tension . . . has generally followed a common pattern. One basic factor has never been lacking: there have always been Baptist immigrants from the South as the cause of tension. . . . The second constant factor has been a dissatisfaction by the southern emigrants with the Northern Convention churches already in the area.[33]

Thus migration, not mission policy, led to the early Southern Baptist churches outside the South. The depression of the 1920s, the dust bowl of the 1930s, and military movements of the 1940s scattered people throughout the country. High wages lured millions of Southerners out of Dixie to work in the vegetable fields of Arizona, the citrus orchards and vineyards

31. Ibid., 1899, p. cxvii.
32. See Kenneth E. Hays, "A Statistical Report on Southern Baptists," *Quarterly Review,* pp. 36 f; see also Jim Lowry, "1983 Statistical Projections," *Baptist Standard,* December 21, 1983, p. 4.
33. Robert A. Baker, *Relations Between Northern and Southern Baptists,* p. 218.

of California, the packing plants of Chicago, and the defense industries of Detroit.

Of course Baptist churches already existed in most of these places, but the migrants found them different. Most differences proved more sociological than theological, which made them, if anything, more a barrier. Northern Baptist churches tended to have beautiful buildings, robed choirs who sang stately anthems, a robed minister who preached from a divided chancel, no Sunday night services, open communion, and an emotional reserve in worship. Somewhat like exiles of an earlier day, Baptists from the South hung their harps away and lamented that they could not sing the Lord's song in a strange land. Unlike the migrations since the 1960s, that of the 1920s and 1930s saw mostly impoverished Southerners moving Northward. Possibly many of them were lost to church life altogether. Whether Northern Baptist churches could have ministered effectively to those lonely exiles might be debated; that most made little effort to do so is beyond doubt.

As a result, little clumps of Southern Baptists in the North met separately for worship, formed home fellowships and then churches, and elected one of their own number or a preacher from the South as pastor. As such churches multiplied, they linked into associations and eventually into state conventions. They soon learned to appeal to the SBC, especially its Sunday School and Home Mission boards for aid, and generally received it. While the SBC did not originally launch the geographical expansion, it undergirded such churches in every way possible. Southern churches in the North were sometimes called "Dixie Clubs," a term perhaps too harsh, but which does point out their early tendency to reach mostly other transplanted Southerners.

Early Expansion

The earliest example of geographical expansion of Southern Baptists in the twentieth century occurred in Illinois. Baptists in northern and southern sections of that state were never firmly bonded. Patterns of migration peopled one section with Northerners, the other with Southerners, a fact demonstrated by divided loyalties during the Civil War. Chicago and Carbondale from the first represented different forms of Baptist life. By 1907 the leaders acknowledged, "Illinois has been the meeting ground of two branches of the Baptist family."[34]

In 1906 William P. Throgmorton, editor of *The Illinois Baptist* and a convinced Landmarker, called for a separation of Baptists basically over events at the University of Chicago. By 1907, 226 churches had answered that call. They formed a separate state convention in 1907 and affiliated with the SBC in 1910. Not everyone was happy with the move. Throgmorton, who might be called "the J. R. Graves of Illinois," wanted to throw

---

34. Lamire H. Moore, *Southern Baptists in Illinois*, p. 70.

in with Ben Bogard and the new BMA movement but could not convince enough churches to go with him. Not all Southern Baptists welcomed the newcomers. An editorial in the *Religious Herald* of Virginia huffed, "We have got as many people . . . of the particular type which constitute the majority of this new Illinois Association as we can take care of."[35] Northern Baptists protested vigorously the new activity of the SBC in a Northern state. However, the switch was made, and the pattern would be repeated elsewhere.

Though late in arriving, Baptists were among the first evangelicals in New Mexico. In 1849 Hiram W. Read settled in Santa Fe, appointed by the Northern Baptist HMS. Within a few years, a string of Northern Baptist churches sprang up along the railroads. Meantime, Southern Baptists eyed New Mexico. In 1894 the SBC voted, "The time has come when this Convention should enter New Mexico as a mission field," but the action was rescinded out of deference to the Fortress Monroe committee.[36] However, while the convention debated, the people acted; multitudes poured across the Llano Estacado into New Mexico. The Lincoln Association was often called the "Texas Association" for its preponderance of Southern Baptists from Texas. Long before any convention voted, migration determined the complexion of Baptist witness in New Mexico.

By 1910 the New Mexico state convention split, with Southerners withdrawing to form a rival convention and appealing to SBC boards for aid. Both groups realized that the competition could not continue. Both conventions disbanded and, in 1912 at Clovis, formed one state body, which sought SBC affiliation. Northern Baptists withdrew all work from the state.

Baptist presence in Arizona Territory dates from 1863 when the HMS sent missionaries to that area. By 1894 there were seven Baptist churches in the territory; by 1904, only fourteen.[37] In 1909 the SBC approved a report which said, "The time will soon come when Arizona and Southern California will be recognized as belonging to the Southern Baptist Convention."[38] In 1917 a schism in the First Baptist Church of Phoenix saw seventy-two members withdraw, mostly Southerners, to form the Calvary Baptist Church. The schismatics, disgruntled over such familiar issues as open communion, alien immersion, and ecumenical cooperation, called C. M. Rock of North Carolina as pastor. In 1921 the Calvary church split, with Rock taking out a group to form the First Southern Baptist Church of Phoenix. The next year the church aligned with the Southwest Association in New Mexico. Soon other Southern Baptist churches sprang up at

35. Cited in *The Illinois Baptist,* March 26, 1910.
36. *Annual,* SBC, 1894, pp. 22, 26.
37. See Leon McBeth, "Expansion of the Southern Baptist Convention to 1951," *Baptist History and Heritage,* p. 37.
38. *Annual,* SBC, 1909, p. 33.

Chandler, Glendale, Willcox, Prescott, Globe, Buckeye, and elsewhere. In 1928 they formed the tiny Baptist General Convention of Arizona and sought SBC affiliation.

Northern Baptists warned, "If the Southern Convention receives this Arizona organization, all fraternal agreements of record between the Southern and Northern Conventions relative to Arizona will be violated." They accused Southern Baptists of furthering an ambition "to extend the work of that Convention to the Pacific Coast," a charge that proved exactly on target.[39] However, the Arizona convention was received and became an aggressive exporter of Southern Baptist views. Southern Baptists issued a "Bulletin" to explain, "Why a New Baptist Convention in Arizona." This piece insisted, "Those accepting the teachings of the New Testament quietly withdrew from the old State Convention in Arizona and organized a State body in which the doctrines of Christ could be taught and safe guarded."[40] Nowhere was the doctrinal issue more bluntly stated.

One area (Arizona) and one man (Willis J. Ray) became the center of one of the most remarkable chapters in SBC expansion. Ray became secretary of the new Arizona convention in 1944 and quickly got the nickname of "Southern Baptist Apostle to the West." The work grew rapidly; at one time the Arizona convention stretched from Mexico to Canada, affiliating churches in at least ten states.

The Comity Agreements

Northern Baptists bitterly opposed Southern encroachments in areas where they already had work. They used precisely the same arguments Southerners had used after 1865 in protesting Northern Baptist work in the South. In defending their expansion, Southern Baptists alleged exactly the same reasons Northerners had used to justify their work in the South. But now the shoe was on the other foot; Baptists in their territorial disputes had come full circle.

In an effort to mediate disputes, Northern and Southern Baptists held a number of comity conferences, the first at Fortress Monroe in 1894. Additional meetings were held in Washington, D.C., (1909) and Old Point Comfort, Virginia, (1911) to work out problems in New Mexico. Perhaps the most important of these comity conferences was at Hot Springs, Arkansas, in 1912. Representatives of the two conventions agreed that there should be only one state convention in each state and that states located in the South and with a majority of Southern inhabitants probably should affiliate with the SBC. They also adopted a statement of basic principles which reaffirmed the advisory nature of all denominational bodies and

39. Cited by H. K. Neely, "The Territorial Expansion of the Southern Baptist Convention 1894-1959," p. 66.
40. Ibid.

protected the autonomy of the local church to choose its own affiliation. Baptist work in Oklahoma was settled on the basis of that agreement. The two state conventions there, Northern and Southern, had merged in 1907, with dual affiliation both North and South. In 1914 the Oklahoma convention dropped the Northern ties and retained single affiliation with the SBC.

The Hot Springs agreement was generally expected to prevent further Southern aggressiveness in Northern territories, but it never worked out that way. Neither convention could control the actions of individuals, and neither could affect migration patterns. The de jure end of comity came in 1944 and 1949 when the SBC voted to remove all territorial limits, but the de facto end dates from the 1942 California decision.

The Turning Point

California proved to be pivotal in the geographical expansion of Southern Baptists. The California decision of 1942 proved a turning point; it effectively ended the comity era and removed all restraints on expansion anywhere. Southern Baptists had entered California with the gold rush of 1849, and in 1855 the HMB appointed J. Lewis Shuck to work among the Chinese there. In 1859 Southern Baptists sponsored a school on Strawberry Point off San Francisco Bay, a century before the Golden Gate Baptist Theological Seminary moved to that beautiful site. However, this early work was curtailed by the Civil War, and Southern Baptists did not reappear in California for over seventy years.

The depression and dust bowl uprooted millions, especially from the tri-state region of Oklahoma, Texas, and Arkansas. In an Anglo version of the "Trail of Tears," best described by John Steinbeck in *The Grapes of Wrath,* the "Oakies" and "Arkies" moved along the asphalt ribbons westward, Model A's and pickups loaded with mattresses and children. One such group settled at Shafter, near Bakersfield, in 1936. They formed the Orthodox Missionary Baptist Church of Shafter in 1936, and by 1939 four such churches formed the San Joaquin Valley Missionary Baptist Association. In 1940, fourteen churches formed a state convention and in 1941 appealed for SBC affiliation. The SBC appointed a committee to study the question. In its 1942 report at San Antonio, the committee made no recommendation but clearly leaned toward refusing the California messengers. However, J. B. Rounds of Oklahoma brought a minority report urging immediate acceptance, and his motion was overwhelmingly approved. Northern Baptists protested vigorously, but to no avail.

Perhaps partly in response to the California decision and the surge of SBC expansion it unleashed, the Northern Convention changed its name in 1950 to the American Baptist Convention and invited other Baptist groups to affiliate under this inclusive umbrella. Perhaps the Southern Convention would have taken that name; a committee appointed to study a name change had agreed to recommend it.[41] Southerners regarded the 1950 name change as an aggressive act but seemed less aware that their own convention meeting sites of Chicago (1950) and San Francisco (1951) could be viewed as aggressive also. In 1951 the SBC voted a tart resolution:

> Whereas the Southern Baptist Convention has defined its territorial position in reports to the Convention in 1944 and 1949 by removing territorial limitations, and whereas the Northern Baptist Convention has changed its name so that it is continental in scope, the Home Mission Board and all other Southern Baptist boards and agencies be free to serve as a source of blessing to any community or any people anywhere in the United States.[42]

Southern Baptists had entered the twentieth century with firmly defined territorial boundaries. They came to mid-century with all limits lifted, all fences down. The familiar term "our Baptist Southland" would become as anachronistic as BYPU.

Later Expansion

Since mid-twentieth century, Southern Baptists have planted churches in every state. These form many stories, yet they boil down basically to one story. Southern Baptists moved to the North, formed churches, linked those churches into fellowships or associations, requested and received aid not only from SBC boards but also from associations and local churches in the South. As the churches multiplied, they formed state conventions, which often included several states. In time, those large regions further subdivided to carve several state conventions out of the larger territory. That basic pattern was repeated from the Pacific Northwest to New England.

The nature of Southern migration, including Baptists, also changed after World War II. In the 1930s, mostly disinherited laborers were on the move; by the 1960s, upwardly mobile corporation executives and white-collar workers made up a sizable part of the Southern Baptist work in the North.

The most thorough state-by-state account of Southern Baptist expansion in the North can be found in Robert A. Baker's *The Southern Baptist Convention and Its People 1607-1982.*[43] Chart 1 shows Southern Baptist churches and membership in all the states as of 1982.[44]

The earliest SBC church in New England was the Screven Memorial Baptist Church, formed in New Hampshire in 1960. That same year there were enough such churches to form the Northeastern Baptist Association. In New York Southern Baptist witness dates from the mid-1950s. The LaSalle Baptist Church was formed in Niagara Falls in 1955, and soon

41. James L. Sullivan, *Baptist Polity as I See It,* p. 104.
42. *Annual,* SBC, 1951, p. 36.
43. Robert A. Baker, *The Southern Baptist Convention and Its People 1607-1982,* pp. 355-389.
44. Hayes, p. 40.

Chart 1
SOUTHERN BAPTISTS IN EVERY STATE—1982

State	Number of Churches	Number of Members*	Percent of Total SBC Membership
Alabama	3,026	998,771	7.1
Alaska	43	16,288	.1
Arizona	236	103,819	.7
Arkansas	1,266	452,872	3.2
California	1,001	357,051	2.6
Colorado	172	61,700	.4
Connecticut	20	4,819	—
Delaware	9	3,784	—
Dist of Col	24	16,467	.1
Florida	1,587	837,453	6.0
Georgia	2,981	1,160,874	8.3
Hawaii	38	11,369	.1
Idaho	45	9,369	.1
Illinois	910	231,605	1.7
Indiana	282	81,186	.6
Iowa	61	10,123	.1
Kansas	196	65,859	.5
Kentucky	2,206	749,319	5.4
Louisiana	1,325	552,893	3.9
Maine	4	862	—
Maryland	274	107,689	.8
Massachusetts	21	3,588	—
Michigan	195	48,433	.3
Minnesota	23	2,989	—
Mississippi	1,938	631,862	4.5
Missouri	1,823	600,371	4.3
Montana	59	7,745	.1
Nebraska	32	8,654	.1
Nevada	51	15,912	.1
New Hampshire	5	1,231	—
New Jersey	47	9,715	.1
New Mexico	263	111,853	.8
New York	115	15,258	.1
North Carolina	3,474	1,134,805	8.1
North Dakota	17	2,975	—
Ohio	479	135,466	1.0
Oklahoma	1,447	700,509	5.0
Oregon	92	23,911	.2
Pennsylvania	90	15,875	.1
Rhode Island	5	1,058	—
South Carolina	1,710	676,766	4.8
South Dakota	37	4,153	—
Tennessee	2,775	1,038,789	7.4
Texas	3,986	2,275,068	16.3
Utah	46	9,938	.1
Vermont	8	695	—
Virginia	1,449	585,472	4.2
Washington	158	42,543	.3
West Virginia	98	26,713	.2
Wisconsin	45	8,964	.1
Wyoming	52	10,786	.1
Canada	29	3,767	—
Other Foreign	2	147	—
Puerto Rico	25	2,629	—
Totals	36,302	13,992,812	100.0

*Membership figures do not include 5,400 members in missions without a sponsoring church.

others sprang up along the East-West corridor at Syracuse, Buffalo, and elsewhere. By far the most influential was the Manhattan Baptist Church, formed in New York City on January 10, 1958. Its first pastor was Paul James from Atlanta, who was also appointed director of all HMB work in the Northeast. When the New York churches formed their own state convention in 1969, James became its first executive secretary. A number of other churches grew out of the Manhattan church, some in New Jersey and others in upstate New York and New England.

One of the strongest Southern Baptist churches in the East was formed at Madison, New Jersey, in 1960, originating as a mission out of the Manhattan church. In 1970 the Baptist Convention of Pennsylvania-South Jersey was formed. Delaware had Southern Baptist work by 1951, the Delaware Baptist Association of six churches and two chapels by 1967, and nine churches with total membership of 3,784 by 1982.

In the East North Central Region, to use the Census Bureau's cumbersome term, Southern Baptist work dates in some cases back to the 1940s but got a better toehold in the 1950s. In Ohio such churches were formed in the late 1930s, five formed an association in 1940, and the State Convention of Baptists in Ohio was formed in 1954, with Ray E. Roberts named first executive secretary. Southern Baptist churches have existed in Indiana since the 1920s, but not until 1958 was the state convention formed, with E. Harmon Moore as executive secretary. In Michigan also Southern Baptist churches existed from the 1920s, perhaps earlier. Their main strength was around Detroit, where an association was formed in 1951. Their state convention was formed in 1952, with Fred D. Hubbs as executive secretary. Southern Baptist work in Wisconsin dates from 1953, when the Midvale Baptist Church was formed in Madison.

Southern Baptists had churches in Minnesota by 1956; Iowa by 1954; North Dakota by 1953; South Dakota by 1953; Nebraska by 1955; and in Kansas by 1910, though the work grew more rapidly after 1940. Military personnel and oilfield workers helped start many of these churches. In the Mountain Region, one finds Southern Baptist churches in Wyoming by 1951; in Montana by 1952; in Colorado from the 1930s; in Utah by 1944; in Idaho by 1951; and in Nevada from 1951. States in the Pacific Region also shared in the Southern Baptist expansion, with churches in Oregon and Washington by the mid-1940s, in Alaska by 1943, and in Hawaii by 1940. Of course, such bare facts alone tell no story, but to scan them will indicate clear trends and the general time frame when Southern Baptists were, as one put it, "outward bound."

Impact of Territorial Expansion

The transformation from regional to national scope has had profound internal impact upon Southern Baptists, leading to new tensions and problems. In his excellent study of SBC expansion, G. Thomas Halbrooks spoke of "growing pains" and analyzed several.[45] Of these resulting tensions, four are noted here.

1. Relation with Northern Baptists. Relations between Northern and Southern Baptists have moved from bitter to better; bitter largely prevailed until about 1960; and better has grown, if not completely prevailed, since then. Some early churches offended by insisting on listing *Southern* as part of their church name, locating near established Baptist churches and trying to siphon off their members, and insisting like Landmarkers (which many of them were) that theirs was the only true church. By the 1960s Southern Baptists had moderated some of their more offensive practices, and Northern Baptists had become more reconciled to Southern presence, realizing there was enough work for all. The two conventions cooperated more cordially than some individuals. Later the development of Southern economy and the attraction of the "Sun Belt" drew Northerners to the South. Baptists among them have established a number of churches and regional conventions in the South.

2. Proposed name change. SBC leaders have long struggled with the anomaly of a regional name with a national constitution. In 1903 the convention heard a proposal to change its name to "The Baptist Convention of the United States," but the next year a counterproposal suggested changing the constitution instead to conform to the facts.[46] From the 1950s the name change has been raised at different times, and for a few years in the 1960s the issue occupied front-page space. Some argued that changing the name would aid Southern Baptist work nationwide; others countered that the SBC had established a doctrinal identity that went beyond mere geography. After an intensive study in the early 1970s, the SBC voted to keep its present name. The issue was complicated by the fact that no acceptable alternate name could be found.

3. Convention representation. According to constitutional by-laws, no area may claim full representation on SBC boards and agencies until it has at least 25,000 Southern Baptist church members. This has created tension in two ways. Some of the newer areas have chafed at the delay in gaining convention representation, feeling themselves, in effect, disenfranchised. Others have felt that the newer areas with relatively few members might be overrepresented on policy-making boards of the SBC.

4. Theological tensions. Two remarkable developments mark the history of Southern Baptists in the twentieth century. The convention has more than doubled its territory and has faced the most severe theological contro-

45. G. Thomas Halbrooks, "Growing Pains: The Impact of Expansion on Southern Baptists Since 1942," *Baptist History and Heritage,* pp. 44 f.
46. *Annual,* SBC, 1903, p. 38.

versies of its history. These two facts are probably related. The territorial expansion of the SBC, especially in the West and Northwest, stirred the fading embers of Landmarkism into a raging fire in Southern Baptist life. Landmarkism, long identified with the Southwest, has found a new empire across the mountains, and it has pipelined controversy back into the older states. Even a cursory glance at this expansion must note the strong Landmarkers associated with it, such as W. P. Throgmorton in Illinois, E. P. Alldredge in New Mexico, R. W. Lackey in California, Willis J. Ray in Arizona, and R. E. Milam in Oregon. Perhaps the isolated and often-disadvantaged Southern Baptists in these pioneer areas felt again the old insecurities that plagued earlier Baptists and helped birth Landmarkism in the first place. While recent SBC controversies have dealt with other issues than just ecclesiology, they have drawn significantly from earlier Landmarkism. That rigid system has provided the background, spirit, and some of the issues for the recent crises.

Territorial expansion has transformed the Southern Baptist Convention. It has increased the convention's numbers, multiplied its institutions, and enlarged its financial and missionary capabilities. It has thrust Southern Baptists into prominence as the nation's largest Protestant denomination and embued them with a national vision.

The expansion has also introduced new tensions and turmoil. Along with new places have come new problems. A new pluralism prevails. The new convention is more massive, less tranquil, more extended, and less united. Just as today's nation of fifty states differs from the Colonial nation of thirteen states, so today's national SBC differs from the 1845 version which was limited to a few states of the old South. Like the nation, the SBC had been forced to cope with new complexities, new diversities, and new opportunities as it forges a new identity.

The General Boards

At the beginning of the twentieth century, the SBC worked through three general boards: the Foreign Mission Board, the Home Mission Board (both formed in 1845), and the Sunday School Board (formed in 1891). The Relief and Annuity Board was added in 1918 to provide pensions for retired or disabled ministers and their families. "Relief" was dropped from its name but not its work in 1960, leaving its present name, Annuity Board. For ten years, 1918 to 1928, the SBC sponsored a fifth general board, the Education Board, but it was abolished in 1928, its work later picked up by the reorganized Education Commission.

The work of these boards expanded rapidly in the twentieth century, in some cases incredibly so. They reflect the growing prosperity, sense of missions, denominational identity, and overall growth patterns which have marked Southern Baptists since 1900. Only the highlights of these ministries can be sketched here.[47]

The Foreign Mission Board (FMB)

To overstate the importance of foreign missions in Southern Baptist history would be difficult. The FMB was the first board formed by the new convention in 1845, and one might argue that it has occupied first place in the hearts and funds of Southern Baptists ever since. More than half of all SBC mission money goes to the FMB, and many regard it as the basic spiritual cohesion which binds a diverse convention together.

The twentieth-century expansion of Southern Baptist foreign mission work staggers the imagination. The FMB now conducts the most extensive Protestant foreign mission program in the world. The far-flung world ministry has had not only an impact abroad but perhaps an even greater impact at home. Much as Southern Baptists have done for the "heathen," it may

Chart 2				
Year	Missionaries under appointment	New Appointees	Nations with SBC missionaries	Lottie Moon Christmas Offering (when reported separately)	Total receipts
1900	94	16	6	$ 5,309	$ 140,102
1910	246	21	7		501,058
1920	341	33	9		2,119,476
1930	345	4	13	190,130	1,222,287
1940	455	42	13	330,424	1,177,418
1950	711	67	23	1,676,914	8,001,107
1960	1,381	144	45	6,778,558	16,144,841
1970	2,490	261	71	15,159,206	31,570,557
1980	3,010	332	95	36,167,418	71,101,418
1983	3,217	406	96	60,000,000	123,000,000

47. More complete histories of these boards exist, though some need to be updated. For the FMB, see Baker James Cauthen, *Advance: A History of Southern Baptist Foreign Missions;* for the HMB, see Arthur B. Rutledge, *Mission to America: A Century and a Quarter of Southern Baptist Home Missions;* for the BSSB, see Robert A. Baker, *The Story of the Sunday School Board* and Walter B. Shurden, *The Sunday School Board: Ninety Years of Service;* for the Annuity Board, see Robert A. Baker, *The Thirteenth Check: Jubilee History of the Annuity Board of the Southern Baptist Convention.* See also appropriate sections in *The Encyclopedia of Southern Baptists.*

be the heathen have done even more for Southern Baptists in helping them to marshal their forces and unify their work.

Between 1900 and 1983 the FMB expanded as follows: Missionaries under appointment, from 94 to 3,217; countries where work was conducted, from 6 to 96; annual Lottie Moon Christmas Offering receipts, from $5,309 to $60 million; in overall annual income, from $140,102 to $123 million. Chart 2 shows approximate statistics at ten-year intervals, and for the most recent year available:[48]

Fields of service. For years the FMB conducted work in just two places, China and Africa. Not until 1870 did it expand into a third area, Italy. It entered the twentieth century with work in six areas: China, Africa, Italy, Mexico, Brazil, and Japan. It regularly recommended entry into other nations, but expansion came slowly. World War II made Americans more world conscious and also brought prosperity which allowed expansion. Southern Baptists developed more of a world vision, with a bold dream to preach the gospel to the whole world. Most of the geographical expansion has come in recent years.

For more efficient operation, the FMB in recent years has divided the world into eight geographical units, each area including a number of nations or other political entities. These are: East Asia; South and Southeast Asia; West Africa; Eastern and Southern Africa; Europe and the Middle East; Eastern South America; Western South America; and Middle America and the Caribbean. Similar divisions have varied over the years, as has the organization within them. However, in general, the FMB maintains area secretaries in Richmond and secretaries on the field for each geographical area. Each nation may have a number of "missions," grouping missionary personnel in regional units, which meet annually. Decisions on personnel, priorities, and funding are shared between Richmond and the missions.

Forms of ministry. The FMB carries on complex ministries but for convenience, it has grouped these in six categories: missionary support; evangelism and church development; schools and student work; publication work; medical ministries; and benevolent ministries. Each covers a multitude of means to convey the gospel, always with the purpose to bring people to faith in Jesus Christ.

---

48. Though copied carefully from FMB reports to the SBC, as listed in SBC *Annuals,* these figures may be inexact for several reasons. Reporting and accounting procedures have changed over the years. Some reports cover the preceding calendar year, some the convention year (June through May). Sometimes the figures include other income (such as interest), sometimes not. During some years WMU funds were reported as a net annual contribution, but in more recent years the Lottie Moon offerings have been reported separately. As to personnel, some reports include only "career" missionaries, but in recent years the figures include also missionary associates, Journeymen, special projects workers, and other categories. Further, the same *Annual* may report one figure at one place and a slightly different one elsewhere for the same year. Income for 1983 shows projected amounts; exact figures were not yet available. While no claims for exactness can be made, these figures do reflect significant trends.

In missionary support, the FMB provides a modest salary, plus cost of living adjustments which vary according to the economy of different nations. Overseas service is punctuated with periodic furloughs, with salary continuing. Most medical needs are provided for the missionary family, educational aid is provided for children through college, and the missionaries are provided retirement benefits. The intention has always been to allow missionaries to devote full attention to their work without undue care for mammon.

Evangelism and church support have always comprised the heart of Southern Baptist missions. The majority of missionaries engage in direct evangelism. Such related work as health care, education, and other benevolent ministries have occupied fewer personnel and even they have kept a central evangelistic thrust. The Crusade of the Americas, 1968-1969, illustrates the FMB commitment to evangelism. In 1983 the FMB reported 12,170 Baptist churches overseas related to its mission work, 79 percent of them self-supporting, plus more preaching points not yet churches. Total overseas membership reached 1,568,098 and 140,844 baptisms were reported in 1982, both all-time highs.[49] The board estimated that in 1982 over 65 million people in the nations heard Baptist radio broadcasts, plus another 29 million who viewed Baptist presentations on television. At least 12 of the foreign conventions or unions related to SBC mission work have foreign mission programs of their own.

In 1982 about 487 SBC missionaries worked in 594 overseas schools, with a combined enrollment of 137,714, ranging from preschool to university levels. Most of the schools were for children. At the adult level, they included 16 colleges and 84 theological schools. However, over 90 percent of the teachers and administrators in the schools were national Christians.[50]

In 1971 the board emphasized a different form of theological training of national church leaders. In addition to fixed schools, where students reside while studying, the missionaries also developed programs of Theological Education by Extension (TEE). Pioneered in Southeast Asia by Ebbie C. Smith, this form of training later spread to other missions. The TEE plan did not bring students to the school but sent teachers to the students, meeting wherever they could. This method was said to be more economical, to raise up indigenous church leaders more quickly, and to fit better into local cultures.

From the beginning, Baptist missionaries have used the printed word, both Bibles and other literature, as part of their witness. The Judsons' need for mission tracts helped bring into being the Tract Society of 1824. Presently the FMB sponsors 25 publishing houses to provide evangelistic, educational, and Christian devotional materials in many languages. Perhaps the best known of these is the Spanish Publishing House, first established in

49. *Annual,* SBC, 1983, p. 104.
50. Ibid., p. 105.

Mexico but later moved to El Paso, Texas. It produces huge amounts of materials for several Latin countries. Others include the Baptist Publishing House (Portuguese) in Rio de Janeiro; the International Publication Services in Nairobi; Baptist Press in Hong Kong; and the Jordan Baptist Press in Japan. These print ministries occupied 148 missionaries in 1982, plus another 95 who distributed the materials.[51] Six out of ten people of the world can now read, and the printed word seems, if anything, more relevant to missions now than a century ago. An astonishing total of 723 different books were printed in 1982 by these various presses, with 56 new titles in Brazil alone. Some bilingual English-national language Bibles and hymnals are offered.

The work of medical missions has always fascinated Southern Baptists. The letters of Dr. Rosewell H. Graves in the 1860s helped channel the missionary awareness of Southern Baptist women. The martyrdom of Dr. Bill Wallace in the Communist takeover of China attracted sympathetic interest as perhaps no missionary has done since Lottie Moon; publicity about Wallace played a major role, no doubt, in the postwar advance of SBC missions.[52] At last report 54 missionary physicians and 57 missionary nurses served on different mission fields, dividing their time between 20 hospitals and 114 clinics sponsored wholly or in part by the FMB. To quote their own report: "Missionary physicians, nurses, dentists, and other medical personnel engaged in curative, primary, and preventive medicine. They cared about whole persons, not just isolated symptoms."[53]

Other forms of benevolent ministries claim attention, for missionaries cannot be blind to human need. Southern Baptist missionaries have worked in community centers, child-care centers, prisons, construction work, disaster relief, and especially in obtaining and distributing food in an all too limited assault on world hunger. Recent reports show at least thirty-eight agricultural missionaries, who seek to improve food production in the various nations. Almost one hundred career missionaries, plus twice that many volunteers, worked in benevolent ministries in the early 1980s.

Funding for foreign missions. From the first Southern Baptists funded foreign missions, and other work too for that matter, in the most informal manner. Many churches and individuals gave, some sacrificially, but others gave nothing, in some cases as much from lack of knowledge as from parsimony. Offerings dribbled in at odd times, the convention boards never knew what to expect and often had to operate on borrowed money until expected funds finally arrived. After 1900, when the new spirit of efficiency

51. Ibid.
52. See the popular book by Jesse C. Fletcher, *Bill Wallace of China,* which has circulated widely. Thousands of Southern Baptists also saw the dramatic movie of Wallace's life and death.
53. *Annual,* SBC, 1983, p. 106.

surfaced in the SBC, almost every FMB report called for some better system of funding its work.

Early in the century, Southern Baptists launched the Judson Centennial Fund, first intended to raise one million dollars for missions by 1912, the centennial anniversary of the sailing of the Judsons. Response was so favorable that the goal was increased and, even so, was exceeded. That showed that concerted support for foreign missions could be raised and provided a warm up for the Seventy-Five Million Campaign that followed.

From 1888 Baptist women of the South took an annual Christmas offering for foreign missions, in addition to their other contributions through the year. Three significant things happened to that offering in the twentieth century. First, it was named for its originator, Lottie Moon, in 1918. Second, whereas it began as a women's project, limited largely to WMU members, by mid-century it had become an all-church affair. Third, and related to the first two, the amount of the offering skyrocketed. From $5,309 in 1900, the Lottie Moon Christmas Offering now approaches $60 million and continues to grow.

However, major support for Southern Baptist foreign missions, as for all their ministries, comes through the Cooperative Program. From 1925 there was a general consensus that the FMB should receive about half of all Cooperative Program receipts, with the Home Mission Board receiving about one-fourth. In recent years that percentage has dropped below 48 percent (and one year as low as 46.4 percent), for which FMB officials complained publicly. Of course, the dollar amounts have risen dramatically, but unlike the other agencies which face inflation only at home, the Foreign Mission Board faces inflation both at home and abroad, sometimes in astronomical dimensions.

Missionary personnel. For years the FMB listed its missionaries in three categories: men, married women, and single women. Though single women were appointed from the early 1850s, the practice was opposed by many and did not become firmly established until the appointment of the Moon sisters in the 1870s. Even before the turn of the century, women missionaries outnumbered the men and still do. In 1900, for example, the 94 missionaries included 41 men and 53 women. Of 711 missionaries reported in 1950, 258 were men and 453 women, of whom 199 were single.[54] However, the percentage of single women appointees has declined from 27 percent in 1948 to about 10 percent in 1968, holding fairly steady since then. The 1982 report shows 8.9 percent of career missionaries as being single; most of these are women. Many Southern Baptists women missionaries function in essentially ministerial roles.

In recent years the board has defined several categories of service. The *career missionary,* now as always, offers lifetime service and represents the

54. Ibid., 1900, Appendix A, p. cxx; 1950, p. 167.

backbone of the work. More recent categories include the *missionary associate,* usually an older person who accepts overseas assignment. The *journeyman* program is designed for young people, usually college students, who accept a temporary overseas term of service similar to the Peace Corps. Many of the journeymen later become career missionaries. The *special projects* category allows the board to appoint persons with needed skills, as in engineering, for variable terms to help with special needs.

Missionary qualifications and preparation are demanding; Southern Baptists are far removed from the day they could appoint an immature twenty-one-year-old innocent like Edmonia Moon in 1872. Appointees must have graduated from college and a Southern Baptist seminary (in some cases, one year of seminary studies will suffice); possess good physical and emotional health; demonstrate Christian conversion and commitment, along with doctrinal stability; and bear testimony to an inner call. Complaints that William Carey himself could not pass such demands are countered by evidence that the FMB does well to screen its applicants carefully.

After appointment, the missionaries are commissioned to their fields, a service functionally equivalent to ordination. In fact, in 1959 the FMB sought and obtained from the IRS a ruling that defined commissioned missionaries, men and women, as ordained ministers in the eyes of the government, a move approved by the SBC.[55] Appointees also undergo intensive orientation and from one to two years of language studies before taking their places on their assigned fields.

Though few missionaries today suffer as did Adoniram and Ann Judson, their hardships are real. Sometimes they are imprisoned, as was David Fite in Cuba under Fidel Castro; they are often caught between opposing forces in political revolutions. Martyrdom sounds old-fashioned, but it still happens; five SBC missionaries met violent deaths in the 1970s.[56] In 1976 the FMB reaffirmed its "long-standing position of non-involvement of its missionary representatives in political affairs" of foreign nations.[57] This grew out of charges that some missionaries had at times supplied information to the Central Intelligence Agency.

Holding the ropes. To administer a world ministry, the FMB has benefited from outstanding home leadership. Seven men have headed the board in this century: Robert J. Willingham, 1893-1914; James F. Love, 1915-1928; T. B. Ray, 1919-1932; Charles E. Maddry, 1933-1944; M. Theron Rankin, 1945-1953; Baker James Cauthen, 1954-1979; and R. Keith Parks, since 1980. Each has dealt with unique challenges and made unique contributions. Willingham led the board to adopt a major ecumenical statement

---

55. See Porter Routh, "Ordination—Contemporary Problems," *Southwestern Journal of Theology,* pp. 77 f. See also Leon McBeth, "The Ordination of Women," *Review and Expositor,* pp. 522 f.

56. See Thomas W. Hill, "Foreign Mission Board, SBC," *ESB,* 4:2208.

57. See Frank K. Means, "Foreign Missions, Directions In," *ESB,* 4:2238.

in 1914 which, while expressing appreciation for others, declined to participate in territorial agreements which would limit Baptists to any particular
fields. Love headed the board during the Fundamentalist crisis of the 1920s
and led the board to adopt, and the missionaries to sign, a moderate doctrinal statement five years before the SBC itself adopted a confession of
faith.[58] Ray kept the board together during the difficult days of the Great
Depression. Few missionaries were appointed during his tenure, but he
managed the retrenchment carefully. Maddry saw better days; he led the
board in recovery and expansion. In his quarter century of leadership,
Cauthen brought both vision and achievements unprecedented in the history of missions. In personnel, funding, fields, and in keeping foreign missions a priority of Southern Baptist life, Cauthen made great strides. Parks,
like his predecessor, came to office from years as a missionary himself and
already has reorganized the work in ways that bode well for the future.

The FMB moved to spacious new headquarters in Richmond in 1959.
The home staff has grown, of course, but the ratio of home versus field costs
seems to confirm the efficiency of the operation. The needs of foreign
missions are kept before Southern Baptist people in church study materials,
through the WMU and Baptist Men's organizations, in special conference
centers at Ridgecrest and Glorieta, through the pages of *The Commission,*
by the speaking of missionaries on furlough, and in many other ways.

The Home Mission Board (HMB)

For Southern Baptists, the home mission task in the twentieth century
has been formidable. It has included the need to provide gospel preaching
where none existed; to plant churches in destitute areas; to strengthen weak
churches by helping support their pastors and providing funds for buildings;
to provide schools, especially in mountain areas, before the coming of public
high schools; to provide social, healing, and helping ministries to those in
need; and to develop an urban mission to share the gospel in the mushrooming cities.

However, if the task was clear, the division of the task was not. Several
Baptist organizations addressed home missions, including associations and
state conventions, as well as the HMB. Added to their work were the efforts
of local churches and itinerant preachers. The result has been overlap and,
at times, tension.

One might think the decision of 1882 to revitalize the home board rather
than abolish it would have settled the issue of its existence, but that was not
the case. Even its role in reclaiming the Southern field between 1882 and
1894, which probably preserved the existence of the SBC itself, did not
guarantee a secure existence to the Home Mission Board. Several times in
the twentieth century, suggestions have surfaced to make radical alterations. Some of the efficiency committees after 1910 wanted to merge the two

58. *Annual,* SBC, 1920, pp. 196 f.

mission boards, making home and foreign work two departments of the same board. During the Great Depression, when the Home Mission Board was saddled with crushing debt, augmented by a case of embezzlement involving almost a million dollars, some wanted simply to abolish the board and turn its work over to the state conventions. Even more threatening were various suggestions which would have preserved the board's formal existence but, by budget and work allocations, would have reduced the board from an active participant in home missions to a role of clearing house for other groups which did the actual work.

The HMB has struggled to maintain its mission and ministry among Southern Baptists. As recently as 1959, its future was in doubt; but the SBC voted that year that "the Home Mission Board should continue to exist as a separate agency of the Convention."[59] No further challenge has arisen about its continued existence.

For years the HMB and state conventions each carried on its own work in the same areas, leading to duplication in some places and neglect in others. In 1959 the convention voted to develop a single mission program for each state, to be operated jointly by the HMB and the state. The two would share in setting goals, appointing missionaries, and directing the work. The proportion of costs borne by the Home Mission Board has varied from 100 percent in areas where the state work was new or weak to as low as 33 percent in stronger states.

The HMB also aided in the geographical expansion of Southern Baptists. When Southern Baptists formed churches outside the South, the HMB was not slow to respond to their appeals for assistance. After 1950 the board launched aggressive mission efforts in the North and West, switching from a regional to a national outlook. During the 1880s Isaac T. Tichenor, head of the HMB, defended the "Southern Baptist territory" in the South. By the 1950s, the board reversed the Tichenor policy; instead of staking out a Southern territory to defend, it planned programs to plant Southern Baptist churches throughout the nation.

New century advance. Like other SBC agencies, the work of the HMB advanced rapidly during the first quarter of the twentieth century. In amounts of money received, number of personnel, and expansion of programs, the HMB flourished under Baron DeKalb Gray, who served as secretary from 1903 to 1928. The board was to receive over twelve million dollars from the Seventy-Five Million Campaign and about 25 percent of Cooperative Program receipts thereafter. The Department of Evangelism was formed in 1906; and though discontinued in 1928, it was restored in 1936 and later raised to division status. In 1894 Baptist women of the South, who had recently launched a special Christmas offering for foreign missions, set aside a "Week of Self-Denial" for prayer and offerings for home

59. Ibid., 1959, p. 61.

missions. In 1903 this took the name of "A Week of Prayer and Special Offering for Home Missions" and in 1934 was named for Miss Annie Armstrong, one of the primary founders of Woman's Missionary Union.[60] That special offering has grown from a few hundred dollars in 1900 to almost twenty million dollars in 1983.

Debilitating debt. By 1917 the Home Mission Board was thirty-eight thousand dollars in debt, due largely to the irregular flow of funds. When the debt exceeded a half million dollars in 1921, many felt concern, but their caution was ignored in the heady optimism of the Seventy-Five Million Campaign. The board rapidly expanded its work on borrowed money. Some of the expansion was in the costly field of health care, with a number of sanitariums launched in the 1920s. The SBC also voted that the home board assume several new responsibilities, such as the proposed Baptist memorial in Washington, without providing adequate funding for those projects. The debts of all SBC agencies reached six and a half million dollars by the end of 1926 and eventually exceeded eighteen million dollars.[61] Of all the agencies, the HMB was perhaps most seriously in debt when the depression struck.

The already serious financial burden was made infinitely worse by the most crucial financial calamity ever to befall any SBC board. In 1928 the HMB discovered that Clinton S. Carnes, its trusted treasurer since 1919, had embezzled a total of $909,461. Carnes had been authorized to draw funds and transfer property on his own signature alone and had for years been diverting funds to his personal use, a fact not revealed due to inadequate accounting procedures. The subsequent investigation revealed that Carnes had a previous prison record for embezzlement, a fact not known before. Because Carnes's misdeeds were committed in several states, he was never tried for all of them. When he was arrested while attempting to flee to Canada, he had on his person about fifty thousand dollars. That, plus the assignment of all his known assets and payment by the bonding company, allowed the board to recover about one-third of its loss. Carnes received a five-year prison term, serving less than three years.

However, the board lost far more than money; it lost the confidence of many Baptists, to say nothing of the loss of trust within the financial community. The Home Mission Board appealed at once for a meeting with the Executive Committee to deal with the crisis. The result was a "crisis committee" made up of members of the Executive Committee and the HMB. The committee's first recommendation was that B. D. Gray, secre-

---

60. Arthur B. Rutledge, *Mission to America: A Century and a Quarter of Southern Baptist Home Missions,* pp. 48-49.
61. Barnes, p. 231.

tary since 1903, be relieved of his duties.[62] They instituted tough retrenchment policies that cut HMB personnel and programs to the bone and made an agreement with the lending institutions to conduct all their work on 60 percent of their income, devoting 40 percent to debt retirement.

Recovery. The Executive Committee designated November 11, 1928, as "Baptist Honor Day." Southern Baptists responded with a special offering of $397,444 to apply to the HMB debt. Undoubtedly this saved the HMB, though it was not debt free until 1943. After over a year of interim leadership, the HMB elected John Benjamin Lawrence as secretary in 1929. He served until 1953. For the first decade, Lawrence was able to do little more than maintain a skeleton mission program while devoting his energies to debt retirement. However, during his last decade, 1943 to 1953, he led in the most remarkable advance the board had known up to that time.

Modern expansion. Three general secretaries have presided over the modern expansion of the Home Mission Board's ministries. They are Samuel Courts Redford, 1954-1964; Arthur Bristow Rutledge, 1964-1976; and William G. Tanner, 1977-1986. During that time the board has enlarged its Atlanta headquarters, vastly increased its personnel, restructured its work, and multiplied its programs. By 1983 the board had 3,430 persons under appointment, including full-time home missionaries; missionary associates; and US2 appointees, student workers who serve for two years.[63] They serve in all fifty states, Puerto Rico, the American Virgin Islands, Canada, and American Samoa. Gradually, the HMB has assumed work in Hawaii and Alaska, while turning over to the Foreign Mission Board its earlier work in Central America and Cuba. In addition to those under regular appointment, the HMB also directs the efforts of more than 40,000 volunteers in mission ventures nationwide each year.

In the 1970s the board reorganized to streamline its operation and to give more emphasis to church extension, language missions, and evangelism. Simply to name some of the programs of the HMB is to indicate the sweep of its ministries: Language Missions, Christian Social Ministries, Black Church Relations, Mission Service Corps, Rural-Urban Missions, Chaplaincy Ministries, Metropolitan Missions, Church Extension, Church Loans, Interfaith Witness, and many others.

In its Department of Language Missions, the board works among eighty-two ethnic groups who speak seventy-nine different languages, providing preaching in most of those languages. Many of the ethnic churches, though affiliated with the SBC, also maintain their own local and regional fellowships. The HMB has assisted in the resettlement of refugees from Cuba and Vietnam in recent years, as well as ministering among "undocumented"

62. Rutledge, p. 58.
63. *Annual,* SBC, 1983, p. 137.

immigrants from Mexico and other countries.[64]

The large cities have provided Southern Baptists with one of their greatest home mission challenges. Their background has been largely rural, with rural life-styles, value systems, and even language (some home missionaries recently made a point to speak of "pavement level" response instead of the old familiar "grassroots"). Under a variety of names, the Home Mission Board has launched missions to urban America. Some of the programs in this area include Mega Focus Cities, attempts to minister in the fifty largest metro areas; Urban Training Cooperative (UTC), an effort to bring needed training to urban ministers; and Project: Assistance for Churches in Transitional Communities (PACT).

The Home Mission Board also sponsors a program of Interfaith Witness, to share an evangelical understanding of the gospel with other religious groups, such as the major cults in modern America. Another major part of the work of this department has been a continuing dialogue with the American Jewish community.

Of course the main thrust of the HMB mission has been to win converts and gather them into churches, or, to use current terms, to "disciple" persons and then "congregationalize" them. The HMB led in the "Thirty Thousand Movement," launched in 1956, an effort to form thirty thousand new SBC churches and missions. More recently, the board has adopted a comprehensive strategy for the remainder of the twentieth century, called "Target: AD 2000." Part of its goal is to have fifty thousand active churches affiliated with the SBC by the turn of the twenty-first century. In 1974 the Home Mission Board launched a program to allow every person the opportunity to share in the witness and fellowship of a local church. The board called this program "Bold Mission Thrust." Others were so attracted to these goals, and especially to the name, that Bold Mission Thrust became the focus of all Southern Baptist ministries in the 1980s.[65] To publicize its various ministries, the HMB issues *Missions USA* (previously, *Home Missions*).

The Baptist Sunday School Board (BSSB)

Though only nine years old in 1900, the BSSB entered the new century with confidence, its value proven and its place in SBC life assured. It had produced excellent materials, showed modest financial success, and largely displaced other suppliers of Sunday School materials, including the highly regarded Publication Society of Northern Baptists. However, no one could have predicted the impact this small publishing board would have upon Baptists in the twentieth century. If the mission boards largely determine

---

64. For more detail, see *Baptist History and Heritage*, July 1983. The entire issue is given to a study of various aspects of "Ethnic Southern Baptist Heritage."
65. Walker L. Knight, "Home Mission Board, SBC," *ESB*, 4:2272.

what Southern Baptists *do,* the Sunday School Board has shaped what Southern Baptists *think.* Among Southern Baptists "Sunday School and church" have become inseparably connected.

Seven men have headed the BSSB in the twentieth century, each making a unique contribution. They are James Marion Frost, 1891-1893 and 1896-1916; I. J. Van Ness, 1917-1935; T. L. Holcomb, 1935-1953; James L. Sullivan, 1953-1974; Grady C. Cothen, 1974-1984; and Lloyd Elder, since 1984. Space allows only the briefest sketch of the work of this complex board.

Shaping the Sunday School. Southern Baptists entered Sunday School work fairly late, inheriting a pattern of organization related only loosely, if at all, to the church. Most Sunday Schools were sponsored by interdenominational agencies like the American Sunday School Union and often used union or nondenominational literature. In the present century, Southern Baptists have recreated the Sunday School in their own image; they have "Southern Baptized" it, to borrow Walter B. Shurden's phrase, and have turned what was an interdenominational agency into a powerful engine for denominational advance.

Lynn E. May has provided a vivid description of Southern Baptist Sunday Schools as of 1900:

> Southern Baptists entered the twentieth century with no tested Sunday School methods, no definite policies of Sunday School work, no field force, and no leadership training course. A majority of Baptists still considered the Sunday School to be a children's organization. Most schools were poorly organized and meagerly attended. Few could boast more than three classes: one for "infants," one for boys and girls, and another for men and women. Most teachers had little training. Church buildings were inadequate for effective Sunday School work. About half of the churches had no Sunday School.[66]

In addition, many Southern Baptists opposed the Sunday School movement, partly because it was new but also because it thrust women into teaching roles and because no such organization was specifically commanded in the Bible. By 1900 about 50 percent of Southern Baptist churches had Sunday Schools, up from only 25 percent in 1857. A surge of growth took place early in the century, with 84 percent of SBC churches showing Sunday Schools by 1926. That percentage peaked at 98.5 percent in 1960 but has since declined to about 97 percent. This means, as William P. Clemmons has observed, "Sunday School is now a nearly universal expression of what it means to be church among Southern Baptists."[67]

Before 1900 the Sunday School Board confined its efforts largely to

66. Lynn E. May, Jr., "The Emerging Role of Sunday Schools in Southern Baptist Life to 1900," *Baptist History and Heritage,* p. 14.

67. William P. Clemmons, "The Contributions of the Sunday School to Southern Baptist Churches," *Baptist History and Heritage,* p. 48.

printing and distributing literature. However, in 1901, the board took an important new direction when Bernard W. Spilman of North Carolina was employed as the first "field worker." That pleasant giant of a man made his office in railroad trains, traveling throughout the South to promote Sunday School work. An oft-told story recounts how Spilman, who was once told it would be impossible to convince Southern Baptists to support the Sunday School and that his work was bound to fail, took up his dictionary and simply crossed out the word *failure.* That dictionary, with a single line through *failure* remains a treasured possession of the Southern Baptist Historical Library and Archives in Nashville.

In field promotion, Spilman did several things for Southern Baptists. He led more churches to form Sunday Schools, led them to adopt more uniform standards, and tied them securely to the denomination by the use of BSSB lesson materials. Whereas earlier Sunday Schools, and especially the large adult classes, had been largely independent, almost like a little church within a church, Spilman insisted that the Sunday School be under church control.

Two books helped shape the Southern Baptist version of the Sunday School: Arthur Flake's *Building a Standard Sunday School* (1919) and *A Church Using Its Sunday School* (1937) by J. N. Barnette. Flake was an active lay leader in Sunday School work before he joined the staff of the BSSB. His famous "Flake's Formula" on how to build an effective Sunday School has become almost legendary among Southern Baptists. His formula had five points: (1) discover prospects, (2) organize to reach the people, (3) enlist and train workers, (4) provide space, and (5) visit and enlist the prospects. At a time when most Sunday School leaders in America sought to make religious education the only purpose of the Sunday School, Flake insisted that outreach and evangelism also ranked as legitimate purposes. The Sunday School must "reach" as well as "teach," he insisted, and Southern Baptists followed his lead.

Sunday School originated as a children's movement, and in most Baptist churches around the world it retains that identification. However, Southern Baptists made a fundamental innovation by extending the Sunday School to include all ages. As early as 1909 the BSSB suggested adult classes, but by 1925 SBC Sunday Schools still catered mostly to children. The introduction of age-group grading and the organization of Sunday School classes for evangelism helped popularize the all-age concept. Nothing has proven more beneficial to Southern Baptists in evangelism and church growth than the effective use of the Sunday School to enlist adults.

In addition to lesson materials for preschool, children, youth, and adults, the BSSB provides specialized literature and teacher training materials for singles, senior adults, handicapped, deaf, and retarded persons. By the 1980s about twenty-four hundred SBC churches sponsored special Sunday

School classes for retarded persons.[68] The board also provides Bible study materials in Braille and in several languages other than English.

At the turn of the century, Southern Baptists reported 636,944 persons enrolled in Sunday Schools; by 1983 that had increased to 7,678,604.[69] Several special campaigns added to that growth, such as the Five Year Plan, 1935-1940; A "Million More in '54," and ACTION in 1976-1977. Between 1976 and 1982, SBC churches added more than one thousand new Sunday Schools each year. Later the BSSB conducted a major promotion called "8.5 by '85," an effort to raise Sunday School enrollment to 8.5 million by 1985. However, the story has not been always growth; the Sunday School showed a period of decline in the early 1970s.

In recent years the BSSB has provided three major sets of curriculum materials for the use of Sunday Schools. The first consisted of the Convention Uniform Series. Although based upon the same Scripture passages studied by other denominations, Southern Baptists enlist their own writers and prepare their own expositions and teacher helps. The board introduced a second series in 1966, known as Life and Work. The L & W materials are more topical and seek to apply the biblical message to contemporary life concerns. Some churches had difficulty choosing between the two series, and some found fault with both. Complaints alleged that the Bible passages seemed to be chosen at random, to lack continuity, and failed over a period of years to impart any connected understanding of the entire Bible. Partly to meet these objections, and partly to provide material for the more conservative churches, the board in 1979 introduced a third curriculum, known as the Bible Book Series. The BBS is based upon the consecutive study of both New Testament and Old Testament books and is intended to give more continuity, more exposition of the Bible with less application, and less use of modern translations. It quickly captured about 13 percent of the market.

Other ministries. In 1956 the Sunday School Board proposed that its name be changed to the Board of Education and Publication, but the convention withheld its approval and the old name remains. However, the ministries of this board extend far beyond Sunday School work, though evangelism and training of lay persons remains the focus of its various programs. Presently, the board sponsors no fewer than fifteen programs in addition to Sunday School.

In the 1890s a youth movement arose in the churches, later taking the name of Baptist Young People's Union, the famous BYPU. It originated on an interdenominational basis but, as in the case of the Sunday School, Southern Baptists "denominationalized" their version of the youth movement, tying it securely to the churches. Quite early the BSSB provided

68. Jerry M. Stubblefield, "Creative Advancements in Southern Baptist Sunday School Work," *Baptist History and Heritage,* p. 48.
69. *Annual,* SBC, 1900, p. 173; 1983, p. 141.

workers and literature for the BYPU movement, which usually met on Sunday evenings. In 1934 they changed the name to Baptist Training Union (BTU) and included classes and materials for all ages. The purpose of BTU was to train church members in the Christian life, to acquaint them with their heritage, and prepare them for church leadership roles. For a generation or more it worked admirably, but more recently the training organization has fallen on difficult times. A name change to Church Training (CT) provided only cosmetic aid. After 1960 enrollment dropped sharply and attendance even more sharply.

The training organization fell victim to several problems, including an unpopular meeting time; competition from television; a less-exciting curriculum; a decline in Sunday night church attendance; competition from other church organizations such as WMU, the Brotherhood, graded choirs, and mission organizations for children; and a prevalent feeling that Southern Baptist churches were "over-programmed" with too many meetings. However, this decline of training has left a serious gap. For all their Sunday School attendance, millions of church members have little grounding in Baptist doctrines and heritage.

The Vacation Bible School (VBS) originated around the turn of the century but was not picked up by Southern Baptists to any great extent until after World War I. One of the earliest such schools among SBC churches was held in 1916 at the Gambrell Street Baptist Church of Fort Worth. Only about three hundred Vacation Bible Schools were held among Southern Baptists in 1925, but this increased to 1,044 in 1935.[70] By 1940 this ministry had grown dramatically; statistics show 5,756 schools that year with over a half-million children enrolled. By the 1960s most SBC churches conducted some form of VBS. Changes in society have affected these summer schools. The employment of women outside the home reduced the pool of available teachers, while a plethora of organized summer activities gave children other options. Some churches have experimented with VBS at night or VBS for all ages, but these have not caught on.

At its formation in 1891, the BSSB was forbidden to publish books, a ban later lifted by the convention. In the 1920s John L. Hill led in the growing book ministry of the board. Noting how Northern Baptists in their publishing ventures capitalized on the name of their famous missionary, Adoniram Judson, Hill suggested Southern Baptists combine the names of two of their early educational leaders, John A. Broadus and Basil Manly, to form Broadman Press, the general publishing arm of the Sunday School Board. The printing of books called for their distribution, which led to the system of Baptist Book Stores scattered throughout the nation.

As early as 1907 B. W. Spilman persuaded the denomination to purchase a beautiful mountain site in North Carolina to provide a place to hold

---

70. Charles F. Treadway, "Vacation Bible School," *ESB,* 2:1440.

workshops to train Sunday School teachers and other lay leaders. Called Ridgecrest Baptist Conference Center, it was sponsored by the Sunday School Board from 1928 (though they obtained title only in 1944). A similar conference center, Glorieta Baptist Conference Center, in Glorieta, New Mexico, was opened in 1952.

The BSSB also sponsors departments for church architecture, church music, church recreation, statistics and research, and many others. Not only has its Bible teaching materials helped shape Baptists' doctrinal views but also its hymnals, especially the *Broadman Hymnal* of 1940, helped shape and standardize Southern Baptist worship. In recent years some Southern Baptist churches have formed their own day schools, and the Sunday School Board has provided some curriculum materials for the study of religion in these schools.

In the early 1980s the BSSB launched a new ministry called Baptist Telecommunication Network, or BTN. This is a satellite television system whereby churches or various church groups can receive programs from denominational leaders. Special programs of Christian training, Bible study, inspiration, and evangelism are projected by means of this system.

Relation to constituency. From the first, Southern Baptists have been a diverse lot and still are. It has been increasingly difficult for the Sunday School Board to provide materials to satisfy the needs of churches large and small, scattered in different regions of the country, and holding doctrines and social views far from uniform. However, the BSSB has made an effort to meet the needs of all and, except during a few periods of special doctrinal or social volatility in this century, has done a fair job of it.

One reason for the three major series of curriculum materials has been the effort to meet the needs of different kinds of churches. For similar reasons, the board has tried to assure that its books, periodicals, and worship materials reflect the diversity that exists among the churches. Even so, some have found fault. In recent years the board has been chastized for views on race relations, the roles of women, and various doctrines as they appear in board publications. The use of the Revised Standard Version, and other modern translations of the Bible, have offended some.

Several recent incidents illustrate the vulnerability of the board to opposition. In the 1960s a pupil's quarterly inadvertently recommended reading from an extremely radical author; and in the early 1970s some churches objected to a photograph in a quarterly for teenagers showing black and white young people talking.[71] Public response to both of these incidents was quick and, for the most part, negative. Numbers of disgruntled churches returned the quarterlies, and many of them took the occasion to purchase non-Baptist literature for their churches. The various independent presses,

71. For a discussion of the photograph incident in "Becoming," see Leon McBeth, "Southern Baptists and Race Since 1947," *Baptist History and Heritage*, pp. 155 *f.*

sensing that the time was right for them to grab a portion of the lucrative Southern Baptist market, went all out to wean churches away from the denominational literature.

Two major publishing ventures also aroused opposition. Broadman Press published *The Message of Genesis,* by Ralph H. Elliott, in 1960. Within weeks opposition had become severe, fanned partly by hostile editorials in several Baptist papers, particularly the *Baptist Standard* of Texas. This "Genesis Controversy" paralyzed the SBC for several months, led to a new confession of faith in 1963, and ultimately resulted in Elliott's dismissal from his teaching post at the Midwestern Baptist Theological Seminary in Kansas City. The BSSB decided not to republish the book when the first edition sold out.

In the late 1960s Broadman released the early volumes of its long-planned *The Broadman Bible Commentary.* Volume 1, on Genesis and Exodus, proved controversial; in fact, the SBC in an angry session at Denver in 1970 voted that it be withdrawn and rewritten from a more conservative viewpoint. Complaints were raised about the entire set, but no other volumes were withdrawn.

Impact of the Sunday School Board. Walter B. Shurden named four ways in which the Sunday School Board has been a force in denominational life.[72] First, the board has provided religious education for Southern Baptists. It has been the teaching arm of the church, or as Sampey put it, "The Sunday School Board is our people's university in the teaching of religion."[73] This board has helped Southern Baptists achieve a level of biblical literacy remarkable in the history of lay religion. Second, the BSSB has been a missionary and evangelistic force. Most converts baptized in Southern Baptist churches still come through the Sunday School. Third, the board has been a financial force by making the Sunday School the primary collecting agency in Baptist churches. The BSSB is the only convention agency which does not receive Cooperative Program funds; instead, it contributes to other causes out of its substantial income. Fourth, the board has brought a measure of unity to Southern Baptist churches. Its literature helped create a commonality of doctrinal outlook (which prevailed until recently), its organizational forms meant members of one Baptist church could feel quite at home if they moved to another, and its hymnals and other worship aids lent a kind of uniformity or at least similarity to Baptist worship services.

To Shurden's list, at least two other contributions might be added. The Sunday School Board has greatly affected Southern Baptist church architecture. Before 1900 most SBC churches, if they had a building at all, had one-room structures. When Sunday Schools made their entrance, the classes usually met in curtained-off corners of the one large room. However,

72. Shurden, *Sunday School Board,* pp. 95 f.
73. Ibid.

in time, Baptist churches designed buildings with both worship space and educational space, the latter at first being little more than a series of rooms for Sunday School classes. Later the development of more elaborate educational departments and classrooms, as well as church libraries, audiovisual centers, and choir rooms can be attributed largely to programs sponsored by the BSSB.

Further, the board has facilitated the development of a plural professional ministry among Southern Baptists. Up to World War II most churches regarded themselves as fully staffed if they had a pastor and a janitor (sometimes the same person), but gradually the "educational director," or "minister of education," emerged out of the Sunday School and other educational work of the church. The earliest known paid Sunday School superintendent was R. H. Coleman of First Baptist Church in Dallas in 1910.[74] By 1915 four SBC churches had paid educational directors, and J. Earl Mead, who joined the staff of First Baptist Church of Beaumont, Texas, in 1919, was apparently the first to bear the title "minister of education."[75] By 1930 almost one hundred persons held paid positions in educational work in SBC churches, and of course the number has escalated since then. A similar enlargement of tasks brought the minister of music and other vocational workers to the churches. Much of this development grew out of the need for trained professionals to oversee programs sponsored by the Sunday School Board.

Though not given to hyperbole, Rober A. Baker gave way to enthusiasm in his history of the Sunday School Board. The record seems to justify his description of the recent history of the board as a "period of splendid maturity."[76]

The Annuity Board (AB)

Southern Baptists lagged behind other denominations in providing some retirement pension plan for their ministers. During the early days, many Southern Baptist pastors received no stated salary, though churches usually provided partial support through occasional offerings. Churches that felt little responsibility to support active pastors felt less to provide for the pastor's inactive years. In fact, the concept of retirement made little headway in the nineteenth century; most people simply worked all their lives or until disability forced them to the sidelines. "Decrepit ministers," as they were sometimes called, either saved for their own declining years, lived with relatives, or in some cases were cared for by a church or some church family. Several state conventions raised benevolent funds for aged ministers

74. Stubblefield, p. 52.
75. Ibid., p. 53.
76. Robert A. Baker, *The Story of the Sunday School Board*, pp. 167 *f.*

and their widows after the Civil War, but eligibility varied from state to state and needs seemed always to outrun available funds.

By the 1850s the Foreign Mission Board faced the question of care for its disabled missionaries. Its announced policy seems harsh, but its actual practice proved more benevolent. In 1859 the board asked, "What is the duty of the Board regarding the support of returned missionaries?" Its answer appears to wash its hands of the ill or disabled: "Should the confirmed ill health of a missionary preclude the possibility of his returning to the foreign field, and his connection with the Board cease, they are no longer under obligation to support him." Lest this sound too cold, the board pointed out, "This principle generally obtains in regard to pastors, agents, and indeed, all classes of persons who labor for regular salaries."[77] However, they softened that statement by agreeing that a missionary who had lost his health in service should be entitled not only to the sympathy of the board but also to some financial support. Gradually that principle gained acceptance in the denomination.

Launching the Annuity Board. The founder of the Annuity Board was William Lunsford, who accepted a Nashville pastorate early in 1914. He became deeply convicted that it was immoral for Baptists to allow their ministers, after a lifetime of selfless service, to finish their days in abject want. He discussed the need with the Nashville Pastor's Conference in 1916, some of whose members served also on the Sunday School Board. They persuaded the BSSB to set aside one hundred thousand dollars for ministerial relief, and in 1917 the SBC authorized a commission "to examine the various plans now being operated for ministerial relief in the various states," with a view to coming up with some united plan. In 1918 the convention voted to establish a Relief and Annuity Board, to be located in Dallas.

The double name was significant; the new body included both relief and annuity. For aged ministers who had made no retirement provisions, the new board worked out a systematic plan of relief allotments. Younger ministers were encouraged to place a certain amount of their earnings into annuity accounts, to build up funds against the day of their old age or illness. Not only pastors but also their widows and dependent children were eligible for aid under these provisions. The board made its relief allotments as generous as possible, sometimes giving an extra monthly check at the end of the year, thus providing Robert A. Baker with the title, *The Thirteenth Check,* for his jubilee history of the Annuity Board.[78]

The board now includes not only retirement plans but also insurance and various savings options. To cite figures seems pointless; they change so rapidly and inflation distorts them. Suffice it to say that most Southern Baptist pastors have enrolled in some phase of the Annuity Board's pro-

77. *Annual,* SBC, 1859, p. 46.
78. Baker, *The Thirteenth Check.*

grams, that the board's resources have grown dramatically, and that most SBC pastors can be assured of at least minimal protection in illness, disability, and retirement.

Impact of the Annuity Board. However, the impact of the Annuity Board has been deeper than dollars. At least three results of its work may be noted. First, and most obviously, the board's programs have provided a financial safety net for the pastor and his family. The fact that the church shares in the dues for the basic retirement program has focused attention on the church's duty to provide for its ministers. Improved benefits may be a factor in the increasing supply of pastors. The SBC in 1918 heard a report on the desperate shortage of pastors and other workers,[79] but more recently one hears reports of an alleged oversupply. Second, the denominational retirement programs, necessary as they are, have probably caused ministers to give more thought to the monetary side of ministry than earlier pastors did (or at least to do so more openly). The rise of retirement programs in industry and government-sponsored Social Security provisions have also focused the attention of ministers, along with other citizens, upon material needs.

A third result of the Annuity Board programs has been its unifying influence upon Southern Baptists. One often hears the remark, "If the convention splits, I'm going with the Annuity Board!" That little jest is always good for a chuckle, but the cohesive impact of the Annuity Board is no laughing matter. The SBC originated in a denominational schism and throughout its history has endured schisms of its own; one thinks, for example, of the Campbell and Landmark schisms. However, since the Annuity Board got its programs in place, the SBC has not experienced a single major schism. Some well-to-do churches and pastors may feel they can do without the Annuity Board, but the average Southern Baptist church and pastor does not have that luxury. Dissident pastors may fulminate against the denomination, but few can afford to bolt. One result has been that the disgruntled, who generations ago would simply have split off as the BMA did in 1905, now stay within the SBC and try to bend the larger body to their own viewpoints. The Annuity Board programs allow ministers to sleep more soundly, but they may also make the convention sessions a lot noisier.

Secretaries who have headed this board include William Lunsford, 1918-1927; Thomas J. Watts, 1927-1947; Walter R. Alexander, 1947-1954; R. Alton Reed, 1955-1971; and Darold H. Morgan, since 1972.

The Commissions

For reasons not entirely clear, the SBC has elected to call its smaller agencies *commissions* rather than *boards*. Their relationship to the conven-

---

79. *Annual,* SBC, 1918, pp. 88-90.

tion and methods of their funding are the same as with boards, but the commissions are smaller and more recent. One observer has compared the work of a board to a shotgun, large and general, while the work of a commission is like a rifle, smaller and more specific.[80] Unlike the boards that are located in different cities, all the commissions but two are located in Nashville; the Brotherhood Commission is headquartered in Memphis and the Radio and Television Commission in Fort Worth.

The Education Commission

Southern Baptists entered the twentieth century with a new surge of educational activity. Already the state conventions sponsored numerous colleges and other schools, but a need was felt for more central planning and coordination. To meet that need, the SBC established the Education Commission in 1915. The new body promptly launched ambitious plans to raise fifteen million dollars for Baptist schools, a plan that seemed so timely and attractive that the SBC took it over and expanded it to encompass the Seventy-Five Million Campaign for all convention causes. In the heady atmosphere of the times, the Education Commission was raised to board status in 1918. Failure of the Seventy-Five Million Campaign to meet its goals combined with the depression to devastate Baptist schools. The Education Board was the first casualty, being abolished in 1928.

However, the Education Commission was restored in 1931, operating for twenty years largely under the leadership of Charles D. Johnson. Though called a commission, its status was that of a convention committee operating with volunteer workers. In 1951 the commission took its present form, chartered "to serve the educational interests of the Southern Baptist Convention."[81] Its first secretary was R. Orin Cornett, who served 1951-1959; followed by Rabun L. Brantley, 1959-1970; Ben C. Fisher, 1970-1978; and Arthur L. Walker, Jr., since 1978.

Though the Baptist colleges and universities are sponsored by state conventions, the Education Commission has served needed functions. In 1972 the convention summarized its work in five points: (1) overall education leadership and coordination, (2) college studies and services, (3) teacher-personnel services, (4) student recruitment, and (5) convention relations. Its overall purpose is to strengthen Baptist higher education in America.[82]

80. Sullivan, pp. 122, 127.

81. R. Orin Cornett, "Education Commission of the Southern Baptist Convention," *ESB,* 1:302.

82. Arthur L. Walker, Jr., "Education Commission, SBC," *ESB,* 4:2191-2192.

Southern Baptist Commission on the
American Baptist Theological Seminary

The American Baptist Seminary in Nashville is jointly operated by the SBC and the National Baptist Convention, Inc. The Southern Baptist Commission is the agency which works from the SBC side in promotion, general funding, and scholarship aid.[83]

By the turn of the century, it became clear that black Baptists in the South needed a theological school to supplement the work being done by black colleges. The National Baptists committed themselves to "the founding and operation of a general Theological Seminary for the education of the negro ministers" and appointed a committee to carry out that commitment.[84] In 1913 the SBC adopted a motion by E. Y. Mullins to appoint a committee to work with the National Baptist group. The resulting agreement in 1914 called for Southern Baptists to raise fifty thousand dollars toward the establishment of such a school.

Several factors delayed the opening of the American Baptist Seminary. Problems arose over the location (Nashville was finally chosen). Promised funds from the SBC came in slowly, and the work was delayed by World War I. Most importantly, a split in the National Baptist Convention in 1915 almost derailed the whole plan. One faction in the National Baptist schism, led by R. H. Boyd, set up a seminary in East Nashville in 1918. However, the larger faction, which took the name of National Baptist Convention, Inc., continued its determination to work jointly with the SBC in founding a seminary.

The American Baptist Seminary opened in 1924. The SBC continues to give financial aid, while the school is governed by a board of trustees equally divided between National and Southern Baptists. By 1980 the school had a well-equipped campus and an enrollment of 190. Through its commission, Southern Baptists provide about 130 scholarships for ministerial students.

Originally, this school was made necessary partly by racial segregation. Since black students now attend whatever seminary they choose, the ABTS by no means represents the entire training picture for black Baptist clergy. However, that school still meets an important need. A recent report said the ABTS "results in theological education for many who plan to fulfill their calling by serving in black Baptist churches. Some of these would not have an opportunity for theological education without the effort of the two conventions."[85]

83. *Annual,* SBC, 1983, p. 327.
84. Ibid., 1914, p. 27.
85. Ibid., 1983, p. 187.

The Brotherhood Commission

The success of Woman's Missionary Union in channeling the energies and efforts of Southern Baptist women led to a desire for a similar agency for Baptist men. In 1907 the Laymen's Missionary Movement was formed, continuing under that name until 1926. From 1927 to 1950 the men's movement was known as the Baptist Brotherhood of the South, and since 1950 as the Brotherhood Commission. The organization in local churches was for years known as the Baptist Brotherhood, and more recently simply as Baptist Men.

The pioneer leader in the Baptist men's program was John T. Henderson, who served as general secretary until 1936. He was succeeded by Lawson H. Cooke, 1936-1951; George W. Schroeder, 1951-1971; W. Glendon McCullough, 1971-1978; and James H. Smith, since 1979. A well-known lay leader in the Brotherhood was Jimmy Carter, governor of Georgia and later president of the United States. Since 1936 the commission has been headquartered in Memphis.

As the name implied, the early purpose of the Laymen's Missionary Movement was to involve men in the support of missions. Later its program expanded to include a number of causes. In 1956 its work was said to be "To seek and discover the talents of the men and boys in Southern Baptist churches, challenge them to action, and utilize their talents for Christ."[86] The men sponsored a number of special programs, including an annual Layman's Day, beginning in 1933; the Man and Boy Movement, begun in 1949; a number of national conferences on men's work; and several programs in the 1970s on lay renewal. In 1954 the work of Royal Ambassadors, the missionary education program for boys, was transferred from WMU to the Brotherhood, a transfer completed in 1957.

The Brotherhood enrolled a total of 529,642 in its programs in 1982, and its Cooperative Program receipts totaled $704,407 for that year.[87] Despite outward success, the men's programs have faced a number of problems. Perhaps the most serious has been the lack of a sharp focus. Unlike the WMU, whose purpose has been specific, the men's organization has served more general purposes, and sometimes the priorities seemed unclear. Whereas Baptist women, who often were restricted from leadership roles in the church, needed WMU as an arena for their own expression and leadership, the men had no such need since they exercised leadership throughout the church. The men have not had the success with the Royal Ambassador program that the women had earlier. Men seemed to put less emphasis on missionary education; and as the RA work turned more toward crafts and outings, it faced serious competition from Boy Scout pro-

86. Cited by Darrell C. Richardson, "Brotherhood, Baptist," *ESB,* 3:1621.
87. *Annual,* SBC, 1983, pp. 189, 322.

grams. In more recent years, men from the Brotherhood have made great contributions in disaster relief work and in helping build new church buildings.

The Christian Life Commission (CLC)

The Southern Baptist Convention was slow to find its voice on social and moral issues. In 1888 the SBC ruled out of order a simple resolution on temperance as not germane to its work. However, early in the twentieth century, Southern Baptists showed greater interest in applying gospel teachings to daily life. In 1907 the SBC appointed the Committee on Civic Righteousness. Its report in 1908 was bold indeed, affirming that

> Civic Righteousness and the Kingdom of God are bound up in each other. We are learning anew that Christ's commission to his followers is not primarily to increase the census of heaven but to make down here a righteousness society in which Christ's will shall be done.[88]

At the same meeting, the convention created a standing committee on temperance, which confined its work largely to the task mentioned in its name, attempting to close every "breathing hole of the devil," as saloons were called. In time Southern Baptists became a major force in effecting national prohibition of alcoholic beverages.

In 1913 some leaders, noting that Southern Baptists might combat other evils as they had alcohol, called for a committee "to deal with other such wrongs which curse society today."[89] The resulting Social Service Commission, chaired by W. L. Poteat, gave its first and last report in 1914. In 1914 the convention combined its two committees dealing with social issues. The combined group took the name of the Social Service Commission but continued mostly the work of the Temperance Committee. For the most part, the more progressive members were dropped from the committee, and calls for broad social reforms were silenced. However, under the leadership of A. J. Barton, the combined committee continued to speak out, primarily on alcohol abuse and lynching.

In the mid-1930s Southern Baptists once again debated their social mission. In 1933 Edwin McNeill Poteat, Jr., proposed that the SBC create "an agency of Social Research" to study social problems and plan concerted action.[90] That suggestion was soundly rejected. However, Southern Baptists' concern with the world around them demanded expression. After the death of Barton, J. B. Weatherspoon became chairman of the Social Service Commission, a role he held until 1955. In 1946 he called for broader social

---

88. Ibid., 1908, pp. 35-36.
89. Ibid., 1913, pp. 73-74.
90. Cited in Leon McBeth, "Origin of the Christian Life Commission," *Baptist History and Heritage,* p. 34.

awareness on the part of Southern Baptists and suggested definite plans to translate that concern into action. In 1947 the SBC strengthened the Social Service Commission, authorizing it to employ a full-time director. Later the name was change to the Christian Life Commission and its work further expanded. The first full-time secretary was Hugh A. Brimm, who served from 1947 to 1953, followed by Acker C. Miller, 1953-1960, and Foy D. Valentine, since 1960.

The SBC assigned two functions to the CLC in 1961 and reaffirmed them in 1968. They are: (1) to assist the churches by helping them understand the moral demands of the gospel and (2) to help Southern Baptists to apply Christian principles to moral and social problems.[91] A widely used motto of the CLC has been, "Helping changed people to change the world."

In a 1983 report, the commission reported that it has

> been at work in support of applied Christianity in such varied areas as family life, race relations, citizenship, economics and daily work, and with such special moral concerns as hunger, peace with justice, alcohol and other drugs, drunk driving, gambling, television programming, pornography, the secular humanism phenomenon, the crisis in public education, and the new religious right.[92]

To focus the biblical message on social issues, the CLC prints and distributes innumerable booklets and pamphlets, holds annual workshops, sponsors special programs at the conference centers, and speaks out for Christian morality on every available forum. The annual budget was set at about $10,000 in 1947, but by 1982 Cooperative Program receipts reached $496,242.[93]

As the Christian Life Commission expanded its work in the 1960s, it aroused renewed opposition. Its early pronouncements for racial equality seemed radical to some, and its stand on peace, world hunger, and abortion further alienated ultraconservatives. Almost every convention since 1965 has seen some effort to abolish, restrict, or reprimand the CLC. While the SBC has not always accepted the CLC's recommendations, it has steadfastly refused to silence the prophetic, though provocative, voice of its agency for moral concerns and social action.

Some opposition has grown out of historic conservatism of Southern Baptists.[94] Some have seen conflict between evangelism and Christian moral concerns where none need exist. Perhaps the recent growth of dispen-

91. Cited in Floyd A. Craig and Foy D. Valentine, "Christian Life Commission," *ESB*, 3:1646.

92. *Annual*, SBC, 1983, p. 189.

93. Ibid., p. 325.

94. See John L. Eighmy, *Church in Cultural Captivity: A History of the Social Attitudes of Southern Baptists;* and Rufus B. Spain, *At Ease in Zion: A Social History of Southern Baptists, 1865-1900* for excellent discussions of the social heritage of Southern Baptists.

sational and premillennial doctrines among Southern Baptists has tended to discourage extensive attention to social issues. One emphasis of apocalyptic teachings is that the world must grow progressively worse. Those who expect the speedy end of the world are usually less concerned to improve it.[95]

The Historical Commission

Delegates at the formation of the Southern Baptist Convention in 1845 seemed aware that they witnessed an historic occasion; at least, they took care to preserve their records. Later the SBC passed resolutions of support for the American Baptist Historical Society, formed in 1853, where several Southerners held membership. A resolution in 1895 asked the Sunday School Board to include more historical emphases in its curriculum materials, a request which seems to have borne little fruit. As early as 1911 the SBC called for a complete history of Baptist work in the South.[96] By 1916 the Sunday School Board engaged an author for such a work, but the resulting manuscript was never published.

In 1921 the SBC voted, "That a Committee be appointed to recommend to the Convention methods and policies for gathering and preserving the historical records of Southern Baptists."[97] The resulting committee recommended that the Sunday School Board establish a department of historical survey and statistics, which was done. It also discovered that several of the older states had flourishing programs for the collection and preservation of their historical records. Out of this SBC action was formed the Southern Baptist Historical Society in 1922, with A. H. Newman as president.[98] That society lapsed after a few years.

Yet another committee on Baptist history was appointed by the SBC in 1936, led by William O. Carver; its work led to formation of the present Historical Commission in 1951. The Southern Baptist Historical Society was also revived in 1947, becoming auxiliary to the commission. The first secretary of the Historical Commission was Norman W. Cox, who served 1951-1959. He was succeeded by Davis C. Woolley, 1959-1971, and Lynn E. May, Jr., since 1971. The assignment given to the Historical Commission at its formation in 1951 was to "conserve and utilize the history interests of the Southern Baptist Convention."[99]

Since it was assigned to collect a library of Baptist historical materials,

95. For a discussion of the impact of premillennialism upon Christian social concerns, see Timothy P. Webber, *Living in the Shadow of the Second Coming* (New York: Oxford University Press, 1979).

96. *Annual,* SBC, 1911, p. 61.

97. Ibid., 1921, p. 29.

98. Ibid., 1922, p. 84.

99. Cited by J. B. Allen, "Historical Commission of the Southern Baptist Convention," *ESB,* 1:625.

the commission formed a cooperative relationship with the Sunday School Board in sponsoring the Dargan-Carver Library, named for E. C. Dargan and W. O. Carver, whose private collections provided its nucleus. Perhaps the most ambitious publishing project of the commission has been the *Encyclopedia of Southern Baptists,* with volumes I and II issued in 1958, III in 1971, and IV plus an Index which came out in 1982. The commission also publishes a quarterly journal, begun in 1965, called *Baptist History and Heritage.* In addition to an extensive collection of books, printed minutes, and periodicals, the commission has also microfilmed available materials in Baptist history, with its "Baptistiana on microfilm" exceeding twelve million pages by 1982.[100] In the later 1960s, the commission launched the Baptist Information Retrieval System (BIRS), to establish a data bank of information on Baptist past and present, available for rapid computer recall. In addition to publications and workshops to help Baptists preserve, understand, and use their heritage, in the early 1980s the commission produced six popular videotapes, entitled "Meet Southern Baptists."

In 1951 the SBC named the Historical Commission as the official archives for the preservation of records of the convention and its agencies, a policy reaffirmed in 1981. Since then several of the boards and agencies have deposited some of their inactive records with the commission for preservation and to be available for research.

At first the commission was funded at about $5,000 a year, but by 1982 its Cooperative Program receipts had grown to $282,060.[101] Since 1951 the commission has occupied space in Sunday School Board facilities, for many years on a rental basis, but moved to the new Southern Baptist Building in Nashville in 1985. This resulted in a division of the Dargan-Carver Library, with the Historical Commission moving its portion of the collection to its new facility, taking the name of Southern Baptist Historical Library and Archives.

Radio and Television Commission

By the 1920s Baptist churches saw the potential for broadcasting the gospel by the new medium of radio, or "wireless telephony" as some called it. One of the earliest churches to begin regular broadcasts was the First Baptist Church of Dallas. However, the equipment was primitive; members recalled that when the church began its broadcasts in 1921 a large metal salad bowl was set on the pulpit to help reflect the sound.[102]

A few state conventions sponsored broadcasts in the 1920s, as did the Home Mission Board, but the organized radio ministry of the SBC dates

---

100. *Annual,* SBC, 1983, p. 201.

101. Ibid., p. 331.

102. Leon McBeth, *The First Baptist Church of Dallas: Centennial History 1868-1968,* pp. 151-152.

from 1938. In that year the convention appointed a committee, chaired by Samuel F. Lowe, to survey the potential for gospel broadcasting, allotting two hundred dollars for expenses. The survey led to a standing Radio Committee (later called the Radio Commission), which operated on a volunteer basis until 1942 when Lowe became the first paid director.

In 1941 the Radio Committee launched a thirteen-week experimental series, called the "Baptist Hour." It has continued ever since as the flagship program of SBC radio ministry. After years of alternating preachers, Herschel H. Hobbs served eighteen years as the regular preacher on the "Baptist Hour." He was succeeded by Frank Pollard, who preached or used the time for interviews. The "Baptist Hour" is the only one of the main radio and television programs to bear the denomination's name.

Lowe served until his death in 1952. He was succeeded by Paul M. Stevens, who headed the work from 1953 to 1979. Jimmy R. Allen took the leadership in 1980. Stevens led the commission to relocate from Atlanta to Fort Worth in 1955 and to adopt the present name, Radio and Television Commission. By 1980 the commission sponsored seven major radio programs and four television productions, heard in ten languages on some three thousand radio and television stations across the country.[103] The first major non-English program, *"La Hora Bautista,"* began in 1958, followed later by *"Momentos de Meditacion."* Other programs are carried in Polish, Portuguese, Chinese, Filipino, Hungarian, Navajo, and others. Recently the commission launched a ministry called American Christian Television System, or ACTS, a cable system to provide Christian programming. In 1982, Cooperative Program receipts by the commission totaled $5,283,534.[104]

The Stewardship Commission

From the 1880s Southern Baptists had called for some systematic plan of raising and dispensing money for the various ministries of the denomination. Such a plan finally emerged from the Seventy-Five Million Campaign. The task of continuing stewardship promotion was committed first to the Conservation Committee and in 1929 to the fledgling Executive Committee. As a result of the Committee to Study the Total Denominational Program, the SBC in 1960 established the Stewardship Commission separate from the Executive Committee. The first secretary was Merrill D. Moore, who served 1960-1971. He was succeeded by James V. Lackey, 1971-1973; and A. R. Fagan, since 1974.

The Stewardship Commission was assigned responsibility for three areas of work: promotion of the Cooperative Program, the development of stewardship awareness and practice by Baptists, and guidance in endowment and capital fund raising. Through its own publications, and by channeling

---

103. Bonita Sparrow, "Radio and Television Commission, SBC," *ESB*, 4:2432.
104. *Annual*, SBC, 1983, p. 337.

emphases to others, the commission keeps before Southern Baptist people the financial needs of SBC ministries and the biblical emphasis upon stewardship and tithing. Stewardship awareness and per capita giving among Southern Baptists have shown impressive increases since mid-century. Total gifts to SBC churches exceeded $3 billion in 1982, with Cooperative Program gifts exceeding the quarter-billion mark. For its own work, the commission received $347,105 in Cooperative Program funds in 1982.[105]

Efforts to abolish the commission and return its tasks to the Executive Committee failed in 1972 and 1973. While continuing its other work, the commission has in recent years intensified its promotion of the Cooperative Program. In 1982 the commission distributed almost ten thousand copies of *The Cooperative Program at Work Around the World* and released a new film entitled *More than Money.*

Convention Committees

In addition to its Executive Committee, the SBC works through a number of other committees. These include standing committees on the Denominational Calendar and Order of Business, whose names explain their work. In addition, the convention somtimes appoints special committees to deal with issues that arise from time to time. Some committees relate to other Baptists, such as the one on the North American Baptist Fellowship, a regional affiliate of the Baptist World Alliance.

The Baptist Joint Committee on Public Affairs (BJCPA) represents a long-standing Baptist concern for safeguarding religious liberty. As early as 1769 the Warren Baptist Association in New England appointed a Grievance Committee to publicize religious persecution and petition the government for relief. Out of World War I, the SBC appointed a standing Committee on Chaplains and in 1936 changed its name to Committee on Public Relations and enlarged its task "to confer, to negotiate, to demand just rights that are threatened or to have other inescapable dealings with the American or others Governments."[106] In 1939 that committee teamed up with a like body from the Northern Baptist Convention, and by 1981 a total of nine Baptist groups in America worked through what was then called the Public Affairs Committee. The SBC funds about 80 percent of the committee's budget, which totaled $492,846 by 1983.[107] They also provide fifteen of the forty-five members of the committee's governing board.

To perform its assigned tasks, the Public Affairs Committee keeps a close eye on developments which might threaten religious liberty and the historic

105. Ibid., 1983, pp. 207, 342.
106. Cited by Walter Pope Binns, "Public Affairs Committee, Baptist Joint," *ESB*, 2:1123.
107. Presnall H. Wood, "The Role of Southern Baptists in Nation's Capital," *Baptist Standard*, February 8, 1984, p. 6.

Baptist emphasis upon separation of church and state. To that end, its members monitor legislation and court cases, testify before congressional committees, issue a monthly paper called *Report from the Capital,* conduct biennial national conferences on religious liberty, and sponsor an annual Religious Liberty Day in Baptist churches. The committee was led by Rufus W. Weaver in the 1930s; but after its expansion, executive secretaries have been Joseph M. Dawson, 1946-1953; C. Emmanuel Carlson, 1954-1971; James E. Wood, 1972-1980; and James M. Dunn, since 1981.

The work of this committee has proven controversial in recent years. The expansion of both government and church programs in education, health care, child care, and other areas means that church and state now interact at far more points than in the simpler days of our early history. The recent aggressiveness of government in intruding into church affairs has challenged the committee, which has also had to face the politicizing of American religion and the efforts of some groups to use government sanction to inculcate their own version of Christian values. The committee has spoken out on government-sponsored prayers in public schools; tuition tax credits and other forms of support for parochial schools; the taxing of churches; efforts in some states to ban clergy from public office; and other issues. In every case, the committee has sought to defend what its leaders regard as historic Baptist principles.

However, opposition has arisen because not all Baptists share the same understanding of religious liberty and separation of church and state nor place the same value upon them. Like the Christian Life Commission, the BJCPA has had to bear its witness in an increasingly pluralistic society. The new factor is that not even Baptists present the same united front they once did on subjects relating to religious liberty.

Woman's Missionary Union

Originating in 1888, the WMU is listed as *auxiliary* to the SBC. While the WMU elects its own trustees and officers, it is represented on the Inter-Agency Council and makes regular reports to the convention. Despite its legal auxiliary status, it relates to the SBC much the same as do the other agencies.

This missionary body has conducted a varied and vigorous ministry in the twentieth century. It was first headquartered in Baltimore for the simple reason that Annie Armstrong, its principal founder, lived there. However, desire for a more central location led the WMU to relocate its national offices in Birmingham in 1921. In almost a century of service, only five executive secretaries have led the union. They are Annie Armstrong, 1888-1906; Edith C. Crane, 1907-1912; Kathleen Mallory, 1912-1948; Alma Hunt, 1948-1974; and Carolyn Weatherford, since 1974.

Related Organizations

Early in the twentieth century, the WMU developed a full program of missionary training for all age groups. They adopted the Sunbeam Band for younger children in 1890 and in 1907 formed the Young Woman's Auxiliary (YWA) for girls over sixteen. Describing children aged twelve to sixteen as "the mission link," in 1908 the WMU formed the Junior Young Woman (in 1914 renamed Girls Auxiliary, or GA) and Royal Ambassadors (RA) for boys. In 1954 the union began the process of transferring the RA work to the Brotherhood.

The Margaret Fund

An initial gift of $10,000 in 1904 launched the Margaret Home in South Carolina, intended as a residence for children of missionaries attending school in this country. Later these resources were made available for scholarships, allowing students to attend schools elsewhere. In 1961 the administration of Margaret Fund scholarships was transferred to the mission boards.[108]

Missionary Training School

Lottie Moon, appointed to China in 1873, had excellent classical education but no specific theological training. While women could attend most Baptist colleges of the time, they could not attend the one SBC seminary. As early as 1902 a trustee committee of The Southern Baptist Theological Seminary in Louisville reported, "We find that there is a necessity, distinct and urgent, for such a school [of theological studies] for Southern Baptist women."[109] As a result, young women were admitted to seminary classes but did not recite or write exams and, upon completion, did not receive degrees. Even so, about thirty-five young women attended classes by 1905.

Eliza S. Broadus, whose father taught at the seminary, helped raise money for a dormitory for the women students. What began as a local project soon engaged the WMU throughout the South, and the initial effort to provide lodging resulted in formation of a separate school for women in Louisville, later named the Carver School of Missions and Social Work. This project failed to win the support of Annie Armstrong, providing one reason for her unhappy resignation in 1906. The school remained a WMU project until 1956, when the SBC began to elect its trustees; in 1962 it was merged into the seminary.

---

108. McBeth, *Women in Baptist Life,* pp. 126 *f.*
109. Cited in Barnes, p. 162.

The WMU and Stewardship

Perhaps in no area except missions has the WMU had a more formative influence upon Southern Baptists than in stewardship. Baptist women took the lead in making the offering a part of worship, when many men felt money should be raised by subscription outside the church. The women pioneered the idea of making regular weekly offerings, however small, when many men were content with two or three big offerings a year. Women adopted the practice, probably borrowed from the Methodist women, of placing their offerings in small envelopes, an idea which later caught on. In their publications, such as the *Baptist Basket* and the *Heathen Helper,* women emphasized tithing at a time when most of the men had either not heard of the practice or opposed it.

Baptist women supported the Seventy-Five Million Campaign whole-heartedly. They pledged about fifteen million dollars of the total and, unlike others, actually paid it; in fact, they gave a bit over sixteen million dollars. During the days of depression and debt in the late 1920s, the women shouldered their full share of debt retirement. At first the WMU voted to concentrate its efforts on paying off the debts of the Foreign Mission Board alone, but the impassioned plea of Louie D. Newton of Georgia persuaded them to distribute their relief among all SBC agencies. That marks a major turning point in the history of the WMU. From its earliest days, it had primarily supported foreign missions, but since that debt retirement decision, the WMU has steadfastly supported the total SBC mission program.

Reports to the Convention

At an early WMU meeting a woman said indignantly, "This is a Woman's Missionary Union, and there is no need for gentlemen to frame our resolutions."[110] Despite the fervent amen of several sisters present, men did read WMU reports to the convention for the first forty years of the union's existence. The WMU president, Mrs. W. J. Cox, was invited to give the report for 1929. A number of men objected and introduced a resolution that "we earnestly protest the president of the W.M.U. or any other woman addressing this Convention."[111] It appeared Mrs. Cox might not be allowed to speak, but the convention president, George W. Truett, said firmly, "Brethren, let us hear the gentlewoman." Truett's powerful personality carried the day, but even so some men walked out. In addition to her report, Mrs. Cox could not refrain from ad-libbing, "No woman went to sleep in the garden. No woman denied Him. No woman betrayed Him. But it was a woman, acting in intuition, who tried to save Him."[112]

---

110. Cited in Alma Hunt, *History of Woman's Missionary Union,* p. 49.
111. *Annual,* SBC, 1929, p. 102.
112. Cited in McBeth, *Women in Baptist Life,* p. 120.

Even so, it was not until 1938 that women regularly gave the WMU report. When the convention met in churches, it was customary to adjourn from the sanctuary and reassemble in a Sunday School hall for the WMU report. This was a precaution against the possibility that in giving the WMU report, a woman might stand in a pulpit.

Changes in WMU

No organization abides unchanged for a century; it should not be surprising that WMU has changed since 1888. The WMU has tried to keep its programs and emphases current, all the while holding firmly to its original purpose. In addition to minor changes, the WMU has reflected a new social awareness on women's rights in recent years. The national president, Christine Gregory, said in 1975, "If a woman feels she is called to be a pastor, this is between her and God, and it should not be our prerogative to deny her."[113] In recent years, the WMU has seemed less "domestic;" it has made common cause, in moderate tones, with women's rights issues. The employment of women outside the home has, of course, played havoc with daytime meetings of the traditional "circles." In 1957 the WMU launched a program of night circles for employed women.

A recent report states that the objective of Women's Missionary Union "is to promote Christian missions . . . in churches of the Southern Baptist Convention."[114] The sharp focus of this purpose and unswerving allegiance to it for almost a century help explain the effectiveness and impact of this organization. To this one end, its many conferences, nine periodicals, annual programs at the conference centers, and other literature lend support.

Enrollment in all WMU organizations stood at 1,149,266 in 1982, down substantially from the all-time high of 1,509,484 in 1964.[115] The decline may be attributed to several factors. Most importantly, the employment of women has reduced their discretionary time. For some young women, the traditional WMU study fare and activities have seemed tame, a condition the WMU has moved to correct. Enrollment in the children's mission groups, included in this total, has faced competition not only from secular groups like Brownies and Camp Fire Girls but also from mushrooming enrollments in the graded choir programs.

Despite these problems, the WMU must be ranked as one of the most successful organizations among Southern Baptists. The declining enrollments, one might argue, are one mark of its success. Whereas mission study was once largely limited to the WMU and its related groups, now it permeates the entire church. From tiny amounts, largely from women's butter and egg money, the Lottie Moon and Annie Armstrong mission offerings now

---

113. Quoted from the *Rocky Mountain Baptist*, June 27, 1975, p. 1.
114. *Annual*, SBC, 1983, p. 219.
115. See statistical reports in *Quarterly Review*, July 1983, pp. 70-71.

enlist the efforts of the entire church membership, raising between them about eighty million dollars a year for missions. In funds and personnel, to say nothing of spiritual commitment, Southern Baptists must be ranked as the most intensely missionary denomination among modern Protestants. The Woman's Missionary Union has probably contributed more to that development than any other SBC organization.

Theological Education

From 1845 to 1950 the Southern Baptist Convention itself established no seminaries but adopted four that had been founded by various Southern Baptist groups. Since 1950 the convention has established two additional seminaries, for a total of six. These schools are as follows, with location, date of origin, and total regular enrollment for the school year 1982-1983.[116]

The Southern Baptist Theological Seminary	Louisville, KY	1859	2,976
Southwestern Baptist Theological Seminary	Fort Worth, TX	1908	4,865
New Orleans Baptist Theological Seminary	New Orleans, LA	1917	2,062
Golden Gate Baptist Theological Seminary	Mill Valley, CA	1944	1,457
Southeastern Baptist Theological Seminary	Wake Forest, NC	1951	1,488
Midwestern Baptist Theological Seminary	Kansas City, MO	1957	809

Overview

The rapid growth of these schools reflects the numerical and geographical expansion of Southern Baptists in the twentieth century. The mushrooming enrollment grows, to some extent, out of the resurgence of evangelical religion in America and specifically out of spiritual awakenings since World War II. All of the schools are accredited by the Association of Theological Schools and most by their regional university accreditation associations as well.

The proliferation of ministries in Christian education, music, childhood religious education, business administration, and other areas prompted the seminaries to offer training in these diverse fields. The pastor's changing role has called for training not only in the classical theological disciplines

116. Enrollment figures as reported in *Annual,* SBC, 1983, p. 196.

but also in such areas as counseling, preaching on radio and television, and church management.

These seminaries also reflect, and have helped to cause, a rising educational standard among Southern Baptist ministers, which, of course, corresponds to similar rising standards in the society generally. The earlier hostility to ministerial training is largely a relic of the past. A study in 1982 showed that about 45 percent of Southern Baptist pastors held seminary degrees, up from about 36 percent a decade earlier.[117] In 1973 72 percent of college-trained pastors had attended Baptist colleges; by 1983 that had declined to 52 percent. However, of those who had attended any seminary, 94 percent had chosen one sponsored by the SBC.

Another emphasis in the seminaries has been the spiritual as well as academic formation of future ministers. Of course, spiritual formation has always been done, but it has received renewed emphasis in recent years, with special programs, courses, and endowed chairs. Studies have emphasized the disciplines of prayer, personal worship, personal Bible reading, meditation, and other devotional practices. The seminaries have struggled, however, to avoid the implication that any one style of spirituality is the only one viable for Southern Baptists.

Since each church calls its own pastor, the seminaries have not developed until recently any formal efforts at placing their graduates. Informal networks of recommendations have operated for years, but in the past decade most seminaries have established offices to help churches and graduates find each other. Most eschew the term *placement*, preferring such terms as *church relations*. Several state conventions have established similar offices, and some think a measure of order may yet emerge from the chaos of ministerial movement among Southern Baptists.

The cost of operating schools, including seminaries, has escalated dramatically. The six SBC seminaries have about $150 million of endowment, divided unequally among them, and thus depend upon the direct support of the denomination. The third largest Cooperative Program allotment, after the mission boards, goes to the seminaries. Even so, direct denominational funds make up a declining percentage of seminary costs, a trend with long-term concern for those who believe that a denomination is best served by schools it supports and controls.

Tensions between the seminaries and the churches have surfaced from time to time. Accusations of teaching "liberalism," a term rarely defined, have been lodged against individual professors and sometimes entire seminaries. Perhaps some professors, though sound in basic theology, have

117. From a questionnaire survey conducted in 1973 by the Home Mission Board. The earlier results are reported in Don F. Mabry and Paul W. Stewart, "A Study of the Educational Attainment of Southern Baptist Pastor," unpublished paper, 1973. The 1982 data is reported in the Statistical Section, Table 3, *Quarterly Review* (April 1984), p. 47.

aggravated these suspicions by incautious terms and "shock-methods" of teaching and preaching. All faculty members in SBC seminaries sign some confessional statement, most of them *The Baptist Faith and Message* adopted in 1963. Faculty at Louisville sign the Abstract of Principles, which dates from 1859, as do faculty at Wake Forest. For years the New Orleans seminary had its own Articles of Religious Belief, but its faculty also affirms *The Baptist Faith and Message.*

The Southern Baptist Theological Seminary (SBTS)

The oldest SBC seminary was founded in 1859 in Greenville and moved in 1877 to Louisville. In 1926 the school moved from downtown to its new campus, known as The Beeches, on Lexington Road. This school has pioneered in a number of areas, including establishment of a department of missions led by William Owen Carver in 1901 and a chair of Sunday School pedagogy founded in 1906 in cooperation with the Sunday School Board. To its theological studies it added a School of Church Music in 1943 and a School of Religious Education in 1952. The James P. Boyce Library was opened in 1959 as part of the school's centennial celebration. Presidents in this century have been Edgar Y. Mullins, 1899-1928; John R. Sampey, 1929-1942; Ellis A. Fuller, 1942-1950; Duke K. McCall, 1952-1981; and Roy L. Honeycutt, since 1981. Every president until Fuller also served as a professor.

In the twentieth century, the seminary has drawn closer to the SBC, thus modifying the society basis of its origin. The convention now elects trustees, allots funding, and sustains basically the same relation to SBTS as to its other institutions.

Occasional periods of turbulence have troubled the seminary. It entered the present century still smarting from the forced resignation of President William H. Whitsitt in 1898. An internal controversy erupted in 1957, which led to the firing of thirteen professors in 1958. Not all agree on the roots of that problem. One historian close to the situation wrote, "A complicated combination of academic and administrative changes generated unrest in the faculty of the School of Theology and prepared conditions for a major rift."[118] Some attribute the conflict to fears that the classical theological disciplines would be diminished by increased attention to skill-oriented studies. Others viewed it as a reaction to leadership styles of the president or as part of the shift from a "chairman of the faculty" to a "president" leadership structure.

In 1982 a senior professor, Dale Moody, came under criticism for views

---

118. Glenn Hinson, "Southern Baptist Theological Seminary," *ESB,* 3:1978. For more information about Southern Seminary see also William A. Mueller, *A History of Southern Baptist Theological Seminary* and *Review and Expositor* (Fall 1984), which includes several articles on the history of this school.

expressed in his book, *The Word of Truth.*[119] In this book Moody affirmed views, which he was said to have taught for years, which seemed to conflict with the Abstract of Principles, particularly on the subject of apostasy. The controversy swirled not only around the doctrine itself but also around the issue of a professor signing the Abstract, which Moody had done, and then allegedly teaching contrary to it. Moody was beyond normal retirement age when the controversy heightened. He was eligible to teach two more years on annual contracts, but those contracts were not renewed.

Southwestern Baptist Theological Seminary (SWBTS)

Southern Baptists established another seminary in 1908, locating it in Fort Worth, Texas. It was sponsored primarily by the Baptist General Convention of Texas, with some aid from neighboring states, until 1925 when it, along with the Baptist Bible Institute in New Orleans, was adopted by the SBC. Southwestern originated out of the Theological Department of Baylor University, much as Southern had come out of Furman a half-century earlier. Six presidents have led the school: B. H. Carroll, 1908-1914; Lee R. Scarborough, 1914-1942; E. D. Head, 1942-1953; J. Howard Williams, 1953-1958; Robert E. Naylor, 1958-1978; and Russell H. Dilday, Jr., since 1978.

More was said than done about ministerial education among early Texas Baptists. Most early preachers did without formal training, though one purpose for the founding of Baylor University at Independence, in the Republic of Texas, in 1845 was to provide ministerial education, and a few young men improved their talents there. However, the real pioneers in ministerial education in Texas, and indeed the Southwest, were the Carroll brothers, Benajah Harvey (1843-1914) and James Milton (1852-1931). As pastor of the First Baptist Church of Waco, B. H. Carroll taught a number of young ministers in his church, in his home, and later in the merged Baylor University at Waco. As a trustee at Baylor, Carroll introduced Bible and other religious studies on the Waco campus, later elevating this to a Theological Department in 1901.[120] S. P. Brooks, president of Baylor, resisted expansion of that department.

In the spring of 1905 on a train near Amarillo, Carroll was seized by a sudden clear idea: Texas needed a theological seminary and God was calling him to establish one. In recounting this experience, Carroll later said:

> I fell to musing. . . . there arose before me a vision of our Baptist situation in the Southwest. I saw multitudes of our preachers with very limited education, with few books and with small skill in using to the best advantage even the books they had. . . . I saw here in the Southwest many institutions for the

119. Dale Moody, *The Word of Truth* (Grand Rapids: Eermans Publishing Co., 1981).
120. Robert A. Baker, *Tell the Generations Following: A History of Southwestern Baptist Theological Seminary 1908-1983* (Nashville: Broadman Press, 1983), p. 115.

professional training of the young teacher, the young lawyer, the young doctor, the young nurse and the young farmer, but not a single institution dedicated to the specific training of the young Baptist preacher. . . . from that hour I knew . . . that God would plant a great school here in the Southwest for the training of our young Baptist preachers.[121]

As a result of that vision, Carroll led in forming Baylor Theological Seminary in 1905. Tensions between the seminary and university made separation necessary; on March 14, 1908, the seminary was chartered as a separate school and took its present name. Two years later it moved to Fort Worth. Perhaps the two men whom Carroll admired most were John A. Broadus, long-time professor and later president of Southern Seminary in Louisville, and Charles H. Spurgeon, famed London pastor and founder of Spurgeon's College. Apparently Carroll took concepts from both in molding the new seminary of the Southwest.

At least three major motives for the founding of Southwestern Baptist Theological Seminary may be noted. First, the spiritual needs of the Southwest called for more and better trained ministers. Second, the distance to Louisville made it next to impossible for that school to serve the needs of the growing Southwest. Besides, as Carroll and others noted repeatedly, young men who went from the Southwest to the Louisville school usually accepted pastorates there and never returned to Texas. A third motive, no doubt, was lingering dissatisfaction over the "Whitsitt Controversy" at Southern. As a trustee of that seminary, Carroll was among those who eventually called for Whitsitt's removal, though he apparently never adopted the doctrinaire Landmark view of Baptist origins which fascinated his younger brother, J. M. Carroll.[122]

Southwestern Seminary pioneered in several areas, including religious education, church music, education for women, and in practical studies in evangelism. From 1910 a course or two in Sunday School work was offered; but in 1915 a Department of Religious Education was formed, with J. M. Price added to the faculty in that area. A young woman graduated in 1917 with a degree in religious education, the first-known degree in that field. In 1921 that department was organized into a separate School of Religious Education, the first such school in America. Also in 1915, I. E. Reynolds joined the faculty to head the new Department of Gospel Music, later organized as the School of Church Music.

From the first, women have been eligible for every degree program at Southwestern, though this may not have been the intention of its founders. From 1908 women attended all classes but received diplomas from the

---

121. Ibid., pp. 24-25.
122. See J. M. Carroll, *The Trail of Blood: Or the History of Baptist Churches from the Time of Christ their Founder to the Present Day* (Lexington, Kentucky: Ashland Avenue Baptist Church, n.d., but first printed in the 1920s).

Woman's Missionary Training School. Not until 1914 did a woman apply for a degree from the seminary. Attorneys who examined the charter noted that Southwestern was authorized to confer degrees "upon any pupil of said Seminary" and ruled that women were included.

In 1915 Lee R. Scarborough, an evangelistic pastor from Abilene who had just been elected president of Southwestern, led the trustees to set up "a department of field evangelism," including students who would both study and serve as field evangelists. The purpose of this work, Scarborough said, was to "tie the gospel onto the work of educating the ministry, winning souls, and otherwise building the kingdom of God."[123] The Department of Evangelism was popularly known as the "Chair of Fire" and has remained a consistent emphasis of the seminary through the years.

Perhaps the most serious controversy Southwestern has faced grew out of the attacks of J. Frank Norris, pastor of First Baptist Church in Fort Worth from 1909 until his death in 1952. A friend of B. H. Carroll, Norris helped sever the seminary from Baylor and was a major factor in its move to Fort Worth, when most people thought it would go to Dallas. However, when Norris became more flamboyant in style and controversial in manner, attacking Texas Baptists on many issues, he broke with Southwestern and became its bitterest foe. Some thought Norris's bitterness stemmed, in part at least, from disappointment at not being chosen Carroll's successor in 1914. For over thirty years, Norris attacked the seminary, seeking to divert students and funds from it to his own school. In his latter years, Norris provided more harassment than real danger.

The campus has grown from just one building in 1910. The most recent building constructed was the A. Webb Roberts Library, with a computerized card catalog and reference center.

New Orleans Baptist Theological Seminary (NOBTS)

Southern Baptist interest in New Orleans goes far back; efforts to provide home missionaries in that area spotlighted the tensions that eventually led to the Baptist division of 1845. After the turn of the century, suggestions surfaced from time to time for a Baptist training center there, and in 1917 the Baptist Bible Institute opened. That school was adopted by the SBC in 1925 and in 1946 changed to its present name and soon thereafter moved to its impressive new campus on Gentilly Boulevard.

Two factors commended New Orleans as a suitable site for a seminary. The mushrooming Baptist growth in the Mississippi Valley called for an ever-increasing supply of ministers and trained home missionaries. Second, the rapid expansion of SBC mission work in the Latin countries made New Orleans seem a logical place not only for training missionaries but also for their embarkation.

123. Baker, *Tell the Generations*, p. 207.

Though expressed somewhat differently from similar sentiments at Southwestern, the New Orleans school also probably embodied a protest against the Whitsitt emphasis at Louisville. John T. Christian, then a pastor in Louisville, was among those who strongly opposed Whitsitt's views. He later became a distinguished professor at New Orleans; his two-volume work, *A History of the Baptists,* provides the most scholarly twentieth-century exposition of the successionist view of Baptist origins.[124]

Presidents who have led the New Orleans school include: B. H. DeMent, 1917-1927; W. W. Hamilton, 1927-1942; Duke K. McCall, 1943-1946; Roland Q. Leavell, 1946-1958; H. Leo Eddleman, 1959-1970; Grady C. Cothen, 1971-1974; and Landrum P. Leavell, since 1975.

Like other SBC seminaries, the NOBTS was for years organized around a trilogy of separate schools of theology, religious education, and church music. In 1972 the school reversed that trend and moved toward school unification by organizing their work around five departments: biblical studies, theological and historical studies, pastoral ministry studies, religious education studies, and church music ministries.[125]

Golden Gate Baptist Theological Seminary (GGBTS)

Southern Baptist presence in California, which diminished after the Civil War, grew rapidly after the 1942 decision affiliating churches in that state with the SBC. Isam B. Hodges became pastor of the Golden Gate Baptist Church of Oakland in 1937 and in 1944 was serving as president of the infant state convention of Southern Baptists in California. By that time, he had a vision of great Baptist growth in the West and conceived the idea that a theological training center could be an important part of that advance. He enlisted the help of Dallas G. Faulkner, pastor of the First Southern Baptist Church of San Francisco. Both men held degrees from SBC seminaries. Hodges established the Golden Gate Baptist Theological Seminary in 1944, with seven students attending classes meeting in his church. At first only the two churches elected trustees, but later the Golden Gate Baptist Association voted to lend "prayerful and moral support" and elected six additional trustees; and five years later, in 1950, the GGBTS was adopted by the SBC.

Presidents include Isam B. Hodges, 1944-1946; B. O. Herring, 1946-1951; Harold K. Graves, 1951-1977; William M. Pinson, Jr., 1977-1981; and Franklin D. Pollard, 1983-1986. In 1959 the seminary occupied its beautiful campus on Strawberry Point in Marin County, with its spectacular view of the city across San Francisco Bay. Mission preparation, particularly for the Asian countries, the education of church workers from the

124. John T. Christian, *A History of the Baptists* (Nashville: Sunday School Board of the Southern Baptist Convention, 1922).

125. Claude L. Howe, Jr., "New Orleans Baptist Theological Seminary," *ESB,* 1:568.

mission fields, and pioneering work in urban evangelism have marked the West Coast seminary.[126]

Southeastern Baptist Theological Seminary (SEBTS)

The removal of Southern Seminary to Louisville in 1877 left the Southeast, the historic center of Southern Baptist strength, without a theological seminary, a loss felt keenly by Baptists in that area. Despite westward expansion, as late as 1950 perhaps one-third of Southern Baptists still resided in the Southeast. Suggestions for a seminary in that area surfaced from time to time but caught hold in 1947 when the SBC authorized a study to determine the need for additional seminaries. As a result, the convention voted to establish two new seminaries as soon as possible, one in the West and one in the East. The adoption of Golden Gate in 1950 seemed to satisfy the need in the West.

In 1951 the Southeastern Baptist Theological Seminary was officially begun, though the convention had authorized it the year before. Fortunately, the move of Wake Forest University to a larger campus made available the old campus in Wake Forest, North Carolina, which was purchased for the new seminary. It has since acquired adjacent lands, making a most attractive and convenient location. In many ways, one might say, the SEBTS was established on the model of Southern Seminary. Its earlier presidents and many of its faculty were Southern graduates, and its curriculum and degree programs tended to pattern those of the older school. Three presidents have served the school, including Sydnor L. Stealey, 1951-1963; Olin T. Binkley, 1963-1974; and W. Randall Lolley, since 1974.

Midwestern Baptist Theological Seminary (MWBTS)

A feeling persisted in the 1950s that Southern Baptists should establish a seminary to provide leadership for their multiplying churches in the North, with Denver, Chicago, and Topeka leading contenders for such a school. After a series of studies dating from 1954, the SBC voted in 1957 to establish the Midwestern Baptist Theological Seminary and, over serious objections, located it at Kansas City, Missouri. Its two presidents have been Millard J. Berquist, 1958-1973; and Milton U. Ferguson, since 1973.

The convention placed restrictions upon the new seminary, forbidding it, for example, to divide into separate schools of theology, religious education, and church music. The convention's preference for one school instead of three expressed no opposition to studies in those areas, but a structural preference for one united school.

Midwestern Seminary opened in 1958 and the next year moved to its spacious campus on rolling hills in north Kansas City. It began with distinct advantages: an impressive campus, though yet undeveloped; a competent

126. William A. Carlton, "Golden Gate Baptist Theological Seminary," *ESB*, 1:568.

and veteran faculty; and a location within access of the heart of Baptist strength in the Midwest. Two shadows, however, clouded its early history: the unfortunate tensions with the Central Baptist Theological Seminary, located in Kansas City since 1901; and the doctrinal crisis which led to the dismissal of Professor Ralph H. Elliott in 1962.

The Kansas City Seminary (later renamed Central) was founded in 1901 largely to provide a theological counterbalance to the University of Chicago, to emphasize training for ministry as well as academics, and to provide pastors for Baptist churches in the Midwest. From the first the school served both Northern and Southern Baptists, drawing students and funds from both groups. Many felt that Northern and Southern conventions might continue to cooperate in this school. However, in the expansive 1950s the SBC voted that it would not support any school whose trustees it did not elect, a policy which, incidentally, also called for adjustments in the Southern Seminary and the Carver School of Missions and Social Work.

In 1956 officials of Central Seminary invited the SBC committee studying a new seminary to visit their campus and discuss bases of possible cooperation. The proposed cooperation failed, and three months later the American Board of Education and Publication recommended that "Central Seminary align itself definitely and positively with the American Baptist Convention" and that henceforth "the entire membership of the Board of Directors be composed of members of American Baptist churches."[127] Several Southern Baptist trustees and teachers resigned, and many Southern Baptist students withdrew. The full story is, of course, more involved. The resulting tension no doubt damaged Midwestern's relationship to area churches. Some observed that many of those agitating the "Elliott Controversy" in the early 1960s were disaffected Baptists sympathetic with Central.

The most serious crisis facing the new seminary was the controversy surrounding Ralph H. Elliott. The popular young professor of Old Testament issued his first major book in 1961, *The Message of Genesis.* Within weeks a fierce controversy raged over viewpoints expressed therein, covering the pages of Baptist papers and dominating the 1962 meeting of the SBC in San Francisco. After several times reaffirming confidence in Elliott and in the historical-grammatical method of biblical study, the trustees of Midwestern voted to dismiss him in late 1962. Elliott was not fired for heresy, indeed was never officially charged with doctrinal deviation. The chairman of the board of trustees that dismissed him said, "The breakdown did not come in the theological area."[128] Elliott declined to agree to a request of the seminary president and a trustee subcommittee that he not submit the book to another publisher, a request Elliott said he would honor

---

127. G. Hugh Wamble, "Midwestern Baptist Theological Seminary," *ESB,* 3:1840.

128. See Leon McBeth, "Fundamentalism in the Southern Baptist Convention in Recent Years," *Review and Expositor,* p. 89.

if it came from the full board. Elliott's dismissal tended to bring suspicion upon all the seminaries.

Extension Studies

For those who want to engage in theological studies but cannot enroll in a seminary, the Seminary External Education Division (SEED) administers two programs. Basic or college level studies are available through home study by correspondence or in extension classes at several hundred locations. Degree level classes are offered at a dozen or more cities, taught by regular seminary faculty who commute. Most are operated and staffed jointly, but a number are sponsored by individual seminaries.

Other Schools

In the early 1980s the convention considered establishing a seventh seminary but declined on the ground that present schools adquately meet the needs. However, there are a number of other schools, mostly supported by Southern Baptists and some bearing the Baptist name, whose graduates seek places of service in Southern Baptist churches. Most of these schools represent ultraconservative theology, and some tension grows out of the fact that they appeal directly to churches for financial aid, while the SBC seminaries cannot.

Theological Developments

Southern Baptists have not been known for their contributions in the field of theology. They have been more active than contemplative; they have produced more doers than thinkers. However, they have produced a number of recognized scholars in various fields, whom one hesitates to list lest a favorite name be excluded. Walter B. Shurden has shown that for the most part pastors, not theologians, have shaped Southern Baptist doctrinal views. For about a century, Shurden argued, from the founding of Southern Seminary to the "Elliott Controversy," Baptist professors and theologians exercised a more determining influence; thereafter pastors resumed their role as doctrinal shapers.[129] The course of Southern Baptist theology may be traced through the work of writing theologians, influential pastors, confessions of faith, and doctrinal controversies.

Writing Theologians

Southern Baptists can list at least five writing theologians who produced systematic theologies.[130] Two wrote in the nineteenth century, and three

129. Walter B. Shurden, "The Pastor as Denominational Theologian," *Baptist History and Heritage*, pp. 15 f. This entire issue explores the theme "Southern Baptist Theologians."

130. Others could be included, depending upon how "systematic theology" is defined. Some argue, for example, for the inclusion of J. R. Graves (1829-1893) who wrote on theology and Carl F. F. Henry, who though a Baptist, has not been closely identified with the SBC.

so far in the twentieth. Their names and major books are: John L. Dagg (1794-1884), *Manual of Theology,* 1858; James P. Boyce (1794-1888), *Abstract of Systematic Theology,* privately printed in 1882, republished in 1899; Edgar Y. Mullins (1860-1928), *The Christian Religion in Its Doctrinal Expression,* 1917; Walter T. Conner (1877-1952), *A System of Christian Doctrine,* 1924; and Dale Moody (1915-   ), *The Word of Truth: A Summary of Christian Doctrine Based on Biblical Revelation,* 1981. Most have gone through several printings, and many of the authors also wrote other books.

Both Dagg and Boyce attended Princeton Theological Seminary, where they came under the influence of Charles Hodge and the "Princeton Theology" generally, including Calvinism and biblical views stemming from Francis Turretin and the Scottish school of theology/philosophy. Mullins modified those views somewhat, giving less emphasis to Princeton rationalism and more to the message of Scripture and the importance of Christian experience. While affirming the full inspiration of the Bible, Mullins preferred a dynamic understanding of inspiration which emphasized its message and magnified the *result* of inspiration more than its *process.*[131] Conner studied with Mullins at Southern and with Augustus H. Strong at the Rochester Theological Seminary. He also studied at the University of Chicago. Known as the "theologian of the Southwest," Conner emphasized Scripture but avoided extremist theories of inspiration. Moody, the latest Southern Baptist to produce a systematic theology, shows the influence not only of Baptist theologians but also of modern theologians of America and Europe.

Pastor-Theologians

Several pastor-theologians have greatly influenced Southern Baptists through their preaching, published sermons, and other publications on theological subjects. Some of the most formative of these include Richard Furman (1755-1825); Basil Manly, Sr. (1798-1868); W. B. Johnson (1782-1862); and J. R. Graves (1820-1893) in the nineteenth century. B. H. Carroll (1843-1914) spanned the centuries and proved one of the most influential thinkers, as well as doers, of his day. In the twentieth century, Southern Baptists have been deeply influenced by such pastors as George W. Truett (1867-1944); M. E. Dodd (1878-1952); and Robert G. Lee (1886-1978). Of several living pastors, surely future historians must take account of Herschel H. Hobbs (1907-   ) and W. A. Criswell (1910-   ), among others.

---

131. E. Y. Mullins, *The Christian Religion in Its Doctrinal Expression* (Nashville: The Sunday School Board of the Southern Baptist Convention, 1917), p. 144. See also Russell H. Dilday, Jr., *The Doctrine of Biblical Authority,* pp. 108-112.

Confessions of Faith

One clue to Baptists' theology is found in their various confessions of faith. These have usually been hammered out on the anvil of some doctrinal dispute. They express consensus and, thus, rarely satisfy extreme partisans on either side. The SBC has spoken a number of times on doctrinal issues, and some of its boards and agencies have done the same. However, the convention itself has adopted only two confessions of faith, in 1925 and again in 1963. Before that time Baptist churches in the South usually adhered to the Philadelphia Confession of 1742, which became the basis for Baptist unification in the South in the 1780s. As that confession receded, Baptists often gave adherence to the New Hampshire Confession, which originated in 1833 and blanketed the South through the work of the Northern Baptist Publication Society.

In 1925 at Memphis, the SBC adopted its first formal confession of faith. Though often called "the Memphis Articles," the confession took the name of *The Baptist Faith and Message.* Two developments led to this confession, one external and one internal. After World War I Southern Baptists, along with others, sought to reestablish communication with the Baptists of Europe. A resolution at the SBC in 1919 called for a committee, chaired by E. Y. Mullins, to prepare a paper to extend "Fraternal Greetings to the Baptists of the World."[132] The report in 1920 took the form of a doctrinal summary, addressed "To Those of 'Like Precious Faith with Us' Scattered Abroad, Beloved in the Lord."[133] Citing a need to reaffirm Baptist principles and practices, the fraternal address was intended not as a complete confession of faith, but a summary of "the things which Southern Baptists believe and practice." The report attracted favorable attention and doubtlessly helped create a climate favorable to the production of a more complete confession later.

The chief internal provocation to frame the 1925 confession was the attacks of J. Frank Norris of Fort Worth, the primary leader of the Southern wing of the Fundamentalist movement. From his pulpit at Fort Worth's First Baptist Church, Norris attacked Southern Baptists for allegedly teaching biological evolution in their colleges, tolerating "modernistic" views of Scripture in their seminaries, and making an idol of the denomination in their churches. At one time a staunch SBC loyalist, Norris broke further with the denomination over the Seventy-Five Million Campaign and spent the rest of his days seeking to undercut the convention and its work. He was eventually excluded from SBC life and formed an independent fundamentalist denomination of his own, remnants of which remain.

132. *Annual,* SBC, 1919, p. 84.
133. Cited in James E. Carter, "The Southern Baptist Convention and Confessions of Faith, 1845-1945," p. 94.

The attacks of Norris attracted wide attention, and partly as a result the SBC voted in 1924 to issue a more complete doctrinal statement. The committee which drew up the confession of 1925 was chaired by E. Y. Mullins and included L. R. Scarborough, C. P. Stealey, W. J. McGlothlin, S. M. Brown, E. C. Dargan, and R. H. Pitt. They used the New Hampshire Confession as their basic framework, adding several articles on practical aspects of the faith, such as religious liberty, evangelism, and Baptist cooperation.

The 1925 confession included no specific article on evolution, and efforts at the convention to add one failed of adoption. Some controversy on that point lingered. At the 1926 convention in his presidential message, George W. McDaniel included a paragraph saying, "This Convention accepts Genesis as teaching that man was a special creation of God and rejects every theory, evolutionary or otherwise, which teaches that man originated in or came by way of lower animal ancestry." The convention immediately adopted this as expressing its view, but it was never officially added to the confession. [134]

The 1925 confession came in an era of renewed Baptist interest in doctrinal statements. In 1922 the Northern Baptist Convention had debated confessionalism and voted not to adopt the New Hampshire Confession. In 1920 the Foreign Mission Board drew up a thirteen-point doctrinal statement to be signed by all its missionaries. Some had advocated in the early 1920s that Northern and Southern Baptists issue a joint statement of faith. At its 1923 meeting in Stockholm, the Baptist World Alliance had issued a doctrinal statement. Baptists of the time were showing a keen interest in publishing their faith to the world.

Somewhat surprisingly, the SBC confession was greeted by almost total silence; what comments were made were favorable. One Southern Baptist leader observed, "We have next to no objections to a statement of our faith set forth by the Southern Baptist Convention. We have felt that there was no great call for such an utterance." [135] That was also the view of E. Y. Mullins, chairman of the committee, who said:

> I do not think the present situation calls for a doctrinal statement, and I am very thoroughly convinced that too much of this sort of thing is very dangerous. The Convention has declared itself most emphatically in recent years and on every vital point. [136]

A number of Baptists warned that adopting such a confession would become a first step on the road to creedalism. They also feared it might turn

134. *Annual,* SBC, 1926, pp. 18, 98.
135. Z. T. Cody, "Issuing a Declaration of Faith," *The Baptist Courier* (October 30, 1924), p. 2; cited in Carter, pp. 114-115.
136. Carter, p. 115.

Baptist attention away from Scripture to human doctrinal statements. Subsequent developments show these fears were not entirely groundless.

The controversy surrounding Ralph H. Elliott, a professor dismissed in late 1962 from the Midwestern Baptist Theological Seminary, provided the occasion for the second major SBC confession. At its 1962 meeting in San Francisco, the SBC debated issues raised by Elliott's book, rejected a motion to ban the book, and adopted resolutions declaring the entire Bible to be the inspired Word of God.[137] The convention also authorized a committee, composed of the presidents of affiliated state conventions of that time and chaired by SBC president Herschel H. Hobbs, to draw up a confessional statement for consideration in 1963. As a result *The Baptist Faith and Message* was adopted at Kansas City in 1963, with a preamble designed to prevent it from becoming a binding creed.

Like the 1925 statement, that of 1963 followed basically the New Hampshire framework. By combining some articles, the 1963 statement reduced the 1925 confession from twenty-five to seventeen articles, modified the earlier Landmark view of the church, and clarified the article on Scripture. Adopted to provide theological guidelines, many have regarded this as a binding declaration of Southern Baptist faith.

Doctrinal Controversies

From their earliest history Baptists have been a contentious lot, a tradition amply upheld by the Southern Baptist portion of the family. The SBC originated in a divisive controversy over slavery, and for the rest of the nineteenth century engaged in external disputes with Northern Baptists over territory, and internal controversies with J. R. Graves (Landmarkism), Crawford H. Toy (biblical inspiration), T. P. Crawford (gospel missionism), and William H. Whitsitt (Baptist origins). It is not surprising, therefore, that several major controversies should mark Southern Baptists in the twentieth century. At least four such controversies, or four phases of one controversy as some prefer, may be noted here. The basic issue has been the nature of the biblical revelation, and it surfaced as early as the 1870s around the teachings of Crawford H. Toy of Southern Seminary in Louisville. Such issues as the documentary hypothesis of Old Testament origins; efforts to harmonize biological evolution with biblical creation; whether the Bible speaks infallibly only in matters of faith and practice or also in details of science, history, and geography; doctrines of millennialism; and which theory of inspiration best explains the origin of Scripture have been at issue.

In the 1920s these issues first resurfaced after a generation of relative quiet. J. Frank Norris of Fort Worth led the attack, alleging that Southern Baptists had accepted "modernistic" teachings on Scripture, evolution, and the church. Norris was also perturbed that Southern Baptists would not

137. *Annual,* SBC, 1962, pp. 64, 68, 72, 73.

accept his own strict views of premillennial eschatology. As the controversy progressed, the intemperate attacks of Norris alienated many. The Seventy-Five Million Campaign, despite failure to reach its financial goals, greatly enhanced denominational solidarity, and the confession of 1925 tended to turn attention away from doctrinal concerns. During the late 1920s and 1930s, Southern Baptists gave more attention to survival than to doctrinal debate.

A second phase of the biblical controversy arose with publication of *The Message of Genesis* in 1961. Described as a "theological interpretation," Ralph H. Elliott's volume advanced what some considered unacceptable views of inspiration. Opposition was immediate and severe. K. Owen White, pastor of First Baptist Church of Houston, initiated the debate in his militant article, "Death in the Pot," which was printed in a number of Baptist papers. White cited selected statements from the book, concluding, "The book from which I have quoted is liberalism, pure and simple. . . . The book in question is poison."[138]

At first the Sunday School Board defended its right to publish books with differing views but later agreed not to publish a second edition. For over a year the Midwestern trustees defended Elliott; but in late 1962, they yielded to mounting pressures to dismiss him. The capitulation of the Sunday School Board and the Midwestern trustees represented a victory for ultraconservative forces in the SBC, and no doubt encouraged them to continue their agitation.

A senior Baptist editor wrote, "Elliott Goes, Problem Remains."[139] Subsequent events proved him right. One reason the controversy lingered was that Elliott was dismissed on a technicality, a fact frustrating to friend and foe alike. Professors in at least three other SBC seminaries came under varying degrees of suspicion of heresy at about the same time. Personal letters of sympathy to Elliott, or recommendations of his book, brought suspicious scrutiny to some; but no other dismissals resulted.

The third phase of the controversy centered around *The Broadman Bible Commentary,* especially volume 1 released in 1969. The editorial committee enlisted G. Henton Davies of England to write the commentary on Genesis. In general, that volume took account of the JEPD documentary hypothesis and used historical-critical methods of interpretation. No specific passage aroused more outcry than comments on Genesis 22 where Davies questioned whether God really commanded Abraham to kill his son Isaac. The controversy raged before and during the Denver convention of 1970. By a wide margin, the messengers voted to ask the Sunday School Board

138. K. Owen White, "Death in the Pot," *Arkansas Baptist* (February 1, 1962), p. 19. See also Leon McBeth, "Fundamentalism," pp. 87 *f.*

139. C. R. Daley, "Elliott Goes, Problem Remains," *Western Recorder* (November 8, 1962), p. 8.

to recall volume 1 and have it rewritten from a more conservative viewpoint.

The elected board first asked Davies to rewrite the work, which he declined to do. They then enlisted Clyde Francisco, respected Old Testament scholar at Southern Seminary in Louisville, to undertake the task. Francisco's new commentary was published in 1973 as "Volume 1, Revised." While using more felicitous language, Francisco's revision, opponents claimed, made only minor changes.

A fourth controversy, or a fourth phase of the same one, erupted at the SBC in Houston in 1979. That meeting was marked by intemperate attacks upon the seminaries at the preceding Pastors' Conference, a hostile spirit at the convention, the most open political maneuvering ever seen at a Baptist convention to that time, and the first-ballot election of a presidential candidate widely regarded as representing ultraconservative viewpoints. However, the buzzword at the Houston convention was *inerrancy.* Although new to most Southern Baptists, that word quickly moved to center stage and dominated the controversy after 1979. "Inerrancy of original autographs" designates a theory of how biblical inspiration is guaranteed. While familiar in American Christianity, particularly out of Princeton Theological Seminary under A. A. Hodge, Charles Hodge, and B. B. Warfield, its roots go further back in Reformed theology. In its Princeton expression, inerrancy was limited to the original autographs of Scripture. Though the term was occasionally used earlier, *inerrancy* became an issue for Southern Baptists with the publication of two books by Harold Lindsell in the 1970s and its appearance at the 1979 convention.[140] Some portrayed inerrancy as the historic Baptist viewpoint, while others contended that the concept has not shown up in any major Southern Baptist theologian, confession, or hymn. They maintained, on the other hand, that the historic Baptist view of biblical inspiration and authority is both older than and better than the Presbyterian view of inerrancy of original autographs.

By regional rallies and Bible conferences, by intense publicity, and by careful political organization, the ultraconservatives, led by a Houston layman, Paul Pressler, and a Dallas minister, Paige Patterson, set out on a frank quest to capture the SBC and turn it to more conservative directions. Targeting the SBC presidency as the key office, since the president appoints the committees which, in turn, name the groups which nominate trustees of SBC boards and institutions, the inerrancy group has been able to elect one of its number since 1979. Some felt the real issue was not belief in the Bible but a political struggle for control of the convention. A loosely organized moderate faction which has resisted such a takeover effort, sometimes called "friends of missions" or "denominational loyalists," was led primarily by Cecil E. Sherman of North Carolina and Kenneth L. Chafin of Texas.

---

140. Harold Lindsell, *The Battle for the Bible,* 1976, and *The Bible in the Balance,* 1979.

During the 1980s Southern Baptists discussed the nature of biblical inspiration. A popular book by Russell H. Dilday, Jr., president of Southwestern Seminary, *The Doctrine of Biblical Authority,* affirmed that Southern Baptists always have and still do accept the Bible as absolute truth without embracing the theory of inerrancy in its Princeton form.[141] James T. Draper, SBC president 1982-1984, tried to be a moderating influence upon the controversy. A recognized conservative himself, Draper did not demand that all use the term *inerrancy* to describe biblical authority, and by his conciliatory spirit sought to heal the breach in the denomination. His book *Authority: the Critical Issue for Southern Baptists* appeared in 1984 in a further effort to find common ground for Southern Baptists.[142]

However, common ground proved elusive. Not only did the controversy not abate but it broadened to include other thorny issues such as ordination of women, the resurgency of Calvinism, prayer in public schools, and social concerns, especially the issue of abortion.

Special Interest Groups

The Elliott controversy led to formation of special interest groups dedicated to certain doctrinal positions. In 1962 a few of the less conservative formed "Baptists for Freedom" to protest the firing of Elliott and to try to stem the fundamentalist tide. In the early 1970s a similar group was formed, taking the name of "E. Y. Mullins Fellowship." Neither group survived; their life was short, their impact minimal. One group that has survived is the "Baptist Faith and Message Fellowship" (BFMF), formed in 1973 to push for more conservative emphases in SBC schools, programs, and literature.[143]

Though no organic continuity can be traced, the BFMF was in some sense a culmination of earlier protest meetings in many places. As early as 1962 a group of "Concerned Baptists" from eight states met in Oklahoma City to plan strategy to push the SBC rightward. Although their immediate purpose was to remove Elliott, their coming together reinforced the emerging conservative movement and convinced them they could by careful strategy and persistent efforts gain control of the convention and its agencies. The inspiration of the BFMF apparently came from loosely organized conservative groups in several states, particularly North Carolina.

From the 1950s onward tensions increased among North Carolina Baptists, centering around two primary issues: the degree of Baptist control over Wake Forest University and certain practices of students there, par-

141. Dilday.

142. James T. Draper, *Authority: the Critical Issue for Southern Baptists* (Old Tappan, N.J.: Fleming H. Revell Co., 1984).

143. C. R. Daley, "The New Conservative Fellowship Raises Questions," *Western Recorder* (April 28, 1973), p. 4.

ticularly dancing on campus; and the allegation that a number of North Carolina churches received members who had not been immersed.[144] Gradually some of the more conservative Baptists coalesced into an informal fellowship, with at least minimal organization, to give direction to their efforts to combat these and other trends they opposed. Similar groups emerged in other states.

Apparently, William A. Powell first suggested a Southwide conservative fellowship on the order of the North Carolina group. M. O. Owens, Jr., pastor in Gastonia and prominent conservative spokesman, and LaVerne Butler, pastor in Louisville, led in the formation of such a group.

The loosely organized "Conservative Fellowship" held meetings at both the 1971 and 1972 conventions, but formal organization of the BFMF came in March 1973 in Atlanta. With striking similarities to the Fundamentalist Fellowship in the Northern Baptist Convention in the 1920s, the BFMF described itself as follows: "The BFMF is a committed group of Southern Baptists concerned about the inroads of Bible-doubting liberalism throughout classrooms and literature. . . . This group believes that the cancer of liberalism within SBC leadership can and should be removed."[145] In November of 1973, the group launched a new paper, called *The Southern Baptist Journal (SBJ),* edited by William A. Powell.

A growing complaint among many SBC conservatives centered on church curriculum materials from the Sunday School Board. Complaints began in the 1950s as the board moved cautiously toward using the Revised Standard Version of the Bible or other modern translations. Dissatisfaction escalated in the 1960s when some writers included mildly progressive materials on race relations. Another complaint was that board publications did not teach a premillennial understanding of Christ's second coming. None of the major writing theologians of Southern Baptists have embraced that viewpoint, and no major Baptist confession of faith, including the two SBC confessions, has embodied it. However, in the twentieth century premillennialism gained adherents in Southern Baptist thought, coming primarily from non-Baptist sources like the Plymouth Brethren, parachurch groups like Campus Crusade, and the popular Scofield Study Bible. In early 1984 the controversy took a new turn, with a request to devote one of the three curriculum series issued by the Sunday School Board to a premillennial viewpoint.

Because of perceived problems in SBC literature, the more conservative Baptists, over the objections of leaders like M. O. Owens, Jr., formed the Baptist Literature Board (BLB) in 1975. While not organically connected with the BFMF, the BLB was composed mostly of the same people, elected

144. See G. McLeod Bryan, ed., *Documents Concerning Baptism and Church Membership: A Controversy among North Carolina Baptists.*
145. "Joining the Baptist Faith and Message Fellowship," undated pamphlet of the BFMF.

the same leaders, and advocated the same principles. The rival literature project was never a real success and, indeed, provided the BFMF one of its most embarrassing setbacks. Brochures clearly implied that the new literature was written by Southern Baptists. The editor of the *SBJ* said the Baptist Literature Board would provide lesson studies "prepared by Southern Baptists who are committed to the fact that the Bible, in its original form, is the infallible and verbally inspired Word of God." The new literature was sometimes referred to as "Verbal Inspiration Literature."[146] However, in 1976 it came to light that the BLB did not prepare the literature but bought it from a nondenominational press, which simply imprinted the Baptist name upon the material. The same materials went to any number of ultraconservative denominations, each with its own name on the cover. Each buyer had freedom to edit the materials to "enhance denominational distinctives," but for the most part the BLB made no changes.[147] This, in effect, substituted nondenominational for Baptist literature in Baptist churches.

The Bible Book Series, the third curriculum line launched by the Sunday School Board in 1980, may have been prompted in part by the interest shown in materials from the BLB. The BFMF also sought to promote other theological schools, particularly the Luther Rice Seminary in Florida and the Mid-America Baptist Seminary, now located in Memphis. The *Southern Baptist Journal* carried frequent articles attacking the SBC seminaries and extolling Luther Rice and Mid-America as the only schools theologically safe for Southern Baptists.

Though it exercised considerable influence during the 1970s, the BFMF later fell upon hard times. Its more moderate leaders, like Owens and Butler, felt the group had made its point, having sharply focused the issues for Southern Baptists, and therefore needed to adopt a less militant stance in its publications. In 1979 the group voted to remove Powell as editor of the *Southern Baptist Journal,* replacing him with Russell Kaemmerling. However, within six months the Powell faction regained control and reinstated Powell as editor. At that point, most of the moderate Fundamentalists withdrew from the BFMF, including its founders, Owens and Butler. Several well-known conservative pastors allowed their membership to lapse. That left the BFMF in the hands of hard-core Fundamentalists, and the tone of their pronouncements became more strident as their impact diminished. The *Southern Baptist Journal* is apparently no longer published on any regular basis.

Meantime, the more moderate Fundamentalists rallied around a new publication, the *Southern Baptist Advocate,* founded in 1980 and now pub-

146. McBeth, "Fundamentalism," p. 94.
147. See Robert O'Brien, "Baptist Literature Board Used Non-Denominational Materials," *Maryland Baptist* (May 27, 1976), p. 1.

lished in Dallas. Edited by Russell Kaemmerling, this paper is supported by conservative organizations, churches, and individuals.

The splintering of the BFMF repeats the well-known tendency for ultraconservatives to argue and divide among themselves. The ultraconservative movement among Southern Baptists is by no means monolithic. Some of the inerrantists favor the resurgent Calvinism in SBC life, while others strongly oppose it. Some ultraconservatives among Southern Baptists seem more attracted to other issues, such as the charismatic movement, divine healing, and prayer in public schools. The BFMF was launched by pastors deeply committed to the local church and to the Southern Baptist Convention and its ministries, but they lost control of the movement. In recent years, some SBC Fundamentalists seemed to place less priority upon the local church, fell unduly under the influence of television evangelists, and reflected a stance more independent than denominational.

Reflections and Impact

This brief survey confirms at least four facts about Southern Baptist theology. First, doctrinal diversity is real. No amount of cordiality can conceal the fact that many Southern Baptists simply do not agree on such questions as the millennium, religious liberty, alien immersion and open communion, and which theory of inspiration best explains the Bible. The famed Southern Baptist unity in the past has been more functional than theological; Southern Baptists have banded together to minister in missions, evangelism, and Christian education. So long as they emphasize functional ministry, the "rope of sand," as one called it, holds; when they switch from function to doctrine, unity is threatened. Second, Southern Baptists have shown a tendency to forget their own heritage. Their own theologians are almost unknown among them; their earlier confessions unfamiliar. This allows some Southern Baptists to claim recent innovations as "the historic Baptist position" on certain issues.

Third, Southern Baptists have shown an openness, or a vulnerability if a more judgmental word is preferred, to non-Baptist viewpoints. Having allowed the roots of their own heritage to wither, they have absorbed a number of emphases from non-Baptist and nondenominational sources. Much of their recent controversy can be traced to that infiltration. A fourth conclusion one reaches from a survey of theological developments is that, despite the cries of alarm, Southern Baptists remain remarkably conservative. Claims that Southern Baptists face widespread defections from the faith are unsubstantiated. The Southern Baptist Convention has never been captured by Fundamentalists, but neither has it ever become the tool of liberals. Most Southern Baptists appear to be where they have always been, in the mainstream of conservative, biblical, evangelical, but not fundamentalist, Christianity.

The controversies of the twentieth century have left an imprint upon

Southern Baptists. At least three areas of impact may be noted. First, the controversies have tended to divert Southern Baptists from their main tasks. Whether Norrisism in the 1920s or inerrancy in the 1970s and 1980s, theological wrangling has eaten up a lot of Baptist ink and paper, claimed a lot of energy and time, and in general represented a distraction from ministry. Second, these times of turbulence have radically changed the office of the SBC president. In addition to being a presider and spokesman, the president can by his appointments, in time, sway the direction of the convention and its agencies. While that power has existed for years, it was only in the 1970s that partisan groups learned how to obtain and use the presidency for their purposes. As a result, the office has been radically politicized.

Third, a rise in creedalism has followed the recent controversies. Both in 1925 and 1963 some warned Southern Baptists that confessions, like day-old manna, can turn sour. At the formation of the Southern Baptist Convention in 1845, W. B. Johnson said, "We have constructed for our basis no new creed; acting in this matter upon a Baptist aversion for all creeds but the Bible."[148] Earlier Separate Baptists in the South cared little for confessions, agreeing with John Leland who asked, "Why this Virgin Mary between the souls of men and the Scriptures?"[149] The Separate Baptists debated the propriety of using any human confessions; and when at last they agreed to merge with Regular Baptists on the basis of the Philadelphia Confession, they took steps "to prevent the confession of faith from usurping a tyrannical power over the conscience of any."[150] With such caution about confessions, it is not surprising that the SBC went eighty years before adopting one.

The preamble to *The Baptist Faith and Message* of 1963, officially adopted along with the confession itself, spells out that the statement represents a consensus, that it is neither complete nor final, that "confessions are only guides in interpretation, having no authority over the conscience," and that they "are not to be used to hamper freedom of thought or investigation in other realms of life."[151]

Despite those safeguards, however, the 1963 confession has become more creedal than any other in Baptist history. Throughout their history, Baptists have claimed to be *confessional* but not *creedal*. While the words mean much the same, they can be used and have been used to mean different things. A confession designates what people *do* believe; a creed what they

148. Cited in Carter, p. 3.

149. Cited by Walter B. Shurden, "Southern Baptist Responses to the 1925 and 1963 Confessions," *Review and Expositor* (Winter 1979), p. 70.

150. David Benedict, *A General History of the Baptist Denomination in America and Other Parts of the World,* 2 vols. (Boston: Manning & Loring, 1813), 1:62.

151. *Annual,* SBC, 1963, p. 269.

must believe. A confession is *voluntary* and serves to inform, educate, and inspire; a creed is *required* and serves to discipline and exclude. A confession offers *guidelines* under the authority of Scripture; a creed tends to become *binding authority,* in subtle ways displacing the Bible. It may be that confessions and creeds do not differ as much today as in the past, but important differences do remain. Southern Baptists in recent years have shown a distinct trend toward creedalism. What they adopted in 1963 was a *confession;* but the way that document has been used has gone far toward hardening it into a *creed.*

Worship in Southern Baptist Churches

If one wished to dramatize the changes in Southern Baptist churches in the twentieth century, perhaps no better way could be found than to contrast styles of worship in 1984 with those prevailing a century earlier. Earlier worship was marked by diversity, spontaneity, and a spirit of warm and informal fervency. Churches used various hymnals, resulting in a patch-work of worship styles and emphases. A printed order of worship would have been practically unknown to SBC churches at the turn of the century, and spontaneity tended to prevail over planning and order.

Toward the end of the twentieth century worship has changed. Most Southern Baptist churches now use the *Baptist Hymnal,* either in its 1956 or 1975 versions, and this has lent a uniformity to worship. A person worshiping in a Southern Baptist church in Alabama or Alaska would likely sing the same hymns, follow a similar order of worship, read similar scriptural responses, and hear a similar sermon. The printed order of service, though varying from a simple listing of hymns to a more formal liturgical order, has become almost universal. Robed choirs and choral responses have become more common, and a more liturgical flavor now marks Southern Baptist worship.

From their earliest history, Baptists inherited an ambiguity about forms of worship. So great was their reaction against the set forms of the Prayer Book of the Church of England that many English Baptists resisted any planning, order, or liturgy. John Smyth would not even allow Bible reading in worship lest that use of written materials hamper the free working of the Spirit. It was not until the late 1680s when Benjamin Keach pioneered in Baptist church music that Particular Baptists allowed singing in church, and the General Baptists resisted it for another generation. Early Baptists in America also opposed singing, and not until the eighteenth century did most of them become comfortable with hymns.

Emerging Tradition

Though not a Baptist, Isaac Watts (1674-1748) shaped church music for a generation, and it was the effort to augment his content that led to the early Baptist hymn anthologies.[152] Baptists like Anne Steele in England (who wrote under the pen name of Theodosia), Caleb Evans of Bristol College, and above all John Rippon of London represent an emerging tradition of Baptist hymnody. Rippon issued his *Selection* of hymns in 1787 and his tunebook, *A Selection of Psalm and Hymn Tunes from the Best Authors,* in 1791. The Wesleyan Revival and the First Great Awakening in America made much of singing and effectively ended opposition to that practice.

Diverging Traditions.

As Baptist hymnody developed in America, it tended to adapt the musical styles of its host culture. As cultural patterns in North and South diverged, so did Baptist worship in the two areas. In 1843 Northern Baptists published *The Psalmist,* probably the first American hymnal issued by a denominational press. Compiled by Baron Stow and S. F. Smith, it adapted the musical heritage represented by Lowell Mason and offered worship music typical of the churchly tradition favored in the urban churches of the North.[153] Designed for "the elevation of evangelical taste," *The Psalmist* never won wide acceptance in the South, despite a supplement by Richard Fuller and J. B. Jeter.

Baptists in the South showed a distinct preference for the *Sacred Harp* tradition, a term which designates not only a hymnal issued in 1844 but also an entire school of music and a characteristic manner of its performance. The *Sacred Harp* represented the revivalist tradition of the Awakening, built upon a Southern folk music tradition in both lyrics and melody. It made room for the more emotional gospel songs, such as "Amazing Grace." Hugh T. McElrath concluded that the *Sacred Harp* movement "constituted a decided turn in Baptist church music, determining the general trend toward the informal spiritual song repertoire that is typical of a large percentage of Baptist congregational singing today."[154] In this same tradition was "Singin' Billy" Walker, a Baptist, who compiled *The Southern Harmony* and helped popularize the "singing school" movement in the South. In his book, *And They All Sang Hallelujah,* a study of camp-meeting singing in the South, Dickson D. Bruce identified the gospel choruses of the *Sacred Harp* tradition as "the common denominator of plain-folk religious belief."[155]

It is not without significance that Baptist styles of worship, North and

---

152. Hugh T. McElrath, "Turning Points in the Story of Baptist Church Music," *Baptist History and Heritage,* p. 5. This entire issue is given to the theme, "Church Music in Baptist History."

153. Ibid., p. 10.

154. Ibid., p. 12.

155. Dickson D. Bruce, *And They All Sang Hallelujah* (Knoxville; University of Tennessee Press, 1973), p. 95.

South, had already taken sharply divergent paths before the denomination itself divided. Those different worship patterns must have made their contribution not only to that division but also to the continued separation of the family.

Changing Traditions

Perhaps nothing has changed Southern Baptist worship in the twentieth century more than the gradual movement away from the *Sacred Harp* tradition. This change was pinpointed by Harry L. Eskew when he remarked, "I. E. Reynolds, long-time director of the School of Sacred Music at Southwestern Seminary, composed gospel songs during his earlier years but then became a crusader for better church music."[156]

Southern Baptists took steps to improve their worship, and especially their church music, early in this century. McElrath identified as one of the "turning points" the formation of the "School of Gospel Music," led by I. E. Reynolds at Southwestern Seminary in 1915, "the first school in the Southern Baptist Convention specifically designed for the training of church music leaders."[157] The convention has made numerous efforts in the twentieth century to provide churches with adequate materials to guide and upgrade their worship. In 1925 the SBC adopted a resolution deploring the prevailing low standards of worship and appointed a committee "for the advancement of music in Southern Baptist Churches."[158] In a longer report on "Church Music and Worship," the convention in 1943 sought to define acceptable worship, established its priority in church life, endorsed the graded choir movement, urged specific training in music and worship for pastors as well as musicians in colleges and seminaries, and concluded with its intention "to prepare and set going a constructive, educational program of Church Music among Southern Baptists."[159]

Two years earlier, in 1941, the Sunday School Board had established its Department of Church Music. It has been headed by B. B. McKinney, 1942-1952; Walter Hines Sims, 1952-1970; William J. Reynolds, 1970-1980; and Wesley L. Forbis, since 1981. In 1940 the board issued the *Broadman Hymnal,* another turning point in Southern Baptist worship history. It captured the allegiance of the churches as no hymnal before it and brought a degree of uniformity to worship which Southern Baptists had not known. Though including many of the gospel songs of the revivalist tradition, the *Broadman Hymnal* also included a number of more churchly hymns, along with choral responses and Scripture readings. Perhaps more than any book

156. Harry L. Eskew, "Southern Baptist Contributions to Hymnody," *Baptist History and Heritage,* p. 33.
157. McElrath, p. 14.
158. *Annual,* SBC, 1925, p. 103.
159. Ibid., 1943, pp. 51-52.

except the Bible, this hymnal shaped the beliefs and worship of Southern Baptists.

The *Baptist Hymnal* came out in 1956, to be replaced by the new *Baptist Hymnal* of 1975. Much of the material in the older *Broadman Hymnal* was not included in the *Baptist Hymnal* of 1975, which has led to some dissatisfaction despite the fact that the 1975 publication has been one of the Board's most widely distributed hymnals.[160] The 1975 hymnal represents an important shift in Southern Baptist worship styles, away from the earlier gospel songs to a more formal and churchly emphasis.

Other trends in Southern Baptist church music include growth of the graded choir program, which dates from the 1930s;[161] the increasing use of musical instruments in church, from handbells to complete orchestras;[162] rapid increase of enrollment in music training programs in Southern Baptist churches, particularly among children and youth, including a 30 percent increase between 1973-1981;[163] a tendency among some churches, slight at present but growing, to use hymnals other than those supplied by denominational sources; and the adaptation of church music to newer musical styles emerging in the general culture, as seen in the popularity of the folk musical *Good News* in 1967.[164]

Changing Roles of Baptist Women

On August 9, 1964, Addie Davis was ordained as a gospel minister at the Watts Street Baptist Church in Durham, North Carolina. So far as the records show, she was the first woman formally ordained to ministry in a Southern Baptist church. In two decades since then, over a hundred other Southern Baptist women have received ministerial ordination, plus countless others who have been ordained as deacons. The changing role of women represents a major trend in Southern Baptist life.[165]

Historical Background

Women served as deacons and deaconesses, and sometimes preached, among the English Baptists from the 1600s. In the American South, the Separate Baptists recognized both deaconesses and eldresses, and some women, like Martha Stearns Marshall, were notable for their fervent

160. Wesley L. Forbis, "The Sunday School Board and Baptist Church Music," *Baptist History and Heritage*, p. 24.

161. See William J. Reynolds, "The Graded Choir Movement Among Southern Baptists," *Baptist History and Heritage*, pp. 55 f.

162. See A. Joseph King, "Instrumental Music in Southern Baptist Life," *Baptist History and Heritage*, pp. 46 f.

163. See Statistical Section, table 6, *Quarterly Review* (January 1984), p. 45.

164. See McElrath, p. 14.

165. See McBeth, *Women in Baptist Life*, for a study of this trend.

preaching and praying in public.[166] Many SBC churches continued to have deaconesses well into the twentieth century. Among most SBC churches, however, the practice diminished largely as a result of adverse reaction to the suffragette movement, the formation of WMU which gave women alternate avenues of service, the changing function of the diaconate from ministry to management, and the rise of the modern church committee structure which allowed women to perform the same work they had done as deaconesses.

New Roles, Old Roles Recovered

While the Christian service of Baptist women is not new, their formal ordination as ministers and deacons is recent.[167] A number of women presently serve as associate pastors in SBC churches and, in that capacity preach, conduct weddings and funerals, and baptize converts. A few women are known to serve as pastors of SBC churches, and others have acted as interim pastors. For years women have been elected directors of missions, especially in North Carolina, where they oversee the cooperative ministries of several churches in their areas.

A recent trend has seen a number of "clergy couples" in SBC churches, in which both husband and wife are ordained ministers and in many cases are called as copastors. Perhaps a dozen such couples were known in the early 1980s, including Anne and Aubrey Rosser of Virginia. Both ordained and holding doctorates, the Rossers were called in 1979 as copastors of a Southern Baptist church in Richmond. They take turns preaching, counseling, and performing other pastoral duties.[168] In 1980 Anne Rosser baptized three converts, the first woman minister known to have baptized in a Southern Baptist church.

By the 1980s women deacons were more numerous, of course, than women preachers among Southern Baptists and less controversial. A number of churches adopted a policy of electing deacons without regard to gender, while some specified that the diaconate be made up equally of men and women. A number of women have been elected to chair the deacon group in their churches.[169] Women emphasize that their role is that of

---

166. See Morgan Edwards, *Materials Toward a History of the Baptists in the Province of North Carolina,* as reprinted in *The North Carolina Historical Review* (July 1930), pp. 389 *f.*

167. Some women may have been ordained in earlier centuries. The early confessions imply as much, and Morgan Edwards, in his 1774 work, *Customs of Primitive Churches,* indicated that eldresses and deaconesses were set apart in similar manner as their male counterparts, though he had never witnessed such a service. Even so, the formal "ordination" of women has been largely a recent development.

168. See Tom Miller, "Women Ministers Find Happiness in the Pastorate," *The Religious Herald* (March 26, 1981), pp. 8-9.

169. "Number of Women Chairing Boards of Deacons," *Biblical Recorder* (November 19, 1977), p. 7. For further information, see Charles W. Deweese, "Deaconesses in Baptist History," *Baptist History and Heritage* (January 1977), pp. 52-57.

deacons, not *deaconesses,* for the latter word has often designated a subordinate role.

Several factors helped lead to changing roles, and in some cases the recovery of ancient roles, for Baptist women. First, changes in society propelled women into the workplace and into leadership in business, education, and government. America's daughters have long been as well educated as her sons, and the churches came to realize that they had an abundance of trained, capable, and highly motivated women available for service. The "liberation" of women in society, and their increasing opportunities for service in other denominations, have doubtlessly affected Southern Baptist women. Second, changes in biblical understandings have affected men and women alike. In the past, many Southern Baptist interpreted the Bible to keep women in silence and subjection. However, in recent years Southern Baptist theologians, pastors, laymen, and laywomen have read the same passages in a new light, professing to find in both Testaments an emphasis upon human equality.

Third, the proliferation of ordination for nonpreaching ministries has encouraged the ordination of women. Even a generation ago, ordination was usually reserved for the preacher or deacon, and workers in education and music were accepted as lay persons. Some of the jobs women have held for years without ordination are now eligible for, and sometimes require, ordination. In some cases, therefore, the real change has not been in the work performed but in the certification required to do the work.

Reactions to Ordained Women

Reaction to ordained women has varied among Southern Baptists, as one might expect from a large denomination with an image for both social and doctrinal conservatism. In 1977 Clay L. Price of the Home Mission Board conducted a study entitled, "A Survey of Southern Baptist Attitudes Toward Women in Church and Society."[170] In this most thorough study to date, Price showed that of Southern Baptists responding, about 17 percent favored women pastors, while over 24 percent favored ordination for women chaplains and over 75 percent favored ordination for women in the fields of religious education, youth ministries, or social work. About two-thirds of those responding thought Southern Baptist attitudes toward ordination of women would change in the next quarter century, probably toward more acceptance.[171] Less extensive surveys at Ridgecrest and Glorieta have shown that many older women are more accepting of church leadership roles for women than are younger women. These informal questionnaires, conducted by Minette Drumwright in 1977, also showed that

170. Clay L. Price, "A Survey of Southern Baptist Attitudes Toward Women in Church and Society" (Master's thesis, West Georgia College, Carrollton, Georgia, 1978).
171. Ibid., p. 100.

women attending Ridgecrest revealed less opposition to women in ministry than did women at Glorieta.[172]

Pronouncements on the role of women have varied among Southern Baptists. Most associations and state conventions have remained silent on the subject, though a few have encouraged the ordination of women.[173] Others have been less tolerant. Associations in several states have excluded churches for ordaining women, and a number of state conventions have done the same and/or adopted resolutions against such ordinations. Up to 1984 the SBC itself steadfastly refused to pronounce on the subject, following the historic Baptist practice of leaving ordination to the authority of the local church. In 1984, however, the SBC adopted a lengthy resolution that opposed women's ordination.[174] This resolution aroused a storm of protest which seemed to center around three ideas. First, a number of Southern Baptists favor ordination for women and thus wanted no resolution against it. Second, many who disapprove such ordinations nevertheless view ordination as a local church issue and regard the convention resolution as an unwarranted violation of local church autonomy. Third, many who disapprove of women's ordination disliked the resolution because they thought its involved explanations insulted women.

Organization of Women

In 1978 the first national Consultation of Women in Church-Related Vocations was sponsored in Nashville by various SBC agencies. Women traced their changing roles in church, expounded biblical teachings on the subject, communicated their earnest desire to serve, and weighed practical suggestions for improvement. Perhaps most importantly, that meeting allowed women who felt a sense of call, but felt isolated, to make contact with other women in similar circumstances and experience the reinforcement of being part of a united group. The women have since effected a more permanent organization and, beginning in 1983, have published *Folio: A Newsletter for Southern Baptist Women in Ministry.*

Recent Trends

To be complete, a history must look at recent trends; but to be honest, it must do so with caution. One lacks perspective to assess recent events, and judgments made in the midst of the facts run the risk of distortion. Therefore, this section will do little more than name a few of the most obvious current trends among Southern Baptists and leave their exposition to future historians.

172. Cited in McBeth, *Women in Baptist Life,* pp. 179-181.
173. See, for example, "D. C. Convention Urges Ordination of Women," *The Southern Baptist Journal* (January 1975), p. 2.
174. *Annual,* SBC, 1984, p. 65.

The Role of Ministers

At the beginning of this century a Baptist "minister" meant either a pastor or missionary or maybe a religion professor. By the 1980s these roles had expanded to include workers in Christian education, music, childhood religious education, church administration, denominational work, workers with youth, and many others. Further, ordination had been extended to most of these expanded forms of ministry.

The training and benefits for ministers has also changed. As recently as the World War I era, only about 20 percent of Southern Baptist pastors served full time, with the 80 percent who were bivocational serving mostly in small rural churches.[175] In 1983 about 46 percent of SBC pastors held earned seminary degrees, up from about 36 percent a decade earlier.[176] In a socioeconomic survey, James E. Carter showed that while many earlier ministers bordered on poverty, by the 1980s an increasing number represented an affluent upper middle class, especially in the larger churches.[177]

Not only has the Baptist ministry changed in role and status but also in function. In many churches the pastor is regarded as the chief executive officer (CEO), as in other corporations of comparable size and budget. Along with this has come a tendency for the pastor to exercise considerable authority in church decisions, much as a corporation president might do. Another trend, quite the opposite, is for some large churches to employ ministers of administration to run the church, leaving the pastor relatively free of day-to-day church life.

The average tenure of SBC pastors declined in the twentieth century, since mid-century averaging only about thirty months. Figures in 1982 showed that about 20 percent of pastors were in the first year of their current pastorates, and only about 5 percent had served the same congregation seventeen years or more.[178] Two factors in society are presently affecting this trend. The employment of pastors' wives outside the home and the trend for churches to provide not a parsonage but a housing allowance for the pastor to purchase his own home have begun to put the brakes on such ministerial mobility.

The forced termination of pastors increased among Southern Baptists in this century, including about twenty-five hundred such cases a year.[179] Described as "a dilemma the denomination does not know how to handle,"

175. Lewis Wingo, "Little Known Facts About the Southern Baptist Convention," *Quarterly Review* (April 1984), p. 42.

176. Ibid., p. 47.

177. James E. Carter, "The Socioeconomic Status of Baptist Ministers in Historical Perspective," *Baptist History and Heritage*, pp. 37 f.

178. Wingo, p. 42.

179. Jim Lowry, "Denomination Struggles with Terminations," *Baptist Standard* (January 11, 1984), p. 11.

the problem of termination has become, along with pastoral placement, one of the most crucial problems facing Baptist ministers. Terminated ministers had difficulty finding another church position, and many left the ministry entirely. Some state conventions have established offices to counsel and aid such pastors and their families, some of them offering limited financial aid for up to three months. The fear of termination, even among those who never experience it, has added to the emotional tension of the pastor's home and family.

The pastor's family has encountered many of the same pressures that confront other American families, including divorce. The number of clergy divorces has increased among Southern Baptists, as for other denominations, and many church members are more tolerant and forgiving. Divorce may damage or even end the pastor's ministry, but it no longer *automatically* does so as was usually the case in earlier years.

Another form of ministry that has mushroomed among Southern Baptists in recent years is that of the professional evangelist. These include both preachers and musicians who travel among the churches conducting revival crusades. This form of ministry was practically unknown among Baptists until about a century ago. William E. Penn, a Texas layman who began itinerant preaching in the 1870s, is considered the first full-time Southern Baptist evangelist.[180] The number of evangelists active in American Protestantism, including Southern Baptists, has increased dramatically since World War II. Evangelists in the SBC formed their own organization in 1965 with only a few members; by 1982 that group reported almost one thousand names of full-time SBC evangelists.[181] Described as "the most fluid of all groups of ministers in the SBC," evangelism shows a high dropout rate, with few remaining in the work more than five years.[182]

Traveling revivalists have proven both popular and controversial among Southern Baptists. Some consider their ministry both biblical and beneficial, citing their effectiveness in publicity, gaining converts, and attracting persons who would not ordinarily attend a church service. Others feel less positive, pointing to such problems as high costs, the "show biz" atmosphere some bring to the churches, the sometimes questionable techniques of gaining converts, and the fact that few of the crusade converts remain active in local church life.[183]

---

180. David W. Music, "Music in Southern Baptist Evangelism," *Baptist History and Heritage* (January 1984), p. 37.

181. *Annual,* SBC, 1982, pp. 746-751.

182. Toby Druin, "The Evangelist Today," *Home Missions* (September 1975), p. 6-7.

183. Ibid., pp. 6-11.

Local Church and Denomination

Court cases in a number of states in the twentieth century have apparently added a new dimension to the historic relationship of the local congregation and its denominational body. Two such cases may be noted. In 1953 the North Rocky Mount Baptist Church in North Carolina voted by about two to one to withdraw from the SBC, the state convention, and the local Baptist association. When a minority of members resisted this action, the state court ultimately ruled that the entire property belonged to the group, however large or small, that continued to adhere to the position and practices of that particular church before the controversy.[184] In effect, those members who wanted to withdraw from the denomination, although a majority, could do so only as individuals and not as a church. At least they could not take the church property with them. The dissidents eventually formed another church and affiliated with a different Baptist denomination.

In 1970 the First Baptist Church of Wichita, Kansas, debated its long-standing affiliation with the American (Northern) Baptist Convention. The majority of members, many of them Southern Baptists who had migrated to Wichita over the years, voted to withdraw. In the resulting lawsuit, the state court ruled that, while members were free to withdraw if they chose, they could not take the church property. Not even a Baptist church, the court ruled, can change its denomination by majority vote. The dissidents later withdrew and formed a Southern Baptist church in Wichita.

The potential impact of these rulings, and others like them, is staggering. At best, this trend can protect the integrity of a Baptist church against an influx of members who want to turn it into something else. At worst, this could give Baptist conventions a kind of vested interest in every affiliated church. It appears that so long as a minority remains to challenge it, with sufficient resources and resolve, a Baptist church may not be able to withdraw from its denominational affiliation.

Another dimension of church-denomination relationship involves recent court rulings in "ascending/descending liability." This means that in certain cases where a convention is sued, the suit may extend to convention-owned institutions (descending); or, where a board or institution is sued, the suit may extend to the sponsoring convention (ascending).

The Charismatic Movement

As early as 1656 the Abingdon Association in England reported, "We doe not now expect, nor sue for, the gifts of tongues."[185] However, some Baptists continue to "sue" for charismatic gifts. While the Pentecostal

---

184. Robert A. Baker, "The North Rocky Mount Baptist Church Decision," *Review and Expositor*, pp. 55-62.

185. B. R. White, ed., *Association Records of Particular Baptists in England, Wales and Ireland to 1660*, Part 3, p. 163.

denominations have flourished in this country from the turn of the century, the charismatic movement, or Neo-Pentecostalism as it was sometimes called, first made inroads into the mainline denominations in the 1960s. These emphases showed up in a number of SBC churches but seemed to have peaked by 1975. At least five associations in four states excluded charismatic churches in the mid-1970s, a policy followed by some state conventions as well.[186] Several others, while not excluding churches, adopted statements of opposition or warning. The National Southern Baptist Charismatic Conference was held in Dallas in 1976 but interest seems to have declined since then.

In his excellent study Claude L. Howe pinpointed several reasons the charismatic movement has appealed less to Southern Baptists than to some others. He said:

> In many respects, a charismatic experience is foreign to Southern Baptist life, stressing a second blessing where Baptists prize the first. Charismatic experience tends to establish a spiritual elite by distinguishing between Christians who have had the experience and those who have not; Baptists stress the equality of all believers in Christ. The focus of the charismatic tends to be inward and upon believers; Southern Baptist concern is outward, directed toward the world. . . . Charismatics often are critical of or indifferent to denominationalism while Southern Baptists are strongly attached to denominational structures and programs.[187]

Baptism and Communion

In the 1860s and following, the Landmark movement made "alien immersion" an issue for Southern Baptists and renewed the long-standing Baptist controversy over open versus closed communion. Those issues have continued in the present century, though since mid-century one rarely hears of closed communion. However, the alien immersion controversy has continued in the spotlight. As in so many issues, Southern Baptist history shows diverse responses; some churches have insisted upon Baptist baptism alone, regarding all others as alien. Other Southern Baptist churches, as the records amply demonstrate, have accepted the immersion of believers upon a profession of faith whether or not performed by Baptists. Some have regarded non-Baptist immersion as irregular but not invalid. The geographical expansion of Southern Baptists since mid-century has revived the issue since much of that expansion, especially in the West and Northwest, proceeded along Landmark lines. Most SBC churches in the old South, by contrast, have little interest in the matter.

The alien immersion issue has been complicated by one fundamental fact: more and more non-Baptist churches have now adopted the practice of

186. Claude L. Howe, *Glimpses of Baptist Heritage,* p. 129.
187. Ibid., p. 122.

believer's immersion. The Baptist witness has borne fruit, so to speak, and others have adopted the Baptist way. Whereas a century ago, few besides Baptists practiced so, now multitudes do. The only way to reject such believers' immersions, it appears, is to retreat to the Landmark insistence that Baptists have the only true churches, and thus the only true baptism, a position not many Southern Baptists today would find comfortable.

Canadian Southern Baptists

Since the early 1950s the number of Southern Baptist churches in Canada has increased to over sixty, most of them affiliated with the Northwest Convention or the Baptist Convention of New England. Though messengers from the Canadian churches have been received in Southern Baptist associations and state conventions, they have not been seated at the SBC. In 1958 the SBC president ruled that Canadian messengers were ineligible, and the next year a motion to change the constitution to admit them was defeated.

In 1957 the convention appointed a Committee on Canadian Cooperation, which worked with a similar group from Canada for a number of years. In 1958 the committee laid down guidelines which affirmed in essence that while Southern Baptists would aid the Canadian churches, they would not seek their affiliation with the SBC. They would instead seek to strengthen indigenous Baptist life in Canada. These guidelines were reaffirmed as late as 1977.

However, from the first many Southern Baptists, both in Canada and the USA, felt this policy was too restrictive. They continued to agitate for full acceptance of the Canadian messengers. At the 1983 convention a motion was made to add two words, "and Canada," to the SBC constitution in Article II on membership. A later motion called for a committee of twenty-five members to study the issue and report to the 1984 convention.

Those who opposed affiliating the Canadian churches pointed out that such an action would make the SBC international, lead to churches in other nations seeking direct affiliation, undercut indigenous Baptist work in other nations, and make Baptists in other nations leery of receiving Southern Baptist workers and assistance lest they be swallowed up. Others spoke in favor of affiliating the Canadians and conducting a full program of mission work in Canada. Supporters argued that this need not lead to wholesale change of relations with other nations and that, despite what the SBC might vote, the fact remained that these churches were already Southern Baptist and intended to remain so. Some regarded this as a mission opportunity that could not be refused; others called it a religious version of "manifest destiny" at its worst. The arguments pro and con sounded remarkably similar to those raised about SBC expansion into the North and Northwest a generation earlier. In 1984 the SBC voted a compromise solution that will not extend direct affiliation to the Canadian churches but will provide for more Southern Baptist activity in Canada.[188]

Resurgence of Calvinism

A new trend among Southern Baptists, still small but growing, represents a resurgence of Calvinistic theology. While related to similar groups among Presbyterians, nondenominationalists and other Baptists, especially the General Association of Regular Baptists, this resurgence by the 1980s represented a strong presence within the SBC. With remarkable similarity to the Strict Baptists of England, and with a pronounced preference for the Particular Baptist confession of 1689, the Southern Baptist Calvinists sought to stem what they regarded as Arminian tendencies in the SBC. They especially objected to typical forms of Southern Baptist evangelism, criticized the "invitation system," and reasserted the priority of predestination.

Calvinists within the SBC have asserted their faith in a number of ways. A strong church in Florida has reprinted and circulated works by John L. Dagg and James P. Boyce, thought by the Calvinists to hold the views they espouse. A number of Calvinists, mostly seminary students, launched a new journal to advocate their viewpoints, and in 1983 a national conference of Southern Baptist Calvinists was held in Memphis.

Three factors help account for this movement. First, there can be no doubt that Calvinism has been a major part of Baptist heritage, an emphasis which has diminished over the years in the activistic American environment. Calvinists wish to reappropriate some of this heritage but, as in all reactions, they run the risk of swinging to the opposite extreme. Second, neither the style nor substance of some Southern Baptist evangelism has been above reproach. In their criticisms of the worst examples of SBC evangelism, the Calvinists have pinpointed shallowness, emotional manipulations, and the distressing tendency of some SBC churches to baptize younger children, including even preschoolers. Some have described this trend as "infant baptism with bigger infants." While most Southern Baptists will not find the Calvinist form of predestination satisfying, they must acknowledge that the movement represents, to some extent, a reaction against shallow evangelism. Third, the Calvinists may be reacting, though unconsciously, to a growing feeling of futility in society. That religious views can be affected by societal trends is beyond doubt. The Calvinist emphasis upon predestination takes responsibility for a person's eternal fate out of one's hands at precisely the moment in American history when many citizens feel helpless to affect their earthly fate. Conversely, the older Calvinism broke down in the ebullient 1800s when the new nation was carving out a new nation in America, full of energy and confidence, first asserting "Manifest Destiny" and then fulfilling it. Pessimistic Calvinism could not

188. *Annual,* SBC, 1984, p. 54.

thrive in that culture, but the threatening 1980s may provide a more fertile field for a theology that says nothing a person does will make any ultimate difference.

Summary

James M. Wall, editor of *The Christian Century,* in 1980 described Southern Baptists as they appear to others, under four images.[189]

Image One: Bible-believers or Inerrancy Dogmatists

At their best, Southern Baptists have unquestionably believed the Bible. According to Wall, others see Southern Baptists as accepting the Bible "not just as a guidebook; it is *the* book." The negative side of this image, Wall said, "is the rigidity of inerrancy," in which Southern Baptist "scholastics are rigidly unbending and intolerant of all who do not accept their exceedingly narrow reading of Scripture."

Image Two: Diligent Missionaries or Arrogant Proselytizers

Nothing puzzles outsiders about Southern Baptists more than their persistent efforts to persuade others to share their faith. Some see this, Wall said, "as arrogance, self-righteousness, and superiority." Some perceive such witnessing as positive; Southern Baptists perceive it as close to the mainsprings of their faith.

Image Three: Rigid Moralists or Defender of Values

"The perception of the Southern Baptist in this area," Wall said, "is one of defender of values based in religion on the positive side; and a rigid, intolerant defender of narrow moral views, on the negative side." Outsiders see Southern Baptists as concerned with issues of personal morality but less aware of what Wall called "societal evils."

Image Four: Defender of Church-State Separation or Anti-Roman Catholic

Religious liberty for all, preserved through separation of church and state, remains one of the earliest and most consistent emphases of Baptists. One could argue that this position has led to greater religious freedom for Baptists and non-Baptists alike. However, the public often perceives a less positive role for Baptists, that of intolerant anti-Catholicism. The religious opposition to the election of John F. Kennedy in 1960 was widely perceived, rightly or not, as spearheaded by Baptists. Opposition to an official ambassador to the Vatican, which surfaced again in 1984, though broadly based

189. See James M. Wall, "Images of Southern Baptists in Contemporary America," *Baptist History and Heritage* (July 1980), pp. 2 *f.*

among American Protestants, was widely perceived as a Baptist phenomenon and in some quarters as a *Southern* Baptist movement. Of more concern to Southern Baptists, perhaps, was evidence that understanding of and commitment to religious liberty might be weakening in their own denomination.

Concluding on a positive note, Wall portrayed Southern Baptists as

> a denomination with a passionate commitment and an unwillingness to conform either to the vagueness of the ecumenical movement or the blandness of the no-offense cultural religion. The Southern Baptist Convention represents the mainline body which has most successfully resisted amalgamation into the secular and church mainstream of the United States.[190]

Time will tell if these images from outsiders have validity and, if so, whether the more negative or positive elements will prevail.

190. Ibid. p. 6.

16

The Larger Baptist Family

Baptists form a large and diverse family, organized into over 150 conventions or unions and scattered unevenly over most of the world. In the United States alone, one could in 1984 identify at least 52 distinct Baptist general bodies with a reported total of 101,683 churches and 30,059,559 members.[1] These various Baptist bodies do not remain constant but are marked by considerable turnover, with some merging, others disbanding, and new ones added. Well over half of the present Baptist groups in the United State have been formed in the twentieth century, and at least 12 have emerged since 1930, though many have roots in earlier times.[2] Baptists have proved more dynamic than static; as they continue to grow and change, they frequently form new structures and alignments, and no doubt that process will continue.

Why such diversity among Baptists? Observers have often puzzled over the Baptist tendency to fragment into many separate structures. Reasons for diversity include religious liberty, which has removed restraints; lack of an official creed to enforce doctrinal uniformity; ethnic diversity; cultural and economic pluralism; doctrinal differences; strong personalities and ego factors; and the fact that mergers often leave unmerged remnants. The process of denominational division is, of course, not new; Baptists were born in diversity and their earliest churches hived off into different groups to push their own doctrines and practices. Baptist fragmentation has reached its zenith in the United States, where over 85 percent of known Baptists live.

Efforts to classify the fifty-two Baptist bodies in the United States have proven difficult. The oldest Baptists in England, General, Particular, and Sabbatarian, each developed continuing groups in the United States, but Baptists have long since outgrown those brief categories. One helpful classification is that developed by Albert W. Wardin, who used geographical/

---

1. For world Baptist statistics, see C. E. Bryant, "Baptist World Alliance Member Bodies," *Encyclopedia of Southern Baptists*, 4 vols. (Nashville: Broadman Press, 1982), 4:2113 f. For a listing of Baptist groups in the USA, see Robert G. Gardner, "Baptist General Bodies in the USA," *Baptist History and Heritage*, April 1977, pp. 92-94. Gardner has also supplied an unpublished update of that listing as of January 31, 1984.
2. Gardner, pp. 92-94.

doctrinal affinities to summarize Baptists in America into four main subgroups.[3] However, for this book a more chronological/topical approach commends itself. Century divisions are not strictly observed since it is necessary to set out the earlier roots of some of these Baptist groups.

No effort is made here to sketch the history of every Baptist group in America. The groups selected are representative of major segments of Baptist life, and no value judgment is intended about those omitted.[4]

Some observers, including Baptists, may assume that those who bear that name believe and practice much the same, but such is not the case. Churches called *Baptist* range over a wide spectrum of doctrinal beliefs, social views and practices, church polity and organization, and priorities in Christian witness. In theology they range from Calvinism to Arminianism, from extreme liberalism to hard-core fundamentalism; on social issues Baptists range from Social Gospel activism to passive silence; in evangelism, from tent revivalism to efforts to redeem society; in Christian living, from strict Puritanism to liberated individualism. Of course, many Baptists embody a happy medium between these extremes. To be called a *Baptist* hardly identifies one amid this denominational pluralism. The name has become so broad and inclusive as to require some preceding adjective to answer the question, What kind of Baptist?

Older Baptist Groups

A number of Baptist groups have their roots in the nineteenth century or before. Most have remained fairly small but have nevertheless exerted influence as a part of the Baptist family in America.

General Baptists

The earliest identifiable Baptist churches of modern history were called *General* for their view of a general atonement. While that name has never been as prominent in America as in England, several Baptist groups in the United States have worn it. They have been called General Baptists, General Six-Principle Baptists, or just Six-Principle Baptists. The "six principles" refer to the list of doctrinal beliefs and practices set out in Hebrews 6:1-2. Many of the early Calvinistic churches were called "Five-Principle" because they omitted the fourth principle, laying hands upon all newly baptized converts. Later the Freewill Baptists expressed another version of General Baptist life, but they will be treated separately.

3. Albert W. Wardin, Jr., *Baptist Atlas*. See chapter III, where he groups Baptists as follows: 1. Regular Baptists, Northern Oriented; 2. Regular Baptists, Southern Oriented; 3. General Baptists; and 4. Reformed Baptists.

4. For further information on the Baptist family in America, see the *Encyclopedia of Southern Baptists;* Frank S. Mead, *Handbook of Denominations in the United States* (Nashville: Abingdon Press, 7th edition, 1980); and Arthur C. Piepkorn, *Profiles of Belief: The Religious Bodies of the United States and Canada,* 7 vols. (New York: Harper and Row, 1978), 2.

General Baptists got an early foothold in America, particularly in Rhode Island and other parts of New England. Even the First Baptist Church of Providence, though established on a Calvinistic basis, adopted General views in the 1650s and was not reclaimed for Calvinism until the coming of President Manning in 1770. The earliest Baptist church in New York followed General views, as did the earliest churches in Virginia and North Carolina. What some regard as the earliest Baptist association in America was formed among the Six-Principle Baptists of Rhode Island, who formed a Yearly Meeting probably in 1670 and almost certainly before 1700.

However, even with an early start, the General Baptists did not prosper in America. They were plagued by internal problems, such as doctrinal ambiguity, lack of aggressive evangelism, and opposition to the First Great Awakening. They also faced continuing conflict over laying on of hands and foot washing. They had few meetinghouses and relied largely on an unpaid and usually untrained ministry. Most General Baptists hesitated to organize at a time when associationalism proved immensely useful among American Baptists. External developments also limited General Baptist progress. Chief among these was formation of the Philadelphia Association in 1707 and adoption of a Calvinist confession in 1742. Ollie Latch, historian of the General Baptists, citing the Philadelphia Association, said, "This organization was to turn the tide of affairs in the Baptist churches of America." Latch continued, "Because of hesitation over associational organizations, dallying over finance, and lack of resolution necessary to take the associational control, General Baptists let the Calvinists carry the day."[5] The thrust of the First Great Awakening was Calvinistic, and it swept all opposition aside.

The Separate Baptists, who translated the Awakening fervor into Baptist life, preached a modified Calvinism which further eroded General Baptist strength. Two strong associations mounted specific campaigns to win the General churches to Calvinism, the Philadelphia working mostly in the South and the Warren working in New England. The Separate Baptists, like Isaac Backus and John Gano, regarded it as a wholesome ministry of "reformation," or reclaiming wayward churches to "the doctrines of grace." The General Baptists, naturally, saw it differently; Latch referred to "raids upon General Baptist churches in the guise of home mission labor."[6] In retrospect, the Calvinists appear to have sometimes used high-handed means to enter autonomous churches, displace their ministers, indict their doctrines, and, in general, invalidate their faith.

The "reformation" of General churches to Calvinist principles represented both a victory and a defeat for the Calvinists. By far the majority of General ministers and churches made the transition to Calvinism, but

5. Ollie Latch, *History of the General Baptists,* p. 102.
6. Ibid., p. 102.

perhaps no more than 5 percent of the members followed them. The remaining 95 percent dropped out of church life, joined other Arminian groups, or tried to maintain the few remaining General Baptist churches.[7] That remnant later provided a seedbed for recruitment among the Freewill Baptists as well as the reconstituted General Baptists.

By 1800 General Baptists had become all but extinct in America, though a few churches may have survived. However, in 1823 Benoni Stinson (1798-1869) founded in Evansville, Indiana, what is now regarded as the oldest surviving General Baptist church in America. Other such churches sprang up, and in 1824 the Liberty Baptist Association of Indiana was formed. Though it clearly represented the same faith and order, no historical link between the older General Baptists and more recent ones has been demonstrated.

The restored General Baptists organized into a number of associations. By the 1860s they expressed a desire for national organization and made overtures to join the Freewill Baptists, with whom they had much in common. These efforts came to nothing. Led by Stinson, they formed the General Association of General Baptists in 1870, with denominational headquarters later removed to Poplar Bluff, Missouri. The founding document said:

> The General Association of General Baptists . . . is designed to comprise all the annual associations . . . to complete the organization of the connection, to consolidate the body by harmonizing its different parts, keeping a common interest in view and producing a unity of sentiment and discipline, to concentrate its strength in a common cause.[8]

The General Baptists' confession of faith could have been composed by John Smyth or Thomas Helwys, whom they claimed as their ultimate founders. They held to general atonement, the necessity to endure in faith to retain salvation, and open communion with all Christians. Foot washing has gradually declined among this group. At its formation in 1870, the General Association listed 9,742 members.[9] Growth has been steady but slow; by 1980, the General Baptists listed 72,764 members in 837 churches, scattered over a 16-state region of the Midwest. They publish a paper, *The General Baptist Messenger;* sponsor a liberal arts college in Oakland City, Indiana; and work through denominational boards for home and foreign missions, Christian publications and Sunday School materials, women's work, and ministerial pensions. The General Baptists have remained Arminian in theology and have benefitted from the softening of Calvinism in America.

7. See William F. Davidson, *An Early History of Free Will Baptists,* p. 119.
8. Latch, p. 197.
9. Ibid., p. 159.

More ordered worship services and rising educational standards for ministry mark their recent history.

Seventh-Day Baptists

The earliest known church of this order was the Mill Yard Seventh Day Baptist Church of London, formed in 1653 and led by the prominent physician, Dr. Peter Chamberlen. He was succeeded by John James, who preached radical millennialism, an emphasis with some affinity for Sabbatarian views. James was hanged in 1661, and his body was drawn and quartered and placed on public display. Despite such brutal persecution, perhaps a dozen or more Sabbatarian churches emerged among English Baptists in the seventeenth century.

Baptists were among those earnest reformers who sought to return from church tradition to the direct authority of the Bible. Some of the more literalist, therefore, reinstituted such practices as laying on of hands, washing feet, baptism by immersion only, and worship on the sabbath. While all of these practices surfaced among Baptists, only one, immersion, became normative. The first-day Baptists accused the Sabbatarians of preferring the Law to the Gospel and receding from Christ to Moses. The Seventh-Day brethren countered that the Bible gives no clear command to change any of the Ten Commandments.

A few Sabbatarian churches have survived among English Baptists, but this group has reached its greatest development in the United States. They might have grown more but for the rise of Seventh-Day Adventism in the 1840s which drew off many of their converts, actual and potential. American religion apparently offers only a limited market for seventh-day worship, and the Adventists have captured the lion's share. Other than their emphasis upon the sabbath, Seventh-Day Baptists closely resemble other Baptist groups. They show the same early adherence to Calvinism, the same moderation of Calvinism in the 1800s, and the gradual rise of a general denominational body with societies for foreign and home missions, Christian education and Sabbath School work. Sabbatarianism surfaced often in Colonial America, as we know from internal discussions of many Baptist churches. Even the First Church of Providence, oldest in the country, had some sharp discussions about the proper day for worship.

Four early centers. One can locate Sabbatarian Baptists in Colonial America in four major centers. The first and strongest such center was Rhode Island. Stephen Mumford, a member of the Bell Lane Seventh Day Baptist Church in London, migrated to Newport in 1665. Finding no church of that order, Mumford joined John Clarke's first-day church. For several years first and seventh-day members coexisted in relative peace. Two developments, both predictable, ended this coexistence. First, Mumford's witness drew a number of others to his views, a fact which alarmed the church. Second, four of the Sabbatarians renounced their Seventh-Day views and "advanced from Moses to Christ," a fact that alarmed the remaining Sabbatarians.

The two groups separated in 1671, when Mumford led seven Sabbatarians to form the First Seventh Day Baptist Church of Newport, the first church of that order in America. They called as pastor William Hiscox, who had been one of Mumford's first converts. No doubt the separation was hastened by Obadiah Holmes, acting pastor in the absence of John Clarke, who preached on "Woe to the world because of offences," and concluded that "offences are such as arise from brethren of the church, such as deny Christ, and have turned to Moses in observing days, times, years, etc., and that it is better that a mill-stone were hanged about the neck of such, and they be cast into the sea."[10] For their part, the Sabbatarians interpreted the first-day preference of the Newport church to represent "the dismal laying aside of the ten precepts altogether."

Seventh-Day Baptists grew by evangelism, church extension, and immigration from England. Within a few years, they had a handful of churches scattered across New England, with the strongest in Hopkinton, Rhode Island. A few Rogerene churches practiced immersion and held the seventh day but never affiliated with Seventh-Day Baptists. The Sabbatarians shared in the struggle for religious liberty, bore witness with other Baptists against religious oppression, and cooperated with mainline Baptists in founding Rhode Island College in 1764. Isaac Backus occasionally preached in Seventh-Day churches on his travels; sometimes they met on the first day to accommodate him.[11]

A second Sabbatarian center arose in Philadelphia. Abel Noble, called "the apostle of Sabbatarianism in Pennsylvania," migrated to that region about 1684 and was later baptized by Thomas Chillingsworth. Noble later embraced Sabbatarian views. A number of Quakers around Philadelphia debated the question of religious authority, whether it be found in "the inner light," as most Quakers said, or in the written Scripture, as George Keith, one of their leaders, maintained. A number of Keithian Quakers broke with the main body, accepted the authority of the Bible, and adopted other Baptist practices. Noble drew a number of Keithians to Seventh-Day Baptist views.

New Jersey, especially around Piscataway, provided a third area of strength for Seventh-Day Baptists. In the 1690s Edmund Dunham, a deacon and lay preacher in the Baptist church at Piscataway, reproved a fellow member for working on Sunday. That member, a Mr. Bonham, replied that Sunday was no special day and challenged Dunham to study the Bible for himself. As a result, Dunham embraced Sabbatarian views and by 1705 had

10. C. F. Randolph, ed., *Seventh Day Baptists in Europe and America,* p. 124.
11. See William G. McLoughlin, ed., *The Diary of Isaac Backus,* 3 vols., 1:335-336.

formed a church of seventeen members at Piscataway. Upon his death, he was succeeded as pastor by his son.

From these three streams, Newport, Philadelphia, and Piscataway, Seventh-Day Baptists spread northward to Connecticut, western New York state, and as far south as Virginia, the Carolinas, and Georgia. By 1802, according to their historian, "There were not less than 20 churches and settlements of Sabbath-keepers, in nine or ten colonies or states, numbering about 2,000 members."[12]

A fourth Sabbatarian center was isolated from the others and had little part in extending the Seventh-Day witness. The Ephrata Community was established in 1735 by John Conrad Beissell (1691-1768). Beissell migrated from Germany to Pennsylvania where he came under the influence of Seventh-Day Baptists. Adding Sabbatarianism to mystical pietism, Beissell founded Ephrata on a semimonastic basis, including celibacy, pacifism, and community of goods. Most of the early converts came from Seventh-Day Baptists. The community declined after Beissell's death, but while it lasted its inhabitants made contributions in printing, hymnology, and the education of children. Apparently their emphasis upon Sabbath School instruction and development of children's curriculum for that purpose influenced the Sunday School movement in America. In 1814 Ephrata was incorporated as the German Religious Society of Seventh Day Baptists but was finally dissolved in 1934. Its cloister remains as a museum of early American pietism.

The General Conference. Like other Baptists, those who held the seventh day found it helpful to hold Yearly Meetings which gathered messengers from their scattered churches to discuss common concerns and plan for united ministry. The Rhode Island group appointed such a meeting as early as 1684, usually meeting in their strongest church at Hopkinton. Some opposed the Yearly Meeting lest it lead to centralization. In 1762 the "General Meeting was laid down" but was restored the next year. The record for 1763 states:

> Our General Meeting was, for sundry good reasons, voted down and to cease last year; but upon considering how necessary it is for brethren to meet together, to stir up one another and likewise to commune together, and in order to provoke one another to Christian love and unity, that the weak may become more strong, that God may have glory and our souls peace, we have thought fit that, for the future, the Sixth-day before the third Sabbath in September be a church meeting, and the Sabbath following an annual communion, that all our distant brethren and sisters may be present, in order to be helpers of our joy.[13]

12. Randolph, p. 133.
13. Ibid., p. 151.

Regional gatherings proved so beneficial that in 1801 the Rhode Island group issued a call for a general conference of all Seventh-Day Baptists to promote fellowship and cooperation in missionary work. The records state that in 1801 about 60 brethren and 12 sisters, led by Elder Henry Clark, "Brought forward a proposition for the several churches of our Union to unite in an institution for propagating our religion in the different parts of the United States; by sending out from the different churches in said Union missionaries, on the expense of the several churches."[14] The ambitious handful formed the General Conference of Seventh Day Baptists (which has endured to the present). Eight affiliated churches represented 1,031 members. The first annual session was held in 1802, with 78 messengers present from 7 churches. At its centennial in 1901, the denomination listed 116 churches, with 9,340 members.[15]

The General Conference soon developed the usual array of related organizations which mark most Baptist groups. The 1852 session asked for clarification, confessing, "We find ourselves embarrassed for want of a clear knowledge of the powers, objects, and purposes of this organization."[16] Over the years the Seventh-Day Baptists formed the Foreign Mission Society (1842), the American Sabbath Tract Society (1843), the Seventh Day Baptist Education Society (1858), the Woman's Executive Board (1884), and the Sabbath School Board (1872). The Sabbatarians were ahead of most Baptists in developing the Sabbath School for religious instruction, and they pioneered in developing suitable curriculum both for children and adults. They sponsored one university (Alfred University, in New York) and two colleges (in Wisconsin and West Virginia). They also supported a number of academies which disbanded as public schools became more available.

The Seventh-Day Baptists have remained theologically conservative. Their "Expose of the Doctrinal Sentiments of the Seventh-Day Baptists," adopted in 1833, differs little from the views of other Baptists except on the sabbath and laying hands upon new converts.[17] In 1980 they heard a proposal to amend the article on Scripture to specify belief in the inerrancy of original autographs, which was referred for further study.[18]

In the 1840s the Seventh-Day Baptists were troubled by inroads of radical millennialism, arising from the Plymouth Brethren movement in England and similar movements in America. From the first, Seventh-Day Baptists proved susceptible to these extremes; many of them were caught up in the Fifth Monarchy Movement in England, and Conrad Beissell emphasized radical millennialism at Ephrata. In 1844 Rachel Preston, a Seventh-Day

14. Ibid., p. 153.
15. Ibid., p. 233n.
16. *Minutes,* Seventh Day Baptist General Conference, Plainfield, New Jersey, 1852, p. 7.
17. *Minutes,* Seventh Day General Conference, 1843, pp. 13-15.
18. *Seventh Day Baptist Yearbook,* 1980, p. 56.

Baptist from Verona, New York, attended a meeting in New Hampshire which dealt with the rising tide of interest in millennialism. While there she distributed tracts and convinced several persons of the validity of sabbath worship, including Ellen G. White and her husband James White, soon to found the Seventh-Day Adventist denomination.[19] Some Seventh-Day Baptists began to speculate about a two-stage second coming of Christ, known as the *rapture.* Most of those who felt drawn to the new doctrine joined the Adventists.

The General Conference carried on an active correspondence with Sabbatarians in England, the emerging Adventist movement in America, and remnants of the Ephrata cloister. The annual meeting of 1849, for example, illustrates the kinds of issues they faced. They passed a series of resolutions on the following topics:

The designating of days numerically;
The beginning of the Sabbath at sunset on Sixth-day;
The better observance of the Sabbath;
The high-handed sin of slavery;
The evils of secret societies;
Recognition of the Seventh-Day Baptist Publishing Society;
The morally bad influence of circus and similar exhibitions;
The importance of having church membership where one lives; and
The need of a denominational college and theological seminary.[20]

The Seventh-Day Baptists often spoke against slavery, the Fugitive Slave Law, excessive use of alcoholic beverages, and secret societies such as the Masonic Lodge. During the 1800s they often entered into cooperative efforts with first-day Baptists and at times challenged other Baptists to Bible study and dialogues.

In 1843 the General Conference published a major treatise on the sabbath. That defense of Sabbatarian views and practices was well written, reflected an irenic tone, and aimed at nothing less than winning mainline Baptists to sabbath observance. Noting that the day of worship "is the only ground of difference between you and us," the Seventh-Day Baptists affirmed, "We are persuaded that the great body of your denomination have dismissed it [the Sabbath] without any particular investigation."[21] That treatise still ranks as one of the better statements of the Sabbatarian point of view.

The twentieth century. For the Seventh-Day Baptists, the twentieth century has brought both advances and reverses. In 1919 the General Confer-

19. Albert N. Rogers, with others, "Seventh Day Baptist General Conference," in Davis C. Woolley, ed., *Baptist Advance,* p. 256.
20. *Minutes,* Seventh Day Baptist General Conference, 1849, pp. 5-7.
21. Thomas B. Brown, Paul Stillman, and Nathan V. Hull, *An Address to the Baptist Denomination of the United States on the Observance of the Sabbath,* p. 6.

ence launched its "Forward Movement," a drive which not only raised funds but also unified the previously independent societies into an overall denominational effort known as "Our World Mission." Like other Baptist groups, the conference created a general board to oversee its work, formed a unified budget, and in 1929 dedicated their new headquarters building at Plainfield, New Jersey. Denominational headquarters were later moved to Janesville, Wisconsin. In 1952 Seventh-Day Baptists created the office of executive secretary to provide overall denominational leadership.

Though small, the denomination has shown an ability to fund its work at a commendable level. Seventh-Day Baptists tend to enlist a large ratio of well-to-do members. Their view of the Old Testament as still binding extends to the practice of tithing. They sponsor a radio ministry called "The Word of Truth," and their major periodical is *The Sabbath Recorder*.

The Seventh-Day Baptists have shown an openness to various ecumenical ventures. The General Conference affiliates with the National Council of Churches, the World Council of Churches, and the Baptist World Alliance. They also helped form the Seventh Day Baptist World Federation, with affiliated bodies in Brazil, Burma, Malawi, England, Germany, Guyana, India, Jamaica, Mexico, Holland, New Zealand, the Philippines, and elsewhere.[22] In 1980 the conference reported only 5,156 members in about 60 churches, which represents about 50 percent loss since the turn of the century.[23] However, worldwide the Seventh-Day Baptists reported 52,155 members in 13 nations, with the largest community in India, with 36,373 members.[24] The numerical decline in America may be partially attributed to the growth of Seventh-Day Adventism, the struggle to maintain a minority witness in a first-day society, and the gradual shift from an evangelistic to a maintenance mentality. However, in 1980 the conference launched its "Decade of Discipleship" program, an effort to double the size of the denomination and its ministries in one decade.[25]

Freewill Baptists

Every person's freedom to believe in Jesus Christ, over against Calvinistic predestination, has provided both the major teaching and the name of the Freewill Baptists.[26] The present denomination emerged on two fronts about a half century apart. Paul Palmer formed General Baptist churches in North Carolina, beginning in 1727, which in time assumed the name of "Free-Willers." Quite independently of the Palmer churches, Benjamin

22. Mead, p. 57.
23. Ibid., p. 56.
24. *Seventh Day Baptist Yearbook,* 1980, p. 149.
25. Ibid., p. 28.
26. The name has been variously written as Free Will, Free-Will, Freewill, or Free Baptist. The modern denomination uses Free Will and Freewill interchangeably.

Randall organized a Freewill Baptist church in New Durham, New Hampshire in 1780. Remnants from both groups merged in 1935 at Nashville, Tennessee, to form the present National Association of Free Will Baptists. That body split in 1962, giving rise to the General Conference of Original Free Will Baptists, headquartered at Ayden, North Carolina. An Evangelical Free Baptist Church, centered in Illinois and numbering about twenty-five hundred members in twenty-two churches, makes up yet another Freewill group. A number of other Freewill churches stand alone without any denominational connection.

The Palmer line. Paul Palmer established a church at Chowan in North Carolina as early as 1727. He was soon joined by Joseph Parker, and other churches followed, all preaching *free will* though that term was no part of their name until about 1800. Most of those churches succumbed to Calvinism in the ''reformation'' after 1750, but a few survived to continue the emphasis upon free will, foot washing, and open communion. In 1807 Jesse Heath found only five such churches left, but 1812 marked the beginning of recovery. In that year, the Free Will Baptist Annual Conference met at Little Creek and adopted "An Abstract of the Former Articles of Faith Confessed by the Original Baptist Church Holding the Doctrine of General Provision with a Proper Code of Discipline."[27] This was an adaptation of the Standard Confession of English General Baptists adopted in 1660. By 1830 the Freewill Baptists had made a remarkable recovery in North Carolina and adjoining states. Their churches were organized into Quarterly Meetings, had a clear sense of self-identity, and claimed continuity from the Palmer group of 1727. They exchanged letters and messengers with Freewill Baptists in New England, and the two branches might have merged but for problems which led to the Civil War.

Despite their claim to continuity from Palmer, historians until recently had been unable to demonstrate a connecting link between the Palmer General Baptist churches and the modern Freewill Baptists of the South. William F. Davidson, in *An Early History of Free Will Baptists,* recently provided that documentation in a convincing manner.[28] He showed that the two movements are connected by the same churches, same pastors, and use of the same confessions. He also showed that the name *Free Will* goes back well before 1800 and was often used interchangeably with *General Baptist.* Davidson concluded, "The evidence has pointed toward the validity of the Free Will Baptist claim that their heritage dates back to 1727."[29]

The Randall line. Another stream of Freewill Baptist life, and by far the larger and more familiar, arose in New Hampshire in 1780. Led by Benja-

27. William F. Davidson, *An Early History of Free Will Baptists 1727-1830,* pp. 166, 170.
28. Ibid.
29. Ibid., p. 214.

min Randall (1749-1808), the New England group represented both a reaction against the stern Calvinism of the time and a Baptist response to the waves of revival which arrived by the late 1770s. Randall had gone to sea with his ship captain father and later worked as a tailor and farmer. Though a pious youth, he delayed joining any church. When he first heard the fiery preaching of George Whitefield, the English evangelist, Randall was critical. He exclaimed to himself, "Ah, thought I, you are a worthless, noisy fellow! All you want is to make the people cry out! My good old minister does not do so, and he is a good a man as you, and much better."[30] Later upon hearing of Whitefield's sudden death in 1770, Randall was smitten with remorse. He thought, "Whitefield is now in heaven and I am on the road to hell." As his concern mounted, Randall said, "My former religion appeared altogether worthless and fled from me as though it had never been."[31] Upon the basis of this conviction, he joined the Congregational Church but found little satisfaction.

Out of doctrinal conviction, Randall joined the Baptists in 1776 but found their strict Calvinism increasingly out of step with views emerging from his own Bible study. In 1779 he was called before a Baptist council and asked why he did not preach the doctrine of election according to John Calvin. Randall's frank reply was, "Because I do not believe it."[32] After extensive discussion, the leader of the council pronounced the Baptist verdict: "I have no fellowship with brother Randall, in his principles." Randall replied, "It makes no odds with me who disowns me, so long as I know that the Lord owns me."[33]

On June 30, 1780, Randall formed a church of seven members at New Durham, New Hampshire, the first of many Freewill churches he and his followers would plant in New England. About a month later he had a traumatic encounter which confirmed his faith and gave an apostolic quality to his preaching. This experience is best described by Randall himself:

> Sometime in July [1780] I was in great trial of mind because of such texts, and, desiring solitude, I walked to a remote place, and entered a field of corn. My soul was in great agony, and I sat down upon a rock, and was praying that my heavenly father would teach me. All at once, it seemed as if the Lord denied my request. This increased my trial, and I cried, "Lord why may I not be taught?" The answer was, "Because thou has too many right hands, and right eyes." I said, "Lord, what are my right hands and right eyes?" Then it appeared to me that they were my old traditions, which I still held, and my old brethren, whose doctrines and opinions I had not fully renounced. I

30. Ibid., p. 31.
31. Ibid., p. 32.
32. Cited in I. D. Stewart, *The History of the Freewill Baptists,* p. 44.
33. Ibid., p. 45.

then saw that I was too much encumbered with natural connections, and that my heart needed much purifying and refining. I said, "Lord, here I am, take me, and do with me as thou wilt."[34]

With this apostolic mandate, Randall traveled widely, establishing other churches in New England. By 1783 enough churches existed to form a Quarterly Meeting, much like an association, and several such Quarterly Meetings formed a Yearly Meeting in 1792. The General Conference of Free Will Baptists took form in 1827, combining the Yearly Meetings and thus completing the denominational structure. At Randall's death in 1808, the movement had about six thousand members.

The Freewill movement grew rapidly in the North, reaping benefits from the waves of revival and the gradual erosion of Calvinism. The Randallites pioneered in several areas. They allowed larger leadership roles for women in their churches; in the 1840s, they became the first Baptist group to send single women as foreign missionaries. They strongly opposed slavery, enlisted many blacks into their membership, and ordained black pastors on an equality with whites. Like the Palmerites, their North Carolina counterparts, the Randall group practiced foot washing, though they made less of laying on of hands. However, in time some outgrew their early enthusiasm and looked toward reunion with Regular Baptists. Others proved vulnerable to the Shaker movement, led first by Mother Ann Lee, which seemed to offer an even more radical Pietism. Other internal problems included occasional outbreaks of Unitarianism, annihilationism, and "angel delusions." A few years later, the Palmerite branch fell victim to the Disciples movement, which decimated them almost as thoroughly as the Calvinist "reformation" had after 1750.

After years of talks, the Freewill Baptists in New England merged into the Northern Baptist Convention in 1911. By that time, both "Regular" and "Free" Baptists had so modified their theology that there appeared little reason to remain separate. The Freewills took with them into Northern Baptist life 857 of their 1,100 churches and all their denominational property, including several colleges. That merger has not proven overly happy. Some attribute the increase of internal tensions among Northern Baptists early in the twentieth century partly to that influx of new churches and viewpoints. By the 1980s, many of the former Freewill churches had withdrawn from American Baptist affiliation, either to join the reconstituted Freewill denomination or to remain independent.

The National Association. Merger in the North and defection in the South greatly weakened Freewill Baptists early in the present century. However, remnants sought to revive the work. Representatives from four churches which refused to go along with the Northern merger met in

---

34. Ibid., p. 54.

Pattonsburg, Missouri, and formed the Cooperative General Association of Free Will Baptists in 1916. They launched a periodical, *The New Morning Star,* and appealed for others to join them. In that way, according to one of their historians, "The scattered remnants of Free Will Baptists slowly began to come back together."[35] Most of their churches were in the West, and the Cooperative Association soon became known as the "Western branch."

Remnants of the Palmer line, meantime, also gathered, forming a General Conference in 1921. Since most of their churches were in the Southeast, they soon became known as the "Eastern branch." Conversations between the two branches revealed much in common. Both were organized into Quarterly Meetings, and they shared the same basic General Baptist faith, though some placed more emphasis upon foot washing. By the 1930s their leaders saw clearly the advantages of a national union.

Messengers from both groups formed the National Association of Free Will Baptists (NAFWB) in 1935, chose Nashville, Tennessee, as their headquarters, set up boards for Sunday School and mission work, and laid plans for a college. They made a giant step toward unity when the associations agreed to a common doctrinal statement adopted in 1935. The editor of *The Free Will Baptist* rejoiced at "adopting a treatise of the faith and practice of our church for all the people." He said, "As a result of this great forward step, we hope to be able to read the same doctrinal statements, or articles of faith, wherever we find Free Will Baptist people."[36]

The Free Will Baptist College, planned since 1935, opened in Nashville in 1942. Though the denomination has discussed the formation of a theological seminary, as yet none has materialized. In 1964 the denomination listed nine seminaries recommended for their ministers, only two of which were Baptist.[37]

In a document on "The Faith of Free Will Baptists," adopted in 1935, the National Association set out doctrinal beliefs and practices which would be familiar to most Baptists for the past three centuries. They accept the freedom of persons to believe in Christ, which gave their name long ago, a point now shared by most other Baptists. Most of their churches practice open communion, foot washing, and some lay hands upon new converts. They believe that the Lord's Supper is open to "all who have spiritual union with Christ" and that "no man has a right to forbid these tokens to the least of His disciples."[38] On washing the saints' feet, the *Treatise on the Faith*

35. Damon C. Dodd, *The Free Will Baptist Story,* p. 115.

36. "The National Association," *The Free Will Baptist,* November 13, 1935, p. 4.

37. "Report of Seminary Study Committee," *Minutes,* National Association of Free Will Baptists, 1964, p. 22, (hereafter cited as *Minutes,* NAFWB).

38. *A Treatise on the Faith and Practices of Free Will Baptists* (Nashville: National Association of Free Will Baptist, Revised 1981), p. 37.

and Practice of Free Will Baptists says, "This is a sacred ordinance, which teaches humility. . . . It is the duty and happy prerogative of every believer to observe this sacred ordinance."[39]

The denomination is organized in stair-step fashion, with delegates from churches to association, association to state meetings, and state to national assemblies. Ministers are always members of the denominational bodies, and each unit may also choose laymen to represent them. While ordination and discipline find their source in local churches, the churches usually delegate these responsibilities to the association.

Freewill Baptists seek to maintain doctrinal conservatism. In 1959 they established the Commission on Theological Liberalism which has become a standing commission, giving annual reports on the doctrinal state of the denomination. Their first report said, "The Free Will Baptist Denomination is greatly blessed in that we have no great problem over modernism at the present time."[40] An amendment to the doctrinal standard, adopted in 1979, affirms, "The Bible is without error and trustworthy in all its teachings, including cosmogony, geology, astronomy, anthropology, history, chronology, etc., as well as in matters of faith and practice."[41]

The Freewill Baptists have enjoyed steady growth through the years. By 1981 they listed 216,848 members, gathered into 2,479 churches and 194 associations. They listed 28 foreign missionaries in 6 nations, plus perhaps twice that many home missionaries. For the year ending in 1981, 6,549 baptisms were reported.[42] Presently the Freewills are distinguished from other Baptists more by their practices, such as foot washing and centralized denominational structure, than by doctrines.

Other Freewill Baptists. In addition to the NAFWB, the largest group, a number of other groupings of Freewill Baptists exist in the United States. Some groups arose independently of either the Palmer or Randall lines, being offspring of Separate Baptist remnants in the South.[43] Pockets of Freewills remain here and there, their churches standing alone without denominational moorings.

The General Conference of Original Free Will Baptists originated in a 1962 schism from the National Association. Located mostly in North Carolina, and headquartered there, these Freewill Baptists reacted against what they regarded as "excessive denominationalism" in the main body and regarded their group as restoring "the traditions and customs of the movement introduced in America by Paul Palmer." They seek to preserve the spirit and simplicity of the Palmer General Baptist background but differ

39. Ibid.

40. *Minutes,* NAFWB, 1960, p. 19.

41. *Treatise,* p. 43.

42. *Minutes,* NAFWB, 1981, p. 139.

43. Robert E. Picarilli, "A Study of Separate, Free Will, Baptist Origins in Middle Tennessee," *Baptist Quarterly* (January-March 1977), pp. 44 *f.*

little in doctrine from the main body. A recent report set membership at about 40,000, gathered in 337 churches.[44]

The United American Free Will Baptist Church, predominantly black, dates from 1867 when a small number of black Baptists formed a church under a brush arbor in Greene County, North Carolina. In the next years several other such churches emerged, enough to form an Annual Meeting by 1887 and a General Conference in 1901. Their organization differs somewhat; their presiding officer, for example, is called "senior bishop." However, their basic beliefs and practices closely resemble other Freewill Baptists. A recent report set membership at 40,100, in about 350 churches.[45]

Primitive Baptists

The Primitive Baptists originated in a protest against the rise of missionary work in the early 1800s. Their extreme Calvinism undercut the theology of missions and their ecclesiology could not make room for the societies and other organizations needed to raise and disburse money for a successful mission operation. Their opposition went beyond missions to include Sunday Schools, Bible societies, theological seminaries, and other "human effort" organizations. While they favored local churches and associations, they opposed the emergence of a more complete denomination.

The names attached to this group reflect their extreme conservatism. They have been called "Primitive," "Old School," "Old Liner," or "Hardshell" Baptists. Some have preferred to be called simply the "Old Baptists." These names reflect those Baptists' conviction that they recapture the original emphases of historic Baptists, whom they seek to trace back to the apostles. They see themselves as descendants of the original Particular Baptists, whose confessions they adopt.

The Primitive churches embrace a strict Calvinism, believing that the elect will inevitably be drawn to salvation, while the nonelect will be left to perish in their sins. Most of their churches are small and generations ago had preaching only once a month. Most of them practice closed communion, and a few practice foot washing. Until recent years, most of their pastors were untrained and served without salary. However, in the twentieth century, a few of the Primitive churches hold weekly worship, led by salaried and, in some cases, by trained pastors.

The Kehuckee Association. Like the Freewills before them, the Primitive Baptists arose from different streams. One major stream came from the Kehuckee Association in North Carolina, which declared against missions in 1826. A church had been formed on Kehuckee Creek in 1742 on General Baptist principles. Soon a number of other General churches sprang up, but

44. Arthur C. Piepkorn, *Profiles of Belief: The Religious Bodies in the United States and Canada,* 2:436.

45. Gardner, p. 94.

after 1750 "reformers" from the Philadelphia Association moved among them, drawing most of them to a moderate Calvinism. The Kehuckee church, for example, was reorganized in 1755 with only ten members. These newly "Calvinized" churches affiliated with the Charleston Association but may have held annual meetings in their own state by the early 1760s. However, it appears the Kehuckee Association was not formed until 1769.[46]

Most of the Kehuckee churches held their recently adopted Calvinism with the zeal of new converts. The influx of Separate Baptists, with their intense evangelism and general invitations to the unconverted, troubled some of the Kehuckee churches. Perhaps the majority wanted to accommodate the newcomers; the Kehuckee Association appointed messengers to meet with Separate leaders with a view to cooperation. However, a few churches could not abide such openness and split off as early as 1775. This indicates that Kehuckee Baptists held their faith strongly and were willing to split if necessary to protect it.

By the early 1800s Baptists in America were caught up in the emerging zeal for missions. Many associations declared in favor of that work and contributed to mission societies. One of those awakened to the potential for missions was Martin Ross, who introduced the following question at the association in 1803:

> Is not the Kehuckee Association, with all her numerous and respectable friends, called on in Providence, in some way to step forward in support of that missionary spirit which the great God is so wonderfully reviving amongst the different denominations of good men in various parts of the world?[47]

G. W. Paschal called this "the first trumpet call of North Carolina Baptists to the work of missions." However, it brought dissension to the churches; one observer said the missionary call of Ross "gave rise to contentions, heartburnings, bickerings, animosities, and strife, broke the peace of the brethren, and was a fire brand in their midst."[48] The next year the association voted "to support the missionary cause," but the churches were split into "missionary" and "anti-missionary" factions. Opposition to missions centered in three areas: theology (predestination), methodology (formation of "societies" outside the churches), and money (offerings to pay missionary salaries). Many of the pastors at that time still served without salaries.

The association had 61 churches and 5,017 members by 1789 and con-

---

46. George W. Paschal, *A History of North Carolina Baptists,* 2 vols., 1:417. In their earlier history Burkitt and Read had set the date at "about 1765," but Paschal later discovered the minutes which pinpointed a later date. See Lemuel Burkitt and Jesse Read, *A Concise History of the Kehuckee Baptist Association* (Philadelphia: Lippincott, Grambo and Company, 1850; reprinted by Arno Press, New York, 1980), p. 36.
47. Paschal, p. 544.
48. Ibid., p. 546.

tinued to grow.[49] When churches in the Chowan area split off to form their own association, most of the antimission churches were left in the old association. They gradually gained the upper hand and in 1826 declared:

> It was agreed that we discard all Missionary Societies, Bible Societies, and Theological Seminaries, and the practices heretofore resorted to for their support, in begging money from the public. . . . we will not invite them [agents of such organizations] into our pulpits, believing these societies and institutions to be the inventions of men and not warranted from the word of God.[50]

With this action of the Kehuckee Association the die was cast; missionary and antimissionary Baptists parted ways. The term *Kehuckeeism* became a synonym for antimissions, and one major stream of Primitive Baptists grew up in the remnants of that association.

Varieties of Primitive Baptists. One can distinguish at least five different groups of Primitive Baptists, divided by doctrine, practice, or ethnic background. The Primitive churches are usually grouped into associations, which, in turn, "correspond" with each other by letter or messenger, but there are no state conventions or general bodies. The Primitives often find their center of unity not in a convention but a periodical.

First in priority and in numbers are the Old Liners, who in 1980 reported 48,980 members in 1,426 churches.[51] While accepting the doctrine of predestination, they make Christians responsible for the way they exercise their salvation. Old Liners are careful not to make God the author of sin. They teach that, while individuals are totally depraved and passive before and in the new birth, they can be active in obedience thereafter. This allows at least a minimum of personal decision, if not in receiving salvation at least in Christian living. Old Liner views are expressed in such journals as the *Advocate and Messenger,* the *Baptist Witness,* and *The Primitive Baptist.*[52]

A second party, known as Absoluters, holds to "the absolute predestination of all things, both good and evil."[53] This means that every human action, whether of the elect or nonelect, before or after salvation, is predestined. This group is concentrated in North Carolina, Virginia, West Virginia, and Kentucky, and it is declining in numbers. In 1980 the group reported 6,495 members in 380 churches.[54] Its views circulate in such papers as *Signs of the Times* and *Zion's Landmark.* Predictably, Absoluters

49. Ibid., p. 494.
50. Cited in Robert A. Baker, ed., *A Baptist Source Book,* p. 82.
51. Wardin, p. 32.
52. Arthur C. Piepkorn, "The Primitive Baptists of North America," *Baptist History and Heritage,* January 1972, p. 46. This article was first published in *Concordia Theological Monthly,* XLII, No. 5, 1971.
53. Ibid., p. 37n.
54. Wardin, p. 32.

often have to defend themselves against charges of antinomianism and making God the author of sin.

In reaction to the strictness of Old Liners and Absoluters, a third group, the Progressive Primitive Baptists, emerged in the early 1900s. The Progressives originated in Georgia but later spread to other states. They accept musical instruments in worship, Sunday Schools, salaried pastors and established a Primitive Baptist college. In recent years their churches have erected attractive buildings, and they often meet weekly rather than monthly, especially in urban areas. Many of their churches sponsor special ministries for youth and women. This group is growing, and its churches tend to be larger than the others. Its membership stood at 11,043 for 1980, gathered in 163 churches.[55]

The Two-Seed-in-the-Spirit Predestinarian Baptists, a fourth group, originated out of the preaching of Daniel Parker. In 1826 Parker published his *Views on the Two Seeds,* based on Genesis 3:15. From the garden of Eden, according to this view, the seed of God and the seed of Satan produce offspring. Children born of God's seed belong to God and will be redeemed; they are the elect. Children born of Satan's seed will be damned, for they are nonelect. No one can control or even predict which seed is in him; thus each person's eternal destiny is predetermined and nothing can change it. Aside from this version of predestination, the Two-Seed group resembles other Primitive Baptists in faith and practice, though the others claim little fellowship with this group.

Parker was reared in Virginia but migrated to Illinois in the 1820s and on to Texas in 1833. Mexican law forbade the organization of a Baptist church in Texas but technically did not prohibit importing an already formed church into the province. Therefore, the shrewd Parker formed the Pilgrim Predestinarian Regular Baptist Church of Jesus Christ (known as the Pilgrim Church) and moved it to Texas in 1833. It may have been the earliest organized Baptist church in the state. Several such churches sprang up and later provided stout competition before yielding to the advance of missionary Baptists who arrived soon afterward.

The Pilgrim Church later formed the nucleus of the Union Primitive Baptist Association of the Old School or Predestinarian Faith and Order, which still functions or at least meets in Texas, though it has dwindled to near extinction. The neighboring South Louisiana Primitive Baptist Association holds similar views. Its story is best told in brief lines from its 1971 associational meeting, which state: "Petitionary Letters from churches desiring membership in the Association were called for. None were received." The next line says, "Petitionary Letters from associations desiring

---

55. Ibid.

correspondence with the Association were called for. None were received."[56]

A fifth group, the National Primitive Baptist Convention of the USA represents black Primitive Baptists. The earliest black Primitive church dates from the 1820s, and in 1869 a group of such churches formed the Indian Creek Primitive Baptist Association in Alabama. In 1907 eighty-eight elders from seven states formed the National Primitive Baptist Convention, headquartered in Huntsville, Alabama.[57] While their statistics remain uncertain, they are evidently growing and may by now constitute the largest Primitive Baptist group in America. The black Primitives have proven less rigid in doctrine than their white brethren.

Primitive beliefs and practices. Despite variations, most of the Primitives follow a common path in belief and behavior. The Fulton Confession of 1900, so called because it was adopted at Fulton, Kentucky, includes twelve doctrinal articles. The *Advocate and Messenger* has frequently reprinted that confession and claimed as early as 1926 that it represented the faith of 90 percent of Primitive Baptists in America.[58] The Fulton Confession specifies a conservative Calvinistic faith which accepts the inspiration of Scripture, a triune God, salvation by grace, predestination, baptism by immersion only, the use of bread and wine in the Lord's Supper, and the complete independence of local churches. Most Primitives hold closed communion, and many also practice foot washing.

Most early Primitives disavowed missions. In 1912 the Union Association of Regular Primitive Baptists of the Predestinarian Faith and Order, held with the Pilgrim Church at Elkhart, Texas, noted that "this Association declares that it has no fellowship with the Baptist Board of Foreign Missions (as so called), nor with the moneyed institutions connected therewith, nor any of the secret institutions of the day."[59] In a similar vein, the Original Upper Canoochee Association of Georgia declared:

> Not being under law, but under grace, we take the New Testament as the rule of our faith and practice, and decline to recognize anything not specifically authorized in the New Testament and practiced by the Apostles. We hold that modern Sunday Schools, religious societies or organizations separate from the church, known as auxiliaries to the church, a salaried ministry, assessing or taxing the members, instrument music in church worship, are unscriptural and, together with oath-bound secret societies, will not be held in fellowship by the association.[60]

56. *Minutes,* South Louisiana Primitive Baptist Association, 1971, Fields, Louisiana, p. 1.
57. Piepkorn, "Primitive Baptists," p. 50.
58. See *Advocate and Messenger* (February 1926), pp. 36-40, which reprinted the confession from the August, 1901, issue of *The Gospel Messenger.*
59. *Minutes,* Union Association, 1912, p. 8.
60. Cited in Piepkorn, "Primitive Baptists," p. 43.

Many of the churches continue to meet monthly, a carry over from frontier days when a scarcity of pastors made that a necessity. Most will not accept the baptism of other Baptist groups. While most Primitives oppose specific training to prepare a minister, they do not necessarily object to an educated ministry. They feel that if God wants a trained person, He will call one already trained. While they embrace predestination, some Primitive Baptists do practice a form of evangelism; some have even spoken in favor of missionary efforts. According to W. A. Pyles of Graham, Texas, a leading elder of Primitive Baptists, they "do not object to missions at home or abroad for the purpose of preaching the gospel for the instruction and edification of children of God." However, they do object "to the idea that the heathen are hell-bound unless we reach them with the preached word."[61]

While most Primitives still object to stated salaries for pastors, many do acknowledge the duty of contributing to the pastor's support. Even the Union Association in Texas, representing the stricter sort, acknowledged in 1912 that "there is a duty enjoined on the church to contribute of their temporal things for the support of the necessities of its Ministers."[62]

Primitive Baptists are mostly rural and concentrated in the South; their churches are small. Their associations meet annually but do little else than publish brief minutes showing that they met. In larger perspective, the Primitives are part of the Old School/New School tensions which marked most denominations in the early nineteenth century.

Regular Baptists

A number of Baptist groups use the term "Regular" as part of their name or description. As a description, the term usually means "true," or "orthodox." Those who incorporate "Regular" into their name tend to be conservative and usually Calvinistic. In Appalachia a group of churches bear the name "Regular Baptists" or "Old Regular Baptists." The "United Baptists," though using a different name, are similar in faith and practice.

The Old Regular Baptists represent surviving remnants of the Regular Baptists in the South who refused to go along with the merger with Separate Baptists in the late 1780s. Their oldest association is the New Salem, formed in 1825 as a United Baptist body. The name was changed to Old Regular in 1870. The Old Regulars are organized into a number of associations but have no state or general conventions. However, the Salem Association functions almost as a general body, with other associations considered

61. Ibid., p. 34n.
62. *Minutes,* Union Association of the Regular Primitive Baptists of the Predestinarian Faith and Order, 1912, p. 8.

"arms" of the parent body. A 1980 report listed 19,770 members, gathered into 24 associations and 366 churches.[63]

The United Baptists, with churches from Kentucky to Missouri, resemble the Old Regulars with whom they share similar origins. Both trace their existence to holdouts who refused to participate in the Regular-Separate merger in the South. Most of the United churches are Calvinistic, though a few hold Arminian views. They also differ on millennialism. The more "progressive" associations, as they call themselves, favor missions, open communion, religious education, and educated pastors, while the "conservative" associations distrust these things. However, all their churches are, as one observer put it, "ruggedly congregational," and the associations do little more than meet and report the fact that they met. In 1964 a few of the United churches formed a general body, the National Association of United Baptists, headquartered in Huntington, West Virginia. Accurate statistics are hard to come by, but clearly most of their churches are small. A recent report placed their membership at 63,641 in 568 churches.[64]

The Duck River Baptists form yet another small denomination. In doctrine and practice they resemble the Old Regulars and United Baptists. The Arminian flavor of Alexander Campbell's preaching in 1826 split the Elk River Association of Primitive Baptists in Tennessee. About a third of the churches withdrew to form the Duck River Baptist Association of Christ. A few years later the phrase "of Christ" was dropped, but this group was often called "the Baptist Church of Christ." The Duck River group split again in 1843 over missions and support of Sunday School publications, leaving two associations claiming the same name, Duck River Baptist Association. The promissionary, propublication faction eventually affiliated with the Southern Baptist Convention and, to avoid confusion, in 1953 added the word *Missionary* to their name.

The old Duck River group declined almost to extinction but later joined with other like-minded associations to form the General Association of Baptists, which recently reported 8,492 members in 81 churches.[65] They also "correspond" with other ultraconservative groups and regard themselves as in some degree of fellowship with Old Regular, United, and Separate Baptists.

These groups, especially the Old Regulars, represent a cultural as well as a religious movement. They have attempted to preserve the rural folkways of an earlier era, with monthly worship, plaintive singing, and sing-song preaching mostly by laymen. Community gatherings, the annual pilgrimage to country cemeteries where their loved ones lie, and emphasis upon fellow-

---

63. Chester R. Young, "Regular Baptist, Old," in *Encyclopedia of Southern Baptists,* 4 vols. (Nashville: Broadman Press, 1982), 4:2435 (hereafter cited as *ESB*).

64. Gardner, p. 94.

65. Piepkorn, *Profiles of Belief,* 2:444.

ship at the annual associations mark this group. Two sources describe the Old Regulars: a book by Rufus Perrigan, *History of Regular Baptist (sic) and Their Ancestors and Accessors,* and a film entitled *In the Good Old Fashioned Way.*[66]

Ethnic Baptists in America

On any given Sunday, Baptists in America will preach and sing in more than eighty different languages. Great diversity marks the Baptists in this country, with churches of every skin pigmentation and most major language and national groups from around the world. Many of these churches are bilingual, but the recent upsurge of immigration has brought new converts who, like their counterparts a century ago, will take time to learn to worship in English.

The term *ethnic* is not entirely apt to describe Baptist groups who stem primarily from European, Hispanic, Asian, or other backgrounds. In a sense, the Anglo-Saxon Baptist majority is no less ethnic than others and, as Franklin D. Roosevelt liked to point out, traced back far enough all Americans are immigrants. However, this history must take account not only of Baptists in other lands but also of Baptists from other lands who have maintained some degree of separate identity in America. The National Baptists, though clearly ethnic, by their size and influence occupy such an important place in Baptist history as to require more extensive treatment elsewhere.

In one sense the ethnic Baptists form many stories in the United States, with different leaders and diverse adjustments to the American scene. In another and perhaps more important sense they form but one story; a common pattern emerges despite local variations. The main outlines of that pattern are as follows: The Baptist immigrants, or immigrants who became Baptists here, banded with others to form churches of their group, using their language and raising up pastors from their ethnic group. They usually formed their own Baptist union or conference to strengthen their churches and launch missions to win other of their countrymen, usually with financial aid from American Baptists. In time they established theological schools or departments to train pastors, all the while jealously guarding their language and national customs and resisting absorption into the "English" churches. Some formed separate ethnic denominations, like the Swedes and Germans, while others contented themselves with a separate conference in some degree of affiliation with American Baptists.

However, no spiritual or linguistic fences erected by one generation could separate the next generation from American culture. Time did its inevitable work, and the gradual Americanization of ethnic Baptists proceeded. Countless individuals simply moved out of the ethnic churches into the

---

66. Rufus Perrigan, *History of Regular Baptist* (sic) *and Their Ancestors and Accessors.* The film, made in 1973 by Herb E. Smith, is available through Appalshop Films, Whitesburg, Ken.

Baptist mainstream; and as the ethnic churches picked up English, many mainline Baptists joined the immigrant churches, further diluting their ethnic distinctiveness. As this process ran its course, some of the ethnic conferences merely disbanded, while others maintained a shadow existence for old times' sake but formed closer ties with mainline conventions. A number of such ethnic fellowships have survived; in some cases, doctrinal disagreements have prompted ethnic groups to draw back and reassert their separate existence.

European immigrants probably made up a larger part of the Baptist family in the nineteenth century than the twentieth. More immigrants arrived then, and more were either already Baptists or candidates for conversion to the Baptist way. By the 1920s many of the immigrant Baptists had been Americanized; and from 1925 to 1975 fewer newcomers arrived, and less of these had any Baptist background or inclinations. However, since the 1970s various world crises have accelerated immigration, both legal and illegal, and many of the newest Americans, especially Asians, have proven open to Baptist witness. Because of location and the strength of its home mission work, Northern Baptists aided most of the European groups in the nineteenth century. Twentieth-century immigrants, particularly Asians, have related more to the Southern Baptist Convention for similar reasons.

The following sketches, though incomplete, provide at least a hint of the ethnic diversity among Baptists in America. They may also serve as an invitation to interested readers to pursue the study in more specialized sources.

European Baptists in America

Europeans "discovered" America in modern times, and the new land proved a magnet which drew settlers from most of the European nations. By 1643 at least eighteen different languages were spoken in what is now New York City. Some of the European newcomers were either already Baptists or converted soon after arrival. Because most points of entry were in the North, the European churches and converts tended to relate to the Northern Baptist societies and after 1907 to the Northern Baptist Convention. In 1983 six European Baptist groups, one predominantly Portuguese, were listed as "Associated Organizations" with the American Baptist churches.[67]

Czechoslovakian Baptists. The Czechoslovak Baptist Convention affiliates churches in the United States and Canada. Czech churches in the United States date from the nineteenth century, and a "Conference" met in Chicago as early as 1909, with the convention formed in 1912. In 1920 Czech Baptists launched a paper, *Pravda (Truth)*, which was later replaced

67. *Directory,* American Baptist Churches in the USA, 1983, pp. 69-70.

by their present publication, *Glorious Hope.* In 1920 they numbered 20 churches with about 1,400 members, but by 1976 that had declined to only 4 reported churches, with 686 members.[68]

Hungarian Baptists. The Hungarian Baptist Union of America was formed in 1902, and by 1920 included about thirty churches and mission stations. They increased 10 percent by baptism in 1920. The churches had to resist Bolshevism and atheism, prevalent among Hungarian immigrants, and to do so the Hungarian Union announced its intention to preach the gospel and "spread a sane Americanization among the Hungarians in this country."[69] At first the Hungarians attempted to support their own training school but later merged with the International Baptist Seminary at East Orange, New Jersey. Their statistics reflect little change since 1920; a 1960 report showed thirty-one churches with 2,216 members.[70]

Polish Baptists. Polish Baptists formed their conference in 1912 and at the 1925 meeting in Milwaukee reported twenty churches and fourteen ministers.[71] By 1960 they reported only eleven churches and about one thousand members.[72]

French Baptists. The work among French Baptists in the United States began in a roundabout way. Swiss evangelicals who migrated to Canada became Baptists in the 1830s under the influence of the famed Grande Ligne Mission. By the 1840s the American Baptist Home Mission Society helped sponsor the French Baptists in Canada and in 1853 appointed its first missionary to preach among French immigrants in New York. As French immigration increased, Baptist churches multiplied among the immigrants. The French-Speaking Baptist Conference of New England was formed in the 1890s, which promoted preaching and tract distribution in that language. However, as the immigrants acquired the use of English, the French Conference declined and in 1960 reported only 405 members in 7 churches.[73]

Scandinavian Baptists. Scandinavian Baptist churches in America date from the 1840s, when Danes and Norwegians immigrated to the Midwest. Hans Valder, newly converted from Lutheranism, formed a Baptist church in Illinois in 1848. The next year he wrote, "My people are nearly all like myself, Norwegians, who have settled in these counties." Noting that the church had increased from seven to nineteen members, most of them by

68. *The Baptist,* January 22, 1921, p. 1740; Gardner, "Baptist General Bodies," p. 92.
69. *The Baptist,* January 22, 1921, p. 1740.
70. Gardner, p. 93.
71. *Watchman-Examiner,* September 17, 1925, p. 1214.
72. Robert G. Torbet, *A History of the Baptists,* 3rd ed., 1973, Appendix B, p. 544.
73. Gardner, p. 92.

baptism, he added, "We ask all to pray for the Norwegians in Illinois."[74]

Church development among the Danes was slowed by several factors. Unlike some immigrant groups, Danes tended to be scattered rather than concentrated. They also tended to merge into the mainline churches more rapidly, drawn especially by the developing young people's programs of the 1890s. According to a 1921 report, this country still had "Danes scattered by the thousands," but their youth "gravitate to American churches."[75]

Many churches included both Danes and Norwegians, and the early Scandinavian Conference included Danish and Norwegian churches. By 1882 it reported thirty churches, twenty-two ministers, and about two thousand members. The conference published a periodical, the *Oliebladet,* as well as a number of tracts and other literature.[76] Surviving churches of this group formed the Danish Baptist General Conference in 1910. A recent report showed 4,025 members in 28 churches.[77] Like several of the European groups, they also affiliate a few churches in Canada.

Romanian Baptists. The Romanians, both in the Old World and the New, have been responsive to the Baptist witness. The Romanian Baptist Association was formed in 1913 and about a half century later reported 1,125 members in 11 churches.[78] Latvian Baptists formed a separate union in this country in 1950 and in 1983 reported 7 churches with 378 members.[79]

Russian Baptists. Baptists emerged as a separate group in Russia in the 1860s, with much of their strength in the Ukraine. A few Baptists were among the Russians who migrated to America, and by 1901 there were enough churches to form the Russian-Ukrainian Evangelical Baptist Union. By 1973 the union reported about two thousand members in thirty-five churches. In 1946 a separate group formed the Ukrainian Evangelical Baptist Convention, and by 1973 its churches numbered twenty with about three thousand members.[80]

As Americanization progressed, most of the separate European groups declined. Some fulfilled their purpose and later disbanded entirely. The Finnish Baptist Mission Union, formed in 1901, is apparently one example, since it no longer appears in lists of Baptist general bodies in America. Perhaps the handwriting was on the wall as early as 1920, when a spokesman reported "nothing specific" going on among the Finnish churches.[81]

---

74. Henry L. Morehouse, ed., *Baptist Home Missions in North America, 1832-1882,* p. 478.
75. *The Baptist,* January 22, 1921, p. 1741.
76. Morehouse, p. 479.
77. Gardner, p. 92.
78. Torbet, p. 544.
79. Gardner, update.
80. Ibid.
81. *The Baptist,* January 22, 1921, p. 1741.

However, two European Baptist groups in America had a lot going on, and their stories require more space. These were the Swedes and Germans.

Swedish Baptists. Swedish Baptist beginnings stem from the 1844 conversion of Gustavus W. Schroeder at a Methodist meeting in New Orleans. The next year while attending the Mariners' Baptist Church in New York, Schroeder became convinced of immersion and was baptized in the East River. The next year he was back in Sweden, where he led Frederick O. Nilsson to Baptist views. Since there was no one in Sweden to immerse him, Nilsson went to Hamburg, Germany, where he was baptized in the Elbe by the German patriarch, Johann G. Oncken.[82] The Hamburg church sent a minister back to Sweden with Nilsson; in 1848 that minister immersed Mrs. Nilsson and four other persons, who formed the first-known Swedish Baptist church.

Persecution drove the Nilssons out of Sweden. They tarried first at Stockholm where Nilsson met Gustaf Palmquist, confirming the latter in his Baptist views. In 1852 Palmquist went to America where he was immersed, ordained, and forty-seven days later formed a Swedish Baptist church at Rock Island, Illinois. That church, the first of its order in America, began with only four members.[83] The Rock Island church disbanded in 1930, leaving the Village Creek church in Iowa, founded in 1853, as the oldest surviving Swedish Baptist church in America.[84]

Nilsson arrived to America in 1853, leader of a band of twenty-one immigrants. Some made their way to Rock Island to augment the Palmquist group, while others went on to Houston, Minnesota, where they formed a church. Nilsson traveled widely, planting new churches and strengthening older ones from New York to the Midwest. He might be called the "apostle of Swedish Baptists in America," though he was an apostle with clay feet. An infidel in his youth, Nilsson during the last decade of his life embraced Unitarianism and denied the inspiration of the Bible. The Baptists in sorrow regarded him as outcast. Only four days before his death in 1881 Nilsson seemed to recover his faith, exclaiming, "Jesus Christ is my only hope; on that rock will I rest, who has saved me."[85]

Another outstanding pioneer of Swedish Baptists was Anders Wiberg, who ministered for a few years in America but made his major mark by stabilizing the Baptist witness in Sweden. Trained as a Lutheran, Wiberg brought an excellent theological education and organizational skills to the Baptist work, making him a competent though sometimes controversial

---

82. Adolf Olson, *A Centenary History as Related to the Baptist General Conference of America,* p. 27.

83. Some sources state erroneously that there were only three members. However, the church minutes in the archives of the Bethel Seminary, give the names of three converts plus Palmquist, who was called as pastor.

84. Olson, p. 48.

85. Ibid., pp. 32-33.

leader. Converted to Baptist views by the witness of Nilsson, Wiberg landed in America in 1852. At his first step upon American soil, he exclaimed, "Oh, my God, what a gift is liberty."[86] After a preaching tour of the Mississippi Valley, Wiberg ministered two years in Philadelphia. In 1855 he was appointed by the Northern Baptists as a missionary to Sweden, but he did not return alone: He recorded happily in his diary that "Sister Caroline promised to go with me to Sweden."[87]

Swedish Baptists came largely from a Pietist background in Europe, and they related well to the evangelical "awakenings" in America. Their letters, diaries, and sermons speak often of prayer and Bible study. While emphasizing Christian experience and spiritual discipline above dogmatic theology, they remained conservative in belief. By the 1920s they drew back sharply from their former alliance with Northern Baptists, the changing theological emphases in the latter group being one reason. A prayer meeting at Village Creek illustrates the Pietist flavor of Swedish Baptist life. A group knelt and prayed at length with Nilsson, who had walked ten miles to attend the meeting. Finally Nilsson arose and pleaded, "Brethren, let us intersperse our prayers with song and testimony. This long posture on aching knees takes the spirit of worship out of us."[88]

The Swedish churches formed a General Conference in 1879. This body still exists, with headquarters in Arlington Heights, Illinois. By 1883 the denominational structure was further refined, with three regional conferences, much like state conventions, relating to the general body. The General Conference has shown steady growth: At the golden anniversary of Swedish Baptists in America in 1902, the denomination listed 324 churches with 21,769 members. By 1982 it had increased to 726 churches and about 131,000 members.[89]

The Swedish Conference conducts a full range of ministries, including home and foreign missions, publications, theological and collegiate education, and special ministries for men, women, and youth. In 1880 the conference appointed its first home missionary, Christopher Silene, whose field was broadly defined as the Midwest. Partially supported by the ABHMS, Silene preached and planted churches from Illinois to Texas. The first Swedish foreign missionary was Johanna Anderson, appointed to Burma in 1888 by the Woman's American Baptist Foreign Mission Society. Many others followed; in the decade from 1910 to 1920, at least twenty-one young people from Swedish churches were appointed to overseas missions. In 1927

86. Ibid., p. 41.
87. Ibid.
88. Ibid., p. 51.
89. Olson, p. 605; Gardner, update.

more than fifty Swedish Baptist foreign missionaries served under the Northern Baptist Society, while sixteen held appointment under other boards.[90]

Many publications antedated the conference. In 1852 Anders Wiberg published an epochal book, *What Is Baptism and Who Should Be Baptized?* By 1865 he edited *Evangelisten,* a monthly periodical which did much to extend the Baptist witness as well as maintain spiritual unity in the group. In 1871 John A. Edgren launched *Zion's Waktare (Watchman of Zion),* but it perished in the Chicago fire. It was followed by *Evangelisk Tidskrift (Evangelical Journal),* and in 1940 two papers were combined to form *The Standard,* issued in English. The denomination also provided books, tracts, and Sunday School literature.

John A. Edgren announced in 1871, "A Theological Seminary for Swedes and others who understand the Swedish language and who intend to devote themselves to preaching, will be opened in the near future in Chicago."[91] Only one student, Christopher Silene, attended the first semester, but that small beginning eventually became the Bethel Theological Seminary, since 1914 located in Saint Paul, Minnesota. Edgren, well-educated in Europe and with devout Pietist leanings, set out firm principles which reveal much about the Swedish Baptist witness:

> 1. Those who are to be admitted into the seminary should be conscious of a real conversion and a call of God to the gospel ministry.
> 2. The preacher should have as good an education as possible, but of all knowledge the most important is to know the Bible. . . . the Bible itself . . . is studied as thoroughly as time will permit.
> 3. To cultivate the mind is important for the preacher, but to cultivate the spiritual life is even more important. . . . spiritual edification must never be lost sight of.
> 4. The relation between teacher and students should not be that of superior and subordinate, but one of real friendship and helpfulness, remembering that One is our Master, and we are all brethren.[92]

For six years the seminary functioned as the Scandinavian Department of the Baptist Union Theological Seminary, itself affiliated with the old University of Chicago. By 1884 a total of eighty-nine students had attended, including sixty-three Swedes, seventeen Danes, and nine Norwegians. Tensions later led the Scandinavian Department to withdraw and resume its separate identity. After several moves and name changes, the seminary settled at Saint Paul in 1914, officially sponsored by the General Conference as of that year. From early days Swedish Baptists also sponsored an academy, which at times operated in conjunction with the seminary. In 1947 the collegiate division rose to senior college level under the name of Bethel

90. Olson, pp. 524-525.
91. Ibid., p. 154.
92. Ibid., p. 155.

College. Carl Emanuel Carlson, a teacher and later dean at Bethel College, served 1954-1971 as executive director of the Baptist Joint Committee on Public Affairs in Washington.

Swedish Baptists have borne a consistent witness in America. Their denomination is relatively small, but highly efficient. They have remained doctrinally conservative but have resisted any extreme tilt toward Fundamentalism. Warm evangelism and a consistent commitment to religious liberty mark their American pilgrimage. Better than most immigrant groups, the Swedes have struck a balance between preserving their old culture and adapting to their new country.

German Baptists. Next to the English, Germany contributed more immigrants to America than did any other nation. Perhaps 250 thousand Germans had arrived by the Revolutionary War, but the flood tide of immigration after the Civil War raised that total to around 8 million.[93] In this "great invasion of Teutonic people," for some years in the 1880s Germans made up over half of all new immigrants to this country.[94] German Baptists formed churches in the United States by 1843 and the beginnings of a denomination within a decade.

Since 1851 German Baptists have maintained their own separate denomination in the United States. Only 8 churches, representing 405 members, formed the first German conference in 1851; by 1977 the North American Baptist Conference (NABC), as it is now called, reported 57,034 members in 356 churches in the USA and Canada. Over two thirds of these are in the United States.[95] Among the German Baptists, none was more famous than Walter Rauschenbusch, pastor and professor, best known as father of the Social Gospel movement. He was a son of August Rauschenbusch, a converted Pietist and one of the founding fathers of German Baptists. From its headquarters in Oakbrook Terrace, Illinois, the NABC oversees a full range of ministries, including home and foreign missions, publication work, homes for children and the aged, a college, and a seminary at Sioux Falls, South Dakota.

For years German Baptists cooperated closely with Northern Baptists, and the Germans sided solidly with the North during the Civil War. The German insistence upon using their own language, the rise of theological differences, and a desire to preserve their cultural heritage prevented the Germans from merging with American Baptists as many other immigrant groups did. Immigration provided enough converts to make a viable German denomination. Some churches offer services in both German and

93. Frank H. Woyke, *Heritage and Ministry of the North American Baptist Conference,* pp. 13-15.
94. Martin L. Leuschner, "North American Baptist General Conference," in Woolley, p. 227.
95. Woyke, p. 10; for 1981, Gardner, update, reported 43,146 members in 260 churches in the USA.

English, though English now predominates. Representing a blend of the Pietist tradition from Europe, the revivalism of early America, and the Social Gospel of Walter Rauschenbusch, the German Baptists have shown slow but steady growth. Like most immigrants, the early Germans congregated in Eastern cities but later fanned out to Kansas, Nebraska, and the Dakotas. This geographical movement had enormous implications for the denomination. After existing for almost a century at Rochester, New York, the seminary moved in 1949 to Sioux Falls. As a major center of cohesion and unity in the denomination, the move to an area of NABC strength has probably reduced the contact between the Germans and ABC churches. It has also tended to diminish the Rauschenbusch tradition within the conference.

German Baptist beginnings in America center around the work of Conrad A. Fleischman. Converted to evangelical views in Switzerland, Fleischman later came under Baptist influence at Bristol, England. By 1839 he felt called of God to preach to his countrymen in the United States. On July 9, 1843, Fleischman and five converts whom he baptized formed the first German Baptist church in America and later affiliated with the Philadelphia Association. This was only one of several independent beginnings; John Eschman formed a German Baptist church in New York City in 1847; Andreas Heinrich laid foundations for similar churches in Buffalo and Rochester; a Prussian immigrant, W. E. Grimm, did the same in Wisconsin by 1850.[96] By these separate beginnings, a number of German churches sprang up from the Atlantic to the Mississippi.

Many of these, however, hesitated to include "Baptist" as part of their name. Fleischman's church of 1843 was called "The German Church of the Lord that meets in Poplar Street." Some called themselves German "Baptized Churches," while others added in small letters after their church name the phrase "usually called Baptist." The first conference of churches in 1851 revealed their Baptist identity only in a tiny parenthesis.[97] This German hesitance to accept the name stems largely from an unfortunate and erroneous identification with the despised Anabaptists of the sixteenth century.

In 1851 Fleischman called "The First Conference of Pastors and Co-Workers of the German Churches of Baptized Christians (usually called Baptists.)"[98] Eight pastors and two laymen attended that first move toward forming the scattered German churches into some kind of denominational cooperation. That early conference, much like an association, laid far-reaching plans. Already Fleischman had launched his paper, *Der Sendbote des Evangeliums* (*Messenger of the Gospel*), which the conference encouraged. The conference also called for a confession of faith, preparation

96. Leuschner, pp. 228-229.
97. Woyke, p. 3.
98. Ibid.

of a German hymnal, continued use of the German language, and the beginning of theological education for German pastors.

The conference learned in 1851 that the Rochester Theological Seminary was willing to offer classes for the German students. It voted hearty thanks to the Rochester Seminary "for their willingness to put forth efforts to train German young men for the ministry," which offer it gladly accepted. However, the Germans cautioned that "care must be taken that the German students in Rochester do not lose the knowledge and use of their mother tongue."[99] Thus began a relationship in 1851 that would provide great strength to the emerging denomination. Operating sometimes as a semiseparate school, and at other times as the "German Department" of the Rochester seminary, this work attracted the talents of such outstanding teachers as August Rauschenbusch, 1858 to 1888, and for a few years his more famous son Walter.

As the churches multiplied, meeting in one conference became increasingly difficult. Not only distance but also doctrinal and sectional tensions led to a division in 1859, when the separate Western Conference came into being. Led by the young and aggressive Philip W. Bickel, the Western Conference formed its own paper, *Die Biene auf dem Missionsfelde* (*The Bee on the Mission Field*). The new conference centered in Ohio but appealed to churches even further west. Though claiming to be two parts of one fellowship, in fact, rivalry and tension marked the relationship of the two conferences. Fleischman in *Der Sendbote* and Bickel in *Die Beine* did not hesitate to air their differences thoroughly.

However, a call for a general conference in 1865 restored unity to the denomination. The two regional conferences came to regard themselves as cooperating wings of the same general body, and they brought a measure of correlation to their home mission and publication work. In 1883 the Western Conference further subdivided into three regional conferences. In time several more regional conferences were formed, functioning much like state conventions. German Baptists in the West proved more conservative, more aggressive, and sought closer relationships with the Baptists of Germany. For years the Western Conference was largely dominated by Bickel, as the Eastern Conference was by Fleischman. Most of the pastors attended the Rochester school. In 1859 the Western Conference formed a pastoral "Protection Committee" to help guard the churches against the intrusion of unworthy or unorthodox pastors.

In 1870 George A. Schulte was appointed by the American Baptist Home Mission Society to serve as a home missionary for the Eastern Conference. Thus developed a close missionary relation between German Baptists and the HMS, which had in fact aided individual German churches and pastors since the 1840s. For the next several years, though Germans contributed

99. Ibid., p. 7.

generously to missions, most of their home and foreign appointees went out under the Northern societies. Later the Germans formed their own societies to send and support their own missionaries. By the 1960s the NABC churches sponsored about one hundred overseas missionaries.

In the twentieth century, the denomination has developed further, with name changes (the terms *German* and *General* were dropped), new denominational headquarters, and the General Council formed in 1934 to function as a kind of executive committee for the denomination. The first full-time executive secretary was Frank H. Woyke, elected in 1946, and area secretaries were first appointed in 1958.

With their Pietist/revivalist background, the German Baptists have remained theologically conservative. Whereas the elder Rauschenbusch had been a major center of unity within the denomination, his son Walter became unwillingly a cause of contention. While appreciating Walter's insightful social teachings, many German Baptists could not accept the more liberal doctrinal views which often accompanied the Social Gospel. Some NABC leaders drew back, but since mid-century much of the Rauschenbusch tradition has been recovered.

What the German Baptists call the "big debate" concerned the location of their theological seminary. This involved far more than the site for a school, since the seminary served as their major center of unity. Over the years the relationship with Rochester grew less satisfactory. Cramped quarters, cramped budgets, refusal of the Rochester Seminary to provide salaries for the German professors, and perhaps above all the constant pressure upon the Germans to abandon their language and enter the English classes created tensions. German Baptists conducted endless discussions about whether to move and if so where and two or three times actually made abortive efforts to remove their training center to some more suitable site. However, the die was cast in 1947 when the conference voted to locate the school far to the west in Sioux Falls, South Dakota. In late 1949 they occupied a handsome new campus in that city.

While the NABC remains predominantly German, most of its services are now conducted in English and many non-Germans have joined its ranks. The new *North American Hymnal* has long since replaced *Die Glaubensharfe*. Though *Der Sendbote* still finds an audience, the main periodical now is the *Gospel Herald*. Classroom instruction in German, once so jealously guarded, has long since yielded to English.

The process of Americanization has been hastened by American hostility to all things German during two world wars in the twentieth century. Although Germans served in the American armies, suspicions remained about their loyalty. Many Americans opposed the teaching and use of the German language. In time the conference dropped the word *German* from its name, published more of its literature in English, and saw its churches pushed, mostly by younger members, to conduct more services in English.

A recent historian has observed that, since the denomination is no longer strictly ethnic, the question arises whether they should merge with some other Baptist denomination. Some feel they should merge but cannot agree with whom. Others maintain that the denomination still has a mission to perform. Their most recent historian concluded, "It appears that the Conference will continue its own program as a separate organization."[100]

Hispanic Baptists in the United States

Persons of Latin heritage now number about 20 million in this country, 20 percent of them in Texas.[101] Hispanics constitute the second largest ethnic minority in the nation, and their numbers continue to increase. By AD 2000 they are expected to form a majority in several Southwestern states. Some have dubbed the 1980s the "Decade of the Hispanic." Estimates say about one million new immigrants per year arrive in America, the highest total in over sixty years. Of these, over half are Hispanic, while a third are Asians. Of Hispanics in America, about 60 percent come from Mexico, while 14 percent are from Puerto Rico and 5 percent from Cuba. The others are mostly from Central and South America.[102]

The term *Hispanic* is used in a broad sense to designate persons whose origin or culture stems from any of a number of Latin countries, such as Spain, Portugal, Mexico, Central or South America, Puerto Rico, or Cuba. Because most Hispanics in this country come from Mexico, many Anglos formed the habit of referring to all Spanish-speaking persons as Mexicans. However, US citizens who come from Mexico are more precisely called Mexican-Americans or, as some prefer, "Americanos." Citizens of Mexico now living in this country are, of course, Mexicans. The term *Mexican* is used in this chapter without political overtones; no distinction is made between Mexican and Mexican-American, and *Hispanic* is used in an inclusive sense.

Hispanics in this country have shown openness to the Baptist witness despite historic ties with Catholicism. By 1982 about 115,000 Hispanic Baptists in the United States were in 1,600 churches. Not surprisingly, their primary strength was in Texas and the Southwest, though they have dispersed throughout the nation since World War II. Texas alone had about 700 Mexican churches and missions by 1982, with 50,000 members, plus at least another 10,000 Mexican Baptists who held membership in Anglo churches.[103] For convenience this brief sketch of Hispanic Baptists takes

100. Ibid., p. 441.

101. Joshua Grijalva, *A History of the Mexican Baptists in Texas 1881-1981,* p. 171.

102. "Hispanics: Fastest Growing Minority," *Fort Worth Star-Telegram,* May 20, 1984, AA 1, 4.

103. Grijalva, p. vii, 171. See also Oscar I. Romo, "Toward a Strategy of Ethnic Missions, A Southern Baptist Perspective," p. 98.

a regional approach, looking at Texas, the Southwest, and the nation. This corresponds largely with the chronological development.

Hispanic Baptists in Texas. The Republic of Texas, having gained independence from Mexico in 1836, remained a separate nation until it joined the United States in 1845. The Treaty of Guadalupe Hidalgo in 1848 established the Rio Grande as the Texas/Mexico border and ceded to the United States much of the present states of Arizona, California, New Mexico, Colorado, and Utah. The largest Hispanic population was in Texas, with about 5,000 Mexicans in 1848.[104]

From early days Baptists saw the need to evangelize among Mexicans in Texas. Thomas J. Pilgrim, who began a Sunday School at San Felipe in South Texas in 1828, attracted the interest of Mexicans despite opposition from the priest.[105] In 1836 the American Baptist Home Mission Society noted that Texas offered a promising field, and a few years later their missionaries, James Huckins and William Tryon, addressed Mexican as well as Anglo hearers in Texas. By the 1850s some of the Anglo associations sought to minister to "the foreigners in our midst," Mexicans and Germans primarily. In 1861 one of the Baptist conventions in Texas appointed J. W. D. Creath to work among Mexicans, apparently the first missionary to that group. Though no church was formed for some years, several Mexican converts joined the Anglo churches; the First Baptist Church of San Antonio, formed in 1861, included as a charter member Angela Maria de Jesus Navarro, daughter of a famous hero of the Alamo.[106] That church formed a Mexican mission, but it survived only six months.

John and Thomas Westrup, Englishmen serving as missionaries in Mexico, crossed the border to preach in Laredo in 1880. The baptism of their first convert in 1881 is considered the beginning of permanent Mexican Baptist work in Texas; this beginning was commemorated in the Mexican Baptist Centennial of 1981. Whether the Laredo converts formed an organized church or only a fellowship is difficult to say. Some sources place the first Mexican Baptist church in Texas at Laredo in 1883, while others find no organized church until San Antonio five years later.[107]

A revival broke out among Mexicans in San Antonio in 1888 under the preaching of W. D. Powell, who had succeeded the martyred John Westrup in Mexico. Powell baptized a number of converts, asking that they be received as members of the church in Saltillo, Mexico. Instead, the Saltillo church authorized Powell to form the *Primera Iglesia Bautista Mexicana*

104. Grijalva, p. 9.
105. Robert A. Baker, *The Blossoming Desert: A Concise History of Texas Baptists*, p. 20.
106. Grijalva, p. 12.
107. For the 1883 date, see Grijalva, pp. 12-13; and L. R. Elliott, ed., *Centennial Story of Texas Baptists*, p. 54. However, an early doctoral dissertation found no organized church before 1888. See William Bricen Miller, "Texas Mexican Baptist History," App. B, p. viii.

of San Antonio in 1888.[108] Other churches sprang up at San Marcos (1889), El Paso (1893), Del Rio (1898), Beeville (1899), and Austin (1899). At least thirteen churches were formed by the turn of the century.

Lack of pastors and buildings hampered the work. Charles D. Daniel wrote that in 1896 Texas had only five Mexican Baptist preachers, serving about two hundred members. "There were neither schools nor meeting houses," Daniel wrote, and the work suffered from poverty and illiteracy of pastors and people alike.[109] A giant step came in 1906 with appointment of Daniel by the Home Mission Board (SBC) as superintendent of Mexican missions in Texas. This marked a new era of Hispanic-Anglo cooperation in Baptist witness. No better choice could have been found; Daniel had served as a missionary in Brazil and Cuba, and few Anglos brought to the work more zeal and insight. By 1907 he launched annual Bible Institutes for training Mexican pastors, led in church extension, persuaded Anglo groups to channel more mission efforts toward Hispanics, and in 1910 led the Mexican churches to form their own state convention.

At a conference of Mexican pastors in 1909, a question arose about linking their churches into some organization. In answer to the pastors' call, twenty-four churches sent thirty-seven messengers to a meeting on May 25, 1910, at the *Primera Iglesia Bautista Mexicana* in San Antonio to "consider the organization of a deliberating body, to be named *Convencion Bautista Mexicana.*"[110] The purpose of the body, according to its first constitution, was "to foster fraternal relations among the churches, associations, and other Mexican Baptist bodies of the State, with the object of cooperation in the evangelization and education of the youth and the publication of Christian literature within its territorial limits."[111] The *convencion* recognized the independence of the churches, adopted a brief confession of faith, and laid plans for evangelism and church extension. The first officers included Charles D. Daniel (who stepped aside after two years so Hispanics could serve), D. C. Barocio, B. C. Perez, and Gil Villarreal. In 1917 a separate women's organization, similar to WMU, came into being, and a few years later the *convencion* launched its own paper, *El Bautista Mexicana.*

By 1921 the churches numbered over fifty, with about two thousand members, but as always the laborers were few. M. C. Garcia, president of the *convencion,* told of poignant experiences with throngs who wanted to hear the gospel. He preached at seven or eight mission points in addition to his own church. When he passed through South Texas towns on the way

108. Joshua Grijalva, "The Story of Hispanic Southern Baptists," *Baptist History and Heritage,* July 1983, p. 41.
109. Miller, p. 177.
110. Romo, p. 87.
111. Miller, p. 64.

to various appointments, throngs of Mexicans would come to the train and entreat him to preach to them. "But I cannot," he said, throwing up his hands in despair, "there are too many invitations and not enough preachers."[112]

In a reversal of the usual order, the Mexican Convention was formed first; the associations came later. Most of the Mexican churches affiliated with Anglo associations, though some participated only minimally. In 1923 Mexican churches formed their first association, the *Asociacion Central de Iglesias Mexicanas*. Several similar associations sprang up elsewhere in the following years. Their historian explained that "ethnic minorities have not always felt at ease in Anglo-American gatherings. Programs often have to be adapted and adjusted within the language, culture, and background of the people. This has been one of the prime reasons for *asociaciones mexicanas*."[113] However, the trend toward separate associations largely ran its course by mid-century; by 1957 the predominantly Anglo association in San Antonio affiliated thirty-nine Mexican churches and missions within its fellowship.

The depression of the 1930s brought decline as some Mexicans had to return to Mexico. The churches had to limit their programs and the HMB reduced its ministries. However, these pressures produced an unexpected result; instead of returning to Mexico, many moved north and west to establish pockets of Hispanic culture throughout the nation. World War II created a labor shortage in the United States, drawing millions from Mexico and other Hispanic countries. Mexican Baptist work surged during the 1940s and after, with aggressive new leaders and dynamic new programs. In the mid-1940s Mexican Baptists divided their work in Texas into four areas, each led by a missions director, and each area expected to develop a school, an encampment, and sponsor field evangelism. In 1943 the leading encampment, *Alto Frio*, became statewide, with special programs for children, youth, adults, singles, families, and other interest groups. In 1941 the *convencion* appointed a state religious education director, whose primary task was to lead the Mexican churches to strengthen their Sunday Schools.

Convention structure also changed in the 1940s. In 1946 for the first time the Mexicans elected a full-time executive secretary, Pascual Hurtiz, who served until 1949. He was succeeded after an interval by Carlos Paredes, 1950-1953; L. D. Wood, 1954-1960; Dallas P. Lee, 1960-1972; Leobardo C. Estrada, 1973-1981; and Roberto Garcia, since 1981. In cooperation with Anglos, Mexican Baptists launched a radio ministry, including *"La Hora Bautista"* in the early 1950s. In 1952 the Mexican Convention sent Miss Esperanza Ramirez as a foreign missionary, and within a few years several others were appointed. During the New Life Crusade of 1964, Rudy Her-

112. Ibid., p. 142.
113. Grijalva, *A History,* pp. 93-94.

nandez, one of the most dynamic Hispanic evangelists, preached not only in several crusades but also over radio and television. In the late 1970s *"La Hora de Proclamacion,"* with Leobardo C. Estrada as speaker, was heard on twenty-nine Texas stations. In 1978 *Himnario Bautista (Baptist Hymnal)* replaced the older *El Himnario Popular.*

The need for education for Mexican pastors in Texas was mentioned as early as 1896, but the first organized action came in 1907. In that year Charles D. Daniel sponsored the first of his annual Bible Institutes, with seventeen pastors attending. The institutes lasted for two or three days and included intense preaching and training sessions in Baptist doctrines, improvement of preaching, and church leadership. The purpose was not only to train but also to motivate and inspire the pastors. After 1910 the institutes were often held just before or after the convention. After a few years they lapsed but later revived as the *Escuela de Profetas* (School of the Prophets), giving rise to the current annual pastors' conferences.

Mexican Baptists made several efforts to launch their own theological training institute. The Baptist Bible Institute, formed at Bastrop in 1926 by Paul C. Bell, lapsed in 1941. A seminary begun in San Antonio moved to El Paso, thence to Torreon, and later to Mexico City where it remains. The Valley Baptist Academy was founded in Brownsville in 1947 to provide both secondary and theological education. First sponsored by the Rio Grande association, the school later moved to a more adequate campus in Harlingen and came under the direction of the Baptist General Convention of Texas (BGCT) in 1956.

Perhaps the most notable school launched by Hispanics in Texas was the Mexican Baptist Bible Institute (MBBI), formed in San Antonio in 1947. First sponsored by the San Antonio association to provide training for local Mexican pastors, the first classes were conducted in a San Antonio church. As the project grew, the BGCT assumed joint sponsorship in 1963. Later the school moved to its beautiful campus south of the city. In 1976 Daniel J. Rivera became president of this unique school, with all instruction in Spanish. Presently, the school enrolls over 150 students for accredited theological training, and the academic dean, Joshua Grijalva, has established satellite programs in 8 other cities.[114] More than half of the Mexican Baptist pastors in Texas are graduates of this school. In 1981, it merged with the Southwestern Baptist Theological Seminary in Fort Worth and took the name of Hispanic Baptist Theological Seminary. Though it continues to operate under its own administration, it is now an extension of Southwestern Seminary.

Hispanics also sponsor the Mexican Baptist Children's Home. The home began in 1944 when three homeless children came to live in the parsonage of *Primera Iglesia Bautista* of Austin. Later a permanent home was estab-

114. Romo, p. 90.

lished in San Antonio and by 1982 had grown to care for more than one hundred children.[115]

Perhaps the most important decision the Mexican Convention faced at its fiftieth anniversary in 1960 was the question of unification with the BGCT, the major Anglo convention. Since Mexicans and Anglos cooperated closely in their Texas witness, the need for a separate Mexican convention was reconsidered in the 1950s. In 1959 a joint proposal was presented to both conventions: "That the Mexican Baptist Convention of Texas enter the Baptist General Convention of Texas as a department of work on the same basis as the Sunday School and Training Union Conventions, with annual meetings, and carried on somewhat the same order as the other conventions."[116] In 1960 both conventions gave tentative approval for a three-year trial and in 1963 made the merger permanent. Some lingering Mexican opposition continues, urging the value of independence. However, the vast majority of both Hispanic and Anglo Baptists have found the closer cooperation helpful. Though an integral part of the larger convention, the Mexican convention retains its identity.

Hispanic Baptists in the Southwest. Southwestern areas of the United States had Hispanic populations before becoming part of the United States, and in some areas Hispanics form the majority. Several of those states have developed a significant Baptist witness among Hispanics.

In New Mexico, Hiram Read arrived in Sante Fe in 1849, appointed by Northern Baptists. Among his early converts were a number of Hispanics, including Blas Chavez who served as a pastor for fifty years. Over the years Hispanic churches emerged at Dona Ana, Carlsbad, Alamogordo, Albuquerque, and elsewhere. In 1923 these churches formed the Hispanic Baptist Convention of New Mexico. A report in 1963 listed 32 churches, 1,770 members, and 50 pastors and missionaries, who had baptized 129 new converts that year.[117] In 1982 they reported about 50 churches.[118] The Hispanic churches have effected a cooperation with the Anglo convention similar to that in Texas. They publish *El Misionero Bautista.*

The First Southern Baptist Church of Tucson, Arizona, began a ministry to Hispanics in 1942, including Bible classes and Vacation Bible Schools. Similar work opened at Chandler, Casa Grande, and elsewhere. In 1944 the HMB appointed workers among the Hispanics and soon organized churches emerged, with Phoenix as a strong Hispanic Baptist center. By 1980 there

115. Ibid., p. 88.
116. Grijalva, *A History,* p. 114.
117. Grijalva, "Hispanic Southern Baptists," pp. 41-42.
118. Romo, p. 99.

were 31 Hispanic churches and missions in Arizona with 1,787 members.[119]

In 1947 Jesus Rios left his pastorate in South Texas to preach among the mushrooming Hispanic population in California. He formed a church at San Jose, then in 1949 moved to Los Angeles where a strong Hispanic church grew up under his ministry. He also formed a string of missions in the Los Angeles area which became churches later. Others who pioneered in the Hispanic witness in California included Lonnie Chavez, Daniel Sotelo, Cristobal Dona, and Leobardo Estrada. In recent years the Golden Gate Baptist Theological Seminary worked with the HMB to form the Multi-Ethnic Theological Association (META) to provide trained Hispanic and other ethnic leadership. Though no complete denominational structures have emerged, Hispanic Baptist pastors formed a statewide fellowship in 1974. In 1979 churches in the Los Angeles area withdrew from the Anglo association to form their own *La Asociacion Bautista de Los Angeles.* By 1982 California reported 130 Hispanic Baptist congregations.

Hispanic work in Colorado dates from 1954 when the Denver Temple Baptist Church established a mission with Julian Ramirez as pastor. In 1956 Joshua Grijalva became pastor of the *Primera Iglesia Bautista* of Denver, and other Hispanic congregations emerged at Pueblo (1965), Colorado Springs (1966), and Greeley (1968). By 1980 Hispanics in Colorado numbered eleven congregations and almost one thousand members.[120]

Hispanic Baptists across the nation. Many still hold the misconception that Hispanics in America are largely limited to the crescent from Texas to California. The fact is Hispanics now live in every part of the United States, with large population centers in New York, other Eastern and Northern cities, and the West Coast. The deep South states have growing Hispanic groups, as do Northern industrial states like Michigan and Illinois. While the story cannot be told with any detail here, the bare outline reveals a modern dispersion of epic proportions, with unequaled opportunity for Baptist witness.

The New York area is characterized by a strong Baptist witness among its three million Hispanics. In 1962 Leobardo Estrada left his pastorate in Los Angeles to begin a new work in New York City. Only three persons attended his first service. Estrada distributed tracts in subway stations and issued personal invitations on the street. He formed a church in 1964; from that beginning, at least twenty-five congregations had grown up in the metro area by 1982.[121]

In 1972 the HMB appointed a missionary couple to work among Hispan-

119. Grijalva, "Hispanic Southern Baptists," p. 43.
120. Ibid., p. 44.
121. Romo, p. 117.

ics in New England, and the same year the *Primera Iglesia Bautista Hispana* was formed in Hartford, Connecticut. Similar congregations grew up at Springfield, Boston, and other places in New England.[122]

Northern Baptists had a missionary in Puerto Rico within two weeks of the raising of the American flag at San Juan in 1899, and the next year a Baptist church was formed there. Over the years several missionaries labored in that area, and enough churches resulted to form a Puerto Rican Baptist Convention. In 1926 the Barranquitas Academy opened, which by mid-century enrolled over one hundred pupils.[123] Puerto Rican Baptists opened a seminary in 1907, which later merged with schools of other denominations to form one training center for Protestant students. Ecumenical cooperation marked the work of early Baptists in Puerto Rico, not only in theological education but also in church planting. Perhaps the most serious internal problem faced by early Baptists in Puerto Rico was the outbreak of Pentecostalism in their churches after World War I.

In 1983 the Board of National Ministries of the American Baptist Churches listed 38 ministers appointed to work among Hispanics.[124] A spokesman for that board reported 210 Hispanic churches related to the ABC, with 24,773 members. Of these congregations, 76 are Puerto Rican.

The earliest Southern Baptist church in Puerto Rico was formed in 1955, the Boringuen Baptist Church which grew up near Ramey Air Force Base. The Anglo pastor launched a work among Hispanics and, as a result, the Spanish-speaking church at Aguadilla was formed that same year. Additional Hispanic churches grew up in San Juan, and the New Life Crusade of 1966 greatly augmented the Baptist witness. The New Orleans Baptist Theological Seminary established a branch training center in Puerto Rico in 1975 under the direction of Miguel Soto. By 1982 Hispanic Baptists in Puerto Rico related to the SBC numbered about 4,300.[125]

In his 1982 study Oscar I. Romo traced the emergence of Hispanic Baptist work throughout the United States. The following sketches come largely from his work.

By the 1940s Hispanic Baptist churches emerged across the Plains states. Pearl Jones, director of the Goodwill Center of the First Baptist Church of Oklahoma City, conducted a Bible study for Hispanics and won several converts. In 1945 the HMB appointed A. V. Alvarado to serve in Oklahoma City, and the next year the First Mexican Baptist Church was formed. By 1980 Oklahoma had about twenty Hispanic churches and missions, gathered into a statewide association. Guillermo E. Benitez began a work in Topeka in 1960; by 1982 Kansas numbered seven Hispanic congregations,

122. Ibid., p. 116.
123. Charles L. White, *A Century of Faith*, p. 193; G. Pitt Beers, *Ministry to Turbulent America*, p. 138.
124. *Directory*, American Baptist Churches in the U.S.A., 1983, p. 93.
125. Grijalva, "Hispanic Southern Baptists," p. 46.

while Nebraska had two. In Missouri, Hispanic churches came earlier; the First Mexican Baptist Church of Kansas City was formed in 1916 by Manuel Urbina, who had come to Missouri to attend William Jewell College.

Jobs in the industrial North drew Hispanic as well as Anglo workers during and after World War II. The Gonzalez and Hernandez families, recently moved from Texas, helped form *Iglesia Bautista Calvario* in 1957 at Adrian, Michigan. By 1982 Michigan had six Hispanic churches and two missions, with a Michigan Spanish Fellowship which met twice a year. In nearby Illinois, Roberto and Evangelina Quiroz, from Galveston, gathered workers for worship under a tree near Chicago. Later Juan Pablo Berlonga formed the First Spanish Baptist Church of South Chicago Heights in 1964. By 1980 Illinois reported twenty-six Hispanic churches, about half in the Chicago area.

Hispanic churches also sprang up across the South, with churches in Alabama by 1970; Georgia, 1970; Mississippi, early 1960s; Virginia, 1961; Kentucky, 1979; South Carolina, 1960s; North Carolina, 1970s. Louisiana has about fifteen Hispanic Baptist churches, dating from the 1950s, with mission impetus as well as training provided by the New Orleans Baptist Theological Seminary. Florida has perhaps the largest Hispanic Baptist community outside of Texas and California, with seventy congregations. The work began in the early 1950s and by 1954 Jose Fleites was pastor of a Spanish church in Miami. The migration of Hispanics to Florida, including at least 700 thousand refugees from Cuba and other Latin countries, has augmented the Baptist challenge there. The Anglo churches have sought to minister to the newcomers, and the New Orleans Seminary located its Ethnic Studies Branch in Miami, with Julio Diaz as director. Currently about fifty students are enrolled, who study, produce materials in Spanish, and preach to the teeming Hispanic population. About half of the churches are concentrated in the Miami area, where they publish *La Voz Bautista.* Juan Pistone provides overall leadership for the Hispanic churches in the Miami association.

Hispanic Baptists have also found a place in the Pacific Northwest, with at least ten churches in Washington and Oregon. The work began in 1960 when Eugene Branch began a Bible study in a labor camp at Crewport, Washington. Fellowship meetings help the various Hispanic groups keep in touch, and seminary extension classes in various locations provide training for both pastors and lay leaders.

Summary. The spread of Hispanic population throughout the United States is a story of epic proportions. Despite historic ties to Catholicism, Hispanics seem open to evangelical Christianity. If present trends continue, one may expect the Baptist family in America to take on an increasing Spanish accent. The Baptist goal of three thousand Hispanic churches by the turn of the century seems on schedule. In 1982 the largest Hispanic congregation was *Primera Iglesia Bautista* in Corpus Christi, with thirteen hundred members.

If Hispanics seem open to Baptists, Anglo Baptists seem more awakened to the opportunities of witness among Hispanics. Both Northern and Southern Baptists have come a long way from the days they considered the Mexicans a minority group along the Rio Grande. Under the leadership of Oscar I. Romo, Southern Baptists have developed a massive, well-directed, and heavily funded effort to share the gospel with over eighty different ethnic groups in America. Himself a Mexican-American, Romo has brought both energy and insight to the task, and results have been impressive under his leadership.

Perhaps the separate Mexican Baptist state conventions, formed earlier in Texas and New Mexico, will not be repeated elsewhere. Present trends seem to call for separate identity in fellowship, pastors' conferences, and sometimes in Hispanic associations, but both Anglo and Hispanic churches seem comfortable with close cooperation in their work. Already many of the Hispanic churches are bilingual and, if history repeats, in time English will become a familiar avenue for their worship. Presently a number of area or state fellowships exist for Hispanic Baptist pastors, and plans are forming for a national fellowship.

Asian Baptists in America

Asians have shown less interest than Europeans in moving to America, and those who did faced severe immigration restrictions. Political events opened China to the West by 1842, and Chinese workers were lured to America by the shipping industry, the gold strike of 1849, and the building of transcontinental railroads. Asians faced more than the usual prejudice against newcomers; the Chinese Exclusion Act of 1882 prohibited any more Chinese from entering America for ten years, and the National Origins Act of 1924 brought further restrictions. The "Chinese Question" greatly agitated nineteenth-century America, but the record shows that Baptists, despite a few unhappy exceptions, rarely embraced the jingoism that marked much of the nation.[126]

Later world crises accelerated the rate of Asian immigration into the United States. The Chinese revolution embracing Communism in the 1940s, the Korean War of the 1950s, the fall of South Vietnam in the 1970s, and continued conflict and social dislocation in Cambodia and Laos have all contributed to the increasing stream of Asians in America. While more Asians live on the West Coast, they may be found anywhere in the country. Local churches of different denominations have helped resettle refugee families so that one might find Cambodians in West Texas or Laotians in

126. Lawrence B. Davis, *Immigrants, Baptists, and the Protestant Mind in America*, p. 36.

Nebraska. Unlike the older immigration, in which people tended to concentrate in large ethnic communities, the new Asians are more scattered.

As always, the Baptists have attempted to minister to the strangers in their midst. As the earlier European newcomers tended to identify with Northern Baptists, the more recent Asians relate more to Southern Baptist structures. That fact helps account for the prominence of SBC witness in this section.

Chinese. John Lewis Shuck, a missionary newly returned from China, attended sessions of the Southern Baptist Convention in 1846. The assembled brethren showed moderate interest in hearing from Shuck, but they eagerly awaited the message from his Chinese convert Yong Seen Sang. They asked the two to delay their return to China, largely that the churches might be inspired by this firstfruits of the Asian mission.[127] Thus, from early days, Baptists have attempted to share the gospel with the Chinese, both there and here.

By 1852 about twenty-two hundred Chinese had arrived, and Northern Baptists reported, "From the commencement of immigration by this people, it has been a favorite plan of the Board to secure a proper missionary to labor among them. . . . We regret to add, as yet without success."[128] Shuck opened work in 1854 among the Chinese in Sacramento where he formed in 1860 the first Chinese Baptist church in America, beginning with nineteen members whom he had baptized.[129] Two of those members, Ah Mooey and Ah Chak, became lay preachers. Meantime, Baptists continued their witness among Chinese in San Francisco with Sunday School classes and street preaching. In 1869 Northern Baptists appointed John Francis to preach in that area, assisted by Fung Seung Nam, and within a year they had formed six Chinese Sunday Schools, meeting in the basement of First Baptist Church. The work looked promising; an early report said, "Chinese converts are already multiplying, inquirers are . . . asking to be taught the way of God more perfectly."[130] By 1874 Francis was assisted by three Chinese preachers who addressed thousands in their native tongue, conducted day schools to help Chinese children learn English, and operated several Sunday Schools in San Francisco and Oakland.

Apparently the first Chinese Baptist church outside California was that formed in Portland, Oregon, in 1874, made up of about forty converts. During his ministry in Sacramento, Shuck also formed a black church and within a short time baptized about sixty persons "representing Europe,

127. *Proceedings,* SBC, 1846, p. 6.
128. Morehouse, p. 485.
129. Ibid., p. 486.
130. Ibid.

Asia, Africa, and both North and Central America."[131] The Civil War interrupted Baptist work among the Chinese, but B. H. Whilden was appointed in 1870 to work in Southern California. Later J. B. Hartwell served in San Francisco from 1878-1884 and in 1880 formed the first Chinese Baptist church in that city with nine members.

Though financial crisis curtailed the work of the mission boards in the 1880s, local churches continued the witness among the Chinese. The First Baptist Church of Augusta, Georgia, started a Chinese Sunday School class in 1885 with one pupil; by 1950 at least one hundred were enrolled, and many had become Christians.[132] The Eutaw Place Baptist Church of Baltimore began a Chinese class in 1888, and by 1898 the First Baptist Church of El Paso had launched a Chinese mission. These were typical of other churches which, wherever Chinese population gathered, sought to minister.

Chak Hoi Lee began a Bible study in New York's Chinatown, which by 1920 was organized as the Trust in God Baptist Church. The First Chinese Baptist Church of Norfolk, Virginia, was formed in 1928 out of a Sunday School class begun years before. The First Chinese Baptist Church of San Antonio, Texas, constituted in 1923 from converts among troops under General John J. "Blackjack" Pershing; their first deacons were Coon Lee Ng, Wong Moon Him, Ng Jan, and Ng Lee. Other Chinese formed Baptist worship meetings, and sometimes organized churches, at Phoenix, New Orleans, Houston, Memphis, Fort Worth, Los Angeles, Miami, and at several points in Hawaii. By 1982 at least 140 Chinese Baptist churches and missions had been established in more than twenty-five states, Western Canada, and Puerto Rico. Most have been formed since 1970.

Japanese. Northern Baptists opened a mission for Japanese in Seattle in 1900. The work soon extended to Tacoma and also to California where over half the Japanese lived. One outstanding leader was Pastor Okasaki who baptized twenty-five converts the day the Japanese church of Seattle was formed and over three hundred during the course of his twenty-four years of ministry there. By 1931 the HMB reported five Japanese missionaries, five churches, with seventy-one baptisms the previous year.[133]

Southern Baptists began a ministry among Japanese in internment camps near Phoenix in 1942 with the appointment of Elizabeth Watkins, former missionary to Japan. Other Japan missionaries forced home by the war joined the work, assisted by a number of Japanese Christians.[134] Bible

---

131. Arthur B. Rutledge, *Mission to America: A Century and a Quarter of Southern Baptist Home Missions,* p. 152.

132. Peter Kung, "The Story of Asian Southern Baptists," *Baptist History and Heritage,* July 1983, p. 49. Much of the material in this section comes from Kung's survey.

133. Charles L. White, *A Century of Faith,* pp. 156-157.

134. Kung, p. 53.

classes, Vacation Bible Schools, and retreats in different cities attracted Japanese youth. Such activities led to a youth revival at the Sawtelle Baptist Church of West Los Angeles in 1947, which involved a number of Japanese. The next year George Fujitas and his wife were appointed to minister among Japanese in California, working mainly out of the Sawtelle church. In another part of Los Angeles summer student missionary Stanley Togikawa started a mission, which grew into the Grandview Baptist Church in 1958. Edwin Dozier opened a witness to Japanese in Hawaii in the early 1940s, including a radio ministry, which led to the formation of churches there.

During the 1950s ministries among the Japanese escalated rapidly. New missions and/or churches sprang up in many places. By 1982 Japanese Southern Baptists reported twenty-eight churches and missions. In addition, a number of Japanese hold membership in the Anglo churches.

Korean. About 1928 Changsoon Kim became a Baptist, but not enough of his Korean countrymen were in the United States or shared his faith to form a church until 1956. In that year Kim helped form the Washington Korean Baptist Church, in Washington, D.C., which called Won Young Kang as pastor. The next year Don and Eisook Kim, natives of Seoul and recent graduates of Southwestern Baptist Seminary, were appointed by the Home Mission Board to minister among Koreans. Kim later became pastor of the Berendo Street Baptist Church of Los Angeles, the largest Korean-speaking Baptist congregation in the country. In 1981 he was elected second vice-president of the Southern Baptist Convention.

Korean churches took a spurt of growth in the 1970s. From only 3 in 1971, these churches increased to 50 in 1976, 203 in 1982, and 253 in 1983. A recent survey showed almost 10,000 Korean Baptists related to the SBC, constituting one of the most rapidly growing Baptist groups in America.

Indochinese. Revolution, war, and social dislocation brought a number of Vietnamese, Laotians, and Cambodians to the United States in the 1970s. Churches have played a major role in their resettlement. The El Cajon Vietnamese Baptist Church, formed in 1975 in California, was the first Baptist church in America composed of Vietnamese. Other groups of Vietnamese Baptists emerged the same year in Washington and Florida. Organized churches grew up in 1976 in Santa Ana, California, and Dallas, Texas. By 1982 there were sixty-seven Baptist churches, missions, and worship groups among Vietnamese in the United States.

In 1975 a group of Laotians formed a Baptist worship group at Selma, Alabama, but the Lao Baptist Church of Des Moines, Iowa, formed in 1977, was the first (and as of 1982 the only) organized Laotian church in America. However, by 1982 there were 63 Lao Baptist worship groups, including both major ethnic groups, Hmong and Yaomienh. Many of these related to Anglo churches. In 1982, 20 of these groups reported 1,681 members with 280 baptisms the previous year.[135]

Lacy, Washington, was the site of the first Cambodian Baptist fellowship in 1976. By 1982 at least twenty-two Cambodian Baptist groups were known in the United States; ten of that number who gave reports listed 882 members, with 390 baptisms for 1981.[136]

Filipinos. The Los Angeles Filipino Baptist Church, the first in the United States, was formed in 1974. By 1982 at least a dozen Filipino Baptist groups were active, over half in California. Their primary leader has been Peol Eduardo, former host of the "Baptist Hour" in the Philippines, who came to the United States in 1970.

Other Asians. By 1973 in Chicago and 1975 in Mill Valley, California, Baptists established a ministry to Asian Indians. That work has since branched out to Doraville, Georgia, and Rochester, New York. The Home Mission Board also sponsors a witness with two Thai groups, two groups of Indonesians, and one Pakistani mission. In 1982 a Baptist witness was begun in a new ethnic group, the Tongans.

Asians make up about one third of new Americans arriving daily in the United States. Churches have played a major role in resettling Asian immigrants, especially those from the war-torn areas of Indochina. These new Americans appear to be open to an evangelical witness, and many are finding their way into Baptist churches or forming churches of their own. Their presence has encouraged about 650 Southern Baptist churches, especially in urban areas, to develop "International Ministry" departments to address the world at their doorsteps.[137] One example is the South Main Baptist Church of Houston. David F. D'Amico, native of Argentina and former professor at Southwestern Baptist Seminary, has served since 1975 as minister to internationals in that church. The church has developed a ministry to language/national groups in Houston, with several separate ethnic churches within South Main, most with their own language pastors.

A little-known aspect of Baptist ministry to Asians in America grew out of Wayland Baptist College (now University) in Plainview, Texas. In 1947 Wayland president J. W. Marshall, a former official with the Foreign Mission Board, inaugurated programs which brought scores of Asian students to Wayland. Over the years this West Texas town became a major training center for Asian Baptists. Among many others, such prominent Asian Baptist leaders as Samuel Choy, Man Pew Lee, Katsuro "Kats" Taura, and Peter Chen, are graduates of Wayland.

135. Ibid., p. 55.
136. Ibid.
137. *Annual,* SBC, 1983, p. 135.

Summary of Ethnic Ministries

Despite a measure of success, the Baptist witness to ethnics in America has not escaped problems. The shortage of ethnic-language ministers has been a continuing concern. Many American-born ethnics have either lost the language or, in some cases, failed to win the confidence of recent immigrants. The prominence of churches in the resettlement of recent Asian refugees, with the trend for immigrants to profess the faith of those churches, has raised questions especially in cases which involved economic aid from the churches.

Perhaps most Anglo Baptists have expected ethnic converts to accept an American or even a regional version of the Baptist faith. However, most of the ethnic Baptists do not come from a culture shaped by Puritan-Separatist traditions, and some of the most recent converts come from cultures with no Christian background at all. Many of the newest Baptists bring new emphases in theology, church practices, and styles of worship which help link their new faith to their old heritage. This process of adaptation to new settings, while as old as the apostle Paul's mission to the first-century Gentiles, continues to trouble some now as it did then.

Landmark Baptists

Landmarkism is a form of Baptist ecclesiology, best expressed in the writings and ministry of J. R. Graves of Tennessee in the nineteenth century. This Baptist exclusivism pervaded many of the Baptist groups of its day, and remnants of its emphases can still be detected among Baptists in America.

A number of small Baptist groups emerged in the early twentieth century to perpetuate those emphases. They are here designated Landmark Baptists, not because they are the only Baptists who hold some Landmark views but because preservation of the Landmark system provided the major reason for their separate existence. Most of the Landmark churches are small, and their historic emphasis upon the local church has retarded the development of general denominational life. Only three of the Landmark groups can be allotted space here.

The Baptist Missionary Association (BMA)

A struggle for the soul of Texas Baptists has been waged at least since the 1840s, and the emergence of the BMA schism in 1900 was but one skirmish in that ongoing conflict. The progressive or "missionary" Baptists formed a convention in 1848 and by the turn of the century had evolved a strong educational and missionary program in Texas, led by such stalwarts as J. B. Gambrell, B. H. Carroll, and George W. Truett. However, the "anticonvention" party, quite numerous in East and North Texas, opposed that denominational program. They had absorbed much of the spirit of Daniel Parker and also embraced the teachings of J. R. Graves. By the 1880s they found their major leader in the person of Samuel A. Hayden, who brought the simmering conflict to the point of schism.

Much of the controversy centered in Dallas, the dividing line between competing state conventions, and leaders of both factions held membership in the First Baptist Church. That church split in 1879 when the majority, composed of more progressive Baptists, excluded fifty-nine members led by R. C. Buckner, founder of the children's homes which still bear his name. The "Memorialists," as the excluded party was called from their memorial of ultimatum, formed the Live Oak Baptist Church as a rival to First Baptist.[138] The Live Oak faction favored Landmarkism, often had Graves as a guest preacher, and opposed the work of the major state convention.

In 1883 the Live Oak church called Samuel A. Hayden as pastor, and within a short time he led the church to reunite with First Baptist. This was a local manifestation of efforts at unification among Texas Baptists which saw the several competing state conventions united in 1886 into the present Baptist General Convention of Texas. Hayden remained in the membership, though not as pastor, finding his main work as editor of the *Texas Baptist and Herald.* Within months the sweet peace, upon which the church was supposedly reunited, went sour. Hayden through his paper bitterly attacked Baptists on the same issues which had provoked the original split in 1879. For several years Hayden's attacks created more diversion than damage, but by 1896 he indicted the convention and its work as unbaptistic and heretical, its leaders as dishonest and corrupt, and used stinging sarcasm to demand changes which if effected would have destroyed the cooperative work of Texas Baptists.

After countless conferences failed to placate Hayden, the convention labeled him a "sower of discord" and in 1897 denied him a seat at the state convention. In 1898 Hayden filed a lawsuit against several Texas Baptist leaders, demanding $100,000 damages. That lawsuit, and the various other litigations it spawned, dragged on for some years, with the attending sensational publicity managed skillfully by Hayden to his own advantage. Finally the matter was settled out of court, but Hayden's attacks probably helped unify the majority of Texas Baptists.

After losing several convention votes, the followers of Hayden held a "rump" session at the state convention of 1899. On June 6, 1900, a number of their leaders, against Hayden's will, met at Troop, Texas, where they formed the East Texas Baptist Convention. This was partly an effort to resurrect the rival state convention which had prevailed in that area before the 1886 unification of Texas Baptists. Within a few months the rival body changed its name to Baptist Missionary Association (BMA).

138. Leon McBeth, *The First Baptist Church of Dallas: Centennial History, 1868-1968,* pp. 73 *f,* 132 *f.*

Most of the BMA churches remained small and retained the Landmark flavor of their origins. Like most Landmarkers, they sought to pursue missionary work only through the local church. In that they resembled T. P. Crawford, whose "Gospel Mission Controversy" raged at about the same time. The BMA objected not to missionary work itself, but the *method* of doing that work through conventions rather than churches. However, the result was that their churches did very little missionary work by any method, and they rapidly acquired the reputation of being antimissionary despite their name. Clearly they absorbed some emphases from the Parker antimission churches which had preceded them in that area.

The conflict between the Hayden group and convention Baptists centered in the doctrine of the church. Hayden contended that the convention was composed of *churches,* not messengers from churches, and for a convention to expel a church elevates the convention above the churches. However, after full discussion, the majority voted that "the Convention is composed of persons chosen by churches, associations, and missionary associations as their messengers, and that when said persons are convened they, and not the churches are the Convention."[139] That ruling was later reaffirmed and expresses the viewpoint of most cooperative Baptists to this day.

Though at first disapproving the 1900 division, Hayden affiliated with the new group. He had a strong following in Texas, though not all of them followed him into schism. Hayden spent the rest of his life bitterly assailing the convention, when he might have done better simply to promote his own group. The BMA group in Texas might have amounted to more but for the rise of a larger Landmark schism in 1905 which tended to preempt the field. In 1924 the BMA group merged with the new group, the American Baptist Association (ABA), but in 1950 a remnant withdrew to reaffirm the BMA heritage.

The American Baptist Association (ABA)

Landmark efforts to capture Southern Baptists took many forms. One of its greatest leaders since Graves was Ben M. Bogard, pastor at Searcy, Arkansas, and leader of the Landmark schism in that state.

Conflict between "convention" and "anticonvention" forces had been building in Arkansas, as in Texas, and came to a head at about the same time. W. A. Clark, editor of the *Arkansas Baptist* and sorely disappointed at not being chosen corresponding secretary of the state convention in 1899, used the paper to attack the convention and the office he had coveted.[140] Landmarkers who opposed the convention met in Little Rock in 1902 to form the General Association of Arkansas Baptists. Their continual agitation divided Baptists in that state and frustrated all efforts at reunion. The

---

139. *Proceedings,* Baptist General Convention of Texas, 1895, p. 36.
140. E. Glenn Hinson, *A History of Baptists in Arkansas, 1818-1978,* pp. 175 *f.*

General Association set the following demands as the price of healing the schism:

1. The scriptural right of individual churches to commission and send forth missionaries.
2. The arranging of missionary methods so that the reports of missionaries shall include only the work actually performed by the missionaries and paid for by missionary contributions.
3. Recognition of each church as a unit and entitled to equal representation with any other church in association or Convention.
4. The absolute abolition of the office and expense of the Corresponding Secretary under whatever title.
5. The right of the churches to instruct their messengers on any subject to be recognized.
6. The abolition of the present plan of cooperation with the Home and Foreign Mission Boards of the Southern Baptist Convention.[141]

The similarity with views of the Hayden movement in Texas is obvious. A few years later a similar movement emerged in southern Illinois under the leadership of W. P. Throgmorton. At first Ben Bogard of Searcy supported the state convention but later switched his allegiance to the General Association; in fact, he completely dominated the body which had been formed to avoid authoritarianism. For over a decade, the various associations in Arkansas were divided in their allegiance, some continuing to support the state convention and others lining up with the General Association.

Had the matter rested there it might have had significance only for one state, but under Bogard's dynamic leadership the issues escalated to challenge the entire Southern Baptist Convention. In early 1905 messengers from fifty-two Arkansas churches met in Texarkana and drafted a memorial to the upcoming meeting of the SBC. Professing love for the Convention and sympathy for its work, the Arkansas faction said, "We have protested against what we honestly believe to be unscriptural principles and methods of work," a reference primarily to the work of the mission boards.[142] They then outlined their ultimatum and concluded, "If you reject this . . . we shall consider that we have done our duty and shall trouble you no more."

Their demands were bold. "First," they said, "we want the money and the associational basis of representation eliminated from the constitution and a purely church basis substituted instead." This would give every church a seat in the convention, with an equal vote regardless of size or contribution. "We object," they continued, "to the power put into the hands

141. Ibid., pp. 177-178.
142. *Annual,* SBC, 1905, p. 43.

of the Boards . . . to appoint and remove missionaries."[143] In their view, that power belonged only to the churches.

The SBC referred the Texarkana Memorial to a committee chaired by W. E. Hatcher of Virginia, no friend of Landmarkism. The committee replied courteously but firmly, rejecting all the Landmark demands. They concluded:

> It would not be in the best interests of the work which the Convention is seeking to do, to accede to the petitions contained in this memorial. These petitions call for action so entirely out of harmony with the principles of our organization, and the methods upon which our work is conducted, that we feel constrained to ask that they be denied. We feel the strongest assurance that the principles upon which the work of our Convention is organized and conducted are in accord with the teachings of God's Word, and in harmony with Baptist history, Baptist usage, and Baptist doctrine.[144]

Thus failing to capture the SBC to their extreme views, the Landmarkers separated and sought to create a rival national organization. They gathered up smaller Landmark groups here and there and narrowly failed to incorporate the Throgmorton schism in Illinois, which in 1910 affiliated with the SBC instead. The branching out of Bogard's movement undercut and eventually absorbed Hayden's BMA movement in Texas. In 1924 the two groups merged under the name of American Baptist Association (ABA).

In *The Baptist Way-Book*, Bogard defended the faith and function of the ABA churches. He popularized the Landmark views which Graves had expounded in greater detail, insisting that Baptists are the only true churches, that they can be traced from New Testament times, and that theirs are the only valid ordinances. Bogard gave a major section to the "Evils of Conventionism," as he saw them, and insisted that churches may not "combine" (as he thought a convention attempted to do), but "they may associate."[145]

The ABA churches tended to be ultraconservative on every issue, refusing to cooperate with other denominations in any way. Though protesting against denominational structure, they set up their own denominational structure at Texarkana, from which they conduct a vigorous publishing ministry. At its height, the movement affiliated 3,570 churches in the United States and Canada, with membership exceeding a million.[146] Despite its antimission image, ABA churches conduct foreign missions in a number of nations.

---

143. Ibid., pp. 43-44.
144. Ibid., p. 42.
145. Ben M. Bogard, *The Baptist Way-Book* (Texarkana: Bogard Press, 1946), pp. 29-39, 44.
146. Piepkorn, 2:420.

The Baptist Missionary Association of America (BMAA)

People who put exclusive emphasis upon doctrine as the essence of their spiritual existence can rarely agree on every subpoint, and so they continue to divide and subdivide. The Landmark Baptists amply illustrate this point, though their divisions often involved personality clashes and regional rivalries as well as doctrine. Tensions increased in the ABA from the first. In 1950 at Little Rock, a dissident group, primarily Texans, withdrew from the ABA and formed a new group called the North American Baptist Association. In 1969 they changed that name to Baptist Missionary Association of America, partly because of misunderstanding about the term *North* in the earlier name and partly perhaps to reassert the earlier BMA heritage in Texas.

The BMAA describes itself as "evangelical, missionary, fundamental, and premillennial."[147] While continuing many of the older emphases, the BMAA represents a more moderate form of Landmarkism. Over the years they have absorbed many emphases of the Fundamentalist movement, in some ways the successor of the Landmark movement among Baptists. Their confession of faith, in twenty-four brief articles, reflects as much modern Fundamentalism as old Landmarkism. This confession also makes "The perpetuity of missionary Baptist churches from Christ's day on earth until His second coming" an article of faith rather than of historical investigation. BMAA Baptists oppose the modern ecumenical movement, and their confession rejects "open communion, alien baptism, pulpit affiliation with heretical churches, modernism, modern tongues movement, and all kindred evils."[148]

The antimission image that clung, often unfairly, to earlier Landmark groups has not attached itself to the BMAA. Louis F. Asher, their major historian, pointed out that they supported 141 missionaries in 1982, of whom 66 served in 19 different nations.[149] The churches maintain a full range of denominational activities, including an aggressive publishing ministry, radio and television programs, three colleges, four homes for children, plus book stores and a modern encampment. Like most Baptist groups, they formed a national Woman's Missionary Auxiliary and a Brotherhood for men. Perhaps their major institution, and the center of denominational unity, is the theological seminary, established in 1965 at Jacksonville, Texas.

Growth of the BMAA has been steady. By 1982 the group had 1,487 affiliated churches in 29 states, reporting 219,697 members.[150] Though more widely distributed than earlier Landmark groups, its main strength

---

147. *Directory and Handbook,* Baptist Missionary Association of America, 1982-1983, p. 7.
148. Ibid., p. 19.
149. Louis F. Asher, "Baptist Missionary Association of America," *ESB,* 4:2105-06.
150. Ibid.

is still the Southwest; Texas leads with about 500 churches, followed by Arkansas with 377.

Fundamentalist Baptists

Fundamentalism arose in America after the Civil War, partly in reaction to modern developments in the physical and social sciences and partly to counteract liberal trends in religion. By the turn of the century, it had coalesced into a definable movement. The sources of Fundamentalism are many, and in some form it affected most denominations, none more than Presbyterians and Northern Baptists. Recent literature on Fundamentalism has sought to trace its origins, analyze its beliefs, and explain its links to the older orthodoxy and the newer evangelical movement.[151] *The Fundamentals,* a series of twelve booklets financed and distributed by wealthy Presbyterian laymen beginning in 1910, helped name and popularize the movement.

However one defines or explains the movement, the fact remains that Fundamentalism greatly affected Baptists, especially in the North. Contrary to popular belief, early Fundamentalism was more native to the urban North than to the rural South; only in recent years could Dallas compete with Detroit as a center of Baptist Fundamentalism. While many Baptists hold some beliefs or practices associated with that movement, some groups owe their existence to fundamentalist schisms. The purpose of this section is not to trace the course of the movement in Baptist life but to summarize the history of those groups which originated out of fundamentalist schisms. These include the General Association of Regular Baptist Churches (GARBC); the Conservative Baptist Association of America (CBAA); the World Baptist Fellowship (WBF); Baptist Bible Fellowship (BBF); and several independent Baptist fellowships.

General Association of Regular Baptist Churches (GARBC)

An earlier chapter traced the growing unrest among Northern Baptists after the turn of the century. Suspicion of liberalism in the schools, rumors of heresy among the missionaries, reports of open membership among the churches, and the growing power of denominational leaders as the societies gave way to a unified convention disturbed the more conservative pastors and led to a right-wing rebellion from which Northern Baptists have never recovered. The Northern Baptist Convention, meeting in Denver in 1919, took four actions which further alienated the conservatives. They launched

---

151. Three recent works may be noted: Ernest R. Sandeen, *The Roots of Fundamentalism and American Culture* (New York: Oxford University Press, 1980); and Jerry Falwell, ed., *The Fundamentalist Phenomenon* (Garden City, New York: Doubleday and Company, 1981); George M. Marsden, *Fundamentalism and American Culture* (New York: Oxford Press, 1980).

the New World Movement to raise 100 million dollars; formed the General Board of Promotion to oversee NBC work; launched a denominational newspaper, *The Baptist;* and voted to join the Interchurch Movement.

The more conservative party saw those actions as entrenching liberal leadership, funding projects they disapproved, erecting massive denominational machinery which threatened the independence of the churches, and giving denominational leaders a monopoly of information through *The Baptist.* In the words of one conservative, "The time had come to fight!"[152] That remark reveals much not only about strategy but also about the spirit of the movement.

The Fundamental Fellowship. At a preconvention rally at Buffalo in 1920 leading critics formed the Fundamental Fellowship of the Northern Baptist Convention. For over a quarter century, that group met annually before the convention to plan strategy and line up votes in what proved to be an unsuccessful effort to gain control of the NBC and its agencies. At first its purpose was to purge the denomination, not leave it, though a few urged separation from the first. That was made clear in a letter of J. C. Massee, one of the more moderate fundamentalist leaders:

> This year [1922] more than ever we must keep the fight going all along the line in order that we may come to the next Convention sufficiently well organized and in forces strong enough to be recognized in the election of Convention officers, the appointment of Convention Committees and the determination of Convention policies. We can never consent to stop short of seeing the denominational machinery in control of the great Conservative Constituency. . . . We must therefore eliminate those men who have put in jeopardy the spiritual life and purpose of the denomination.[153]

Despite these plans, 1922 proved disastrous for the Fundamentalists. They were soundly defeated in every vote, and the convention refused to adopt the New Hampshire Confession, which was the keystone of the Fundamentalist reform program.

The Baptist Bible Union. From the first the Fundamental Fellowship contained two groups; the moderate conservatives who wanted to remain within the convention and militant separatists who wanted to split off. The defeat at the 1922 convention led the militants to issue a call of their own for a meeting in 1923 at Kansas City, at which they formed the Baptist Bible Union, clearly separating from Northern Baptists. In light of Northern Baptist apostasy, they said, "Further delay . . . would be not only perilous but deadly."[154] Their major leaders included W. B. Riley, A. C. Dixon, J. Frank Norris, and T. T. Shields.

152. Joseph M. Stowell, *Background and History of the General Association of Regular Baptist Churches,* p. 12.
153. Ibid., p. 18.
154. Ibid., p. 20.

The new Bible Union differed significantly from the more moderate Fundamental Fellowship. The union included Baptists in Canada and the South; one of its founders was J. Frank Norris of Fort Worth, leader of Southern Baptist Fundamentalism, and its first president was T. T. Shields of Toronto. The new group took a more militant and separatist stance, put more emphasis upon premillennialism, and at times lost all sense of restraint in their attacks upon Northern Baptists. For some years they held their own preconvention rally, separate from the Fundamental Fellowship, and often hampered efforts at cooperation between moderate Fundamentalists and convention loyalists.

The Bible Union adopted the New Hampshire Confession, with a premillennial revision of the article on eschatology. A major part of its protest focused on the denominational machinery which accompanied formation of the Northern Baptist Convention. T. T. Shields called it "ecclesiasticism," and Bible Unioners announced they would never again come under denominational "overlordship."[155] For their own organization, they intended "the minimum of organization and the maximum of fellowship."[156] However, it never worked out that way. The dissident group in an amazingly short time erected almost all the features they had complained about in the Northern convention, including a tightly controlled paper, denominational machinery with far more power over local churches, and leaders who bore different titles but exercised the same or even stronger leadership.

True to its separatist purpose, the BBU launched its own programs. Its churches attempted to form their own foreign mission agency and did launch a Sunday School literature work in which they purchased lesson quarterlies from a nondenominational press, did minor editing, and resold them to Fundamentalist Baptist churches. In 1927 they obtained title to a school in Des Moines, but it proved their ruin. When the trustees fired the entire faculty and administration, a campus riot erupted which required police to control. The publicity was damaging, the school was bankrupt, and the divisive spirit of the Bible Union lay exposed to the world. That riot destroyed more than a school; it also destroyed the Baptist Bible Union. Whereas hundreds had attended its annual meetings, the 1932 session drew only thirty-four dispirited delegates.

A new organization. In 1932 the Baptist Bible Union adopted a report recommending that it be transformed into the General Association of Regular Baptist Churches. By the next year, its affiliated churches ratified that action and 1933 is usually accepted as the origin of the GARBC. However, it might as easily claim 1923, for the GARBC was a direct outgrowth and continuation of the BBU.

A decade of hard experience led the Fundamentalists to make changes

155. Ibid., pp. 23, 33.
156. Ibid., p. 57.

in the new structure. For one thing, they allowed membership of churches as well as individuals. Instead of forming their own mission agencies and schools, they worked through agencies independent of the new denomination, but on its approved list. Their 1952 annual, for example, lists five independent mission agencies as "approved by the G.A.R.B.C." Perhaps the best known of these, and the one through which many GARBC churches channel their mission gifts, is Baptist Mid-Missions. A lesser-known, but still approved, agency at that time was the Hiawatha-Land Independent Baptist Missions, Inc.[157] The same annual lists five approved schools, all sponsored by Baptists but not officially connected with any Baptist body.

By working through independent agencies, the GARBC saved itself the burdens of financing and managing denominational ministries in missions, publications, and education. They could also exercise maximum doctrinal control over the "approved" agencies with a minimum of financial investment. In Baptist polity, this amounted to a shrinking from the concept of a *denomination* and, in effect, restored the independent society concept of Northern Baptists before 1900. In methods, if not in doctrines, the GARBC harked back to Francis Wayland, while rejecting Luther Rice.

While composed of more militant Fundamentalists, the GARBC has over the years moderated somewhat. In early days its paper, *The Baptist Bulletin,* was known for lurid headlines and angry articles, and its preachers sounded more polemical than pastoral. However, time has done its work and the GARBC churches seem more sedate, its ministers less angry, and its doctrinal convictions, while still strong, find expression in calmer tones.

The GARBC has grown rapidly. By 1978 it reported 1,544 churches, with 236,000 members. As early as 1958 it reported 989 foreign missionaries, about half appointed through Baptist Mid-Missions.[158]

Conservative Baptist Association of America (CBAA)

From the first the Fundamental Fellowship of 1920 included both militant and moderate Fundamentalists. As noted, the more militant split off in 1923 to form the Baptist Bible Union, which in a decade became the GARBC. The more moderate Fundamentalists, meanwhile, remained within the Northern Convention for another twenty years. Led by men like Frank M. Goodchild, J. C. Massee, and Curtis Lee Laws, they worked from within to effect reforms, but despite their protests and strategies, the group never won a major convention victory. They moved reluctantly toward separation, forming the Conservative Baptist Foreign Mission Society in 1943 and the general body, the CBAA, in 1947.

In addition to the broad range of Fundamentalist concerns, two issues

---

157. *Annual,* General Association of Regular Baptist Churches, 1952, no page number.
158. Mead, p. 51; William J. Hopewell, *The Missionary Emphasis of the General Association of Regular Baptist Churches,* p. 152.

finally led to schism: dissatisfaction with the foreign mission work of the NBC and the growth of what Fundamentalists considered an excessive denominational bureaucracy. Fundamentalists claimed that the Foreign Mission Society continued to follow an "inclusive policy," which they interpreted to mean appointment of both liberals and conservatives. The society, however, maintained that it followed an "evangelical policy" of appointing only those who held evangelical doctrines, though their understandings might vary at points.

Formation of the Northern Baptist Convention in 1908 represented a major change for a denomination that had worked through a series of independent societies. The NBC formed a unified budget and elected a central administrative board. To some this seemed only prudent and necessary to guide large programs, but to others it appeared as excessive bureaucracy. C. L. Laws spoke for many, no doubt, when he observed that formation of such a general board "creates a piece of machinery that may be effective but it is certainly not democratic nor in harmony with Baptist traditions."[159] Between the schisms of 1933 and 1947, the focus seemed to shift from theology to complaints about denominational structure. Even in the missions controversy, the doctrinal issue seemed to recede as Fundamentalists became more frustrated with their failure to control the structures.

Conservative Baptist Foreign Mission Society. The election of Elmer A. Fridell, despite strong Fundamentalist objections, as secretary of the convention's foreign board in early 1943 triggered the break. Fundamentalists adopted a "Directive" to the foreign society, which became a sort of ultimatum:

> We, representing the Fundamentalist Fellowship of the Northern Baptist Convention, declare we will no longer give funds to the American Baptist Foreign Mission Society that can in any way be appropriated for the support of missionaries who do not affirm faith in the Bible as the inspired Word of God; the deity of our Lord Jesus Christ, which includes His preexistence, virgin birth, miracles, and His bodily resurrection from the dead; the substitutionary death of our Lord for sinners in atonement for their sins; His high priestly intercession at the right hand of God and His eternal sovereignty.[160]

The mission society regarded the "Directive" as a creedal statement and argued that, since the convention had refused to adopt a creed, the mission society could not do so. Instead it voted to reaffirm the evangelical policy. Apparently the leadership underestimated the depth of dissatisfaction and later seemed genuinely surprised at the extent of the ensuing schism.

When the Conservative Baptist Foreign Mission Society was formed in

159. Bruce L. Shelley, *A History of Conservative Baptists,* p. 22.
160. Ibid., p. 32.

late 1943, immediately the question arose as to its relation to the NBC. Convention leaders from the first regarded it as a separatist structure, but Fundamentalists viewed it simply as one more agency related to overall convention work. The convention had both liberal and conservative seminaries, they argued, so why not diverse mission societies? However, a convention committee ruled the new society "a divisive and competing organization," refusing to acknowledge them as an approved agency. Further, in 1946 the bylaws were changed to make convention representation dependent upon funds contributed. That meant fundamentalist churches could no longer send their contributions to nonconvention agencies and expect to maintain full voting rights in the convention. "The amendment was eminently just," according to one analysis, "in everything but intention, which was clearly to weaken the forces of the fundamentalists without joining in serious theological debate."[161]

Final separation. By 1946 "it became apparent to all except a blind man that the Conservatives were heading for complete separation" from the Northern Convention.[162] One observer said, "Two opposing elements have been trying to get along with each other for years. It has not succeeded."[163] Of course, the two sides viewed the separation of 1947 differently. Convention leaders felt they had been harassed long enough, and while they deplored schism they hoped it would end a generation of wrangling. Fundamentalists felt that their sincere efforts at reform had been rejected and that their exit was not by choice but by coercion.

Having decided to split, the conservative group first explored and then rejected the idea of merger with either the GARBC or the Swedish General Conference. Instead they formed their own group, the CBAA, in 1947.

The new denomination received a surge of support. They not only enlisted the affiliation of scores (and eventually hundreds) of NBC churches but also gathered up a number of churches which had withdrawn from the NBC but had not linked up with any other fundamentalist group. Within a few years, the CBAA had its own structures completed. In 1950 it formed a Conservative Baptist Home Mission Society; the delay can be largely explained by the fact that home mission work created less controversy than the foreign work. Also in 1950 the CBAA established the Conservative Baptist Theological Seminary in Denver and the next year adopted a seminary that had been established in Portland in 1927. By the 1940s, the moderate group preferred to be called conservatives, perhaps to escape the negative overtones which still attach to Fundamentalism. Even the old Fundamental Fellowship renamed itself the Conservative Fellowship in

161. Paul M. Harrison, *Authority and Power in the Free Church Tradition* (Princeton University Press, 1959), p. 154.
162. Shelley, p. 51.
163. Ibid., p. 26.

1946. In time the CBAA sponsored colleges in Portland and Phoenix and created the usual denominational offices for promotion and publication. Several smaller papers combined to form *The Conservative Baptist.*

All of these denominational agencies were, at least in theory, independent of each other and of the CBAA. Norman Cox observed that "they [the CBAA] have recreated the organizational structure that they obtained from Northern Baptists prior to the organization of the Northern Baptist Convention in 1907."[164] Bruce L. Shelley, major historian of the movement, said, "Conservative Baptists are a hybrid of denominational values and interdenominational ones."[165] This left unclear the relationship, if any, between the various agencies and between the agencies and the churches. The main issue, never finally settled, was whether the mission societies were arms of the CBAA or separate and equal organizations.

The CBAA was founded upon a broad base, but over the years that base tended to narrow. At first churches affiliated with the new group could continue to hold dual affiliation in the NBC or any other Baptist body. Like the Fundamental Fellowship out of which it came, the CBAA from the first included a "moderate majority" and what came to be called a "militant minority" or hard-core Fundamentalists. It seems ironic that within a decade the new denomination faced many of the same problems it had sought to escape in the old and, what is more ironic still, adopted some of the same tactics to try to control its own militant minority.

Problems erupted at three points: polity, degree of separatism, and premillennialism. As to polity, the CBAA over the years took on more and more the character of a denominational body, with the mission agencies regarded as its boards. In time the separatism became more rigid, with dual affiliation suspect. Many churches, long affiliated with the CBAA, reluctantly pulled back when it became clear that to continue they would have to sever their historic ties with Northern Baptists.

The issue of premillennialism became more divisive. At its formation in 1943, the Conservative Baptist Foreign Mission Society, first agency of the new denomination, adopted articles of faith and voted that "they shall never be changed, altered, modified or revoked."[166] While conservative in tone, that confession did not specify a belief in premillennialism. Most of the new group probably held that view, though some did not, and at the time the doctrine did not appear significant enough to require it for fellowship. Over the years, however, as hard-core Fundamentalists displaced moderates, many wanted to require premillennialism as the price of affiliation. The home society voted such a requirement in 1953, and it appeared the foreign

---

164. Norman W. Cox, "Conservative Baptist Association of America," *The Quarterly Review* (April-June 1959), p. 25.
165. Shelley, p. 3.
166. Ibid., p. 80.

society might do likewise. However, legal counsel advised that such a change was illegal and probably would not stand in a court of law. Later the adamant premillennialists sneaked in the back door, inserting a clause not in the confession but in the constitution, saying, "The purpose of this Society is to provide a channel for *premillennial* Bible-believing Baptists to cooperate."[167]

Despite a distinct shift from conservative to more fundamentalist positions on a number of issues, the hard-core Fundamentalists did not rest. Not content with premillennialism, some wanted to require a pretribulation rapture; the remnants of the old Fundamental Fellowship had already voted such a change. In the 1960s these and other tensions led to further schism, with hard-core Fundamentalists pulling out of the CBF to form the World Conservative Baptist Mission. Later the New Testament Association of Independent Baptist Churches split off from the CBAA.[168] If history repeats, one may expect further divisions for fragmentation seems to follow Fundamentalism.

Recent reports mention about 1,200 churches affiliated with the CBAA, involving probably over 300,000 members. Statistics are tenuous, for churches affiliate and disaffiliate with some regularity. By 1980 the group sponsored about 600 foreign missionaries and 250 missionaries in the homeland.[169] Its motto has been from the first, "Every Baptist a missionary; every church a Bible institute." Generally regarded as one of the more balanced fundamentalist groups, it has been described as people "in a hurry to serve the Lord."[170]

World Baptist Fellowship (WBF)

A series of divisive movements sprang up around John Franklyn Norris (1877-1952), colorful pastor for over forty years of the First Baptist Church in Fort Worth, Texas, and the acknowledged leader of the Southern wing of the fundamentalist movement. Norris, who had been a loyal Southern Baptist, by 1917 had become a militant Fundamentalist. The "Texas Cyclone," as he was called, delivered the same kinds of attacks upon the SBC that W. B. Riley and others leveled against the NBC and with less reason. After showing extraordinary patience for a number of years, Southern Baptists excluded Norris from the local association, the state convention, and the SBC.

When the Baptist Bible Union collapsed, Norris along with C. P. Stealey, formed the Premillennial Baptist Missionary Fellowship in Fort Worth. A

167. Ibid., p. 87.

168. Ibid., p. 94.

169. Piepkorn, *Profiles* 2:424; Bruce L. Shelley, "Conservative Baptist Association of America," *ESB*, 4:2171.

170. Cox, p. 26.

few years later that body was chartered under a slightly different name, and in 1950 the name was changed to World Baptist Fellowship. Most of its early churches were in Texas because Norris was there. The dramatic personality of Norris, along with his powerful preaching and sensational methods, attracted widespread attention, especially through the pages of his paper, *The Fundamentalist.* C. Allyn Russell described Norris as a "violent fundamentalist." During his ministry Norris was at different times indicted and tried for murder, perjury, and arson.[171] In 1939 he founded at his church the Bible Baptist Seminary, later restructured as Arlington Baptist College, Arlington, Texas. The WBF formed its own mission agencies and by 1982 reported 80 missionary families at work in 24 nations. By that time, it had about 1,250 affiliated churches.[172]

"Norrisism," as some called the movement, prospered as long as Norris lived, but its growth has slowed since his death. Though he preached independence, Norris totally dominated the movement. Some found that stifling during his lifetime, and after his death in 1952, no comparable successor emerged. The WBF has suffered two major schisms, one in 1950 when a group split off to form the present Baptist Bible Fellowship of Springfield, Missouri. In 1984 the embattled remnants of the Norris movement split again over a dispute in the Arlington Baptist College. One group pulled out to form another fundamentalist body, with plans to launch a new school expected to bear the name of J. Frank Norris.[173]

Baptist Bible Fellowship (BBF)

The BBF movement split off from J. Frank Norris in 1950, set up headquarters at Springfield, Missouri, and over the years developed a full range of denominational ministries. By 1983 it reported 3,164 affiliated churches, making it apparently the largest of the Baptist fundamentalist groups.[174] Of these churches, about 2,500 are said to be "firm," while others support portions of the BBF work; many hold dual or even multiple affiliations with other Fundamentalist bodies.

The issues. A growing uneasiness in the Norris movement threatened division for some years and finally led to what insiders call the "big fight" of 1950. Three major issues led to the division of 1950, none of them doctrinal. First, the personality and methods of Norris had alienated many followers, even some of his friends. A recent fundamentalist historian has pictured Norris in his later years as erratic, domineering, devious, and under suspicion of having diverted funds intended for the seminary to other

171. C. Allyn Russell, *Voices of American Fundamentalism,* p. 20.
172. Wayne Martin, "World Baptist Fellowship," *ESB,* 4:2562.
173. Jim Jones, "Baptist College Feud Leads to Split," *Fort Worth Star-Telegram,* April 7, 1984, p. 1.
174. *Baptist Bible Tribune,* August 5, 1983, p. 1.

purposes.[175] Noel Smith, a leader of the schism, said, "This thing is an accumulation of grievances and outrages." Smith noted the egotistical and possessive attitudes of Norris, complaining that Norris frequently spoke of "my Seminary, my churches, my fellowship."[176] Others accused Norris of using both threats and promise of rewards to keep followers in line. Continuing bad publicity about Norris's murder and arson trials, the defection of his son to form the Gideon Baptist Church in 1945, and Norris's stroke the next year weakened his leadership. Some of the more moderate Fundamentalists were embarrassed by the Norris tactics and the lack of educational standards in the seminary. Pastors complained that they often had to apologize for the seminary and for Norris. One concluded, "He [Norris] has arranged his own disaster."[177]

A second issue revolved around control of the Bible Baptist Seminary which Norris had set up in his church in 1939 and had later turned over to the fellowship. Just how much control Norris and his church retained and how much belonged to trustees elected by the fellowship was the issue. By all accounts, the school had not been overly successful, had run about $253,000 in debt, and allegedly had no curriculum in the usual sense of that word. Classes met spasmodically, often with all the students gathered in one large room to hear fiery sermons by Norris when he was in town. In 1948 Norris installed George Beauchamp Vick as the new president of the seminary. Vick had worked with Norris for years at Temple Baptist Church in Detroit. Vick demanded and received full authority to run the seminary, with the counsel of trustees duly elected by the denomination. Though no schoolman, Vick proceeded with integrity and common sense and, by 1950, had made vast improvements in the school and had reduced the debt to $115,000.

Early in 1950 Norris suddenly resumed personal control of the seminary. He fired the president and some teachers, replaced the trustees, and "cooked-up," his opponents said, a new set of bylaws, returning full seminary control to Norris and First Baptist Church. Clearly Norris felt the school was his, and he wanted to return to its original status before the fellowship assumed its sponsorship. Norris also feared, with some reason, that his opponents intended either to move the school to Springfield or found an alternate school there. Since schools have formed such a unitive center for Fundamentalism, Norris rightly feared that such a move would erode his domination of the movement. The Norris opponents felt that the seminary belonged to the denomination and, noting the fact that the fellow-

175. Billy Vick Bartlett, *The Beginnings: A Pictorial History of the Baptist Bible Fellowship.*
176. *Transcript of Minutes and Records of Formation of Baptist Bible Fellowship,* May 1950, stenographically recorded by Miss Jerry Hayles. Section A, p. 6 (hereafter cited as *Transcript*).
177. Ibid.

ship had generously supported the school, demanded a voice in its governance.

The third divisive issue concerned an overall power struggle within the Norris movement. This could be seen as a struggle between two Norris lieutenants, Louis Entzminger of Fort Worth and G. Beauchamp Vick of Detroit. It could be viewed regionally, as a struggle between Northern and Southern wings of the Norris movement, or even narrowed to the question of dominance between two great churches, First Baptist of Fort Worth and Temple Baptist of Detroit, both pastored by Norris. The conflict also appears in retrospect as a struggle between the more moderate Fundamentalists, mostly in the Midwest, and the more sensational group, centered in Texas and the South.

When Vick became seminary president in 1948, with Entzminger on the faculty, the two veteran Norris lieutenants faced inevitable conflict. Apparently "Entz," as he was called, helped engineer Vick's removal in 1950. At the 1950 meeting of the denominational fellowship, Norris appeared as an embattled monarch trying, unsuccessfully as it turned out, to put down rebellion between rival factions of his own kingdom.

A new fellowship formed. Before most pastors had arrived for the annual meeting of 1950, Norris convened a meeting of mostly students and led them to vote for new bylaws which returned control of the seminary to First Baptist Church. A few students from Detroit who refused to vote were expelled and given twenty-four hours to vacate their rooms. By the next day when more pastors had arrived, after a shouting and shoving match for access to the platform, some demanded a committee investigation of seminary affairs. According to one report, Norris angrily responded: "We are going to follow these by-laws regardless of any investigation. You can appoint all the committees you want to. We are going to follow these by-laws. . . . They cannot be changed. They are on record in Austin. And that is final."[178]

As it turned out, that action indeed proved final. About a hundred pastors met the next day, May 24, at the Texas Hotel in Fort Worth. Their purpose was to form an alternate school, but by 3:30 PM they had formed an entire alternate denomination. James O. Combs, a young pastor and later editor of the *Baptist Bible Tribune,* suggested the name Baptist Bible Fellowship. That night and the next day in meetings at the Central Baptist Church of Denton, the group elected W. E. Dowell as president, named a seven-member board of directors and a slate of college trustees, and made plans to open a school in Springfield by that summer. In an amazingly short time, the new BBF put in place a three-pronged denominational program with a college, newspaper, and mission agency. Beginning with no more

178. "Reasons for Baptist Bible Fellowship," *Baptist Bible Tribune,* June 23, 1950, p. 3.

than fifty affiliated churches, within months they had grown to one hundred or more. Growth since then has been steady and at times startling.

Within two months, the BBF had its Baptist Bible College in Springfield in operation, with G. B. Vick as president. Apparently Norris had good reason to fear his opposition intended either to move his school or form a rival. Even before the Fort Worth meeting, some leaders had raised eleven thousand dollars for a new school, had looked at prospective sites, had negotiated for purchase of movable army barracks for temporary buildings, and had discussed curriculum. The school began with a handful of students but has grown steadily over the years to enroll currently more than twenty-four hundred students. Perhaps its most illustrious graduate is Jerry Falwell, television evangelist and pastor of the Thomas Road Baptist Church of Lynchburg, Virginia.

The second agency established by the BBF was the paper, *Baptist Bible Tribune.* Wendell Zimmerman, who at the Texas Hotel meeting insisted, "We need a clean break," moved that "we organize a separate distinct new independent Fundamental, premillennial, old-fashioned, Baptist, missionary fellowship." Zimmerman's second motion asked that the group "form a committee to prepare a paper."[179] Within days the thing was done, and the *Tribune* put out its first issue on June 23, 1950.

As for missions, the third agency, the new BBF largely took over the foreign mission work of the Norris group, which it described as "defunct." Beginning in 1951, Fred S. Donnelson, veteran missionary to China, headed the mission program and became known in the new denomination as "Mr. Missions."[180]

What began as a fellowship has over the years become in effect a denomination, though some object to that term. A number of state fellowships function much as state conventions do in other Baptist groups. Several other colleges and seminaries have grown up, none more prominent than the Liberty Baptist College and Seminary at Lynchburg, Virginia, founded by Jerry Falwell. The BBF has made ambitious plans for the future, and thoughtful leaders like Elmer Towns have warned them to beware of traditional pitfalls of Fundamentalist Baptists, such as identification with right-wing politics, personality-cult leadership, a "black/white mentality" that gives easy answers to complex questions, concentration on sins of the flesh to the exclusion of sins of the spirit, and the blindness of Fundamentalists to their own weaknesses and their historic "little capacity for self-criticism."[181]

Some observers feel that the Baptist Bible Fellowship represents the moderate wing of Southern Fundamentalism, as the Conservative Baptist

179. *Transcript,* Section D, p. 1.
180. James O. Combs, ed., *The Roots and Origins of Baptist Fundamentalism,* p. 102.
181. Ibid., pp. 126-129.

Association represents the moderate wing of Baptist Fundamentalism in the North. Conversely, the World Baptist Fellowship, the remnants of the old Norris movement, reflects the more militant Southern Fundamentalism, finding its Northern counterpart in the GARBC.

In 1982 a group of Baptist Fundamentalists, including Jerry Falwell, launched an attractive new national periodical, the *Fundamentalist Journal,* with news and reports from several Baptist groups. This group also sponsored a giant rally in Washington, D. C., called "Baptist Fundamentalism '84." While the rally drew smaller crowds than expected, it was one of the largest gatherings of Baptist Fundamentalists in history. If Falwell and his followers hoped to unite Baptist Fundamentalists, they had a way to go. At its 1983 meeting the GARBC voted to "go on record as stating that this Congress does not represent the historic heritage and militant convictions of Baptist Fundamentalism."[182]

The Southwide Baptist Fellowship (SBF)

In 1956 Lee Robertson, pastor of the Highland Park Baptist Church in Chattanooga, Tennessee, formed the Southern Baptist Fellowship, composed mostly of independents and a number of disgruntled Southern Baptists. The group, whose name was later changed to "Southwide," has become known for its intense evangelism, massive church bus ministries, fundamentalist beliefs and behavior, and a spirit perhaps more independent than most fundamentalist groups. The First Baptist Church of Hammond, Indiana, said to include about fifty thousand members, has cooperated at times with the SBF.

Another independent Baptist who helped form the Southwide Baptist Fellowship was John R. Rice. A former Southern Baptist and colleague of J. Frank Norris, Rice founded the *Sword of the Lord* in Dallas in 1934. Before his death, Rice built it into the most widely circulated fundamentalist paper in America. Through the *Sword* and various Bible conferences, Rice exerted vast influence and enlisted the aid of a circle of churches, though no new denominational structure resulted. Rice cooperated with most Fundamentalists but joined none. More than half of Rice's conferences were under the auspices of the Baptist Bible Fellowship; and Jerry Falwell, according to one report, worked closely with Rice in the 1970s.[183]

Baptist Fundamentalism in Perspective

Baptist Fundamentalism needs to be set in some kind of context. First, Fundamentalism involves more than doctrine. Everyone knows that Fundamentalists hold ultraconservative doctrines; they are often identified with

---

182. *Fundamentalist Journal,* September, 1983, p. 58.
183. Personal letter, James O. Combs to Harry Leon McBeth, undated but received May 16, 1984. Used by permission of James O. Combs.

belief in the inerrant teachings of the Bible, the virgin birth of Christ, His bodily second coming, and similar doctrines. However, many non-Fundamentalists believe these same doctrines. Fundamentalism involves a *mindset* as well as a *set of beliefs;* it includes attitudes as much as beliefs; it is perhaps as much a psychology as a theology. The Fundamentalist tends to see issues in terms of black and white, either absolutely right or completely wrong. The Fundamentalist must be *absolutely certain* even in areas where human certainty is suspect. The seeking for extreme certainty may in fact mask a deeper level of doubt. This kind of mind-set can often tolerate error better than ambiguity; at least a known evil can be confronted. Fundamentalists also tend to be 100 percenters, a trait commendable at times but with a potential for excessive actions which at times may border on fanaticism. Perhaps J. Frank Norris in his later embattled years best exemplified these negative features of Fundamentalism.

Second, it appears that for the Baptist version of Fundamentalism the bedrock doctrine is premillennialism. While beliefs about the Bible and Christ are vitally important, history shows that the millennial question time and time again has determined the lines of fellowship among Baptist Fundamentalists. A few early leaders of Northern Baptist Fundamentalism held amillennial views, but they soon left or were driven out. The Bible Union movement of 1923 expressed militant premillennialism, as did the GARBC movement of 1933. Even the Conservative Baptist Association struggled for years and eventually split over whether to require premillennialism. From its origin, the Norris movement of the South was based on that doctrine; before the Norris movement became the World Baptist Fellowship, it was known as the Premillennial Fellowship. The refusal of Southern Baptists to embrace premillennialism, or to write that view into their first major confession of 1925, was one reason for the final split between Norris and the SBC. Premillennialism provides a major issue in fundamentalist agitation within the Southern Baptist Convention in recent years. Premillennialism is *the* fundamentalist doctrine.

Third, another key word for Fundamentalists is *independent.* Many incorporate the word into their church names and the concept into their denominational structures. In fact, many fear the concept of *denominationalism* almost as much as the apostasy they often identify with denominations. Hierarchy, ecclesiasticism, and conventionism are among the evils which many Fundamentalists equate with a cooperative denomination. Of course, the independence of every local Baptist church has stood for centuries as a primary principle of the Baptist way. However, Fundamentalists seem unconvinced that churches can voluntarily cooperate with others without losing their freedom, and many fail to see that their own fellowships often exert more actual control over affiliated churches and pastors than do the conventions against which they rebel.

This fear of denominationalism goes far back in Baptist history. One recalls the reluctance of English Particular Baptists to organize; it took them 174 years to form a general body. In 1767 even Isaac Backus refused at first to line up with the Warren Baptist Association in New England. In the early 1800s Baptists in the North formed a series of independent mission societies, but in 1826 they firmly rejected the growing denominational unification led by Luther Rice, Richard Furman, and W. B. Johnson. It is significant that both major branches of Northern Baptist Fundamentalism, the GARBC (1933) and the CBAA (1947) reproduced essentially the independent society system of Northern Baptists before formation of the Northern Baptist Convention. The conflict between Norris and the SBC included blistering barrages against *conventionism,* a word Norris could make sound like a curse. Fundamentalists prefer to name their groups associations or fellowships, and feel uncomfortable with the term *denomination.*

This does not, of course, change the fact that most such groups are denominations in every sense. Despite their emphasis upon independence, Fundamentalists often enjoy less of it than most cooperative Baptists. Fundamentalist churches are more totally dominated by the pastors, and pastors and churches are subject to both structured and subtle control by the denomination. Of course such pastors and churches have the freedom to withdraw from the movement; but if they remain, they must toe the mark.

A fourth characteristic of Fundamentalism is its militant spirit. Fundamentalists are often called "fighting Fundamentalists." Their vocabulary is sprinkled with combative terms: they do "battle royal," they are ready to "fight to the finish," they see themselves in constant "warfare," and their followers are "troops" or "good soldiers." A recent writer said, "Fundamentalism represents religion under siege, religion on the defensive."[184] Even some Fundamentalists recognize this; a recent article by an insider asked if they are "contentious for the faith, or just contentious?"[185] Though happy exceptions abound, it is impossible to escape the fact that Fundamentalists have often been marked by a narrow, rigid, and angry spirit.

Many of these fundamentalist views are at heart virtues taken to extremes. Not content to believe the Bible, the Fundamentalists often buttress it by various human theories of inspiration which prove harder to explain than the Bible itself. Beyond believing in Christ's return, they make it premillennial or even dispensational; some go beyond that to require pretribulation, midtribulation, or posttribulation views; and at times, fellowship has been ruptured over a doctrine called, ironically enough, the "rapture."

The tendency to extremism is nowhere more evident than in fundamen-

184. Leon McBeth, "Baptist Fundamentalism: A Cultural Interpretation," *Baptist History and Heritage* (July 1978), p. 17.
185. Nelson Keener, "Contending for the Faith or Just Contentious?" *Fundamentalist Journal* (September 1983), p. 66.

talist journalism. One cannot pick up a Fundamentalist paper, past or present, without being struck by the abundance of capital letters, extensive underlining and italics, and the tendency to end sentences with a series of exclamation points. Some Fundamentalists noted this, for founders of the *Bible Baptist Tribune* said in their first issue "We are going easy on the caps."[186] Far more is involved here than a mere question of literary style. The intensity of print reveals the intensity of spirit in Fundamentalism. Every minor achievement must be presented as the greatest victory since Pentecost, and the most trivial disagreement ranks with the betrayal by Judas. In time, as these movements gain more spiritual balance, their type-setting tends to reflect that balance.

Despite characteristics which appear negative to many observers, the Baptist Fundamentalists must be given credit for their virtues. They have held to doctrinal convictions when many not only lost faith but also lost interest in "beliefs." While not all would agree with what Elmer Towns called their "blazing evangelism," they have not lost sight of the Christian commission to win new converts to Christ.[187] No one can accuse the Fundamentalists of hiding their light under a bushel; they have sought aggressively to share their faith and way of life by every means, while their opponents who called for more tasteful ways of witness have too often settled for no witness at all.

The various Baptist fundamentalist groups are said to command the allegiance, more or less, of about ten thousand churches in the United States, gathered into any number of separate general bodies.[188]

The Calvinistic Baptists

The labels assigned various groups in this chapter are not always precise, and often the categories overlap. Some Calvinists are also Fundamentalists, and some are not; conversely, some Fundamentalists are Calvinists, but not all. Most Landmark Baptists are Fundamentalists, but not all Fundamentalists are Landmarkers, and many ethnic Baptists could fit doctrinally into one or more of the other categories. A recent movement has emerged among Baptists to emphasize Calvinistic beliefs and behavior patterns. This section can only summarize the highlights of that movement and point to more detailed sources for further study. The movement is still emerging and one may expect further groupings to take shape in the future.

The Pioneer

The evangelist Rolfe P. Barnard (1904-1969) is often called "the Pioneer" of Calvinist resurgence among Baptists. He claimed that his early interest

---

186. June 23, 1950, p. 4.
187. Cited in Combs, p. 130.
188. Ibid., p. 88.

in that system was kindled in theology classes of Professor W. T. Conner at Southwestern Baptist Theological Seminary in 1927, though Conner's published works show no such emphases as Barnard developed. Barnard worked closely with J. Frank Norris, to his later regret, and by the late 1940s had become a close associate of the independent Fundamentalist, John R. Rice.[189] At a Bible conference in Greenville, Mississippi, Barnard's sermon revealed his Calvinistic convictions. John R. Rice, who was present, reacted adversely. The word went out that Barnard had departed the faith, and he was quickly ostracized from Fundamentalist circles.

In 1950 Barnard preached a revival at a Southern Baptist church in Ashland, Kentucky. By that time he considered Southern Baptist methods of evangelism nothing more than "programmed professionalism," with no lasting results because the converts resulted not from divine grace but human persuasion.[190] He preached, "Jesus is Lord, as well as Savior," emphasizing such Calvinistic doctrines as total depravity, bondage of the will, and particular election. That revival attracted widespread attention, not all favorable, though it called out a number of other Southern Baptist preachers who had either already embraced Calvinism or showed an interest. The next year Barnard was back in Ashland for a tent revival; the church and its pastor, Henry Mahan, embraced the Calvinist system. In 1954 Mahan led the church to sponsor the "Sovereign Grace Bible Conference" which attracted a number of other pastors.

The pioneer ministry of Barnard enlisted a number of churches in Calvinism but led to no formal organization beyond annual Bible conferences. Like the Particular Baptists of old, whom they imitate, the new Calvinists are reluctant to organize. Recently a volume of Barnard's sermons has appeared.[191]

Reformed Baptists

A similar group of Calvinistic Baptists arose in the Northeast in the 1960s, but with little connection with Barnard's movement. They drew inspiration from England, where in the late 1940s an interdenominational group formed the Banner of Truth Foundation to revitalize Fundamentalist Calvinism. The name comes from C. H. Spurgeon's note in the preface of his reprint of the 1689 Baptist confession, "We need a banner because of the truth."[192] The English group founded the *Banner of Truth* magazine,

189. John F. Thornbury, "Evangelist Rolfe Barnard, 1904-1969," *Reformation Today* (September-October 1978).

190. Mark McCulley, *Studies in History and Ethics* (Malin, Ore.: Searching Together, 1983), p. 23.

191. Eulala Bullock, comp., *Sermons of Evangelist Rolfe Barnard* (Greenville, S.C.: Printed for Compiler, 1982).

192. *Things Most Surely Believed Among Us* (Essex Fells, N.J.: Trinity Baptist Church, n.d.), p. 5.

edited by Iain Murray, and republished Calvinistic works of A. W. Pink, C. H. Spurgeon, and others. They also sponsored a series of Calvinism conferences.

This reform movement leaped the Atlantic; in June, 1967, the Grace Baptist Church of Carlisle, Pennsylvania, sponsored a "conference of Baptists of Reformed and Calvinistic persuasion."[193] The Trinity Church was formed at Essex Fells, New Jersey, in 1967, destined to become one of the leading centers of the new Calvinism. At first unaffiliated, the Trinity Church added "Baptist" to its name in 1971. These two strong churches, Grace in Pennsylvania and Trinity in New Jersey, anchor the Calvinist movement in the Northeast. They are led by Walter J. Chantry (Grace) and Albert N. Martin (Trinity). In 1967 they organized the Reformed Baptist Association, actually more a fellowship of ministers than an association in the usual Baptist sense of that term. Some non-Baptist churches participate in this loose fellowship, a fact which illustrates the interdenominational nature of the new Calvinism.

Trinity has established the Trinity Ministerial Academy, the strongest training center of the movement. That church also publishes *Trinity Times* and conducts a nationwide ministry by means of cassette recordings. Classes are held in the church building, and academy students are expected to become active members during their three-year stay. With only one full-time professor in 1983, aided by other ministers who taught part time, the academy prospectus listed a full three-year course in the usual theological disciplines.[194]

The Banner of Truth Baptists hold to the usual Calvinistic emphases on sovereign grace, particular election, and plural eldership in the church. They adhere to the Baptist confession of 1689 and tend toward Sabbatarianism in their views of the Old Testament. Much like the Presbyterians, who also have resurgent Calvinist groups in their midst, the Banner of Truth Baptists hold "Covenant Theology."

Though firm statistics are scarce, the movement appears to be growing. Albert Wardin estimated that Reformed Baptists by 1980 included about 7,000 of the elect in 150 churches.[195]

Continental Baptist Churches (CBC)

"There has been no great unity" among American Calvinists, according to one of their writers, who explained that "most Sovereign Grace pastors are . . . not sure that close fellowships or mutual enterprises with other

193. Personal letter, Paul C. Clarke to Leon McBeth, January 31, 1984. Used by permission of Paul C. Clarke.

194. *Trinity Times* (October 1983), p. 1.

195. Wardin, p. 39.

like-minded churches are either necessary or desirable."[196] While Calvinist groups spring up here and there, as yet no national or unified movement has coalesced.

A slightly different form of Calvinism emerged in the Dallas area in 1981, but its roots go back at least a decade. In 1972 Norbert Ward founded the *Baptist Reformation Review,* a Calvinist paper, in Nashville. According to one historian, "Norbert Ward had been a Primitive Baptist," where he had learned the usual Calvinist teachings.[197] However, feeling that Primitivism could not speak to the modern world, he sought a more relevant faith without forsaking Calvinist moorings. In his paper, Ward explored the question of the "continuity of Covenants,"which Calvinists find controversial.

Meantime, Ron McKinney had assumed editorship of the *Sword and Trowel,* named for Spurgeon's old paper and since the late 1970s published in the Dallas area. The *Sword and Trowel* leaders, beginning in 1979, sponsored an annual Council on Baptist Theology. Gradually it became clear that the Dallas group, while in touch with New Jersey Calvinists, held different understandings. The Dallas group preferred the 1646 confession, put less emphasis upon covenant theology, and in general represented a milder form of Calvinism. They were said to emphasize a more inclusive ecclesiology, the centrality of preaching, and "covenantal discontinuity for ethics," which put them out of step with Reformed Baptists of the Northeast.[198]

The *Sword and Trowel* Calvinists decided to form their own association, and a constitution was adopted in 1983, creating a new body called Continental Baptist Churches (CBC). They provided for regional associations, and the first is called the Continental Association. The new group began with about twenty churches.

Another Calvinistic group may be ready to emerge in the Great Lakes area. A group of churches there announced plans to form the Great Lakes Baptist Association in 1984. Most of these churches have links to the GARBC movement, which has long held Calvinist views.

Calvinists in the Southern Baptist Convention

In addition to separate Calvinist groups, a number of Southern Baptists have embraced the new Calvinism. The group had enough cohesion to form a journal, distribute literature, and sponsor a national conference on Calvinism in 1983. Ernest C. Reisinger, pastor in Florida, is one leader of this group. Others include Tom J. Nettles, professor at the Mid-America Baptist Seminary in Memphis and one founder of *The Wicket Gate,* and Carl

196. McCulley, pp. 23, 26.
197. Ibid., p. 23.
198. Ibid., p. 25.

Benjamin Mitchell, pastor in Louisville. No statistics are available, but estimates suggest there may be about four hundred Southern Baptist pastors who have some degree of allegiance to the new Calvinist movement.

Calvinism in Perspective

There can be no doubt that the theology of John Calvin has played a large role in Baptist history. The earliest Particular Baptist churches embraced Calvin's views by 1638 and in time, unfortunately, took them to damaging extremes. Many Baptists in early America held some form of that system. The Philadelphia Confession of 1742 and the New Hampshire Confession of 1833 also reflected Calvinism. The two Southern Baptist confessions of 1925 and 1963 retained some Calvinistic emphases, though these were muted somewhat and balanced by heavy emphasis upon evangelism, missions, and Christian responsibility in the world.

For reasons too lengthy and complex to fit this limited space, Baptists softened their Calvinism in the nineteenth century. That process of redefinition was not new; Andrew Fuller of England led a modification of Calvinism in the eighteenth century which made the modern mission movement possible. In America the Philadelphia Association by their work if not their confession put Calvinism in a new light. The American frontier with its "can do" spirit, American revivalism, and Calvinistic extremes all contributed to the softening of that system. Nor is the contemporary movement the only effort to recover Calvinism among Baptists. The Strict Baptists of England and the Primitive or "Hardshell" Baptists in America had the same purpose, and the contemporary movement has been influenced, if only indirectly, by both of these.

In 1928 W. T. Whitley wrote of English Baptists, "The great mass of Baptists no longer attend to the question at all. . . . For the majority the truth or falsity of Calvinism is a vanished condition."[199] The same statement, with a bit less emphasis, might be made of Baptists in America. Calvinism among Northern Baptists, already fading, was further diluted by absorption of the Freewill Baptists in 1911. Southern Baptists have retained some Calvinism, but their doctrinal inheritance from General Baptists of England and Separate Baptists of the South, plus their commitment to evangelism and missions, have muted the Calvinistic part of their background. Not traditionally a doctrinaire people, Southern Baptists have found their primary emphasis in ministry and fellowship, not in theological reflection upon Calvinism or any other doctrinal system.

At least four factors have contributed to the recent resurgence of Calvinism among Baptists. First, the Calvinists feel they are going back to original Baptist roots, recovering the authentic Baptist heritage. Actually, Calvinism accounts for only a part of early Baptists; the earliest, and for

199. W. T. Whitley, *The Baptists of London 1612-1928*, p. 27.

years the larger, Baptist group came out of non-Calvinist influences. Second, the Calvinists react against what they consider shallow evangelism, especially as practiced by Southern Baptists. The "Simultaneous Revivals" of the late 1940s provided an early stimulus to the Calvinist awakening. The tactics of evangelists, the baptism of young children, and use of various techniques to promote "decisions for Christ" have disturbed many thoughtful Baptists. Some of these Baptists have found relief in Calvinism, which downplays the role of human decision or human effort.

Third, Calvinism represents to some extent another expression of the contemporary fundamentalist movement. One of their historians said, "Most Particular Baptists used to be Fundamentalists"; the evidence confirms that many come to Calvinism by that route.[200] Modern Calvinists embrace many of the views that bind modern Fundamentalists, such as extreme local church independence, biblical inerrancy, and a sense of alienation from the world. Calvinists do not generally hold premillennialism, as most Fundamentalists do. However, links between Calvinists and Fundamentalists, both past and present, cannot be avoided.

Fourth, Calvinism probably reflects emphases from contemporary society. That religious teachings may be influenced by environment is beyond doubt and can be documented throughout history. Calvinism includes an emphasis upon the *inevitable;* some have understood this in an almost fatalistic sense. The Calvinist who really follows the Geneva Reformer must believe that each person's eternal fate is determined before birth and that no human decision can change that predetermined destiny.

Calvinism faded in the optimism of the nineteenth century, when American society seemed so hopeful. Americans were busy carving an empire out of the wilderness, developing an economy and standard of living to amaze the world, winning all their wars, and early in the twentieth century, fighting a "war to end all wars" in order to "make the world safe for democracy." In that heady optimism, liberal theology and the Social Gospel flourished. Since then, however, storm clouds have darkened the American dream. America has lost recent wars, suffered economic reversals, faced massive and seemingly insoluble problems of crime, pollution of the environment, racial tension, and erosion of traditional values. The bright optimism of the past has been chastened by present reality. It seems that we have little control over our world.

Religion has responded to these changes in different ways. The old liberalism and Social Gospel faded quickly, to be replaced by more sober, if still liberal, views. Fundamentalism arose to reassert what it regarded as unchanging truths for changing times. The resurgent Calvinism fits the new environment. The secular society seems beyond human control; Calvinism provides a religious doctrine that says the same of eternal destiny. This is

200. McCulley, p. 27.

not to reduce religion to sociology, nor to overlook the theological content of the Calvinist system. It does acknowledge, however, that religion is influenced by its environment and that the recent American environment has created conditions in which doctrines of human helplessness can flourish.

The National Baptists

Black believers make up a major part of the Baptist family in the United States, reporting about ten million members by 1982.[201] Most black churches affiliate with one of the three National Baptist Conventions, though a few form their own Primitive, Freewill, or other smaller Baptist groups.

Most blacks who came to America in slavery had no interest in embracing Christianity, a religion which they identified with their oppressors. The American churches were slow to evangelize among the blacks, partly from language barriers and partly from a prejudice among some who doubted whether blacks had souls to be saved. Some slave owners also hesitated because of economic concern; an ancient tradition asserted that a slave converted could no longer be held in servitude, having become a brother beloved in Christ. However, by 1660 Colonial legislatures had passed laws that Christian conversion did not affect the outward state or condition of slaves.

Only in the revival "awakenings" after the American Revolution did blacks in great numbers turn to Christianity. Several factors help account for that upsurge of conversions. By the 1780s many of the slaves were American-born. Language no longer posed a barrier to prevent them from hearing the gospel. The native African religions were only memories to many, stories heard but never experienced to most. As a result, blacks were open to a new meaning structure; the fading of their ancestral religions opened them to conversion to a new religion. The revival fervor of the various awakenings reached to the blacks as well as to the whites. A few blacks responded during the First Great Awakening of the 1740s, but the floodtide of black conversions came after the Revolution.

The earliest known black Baptist was "Jack, a colored man," a slave baptized into the First Baptist Church of Newport, Rhode Island, in 1652.[202] The first free black Baptist of record was Peggy Arnold, who joined the Newport Seventh Day church in 1719. Only six black Baptists show up in church records before 1750, but there may have been others not recorded. Such records as remain reveal that blacks joined Baptist churches in both the North and South after the Great Awakening, with such members showing up in New Jersey by 1747 and New York by the 1750s.

201. Maynard P. Turner, "National Baptist Convention, USA, Inc.," *ESB*, 4:2363.
202. Robert G. Gardner, *Baptists of Early America: A Statistical History, 1639-1790*, p. 39.

Predominantly white churches in Virginia were known to have black members by the 1750s, and by 1790 almost one third of all Virginia Baptists were black.[203] Black converts received immersion in South Carolina at least as early as 1737; in the years following blacks were members of churches in most of the Southern states. John Asplund, who attempted to compile a "Universal Register" of Baptist statistics, said in 1790, "In the Southern States, viz. south and west of Maryland, [a] great many Negroes belong to the churches, about 2 blacks to 5 whites."[204]

Most of the growth came late in the century. In 1780 blacks made up only about 10 percent of Baptists in America, but by 1790 they had doubled that ratio to about 20 percent. This growth is even more remarkable in that it came during a time of rapid growth among the white Baptists, indicating that the increase among black Baptists was even more rapid. Black Baptist growth was most rapid in the South; in 1770 about 76 percent of all black Baptists lived in the South, but by 1790 that had risen to 97 percent.[205] Most of these joined predominantly white churches.

Early Black Churches

Extant records do not settle conclusively the identity of the earliest organized black Baptist church in America. Several all-black worship groups were known to have met from the late 1750s, but most never became organized churches. Most historians have recognized the Silver Bluff church, formed in 1773 (some sources say 1775) in Aiken County, South Carolina, as the earliest organized black Baptist church.[206] Recent research, however, has challenged that view.

In an important work entitled *Trabelin' On,* Mechel Sobel contended that Silver Bluff was not the first but that a black congregation existed by 1758.[207] She based this partly on a statement in Robert B. Semple's early history of Virginia Baptists that William Murphy and Philip Mulkey preached in the Bluestone community of Mecklenburg County, Virginia. Semple said, "Their labors were very successful, and in 1758 or 1759 they were sufficiently numerous to exercise the rights of a church. There were several white members besides a large number of blacks."[208] Most of the blacks came from the William Byrd plantation. When that plantation broke

203. Ibid., p. 102.

204. Ibid., p. 42.

205. Ibid., p. 43.

206. Owen D. Pelt and Ralph L. Smith, *The Story of the National Baptists,* p. 29. See also Lewis G. Jordan, *Negro Baptist History, U.S.A.* pp. 58, 361 f. For other helpful studies of black Baptists, see Leroy Fitts, *Lott Carey: First Black Missionary to Africa* and James M. Washington, *The Origins and Emergence of Black Baptist Separatism, 1863-1897.*

207. Mechal Sobel, *Trabelin' On: The Slave Journey to an Afro-Baptist Faith,* p. 102.

208. Robert B. Semple, *History of Baptists in Virginia* (Reprint, Lafayette, Tenn.: Church History Research Archives, 1976), pp. 291-292.

up a few years later, most of the blacks were scattered but, according to Semple, this "did not rob them of their religion." Remnants of this congregation formed a new church in 1772, apparently first led by whites but later relinquished to blacks.

In a comment upon Sobel's findings, Sid Smith said,

> I am convinced that, based on evidence, there was a predominantly Black congregation as early as 1758 on the plantation of William Byrd III on the Bluestone River in Mecklenburg County, Virginia. This church struggled, many members scattered, but the congregation revived in 1772. . . . That church can trace its unbroken history to the First Baptist Church, Petersburg, Virginia, a Black congregation today that claims the title: "The Oldest Black Church in America."[209]

The conclusion as to which church is earlier rests to some extent upon one's definition of a black church. Must the church be all black, or must it have a black pastor? Clearly the Bluestone church began as a racially mixed congregation, though blacks formed the large majority of members. Apparently its founders and early pastors were white, and even the reconstituted church of 1772 was for a time under white leadership. There is no doubt that a church was formed in Virginia in 1758 or 1759 with predominantly black membership, but it was under white leadership. Most historians, black as well as white, have applied the description "black church" only to those congregations under black control. It is quite likely that other churches had a majority of black members, even earlier. Evidence also suggests that there may have been informal worship meetings of black Baptists that functioned essentially as churches but never achieved formal organization.

As research continues, new evidence may come to light and new conclusions result. The most one can say at present is that a church made up mostly of black converts to the Baptist way emerged in Virginia by 1758 or 1759. However, the earliest-known organized Baptist church composed of all black members, founded by and led by blacks, was that formed at Silver Bluff in 1773. Lewis G. Jordan, a pioneer black historian, listed several other black churches before the turn of the century, including three in Virginia—Petersburg, 1776; Richmond, 1780, and Williamsburg, 1785; one at Lexington, Kentucky in 1790; and one in Augusta, Georgia in 1793.[210] While some of those remained unassociated, two or three joined the white associations.

Jordan distinguished several types of black churches. In addition to those with black pastors and membership, he mentioned that some had white

209. Sid Smith, "In Search of the First Black Baptist Church in America," *Ethnicity* (Spring 1984), p. 8.
210. Jordan, p. 61.

pastors. For over twenty-five years, for example, a white pastor led the First Colored Baptist Church of Richmond. Jordan also described the "Colored Branch" pattern, in which black and white sections of the same church coexisted. Such churches sometimes met together, usually with the blacks segregated in balconies, but at other times the white congregation met on Sunday morning while the blacks met in the afternoon. Often the black branch would have their own deacons, their own discipline, and occasionally their own pastors. A few predominantly white churches chose black pastors, defending that choice on the grounds that they wanted the best available preacher and the black fit that description.

The Silver Bluff church was formed by an itinerant black preacher known only as "Brother Palmer." Palmer began preaching to the slaves on John Galphin's plantation in Jasper County, South Carolina, just across the river from Augusta, Georgia. Soon Palmer had gathered eight converts, one of whom, David George, said, "Brother Palmer appointed Saturday evening to hear what the Lord had done for us, and the next day he baptized us in the mill stream. Brother Palmer formed us into a church, and gave us the Lord's Supper at Silver Bluff."[211] After Palmer's itineration took him elsewhere, George continued as pastor of the Silver Bluff church until the Revolution disrupted the group. He later fled to Savannah, taking many of the Silver Bluff members with him. They later merged into the African Baptist Church of Savannah.

Another who preached occasionally at Silver Bluff was George Lisle (sometimes spelled Leile). Born in Virginia about 1750, Lisle was a slave of a Baptist deacon named Henry Sharpe. Lisle was converted as a youth and early showed both interest and aptitude for preaching. Seeing his gifts and commitment, Sharpe gave Lisle his freedom and encouraged him to preach. Lisle preached off and on at Silver Bluff and later in Savannah. By 1777 he had formed the African Baptist Church in Savannah and served as its pastor. After Sharpe's death, his heirs sought to reenslave Lisle who fled to the British for protection. After the British left Savannah, Lisle and his family moved to Jamaica where he established a strong Baptist church. Though not appointed by any board or society, Lisle was one of the earliest Baptist missionaries to go to a foreign field to preach the gospel, antedating William Carey by a decade.

In addition to David George and George Lisle, another black leader active in the Savannah church was Andrew Bryan. Later Bryan became pastor of the Savannah church and led in erecting its first building in Yamacraw, on the outskirts of Savannah. That was probably the first building of any black church in America. The church grew rapidly, reaching about seven hundred members by 1800. Such expansion frightened many whites who suspected that the black churches would foment rebellion.

211. Pelt and Smith, p. 30.

This brought on a period of severe persecution in which Andrew Bryan and his brother Samson, both gentle and compassionate Christians, were brutally beaten and the church forbidden to meet. Jonathan Bryan, their owner, at last came to their legal aid and secured their release from jail and made it possible for the church to meet again. The brothers came to enjoy the respect and esteem of both white and black communities. Perhaps the turning point came when white patrols, eavesdropping on a black church meeting in a barn, were deeply moved by hearing Andrew and Samson Bryan praying earnestly for their white oppressors.

By 1800 black Baptists had become numerous, but their churches were still few. Most of them held membership in white-controlled churches. Of the separate black churches that emerged before 1800, all were in the South. Shortly after the turn of the century, however, black churches also emerged in the North. Thomas Paul, a free black from New Hampshire, formed the Joy Street Baptist Church in Boston in 1804 and served as its pastor for about twenty-five years. Some of the black members in the predominantly white Gold Street Baptist Church in New York City heard of Paul's ministry and invited him to New York to help them. He led the black members to separate and form their own church. They later purchased a vacant church building in the Harlem section of New York and in 1809 took the name of Abyssinian Baptist Church. The first members consisted of four men and twelve women from the Gold Street church, plus three new converts. After a period as their pastor, Paul was appointed and served briefly as a missionary in Haiti. The Abyssinian church later became one of the largest and most influential black churches in America. Perhaps its most prominent pastor in the twentieth century has been Adam Clayton Powell, Jr., who served also several terms in the United States Congress.

In 1809 thirteen black members of First Baptist Church of Philadelphia formed the First African Baptist Church, with Henry Cunningham as pastor. Within a few years, other black churches appeared in several Northern states. The first black Baptist associations and conventions also appeared in the North, due no doubt to the greater freedom existing there.

Early Black Organizations

Most of the early black churches stood alone or joined the white associations. Conditions of the time did not encourage or facilitate the emergence of black organizations beyond the local church level. The First African Baptist Church of Savannah joined the Georgia association in 1790 and became a founding member of the Savannah River Association in 1802, both of which were predominantly white. When the Savannah River association divided a few years later, the resulting Sunbury association was made up mostly of black churches. Of the eleven churches in the early Sunbury association, five were black and six had racially mixed memberships, but overall the associational membership was predominantly black.

At first the churches and messengers operated with equality, but in time the smaller white churches came to control the association. By the 1830s the blacks noted, "We had a vote, and at most times timidly used it, but never had a voice in the body unless answering some question asked."[212]

The earliest Baptist association of black churches originated in Ohio in 1836 when six churches formed the Providence association. The six churches totaled fewer than two hundred members, most of them ex-slaves from the South who took the occasion to express their new freedom. Despite their small numbers, black Baptists in Ohio formed a second association, the Union, in 1840. The Union association by 1845 included fifteen churches in Ohio, Indiana, and Illinois. The Colored Baptist Association, Friends to Humanity, was formed in Illinois in 1839 on a strong antislavery basis. At first that association had only three churches, all pastored by John Livingston, with perhaps no more than forty total members. At least six black Baptist associations had been formed before the Civil War, two in Ohio, two in Illinois, and one each in Indiana and Canada.

Like their white counterparts, the black Baptists sought to link their churches into larger associations and conventions. No doubt, similar motives moved both groups as they sought fellowship, a sense of belonging, and opportunity for mutual encouragement. The black churches also sought to combine their resources for ministry beyond the local level and find a forum to express their united voice on social and moral issues.

A different type of organization emerged in Richmond in 1815 where blacks formed the African Baptist Missionary Society. The first president was William Crane, a white, but most of the members and primary leaders were black, including Collin Teague and Lott Cary. Both were slaves who became skilled craftsmen and earned enough to purchase their own freedom and that of their families. Both became devout Baptists and served for a time as assistant pastors of the African church in Richmond. Cary absorbed much of the missionary zeal which had aroused white Baptists at the time and formed a dream of taking the gospel to Africa. He also became interested in the colonization movement of the times, an ill-conceived effort to repatriate American blacks to their native Africa. The movement was impractical, racially motivated, and overlooked the basic fact that blacks were as much Americans as anybody. If not all blacks would have agreed with the black poetess, Phillis Wheatley, who wrote, "Africa? What Is Africa to me?" the fact remained that most blacks had no desire to move to Africa. Yet the movement appealed to many whites, and colonization and foreign missions were combined in several societies, including the one in Richmond.

That society, with some white assistance, sent Cary and Teague with their families to Africa in 1821. Cary became an outstanding missionary and statesman, establishing the African nation of Liberia, named from the

212. Sobel, p. 358.

concept of liberty. To this day that land has had a strong Baptist witness. That was the first venture of black Baptists into organized foreign missions, though George Lisle had gone to Jamaica as an individual a generation earlier. The Liberian venture also established Africa as the primary object of black Baptist foreign mission interest, a concentration which has continued. Other societies similar to the one in Richmond also emerged at other places.

Regional Conventions

In addition to associations and mission societies, black churches quite early formed regional conventions. Perhaps these were premature, for the earliest ones failed to enlist the consistent support of the churches and did not long endure. In 1840 messengers from three churches met in the Abyssinian church in New York and formed the American Baptist Missionary Convention. This was the first recorded effort of black Baptists to form a general body. The convention could not by law work in the South, though a few Southern churches did affiliate. By its meetings, sharing of information, and promoting of missions, this early convention did much to create awareness among the black churches and solidify their identity as a distinct religious community. It was limited in geography primarily to the North and in function to foreign missions. They opened a mission in Haiti and planted the dream of a major mission in Africa.

In 1864 the Western and Southern Missionary Baptist Convention was formed in Richmond to work in areas not covered by the 1840 body. In 1866 the two regional conventions merged into the Consolidated American Baptist Convention. This was the first effort at a truly national convention, but it came on evil times just after the Civil War. The consolidated convention lapsed in 1877, but perhaps remnants were gathered up in the African Mission Convention, a group of which little is known except that they did not long survive.

Forerunners of National Organization

Clearly black Baptists had a dream of national organization, but they had not yet found a vehicle for that goal. The next steps toward national structure came with the formation of three conventions between 1880 and 1893. In 1895 these three were combined, along with remnants from the earlier regional conventions, to form the National Baptist Convention. Though it has suffered some schisms, the National Baptist Convention remains to this day as the major structure for the affiliation of black churches in America. The three "forerunner" groups that made up that convention must be sketched.

In 1880 W. W. Colley led in forming the Baptist Missionary Convention in Montgomery. Colley had served five years as a missionary to Africa under the Southern Baptist Convention and shared the vision of a major mission to that continent. Concerned at the collapse of the consolidated convention, leaving black Baptists with no viable missionary organization, Colley returned to America to stir up his own people to greater missionary effort. Foreign missions became the primary focus of the Montgomery group, and a few years later Colley returned to Africa as their missionary.

The second forerunner group was formed in Saint Louis in 1886, led by W. J. Simmons. Called the American National Baptist Convention, it attempted to gather the churches into a full denominational program but could not compete with the Colley group in foreign missions. Therefore, in time the Simmons group concentrated more upon home missions.

A third forerunner group emerged in 1893 in Washington, D. C., taking the name of National Baptist Educational Convention. It addressed the need for better trained black pastors and missionaries and sought to give guidance to the numerous black schools and colleges, primarily in the South.

These three groups proved both complementary and competitive. In a sense they were rivals in that all tried to become a general body, but in time they became more cooperative as each concentrated on its own specialty. Despite their "convention" name, they followed basically the single-barreled society approach long popular among Baptists in the North. The need for correlation in time pulled the three groups together.

Working separately the three bodies showed no great success. Amid much discouragement, the three groups met jointly in Montgomery in 1894. At that meeting A. W. Pegues, a graduate of Bucknell University and a well-known scholar, offered the following resolution:

> Whereas, The interests and purposes of the three National bodies, namely, the Foreign Mission, the National, and Educational conventions, can be conserved and fostered under the auspices of one body; and whereas, the consolidation of the above-named bodies will economize both time and money; Therefore, be it resolved, that the Foreign Mission Convention appoint a committee of nine, who shall enter immediately into consultation with executive boards of the National and Educational conventions for the purpose of effecting a consolidation of the three bodies upon the following plan:
>
> 1. That there shall be one national organization of American Baptists.
>
> 2. Under this, there shall be a Foreign Mission Board, with authority to plan and execute the foreign mission work according to the spirit and purpose set forth by the Foreign Mission Convention of the United States of America.
>
> 3. That there shall be a Board of Education and a Board of Missions to carry into effect the spirit and purpose of the National and Educational conventions, respectively.[213]

The response was overwhelmingly favorable, and the three groups merged in 1895 as the National Baptist Convention. Unification was in the

213. E. A. Freeman, "National Baptist Convention, U.S.A., Inc.," *Baptist Advance,* p. 206.

air, for the foreign mission group had already absorbed some remnants of the earlier regional conventions in what was called a "Tripartite Union." In the 1895 merger, the three separate groups became, in effect, program boards of the united convention. Though merged in 1895, the national convention claims a founding date of 1880 since that is the date of the oldest group in the merger. E. C. Morris of Arkansas was elected the first president. The newly adopted constitution said in part:

> Whereas, It is the sense of the Colored Baptists of the United States of America, convened in the city of Atlanta, Ga., Sept. 28, 1895, in the several organizations as "The Baptist Foreign Mission Convention of the United States of America," hitherto engaged in mission work on the West Coast of Africa; and the "National Baptist Convention," which has been engaged in mission work in the United States of America; and the "National Baptist Educational Convention," which has sought to look after the educational interest that the interest of the way of the Kingdom of God required that the several bodies above named should, and do now, unite in one body, Therefore, we do now agree to and adopt the following constitution:
>
> Article I
> Name
>
> This body shall become known and styled The National Baptist Convention of the United States of America.
>
> ....
>
> Article II
> The Object
>
> The Object of this Convention shall be to do mission work in the United States of America, in Africa, and elsewhere, and to foster the cause of education.[214]

The National Baptist Convention, 1895-1915

After the 1895 merger, Lewis G. Jordan was elected to head the Foreign Mission Board. He found an empty treasury, an office equipped with only three chairs and a record book, limited cooperation from the churches, and a persistent image of prior mismanagement. To the dismay of some Eastern leaders, Jordan led in relocating the board from Richmond to Louisville. He went to work with vigor and within a few years had built up the agency to one of the major foreign mission boards of any denomination in America. Jordan constantly emphasized the priority of world missions, the need for denominational cooperation, and pledged careful management of mission resources.

The Home Mission Board, headed by R. H. Boyd, was first located in Little Rock. Its early home mission efforts proved minimal, but the board soon found an exciting new interest. At the 1895 merger, the black Baptists considered whether to launch a publication board to produce their own

214. Ibid., p. 207.

literature but decided against it. Some wanted to continue to buy materials from Northern Baptists, and by then a few churches patronized the new Sunday School Board of the SBC. The expense of launching their own publication ministry also moved the leaders to caution.

However, the issue would not die. Eloquent black speakers, like President E. C. Morris, pointed out that a people must make their own literature in order to interpret and perpetuate their own traditions. Morris said, "The sun has forever gone down on any race of people who will not encourage and employ their literary talent."[215] The move to publish their own materials was further hastened by the unseemly withdrawal of an invitation earlier extended to some black scholars to prepare lesson materials for quarterlies of the American Baptist Publication Society.

In response to these trends, and a persistent feeling that the materials from the white presses North or South did not meet the needs of black churches, the national convention formed its own Publication Board. The name might imply a separate board, but in fact the convention placed this work under the wing of the Home Mission Board, headed by R. H. Boyd. The new publication work got off to an excellent start. Within three years, it issued nine titles, distributed over six million copies of quarterly materials, and took over publication of *The National Baptist Magazine*. This work absorbed most of Boyd's energy and soon overshadowed the home mission work, which tended to languish. A part of this imbalance resulted because the home mission work *cost* money and the publication work *made* money.

The publication work also provoked a minor schism in 1897. Some Eastern leaders never favored the 1895 merger, fearing that a general denominational program might detract from foreign missions. They also opposed separatism, hoping that black and white Baptists might work more closely together. They saw the Publication Board as a further separation from white Baptists. Some of their leaders were employed by the ABPS and thus had vested interests in continuing to use the Northern Baptist literature. They also had regional concerns, deploring the shift of the Foreign Mission Board to Louisville with its reduction of their voices in denominational life. For all these reasons, a group withdrew in 1897 and formed the Lott Cary Baptist Foreign Mission Convention. It has operated on a society basis, sponsoring foreign missions only, but in recent years has cooperated with the national convention.

The Schism of 1915

In establishing the Publication Board, the convention neglected to add the customary phrase "of the National Baptist Convention," a phrase which did appear in the charters of the other boards and anchored them firmly

---

215. E. C. Morris, "Presidential Address," *National Baptist Magazine* (September 1899), pp. 71-72.

to convention ownership and control. The Publication Board had enjoyed startling success, constantly enlarging its property and presses which had been moved to Nashville, Tennessee. Problems arose when E. C. Morris, convention president, attempted to separate the Publication Board from the Home Mission Board. That was, no doubt, an effort to remove the publications from the control of R. H. Boyd who headed both boards.

Boyd resisted the separation, and the convention filed a lawsuit to gain control of the Publication Board. Convention leaders regarded the board as established by the convention for convention purposes and assumed that its property and copyrights belonged to the convention. However, the court case revealed that Boyd had bought property and enlarged buildings and printing facilities with his own money and had kept title deeds and copyrights in his own name. That allowed Boyd to retain ownership and control of the Publication Board. He achieved among National Baptists what J. R. Graves had tried so hard to achieve among Southern Baptists, namely cornering the market for Sunday School literature in his denomination for personal profit.

The Boyd faction pulled out and formed their own convention, taking the name of National Baptist Convention, USA. Sometimes called the "Boyd Convention," they were also called in verbal shorthand the "Unincorporated Convention" for their refusal to incorporate. From the first, their work centered around publications, though in time they formed boards for other forms of ministry.

The National Baptist Convention, Incorporated

After it lost its Publication Board in the schism of 1915, the NBC not only formed a new publication work but also took the occasion to tighten its entire operation. A part of that reorganization was legal incorporation of the convention, fixing legal guarantees that ownership and control of all the boards and their properties are vested in the convention. As a result this group, by far the largest of the black conventions, has been called the "Incorporated Convention." It has also been called the "Townsend Convention," from Arthur M. Townsend, who headed the new Publication Board in Nashville for many years. In more recent years, this has sometimes been called the "Jackson Convention," from Joseph H. Jackson who served as president from 1953 to 1982.

Now headquartered in Chicago, the NBC, Incorporated works through seven general boards, including Foreign Mission Board, Home Mission Board, Evangelistic Board, Benefit Board, Educational Board, Sunday School Publishing Board, and the Training Union Board. There are also organizations for women and youth.

Despite incorporation, the relationship of the boards to the convention has remained problematical. At times the boards have sought to act independently of the convention or assert control over their own property.

Part of the problem lies in the fact that some of the boards antedate the convention; the convention did not give birth to the boards, but instead the boards formed the convention. As recently as 1981, strong President J. H. Jackson firmly reminded the boards that they owned and controlled no property.[216]

The incorporated convention has a history of strong presidents. Usually the presidents serve for life or until poor health sidelines them. The convention has no executive secretary; the president serves as the chief executive officer, and over the years that office has acquired enormous power. Virtually singlehandedly the president controls the convention. Presidents in this century have included E. C. Morris, 1894-1922; L. K. Williams, 1924-1940; D. V. Jemison, 1941-1952; Joseph H. Jackson, 1953-1982; and Theodore J. Jemison, since 1982.

Without doubt the most influential president of this century was J. H. Jackson. Jackson first rose to prominence in 1940 as head of the Foreign Mission Board, the strong agency of the convention. In 1942 he became pastor of the Olivet Baptist Church of Chicago, a church he has transformed into one of the most influential in the denomination. In 1958 the church voted him life tenure. When Jackson was elected president in 1953, many voices were clamoring for reform. However, he rode out flurries of opposition in the early years and consolidated his power beyond any convention president before or since.

Many of the reform faction objected to lifetime tenure for the president. In fact, in 1955 the NBC voted to limit the president to a four-year term. Many expected that Jackson would step aside when he had completed the allotted years, but he refused. Convention by-laws provided that no constitutional changes could be voted after the second day of the convention, and the tenure limitation was voted on the third day. Jackson challenged the rule and won; and by that time, he had so consolidated his power that such a change could no longer be voted.

The Progressive National Baptist Convention

Like others who bear the Baptist name, the black Baptists have been prone to controversy and division. The union of 1895 has been marked by recurring tensions and occasional schisms. A number of tensions intensified in the 1950s and led to a new schism in 1961 which produced the National Progressive Baptist Convention. Perhaps the three major sources of tension were dissatisfaction with J. H. Jackson's autocratic leadership, disagreement over the structure of the convention, and different approaches to the civil rights movement of the time.

Jackson's tenacious leadership alienated many. At the close of D. V.

---

216. *Minutes,* Annual Session of the National Baptist Convention, U.S.A., Inc. (Detroit, 1981), p. 65.

Jemison's presidency in 1953 a strong faction tried, with apparent success, to move the convention to limit the tenure and power of the president. As noted earlier that provision was invalidated on a technicality, and Jackson survived all efforts to oust him. After 1961 most of his opponents either left the convention or gave up the struggle.

The effort to limit the presidency was only one part of a larger effort to restructure the NBC. From the first, the president had functioned as chief executive officer, but some preferred to elect a full-time executive secretary. Had that change been effected, it would have reduced the presidency to a more ceremonial role, while placing real power elsewhere. The presidents, not surprisingly, have resisted such a change.

Perhaps the sharpest tensions within the NBC in the 1950s centered around the civil rights movement and the methods of Martin Luther King, Jr. That young National Baptist pastor in Montgomery led a bus boycott in 1955 that attracted nationwide attention. Out of that movement, King formed the Southern Christian Leadership Conference (SCLC) to guide the emerging civil rights struggle. Drawing inspiration from the Bible and much of his method from Mahatma Gandhi of India, King developed a movement that emphasized nonviolence but challenged the racial mores and practices of the South. From this evolved such tactics as sit-ins, freedom rides and marches, and economic boycotts. The civil rights movement was to some extent an outgrowth of the black church. Ministers were its leaders, churches its launching pads, and the Bible the source of its major emphases and symbols; the Old Testament saying of "Let my people go" took on a renewed meaning in the South.

President Jackson, as it turned out, had little sympathy with King or his methods, though he professed to be committed to the same goal of ultimate racial equality in America. Perhaps King and his new organization seemed a threat or challenge to the convention and its president. Jackson preferred to work through the older National Association for the Advancement of Colored People (NAACP) and to use less confrontive methods. "It was not our purpose," Jackson wrote, "to join with any group, or groups, to become hostile to and work in opposition to the National Association for the Advancement of Colored People."[217] He rejected King's philosophy of civil disobedience, calling it "a form of lawlessness." He urged the government to "no longer pamper those who break the law be they Negro or white."

In addition to these areas of disagreement, some sought more freedom for women, a move the Jackson faction abhorred. The new group said that women had been too long hampered by "the begrudging prejudices of the

217. Joseph H. Jackson, *Unholy Shadows and Freedom's Holy Light,* pp. 77-78.

Negro preachers" and asked "why should our women be hog-tied to the men's control?"[218]

Those who wanted reforms gathered around Gardiner C. Taylor, whom they sought to elect president in place of Jackson. In 1960 the Taylor faction held a rival convention, elected their own slate of officers with Taylor as president, and proclaimed themselves the true National Baptist Convention. At the 1961 meeting of the NBC, the Taylor people sought to occupy the platform by force, and a violent confrontation resulted in which one man was accidentally killed. Take-over efforts ultimately failed, and Jackson maintained control. At that point, most of the dissidents gave up the struggle.

In late 1961 a call was issued for a meeting to consider forming a new convention. A total of thirty-three delegates from fourteen states met in Cincinnati and voted to separate. They formed the Progressive National Baptist Convention (PNBC) and adopted a constitution which effected the major reforms they had sought within the NBC. They chose Washington, D. C., for their headquarters. The group reported only 290 churches affiliated in 1963 but had increased to 1,420 in 1977. This convention has entered into formal cooperation with the American Baptist Churches, and many of the progressive churches are dually aligned with both PNBC and ABC.

Relation of Black and White Baptists

How to relate to white Baptists has been a persistent question for black Baptists in America. Many early black churches affiliated with predominantly white associations, while others pioneered in founding black associations. After 1865 most black Baptists withdrew from white churches to form their own, and formation of the National Baptist Convention in 1895 provided their own general body. However, from the first they have welcomed mutual cooperation with the major white conventions.

From early times both Northern and Southern Baptists have entered into various cooperative ministries with black Baptists. The Home Mission Society of the North was most active in educational work, while Southern Baptists shared more in evangelistic efforts. A recent trend shows numerous black churches seeking dual alignment, retaining their ties to the National Baptist Convention but affiliating also with one of the major white groups. The American Baptist Churches include many black congregations; recent reports affirm that perhaps one third of ABC membership is black.

The first black congregation affiliated with the SBC in 1951. By 1984 the SBC included over 800 black churches, with a membership of about 250,000 members. At least 95 percent of these churches were also aligned with the

218. *Minutes,* First Annual Session of the Progressive National Baptist Convention, Inc. (Philadelphia, 1962), p. 5.

National Baptist Convention. Perhaps another 50,000 or more blacks hold membership in some 3,000 predominantly white SBC churches. Not all black Baptist leaders favor this trend to dual affiliation. While welcoming every opportunity to demonstrate brotherhood, they feel this has potential to weaken their own National Baptist Convention.

17

Baptists in Europe

Baptists in Europe comprise "a vital Christian leaven in a secularized society," according to a recent study which further described them as "a magnificent minority."[1] They have shown magnificent courage against great obstacles in the twentieth century, including some of the most severe persecution any Baptists have ever faced, especially in Eastern Europe. They have remained a numerical minority, with about one million Baptists reported on the Continent in 1981.[2] Baptist communities vary in size from Greece, which reported only one Baptist church with a total of twenty-eight members, to the Soviet Union, which reported about five thousand churches and over a half million members.[3] About two thirds of these Baptists live in Eastern Europe, and reports indicate that they show more spiritual vitality and numerical growth than their less-harassed fellow Baptists in Western Europe.

In 1950 Baptists on the Continent formed the European Baptist Federation (EBF), which affiliates about twenty-five Baptist unions in the various countries throughout Europe. Ties are still fragile, but the EBF affords a forum for communication, fellowship, and mutual encouragement. Like Baptists elsewhere, those in Europe reflect considerable diversity in doctrine and practice. Except in Germany, they have largely outgrown the Anabaptist image that attached to them in the nineteenth century, though they remain more quietist and less activistic than Baptists in America. While participating in the Baptist World Alliance and the World Council of Churches, many European Baptists have also formed cooperative work with local evangelical groups, thus giving a kind of grass-roots ecumenism to their witness. In some European countries, one must distinguish between those who are specifically "Baptist" and those who immerse believers but represent a more nondenominational stance. Both may share membership

1. Dean R. Kirkwood, *European Baptists: A Magnificent Minority*, p. 9.
2. *Yearbook*, American Baptist Churches in the USA, 1982, p. 133. Other sources give slightly different statistics, depending upon whether Baptists in Great Britain are included, and whether the sources report all known Baptists or only those affiliated with the Baptist World Alliance.
3. G. Keith Parker, *Baptists in Europe*, pp. 278-279.

in the same local churches, and churches of both kinds may be affiliated in the same Baptist union.

The Twentieth-Century Setting

The spiritual climate of Europe has changed dramatically since the nineteenth century. The surge of Pietism which swept over Europe in the nineteenth century and fueled Baptist growth throughout the Continent ran its course and waned. The twentieth century has seen no such evangelical movement on so wide a scale. Instead, Europe has been engulfed by some of the most rampant secularism the world has ever seen. Keith Parker called secularism a "major obstacle" to the advance of Baptists and other evangelical Christians in Europe in recent years.[4]

The Rise of Communism

The confrontation of Christianity and Communism is one of the most important historical realities of the twentieth century. Government persecution of Christians in Communist lands has attracted world notice and has become a part of the human rights discussion between the political superpowers of East and West. Not since the Roman Empire, perhaps, has the world seen a more determined government attempt to stamp out or at least severely limit Christianity. The Communist countries, led by the Union of Soviet Socialist Republics, have alternately permitted or proscribed evangelical churches as suited their purpose. They also forced upon Baptists first a complete decentralization then some years later an episcopal kind of centralization, thus using different methods for one purpose, control of the churches.

The Russian Revolution toppled the tsarist regime and brought to power a government which embodied the teachings of Karl Marx. Nikolai Lenin headed the radical Bolshevik party which had fomented rebellion since the turn of the century and eventually came to power in 1917. Under the label of "dictatorship of the proletariat," Lenin and his followers forged a radical Socialist government which forced social and political reforms throughout the Soviet Union. Discontent had been building for years against both the tsars and the Orthodox Church, who were perceived as partners in exploiting the Russian people.

The fall of the tsars also meant the fall of the Orthodox Church. At first the new Communist regime dealt more harshly with the Orthodox Church than with the evangelical churches. Marxist historians tended to identify Orthodoxy with exploitation, while they portrayed the emergence of evangelical groups as part of the class struggle which would lead to a Socialist

4. Personal interview with G. Keith Parker at the *Baptistische Theologische Hochschule,* Ruschlikon, Switzerland, June 12, 1984.

society.[5] Therefore, for some years Baptists and other Evangelicals enjoyed more freedom under Communism than they had ever known under the tsars. This does not mean that the Marxist regime favored evangelical Christianity, but they sought to use its strength to help break the stranglehold of the established Orthodox Church. The impact of the rise of Communism extended far beyond the Soviet Union, affecting religion in all the Eastern European countries and, with a ripple effect, in Western Europe as well.

By 1928 the government of the Soviet Union abandoned its policy of toleration of Evangelicals, including Baptists, and introduced severe persecution which lasted for over a generation under the leadership of Joseph Stalin. The churches were badly crippled, though by the middle of World War II it was clear that they had not been totally eradicated as the government had hoped. The limited concessions to religion which the Soviets put into effect in the 1940s forced some strange structural combinations, with Baptists, Brethren, and Pentecostals grouped into the same unions. Government policy also forced some un-Baptistic leadership methods, when government agencies for religious affairs determined the election and defined the duties of pastors, presbyters, and Baptist union leadership. It was in the government's interest to encourage a semiepiscopal style of leadership among Baptists so the government could more easily control the churches through control of the leaders.

The rise of Communism and its strict regulation of religious affairs in several Eastern European countries raised again the troublesome issue of the relationship of church and state. Some believers advocated a firm adherence to the historic Baptist witness for separation of church and state, while others bowed to the inevitable and tried to carry on the Baptist witness as best they could within the context of government control.

Two World Wars

During 1914-1918 and again in 1939-1945 great wars raged, involving European, Asian, and American powers. One historian spoke of "the repatterning of Europe" after World War II which drew new political lines in a way that isolated many Baptists.[6] The privation and suffering, dislocation of people, and destruction wrought by the war left both physical and spiritual scars upon the people and lands affected. Those wars were notable for their world scope, severity, use of advanced weapons, and number of casualties. In World War II, for example, the Soviet Union lost about twenty million men.

The twentieth-century wars have had a great impact upon religion. In

5. For example, see A. I. Klibanov, *History of Religious Sectarianism in Russia, 1860s-1917,* Ethel Dunn, trans.

6. Kirkwood, p. 132.

many parts of Europe, churches were closed, buildings destroyed or diverted to nonreligious use, congregations scattered, schools abandoned, church unions lapsed, and leaders killed or imprisoned. It was not possible to continue the preparation of an adequate supply of pastors under wartime conditions, nor could such pastors have functioned had they been prepared. In many places in Europe after World War II, only a fraction of the Baptists who had been active before the war could be found. Many areas have not to this day attained the number of Baptist churches and members and the level of personal and pastoral witness that marked their areas before World War II.

Struggle for Religious Freedom

Not since their earliest days when they populated the prisons of England have Baptists faced such intense and prolonged persecution as they have confronted in Europe in the twentieth century. While the worst of persecution eased off in Western Europe, leaving remnants of subtle discrimination, in much of Eastern Europe Baptists have suffered severely. Hundreds of Baptists have languished in prison, scores have died under mysterious circumstances, pastors have been separated from their flocks, and countless churches have been closed.

This modern persecution has come almost entirely from civil governments. Most of the state churches, where they still exist, have lost the means and much of the will to inflict serious damage upon other religious groups. Perhaps the major government weapon against evangelical churches in Europe during this century has been their control of church registration. This is a process by which churches gain official government sanction for their existence and meetings. By extending or withholding registration, the governments exercise effective control. They have also sought to control the churches by limiting the age of baptism, forbidding religious instruction of children and youth, refusing permission for buildings or needed enlargement, restricting the supply of clergy, limiting the supply of Bibles and other religious literature, refusing Christians admission to higher education, imprisonment of church leaders, and loss of jobs and other harassment to church members. One of the most severe forms of control, often threatened but less often actually done, was forcible separation of children from Christian parents.

In addition to these forms of restriction, a number of European governments have attempted to encourage and spread the teaching of atheism in homes and schools. They also devised substitute ceremonies and organizations to wean young people away from the churches. At times the harsh treatment of Christians has led to a reaction of sympathy for suffering people whose outward lives seemed exemplary. In this way, persecution has sometimes backfired, and European governments have had to ease up on Christians because of adverse public opinion within Europe and beyond.

Like the persecutions of the early church, these periods of suffering have pruned and perhaps purified the Baptist churches and have discouraged casual membership. However, they have also led to abberations from historic Baptist practices and have given to some Baptists in Europe a kind of fortress or siege mentality.

One result of such sustained opposition has been the framing of Baptist confessions of faith. European Baptists have devised more confessions in the twentieth century than British and American Baptists combined. These have been designed partly to define and defend the Baptist faith within their own communion and partly to try to win acceptance from civil governments as officially registered religious groups.

Work of the Baptist World Alliance

The Baptist World Alliance was formed in London in 1905 and quite early showed an interest in Baptist work on the Continent. The BWA held regional meetings in Berlin in 1908 and Stockholm in 1913; several times its general congress has met in Europe, beginning in 1923. In time this organization opened a European headquarters, now at Copenhagen, and from 1923 James H. Rushbrooke worked full time as the BWA secretary for Europe. The BWA brought together Baptists from Allied and Axis countries after the world wars, providing a forum for discussion and a structure to restore fellowship. This world Baptist organization also provided significant leadership in war relief work, the struggle for religious freedom, and the gathering of statistics on European Baptists.

In these ways, the Baptist World Alliance has influenced the course of European Baptist history. It encouraged the formation of Baptist unions in the various countries and fostered a spirit of cooperation at both national and international levels. The European Baptist Federation grew out of postwar meetings which began in 1948 under the sponsorship of the BWA. At times rival Baptist groups in various countries have attempted to make polemic use of their BWA membership to gain legitimacy in the eyes of the world Baptist community, their own civil government, or both. On balance, it appears that membership in the Baptist World Alliance has been even more important to Europeans than to their fellow Baptists in the Western world.

The American Presence

When Thomas Jefferson served as American ambassador to France in the 1780s, the visit of other Americans to Paris could still elicit interest and comment. Two centuries later, however, the presence of numerous Americans in Europe was so commonplace as to be hardly noticed. Large numbers of Americans now live in Europe for longer or lesser periods, drawn there by military assignment, universities which attract American students and teachers, business enterprises, government representation, and opportunities in the various fields of art. Estimates place the number of Americans living in Europe at about one million. Kaiserslautern, West Germany, has an estimated American population of 100 thousand persons, which comprises the largest concentration of Americans outside the United States.[7] In some areas the American presence is enough to make at least a mild blip upon the economic scene and to further the multilingual and multicultural flavor of Europe.

Many of the Americans in Europe are Baptists and wish to continue in active churchmanship while living there. For the most part, language barriers have kept them out of the European Baptist churches. American servicemen formed their own Baptist church at Wiesbaden, West Germany, in 1957. In 1958 the churches at Wiesbaden and Frankfort led in forming the Association of Baptists in Continental Europe (ABCE) to link churches composed primarily of American members. As the work continued to develop, the association was restructured in 1964 as the European Baptist Convention (EBC). By 1984, it had 46 affiliated churches, with 3,737 members in 11 countries of Europe.[8] Only 5 of these churches were in England; the rest were on the Continent.

While not officially connected with the Southern Baptist Convention, the EBC carries on its work with a distinctly Southern Baptist flavor. In 1984 fifteen of its pastors were under appointment by the Foreign Mission Board of the SBC. Its executive secretary, John W. Merritt, was appointed a missionary to Italy in 1964 and has served the EBC since 1972. The EBC channels its foreign mission funds through the SBC and also raises an annual offering to assist European Baptist churches in obtaining their own buildings. The convention publishes a monthly paper, *Highlights,* from its offices in Wiesbaden. In 1984 the EBC called for a Baptist Book Store in the Wiesbaden or Frankfort area with Southern Baptist missionary personnel to operate it.

Churches of the EBC have ministered primarily to Americans living in Europe. Even so, the EBC is not always warmly regarded by European Baptists. They sometimes regard its methods as too Americanized and its worship as culturally insulated against the European heritage. The confident and aggressive spirit which often marks these churches seems to border on spiritual pride, and Europeans often think the Americans not only fail to understand the situation of European Baptists but, what is perhaps worse, fail even to try. Despite its organizational independence, the EBC must be regarded as an extension of Southern Baptist work on the Continent. Most Baptists from America who are active in church life in Europe are Southern Baptists. In general one could say that Northern Baptists were

---

7. Reginald M. McDonough, "A Sister Convention Across the Sea," *Baptist Program* (September 1984), p. 35.

8. *Yearbook,* European Baptist Convention, 1983, pp. 62-63.

more active in Europe, in both personnel and funds, in the nineteenth century, but Southern Baptists have been more involved in the twentieth century.

Baptists in Europe: A Geographical Survey

This section will trace Baptists in various countries of Europe during the twentieth century. While no complete picture can be given here, these selected snapshots will reveal at least the highlights of the continental contingent of the Baptist family since 1900.

Central Europe

From the first, Central Europe served as a staging ground for expansion of the Baptist witness to the rest of the Continent. However, the two world wars took a heavy toll in this area, especially in Germany, and Baptist work suffered severe setbacks.

Germany. In 1984 the European Baptist Federation met in Hamburg to join in celebration of the one hundred fiftieth anniversary of the Johann Gerhard Oncken Baptist Church where Oncken was baptized in 1834. This oldest surviving Baptist church on the Continent forms a strong center of Baptist witness, along with twelve other Baptist churches in the city. Hamburg is also the site of the oldest Baptist seminary in Europe and has long been a major center for theological training and missionary outreach.

German Baptists entered the twentieth century on an upbeat, still benefiting from the Oncken legacy. Their optimism was best expressed by an influential preacher who pronounced, "Baptists have a future."[9] However, two world wars have clouded that future. World War I depleted their leadership, but they increased their witness by publication and experienced considerable growth in the early 1920s.

The rise of Adolf Hitler and his Nazi party provoked little response from the Baptists who either did not realize what was happening or tried to ignore it. They hosted the Baptist World Alliance Congress in Berlin in 1934 without incident, and some reassured themselves that Hitler represented no threat since he had not interfered with Baptist work. Some accused the German Baptists of hiding from the burning issues of the day.[10] At the Hamburg meeting of the European Baptist Federation in 1984, the German Baptists acknowledged their fault in not speaking out earlier and more strongly against Hitler.

The war devastated the Baptists. Many of their leaders died and fully half of their 275 church buildings were destroyed, including all those in the eastern part of Germany. The Hamburg seminary was reduced to ruins, and

9. J. H. Rushbrooke, *The Baptist Movement in the Continent of Europe* (London: Kingsgate Press: 1923), p. 44.
10. Robert G. Torbet, *A History of the Baptists,* 3rd ed., p. 175.

the printing facilities built up by Oncken were destroyed. During the war, Baptists merged into the Union of Evangelical Free Churches which included Brethren and Pentecostal churches. Later most of the Pentecostals withdrew to form their own group, and the union took on a more Baptist identity as shown by the inclusion of the name *Baptisten* in parenthesis as part of the union name. By 1950 German Baptists numbered about 100,219 members in 559 churches.[11]

One result of the war was the division of Germany, thus creating two German nations. The Federal Republic of Germany (FRG), with its capital in Bonn, affiliated with the West, while the German Democratic Republic (GDR) lined up with the Communist powers of Eastern Europe. The two nations divided Berlin between them, and the infamous Berlin Wall became the most dramatic symbol not only of Germany's division but also the entire division of East and West. By 1959 Baptists in East Germany formed their own seminary at Buckow and a few years later in 1970 organized their own Baptist union. Bibles have been readily available in East Germany, sold openly in the Baptist Book Store in East Berlin.

Baptists in West Germany rebuilt the Hamburg seminary and restored their publication ministry, but in recent years they have faced a number of internal tensions which have reduced their growth. These tensions have included such issues as authority of Scripture, the role of women in church, the relationship of local churches and denomination, and the authority of pastors. Like Baptists in most places, those in West Germany have persistent doctrinal disagreements.

In 1974 an effort was begun to devise a confession of faith acceptable to Baptists of East and West Germany, as well as other German-speaking Baptists in Austria and Switzerland. The resulting confession, known as "An Account of Our Faith," was accepted in 1977. While all hold to baptism by immersion, the East Germans insisted upon adding the following sentences to their version of the confession: "Others see in baptism received through faith not only an act of man but also an act of God. The person is conveyed to his Lord in his baptism." That accommodates those who hold to some form of baptismal regeneration. The confession is fairly lengthy and deals not only with theology but also with the Christian life in its personal, social, and family dimensions.[12]

East Germany had in 1980 less than one third as many Baptists as West Germany. They operate under severe restrictions, while those in the West enjoy a high degree of freedom. Their combined strength does not approach what it was before World War II. Both tend to call their churches "Evangelical" and seem quite reluctant for the name "Baptist" to be listed publicly as part of their church name.

11. Ibid., 176.
12. The confession is printed in Parker, pp. 57-76.

Switzerland. After World War I, the Baptists in Switzerland formed their own union, along with such related ministries as publications, a deaconess house, and mission outreach. Some churches have not affiliated with the Swiss Baptist Union, preferring to remain in the more conservative Evangelical Association of French-Speaking Baptist Churches. Almost half of Swiss Baptists are found in one dynamic church in Zurich, notable for its preaching and over forty home study groups. Most of the Swiss churches, however, have not developed any effective evangelistic outreach.

The Baptist Theological Seminary, an international school at Ruschlikon, forms an important part of the Baptist witness in Europe. Located on a beautiful hillside overlooking Lake Zurich, this seminary trains Baptist leaders from all parts of Europe, including many of the Eastern countries. In addition, many students from Britain and America attend its classes. The seminary was formed in 1949 and has been described as "the most significant step in the unifying of Baptist life in Europe."[13] The school grew out of efforts of the Baptist World Alliance to help reconstruct the Baptist life of Europe shattered by the Second World War. At first jointly sponsored by both American and Southern conventions in America, the financial support of the Ruschlikon school has been more and more assumed by the Foreign Mission Board of the SBC, which currently provides about 80 percent of its financial support. The faculty is made up of scholars appointed by the European Baptists as well as by the Foreign Mission Board. At times tensions have surfaced between Americans and Europeans on the faculty, revealing underlying differences about the directions the school should take.

In 1980 Denton Lotz, a professor from the American Baptist Convention, devised and directed an innovative summer program at Ruschlikon which has become an important part of its annual schedule. Lotz developed the Summer Institute of Theological Education (SITE), involving study in residence at Ruschlikon for one month. The target group included especially pastors from Eastern Europe, ministering in lands that for the most part had no provisions for theological study. The Ruschlikon seminary provided compact conferences in biblical, theological, and pastoral studies. It also provided a minilibrary of about ten basic books to aid the pastors in continuing study. The costs of this program have been borne entirely by the seminary, for the Eastern countries will not allow their citizens to bring any money out. Food and lodging, transportation, and even a spending allowance is provided by the seminary. Observers regard the SITE program as a great success and say it meets a serious need.

The Ruschlikon seminary probably maintains the highest academic standards of any Baptist school in Europe, surpassing perhaps even such reputable seminaries as those in Hamburg and Stockholm. However, some

13. Kirkwood, p. 118.

complain that this school seems to place more emphasis upon academics than upon practical and pastoral training for ministry.

Austria. Like their neighbors in Switzerland, the Austrian Baptists have not achieved great numerical growth. In 1953 seven churches formed the Union of Baptist Churches in Austria, and they later endorsed the German confession of 1977. As of 1980 they had only nine churches with fewer than seven hundred members.[14] Most of the Baptists are concentrated in Salzburg and Vienna. In recent years, a Baptist witness has been opened among students who flock to Austria, with a new church opening at the famous resort city of Innsbruck.

The Netherlands. From 1900 to 1980 Baptists in the Netherlands grew from thirteen to eighty-one churches. Their membership increased almost 25 percent in the decade of the 1970s, to total about twelve hundred as of 1980.[15] They are the only Baptists in Europe to register a membership gain for every year from 1900 to 1980. The Dutch Baptists have carried on an effective publication ministry, as well as progressive ministries among women and youth. Their seminary, *De Vinkenhof,* opened in 1958 near Utrecht. Though Amsterdam was occupied by the Nazis in 1945, the Netherlands and the Baptists escaped the devastation which came to their neighbors in Germany. The exemplary conduct of Baptists during the war greatly enhanced their image and, after the war, they found open doors for work and witness.

In the 1940s the Union of Baptist Churches in the Netherlands affiliated with the major ecumenical structure of the Netherlands and also with the newly formed World Council of Churches, formed in 1948 in Amsterdam. This ecumenical relation provoked intense controversy, and in 1963 the Baptist union voted to withdraw from both bodies. The Dutch churches are generally conservative in theology. Their confession, which dates back to the turn of the century, was most recently revised in 1953. It reflects an evangelical tone, though it is little known or used. It proclaims the Bible as "the infallible Word of God" and includes five brief paragraphs about different aspects of the Christian faith.[16] Some Dutch Baptists have suggested they draw up a more complete confession, to include guidance for Christians not only in doctrine but also in pressing social and moral issues.

Northern Europe

Although Baptists are the oldest of the free church groups in Scandinavia, they have remained a numerical minority. Their great strength, as always, has been in Sweden. While the Scandinavian countries figured

14. Parker, p. 278.
15. Ibid., p. 278.
16. The confession is printed in Parker, pp. 88-89.

largely in World War II, particularly the invasion of Norway, they did not sustain the physical destruction of some other parts of Europe.

Denmark. Though the Baptists of Copenhagen hosted a meeting of the Baptist World Alliance in 1947, Danish Baptists did not achieve government status as a recognized religion entitled to toleration until 1952. At their beginnings, Danish Baptists were reluctant to accept human confessions of faith, though they did for a time use a modified version of Oncken's German statement of doctrines. To this day, they have no specific confession, though they are conservative. For a time, they operated a seminary at Tølløse but have sent a number of students to schools at Stockholm, Hamburg, and in recent years to Ruschlikon.

Norway. As of 1980 the Norwegian Baptist Union had 64 affiliated churches with 6,299 members. They conducted a full range of ministries, including publications, youth ministries, and mission work. As early as 1910 they opened a theological school at Christiana; but after World War II, with the aid of Baptists in America, they obtained property for a new seminary at Oslo. Because the government required a confession as a prerequisite to recognized status, the Norwegian Baptists adopted a confession in 1963. It reflects clear evangelical emphases. After considerable debate in the late 1960s, the Norwegians issued a further statement on the Bible as "God's inspired word." The added statement, though never officially adopted, is generally considered a part of the doctrinal statement of Norwegian Baptists.[17]

Sweden. The largest Baptist population in Scandinavia is in Sweden, which in 1980 reported over 40 thousand members in 656 churches. Since the nineteenth century, Baptist work has been divided between the Baptist Union of Sweden, with offices in Stockholm, and the Orebro Mission, located in the city of the same name. The division occurred late in the nineteenth century when Baptists in Orebro adopted Pentecostal views and practices, while the Baptist union group maintained more traditional Baptist emphases. The two groups are about equal in number, though the union group has more churches. The Baptist union maintains its well-known Bethel Seminary at Stockholm, while the Orebro Mission conducts its own seminary at Orebro. The Baptist union long ago adopted a confession of faith, expressing conservative Calvinistic views, but it has fallen into disuse. The Orebro Mission maintains a fervent and conservative theology but has adopted no confessional statement. While many of the original differences have moderated, the Baptist union maintains a more strictly Baptist image while the Orebro group maintains a more Pentecostal stance.

Finland. Baptists in this northern land, few as they are, maintain two separate Baptist unions, the Finnish Baptist Union (Finnish-speaking) and the Swedish-speaking Baptist Union of Finland. Their differences are

17. The confession is printed in Parker, pp. 97-98; the supplement, on pages pp. 256-257.

primarily linguistic and cultural. Neither has experienced much numerical growth. After more than a century of witness, the Finnish-speakers have only ten churches while the Swedish language group numbers twenty-four, and both groups combined numbered only 2,483 members in 1980. A Finnish law of 1922 gave the status of "religious communities" to recognized religious groups, while others had the lower status of "religious associations," which allowed less freedom. For years the Finnish-speaking Baptists have had the higher status, based upon a confession from the nineteenth century. Only in 1979 did the Swedish-speaking group present a confession, which elevated their official status. The 1979 confession is extremely brief, affirming the Apostles' Creed, personal faith in Christ, baptism by immersion, and the priority of missions. Most major doctrines are not mentioned, and the framers contented themselves by saying, "Concerning founding churches, dedication of children, baptismals and the Holy Communion the Union follows . . . the New Testament."[18] They give no hint, however, about what they believe the New Testament teaches on these subjects.

Southern Europe

The southern countries of Europe have never provided a favorable climate for Baptist growth. Baptists have been present in that area from early times; in fact, the earliest appearance of Baptists in modern Europe was in France, though the work did not survive. The strong Roman Catholic presence, lack of a strong evangelical tradition in the culture, and the unfortunate tendency of Baptists to attract a bad image have combined to make their witness in the sunny parts of Europe less successful.

Italy. The Southern Baptist Convention helped open work in Italy in the nineteenth century. In an effort after World War I to help the Baptists of Europe to recover, a committee of the Baptist World Alliance suggested that the SBC continue its relation to the Italian Baptists. In 1939 the Italian churches formed the Baptist Federation, but it suffered severely during World War II. A few years later the Italian Baptist Union was formed, now known as the Baptist Christian Union of Italy. Italian Baptists now number about forty-two hundred members in eighty churches and sponsor a number of ministries, including a Baptist paper, various mission centers, and a girls' training school in Rome, known as *Villa Betania,* founded and funded largely by the Woman's Missionary Union of the SBC.

Spain. Only in the "iron curtain" countries have European Baptists had a harder time winning religious liberty than in Spain. The Franco regime which began in 1939 took a harsh attitude toward evangelical religion and many churches were closed. A 1945 agreement between the Spanish government and the Roman Catholic Church allowed only private worship to

18. Ibid., p. 112.

Protestants and prescribed that only Catholic services or symbols could be public. The official agreement said, "This law expressly forbids public worship outside private houses or chapels which must show no signs on the outside; it also forbids proselytizing through the written or spoken word."[19]

Though tensions eased somewhat in later years, in the 1960s Baptist pastors and people still experienced restriction, harassment, and some times imprisonment for their efforts to worship openly. However, the new Spanish constitution of 1978 allowed much broader freedom, and Baptist churches have grown dramatically since then. They have formed a Baptist Evangelical Union of Spain, sponsor publications, operate a seminary near Madrid, and offer specialized ministries among women and youth. Baptists in Spain are in close cooperation with the Southern Baptist Convention, and in 1970 they officially adopted *The Baptist Faith and Message,* a confessional statement drawn up by the SBC in 1963.

Portugal. Baptist witness in Portugal owes much to the work of Robert Reginald Young, a Canadian Baptist who went with his bride to Orporto, Portugal, about 1902. Though basically independent missionaries, they sustained some relation to the Tremont Temple Baptist Church of Boston. Later, Southern Baptist missionaries in Brazil, including Zachary C. Taylor and the intrepid Solomon L. Ginsburg, visited Portugal to see if a Brazilian Baptist mission seemed feasible. By 1913 Southern Baptists were quite active in Portugal. When Brazilian Baptists had to reduce their missionary presence in Portugal, the Southern Baptist Convention voted to "enter Portugal in strength."[20] In 1960 the Grayson Tennisons became the first SBC missionaries appointed permanently to Portugal, and by the mid-1980s ten such couples were in that land.[21]

The Portuguese Baptist Convention was formed in 1920 and has worked in such areas as church extension, publications, and theological education. Not all churches affiliate with this convention, however. Several other Baptist groups in the United States have sponsored work in Portugal, including the Conservative Baptists of America and the Baptist Missionary Association of Texas, and a few churches adhere to these groups. In 1975 the Portuguese Baptists adopted the "Statement of Principles of the Baptist Faith," a slightly modified version of *The Baptist Faith and Message* of the SBC.

France. Baptists in France have prospered little until recently and have faced a continuing struggle for unity. A step in that direction was taken in 1919 with formation of the French Baptist Federation. The French Baptists have adopted no new confession in the present century but still make considerable use of a doctrinal statement last revised in 1895. Though

19. Cited in Parker, p. 119.
20. *Minutes,* Foreign Mission Board, SBC, September, 1958, p. 2.
21. Norman Harrell, "The Establishment of Baptist Work in Portugal," p. 25.

strikingly similar to the New Hampshire Confession in America, this French confession is also remarkable for limiting the authority of the pastors, providing for both men and women deacons, and the public consecration of children.[22] A postscript distinguishes between baptized members of the church and members of the congregation and spells out the rights and privileges of each. This confession emphasizes life-style as well as theology, admonishing Christians to "live warily in this world."

The decade of the 1970s saw remarkable growth among French Baptists, with twenty-three new churches formed during that time.[23] Membership increased by about 20 percent in that decade, while the number of congregations almost doubled and financial contributions more than quadrupled. During that time, the French Baptists made more progress in the cities, including Paris. In 1970 they completed their new study center, *Les Cedres,* located in a Paris suburb. While they do not have a seminary, the study center can accommodate about forty persons in residence and is used for a variety of conferences and retreats. It is also used for orientation of French pastors who have graduated from seminaries outside the country and for continuing education conferences for active pastors. The center also houses a publishing ministry and a recording studio for radio ministry not only in France but also for mission stations sponsored by the French Baptists.[24]

Baptists from America have been active in France. The earliest church established primarily for Baptists from America was on the Left Bank in Paris, at 48 *Rue de Lille.* Later the French Baptist Federation was formed there and used the location as its headquarters. The European Baptist Federation was also formed there.

In 1921 a number of more conservative churches separated to form the Evangelical Association of French-Speaking Baptist Churches, and to this day they remain separate from the French Baptist Federation. The Evangelical Association also affiliates a few French-speaking churches in Switzerland and Belgium. Their overseas contacts are primarily with ultraconservative groups, such as Strict Baptists in England and the Regular Baptists of Canada. The association publishes a paper, *Lien Fraternel,* as well as Bible study materials. While providing communication between the churches, the association has emphasized local church autonomy. Perhaps their most effective leader was Robert Dubarry (d. 1970), who helped form the association and during his lifetime set its doctrinal standards and witness methods. He served as president of the association from 1921 to 1960. The association has a rather complete confession of faith, last modified in 1979, which expresses generally evangelical Baptist views. This

22. Parker, pp. 123-134.
23. Kirkwood, p. 163.
24. Ibid., p. 164.

confession provides for both deacons and deaconesses.[25]

Belgium. Next to Greece, with only one church, Belgium has the smallest Baptist community in Europe, with eight churches and 512 members in 1980.[26] The three largest congregations are either English- or Polish-language churches, and large sections of Belgium have no Baptist witness at all. Only in 1970 did some of the churches obtain their own buildings, and most of their pastors are bivocational. Despite limited numbers, the churches formed the Belgium Baptist Union in 1922, but it did not survive the devastation of World War II. A number of other evangelical congregations in Belgium baptize believers by immersion. Baptists in many other European countries have merged with evangelical churches far less "Baptist" than these, and some observers recommend that the handful of Belgium Baptist churches do the same.[27]

Eastern Europe

About two-thirds of all Baptists on the Continent live in Eastern Europe. Paradoxically, these Baptists have suffered severely in the twentieth century, yet their churches show the greatest spiritual vitality and the highest rates of numerical growth. Their greatest assets are their spiritual zeal, the spiritual hunger which pervades their lands, and their courageous commitment to the gospel. Their major handicaps are found in hostile governments, difficulties in obtaining or enlarging church buildings, the shortage of Bibles and Christian literature, and the difficulties for pastors to obtain adequate training. While churches in Eastern Europe are growing, they have few theological schools. Of course, the rise of Communism is the one dominant historical reality which has most influenced Baptist life in the twentieth century, as it has influenced everything else in Eastern Europe. However, despite intense persecution, and some might even say because of it, Baptists there have won the respect of the world and grudging concessions from their own governments.

Baptists in Communist countries have had to adjust to restrictions which are unknown to Baptists elsewhere. Some have been criticized for capitulating too much to atheistic governments, but they have had to choose at times between a limited witness or no witness at all. One Eastern European leader said, "While we have the freedom to preach the gospel and to make converts and baptize them, we are happy; and we are prepared to accept the restrictions." He concluded, "While the door is open wide enough for us to do this, we will not push it in case it should come back in our faces and what

25. Parker, p. 143.
26. Ibid., p. 279.
27. Kirkwood, pp. 170-171.

we have should be lost."[28] Most Baptists in the Eastern countries readily accept Socialist viewpoints and profess political loyalty to their countries but, of course, reject the official atheism that often accompanies the system.

Poland. A report in 1920 observed that the Baptist cause in Poland lay in "misery and wretchedness."[29] Most of the churches lacked pastors, and Baptists carried a foreign image which proved a barrier in reaching the Polish population. World War II added to the wretchedness. The people of Poland stoutly resisted Adolf Hitler, as they later resisted domination by the Soviet Union, for which they have paid a heavy price. Though historically Poland has been strongly Catholic, evangelical religion has shown great vitality there as well. As of 1980 the Baptists numbered 55 churches with about 2,539 members, along with numerous home fellowships and preaching points scattered throughout Poland.[30]

For years two Baptist unions, one for German-speaking members and one for the Polish-speaking, existed side by side. During the war, they were forced into a merger with other similar Evangelicals, but after the war few Baptists remained or could be found. In 1947 the non-Baptists withdrew from this artificial union, allowing the Baptists to resume their Polish Baptist Federation. Constitutional changes brought greater religious freedom, and they were able to make a comeback from the devastation of the war years. They carry on youth ministries, publish a Baptist paper, and sponsor a radio program. They have made only slight changes in their 1930 confession, which is still accepted by the churches. This confession deals with the usual biblical and doctrinal subjects and includes a strong affirmation of political loyalty, including the obligation "to place ourselves at our country's disposal in the times of war if we are called to do so."[31]

The warm reception and overflow crowds which attended the visit of Billy Graham to Poland in 1979 indicate something of the spiritual openness of the Polish people. Years later Baptists were said to be still benefiting from the interest and favorable impressions from Graham's preaching.

Hungary. Building on the nineteenth-century work of the "peasant prophets" Kornya and Toth, Baptists in Hungary continued to grow in the present century. However, the familiar tensions erupted between the two major language groups, with German and Hungarian churches splitting into separate unions in 1905. Not until 1920 did they iron out their differences, which were more cultural than doctrinal, and join together in the Union of Hungarian Baptist Churches. In 1955 they changed the name to Hungarian Baptist Church. By 1980 they numbered about twelve thousand

28. Ibid., pp. 142-143.
29. *The Baptist,* January 22, 1921, p. 1746.
30. Parker, p. 279.
31. Ibid., p. 183.

members gathered into two hundred churches.[32]

The Hungarian Baptist confession of 1902 was updated in 1967 and remains the doctrinal basis of Hungarian Baptist life. Though phrased somewhat differently than many Baptist confessions, it expresses generally evangelical convictions. The confession affirms that the Bible was "written by divinely inspired men, was put together by the Church under the impulse and guidance of the Holy Spirit." It concludes that "the providence of God has saved the Holy Scripture—both in its origin and in its transmission—from all essential errors."[33] This doctrine of "functional inerrancy" is applied to the present Bible rather than being restricted to original manuscripts. The confession also speaks on moral issues; and while it allows divorce, it urges divorced persons not to remarry. Unlike many Baptist groups in Europe, the Hungarians have few Brethren members in their churches. This may be one reason their confession shows no emphasis upon premillennialism or nondenominationalism.

Czechoslovakia. The Baptist Union of Czechoslovakia dates from 1919, and by 1980 it had 28 affiliated churches with 3,978 members.[34] The major symbol of the Czech churches is a communion cup over an open Bible, by which Baptists seek to identify with the historic Reformed traditions of that land. A modern-language edition of the Czech Bible has led to numerous Bible study groups, which, in turn, has led some people to Baptist viewpoints. Though they have no confession of their own, the Czech Baptists have accepted the German confession of 1977.

Due perhaps to repeated political uprisings against the Communist regime, the Czech government requires all clergy to take an oath of political allegiance. The government also regulates and pays pastors' salaries, including Baptists. Though Baptists have now gained recognized status and enjoy a measure of freedom, at times harsh restrictions have been enforced against them. A number of younger Baptist pastors have managed to flee from Czechoslovakia to carry on their ministries in Western countries.

Bulgaria. The land that is now called Bulgaria has been dominated for centuries by two religious forces: Orthodox Christianity and Islam. These have left little room for the growth of evangelical forms of faith. The Baptist community in Bulgaria can be described as small and relatively isolated, but it nevertheless show a spirit of vitality. With only 10 churches and 650 members, Bulgarian Baptists formed a union. Their pastors and churches have participated little in either the European Baptist Federation or the Baptist World Alliance. Their churches operate under several restrictions, and they lack Bibles and other needed Christian literature. The most one

32. Ibid., p. 279.
33. Ibid., p. 188.
34. Ibid., p. 279.

can say is that the Bulgarian Baptists, few as they are, courageously maintain their witness.

Yugoslavia. The greatest leader of Yugoslavian Baptists in this century was Vinko Vacek; since his death in 1939, no comparable leader has arisen. In 1941 Yugoslavia was divided between several neighboring nations and the Baptist union, being dismembered, perished. Rebuilding was slow after the war, but in time the seminary and many of the churches destroyed by war were restored. Baptists in Yugoslavia drew up a new confession in 1948, partly for the unity and instruction of their own members and partly to meet government requirements as a recognized religious group. The confession includes a rather militant defense of Baptists, directed against those who considered them an insignificant sect with dangerous teachings. The confession also emphasizes that, while their numbers might be few in Yugoslavia, they belonged to a world family that represents millions of Baptists who claim a place not as a sect but as a legitimate part of the historic Christian faith.[35]

Romania. Next to the Soviet Union, Romania has the largest Baptist community in Eastern Europe. Some observers suggest Romanian Baptists also show the most spiritual vitality, since they have been in the midst of an intense religious revival for several years. By the late 1970s, they were baptizing about 10,000 new converts each year, and by 1980 numbered about 160,000 members in 662 churches. This represents remarkable growth for a people who numbered scarcely 1,000 at the turn of the century.

The Romanian Baptist churches include many dynamic and educated young couples, professional people, and community leaders. Many Baptist groups in Europe have not enlisted this kind of constituency. With such people representing Romanian Baptists, the Baptist image has been vastly improved. With such rapid growth, the Baptists have not been able to provide enough pastors, though they send a number of students to study in England, America, or elsewhere in Europe. They also operate their own seminary in Bucharest; but as of the mid-1980s, they still had a serious shortage of trained ministers.

Baptists in Romania have not always enjoyed the rapid progress which has marked them in recent years. Around the turn of the century, they numbered scarcely a thousand members, divided into different language groups and with little promise of progress. They formed a Baptist union in 1920 and a seminary the year after, but World War II decimated them. A law passed in 1942 was interpreted as calling for the complete abolition of Baptists in Romania, and for a time all their churches were closed. That total prohibition was never effective, and efforts to enforce it lasted only two years. In 1944 the Baptists regained the right of legal existence, though they have been repeatedly persecuted and harassed since then.

35. This confession is printed in Parker, pp. 204-215.

The Romanian Baptist confession of faith, like most of those in Europe, speaks on both theological beliefs and daily Christian living in the family and in society. Some parts are vividly stated; without a new birth, the confession affirms, "we are like a wild tree which cannot bring forth good fruits."[36] The statement insists that though marriage is basically a civil contract, Baptists should not forego a church as well as a civil ceremony. It makes room for divorce and specifically allows the right of remarriage to divorced persons. The confession offers a strong affirmation of Christian obedience to the government. It makes no mention of millennialism but does affirm a belief that Christians can renounce their faith and thus lose their salvation.

Like most of the Communist countries, Romania provides for freedom of religion in its constitution but, again like other such countries, finds countless ways to subvert that provision. Government officials have kept the Baptists under careful watch, apparently feeling threatened by their vitality and growth. State officials have tried to prevent the formation of new churches, have delayed or denied permits to erect or enlarge church buildings, and have limited theological education in an effort to dry up the supply of pastors. Pastors have been a special target of government opposition. Many have been arrested, subjected to beatings and other abuse, and often imprisoned. Despite these hardships, Romanian Baptists continue to maintain their faithful witness. More than most iron-curtain Baptists, those in Romania have been able to print Bibles and other Christian literature. In the 1980s they even translated the twelve-volume *The Broadman Bible Commentary* into Romanian.

Union of Soviet Socialist Republics (USSR). The Soviet Union is hardly the atheistic empire which many Westerners imagine or that the Communist regime has tried so hard to create. The two largest religious groups, the Eastern Orthodox Church and Muslims, are said to include about fifty million adherents each. Smaller religious groups, who number in the millions, include Roman Catholics, Jews, and Lutherans. A recent Soviet writer spoke of "more than 400 religious sects" in the USSR.[37] Knowledgeable sources estimate that about 20 percent of the Soviet population remains actively Christian and that weekly church attendance in the USSR runs over four times that of Great Britain.[38] Renewed interest in religion was reported in the Soviet Union in the 1980s, especially among young people. Some did not hesitate to call this a religious revival and noted that it included some members of the Communist Party.

Through the twentieth century, the Communist government has changed

36. Ibid., p. 220.

37. Cited in Michael Bourdeaux, *Religious Ferment in Russia*, p. 1.

38. Walter Sawatsky, *Soviet Evangelicals Since World War II* (Scottdale, Penn.: Herald Press, 1981), p. 14.

its tactics many times but has never swerved from its announced goal to stamp out all religion and to create an atheistic society. Christianity has proven remarkably durable. With all its resources and power, the Soviet state has not been able to fix atheism upon the whole population. In fact, in the 1980s the Baptists in the Soviet Union probably outnumbered members of the Communist Party. Amid such a struggle between belief and unbelief, Soviet Baptists have lived their witness. Baptists and Evangelical Christians in the USSR number at least a half million baptized members, and the total community is estimated at several times that number.

Diversity among Soviet Baptists. The term "Russian Baptists" can be misleading. Of churches in the major Baptist union, not all are Russian and not all are Baptist. Soviet society includes Russians, Ukrainians, Belorussians, Latvians, Estonians, Lithuanians, Moldavians, Georgians, Armenians and others stretched over vast territories from the Baltic to the Black Seas. One finds a wide diversity of languages, national origins, and ethnic stocks in this collection of countries. Although Russian is the official language of the USSR, fully 20 percent of the population cannot speak it. Baptists share in the diversity which marks the Soviet Union; at their 1966 meeting, they described their union as "multi-national" and "multi-denominational."[39]

Russian Evangelicals entered the twentieth century grouped into two major denominations. The more distinctly Baptist group of the Ukraine formed the All-Russian Baptist Union in 1881. They centered around Kiev and represented mostly the Oncken tradition from which they sprang. A major and sometimes militant spokesman for these strict Baptists was D. I. Mazaev, who served as president of the Baptist union from 1887 to 1920. The "Evangelical Christians" of the North, centering around Saint Petersburg, also immersed but eschewed the name Baptist. Their origins were from the Plymouth Brethren in England, through the ministry of Lord Radstock and Vasili Pashkov. Though sometimes called "Pashkovites," they preferred the name Evangelical Christians. Led by Ivan Stepanovich Prokhanov, they formed the Russian Union of Evangelical Christians in 1907. Both groups affiliated with the Baptist World Alliance in 1905, and in 1911 Prokhanov was elected a vice-president of the BWA.

Degrees of restriction. The Easter Proclamation of 1905 allowed a measure of religious toleration in the USSR, and both the Baptists and Evangelical Christians entered a period of rapid growth. Despite their differences, the two groups explored the possibility of merger, but after countless conferences they could never find common ground. The Baptists took a more conservative, denominational stance, while the Evangelicals were more liberal and nondenominational. At times hostility erupted between the two

---

39. *Documents of Moscow, 1966. All Union Conference of Evangelical Christian-Baptists,* p. 8.

groups, as when the Baptists called the Evangelical Christian Council "a house of prostitution," and Prokhanov, leader of the Evangelicals, solemnly swore, "I will not die until I step over the corpse of the Baptist organization."[40]

Despite the toleration of 1905, both groups remained under the watchful and sometimes hostile eye of the government. Their tendency to pacifism, inherited partly from the Mennonites in the Ukraine, led to government opposition. By the 1920s perhaps half the Soviet Evangelicals were pacifists. At one meeting, the Evangelical Christians described "the shedding of blood under every state system" as "a crime against conscience and the exact teaching and spirit of the Holy Scriptures." They concluded that it was their "sacred obligation openly to refuse military service in all its forms."[41] However, other Evangelicals, and especially their leaders, took a more militarist stance and pointed to their costly participation in World War I as evidence of total loyalty to their country. A later Evangelical Christian report "emphatically condemns such [pacifist] actions and declares that such persons will not be considered as members." In more recent years Soviet Evangelicals have become deeply involved in the organized peace movement, led to that stance partly by government pressure and partly by conviction. Evidence suggests that more than a trace of their historic pacifism remains, especially among the strict Baptists.

The October Revolution of 1917 crippled the Orthodox Church but opened a "golden decade" of growth for the Evangelicals. Though atheist from the first, the early Lenin government lacked the obsessive fear of religion which marked later years. It probably sought to use the Evangelicals to help break the 900-year domination of Orthodoxy. For whatever reasons, Baptists enjoyed more freedom during the first decade of Communism than they ever had under the tsars. Baptists expanded their union, sent out many evangelists, and formed numerous new churches between 1917 and 1928. In 1922 the Baptist union reorganized its work to include departments for evangelism, literature and publishing, music, preparation of pastors and evangelists, moral education, and church order.[42] Ivan S. Prokhanov and Jacob Zhidkov of the Evangelical Christians raised money in America to print about twenty-five thousand Bibles in Russian in 1926, plus about as many more New Testaments and other Scripture portions. A pamphlet widely circulated in America in the 1920s, entitled "A New Religious Reformation in Russia," painted a hopeful picture of winning that

40. Cited in A. I. Klibanov, *History of Religious Sectarianism in Russia, 1860s-1917,* Ethel Dunn, trans., pp. 289-290.

41. Sawatsky, p. 116.

42. Ibid., p. 40.

land to evangelical faith.[43] An evangelical monthly in Philadelphia, sponsored by one of several Russian missionary societies, reported in 1920, "Whole districts are being brought to Christ, and the demand for Bibles and spiritual literature is growing. . . . A great awakening is coming on in the population."[44] The same issue carried a report by Ivan Shiloff, a Russian pastor, that the "great harlot" (by which he meant the Orthodox Church) had been put to nought "and the true church of Jesus is flourishing here now." Not only spiritual revival but also financial prosperity marked the Baptist churches in the 1920s. Pastor Shiloff reported, "At the end of 1918 I received the treasury of the church with only 38 rubles balance, but at the end of 1919 we had in the treasury 38,000 rubles. Now I am busy with repairing the buildings."[45]

Baptist progress ended abruptly and disastrously with the rise to power of Joseph Stalin, who inaugurated a crackdown on religion to rival any persecution in history. The Law of Religious Cults in 1929 stripped the Evangelical churches of most of their liberties. The government outlawed most of the evangelistic methods by which the Evangelicals had grown, closed and/or confiscated many church buildings, imprisoned countless leaders, curtailed practically all printing and distribution of religious literature, and forbade religious teaching for children. Stalin had studied for a time in a religious school in Russian Georgia, but that apparently only increased his bitter hatred for Christianity.

The impact upon Baptists was immediate and devastating. One historian wrote, "By the late thirties, the churches had virtually ceased to exist as institutions."[46] The worst of the hard times lasted until 1944, but by then the Baptists had been wasted numerically and spiritually. The Baptist union collapsed in 1935; the Evangelical union, though it never formally went out of existence, also ceased all activity by the late 1930s. A spirit of death rested upon the land so far as evangelical religion was concerned.

However, religious interest surfaced again during the war. The loyal and even heroic participation of Soviet Evangelicals in World War II, despite some lingering pacificist ideas, won them the grudging respect of the government. By the mid-1940s the worst of the Stalin persecution eased a bit. As Baptists cautiously reemerged into the light of what they hoped would be a new day, it became obvious that while they had not flourished during the hard years they had at least survived.

United under pressure. In 1944 the Baptists and Evangelical Christians finally merged into a common union, thus creating the most influential

43. Published by the Russian Evangelization Society, New York, 1925.
44. William Fetler, ed., *The Friend of Russia* (Philadelphia: Russian Missionary and Educational Society, 1920), p. 60.
45. Ibid., p. 69.
46. Sawatsky, p. 16.

Protestant group in the Soviet Union. A goal pursued by their leaders since the 1880s at last came to fruition. However, the new body, called the All Union Council of Evangelicals-Baptists, was clearly forced upon the churches by the Soviet government.[47] The churches never voted to form such a union; in fact, for years after 1944, many of the leading churches of both groups had not yet even heard that such a union had been formed. The new body, sometimes called the All Union Council, was more often known by its initials of AUCECB. This new union set senior presbyters over the churches of various regions and elected the Union Council of about thirty persons. They also elected a presidium, a smaller executive committee of about a dozen members, and a general secretary and president. The first general secretary was Alexander Karev, and Jacob Zhidkov was elected president. Both served for life.

There is every evidence that the government not only forced the formation of such a union but also closely monitored and, at times, even controlled its decisions. In 1945 the Mennonites joined the union, apparently more from government pressure than any sense of belonging. It was their only avenue for legal existence. Some years later a fourth group, the Pentecostals, joined. They were also pressured by the government. The Pentecostals had to promise not to practice *glossolalia* in public worship and to tone down some of their worship practices. They had to subdue their convictions and practices and act, in public at least, like Baptists. Ultimately the All Union Council contained four distinct denominational groups: the Baptists, who were probably most numerous at first; the Evangelical Christians; the Mennonites; and the Pentecostals. Not surprisingly, such a diverse grouping, formed more from government pressure than church desires, continues to reveal tensions and disagreements. In time most of the Mennonites withdrew, their historic pacifist leanings offended by the militaristic tone of the union. Many of the Pentecostals also withdrew, though neither they nor the Mennonites were allowed to form their own union. There was also a steady drain of strength from the Baptists to the Evangelicals. The Baptists represented a lower socioeconomic group from the Ukraine. Their leaders had lower educational attainments, stricter and more militant views on doctrines and practices, and a distinct suspicion of Moscow. The Evangelical Christians, on the other hand, represented a higher culture, a more educated and urbane constituency, and more relaxed doctrinal teachings. This group steadily increased as many Baptists came into their ranks. Clearly the government preferred that the strict Baptists decrease, preferring to deal with the more manageable Evangelicals.

Baptist statistics in the USSR. Statistical reports on Soviet Baptist mem-

47. The name has varied somewhat through the years, but to avoid confusion it seems best to use the more recent name.

bership must be taken with a large grain of salt.[48] Baptist membership in the twentieth century has been reported as low as 40 thousand and as high as 4 million. Such reports are of little value. Both the union and the government have manipulated figures when it suited their purposes to do so. Many of the Baptist and Evangelical churches are so isolated that they have never been included in any statistical survey. Among the Evangelicals, a persistent conviction has opposed even keeping a membership roll. They have felt that, since God keeps account of His own, the churches need not trouble themselves with statistics. The All Union Council report of 1966 acknowledged "the vagueness of [their] statistics" and noted that "our Brotherhood has deemed it unnecessary to keep exact count of the number of its communicants."[49]

The result is that Baptists themselves do not know how many members they have. Even if they did, it is hardly likely they would want the government to know their full strength. In 1963, for example, the president of the AUCEBC sought to downplay their growth, offering the view that they probably had only about half of the reported membership at that time. The picture is further complicated by the fact that some reports include only members of churches registered with the government, and such registered churches comprise perhaps less than half of the Baptist-Evangelical churches in the USSR. Of course, only baptized members are reported and, given age restrictions for baptism, the community of Baptist believers and regular worshipers would probably be several times as large as the baptized membership. After 1960 Soviet Evangelicals found yet another way to get around the law that restricted church membership to those over a certain age; they separated baptism from formal church membership. Thus in recent years a person, a teenager for example, could be converted and baptized and yet not be presented for official church membership for some years. This would mean a sizeable group of baptized converts who would not show up on any membership reports.

The bottom line is that nobody knows how many Baptists-Evangelicals there are in the Soviet Union. At times the government has sought to minimize their strength. Government sources reported that Baptists had declined by over 50 percent in the 1920s and that in 1961 they had only about 25 percent as many members as in 1928.[50] Other sources, however, confirm that the 1920s was a time of rapid growth; Rushbrooke, for example, reported a Baptist community of more than 3 million in the early

48. An excellent discussion of evangelical statistics in the USSR is found in William C. Fletcher and Anthony J. Strover, eds., *Religion and the Search for New Ideals in the USSR*, pp. 62-65.
49. *Documents, 1966*, p. 9.
50. Fletcher, p. 63.

1920s.[51] Despite the devastation of World War II, by 1950 Baptists again reported their usual 550,000 members, a figure which has not changed in more than thirty years. Many observers are convinced that baptized Evangelicals in the USSR may, indeed, reach the half-million mark but that the believing community greatly exceeds that figure.

Perhaps William C. Fletcher was right in saying that the Soviet government reaction to Baptists-Evangelicals is a more accurate gauge of their strength than are statistical reports.[52] The government has shown an obsessive fear of Baptists completely out of proportion to their reported numbers and has singled them out for special restrictions. In 1972 a Moscow newspaper reported "a severe outbreak" of Baptist faith among Russian youth and warned that "Baptists are particularly dangerous, for among them the laymen are also evangelists. Every Russian Baptist tries to win adherents to his faith."[53] This confirms an earlier Soviet assessment of Baptists as "the most dangerous and militant representatives of sectarianism."[54]

After a few years of relative peace, the Soviet government under Nikita Khrushchev launched a major crackdown on Baptists in 1959. The government escalated the official teaching of atheism in schools and universities, invented atheistic rituals to replace Christian ordinances, closed many churches, and made it increasingly difficult for others to register or carry on the Baptist work. In some areas, all churches but one were closed and in many cases the one church allowed to exist was reassigned to distant and isolated meeting places that meant, in effect, their death as a church. Article 227 of the revised penal code of the Russian Republic was so vaguely worded that the government could arrest and imprison virtually any minister at any time it chose.[55] At the same time, the government launched a heavy barrage of propaganda against religion and Baptists in particular.

Soviet Baptist schism. The response of the union leadership to renewed persecution provoked a schism which endures to the present. Under severe government pressure, the union leadership capitulated to most of the government's demands to curtail activities and preaching. The Union Council in 1960, led by Alexander Karev and Jacob Zhidkov, issued a list of "New Statutes" and a "Letter of Instruction" about what churches and ministers could and could not do. Apparently the letter represented a complete capitulation to the government demands. Perhaps the most serious provision was that pastors had to stop evangelizing and confine their preaching and ministry entirely to the maintenance of the present membership. Young

51. Rushbrooke, p. 143.
52. Fletcher, p. 63.
53. Cited by C. E. Bryant, "East European Baptists Still Growing," *Baptist Standard,* June 7, 1972, p. 18.
54. Klibanov, p. 279.
55. Bourdeaux, p. 12.

people were not to be taught religion, in fact were not allowed to attend church younger than the age of eighteen, and were not to be baptized until the age of thirty. All baptisms were to be discouraged and pastors had to be careful "to check unhealthy missionary tendencies."[56]

The Evangelical Christians tended to accept these restrictions and try to make the best of them; a union official even went so far as to rejoice publicly that there were fewer and fewer baptisms. The Baptists within the union, however, refused to knuckle under and that provoked the schism. The union leaders took a position of political loyalty to the government; they refused in speech or print to criticize the new restrictions. They felt they were facing reality and tried to do the best they could to keep their witness alive despite the desperate turn of events. As one put it, "If we have sugar, we will drink tea with sugar. If we have no sugar, we will drink tea without sugar." They felt it was better to keep at least some witness alive rather than to run the risk of total extinction at the hands of the atheistic government. Perhaps Ernest A. Payne put the most charitable construction upon their pronouncements, calling them "unhappily expressed and inadequately understood."[57]

A group of militant Baptists rejected the union approach as compromise with the world and formed a splinter group in 1961. At first they were called *Initsiativniki,* or the Initiative Group. Led by A. F. Prokofiev, the dissenting Baptists formed an *Orgkomitet* or Organizing Committee. They demanded that the All Union Council renounce the Letter of Instruction, acknowledge their sin of capitulation to a pagan government, and publicly repent. The All Union Council refused, and the government responded by wholesale arrests among the dissenting group. After the imprisonment of Prokofiev, Georgi Petrovich Vins became leader of the dissenting group. Born in Siberia and trained as an engineer, Vins was then pastor in Kiev. He later suffered several imprisonments and beatings, as had his father before him and his son after him, thus being a part of three generations of Baptist suffering. By 1963 the schism was complete, and the dissenting group formed their own union, the Council of Churches of Evangelical Christians-Baptists (CCECB). One of the new union's first actions was to excommunicate Zhidkov and Karev, along with several other leaders. However, it has not been recognized by the government, nor have most of its churches been allowed to register. The new group advocates a more strictly Baptist theology; some call them the Pure Baptists or Reform Baptists. Their paper, *Bratskii Listok,* provides a center of unity for the group.

At its height about 1965 the Reform Baptists represented perhaps 155,000 members, some say, but they have steadily lost support since then. By the 1980s Georgi Vins, then living in the United States, claimed 100,000 adherents for the movement, but others estimated it at much less. Since

---

56. Cited in Bourdeaux, p. 21.
57. Ernest A. Payne, *Out of Great Tribulation: Baptists in the U.S.S.R.,* p. 42.

1965 there has been a steady move from the reform group back to the main union, and that trend accelerated sharply in the 1980s.

The issues in the 1961 schism defy simple analysis. Perhaps the role of young people in the church comes close to the basic concern of 1961; the Baptists could not abide the government refusal to allow their youth to learn the gospel. But the issues go far beyond 1961. They afford a vivid reminder that the union of 1944 was artificial from the first, forced by the government, and that it yoked quite diverse denominations into an unwilling partnership. The Baptists of the Oncken heritage have never been happy in this amalgamated group, nor have they participated fully. Perhaps the release of scores of Baptists from prison in the mid 1950s brought back into the churches a new intensity that helped prepare for the schism a few years later.[58] Most of the Baptists are located in the Ukraine, and the All Council Union was from the first headquartered in Moscow and staffed mostly by Moscow leaders of a Russian heritage. Most of the All Union churches felt comfortable with open communion, Arminian theology, freedom for Mennonites to immerse or sprinkle as they preferred, and avoidance of the name Baptist as far as possible. They put less emphasis on evangelism and often delayed baptism of new converts until after a lengthy probation period. The Baptists, on the other hand, treasured their name and its heritage, preferred closed communion, more conservative doctrines generally, insisted upon immersion as the only form of baptism, and usually baptized converts promptly. They also represented a more militant stance toward the government and made rather self-righteous demands that the union leadership admit their "grievous sin" of capitulation to paganism in 1961. Many Reform Baptists have also cultivated the unfortunate habit of referring to union leaders as "mouthpieces of Satan," and warning that all who follow them will forfeit their salvation. Given these factors, one is not surprised that the schism occurred or that it has thus far proven resistant to any healing.

In 1964 the Reform Baptists complained that "they condemn us not for evil deeds or for breaking the law but for good deeds, for non-recognition of the AUCECB and its 'constitution' which destroys the church." They boldly affirmed that "the AUCECB has destroyed the church and its true servants" and claim that "hundreds of brothers and sisters suffer in prison and exile because of the AUCECB."[59] Since the early 1960s the number of Reform Baptists imprisoned in the USSR has varied from 150 to perhaps as many as 200; by 1984 about 175 were said to be imprisoned.

The AUCECB churches, meanwhile, from the first sought reconciliation and reunion with the alienated Reform Baptists. By 1963 they largely ignored the offensive Letter of Instruction and by 1966 directly repudiated

58. Fletcher, p. 66.
59. Ibid., p. 74.

it. They claimed the letter contained only suggestions for discussion and since its provisions were never adopted they carried no force. That puts the best face on a difficult situation, but unfortunately does not accord with the facts. Further, the union leaders were willing to admit "some errors and shortcomings" in 1960 but balked at repenting of "grievous sins."[60] All overtures for reconciliation were rejected by the reform group, often with blunt and unbrotherly rebuff. One wonders if the reformers wanted reunion. Repeatedly since 1884, when the Baptists had an option, they had consistently declined union with the Evangelicals. The merger of 1944 was forced upon them, and one suspects that many welcomed the occasion to resume their independent status.

However, a number of Baptist individuals and churches have returned to the union. Even Vins's church at Kiev, bellwether church of the Pure Baptists, registered with the government. The change of leadership in the course of time, which replaced those personally involved in the 1960 policies, enabled many dissenters to return. By 1984 the prospects of reunion looked bright. Over the years the union has conceded many of the reforms the Pure Baptists demanded. Some see this as an evidence of Baptist influence in the USSR, for clearly the Baptists have forced important concessions from the government. The Khrushchev crackdown, as it turned out, did not succeed and much of it had to be reversed.

The question often arises about the degree of freedom enjoyed by Baptists in the Soviet Union. The major union conducts its own public relations through the Baptist World Alliance and the World Council of Churches to convince the West that they have extensive religious liberty. In 1982 the American evangelist Billy Graham made a preaching tour of the USSR and upon his return reported that he had encountered a generous amount of religious freedom. Some harshly criticized Graham's remarks, pointing out that 170 to 180 Baptists were then in prison in Russia, others were in hiding, and countless churches had been suspended or met in secret. It appears that the registered churches of the major union, while they behave circumspectly and do not push their luck, have freedom to hold stated services. However, they are not allowed to have Sunday Schools or give open religious instruction to youth. They have a perpetual shortage of Bibles and other religious literature and are not allowed to conduct a theological seminary. For the Reform Baptists and other unregistered churches, however, life in the USSR can still be quite chancy.

Early in the twentieth century the Soviet Baptists conducted a seminary at Leningrad, but it has long since closed. For a time Russian pastors studied elsewhere in Europe, in England, or the United States; but most of those doors have also closed. Beginning in 1968, the union has been allowed to operate a correspondence training school in Moscow, to accommodate

60. *Documents, 1966*, p. 77.

up to one hundred students who study in residence about one month a year and by correspondence thereafter. At times the school has included up to two hundred, which the government has winked at, and a select few have been allowed to study abroad. The *Bratskii Vestnik (Fraternal Messenger)*, official paper of the union, contains articles of substance on theology, biblical exposition, and guidance for pastoral ministry. Unfortunately, it does not go to all the pastors. For years the Soviet government has promised to allow a theological seminary, but thus far they have balked at fulfilling the promise.

Many of the Baptists pastors in Russia are retired pensioners, though a recent trend shows younger pastors emerging, especially among the Reform Baptists. The union appoints senior presbyters over large districts, who function essentially as bishops. Some churches call their own pastors, while others are appointed by the senior presbyters. Churches must report all financial affairs to the government, and the amount of the pastor's salary is regulated by the government.

For most Baptists the church is the major source of social life. The services tend to be long, with additional meetings through the week for choir practice, band and musical ensemble work, and even church outings and picnics. The government calls church buildings "prayer houses," an apt name. The Russians make much of music, which they call the "second pulpit." Second only to their hunger for the Bible is their hunger for hymnals. Many churches have several choirs and musical groups which attract young people. Choir practice includes a time of Bible study, another way the churches get around government restrictions. The government has also had to back off from its earlier requirement that all choir and church band members be baptized members of the church, which was an effort to limit the participation of youth. The churches require all choir members to be "believers," but many are not yet baptized.

Even the Communists admit grudgingly that most Baptists live quiet, hard-working lives and that their patriotism is beyond reproach. For the most part, they reflect faithful marriages, wholesome family life, and clean-cut living that borders on Puritanism. They live sober lives in a land plagued by drunkenness; one Baptist claim is, "We however do not slop around in taverns."[61]

Many observers point out that Baptists and the Communist Party tend to appeal to the same kind of people, which may help explain the intensity of conflict between the two groups.[62] Despite their enormous advantage in control of media and money, the Communists have not succeeded in destroying religion or winning the entire populace to atheism. To make matters even worse, some nonbelievers have begun to ask why there should be

---

61. Klibanov, p. 258.
62. Fletcher, p. 81.

such intense persecution of hard-working, patriotic citizens. This fact has led to a renewed interest in religion. Of course, the government has not altered its atheistic program or goals, and Baptists realize that the government could turn on them at any moment with total extermination in mind.

Soviet Baptists-Evangelicals approach the twenty-first century with both pluses and minuses. They are divided into dissident factions, their major union includes diverse denominations, they need more trained pastors, and their need for Bibles and other Christian literature seems boundless. On the other hand, they have numerous churches, courageous leaders who bear the scars of faithful witness, the sympathetic attention of the worldwide Christian community, and what appears to be a rising tide of interest in evangelical religion in the Soviet Union. They do not lack self-confidence; a recent report noted, "It can safely be said that our Evangelical Church remains the sole exponent of apostolic Christianity in the whole world . . . and it should be their [Union leaders'] mission to be messengers of this apostolic Christianity in the West where it has been forgotten."[63]

Baptists in Europe: The Larger Picture

These sketches of Baptists in various parts of Europe have been necessarily brief, although the Soviet section seemed to require more attention. Despite their diversity, a few observations may pertain to the entire Baptist family on the Continent and serve to place them in their larger cultural and historical context.

A Minority in the Midst of Secularism

The description of Baptists as a minority in the midst of secularism might fit Baptists almost anywhere in the modern world, but it seems especially true of Europe. Most observers agree that secularism is far advanced in Western Europe and Britain and that it constitutes one of the most serious challenges to evangelical Christianity. Even persecution, which has been especially intense in parts of Eastern Europe during the twentieth century, probably does not in the long run threaten evangelical Christianity as much as secularism does. Secularism is hard to define, but it clearly differs from the atheism which constitutes the official religion of the Soviet Union. The church can confront atheism; and if history offers any guidelines, atheism meets its match in committed and believing Christian faith. Because atheism is itself a religious viewpoint, though a negative one, it may be less harmful than secularism. For the most part, modern secularism would not oppose Christianity; it would not have that much interest one way or another. In the secular context, religion is not considered dangerous, as in the Soviet Union; it is considered irrelevant. That spirit, as European Bap-

63. *Documents, 1966,* p. 28.

tists have learned, provides a more difficult field for Christian witness than hostile persecution.

Life and Work

Most European Baptist pastors are bivocational, to use an American term. Many pastors and families live in apartments within the church building itself. Few European Baptist churches have Sunday Schools or any specific Bible study-teaching programs for either children or adults; those which sponsor Sunday Schools provide only for children. Many of the churches, especially in Western Europe, have beautiful and well-appointed buildings, but whether from memories of ancient persecution or from habit, they still show a reluctance to have the name *Baptist* attached to the buildings.

A few women have been ordained to the preaching ministry among the Europeans. Of course, almost all European Baptist churches have had women deacons or deaconesses since the nineteenth century. In most areas church and state remain separate, but the relationship evolved differently and does not always match the American pattern. Many European Baptists can comfortably accept government aid for such ministries as summer camps for children and youth, programs for religious education of children in some areas, and in a few cases government supplement to the pastor's salary. In Eastern Europe separation of church and state, and separation of church and school, is spelled out most clearly in the constitutions and violated most consistently in reality. As one perceptive Baptist put it, the church is separated from the state, but the state is not separated from the church.

Faith and Order

European Baptists are doctrinally diverse. In general, one can say that Baptists in Western Europe tend to be more liberal doctrinally, while those in Eastern Europe tend to be more conservative. In the West, doctrinal issues that are familiar to Baptists in America often surface, such as the nature of biblical inspiration and authority, the role and form of baptism, open communion, the role of women in the church, the nature of salvation, and alternate understandings of eschatology. The doctrine of the church among Baptists in Western Europe usually makes room for the ecumenical vision. While Baptists in the East share some of these viewpoints, many of them prefer more conservative views.

Theological Education

Few subjects are of greater long-range concern to Baptists than a continuing supply of qualified ministers. Most of the churches in the West have pastors, and the pastors have reasonable access to theological training. Excellent seminaries exist at Hamburg, Germany; Stockholm, Sweden;

Ruschlikon, Switzerland, and elsewhere. In addition, almost every country in Western Europe has some kind of Baptist school where ministers can study. Theological books and commentaries are readily available for serious programs of self-study.

Unfortunately, comparable opportunities do not presently exist in Eastern Europe. A few countries have theological schools, but they are small, can take only a limited number of students, and most are severely restricted in who can teach and what can be taught. Some countries, like the Soviet Union, have no theological seminaries but do allow correspondence study programs for Baptists. Several of the Eastern European countries allow a select few students to study abroad. Further, theological books and commentaries are almost nonexistent in many of the lands and languages of Eastern Europe. Consequently the level of theological preparation is quite limited, and the supply of effective pastors is never adequate at a time when signs of unusual opportunity for witness appear. To compensate, the Eastern European pastors make the most of self-study, reading, and such limited group study as may exist.

Areas of Strength and Weakness

Like Baptists the world over, those in Europe reveal both strengths and weaknesses. Perhaps their greatest strengths lie in their capable lay membership and their faithful commitment to the gospel light in a dark world. They have preserved their witness against great odds, and some have suffered persecution for the cross. Their courage and constancy forms a worthy badge of discipleship.

Among the less positive aspects of European Baptist life, perhaps three stand out: the widespread failure to develop for children or adults any effective system of Bible study; lack of teaching and practice of financial stewardship; and the failure to develop, especially in Western Europe, any effective evangelistic outreach ministry. A number of their own leaders have sought to address these needs, of course, and one can hope for more effective ministries in these areas for the future.

Bibliography

The following represents a selective bibliography in Baptist studies. It is by no means complete, but does include representative examples of both primary and secondary sources used in preparation of this volume. I have also used, but have not listed separately, the innumerable minutes, annuals, proceedings, etc. which constitute the periodic reports of various Baptist groups. Neither have I listed the many Baptist newspapers in Britain, Canada, the United States, and Europe, though they form important sources for information about Baptists past and present.

The serious researcher in Baptist history will find some historical collections extremely helpful. Among these I would name the American Baptist Historical Society collection, Rochester, NY; the Southern Baptist Historical Library and Archives, Nashville, TN; the Baptist collection in the A. Webb Roberts Library, Southwestern Baptist Theological Seminary, Fort Worth, TX; the James P. Boyce Library, The Southern Baptist Theological Seminary, Louisville, KY; the Angus Collection, Regent's Park College, Oxford; the Historical Archives, Freewill Baptist College, Nashville, TN; and the European Baptist Collection, International Baptist Seminary, Ruschlikon, Switzerland; Baptist Church House, Swansea (Wales); Baptist Church House, Glasgow (Scotland); and Baptist Church House, London. I have been cordially admitted to all of these collections and have found them, and their staff members, most helpful.

Reference

Burgess, G. A. and Ward, J. T., eds. *Free Baptist Cyclopaedia, Historical and Biographical.* Boston: Free Baptist Cyclopaedia Co., 1889.

Cathcart, William, ed. *The Baptist Encyclopedia* (Philadelphia: Louis H. Everts, 1881).

Encyclopedia of Southern Baptists. 4 vols. and index. Nashville: Broadman, 1958, 1971, 1982.

Lippy, Charles H. *Bibliography of Religion in the South.* Macon, Ga: Mercer University Press, 1985.

Starr, Edward C., ed. *A Baptist Bibliography: Being a Register of Printed Material by and about Baptists; Including Works Written Against the Baptists.* 17 vols. Philadelphia: Judson Press, 1947.

Whitley, W. T., ed. *A Baptist Bibliography: Being a Register of the Chief Materials for Baptist History, Whether in Manuscript or in Print, Preserved in Great Britain, Ireland, and the Colonies (1526-1837).* 2 vols. London: Kingsgate Press, 1916-1922.

Periodicals

Baker, Robert A. "More Light on William Screven." *Journal of the South Carolina Baptist Historical Society* November 1980.

————. "The North Rocky Mount Baptist Church Decision." *Review and Expositor* January 1955.

————. "The Southern Baptist Convention, 1845-1970." *Review and Expositor* Spring 1970.

Bollen, J. D. "English-Australian Baptist Relations 1830-1860." *The Baptist Quarterly* July, 1974.

Carter, James E. "The Socioeconomic Status of Baptist Ministers in Historical Perspective." *Baptist History and Heritage* January 1980.

Clemmons, William P. "The Contributions of the Sunday School to Southern Baptist Churches." *Baptist History and Heritage* January 1984.

Deweese, Charles W. "Deaconesses in Baptist History." *Baptist History and Heritage* January 1977.

Eskew, Harry L. "Southern Baptist Contributions to Hymnody." *Baptist History and Heritage* January 1984.

Estep, William R. "Anabaptists and the Rise of English Baptists." *The Quarterly Review* October-December, 1968; January-March, 1969.

Forbis, Wesley L. "The Sunday School Board and Baptist Church Music." *Baptist History and Heritage* January 1984.

Garrett, James Leo. "Restitution and Dissent Among Early English Baptists." *Baptist History and Heritage* April 1978.

Grijalva, Joshua. "The Story of Hispanic Southern Baptists." *Baptist History and Heritage* July 1983.

Halbrooks, G. Thomas. "Growing Pains: The Impact of Expansion on Southern Baptists Since 1942." *Baptist History and Heritage* July 1982.

Handy, Robert T. "American Baptist Polity: What's Happening and Why." *Baptist History and Heritage* July 1979.

Hayden, Roger. "Kettering 1792 and Philadelphia 1814." *Baptist Quarterly* 2 parts January 1965 and April 1965.

————. "William Staughton: Baptist Educator and Missionary Advocate." *Foundations* January-March, 1967.

Hays, Kenneth E. "A Statistical Report on Southern Baptists." *Quarterly Review* January-March 1984.

Howe, Claude L. "William Newton Clarke: Systematic Theologian of Theological Liberalism." *Foundations* April 1963.

Hudson, Winthrop S. "Baptist Were Not Anabaptists." *The Chronicle* October 1953.

————. "Stumbling into Disorder." *Foundations* April 1958.

Jenks, Philip E. "In SCODS We Trusted." *American Baptist Quarterly* December 1983.

Jennings, Ray. "The Biennial as 'Family Gathering.' " *American Baptist Quarterly* December 1983.

Kingdon, D. P. "Irish Baptists and the Revival of 1859." *Irish Baptist Historical Society Journal* 1968-1969.

Kliever, Lonnie D. "General Baptist Origins: The Question of Anabaptist Influence." *The Mennonite Quarterly Review* October 1962.

Kung, Peter. "The Story of Asian Southern Baptists." *Baptist History and Heritage* July 1983.

Langley, Arthur S. "Seventeenth Century Baptist Disputes." *Transactions of the Baptist Historical Society* 5: 1916-1917.

Laws, Curtis Lee. "As to Union with the Disciples." *Watchman-Examiner* July 15, 1929.

Mallard, Ian. "The Hymns of Katherine Sutton." *The Baptist Quarterly* January 1963.

Maring, Norman H. "Notes from Religious Journals." *Foundations* July 1958.

Martin, Hugh. "The Baptist Contributions to Early English Hymnody." *The Baptist Quarterly* January 1962.

Mattingly, Terry. "Old Baptists, New Baptists: A Reporter Looks at the Battle to Control the SBC." *Southwestern Journal of Theology* Summer 1986.

May, Lynn E., Jr. "The Emerging Role of Sunday Schools in Southern Baptist Life to 1900." *Baptist History and Heritage* January 1984.

McBeth, Leon. "Baptist Fundamentalism: A Cultural Interpretation." *Baptist History and Heritage* July 1978.

————. "Expansion of the Southern Baptist Convention to 1951." *Baptist History and Heritage* July 1982.

————. "Fundamentalism in the Southern Baptist Convention in Recent Years." *Review and Expositor* Winter 1982.

————. "The Ordination of Women." *Review and Expositor* Fall 1982.

————. "Origin of the Christian Life Commission." *Baptist History and Heritage* October 1966.

————. "Southern Baptists and Race Since 1947." *Baptist History and Heritage* July 1972.

McElrath, Hugh T. "Turning Points in the Story of Baptist Church Music." *Baptist History and Heritage* January 1984.

McMullan, R. C. "Baptist Education in Ireland." *Irish Baptist Historical Society Journal* 1970-1971.

Mosteller, James D. "Baptists and Anabaptists." *The Chronicle* January 1957; July 1957.

Oakley, I. J. W. "A History of the Baptist Irish Society." *Irish Baptist Historical Society Journal* 1970-1971.

Patterson, W. Morgan. "The Influence of Landmarkism Among Baptists." *Baptist History and Heritage* January 1975.

Payne, Ernest A. "Contacts Between Mennonites and Baptists." *Foundations* January 1961.

————. "Who Were the Baptists?" *The Baptist Quarterly* October 1956.

Picarilli, Robert E. "A Study of Separate, Free Will, Baptist Origins, in Middle Tennessee." *Baptist Quarterly* January-March 1977.

Pierce, Earle V. "Northern Baptist Foreign Missions—Part I." *Watchman-Examiner* August 19, 1943.

————. "Northern Baptist Foreign Missions—Part II." *Watchman-Examiner* August 26, 1943.

Pousett, Gordon H. "Formative Influence on Baptists in British Columbia, 1876-1918." *Baptist History and Heritage* April 1980.

Reynolds, William J. "The Graded Choir Movement Among Southern Baptists." *Baptist History and Heritage* January 1984.

Riley, W. B. "The Foreign Mission Board Controversy." *Watchman-Examiner* November 15, 1943.

————. "To All Baptists Who Believe the Bible to Be God's Word." *Watchman-Examiner* November 19, 1925.

Routh, Porter. "Ordination—Contemporary Problems." *Southwestern Journal of Theology* Spring 1969.

Shurden, Walter B. "The Pastor as Denominational Theologian." *Baptist History and Heritage* July 1980.

————. "The Southern Baptist Synthesis: Is It Cracking?" *Baptist History and Heritage* April, 1981.

Smith, Sid. "In Search of The First Black Baptist Church in America." *Ethnicity* Spring 1984.

Stanley, Brian. "Spurgeon and the Baptist Missionary Society, 1863-1866." *The Baptist Quarterly* July 1982.

Stassen, Glen H. "Anabaptist Influence in the Origin of the Particular Baptists." *The Mennonite Quarterly Review* October 1962.

Stell, C. F. "The Eastern Association of Baptist Churches, 1775-1782." *The Baptist Quarterly* January 1977.

Stubblefield, Jerry M. "Creative Advancements in Southern Baptist Sunday School Work." *Baptist History and Heritage* January 1984.

Taulman, James E. "The Life and Writings of Amos Cooper Dayton 1813-1865." *Baptist History and Heritage* January 1975.

Thompson, Joshua. "The Origin of the Irish Baptist Foreign Mission." *The Irish Baptist Historical Society Journal* 1969-1970.

Tonks, A. Ronald. "Highlight of the Relationships of Southern Baptists With Canadian Baptists." *Baptist History and Heritage* April 1980.

White, B. R. "The Organization of the Particular Baptists, 1644-1660." *Journal of Ecclesiastical History* October 1966.

———. "Thomas Patient in England and Ireland." *Irish Baptist Historical Society Journal* 1969-1970.

Whitley, W. T. "Leonard Busher Dutchman." *Transactions of the Baptist Historical Society* 1908-1909.

Primary

An Apology of some call'd Anabaptists, in and about the city of London, in behalf of themselves and others of the same judgment with them. London: 1660.

Asplund, John, ed. *The Annual Register of the Baptist Denomination in North America.* 1790-1794. New York: Arno Press, 1980. First published 1794.

Babcock, Rufus, ed. *Memoir of John Mason Peck.* Carbondale: Southern Illinois University Press, 1965.

Baker, Robert A., ed. *A Baptist Source Book.* Nashville: Broadman Press, 1966.

Barber, Edward. *To the Kings Majesty: The Petition of Many of His Subjects, Some of Which Having Beene Miserably Persecuted.* London: n.p., 1641.

Barrows, C. Edwin, ed. *The Diary of John Comer.* Philadelphia: American Baptist Publication Society, 1892.

Behold a Cry; or, a true relation of the unhuman and violent outrages of divers Soldiers, Constables and others, practiced upon many of the Lord's people, commonly, tho' falsely called Anabaptists, at their several meetings in and about London. London: 1662.

Belcher, Joseph, ed. *The Complete Works of the Rev. Andrew Fuller.* 3 vols. Philadelphia: American Baptist Publication Society, 1845.

Berry, W. J., comp. *The Kehuckee Declaration and Black Rock Address, with Other Writings Relative to the Baptist Separation between 1825-1840.* Elon College, N.C.: Primitive Publications, n.d.

Blackwood, Christopher. *Apostolicall Baptisme, or, a sober rejoinder to a treatise by Thomas Blake, intituled, Infants baptisme freed from Antichristianisme.* London: 1645.

———. *The Storming of Antichrist, in His Two Last and Strongest Garrisions: of Compulsion of Conscience and Infants Baptisme.* London: n.p., 1644.

Booth, Abraham. *Commerce in the Human Species.* London: n.p., 1792.

Brackney, William H., ed. *Baptist Life and Thought: 1600-1980.* Valley Forge: Judson Press, 1983.

———. *Dispensations of Providence: The Journal and Selected Letters of Luther Rice, 1803-1830.* Rochester, New York: American Baptist Historical Society, 1984.

Briggs, John H. Y. *Signs of Hope: The Report of the Denominational Enquiry Group.* London: Baptist Union, 1979.

Brown, Thomas B., Stillman, Paul, and Hull, Nathan V. *An Address to the Baptist Denomination of the United States on the Observance of the Sabbath.* New York: J. Winchester, New World Press, 1843.

Bryan, G. McLeod, ed. *Documents Concerning Baptism and Church Membership: A Controversy among North Carolina Baptists.* No place of publication named: Association of Baptist Professors of Religion, 1977.

Bunyan, John. *Complete Works.* Philadelphia: J. W. Bradley, 1861.

Busher, Leonard. *Religions Peace; or a plea for liberty of conscience.* No place of publication: n.p., 1614.

Cheyney, Edward P., ed. *Readings in English History Drawn from the Original Sources.* New York: Ginn and Company, 1922.

Clarke, John. *Ill Newes from New-England: or a Narrative of New-England's Persecution.* London: 1652.

Collier, Thomas. *A General Epistle to the Universal Church of the First-Born.* London: n.p., 1652.

_____. *The Glory of Christ and the Ruine of Antichrist.* No place of publication: n.p., 1647.

_____. *The Marrow of Christianity,* London: 1647.

_____. *The Works of Thomas Collier, Preacher in the West of England.* No editor indicated. London: n.p., 1652.

Collins, Hercules. *The Temple Repair'd: or, An Essay to revive the long-neglected Ordinances, or exercising the spiritual Gift of Prophecy for the Edification of the Churches; and of ordaining Ministers duly qualified.* London: Printed for William and Joseph Marshal, 1702.

Cotton, John. *The Bloudy Tenent Washed and Made White in the Bloud of the Lamb.* London: n.p., 1647.

Crisp, Tobias. *Christ Alone Exalted: Being the Compleat Works of Tobias Crisp.* London: 1690.

Delaune, Thomas, *A Narrative of the Sufferings of Tho. Delaune.* No place of publication: n.p., 1684.

_____. *A Plea for Nonconformists.* No place of publication: n.p., 1684.

Denne, Henry. *The Quaker No Papist.* London: Printed by Francis Smith, 1659.

Documents of Moscow, 1966. All Union Conference of Evangelical Christian-Baptists, 1966.

Edwards, Morgan. *Customs of Primitive Churches.* No place of publication: n.p., 1774.

_____. *Materials Towards a History of Baptists.* 2 vols. Danielsville, Georgia: Heritage Papers, 1984. Prepared by Eva B. Weeks and Mary B. Warren.

Edwards, Thomas. *The casting down of the last and strongest hold of Satan, or a treatise against toleration and pretended liberty of conscience.* London: 1647.

_____. *Gangraena: or a Catalogue of Many of the Errours, Heresies and Pernicious Practices of the Sectaries of this Time.* London: Printed for Ralph Smith, 1646.

Featley, Daniel. *The Dippers dipt. or, The Anabaptists Dunk'd and Plung'd Over Head and Eares.* London: 1645.

_____. *A Warning for England, especially for London, in the famous history of the frantick Anabaptists.* London: n.p., 1647.

First Annual Report of the Baptist Board of Foreign Missions. Philadelphia: n.p., 1815.

Fuller, Andrew. *The Atonement of Christ, and the Justification of the Sinner.* New York: American Tract Society, 1854.

Fuller, Richard, and Wayland, Francis. *Domestic Slavery Considered As a Scriptural Institution.* New York: Lewis Colby, 1845.

Gaustad, Edwin S., ed. *A Documentary History of Religion in America Since 1865.* Grand Rapids: William B. Eerdmans, 1983.

Gee, Henry, and Hardy, William J. *Documents Illustrative of English Church History.* London: Macmillan and Company, 1892.

Gill, John. *A Body of Doctrinal Divinity.* 3 vols. London: Printed for the author, 1769.

Gillette, A. D., ed. *Minutes of the Philadelphia Baptist Association, From A. D. 1707 to A. D. 1807.* Philadelphia: American Baptist Publication Society, 1851.

Grantham, Thomas. *Christianismus Primitivus.* London: n.p., 1678.

_____. *The Loyal Baptist, or an apology for the baptized believers.* London: Thomas Fabian, 1674.

_____. *The Successors of the Apostles.* London: n.p., 1674.

Graves, J. R. *Old Landmarkism: What is It?* Texarkana: Baptist Sunday School Committee, 1928 ed.

_____. *The Trilemma; or Death by Three Horns.* Memphis: J. R. Graves & Son, 1890.

Greene, L. F., ed. *The Writings of the Late Elder John Leland.* New York: G. W. Wood, 1845.

Hayden, Roger, ed. *Baptist Union Documents 1948-1977.* London: Baptist Historical Society, 1980.

_____. *The Records of a Church of Christ in Bristol 1640 to 1687.* Bristol: Bristol Record Society, 1974.

Heart-Bleedings for Professors Abominations, By the Churches of Christ in London, Baptized. London: for Francis Tyton, 1650.

Helwys, Thomas. *A Short Declaration of the Mistery of Iniquity.* London: n.p., 1612. Reprinted by Kingsgate Press, London, 1935.

Jessey, Henry. *The Lord's Loud Call to England.* London: Printed for Francis Smith, 1660.

Keach, Benjamin. *Antichrist Stormed.* London: n.p., 1689.

_____. *Distressed Zion Relieved.* London: Printed for Nath. Crouch, 1689.

Lumpkin, William L., ed. *Baptist Confessions of Faith.* Valley Forge: Judson Press, 1959.

McLoughlin, William G., ed. *Issaac Backus on Church, State, and Calvinism: Pamphlets, 1754-1789.* Cambridge, Mass.: Harvard University Press, 1968.

_____. *The Diary of Isaac Backus.* 3 vols. Providence: Brown University Press, 1979.

Mode, Peter G., ed. *Source Book and Bibliographical Guide for American Church History.* Boston: J. S. Canner and Company, Inc., 1964.

Narrative of the General Assembly in London, 1689. No publication data. Available in Angus Collection, Regent's Park College, Oxford University.

Nettles, Tom J. *Baptist Catechisms.* Fort Worth: For the author, 1982.

Nordenhaug, Josef, ed. *The Truth that Makes Men Free: Official Report of the Eleventh Congress, Baptist World Alliance, 1965.* Nashville: Broadman Press, 1966.

Owen, J. M. G., ed. *Records of an Old Association.* No place or publisher named, n.d.

Parker, Daniel. *Views on the Two Seeds.* Vandalia, Ill.: Robert Blackwell, 1826. Republished by S. L. and S. J. Clark, 1923.

Pendleton, J. M. *An Old Landmark Re-Set.* Fulton, Ken.: National Baptist Publishing House, 1899.

Proceedings of the Baptist Convention for Missionary Purposes. Philadelphia: n.p., 1814.

Proceedings of the Convention Held in the City of New York for the Formation of the American Baptist Home Mission Society. 1832.

Records of the Welsh Tract Baptist Meeting. Two Parts. Wilmington: The Historical Society of Delaware, 1904.

Richardson, Samuel. *The Necessity of Toleration in matters of Religion: or, Certain questions propounded to the Synod, tending to prove that Corporall Punishments ought not to be inflicted upon such as hold Errors in Religion, and that in matters of Religion men ought not to be compelled, but have liberty and freedom.* London: n.p., 1647.

_____. *Some Brief Considerations on Doctor Featley His Book, intituled, The Dipper Dipt.* London: n.p., 1645.

Robinson, John. *An Answer to a Censorious Epistle.* No place of publication: n.p., 1610.

Second Annual Report of the Baptist Board of Missions. Philadelphia: n.p., 1816.

Shurden, Walter B., ed. *The Life of Baptists in the Life of the World.* Nashville: Broadman Press, 1985.

Skepp, John. *Divine Energy: or the efficacious Operations of the Spirit of God upon the Soul of Man.* London: n.p., 1815.

Smith, Shelton H., Handy, Robert T., and Loetscher, Lefferts A., eds. *American Christianity: An Historical Interpretation with Representative Documents.* 2 vols. New York: Charles Scribner's Sons, 1960.

Smyth, John. *The Character of the Beast of the False Constitution of the Church,* 1609.

_____. *The Last Booke of John Smyth, Called the Retractions of His Errours, and the Confirmation of the Truth.*

Spurgeon, Charles Haddon. *The "Down Grade" Controversy: Collected Materials Which Reveal the Viewpoint of the Late Charles Haddon Spurgeon.* Pasadena, Tex.: Pilgrim Publications, n.d.

Stealey, Sydnor L., ed. *A Baptist Treasury.* New York: Thomas Y. Crowell Company, 1958.

Stovel, Charles. *The Duty of the Church in Relation to the Evils of Intemperance.* London: n.p., 1859.

_____. *The Sin of Exacting Excessive Labour.* London: n.p., 1852.

Sweet, William Warren, ed. *Religion on the American Frontier: The Baptists 1783-1830.* New York: Cooper Square Publishers, Inc., 1964.

Taylor, Dan. *A Dissertation on Singing in the Worship of God.* London: Printed for the author, 1786.

Taylor, John. *Thoughts on Missions.* No place of publication: n.p., 1820.

Taylor, Michael H. *A Plain Man's Guide to the Incarnation.* No place of publication: n.p., 1971.

The Clergyes Bill of Complaint. Oxford: Leonard Lichfield, 1643.

Tombes, John. *The Ancient Bounds: or liberty of conscience tenderly stated, modestly asserted, and mildly vindicated.* London: n.p., 1645.

_____. *Saints no smiters; or smiting the civil powers not the work of saints.* London: n.p., 1664.

Transcript of Minutes and Records of Formation of Baptist Bible Fellowship, May 1950, stenographically recorded by Miss Jerry Hayles.

Trestrail, Fred. *The Past and Present.* London: n.p., 1884.

Truett, George W. *Baptists and Religious Liberty.* Nashville: Sunday School Board of the Southern Baptist Convention, 1920.

Underhill, Edward Bean, ed. *The Records of a Church of Christ Meeting in Broadmead.* Bristol: n.p., 1640-1687.

_____. *Records of the Churches of Christ gathered at Fenstanton, Warboys, and Hexam, 1644-1720.* London: Haddon, Brothers and Company, 1854.

_____. *Tracts on Liberty of Conscience, 1614-1661.* London: J. Haddon, 1846.

White, B. R., ed. *Association Records of the Particular Baptists of England, Wales and Ireland to 1660.* London: The Baptist Historical Society, 1974.

Whitley, William T., ed. *Minutes of the General Assembly of the General Baptist Churches in England.* 2 vols. London: Kingsgate Press, 1909.

_____. ed. *The Works of John Smyth.* 2 vols. Cambridge: University Press, 1915.

Williams, Roger. *The Bloudy Tenent Yet More Bloudy.* London: Printed for Giles Calvert, 1652.

_____. *The Bloudy Tenent of Persecution for Cause of Conscience Discussed in a Conference Between Peace and Truth.* London: n.p., 1644. Edited and reprinted by Edward Bean Underhill. London: J. Haddon, 1848.

_____. *Christenings make not Christians.* London: Printed for Iane Coe, 1645; included in *The Complete Writings of Roger Williams.* 7 vols. Perry Miller, ed. New York: Russell and Russell, Inc., 1963.

_____. *Mr. Cottons Letter Lately Printed, Examined and Answered.* London: n.p., 1644.

Winthrop's Journal: History of New England 1630-1649. 2 vols. Edited by James K. Hosmer. New York: Charles Scribner's Sons, 1908.

Secondary

Allen, Catherine B. *The New Lottie Moon Story.* Nashville, Broadman Press, 1980.

Alley, Reuben Edward. *A History of Baptists in Virginia.* Richmond: Virginia Baptist General Board, 1973.

Armitage, Thomas. *A History of the Baptists: Traced by Their Vital Principles and Practices from the Time of Our Lord and Saviour Jesus Christ to the Year 1886.* New York: Bryan, Taylor, and Co., 1887.

Backus, Isaac. *A History of New England with Particular Reference to the Denomination of Christians Called Baptists.* 2 vols. Newton: Massachusetts, 1871.

Bacon, Ernest W. *Spurgeon, Heir of the Puritans.* Grand Rapids: William B. Eerdmans Publishing Company, 1968.

Baker, Robert A. *The Blossoming Desert: A Concise History of Texas Baptists.* Waco: Word Books, 1970.

_____. *The First Southern Baptists.* Nashville: Broadman Press, 1966.

_____. *Relations Between Northern and Southern Baptists.* Fort Worth: Evans Press, 1948.

_____. *The Southern Baptist Convention and Its People 1607-1972.* Nashville: Broadman Press, 1974.

_____. *The Story of the Sunday School Board.* Nashville: Convention Press, 1966.

_____. *Tell The Generations Following: A History of Southwestern Baptist Theological Seminary 1908-1983.* Nashville: Broadman Press, 1983.

_____. *The Thirteenth Check: Jubilee History of the Annuity Board of the Southern Baptist Convention.* Nashville: Broadman Press, 1968.

Baker, Robert A. and Craven, Jr., Paul J. *Adventure in Faith: The First 300 Years of First Baptist Church, Charleston, South Carolina.* Nashville: Broadman Press, 1982.

Barnes, William Wright. *The Southern Baptist Convention: 1845-1953.* Nashville: Broadman Press, 1954.

Bartlett, Billy Vick. *The Beginnings: A Pictorial History of the Baptist Bible Fellowship.* Springfield, Mo.: Baptist Bible College, 1975.

Bassett, Thomas Myrfin. *The Welsh Baptists.* Swansea: Ilston House, 1977.

Beaver, R. Pierce. *All Loves Excelling: American Protestant Women in World Missions.* Grand Rapids: William B. Eerdmans, 1968.

Beers, G. Pitt. *Ministry to Turbulent America: A History of the American Baptist Home Mission Society Covering its Fifth Quarter Century, 1932-1957.* Philadelphia: Judson Press, 1957.

Belcher, Joseph, et al., *The Baptist Irish Society; its Origin, History, and Prospects: with an outline of the Ecclesiastical History of Ireland, and a Lecture, enforcing its claims on the Sympathy and Efforts of Christians in England.* London: Printed for the Baptist Irish Society, 1845.

Benedict, David. *A General History of the Baptist Denomination in America and Other Parts of the World.* 2 vols. Boston: Lincoln and Edmands, 1813.

_____. *Fifty Years Among the Baptists.* Glen Rose, Tex.: Newman and Collins, 1913.

Bloomfield, W. E. *The Baptists of Yorkshire.* London: Kingsgate Press, 1912.

Bogard, Ben M. *The Baptist Way-Book.* Texarkana: Bogard Press, 1946.

Bollen J. D. *Australian Baptists: A Religious Minority.* London: Baptist Historical Society, 1975.

Bourdeaux, Michael. *Religious Ferment in Russia.* London: Macmillan, 1968.

Broadus, John A. *Memoir of James Petigru Boyce.* Nashville: Sunday School Board, 1927.

Bronson, Walter C. *The History of Brown University, 1764-1914.* Providence: Brown University, 1914.

Brown, Basil S. *Members One of Another: The Baptist Union of Victoria 1862-1962.* Melbourne: Baptist Union of Victoria, 1962.

Brown, J. Newton. *History of the American Baptist Publication Society, from its Origin in 1824 to 1856.* Philadelphia: American Baptist Publication Society, n.d.

Brown, John. *The Stundists: The Story of a Great Religious Revolt.* London: James Clarke & Co., Fleet Street, 1893.

Brown, Louis Fargo. *Baptists and the Fifth Monarchy Men in England.* Oxford: University Press, 1912.

Browne, Benjamin P. *Tales of Baptist Daring.* Philadelphia: Judson Press, 1961.

Burkitt, Lemuel, and Read, Jesse. *A Concise History of the Kehukee Baptist Association.* Halifax: A Hodge, 1803.

Burgess, Walter H. *John Smyth the Se-Baptist, Thomas Helwys and the First Baptist Church in England.* London: James Clarke & Co., 1911.

Burrage, Champlin. *The Early English Dissenters in the Light of Recent Research.* 2 vols. New York: Russell and Russell, 1967. First published 1912.

Burrage, Henry S. *Baptist Hymn Writers and Their Hymns.* Portland, Me.: Brown Thurston & Company, 1888.

Burton, Joe W. *Road to Augusta: R. C. B. Howell and the Formation of the Southern Baptist Convention.* Nashville: Broadman Press, 1976.

Bush, L. Russ and Nettles, Tom J. *Baptists and the Bible.* Chicago: Moody Press, 1980.

Capp, B. S. *The Fifth Monarchy Men.* Totowa, N.J.: Rowman and Littlefield, 1972.

Carey, S. P. *William Carey.* Philadelphia: Judson Press, 1923.

Carroll, B. H., Jr. *The Genesis of American Anti-Missionism.* Louisville: Baptist Book Concern, 1902.

Carroll, J. M. *A History of Texas Baptists.* Dallas: Baptist Standard Publishing Co., 1923.

————. *Texas Baptist Statistics.* Houston: J. J. Pastoriza, 1895.

————. *The Trail of Blood.* Lexington, Ken.: Ashland Avenue Baptist Church, 1931.

Cauthen, Baker James. *Advance: A History of Southern Baptist Foreign Missions.* Nashville: Broadman Press, 1970.

Chiminelli, Peter. *The Baptists in Italy: Their History and Work.* Nashville: Sunday School Board of the Southern Baptist Convention, 1923.

Clarke, William Newton. *Sixty Years with the Bible.* New York: Charles Scribners, 1909.

Clements, K. W., ed. *Baptists in the Twentieth Century.* London: Baptist Historical Society, 1983.

Clifford, J. Ayson. *A Handful of Grain: The Centenary History of the Baptist Union of New Zealand.* 2: 1882-1914. Wellington: New Zealand Baptist Historical Society, 1982.

Cole, Stewart G. *History of Fundamentalism.* New York: Richard R. Smith, Inc., 1931.

Combs, James O., ed. *The Roots and Origins of Baptist Fundamentalism.* Springfield: John the Baptist Press, 1984.

Compolo, Anthony. *A Denomination Looks at Itself.* Valley Forge: Judson Press, 1971.

Cook, Henry. *What Baptists Stand For.* London: Carey Kingsgate Press, 1958.

Cox, F. A. and Hoby, J. *The Baptists in America.* New York: Leavitt, Lord and Co., 1836.

Crosby, Thomas. *The History of the English Baptists.* 4 vols. London: n.p., 1738-1740.

Davidson, William F. *An Early History of Free Will Baptists 1727-1830.* Nashville: Randall House Publications, 1974.

————. *The Free Will Baptists in America 1727-1984.* Nashville: Randall House Publications, 1985.

Davies, Horton. *Worship and Theology in England.* Princeton: Princeton University Press, 1961.

Davis, Lawrence B. *Immigrants, Baptists, and the Protestant Mind in America.* Chicago: University of Chicago Press, 1973.

Dawson, Joseph M. *Baptists and the American Republic.* Nashville: Broadman Press, 1956.

Day, Richard Ellsworth. *The Shadow of the Broad Brim.* Philadelphia: The Judson Press, 1934.

Devin, Robert I. *A History of Grassy Creek Baptist Church.* Raleigh: Edward Broughton and Company, 1880.

Dexter, Henry Martyn. *As to Roger Williams, and his 'Banishment' from Massachusetts Plantation.* Boston: Congregational Publishing Society, 1876.

_____. *The True Story of John Smyth.* Boston: Lee and Shepard, 1881.

Dilday, Russell H., Jr. *The Doctrine of Biblical Authority.* Nashville: Convention Press, 1982.

Dodd, Damon C. *The Free Will Baptist Story.* Nashville: National Association of Free Will Baptists, 1956.

Edgar, S. L. *A Handful of Grain: The Centenary History of the Baptist Union of New Zealand.* 4: 1945-1982. Wellington: New Zealand Baptist Historical Society, 1982.

Eighmy, John Lee. *Churches in Cultural Captivity: A History of the Social Attitudes of Southern Baptists.* Knoxville: University of Tennessee Press, 1972.

Elliott, L. R., ed. *Centennial Story of Texas Baptists.* Dallas: Baptist General Convention of Texas, 1936.

Ellis, William E. *A Man of Books and a Man of the People: E. Y. Mullins and the Crisis of Moderate Southern Baptist Leadership.* Macon, Ga.: Mercer University Press, 1985.

Ernst, James. *Roger Williams: New England Firebrand.* New York: The Macmillan Company, 1932.

Estep, William R. *The Anabaptist Story.* Nashville: Broadman Press, 1963.

_____., ed. *The Lord's Free People in a Free Land: Essays in Baptist History in Honor of Robert A. Baker.* Fort Worth: Evans Press, 1976.

Evans, B. *The Early English Baptists.* 2 vols. London: J. Heaton & Son, 1862-1864.

Fitts, Leroy. *A History of Black Baptists.* Nashville: Broadman Press, 1985.

_____. *Lott Carey: First Black Missionary to Africa.* Valley Forge: Judson Press, 1978.

Fletcher, Jesse C. *Bill Wallace of China.* Nashville: Broadman Press, 1963.

Fletcher, William C. and Strover, Anthony J., eds. *Religion and the Search for New Ideals in the USSR.* New York: Frederick A. Praeger, 1967.

Foss, A. T. and Matthews, E. *Facts for Baptist Churches.* Utica: American Baptist Free Mission Society, 1850.

Frost, James M. *The Sunday School Board of the Southern Baptist Convention: Its History and Work.* Nashville: Sunday School Board, n.d.

Furman, Wood. *A History of the Charleston Association of Baptist Churches in the State of South Carolina.* Charleston: J. Hoff, 1811.

Gardner, Robert G. *Baptists of Early America: A Statistical History, 1639-1790.* Atlanta: Georgia Baptist Historical Society, 1983.

Garrett, James Leo and Hinson, E. Glenn. *Are Southern Baptists "Evangelicals"?* Macon, Ga.: Mercer University Press, 1983.

Gaustad, Edwin S., ed. *Baptist Piety: The Last Will and Testimony of Obadiah Holmes.* Grand Rapids: William B. Eerdmans, 1978.

George, Timothy. *John Robinson and the English Separatist Tradition.* Macon, Ga.: Mercer University Press, 1982.

Gilbert, Alan D. *The Making of Post-Christian Britain.* London: Longman House, 1980.

Gilmore, Alex, ed. *The Pattern of the Church.* London: Lutterworth Press, 1963.

Goen, Clarence C. *Revivalism and Separatism in New England, 1740-1800.* New Haven: Yale University Press, 1962.

Greaves, Richard L. *John Bunyan.* Grand Rapids: William B. Eerdmans Publishing Company, 1969.

Grijalva, Joshua. *A History of the Mexican Baptists in Texas 1881-1981.* Dallas: Baptist General Convention of Texas, 1982.

Guild, Reuben A. *Chaplain Smith and the Baptists.* Philadelphia: American Baptist Publication Society, 1885.

_____. *Life, Times, and Correspondence of James Manning, and the Early History of Brown University.* Boston: Gould and Lincoln, 1864.

Harrison, Paul M. *Authority and Power in the Free Church Tradition.* Princeton: Princeton University Press, 1959.

Hartshorne, Hugh and Froyd, Milton C., eds. *Theological Education in the Northern Baptist Convention.* Philadelphia: Judson Press, 1945.

Hayden, Roger. *William Staughton: Baptist Educator, Missionary Advocate and Pastor.* London: Baptist Union Library, 1965.

Hester, H. I. *Southern Baptists in Christian Education.* Murfreesboro, N.C.: Chowan College School of Graphic Arts, 1968.

Himbury, D. Mervyn. *British Baptists: A Short History.* London: Carey Kingsgate Press Limited, 1962.

Hinson, E. Glenn. *A History of Baptists in Arkansas, 1818-1978.* Little Rock: Arkansas Baptist State Convention, 1979.

Hiscox, Edward T. *The New Directory for Baptist Churches.* Philadelphia: American Baptist Publication Society, 1894.

Hocking, William E. *Re-Thinking Missions: A Laymen's Inquiry after One Hundred Years.* New York: Harper and Brother, 1932.

Hood, Roland P. *Southern Baptist Work in Canada.* Portland: Baptist General Convention of Oregon-Washington, 1968.

Hopewell, William J. *The Missionary Emphasis of the General Association of Regular Baptist Churches.* Chicago: Regular Baptist Press, 1963.

Hovey, Alvah. *A Memoir of the Life and Times of the Reverend Isaac Backus.* Boston: Gould and Lincoln, 1859.

Howe, Claude L. *Glimpses of Baptist Heritage.* Nashville: Broadman Press, 1981.

Hudson, Winthrop S., ed. *Baptist Concepts of the Church.* Chicago: Judson Press, 1959.

_____. *Religion in America.* 3rd ed. New York: Charles Scribner's Sons, 1981.

Hudson-Reed, Sydney, ed. *Together for a Century: The History of the Baptist Union of South Africa 1877-1977.* Pietermaritzburg: South Africa Baptist Historical Society, n.d.

Hughes, H. Estcourt. *Our First Hundred Years: The Baptist Church of South Australia.* Adelaide, Australia: South Australian Baptist Union, 1937.

Hunt, Alma. *History of Woman's Missionary Union.* Nashville: Convention Press, 1964.

Hyatt, Irwin T., Jr. *Our Ordered Lives Confess.* Cambridge: Harvard University Press, 1976.

Ivimey, Joseph. *A History of the English Baptists.* 4 vols. London: Printed for the author, 1811.

Jackson, Joseph H. *Unholy Shadows and Freedom's Holy Light.* Nashville: Townsend Press, 1967.

James, Charles F. *Documentary History of the Struggle for Religious Liberty in Virginia.* Lynchburg, Va.: J. P. Bell Company, 1900.

John, Mansel, ed. *Welsh Baptist Studies.* Llandysul: Gomer Press, 1976.

Jordan, Lewis G. *Negro Baptist History, U.S.A.* Nashville: Sunday School Publishing Board, N.B.C., 1930.

Jordan, Wilbur K. *The Development of Religious Toleration in England.* 4 vols. London: George Allen and Unwin Ltd., 1932-1940.

King, Henry Melville. *The Baptism of Roger Williams.* Providence: Preston and Rounds, 1897.

King, Joe M. *A History of South Carolina Baptists.* Columbia: General Board of the South Carolina Baptist Convention, 1964.

Kirkwood, Dean R. *European Baptists: A Magnificent Minority.* New York: Houghton Mifflin Company, 1972.

Klibanov, A. I. *History of Religious Sectarianism in Russia, 1860s-1917.* Ethel Dunn, trans. Elmsford, N.Y.: Pergamon Press, 1982.

Latch, Ollie. *History of the General Baptists.* Poplar Bluff, Mo: The General Baptist Press, 1954.

Lawrence, J. B. *History of the Home Mission Board.* Nashville: Broadman Press, 1958.

Lerrigo, Peter Hughes James, ed. *Northern Baptists Rethink Missions: A Study of the Report of the Layman's Foreign Missions Inquiry.* New York: Baptist Board of Education, Department of Missionary Education, 1933.

Levy, George E. *The Baptists of the Maritime Provinces, 1753-1946.* St. John, New Brunswick: Barnes-Hopkins, Ltd., 1946.

Little, Lewis P. *Imprisoned Preachers and Religious Liberty in Virginia.* Lynchburg, Va.: J. P. Bell Company, Inc., 1938.

Looney, Floyd. *History of California Southern Baptists.* Fresno: Board of Directors of The Southern Baptist General Convention of California, 1954.

Lord, F. Townley. *Achievement: A Short History of the Baptist Missionary Society, 1792-1942.* London: The Carey Press, 1942.

_____. *Baptist World Fellowship: A Short History of the Baptist World Alliance.* Nashville: Broadman Press, 1955.

Lumpkin, William L. *Baptist Foundations in the South.* Nashville: Broadman Press, 1961.

_____. *A History of Immersion.* Nashville, Tennessee: Broadman Press, 1962.

Lyon, T. *The Theory of Religious Liberty in England: 1603-39.* Cambridge: University Press, 1937.

Manley, Ken R. and Petras, Michael. *The First Australian Baptists.* Eastwood: Baptist Historical Society of New South Wales, 1981.

Maring, Norman H. *Baptists in New Jersey.* Valley Forge: Judson Press, 1964.

Maring, Norman H., and Hudson, Winthrop S. *A Baptist Manual of Polity and Practice.* Valley Forge: Judson Press, 1963.

May, Lynn E., Jr. *The First Baptist Church of Nashville, Tennessee 1820-1970.* Nashville: First Baptist Church, 1970.

McBeth, Leon. *English Baptist Literature on Religious Liberty to 1689.* New York: Arno Press, 1980.

_____. *The First Baptist Church of Dallas: Centennial History 1868-1968.* Grand Rapids: Zondervan Publishing House, 1968.

_____. *Women in Baptist Life.* Nashville: Broadman Press, 1979.

McCall, Duke K., ed. *What is the Church?* Nashville: Broadman Press, 1958.

McClellan, Albert. *The Executive Committee of the Southern Baptist Convention 1917-1984.* Nashville: Broadman Press, 1985.

McGlothlin, William J. *Baptist Beginnings in Education.* Nashville: Sunday School Board, 1926.

McLemore, R. A. *A History of Mississippi Baptists, 1780-1970.* Jackson: Mississippi Baptist Convention Board, 1971.

McLoughlin, William G. *New England Dissent 1630-1833: The Baptists and the Separation of Church and State.* 2 vols. Cambridge, Mass.: Harvard University Press, 1971.

Miller, Glenn T. *Religious Liberty in America.* Philadelphia: Westminster Press, 1976.

Moody, Barry M., ed. *Repent and Believe: The Baptist Experience in Maritime Canada.* Hantsport, N.S.: Lancelot Press, Ltd., 1980.

Moon, Norman S. *Education for Ministry: Bristol Baptist College 1679-1979.* Bristol: Bristol Baptist College, 1979.

Moore, Lamire H. *Southern Baptists in Illinois.* Nashville: Benson Printing Co., 1957.

Morehouse, Henry L., ed. *Baptist Home Missions in North America, 1832-1882.* New York: Baptist Home Mission Society, 1883.

Morrell, Z. N. *Flowers and Fruits in the Wilderness.* St. Louis: Commercial Printing Company, 1882.

Mueller, William A. *A History of Southern Baptist Theological Seminary.* Nashville: Broadman Press, 1959.

Mullins, E. Y. *The Christian Religion in Its Doctrinal Expression.* Nashville: The Sunday School Board of the Southern Baptist Convention, 1917.

Murdock, John M., ed. *The Missionary Jubilee: An Account of the Fiftieth Anniversary of the American Baptist Missionary Union.* New York: Sheldon and Company, 1865.

Murray, Derek B. *The First Hundred years: The Baptist Union of Scotland.* Dundee: Baptist Union of Scotland, 1969.

Neal, Daniel. *The History of the Puritans.* 4 vols. London: Richard Hett, 1732-1738.

Newman, A. H., ed. *A Century of Baptist Achievement.* Philadelphia: American Baptist Publication Society, 1901.

_____. *A History of the Baptist Churches in the United States.* Philadelphia: American Baptist Publication Society, 1898.

Olson, Adolf. *A Centenary History as Related to the Baptist General Conference of America.* Chicago: Baptist Conference Press, 1952.

Owens, Loulie Latimer. *Saints of Clay: The Shaping of South Carolina Baptists.* Columbia: R. L. Bryan Company, 1971.

Parker, G. Keith. *Baptists in Europe.* Nashville: Broadman Press, 1982.

Paschal, George W. *A History of North Carolina Baptists.* 2 vols. Raleigh: General Board, North Carolina Baptist State Convention, 1930, 1955.

Patterson, Morgan W. *Baptist Successionism.* Valley Forge: Judson Press, 1969.

Paul, S. F. *Historical Sketch of the Gospel Standard Baptists.* London: Gospel Standard Publications, 1945.

Payne, Ernest A. *The Baptist Union: A Short History.* London: The Carey Kingsgate Press, 1959.

_____. *The Fellowship of Believers: Baptist Thought and Practice Yesterday and Today.* Enlarged ed. London: The Carey Kingsgate Press, 1952.

_____. *The Free Church Tradition in the Life of England.* London: SCM Press Ltd., 1951.

_____. *James Henry Rushbrooke.* London: Carey Kingsgate Press Limited, 1954.

_____. *Out of Great Tribulation: Baptists in the U.S.S.R.* London: Baptist Union, 1974.

Pelt, Owen D. and Smith, Ralph L. *The Story of the National Baptists.* New York: Vantage Press, 1960.

Perrigan, Rufus. *History of Regular Baptist (sic) and Their Ancestors and Accessors.* Hayse, Va.: Published by the author, 1961.

Petras, Michael. *Extension or Extinction: Baptist Growth in New South Wales 1900-1939.* Eastwood, NSW: Baptist Historical Society of New South Wales, 1983.

Posey, Walter B. *The Baptist Church in the Lower Mississippi Valley 1776-1845.* Lexington: University Press of Kentucky, 1957.

Prior, Alan C. *Some Fell on Good Ground: A History of the Beginning and Development of the Baptist Church in New South Wales, Australia, 1831-1965.* Sidney: The Baptist Union of New South Wales, 1966.

Purefoy, George W. *A History of the Sandy Creek Association.* New York: Sheldon and Company, Publishers, 1859.

Randolph, C. F., ed. *Seventh Day Baptists in Europe and America.* Plainfield, N.J.: American Sabbath Tract Society, 1910.

Rauschenbusch, Walter. *A Theology for the Social Gospel.* Nashville: Abingdon Press, 1945.

Rippon, John, ed. *Baptist Annual Register.* London: 1790-1802.

_____. *A Brief Memoir of the Life and Writings of the Late Rev. John Gill.* London: John Bennett, 1838.

Robertson, A. T. *Life and Letters of John Albert Broadus.* Philadelphia: American Baptist Publication Society, 1901.

Robinson, H. Wheeler. *Baptists in Britain.* London: Baptist Union Publication Department, 1937.

_____. *The Life and Faith of the Baptists.* London: Kingsgate Press, 1946.

Robinson, Robert. *Ecclesiastical Researches.* Cambridge: Francis Hodson, 1792.

Rogers, James A. *Richard Furman: Life and Legacy.* Macon, Ga: Mercer University Press, 1985.

Russell, C. Allyn. *Voices of American Fundamentalism.* Philadelphia: Westminster Press, 1976.

Rutledge, Arthur B. *Mission to America: A Century and a Quarter of Southern Baptist Home Missions.* Nashville: Broadman Press, 1969.

Ryland, Garnett. *The Baptists of Virginia 1699-1926.* Richmond: The Virginia Baptist Board of Missions and Education, 1955.

Ryland, John. *The Life and Death of the Rev. Andrew Fuller.* Charleston: Printed by Samuel Ethridge, 1818.

Sandeen, Ernest R. *The Roots of Fundamentalism: British and American Millenarianism 1800-1930.* Chicago: The University of Chicago Press, 1970.

Sawatsky, Walter. *Soviet Evangelicals Since World War II.* Scottdale, Penn.: Herald Press, 1981.

Semple, Robert Baylor. *History of Baptists in Virginia.* Originally published 1810; reprinted at Lafayette, Tenn.: Church History Research and Archives, 1976.

Shakespeare, J. H. *Baptist and Congregational Pioneers.* London: The Kingsgate Press, 1906.

————. *The Churches at the Crossroads: A Study in Church Unity.* London: Williams and Norgate, 1918.

————. *The Story of the Twentieth Century Fund.* London: Baptist Union Publication Department, 1904.

Sheets, Henry. *Who Are Primitive Baptists?* Raleigh: Edwards and Broughton Printing Co., 1908.

Shelley, Bruce L. *Conservative Baptists. A Story of Twentieth-Century Dissent.* Denver: Conservative Baptist Theological Seminary, 1960.

————. *A History of Conservative Baptists.* Wheaton, Illinois: Conservative Baptist Press, 1971.

Shurden, Walter B. *Associationalism Among Baptists in America: 1707-1814.* New York: Arno Press, 1980.

————. *Not a Silent People.* Nashville: Broadman Press, 1972.

————. *The Sunday School Board: Ninety Years of Service.* Nashville: Broadman Press, 1981.

Slaght, Lawrence T. *Multiplying the Witness: 150 Years of American Baptist Educational Ministries.* Valley Forge: Judson Press, 1974.

Smith, H. Shelton. *In His Image, But . . . : Racism in Southern Religion, 1780-1910.* Durham, N.C.: Duke University Press, 1972.

Sobel, Mechal. *Trabelin' On: The Slave Journey to an Afro-Baptist Faith.* Westport, Conn.: Greenwood Press, 1979.

Sorrill, Bobbie. *Annie Armstrong: Dreamer in Action.* Nashville: Broadman Press, 1984.

Spain, Rufus B. *At Ease in Zion: Social History of Southern Baptists 1865-1900.* Nashville: Vanderbilt University Press, 1961, 1967.

Spencer, J. H. *A History of Kentucky Baptists, from 1769 to 1885 Including More than 800 Biographical Sketches.* 2 vols. Cincinnati: T. R. Baumes, 1885.

Sprunger, Keith L. *Dutch Puritanism.* Leidon: E. J. Brill, 1982.

Spurgeon, Susannah and Harrald, Joseph, comp. *C. H. Spurgeon: Autobiography.* 2 vols. Edinburgh: The Banner of Truth Trust, 1981.

Stevens, Daniel G. *The First Hundred Years of the American Baptist Publication Society.* Philadelphia: ABPU, n.d.

Stewart, I. D. *The History of the Freewill Baptists.* Dover, N.H.: Freewill Baptist Printing Establishment, 1862.

Stowell, Joseph M. *Background and History of the General Association of Regular Baptist Churches.* Hayward, Calif.: General Tracts Unlimited, 1949.

Sullivan, James L. *Baptist Polity as I See It.* Nashville: Broadman Press, 1983.

Tatum, E. Ray. *Conquest or Failure? Biography of J. Frank Norris.* Dallas: Baptist Historical Foundation, 1966.

Taylor, Adam. *The History of the English General Baptists.* 2 vols. London: T. Bore, 1818.

_____. *Memoirs of the Rev. Dan Taylor.* London: Printed for the author, 1820.

Taylor, James B. *Memoir of Luther Rice.* 2nd ed. Baltimore: Armstrong and Berry, 1841.

Taylor, John. *A History of Ten Baptist Churches.* Frankfort, Ken.: J. H. Holeman, 1823.

Thompson, Evelyn Wingo. *Luther Rice: Believer in Tomorrow.* Nashville: Broadman Press, 1967.

Thompson, Margaret E. *The Baptist Story in Western Canada.* Calgary, Alberta: The Baptist Union of Western Canada, 1974.

Thomson, Ronald W. *The Story of the Ter-Jubilee of the Baptist Union.* London: The Baptist Union, 1964.

Tiller, Carl W. *The Twentieth Century Baptist.* Valley Forge: Judson Press, 1980.

Tolmie, Murray. *The Triumph of the Saints: The Separate Churches of London 1616-1649.* Cambridge: Cambridge University Press, 1977.

Tonson, Paul. *A Handful of Grain: The Centenary History of the Baptist Union of New Zealand.* 1: 1851-1882. Wellington: New Zealand Baptist Historical Society, 1982.

Torbet, Robert G. *The Baptist Ministry: Then and Now.* Philadelphia: The Judson Press, 1953.

_____. *A History of Baptists.* 3rd ed. Valley Forge: Judson Press, 1973.

_____. *A Social History of the Philadelphia Baptist Association, 1707-1940.* Philadelphia: Westbrook Publishing Co., 1944.

_____. *Venture of Faith.* Philadelphia: Judson Press, 1955.

Townsend, Leah. *South Carolina Baptists 1670-1805.* First published 1935, republished at Baltimore: Genealogical Publishing Company, Inc., 1978.

Tull, James E. *Shapers of Baptist Thought.* Valley Forge: Judson Press, 1972.

Underwood, A. C. *A History of English Baptists.* London: Carey Kingsgate Press, 1947.

Vail, Albert L. *The Morning Hour of American Baptist Missions.* Philadelphia: American Baptist Publication Society, 1907.

Wagner, William L. *Growth Patterns of Baptists in Europe.* South Pasadena, Calif.: William Carey Library, 1978.

Walton, Robert C. *The Gathered Community.* London: Carey Press, 1946.

Wardin, Albert W., Jr. *Baptist Atlas.* Nashville: Broadman Press, 1980.

Watts, Michael R. *The Dissenters.* Oxford: Clarendon Press, 1978.

Wayland, Francis. *Notes on the Principles and Practices of Baptist Churches.* Boston: Gould and Lincoln, 1856.

West, W. M. S. *To Be a Pilgrim: A Memoir of Ernest A. Payne.* Guildford, Surrey: Lutterworth Press, 1983.

White, Barrington R. *The English Separatist Tradition.* Oxford: Oxford University Press, 1971.

White, Charles L. *A Century of Faith.* Philadelphia: Judson Press, 1932.

Whitley, W. T. *The Baptists of London 1612-1928.* London: Kingsgate Press, 1928.

_____. *Calvinism and Evangelism in England.* London: Kingsgate Press, n.d.

_____. *A History of British Baptists.* London: Charles Griffin & Company, 1923.

Whitsitt, William Heth. *A Question in Baptist History.* Louisville: Charles T. Dearing, 1896.

Williams, Gwyn A. *The Search for Beulah Land: The Welsh and the Atlantic Revolution.* New York: Holmes and Meier Publishers, Inc., 1980.

Winslow, Ola Elizabeth. *Master Roger Williams.* New York: The Macmillan Company, 1957.

Woolley, Davis C., ed. *Baptist Advance.* Nashville: Broadman Press, 1964.

Woyke, Frank H. *Heritage and Ministry of the North American Baptist Conference.* Oakbrook Terrace, Ill.: North American Baptist Conference, 1979.

Yuille, George. *History of the Baptists in Scotland.* Glasgow: Baptist Union Publication Committee, 1926.

Zeman, Jarold K. *Baptists in Canada: Search for Identity Amidst Diversity.* Burlington, Ont.: G. R. Welch Company, Ltd., 1980.

————. *Baptist Roots and Identity.* No place of publication: Baptist Convention of Ontario and Quebec.

Unpublished

Carter, James E. "The Southern Baptist Convention and Confessions of Faith, 1845-1945." Th.D. dissertation, Southwestern Baptist Theological Seminary, Fort Worth, Texas, 1964.

Carter, Terry G. "Baptist Participation in Anti-Catholic Sentiment and Activities, 1830-1860." Ph.D. dissertation, Southwestern Baptist Theological Seminary, Fort Worth, Texas, 1983.

Estep, William R. "On the Origin of English Baptists." Article, 1980.

Harrell, Norman. "The Establishment of Baptist Work in Portugal." Paper, 1984.

Lee, O. Max. "Daniel Parker's Doctrine of the Two Seeds." Th.M. thesis, Southern Baptist Theological Seminary, Louisville, Kentucky, 1962.

Melton, Donnie Gerald. "The Seventy-Five Million Campaign and Its Effects upon the Southern Baptist Convention." Th.D. dissertation, Southwestern Baptist Theological Seminary, Fort Worth, Texas, 1975.

Miller, William Bricen. "Texas Mexican Baptist History." Th.D. dissertation, Southwestern Baptist Theological Seminary, Fort Worth, Texas, 1931.

Neely, H. K. "The Territorial Expansion of the Southern Baptist Convention 1894-1959." Th.D. dissertation, Southwestern Baptist Theological Seminary, Fort Worth, Texas, 1963.

O'Kelly, Steve. "The Influence of Separate Baptists on Revivalistic Evangelism and Worship." Ph.D. Dissertation, Southwestern Baptist Theological Seminary, Fort Worth, Texas, 1978.

Patterson, T. A. "The Theology of J. R. Graves and Its Influence on Southern Baptist Life." Th.D. dissertation, Southwestern Baptist Theological Seminary, Fort Worth, Texas, 1944.

Romo, Oscar I. "Toward a Strategy of Ethnic Missions, A Southern Baptist Perspective." D.Min. dissertation, Austin Presbyterian Seminary, Austin, Texas, 1982.

Smith, Harold Stewart. "A Critical Analysis of the Theology of J. R. Graves." Ph.D. dissertation, Southern Baptist Theological Seminary, Louisville, Kentucky, 1966.

Tull, James E. "A Study of Southern Baptist Landmarkism in the Light of Historical Baptist Ecclesiology." Privately published Ph.D. dissertation, Columbia University, New York, 1960.

Washington, James M. "The Origins and Emergence of Black Baptist Separatism, 1863-1897." Ph.D. dissertation, Yale University, 1979.

Yarbrough, Slayden A. "Henry Jacob, A Moderate Separatist, and his Influence on Early English Congregationalism." Ph.D. dissertation, Baylor University, 1972.

Index